THE NATIONAL
CYCLOPÆDIA OF AMERICAN
BIOGRAPHY

BEING THE

HISTORY OF THE UNITED STATES

AS ILLUSTRATED IN THE LIVES OF THE FOUNDERS, BUILDERS, AND DEFENDERS
OF THE REPUBLIC, AND OF THE MEN AND WOMEN WHO ARE
DOING THE WORK AND MOULDING THE
THOUGHT OF THE PRES-
ENT TIME

EDITED BY

DISTINGUISHED BIOGRAPHERS, SELECTED FROM EACH STATE
REVISED AND APPROVED BY THE MOST EMINENT HISTORIANS, SCHOLARS, AND
STATESMEN OF THE DAY

VOLUME XV

NEW YORK
JAMES T. WHITE & COMPANY
1916

INTRODUCTION

This new volume of THE NATIONAL CYCLOPEDIA OF AMERICAN BIOGRAPHY is presented with confidence that the high standard of completeness, as well as of accuracy, which has been persistently striven for in the preceding numbers will be found to be fully attained. The following paragraph, quoted from the introduction to the preceding volume, defines the general plan and scope:

"In compiling a Cyclopedia of Biography that should be truly national, that should comprehend every period of American history, and that should be representative of every section of the country, it was decided to make it absolutely complete along certain well-defined lines. Whatever else it might contain, it was decided that such a Cyclopedia should include all the high government officials: the presidents of the United States and their cabinet officials, the heads of the various departments in Washington, all the United States senators, all the United States ministers and ambassadors to foreign countries, the governors of all the states, the chief justices of the highest state courts, the justices of the United States Supreme Court, the heads of the various departments of the army, commissioners and delegates to important national congresses, conferences, etc.; presidents of the universities and colleges, bishops of the various churches, directors of astronomical observatories, presidents of the leading scientific and learned societies and religious organizations, as well as clubs and social institutions of more than a local fame."

Besides the official names mentioned above, there have been included the biographies of distinguished men and representatives of leading American families who have recently passed away; a list of contemporaries who have become distinguished in the church, at the bar, in literature, in the arts and sciences, and in the commercial and industrial world, and of whose particular efforts for the progress of civilization the public will be eager to learn. The details regarding such work have been obtained mainly from original sources, and are given to the world for the first time in authoritative, comprehensive form, and no pains have been spared to insure absolute correctness in all statements of fact. In dealing with scientific subjects great care has been taken to secure accuracy and reasonable fullness of treatment.

The new styles of the portrait illustrations and the increased space devoted to them will be appreciated by all students of history and biography. The life-like and characteristic pictures accompanying the biographical sketches have become a most important and valuable feature of this Cyclopedia, and the liberal co-operation of the American public which has made this portrait feature possible is hereby acknowledged.

The human face is the most fascinating study in the world. It is an indelible record of thought, feeling and experience which is open to all those who have learned by observation and study how to translate its various lineaments. It will be admitted by all that the preservation of a faithful and characteristic likeness of our notable Americans in some permanent repository, safe from loss or destruction, for the benefit of posterity, is a matter deserving universal approval.

Unquestionably there is no better medium for preserving such a collection of portraits than a great historical compilation designed to perpetuate the personal achievements and family records in the historical archives of the nation for the instruction and benefit of the generations to come. Just such a compilation is THE NATIONAL CYCLOPEDIA OF AMERICAN BIOGRAPHY. As it was planned to cover the entire field of American history and biography with a degree of completeness never before attempted, the Publishers felt justified in offering its pages as a repository for a National Collection of Portraits, and to invite the public's co-operation to make of this feature a veritable National Portrait Gallery. Without some plan of individual contribution such a comprehensive collection of portraits manifestly would have been impossible. In precisely the same way the British Government furnished the building, and the English people contributed the portraits that comprise the famous National Portrait Gallery of Great Britain.

The idea of such a National Portrait Gallery has met with universal enthusiastic and patriotic approval, and the general acceptance of the plan has been most widespread and liberal, permitting the publication of some 12,000 portraits, which is by far the largest collection of the kind in the world.

In the preparation of the portrait plates every endeavor has been put forth to secure the best likenesses. Oil paintings have been photographed; steel engravings, old prints, daguerreotypes and early photographs reproduced, and many hundreds of original photographs taken from life especially for the Cyclopedia. Moreover, in the great majority of cases the engravings and plates were made under the direct supervision of the families themselves.

Gathered together for permanent preservation in this convenient form, and made accessible to the whole world, THE NATIONAL CYCLOPEDIA OF AMERICAN BIOGRAPHY presents as could be done in no other way a portrait collection so complete and representative that it may truly be called the National Portrait Gallery of America.

JAMES T. WHITE & CO.

THE NATIONAL
CYCLOPÆDIA OF AMERICAN BIOGRAPHY.

VOLUME XV.

THE NATIONAL
CYCLOPÆDIA OF AMERICAN BIOGRAPHY.

HARRIS, William Torrey, philosopher, sociologist, philologist, educator and author, was born at North Killingly, Conn., Sept. 10, 1835, son of William and Zilpah (Torrey) Harris. His father was a farmer. His first paternal American ancestor was Thomas Harris who, in 1630, sailed from Bristol, England, with Roger Williams in the ship Lyon, landed at Salem, Mass., and in 1637 settled at Providence, R. I. From him the line descends through his son Thomas and the latter's wife, Elnathan Tew; their son Richard, and his wife Ruth King; their son Jonathan, and his wife Anna Whipple Mowry; their son Jabez, and his wife Mercy Arnold; their son Stephen and his wife Ruth Aldrich; their son John and his wife Amy Wilkinson, who were the grandparents of William Torrey Harris. Thomas Harris, settler, was in 1640 one of thirty-nine to sign an agreement for a form of government for Providence. He held the offices of commissioner, lieutenant, surveyor, deputy to the general court, and member of town council. His son Thomas, was likewise deputy to the general court and member of town council. The maternal grandparents of William Torrey Harris were William and Zilpah (Davison) Torrey, the former a descendant of William Torrey, a native of Combe St. Nicholas, Somersetshire, England, who emigrated in 1640, settled at Weymouth, Mass., became "captain of the trainband," was for many years representative for Weymouth in the general court, which he served as secretary; was a member of the committee to examine Eliot's Bible; wrote a book on the millenium entitled "A Discourse Concerning Futurities," and was the author of various other literary productions. William Torrey Harris received his preparatory education at various academies, among them Woodstock (Conn.) Academy, and Phillips Academy, Andover, Mass. He entered Yale College in the class of 1858, but after spending two and a half years at that institution, he removed, in 1857 to St. Louis, Mo., and began his professional career as a teacher in a phonographic institute, acting also as a private tutor. In 1858 he became an assistant teacher in the public schools of St. Louis, and for twenty-three years was associated with them as teacher, principal, assistant superintendent and superintendent, holding the latter position from 1867-80. During that period the increase of pupils rose from 17,000 to 55,000, and he also published thirteen volumes of reports which were contributed to the educational exhibit of the U. S. government at the Paris exposition of 1878 where they attracted such attention as to cause to be conferred upon him the honorary title of

Officer of the Academy, while the reports themselves were placed in the pedagogical library of the ministry of public instruction, then being organized in the Palais Bourbon. In 1889 he received the title of Officer of Public Instruction from the French government. Resigning the superintendency of the St. Louis schools in 1880 because of impaired health, he was presented with a $500 gold medal and a purse of $1,000 by the citizens of the city in recognition of his faithful and distinguished service. He then visited Europe, representing the U. S. Bureau of Education at the International Congress of Educators in Brussels in 1880. Upon his return he settled at Concord, Mass., where he took a prominent place as a member of the School of Philosophy with Bronson Alcott, Ralph Waldo Emerson and Thomas Davidson. In 1889 he again represented the U. S. Bureau of Education at the Paris exposition, and in the same year was appointed by Pres. Harrison U. S. Commissioner of Education, and removed to Washington, holding that position until 1906. He founded in 1867 the "Journal of Speculative Philosophy," the first attempt of its kind, editing and publishing twenty-two volumes, the last of which appeared in 1893. He was assistant editor of "Johnson's Cyclopedia," contributing articles to the departments of philosophy and psychology; in co-operation with Mr. and Mrs. A. J. Rickoff and J. Mark Bailey he made the "Appleton School Readers" (1877); edited "Appleton's International Education Series," the fifty-eighth volume of which appeared in 1908; published a translation of the second volume of "Hegel's Larger Logic," under the title of "Hegel's Doctrine of Reflection" (1881); "The Spiritual Sense of Dante's Divina Commedia" (1889; second edition (1896); "Introduction to the Study of Philosophy" (1889); "Hegel's Logic, or the Genesis of the Categories of the Mind" (1890); chapters on "The Philosophy of A. Bronson Alcott" in Sanborn's "Memoir of A. Bronson Alcott" (1893); "Psychologic Foundations of Education," in "International Education Series" (1898); "Monograph on Elementary Education in the United States," for series edited by Nicholas Murray Butler and contributed by the state of New York to the United States educational exhibit at Paris exposition of 1900; "Social Culture in the Form of Education and Religion," read before the International Congress of Arts and Science, Louisiana Purchase exposition, 1904; convocation address at the educational congress held at Lewis and Clarke exposition, Portland, Ore., 1905; editor-in-chief of

"Webster's International Dictionary," edition of 1900, and continued in that capacity during revision of entire book, when the "New International" was prepared. He invented the divided page that made possible the insertion of a larger vocabulary and fuller definitions and of more encyclopædic matter than had previously been found in a one-volume dictionary, and also contributed many signed articles and definitions in the departments of philosophy and psychology. In 1866 he founded the Philosophical Society of St. Louis; was a life director in the National Educational Association, and its president in 1875; president of the National Association of School Superintendents in 1873; for fifteen years an officer in the American Social Science Association; member of various educational and scientific bodies. among them the American Philosophical Association to which he contributed numerous papers. Many distinguished honors were conferred upon Dr. Harris. In 1894 he received from the King of Italy the degree of the Commander of the Order of St. Maurice and Lazarus. In 1869 Yale College bestowed upon him the degree of A.M. and in 1895 that of LL.D., which latter he likewise received from the University of Missouri in 1870, the University of Pennsylvania in 1894 and Princeton University in 1896. He received the degree of Ph.D. from Brown University in 1893, and from the University of Jena, Germany, in 1899. In 1906 the Carnegie Foundation for the Advancement of Teaching conferred upon him "as the first man to whom such recognition for meritorious service is given, the highest retiring allowance which our rules will allow, an annual income of $3,000." In the generation following 1867, Dr. Harris, by his "Journal of Speculative Philosophy," stood at the head of American idealistic thought. Prime Minister Balfour declared that he had read all of the twenty-two volumes published and that their existence was a high tribute to America. The work was of the first importance in German circles, as well as with the Wallaces in Oxford and the Cairds and Stirling of Scotland. Dr. Harris was the indefatigable torch-bearer of high philosophy and was forever lighting up those four great watch-towers, Kant, Hegel, Aristotle and Plato, holding their importance in the order named. His final word to young America is the little essay "Platonism" in Webster's Dictionary." It is by this essay and his "Hegel's Logic" that he wished to be remembered. He has been called our first philosopher, and he was the first one with conscious knowledge of what it is to be a philosopher, and with ability to cover the whole field, applying the highest German theories to practice. He was married in Providence, R. I., Dec. 27, 1858, to Sarah Tully, daughter of James Bugbee of Thompson, Conn. There are two surviving children: Theodore Harris, a lawyer of San Antonio, Tex., and Edith Davidson Harris. Dr. Harris died in Providence, R. I., Nov. 5, 1909.

ROTCH, A[bbott] Lawrence, meteorologist, was born in Boston, Mass., Jan. 6, 1861, son of Benjamin Smith and Annie Bigelow (Lawrence) Rotch. He was descended from William Rotch, who came from Salisbury, England, in 1710, and settled in Provincetown, Mass., through William's son Joseph, who married Love Macy; their son William, who married Elizabeth Barney; their son William, Jr., who married Elizabeth Rodman, and their son Joseph, who married Ann Smith and was the grandfather of Abbott Lawrence Rotch. His father (1817-82) was a successful merchant of Boston and the founder of the New

Bedford Cordage Co., who married a daughter of Abbott Lawrence. The son received his early education in Europe and the Chauncy Hall School, Boston. He was graduated in the department of mechanical engineering of the Massachusetts Institute of Technology in 1884. He early developed an absorbing interest in meteorology, and determined to devote his life to the advancement of that science. Inheriting ample means, he built at Great Blue Hill, near Hyde Park, Mass., which is the highest point on the Atlantic coast south of New Hampshire (635 feet), an observatory for meteorological research, which he not only fully equipped and maintained during his lifetime, but for the continuation of which he provided in his will. It was the first private institution for the study of that science, and with the exception of the municipal station in New York city, it was the first to be equipped with self-recording instruments. It is one of the comparatively few observatories in the world where nearly every meteorological element is continuously recorded, and there is probably no establishment of any kind which is better known for the high standard of its work. Beginning in 1885, Prof. Rotch made frequent trips to Europe to study the

meteorological stations, and he wrote articles describing these stations for the "American Meteorological Journal," of which he was editor or associate editor from 1886 until his death. Prof. Rotch began making regular observations Feb. 1, 1885. These included amount of rainfall, velocity and direction of the wind, maximum and minimum temperatures, and the paths of thunder and other storms. Local weather predictions were made here and continued until the government commenced similar forecasts in Boston in 1891. He originated the method of recording local observations on a map, which is now in practice by the United States weather bureau. In 1890 he began a series of measurements of the height and velocity of clouds by trigonometrical and other methods. These measurements were resumed in 1896 as a part of an international system, and embodied perhaps the most complete investigation of cloud heights, velocities and movements ever undertaken. In 1894, at the suggestion of W. A. Eddy, he began to use kites for obtaining records of the upper atmosphere, the kites lifting self-recording instruments a great distance into the free air. He originated the use of cellular kites flown with steel wire and controlled by a power windlass for meteorological purposes. The unprecedented height of three miles was reached by kites in 1900, and kite flights are still made once a month to obtain temperatures at much greater heights. In 1901, during a voyage across the Atlantic, he obtained the first meteorological observations by means of kites carrying self-recording instruments

W.T. Harris

flown from the deck of a moving steamer, thus pointing out a new way of obtaining information concerning the conditions of the free air over oceans and lakes. At this time also he invented a device for determining the true direction and velocity of the wind at sea. In 1904 Prof. Rotch first sent up free balloons carrying self-recording instruments from the grounds of the St. Louis Exposition, and he continued these experiments for four years. Of seventy-six such balloons sent up from St. Louis, seventy-two were recovered. In 1908 a height of eleven miles was attained in this way. The lowest temperature was found to be at a height of about eight miles, above which the temperature increased or remained stationary. A temperature of 110 degrees below zero, recorded in winter above St. Louis, Mo., at a height of nine miles, is nearly the lowest natural temperature yet found. In 1909 he made the first trigonometrical measurements of the flight of pilot balloons in the United States. With Teisserenc de Bort he fitted out and took part in an expedition in 1905-6 to explore the tropical atmosphere over the Atlantic ocean by means of kites and pilot balloons and collected much valuable data concerning the temperatures and movements of the upper air in the tropics. In his enthusiastic pursuit of meteorological knowledge Prof. Rotch became an expert mountain climber. He ascended the summit of Mont Blanc at least five times, and climbed some of the highest mountains in North and South America to make important observations on the physiological effects of diminished atmospheric pressure. He was a member of several solar eclipse expeditions and made some of the most complete studies ever made of eclipse meteorology. He also took part in a number of balloon ascents. He served on the international jury of awards for instruments of precision at the Paris Exposition in 1889, and received from the French government the decoration of chevalier of the Legion of Honor. During the winter of 1889-90 he made magnetical and meteorological observations with M. L. Teisserenc de Bort in the northern portion of the Algerian desert. He showed an enthusiastic interest in the development of aeronautics, and among his last publications was a set of "Charts of the Atmosphere for Aeronauts and Aviators" (1911), embodying in practical form many of the valuable results of his meteorological observations at Blue Hill. The relations between the Blue Hill Observatory and Harvard University have been very close, practically from the establishment of the former. From 1888 to 1891 and from 1902 to 1906 Prof. Rotch held the honorary position of assistant in meteorology at Harvard, and in 1906 he was appointed professor of meteorology, the first man to hold that position at Harvard. In 1908–09 he placed the Blue Hill Observatory at the service of Harvard University by offering a research course to students in the department of geology and geography who were competent to carry on investigations in advanced meteorology. In 1891 the university conferred upon him the honorary degree of A.M. Besides his "Charts" mentioned above, Prof. Rotch wrote "Sounding the Ocean of Air" (1900) and "The Conquest of the Air, or the Advent of Aerial Navigation" (1909), and a large list of papers covering a variety of subjects other than his particular science. He was one of the pioneers of the New England Meteorological Society, a fellow and librarian of the American Academy of Arts and Sciences, a member and trustee of the Boston Society of Natural History, a fellow of the Royal Meteorological Society (London) and a member of the Astronomical and Astrophysical Society of America, American Philosophical Society, Physical Society of London, International Solar Commission, International Commission for Scientific Aeronautics, International Meteorological Committee, Société Météorologique de France and Deutsche Meteorologische Gesellschaft. He was married in Savannah, Ga., Nov. 22, 1893, to Margaret Randolph, daughter of Col. E. C. Anderson, who survived him, with three children: Margaret Randolph, Arthur and Katharine Lawrence Rotch. He died in Boston, Mass., Apr. 7, 1912.

O'REILLY, Charles J., first Roman Catholic bishop of the diocese of Baker City, Ore., was born at St. John, New Brunswick, Can., Jan. 4, 1860. His primary and classical studies were made at the Christian Brothers' School, St. John, and at St. Joseph's College, Memramcook; his theological course at the Grand Seminary of the Sulpicians, at Montreal. He was ordained priest at Portland, Ore., June 29, 1890, and for four years attended the mission of Oswego and Tegardville. In February, 1894, he was appointed rector of the Church of the Immaculate Heart of Mary at Portland and continued in charge there until he was chosen bishop of the new diocese of Baker City, established in 1903 to include fifteen counties of the state of Oregon, an area of 68,000 square miles. He was consecrated on Aug. 25, 1903. The diocese has a Catholic population of about 6,500, with thirty-three priests, and fifty-two churches, chapels and missions. During his pastorate in Portland Bishop O'Reilly acted for several years as editor of the local weekly, the "Catholic Sentinel," during which time he taught himself to set type.

LEONARD, [Harry] Ward, electrical engineer and inventor, was born in Cincinnati, O., Feb. 8, 1861, son of Ezra G. and Henrietta (Ward) Leonard. His first paternal American ancestor was Solomon Leonard, who came from England in 1629, and was one of the party with Miles Standish and John Alden who established the town of Duxbury, the first settlement out of Plymouth; from him the line of descent is traced through his son Jacob, who married Phœbe Chandler; their son Joseph and his wife, Martha Orcutt; their son Joseph and his wife, Mary Packard; their son David and his wife, Mary Hall; their son George W. and his wife, Sarah Tucker Baker, who were the grandparents of the subject of this sketch. Mr. Leonard is a descendant, through his mother's family, of Gen. Artemus Ward, the first commander-in-chief of the revolutionary forces, and also of John Alden of the Mayflower. He was educated at the public schools and the Massachusetts Institute of Technology, and after a year in the service of the Western Electric Light Co. in Chicago, Ill., as general superintendent, he established the important electric contracting business of Leonard & Izard. In 1889 the firm was bought out by the Edison interests, and Mr. Leonard became manager of the light and power departments of the combined Edison interests for the United States and Canada, with headquarters in New York city. Meanwhile he had devoted considerable attention to experimental work. His first important invention was a method of electric lighting for railway trains. It provided for a dynamo in the forward part of the train operated by steam from the locomotive, and by running both wires of the electric circuit the length of the train and back again, he secured a uniform brilliancy of every lamp on the circuit throughout the train. The system was first installed in 1888, and is now in general use throughout the railway world. Another important invention is what is known as the "Ward Leonard system of motor control," regarded by the English courts as "a triumph on which electric engineering may well congratulate itself." Previous to this important invention the voltage at the motor was that of a constant potential line less a certain amount absorbed by a rheostat. The voltage absorbed by the rheostat multiplied by the ampere load taken by the motor, appeared as heat watts in the rheostat and was dissipated without doing any useful work. For instance, if the motor was reduced to half speed by absorbing half the voltage in the rheostat, and the other half was applied at the armature, then the rheostat dissipated in useless heat one-half the power of the motor. Realizing the tremendous inefficiency of this method of control, Mr. Leonard conceived the idea of varying the voltage of the dynamo supplying the motor by means of a small field rheostat in the generator field circuit, instead of varying the voltage at the aramature terminals by means of a rheostat in series with the motor armature. As a result the watt loss in the little field rheostat was only a fraction of 1 per cent. of the total output, instead of the large amount lost when the rheostat was placed in series with the motor armature. Going a step further he conceived the idea of running a number of dynamos of constant potential at the power house, and having a set of wires for each one running through such a place as a machine shop, so that a motor driving a machine tool or other piece of apparatus could be tapped across the voltage of one dynamo to run at slow speed, and then put across two in series to run at higher speed, three in series to go at still higher speed, etc., thus getting a voltage control without resistance in series with the armature, and without making it necessary to have a separate dynamo to supply energy to each motor. By this method it is possible to reverse smoothly and efficiently a large motor from full speed in one direction to full speed in the opposite, and it is now used all over the world. Among his other inventions were a multiple voltage system for regulating the speed of operating motors (1892); the "Ward Leonard double-arm circuit breaker," which is now in almost universal use; a system of regenerative braking, by which a railway train can be stopped more efficiently and quickly than by air brakes; a single-phase railway system, by which the locomotives are located in different parts of a long train, but are under the control of the engineer or operator in the first locomotive, and by which a perfect, smooth and rapid acceleration can be obtained with minimum energy from the source of supply. This is now recognized as the best form of trunk-line electrification, and is being installed for railway use in all parts of the world. He designed an automatic dynamo lighting and starting system for automobiles, consisting of a shunt wound dynamo, which is automatically controlled to keep a constant current at all running speed for supplying the battery and lamp of the car, and he also invented the form of change gear for automobiles which is now used in nine out of every ten high-grade motor cars. Mr. Leonard was a prolific inventor, and his inventions were not only practical but were epoch-making in the history of electricity. In 1891 he resigned from the Edison Co. and organized the Ward Leonard Electric Co., with a factory at Bronxville, N. Y., for manufacturing and marketing his inventions. He was awarded the John Scott medal by the Frank-

lin Institute of Philadelphia in 1903 for his work in electrical research. He was president of the Inventors' Guild (1913-14), Fellow of the American Institute of Electrical Engineers, of which he was vice-president in 1892, member of the Union League, Engineers' and Technology clubs of New York and the New York Electrical Society. He was a director of the Mount Morris Bank of New York, president of the Sagamore Development Co., and was president of the village of Bronxville, N. Y., in 1902. Mr. Leonard was married, Aug. 24, 1895, to Carolyn, daughter of J. W. Good, of New York City. He died at Bronxville, N. Y., Feb. 18, 1915.

MONETTE, John Wesley, physician, was born in Staunton, Va., Apr. 5, 1803, son of Dr. Samuel Monette, of Huguenot descent. He was educated at an academy in Chillicothe, O., where the family lived until 1821, when it removed to Washington, Miss. Here he began his professional practice after graduating M. D. at the Transylvania University, Lexington, Ky., in 1825. He made a careful investigation of yellow fever, epidemics of which had visited Natchez and Washington on two occasions, and in 1837 he read a paper before the Jefferson College, in which he suggested the use of quarantines in restricting the disease. When yellow fever broke out in New Orleans soon afterward, Dr. Monette had the pleasure of seeing his quarantine theory put to the test, it being the first time that an attempt was made to control the spread of the fever. He was regarded as the leading authority on the subject and contributed a series of papers on it to the "Western Journal of Medicine and Surgery," during 1842–43. Dr. Monette was a life-long student and in addition to his medical practice, devoted considerable time to literary work. He wrote a paper, in 1824, on the "Causes of the Variety of the Complexion and Form of the Human Species," in which he gave, in a hypothetical way, many of the principles published by Darwin thirty-five years later. He was the author of "Geography and History of the Mississippi Valley" (1833), "Essay on the Improbability of Spontaneous Production of Animals and Plants," and a number of poems and articles on literary topics, which he contributed to the press anonymously. He was married Dec. 10, 1828, to Cornelia Jane, daughter of George Newman, and of their ten children four lived to maturity: George N., A. C., Anna Maria and Louise Monette. He died in Washington, Miss., Mar. 1, 1851.

HOLLAND, John Philip, inventor of the submarine, was born at Liscannor, County Clare, Ireland, Feb. 24, 1842, son of John and Mary (Scanlan) Holland. He was educated at the Christian Brothers' School in Limerick. After teaching for some time in Ireland he came to this country, in 1875, and continued his vocation in St. John's Parochial School, Paterson, N. J. He was an ardent Irish patriot who wanted to see his native land freed from English rule, and it was the desire to find some means of crushing England's sea-power that first directed his thoughts to the construction of a submarine boat. Though he had made a number of designs before coming to America, he was unable to obtain much progress, owing to lack of capital. Soon after settling at Paterson, however, he secured funds from the Fenian agitators and began the construction of a submarine boat in Todd & Rafferty's shop in that city. This cigar-shaped vessel was launched in the Passaic river, and Holland had the satisfaction of seeing his early dreams substantially realized. She de-

John P Holland.

veloped certain faults in construction, and he sank her in the river and built his second boat in 1881, known as the "Fenian Ram." This vessel quite surpassed his expectations, diving almost daily without mishap in New York bay and proving conclusively that his principles were sound and practical. Though Holland continued experiments, the world heard little more of his submarine until 1895, when the United States navy advertised for bids and plans for submarines, and he submitted a set of drawings which won the competition. These drawings embodied the specifications of his third boat, the "Plunger," which was built at the Columbian Iron Works, Baltimore, Md., and, unlike its predecessors, which were equipped with a Brayton petroleum engine, was propelled by steam. He was considerably hampered in his work for the government by the interference of interested parties who were totally ignorant of submarine construction, and, as a result, he abandoned the "Plunger" and returned the government appropriation. In 1898 he built the "Holland" in the Crescent shipyards at Elizabeth, N. J., the dimensions of which were: length, 53 feet 10 in.; diameter, 10 feet 3 in.; submerged displacement, 53 tons, and armament, one bow torpedo tube, one bow pneumatic dynamite gun and three short Whitehead torpedoes. She was propelled on the surface by an Otto gasoline engine of 50 h. p., and, when submerged, by a 50 h. p. electric motor, fed by a battery of sixty cells with a capacity of 1,500 ampere hours at a four-hour rate of discharge. A double commutator was fitted on the motor, so that 150 h. p. could safely be developed. Her surface speeds were six knots with the gasoline engine and about eight k.ots with the motor, while her submerged speed was five and one-half knots with the motor. A single pair of horizontal rudders, operated by air-engines at the stern, served to control her in the vertical plane. The engine, however, was hardly ever used. Air reservoirs and compressors furnished air for steering and driving engines, tank and torpedo service, as well as for breathing purposes. The "Holland" is recognized in the naval world as the first of modern submarines. It amazed everybody by its mobility and rapidity of submersion; it could rise to the surface and disappear again in five seconds. After a number of the most searching tests, the United States government purchased the "Holland" in 1900, and ordered six more from the J. P. Holland Submarine Boat Co., which had taken over the patents. Disagreements with this company became so frequent that Holland withdrew in 1904 and devoted the last years of his life to the development of the flying machine. He was married in Brooklyn, N. Y., Jan. 17, 1887, to Margaret, daughter of John Foley, of Paterson, N. J., and had five children: John P., Jr., Robert C., Joseph F., Margaret D. and Julia Holland. He died in Newark, N. J., Aug. 12, 1914.

LAKE, Simon, inventor, was born in Pleasantville, N. J., Sept. 4, 1866, son of John Christopher and Miriam (Adams) Lake. His earliest paternal American ancestor was John Lake, one of the patentees of Gravesend (now South Brooklyn, N. Y.), who first settled in Massachusetts early in the seventeenth century. The tradition is that the name was of Welsh origin (Leake), and that the family emigrated from Wales to England in the thirteenth century. From John Lake the line runs through his son William, who married Sarah Golden; their son Daniel, who married Gartara Steelman; their son Daniel, who married Sarah Lucas; their son John, who married Abigail Adams, and their son Simon, who married Sarah Blake, and was the grandfather of the inventor. This Simon Lake was a member of the New Jersey legislature, internal revenue collector, organizer of a company of South Jersey troops in the civil war, founder (with his sons) of Ocean City, N. J. His son, John Christopher Lake, father of the present Simon Lake, was the inventor and manufacturer of shade rollers and the proprietor of an iron foundry and machine shops at Ocean City, N. J. Simon Lake was educated in the public schools of Philadelphia, Pa., and Toms River, N. J., and at the Clinton Liberal Institute, Fort Plain, N. Y. After a course in mechanical drawing at Franklin Institute, Philadelphia, he became a partner in his father's foundry. In 1889 he began the manufacture of his patented steering gear, dredges and other vessel appliances at Baltimore, Md. While there he invented and designed his first submarine boat, which is applicable for use as a torpedo boat for offensive and defensive purposes and for various kinds of submarine engineering work. The United States government had previously designated various requirements for submarine vessels in the following order: Safety, facility and certainty of action when submerged, speed when running on the surface, speed when submerged, endurance, both submerged and on the surface; offensive power, stability and visibility of object to be attacked. Mr. Lake submitted a design for an even keel submersible eighty-five feet long, with oil-burning boilers and triple expansion steam engines for navigating on the surface and motors deriving their power from storage batteries while submerged; she was of double hull construction, the spaces between the hulls to be utilized for water ballast; had a drop keel and various automatic devices for maintenance of a level keel; her depth was to be controlled by hydroplanes; she was also to be fitted with a diving compartment and had wheels for navigating over the water bed; she was designed to meet the United States navy department requirements and contained all the elements that have later worked out as successful in the Lake type of submarine torpedo boats, but as Mr. Lake was only a young man at this time with no financial backing, the government finally decided to place the contract based upon certain guarantees of performance of another type. A vessel of this other type was built, but after spending several years in its construction it was abandoned as a failure. Mr. Lake was not discouraged by his failure to win recognition, and he determined to build a small boat himself to demonstrate the new features and novel principles of his type of boat. Accordingly he built the Argonaut, Jr. It was a crude, coffin-shaped vessel, or box, designed simply to demonstrate the practicability of navigating on the waterbed and permitting divers to leave the vessel through the open door of a diving compartment, or of permitting operations on the bottom without recourse to diving dress or risk of water entering the boat through that opening. The craft was propelled by hand power, which revolved toothed wheels resting with sufficient weight upon the waterbed to give the necessary tractive force when submerged. In 1899, six years after Mr. Lake submitted his plans to the United States government, the French government launched the Narval, which was their first submersible, and this vessel contained the distinguishing features of the Lake boat, viz.: hydroplanes for controlling her submergence, a double hull, and by raising the center of buoyancy had sufficient longitudinal stability to submerge more nearly on an even keel. His experiments with the Argonaut Jr. enabled him to secure sufficient aid to build the Argonaut 1, the first submarine vessel to navigate successfully in the open sea. She was designed to run either on the surface or under water, using her main engines at all times for propulsion. She was intended for submarine exploration work and was navigated over the bottom on wheels. Owing to the lifting effect of submarine waves, and to keep the boat from bounding on the bottom, it was found necessary to give her a negative buoyancy of about 1,500 pounds, when it was found possible to navigate her easily upon the waterbed of hard sand. This resulted in modification of the boat in the form of smaller wheels, fitted to swinging arms. These allowed the boat to lie at rest, or buoyant, a short distance above the bottom to which she was anchored by the weight of the wheels, which were free to move up or down, thus permitting the hull of the vessel to rise and fall without fear of the body of the craft being brought in contact with the bottom. The vertical movement thus permitted was a rise and fall of three feet before the keel could reach the bottom. The Lake boats do not themselves touch the bottom or "run on wheels." When the wheels come in contact with the bottom the boats lose the negative buoyancy which carried them down and the wheels absorb their own dead weight, the vessel held in suspension above them. In practice it has been found possible to navigate over bottoms consisting of soft mud, sand, shale, or even that of a moderately rock nature. Boats of this type have gone over obstructions rising ten feet from the bottom and have suffered no shock whatever. In the Lake vessels all gasoline tanks are carried outside the main hull and within the superstructure, thus enormously reducing the dangers incident to the use of gasoline as a fuel. The Argonaut 1 traveled several thousand miles under her own power along the Atlantic coast, on the surface, and ran several hundreds of miles totally submerged upon the bottom. The achievements of the Argonaut 1 were a most remarkable advance in the science of submarine navigation. Submarine boats are exposed to more danger of collision when running submerged than are surface craft, hence Mr. Lake invented the "omniscope," which gives an all-round view of the horizon on being rotated in either direction only thirty degrees. With this instrument a submarine vessel, while running submerged, may keep a continual check upon the movements of other vessels in the neighborhood. In 1901 he built the Protector, combining the results of the experiences with the preceding vessels of the Lake type. Official consideration of the Protector by the United States naval authorities was suspended pending the completion of a rival boat, and meanwhile she was sold to the Russian government. The Lake Torpedo Boat Co., whose plant is at Bridgeport, Conn., has also built submarines for Austria, and the "Seal" G-1 for the United States navy, the latter being the largest and fastest submarine in this country. In addition to usual fixed torpedo tubes arranged in the bow of the vessel which require the vessel herself to be trained, the G-1 carries four torpedo tubes on her deck which may be trained while the vessel is submerged, in the same manner as a deck gun on a surface vessel is trained, and thus fire to either broadside, which gives many technical advantages. She was submerged to a depth of 256 feet, a world's record, exceeding her contract requirements, and proving beyond question the capability of the Lake type

in meeting any demands that submarines might be called upon to fulfill. The United States government has adopted the Lake type of submarine torpedo boat to be built in the navy yards under royalty to the Lake company. In 1895 the Lake Submarine Co. was organized for the purpose of developing certain phases of submarine engineering work. It is not a working company, i. e., it does not engage in the actual recovery of vessels or their cargoes, but grants to others licenses for the exclusive use of the apparatus and methods covered by the patents of the company. The field embraces the location and recovery of sunken ships and their cargoes, removing or floating stranded vessels, construction of breakwaters, etc.; the deepening and improving of waterways and harbors, subaqueous tunnels, gold dredging from river beds and seacoast bottoms, sponge and pearl fishing, scientific investigations under water and hydrographic work of various sorts. Mr. Lake has spent several years in Germany, England, Russia and Austria in designing, building and acting as advisory engineer regarding submarine torpedo boats. He invented and designed a special type of submarine tunnel to form connection between France and England, which was submitted in 1906 and which has been highly recommended by prominent engineers. He has taken out over eighty patents in the United States, many of which are now in use, while others are still to be developed. Among them are a new type of heat engine, life-saving apparatus for vessels and a method of treating certain diseases by air pressure. Mr. Lake is a member of the Institution of Naval Architects of London, Schiffsbautechnische Gesellschaft of Berlin, American Society of Mechanical Engineers, Society of Naval Architects and Marine Engineers of America and an associate member of the American Society of Naval Engineers. He is a member of the Engineers' Club, New York city, and the Algonquin Club of Bridgeport, Conn. He is also a member of the Society of the Sons of the American Revolution. He was married, June 9, 1890, to Margaret C., daughter of John Vogel of Baltimore, Md., and has three children: Miriam, Thomas E. and Margaret Lake.

QUINCY, Henry Parker, physician, was born in Boston, Mass., Oct. 28, 1838, son of Edmund and Lucilla Pinckney (Parker) Quincy, and a member of the famous Massachusetts family of Quincy. He was educated at Dixwell's private school in Boston, and was graduated at Harvard College in 1862. He began the study of medicine with Prof. Wyman, of Cambridge, Mass., was graduated M.D. at the Harvard Medical School in 1867, and then spent four years studying at some of the leading European medical schools and clinics. After his return from Europe he was appointed professor of histology at the Harvard Medical School, a position which he held for twenty years. The teaching of histology and the advancement of that branch of study to a recognized place among the essentials of a medical training constituted the chief life work of Dr. Quincy. "At the beginning of his long period of service," said Prof. Minot, of Harvard, "histology was barely recognized. The study was not required, the only equipment was a few inferior microscopes, and his only work-place was a corner hospitably allotted to him in the physiological laboratory of the old building on North Grove street. When he retired in 1898 he left a large, well-equipped laboratory, giving a required course in histology, attended by over 200 students." The value of this service to the cause of medical science is without measure. To appreciate it fully, it should be known that a professional career for Dr. Quincy was not necessary as a means of livelihood. He was a man of independent means and might have led a life of ease, but he chose an exacting career and devoted himself systematically and untiringly to a new branch of medical science which by its very nature was unnoticeable to any but a few. He was a citizen of the highest type and was continuously active and liberal in the support of every good cause and institution in the communities with which he was identified. He gave freely both of his time and his money to educational, philanthropic and religious institutions, and never failed to interest himself actively in every movement for the welfare of his fellow citizens. Dr. Quincy was a member of the Massachusetts Medical Society and the Norfolk District Medical Society, the Massachusetts Colonial Society, a warden of St. Paul's Episcopal Church, of Dedham, Mass., and a trustee of the Dedham public library. He was married in Quincy, Mass., June 20, 1877, to Mary, daughter of Charles Francis Adams, and had two daughters: Dorothy and Elinor Quincy. He died in Boston, Mar. 11, 1899.

LANGLEY, Samuel Pierpont, scientist, was born at Roxbury, Mass., Aug. 24, 1834, son of Samuel and Mary Sumner (Williams) Langley. His earliest paternal American ancestor was presumably Nathaniel Langley, who was at Roxbury, Mass., prior to 1660. From him the line of descent is traced through his son John, who married Mary Adams; their son Nathaniel, who married Ann Pierce; their son Samuel, who married Esther Mayo, and their son Samuel, who married Emily Montague Pierpont, and who was the grandfather of Samuel Pierpont Langley. Capt. Samuel Langley, his great-grandfather, was a soldier in the war of the revolution. His father, Samuel Langley, was a merchant and a promoter and initial stockholder of the Boston Atheneum. (For an account of Prof. Langley's work at the Allegheny Observatory, his inauguration of a standard time system, his researches on the sun and his bolometer, see Vol. III, p. 338.) The subject of flying had been of interest to him throughout his life, but it was not until 1887 that he began to give it serious thought. In that year he constructed at the Allegheny Observatory a turntable operated by steam power which furnished the air currents for a series of experiments and studies on the lifting force and resistance of various plane surfaces set at different angles. The results were recorded in "Experiments in Aerodynamics" (1891), published by the Smithsonian Institution, and "The Internal Work of the Wind" (1893). They gave to physicists perhaps for the first time firm ground on which to stand as to the long-disputed question of air resistance and reactions. They established (1) a more reliable coefficient for rectangular pressures than that of Smeaton; they proved (2) that upon inclined planes the air pressures were really normal to the surface; they disproved (3) the "Newtonian law" that the normal pressure varied as the square of the angle of incidence on inclined planes; they showed (4) that the empirical formula of Duchemin, proposed in 1836 and ignored for fifty years, was approximately correct; that (5) the position of the center of pressure varied with the angle of inclination, and that on planes its movements approximately followed the law formulated by Joessel; that (6) oblong planes presented with their longest dimension to the line of motion were more effective for support than when presented

with their narrower side; that (7) planes might be superposed without loss of supporting power if spaced apart certain distances which varied with the speed; and (8) that thin planes consumed less power for support at high speeds than at low speeds. This last has been called "Langley's law." It resulted from the fact that the higher the speed the less need be the angle of inclination to sustain a given weight, and the less, therefore, the horizontal component of the air pressure. These studies of mechanical flight were more elaborate, more profound and more instructive than those of any of his contemporaries and predecessors, and they proved to be of immense value to Messrs. Chanute, Wright and others who continued the work where he left off. Langley now undertook to apply this knowledge practically to the problem of actual flight. For this purpose he built, during 1891-95, four model flying machines, one driven by carbonic acid gas and three by steam engines. He encountered a series of disappointments and failures, of which he has given an interesting account in the "Aeronautical Annual" for 1897, but on May 6, 1896, he had the satisfaction of seeing his "Aerodrome No. 5" fly a distance of about 3,000 feet on the Potomac river. This was followed by the successful flight of another aerodrome on Nov. 28, 1896, and on subsequent occasions, of which no public accounts have been given. The miniature aeroplane weighed but thirty pounds and could carry only enough fuel to run its engine a very few minutes, but it sustained itself in the air, covering half a mile on each trip, and it proved to Langley at least that the riddle of the air had been solved. These experiments in flying having attracted the attention of the army and navy, a board of officers recommended, in 1898, that a full-size man-carrying machine be developed for war purposes. The board of ordnance and fortifications of the U. S. army appropriated $50,000 for the purpose, and Langley agreed to supervise the work without remuneration to himself. The engine was built in the shops of the Smithsonian Institution. It was a gasoline motor of 52 brake horse-power, weighing with cooling water, carbureter, battery, etc., somewhat less than five pounds to the horsepower, an achievement which had not been paralleled by the lightest gasoline motors of European builders. The flying weight of the machine complete with the aeronaut aboard was 830 pounds, its sustaining surfaces were 1,040 square feet, and it was intended to be launched from a catapult placed on the deck of a houseboat, precisely in the same manner as his previous models. Attempts were made to launch this machine with Charles M. Manley as pilot on Oct. 7th and Dec. 8, 1903. Both trials were failures in consequence of a defect in the launching gear, causing considerable injury to the machine before it could get under way. The press, not knowing all the facts, cast ridicule on the experiment and decried such useless expenditure of public money, and the funds allotted by the board of ordnance having been expended, additional grants were now refused. Thus was Langley, with success in sight, finally defeated and deprived of the honor which he craved of being the first to achieve dynamic man-flight in the air. The irony of this failure is shown when, eleven years later, Glenn H. Curtiss took the same machine just as Langley left it in the Smithsonian Institution and flew with it over Lake Keuka, at Hammondsport, N. Y., May 28, 1914. On that occasion it arose from the surface of the lake under its own power on its first trial and sailed steadily along despite a puffy wind, maintaining remarkable stability. This vindication of what was called "Langley's folly" proves the truth of the statement he made eleven years before that "the machine never had a chance to fly at all," and it establishes Samuel P. Langley as the first inventor of the heavier-than-air flying machine. Meanwhile he was continuing his researches in astrophysics and making improvements in his bolometer. In 1900 he organized an expedition to observe the eclipse of the sun at Wadesboro, N. C., and so complete were his preparations and so successful his methods that he was able to procure invaluable data and material for the benefit of other scientists. Because of the unfortunate termination of his experiments in flying, he will be best remembered for his solar studies, and it is probably no exaggeration to say that in his handling of the problems which these have raised in the minds of astronomers his best service to the world was performed. He sought to learn something about the complicated structure of the light-giving cloud-shell of the sun. He attempted to determine the amount of heat radiated by that body, and the proportion of it which is subtracted by the earth's atmosphere. He examined the visible spectrum to find which part of it emitted the most energy. He also investigated the invisible extension beyond the red end of the spectrum, and mapped a region that was practically unknown before his day. In this and certain other undertakings he made use of an instrument whose delicacy he himself increased to a marvelous extreme. His perfected bolometer measured differences of temperature to a millionth of a degree. A distinguishing characteristic of Prof. Langley was his great diversity of interests, not only in the realm of science, but in literature and the arts as well. He loved art with a deep and abiding love, and he was competent to discuss it in its highest manifestations. History and literature he had so thoroughly studied in some of their most fruitful fields that he would have done honor to any institution as a professor in them, so much so that at one time he was consulted by no less a literary center than Oxford University on questions of English history and literature. His deep concern in religion was manifest in his frequent discussions with men of positive religious views, whether Jesuit, Jew, Buddhist or Mohammedan. He took particular interest in the welfare of the city of Washington, especially in the development of its National park and the zoological garden, for which he was largely responsible. Personally, he was described as reserved and even shy. Concentrating his mind upon the problems before him, an aloofness arose from much of the work of others, and he lived in seclusion, not accessible in his own home save to very few. He inherited from his New England ancestry a strong sense of duty, and his labor, his thought, his efforts in every field had as their one object the establishment of truth for truth's sake. He was a corresponding member of the Institute of France; foreign member of the Royal Society of London, the Royal Society of Edinburgh and Academia dei Lincei, Rome; a fellow of the Royal Astronomical Society of London; a member of the Royal Institution of London, the National Academy of Sciences, and of many other American and foreign scientific societies. He received the honorary degrees of D. C. L. from Oxford University in 1894; D.Sc. from Cambridge University in 1900; LL.D. from Harvard, Princeton, University of Michigan and the University of Wisconsin, and he was awarded the Henry Draper medal by the National Academy of Sciences; the Rumford medal by the Royal Society of London;

the Rumford medal by the American Academy of Arts and Sciences; the Janssen medal by the Institute of France, and a special medal by the Astronomical Society of France. He was unmarried, and died in Aiken, S. C., Feb. 27, 1906.

LANGLEY, John Williams, chemist, electrical engineer and educator, was born in Boston, Mass., Oct. 21, 1841, son of Samuel and Mary (Sumner) Williams Langley and brother of Samuel P. Langley, above. He was educated at Chauncey Hall school, Boston, and was graduated at the Lawrence Scientific School of Harvard University in 1861 with the degree B. S. In 1890 the University of Michigan gave him the degree Ph. D. He remained at Harvard for six months as an assistant in chemistry, and then entered the U. S. navy as an assistant surgeon, serving until 1864, when he resigned to travel for a year in Europe and to study chemistry and physics. In 1866 he became assistant professor of chemistry and natural science at Antioch College, Ohio, where he remained until the reorganization of that institution, in 1867. After further study in Boston and Cambridge, Mass., he was appointed professor of mathematics and natural philosophy in the U. S. Naval Academy, Annapolis. He resigned, in 1871, to take a business position, but his preference was for a scientific rather than a commercial career, and he accepted an appointment as professor of chemistry and allied sciences at Western University of Pennsylvania. He was professor of chemistry and physics at the University of Michigan during 1875–90; was consulting electrician and metallurgist in Pittsburgh 1890–92, and in 1892 was professor of electrical engineering in the Case School of Applied Science, Cleveland, Ohio, during 1892–06, when he was made professor emeritus. In his scientific work he has specialized in the chemistry of iron and steel, and the results of his researches have been published in the "American Journal of Science" and elsewhere. He is author of many scientific papers and monographs on chemistry and metallurgy. He is a member of the American Association for the Advancement of Science (vice-president, 1884), the British Association for the Advancement of Science, the American Electro-chemical Society, and the Society of Engineers of Western Pennsylvania, the University Club of Cleveland, and various other scientific and social societies and clubs. He was married at Charlestown, Mass., Sept. 12, 1871, to Martica Irene, daughter José Carret, a Cuban planter, and has four children: Mary W., wife of H. Burt Herrick; Martica I., wife of Paul S. Whitman; Annie W., and Samuel P. Langley. Portrait opposite page 9.

HAINES, John Michener, governor of Idaho, was born in Jasper county, Ia., Jan. 1, 1863, son of Isaac L. and Eliza (Bushong) Haines. His boyhood was spent on his father's farm. At the age of seventeen he entered Penn College at Oskaloosa, Ia., a sectarian institution of the Quaker faith, to which his parents belonged, but after three years his health failed and he was obliged to relinquish his studies. In 1883 he located at Friend, Neb., where he was connected with the Merchants' and Farmers' Bank for two years. He then removed to Richfield, Kan., and engaged in the real estate business, meeting also in that place W. E. Pierce and L. H. Cox, his present business associates. Reverses came, due to a wide-spread business depression occasioned by a severe drouth in that section, and he removed to Boise, Idaho, Aug. 10, 1890. Before leaving Kansas he entered into an agreement with Messrs. Pierce and Cox to engage

S. P. Langley

JOHN W. LANGLEY
SCIENTIST

JOHN M. HAINES
GOVERNOR

FRANKLIN H. GIDDINGS
SOCIOLOGIST

JAMES E. FERGUSON
GOVERNOR

in the real estate business in Boise, and a partnership was formed which has continued until the present time under the firm name of W. E. Pierce & Co. The enterprise was reasonably successful from the outset, and may be regarded as unique from the fact that there has been no change whatever in the personnel of the partnership for twenty-five years. He and his associates originated and fostered many enterprises, and assisted in whatever tended to advance not only Boise but the state as well, and are at the present time heavily interested in many enterprises throughout the commonwealth. In 1907 he was elected mayor of Boise, and filled his term of two years with great satisfaction to his friends and to himself. In July, 1912, he was nominated by the Republicans of Idaho as their candidate for governor, and in the following November was elected to that office. He was married, May 20, 1883, to Mary, daughter of Aaron Symons, a Quaker minister of Jasper county, Ia.

GIDDINGS, Franklin Henry, sociologist, was born in Sherman, Conn., Mar. 23, 1855, son of Rev. Edward Jonathan and Rebecca Jane (Fuller) Giddings, and a descendant of George Giddings, who emigrated from St. Albans, England, in 1635 and settled in Ipswich, Mass. George Giddings' wife was Jane Lawrence, and the line is through their son John and wife, Sarah Alcock; their son Thomas and wife, Sarah Andrews; their son Joseph and wife, Eunice Andrews; their son Jonathan and wife, Mary Baldwin; their son Jonathan and wife, Lydia Salmon, and their son Augustine and wife, Olive Lydia Millard, who were the grandparents of Prof. Giddings. His father (1832–94) was a prominent Congregational clergyman of Massachusetts and the author of "American Christian Rulers" (1889). After a preparatory course at the Great Barrington High School, he entered Union College in 1873, but left after two years to take charge of the academy at Goshen, Conn., continuing his studies privately and covering much more ground than was required by the college course. In 1888 he was graduated A.B. by Union College as of the class of 1877, and in 1889 the degree of A.M. was conferred upon him by the same institution. During 1876–78 he was associate editor on the Winsted (Conn.) "Herald," and in the latter year he was also an editorial writer on the Springfield "Republican." He was later an editor of the Berkshire "Courier," of Great Barrington, Mass., editor of the New Milford "Gazette," and editorial writer and literary critic on the Springfield "Union." In 1885 he conducted an investigation on coöperation and profit-sharing in the United States for the Massachusetts Bureau of Labor, and his report was widely translated and circulated. In 1888 he was chosen lecturer on political science at Bryn Mawr College, and in the following year was made associate, advancing to associate professor in 1890 and professor in 1892. Two years later he left Bryn Mawr to become professor of sociology at Columbia University, where he had served as a lecturer since 1891. Prof. Giddings is the author of many articles and monographs on economic and sociological theories which have attracted much attention, and "The Modern Distributive Process" (in collaboration with John B. Clark, 1888); "The Theory of Sociology" (1894); "The Principles of Sociology" (1896), which has been translated into French, Russian, Spanish, Hebrew, Czech and Japanese, and secured him the degree of Ph.D. from his alma mater; "The Theory of Socialization" (1897); "Elements of Sociology" (1898); "Democracy and Empire" (1900); "Inductive Sociology" (1901), "Descriptive and Historical Sociol-

ogy" (1906); "Pagan Poems" (1914), and "The Western Hemisphere in the World of Tomorrow" (1915). The working principle by which he seeks to explain the fundamental sociological phenomena is psychical in its nature—"consciousness of kind" in his earlier works, "like response to like stimuli" in the "Inductive Sociology." In this he differs radically from the school of contemporary writers, who seek to explain sociological facts in terms of environment. His later works are characterized by the ingenious application of statistical method to sociological material. He was editor of the annals of the American Academy of Political and Social Science during 1890–94 and editor of publications of the American Economic Association, 1891–93. Oberlin College conferred the degree of LL.D. upon him in 1900. Prof. Giddings is a fellow of the American Geographical Society and a member of the American Academy of Political and Social Science, of which he was a founder; the American Economic Association, the American Sociological Society (president in 1910-11), the Charity Organization Society, the Academy of Natural Sciences, Philadelphia, the Academy of Sciences of New York, and l'Institute International de Sociologie, Paris, of which he was president in 1913, and of the Authors' and Century clubs of New York. He is a trustee of Union College, and since 1915 has been a member of the board of education of New York city. He was married at Housatonic, Mass., Nov. 8, 1876, to Elizabeth Patience, daughter of Stephen Starr Hawes, of Great Barrington, Mass., and has three children: Henry Starr, Elizabeth Rebecca and Lorinda Margaret Giddings.

FERGUSON, James Edward, governor of Texas, was born on a farm near Temple, Bell co., Tex., Aug. 31, 1871, son of James Edward and Fannie (Fitzpatrick) Ferguson, both of Scotch-Irish descent. His father was a Methodist minister, who preached, farmed and operated a grist mill on Salado creek, and was widely known for his beneficent life. He died when our subject was four years old and the latter's educational opportunities were meagre. At the age of sixteen he left Texas for the far West, where he was variously engaged as a laborer in the vineyards of California, a teamster on some of the largest ranches in the world, a helper to placer miners in the Rocky Mountains, a roustabout in a barb wire factory in San Francisco, and a workman in the lumber regions of Washington territory and in the quartz mines of Nevada and Colorado. Returning to Texas, he was employed as a bridge-builder and foreman of construction crews. While farming he began to devote his spare hours to the study of law, was admitted to the bar in 1897, and for seven years successfully practiced his profession at Belton, Texas. He also established a small bank at Belton, and for two years made a close study of banking systems and methods. Removing to Temple, he organized the Temple State Bank, which is one of the chief factors in the "greater Temple" of to-day. Previous to announcing himself as a candidate for the governorship he had never aspired to political office. A study of the political and business conditions of the state led him to point out the remedy. With a platform of his own he went before the people, and in a hotly contested campaign was nominated and elected on the Democratic ticket by one of the greatest majorities ever received by a candidate for governor of the state of Texas. It is probable that the records of no other gubernatorial contest will show such a victory of a man personally known to but few outside the bounds of his home county, of humble birth, a stranger to fame, never having sought or held public office, overcoming enormous obstacles, and defeating the schemes of every combination or astute politicians that aimed to curb his ambition and determination to give Texas a business man's administration. Gov. Ferguson finds his greatest pleasure in the domestic circle, with his wife and children surrounding him, content in the knowledge that his daily life is of benefit to his fellowmen. He was married, Dec. 31, 1899, to Miriam, daughter of Joseph L. Wallace, a prominent pioneer Bell county farmer; Mrs. Ferguson is cultured, refined and witty, and is possessed of a charmingly frank personality; two children are the fruit of this union: Ouida and Dorrace Ferguson.

FARRELLY, John P., fourth Roman Catholic bishop of Cleveland, was born at Memphis, Tenn., Mar. 15, 1856, son of John P. and Martha (Clay) Farrelly. His father was a well-to-do merchant of Nashville, Tenn. The son was educated at the public schools of Nashville, at Georgetown College, D. C., at Notre Dame de la Paix, Belgium, and was prepared for the priesthood at the North American College in Rome, where he was ordained a priest May 22, 1880. From the time of his ordination until his consecration as bishop, Father Farrelly spent but two years in America, 1884–86, during which he served as secretary and chancellor to Bishop Rademacher, then bishop of Nashville. During his student years, and after his ordination, he made a specialty of Scripture and Biblical exegesis, supplementing his studies in Rome by a year's study in the Holy Land. He remained in the American College as one of the faculty for several years, becoming its spiritual director in 1883. He is recognized as an authority on the topography of Palestine and on Biblical interpretation. He is an archæologist of note and one of the best informed men on the art and architecture of later pagan and early Christian times. Upon the death of Bishop Horstmann in 1908 Dr. Farrelly was appointed his successor and was consecrated bishop of Cleveland May 1, 1909. Cleveland is the diocese in the northern section of Ohio, covering thirty-six counties in an area of 8,034 square miles. It has a Catholic population of about 400,000, 380 priests, 286 churches, 165 schools with 48,000 pupils.

FLAGLER, Henry Morrison, financier, was born at Hopewell, N. Y., Jan. 2, 1830. His father, of old Dutch and Yankee stock, was a Presbyterian pioneer missionary preacher, one of the men who put the stamp of God upon the middle West. Laboring for a salary of $300 or $400 a year, he had no means with which to send his child to school and college. When the boy was fourteen years old, after a journey on the Erie canal to Buffalo, and a lake voyage from Buffalo to Sandusky, O., he finally arrived at Republic, O., and found employment in a general store at five dollars a month and "found." Those were years of great hardship, but he accumulated a little money, and before he was twenty-one he moved to Bellevue, O., where he established himself as a dealer in grain. John D. Rockefeller was a commission merchant in Cleveland at the time, and Mr. Flagler sent to him many carloads of wheat, which Rockefeller sold as Flagler's agent. Mr. Flagler also had an interest in a distillery, but gave it up because of conscientious scruples regarding the business. Having saved $50,000 in Bellevue, he went to Saginaw, Mich., where he engaged in the manufacture of salt, but he lost his fortune in this venture, and after three years was

about $40,000 in debt. From Saginaw he moved to Cleveland, O., and started a grain and produce commission business. In 1867, having borrowed money from a relative, he entered into partnership with John D. and William Rockefeller, Samuel Andrews and Stephen V. Harkness, who then owned several oil refineries. In 1870 the Standard Oil Co. was incorporated, with Mr. Flagler, who was responsible for its actual organization, as a member of the corporation, which was capitalized at $1,000,000. Mr. Flagler will be chiefly remembered for his pioneer development of the state of Florida. Visiting the state in 1883, he was quick to perceive the possibilities for a series of winter resorts. In 1885 he began the erection of the Ponce de Leon and Alcazar hotels at St. Augustine, which was the first step in a series of lavish expenditures for the development of tourist travel on the east coast of the state. The Ponce de Leon cost $2,000,000 and was said to be the finest hotel in the world. He also built the first railroad into St. Augustine. The hotels were both successful, and, finding his judgment correct, he acquired other hotels at Ormond and Daytona on the Halifax river, and extended his railroad to those points. Later he built the Royal Poinciana hotel at Palm Beach, and after that the Breakers and the Royal Palm in Miami, extending the railroad to accommodate the patrons. Thus was gradually built the Florida East Coast line, a trunk line extending nearly the full length of Florida, from Jacksonville to Miami, 366 miles, with various branches to the beaches and other winter resorts. In all, ten hotels served by 700 miles of railroad were the realization of Mr. Flagler's efforts to develop the state. He made the city of Miami an important railroad terminal by dredging the harbor, thus allowing a line of steamers to run between Miami and Key West and Nassau. In 1905 he began work on his Ocean railroad, which is an extension of his East Coast line across the Florida keys to Key West, a distance of 166 miles from Miami, and known as the "railroad over the sea." The first train was run to Key West on Jan. 22, 1912, after seven years' construction. The road spans the chain of islands between the mainland and Key West with a number of concrete bridges and arches, constituting some of the most remarkable engineering feats of the present age. The longest of these bridges, the Flagler viaduct, is seven miles in length, and is the longest bridge in the world. At some points the railroad crosses deep water, and huge drawbridges have been erected to accommodate shipping, while at other points a solid roadbed has been filled in by hydraulic dredges. The completion of the Ocean railroad, as it is called, enables tourists to be carried within six hours' sailing distance of Cuba. The Florida of to-day is a radically different commonwealth from the Florida in which Mr. Flagler first became interested. The transformation that has been effected in the 300 miles between St. Augustine and Miami has been the practical creation of a state out of a wilderness. In the more than a quarter of a century which he devoted to Florida he spent there nearly $50,000,000. He invested twelve millions in hotels, eighteen millions in the improvement of old railroads, more than a million in steamships, and the remainder in the Key West Extension. Mr. Flagler was a guiding spirit in the Standard Oil Co. for many years. With H. H. Rogers, William Rockefeller and John D. Archbold, he remained a vice-president until June, 1908, and it was not until the latter part of 1911 that he resigned his directorship. He was a director of the Chicago, Rock Island and Pacific railway, the Duluth and Iron Range railroad, the Western Union Telegraph Co., the Jacksonville, Tampa and Key West railway, The Cuba, and many other corporations. Mr. Flagler was a man of vigor, grasping the most abstruse problems and reducing them to a basis of simplicity. Many extremely discouraging difficulties were surmounted by his determination, self-reliance and indefatigable energy. Though not a politician, he was more powerful in the politics and legislation of Florida than any other man; he had justly earned that power, however, by all the common American standards of social value and integrity. In the annals of American history his name will be classed with those empire builders like Com. Vanderbilt, Collis P. Huntington, Frederick Meyerhaeuser, James J. Hill and others, who, by their genius and wonderful foresight, have built up the commonwealth and created vast fortunes for the countless thousands who are to follow and reap the benefit of their far-reaching activities. His private benefactions were very large, and almost always were made upon the condition that their source should remain unknown. He devoted much attention to philanthropic work, and endowed a number of hospitals in the state of Florida. His outlook upon life was very broad. He knew by experience the lessons of poverty and hard work, and used to say that his only schooling had been that of adversity. An unusual combination of strength and weakness, of boldness and modesty, of fearlessness and bashfulness, he was yet strong with the strength which is often unyielding, as was necessary to be the organizer of the greatest business of history. He was a born leader of men, a captain of industry, and endowed with one of the most constructive minds America has ever known. With sloth and indolence he had no patience, because, an indefatigable worker himself, he had no appreciation of idleness. He loved to overcome obstacles, and once they were conquered, he looked for still others to surmount. Methodical in all things, he was an economist of time, and proud of keeping his word. His ability to retain his subordinates was phenomenal; his men never left him. A wide reader, with an extensive knowledge of the Bible, he possessed a keen sense of humor, and a devotion that never wavered toward those who loved and trusted him. His voice was low and musical, and he was quiet, dignified and unobtrusive in manner. His matured career was nobly creditable to himself and America. He was a man who could do things of permanent significance to state and commonwealth, and of all the monuments to his memory erected by his life and labors, he valued most the love and gratitude that he won from the people of Florida and kept to the end. He was married Nov. 9, 1853, to Mary Harkness, daughter of Dr. Lamon G. and Julia (Follett) Harkness, of Bellevue, O., who bore him two daughters, Jennie Louise and Carrie Harkness, and one son, Harry Harkness Flagler. The two daughters are deceased, and Mrs. Flagler died May 18, 1881. He was married the second time June 5, 1883, to Ida A. Shourds; and, third, Aug. 24, 1901, to Mary Lily, daughter of William R. and Mary (Hargrave) Kenan, of Wilmington, N. C. Mr. Flagler died at West Palm Beach, Fla., May 20, 1913.

WIDENER, Peter Arrell Brown, financier and philanthropist, was born in Philadelphia, Pa., Nov. 13, 1834, the son of John and Sarah (Fulmer) Widener. The quest for religious freedom led the first American Wideners to join the Penn colony in 1740, and since then the family has been prominently identified with the history of Pennsylvania, and especially of Philadelphia, while offshoots of it are found in New Jersey, New York and Canada. Peter A. B. Widener received his education at the public schools of Philadelphia, and during those years spent his spare time in a printing office, indulging a taste for letters which never deserted him. Beginning business as his brother's butcher boy, he saved enough to start a meat market of his own, and soon afterward organized a chain of meat stores, one of the first in the country. He took an active interest in local politics and for some twenty years was identified with the important political movements of the city. He held the office of city treasurer in 1873–74. About 1862, in association with his friend, William L. Elkins (q. v.), he became interested in street railways, and in 1864 he abandoned his other enterprises to devote himself entirely to the promotion of transit projects in Philadelphia and other cities. His activities in Philadelphia were specially important and comprehensive, and he is in effect the father of the present Philadelphia street railway system. Widener and Elkins bought gradually into the street car lines of Philadelphia until eventually they gained control of all the public transportation lines in that city. These they improved by abolishing the horse-drawn cars and introducing the first cable system and subsequently electricity. They then extended their operations to Chicago, where they finally bought out the Yerkes street railway lines. In the meantime they had been joined by Thomas Dolan, and in 1886 they came into the traction situation in New York city, where they became associated with Thomas F. Ryan, William C. Whitney and Anthony N. Brady. This group acquired control of the old Metropolitan Traction Co., later known as the Metropolitan Street Railway Co., which by 1893 had taken to itself a network of unrelated lines of the city. After the merger of the Metropolitan with the Interborough Rapid Transit Co., Widener withdrew from the New York transit situation. Over a period of thirty years, working separately or together, the Widener-Elkins syndicate entered city after city, state after state, acquiring street railways, gas and electric lighting companies and developing them on an enormous scale. Besides their share in the transit development of Philadelphia, New York and Chicago, they also built up the street railway systems of Pittsburgh and other cities and towns in the states of Pennsylvania, Massachusetts, Ohio, Indiana. They carried their activities into the gas and electric lighting business of Philadelphia, Reading, Harrisburg, Concord, Atlanta, Savannah, Vicksburg, St. Augustine, Minneapolis, Omaha, Des Moines, Kansas City and elsewhere until the united capitalization of the street railways and other public utility corporations they controlled amounted to $1,500,000,000. In addition to these enterprises, Widener took part in the organization of the United States Steel Corporation, the International Mercantile Marine Co., and the American Tobacco Co. He owned a controlling interest in the Jarden Brick Co. of Philadelphia and was a director of the United Gas Improvement Co. of Philadelphia, the New Jersey Central, Philadelphia and Reading, and Lehigh Valley railroads, besides a number of other corporations. Gradually, during the last years of his life, he turned his large traction interests over to his son, George D. Widener, and devoted himself more and more to the gratification of his love for art and literature and to the many philanthropic activities which formed not the least part of his valuable service to the city of Philadelphia. His art gallery was one of the finest private collections in the country, both in size and in selection. Among its most notable treasures were Raphael's "Madonna and Child," three Cattanso Van Dycks and Rembrandt's "The Mill," important examples of El Greco, Velasquez, Murillo, Titian, Del Sarto, Albrecht Durer, Rubens, Paul Veronese, Jan Steen, Van der Meer, Hobdema, Cuyp, Adriæn Van de Velde, Isaak Van Ostade, Paul Potter, Pieter de Hooghe, Frans Hals, Watteau, Corot, Troyon, Diaz, Dupre, Courbet, Maris, Puvis de Chavannes, Hogarth, Romney, Gainsborough, Sir Joshua Reynolds, Hoppner, Turner, Constable and Whistler. In addition, the Widener galleries contained a large amount of rare tapestries, old furniture, bronzes, statuary and china ware. The Widener collection of Chinese porcelains was rated as one of the finest in the world. He was, besides, a generous and discriminating patron of artists, many of them, by material as well as moral encouragement, he helped from obscurity to success. His benefactions were very extensive, and most of them were made in memory of his wife. As a memorial to her he gave to the city of Philadelphia his town house at the corner of Broad street and Girard avenue for the Josephine Widener Branch of the Free Library. Her influence, too, was the inspiration of the Widener Home for Crippled Children, which he built and endowed at a cost of $2,000,000. This is one of the most valuable single charities in the country. The home covers thirty-six acres and includes medical and operating wards, lecture halls, winter and summer playgrounds, workshops, etc. The inmates are instructed in such light work as typewriting, stenography, serving and the construction of small tools and instruments. Many other substantial public gifts came from his ready hand, and his private benefactions were beyond count. He was a fine exemplar of a type which is peculiarly American— the private citizen of wealth who takes upon his shoulders many tasks which are undertaken by governments or municipalities in other countries. P. A. B. Widener was a member of the Philadelphia board of education during 1867–70, city and county treasurer during 1870–77 and park commissioner during 1890–95. He was decorated by the Kaiser of Germany with the order of the Red Eagle in 1902. He was married, Aug. 18, 1858, to H. Josephine Dunton, and had three children: Harry Kern, George D. and Joseph Early. He died at Elkins Park, Pa., Nov. 6, 1915.

WIDENER, George Dunton, financier, was born in Philadelphia, Pa., June 16, 1861, son of P. A. B. and Josephine (Dunton) Widener. He was educated in private schools of Philadelphia and began his business career in a grocery store in that city. Later he entered the office of his father, and thus had the opportunity of studying large transit problems at first hand. He was soon recognized throughout the country as a traction expert and it was not long before the management of his father's interests was placed almost entirely in his hands. The ability with which he managed the business is an important part of the history of the Philadelphia street railway system. Like his father, he was of the constructive type, a builder rather than a financier. He supervised and largely worked out the details of the change in the street railway system from horses to cable propulsion and again to electric power, and in each case the change was accomplished with remarkable speed and little inconvenience to the

public. He was not only a good business man with a thorough knowledge of his business, but he was also imbued with a conscientious feeling of his obligations toward the public he served. At the time of his death he was president and director of the Philadelphia Traction Co., the Catherine and Bambridge Street Railway Co., the Continental Passenger railway, the Fairmount Park Passenger railway, the Huntingdon Street Connecting railway, the Park Avenue and Carlisle Street railway, the Ridge Avenue Passenger railway, the Seventeenth and Nineteenth Streets railway, the Tioga and Venengo Streets Passenger railway, the Twenty-second street and Allegheny Avenue railway, the Union Passenger railway, the Walnut Street Connecting railway, the West Philadelphia Passenger railway, and the Doylestown and Willow Grove Turnpike Co. At one time he was vice-president of the company controlling the "L" and subway system, but resigned from the directorate upon the entrance of E. T. Stotesbury, though he still retained his holdings in the company. Besides his traction connections he was director of the Land Title and Trust Co., the Electric Storage Battery Co., the Jarden Brick Co. and the Vulcanite and Portland Cement Co., and was president of the company that built the Ritz-Carlton hotel in Philadelphia. He was interested in a number of philanthropies, but especially in the Widener Memorial Home, founded by his father, and he superintended its building and organization. The institution was not to him a mere vehicle for the charitable disposition of surplus wealth; it was rather an opportunity for exercising the great generosity and tenderness which were such conspicuous qualities of his splendid character. A director of the Philadelphia Academy of Fine Arts, he was a connoisseur of art and a discriminating collector of old books, and he left behind him valuable collections of both pictures and books. He was a member of the Union League, Philadelphia Country, Rose Tree Hunt, Art, Racquet, Huntingdon Valley, Corinthian Yacht and Germantown Cricket clubs. He was married in 1883 to Eleanor, daughter of William L. Elkins, Philadelphia, and had three children: Eleanor, George D., Jr., and Harry Elkins Widener. He and his son Harry were lost on the Titanic, which collided with an iceberg while returning from Europe, and sank with most of her passengers on April 15, 1912.

WIDENER, Harry Elkins, bibliophile, was born in Philadelphia, Pa., Jan. 3, 1885, son of George D. and Eleanor (Elkins) Widener. He was graduated at Harvard University in 1907 and subsequently became identified with the business interests of his father and grandfather. Like them he also engaged actively in philanthropic work. A natural taste for literature was the chief factor in his extraordinary success as a book collector. He was an intense student of books, and he pursued his quest for rare books with persistence and diligence. He was fortunate in securing the scholarly co-operation of Dr. A. S. W. Rosenbach, of Philadelphia, and Mr. Bernard Quaritch, of London, and his enthusiasm and winning personality gained him such friendly assistance from book-dealers and collectors as money alone could never purchase. In his will he made provisions for the transfer of his collection in toto to Harvard University and after his untimely death his mother erected the Cambridge building specially to contain them. The Widener books are primarily a library of English literature, including first editions of Shakespeare, Milton, Spencer,

Johnson, Goldsmith, Gray, Keats, Shelley, Dickens, Thackeray and Meredith, and a unique collection of books by and about Stevenson. Among the choice items of the collection are a copy of Sidney's "Arcadia," originally owned by the author's sister, the Countess of Pembroke; presentation copies of "David Copperfield," "Martin Chuzzlewit" and "Oliver Twist"; a dedication copy to Macready of "Nicholas Nickelby"; a presentation copy of "Ingoldsby Legends," to E. R. Moran, with a verse in Barham's autograph; a presentation copy of Boswell's "Life of Johnson"; the "Anatomy of Melancholy," in the original binding; the Shakespeare folios; Thackeray's copy of "Poems of Cowper"; an inscribed copy of "Romola"; and a presentation copy of Butler's "Hudibras." There is also a notable collection of drawings by William Blake, George and Robert Cruikshank, Thomas Rowlandson and Aubrey Beardsley. The Cruikshank drawings include illustrations of "Oliver Twist," on which Cruikshank based his claim that it was he who had supplied the ideas which Dickens elaborated in the novel. There are about 150 Rowlandson water-color drawings, an interesting volume of unpublished sketches by Aubrey Beardsley. Altogether the collection is perhaps the most fascinating of its kind to be found in America. Mr. Widener was with his father on the fatal voyage of the Titanic, which sank in mid-Atlantic Apr. 15, 1912.

ALEY, Robert Judson, mathematician and fifth president of the University of Maine, was born near Coal City, Ind., May 11, 1863, the son of Jesse Jackson and Paulina (Moyer) Aley, and grandson of Solomon Aley, who was born on the high seas when his parents were on their way to America in 1800. He was brought up on his father's farm, and received his early education in the country school. He began teaching shortly after he was fourteen years old and finished his first term of five months before he was fifteen. For two summers he attended a select school in Patricksburg, Ind., taught by Robert Spear. The summers of 1879–82 were spent in the Northern Indiana Normal School, now Valparaiso University, while he taught district schools in his native township during the winters. In 1882 he became principal of the Spencer (Ind.) High School and held that position five years, excepting the year (1885) when he took a special course in Indiana University. In the fall of 1887 he returned to Indiana University as instructor in the department of mathematics and was graduated in 1888, being the first graduate with mathematics as a major. He was professor of mathematics in Vincennes University during 1889–91, and at his alma mater from 1891–1910. The year 1894–95 was spent on leave of absence at Stanford University as acting associate professor of mathematics, and the year 1896–97 as Harrison fellow at the University of Pennsylvania, where he received the degree of Ph.D., his thesis being, "Some Contributions to the Geometry of the Triangle." Prof. Aley was married Aug. 28, 1884, to Nellie, daughter of J. W. Archer, of Spencer, Ind., and has one son, Max Aley. He has always taken an active interest in the educational affairs of his state, having been a member of the State Teachers' Association for over twenty five years, a member of the National Educational Association, and of the National Council of Education. He was president of the Southern Indiana Teachers Association in 1908, and of the Indiana State Teachers Association in 1909. He was for a number of years the editor of

the "Educator Journal," the leading educational journal of the state. In 1906 he was the Democratic nominee for superintendent of public instruction, but was defeated. Two years later he was elected, and served in this position from March 15, 1909, to Nov. 12, 1910, when he resigned to become president of the University of Maine. He is a fellow of the Indiana Academy of Science, and the American Association for the Advancement of Science, a member of the American Mathematical Society, the London Mathematical Society, the Edinburgh Mathematical Society, the English Mathematical Association, and der Deutsche Mathematiche Vereiniegung. He is a member of the societies of Sigma Xi, Phi Kappa Phi, and Phi Beta Kappa; a Knights Templar and a Scottish Rite Mason. While he was connected with the University of Indiana he taught a Sunday-school class of about 150 young men and women, and during his official residence in Indianapolis he was teacher of the Mens' Bible Class of the Third Christian Church. He writes much for the educational press of the country, and is the author of numerous mathematical pamphlets, and joint author with O. L. Kelso of an arithmetic, and with D. A. Rothrock of a high school algebra.

O'GORMAN, James Aloysius, U. S. senator, was born in New York city, May 5, 1860, son of Thomas and Ellen (Callan) O'Gorman, both natives of Ireland. After attending the public schools and the College of the City of New York, he was graduated at the law department of New York University in 1882. In that year he was admitted to the bar of New York and began the practice of his profession in New York city. In 1911, after his retirement from the bench, he became the senior partner of the firm of O'Gorman, Battle & Marshall, his associates being George Gordon Battle and H. Snowden Marshall. On the appointment of the latter as U. S. district attorney of the southern district of New York in 1913 the firm name was changed to O'Gorman, Battle & Vandiver. Early in his career he took an active interest in politics and identified himself with the Democratic party, in which he was an energetic worker and campaigner. He was prominent in the Anti-Monopoly League in the early eighties, and in 1887 was nominated by the United Labor party as judge of the district court of the city of New York, but was defeated. Six years later he received the Democratic nomination as district court judge and was elected for the term of six years. When his term expired in 1899 he was elected justice of the supreme court of the state of New York for a term of fourteen years. As a testimonial to the esteem in which he was held by his professional brethren of all parties, it may be mentioned that his candidacy was supported by the entire Bar Association. His record as a judge is without blemish, and while holding that office he neither made a speech, wrote a political letter nor participated in a campaign, convention or even a conference. In his service of eighteen years on the bench Judge O'Gorman tried many important cases. In January, 1911, he reluctantly declined a unanimous request from the judges of the court of appeals to accept an assignment on that bench. In the same year a contest occurred in the New York legislature over the election of a successor to Senator Depew in the U. S. senate, which resulted in a deadlock lasting over two and a half months. Technically, it was a fight between the regular and independent Democrats, and it was broken only when Judge O'Gorman's name was presented without solicitation or candidacy on his part. He was elected on the sixty-fourth ballot and took his seat in the senate on March 31, 1911. He resigned from the supreme court on the same day. "The state of New York," said Gov. John A. Dix, on hearing the result, "has elected for its representative in the Federal senate an eminent jurist, a man of pronounced ability, of great attainments and of the highest character. He will rank with the ablest statesmen the senate has known, will well represent the Empire State and bestow honor upon the party that elected him." Since entering the upper house of the national congress Sen. O'Gorman has fully justified this prophecy. He has been a member of various important committees, such as the committees on rules, judiciary and foreign relations. He is chairman of the committee on inter-oceanic canals, charged especially with legislation affecting the control and regulation of the Panama canal. When he was elected he announced himself in favor of the election of U. S. senators by popular vote and the passage of a constitutional amendment providing for a Federal income tax "free from mischievous interference with the governmental instrumentalities of the several states." He expressed his belief in the urgent need of an immediate reduction of tariff rates, advocated the establishment of the parcels post and heartily approved a reciprocity treaty with Canada. As a leader of the liberal wing of his party, Sen. O'Gorman has strengthened his former enviable reputation for character and ability, and has become a tremendous force in the rehabilitation of the Democratic party. He was an early advocate of the nomination of Woodrow Wilson for the presidency, and was one of the few delegates from New York who supported Mr. Wilson in the Baltimore convention. He has advocated many important measures, among them the following: to increase the efficiency of diplomatic and consular service; to establish a parcels post (included in the bill to reduce postal rates, improve postal service and increase postal revenue); to promote safety of passengers and others upon railroads by compelling common carriers engaged in interstate commerce to use cars constructed of steel; to acquire a site for the Federal court house in New York; to establish a fish cultural station on Long Island; to issue medals to the survivors of the battle of Gettysburg, and to pay specified war claims. He has also been interested in the question of securing a replica of John Q. A. Ward's statue of Washington, to be erected in the national capital. The original is in front of the U. S. Sub Treasury building in New York city. He was a member of the senate committee on banking and currency that framed the new national banking law. Sen. O'Gorman was active in securing the free toll provision of the Panama Canal act during Pres. Taft's administration and vigorously opposed Pres. Wilson's recommendation to repeal this provision in 1914. He, with six other Democrats, in 1915 prevented the passage of the so-called Ship Purchase bill, which empowered the government to engage in the purchase and operation of ships in foreign trade. It was claimed that this legislation, strongly urged by the administration, would enable the government to purchase the ships of belligerent nations then interned in American ports, and grave fears were entertained that our country would thereby become involved in serious foreign complications. In March, 1915, Col. Harvey, in the "North American Review," in his appeal to the people of Great Britain, declared that this bill "was defeated through the exertions of Sen. James A. O'Gorman, a Tammany Democrat and the foremost statesman

of Irish extraction now in American public life." During his long public career Sen. O'Gorman has become widely known as a distinguished public speaker, and he has written much that is scholarly, philosophical in tone and of exceptional weight and interest. A member of the Catholic church, he occupies a high place in the laity, and is a personal friend of Cardinal Gibbons. He is a member of the National Democratic, Manhattan, Lawyers', Catholic, New York Athletic and Oakland Golf clubs of New York, and the Army and Navy, Chevy Chase and Columbia Country clubs of Washington, D. C. In 1903 he was elected grand sachem of the Columbian Order or Society of Tammany and held the office until 1905. The Columbian Order is a patriotic society sometimes confounded with the well-known political organization. An excellent portrait of him in his robes as a judge was painted by Benziger in 1910. He was married in New York, Jan. 2, 1884, to Anne M., daughter of William H. Leslie, of Westchester, N. Y., and has seven children: Mary, wife of Hon. Dudley Field Malone, collector of the port of New York; Ellen, wife of W. Lee Duffy; Dolorita, wife of John A. Maher; Alice, Anna, Agnes and James A. O'Gorman, Jr.

GOODNOW, Frank Johnson, third president of Johns Hopkins University (1914——), was born in Brooklyn, N. Y., Jan. 18, 1859, son of Abel F. and Jane M. (Root) Goodnow, and a descendant of Thomas Goodnow, who came from Shasbury, England, in 1638, and settled in Massachusetts. His father was a successful manufacturer near Worcester, Mass., and after his retirement from business settled in Brooklyn, N. Y., where he was identified with the development of the Brooklyn Institute of Arts and Sciences. He was educated in private schools in Brooklyn, and was graduated at Amherst College in 1879. After a year in a broker's office in New York, he entered the law school of Columbia University, where he was graduated in 1882. Subsequently he spent some time in the law office of Judge Dillon, in New York, and studied for a year at the Ecole Libre des Sciences Politiques, Paris, and at the University of Berlin. In 1883 he became instructor in history and lecturer on the administrative law of the United States, at Columbia University. He was adjunct professor of the same during 1887–91, professor of administrative law during 1891–1903, Eaton professor of administrative law and political science in 1903, and acting dean of political science in 1906–07. In addition to his work at the university, Dr. Goodnow held many important outside appointments. For several years he was interested, through the City Club of New York, in drafting and proposing new legislation for the improvement of the condition of the poor, for overcoming congestion of population and for child welfare. Gov. Roosevelt appointed him a member of the New York Charter Revision Committee, and he went to England in 1906 as a member of the National Civic Federation to report on the question of municipal ownership of public utilities. In 1910 he was a representative of the U. S. government to the convention on administrative science, held at the Brussels Exposition. He was a member of Pres. Taft's Economy and Efficiency Commission in 1911–12, and made an exhaustive investigation of certain of the government departments for the purpose of instituting modern business methods. His reputation as an authority on government administration led to his appointment, in 1913, as expert legal advisor to the republic of China for a term of three years and, at the request of Yuan Shih Kai, he aided in drafting the new

James A. O'Gorman

Chinese Constitution. He resigned after a year to accept the presidency of Johns Hopkins University. At that time Prof. Munroe Smith wrote of him in the "Independent": "Mr. Goodnow has been and is primarily a teacher and writer. Although he has only just completed his fifty-fifth year, he has for thirty years taught American and European public law in Columbia University and has trained many students to research in these fields. Not a few of these hold chairs in American colleges and universities. . . . He has published a number of books on municipal, state, and national administration. Several of these broke new ground —new at least to Anglo-American lawyers—and in some of them Mr. Goodnow went back of the law to study the political and social factors by which law is moulded. . . . Practical experience has been gained in many fields. . . . In his special field of study he has supplemented his reading by observation in extended service in governmental commissions. . . . He works easily. . . . His mind goes quickly to the core of a problem, and his tentative conclusions are usually corroborated by more deliberate consideration. In forming his judgments he is exceptionally independent of prevailing currents of opinion; in stating them he is fearless but not aggressive. In his special field of politics he has always distrusted theories and principles: to quote a favorite phrase of his, he always wishes to 'get down to brass tacks.' . . . At Columbia he has always approached educational problems in the same spirit. . . . His personal qualities have won him many friends. No Columbia professor is more generally liked or more highly esteemed by his colleagues, and his withdrawal from Columbia has aroused keen regret." Dr. Goodnow is the author of "Comparative Administrative Law" (1893); "Municipal Home Rule" (1895); "Municipal Problems" (1897); "Politics and Administration" (1900); "City Government in the United States" (1904); "Principles of the Administrative Law of the United States" (1905); and editor of "Selected Cases on the Law of Taxation" (1905); "Selected Cases on Government and Administration" (1906); "Selected Cases on the Law of Officers" (1906); "Municipal Government" (1910); and "Social Reform and the Constitution" (1911). He was the first president of the American Political Science Association, and he is a member of the American Economic Association, the Association of the Bar of the City of New York, the Cosmos Club of Washington, D. C., the Peking Club of Peking, the Century, University and City clubs of New York, the Maryland and Baltimore clubs of Baltimore. The degree of LL.D. was conferred upon him by Amherst in 1897, Columbia in 1904, Harvard in 1909, and Brown in 1914. He was married in Brooklyn, N. Y., June 2, 1886, to Elizabeth, daughter of David C. Lyall, and has three children: David, Isabel, wife of E. Kendall Gillett, of New York, and Lois, wife of J. V. MacMurray.

HUNTINGTON, Collis Potter, railroad builder, was born at Harwinton, Conn., Oct. 28, 1821, son of William and Elizabeth (Vincent) Huntington. His father was a farmer, energetic, hard-working, and as financially comfortable as the average New England farmer at that time. At the age of fourteen the son left school, and after working on a farm for two years went to New York, determined to branch out for himself in a broader field. He had a strong instinct for business. His first venture, a deal in watch findings, was very successful, after which he traveled in the South collecting a number of notes which had been given to New York clock dealers for goods, and which he had purchased at a heavy discount. At the age of twenty-one he formed a partnership with his brother, Solon Huntington, in general merchandising at Oneonta, N. Y. He had a perfect craving for work, and no amount of it seemed to present any difficulties to him. He was beginning to chafe under the monotonous life of a country storekeeper when gold was discovered in California, and a number of parties from Oneonta left for the new Eldorado. Shrewd and far-sighted beyond his years, he realized that the thousands of gold-seekers would require many articles that were not made in California, and, moreover, that they would pay well for them. He had the peculiar faculty of calculating the possibilities of a business proposition to a nicety, and reducing the percentage of chance to a minimum, and he believed that he could gain wealth more rapidly by selling goods to miners than by digging gold from the mines. In October, 1848, he made a shipment of goods to California, and in March of the following year went out himself with $1,200 in cash. Incidentally, while waiting on the Isthmus of Panama for a vessel to take him up the Pacific, he added $4,000 to his capital by buying and selling goods across the isthmus. Settling in Sacramento, Cal., he soon became one of the most successful traders on the coast, dealing chiefly in hardware, but overlooking nothing in which he saw a likelihood of profit. In 1854 he formed a partnership with Mark Hopkins, which lasted until the latter's death. Never were two men better fitted for such a union. Hopkins was the office-man and Huntington the buyer and dictator of the firm's policy. They did an enormous business and had few losses, becoming wealthy men as wealth was rated in those days. In 1861 he became interested in the question of a transcontinental railway, a project which owes its accomplishment to him more than to any other one man. To whom the honor of first proposing a transcontinental road belongs can hardly be stated reliably. Smalley, in his history of the Northern Pacific Railroad, claims that Dr. Samuel Bancroft, of Granville, Mass., advocated one as early as 1834, recommending its construction by direct appropriations from the U. S. treasury. In 1836 John Plumme, a Welshman by birth and a civil engineer by profession, called the first public meeting at Dubuque, Ia., to agitate the subject. In 1837 Dr. Hartley Carver published in the New York "Courier and Inquirer" an article advocating such a construction. But the first to formulate a practicable scheme was Asa Whitney, who between 1844 and 1850 agitated the question in addresses to legislatures and public meetings, his proposition being to construct from Prairie du Chien on the Mississippi across the Rocky Mountains by way of South Pass to a terminus on the Columbia river at Vancouver, with a branch to San Francisco, the point being to make a route for Asiatic commerce to Europe through the United States. So many propositions were made to legislatures in the next twenty years that they defeated their own purpose. In 1851 Sen. W. M. Gwin introduced a bill, and in 1852 Sen. Douglas introduced another. In the latter year the California legislature passed an act granting a right of way through the state and the next year congress appropriated $150,000 for the expense of surveying parties to be sent out by the war department. In 1854 it made two more of $40,000 and $150,000, respectively, and three more parties were sent out. Both the Republican and Democratic conventions in their platforms pledged aid in appropriate legislation. Prior to 1860 the legislatures of eighteen states had passed resolutions to similar effect. In California it only needed an enthusiast to bring the question to a head and he appeared in the person of Theodore Judah, an engineer who was dubbed "Pacific Railroad Crazy." One day he startled the people of Sacramento by announcing that he had found a long and easy ascent of the Sierra Nevada Mountains by way of Dutch Flat which was practicable for a railroad. He called public meetings, arousing great enthusiasm, and at one of them in Sacramento Huntington was present. Arranging for an interview with Judah, Huntington agreed to secure six men who would pledge themselves to pay the expense of a thorough survey across the mountains, which Judah then estimated would cost about $35,000. This may be said to be the real inception of the Central Pacific Railroad. The seven men were Huntington and his partner Hopkins, Leland Stanford, Theodore Judah, L. A. Booth, Charles Marsh and James Bailey. They caused five preliminary surveys to be made and at last settled upon the Dutch Flat or Donner Lake route. On June 8, 1861, they organized the Central Pacific Railroad Company of California, with a nominal capital of $8,000,000, to construct a railroad from Sacramento to the eastern boundary of the state. These organizers were Huntington, Stanford, Hopkins, Charles Crocker, and James Bailey, E. B. Crocker coming in later. They went to Nevada and obtained consent to cross the deserts. Huntington then went to Washington to interest the authorities in the project, and on July 1, 1862, congress passed an enabling act which embodied a contract by which the Central Pacific railway undertook to construct a road and telegraph line from the Pacific coast to the eastern boundary of California, and also permission to continue building eastward until it should meet the tracks of the Union Pacific Co., which by the same act was given permission to continue building from the east westward. The Union Pacific declined to accept the act of 1862, because its terms were not inviting enough, but the Central Pacific formally accepted the act in the following October, feeling that it was obliged to do so because its projectors had made many preliminary surveys, had completed the organization of a California corporation, put in large sums of money and secured aid from the state and other sources, and it felt bound to accept this act of congress or abandon the scheme entirely. But there were some conditions of the first enabling act that proved so unsatisfactory that Huntington went to Washington in 1864 and secured by another act of congress a modification of the terms. The modified terms were as follows: The United States agreed to donate every alternate section of public land designated by odd numbers to the amount of ten sections per mile on each side of the road within ten miles of each side of the road not sold, reserved or otherwise disposed of, the title of said land to be vested in the company when it should have completed twenty consecutive miles; that on completion of each twenty miles the secretary of the treasury should issue to the company United States bonds payable thirty years after date at 6 per cent. interest to the amount of sixteen bonds per mile, and from the western base of the Sierra Nevadas the bonds should be $48,000 per mile for 150 miles eastwardly, and between the mountainous sections at the rate of $32,000 per mile. The Central Pacific was to complete fifty miles within two years and twenty miles each year thereafter. The capital stock of the company could be increased to $100,000,000. The grants of lands and bonds were made upon condition that the company should pay the bonds at maturity, but it had authority to issue first mortgage bonds of its own; the company should keep its line in repair, at all times transmit despatches, transport mails, troops and munitions of war, supplies and public stores for the government whenever required to do so; the government to have the preference in the use of the road at a fair and reasonable rate of compensation, said compensation for such services to be applied to the payment of the bonds and interest until the whole amount should be fully paid, and after the railroad was completed at least five per cent. of the net earnings should be annually applied in payment thereof. On Jan. 8, 1863, the first shovelful of earth was turned at Sacramento. The company labored under great disadvantages in procuring supplies, which were not shared by the Union Pacific. The former was obliged to ship such supplies by water and to pay enormous war risks of insurance, while the latter obtained its supplies overland in much quicker time and at less expense. But the dynamic energy and relentless determination of Huntington, who was the master mind of the men back of the enterprise, overcame all obstacles. Once across the state line the race between the Central Pacific and the Union Pacific became a heart-breaking, nerve-racking struggle. Nothing just like it has ever been known in the whole history of railroad building. On the last day it is said that rails were laid on more than ten miles of track. It was the aim of the company to reach Ogden, Utah, before its rival and so get a terminal of commercial importance, but it was some fifty miles short of it when the Union Pacific got there. Each company kept on building and paralleling each other, until finally Pres. Lincoln fixed the point of junction five miles west of Ogden, and the Central, abandoning its parallel grade, purchased 47½ miles of the Union's line. The ceremony of joining the tracks, which has been so often described in prose and poetry, took place May 10, 1869, at Promontory. In 1870 there began to be discussed the question of a railroad through the southern states to California. Col. Thomas A. Scott, president of the Pennsylvania railroad, wanted government aid to enable him to build his Texas Pacific into California, and in 1871 congress passed an act subsidizing a road to be built on the southern line. Mr. Huntington went to Washington as the representative of his associates in opposition to this bill. It was realized that if the Pennsylvania Co. should get a road to California the value of the Central Pacific as a carrier would be vitally lessened. The Central Pacific officials had by this time acquired by purchase and consolidation the Western Pacific, the San Francisco, Oakland and Alameda, and the San Joaquin Valley roads, and had already begun building a line down towards Yuma. They now bent their energies to extending to Los Angeles; they reached and passed Ft. Yuma, and pushed across the territories of Arizona and New Mexico under three separate corporations, the Southern Pacific Railroad Co. of California, Arizona and New Mexico respectively. In Washington Huntington obtained aid from congress similar to that granted to the Central Pacific. The Texas Pacific was met at El Paso, and connection between the two lines was made in 1883. By the acquisition of several short lines in Texas and more construction the way was cleared into New Orleans by the purchase of Morgan's Louisiana and Texas railroad, a purchase which carried with it the Morgan Line of steamboats from New Orleans and Galveston to New York. Having reached

New Orleans, Huntington, still too vigorous and ambitious to be satisfied, proposed to his associates that they go still further and continue building right through to the Atlantic coast; but they had had enough of the long-continued strain and they called a halt at New Orleans. Huntington, however, kept on. In New York, he had been seriously figuring on a subway for New York city; but the Chesapeake and Ohio Railway, the attempt to build which had ruined a number of contractors, was offered to him and he finally took hold of the proposition. That completed, he added to his conquests other roads in Kentucky and Tennessee and finally, with the building of the Louisville, New Orleans and Texas R. R., between Memphis and New Orleans, he at last reached the summit of railroad enterprise in having a continuous line of track controlled by him, from the Atlantic to the Pacific, a feat which is still unparalleled in a country the most marvellous in the world for its achievements in railway construction. In 1884, the Southern Pacific Company of Kentucky was formed to take over the stock of the various roads which by purchase or consolidation had been absorbed into the control and ownership of the Central and Southern Pacific railroads, viz., the Central, the Southern, the California Pacific, California, and Oregon, Oregon and California, Mexican International, New York, Texas and Mexican, and many other feeders, the Pacific Mail S. S. Co., and the Occidental and Oriental S. S. Co. Huntington was the prime mover in all those operations. He was the biggest man of the Central Pacific quartet and became president, not only of the Central Pacific and Southern Pacific, but of most of the other companies as well. Huntington now controlled a continuous railroad from Portland, Ore., to Newport News, Va., with over 3,000 miles of ramifications and over 20,000 miles of continuous water routes. The crowning achievement of his career was the shipyard and dry dock at Newport News, Va. He practically built the town of Newport News as an Atlantic tide-water terminal to his great railroad system. There he built a shipyard with a water frontage of half a mile and a dry dock, 600 feet in length, capable of taking in the largest vessels then afloat. He not only made his shipyard the largest in America, but he also made it one of the best-equipped in the world. To the town of Newport News, he was a most valuable benefactor. He founded the city, he built it up, he held hundreds of thousands of dollars worth of property, exclusive of the shipyard, and he made it an important port, as well as the seat of a great industry. The domestic side of C. P. Huntington's character exhibits an interesting personality. He was twice married, his first wife having died in 1884. He had no children, but adopted a son and daughter—Archer M. Huntington of New York, and Clara Huntington, who married Prince Francis Hatzfeldt Wildenburg of Germany. While Mr. Huntington was counted by some who only knew him through the columns of the newspapers as an unyielding personality, a blunt, massive, unbreakable and perfectly efficient instrument of destiny, his intimates knew him as a most genial, good-humored and companionable man, absolutely without pretensions, simple and abstemious in his habits, unsoured by prejudice and exceedingly tolerant of the weaknesses of others, except in one particular—he had undisguised contempt for a man who could not or would not live within his income. That his nature was tinged with not a little tenderness for the weak and down-trodden is shown by his deep and substantial interest in the so-called inferior races—the negro and the Indian. He contributed liberally to institutions and organizations for their benefit and was one of the chief supporters of the Hampton (Va.) Normal and Industrial School for Negroes and Indians, as well as a giver of many thousands to the Tuskegee School. Though he spent largely for charity, particularly in the latter years of his life, he exercised a most careful judgment in his distribution, believing that the most useful help is generally not in money, but in furnishing the opportunity to earn it. Besides his mansion on "Nob Hill," San Francisco, and his residence in New York city, he had a beautiful country place at Throggs Neck, on Long Island Sound. He died at his camp on Raquette Lake, known as "Pine Knot Camp," Aug. 13, 1900.

HUNTINGTON, Henry Edwards, capitalist, was born at Oneonta, N. Y., Feb. 27, 1850, son of Solon and Harriet (Sanders) Huntington. His father was a successful merchant of Oneonta and for many years was in business there in partnership with his brother, Collis P. Huntington (q. v.). After a public school education he began his business career as a clerk in a hardware store in Oneonta, but later obtained a position with the hardware firm of Sargent & Co. in New York. At this time Collis P. Huntington, who in 1869 had with his three California associates achieved the tremendous feat of building the Central Pacific railroad across the continent and was the moving spirit in the organization of what was finally to become the great Southern Pacific system of railroads, was established in New York and had just acquired what was known as the Chesapeake and Ohio railroad in Virginia. Learning of a combination formed among certain dealers in lumber supplies to put up the price of railroad ties he promptly set to work to checkmate the move. Having perceived in his nephew the unmistakable traits of thrift, energy and economy, he sent him to St. Albans, W. Va., as manager of a sawmill which supplied railroad ties to new lines in process of construction. Young Huntington, untrained as he was, ran the mill so successfully that he reduced the price of ties to 28 cents, a particularly low price. Early in the seventies the elder Huntington sold the mill and discovered that his nephew was one of the buyers. Later he became the sole owner, and in three years retired from the business with the foundation of his fortune soundly laid. When in 1800 the building of the Chesapeake, Ohio and Southwestern railroad between Louisville and Memphis was under way the elder Huntington appointed his nephew superintendent of construction. In this new line of work, without previous experience, he also made a success and completed the work ahead of schedule time. One by one the elder Huntington had acquired various lines forming links and feeders in the great chain of railroads that was ultimately to reach from the Atlantic to the Pacific. Among these was the Kentucky Central, running from Covington, Ky., to Lexington. He offered to his nephew the post of vice-president and general manager, and told him to go ahead and run it his own way. The young man found the property burdened with a load of debt, with broken-down equipment, and less than 10 per cent. of the business to Lexington. He added more debt by overhauling the property thoroughly, putting in new equipment and making the roadbed safer. The road went into the hands of a receiver, who was H. E. Huntington himself, and in four years he not only had a surplus but was getting 90 per cent. of the business between Lexington and Cincinnati. It was during his connection with the Kentucky Central that he supervised the building of the railroad between Ashland, Ky., and Covington (known then as the Maysville and Big Sandy railroad), and the Ohio bridge between Covington and Cincinnati, and his reputation as a successful railroad builder became established. He displayed such unusual executive ability that C. P. Huntington decided to make his nephew his representative in the vast interests connected with and allied to the Southern Pacific system of railroads, which dominated the territory from Portland, Ore., south to Los Angeles and thence to New Orleans, as well as the great pioneer line from San Francisco to Ogden. The young man was made assistant to the president of the Southern Pacific Co., becoming in turn second vice-president and (in June, 1900,) first vice-president of the whole system. He was made president of the Southern Pacific railroads of Arizona and New Mexico and California, of the Carson and Colorado railroad in Nevada, of the South Pacific Coast railway and of the Market Street Cable Railway Co. of San Francisco. His uncle, C. P. Huntington died in August, 1900, leaving a vast estate, of which the widow and Henry E. Huntington were made residuary legatees. While Henry Huntington was the logical successor of his uncle as head of the Southern Pacific system this promotion failed to come to him for reasons quite human in their nature, and another great man, Edward H. Harriman (q. v.), became president. H. E. Huntington was, however, retained as vice-president and director. He was now free to realize his dream in a new line of constructive endeavor, viz., electric railroading, the exploitation of which was destined to make him the greatest electric railroad builder in the world. He had already acquired substantial holdings in the three street car lines of Los Angeles. After he had obtained control, the separate properties were unified under the name of the Los Angeles railway, their equipment and service were brought up to date and extensions were undertaken which in time gridironed the whole city. Lines were established over every available route to outlying districts within a radius of seventy miles. He also built lines to the beach resorts twenty and forty miles away and brought them up to the Huntington standard of efficiency, making altogether the largest interurban system in the world, comprising nearly 1,000 miles of double and quadruple tracks, and valued at approximately $100,000,000. In addition he secured the properties of the San Bernardino Valley Traction Co., the San Bernardino Interurban Co., the Redlands Central and the Riverside and Arlington, with their scores of miles of electrically-equipped lines throughout the "Orange Belt," with the intention of connecting them with his Los Angeles lines. Realizing that patronage alone could support such a network of suburban lines, he gave every impetus to the development of traffic, hand-in-hand with the extension of the tracks. To accomplish this he bought large areas of city property and tract after tract in terminal localities, as well as at promising way points. He constructed a nineteen-story office building in Los Angeles containing eleven acres of floor space; he built resorts by the sea and at conspicuous viewpoints in the mountains, laid out residence subdivisions, roads, parks and townsites; developed suburban cities, encouraging home-building and travel alike. Near the culmination of his great interurban traction plan his desire for the freedom of entire ownership again became dominant. In a position where he

owned half of the Pacific Electric and 55 per cent. of the city systems by exchanging in 1910 his holdings in the former to the Southern Pacific Co., he secured complete control of the more compact Los Angeles properties, and also retained his immense land holdings. These now comprise, besides many city properties, thousands of acres in the adjacent country with a total present value approximated at twenty millions and make him the largest owner of realty in southern California. Another enterprise of great magnitude undertaken by Mr. Huntington was the Pacific Light and Power Co. (now the Pacific Light and Power Corporation), which was organized for the manufacture and sale of electricity for light and power purposes in southern California. In the extent and value of its properties and in the volume of sales it ranks as one of the largest and most successful public utility corporations on the entire Pacific coast. Coincident with the growth of Los Angeles itself, whose population of 210,000 in 1905 has risen to 500,000, the Pacific Light and Power Corporation's earnings have expanded in the same period from approximately $1,000,000 to $2,750,000 per annum. The principal difficulty thus far has been to keep pace with the remarkable development of the territory served. With the plants operated at practically full capacity in 1911 additional facilities became imperative, and it was also desirable that the steam plants for generating power should be replaced with hydro-electric current, which was cheaper in the end than steam. Accordingly, in 1912 the company began the construction of a comprehensive power development at Big Creek in the mountains of Fresno county. The completion of what was called in 1914 the initial development is noteworthy because it involved unusual natural conditions, unusual engineering problems and an unusual commercial accomplishment. It is by far the largest high head development in this country and the most powerful impulse wheels ever built drive the largest electric generators of their type. The transmission line is the longest "express" line in existence and will operate at the highest voltage ever used commercially. It carries power 240 miles to Los Angeles. The work included the making of a reservoir 7,000 feet above the sea, the erection of three concrete dams, the construction of two power houses and a substation, the boring of five miles of tunnel through granite, the setting of over 3,000 steel towers over the mountains and across the desert and the stringing of 5,000,000 pounds of aluminum cable. In each power house are two main generators of 17,500 kilowatts capacity each and more are to be added as business necessities demand. Current is generated at 6,600 volts pressure and raised by the transformer to 150,000 volts for its long journey to Los Angeles. A summary of the company's work shows the importance of it. With its Big Creek and other plants it shows a horse-power capacity of 155,550; it has 938 miles of transmission lines and 1,876 miles of distributing lines. Seventy-eight per cent. of the power sold is used by the Los Angeles (operating 335 miles) and Pacific Electric (operating 868 miles) railway systems. Substantially all of the $23,591,500 capital stock is owned or controlled by Mr. Huntington, who also owns the entire $20,000,000 capital stock of the Los Angeles Railway Corporation. Not only did Mr. Huntington's personal fortune grow apace, but with his marriage to the widow and co-heir of his uncle the combined family wealth was enormously increased. In five corporations alone they own practically every share of stock. These are the Pacific Light and Power Corporation, the Los Angeles Railway Corporation, the Huntington Land and Improvement Co., the Safety Insulated Wire and Cable Co., of all of which Mr. Huntington is president, and the Newport News Shipbuilding and Drydock Co., in which he is chairman of the board of directors. This latter industry, created and developed by his uncle, has built and fitted out many of the fastest battleships and cruisers in the United States navy, besides constructing many vessels of the merchant marine. Mr. Huntington is a director of Alhambra Addition Water, City Railway Co. of Los Angeles (president), Covina City Water, Dolgeville Land, Donner Boom and Lumber, Hammond Lumber, Huntington Beach, Huntington Land and Improvement, Los Angeles Land, Los Angeles Railway Land, Los Angeles Railway (president), Oak Knoll, Pacific Light and Power (president), San Gabriel Wine and San Marino Land companies. He is also a director of the Chesapeake and Ohio Railway (executive committee), Equitable Trust Co., Chesapeake and Ohio, Northern Railway, Des Moines and Fort Dodge Railway, Hocking Valley Railway, Missouri, Kansas and Texas Railway, Newport News (Va.) Shipbuilding and Dry Dock, Newport News (Va.) Light and Water, Old Dominion (Va.) Land, National Surety (N. Y.), Southern Pacific, Wells Fargo & Co. Express and many other companies. Of clubs and societies he is a member of the following: Annandale Country (Cal.), California (Los Angeles), Chamber of Commerce (Los Angeles), Gamut (Los Angeles), Jonathan (Los Angeles), Los Angeles Country, Midwick Country (Los Angeles), Pasadena Country, Pasadena Polo, Pasadena Board of Trade, Pasadena Music and Art Association, Tournament of Roses Association (Pasadena), Southwest Museum (Los Angeles), Alhambra (Cal.) Board of Trade, Geographical Society (Los Angeles), Humane Association of the State of California. In New York: City Midday, Union League, Chamber of Commerce, Concordance Society, Economic, Grolier, Hobby, Lotus Magazine, Metropolitan, Museum of Peaceful Arts, New England, Oneonta (N. Y.), Sleepy Hollow Country and American Museum of Natural History; also Chamber of Commerce (Newport News), Bibliophile Society (Boston), Fairbanks Family in America, Huntington Family in America. Many years ago Mr. Huntington declared that he should retire from active work in 1910, but what he really did was to change his occupation and continue along a new line of activity. Nine miles northwest of Los Angeles on the apex of a bench that overlooks the beautiful San Gabriel Valley he began the building of a splendid mansion of reinforced cement. In its completed state it stands forth as about the last word in comfort and stately magnificence. There are between four and five hundred acres in the ranch property, with upwards of nine miles of well-made scenic drives upon it. Simple in its grandeur its interior is a marvel of artistic workmanship and its walls are graced with beautiful paintings and tapestries. The five famous Boucher tapestries, of historical distinction and undoubtedly the only perfect set in existence, are seen here. His library of rare editions is said to include the finest private collection of English literature and Americana in the whole world. It contains such prizes as the almost priceless original manuscript of Benjamin Franklin's biography; that rarest of law books, "The Bradford-New York"; the first laws of Massachusetts, the largest private collection (the only copy) and the first

collection of Washington manuscripts, and the laws of nearly all the states; the largest private Lincoln letters and manuscripts; the complete papers of the Dutch West India Co. and the most numerous and valuable aggregation of primers and almanacs ever collected. It also contains the famous Guttenberg Bible, the first book printed in color, for which he paid $50,000; the rare folios and quartos of Shakespeare, and innumerable other first editions from Homer down, altogether furnishing an inexhaustible source of delight to the bibliophile.

HUNTINGTON, Archer Milton, author and founder of The Hispanic Society of America, was born in New York city, Mar. 10, 1870, son of Collis P. Huntington. He was educated chiefly under private tutors. He studied and traveled in Spain for several years, imbibing the history and traditions of that once glorious land and making a collection of rare books, manuscripts and paintings, and of literary, artistic and archæological interest. He continued to add to his relics until it became the greatest collection of its kind possessed by any private individual in the world. In 1904 his library alone contained over 40,000 volumes, and deciding to place his collection at the disposal of the American public, he founded the Hispanic Society of America, with a liberal endowment of land and money. The deed of gift provides for the establishment in New York city of a free Spanish and Portuguese library, museum and educational institution, having for its object the study of the Spanish and Portuguese languages, literature and history, and the advancement of the study of countries wherein Spanish and Portuguese are or have been spoken languages. It aims to promote the public welfare by actively advancing learning and providing means for encouraging and carrying on the before-mentioned work within the state of New York, also by issuing publications from time to time, and by otherwise doing such things as may be necessary fully to accomplish its work. The building erected in Audubon Park in 1904 as a memorial to Collis P. Huntington contains the most valuable and interesting collection of Hispanic material ever brought together under one roof. There is a reference library of over fifty thousand books relating to Spain, Portugal and Latin-America, besides the chief periodicals of the Hispanic countries. The library contains about 170 Spanish and other incunabula, beginning with the works of Lambert Palmart, of Valencia, the earliest known printer in Spain; Latin and Hebrew manuscripts of great antiquity; first editions of all the notable Spanish authors; Vierge's illustrations of "Don Quixote," and a large collection of ancient maps, portolan charts, prints and fac-similes. The art collection includes "Portrait of the Duke of Olivares" and a "Portrait of a Little Girl," by Velasquez; paintings by Murillo, El Greco, Goya, Ribera, Morales, and modern painters, such as Sorolla, Zuloaga, Jiminez Aranda, Anglada, Madrazo, etc. It may be mentioned here that The Hispanic Society's exhibition of paintings by Sorolla and Zuloaga in 1910 was one of the most notable art exhibitions ever held in this country. The general collection includes wood carvings, silver and iron work, ivory plaques and objects of Phœnician origin, neolithic and Roman pottery, Roman mosaics and objects of domestic use from the Roman Italica, examples of Buen Retiro ware, Hispano-Moresque plaques, "Azulejos" or iridescent tiles, a general Spanish numismatic collection, ecclesiastical vestments and embroideries, and sculptured tombs illustrating the development of Gothic and Renaissance ecclesiastical sculpture. The museum is open free to the public every day in the year except Christmas and Thanksgiving. A special welcome and special assistance is given to students of the subjects to which the library is devoted and everything possible is done to encourage and promote new and original investigation of such subjects. While the society was founded and has its headquarters here, it is international in its membership and in the scope and character of its work. It issues an official organ, the ''Revue Hispanique,'' published quadrennially in Paris, and has also issued one hundred distinct publications. These include fac-similes of rare books, maps and documents in Spanish, Catalan, Portuguese, English, Dutch and Latin, and archæological and literary treatises. It has published editions of the books of Cervantes, Lope de Vega and Camoens. One of the most notable publishing enterprises ever undertaken in America is its critical edition of ''Don Quixote,'' containing fac-simile reproductions of the first Madrid edition of the first part (1605), of the first edition of the second part (Madrid, 1615), and of the fourth Madrid edition (1605), forming three volumes, and a critical text and glossary in four more.

MARTIN, Winfred Robert, orientalist, was born in Ningpo, China, Mar. 22, 1852, son of William Alexander Parsons and Jane (Vansant) Martin. His father was at first a Presbyterian missionary at Ningpo, China, 1850-60, and at Peking, 1863-68. During 1867-92 he was president of Tung-wen College (the government college for training diplomats) at Peking and professor of international law. In 1898 he became first president of the New Imperial University in the same city, and was president of Viceroy's University, Wuchang, 1902-05. He also served as adviser to the Chinese foreign office on questions of international law, and he was made a mandarin of the third class, 1885, by the Chinese government, and of the second, 1898. He translated into both Chinese and Japanese a number of important works on international law by American and European authors, thus introducing the subject to the Chinese, and he also wrote some notable books in Chinese on the evidence of Christianity, a broadly philosophical treatise on natural philosophy and chemistry and works in English on Chinese history and philosophy. The son was educated at Phillips Academy, Andover, Mass., and entering Princeton College was graduated in the class of 1872. He held the classical fellowship of his class at Princeton, and soon after graduation went abroad, spending one semester at Berlin and one at Leipsic. Returning to the United States in 1874 he was for several years instructor in Latin and Greek at the Jersey City High School, and later in the Hartford (Conn.) High School. While teaching at the latter he took up the study of Sanskrit under Prof. Whitney, of Yale University, and made a second trip abroad in 1885 to pursue its further study. He was professor of Oriental languages and co-ordinate professor of modern languages at Trinity College during 1888-1907, when he was appointed librarian of the Hispanic Society of America, which had recently been organized by Archer M. Huntington. Meanwhile he was also instructor of Sanskrit at the Hartford Theological Seminary. Prof. Martin was a member of the American Oriental Society, the American Philological Association, the Society of Biblical Literature and Exegesis, the American Geograph-

ical, the American Numismatic Society and the Hispanic Society of America, but he made it his business to promote the studies of these rather than to publish. He received the degrees of A.M. from Princeton in 1875, LL.B. from the New York University in 1878, Ph.D. from the University of Tübingen in 1887, and LL.D. from Trinity College in 1907 in recognition of long educational service. As librarian of the Hispanic Society of America, a place of somewhat varied functions, he received the decoration of Knight of the Order of Isabella the Catholic. In the material for original research in the special field the library is one of the richest existing. He was unmarried, and died in New York, Feb. 21, 1915. Portrait opposite page 22.

BLISS, Eliphalet Williams, inventor and manufacturer, was born at Fly Creek, near Cooperstown, N. Y., Apr. 12, 1836, son of Dr. John Stebbins and Ruby Ann (Williams) Bliss. He was descended from Nathaniel Bliss, who came to America from England with his father in 1635, settling at Springfield, Mass., the line running through Nathaniel's son, Williams, his son, Gad, and his son, John, the grandfather of Eliphalet W. Bliss. In his sixteenth year he was apprenticed to a machinist and at the age of twenty-one, having served his time, he was employed in the shops of the New York Central railroad at Syracuse, N. Y. Subsequently he entered the employ of the Charles Parker Gun Co., at Meriden, Conn., and he was manager of the company's factory at the outbreak of the civil war. He enlisted in Company I of the Third Connecticut regiment and was in action at the first battle of Bull Run. After being mustered out of service as corporal, he returned to the gun factory in Meriden, but in February, 1866, removed to Brooklyn, N. Y., and worked one year for Andrew Campbell, inventor of the Campbell printing press. A year later he formed a partnership with John Mays under the name of Mays & Bliss to engage in the press and die business. In 1871 John Mays sold his share to Mr. Bliss' cousin, J. H. Williams, and later Mr. Bliss purchased Williams' interest and conducted the business alone. He devised special machinery for stamping out cans for holding kerosene oil and paints. In 1886 he formed a stock company admitting eleven of his employees to a share in the profits, and in 1890 the present E. W. Bliss Co. was incorporated with a capital of $1,250,000, which was afterwards increased to $2,000,000. The company manufactures a line of special presses adapted for sheet metal work. It bought out the business of the Styles & Parker Press Co. and later the U. S. Projectile Co., of which Mr. Bliss was president, and since then his company has been producing the Bliss-Leavitt torpedo. (See Leavitt, Frank M., below.) The E. W. Bliss company manufactures a line of special power stamping machines, automobile parts, torpedoes, shrapnel and armor-piercing projectiles. At the time of his death the company's plant covered eighty-five city lots and employed 13,000 men. In addition to the above enterprises, he was for many years a director of the Brooklyn City Railroad Co., the Kings County Trust Co. and the Brooklyn Bank. He was married June 19, 1865, to Annie Elizabeth, daughter of Charles H. Metcalf, his former employer in Fly Creek, and had one daughter, Eva Metcalf, wife of James Warren Lane, who succeeded to the presidency of the Bliss company. Mr. Bliss died in Brooklyn, N. Y., July 21, 1903. Portrait opposite page 22.

LEAVITT, Frank McDowell, inventor, was born at Athens, O., Mar. 3, 1856, son of Rev. John

McDowell and Bithia (Brooks) Leavitt, and a descendant of John Leavitt, an Englishman, who emigrated with the Puritans from Norfolk county, England, in 1628, and settled at Hingham, Mass. His father (q.v.) was president of Lehigh University and later of St. John's College at Annapolis, Md., and his grandfather, Humphrey H. Leavitt, was a U. S. district judge of Cincinnati, O., by appointment of Andrew Jackson. His noteworthy decision rendered in the famous Vallandigham habeas corpus case during the civil war was of such interest that Pres. Lincoln immediately telegraphed him that it was as important to the Federal cause as the winning of ten battles. Another notable decision was rendered in the famous Methodist Book Concern case. He also served two terms in congress (1831-35). His father, John Leavitt, moved to Ohio from Suffield, Conn., about the close of the eighteenth century. Early in life Frank M. Leavitt displayed an interest in and aptitude for mechanics. He took a course at the Stevens Institute of Technology, and after being graduated in 1875 began his scientific career with Frederic Sickels in New York, who was the pioneer inventor of the steam steering gear for ships. In 1876 he entered the employ of the firm of Bliss & Williams, which at that time was engaged in the press and die business. While there he invented an automatic can-making machine, which enormously reduced the cost of manufacturing tin cans, and practically revolutionized the can business. He also invented the toggle drawing-press for producing all kinds of hollow pressed ware, such as pails, cooking utensils and hollow dishes of all kinds. The business grew steadily until it became one of the largest of the kind in the United States. Mr. Eliphalet W. Bliss bought out his partner in 1881, conducting it under his own name until in 1890 it was incorporated as the E. W. Bliss Co., its present title, with a capital of $1,250,000, and at that time Mr. Leavitt was given an interest in the concern. In 1890 the E. W. Bliss Co. purchased the U. S. Projectile Co., manufacturers of shells and other projectiles for war purposes. It was continued as a department of the Bliss Co., and now manufactures the celebrated Bliss-Leavitt torpedo used by the U. S. navy. The Bliss-Leavitt torpedo is a wonderfully ingenious and delicately constructed mechanism, almost human in its operations. It is cigar shaped, from fifteen to twenty-one feet long, and eighteen to twenty-one inches in diameter, propelled by a compressed-air motor, and carries in its head from 200 to 300 pounds of gun cotton, which is exploded by contact. It is equipped with a mechanical device that by hydrostatic pressure regulates its depth below the surface, and it has a gyroscope connected with its rudders to hold the torpedo in a straight course. Its original range was 800 yards in a straight line, with a speed of twenty-eight knots an hour. Mr. Leavitt conceived the idea of increasing its propulsive capacity by heating the compressed air, and he also substituted a turbine for the piston engine formerly used, with the result that the range of the Bliss-Leavitt torpedo has been increased to 10,000 yards. At that distance it is possible to hit a target only 600 feet long. Another notable improvement devised by Mr. Leavitt is an ingenious mechanism for changing the course of the torpedo after it leaves the submerged discharge tube to the right or left at will. Torpedoes may be fired from above the surface or below. A submerged torpedo tube cannot be swiveled or swung around to be aimed, as is possible when above the surface. The tube is fixed in the side of a battleship or the bow of a torpedo boat, and to bring it to bear on the target it is necessary to move the entire vessel until the launching tube is aimed in the right direction. Mr. Leavitt obviated this difficulty by inventing a device for regulating the gyroscopic steering gear, so that when launched the torpedo, instead of pursuing its flight in a straight line, will first turn in any part of a circle previously determined upon and then continue in a straight course toward the point of attack. It is thus possible to fire the Bliss-Leavitt torpedo from below the surface in any desired direction, without regard to the position of the ship. The effectiveness and deadliness of the modern torpedo have been demonstrated in the European war, and it has been predicted that when used in conjunction with the submarine boat, of which it is the sole offensive weapon, it will make the massive battleship obsolete. Mr. Leavitt is a member of the American Society of Mechanical Engineers, the American Society of Civil Engineers, the Society of Naval Architects and Marine Engineers, and the American Association for the Advancement of Science. He was married Nov. 8, 1893, to Gertrude, daughter of Charles Goodsell, founder and editor of the New York "Graphic," and has one daughter, Beatrice Leavitt.

FESSENDEN, Reginald Aubrey, electrician and inventor, was born at Bolton, Quebec, Can., Oct. 6, 1866, son of Elisha Joseph and Clementina (Trenholm) Fessenden. He is seventh in descent from Nicholas Fessenden, an Englishman, who settled at Cambridge, Mass., in 1674, and was the ancestor of the well-known Maine family to which belong Hon. William Pitt Fessenden and Gen. Samuel Fessenden. Nicholas Fessenden's wife was Margaret Cheney, and the line runs through their son, William Fessenden, who married Martha Wyeth; their son Peter, who married Mary Oliver; their son Ebenezer, who married Hannah Moss; their son Elisha Moss, who married Elsie Tibbetts, and their son Elisha Joseph Fessenden. The latter was a clergyman of the Church of England. Reginald A. Fessenden was educated in private schools and at Trinity College School, Port Hope, Ont. For a short time he was senior classical master in Bishop's College School, Lenoxville, Can., and for one year was principal of Whitney Institute in Bermuda. Having made a special study of electricity, he obtained a position with the Edison Co. as inspecting engineer in New York (1886) and in the following year was made head chemist of the Edison laboratory at Orange, N. J. He conducted experiments to discover some substance which should have the properties of India rubber but be fireproof. He found that the existing mathematical treatises on the theory of elasticity were not in accordance with the facts, and attacking the problem on a new line, he finally discovered that (1) cohesion was due to the fact that the molecules of the elements formed electrostatic doublets, with ionic charges; (2) cohesion varied with the inverse fourth power of the distance; (3) from these laws formulæ could be derived which gave the elastic constants of metals more accurately than the probability of error in observation; (4) Van der Waal's equation for gases must be modified; (5) electric conductivity and velocity of sound were related to each other in a simple manner. These discoveries were published in a series of scientific papers but they attracted no attention until twenty years later Sutherland, J. J. Thomson and others corroborated Fessenden's theories in detail. In 1890 he went to the Westinghouse Electric and Manufacturing Co. as chief electrician of the eastern works.

After a short time in a chemical laboratory at Pittsfield he was appointed professor of physics at Purdue University. From there he became professor of electrical engineering and post-graduate mathematics at Pittsburgh University, and while holding that chair (1894–1900) he did considerable original work in the study of molecular physics, electricity, magnetism, inertia, gravitation and electro-magnetic theory. He was the first to show that inertia is an electrical effect ("Electrical World" Apr. 7, 1900). In 1900 he became a special agent of the United States Weather Bureau to conduct original experiments in wireless telegraphy, resulting in the perfection of the oscillation method now used in connection with microphone detection systems, for which he obtained a patent May 29, 1901. He operated his wireless telegraph system between Brant Rock, Mass., and Machrihanish, Scotland. He also invented the high-frequency alternator (covered by the sustained oscillation patent); the high-frequency arc, patented June 6, 1902, and Apr. 9, 1903, and the quenched gap method, patented Jan. 9, 1907. The National Electric Signalling Co. was organized in Washington, D. C., in 1903, to exploit these inventions, and some $500,000 worth of apparatus based on his patents were sold to the United States government, the United Fruit Co. and others for non-commercial use. The Fessenden wireless telegraph system is to-day in successful operation on many steamship lines. Meanwhile he had been experimenting with wireless telephony. He invented an improved receiver, patented Dec. 15, 1899, and a system of generating waves continuously (in contradiction to Marconi's induction coil method with its interval of no waves between sparks, making telephony impossible), patented May 29, 1901, and Sept. 28, 1901. The latter patent covers broadly the method of generating waves continuously and modifying their characteristics, i.e., frequency or intensity in accordance with sound waves. It shows three alternative methods, all of which are in practical use, one by the Bell Telephone Company in its operation across the continent. He made the first actual transmission of speech by wireless Dec. 23, 1900, and gradually improved his apparatus until in 1905 it operated for twenty-five miles. In 1907 he talked by wireless between Brant Rock and Brooklyn, N. Y. (190 miles), and Brant Rock and Washington, D. C. (400 miles). On May 13, 1913, Mr. Fessenden obtained a patent for submarine telephoning and telegraphing, a device which could also be used as a position finder and fog signal, and after the sinking of the Titanic in mid-Atlantic from a collision with an iceberg, he invented an iceberg detector and sounding apparatus, patented Apr. 2, 1914. Some of his other inventions are: a compressed air condenser; a wave meter; umbrella antenna; a phantom antenna for wireless telegraphy; a subterranean water reservoir method of storing power; a low-pressure steam method of generating energy from solar and space radiation; a coal dust engine and apparatus for the mining and transportation of coal dust; an outside piston engine; turbo-electric drive for battleships, which he did not patent, but instead turned over to the United States navy; method of running submarines submerged without batteries, patented June 1, 1915; an induction furnace; visible record phonograph; dirigible torpedoes; gun sights, etc. In all he has obtained 150 patents. His mathematical studies resulted in the development of a new branch of mathematics called "Qualitative Mathematics." Prof. Fessenden's contributions to scientific literature include:

"Laws and Nature of Cohesion" in "Electrical World" and "Science" (1891–92); "Outline of Electrical Theory of Comets' Tails" in "Astrophysical Journal" (1896); "Nature of Electric and Magnetic Quantities and the Density and Elasticity of Ether" in "Physical Review" (1900); "Nature of Inertia" and "Nature and Velocity of Gravitation" in "Electrical World" and "Science" (1900). Among papers read before learned bodies are: "Recent Work of Molecular Physics" (Franklin Institute, 1896); "Conduction and Insulation" (Institute of Electrical Engineering, 1898); "Electro-magnetic Mechanism with Special Reference to High Speed Telegraphy" (Franklin Institute, 1899); "Wireless Telegraphy" (American Institute of Electrical Engineers, 1899); "Wireless Telegraphy" (American Institute of Electrical Engineers, 1908); "Submarine Telegraphy and Telephony" (American Academy of Science, 1914). Prof. Fessenden was married in New York, Sept. 21, 1889, to Helen May, daughter of Thaddeus Trott, of Bermuda, and has one son, Reginald Kennelly Fessenden.

SPERRY, Elmer Ambrose, inventor, was born in Cortland, N. Y., Oct. 12, 1860, son of Stephen Decatur and Mary (Borst) Sperry. His first American ancestor was Richard Sperry, a native of England, who emigrated from England in 1634 and became one of the early settlers of the New Haven colony in Connecticut. As recorded in Stiles' History, he afforded protection for a considerable time to the "Regicide Judges," Goffee, Whalley and Dixwell, by secreting them in a cave on his farm at West Rock, known now as the "Judges' Cave," and his children carried food and left it at a designated place in the forest where the hunted men would secure it at night. They were safely kept until the pursuit died away, although large rewards were offered for their capture, and Sperry's house was searched twice by the "redcoats" for them. Richard Sperry's son Richard built upon the Sperry farm near New Haven a stone house which is still occupied by his descendants, having never been out of the family. From Richard Sperry, the emigrant, the line of descent runs through his son Richard, who married Martha Mansfield; their son Jonathan, who married Mehitabel Collins; their son Richard, who married Abigail Northrop; their son Medad, who married Elizabeth Hine, and their son Ambrose, who married Mary B. Corwin and was the grandfather of the inventor. Elmer A. Sperry was educated in the state normal school of his native town and for one year attended Cornell University (1879–80). Like most pioneers, his training in the lines of special endeavor in after life came through his own efforts and interest. As early as 1879 he perfected one of the first electric arc lights in America, and although not yet of age, founded the Sperry Electric Co., in Chicago, to manufacture arc lamps, dynamos, motors and other electrical appliances. His early activities were as various as they were numerous, embracing nearly every branch of electrical science. In 1883 he erected on the shore of Lake Michigan the highest electric beacon in the world, 350 feet in height, and equipped it with 40,000 candle-power arc lights. Directing his attention to electrical mining machinery, he invented in 1888 a wide range of appliances, from reciprocating mining machinery to rotary and chain-cutting equipment and electric locomotives for mines. Since the date of their first appearance, the Sperry mining appliances have ranked among the best-known and most widely used of their class, and have repre-

WINFRED R. MARTIN
ORIENTALIST

ELIPHALET W. BLISS
MANUFACTURER

FRANK M. LEAVITT
INVENTOR

REGINALD A. FESSENDEN
ELECTRICIAN

Elmer A. Sperry.

sented a profitable field of business. Following this he appeared as a practical designer of electrical street railway cars, which were just beginning to achieve the success and popularity that they afterwards attained. In 1894 he founded the Sperry Electric Railway Co. of Cleveland, O., to manufacture his cars. The business and patents are now the property of the General Electric Co. of New York. The transition from electric street railway car to the electric motor vehicle was easy and natural. In 1895 he designed a successful electric carriage, and manufactured it for several years. He also drove the first American-built automobile in the streets of Paris in 1896 and 1897, where a large number of these automobiles were sold and delivered. In the field of electro-chemistry Mr. Sperry discovered an important commercial process for producing caustic soda and bleach, now used by the Hooker Electro-Chemical Co. of Niagara Falls, N. Y. Among other minor inventions may be mentioned his detinning process, now used by extensive detinning interests, and also his machinery for producing fuse wires, on which was based the Chicago Fuse Wire Co. He was instrumental, also, in designing several varieties of machinery for the General Electric Company, the Goodman Manufacturing Co. and others. At the present time there are four industrial corporations founded to manufacture his inventions, doing in the aggregate an annual business of ten million dollars, with all of which he has been actively connected in engineering and executive capacities. In 1890 Mr. Sperry first turned his attention seriously to the possibilities of the gyroscope, which, since its first demonstration by the French scientist, Foucault, in 1851, had been little more than a scientific curiosity. He is one of several inventors both in America and in Europe who have attacked the problem of adapting the gyroscope to practical uses, but no one has gone as far and attained as satisfactory results as he. He is the inventor of the gyroscopic compass, which is now in practical use, and is destined to supersede entirely the ancient magnetic compass. Respecting the motions of the gyroscope Foucault discovered the following laws: ''First, that the inertia of a rapidly rotating wheel, suspended with freedom to move upon all axes, is relative to space, and consequently that a gyroscope suspended in that manner will maintain its plane of rotation in space; second, that a gyroscope suspended with its axis of rotation horizontal, and with freedom about the horizontal axis partly or wholly suppressed, will tend to precess, or turn, about the vertical axis in an effort to place its plane or rotation coincident with that of the earth.'' Thus its action is precisely that of a mechanical magnet in which the rapid rotation of the axis is analogous to the interatomic ''circulation'' of the magnetic forces in a bar of magnetized steel, and it has the same ''polarity'' effect, since the direction of rotation ''clockwise'' or ''counter-clockwise'' determines precisely which end of the rotating axis shall point to the north. To drive his gyroscope, Mr. Sperry used the wheel rim as the rotor of a three-phase electric motor. His invention consists of a master compass which may be placed in a ship's hold for safety, and a number of repeating instruments in electrical connection with it in other parts of the vessel. The gyro-compass does not have to be adjusted at every voyage; it points absolutely north, and any deflection caused by external circumstances is adjusted automatically. In 1914 he received the gold medal of the Franklin Institute for this invention. He next attacked the problem of stabilizing ships with the use of the gyroscope, and invented a gyro-stabilizer, which entirely prevents the rolling of vessels at sea and which is being introduced on large vessels and the warships of the United States. In Mr. Sperry's instrument the gyros are mounted with their axes horizontal and normally athwartship and with their precession rings pivoted about a vertical axis. Movements about the vertical axis are controlled by an engine, which in turn is controlled by a small gyroscopic pendulum which maintains a fixed base line. A tendency to roll, of even so small an amount as one-tenth of a degree, is immediately felt by the gyro-pendulum, which causes the precession engine to move the gyros in such a manner as to deliver an impulse to the ship about its longitudinal axis which will exactly counteract the tendency to roll. This prevents any motion, and, as the ship is kept on an even keel, very little power is required. A modification of his stabilizer has been adapted to aeroplanes. It consists of four gyroscopes driven by the aeroplane engine. One set of gyroscopes is attached to the elevating planes in such a way that when the flying machine reaches a dangerous angle, the planes are automatically thrown back into a horizontal position; the other set keeping up an automatic lateral balance. It has proved entirely practicable, and after the public tests in France in 1914, which won for Mr. Sperry the Collier trophy and the first prize of the Aero Club of France, he received large orders from the governments at war in Europe. He is a member of the American Institute of Electrical Engineers, the American Electro-Chemical Society, the American Society of Mechanical engineers, the American Chemical Society, the Society of Naval Architects and Marine Engineers, the Aero Club of America and the Engineers' Club of New York city. In 1915 he was selected to serve on the advisory board of engineers and inventors of the U. S. navy. He was married June 28, 1887, to Zula Augusta, daughter of Edward Goodman, proprietor of the "Standard" of Chicago, and has one daughter and three sons: Helen Marguerite, Edward Goodman, Lawrence Borst and Elmer Ambrose Sperry, Jr. Lawrence Sperry early mastered the aeroplane, constructing one of his own design when only eighteen years of age, and flying with it at Brighton Beach, N. Y. He has made many flights while conducting experiments with his father's stabilizer, including official tests in France.

NELSON, Richard Henry, Protestant Episcopal Bishop of Albany, was born in New York city, Nov. 10, 1859, son of Edward Delavan and Susan Blanchard (Macdonald Nelson). His father (1821-71) was an artist of note, and a descendant of John Nelson, a resident of Flatbush, L. I., as early as 1670, who purchased lands at Scarsdale, Westchester co., in 1683. From this John Nelson and his wife, Hendrica Vander Vliet, the line is traced through their son Francis and his wife, Mary Skinner; their son John and his wife, Elizabeth Davenport; their son Thomas and his wife, Sarah Wright; their son John and his wife, Celia Pele; their son Richard and his wife, Cordelia Adams, and their son Edward Delavan, father of the bishop. Richard Henry Nelson was graduated at St. John's school, Sing Sing, and at Trinity College, Hartford, Conn., in 1880. He subsequently studied at the University of Leipzig and the Berkeley Divinity School, and in 1883 was ordained deacon in the Protestant Episcopal church. In the following year he was ordained a priest. He served as curate of St. John's Church, Stamford, Conn., 1883-84, and was rector successively of Grace Church, Waterville, N. Y., 1884-87; Christ Church, Norwich, Conn., 1887-97; and St. Peter's Church, Philadelphia, in 1897-1904. On May 19th of the latter year he was consecrated bishop coadjutor of Albany, and in the same year received the degree of S.T.D. from the University of Pennsylvania and the Berkeley Divinity School, and the degree of D.D. from Trinity College. In 1914 he succeeded Bishop Doane as Bishop of Albany. Bishop Nelson's activities have been varied and many-sided. He has taken a special interest and done much valuable work in the cause of education. He was for seven years an elected member of the board of education of Norwich, Conn., and was chairman of the committee for the examination and selection of teachers. During his seven years in St. Peter's Church, Philadelphia, he did a vast amount of religious, charitable and educational work among the poor of the city, although his congregation included some of the wealthiest and most noted families. He was a member of the standing committee of the diocese of Pennsylvania and served on the boards of trustees of several charitable and educational institutions. In 1902 he was defeated by a narrow margin in the election for Bishop coadjutor of Pennsylvania and in the same year received an equally large vote relatively for Bishop coadjutor of central New York. During his incumbency of the office of bishop coadjutor of Albany, he showed marked ability in the administration of a large diocese which includes the Adirondack and Catskill Mountains. Perhaps his most valuable work, from a social viewpoint, has been done in connection with the campaign against tuberculosis. He is chairman of the Albany committee on education and publicity and is a member of the state committee (of the State Charities Aid Association) for the prevention and cure of tuberculosis. Dr. Nelson was instrumental in arousing the Central Federation of Labor in Albany to establish a hospital for consumptives, a valuable precedent that has been followed in other cities, and has led the leaders of organized labor to devote considerable thought to the matter of public health. Bishop Nelson has won the affection and respect of both the clergy and laity of the diocese by his fidelity and kindliness, his discernment of men and circumstances, his fine intellectual and spiritual quality, his poise and sense of justice, his public spirit and interest in the moral and humanitarian issues of the day. He was married Jan. 20, 1885, to Harriet Schuyler, daughter of Smith W. Anderson, of New York city, and has two sons: Richard Macdonald and John Low Nelson.

BROWN, Ernest William, mathematician, was born in Hull, England, Nov. 29, 1866, son of William and Emma (Martin) Brown. He entered Christ's College, Cambridge, in 1884, when he obtained a scholarship in open competition in mathematics. In 1887 he received his degree of A.B., as sixth wrangler in the mathematical tripos. In 1889 he was elected to a fellowship in the same college, holding it for six years, and received his degree of M.A. in 1891. As soon as regulations permitted he proceeded to the degree of Sc.D. in Cambridge in 1896. In 1891 he was appointed instructor, and two years later professor, of applied mathematics in Haverford College, Pa., retaining that position until 1907, when he was called to occupy the same chair at Yale University. In 1899 he was appointed one of the three editors of

the "Transactions of the American Mathematical Society." His chief work has been on the theory of the motion of the moon as deducted from the law of gravitation. In a series of memoirs written between 1891 and 1895 a new method, due in the first instance to L. Euler and later to Dr. G. W. Hill, was developed for the purpose of obtaining results from which Tables of the Moon could be ultimately constructed. These culminated in a paper, "Investigations on the Lunar Theory" ("American Journal of Mathematics," 1895) in which a complete plan was outlined for carrying on the necessary numerical work. The following year the latter was started, and with the aid of one computer was finished in the summer of 1904. The results have been published in four parts in the "Memoirs of the Royal Astronomical Society." One interesting result was the proof of the fact that Newton's law of gravitation is accurate so far as the moon is concerned within one-two-hundred-fifty-thousandths of one per cent. At various times he has published papers dealing with the mathematical theories of dynamical problems in general, and of the problem of three or more bodies in particular. In one of these application is made to the famous problem of determining the theoretical value of the slow increase in the average rate at which the observations show the moon revolves round the earth; this is known as the secular acceleration of the moon's mean motion. The determination of this quantity, which had previously been laborious and difficult, was obtained accurately by a few simple and short processes by means of a newly discovered relation. The results of Prof. Brown's researches are being put into the form of numerical tables which will be used to obtain the position of the moon at every hour throughout the year in most of the national nautical almanacs. He has also published investigations on the motions of the planets and the asteroids, more particularly those known as the Trojan group. In addition he has published many reviews of books on astronomy, hydronamics, theory of tides, and other subjects in applied mathematics, chiefly in the "Bulletin of the American Mathematical Society." He has written popular articles on various subjects from time to time, and he has occasionally delivered addresses and popular scientific lectures. In 1898 he was elected a fellow of the Royal Society, England; he is also a fellow of the Royal Astronomical Society, from which he received a gold medal in 1907; member of the London Mathematical Society; Cambridge Philosophical Society; American Philosophical Society; American Mathematical Society, president (1914–16); and American Association for the Advancement of Science (vice-president section A, 1910). He is now editor of the "Bulletin of the American Mathematical Society," and associate editor of the "Astronomical Journal." He received the honorary degree of Sc.D. from Adelaide University in 1914, also that same year a royal medal for researches in astronomy awarded on the recommendation of the Royal Society of London. He is fond of all out-door activities, especially of country life; he also takes pleasure in working with his hands. His indoor enjoyments are chiefly chess and music. While at college he rowed in the college boat. He visited Switzerland for high climbing several seasons, and has traveled in Africa, Australia and New Zealand. He is unmarried.

ARBUCKLE, John, merchant and philanthropist, was born in Allegheny City, Pa., in 1838, son of Thomas Arbuckle, who was of Scotch-Irish descent. The father came to America as a young man and settled in western Pennsylvania, where he became the proprietor of a cotton mill. The son John attended the public schools of Allegheny and Pittsburgh, and in the latter shared a desk with Henry Phipps, the banker. In 1856 he became a student at Washington and Jefferson College, but left to engage in the coffee roasting business with his younger brother Charles under the name of Arbuckle Brothers, and by ambition and economy built up a highly prosperous trade. In 1871 they moved their establishment to Brooklyn, N. Y. In his boyhood John Arbuckle had a strong bent for science and machinery, and although he chose the coffee instead of the steel business for his career, the basis of success was an invention. His business in those days was the selling of roasted coffee in packages, in which his firm was the pioneer. It required five hundred girls to wrap up the packages of coffee the firm sold. With the aid of a draftsman and machinist he invented a machine which filled, weighed, sealed and labeled coffee in paper packages as fast as it came from the hopper. This gave the Arbuckle Brothers the control of the package coffee trade of the world. They stuck to one particular brand from the beginning, and through judicious and extensive advertising their ''Arbuckle Ariosa'' coffee came to be used all over the country. After the death of Charles Arbuckle, in 1890, John Arbuckle continued the coffee business under the old firm name of Arbuckle Brothers, although other partners were taken in from time to time as the business continued to grow. The concern finally became the largest importer of coffee on the continent, and because of its purchasing power and firmly established selling trade it was able practically to control the price of coffee in the markets of the world. Although John Arbuckle purchased green coffee by the shipload and sent it out of Brooklyn in pound packages by the trainload, yet the capacity of the plant was never overtaxed, nor was the retail market oversupplied. Accordingly he determined to pack and sell sugar the same way. Refined sugar was used for this purpose and at first it was purchased from the Havemeyer interests. It was a good move financially for John Arbuckle and soon doubled his income, but it was the beginning of the historic Arbuckle-Havemeyer trade battle that cost the combined sugar and coffee forces $25,000,000. John Arbuckle, noticing that while the price of raw sugar had declined there was no corresponding drop in the refined article to him, remonstrated with Henry O. Havemeyer, who he believed regarded him as a valued customer. But the Havemeyers considered the Arbuckle trade in sugar a menace to their own interests, and had vainly attempted to stop the sale of sugar in packages, inasmuch as their efforts to secure the Arbuckle patented packing machine had proved futile. When, therefore, the Havemeyers raised the price of sugar Mr. Arbuckle announced that he would establish a refinery of his own, although he knew nothing about sugar refining. On the other hand the sugar people tried to ruin their rivals by securing control of the Woolson Spice Mills of Toledo, with their established ''Lion Brand'' of coffee. The resulting competition was hard for both. There were suits and countersuits, enormous competitive expenses, and the losses grew to frightful proportions, making one of the most spectacular controversies in the history of American industry. After a long and bitter war an agreement was finally signed ending the strife. John Arbuckle

was a unique figure among American merchants. He was as modest and unostentatious in his commercial activities as in his remarkable humanitarian efforts. Even at the time of his death it was not generally known that he had been the largest individual ship owner in America. In truth his name was better known in that respect in Rio Janiero and Buenos Ayres than in his home city. Practically every merchant ship engaged in the South American coffee trade was his, or controlled by his firm. In 1906 he turned his attention to the salvage of vessels, and conceived a system for raising sunken vessels. The Arbuckle Wrecking Company which he established acquired a floating equipment, among which was the Arctic ship Roosevelt, and raised the stranded U. S. vessels Yankee and Nero. He likewise formulated a plan to meet the needs of passenger vessels in danger from shipwreck, fire or other accidents. This was the maintenance at his personal expense of a fleet of ocean-going tugs equipped with wireless telegraphy which would respond to alarms received at government life-saving stations. To act in conjunction with them he built barges equipped with breeches buoys and oil tanks. He also did great humanitarian work by purchasing vessels for use as floating homes or hotels. For this purpose he acquired the old ship, Jacob A. Stamler, and the schooner yacht, Sitana, and mooring them at piers in New York, admitted persons who could not afford to pay forty or fifty cents a day for board and lodging. He also used the vessels to take mothers and their babies down the bay; and he converted another boat into the ''Riverside Home for Crippled Children,'' fitted it with every convenience for their comfort, and provided simple employment which enabled them to earn money, and which enabled them to get board and lodging aboard at actual cost. Much the same plan is observed in the conduct of an 800-acre farm at New Paltz, N. Y., founded by him, where in the clear mountain atmosphere on the shores of Lake Mohonk is maintained a fresh air home for the children of the crowded city. There, too, he built a splendid home for the aged. A gift to Plymouth Church and the people of Brooklyn in honor of Henry Ward Beecher was the memorial institute and arcade, planned during his last days and carried out by his sisters after his death. The institute is provided with all the appurtenances of a modern clubhouse, with library, writing room, assembly room, gymnasium, swimming pool and lockers. In its classrooms members may be instructed in typewriting, stenography, bookkeeping, dressmaking, millinery, and other subjects. Mr. Arbuckle was a director of the Importers and Traders Bank, Kings County Trust Company of Brooklyn, Lawyers Title Insurance and Trust Company, and the Mortgage Bond Company, New York. He was president of the Royal Horse Association, which has ranches in Wyoming. He owned the magazine called ''Sunshine,'' which was conducted in the benevolent interests of children. John Arbuckle's affability was a byword in the shipping district, and he would meet personally any one who called at his office at Old Slip and Water street. His geniality was of the proverbial Scottish kind and his modesty was a strong characteristic. Loath to speak of his deeds, he would not even bother to dispel the myths circulated about him, and he attended to business to within a few days of his death. An interesting glimpse of his personality is afforded by the following motto which he personally gave to hundreds of persons, printed on a bit of cardboard: ''Politeness is the cheapest commodity on God's earth. It costs nothing and will carry you farther and pleasanter through life than any other ticket you can travel on." A plain business man, strong, quiet and retiring, he was little known by the world at large. He held membership in none of the fashionable clubs of Fifth avenue and he cared not at all for the blandishments of so-called society. Outwardly his speech was blunt and abrupt, inwardly his heart was kind and gentle. His benevolences toward the poor and weak were largely personal, individual and self-directed. The abiding interest of his life was his enthusiasm for Henry Ward Beecher and old Plymouth Church, to whom and to his parents he said he owed more than any other influence of his life. He was married in Pittsburgh, Pa., in 1868, to Mary Alice, daughter of David Kerr. He died without issue in Brooklyn, N. Y., Mar. 11, 1912.

DIX, John Alden, 41st governor of New York (1911–13), was born at Glens Falls, N. Y., Dec. 25, 1860, the son of James Lawton and Laura (Stevens) Dix. His father was the son of Samuel Dix, of Wilmington, Vt., and a descendant of the original Dyks family who came from Holland and located in New England in 1660. He was educated at Glens Falls Academy and at Cornell University, but was not graduated. At college he was a leader in athletics as well as in his studies and in social affairs. He was in the black marble business under the firm name of Reynolds & Dix from 1882 to 1887, when he became a partner of Lemon Thomson (q. v.), of Albany, in the lumber trade. The firm of Thomson & Dix also did a large wood pulp manufacturing business and later developed into one of the largest and best wall-paper plants in the country. To supply his own mills Gov. Dix acquired a tract of 17,000 acres of timber land, and he early made it a rule that for every tree that was cut down, another should be planted, thus inaugurating a very practical plan of conservation of natural resources that is to-day bearing result. Besides being the head of the firm of Thomson & Dix, of Thomson, N. Y., he is president of the Iroquois Pulp and Paper Co., treasurer of the American Wood Board Co., vice-president of the First National Bank of Albany, vice-president of the Bandy Paper Co. of Greenwich, treasurer of the American Wood Board Co. of Thomson, and a director of the Albany Trust Co., the Glens Falls Trust Co., the National Bank of Schuylerville, the Hudson Falls and Adirondack Trust Co. of Saratoga, and the Standard Wall Paper Co. of Hudson Falls. As a banker, Gov. Dix achieved a notable reform in securing to the state an increase in the rate of interest on the state's bank deposits, which he accomplished after he had effected a combination between the Exchange and First National banks of Albany, in 1906. His prominence in local politics dates from 1904, when he was a delegate to the Democratic national convention at St. Louis. As Democratic county chairman for Washington county in 1906, he inaugurated new methods which proved very successful and acceptable. In that year he was mentioned for governor, but withdrew his name when the Independent party's candidate was nominated, declaring that while he could not vote for the candidate nominated, he would remain steadfast to the principles of his party. He was nominated for lieutenant-governor two years later, but was defeated. However, during this time he was constantly gaining strength in his party, and in 1910 he was made chairman of the Democratic and state committee. This was followed by his nomination for governor, he being

regarded as the strongest man available to run against the Roosevelt candidate, Henry L. Stimson. In the following election he received 689,700 votes to Stimson's 622,299. He carried the ticket with him and the Democratic party had a majority in both houses at Albany for the first time since Gov. Hill held the office. In his first message he emphasized the necessity for economy and the abolition of unnecessary boards and the combination of others; he recommended a system of state-wide nominations which should ensure the people the right to choose members of political committees and nominate candidates for public office, and declared in favor of an income tax. The practical business training of the governor was soon evidenced in his methods of conducting the affairs of the office. His was notably a business administration, during which many reforms resulting in improved methods and rigid economies were inaugurated. These reforms included a new election law providing for primary elections, the first primary election being held Mar. 26, 1912, for delegates to the Republican state convention. The legislation of 1912 embraced an unusual number of measures of first importance; amendments were made to the banking law, providing for the removal of the bank and insurance departments from political control and inaugurating new methods in the finance department; amendments in the state's highway laws, pure food laws and the labor laws. At the beginning of his administration there was a deficit of $1,500,000 in the state treasury and at the close there was a workable surplus approximating $4,000,000. An incident of his term which attracted wide attention and no little criticism was the pardoning of Albert D. Patrick, after what was probably the most remarkable fight ever made by a convict in the United States. Patrick was under sentence of death for murder during four years and seven months, and after a series of legal proceedings involving many difficult legal and medical complications, his sentence had been commuted by Gov. Higgins to life imprisonment. The honorary degree of LL.D. was conferred on Gov. Dix by Hamilton College in June, 1912. He was married in Albany, N. Y., Apr. 24, 1889, to Gertrude Alden, daughter of his former business associate, Lemon Thomson. Portrait opposite page 27.

HOWARD, Edward Lloyd, physician, was born in Baltimore, Md., Jan. 14, 1837, son of William and Rebecca (Key) Howard. His maternal grandfather was Francis Scott Key, author of the "Star Spangled Banner," and his paternal grandfather was Col. John Eager Howard of revolutionary fame. The boy received a liberal training at home under private tutors, and studied medicine at the University of Maryland, where he was graduated M. D. in 1861. He served in the Confederate army during the civil war, both as a soldier and a surgeon. He was subsequently professor of anatomy at the Baltimore College of Dental Surgery, and in 1870, in association with Dr. Thomas Latimer, he founded the "Baltimore Medical Journal," of which he was editor. In 1872 he became professor of anatomy and later physiology at the Baltimore College of Physicians and Surgeons. He made a special study of legal medicine; read a paper, "The Legal Relations of Emotional Insanity," before the American Medical Association in 1874, and in the same year secured the establishment of a state board of health. He died by drowning, Sept. 5, 1881.

LEA, Luke, U. S. senator, was born near Nashville, Tenn., Apr. 12, 1879, son of Overton and

John Arbuckle

JOHN A. DIX
GOVERNOR

LUKE LEA
U. S. SENATOR

THOMAS B. HOWARD
NAVAL OFFICER

MONTGOMERY SCHUYLER
JOURNALIST

Ella (Cocke) Lea, and grandson of Luke Lea, a member of congress. He was graduated at the University of the South in 1900 and at the law school of Columbia University, New York, in 1903. In the same year he was admitted to the bar of Tennessee and began the practice of his profession at Nashville. He first came into prominence in 1905 when he took charge of the Home Telephone Co.'s fight for a franchise in Nashville against the Cumberland Telephone Co. In the following year he stampeded the state Democratic convention and secured the nomination of M. R. Patterson for governor of Tennessee. From that time he has been a conspicuous figure in Tennessee politics. Dissatisfied with Patterson's subservience to the party machine, he espoused the cause of Carmack and carried on the fight through the columns of the "Tennesseean," which he founded and of which he made Carmack editor. The murder of Carmack almost caused an armed revolution in the state. It resulted in the political demise of Gov. Patterson and, temporarily, of the Democratic party. Lea elected a Republican governor, the first in Tennessee for twenty-five years. In the course of the fight he purchased the "American," the oldest newspaper in Tennessee and the chief organ of his opponents, which he consolidated with the "Tennessean" under the name of the "Tennessean and American." He led the winning fight for prohibition in Tennessee, and in 1911, despite his youth and the fact that he had so far held no public office, the overwhelming sentiment of the public in his favor resulted in his election to the U. S. senate. He has served as chairman of the committee on the Library of the Senate and chairman of the joint committee on the Library of Congress, and at the present time is chairman of the committee to Audit and Control the Contingent Expenses of the Senate. He is a member of the following committees: Appropriations, Military Affairs, Post Offices and Post Roads, Privileges and Elections, Rules, Expenditures in the Treasury Department, and the committee to examine the several branches of the civil service. He was a member of the Democratic Steering Committee of the senate during the 63d congress. Sen. Lea was prominent in the election cases of Sen. Lorimer of Illinois and Sen. Stephenson of Wisconsin. He has been and is at present interested in the investigation of the affairs of the Louisville and Nashville and the Nashville, Chattanooga and St. Louis railroads which he instigated in the senate, before the Interstate Commerce Commission and before the Railroad Commission of Tennessee. Sen. Lea is a big, strong, boyish man with a vast amount of force, enthusiasm, earnestness and fighting spirit, and withal a ready geniality and a sunny temper that win him friends among all sorts of people. He is one of the youngest, one of the most picturesque and one of the most popular men who have ever sat in the U. S. senate. He was married in 1906, to Mary Louise, daughter of Percy Warner, of Nashville, Tenn.

HOWARD, Thomas Benton, naval officer, was born at Galena, Ill., Aug. 10, 1854, son of Bushrod Brush and Elizabeth (Mackay) Howard. His great-grandfather, Maj. T. C. Legate, served in the war of 1812; his grandfather, Col. Aeneas Mackay, served in the Mexican war and the war of 1812, and his father was a lieutenant in the Mexican war and a captain in the civil war. He was educated in the Galena public schools, and by appointment of Pres. Grant entered the U. S. Naval Academy where he was graduated in 1873. He became ensign in July, 1874;

master in June, 1879; lieutenant in November, 1885; lieutenant-commander in March, 1899; commander in June, 1902; captain in February, 1907, and rear-admiral in November, 1910. He served on the Alaska on the European station in 1873; was transferred to the Wabash in 1874, and to the Franklin in 1875. He was on duty at the naval academy during 1876–78, and was then assigned to the Plymouth of the North Atlantic squadron, 1878–79, and to the Kearsarge, 1879–81, when he returned to the naval academy for another term of three years. He was on the practice ship Dale in 1881 and again in 1883. He was on the Saratoga of the training squadron during 1884–87, and on the Constellation, 1887–89. In 1893 he crossed the Atlantic on the caravel Pinta from Barcelona to Havana, when that fac-simile of Columbus' ship was sent to the Chicago Exposition. On the 1st of May, 1898, he sailed with Dewey into Manila Bay and was present at the surrender of the city. During the insurrection he took part in the battles of Manila and Caloocan and in the bombardment of Cebu, and in 1900 preceded Capt. Strong in command of the old monitor Monadnock on the Philippine station. He has served four terms at various times at Annapolis, and has commanded in order the Chesapeake, Nevada, Olympia, Tennessee and Ohio. He accompanied Admiral Sperry's fleet on its cruise around the world in 1908–09, has had duty as member of the General Board, and was in command of the fourth division of the Atlantic fleet from October, 1910, to January, 1912, and of the third division of the Atlantic fleet from January to April of the latter year. From April, 1912, to December, 1913, he served as president oɪ the Naval Examining and Retiring Board, and in January, 1914, was ordered commander of the Pacific fleet, holding the rank of admiral from March to September, 1915. This fleet protected American interests and shipping in Mexico after the Vera Cruz trouble without the loss of a single life. He commanded the expedition in June, 1915, to protect Americans in Mexico from the Yaqui Indians. Admiral Howard is a member of the Military Order of the Loyal Legion; the Society of Manila Bay; the Military Order of Carabao (Grand Paramount Carabao, 1914–16), and the American Society of International Law. He was married May 13, 1879, to Anne J., daughter of Dr. Abram Claude of Annapolis, Md., and has four children: Abram Claude, graduate of the U. S. Naval Academy, gas engineer; Grace Laurens, wife of Commander James P. Morton, U. S. N.; Douglas Legate, lieutenant, U. S. N., and Bushrod B. Howard, lieutenant, U. S. N.

SCHUYLER, Montgomery, journalist and author, was born at Ithaca, N. Y., Aug. 19, 1843, son of Anthony and Eleanor (Johnson) Schuyler, and a descendant of Philip Schuyler, who came from Amsterdam, Holland, to Albany, N. Y., about 1645, the line descending through Arent, Casparus, Arent, Aaron, Anthony and Montgomery Schuyler. His father was an Episcopal clergyman and rector of Grace Church, Orange, N. J. The son entered Hobart College in 1858, but did not graduate, receiving, however, the honorary degree of A.M. later. Shortly after removing to New York in 1865, he joined the brilliant group of writers and artists who were beginning to find themselves at that day. He was on the staff of the New York "World" during 1866–83 when Manton Marble was editor, was on the staff of the New York "Times" during 1883–1907, and from 1912 until his death was connected with the New York "Sun." During

1885–87 he was managing editor of "Harper's Weekly," and from 1887 to 1894 was reader for Harper & Bros. He was one of the founders and a regular contributor to the "Architectural Record." He was the author of "The Brooklyn Bridge," with W. C. Conant (1883); "Studies in American Architecture" (1892); and "Westward the Course of Empire" (1906) and numerous articles on literary and art subjects in "Scribner's," "Putnam's," "The Forum," "North American Review" and other magazines. American journalism has developed few men of the brilliant gifts of Mr. Schuyler. As an editorial writer he belonged to the school of Raymond, Marble and Hurlbert, imparting to the discussion of subjects of importance in the news of the day literary grace of an uncommon sort and the charm of a cultivated and genial mind. His field was broad, for besides the equipment, derived from long years of newspaper training, for the discussion of civic and political matters, he was an authoritative writer on architecture, music and the fine arts. He was an omnivorous reader with a preference for the classics and possessed the happy faculty of apposite quotation. Any group of which he formed a part never lacked for spontaneity of wit. In his gift for repartee his wife rivaled him, and they were inseparable. On his retirement from the "Times" in 1907 he moved to New Rochelle, N. Y. He was a member of the Century Association, the American Institute of Arts and Sciences and the American Institute of Architects. He was married, Sept. 16, 1876, to Katherine Beeckman, daughter of Robert Dwight Livingston. Mrs. Schuyler was president of the Dames of the Revolution for many years. She was once a prominent soprano singer, and was also a painter and sculptor. Two sons were the issue of this marriage: Montgomery, Jr., formerly U. S. minister to Ecuador, and Robert Livingston Schuyler, assistant professor of history in Columbia University. Montgomery Schuyler died at New Rochelle, N. Y., July 16, 1914.

SCRIPPS, James E., journalist, was born in London, England, Mar. 19, 1835, son of James M. and Ellen M. (Saunders) Scripps. His father, one of the leading bookbinders of London, brought his family to the United States in 1844 and settled in Illinois. The son began his journalistic career on the Chicago "Tribune" in 1857 and two years later went to the Detroit "Advertiser." He effected a consolidation of the "Advertiser" and "Tribune" in 1862, and under his management the paper entered upon a career of great prosperity. He had long advocated a cheap priced paper, and as his associates opposed the reduction of the price of the "Tribune," he established the "Evening News," which is now known as "Detroit News," on Aug. 23, 1873, to be sold at two cents. Its success was immediate and it became the leading newspaper in Michigan. In 1878 with his brothers, Mr. Scripps founded the Cleveland "Press," and later the Cincinnati "Post," and St. Louis "Chronicle." He bought the Detroit "Tribune" in 1891, and in 1900 he acquired a controlling interest in the Chicago "Journal." He was one of the founders of the Detroit Museum of Art, to which he contributed $80,000; was a member of the Detroit board of park commissioners and a public library commissioner and in 1902 was elected to the state senate on both Republican and Democratic tickets. He was the author of a number of pamphlets and two books: "Five Months Abroad" (1882) and "Memorials of the Scripps Family" (1891). In politics he was a Republican, and an advocate of free trade and civil service reform. He was married, Sept. 16, 1862, to Harriet Josephine,

daughter of Hiram King Messenger; his son, William Edmund Scripps is vice-president and managing director of the "Detroit News," and is identified with the automobile industry in Detroit.

STILLMAN, James, financier, was born at Brownsville, Tex., June 9, 1850, son of Charles and Elizabeth Pamila (Goodrich) Stillman, and a descendant of George Stillman, who came over from England in 1680 and settled in Massachusetts. His father was a man of unusual business sagacity and force of character, who acquired a fortune in mercantile pursuits and increased it by judicious investments in railroad property and real estate. The son spent his youth at Hartford, Conn., and was educated in a private school in Sing Sing, N. Y. Entering the employ of Smith & Dunning, commission merchants of New York, he was admitted to the firm in 1871 under the name of Smith, Woodward & Stillman. In 1883 James Smith retired and the business was continued by Mr. Stillman and William Woodward, a brother of James T. Woodward, president of the Hanover National Bank. Upon the death of Mr. Woodward, Mr. Stillman became head of the firm, though the name is still (1916) Woodward & Stillman. Early in his career he won the confidence of Moses Taylor (q. v.), a millionaire merchant and banker, and became associated with him in several large projects, including the organization of the Houston & Texas Central Railroad. Through Mr. Taylor he also became interested in a number of large corporations, and was a recognized factor in all the important branches of the extensive Moses Taylor estate. In November, 1891, Mr. Stillman succeeded Percy R. Pyne, a son-in-law of Moses Taylor, as president of the National City Bank. His election to this position meant the choice of a banking genius, as well as the acquisition of the tremendously valuable business of the Standard Oil Co. The City bank and the Standard Oil Co. had always had one policy in common, a big cash reserve. Mr. Stillman and Mr. William Rockefeller equally appreciated the value of such a policy and when the panic of 1893 came the National City Bank had millions of dollars of ready resources while other banks were drained of cash. In 1892 the bank had increased its deposits from $12,000,000 to $16,000,000 and before the panic was over it had $31,000,000, making it the largest bank in New York and the greatest reservoir of cash in America. In 1897 it was further strengthened by the addition to its federation of the Union Pacific Railroad. Kuhn, Loeb & Company, who reorganized the road, had had no previous affiliations with the Taylor-Stillman-Rockefeller triumvirate. They came to the City bank because it was the only institution capable of financing the reorganization, with its payment of $45,000,000 to the U. S. Government. In that year it absorbed the Third National Bank of New York, and its deposits rose to $95,000,000. In 1900 they touched $120,000,000 and its capital was increased to $10,000,000. In 1902 the capital was increased to $25,000,000 and its surplus to $15,000,000. In 1916 its surplus and undivided profits had increased to $35,000,000. In 1898 the directors purchased the old U. S. Custom House at 55 Wall street, which was converted by Messrs. McKim, Mead and White into the beautiful structure which it now occupies, the finest bank building in the United States. The original Ionic colonnade on Wall street was preserved practically intact, and to it was added a Corinthian colonnade, increasing the height of the old building by four stories. Mr. Stillman retired from the presidency in 1909

JAMES STILLMAN

Frank Arthur Vanderlip

and became chairman of the board of directors. He withdrew from all business connections in 1915 and took up his residence in Paris, France. He was a director or trustee of the United States Trust Co., Chicago and Northwestern Railway Co., Baltimore & Ohio Railroad Co., Delaware, Lackawanna & Western Railroad Co., Western Union Telegraph Co., North British & Mercantile Insurance Co., Queen Insurance Co., Hanover National Bank and New York Trust Co. He is a member of the Cotton Exchange and the Chamber of Commerce. He is also a member of the Union, Metropolitan, Century, Union League, Manhattan, Reform, Tuxedo and City clubs, and Down Town Association; the New York, Seawanhaka-Corinthian, Eastern and St. Augustine Yacht clubs, the Jekyl Island and Storm King clubs, the New York Historical Society and the Metropolitan Club of Washington, D. C. In 1898 he presented to Harvard the Stillman Infirmary. He was married to Elizabeth Rumrill, and his children are Elsie, wife of William G. Rockefeller, James A., Isabel Goodrich, Charles Chauncey and Ernest G.

VANDERLIP, Frank Arthur, financier, was born at Aurora, Kane co., Ill., Nov. 17, 1864, son of Charles and Charlotte (Woodworth) Vanderlip. The founder of his family in America was William Vanderlip, a native of Holland, who came over to the colonies in 1756 and settled in southern Pennsylvania. From him the line of descent is traced through his son William and the latter's wife, Anna Woodburn Taggart; their son, Harmon Blackmore, and his wife, Hannah Smith, who were the grandparents of Frank A. Vanderlip. The subject of this sketch lost his father at an early age, and thus being thrown upon his own resources, obtained employment in a machine shop at Aurora. His early education was obtained in the public schools of the neighborhood, and he completed his studies at the University of Illinois and the University of Chicago. He devoted his spare moments to the study of stenography, and was employed in the Investors' Agency in Chicago for a short period. In 1889 he became a financial reporter on the "Tribune," and a year later was made its financial editor. Thus early in his business life he began to make a study of finance, a sphere in which he was destined to attain a pre-eminent position. Under his editorship the financial section of the Chicago "Tribune" became a recognized authority on financial matters. In 1895 Mr. Vanderlip resigned from the Chicago "Tribune" to devote his time to the editorial work on the Chicago "Economist," a weekly financial journal in which he was interested. During this period Mr. Vanderlip was closely associated with educational work, and he delivered many lectures on finance in colleges and universities throughout the Middle West. After the election of Mr. McKinley he became the private secretary to Lyman J. Gage, secretary of the treasury. On June 1, 1897, he was appointed by the president assistant secretary of the treasury. In this position he had charge of the floating of the Spanish war loan, and of the operations connected with the refunding of the 3 per cent. and 4 per cent. bonds into the 2 per cent. gold consols of 1930, as authorized under the act of Mar. 4, 1890. He instituted many reforms in the management of the Bureau of Engraving and Printing, and made improvements in the government mints at New Orleans and Philadelphia. Upon his resignation in 1901 he was elected vice-president of the National City Bank of New York under James Stillman. Before entering upon the duties of this office he made an extended trip abroad in the interests of the bank, visiting all the important cities, conferring with the finance ministers and public men in the European countries, and studying at first hand the banking methods and financial policies and practices of the leading commercial nations. While in Belgium he attended as delegate from the United States the international conference of commerce and industry at Ostend. The result of this investigation of European conditions was embodied in a work entitled "The American Commercial Invasion of Europe" (1902). He remained vice-president of the National City Bank until 1909, when he was elected its president. The National City Bank is now recognized as the foremost banking institution in the United States. It has been said of Mr. Vanderlip that few bank presidents know as many phases of American life as he does, and few have such broad sympathies. He has delivered numerous addresses on financial subjects that have attracted national attention, and his contributions to current financial literature, which have appeared in the "Outlook," the New York "Independent," the "North American Review," the "World's Work," "Scribner's" and other publications have been exceedingly valuable and constitute the highest authority upon the most important branches and aspects of international finance. Mr. Vanderlip received the honorary degree of A. M. from the University of Illinois and of LL.D. from Jacksonville College in 1905, and that of LL.D. from Colgate University in 1911. He is a trustee of the Carnegie Foundation, a trustee of New York University, and a director of the Farmers' Loan and Trust Company, the National Bank of Commerce in New York, the National City Bank of New York, the New York Edison Co., the Union Pacific Railroad Co., Riggs National Bank of Washington, D. C., and the United States Realty and Improvement Co. of New York. He is a member of the Metropolitan, Century and Union League clubs of New York, the Cosmos Club of Washington, and the Sleepy Hollow Country Club. He was married May 19, 1903, to Narcissa, daughter of Charles Epperson Cox, of Chicago, Ill., and has five children: Narcissa, Charlotte Delight, Frank Arthur, Virginia Jocelyn and Kelvin Cox.

GRAY, John Henry, economist, was born in Charlestown, Ill., Mar. 11, 1859, son of James Cowan and Mary A. (Mitchell) Gray. He was prepared for college in the high school department of the Illinois State Normal University, and was graduated at Harvard University in 1887 with special honors in political science. He was instructor in political economy at Harvard in 1888–89 and having received a Harvard traveling fellowship, he spent two semesters at Halle, one semester at Paris, and one at Vienna, and the next two semesters at Berlin. In May, 1892, he took the degree of Ph.D. at the University of Halle, magna cum laude. During 1892–1907 he was professor of political and social science in Northwestern University. In the latter year he became professor of economics and head of the department of economics and political science in the University of Minnesota, continuing thus until 1913, when he became head of the department of economics in the same institution, and has so remained until the present time (1916). He was chairman of the committee of the congress on political and social science in connection with the Columbian exposition at Chicago in 1893. In 1897–98, 1903–04 and 1913–14 he was first vice-president of the American Economic Association, and was its president in 1913–14. He was appointed an expert of the U. S. department of labor in 1902 to investigate the restriction of output in Great Britain, and represented that department at the International Coöperative Congress, held at Manchester, England, in July, 1902. That same year he represented the United States at the international congress on the insurance of workingmen, at Düsseldorf, Germany, and also the international congress on commerce and industry, at Ostend, Belgium. He was a member of the National Civic Federation Commission on Municipal Ownership in 1905, and was expert to the commission for the American investigation. In 1913–14 he was a member of the executive council of the department of the National Civic Federation, to investigate the regulation of public service corporations, and served as secretary of the department and director of the investigation. Prof. Gray is associate editor of the "Journal of Accountancy." Among his most important publications are: "Die Stellung der Privaten Beleuchtungsgesellshaften zu Stadt und Staat" (1893); "Difficulties of Controlling Corporations" (1900); "Capitalization, as Controlled by the Massachusetts Gas Commission" (1901); "Regulation and Restriction of Output in Great Britain," in the eleventh special report of the United States commissioner of labor, and a large part of Part II, Volume I, Reports of Experts in the National Civic Federation Report on Municipal and Private Operation of Public Utilities. He has been a liberal contributor to the current press, and notably to the "Quarterly Journal of Economics," and has published many papers having particular reference to public utilities. He was married, June 14, 1894, to Helen Rockwell, daughter of Franklin Remington Bliss, of New Haven, Conn., and their children are: James Bliss and Evelyn Gray.

GOODSPEED, Arthur Willis, physicist, was born in Hopkinton, N. H., Aug. 8, 1860, son of Obed and Helen Bruce (Morse) Goodspeed. He was graduated at the Boston Latin School in 1880, the winner of the Franklin medal, and in the following autumn entered Harvard College, where, after taking second year honors in mathematics, he was graduated A.B. in 1884, "summa cum laude," with highest honors in physics. He was appointed assistant in physics the same year at the University of Pennsylvania, becoming instructor in physics a year later, and assistant professor in 1889, taking at that time also the degree of Ph.D. at the same institution. In 1904 he was appointed professor of physics at the University of Pennsylvania and director of the laboratory of physics and has held these positions until the present time (1916). His special line of investigation has been regarding the Röntgen rays and their applications and radioactivity. He was a member of the jury of awards at the National Export Exposition in 1899. He has written numerous articles on Röntgen rays and other scientific subjects, and has frequently lectured in university extension work. He is a fellow of the American Association for the Advancement of Science; a member of the Franklin Institute, the American Röntgen Ray Society (president 1902–03), the Royal Society of Arts (London), the American Philosophical Society, of which he is a secretary, the American Physical Society, and Société Français de Physique. In 1901 he was elected vice-president of the New Hampshire Antiquarian Society and president in 1914. Dr. Goodspeed has been twice married: (1) June 24, 1896, to Annie Howe, daughter of Joseph Bailey, of Hyde Park, Mass., and their children were: Frederick Long, Willis Bailey, and Helen Gertrude Goodspeed; Mrs. Goodspeed died in May, 1910,

and he was married (2), Aug. 19, 1913, to Ethel W., daughter of William T. Mitchell, of Staunton, Va. From the second marriage there is one son, Arthur Willis Goodspeed, Jr.

HEPBURN, Alonzo Barton, banker, was born at Colton, N. Y., July 24, 1846, son of Zina Earl and Beulah (Gray) Hepburn, and a descendant of Patrick Hepburn, who came from Abbey Mill, Scotland, and settled at Stratford, Conn., in 1736. From Patrick Hepburn the line descends through his son Peter and the latter's wife, Sarah Hubbell; their son Joseph and his wife, Eunice Barton; their son Joseph and his wife, Helen Lobdell, who were the grandparents of Alonzo Barton Hepburn. The son was graduated at Middlebury College, Vt., in 1871. After leaving college he became for a time instructor in mathematics at St. Lawrence Academy, and later was principal of Ogdensburg Educational Institute. He studied law, was admitted to the bar, and for ten years practiced his profession at Colton, N. Y. In 1874 he was elected to the assembly, where he served five years. He began his banking career in 1880, when he was appointed superintendent of the banking department of the State of New York, and held that office for three years. In 1888 he was made U. S. bank examiner for New York, and served until 1892, when he became comptroller of the currency. In the following year he resigned to accept the presidency of the Third National Bank, and he remained there until 1897, leaving to accept the vice-presidency of the National City Bank, which he held until 1899. In 1900 he was chosen president of the Chase National Bank, which post he filled until 1911, when he became chairman of the board of directors. In addition to these activities he is a director of the Bankers' Trust Co., Columbus Trust Co., Fidelity Trust Co. of Newark, Maryland Trust Co. (Baltimore), New York Life Insurance Co., First National Bank, First Security Co., American Car and Foundry Co., American Agricultural Chemical Co., American Cotton Oil Co., Safety Car Heating and Lighting Co., Sears, Roebuck & Co. (Chicago), United Cigar Manufacturers Co., Studebaker Corporation, Texas Co. and the Woolworth Co. He is a member of the New York Chamber of Commerce (president 1910), New England Society (former president), St. Andrew's Society (former president), The Pilgrims, Burns Society, Germanistic Society, Academy of Political Science (former president), and National Currency Association (former president). He has written much on financial subjects and is the author of: "History of Coinage and Currency" (1903); "Artificial Waterways and Commercial Development" (1909); "Artificial Waterways of the World" (revision of his former "Artificial Waterways" and "Commercial Development") (1914), and "The Story of An Outing" (1913). Mr. Hepburn is a trustee of the Rockefeller Foundation, and of Middlebury College, which bestowed upon him the degree of LL.D. in 1894. He received the same degree from Columbia and from Williams in 1911, and that of D. C. L. from St. Lawrence University in 1911. In 1912 he was made an officer of the Legion of Honor, France. His clubs include the University, Metropolitan, Union League, City, Barnard, Economic (former president), Camp Fire, St. John's Salmon (Gaspe, Quebec), Long Island Country, Automobile, Ridgefield, Ridgefield Country, McDowell, Faculty (Columbia University), Press, Recess, St. Andrew's Golf and National Golf Links of America. Mr. Hepburn's favorite pursuits are golf and hunting, and he has hunted big game in all parts of the North American continent and in Africa. He was married (1) Dec. 10, 1873, to Hattie A. Fisher, of St. Albans, Vt., by whom he had one son, Charles Fisher; (2) to Emily L. Eaton, of Montpelier, Vt. There are two children of the second union: Beulah E., wife of Lieut. Robert R. M. Emmett, U. S. N., and Cordelia Susan Hepburn.

MILLER, Spencer, engineer and inventor, was born at Waukegan, Ill., Apr. 25, 1859, son of Samuel Fisher and Charlotte (Howe) Miller, grandson of Rev. Moses and Bertha (Ware) Miller, and great grandson of Moses Miller, of Worcester, Mass. He was graduated at the Worcester Polytechnic Institute in 1879. After tutoring in mathematics at Amherst College, he became an illustrator for the "Western Manufacturer," Chicago, and then began his professional career as draughtsman with the Link-Belt Machinery Co., Chicago. While there he designed a number of rope drives, and a novel equipment for handling cargoes by continuous systems of conveying for the Union Steamboat Co. It was in connection with the use of rope driving with grooved pulleys of different diameters that he devised the method of equalizing the strain in the strands of rope by enlarging the angle of the grooves in the larger pulley sufficiently to compensate for the extra hold of the rope in the groove incident to the larger arc of contact. He invented a bicycle lamp in 1882, to be suspended from the hub of the large wheel so as to destroy the shadow cast by the rim, but the high wheel bicycle was soon after superseded by the "safety." In 1888 he associated himself with the Lidgerwood Manufacturing Co., of New York, which was then manufacturing a crude overhead cable system involving fall-rope carriers of the chain connected type. He perfected an entirely new fall-rope carrier system which is now an important part of the Lidgerwood cableway of commerce. It was immediately adopted in various parts of the world for use in the construction of government fortifications, dams, filtration beds, sewers and similar work as in open mining. The thirteen cableways installed by his company at Panama for the construction of the Gatun locks proved a dominant factor in successful completion of that great work. There the buckets filled with concrete sped along the suspended cable at the rate of 2,000 feet per minute. One of the most stubborn engineering problems solved by Mr. Miller was the removal of cypress logs from Louisiana swamps. Owing to the difficulties formerly encountered in handling these logs an acre of timber land containing 50,000 feet of lumber was valued at only one dollar. His invention of a log-skidding cableway (1893) reduced the cost of logs at the mill more than 50% and increased the capacity of the sawmills 400 per cent. The timber lands of that section consequently increased in value fifty fold, and the success of the apparatus led to its use in the lumber camps of the world. One of the early problems of the Spanish-American war was presented to the navy department in the question of coaling ships at sea. The Lidgerwood Manufacturing Co. entered into a contract with the government to handle this problem, and Mr. Miller designed a marine cableway that made it possible to transship coal under headway at sea. A cable, over which the coal bags are run, is suspended between the ship and the collier and is kept uniformly taut by an automatic steam reel on one vessel that automatically takes up or pays out the cable as the motion of the vessels requires. By this device ships can be coaled at the rate of 100 tons per hour. It has been adopted by the United States navy and has been used by

several governments in Europe. In coaling ships in harbor his method of broadside handling has increased the capacity from twenty-five to 150 tons per hour, and one man now does the work which under the old system required eighty. Many new colliers of the United States navy, notably the Jason, Orion and Neptune, are equipped with this transfer system for delivering coal to ships at sea. In a smooth sea one of these colliers can coal three battleships broadside in a day, using clamshell buckets, while if the sea is moderate or not too rough it will deliver 600 tons in ten hours with the marine cableway, the collier towing the battleship. The same idea has been applied by Mr. Miller to his breeches buoy cableway apparatus in use by the United States revenue cutter service. With it any ship can rescue passengers from another ship in the heaviest sea over a cable kept taut at all times and notwithstanding the roll of the ships. The Lidgerwood Manufacturing Co., with main works in Brooklyn, foundry department in Newark, and general offices in New York, manufactures hoisting engines, electric hoists, cableways and logging machinery, and has branch offices in seven American cities. Aside from his engineering activities Mr. Miller is greatly interested in civic and municipal improvement, especially in the establishment of public libraries, parks and playgrounds in his home town, South Orange, N. J. He is a director of the South Orange public library and past president of the local playground commission. He was vice-president of the Essex County Mosquito Extermination Commission, and read a paper, "Prevention of Mosquito Breeding," before the American Society of Civil Engineers in 1912. He is a member of the council of the American Society of Mechanical Engineers; member American Society of Civil Engineers, American Institute of Mining Engineers, Society of Naval Architects and Marine Engineers, and the Canadian Institute of Mining Engineers, and was appointed a member of the Civilian Naval Consulting Board in 1905, of which Thomas A. Edison is president. He is also a member of the Engineers' Club, New York, and the Metropolitan Club and University Club of Washington, and wears the gold key Sigma Xi. He was married at Worcester, Mass., Jan. 1, 1884, to Hattie M., daughter of Willard G. Ruggles, and has three children: Marguerite R. Miller, wife of P. E. Grannis, of New York; Spencer Miller, Jr., deputy warden Sing Sing Prison, and Helen Emerson Miller. Portrait opposite page 32.

PARKER, Henry William, librarian, was born in New York city, May 28, 1860, son of James and Mary Louisa (Dewland) Parker. From William Macclesfield Parker, a native of England, who settled at Charlestown, Mass., about 1718, he descends through the latter's son James, his son William M., who married Amanda Patterson; and their son William H. M., who married Lucy Van Arsdale, and who was the grandfather of Henry William Parker. William M. Parker served as a lieutenant in the revolutionary war. William H. M. Parker was a soldier in the war of 1812, and our subject's father, and was a naval officer in the Mexican war. The son was educated privately and at Trinity School, New York city. He was chorister of Trinity Protestant Episcopal church and first boy soprano in the quartette at Grace Church, New York, during 1872–74. In 1874 he began library work by becoming page in the Apprentice's (now Mechanics') Library. He was advanced to a clerkship in 1878; became a cataloguer in 1885; assistant librarian in 1898, and librarian in 1900, a position he still holds. He is the originator of a library classification system which, in many respects, is a marked improvement over Dewey's numerical system. It is as nearly mnemonic as possible, intending to aid both the public and the library employees. All books have an individual number representing (1) a general classification, (2) the author's numbered combination, and (3) the initial letter of the title of the book. General subjects are represented by capital letters: A for agriculture, B for biography, C for commerce, etc.; subclasses by small letters, for instance "Af" indicates books on farming, a subdivision of A, agriculture, and divisions of the subclasses have distinguishing numbers. Authors' numbers begin with 1001 for A and cover nearly 10,000 names, or parts of names, to 9999 for Zwir; for example, the shelf number of John Fiske's "American Revolution" is "Hu. 44059a": H, history; u, United States; 4, revolutionary period; 4059, the author's number, and a the initial letter of book. In the case of general reference books with no individual author, the author's number is given to the title. Thus this publication, "The National Cyclopedia of American Biography," is represented by "Bc. 16815": B, biography; c, collective; 1, dictionaries and annuals, and 6815, national. This system, the outcome of thirty-six years of his practical library work, was published in book form in 1901 and 1910 without copyright, "so that the library may become more useful as a public institution," and has been adopted by nearly fifty libraries here and in Europe. Mr. Parker possesses a large private collection of rare volumes, as well as of book-plates. Aside from this intellectual pursuit, he finds recreation in fishing, boating, mechanics and lathe work. He is a member of the Royal Arcanum, Masons, Odd Fellows and Loyal Association, Friday Night and New York Library clubs, and National Geographic Society. During 1878–85 he was a member of the 9th regiment of N. G. N. J. He was married in Jersey city, N. J., Aug. 20, 1883, to Mary Louisa, daughter of Nicholas Rouse, and has one child, Arthur Sidney Parker.

FEWKES, Jesse Walter, ethnologist, was born at Newton, Mass., Nov. 14, 1850, son of Jesse and Susan Emeline (Jewett) Fewkes. His first paternal American ancestor was Benjamin Fewkes, who came from Loughborough, England, and settled in Boston, Mass., in 1818; his wife was Elizabeth Smith, and they were the grandparents of the subject of this sketch. He received his preliminary education at the Newton High School, Newton, Mass., and was graduated at Harvard University in 1875, receiving the degrees of A.M. and Ph.D. at the same institution two years later. He received the degree of LL.D. from the University of Arizona in 1915. He prepared for his scientific career at Harvard and the University at Leipzig, studying zoology at the last named university during 1878-80. On his return to America he was appointed assistant curator in the Museum of Comparative Zoology at Cambridge, Mass., which position he held until 1889. He was also secretary of the Boston Society of Natural History during 1888-91. In the summers of 1880-89 he had charge of the Marine Laboratory of Prof. Alexander Agassiz at Newport, R. I., where he made extensive researches of marine animals, especially the jellyfishes and starfishes. He was editor of the "Journal of American Ethnology and Archaeology" during 1890-94, and had charge of the work of the Hemenway Expedition in Arizona until that time.

He was the first to use the phonograph in the study of Indian music, taking this instrument to the Passamaquoddy Indians in 1889 and to the Zuñi and Hopi Indians in 1890 and 1891. The records obtained by him on the last mentioned excursions were published in the "Journal of American Ethnology and Archæology," by B. I. Gilman under the titles "Zuni Melodies" and "Hopi Songs." In 1891 he made the first scientific studies of the Hopi Snake Dance, an account of which was published in the same journal. In 1895 he undertook archæological work in Arizona for the Bureau of American Ethnology of the Smithsonian Institution; he was officially appointed ethnologist on the staff of the bureau in the following year. Extensive collections, the best specimens of which are now on exhibition in the National Museum, were made from the ruins in Arizona during the years 1895-1905. In 1905-7 extensive studies were made in Porto Rico and the other West Indian islands, the results of which appeared in a monograph entitled "The Aborigines of Porto Rico," published in one of the reports of the bureau. In 1908-9 Dr. Fewkes was in charge of the excavation and repair of Casa Grande in Arizona and Cliff Palace and Spruce Tree House, two of the largest cliff dwellings in Colorado. In 1915 he excavated and repaired Sun Temple, a new type of ruin situated in the Mesa Verde, National Park, Colorado. Dr. Fewkes is a member of the National Academy of Sciences, American Academy of Arts and Sciences, the Antiquarian Society, the Anthropological Association (president, 1912–13), the American Association for the Advancement of Science (vice-president, 1905, 1912–13), the Boston Society of Natural History, the Essex Institute, Salem, the Brooklyn Institute and other scientific bodies. He is also corresponding member of the Berlin Anthropological Society, the Royal Society of Florence, the Antonio Alzate, and the Société des Americanistes, Paris. He was knighted by the Queen Regent of Spain with the order of "Isabela la Catolica" in 1892, and received a gold medal from King Oscar of Sweden in 1893 for scientific research. He was in charge of the Hemenway exhibit in the exposition commemorative of the discovery of America in Madrid in 1893, and was awarded a gold and silver medal for the installation. Dr. Fewkes is the author of various pamphlets and articles on marine zoology, American ethnology and archæology, He is particularly interested in the lower marine animals, especially the Medusae. His various publications on natural history may be found in the bulletins and memoirs of the Museum of Comparative Zoology at Cambridge, Mass. In anthropology he is deeply interested in the religious ceremonials and the archæology of the Hopi and other Indian tribes of the Southwest, and also in the prehistoric people of the West Indies. His publications on anthropology may be found in various reports of the Bureau of American Ethnology and the Smithsonian Institution. The most important among them are his papers on the Snake Dance ceremonials at Walpi, which contain the first scientific study of this weird dance of the Hopi Indians; an "Archæological expedition to Arizona in 1895," which contains an account elaborately illustrated with colored plates of the beautiful pottery obtained by excavation of a ruin in northern Arizona; "Aborigines of Porto Rico and Neighboring Islands," containing a monographic exposition of the archæology of the West Indies; and monographs on Casa Grande,

SPENCER MILLER
ENGINEER

HENRY W. PARKER
LIBRARIAN

JESSE W. FEWKES
ETHNOLOGIST

JAMES A. FARRELL
MERCHANT

Cliff Palace, and Spruce Tree House. Dr. Fewkes was married (1) in 1883, to Florence Georges, daughter of George Eastman, of Newton, Mass; (2) April 4, 1893, to Harriet O., daughter of James Cutler, of Cambridge, Mass.

FARRELL, James Augustine, president of the U. S. Steel Corporation, was born in New Haven, Conn., Feb. 15, 1863, son of John G. Farrell and Catherine Farrell. His father was a native of Ireland, who early came to the United States and became a merchant and shipowner of South Norwalk, Conn. His death occurred during the son's boyhood, and the latter began his business career at the age of sixteen in the employ of a New Haven wire mill. In 1888 he transferred his services to the Pittsburgh Wire Co. of Pittsburgh, Pa., becoming soon afterwards assistant superintendent and later superintendent of the factory. He displayed unusual intelligence and executive ability, and it was not long before he was made general manager of the business, devoting himself especially to improving the efficiency of the works. Following this he was manager of the Oliver Steel Co. of Pittsburgh, and while holding this position he was invited to participate in the organization of the Pittsburgh Steel Co., of which he was made manager. He had charge of the erection of the company's plant at Braddock, Pa. The next step in his career was to be manager of the foreign department of the American Steel and Wire Co., a position he assumed in 1899. The steel interests were just beginning to devote attention to export trade. He was one of the organizers of the United States Steel Products Export Co. in 1902, which a year later became the United States Steel Products Co., which is the general selling agency of the United States Steel Corporation, and during the eight years that he was its president he developed almost single-handed an enormous foreign business, which has made for the wonderful success of the entire American steel industry. He established as many as fifty-five agencies abroad. By 1909 the company of which he was president was doing an export business of ten per cent. of the total sales of the United States Steel Corporation, and at the close of that year its unfilled orders for foreign shipments amounted to 462,600 tons. In January, 1911, Mr. Farrell succeeded William Ellis Corey as president of the United States Steel Corporation. His selection for this, probably the greatest executive office in the industrial world, was due to his thorough training as a workman and his practical knowledge of the manufacturing of iron and steel, as well as his experience and ability in the sales department. During Mr. Farrell's administration the United States Steel Corporation has developed to a high state of efficiency its welfare work for the benefit of its 200,000 employees. A great part of the improvement effected has been carried on by the corporation in conjunction with the American Iron and Steel Institute. The latter is an organization composed of leading steel manufacturers of the country, and in 1910 Mr. Farrell was chairman of its committee on foreign relations. Mr. Farrell is known as an ardent yachtsman and a lover of outdoor life. Besides his residence in Brooklyn he has a country estate at South Norwalk on Long Island Sound. He is a communicant of St. Francis Xavier Church of Brooklyn, and a member of the Metropolitan Club, the Railroad Club of New York, the Manufacturers' Association, the Manufacturers' Export Association and the Montauk Club of Brooklyn. He was married in 1889 to Catherine McDermott, and has five children: John J. Farrell, Mary Theresa Farrell, Catherine Farrell, James A. Farrell, Jr., and Rosamond Farrell. Portrait opposite page 32.

LOWELL, Guy, architect, was born in Boston, Mass., Aug. 6, 1870, son of Edward Jackson and Mary Wolcott (Goodrich) Lowell, grandson of Francis Cabot Lowell, and great-grandson of Francis Cabot Lowell (q. v.), founder of Lowell, Mass. His mother was the daughter of Samuel G. Goodrich, the author known as "Peter Parley." He was graduated at Harvard University in 1892. He took the course in architecture at the Massachusetts Institute of Technology, and after receiving the degree of B.S. in 1894, entered the Ecole des Beaux Arts, Paris, in order to complete his architectural education. Here he won the Jean Le Clair prize and was graduated in 1899. He has since practiced his chosen profession in Boston and New York. He designed a great many country residences, and in a short period of time he became known as one of the most prominent of the younger men in his profession. He designed the Lecture Hall and Emerson Hall at Harvard University; the Memorial tower of Brown University; two dormitories and a refectory for Simmons College; the Stevens Memorial Library at North Andover; the gymnasium at North Easton, memorial fountains and park gates for the Boston Common; the Unitarian church of Barnstable; the arts building of Bar Harbor, Me.; the courthouse of Portland, Me.; the Museum of Fine Arts, Boston; the architectural work of the Charles river basin; the Museum of Archæology, several dormitories and clubhouses at Andover, Mass.; the Iowa State Memorial, Vicksburg, Miss.; the Canby Memorial of Wilmington, Del., and the Memorial Hospital of Pawtucket, R. I. The most notable of his more recent buildings are the museum of the New Hampshire Historical Society at Concord, N. H.; the Evans Memorial Gallery, Boston; the county courthouse, New York city; buildings for Andover (Mass.) Academy; Framingham (Mass.) Normal School, and a number of private residences, stables, etc., for country estates. Mr. Lowell has done considerable landscape work, notably the grounds for Radcliffe College, Cambridge; the gardens for the homes of Andrew Carnegie and J. Pierpont Morgan in New York, and gardens at the country homes for Payne Whitney at Manhasset, L. I.; Nathaniel Thayer at Lancaster, Mass.; T. Jefferson Coolidge at Beverly, Mass.; F. L. Ames at North Easton, Mass., and Mortimer F. Plant at Groton, Conn. Unlike many American architects trained in the French school, Mr. Lowell's work shows a distinctly American character, far different from the modern French work, although the academic tendency of French architecture, which is an essential part of the Ecole training, is always evident, even in the planning of his comparatively small houses. Combined with this academic feeling there is always found that quality, difficult of analysis and perhaps still more difficult of attainment, which shall eventually produce an American style of architecture. He taught architecture for fifteen years at the Massachusetts Institute of Technology, and has written two books, "American Gardens" (1902) and "Smaller Italian Villas and Farmhouses" (1916). He was married, May 17, 1898, at Brookline, Mass., to Henrietta, daughter of Charles Sprague Sargent.

PERKINS, George Walbridge, financier, was born in Chicago, Ill., Jan. 31, 1862, son of George Walbridge and Sarah Louise (Mills) Perkins. His earliest paternal American ancestor was Jacob Perkins, who came from England in 1631 and settled first in Boston and subsequently at Ipswich,

Mass. From him the line of descent is traced through his son Joseph and his wife, Martha Morgan; their son Joseph and his second wife, Maria Bushnell; their son Joseph and his wife, Joanna Burnham; their son Elijah and his son William W. and his wife, Lucy Walbridge, who were the grandparents of George W. Perkins. His father, George Walbridge Perkins, was engaged in shipping on the Great Lakes at Buffalo, and was a pioneer in the American life insurance field. Later he was greatly interested in the philanthropic and civic life of Chicago. Geo. W. Perkins received a public school education, and at the age of fifteen entered the Chicago office of the New York Life Insurance Co. as clerk. Two years later he was made assistant bookkeeper in the Cleveland office of the company, and in 1883 was promoted to be cashier. He was a solicitor of the company for two years, and in 1888 was appointed agency director, with headquarters in Denver, Colo. In the following year he became inspector of agencies in the Rocky Mountain district, with supervision over eight states. When the office of third vice-president was created Mr. Perkins was given the position and at the same time was placed in charge of the company's agencies throughout the world. In 1898 he succeeded to the second vice-presidency, and subsequently became chairman of the finance committee. In 1903 he was made vice-president. As a result of his unusual executive ability the company wrote a larger business, by considerable of a margin, than any other insurance company in the world. His achievements attracted the attention of J. Pierpont Morgan, who made him an offer, which resulted in his becoming a partner (1900) in the firms of J. P. Morgan & Co., of New York; Drexel, Morgan & Co., of Philadelphia, and Morgan, Harjes & Co., of Paris. In this new connection he had even greater opportunity to exercise his gift of independent action in large transactions. To understand fully the attitude which Mr. Perkins took toward the industrial and banking problems which faced him it must be borne in mind that, according to his view, the world of business is built on what he calls the three M's—Men, Money and Machinery. While inventive and financial skill has dealt satisfactorily with the last two, he believed the first had been comparatively neglected. He set about to remedy conditions and to show the money-kings, with whom he was associated in various enterprises, that any great business was a partnership between directors and workmen and that the denial of that partnership was the cause of all industrial unrest. For years he had looked about him and had seen as much discontent among the men who had made the millions as among the working classes. Meanwhile he had become a director and member of the finance committee of the United States Steel Corporation, International Harvester Corporation, International Harvester Co., of New Jersey; German-American Insurance Co., and German Alliance Insurance Co.; director and member of the executive committee New York Trust Co., and director Cincinnati, Hamilton and Dayton Ry., Erie Railroad Co., Florida East Coast Ry., International Mercantile Marine Co., and the New York State Bankers' Association. He first suggested profit-sharing insurance, sick benefits and old-age pensions, also service bonuses in the steel trust and the harvester trust, and he inaugurated the plan which permitted employees of these corporations to purchase stock at less than market value, believing that industrial justice is the most profitable of investments, that justice promotes peace, peace promotes prosperity, and that the workmen's prosperity is necessary to the prosperity of the business man. For the purpose of devoting more time to this and other work of a public and semi-public nature he retired from the firm of J. P. Morgan & Co. in 1910. Having ever been a progressive among conservatives, it was natural that he should throw his political fortunes with the Progressive party at a time when he was working independently, writing and speaking on subjects of industrial justice. He saw that in Roosevelt's principles lay the practical accomplishment of the very ideas which had been closest to him. He threw his own energies and time into the work as chairman of the national executive committee of the party. He has, however, never sought a political office. He was, however, nominated as delegate to the constitutional convention of the State of New York, in 1914, from the County of Bronx, but was defeated by his Democratic opponent. He is president of the New York Palisades Interstate Park Commission; member of the board of managers and executive committee New York Botanical Gardens; honorary vice-president of the Park District Protective League; director and member of the finance committee of the Young Men's Christian Association; trustee of the New York Scenic and Historic Preservation Society, Vassar College and Berry School, Rome, Ga.; member of the arbitration committee of the New York Chamber of Commerce, and member of the New York Zoological Society, the Metropolitan Museum of Art, the Horticultural Society of New York, the American Museum of Natural History, the American Academy of Political Science, the American Iron and Steel Institute, the American Federation of Arts, the American Society for Judicial Settlement of International Disputes, the Peace Society of New York, the National Geographic Society, the National Kindergarten Association, the National Institute of Social Sciences, the National Civic Federation, the American Board of Home Missions, the Society for the Prevention of Cruelty to Animals, the Museum of Safety and Sanitation, the Lincoln Memorial Road Association, the New York State Forestry Association, the Luther Burbank Society, the Municipal Art Society of New York, the Society of the Lying-in Hospital, the Franco-American Committee, the Civil Service Reform Association, the Honest Ballot Association, the Milwaukee Art Society, the Japan Society, the Ohio Society of New York, the Illinois Society of New York, the Pilgrims of the United States, and of the following clubs: Metropolitan, New York Yacht, Union League, Army and Navy, Railroad, Automobile of America, Quill, Economic India House and The Recess, New York city; Union League and Chicago, Chicago; Country Club of Westchester, Ardsley Country, St. Andrew's Golf and Sleepy Hollow Country. Active in civic affairs, he is chairman of Mayor Mitchell's committee on pensions and food supply. He received the honorary degree of LL.D. from the University of Wooster and the University of Vermont in 1911. He was married at Cleveland, O., in 1889, to Evelina, daughter of Flamen Ball, of Cleveland, O., and has two children, Dorothy and George W. Perkins, Jr.

WADSWORTH, James Wolcott, Jr., U. S. senator, was born at Geneseo, N. Y., Aug. 12, 1877, son of James and Louise (Travers) Wadsworth. William Wadsworth, the progenitor of the family in America, came over in the ship Lyon, which anchored in Boston harbor Sept. 16, 1632. William Wadsworth was accompanied by his family of four

Geo. W. Perkins.

and settled in Newtown (now Cambridge), Mass., subsequently removing to Hartford, Conn. His second wife was Elizabeth Stone, and the line of descent is traced through their son, Sergeant John, brother of Joseph Wadsworth, who seized the original Connecticut charter and secreted it in the historic oak tree and who married Sarah Stanley; their son, Capt. James Wadsworth, who married Ruth Noyes; their son James Wadsworth, who married Abigail Penfield; their son John Noyes, who married Esther Parsons; their son James, who married Naomi Wolcott; their son, Gen. James Samuel (q. v.), who married Mary Craig Wharton and was the grandfather of the senator. His father (b. 1846) was aide-de-camp on the staff of Gouveneur K. Warren, commanding the 5th army corps of the army of the Potomac and was brevetted major of volunteers in April, 1865, for gallant and meritorious services at the battle of Five Forks, Va., in the civil war. He was elected state comptroller in 1879 with Gov. Cornell, being the youngest incumbent of that office, and served in the national congress. The son was educated at St. Mark's School, Southboro, Mass., and was graduated at Yale University in 1898. At college he was a member of the Delta Kappa Epsilon fraternity and the Skull and Bones Society. At the time of his graduation the Spanish-American war was in progress, and he enlisted in battery A of the Pennsylvania light artillery, under Gen. Frederick D. Grant. At the termination of the war he was discharged from the volunteer service, but early in 1899 made a voyage with three classmates to the Philippine Islands and saw active service there. Upon his return to the United States he took up scientific farming on his estate at Mt. Morris, N. Y., a subject in which he had taken deep interest during his whole career. His political life began in 1904, when he was elected on the Republican ticket to the state assembly, serving by re-election until 1910, at each term being speaker of the assembly. He was a delegate to the Republican national convention in 1908 and again in 1912. In 1914 he was elected to the U. S. senate. Sen. Wadsworth is a director of the Genesee Valley National Bank at Geneseo, N. Y., and was the manager of a large ranch at Paloduro, Tex., during 1911–15. He is a member of the Loyal Legion, Spanish War Veterans, Grange, and the Delta Kappa Epsilon college fraternity. He is a member of the Metropolitan Club of Washington, D. C., the Racquet and Tennis, Union League and Yale clubs of New York city, and Fort Orange club of Albany. Sen. Wadsworth was married, Sept. 30, 1902, to Alice, daughter of Hon. John Hay (q. v.), secretary of state in the cabinets of Pres. McKinley and Pres. Roosevelt, and has three children: Evelyn, James Jeremiah and Reverdy Wadsworth.

BAKER, William Henry, physician and surgeon, was born at Medford, Mass., Mar. 11, 1845, son of Abijah Richardson and Harriet Newell (Woods) Baker, and a descendant of Richard Baker who came from England and settled in Dorchester, Mass., in 1635. Richard Baker married Faith Withington, and the line is traced through their son John, who married Preserved Trott; their son Abijah, who married Hannah Lyon; their son Abijah, who married Esther Hill; their son Abijah, who married Esther Parker, and their son David, who married Jemima Richardson, and was the grandfather of Dr. Baker. His mother, under the pseudonym, "Madge Leslie," was the author of the series of "Tim" books, and was the daughter of Rev. Leonard Wood, president of

the Theological Seminary at Andover, Mass. William H. Baker left school at eighteen years of age, and was engaged for six years in business in New York city. He was graduated M.D. at the Harvard medical school in 1872, and after serving one year in the Boston City Hospital became interne to the Woman's Hospital in New York, and was assistant for eighteen months to Drs. H. Marion Sims, T. Addis Emmet, T. Gaillard Thomas and E. R. Peaslee, while pursuing special studies in gynecology. He returned to Boston in 1874 and began to specialize in gynecology, being the first specialist in his particular field in that city. For twenty years he was clinical instructor of the diseases of women at the Harvard medical school. He virtually created that department in the college. In 1882 he was appointed assistant professor of gynecology in Harvard University, and in 1888 full professor, a position he held for seven years, when he resigned to devote more time to special medical researches and also to his work at the Free Hospital for Women, a charity which owed its inception, organization and success to him more than any other. Every detail of the hospital was under his personal supervision, and he held the dual post of surgeon-in-chief and member of the board of trustees until 1907, when he retired and was made surgeon emeritus. Early in his career he manifested that unusual dexterity and delicacy of touch which afterward marked his work, the most remarkable features of which were in plastic surgery, while his abdominal surgery was especially noted for its thoroughness. Among the best of his professional papers are: "Amenorrhoea, Its Causes and Treatment"; "Amenorrhoea from Undeveloped Uterus"; "Mechanical Appliances in Uterine Surgery"; "Lacerations of the Cervix Uteri, as a Cause of Uterine Disease"; "Malpositions of the Uterus"; "Vaginal Ovariotomy"; "Drainage in the Removal of Submucous Fibroids"; "The Treatment of Cancer of the Uterus"; "Hyperaemia of the Vesico-Urethral Membrane"; "Cancer of the Uterus, Its Treatment by High Amputation Compared with the Total Extirpation"; "Diseases of the Urethra and Bladder"; "Cancer of the Cervix Uteri—Results of Its Treatment by High Amputation." Dr. Baker's chief characteristic perhaps was an unfailing courtesy and kindliness of manner, together with genuineness in every word and act. Toward his patients he was very sympathetic, and shrank from no exertion in their behalf. His clinics were always crowded, and his lectures abounded in practical teaching. In his will he founded the Baker Chair of Gynecology at the Harvard medical school. He was a fellow of the American and British Gynecological societies; member of the Boston Obstetrical Society and the Massachusetts Medical Society; the American Gynecological Society (vice-president); and honorary president of the International Congress in Belgium. He was married Oct. 21, 1874, to Charlotte, daughter of Jonas Ball, one of the trustees of the Boston City Hospital, and had two sons: Roy Ball and Harold Woods Baker. Dr. Baker died in Boston, Mass., Nov. 26, 1914.

DEMAREST, William Henry Steele, president of Rutgers College (1906–), was born at Hudson, N. Y., May 12, 1863, son of David D. and Catherine L. (Nevius) Demarest, and a descendant of David des Marest, a native of France, who came through Holland to America in 1663, settling first on Staten Island and later (1678) removing to a patent on the Hackensack. From this ancestor and his wife, Marie Sohier, the line is traced through their son David and his wife, Rachel Cresson; their son Daniel and his wife, Rebecca De Groot; their son Peter D. and his wife, Osseltie Vander Linde; their son Peter P. and his wife, Lydia Hopper; their son Peter P. and his wife, Lea Demarest, and their son Daniel P. and his wife, Leah Bogert, who were the grandparents of Pres. Demarest. His father, David D. Demarest, D.D. LL.D., was a clergyman of the Reformed Church in America and a theological professor at the seminary of that church in New Brunswick, N. J. The son was graduated at Rutgers College in 1883, receiving the degree of A. M. from the same institution three years later. During 1883–86 he was engaged in teaching and in 1888 he was graduated at the New Brunswick Seminary preparatory to entering the ministry of the Reformed Church in America. He was pastor at Walden, N. Y., 1888–97, and at Catskill, N. Y., 1897–1901. In the latter year he became professor of church history in the New Brunswick Theological Seminary, remaining in that relation until 1906, when he was elected president of Rutgers College. During the ten years of his administration Rutgers College has had constant and substantial progress. The number of professors and instructors has increased from thirty to sixty and the number of students has increased from 245 to 485. The courses of instruction have been greatly developed, especially in the departments of applied science, the technical courses in engineering, chemistry, biology and agriculture. The department of education also has been definitely organized and advanced. The growth in the number of students in attendance on the more general courses has kept pace, however, with the growth of attendance on the technical courses. The property of the college in land, buildings and equipment has increased in value from about $750,000 to $1,500,000. The college campus with adjacent college land has increased from six acres to twenty acres and the college farm now consists of 300 acres instead of ninety five acres. The new buildings erected during the decade are the Engineering building, the Chemistry building, the swimming pool, the John Howard Ford dormitory, the Entomology building, and, at the farm, the Short Course building, the Agricultural building, small department buildings, and greenhouses. The endowment of the college now amounts to about $750,000 and the Federal and state appropriations to the trustees of Rutgers for the maintenance of the State College of New Jersey are much greater than ten years ago. In addition to the regular undergraduate work, short courses in agriculture have been maintained since 1906, and a summer session has been held since 1913; in the former there are about 200 students and in the latter about 500 each year. Post graduate work is also growing and about twenty-five of the 485 students in degree courses in 1915 are post-graduates. The work of the experiment station attached with the college has developed largely in scope and results. Under the Smith-Lever act of the National congress a large extension work has also been recently undertaken. The honorary degree of D.D. was conferred on Pres. Demarest by his alma mater in 1901, and that of LL.D. by Columbia University in 1910, by Union College in 1911, and by the University of Pittsburgh in 1912. He is a member of the Holland Society, the Huguenot Society, the University Club of New York, and the Delta Phi and Phi Beta Kappa college fraternities. He is unmarried.

MUNDELEIN, George William, third archbishop of Chicago, was born in New York city July 2, 1872, son of Francis and Mary (Goetz) Mundelein. He was graduated at Manhattan College in 1889, and after preparatory theological studies at St. Vincent's Seminary, Westmoreland, Pa., was sent as a student from the diocese of Brooklyn to the College of the Propaganda, Rome, Italy, where he was ordained priest June 8, 1895. Returning to Brooklyn, he was appointed secretary to Bishop McDonnell and pastor of a Lithuanian church. In 1898 he was made chancellor of the diocese, and in 1906 a domestic prelate of the Pope, two years later representing the diocese in Rome at the Pope's jubilee, and receiving then the degree of doctor of theology from the Propaganda. On Sept. 21, 1909, he was consecrated titular bishop of Loryma to act as auxiliary bishop of Brooklyn, and his election was followed by a special audience with the Pope. He is conversant with several languages, and as chancellor of the diocese of Brooklyn he managed the office with a skill and discretion that won not only the approbation of Bishop McDonnell, but the esteem of every priest in the diocese. He founded the preparatory seminary of the Immaculate Conception in 1913, and was its first president. In the same year he completed the Church of the Queen of All Saints and also its parish school, two of the most beautiful Gothic buildings in the country. The Church of St. Mary of the Isle, at Long Beach, L. I., was also his work. For his brilliant defense of Pope Pius X's condemnation of Modernism he was made, in 1907, a member of the ancient Roman Academy of Arcadi, an honor never before given to an American. He was appointed archbishop of Chicago Nov. 30, 1915, to succeed Archbishop Quigley, the youngest prelate attaining that rank. He had previously been nominated, in 1909, by the bishops of the Province of Cincinnati for the vacant bishopric of Louisville, Ky. Few men have been more rapidly promoted in the service of a church which recognizes force and character in its priesthood very promptly, and owes much of its strength to such recognition. He is a very forceful speaker and executive and is noted for the sturdy and aggressive Americanism which he has manifested on a number of occasions in his public addresses. Chicago is one of the largest Catholic communities in the country, having 1,150,000 Catholics, 800 priests, 400 churches, 324 schools with 127,000 pupils.

JAMESON, Horatio Gates, physician and surgeon, was born in York, Pa., in 1778, son of Dr. David Jameson, who had emigrated to Charleston, S. C., in 1740, in company with Dr. Hugh Mercer. He studied medicine under his father, and began practicing in Pennsylvania at the early age of seventeen. Removing to Baltimore, Md., in 1810, he attended lectures at the College of Medicine of the University of Maryland and was graduated M.D. in 1813. During the war of 1812 he was surgeon to the United States troops in Baltimore. He was surgeon to the Baltimore Hospital and consulting physician to the board of health. In 1830 he read a paper on the "Non-contagiousness of Yellow Fever" before the Society of German Naturalists and Physicians at Hamburg, Germany, being the first American to attend these meetings. In 1832 he was appointed superintendent of vaccination, and was in charge of the cholera hospitals during the epidemic in that city. He was president of the Ohio Medical College at Cincinnati for a short time, but owing to his wife's ill health he returned to Baltimore and his last years were spent in Philadelphia. He performed a number of valuable and original operations, including the extirpa-

G. W. Mundelein

C. W. Amory

tion of upper jaw with preliminary ligation of the carotid artery in 1820. During 1829—32 he published a quarterly journal entitled the "Maryland Medical Recorder." He also published two lectures, "Fevers in General" (1817) and "American Domestic Medicine" (1817), and a "Treatise on Epidemic Cholera" (1854). He was twice married, first in 1797 to Catherine Shevell, of Somerset county, Pa., by whom he had nine children; she died in 1837, and his second wife was a widow Ely. He died in New York city, Aug. 24, 1855.

MacVICAR, John, political reformer, was born in Galt, Canada, July 4, 1859, son of John and Mary (McEwen) MacVicar. His father, a native of Peterhead, Scotland, emigrated to America in 1852, and settled in Galt, Canada. After his son's birth he removed to Guelph, and later to Erie, Pa., where John MacVicar attended the public schools. He began his business career in the employ of a mercantile business in Erie in 1872. Ten years later he went to Des Moines, Ia., to be manager of the wall paper department of the firm of Redhead, Norton, Lathrop & Co., and in 1893 he organized a wall paper business of his own, the John MacVicar Co., which he conducted in 1900. Early in his career he became interested in local politics, and has devoted much time to the study of municipal problems. He served as town clerk of North Des Moines in 1888, and was elected mayor in the following year. After the consolidation of North Des Moines with Des Moines he was elected mayor of the latter in 1896, serving for two terms or four years. He was one of the originators of the commission form of city government, developing what became known as the "Des Moines Plan," so called because Des Moines was the first city of size in the city to adopt the idea. The Iowa legislature passed a bill Mar. 29, 1907, enabling cities of 25,000 population and over to use a commission form of government on petition of 25 per cent. of the voters (subsequently amended to include cities of 7,000 population). By it the government of the city is vested in a council consisting of the mayor and two others if it has less than 25,000 population, and four others if over 25,000, the councillors to be elected by the voters and they are to be subject to removal on recall. The council is to have all the executive, legislative and administrative powers formerly exercised by the mayor, city council, board of public works, park, police and water departments, solicitor, assessor, treasurer, auditor and city engineer, with authority to appoint the necessary heads or managers of such departments. Based on modern scientific business methods, the "Des Moines Plan" gives no heed to pleas of partisanship, and recognizes neither personal element nor political party. The plan was quickly copied by other cities in Iowa, and has been taken up with modifications elsewhere throughout the United States. Mr. MacVicar served on the "Des Moines Plan" council during 1908–12. He was the dominant figure during the commission's first term and was re-elected two years later. He was married, June 14, 1884, at Des Moines, to Nettie, daughter of John A. Nash, a pioneer clergyman of the Baptist church. To this union were born four children: Mary Hepburn, Marjorie Nash, John Nash and Dorothy MacVicar.

AMORY, Charles Walter, soldier and capitalist, was born in Boston, Mass., Oct. 16, 1842, son of William and Anna (Sears) Amory. His first American ancestor was Jonathan Amory, a native of Somersetshire, England, who settled in South Carolina about 1692. His wife was Rebecca Houston Dublin, and from them the line of descent is traced through their son Thomas and his wife, Rebecca Holmes; their son Thomas and his wife, Elizabeth Coffin, and their son Thomas Coffin and his wife, Hannah Rowe Linzee, who were the grandparents of Charles Walter Amory. The first Thomas Amory moved to Boston, Mass., from South Carolina in 1720, and the family have ever since been identified with the mercantile and manufacturing interests of New England. His father was treasurer of the Amoskeag Cotton Mill, of Manchester, N. H., and under his management it grew from one small mill and 2,000 spindles to 137,000 spindles. When he first took it the town had no railroad, no schools, no churches nor waterworks; on his retiring it was a large and thriving city. The Amory mills, at Manchester, were named for him. Charles Walter Amory attended the Boston Latin School, and was graduated at Harvard College in 1863. On Apr. 24, 1864, he was appointed second lieutenant in the 2d Mass. volunteer cavalry, which guarded the region near Washington, D. C., and during the ensuing three months was engaged with the Confederate cavalry at Rectortown, Difficult Run and Mt. Zion Church, near Aldie. He was captured soon after and suffered untold hardships in Confederate prisons until he was exchanged in October and returned to Boston an emaciated wreck. His prison experience was the cause of an illness which lasted a lifetime. In January, 1865, he was in the South seeking his regiment, which he joined in time to participate in the siege of Petersburg and Richmond. In April he was with Gen. Sheridan and was sent to City Point in command of 230 men, the remainder of his regiment, consisting of 130 men, being in the field with Col. Crowninshield. After Appomattox he was assigned, with other troops, to look for Gen. Johnson, who, however, surrendered before they reached his command. At this period he wrote home that he congratulated himself that he "did not take the advice of family and friends and let the war come to a close without taking some part in it. My part has been small, but still I feel a sort of right to claim a share of the glory." A trip to Europe helped to restore his health, and in 1868 he formed a partnership with H. C. Wainwright, under the name of Wainwright & Amory, stock brokers. In 1880 he was elected treasurer of the Amory Manufacturing Co., which, in 1882, absorbed the Langdon Mills. In 1898 he was also made treasurer of the Amoskeag Manufacturing Co., which, in 1905, purchased the Manchester Mills and the Amory Mills, consolidating them into the largest cotton manufacturing company in the country, if not in the world. The directors wished him to take charge of this large concern, but his health would not permit. He was made president, and held the position until confined to his house. He was also president of the Great Falls Manufacturing Co., and of the Fifty Associates; vice-president of the Provident Institution for Savings, director and member of the executive committee of the American Telephone and Telegraph Co., director of the American Bell Telephone Co., Western Telephone and Telegraph Co., Bay State Trust Co., Old Colony Trust Co., Merchants' National Bank, Western Electric Co., Edison Electric Illuminating Co. of Boston, Boston Manufacturers' Mutual Fire Insurance, Cocheco Manufacturing Co., Lawrence Manufacturing Co., Lyman Mills and the Massachusetts Hospital Life Insurance Co. He had also served as a trustee of the Boston Block Trust of Minneapolis, the Merrimack Manufacturing Co. and the Walter Baker Co. He was a member of the Society of the Loyal

Legion and of the Massachusetts Humane Society. His clubs were: Somerset, Exchange and Eastern Yacht, of Boston; Country, of Brookline, and the Myopia Hunt, of Hamilton, Mass. He seemed to desire to fulfill his rôle acceptably in life, rather than to acquire wealth. Frugal with himself, he was most liberal to others and gave generously to any worthy object. His life is an example of sterling worth and integrity, in which his business associates, his classmates, his friends and family, may justly take pride. He was married Oct. 23, 1867, to Elizabeth, daughter of George Gardner, of Boston, and had four children: William, Clara, wife of T. Jefferson Coolidge; George Gardner and Dorothy, wife of Frederic Winthrop. Mr. Amory died in Boston, Mass., Nov. 5, 1913.

HILL, Frederic Stanhope, naval officer and author, was born in Boston, Mass., Aug. 4, 1829, son of Frederic Stanhope and Mary Welland (Blake) Hill and a descendant of Samuel Hill, a native of England, who early settled at Machias, Me. His father was a playwright and poet. He was educated at a private school in Brattleboro and at the Friends' Academy, Providence, R. I., after which he followed the sea for several years, becoming skipper of a number of famous sailing ships. He went to California at the time of the gold rush in 1849, but after two years returned to his native city and accepted a position in the local post-office. He was employed in the U. S. Custom House, Boston, for four years, during which he also engaged in journalism, and was Boston correspondent of the "New Yorker." During the civil war he was an officer in the U. S. navy, and participated in many of the most important naval conflicts of the war. He was with Adm. Farragut at the capture of New Orleans; was present at the fall of Vicksburg, and served on the coast of Texas and in the Mississippi squadron, where he was in command of the Benton and Tyler respectively. He was mustered out of the naval service in 1865 with the rank of captain and then began his literary career. In 1886 he purchased the Cambridge (Mass.) "Chronicle," and subsequently became editor of the "Tribune," of that city. During 1892–1908 he was secretary of the Massachusetts Nautical Training School Commission. His best books are "Twenty Years at Sea, or Leaves from My Old Log Book," a story for boys (1896); "The Story of the 'Lucky Little Enterprise' " (1900); "The Continuity of the Anglican Church, A. D. 61–1900" (1900); "Twenty-six Historic Ships" (1903); and "The Romance of the American Navy" (1909). Capt. Hill possessed a genuine wit and great dexterity in phrase-making. He was swift to seize a point and extraordinarily apt in anecdotes and illustrations. He was remarkably alert of mind and body and a pleasing conversationalist, with quick sympathy, keen interest in the world's work and ways, the happiest choice of words, and a never-failing humor as genial as it was pungent. He could talk art, war, sport, politics and books, but notwithstanding his erudition and marvelous grasp of mind, his social demeanor was quiet and unobtrusive almost to the point of affectation. His singular gentleness of speech gave a special piquancy to his keen and delicate satire, to which was added readiness in repartee and subtle irony. He was married, Sept. 3, 1860, to Caroline M., daughter of Samuel H. Tyson, of Philadelphia, Pa., and had one daughter, Gertrude Blake, wife of Lawrence M. Stanton, M.D., of New York city. Capt. Hill died in Cambridge, Mass., Sept. 24, 1913.

SMILEY, Albert Keith, educator and reformer, was born at Vassalborough, Kennebec co., Me., Mar. 17, 1828, son of Daniel and Phoebe (Howland) Smiley. He was of Scotch descent on the paternal side and of English Puritan stock on the maternal side. He was brought up on his father's farm on the Kennebec river and was graduated at Haverford College (Pa.) in 1849. He remained at Haverford as instructor in English until 1853 when, with his twin brother, Alfred H., he established the English and Classical Academy in Philadelphia, which he conducted for four years. He was principal of Oak Grove Seminary in Vassalborough, Me., in 1858–60 and principal of the Friends' School, now Moses Brown School, Providence, R. I., for nineteen years. In 1869 he acquired the property surrounding Lake Mohonk, some 300 acres, sixteen miles west of Poughkeepsie, N. Y., which was the scene of the crowning achievement of his life. Here he built a summer resort and filled it with guests who desired and enjoyed the environment which has fitted Lake Mohonk to become the center of great world movements. Year after year the profits of the summer's business went back into the estate in the form of landscape gardening, forestry, good roads, paths and finally a modern hotel of 350 rooms. The world-wide reputation that Lake Mohonk has enjoyed for many years may be attributed not so much to its natural scenic beauty and healthful climate or to the proprietor's observance of the Sabbath and the absence of all liquor-selling as to the series of annual conferences on matters of weight which Mr. Smiley instituted as early as 1883, when his interest in the Indian question led him to invite as his personal guests a coterie of men and women familiar with Indian affairs for a three days' discussion of that great problem. It became known as the Lake Mohonk Conference of Friends of the Indians, and similar conferences have been held annually ever since to the present time. Much of the constructive legislation of recent years for Indians throughout the nation has had its inception in these conferences. Since 1904 the conferences have also discussed affairs in the Philippines, Porto Rico and other outlying territories and dependencies of this country. In 1890 and 1891 two meetings were held there for discussion of the negro problem, and beginning in 1895 Mr. Smiley started an unbroken series of spring conferences on international arbitration which have come to be a world-force in the molding of public opinion concerning the substitution of arbitral and judicial agencies for war. On these occasions Mr. and Mrs. Smiley entertained between two and three hundred persons as their personal guests, among whom have been hundreds of the most prominent men and women in this and foreign countries. His interest in this movement is indicated by a devout wish for its continuance expressed in his will conveying the property to his younger brother and successor, Daniel Smiley, who has long shared in the maintenance of and is now continuing the conferences. As a hotel proprietor Mr. Smiley was able to create a homelike atmosphere which buried all idea of financial relations in a spirit of whole-hearted hospitality. He was his guests' friend and companion, sharing their pleasures and their troubles. As a mark of the esteem in which he and his wife were held, some 2,000 of their guests united in erecting the so-called "Smiley Testimonial Gateway" at the entrance to the Mohonk grounds on the occasion of their golden wedding in 1907. In 1889 Albert and Alfred Smiley purchased a winter residence in Redlands, Cal., developing the property commonly known as "Smiley Heights" into a place of great natural beauty and throwing it freely open to the public. It is visited annually by many thousands of tourists. In 1898 he presented to the city of Redlands an additional park and a library building costing $60,000. Next to his love for humanity was his love of nature. He was his own landscape artist, and the enhanced scenic beauty of his estates at Lake Mohonk and Redlands testify to his exceptional skill. His aim was ever to assist, not supplant the beauties of nature, just as, in the larger field, he strove to assist the great forces for the welfare of mankind. His was a beautiful character which ennobled those about him and lent far more than the ordinary contribution of one man to the world's betterment. His sympathy was genuine, and his intellectual attainments made him a rare and charming companion and conversationalist; but more than these, he was a man of large mind, with an unusual grasp of events and relative values, and an interest in public affairs that looked beyond the individual or the group to the welfare of all. A man of keen sympathies and generous impulses, his many charities were prompted by careful thought and practical common sense. By birth and training a member of the Society of Friends, and in the family circle observing the society's modes of expression, he was an example of the larger religion which overlooks creeds and factional differences. In the religious services held daily in his hotel, denominations played no part, and his own Quaker faith was completely concealed in contact with those of other religious beliefs. While a firm advocate of international peace, he did not fully accept the Quaker doctrine of absolute non-resistance, but believed in reasonable armies and navies. A great idealist, he differed from most idealists in being able to guide idealism along lines of practical logic for the improvement of humankind. He was married, July 8, 1857, to Eliza Phelps, daughter of Richard Cornell, of New York, and a woman of brilliant mind, sharing in a marked degree her husband's charm of manner and his interest in human betterment. Mr. Smiley was a member of the board of trustees of Bryn Mawr College, president of the board of trustees of the New York State Normal School at New Paltz, and trustee of Pomona College, Cal. He received the honorary degrees of A.M. from Brown University in 1877 and LL.D. from Haverford College in 1906. He died at his winter home in Redlands, Cal., Dec. 2, 1912.

STANG, William, first Roman Catholic Bishop of Fall River, Mass., was born in Langenbrüken, grand duchy of Baden, Germany, in 1854. His education, begun in the gymnasia of his native land, was completed at the American College, Louvain, Belgium, where he was ordained priest in 1878. He then emigrated to the United States and became affiliated with the diocese of Providence, R. I., serving as an assistant at the cathedral. In 1884 he was appointed pastor of Cranston, and shortly after was promoted to the pastorate of the Cathedral in Providence and chancellor of the diocese. In April, 1895, he returned to the American College, Louvain, to be its vice-rector, and in that office he displayed marked administrative abilities. The faculty of the University of Louvain appointed him professor of fundamental moral theology in August, 1898. He returned to Providence the following April, and became head of the Diocesan Mission Band and pastor of St. Edward's Church, Providence. On Mar. 12, 1904 the new diocese of Fall River was established, to take in an area of 1,194 square miles in Bristol, Barnstable, Dukes, Nantucket and Plymouth counties, Mass., and Dr. Stang was appointed its first bishop, being consecrated in the Providence Cathedral May 1, 1904. He began a most zealous career of episcopal activities, but it lasted only a little over two years. He was the author of "Pastoral Theology" (1896); "Historio-graphica Ecclesiastica" (1897); "Business Guide for Priests" (1899); "Pepper and Salt" (1901); "Socialism and Christianity" (1905); "Medulla Fundamentalis Theologiæ Moralis" (1906), besides many pamphlets, essays, and contributions to ecclesiastical periodicals. He died in St. Mary's Hospital, Rochester, Minn., Feb. 2, 1907.

SOUTHMAYD, Charles Ferdinand, lawyer, was born in New York city, Nov. 27, 1824, son of Samuel Dwight and Mary (Ogden) Southmayd. His first American ancestor was William Southmead or Southmate, who came from England about 1640 and settled first at Gloucester and later at Salem, Mass.; from him and his wife, Millicent Addis, the line of descent is traced through their son William and his wife, Margaret Allyn; their son William and his wife, Mehitabel Dwight and their son Partridge Samuel or Samuel Partridge and his wife, Hannah Fanning, who were the grandparents of Charles F. Southmayd. He was educated at private schools in New York city, and entered the law office of Elisha P. Hurlbut, of the firm of Hurlbut & Owen, where he remained as student clerk and then as partner until 1847, when Mr. Hurlbut went on the bench. Subsequently he was in partnership with Alexander S. Johnson until the latter was appointed a judge of the court of appeals in 1851, and then was a member of the firm of Butler, Evarts & Southmayd and its successor, Evarts, Southmayd & Choate. He retired from active practice in 1884. Of the many important cases with which Mr. Southmayd was identified during his long career especial mention should be made of Ogden *vs.* Astor; Iddings *vs.* Bruen; the Delaware & Hudson Canal Co. *vs.* the Pennsylvania Coal Co.; the Tennessee Bond case, and Langdon *vs.* the city of New York, all of which were of important public concern, and in which the most eminent counsel were engaged on both sides. Mr. Southmayd was one of the great lawyers of his day. He had wonderful powers of concentration. His mind was naturally adapted to the principles of equity law, of which he became master, and during the entire period of his connection with his several law firms he was the mainstay of the whole concern. If there was a knotty point of law or practice to be decided, a difficult will, trust or contract to be drawn, an important opinion to be prepared, it was almost always left to him and he would never give in till the problem was solved. He had, in fact, a genius for the law, and there was no department of it to which he was not fully equal, except trial by jury, for which he had no taste. It was said that the great lawyers of the city sought his opinion upon questions that arose in their own practice, and notwithstanding many eccentricities he had an absolutely honest and straight mind. Said Joseph H. Choate, "In addition to great learning and inexhaustible power of labor, untiring patience and common sense, he had the great and unspeakable gift of character which is more than all the rest combined in the formation of a great lawyer, stooping to nothing, tolerating nothing small or mean or low, maintaining always the highest standard of personal and professional conduct, and putting everything to the test of his own good and clear conscience." Mr. Southmayd received the degree of LL.D. from Yale in 1884.

He was one of the founders, and at one time a vice-president, of the Association of the Bar of the City of New York. At the time of his death he was the earliest living member of the Century Club, and he was also a member of the Society Library, New York. He died unmarried, in New York city, July 11, 1911.

MATTHEWS, J[oseph] Merritt, chemist and author, was born in Philadelphia, Pa., June 9, 1874, son of Joseph Merritt and Blanche (Fowler) Matthews. The first of the family in America was Thomas Matthews, who had served under Cromwell and was afterwards a public preacher among the Friends in the north of England, and who came to this country about 1650, settling in Centre, New Castle co., Del. The line of descent is traced through Oliver, Thomas, Daniel, Thomas and Thomas Johnson Matthews, who was the grandfather of the subject of this sketch. He was educated in the public schools of Philadelphia and was graduated at the University of Pennsylvania in 1895 with the degree of B.Sc. After a post-graduate course, receiving the Ph.D. degree in 1898, he became head of the department of chemistry and dyeing of the Philadelphia Textile School. In 1907 he accepted the position of manager of the dyeing department of the New England Cotton Yarn Co. at Taunton, Mass., where he remained three years and then opened an office in New York city as consulting chemist and expert in patent causes and chemical jurisprudence. Dr. Matthews has delivered many addresses before scientific bodies on technical subjects, and has contributed to technical journals numerous articles relating to textile chemistry. Since its establishment in 1908 he has been assistant editor of the "Journal of Industrial and Engineering Chemistry," to which he is a regular contributor. He is the author of Volume III., Part I. of "Allen's Commercial Organic Analysis" (1900); "Textile Fibres" (1904, 1907, 1913); "Laboratory Manual Dyeing and Textile Chemistry" (1909), and has translated Alexieff's "General Principles of Organic Syntheses" (1906). Dr. Matthews has devised many methods and improvements in bleaching and dyeing in the line of textile chemistry, one of the most radical being the displacement of bleaching powder by liquid chlorin. Notwithstanding many improvements in connection with the textile industry made by Dr. Matthews for greater efficiency and economy, he has applied for only one patent, that for a process of making carbon tetra chloride, which was issued Nov. 6, 1906. He is a fellow of the American Association for the Advancement of Science; member of the American Chemical Society (vice-president, 1902), the Society of Chemical Industry, the Society of Dyers and Colorists of England, the American Institute of Chemical Engineers, the American Society for Testing Materials, the National Geographic Society, the American Legion, the Chemists' Club of New York, and the Authors' Club of London. He was formerly a member of the Franklin Institute of Philadelphia, and was a member of the International Congresses of Applied Chemistry in 1903, 1906, 1909 and 1912. He was married May 15, 1903, to Augusta Spaulding, daughter of John Edgar Gould, of Philadelphia, Pa.

GAZZAM, Joseph Murphy, lawyer, was born in Pittsburgh, Pa., Dec. 2, 1842, son of Edward Despard and Elizabeth Antoinette de Beelen (de Bertholff) Gazzam. His grandfather, William Gazzam, an English journalist, in 1792, through the resentment of the king, was compelled to seek refuge in the United States, whose rights he had openly defended. Settling first in Philadelphia, later in Carlisle, and finally in Pittsburgh he was appointed a magistrate by Gov. Snyder, served as collector of the port under Pres. Madison, and died there in 1811. His father, Edward D. Gazzam, was a prominent physician and lawyer. Mr. Gazzam was educated at home under private tutors, was graduated at the Western University in Pennsylvania, studied law in the office of David Reed, and was admitted to the bar in Pittsburgh in 1864. He was admitted to the state supreme court in 1867, to the U. S. circuit and district courts in 1869, and the U. S. supreme court in 1870. In 1871 he was elected a director for Pennsylvania in the U. S. Law Association, and in 1872 he entered into a law partnership with Hon. Alexander G. Cochran. Mr. Gazzam was a member of the common council of Pittsburgh during 1869–73, and was elected state senator in 1876. He was the author of a number of important measures, among them the law which abolished special elections for state officers, thereby making a great saving to the taxpayers. He also introduced a bill for a marriage-license law almost identical with the one now in operation, passed many years later. In 1879 Mr. Gazzam removed to Philadelphia, where he practiced law for a number of years, being the senior member of the firm of Gazzam, Wallace & Lukens. Mr. Gazzam occupies a prominent position in the financial and industrial realms. He was one of the projectors of the Beech Creek Railroad, now under the Vanderbilt system, and the town of Gazzam was named for him. One of the organizers of the Quaker City National Bank, of Philadelphia, he served as vice-president of that institution for fourteen years. He is president of the Ames-Bonner Co., brush and mirror manufacturers of Toledo, O., and of the Rees-Welsh Digest and Law Publishing Co., of Philadelphia; vice-president of the Dent's Run (Pa.) Coal Co.; chairman of the Board of Directors of Peale, Peacock & Kerr, Inc., and Toledo Web Press Manufacturing Co.; a director of the Delaware Co., and an officer or director in a long list of others. Among the numerous positions of trust held by Mr. Gazzam was that of commissioner from Pennsylvania to the South Carolina Inter-State and West Indian Exposition of 1902; he was also a member of the Pennsylvania commission to the Louisiana Purchase Exposition at St. Louis in 1904. His interest in arts and letters has been dominant throughout his life. He is a life member of the Pennsylvania Historical Society; Fairmount Park (Philadelphia) Art Association; Franklin Institute; Horticultural Association; Pennsylvania Academy of Fine Arts; Zoological Society; American Academy of Political and Social Science; Genealogical Society of Pennsylvania; Archæological and Paleontological Society of Pennsylvania; and the Geographical Society. He is also a life member of the Union League and Lawyers' Club of Philadelphia, the National Arts and City clubs of New York city, and of the Toledo and Toledo Yacht clubs, of Toledo, O. For three years he served as president of Pennsylvania Club, of which he is a member. Mr. Gazzam has been twice married; first, Oct. 30, 1878, to Mary Anna, daughter of the late John Grandin Reading of Philadelphia; two children were born of this union, Sada (deceased), and Antoinette Elizabeth Gazzam, wife of Charles B. Galvin; second, Sept. 7, 1893, to Nellie May, daughter of Benjamin Andrews, of New Orleans, one of the pioneer cotton-seed oil men of the south; two children have been the issue of this union, Joseph, and Olivia Mary de Beelen Gazzam.

BELL, James Stroud, miller and capitalist, was born in Philadelphia, Pa., June 30, 1847, son of Samuel and Elizabeth (Faust) Bell, and great-great-grandson of Henry Bell, a miller of Carlyle, England, who came to America in 1770. For five generations, or nearly 200 years, the Bell family were engaged in the milling industry in England and the United States. In 1837 his father became a flour commission merchant of Philadelphia, operating first as W. & S. Bell, then as Samuel Bell, and subsequently as Samuel Bell & Son. James S. Bell was educated in the public schools of Philadelphia, and entering his father's flour business, became a partner in 1868, the name of the firm becoming Samuel Bell & Son. It was sales-agent for Washburn, Crosby & Co., one of the great milling companies of Minneapolis, and when the latter was reorganized in 1888 he entered the firm and removed to Minneapolis. A year later it was incorporated as the Washburn-Crosby Co., and he was president of this the largest flour milling concern in the world during the remainder of his life. These mills now have a total daily capacity of approximately 50,000 barrels. They embrace in addition to the great Minneapolis plant, huge mills in Buffalo, N. Y., Louisville, Ky., Great Falls and Kalispell, Mont. It was due to his extraordinary acumen and insight into the peculiar demands of the trade, its strategy and vantage points of competition, that these mills were added to the plant of the company, which is not only an acknowledged leader in American flour milling, but a commanding figure in the grain trade and financial field of this country and Canada, pointing the way of large traders in the Minneapolis Chamber of Commerce. In 1905, when there was a shortage of hard wheat, Mr. Bell imported 3,000,000 bushels of West Canadian wheat in bond, and milled it in Minneapolis, thus making new history in the industry. In the original draft of the new tariff bill of the Woodrow Wilson administration, it was proposed to make flour free of import duty and retain a duty on wheat. Mr. Bell was the spokesman for the milling industry of the entire country in opposition to this change, and his proposal that the tariff on wheat be either maintained, or both wheat and flour made free, was finally adopted. He was president of the St. Anthony and Dakota Elevator Co., St. Anthony Elevator Co., Barnum Grain Co., Royal Milling Co., Rocky Mountain Elevator Co., and Brown Grain Co., vice-president of the Minneapolis Trust Co., and a director of the Northwestern National Bank, the old National Bank of Commerce, and the Chicago, Great Western Railway Co. Mr. Bell was a Republican in politics, and for many years a member of the Westminster Presbyterian church. His clubs were the Minneapolis and the Minikanda of Mineapolis, and the Union League of Philadelphia. He was twice married: (1) Jan. 8, 1873, to Sallie Montgomery, daughter of Edwin Ford, of Philadelphia, and had one son, James Ford Bell. Mrs. Bell died in 1905, and he was married (2), Sept. 28, 1912, to Mrs. Mabel Sargent, of Boston, Mass. He died in Minneapolis, Minn., Apr. 5, 1915.

WESTINGHOUSE, George, inventor and manufacturer, was born at Central Bridge, Schoharie co., N. Y., Oct. 6, 1846, son of George Westinghouse and his wife, Emmeline Vedder. As early as the ninth century the ''Westinghausen'' family was prominent in Westphalia, Germany, and in the 14th century a branch of the family emigrated to England. From this English branch originated the American families of the name. In the early part of the nineteenth century the father of George Westinghouse removed from Vermont to Ohio, but the unsettled condition of that country prompted his return to New York state, and he settled at Central Bridge as a farmer. Being of an inventive mind he made various valuable improvements in farming implements, for the manufacture of which he formed the firm of G. Westinghouse & Co. at Schenectady, N. Y., in 1856. His son, George, made a playground of his father's machine shop, where he imbibed an early love for machinery and mechanics. He had a special fondness for mathematics and power problems, and at the age of fifteen he invented and built a rotary engine. Between school and college he served in the civil war, first in the 12th regiment, N. G. N. Y., and later in the 16th regiment, New York volunteer cavalry. In December, 1864, he exchanged from the army to the navy, and was appointed third assistant engineer on the U. S. S. Muscoota. Resigning at the end of the war, he entered Union College, Schenectady, N. Y., class of 1869, but upon the advice of President Hickok left in his sophomore year to devote himself to the completion and introduction of his inventions, which President Hickok foresaw would be of far greater importance than further study at college. Meanwhile, in 1866, he had perfected two inventions—a device for replacing derailed cars upon the track, and a reversible steel railroad frog. The formation of a partnership in Schenectady and the building of a foundry for the manufacture of these inventions proved unsuccessful through lack of capital. It is interesting to note, however, that this was probably the first effective attempt in this country to make steel castings. Subsequently he went to Pittsburgh, Pa., and arranged with a steel firm in that city to manufacture the articles for him while he went on the road to sell them to railroad companies. This was the beginning of his wonderful career of forty-seven years in that city. At the time of his arrival in Pittsburgh he had already conceived the idea for the air brake, which was suggested to him by a collision between two freight trains. His experiments were without practical results until an article in a paper suggested to him the idea of using compressed air to operate his brake. This idea solved the problem, and he perfected a complete brake apparatus that was destined to revolutionize the operation of steam trains. The operation of the Westinghouse air brake is as follows: Air at about eighty pounds pressure is compressed and stored on the locomotive and under this pressure is conveyed by means of pipes and flexible hose to reservoirs placed under each car of the train. Each car has a cylinder with a piston so arranged that when air pressure is admitted to the cylinder its piston will force the brake shoes against the wheels of the car. After the desired braking effect has been secured, it can be released by permitting the compressed air to escape from the brake cylinder. A ''triple valve'' on each car controls the flow of air from the supply pipe to the storage reservoir, from the reservoir to the brake cylinder to apply brakes, and from the brake cylinder to the atmosphere to release them. It is actuated by variations of pressure in the supply pipe, which are produced by the engineer on the locomotive when it is desired to operate the brakes. The latter can be set from the locomotive, or from the cars by means of the ''conductor's valve,'' or automatically by the reduction of pressure in the supply pipe such as would be caused by an accidental rupture or serious leakage. From this important feature the device has derived the title of ''automatic brake.'' The air brake was tested for the first time in December, 1868, on the Steubenville division of the Pittsburgh, Columbus, Cincinnati and St. Louis railroad (the Panhandle), and it is interesting to record that the initial application of the air brake was to save the life of a man. A driver of a coal wagon crossing the tracks had been thrown from the seat just as the engine appeared at the mouth of the tunnel. The brakes were applied quickly, and the man was saved. On Apr. 13, 1869, Mr. Westinghouse received his first air-brake patent, and in the following July he organized the Westinghouse Air Brake Co. The company proved a great success from the start, and after the brake had become generally known in this country he went abroad in 1870 to introduce the apparatus to the railroads of Europe. Here he met with many disappointments, especially in England. For over ten years he spent half his time in Europe. Reward finally came to him, and the demand for the Westinghouse air-brake in Europe necessitated the establishment of factories in England, France, Germany, Russia and Italy. Seeking other uses for the compressed-air principle in his brake, and following certain experiments with electricity he invented a pneumatic system of interlocking signals for railroads, operated by compressed air and electricity combined. For the purpose of manufacturing this invention he organized in 1881 The Union Switch and Signal Co., which also developed into an industry of important proportions. In 1888 he invented the Westinghouse friction draft gear, which is now in use on thousands of cars and has a special value on account of the general introduction of steel cars. Electricity had now begun to fascinate him, and the more he worked with it the deeper his interest grew. As early as 1877 he had invented an automatic telephone exchange system, but its utility and value were not then understood, and his patents expired before the telephone people and the public could be persuaded to adopt it. In 1885 he engaged William Stanley to assist him in electrical development. During that year he purchased the Gaulard and Gibbs transformer patents for the distribution of electricity by alternating currents, and remodelled and improved the designs; and in the following year he organized the Westinghouse Electric Co. for the manufacture of electric lighting apparatus. The success of the alternating current system precipitated a bitter controversy which lasted for over ten years. It was claimed by its opponents that the high voltage of the alternating current was dangerous to life, and efforts were made to have laws passed to prohibit its use. The execution of criminals by electricity, it has been said, was introduced in New York State for the sole purpose of terrifying the public so that the use of the alternating current would be prohibited. It is now generally conceded that George Westinghouse, by the introduction and development of the alternating current, laid the foundation for the marvelous extension of electrical achievements which have been made within the last thirty years. Recognition came to him in 1912, when he was awarded the Edison gold medal by the American Institute of Electrical Engineers for ''Meritorious achievements in the development of the alternating current system.'' In 1887 he purchased and

developed the inventions of Nicola Tesla that made practicable the use of alternating current to drive electric motors. Four years later the Electric company was reorganized under the name of the Westinghouse Electric and Manufacturing Co., now one of the leading manufacturing companies of electrical apparatus in the world. In 1893 he built the generators to supply the World's Columbian exposition in Chicago with electric lights. Subsequently his company furnished the first ten generators to the Niagara Falls Power Co. for transmitting electrically the power of Niagara Falls, and it also built the dynamos for the elevated and subway roads in New York city, for the Metropolitan Railway in London, and for the Subway of Paris. In 1884 his attention was drawn to the natural gas in the vicinity of Pittsburgh. A well drilled on his own property produced a very large flow of gas, and this led him to experiments with natural gas apparatus. He invented a complete system for conducting natural gas into homes, mills and factories. As natural gas became more and more used in the manufacture of steel and glass, his inventions in that field did much to establish the supremacy of Pittsburgh for those products. In 1885 he purchased the charter of the Philadelphia Co., and with it supplied gas to thousands of private houses in Pittsburgh through many miles of pipe lines from the surrounding country. In 1888 he organized the East Pittsburgh Improvement Co. and inaugurated the development of the Turtle Creek Valley by erecting in 1890 the works of the Westinghouse Air Brake Co., in 1891 the plant of the Pittsburgh Meter Co., in 1894 the immense factories of the Westinghouse Electric and Manufacturing Co. and the Westinghouse Machine Co., and in 1902 the Westinghouse Foundries at Trafford, Pa. In 1895 he began the development of gas engines of large capacity in conjunction with the engineering department of the Westinghouse Machine Co. organized in 1880 to build high-speed steam engines, designed by his brother, Henry Herman Westinghouse, and he subsequently turned out apparatus of this type in units of 4,000 horsepower each. Acquiring the American rights of the Parsons steam turbines in 1896, he made many improvements in turbine construction along entirely new lines. In collaboration with Adm. George W. Melville, and the latter's partner, John H. Macalpine, he developed a mechanical reduction gear for the purpose of adapting high-speed turbines to marine service. Its characteristic feature, invented by these men and improved by Westinghouse, is a self-adjusting floating frame which is designed to keep the gears and pinions in perfect alignment. His last invention was an air spring to be used on automobile and motor trucks, which was completed in 1912. At various times Mr. Westinghouse was in control of the following industrial companies: the Westinghouse Co. of Schenectady, N. Y.; the Westinghouse Air Brake Co., the Westinghouse Electric and Manufacturing Co., the Westinghouse Machine Co., the Union Switch and Signal Co., the R. D. Nuttall Co., the Standard Underground Cable Co., the Westinghouse Friction Draft Gear Co., the Trafford Real Estate Co., the Philadelphia Co., the Alleghany Heating Co., the Allegheny County Light Co., the Security Investment Co., the Westinghouse Traction Brake Co., the Nernst Lamp Co., the Fuel Gas and Manufacturing Co., the Westinghouse Foundry Co., the Westinghouse Inter-Works Railway Co., the Westinghouse Glass Co., the Pittsburgh Meter Co., the

Sawyer-Man Electric Co., the Westinghouse Air Spring Co., the East Pittsburgh Improvement Co., all of Pittsburgh, Pa., the Cooper Hewitt Electric Co., Westinghouse, Church, Kerr & Co., and the United Electric Light and Power Co. of New York; the American Air Brake Co. of St. Louis, Mo.; the Bryant Electric Co., and the Perkins Electric Switch Manufacturing Co. of Bridgeport, Conn.; the Westinghouse Lamp Co. of Bloomfield, N. J.; the Canadian Westinghouse Co. of Hamilton, Ontario, Canada; the British Westinghouse Electric and Manufacturing Co. of Manchester, England; the Traction and Power Securities Co., Ltd., London; the Société Anonyme Westinghouse, France; the Société Anonyme Westinghouse, Russia; the Westinghouse Brake Co., London, England; Die Westinghouse Luft Bremsen Gesellschaft, Hanover, Germany; the Societa Italiana Westinghouse, Italy; the Westinghouse Metallfaden Gluehlampen Actien Gesellschaft, Vienna, Austria; the Westinghouse Electricitaets Actien Gesellschaft, Berlin, Germany. The combined capitalization of all these companies was about $200,000,000, giving employment to over 50,000 persons. He was one of the largest employers of labor in the world, and he took the utmost interest in the welfare of his employees. He was the originator in the United States of the Saturday half holiday for workmen, in 1871. He was most helpful to the striving inventor, and always ready to give advice and financial aid to others. He received many honors both at home and abroad. In 1874 the Franklin Institute awarded to him the Scott premium and medal for his improvements in air brake construction; in 1884 the king of Belgium decorated him with the Order of Leopold, and later he was made an officer of that order; in 1889 King Victor Emmanuel presented him with the decoration of the Order of the Crown of Italy, and in 1891 he was made a member of the Legion of Honor of France. His alma mater, Union College, conferred upon him the degree of Ph.D. in 1891, and the Koenigliche Technische Hochschule of Berlin, Germany, gave him the degree of Doctor of Engineering in 1906. In 1913 the Society of German Engineers presented him with the Grashof medal, he being the first American so honored by that body. Besides the Edison gold medal, already mentioned, he also received the John Fritz medal in 1906. He was one of the two honorary members of the American Association for the Advancement of Science, honorary member of the National Electric Light Association of America, and was president of the American Society of Mechanical Engineers in 1910. In 1905 he was chosen, with ex-Pres. Cleveland and Justice Morgan J. O'Brien, one of three trustees of the Equitable Life Assurance Society at a time of general unrest in insurance and financial conditions. He was a member of the Royal Institute of Great Britain; American Academy of Political and Social Science, Philadelphia; Franklin Institute; American Association for the Conservation of Vision; American Institute of Electrical Engineers; American Institute of Mining Engineers; American Society of Automobile Engineers; American Society of Civil Engineers; American Society of Naval Engineers; American Protective Tariff League; National Geographic Society; American Society of the Fine Arts; American Museum of Natural History; Metropolitan Museum of Art; New York Zoological and Botanical Society; Pilgrims of the United States; Japan Society; Pan-American Society of the United States; New York Chamber of Commerce, and Western Pennsylvania Exposition Society. He was also a member of the following clubs: Automobile Club of America, City, Midday, Economic, Metropolitan, Railroad, Lawyers and Union League, New York city; Duquesne, University, Union, Pittsburgh, Pittsburg Country and Oakmont Country, Pittsburgh; Chevy Chase, Washington, D. C.; Lenox, Lenox, Mass., and Sleepy Hollow Country, Westchester County, N. Y. George Westinghouse holds a conspicuous place in American biography. Great as were his achievements as an original inventor, a deep thinker, a successful manufacturer and a masterly organizer, they were matched by his noble character as a man. Tireless energy, extraordinary foresight, inspiring enthusiasm, indomitable courage, inflexible integrity and benevolence of purpose were his dominant traits. From association with him men caught inspiration. He radiated enthusiasm and energy; he demanded honest work and honest dealing; all that was in him he gave freely to whatever work he had in hand; he imposed no limitations upon his own hours nor upon his own resources of energy; he believed sincerely that his mission was to be useful; and he was useful to an extent beyond even the dream of most men. Considerate of others, his greatest satisfaction was the knowledge that what he had accomplished contributed so largely to the benefit and comfort of his fellow men. His greatest monument is the worldwide use of the invention which gave passenger travel delightful security, developed the transportation of freight, the rapidity of commercial transactions, and so largely assisted in removing the growing obstacles to trade and manufacture. He thought in flashes, and his action seemed almost as quick as his thought. He was untiring, and he had the rare faculty of concentration joined to the still rarer faculty of switching his concentration from one undertaking to another. His memory was astonishingly comprehensive and accurate. It absorbed and classified details, and it was so retentive that he was scarcely ever known to make a note, and he never used a memorandum book. In social life he was gentle, unaffected, accessible and delightful in manner. In all circumstances he stood for high manhood, a true patriotism, and the graces of a noble character. He was married Aug. 8, 1867, in Brooklyn, N. Y., to Marguerite Erskine, daughter of Daniel Lynch and Eliza Smart (Burhans) Walker of Roxbury, Delaware Co., N. Y. Mrs. Westinghouse was in close accord with his ambitions and struggles, and he himself said that any success he may have had in life was due entirely to her inspiration and encouragement. They had one child, George Westinghouse, 3rd, who resides at Lenox, Mass. Mr. Westinghouse died in New York city, Mar. 12, 1914. His widow died June 23 of the same year.

WESTINGHOUSE, Marguerite Erskine Walker (Mrs. George Westinghouse), was born at Roxbury, Delaware co., N. Y., Mar. 1, 1842, daughter of Capt. Daniel Lynch and Eliza Smart (Burhans) Walker, and a descendant of Philip Walker of Rehoboth, Mass., who served in the war of the revolution. She was educated at home and at Roxbury Academy, and early developed a marked talent for sculpture, executing some work of exceptional merit, both before and after her marriage. Among her most notable creations are a life-size bust of her husband (the only one extant), done in 1878, and a bust of the famous Dr. Diomedi C. Pantaleoni, of Rome, known as Garibaldi's right-hand man, which is said to be the best likeness of him ever made. Her artistic talents found further expression in planning the Westinghouse summer home, "Erskine Park," at Lenox, Mass. The house and the landscape effects were built and laid out according to her own designs and under her personal supervision. "Erskine Park" was the show place of Lenox, and was aptly described as "A poem in green and white." "Solitude," the Westinghouse residence in Pittsburgh and for many years the show place of that city, was also a concrete testimony to her artistic talents. But, great as were her abilities, they were dwarfed by her virtues. It would be hard to find a woman who was to such a degree the incarnation of the qualities enshrined in our ideal of womanhood. Charity, in its broadest sense, sympathy, tenderness, devotion, thoughtfulness, helpfulness and unselfishness informed all the relations of her life, while she had to a remarkable extent the faculty of imparting encouragement and inspiration, which is, perhaps, woman's noblest and most valuable function. It was in the home especially that these qualities were exemplified. How much of Mr. Westinghouse's distinguished achievement was due to her help and inspiration it would be impossible to measure, but he probably was not overstating the case when he attributed his success in life to his wife. During forty-seven years of married life they remained devoted lovers, and the atmosphere of their home was cheering and stimulating beyond description. The Westinghouse entertainments were social events of their time in Pittsburgh, Washington and Lenox. And behind all this gaiety and brilliance there was constantly felt the peace, harmony, love and high seriousness which made the home everything that an ideal home could be. None knew and few guess the full extent of her kindness. Her charity did not consist merely in giving abundantly of her means; she also gave generously of herself, of her strength and the rich store of her love and sympathy. It was well said of her that "she lived as others preached." Her interest went out not only to individual cases of suffering and need, but to all movements and institutions of worthy and beneficent purposes. She was an active member of the boards of managers of numerous hospitals in Pittsburgh, Pa., and Washington, D. C., giving freely to them of her time and means. She was a life member of the National Geographic Society, and a member of the National Society of Fine Arts, the American Social Science Association, the American Forestry Association, the Archeological Institute of America, the American Red Cross, Pittsburgh Chapter, Daughters of the American Revolution, and the Twentieth Century Club of Pittsburgh, the Lenox Garden Club, the Lenox Golf Club, the MahKeenac Boating Club of Lenox and the Berkshire Hunt Club. Her religious affiliation was with the Presbyterian church. The date of her marriage was Aug. 8, 1867, and she had one son, George Westinghouse, Jr. She survived her husband but a few months, dying at "Erskine Park," Lenox, Mass., June 23, 1914.

MAYO, Henry Thomas, naval officer, was born in Burlington, Vt., Dec. 8, 1856, son of Henry and Elizabeth (Eldridge) Mayo. His first American ancestor was John Mayo, who came from West Malling, Kent co., England, to Massachusetts in 1632 on the ship William and Mary, and settled in Roxbury. From this John Mayo and his wife, Hannah Graves, the line of descent is traced through their son Thomas, who married Elizabeth Davis; through their son Maj. Joseph, who married Esther Kenrick; their son Col. Joseph, who married Lucy Richards; their son Col. Nathaniel, who married Hannah Simonds, and who was the grandfather of the subject of this sketch. Maj. Joseph Mayo and his son, Col. Joseph Mayo, served in the revolutionary war. Our subject's father, Capt. Henry Mayo, was prominently identified with navigation on Lake Champlain, commanding the lake steamers Boston, Montreal, Saranac, A. Williams and United States, retiring in 1883 after a continuous service of fifty-eight years. The son entered the U. S. naval academy at the early age of fifteen, and was graduated in 1876. He was at sea as passed midshipman for two years, and during 1879–82 as ensign was engaged in scientific work with the Coast and Geodetic Survey. This continued until 1889, excepting three years, when he was assigned to the U. S. naval observatory, where he had further opportunity to develop his scientific bent. Three years on the training-ship Jamestown were followed by another period of scientific work in the naval branch hydrographic office at Port Townsend, Wash. During the Spanish war in 1898 he served inconspicuously on the gunboat Bennington. He was appointed lieutenant-commander in June, 1899, and commander in February, 1905, being assigned soon after to the lighthouse inspection service on the California coast. In September, 1908, he was promoted to be captain, and was given command of the Albany, and later the cruiser California on the Pacific coast. He was secretary of the lighthouse board in 1908–09, and commanded the navy yard at Mare Island, Cal., during 1911–13. In June, 1913, he was made rear-admiral, and soon after was appointed aid to Secretary of Navy Daniels. There are four such aids, and they occupy very important, responsible and influential positions. They are the secretary of the navy's cabinet and were instituted under the reorganization effected by George von L. Meyer when he held the naval portfolio, mainly for the purpose of overcoming the power of the chiefs of naval bureaus who held their offices by statutory authority. Sec. Daniels was so impressed with the high qualifications of Capt. Mayo that he appointed him to take charge of the personnel branch of the work assigned to the so-called aids. In December, 1913, he was placed in command of first and fourth divisions of the Atlantic fleet then in Mexican waters, his flagship being the Connecticut. At this time occurred the incident that greatly aggravated the then strained relations with Mexico. The crew of one of the Dolphin's launches going ashore at Tampico, Mexico, for gasoline, was arrested and imprisoned. Mayo, with commendable promptness, and acting on his own initiative, demanded of the Mexican commander, Gen. Zaragosa, the immediate release of the American sailors, an apology to the United States, and a salute of twenty-one guns to the United States flag before sundown. The first two demands were complied with, but not the third. The United States government pressed the point by sending the entire navy to Mexican waters; the city of Vera Cruz, Mexico, was taken and held by American forces for a number of weeks; several lives were lost in skirmishes with Mexican troops, and for a time relations with Mexico were near the breaking point. (See Fletcher, F. F.) Since then Adm. Mayo has commanded in turn the Minnesota, Kansas, Vermont, Arkansas and New York. In June, 1915, he was made vice-admiral, the first incumbent of that rank since Rowan in 1870, and was placed in command of the battleship squadrons and first division of the Atlantic fleet. Adm. Mayo is a

man of decision and a strict disciplinarian on shipboard. Off duty he is quiet and unassuming, genial and affable, and has been characterized as "one of the biggest-hearted men in the navy, and one of the most popular among its officers." He is a member of the Army and Navy Club of Washington, and the New York Yacht Club of New York city. He was married Mar. 9, 1881, to Mary C., daughter of H. R. Wing, of Burlington, Vt., and has two sons: Chester Garst, a paymaster in the United States navy, and George Mayo, a lieutenant in the corps of engineers, United States army.

HARTY, Jeremiah J., first American archbishop of Manila, Philippine Islands, was born in St. Louis, Mo., Nov. 1, 1853, son of Andrew and Julia (Murphy) Harty. After attending St. Louis University he took his theological course at St. Vincent's Seminary, Cape Girardeau, and was ordained Apr. 28, 1878. His work as a pastor was most efficient. While he was in charge of St. Leo's Church in St. Louis he was selected by the Pope to be the first American archbishop of Manila in the reconstruction of the affairs of the church in the islands after their acquisition by the United States. He was consecrated Aug. 15, 1903, and went at once to his charge, where his efforts to restore the order and discipline upset by the war and the departure of the old Spanish ecclesiastics met with special success. He placed priests in ninety-seven parishes; saw eight suffragan bishops appointed in dioceses stretching over 2,000 miles with 2,000 parishes and 1,700 priests; founded St. Paul's Hospital, Manila; renovated the Hospicio of San Jose; built an insane asylum at Cavite, an industrial school for boys, an orphanage at Tondo, and a college at Tayum. In promoting the harmonious adjustment of the civil affairs of the islands he was also of great service to the government. There are 9,000,000 Catholics in the Philippines. In 1914 Archbishop Harty returned to the United States on a short visit to report the progress of his work and secure help for its further extension.

JONES, William Richard, manufacturer, was born in Scranton, Pa., Feb. 23, 1839, son of Rev. John G. and Magdalene (Davis) Jones. His father was a Welsh pattern-maker, and the religious and intellectual leader of the Welshmen in the village of Catasauqua, Pa. When William was eight years old his mother died and he lost his father at fourteen. Having little regard for books or for the schoolroom, he received but a limited education, although from his early years he possessed a taste for the best literature. In 1849 he entered the employ of David Thomas, of Catasauqua, called "the father of the American iron trade." From boyhood young Jones was absolutely indifferent to danger or pain. In the civil war he fought as captain at Fredericksburg, Chancellorsville and the storming of Fort Fisher, and after the war was employed by the Cambria Iron Co. at Johnstown, Pa. Becoming dissatisfied with his employment there, he accepted an offer from Andrew Carnegie to become manager for the new works at Braddock, near Pittsburgh, and having always been popular with his men, Jones induced many of his most skillful workmen in Johnstown to join him. This enabled the new works at once to take the lead. In the first three months he broke all records by nearly doubling the output of similar mills. A year later he made more steel in a week than the average plant had been producing in six weeks. While every one in the steel world was astounded at the news, Jones

nerved himself for greater efforts, and actually doubled this remarkable output, bringing it up to 3,300 tons a week, which sold readily at fifty dollars a ton. Ambitious to surpass the world in making steel, he also possessed the power of inspiring his workmen to exert their best efforts to outstrip all others in the business. Accurate accounts of his work, written by himself, were read before American and English associations of ironmasters and they were astonished at the array of figures. Among all the partners and employees of the Carnegie Company, Jones earned the most and received the least. This was mainly his own fault, as he refused to be a shareholder, saying he had trouble enough without bothering himself with business cares. Carnegie then told him that in the future he should receive the same salary as the president of the United States, $25,000 a year. Much of his success was due to his genius for invention. One of his patents, the Jones mixer, is still used exclusively by the successors of those for whom it was built. James Gayley, the first vice-president of the United States Steel Corporation, said that "Capt. Jones, through his mechanical contributions to the development of the steel-making industry, accomplished fully as much as Mushet or Sir Henry Bessemer." Practical suggestions flashed from him like sparks. "See here, why can't we armor-plate that hose?" he asked one day. "Get a coil of wire and wind it around the hose to keep it from bursting." The idea has been generally adopted. Capt. Jones was very charitable, and scattered his thousands with a free hand among his men and their families, accumulating comparatively little for himself. The day following the Johnstown flood, he took 300 of his men to the wrecked city at his own expense and worked for two weeks to restore the property that had been destroyed. Others sent money and sympathy, he gave himself. To him more than any other the importance of the iron and steel trade of America, and especially of Pittsburgh, should be ascribed. His death was due to an accident at one of the Braddock furnaces, which fractured his skull. He was married Apr. 14, 1861, to Harriet, daughter of William Lloyd, of Chattanooga, Tenn., and they had four children: Ella, William M., Cora M., wife of Daniel D. Gage, and Charles K. Jones. He died in Pittsburgh, Pa., Sept. 28, 1889.

BAKER, Martha Sue, artist, was born at Evansville, Ind., Dec. 25, 1871, daughter of Charles Elbert and Susan Howard (Stevenson) Baker and a descendant of Francis Baker, of St. Albans, Hertfordshire, England, who came over in 1635 and settled at Yarmouth, Mass. She studied at the Art Institute of Chicago, where she was subsequently instructor for several years. During her later years she lived chiefly in Paris, where she enjoyed the friendship of Rafaelli and other distinguished modern painters. She specialized in portraits and worked in oil, pastel and water color. In the last she was particularly skilful, but it was in miniature painting that she made her most notable successes. She is represented at the Chicago Art Institute by two large oil portraits and a group of miniatures, one of her miniatures is in the Metropolitan Museum of Art, New York, and another in the Luxembourg Gallery, Paris. Miss Baker died in Chicago, Ill., Dec. 21, 1911.

MARBURG, Theodore, publicist and diplomat, was born in Baltimore, Md., July 10, 1862, youngest son of William A. and Christine (Munder) Marburg. His father, a native of Nassau, Germany, came to the United States in 1857 and engaged in the tobacco business in Baltimore. He was said to be the largest importer of cigars before the civil war. The son was educated at Princeton Preparatory School, Johns Hopkins University, Oxford University, Ecole Libre de la Science Politique, Paris, and the University of Heidelberg. He received an honorary A.M. from Johns Hopkins in 1902. In 1885 he joined his brothers, Charles L. and Louis H. Marburg, in the firm of Marburg Bros., manufacturers of smoking tobacco, and continued until they sold out to the American Tobacco Co. in 1891. His lifelong interests have been along the lines of political science, political economy and international peace. He was one of the organizers of the Municipal Art Society of Baltimore, 1899, which held its first meeting at his home. The Maryland Peace Society and the American Society for the Judicial Settlement of International Disputes, of which he was secretary, were also organized at his home in Baltimore. He is the author of: "In the Hills" (poem, 1895); "World's Money Problem" (1896); "The War with Spain" (1898); "Expansion" (1900); "The Peace Movement Practical" (1910); "Salient Thoughts on Judicial Settlement" (1911); "Philosophy of the Third American Peace Congress" (1911). Of his many public addresses the following have been printed: "Shorter Hours," "State Interference," "The Financial Crisis," "The International Court of Justice," "The Regulation of Industrial Combination," and he translated Levasseur's "Elements of Political Economy." Mr. Marburg is of the Unitarian faith and in politics a Republican. Pres. Taft appointed him U. S. minister to Belgium in 1912. He is a member of the American Economic Association (vice-president 1899–1901), the American Political Science Association, the American Society of International Law (chairman of the executive committee), the Metropolitan Club of Washington, the Century, Pilgrims, National Arts and Grolier clubs of New York, the Bibliophile Club of Boston, and the Maryland and University clubs of Baltimore. Mr. Marburg was married, Nov. 6, 1889, to Fannie, daughter of Thomas Grainger, of Wilmington, N. C., and his children are: Christine, Theodore, Francis, Grainger and Charles Louis Marburg.

CABOT, Arthur Tracy, physician and surgeon, was born in Boston, Mass., Jan. 5, 1852, son of Samuel and Hannah Lowell (Jackson) Cabot. His father was a noted surgeon. The first of the family in America was Jean Cabot or Chabot, probably a native of the Island of Jersey, who came to this country in 1700. From him and his wife, Anne Orne, the line of descent is traced through their son Samuel and his wife, Elizabeth Higginson; their son Samuel and his wife, Sally Barrett; their son Samuel and his wife, Elizabeth Perkins; their son Samuel and his wife, Hannah Lowell Jackson. Arthur T. Cabot was a great-grandson of Thomas H. Perkins (q. v.) and his maternal grandfather was Patrick Tracy Jackson, a pioneer cotton manufacturer, who introduced the power loom into American cotton manufacture, and in 1813 built at Waltham the first factory in the United States combining under one roof the various processes used in converting cotton into the finished cloth. Arthur T. Cabot received his elementary education at the Boston Latin School and was graduated at Harvard University in 1872. Subsequently he entered the Harvard Medical School, where he was graduated at the head of his class in 1876. In the same year he went to Europe, and during the next fourteen months studied in Vienna

and Berlin. He received the degree of A.M. from Harvard in 1878, and became instructor in oral pathology and surgery at the Harvard Medical School, holding that position until 1880. In 1885 he became instructor in genito-urinary surgery (clinical), and in 1894-96 was instructor in genito-urinary and clinical surgery. He began general practice in 1877, but after about ten years he devoted his attention altogether to surgery. As a general surgeon he soon won a position of recognized eminence, both for his skill in operation and for his contributions to operative methods. Among the latter may be mentioned his use of valve acting dressing and chlorinated soda irrigation for empyema operations. His wire splint for fractures of the lower leg has met with wide use throughout the world. It is as a genito-urinary surgeon, however, that he attained special fame, and he was generally accepted as perhaps the leading American specialist in that branch of surgical science. Dr. Cabot was attached at different times to the surgical staffs of the Massachusetts General Hospital, Carney Hospital, the New England Hospital for Women and Children, and the Children's Hospital. He was a prolific writer on medical science, and during about thirty otherwise extremely busy years published one hundred and twenty papers on various subjects of professional interest. Of especial note is his "Realism in Medicine," a discourse first delivered before the Massachusetts Medical Society in 1900. Subsequent to 1904 Dr. Cabot devoted much time and attention to the problem of preventing tuberculosis. In 1910 he gave up his private practice to devote himself entirely to this important field of labor. As chairman of the Associated Committees for the Prevention and Control of Tuberculosis, and also chairman of the Massachusetts Commission on Consumptive Hospitals, he had a hand in organizing and directing the anti-tuberculosis work throughout the state. In 1904-06 he was president of the Massachusetts Medical Society. He was also honorary president of the American School Hygiene Association; a trustee of the Boston Museum of Fine Arts; a sustaining member of the American Health League, and a member of the American Academy of Arts and Sciences, the American Medical Association, the American Surgical Association, the International Surgical Association, the Boston Society for Medical Improvement, the Boston Society of Medical Sciences and the Boston Chamber of Commerce. He was made a member of the corporation of Harvard in 1896. He was interested in all forms of active outdoor sport, and was fond of boating, polo, hunting and fishing. In pursuit of the two last-named recreations he traveled extensively. His clubs were the Union, Tavern, St. Botolph, Economic and Harvard, of Boston; the University and Harvard, of New York; the Dedham Polo, Hoosic-Whisic, Kippewa Fishing and Hunting, Norfolk Hunt, Country, of Brookline. In politics Dr. Cabot was a Republican with independent views and he was affiliated with the Unitarian church. An indefatigable worker and one of the really great surgeons of his time, he possessed exceptional qualities of character and held a position of honor and eminence both in and out of his profession. In his will Dr. Cabot provided for the establishment of a fund of $100,000 to be paid after the death of his widow to Harvard College. Half of the fund is to be used for the purchase of books and other articles for the libraries; the income of the other half is to be used for the general purpose of the medical school. Dr. Cabot was married in Boston, Aug. 16, 1882, to Susan,

Arthur T. Cabot.

daughter of George O. Shattuck, of that city. He died in Boston, Nov. 4, 1912.

WOODWARD, John Blackburne, soldier, was born in Brooklyn, N. Y., May 31, 1835, son of Thomas and Mary Barrow (Blackburne) Woodward and grandson of Isaac Woodward, who came to the United States in 1818. His father, Thomas Woodward, learned the silversmith's trade, and with two brothers conducted a business in New York under the firm name of Woodward & Bros. for nearly forty years. He invented the "Diamond Pointed Gold Pen," the "Ever Pointed Pencil," and the "Shielded Safety Pin." The son John was educated in private schools. In 1859 he entered an export business, became a partner and in 1881 sole proprietor. He was a member of the Thirteenth regiment New York state militia, with which he served throughout the civil war In March, 1869, he was appointed major-general commanding the second division, N. G. N. Y., and resigned in 1874 to take the place of inspector-general of the state, where he ranked as brigadier-general. The members of his old staff converted the membership into a fraternal society called "The General Woodward Staff." He was the originator of the "Brooklyn Citizens' League," to secure non-partisan municipal government for Brooklyn, was president of the Brooklyn Art Association, president of the department of parks, and president and director of the Brooklyn Institute of Arts and Sciences. A statue of him by MacMonnies stands in the Institute museum. He was married May 31, 1870, to Elizabeth Cook, daughter of Rollins Cook Blackburne and had four children. His brother, Robert Budicome Woodward (1840–1915), was a prominent financier of New York, and was also a large contributor to the upbuilding of the Brooklyn Institute of Arts and Sciences, of which he was a vice-president and trustee; his gifts to the institute amounted to over $100,000, and in acknowledgment he was given the title of "Benefactor" of the institute. He was vice-president and director of the Nassau National Bank of Brooklyn, and a trustee of the Bowery Savings Bank, the Franklin Safe Deposit Co., the Franklin Trust Co. and the Mutual Life Insurance Co. of New York. John B. Woodward died in Brooklyn, N. Y., Mar. 6, 1896.

PROCTOR, Joseph, actor, was born at Marlboro, Mass., May 7, 1816, son of Nicholson Broughton and Lucy (Bond) Proctor. He was descended from John Proctor, a native of England, who emigrated in 1635 and settled at Ipswich, Mass., the line being traced through his son John, who married Widow Elizabeth Bassett; their son Joseph, who married ———, and their son, Capt. Joseph, who married Anna Broughton and was the grandfather of the actor. He was educated in the public schools and the Gates Academy of Marlboro. At the age of sixteen he went to Boston to begin a business career. He made the acquaintance of the members of an amateur dramatic club, and having developed marked talents in this direction determined to abandon commercial life for the stage. He made his first appearance at the Warren Theater, Nov. 17, 1833, in "Damon and Pythias." His next appearances were as Rolla in "Pizarro" and Carwin in "Therese, the Orphan of Geneva," and the title role in "Macbeth." He had the good fortune to be associated with many of the leaders of his profession, such as James Sheridan Knowles, Thomas A. Cooper and the elder Booth. While under the management of Thomas Hamlin, of the Bowery Theater, New York, he achieved his first great success by creating the part of Jibbenainosay in "Nick of the Woods." For years Proctor was identified with this play, and it made him famous not only in America, but also abroad. It was to him what Matamora was to Forrest and Lord Dundreary was to Sothern. In 1844, while visiting in the South, he played an engagement in New Orleans and other southern cities, and after an engagement in Philadelphia, New York and Boston he assumed the management of the Beach Street Museum in Boston, Mass. (1848). A year later he opened a new theater in Portland, Me., but he soon found that such an undertaking would not be financially successful, and he resumed his starring tours. During 1851–59 he made a series of tours throughout the country, going as far west as California. In 1859 he went to Europe for two and a half years, during which he made a prolonged tour of the provinces and played a large variety of roles, including Shakespearian parts. In 1878 he produced at the Music Hall, Boston, a religious play called "Saul," which he himself had adapted for the stage in the form of a musical drama. The music was written by W. J. D. Leavett, and the performance was received by the critics with high praise. In 1883 a complimentary benefit by his friends was tendered him on the fiftieth anniversary of his début. He now practically retired from the stage, and in 1885 established a school of elocution and dramatic art in Boston, which he conducted successfully until a short time before his death. Mr. Proctor possessed a fine physique and a rich and powerful voice capable of the strongest emotion or the gentlest pathos. He was above the average in height, and retained until the end an erect and dignified bearing. He was a member of the Boston Commandery of Knights Templars and was an honorary member of the Players' Club of New York and the Playgoers' Club of Boston. He was married in June, 1837, to Hettie Willis, daughter of William Warren, of Philadelphia, and sister of the popular comedian, William Warren. She died in 1841, and he was married again, Feb. 1, 1851, to Mrs. Elizabeth Wakeman Currier, daughter of Bradley Wakeman, of Baltimore, Md. Mr. Proctor died at his home in Boston, Mass., Oct. 2, 1897, survived by his wife and one daughter, Anna E. Proctor.

INGERSOLL, Edward, soldier, was born in Westfield, Mass., Dec. 18, 1812, son of John and Elizabeth (Martin) Ingersoll, and a descendant through six generations from John Ingersoll, one of two brothers who emigrated from Bedfordshire, England, in 1629, and settled in Salem, Mass. Maj. Ingersoll's parents moved to Springfield, Mass., and he was educated in the public schools there. After a trip to Michigan he obtained employment in the drygoods house of Ralph Snow, in Northampton, and subsequently entered the employ of William Child, of Springfield. In 1835 he removed to Savannah, Ga., to engage in a mercantile business with his brother, and, although at first successful, met with reverses as a result of the panic of 1837, and failed. In 1841 congress decided to restore the armory at Springfield, and he was appointed storekeeper and disbursing officer of the national armory, as it was called. He held the position, which was one of great responsibility, until 1882, during which time he disbursed over $100,000,000, and maintained the armory in a state of such efficiency that he was able to fill any rush order with dispatch. On account of meritorious service he was given the rank of major. He took much pride in the beautifying of Springfield. He transformed the armory grounds from a barren desert into a garden of flowers and planted the elm trees on Court square. "Ingersoll Grove" in the city perpetuates his name. Tall and slender, he had finely-cut features and penetrating blue eyes, and was long regarded as the father of Springfield. He was married Oct. 29, 1834, to Harriet J. Child, daughter of his former employer, and had six children. He died in Springfield, Mass., Jan. 28, 1891.

JACKSON, William Purnell, U. S. senator, was born at Salisbury, Md., Jan. 11, 1868, son of William Humphreys and Arabella (Humphreys) Jackson, of English and Scotch descent. His father was a prominent lumber dealer of Maryland and a member of the 57th, 58th and 60th congresses, and his uncle, Elihu E. Jackson (q. v.), was governor of Maryland during 1888–92. He was educated at the public schools of Salisbury and the Wilmington Conference Academy, Dover, Del. He spent his vacations in industrial occupations, working first in his father's lumber mill, and in 1886 entered the employ of E. E. Jackson & Co., Washington, D. C., remaining with the firm until it was dissolved in 1889. He then formed a partnership with his father in the lumber business in Salisbury under the firm name of W. H. Jackson & Son. In 1903 the firm became Jackson Bros. Co., of which he was secretary and treasurer. Sen. Jackson is a signally shrewd business man, and his judgment in a business deal is considered remarkable by men who are associated with him. Though he is one of the wealthiest men in the state, he is unostentatious and is genuinely popular in Wicomico county. He has a reputation for square dealing and integrity as well as for business acumen. He and his father have done much to develop Salisbury and Wicomico county. Among the positions of importance in the business world which are occupied by him are: president of the Citizens Gas Co. of Salisbury, the Salisbury National Bank, and the Jackson-Gutman Co., shirt manufacturers, and directing head of the Jackson Brothers Co., whose operations extend throughout the country. He is also president of the Peninsular General Hospital, located at Salisbury. Interested in public affairs, Mr. Jackson became a member of the Salisbury city council in 1900, and occupied the position for the four years during which it was regarded as a non-political office. Having demonstrated his adaptability for public life, he was made national Republican committeeman for the state in 1908, and was reappointed in 1912. In this field he obtained a thorough acquaintance with the political trend of his state and helped to shape his party's policies. Prominent in business affairs, in which he had long demonstrated his capacity, and in which he had obtained a wide and practical experience, with sound and mature views and forceful character, possessing as he did an active as well as logical mind, he became marked as exceptionally well fitted for the conduct of public affairs and was recognized throughout the state as a man worthy of representing it in any position. Therefore, no surprise was expressed when Gov. Goldsborough appointed him U. S. senator on Dec. 3, 1912, to fill the vacancy caused by the death of Isidor Rayner. He is a member of the Maryland Club of Baltimore, the Union League, Racquet and Manufacturers' clubs of Philadelphia, and is an Elk, a Knight Templar, and a Shriner. He was married, first, in 1890, to Sallie, daughter of A. P. McCombe, of Havre de Grace, Md. She died in 1897, leaving one son, William Newton Jackson, and one daughter, Belle; and second, in 1900 to Katherine, daughter of George C. Shelmerdine, of Philadelphia, Pa. By the second marriage there are two children, Elizabeth and William Jackson.

MYERS, Henry Lee, U. S. senator, was born in Cooper county, Mo., Oct. 9, 1862, the son of Henry Marks and Maria Moss (Adams) Myers, of German descent. His father was born on a farm in Virginia, and on reaching manhood, moved to Cooper county, Mo., to engage in farming. The son was educated in private schools at Bonneville, Mo. After teaching in public schools in Missouri for several years he studied law and was admitted to the bar in 1884. But he continued teaching and was also engaged in newspaper work as a reporter and editorial writer until 1890, when he opened a law office in West Plains, Mo. Three years later he moved to Hamilton, Mont., where he settled permanently and built up an extensive practice. He was prosecuting attorney for Ravalli county for two terms, and was subsequently elected state senator. In one of his law cases before the supreme court of Montana he secured a ruling in an appeal case that there was no right of compulsory physical examination in cases of personal injury. In 1907 he was appointed district judge to fill an unexpired term, and in 1908 was elected for the full term of four years. He was elected to the U. S. senate by the state legislature in March, 1911, to fill the unexpired term of Sen. Carter, for the full term of six years. In the senate he was appointed a member of the Irrigation and Reclamation of Arid Lands, Mines and Mining, Public Lands, Indian Affairs, Civil Service and Entrenchment committees. He was married, July 10, 1896, at Hamilton, Mont., to Nora S., daughter of Thomas M. Doran, and has one daughter, Mary.

BLAIR, Charles Austin, jurist, was born in Jackson, Mich., Apr. 10, 1854, son of Austin and Sarah (Horton) Blair, of Scotch descent. His father was the famous "war governor" of Michigan. He was graduated at the Jackson high school in 1872, and in the literary department of the University of Michigan in 1876, taking high honors as an unusually accomplished student, a philosophical thinker and a logical and exact reasoner; he was also the poet of his class. After graduation he studied law in his father's office and was admitted to the bar in 1878. He formed a partnership with his father and George S. Wilson, under the firm name of Blair, Wilson & Blair, later with Thomas E. Barkworth, and still later with Charles H. Smith and Charles E. Townsend, under the style of Blair, Smith & Townsend. Upon the dissolution of this firm he entered into partnership with Benjamin W. Williams. He was at one time city attorney for Jackson, and later prosecuting attorney for his county, positions which he held with credit and distinction. In 1902 he was elected attorney-general, and was nominated for a second term but withdrew his name to become a candidate for justice of the supreme court. He was elected to the supreme bench and was re-elected in April, 1909. He served as chief justice in 1909. His opinions in the supreme court bore evidence of great learning, industry and painstaking efforts to arrive at the right and truth of a controversy. He had a pleasing personality and was a just, fearless and upright judge. The University of Michigan conferred upon him the degree of LL.D. in 1909. He was a member of the Benevolent and Protective Order of Elks and of the Alpha Delta Phi college fraternity. He was married, Oct. 8, 1879, to Effie C., daughter of Guy F. North, of Jackson, Mich., and had four children, of whom two survived: George F. and Helen Blair. Judge Blair died in Lansing, Mich., Aug. 30, 1912.

EDWARD INGERSOLL
SOLDIER

WILLIAM PURNELL JACKSON
U. S. SENATOR

HENRY LEE MYERS
U. S. SENATOR

CHARLES AUSTIN BLAIR
JURIST

BURNS, William John, detective, was born in Baltimore, Md., Oct. 19, 1861, son of Michael and Bridget (Trahey) Burns. While he was still a child his parents moved to Ohio, settling first at Zanesville and in 1873 at Columbus, where his father engaged in business as a merchant tailor. After a public school education William attended a business college in Columbus and then joined his father in the merchant tailoring business. But his remarkable talents soon pointed the way to a very different vocation. When his father became police commissioner of Columbus young Burns eagerly grasped the opportunity of gratifying his taste and exercising his talent for criminal investigation. Though he was never officially connected with the police department of Columbus he was for a time practically the brains of its detective branch, and time and again his unerring genius lighted the way for the perplexed police officials through the dark ages of seemingly impossible problems. His fame in this respect grew so quickly and widely that when the famous tally-sheet forgeries occurred in Ohio in 1885 and the methods of the best trained investigators resulted in absolute failure he was called upon to take up the investigation by the prosecuting attorney, Cyrus Huling. His efforts were crowned with complete success, and this achievement attracted so much notice that many of the largest corporations in Ohio eagerly sought his services as a detective. In the year 1889 Mr. Burns was asked to join the United States secret service, and was appointed to the headquarters at St. Louis, Mo. Five years later he was promoted to the Washington office. The United States secret service has charge of all kinds of crimes against the United States government, except those within the scope of the post office, which maintains its own detective service. Its work includes the pursuit of criminals in general, search for counterfeiters, investigations of customs frauds, defalcations in national banks, dishonesty of government employes—in fact every kind of detective work required in the investigation of offenses against the Federal statutes. The advent of William J. Burns in the United States secret service marked the beginning of a notable epoch in its history. Never before, even in the picturesque days of the civil war, did the secret service attract so much public attention as it did when the mind of the remarkable detective set to work on its big problems, and never before outside of fiction was the public regaled with such brilliant feats of investigation as he accomplished. Even the dry newspaper accounts of his exploits read like the imaginative pages of Poe, Gaboriau and Conan Doyle. Indeed, Sherlock Holmes, the greatest detective of fiction, never handled problems of such magnitude and nation-wide importance as did William J. Burns, the greatest detective of fact, and those he did handle were worked with more frills but less brilliancy. It is putting it mildly to say that William J. Burns was the star of the secret service; John E. Wilkie, the present head of the department, referred to him as the best detective he ever knew; and press and public have been practically unanimous in acclaiming him the greatest of all detectives. Many of the high cases handled by Burns are part of the history of the country. The celebrated Costa Rican case is one of these. In 1896 De Requesons, De Costa and others undertook to foment a revolution in Costa Rica and began operations by counterfeiting the currency of that country in the United States.

Their object was the double one of discrediting the monetary system of Costa Rica and acquiring funds with which to carry out their plans. Burns handled the difficult case throughout and obtained the evidence which sent both men to prison. Big as the case was it was entirely overshadowed by the famous Brockway case and the Monroe-head silver $100 certificate case. Clever counterfeiters have always been about the most difficult game a detective can stalk, and Brockway was perhaps the cleverest of them all. He took a special course in chemistry at Harvard University for the special purpose of perfecting himself in that particular branch of his counterfeiting work. He was known to the government for over twenty-five years but the Federal authorities were always glad to compromise with him, every time he was arrested in return for the surrender of his plates. They never could obtain sufficient evidence to convict him and round up to his gang until Burns took hold of the case in 1894 and obtained the evidence which sent him and his gang to jail. So skillfully was the counterfeited Monroe-head silver $100 certificate printed that even the treasury experts were deceived and it was of vital importance that the printing of them should be stopped. Not the slightest clue to the identity of the counterfeiters was in the hands of the government and the mere task of establishing their identity was a stupendous one. Burns conducted the investigation with characteristic thoroughness. He looked up every engraving establishment in the country and made a list of all the expert engravers who could possibly have done such clever work. He obtained a list of plate makers and finally a list of those concerns that used the photo-mechanical process, and by elimination his suspicions were narrowed down to three men in Philadelphia, two of whom proved to be the culprits, Taylor and Bredell. A piece of remarkably clever detective work of an entirely different nature was his investigation of a lynching that occurred at Versailles, Ind., in 1897, when five prisoners were taken from the county jail and hanged or shot by a mob. Public opinion was aroused to such a high pitch that the local officers failed or refused to act and Gov. Mount of Indiana appealed to the Federal authorities for aid in enforcing the law. Because of the dangerous state of affairs Secretary Lyman J. Gage declined to assign any of his men on the case, but offered a leave of absence to Detective Burns if he would volunteer. Not long after he appeared on the scene in the guise of an insurance agent, and by associating with the natives and ingratiating himself in their good graces for a number of months, he succeeded in obtaining a list of the perpetrators of the crime with proofs which he turned over to the authorities. In 1903 he resigned from the secret service and was appointed by Secretary E. O. Hitchcock of the Interior Department to take charge of the investigation of the Oregon, Washington and California land fraud cases, which were probably the most gigantic swindle that has ever been attempted against the United States government. For years and years vast areas of valuable government lands in the far West had been systematically stolen by the thousands and millions of acres. The secretary of the interior had made several attempts to get at the bottom of the frauds, but his special agents were never able to solve the problem and in addition they were bought off and bribed by the rich and powerful men involved in the frauds. But Mr. Burns is no respector of persons. He follows his leads in the performance of his duties, no matter how high up they go. He pursues his investigations without fear or favor, and in this case his disclosures resulted in the prosecution and conviction of a number of Federal, state and city officials, including U. S. senator John H. Mitchell of Oregon. The prosecuting officer in the land fraud cases was Francis J. Heney, who was to come more prominently before the public in the graft prosecution in San Francisco, Cal. It was Mr. Heney's acquaintance with Mr. Burns and his knowledge of the latter's exceptional ability that prompted him to urge Mr. Burns to accept the offer from prominent citizens of San Francisco to gather the evidence in the latter case. After the completion of his work there Burns went to New York to complete the plan his son George E. Burns, now deceased, had long cherished of establishing a detective agency of his own. The William J. Burns National Detective Agency was organized in New York in 1909, and it at once took over the protection of the 12,000 bank members of the American Bankers' Association. Mr. Burns brought to the work the latest and most modern methods for preventing crime and apprehending criminals. His agency has branch offices in Boston, New York, Philadelphia, Pittsburg, Cleveland, Chicago, St. Louis, Kansas City, Denver, Minneapolis, Seattle, Portland, San Francisco, Los Angeles, New Orleans, Atlanta, Ga., Detroit, Mich., and Dallas, Tex., and employs a staff of over 600 men. It was shortly after his agency was organized that Mr. Burns was assigned the most difficult piece of work in his entire career, the successful outcome of which has given him a world-wide reputation and led the New York "Times" to characterize him as "the greatest detective certainly, and perhaps the only really great detective, the only detective of genius, whom this country has produced." This was the discovery and apprehension of the labor union dynamiters in 1911, which terminated a seven-years' reign of terror in the building trades all over the United States. The Bridge and Structural Iron Workers' Union had demanded the closed shop and had instigated a strike to enforce those demands. The building employers held out for the open shop, and thereafter all kinds of iron structural work in process of building was attacked by dynamite, sometimes with loss of life. During the seven years hundreds of lives had been lost and millions of dollars worth of property destroyed as the result of these outrages. The climax of these attacks was the destruction of the Los Angeles "Times" building in 1910, when twenty-one men were killed. The mayor of Los Angeles sought the services of Mr. Burns. The Burns agency had already been retained to investigate a previous dynamite explosion occurring in some property under construction belonging to McClintic, Marshall & Co., at Peoria, Ill. The outcome was the arrest of John J. McNamara, secretary and treasurer of the National Association of Structural Iron and Bridge Workers; his brother, James B. McNamara, and Ortie McManigal, and the revelation of a most shameful conspiracy against building concerns all over the country, traced to the very door of organized labor. His evidence was so overwhelming that McManigal confessed before trial and both McNamaras pleaded guilty. It was such an appalling mass of absolutely unimpeachable evidence that it created consternation in the ranks of the unions, and shortly after the

confessions of the McNamaras a concerted movement was started to immediately call off all pending strikes among organized labor. Nothing has so stirred the American people since the civil war, and Mr. Burns won the everlasting gratitude of the entire nation for the thoroughness and fearlessness with which he laid bare the truth. Ex-President Roosevelt well expressed the sentiment of the American public on the conclusion of the Los Angeles case when he telegraphed to Mr. Burns: "All good American citizens feel that they owe you a debt of gratitude for your signal service to American citizenship." Personally Mr. Burns is affable and unassuming, with the general appearance of a prosperous and contented business man. No one would ever suspect his calling from his appearance. He is as far from the typical police detective as he is from the pale and penetrating Sherlock Holmes. But behind those external characteristics lies the unusual combination of attributes which have made him the greatest detective in the world. He is aggressive, dominating, assured, forceful and convincing, possessing dauntless courage, a remarkable mental alertness and the necessary self-assurance to carry him through any emergency. He has been successful as a great detective because he is in many respects a great character. There is probably no individual in the entire country with more inside information regarding municipal affairs, and he has been frequently called upon to deliver addresses in various cities of the country and before colleges on municipal problems of the day. He has addressed Columbia University, Ann Arbor University, and many other leading colleges, and has shown in his public addresses that he possesses oratorical ability of a high order.

MASON, John (Hill Belcher), actor, was born at Orange, N. J., Oct. 28, 1858, son of Daniel Gregory and Susan W. (Belcher) Mason, and a grandson of the well-known musical educator, Dr. Lowell Mason. He is descended from Robert Mason, an Englishman, who settled in Salem, Mass., in 1630, the line being traced through Robert's son Thomas, who married Margery Partridge; their son Ebenezer, who married Hannah Clark; their son Thomas, who married Mary Arnold; their son Barachias, who married Love Battelle; their son Johnson, who married Caty Hartshorn; their son Lowell, who married Abigail Gregory, and their son Daniel Gregory, who was the father of the subject of this sketch. On his mother's side he is a direct descendant of Gov. Belcher of Massachusetts. John Mason is a cousin of Daniel Gregory Mason (q. v.), the well-known author of standard musical books. He was educated in private schools at home and at the Frankfort Gymnasium, and entered Columbia University, New York, in 1876. He began his career on the stage at the age of twenty, making his first appearance at the Walnut Street theatre, Philadelphia. During that season he appeared in a number of notable plays, supporting such well-known stars as Lawrence Barrett, Mary Anderson, Lotta Crabtree, James K. Emmet, James C. Williamson, Mme. Janauschek, Fanny Davenport and Frank C. Bangs. From Philadelphia he went to the Boston Museum (1879), and while there played with William Warren, Dion Boucicault, Lester Wallack and other well-known actors, continuing there until 1889, with the exception of two seasons, when he was a member of A. M. Palmer's Union Square Theatre Co., of New York. During that interim in New York he

GUSTAV L. BECKER
MUSICIAN

JOHANNES W. W. HOVING
PHYSICIAN

MAUD NATHAN
REFORMER

MATTHEW BIRCHARD
JURIST

took part in the dedication performance of what subsequently became Daniel Frohman's Lyceum theatre. By this time Mr. Mason had served an apprenticeship under the best masters in the profession, and had become thoroughly schooled in every line of business known to the stage excepting grand opera. He was seen in all the Gilbert and Sullivan operas that appeared in this country, having originated the character of the Colonel in "Patience" and that of Florian in "Princess Ida," and he created the leading parts in such well-known melodramas as "Hands Across the Sea" and "The English Rose." When Bronson Howard's war play, "Shenandoah," was first brought out in 1889, at the Boston Museum, he created the character of Kerchival West. In 1890, after the death of his mother, Mr. Mason went to London and made a great success with Sir George Alexander at St. James theatre as Simeon Strong in Haddon Chamber's great play, "The Idler." Returning to America, he starred for three years with Marion Manola, then the queen of comic opera, appearing in an adaptation of the French classic, "L'Ami Fritz." At this period Mr. Mason was attracted by the glamour of the vaudeville stage, and succumbed to the flattering offers of vaudeville managers. But after playing in vaudeville for two years in company with his wife, Marion Manola, he returned to the legitimate drama in 1896, appearing first in London in his old part in "The Idler," and afterward with Edward S. Willard at the Garrick theatre in the part of Col. Moberly in Augustus Thomas's "Alabama." The following season was spent on tour in the United States in the Mason-Manola Co. in his former success, "L'Ami Fritz," and in 1898 he added to his laurels by creating the character of Horatio Drake in Hall Caine's "The Christian," at the Knickerbocker theatre, New York. After two seasons as the leading man in Frohman's Lyceum Theatre Co., he went on tour under the management of Jacob Litt in "The Altar of Friendship," which was followed by a season with Elsie De Wolfe in Clyde Fitch's "The Way of the World" and with Annie Russell in "Mice and Men." In 1905 he became a member of Minnie Maddern Fiske's company in New York, and was leading man in all her notable plays, which included "Becky Sharp," "Hedda Gabbler," "Leah Kleschna;" her own play, "A Light from St. Agnes," and John Luther Long's "Dolce." Of all the many teachers to whom Mr. Mason is indebted for advice, instruction and inspiration, he considers Mrs. Fiske the kindest, the most intelligent and the most effective. By this time Mr. Mason had achieved a national reputation as one of America's foremost actors. Subsequently he was seen in "The Liars," "Jane," "The Tyranny of Tears" and "Anna Karenia," and in September, 1907, he made one of his best hits as Jack Brookfield in Augustus Thomas's great play, "The Witching Hour." He appeared in "The Witching Hour" 970 times. Next in his career were two plays, "None So Blind" and "A Son of the People," and in the latter play a notable tribute was paid him when he was invited to produce it at the New theatre in New York. As Mark Aaron he was the first star to appear in the New theatre with his own company, Feb. 28, 1910. His phenomenal success in "The Witching Hour" was duplicated in a new play by Augustus Thomas entitled, "As a Man Thinks," which was first brought out Mar. 13, 1911, at the 39th Street theatre. This play ran the remainder of the season, and he opened the

season of 1911-12 with it. As an actor John Mason has displayed talents of an unusual order. He has been compared with the famous French actor, Guitry, by no less an authority than Augustus Thomas, who said: "He has all that Guitry has and in addition he has the ability to wear a dress suit and to conduct himself in a salon with the grace of a nobleman. It is a safe prediction that whenever he (Guitry) does come to America there will be an inevitable comparison between him and Mason and that America will then wake up to the fact that she possesses the greatest and most powerful actor of modern intellectual and emotional roles." Mr. Mason is a man of quiet disposition, whose friends are few and select, two of the closest and most cherished of them being William Winter, the critic, and Col. Henry Watterson, of the Louisville "Courier-Journal." And, in long perspective, another should be mentioned, who has ever remained his inspiration and his standard as an actor, teacher and friend—Edwin Booth. He was twice married: first to Marion Manola, and, second, to Katherine Grey, both actresses of note.

BECKER, Gustav Louis, pianist and composer, was born at Richmond, Tex., May 22, 1861, son of Francis Louis and Maria A. T. (Langhammer) Becker, natives, respectively, of Germany and Austro-Hungary. His father, who settled in Texas in 1851, was a musician and inventor, having devised an improved piano action, a music-leaf turner, and a pianist's finger exercising machine. Perhaps the best known of his creations is the violin chin and shoulder rest, which is used by violinists practically all over the world. After the civil war in which he served as bugler and bandmaster, he settled in Galveston, Tex., but spent the later years of his life in New York city. The son was educated in private schools in Galveston. Inheriting his father's musical genius he determined to follow that profession and began his studies under Emil Zavadil (a pupil of Czerny) at Galveston, Tex., making his first appearance as a piano player at that city at the early age of eleven years. After removing to New York in 1881, he continued his studies with S. B. Mills, C. C. Muller, Constantin von Sternberg, Dr. Robt. Goldbeck, and Horace Wadham Nicholl. To complete his musical education he went abroad in 1888 and studied under such well-known masters as M. Moszkowski, Ph. Scharwenka, W. Bargiel, E. Rudorff, supplementing this upon his return by a course of criticism under R. Joseffy. He gave his first music lesson in 1878, and has taught almost constantly since then. Settling in New York city, he opened a private studio and before long was appointed professor of music at the Hasbrouck Institute, Jersey City, N. J. He has ever since been identified with this institution, having been superintendent of the Hasbrouck School of Music since 1903. While enjoying a national reputation as a teacher of music, Mr. Becker is best known for his exposition and theories of musical education. He has personally investigated every system of teaching and studied with its foremost representatives whenever he felt that there was something distinctively worth learning. The result has been an original method of his own, which has proved very successful when carried out in practice. Briefly summarized Mr. Becker believes that the pupil should be trained for efficient musicianship through the three-fold development of the ear, the eye and the hand, and at the same time there must be developed and trained the faculty of musical thought and musical emotion; the first by constant analysis of the structure of music, and the second by aesthetic analysis. In his teaching Mr. Becker sees to it that all this is done from the very first by methods adapted to the age and needs of the individual pupil, always along with the direct piano teaching and always made an integral part of it. His pupils are also afforded the opportunity for ensemble playing both for two pianos and with other instruments for trios and quartets. This last opportunity is made possible through his lecture musicales, which have been a regular feature of the New York musical season for the past seventeen years. These lectures are scholarly, instructive and full of interest and mark their author as a man of more than the usual intellectual attainments and a thorough master of the subject of which he has made a life study. Another advantage which he offers his pupils, and one probably not equaled by any other private instructor, is access to a lending library of over 500 volumes of music and books on musical subjects. He is the author of various articles of merit contributed to musical publications, and in 1911 wrote a book, "The Requisites of Musicianship." As a composer he will be remembered for his clever piano pieces and songs and his "Festival March" (1890), composed for full orchestra. His compositions have been favorably received on both sides of the Atlantic, and are invariably characterized by refinement in conception of theme and by harmonious tone color. Mr. Becker is a member of the Manuscript Society of New York, and served on its board of directors and as its librarian. He is also a member of the New York State Music Teachers' Association, (twice chairman of the program committee and in 1911 elected president), the Bohemian Club (member board of directors), the Fraternal Association of Musicians (treasurer), and the Tonkunstler Society. He was twice married: first, June 20, 1894, to Mary B. Lamberton, and second, Feb. 11, 1911, to Fannie Granger, daughter of Col. Edwin B. Dow of New York, and has one daughter by his first wife, Beatrice L. Becker.

HOVING, Johannes Walter Wilhelm, physician, was born in Wiborg, Finland, Apr. 17, 1868, son of Walter and Bertha (Boldt) Hoving. His father, who was born in Stockholm, Sweden, in 1841, was president of the Savings Bank, ex-president of the board of aldermen in Wiborg and for several years member of the "Landtdag" (House of Representatives) in Finland. His mother was of German stock, her father having removed from Holstein, Germany, to Helsingfors, Finland. The subject of this sketch attended the Classical Lyceum and Gymnasium of Wiborg, and was graduated as a magister (Dr.) of Philosophy at the University of Helsingfors in 1889. The following year he studied anatomy, histology and dentistry at the Friedrich Wilhelm University in Berlin, and in 1891 continued his studies at the "Karolinska Medico-Chirurgiska Institutet," in Stockholm, receiving his M.D. degree in 1898. In the same year he studied hydrotherapy, mechanotherapy, inhalation treatment, etc., in nearly all the baths of Germany, Austria, Hungary, Belgium, Holland, Norway, Denmark, Sweden and Finland. Previously he had made an exhaustive study of cholera asiatica in Russia. Dr. Hoving was special assistant to Prof. Oscar Medin in Stockholm at the Children's Hospital and Asylum during 1897-98, and in the latter year located for private practice in Hel-

singfors. In 1898 also he was elected chief physician in the Baths and Medical Institute of Aland Islands, between Sweden and Finland, and was superintendent there during 1899-1903. The baths of Mariehamm, Aland, were known all over the north of Europe as the finest and largest, but Dr. Hoving did not admit any Russians, and as a consequence came into collision with their government, and was compelled to leave Finland in 1903. He had also during these six years a medical institute in Helsingfors with an inhalaratorium and apparatus for mechano-therapeutic, dry heat, electrical and massage treatment, one of the largest of its kind in northern Europe. Dr. Hoving emigrated to the United States in 1903 and settled in New York city, where he has built up a large and lucrative practice. He was a member of the visiting staff of the Sydenham Hospital, 1908-10, and in the year 1911 established a private hospital of his own. He is the author and translator of several professional and other essays in Swedish, German, Finnish and English. Dr. Hoving is vice-president of the Swedish Home for Aged People and of the United Swedish Societies of New York, honorary member of the Swedish Gymnastic Society of New York, and life member of the Swedish Medical Society of Stockholm. He is also a member of the National Association for the Prevention of Tuberculosis, American Association for the Advancement of Science, the Physicians' Mutual Aid Society, the United German Societies of New York, the Association of German Authors of America, of which he is a trustee, American Society of Swedish Engineers, Union of Old German Students of America, American-Scandinavian Society of New York, Peace Society of New York, Swedish Historical Society of America, Swedish Aid Society and the order of Odd Fellows. He is also knight of the Grand Lodge of Freemasons in Sweden, and has given several very interesting lectures in the lodges in New York. Dr. Hoving was married June 17 1894, to Helga Adamsen, of Copenhagen, Denmark, and has three children: Hannes, Walter and Greta Hoving. Portrait opposite page 51.

NATHAN, Maud, reformer, was born in New York city, Oct. 20, 1862, daughter of Robert Weeks and Anne Augusta (Florence) Nathan, granddaughter of Seixas Nathan, and great-granddaughter of Simon Nathan, who came from Somersetshire, England. Her father (1831-88) was a member of the New York stock exchange, and her mother was a daughter of William Florance of New Orleans. Her maternal grandfather was Gersham Seixas, a prominent Rabbi of New York, and a trustee of Kings College (Columbia) for twenty-eight years. Mrs. Nathan was educated in Mrs. Ogden Hoffman's school, in the Gardiner Institute of New York, and the Green Bay (Wis.) high school. She was married April 7, 1880, to Frederick Nathan of New York and spent a year and a half in travel throughout France, Switzerland, Austria, Germany, England and Italy. Upon returning to New York she began to take an interest in many educational and philanthropic movements. She was the first woman to speak in a Jewish synagogue at a regular Sabbath evening service, the subject of her address being the "Heart of Judaism," and she has occupied pulpits of synagogues and churches in New York, Chicago and Boston. She was a speaker before the International Congress of Women in London in 1899, in Berlin, Germany (in German), in 1904, before the International Peace Congress in New York in 1907, before the International Conference of Consumers' Leagues in Geneva, Switzerland (in French), in 1898, and before the International Woman Suffrage Congress held at Stockholm, Sweden, in 1911. She was a delegate to the International Congress for Labor Legislation in Lucerne in 1908, and has been vice-president of the National Consumers' League since its organization. In 1897 Mrs. Nathan was elected president of the Consumers' League of the City of New York. This movement was organized in 1891 as the outcome of an inquiry made by the Working Women's Society into the conditions under which saleswomen and cash-children were treated in the retail stores of that city. Recognizing the fact that the majority of employers are virtually helpless to improve conditions as to hours and wages unless sustained by public opinion and by law, the League accordingly had for its object the amelioration of the condition of women and children employed in New York by helping to form a public opinion which would lead consumers and customers of these retail stores to recognize their responsibilities. Its method of accomplishing this was to prepare a list of conditions insuring just treatment of employees, to be used as a standard, and to publish what was called a "White List," consisting of the names of those retailers who had put into practice those conditions. What is called a "Fair House" on the "White List" consists of one in which equal pay is given for work of equal value, irrespective of sex, and in which no saleswoman who is eighteen years of age or over receives less than $6.00 per week, with a minimum wage for cash-children of $3.50 per week, wages to be paid by the week, the number of working hours not to exceed nine, with at least three-quarters of an hour for lunch and a general half holiday during at least two summer months, a vacation of not less than one week during the summer season, and compensation for all overtime; also where the work, lunch and retiring rooms are apart from each other, and conform in all respects to the present sanitary laws. The league was instrumental in securing the passage of the mercantile employers' bill by the New York legislature. The original consumers' league confined its work to New York city, but its success was such that interest in the movement was aroused in other cities, and similar leagues were organized in other cities and states. In 1898 the National Consumers' League was organized, and from a general adoption of its principles throughout the entire United States, the movement has now spread to foreign countries, and permanent reforms in the treatment of women workers throughout the business world have been generally established. The Consumers' League of the City of New York, of which Mrs. Nathan is president, is the parent of all the other movements, and it may be considered the most important of them all, since it has had a formative influence on those others, while it still exercises a deep influence for good in the metropolis of the country. Mrs. Nathan was active in three municipal campaigns in New York city, and was one of the first vice-presidents of the Woman's Municipal League. She is the author of various articles contributed to magazines and newspapers, on the social, economic and religious questions of the day. She was first vice-president of the New York City Federation of Women's Clubs for two years and for two years was chairman of the

Committee on Industry of Women and Children, National Federation of Women's Clubs. She is first vice-president of the Equal Suffrage League of New York, vice-president of the Equal Franchise Society, and a member of the League for Political Education, the Woman's Municipal League, the Free Kindergarten Society, the National Peace Society, the Daughters of the American Revolution, and the Lyceum Club of Paris, France, the Barnard and National Arts clubs of New York, and the Cedar Park Country Club.

BIRCHARD, Matthew, jurist, was born at Becket, Mass., Jan. 19, 1804, son of Nathan and Mary (Ashley) Birchard. When he was eight years of age his parents settled in Windham, Portage co., O., and at the age of twenty he began the study of law with Roswell Stone. He was admitted to the bar in 1827, and at once entered into partnership with David Tod (q. v.), under the firm name of Birchard & Tod. In 1829 he was appointed postmaster at Warren by Pres. Jackson, but resigned in 1833 to accept the position of Common Pleas judge, which latter position he held for four years. He was Solicitor of the general land office at Washington during 1836-39, and was then appointed Solicitor of the U. S. treasury by Martin Van Buren, and held the office throughout the balance of Van Buren's administration and during the short rule of Gen. Harrison, when he retired. It was during this period that the celebrated "Florida claims" were pressed upon the government, in the adjustment of which Mr. Birchard took a leading part, his management of the same being so able and honorable as to call forth high praise from the leading men of the nation. Returning to Warren he resumed his law practice with Mr. Tod, continuing it until 1842, when he was elected to the supreme bench of the state for seven years, being chief justice for the last two. At the expiration of his term Judge Birchard again practiced at the bar in Trumbull county until 1853, when he was nominated by the Democratic party for the general assembly, and was elected in what had always been regarded as one of the strongest Whig counties in the state. His last years were devoted to the practice of his profession, finding peculiar delight in the pursuit of that which was so congenial to his feelings and tastes. As a lawyer Judge Birchard ranked high in his profession. His knowledge of the fundamental principles of law was exceedingly clear, whilst his tact in their application was unsurpassed. His cool reflection and matured judgment made him eminently safe as a counsellor. As chief justice of the supreme court of Ohio, Judge Birchard did ample honor to himself, the bench and the state, his decisions being regarded as standard authority, not only in this country but in the English courts as well. His decisions were always made with the greatest circumspection, prudence and diligent research. He was ever public-spirited, working for the advancement of the educational, the material and religious interests of his community. His kindness of heart, his sympathy for the suffering or afflicted, his generosity toward the poor, and his leniency towards his debtors were proverbial. He was married at Bella Vista, Va., in 1841, to Jane E., daughter of Lieut. William A. Weaver of the United States navy, and she survived him with one daughter, Jane Van Wyck, wife of Frank H. Mason, and one son, William Augustus. Judge Birchard died at Warren, O., June 16, 1876. Portrait opposite page 51.

SULLIVAN, James Edward, founder of the American Amateur Athletic Union, was born in New York city, Nov. 18, 1861, son of Daniel J. and Julia (Halpin) O'Sullivan, both natives of Ireland. His father built the Fourth Avenue railroad. He received his education in the public schools, and at the age of sixteen entered the publishing house of Frank Leslie. After the death of the latter he was associated with Mrs. Leslie in the publishing business. In 1880 he started "The Athletic News." Later he was for a time at the head of the sporting department of the New York "Morning Journal," and at one time was associated with John P. Day in the publication of the New York "Sporting Times." He was connected with the American Sports Publishing Co. from its inception and at the time of his death was president of that concern and editor of its numerous publications. From his youth he was an active worker in the promotion of athletics, and for many years before his death he was recognized as the leader of amateur athletics in America. From 1877 he was a member of the Pastime Athletic Club, of which he became president in 1885. In the latter year he represented his club as delegate to the old National Association of Amateur Athletes of America, of which he became vice-president in 1887. In 1888 he organized the American Amateur Athletic Union and became its first secretary. He was made chairman of the amateur athletic committee which had charge of the athletic competitions at the World's Fair, Chicago, in 1893, and in 1900 he was appointed assistant director of the second Olympic Games held in Paris. In 1904 he was chief of the department of physical culture at the Olympic Games in St. Louis. President Roosevelt appointed him special commissioner to Greece in 1906 and to England in 1908, and for the help he rendered the Greek committee at Athens he was decorated by King George I with the golden cross of the Royal Order of the Savior. He was honorary director of the Jamestown Exposition in 1907, and in 1912 was the American commissioner at the Olympic Games in Stockholm. At his death he was athletic director for the Panama-Pacific Exposition and had made the arrangements for the contests to be held there in 1915. He was a vital factor in the promotion of clean sport in America, and it was due to his exertions in this respect in the Amateur Athletic Union and many other organizations in which he was prominent that the sharp dividing line between the amateur and professional which is so marked in the athlete of this country has been established and maintained. He was first to advocate the establishment of public playgrounds in New York city, his services in this respect leading to his appointment by Mayor Gaynor as president of the Public Recreation Commission of New York. His interest in the health and happiness of school children caused him to be prominent in the organization of the Public Schools Athletic League in 1903, and from that time until his death he was one of its executive committee and chairman of its committee on games. His thorough knowledge and vast experience in every branch of athletics, his deep interest in the objects of the league, his great executive capacity and untiring, unselfish industry made him one of the important factors in the great work accomplished by the league, which is the largest athletic organization in the world, and which has immensely improved the health and physique of school children and caused its methods and rules to be adopted in many cities in this and other countries. From 1908 until his death he was a member of the board of education and member and chairman of various committees of that board. At his death he was also secretary and treasurer of the Amateur Athletic Union, president of the Metropolitan Association of the Amateur Athletic Union and a member of the New York Athletic Club. He received the Olympic medal at St. Louis in 1904, the first American, excepting President McKinley, to receive this honor. At the Stockholm Olympic Games in 1912 he was decorated by the king of Sweden. When the New York State Athletic Commission was organized in 1911 he was appointed chairman. His latest work on behalf of amateur athletics was as one of the American delegates to the International Olympic Games and Federation in France, where he was instrumental in originating much new international athletic legislation. He was past president of the Knickerbocker Athletic Club and of the old Outdoor Recreation League, and he was an honorary member of various athletic clubs and associations in other American cities and abroad. Mr. Sullivan was married in New York city, Apr. 4, 1882, to Margaret Eugenie, daughter of Peter Byrne, of New York city, and is survived by two children: Julie Ellsbee, wife of Joseph A. Abel, and James Stacey. He died in New York city, Sept. 16, 1914.

FULLER, Gardner, educator, was born at Fullerville, St. Lawrence county, N. Y., Nov. 21, 1833, son of Ashbel and Catherine (Dawley) Fuller, and a descendant of Edward Fuller, who came over in the Mayflower in 1620; from him and his wife, Ann ———, the line descends through their son Samuel and his wife, Jane Lothrop; their son John and his wife, Mehitable Rowley; their son Joseph and his wife, Lydia Day; their son Abraham (a lieutenant in the colonial wars, afterward captain in the revolutionary war, and guardian of the Scatacook Indians) and his wife, Lydia Gillette; their son Ashbel (fifer in his father's company during the war of the revolution) and his wife, Lorain Millard, who were the grandparents of Gardner Fuller. His maternal grandparents were Job and Lovisa (Trumbull) Dawley of Florence, N. Y. His father removed from Vermont to New York state about 1820, and built iron furnaces on the Oswegatchie river in St. Lawrence county, from which fact the place still bears the name Fullerville Iron Works, or Fullerville. He attended Cazenovia and Falley seminaries, and was graduated with honors at Wesleyan University, Middletown, Conn., in 1858, receiving the degree of A.M. from that institution in 1861, and being elected a member of the Phi Beta Kappa Society. He entered upon his professional career as a teacher in private schools in Massachusetts and Connecticut, and at Macedon Academy in New York state. In 1867 he became principal of the Batavia Union School, afterward the high school of Batavia, which position carried with it later the superintendency of the city schools, and he continued in that relation for twenty-three years. Resigning in 1890 he spent several years in European travel and on the Pacific coast of the United States. In 1895 he returned to Batavia and within a month received the appointment of superintendent of the New York State School for the Blind, located there. During the years of his superintendency he laid foundations upon which were builded lives of great usefulness, some of his blind pupils working their way through college. He introduced into the school the system of regent's examinations, and greatly raised the standard of scholarship. A gymnasium was erected and systematic physical instruction given for the first time in

Gardner Fuller

Henry H. Windsor

the history of the school. He resigned that position in 1901, and again spent a period in foreign travel. He was a man of striking physical and intellectual characteristics; his knowledge of men, of events, and of scholastic subjects was broad and accurate; his opinions were carefully formed, just and positive, and while liberal and tolerant in his views, his nature was free from vanity or pretence. Mr. Fuller was married Aug. 4, 1868, to Julia, daughter of Henry Tarbox of Scottsville, N. Y. He died at Williamsville, N. Y., Jan. 1, 1914.

WINDSOR, Henry Haven, editor and publisher, was born at Mitchell, Ia., Nov. 13, 1859, son of William and Harriet Butler (Holmes) Windsor and grandson of John Wesley and Mary Anne (Hill) Windsor. His paternal grandfather came from Petersfield, England, in 1844 and settled at Dubuque, Ia., having joined the British navy at the age of twelve and participated in the celebrated sea fight between the British man-of-war Levant and the U. S. frigate Constitution; he subsequently studied for the ministry, becoming a noted Congregational divine in Dubuque. His father, also a native of Petersfield, England, was a pastor of the Edwards Congregational Church in Davenport, Ia., and during the civil war served as chaplain in the hospitals and camps of the Federal troops in Iowa. The son was conducting a profitable job-printing office at the age of fourteen. Later he attended Iowa College, leaving at the age of twenty to become city editor of the daily ''Times-Republican,'' Marshalltown, Ia. In 1880 he was appointed private secretary to the general passenger agent of the Northern Pacific Railway Co., St. Paul, and edited the ''Land Seekers' Guide,'' which was devoted to the development of lands and towns along the company's lines in Minnesota, North Dakota and Montana. Three years later he became secretary of the Chicago City Railway Co., and while in that position published a volume on the construction and operation of the cable road system, then at its zenith. He resigned in 1890 to organize the publishing house of Windsor & Kenfield and founded the ''Street Railway Review,'' a large corporation monthly devoted to street railway construction and operation, and of which he was the editor. In 1892 the firm founded a technical journal devoted to all branches of clay working and which he likewise edited. In addition to his editorial duties he organized and built a fifteen-mile steam railroad in Illinois in 1894. In 1900 he sold his publishing interest to found ''Popular Mechanics Magazine,'' of Chicago, of which he is editor and publisher. This periodical has achieved a national reputation for its interesting description of mechanical devices and its popular accounts of recent events in the world of science. In 1903 he founded the ''Rural Free Delivery News,'' and personally organized the National Rural Letter Carriers' Association and many of their state associations. Mr. Windsor is a member of the Chicago Athletic Association, and of the Union League, South Shore Country and Press clubs, Chicago; National Press Club, Washington; Atlantic Yacht Club, New York, and Camden Yacht Club, Camden, Me. He was married at Marengo, Ill., June 25, 1889, to Lina Bradt, daughter of Samuel Jackson, a manufacturer of Chicago, and has one son, Henry Haven, Jr.

PILLING, James Constantine, ethnologist, was born in Washington, D. C., Nov. 16, 1846, son of James and Susan (Richards) Pilling, and a descendant of John Pilling, a native of Huddersfield, Yorkshire, England. He was educated in the public schools and at Gonzaga College. Entering the employ of a book store in Washington, he devoted his spare moments in perfecting himself in the then novel art of stenography. He secured positions as stenographer in court work; in committee work in congress, and in the various commissions established by congress for the settlement of civil war claims, and consequently gained not only a wide acquaintance, but a reputation as a brilliant and industrious worker. He was regarded as one of the most expert shorthand writers in the country. In 1875 he joined the survey of the Rocky Mountain region, under Maj. Powell, which gave a large share of attention to the Western Indians. He lived five years among the native tribes, engaged in tabulating vocabularies of their languages, and collecting tales of their weird mythology. When, in 1881, his chief succeeded to the head of the U. S. geological survey, he was made chief clerk. Continuing his ethnological researches as a member of the bureau of ethnology, he catalogued and indexed the literature relating to the languages of nearly all the Indians of North America, including bibliographies of the Siouan, Eskimo, Iroquoian, Muskhogean, Athapascan, Wakashan, Salishan, Chinookan and Algonquin languages. The last is one of the most important ethnological works in existence, and the portion of it published separately and devoted to Eliot's Indian Bible is highly regarded by scholars. At the time of his death he had just completed a bibliography of the ancient Mexican languages, which was published as soon as it was indexed. He was married in Washington, Feb. 11, 1888, to Minnie, daughter of John Randolph Harper, of Georgia, and stepdaughter of Judge George W. Paschal, of Washington, and had one daughter, Ruth Harper. He died at Olney, Md., July 26, 1895.

CASSELBERRY, William Evans, physician, was born in Philadelphia, Pa., Sept. 6, 1858, son of Jacob Rush and Ellen Lane (Evans) Casselberry. His father, a prominent dry-goods merchant of Philadelphia, was a descendant of Hendrick Kasselberg, one of the early settlers of Germantown, Pa., who emigrated from Bakersdorf, Bruggen, Germany, in 1691. From him the line of descent is traced through Paul, Jacob, Benjamin, Isaac and Jacob Rush Casselberry. The name Kasselberg was gradually anglicized to its present form, which has since remained unchanged except by a collateral branch of the family in the South, which established the town of Castleberry in Mississippi. Dr. Casselberry's mother was a daughter of William Evans of Evansburg, Pa. The son was educated in the public schools of Philadelphia, and studied medicine at the University of Pennsylvania under the preceptorship of Dr. William Pepper (q. v.), where he was graduated M.D. in 1879 with high honors. After serving two years as interne at the Germantown Hospital, he decided to make a specialty of diseases of the ear, nose and throat, and went to Europe to continue his studies, taking a special course at the University of Vienna under Prof. Leopold von Schrotter, and at the London Throat Hospital under Sir Morell Mackenzie. On his return to the United States he located in Chicago, Ill., which became his permanent residence. In 1883 he founded the department of the throat and nose at the Northwestern University Medical School, and acted as its chief of clinic and professor of therapeutics and laryngology for twenty-five years, becoming professor emeritus in

1908. This was during the formative period of a new specialty in surgery, and Dr. Casselberry was obliged to train his own assistants. At this new clinic thousands of destitute sufferers were afforded the most advanced relief, which could not be obtained elsewhere. There, also, under his direction and instruction, many hundreds of students were made familiar with the difficult technique of this surgery. He was also professor of laryngology and climatology at the Northwestern University Woman's Medical School during 1898-1901. Dr. Casselberry has written many monographs and addresses making known to various medical societies the original information, methods and devices afforded by his wide and varied experience. He is also senior laryngologist on the medical boards of St. Luke's and Wesley hospitals, and it was through his influence that a special throat department was first established at Wesley Hospital in 1889 and at St. Luke's in 1895. Dr. Casselberry is a member of the American Laryngological Association (president 1898-99), the Chicago Academy of Science, the Chicago Laryngological and Otological Society, the American Climatological Association, the Chicago Medical Society, the Mississippi Valley Medical Association, the American Academy Oto-Laryngo, and the National Tuberculosis Association. He is the author of various publications and papers upon subjects connected with his specialty, the most prominent of which are: "A New Method of Feeding in Cases of Intubation of the Larynx" in the "Chicago Medical Journal and Examiner" (1887); the chapters on "Diseases of the Nose, Pharynx and Naso-Pharynx" in the "American Textbook of Diseases of Children" (1894); "A New Suggestion Concerning Uvulotomy, Nitrous Oxide and Ether Anæsthesia" (1900); "Neoplasms of the Nose and Larnyx," being a chapter in Wright's "Treatise on the Nose and Throat"; "The Indications for Surgical Interference in Disease of the Faucial Tonsils and the Methods of Choice in Operating," in "The Laryngoscope" (1906); "Laryngeal Disturbances Produced by Voice Use," in the "British Medical Journal" (1906). Dr. Casselberry was married June 23, 1891, to Lillian, daughter of William G. Hibbard of Chicago, and they have three children, Hibbard, Catherine and William Evans Casselberry, Jr.

STIEGLITZ, Julius Oscar, chemist, was born in Hoboken, N. J., May 26, 1867, son of Edward and Hedwig (Werner) Stieglitz. His father, a native of Thuringia, Germany, came to this country in 1849, established himself in New York city as an importer and wholesale merchant, and served as lieutenant in the 6th regiment, N. Y. militia, during the civil war. The son was graduated at the Realgymnasium, Karlsruhe, Germany, in 1886, and at the universities of Goettingen and Berlin, receiving from the latter the degree of A.M. and Ph.D. in 1889; subsequently he attended Clark University, from which he received the honorary degree of Sc.D. in 1909. In 1890 he was chemist for Parke, Davis & Co., at Detroit, Mich.; was docent in chemistry at the University of Chicago during 1892-1893, assistant instructor 1893-1894, instructor 1894-1897, assistant professor 1897-1902, associate professor 1902-1905, and professor of chemistry there since 1905. He has also served as director of analytical chemistry in the same institution since 1909, and director of the university laboratories since 1912. Prof. Stieglitz has conducted important researches in organic and physico-organic chemistry, the results of which have been published in many scientific articles contributed to the "American Chemical Journal," "Journal of the American Chemical Society," and "Berichte der Deutschen Chemischen Gesellschaft." In 1904 he delivered an address at the International Congress of Arts and Sciences, St. Louis, on "The Relations of Organic Chemistry to Other Sciences." He was Hitchcock lecturer at the University of California in 1909, has been associate editor of the "Journal of the American Chemical Society" since 1912, and a member of the council on chemistry and pharmacy of the American Medical Association since 1905. He has been a member of the international commission on Annual Tables of Constants since 1911. Prof. Stieglitz is a member of the National Academy of Sciences, American Academy of Arts and Sciences, Washington Academy of Science, American Chemical Society, Deutsche Chemische Gesellschaft, Société Chimique de Paris, and other scientific organizations. His clubs are: The Quadrangle, of Chicago, and the Chemists', of New York. He was married at Lake George, N. Y., Aug. 27, 1891, to Anna, daughter of Julius Stieffel, an official of Karlsruhe, Germany, and they have two children, Hedwig and Edward Julius Stieglitz.

KELLER, Herbert Paist, lawyer, was born in St. Paul, Minn., Feb. 7, 1875, son of John M. and Annice Elizabeth (Scott) Keller. His paternal grandfather was hereditary mayor of Ostheim, Saxe-Weimar, Germany, but having participated in the revolution of 1848, was one of the refugees that fled from Germany, coming to America in 1849 with Carl Schurz and others, and settling in Baltimore, Md. He was graduated at the law department of the University of Minnesota in 1896, and began the practice of his profession in St. Paul in 1900 as senior member of the firm of Keller & Kimball. This partnership was dissolved in the same year, and he practiced alone until 1910, when he became associated with Frederick N. Dickson and Louis B. Schwartz under the name of Dickson, Keller & Schwartz. Mr. Dickson withdrew from the firm in 1911, and Harry Loomis took his place, the name becoming Loomis, Keller & Schwartz. Another change was made in 1914, when the firm became Keller & Loomis. Mr. Keller served as third assistant corporation attorney of St. Paul in 1902-03. He was a member of the assembly, one of the branches of the assembly, one of the branches of the bi-cameral council of the city of St. Paul, for three terms (1904-10), and mayor of the city during 1910-14. As mayor he inaugurated and pushed through an investigation of gas and electric rates which resulted in substantial reductions, and he opposed the efforts of the St. Paul City Railway Co. to impede the rights of the city in reference to street car extensions, which case went to the United States supreme court and was won by the city. He inaugurated the sale of participating certificates to small savers in the financing of great municipal projects as the linking of several Ramsey county lakes by a system of canals; the widening and paving of business streets and also University avenue connecting St. Paul and Minneapolis, as well as the paving of Summit avenue; establishment of municipal testing and analyzing laboratories; also the start toward building the present library. Mr. Keller is a member of the American Bar Association, the Ramsey County Bar Association, the Association of Commerce, University Club, Commercial Club, Daytons Bluff Commercial Club, Damascus Commandery, Minnesota

WILLIAM E. CASSELBERRY
PHYSICIAN

JULIUS O. STIEGLITZ
CHEMIST

HERBERT P. KELLER
LAWYER

WILLIAM H. THOMPSON
JUDGE AND SENATOR

Chapter; Royal Arch, Braden Lodge, A. F. and A. M.; Knights of Pythias, Benevolent and Protective Order of Elks, Automobile Club and White Bear Yacht Club. He was married, Dec. 20, 1905, to Carrie S., daughter of Albert Johnston, of St. Paul, Minn.

THOMPSON, William Howard, judge and U. S. senator, was born in Crawfordsville, Ind., Oct. 14, 1871, son of John Franklin and Dora Emma (McGriff) Thompson. His parents removed to Kansas when he was eight years old, and he was brought up on a farm in Nemaha county. He was educated in the public schools of Seneca, and studied law in the office of his father, who was a district judge at Sabetha. While thus engaged in his law studies, he was appointed register of deeds of Nemaha county. He taught school one term, and in 1889, though still under age, was appointed deputy treasurer of Nemaha county, and for part of the time had exclusive charge of that office. At the age of twenty he was appointed official court reporter for the 22d judicial district, of which his father was judge. He was appointed clerk of the court of appeals in January, 1897, and while in this office inaugurated radical reforms, changing the office from one of the poorest under his predecessor's administration to the best-paying office of the kind in the whole state, yielding a large sum of money to the state each year, instead of leaving a deficit as had been the case previously. He was meanwhile improving every opportunity to acquire a thorough legal training. In 1894 he was admitted to the bar and since then he has acquired a large and lucrative practice. After serving four years in Topeka, Kan., he became associated with his father in Iola, Kan. In 1905 he removed to Garden City, and has made that his permanent residence. He served six years as district judge, during which his decisions were characterized as being absolutely fair and non-partisan. He was the first Democrat to be elected judge in his district, and so well was his work performed that he was re-elected at the expiration of his first term, defeating his Republican opponent by an overwhelming majority. In 1912 he was nominated for the U. S. senate on the Democratic ticket, and in the following election received the largest popular vote as well as the largest vote in the legislature ever given to any U. S. senator in Kansas, Democrats, Republicans and Socialists alike voting for him almost unanimously. Entering the senate at the time his party came into power under Pres. Wilson, Sen. Thompson at once identified himself with the majority organization and took a prominent part in support of the reform legislation accomplished by the new administration. The tariff, federal reserve, Clayton anti-trust, federal trade commission and Philippine independence acts are among the important laws that he aided in framing. He is a man of power and of action and is regarded as one of the able advisers of the administration in matters of legislation and foreign affairs. He is a strong advocate of national prohibition and woman suffrage. Sen. Thompson is the author of a number of articles on judicial reforms, which have attracted much notice throughout the country. The most notable of these are: "Jack Rabbit Justice"; "Tricks of the Trade"; "Impaneling a Jury Speedily in Criminal Cases." He is a man of great energy and capacity for work. He was married Aug. 29, 1894, to Bertha, daughter of Andrew J. Felt of Seneca, Kan., a lieutenant-governor of the state. They have three children: Thelma Bertha, Wilbert Felt and William Howard Thompson. Portrait opposite page 56.

CRAFTS, Leo Melville, physician and surgeon, was born in Minneapolis, Minn., Oct. 3, 1863, son of Amasa and Mary Jane (Henry) Crafts. His earliest paternal American ancestor was Griffin Craft, who came from England in 1630 as a member of John Winthrop's expedition, settled first at Roxbury, Mass., and was one of the founders of Boston. From him the line of descent is traced through his son Samuel and his wife, Elizabeth Seaver; their son Samuel and his wife, Elizabeth Sharp; their son Moses and his wife, Esther Woodward; their son Samuel and his wife, Rebecca Parker; their son Moses and his wife, Hadassa Mills, to their son Moses Mills and his wife, Rhoda Stone, who were the grandparents of Leo Melville Crafts. His grandfather was a captain in the war of 1812, and his great-grandfather served in the revolution. Maj. Amasa Crafts, his father, was a merchant of Boston, Portland and Minneapolis, being one of the pioneers and active builders of the latter city. The son was graduated B.L. at the University of Minnesota in 1886, and M.D. at the Harvard Medical School in 1890. During 1889-91 he was house physician at the Boston City Hospital. He began active practice in Minneapolis in 1892, making a specialty of neurology and psychiatry. He was professor of neurology and mental diseases at Hamline University Medical School during 1893-1909, and dean of the faculty of that institution during 1897-1904, when he was instrumental in securing a new plant, new grounds and new equipment for the institution. At various times he was visiting neurologist on the staffs of the City, Asbury Methodist, St. Barnabas and Swedish hospitals. He has been a frequent contributor to the medical and scientific press, and is the author of numerous monographs and addresses, including "The Physician in Practice," "The Problem of the Insane and the Defective," "Expert Testimony and the Medical Witness," "Possibilities in the Treatment of Epilepsy," "Medical Education," etc., also "The Song of the Pines," a descriptive article on forestry. He was a member of the board of directors of the Minnesota National Park and Forestry Association during 1898-99, and secretary-general of the executive committee of all organizations combined for a national park and reserve in the state. In 1895 he was treasurer of the Minnesota branch of the Western Society for the Suppression of Vice. He was president of the Minnesota State Sunday-School Association during 1893-96; a member of its board since 1893; was president of the Minneapolis Sunday-School Officials' Association, 1895-96 and 1902-03; is past president (1906) of the Native Sons of Minnesota, member of the Minneapolis Athletic Club, and formerly a member of the American Academy of Political and Social Science, and American Academy of Medicine. He is past chairman, nerve section, Minnesota State Medical Association; past treasurer Hennepin County Medical Association; past president (1910) Minnesota Neurological Society; fellow Massachusetts Medical Society and American Medical Association; member Mississippi Valley Medical Association, American Association of Railway Surgeons, Boston City Hospital Alumni Association, Minneapolis Society of Fine Arts, and the Sons of the American Revolution. He is also a member of the Commercial Club. He is vice-chairman of the state central committee of the progressive party, and past president (1913) of the Progressive Club of Hennepin County. He is noted for his after-dinner speeches and addresses, and has acquired no little fame through his impromptu orations. Dr. Crafts is an authority on legal medicine, in the neurological field, and a leading medico-legal expert. Special mention may be made of his monographs on "The Influence of the Ductless Glands over Metabolism" and "A Fifth Case of Family Periodic Analysis." The former was one of the early papers throwing light on our knowledge of the ductless glands; the latter relates to an exceedingly rare disease—Dr. Crafts' case being the fifth ever reported in literature in this country. He was married in Minneapolis, Minn., Sept. 4, 1901, to Amelia I., daughter of Thomas Burgess, a marine engineer, formerly of Portland, Me., now of Minneapolis.

HICKEY, Thomas Francis, second Roman Catholic bishop of Rochester, N. Y., was born in Rochester, Feb. 4, 1861, son of Jeremiah and Margaret Hickey. His studies were made at St. Andrew's Seminary, Rochester, and at St. Joseph's, Troy, N. Y. He was ordained priest Mar. 25, 1884, and in the early years of his ministry served at Geneva and Moravia, and was chaplain of the State Industrial School in Rochester. In 1893 he was made rector of the cathedral and then vicar-general, and on May 24, 1905, at the request of Bishop McQuaid, was consecrated his conductor with the right of succession. Intimately associated with that prelate in these offices for many years, he was responsible in no small degree for the great progress made in the diocese, especially in the building up of St. Andrew's Seminary, which is regarded as one of the model institutions of its kind in the country. When Bishop McQuaid died, Jan. 18, 1909, he at once succeeded to the charge 155,000, with 203 priests, 167 churches, sixty-five schools and 23,000 pupils.

RUSSELL, William Worthington, diplomat, was born in Washington, D. C., Dec. 3, 1859, son of Maj. William Worthington and Virginia (Fletcher) Russell. He was educated in the Rockville (Me.) Academy and the United States Naval Academy, Annapolis, Md. He was appointed a midshipman Sept. 18, 1875, but remained at the academy only till May 17, 1876, when he resigned to take up the engineering profession. He was connected with several surveys of railroad routes in South America, Mexico and the United States and was assistant engineer in locating the route of the Eads ship-railway across the Isthmus of Tehuantepec. He was senior watch officer of the Brazilian cruiser America, which was delivered to that nation at the time of the Mello revolution in 1893. In 1895 Mr. Russell was appointed secretary of legation at Caracas, Venezuela, and in January, 1904, was transferred to Panama City, where he was secretary of legation until Mar. 17, 1904, and charge d'affaires ad interim from Feb. 13th to Mar. 17, 1904. In fact, Mr. Russell was the first accredited diplomatic officer of the United States government to Panama after the withdrawal of the special commissioner, William I. Buchanan, who concluded the treaties and conventions between the new republic and the United States. He raised the American flag over the buildings transferred to the United States by the French-Panama Canal Co., and negotiated the existing extradition treaty between the two countries. In March, 1904, he was appointed envoy extraordinary and minister plenipotentiary to Colombia, and in June, 1905, was transferred to Venezuela in the same capacity. He was recalled in June, 1908, when the state department terminated diplomatic relations with Venezuela on account of cancellation by the government of that country of various concessions to American corporations and individuals, notably the Asphalt claim, the Critchfield claim and that of the Orinoco Steam Navigation Co. From August, 1908, to January, 1909, he was commissioner to the national exposition at Quito, Ecuador, and in 1910, after the difficulties had been settled, he returned to his post in Venezuela. A few months later he was appointed minister to Santo Domingo, being known as minister-resident and consul-general. Shortly after taking this office he was made an envoy with the title of minister only, and held this position until August, 1913, when he was retired. In 1915 he was again appointed minister to the Dominican republic to succeed James M. Sullivan. Mr. Russell was married, May 24, 1905, to Grace C., daughter of James M. Lidstone, of London, England.

FORD, Henry, manufacturer, was born at Greenfield, near Detroit, Mich., July 30, 1863, son of William and Mary (Litogot) Ford. He early developed a natural bent for mechanics, and at the age of fifteen constructed a steam engine that worked successfully. Finding farm life distasteful, he ran away to Detroit and obtained employment in a machine shop where he quickly mastered all the details of the making of machinery, and gave evidence of a natural gift for devising more expeditious and efficient methods of getting work done. It was this innate faculty of producing the greatest result with the least expenditure of effort and material that proved the most important factor in his subsequent remarkable success. In the early 90s he became manager of the mechanical department of the Edison Illuminating Co., and while here he applied practically his genius for efficiency by inaugurating an eight-hour day for the men without increasing the payroll. Before entering the employ of the Edison Illuminating Co. he had worked out detailed plans for the manufacture of watches in enormous quantities at a very small price. He had gone so far as to make plans for a factory when his mind was diverted to the subject of self-propelled vehicles by the sight of a steam fire engine on the streets of Detroit. He may have seen also the steam automobiles of R. E. Olds and others, for the idea of a self-propelling road vehicle now took entire possession of him, and he determined to build such an engine of his own and apply it to a carriage. For nearly two years he worked on his first model, devoting to it all his spare time outside the working hours of the Edison Co. The result of his efforts was a vehicle scarcely larger than a tricycle with a very crude steering apparatus, and driven by a small one-cylinder engine with a pulley clutch (1892). He gained some prestige by entering a local race with his crude machine and winning the race. In 1898 he interested some capitalists who organized the Detroit Automobile Co., which financed the experiments that Mr. Ford was making. In this experimental work he was assisted by Mr. Olds, the Dodge brothers and other engineers. It was Mr. Ford's ambition to produce a low-priced car within reach of people of moderate means; but this idea did not appeal to the capitalists who preferred to manufacture fewer cars at a larger profit, and he accordingly withdrew from the original company. He now resolved to enter another race, and with a special car designed by Oliver E. Barthel and equipped with a 7 x 7 in. two-cylinder motor, he defeated Alexander Winton at the Detroit Driving Club track in 1901. Subsequently with a four-cylinder engine he ran a race on the ice of Lake St. Claire, and made a record of one mile in 39⅕ seconds, beating the world's record at that time by seven seconds. The Detroit Automobile Co. was reorganized into the Henry Ford Co., which was still experimenting on two-cylinder gasoline cars, and by 1902 a two-cylinder automobile, similar in appearance to the Cadillac, was developed. In June, 1903, the Ford Motor Co. was capitalized at $100,000, and this was the beginning of what became the largest automobile company of the world. The original factory was a little frame building on Mack avenue, Detroit, where $195,000 worth of product was turned out the first year. At the outset of its career the company came into collision with a serious obstacle in the shape of the Selden patent. This was a blanket patent obtained by George B. Selden of Rochester, N. Y., in November, 1895, covering very broadly the combination with a road locomotive, including running gear, propelling wheel and steering mechanism, of a so-called liquid hydrocarbon gas engine of the compression type. In 1901 suit had been brought on this patent against the Winton Motor Car Co. of Cleveland, O., and the outcome of it was the organization of the "Licensed Association of Automobile Manufacturers," whose members paid a license under the Selden patent, and undertook to prosecute all infringers. Soon after the organization of the Ford company suits were brought in October, 1903, against it as manufacturer, against John Wanamaker & Co. of New York as selling agent, and against O. J. Gude Co. of New York as purchaser of a Ford car. Advertisements were scattered throughout the country announcing the suits and threatening similar action against all the Ford company's customers; but the latter advertised just as extensively that it would defend all such suits, and it did so. This suit was one of the most gigantic in the legal annals of the United States. On one side the Licensed Association was fighting to save patent rights for which its members had paid vast sums of money, and on the other side Ford was fighting to release the industry from paying tribute to a patent which he believed was unsound, and incidentally to keep down the retail price of his automobile. A year was consumed in taking testimony for the complainant and another year for the defendant. During the trial it was shown that similar engines had been in operation previous to Selden's application for a patent. The decision of the United States circuit court in 1909 affirmed the validity of the patent, holding that the Ford Co. and others were infringers; but this decision was reversed on appeal, and both the litigation and the existence of the Licensed Association were terminated accordingly. The cost of the lawsuit to the Ford Co. was about $155,000. The business, however now entered upon an era of phenomenal prosperity. In 1908 the company sold over 6,300 Ford cars; a larger factory was erected to supply the demand, and in 1909, 10,600 cars were sold. In the latter year the company bought 276 acres on the outskirts of Detroit and built the present enormous establishment, covering forty-seven acres. Apart from its small price ($385.), the principal characteristics of the Ford car are its durability and its simplicity of construction. The engine, which is of the "Otto" four-cycle type, has no especially distinctive features except the magneto, which was invented by Edward S. Huff. In the ordinary magneto the magnets are fixed and the armature revolves, but in the Ford magneto, which is built in the flywheel and forms a part thereof, the magnets revolve and the armature is fixed. The Ford cylinders are cast all together in one block bored out by one machine, so that the axes coincide, with a block head covering all four cylinders and carrying the spark plugs. As an accessory to the engine the transmission contains a planetary change-speed gear and disk clutch coupling, the principle of which is that the disks and clutches are compressed to give a solid drive through from the engine shaft to the rear axle for the high gear. On low gear the parts are unclutched. A drum is held rigidly by a band like a brake, compelling the internal gears to revolve so that the high speed of the crank-shaft is transmitted to the shaft drive through gearing, which reduces that speed to a ratio of between 11 and 12 to 1. The extraordinary success of the Ford company is due to Henry Ford's genius for system. The factory at Detroit is a perfect model of organized efficiency, where every possible waste of time, labor and material has been completely eliminated. The making of a Ford car resembles the easy, uninterrupted confluence of a number of streams from widely different sources, each part taking shape in its own special department, and all flowing together, as it were, naturally into the completed whole. In the vast machine shop, where the different parts come into being, the visitor familiar with machine-shop practice is at once struck by the peculiar location and setting of the machinery. The machines of a class, or type, are not all located in a single group or unit. Each department contains all of the necessary machinery to complete every operation on each part or piece it produces. For example, a rough forging or casting is started in a department at one point, and after passing through the machines doing the required operations, it leaves this department in a finished condition, ready to be assembled into the car. Such a system necessitates the grouping together of many different kinds of machines, as well as including brazing furnaces, cyanide furnaces and other special units generally found in separate buildings. Then chutes, conveyors and endless belts are freely used and make a considerable saving in time, trucking expense and loss of material. The assembled units pass from their separate departments into the final assembly department. The first units to be assembled (front axle, rear axle and frame) are brought together first on a chain conveyor on which they travel through the department, meeting the other units at the points where those units are needed. The chain conveyor moves through the department at a constant speed of eight feet per minute, and each man assembles one part or does one operation which is assigned to him, so that when the chassis reaches the end of the line it is ready to run on its own power. The complete chassis is then driven out into the final inspection line, where it is taken in charge by a corps of inspectors, one man being responsible for the examination of each part. On an average a completed car leaves the assembly line every twenty-five seconds. The average daily product of the Ford factory is now over 2,000 automobiles, this tremendous output being made possible by the maintenance of twenty-eight Ford assembling plants and fifty-one branch houses in the United States, as well as fifteen branch houses in foreign countries. The total number of employees in 1915 averaged 31,500, and the annual business was $150,000,000. The Ford efficiency system is not confined to methods and machinery; it applies also to men. The relations established by the company toward its employees, through its sociological department and its profit-sharing plan, constitute one of the most notable and significant developments in recent industrial history. It is a sociological experiment of great importance, the magnitude of which may be gauged from the fact that the average number of employees in the Ford plant at Detroit is about 28,000 and includes fifty-three nationalities, speaking more than 100 languages and dialects. Its predominant feature is a profit-sharing plan which was inaugurated by Mr. Ford in 1908. In 1914 it was announced that thenceforth a percentage of the company's net profits would be distributed in the regular pay envelopes to every married employee living with and taking good care of his family; to every single man more than twenty-two years of age, of good habits, and to every man less than twenty-two years of age and every woman who is the sole support of next of kin or blood relation. The share of profits that each employee receives is distinct from his wages and is in inverse ratio to his wage rate. Simultaneously with the installation of the profit-sharing plan, the working day was cut from nine to eight hours. Where it is necessary to work more than eight hours extra shifts are put on. Moreover, social workers are employed to look after the welfare of the men and their families. Instruction and advice are given in sanitation, hygiene, cooking, living habits, handling of money, etc., resulting in a vast improvement in living conditions among the employees in comfort, sanitation and even in æsthetic attractiveness. The health of the employees is the special care of a large and thoroughly equipped medical department, and the services of the legal department, such as advice on matter of law, the inspection of contracts, the appraisement of property values, the examination of titles to property and such matters has proved a valuable and much-needed protection, especially to the foreign-born. Both services are free. For the further benefit of the foreign-born employees the company has organized an English school, where classes in the languages are taught according to a system similar to the Berlitz method. The school at present has more than 100 instructors and over 1,600 students. All this, according to Mr. Ford, is done simply in the interest of greater efficiency, and is not in any sense an attempt at paternalism. As in the case of other American millionaires Mr. Ford found a serious problem in the best uses to be made with his rapidly acquired wealth. He built the Henry Ford Hospital in Detroit at an expense of $2,000,000. In November, 1915, he made the startling announcement that he would conduct a peace mission to end the great European war and have the troops out of the trenches by Christmas. With no more definite plans than a possible conference of neutral nations and with no conception, seemingly, of the deeper underlying questions involved in the titanic struggle, he chartered a steamer and with about 160 invited guests, newspaper correspondents and moving picture photographers, sailed from New York city, Dec. 4, 1915, for Christiana. Disagreements and dissentions among the peace-makers while at sea were reported, no official recognition was accorded in any country, and gradually realizing the futility of the venture, Mr. Ford was among the first to leave the expedition. Mr. Ford's hobby is farming and the care and conservation of wild creatures, particularly birds, and he finds his chief recreation on the farm on which he was born. Throughout his 2,000-acre estate are scattered houses for birds and means of feeding them. He has taken an active interest in legislation in both the United States and Canada,

designed to protect wild birds. In 1914 he brought to America six species of English song birds and turned 400 of them loose on his estate. He is a member of the Detroit board of commerce, the Society of Automobile Engineers, the Free and Accepted Masons, and the Detroit Country, Bloomfield Hills Country, Detroit Golf, Detroit Boat, Wolverine Automobile, Bankers', Fellowcraft and Detroit Athletic clubs of Detroit, and the Automobile Club of America. He was married at Greenfield, Mich., Apr. 11, 1888, to Clara J., daughter of Melvin S. Bryant, and has one son, Edsel B. Ford.

CREW, Henry, physicist, was born at Richmond, Jefferson co., O., June 4, 1859, son of William Henry and Deborah Ann (Hargrave) Crew. His father (1828–1870) was a merchant. His grandfather, Henry Crew, who married Margaret Bailey, removed from Virginia to Richmond, O., in 1816, opened a store for general merchandise, accumulated considerable wealth, did a large commission business with Baltimore and Philadelphia, and was a leading Quaker. The grandson and namesake received his preparatory education at Wilmington, O., was graduated (A.B.) at Princeton in 1884, and at Johns Hopkins (Ph.D.) in 1887, and pursued a course of study at Berlin University. He began the teaching of physics as assistant at Johns Hopkins University in 1887, and during 1888–91 was instructor in physics at Haverford College. In 1891–92 he was astronomer at Lick Observatory, and from 1892 until the present time he has been professor of physics at Northwestern University. Among Prof. Crew's most notable achievements in science is the discovery of the effect of change in the gaseous medium surrounding an arc upon the lines of the spectrum of that arc (Phil. Mag., 1900). He was consulting engineer for the American Luxfer Prism Co. (1898–99), and has been assistant editor of the "Astrophysical Journal" since 1892. In 1900 he served as delegate to the congress of physicists at Paris. He is the author of "Elements of Physics" (1899); "Laboratory Manual of Physics," joint author with R. R. Tatnall (1909); "Principles of Mechanics" (1908); and "General Physics" (1908), and has contributed to various scientific journals for many years. He is a member of the National Academy of Science, American Academy of Arts and Sciences, American Physical Society (president 1909), Illinois Academy of Science (president 1912), and the American Association for the Advancement of Science (vice-president 1914). His clubs are: University of Chicago and University of Evanston. Prof. Crew was married, July 17, 1890, to Helen C., daughter of Thomas E. Coale, of Baltimore; their children are: Alice Hargrave, Mildred and William Henry Crew.

LAZEAR, Jesse William, scientist, was born in Baltimore, Md., May 2, 1866. He was graduated at Johns Hopkins University in 1889; studied medicine at the College of Physicians and Surgeons of Columbia University, New York, and after receiving his degree in 1892 was an interne at Bellevue Hospital for two years. He spent a year in Europe, part of which was passed at the Pasteur Institute in Paris, and upon his return was appointed bacteriologist to the medical staff of the Johns Hopkins Hospital. He displayed brilliant promise in research. It was he who first succeeded in isolating the diplococcus of Neisser in pure culture in the circulating blood in a case of ulcerated endocarditis, and he was the first person in this country to confirm and elaborate the studies of Romanovsky and others concerning the intimate

Matthew H Walker

structure of the hematozoa of malaria. In 1900 when the United States Army Yellow Fever Commission was appointed he was made a member and reached Cuba several months before his colleagues. This time he spent in investigating the pathological and bacteriological side of the disease, so that when the commission met he was able to say with confidence that cultures and blood examinations promised nothing of special importance. The board, the other members of which were Maj. Walter Reed, Dr. James Carroll and Dr. Aristides Azramonte, made careful inquiry into the theory of the transmission of yellow fever from man to man by the mosquito. Early misgivings due to lack of results finally gave way to positive proof that yellow fever is not contagious, but is spread largely through the bite of mosquitoes. Dr. Carroll allowed himself to be bitten by a mosquito that had previously bitten a fever patient, and in due time he was stricken but he recovered. Dr. Lazear was accidentally bitten shortly afterwards and in his case the disease proved fatal. His colleague, Dr. Walter Reed (q. v.), when speaking of him before the Medical and Chirurgical Society of Maryland said: ''It is my earnest wish that what ever credit may hereafter be given to the work of the American Commission in Cuba, the name of my late colleague, Dr. Lazear, may always be associated therewith.'' He died in Cuba, Sept. 25, 1900, and a tablet was erected to his memory at the Johns Hopkins Hospital.

WALKER, Matthew Henry, banker, was born at Yeadon, England, Jan. 16, 1845, son of Matthew and Mercy (Long) Walker. His parents came to America in 1850, locating at St. Louis, Mo., where his father soon afterwards died; two years later his mother with her sons removed to Salt Lake City, Utah. Young Walker was educated in the common schools, and at the age of twenty started in partnership with his brothers, Joseph R., Samuel S. and David F. Walker, in a commercial venture, which is still continued by the two sons of the first-named. In 1859 they entered the banking business under the firm name of Walker Bros., and in 1885 they founded the Union National Bank of Salt Lake. In the course of their business operations they have become largely interested in real estate and have erected numerous large buildings in the city, among them the Walker House, Mercantile Central black, Union block, Alta block, and others. Mr. Walker was vice-president of the Union National Bank until it gave up its charter in 1894 and became a private bank, of which he was vice-president. In 1903 it was incorporated as a state bank, of which Mr. Walker became president and has held that position to the present time (1916). In the highest sense of the word, he is self-made, and is one of the most responsible and highly respected business men of Utah. His bank is one of the strongest financial concerns in the West, and the oldest in the state. He is a stockholder in Walker Bros. Dry Goods Co. and is actively connected with many mining companies throughout the inter-mountain region. He is also a director and stockholder in the Independent Coal and Coke Co. During 1898-1902 he served as member of the board of education—the only public office which he has ever occupied. Mr. Walker has seen the development of Salt Lake City from a mere wilderness to the great and beautiful city which it is to-day and has been identified with its splendid progress from the beginning. He is one of Utah's most distinguished and successful citizens and holds a position in the financial and mercantile world second to none in the inter-

mountain region. He is a member of the Masonic fraternity, the Alta, Commercial and Country clubs or Salt Lake, and the Young Men's Christian Association. His favorite diversions are hunting, fishing and golf. He was married, (1) Jan. 16, 1865, to Elizabeth, daughter of Bishop John Carson, of Fairfield, Utah; (2) Jan. 23, 1897, to Angelina, daughter of John Andrews, of London, England. His children are: John Henry and Francesca Glenn Walker.

PITNEY, Mahlon, associate justice of the U. S. supreme court, was born in Morristown, N. J., Feb. 5, 1858, son of Henry Cooper and Sarah Louisa (Halsted) Pitney. The founder of the family in America was James Pitney, who is said to have been a button manufacturer in London, and emigrated to America before 1722, settling first in New Brunswick, N. J., and later at Basking Ridge. The line of descent is traced through his son James, who married Deziah Thompson; their son Mahlon, who married his cousin, Sarah Pitney; their son Mahlon, who married Lucetta Cooper, and their son, Henry Cooper Pitney, the father of the justice. His great-grandfather, Mahlon Pitney, was a soldier in the revolutionary war. His father was a prominent lawyer and judge, one of the founders of the National Iron Bank and the Morris County Savings Bank of Morristown, and served as vice-chancellor of the state from 1889 until 1907. The son was graduated at Princeton College in 1879. Taking up the study of law in his father's office at Morristown, he was admitted to the bar in 1882 and opened an office in Dover, Morris co., N. J., where he practiced for seven years. In 1889 he returned to Morristown, which has since been his permanent address. He early became active in state politics, and was a recognized leader of the Republican party in his section of the state. He was temporary chairman of the Republican state convention of 1895, which nominated John W. Griggs for governor and gave the state of New Jersey the first Republican governor that it had had in nearly thirty years. In 1894 he was elected to the national congress on the Republican ticket in a district that was largely Democratic and was re-elected by an increased plurality in 1896. His course in congress won him the commendation not only of his home district, but also of many of the ablest members of the house. During his first term the Alaska boundary dispute was up before congress for settlement. As a member of the Foreign Relations committee he was asked to submit a brief on the subject, and his report was so thorough and exhaustive that his committee assigned to him the duty of managing the passage of the report after its presentation to the house, and he added to his reputation as a parliamentarian and as a debater in the discussions which followed. He resigned from the 55th congress in January, 1899 to take his seat in the New Jersey senate to which he had been elected in 1898. He was the majority leader on the floor, and was president of the senate in 1901. In February, 1901, he was appointed by Gov. Voorhees a justice of the New Jersey supreme court to succeed Justice William S. Gummere, who had resigned. Seven years later (1908) he was appointed by Gov. Fort chancellor of New Jersey to succeed Chancellor Magie for a term of seven years, but resigned in March, 1912, to accept the appointment of associate justice of the United States supreme court to succeed John M. Harlan, deceased. The degree of A.M. was conferred on him by his alma mater in 1882, and he received the honorary degree of LL.D. in 1908. He is a Mason and member of the Presbyterian church. He was married, Nov. 14, 1891, to Florence T. Shelton, of Morristown, and has three children: Shelton, Mahlon, Jr., and Beatrice Pitney. Justice Pitney is a man of fine presence, six feet high, of athletic frame, fond of outdoor sports. He is a forcible, earnest and convincing speaker, and his written decisions reflect the literary finish of the scholar as well as the eloquence of the orator.

HORNE, Ashley, soldier, farmer, merchant and capitalist, was born in Clayton, N. C., Mar. 27, 1841, son of Benajah and Elizabeth (Tarver) Horne, of Scotch descent. His father, son of William Henry Horne, was a magistrate and the general business man of his community. Volunteering for the civil war, the son was first assigned to company C, 50th North Carolina regiment, but later was transferred to the 53d regiment, of which his older brother, Samuel, was lieutenant. Except for a brief period in eastern North Carolina, his service was with Gen. Lee in the army of Northern Virginia. Returning home after the war, he engaged in farming and traded in tobacco. He was among the first to see that the South was at the turning point of its history and that its development must now be commercial as well as agricultural. He did not entirely forsake farming, but kept it as his diversion and relaxation. Mr. Horne came to be numbered among the busiest, largest and wealthiest farmers, merchants and manufacturers in the state. The more important of his positions as industrial leader included the presidencies of the Clayton Banking Co., the Clayton Cotton Mill, the North Carolina Agricultural Society and the Capudine Chemical Co. He was also vice-president and director of the Caraleigh Phosphate and Fertilizer Mills from its organization in 1890 and was director of the Raleigh Standard Oil Mill, the Raleigh Commercial and Farmers Bank, the Caraleigh Cotton Mill Co., the Wilson Farmer's Oil Mill, the Goldsboro and Seven Springs Securities Co. and the Eastern Life Insurance Co. He served as state senator during 1884–85, and as member of the finance committee aided in establishing the Agricultural and Mechanical College. While in the house of representatives (1911–12), he was instrumental in securing the appropriation for the state administration building. His private philanthropies were many, large and generally unknown except to the recipients. He was for several years colonel of the Walter Moore camp of the United Confederate Veterans, being the only man who ever held this offie more than one year. He was also brigadier-general on Gen. William E. Mickle's staff of the United Confederate Veterans. Mr. Horne was twice married; first, on Mar. 27, 1871, to Cornelia Frances, daughter of Charles Lee, of Clayton, N. C., and second, Jan. 31, 1889, to Rena Hasseltine, daughter of Calvin Beckwith, of Raleigh, N. C. He had one daughter, Nellie, wife of Dr. E. H. McCullen, of Clayton, N. C. Mr. Horne died at Clayton, Oct. 22, 1913.

THOMPSON, George Smith, capitalist, was born in Troy, N. Y., Feb. 14, 1840, son of John Leland and Mary (Perkins) Thompson, and a descendant of Anthony Thompson, a native of England. His father was a wholesale druggist. He began his business career as a clerk in a wholesale grocery firm, and in 1869, with S. S. Stevens, purchased a half interest in the North Hoosick (N. Y.) paper mill under the firm name of Stevens & Thompson. In 1874 the partners, with Mr. Thompson's brother, Robert H., bought the Walloomsac (N. Y.) paper mill, and conducted it under the name of the Walloomsac Paper Co. In 1885 he and Mr. Stevens increased their paper manufacturing interests by the purchase of a wood-pulp mill at Middle Falls, and in 1901 the Ondawa paper mill at Middle Falls, incorporating them as the Stevens & Thompson Paper Co. He was president and treasurer of the Stevens & Thompson Co., Inc., North Hoosick, and the Stevens & Thompson Paper Co., Middle Falls; director of the Walloomsac Paper Co., the International Pulp Co., New York; the Troy Savings Bank, Security Trust Co., of Troy, Troy and Greenbush Railroad Co., Troy and Bennington Railroad Co., Albany and Vermont Railroad Co., and the Walter A. Wood Mowing and Reaping Machine Co. He had been a captain of the old 24th regiment, N. G. N. Y., and had served as a member of the old Troy volunteer fire department. He was a member of the Troy Club, the Hoosac and Hoosick Falls Country clubs, Mt. Zion Lodge, F. & A. M., Troy, and his religious affiliation was with St. John's Protestant Episcopal Church. He was married in Troy, N. Y., Dec. 23, 1874, to Abby Shepherd, daughter of Peter Burden, and granddaughter of Henry Burden (q. v.). She survived him with three children: Mary Burden, Gertrude Shepherd and Howard Burden Thompson, treasurer of the Stevens & Thompson Co., Inc., and treasurer and secretary of the Stevens & Thompson Paper Co. He died in North Hoosick, N. Y., Aug. 24, 1913.

FERRIN, Augustin William, publisher, was born at Little Valley, N. Y., Sept. 1, 1875, son of Augustin William and Flavilla (Van Hoesen) Ferrin. The founder of the Ferrin family in America was Lieut. Jonathan Ferrin, who served in the colonial wars and after the separation of New Hampshire from Massachusetts, settled in Hebron, N. H., where part of the family has continued to live to the present day. He was married in 1719 to Sarah, daughter of Titus Wells and grand-daughter of Rev. Thomas Wells, the first settled minister in Amesbury, Mass., and the first graduate of Harvard College. Mr. Ferrin's father entered the Federal army at the age of nineteen, but was retired because of sickness contracted at the siege of Port Hudson. After the war he founded the Cataraugus "Republican," which was for fifty years the leading Republican weekly in western New York, and he continued to publish this until his death in 1903. He also founded the Bradford, Pa., "Era," and the "Buffalo Christian Advocate," and at the time of his death was editor and publisher of the Olean (N. Y.) "Daily Times," as well as the "Cataraugus Republican," at that time published in Salamanca, N. Y. The son was prepared for college in the public schools and by tutor at Salamanca and was graduated at Yale University in 1897. He served a short apprenticeship as reporter on the "Buffalo Express" and then removed to New York as news editor of the American Press Association, a position he held until 1908. After travelling in Europe for some time he returned to New York and purchased a controlling interest in Moody's Magazine a monthly financial publication established in 1905 by John Moody, founder of "Moody's Manual," and Byron W. Holt, the well-known economist, as a forum for the discussion of the economic principles governing finance. The scope of the magazine has since been increased to include the analysis of corporations and railroad reports and general investment subjects. "Moody's Magazine" is the only publication of its kind in the United States and has the largest circulation among investors of any American financial periodical with the excep-

MAHLON PITNEY
JURIST

ASHLEY HORNE
CAPITALIST

GEORGE S. THOMPSON
CAPITALIST

AUGUSTIN W. FERRIN
EDITOR

J. HAMILTON LEWIS
U. S. SENATOR

DAVID C. McCORMICK
MANUFACTURER

EDWIN BONNELL
BANKER

GEORGE E. HUNT
DENTAL SURGEON

tion of "The Commercial and Financial Chronicle," which is mainly statistical. On the formation of the Moody Magazine & Book Company in 1913 he was elected its president and is now devoting himself to the publication of "Moody's Magazine," of which he is editor, and of books on finance and economics. He is a member of the Salamagundi Club and belongs to the Episcopal Church. He is unmarried.

LEWIS, James Hamilton, U. S. senator, was born at Danville, Va., May 18, 1866. His education was obtained in the schools of Georgia and the University of Virginia. After leaving college he went to Seattle, Wash., where he was admitted to the bar as a practicing attorney. In 1889 he was elected as a Democratic territorial senator for the Seattle district. In 1894 he was one of the caucus candidates chosen by the Democratic minority of the legislature for the U. S. senate, and two years later was elected Democratic congressman-at-large for the state of Washington. He was the author of the resolution which eventually became the foundation of the resolution upon which war with Spain was declared. When he entered congress he was a lieutenant-colonel in the national guard of the state of Washington. At the outbreak of the Spanish-American war he offered his services to the government, and was assigned to Gen. John R. Brooks' staff, but was subsequently transferred to the staff of Gen. F. D. Grant, where he served as inspector-general with the rank of colonel. Sen. Lewis was appointed to represent American interests at the conference of the joint high commission in London regarding the temporary settlement of the border line of Alaska, Canada and the United States. He opposed the temporary agreement entered into by representatives of England and the United States, and returning home, voiced his protest to his government. Later he was elected congressman-at-large for the state of Washington. In 1900 he was presented as the candidate of the states of Washington, Oregon and Idaho for vice-president, receiving 110 votes in the convention. Col. Lewis removed to Chicago in 1903, where he served as corporation counsel from 1905-07. In 1908 he was the Democratic candidate for governor of Illinois, and in 1913 was unanimously nominated at the primaries for U. S. senator. He was nominated by Pres. Wilson as senate member at the international conference to prepare the international treaty for laws for safety at sea, held in London in January, 1914. He is joint author with Prof. A. H. Putney of ' Laws and Decisions Upon Elections" and of "Constitutions, Statutes and Their Construction"; and author of "The Two Great Republics, Rome and the United States." He has served as lecturer in the law department of Northwestern University and as president and lecturer of Webster College of Law, Chicago, and is a member of the Geographical and Historical Society of Paris. He was married Nov. 16, 1898, to Rose Lawton Douglas, of Georgia.

McCORMICK, David Cummings, manufacturer, was born near Savannah, Ga., Aug. 22, 1832, son of Pollard and Rebecca (Shoenberger) McCormick. His mother was a daughter of Dr. Peter Shoenberger, who came from Germany at the beginning of the nineteenth century and founded the famous iron firm of the Shoenbergers in Pittsburgh, erecting a number of furnaces which he called by the names of his daughters—the Sarah Furnace, the Martha Furnace, the Maria Furnace and the Rebecca Furnace. He also owned the Juniata Forge in Huntingdon county and erected the Juniata works, the first rolling mill in Pittsburgh. Associated with him in the conduct of the

business were his son, John H. Shoenberger, and his son-in-law, Pollard McCormick. David C. McCormick was educated at old Carlisle College, Carlisle, Pa., and at Yale College. He engaged in the manufacture of pig iron at Holidaysburg, Pa., under the name of the Sarah Furnace Co., being the first to manufacture pig iron for the supply of Pittsburg mills and, during the fifteen years of his connection with this business, he was a conspicuous figure in the industry. During the last twenty-five years of his life he lived in retirement, devoting himself to promoting the welfare of his community and to a generous participation in philanthropic activities. He was a man of forceful personality, keen mentality, kindly and a liberal disposition and stainless character. He was married in Pittsburgh, Pa., June 16, 1860, to Cecelia, daughter of George Grant, of Boston, Mass., and is survived by two children: Sophia Grant and John Shoenberger McCormick. He died in Pittsburgh, Pa., Mar. 12, 1910.

BONNELL, Edwin, banker, was born in Cincinnati, O., Sept. 23, 1836, son of Allison Clarke and Catharine Hough (Looker) Bonnell, and grandson of Aaron Bonnell, who married Rachel Clarke and was a soldier in the New Jersey troops during the revolution. During the gold excitement of 1849 Allison C. Bonnell went to California and later settled in Portland, Ore., of which he was one of the early mayors. He was also a mill owner and lumber dealer, but a disastrous fire deprived him of his fortune, and in 1852 he removed to San Francisco, Cal., where for many years he was cashier of the San Francisco "Bulletin." Edwin Bonnell received his education in the district schools of Ohio, and at the age of sixteen joined his father at Portland and was for a time engaged in scaling logs. He became an accomplished accountant and was steadily employed. In 1873 he accepted a position with the Savings and Loan Society, the pioneer savings bank of San Francisco, and for thirty-five years was with that institution, first as secretary and for the last six years as cashier. He retired in 1909, when the Savings and Loan Society was amalgamated with the Savings Union. He was secretary of the California School of Mechanical Arts, of the Sons of the American Revolution and the Unitarian Club, and a member of the California Pioneers' Association. He was treasurer and trustee of the William and Alice Hinckley Fund, and held many other positions of trust. He was known among his intimate friends for his ability as an artist in oil, although he never exhibited publicly. A close friend of William Keith, the artist, he had studied for some time under that noted painter, and Bonnell's canvases of California scenes and landscape show the influence of Keith's teaching. When Keith died he appointed him executor of his estate. He was a member of the Unitarian Church. He was married in San Francisco Dec. 22, 1861, to Mary Angelina, daughter of James Haley, of New York, and had two children: Allison Clarke and Edith, wife of Judge F. H. Dunne, of the superoir court. He died in San Francisco, Cal., Nov. 28, 1912.

HUNT, George Edwin, physician, dental surgeon, author and editor, was born in Indianapolis, Ind., Apr. 29, 1864, son of Phineas George Canning and Hannah Mary (Phipps) Hunt. His father, a native of Urbana, O., was a dental surgeon of Indianapolis. He received his preliminary education at the public schools of Indianapolis; completed a two years' course in civil engineering at Asbury, now De Pauw University, and was a student at the University of Michigan for one year. During the ensuing four years he was engaged in railroad construction and location work in Florida. He was graduated at Indiana Dental College in 1890, with the degree D.D.S., and at the Medical College of Indiana in 1892, with the degree M.D. He then began the practice of dentistry in association with his father. In 1891 he became a member of the board of trustees of Indiana Dental College. He was appointed secretary in 1895 and was dean from 1896 until his death. Upon the death of his father in 1896 he closed his dental office and gave his entire time to college work. In 1904 he was vice-president of the Fourth International Dental Congress, St. Louis. He was past president of the Institute of Dental Pedagogics; past president and past secretary of the Indiana State Dental Association; past vice-president of the National Dental Association, and past secretary of the National Association of Dental Faculties, of which he was president at the time of his death. He was secretary (in 1900) of the board of trustees of the University of Indianapolis; past secretary of the Indiana State Board of Commerce, the Citizens' League of Indianapolis and the Commercial Club, a thirty-second degree Mason and a member of the Ancient Arabic Order of the Nobles of the Mystic Shrine, the Delta Tau Delta and Delta Sigma Delta fraternities, and the German House, Columbia and Highland Golf clubs of Indianapolis. He had a distinctive literary talent and was the author of numerous short stories which appeared in the magazines. He was also a contributor to professional journals; was the founder, and until 1900 the editor, of the "Indiana Dental Journal"; was for fourteen years editor of "Desmos," a dental fraternal journal, and from 1911 to his death was editor of "Oral Hygiene." Dr. Hunt's dominating personal characteristics were his capacity for making and keeping friends, and his sparkling geniality. He was married (first) in Indianapolis, Ind., Nov. 16, 1892, to Grace, daughter of William H. Morrison, of that city; (second) in Indianapolis, June 23, 1908, to (Mrs.) Maria (Foster) Buchanan, widow of Russel R. Buchanan and daughter of Edgar J. Foster, of Indianapolis. He died in Indianapolis July 11, 1914.

GLASPELL, Susan (Mrs. George Cram Cook), author, was born in Davenport, Ia., July 1, 1882, daughter of Elmer S. and Alice (Keating) Glaspell. She is of English and Irish ancestry, her father's people having come from England in Colonial days, first settling in New England, but removing as early as 1810 to the Middle West, with which part of the country they have since been identified. Her mother's people were from Dublin, Ireland. She attended the public schools of Davenport and was graduated Ph.B. from Drake University, Des Moines, Ia. Later she pursued a brief course in English at the University of Chicago. For a time she was engaged in newspaper reporting in Des Moines, her work being of a political nature, as she had the state house and legislative assignments. The stories she came in touch with there first awakened in her a desire to try short stories for the magazines, and her work appeared in "Harper's," "The American" and several other American periodicals. Her earliest novel, "The Glory of the Conquered," was published in 1909 and found a large public. Her succeeding books are: "The Visioning" (1911), "Lifted Masks" (1912) and "Fidelity" (1915). Miss Glaspell's work has been compared with the best of contemporary English fiction, and of "Fidelity" the New York "Tribune" wrote: "In the admirable quality of its workmanship it is probably the best American novel published this year." She was married, April 13, 1913, to George Cram Cook.

LITTLE, Arthur Dehon, chemist, was born in Boston, Mass., Dec. 15, 1863, son of Thomas J. and Amelia (Hixon) Little. His early education was obtained in Portland, Me., and at Berkeley School, New York city. He took a special course at the Massachusetts Institute of Technology, after which he obtained a position as chemist and superintendent of the Richmond Paper Co., at Providence, R. I. Having acquired a thorough knowledge of the details of paper-making by the sulphite process, he brought into operation pulp mills in Wisconsin and North Carolina, where the new process was installed. In 1886 he opened an office in Boston, Mass., as a consulting chemical engineer, first in association with Roger B. Griffin and later with Dr. William H. Walker. In 1905 the business was incorporated under the firm name of Arthur D. Little, Inc. Mr. Little has been retained as consulting chemist by many large corporations such as the American Pulp & Paper Association, General Motors Co., United Shoe Machinery Co., International Paper Co., Union Bag & Paper Co., United Fruit Co., Great Southern Lumber Co., General Chemical Co., and Plymouth Cordage Co. Mr. Little is the author of numerous addresses dealing with the broader aspects of the application of chemistry to industry. He has made a specialty of the chemistry of cellulose, fibres, and paper-making, on which he is probably the foremost authority in America. In 1912 he erected an experimental plant in Boston for carrying out on a semi-commercial scale studies in paper-making and solving practical problems in connection with pulp and paper mill operation. The plant is a complete pulp and paper mill on a small scale. He is member of the corporation of the Mass. Institute of Technology, fellow of the American Association for the Advancement of Science, a member of the American Chemical Society (president, 1912–14), the Society of Chemical Industry, the American Electrochemical Society, the American Institute of Chemical Engineers, the American Society of Mechanical Engineers, and the Union Engineers', Chemists, Bankers, and St. Botolph clubs. He was married Jan. 22, 1901, to Henrietta Rogers, daughter of Nathan Anthony, of Boston.

CRANE, Caroline Bartlett, minister and municipal expert, was born at Hudson, Wis., Aug. 17, 1858, daughter of Lorenzo Dow and Julia A. (Brown) Bartlett. Her father was a physician. She was graduated at Carthage College, Ill., in 1879, and subsequently did post-graduate work at the University of Chicago. During 1879–83 she was engaged as a teacher, and during 1883–86 she was a newspaper writer and city editor with the Minneapolis "Tribune." During 1886–89 she was pastor of All-Souls' Church at Sioux Falls, S. D. In the latter year she was called to the First Unitarian Church at Kalamazoo, Mich., where she was ordained as a minister of liberal religion. There she found a small handful of elderly people and four children. She at once started a Sunday-school, and gradually both Sunday-school and congregation increased remarkably in numbers. After a time, under the influence of their pastor, they began to hold mid-weekly meetings to study the needs of their town. As a result, when the growth of the congregation necessitated the building of a new church, there was included with it a kindergarten, a gymnasium for women, a manual training department, and a domestic science department. The new church was named the People's Church, and recognized no sectarian boundaries. In the course of time the people of Kalamazoo found that kindergartens, cooking courses and manual training were such good things that they incorporated them in the public schools. After she had her church work running smoothly, Mrs. Crane began to investigate other matters of public interest, and, finding many conditions in Kalamazoo that needed attention, she organized a Civic Improvement League. The first work of this body, most of which was supervised personally by Mrs. Crane, was to clean the backyards and alleys, and then the streets, of the city. She then organized a Charity Organization Branch of the Civic Improvement League, which quickly put a check on vagabondage and miscellaneous begging, found work for the needy who were willing and able to work, and induced the poor to save by arranging with a local savings bank to accept small accounts, from one penny upward. The Charity Organization Branch also works for the settlement of domestic relations, supplies trained nurses for poor homes where nurses are needed, employs savings collectors to keep the people stirred up to the need of putting money in their accounts, and sends visitors around to dispense sympathy, advice and good cheer. In 1903 Mrs. Crane, as chairman of the committee on household economics of the Twentieth Century Club of Kalamazoo, tried to secure a speaker on meat inspection. Failing to find one, she decided to speak on the subject herself. A first-hand investigation of the abattoirs of the city revealed a shocking state of affairs. The city government could do nothing in the matter, as the slaughter houses were outside the city limits. Mrs. Crane then investigated the slaughter houses of Grand Rapids, Owosso and Lansing to see if conditions were as bad in those cities as in Kalamazoo, and, finding that they were, she framed a law, which she succeeded in having passed by the state legislature, providing that the cities of the state could frame their own meat inspection ordinances. She then drafted an ordinance for Kalamazoo which, in spite of violent opposition, was finally passed by the city council. By this time Mrs. Crane's reputation had spread throughout the state, and she was invited to visit and inspect Saginaw, Big Rapids, Calumet, Hastings and Bay City. As demands for inspections grew, she put a price upon her services and adopted sanitary inspection as a profession. Calls began to come from other states, and up to the present time she has made sanitary surveys, as she calls them, of over fifty cities in all parts of the United States. Her investigation is very thorough, embracing the city's resources and everything connected with community life. Her reports and suggestions for improvements and reforms are printed and serve as a municipal text-book for years to come. The result of her work as a professional sanitarian has been the organization of local civic leagues, the enactment of new health laws by state legislatures, and the adoption of radical sanitary reforms. In addition to numerous reports, Mrs. Crane is the author of "U. S. Inspected and Passed" (1913), a criticism of federal meat inspection. She is a member of the executive board of the National American Woman Suffrage Association and the American Civic Association. She was married at Kalamazoo, Mich., Dec. 31, 1896, to Dr. Augustus Warren Crane.

O'CONNELL, Denis Joseph, seventh Roman Catholic bishop of Richmond, Va., was born at Donoughmore, County Cork, Ireland, Jan. 28, 1849.

He came to this country in childhood with his parents, who settled in South Carolina, where his uncle was a distinguished member of the clergy in the Columbia section. He was educated at St. Mary's College and at St. Charles' Seminary, Columbia, and finished at the North American College, Rome, being ordained priest May 26, 1877. On his return home Cardinal Gibbons made him his secretary, and in this capacity he was prominent in the proceedings of the third plenary council of Baltimore and carried its decrees to Rome for the approval of the pope. He was made a domestic prelate Mar. 20, 1887, and was appointed rector of the North American College, Rome, after the death of Mgr. Hostlot in 1884. He resigned in July, 1895, but remained in Rome as the vicar of Cardinal Gibbons for his titular church, S. Maria in Trastevere. In 1903 he returned to the United States to become rector of the Catholic University at Washington, D. C. His administration during a period of five years contributed materially to the progress of that institution. He was consecrated titular bishop of Sebaste May 3, 1908, by Cardinal Falconio, and on Dec. 24th, following, was appointed auxiliary bishop of San Francisco. Here he remained assisting Archbishop Riordan until Jan. 19, 1912, when he was transferred to the vacant see of Richmond, Va., in succession to Bishop Van de Vyver. Richmond diocese has a Catholic population of 45,000, with sixty-seven priests, 184 churches, chapels and stations, thirty-five schools and 5,379 pupils. He is a noted student of Dante and was president of the Catholic Educational Association.

PIERSON, Lewis Eugene, banker and merchant, was born at Metuchen, N. J., Mar. 12, 1870, son of Edgar L. and Anna (Southard) Pierson. He received a public school education and at the age of fifteen began his business career as a messenger in the Hanover National Bank of New York city. In 1898 he became cashier of the National Exchange Bank and for six years held the dual position of cashier and vice-president and was then made president. In 1906 the National Exchange Bank was consolidated with the Irving National Bank, and Mr. Pierson became president of the new institution, the Irving National Exchange Bank. His administration, covering a period of six years, was one of development and prosperity, largely on account of his own personal efforts. To increase the bank's influence and efficiency, he developed a service that afforded unique facilities in bill-of-lading business, so that the bank adopted the trade-mark, "B. L." He introduced a new system of collection, and was the first to give customers a statement instead of the old plan of balancing pass-books. He inaugurated a publicity campaign, which included a unique, clear and intelligible "quick assets" statement. For the directors he prepared typewritten lists of transactions in place of the customary oral reports, and he arranged "directors' dinners" which became famous in banking circles. Thus his bank steadily increased in business, power and influence until its earning capacity ranked with the five leading national banks of New York, and when Mr. Pierson retired from the presidency the assets of the institution were $53,000,000. In 1912 Mr. Pierson became president of the firm of Austin, Nichols & Co., wholesale grocers. He immediately introduced new methods whereby the efficiency in transacting its business was greatly enhanced. The simplification of procedures, the placing of definite responsibilities, and the reorganization of departments in the interests of economy and betterment of service were among the reforms which he established. The corporation of Austin, Nichols & Co. now includes the houses of Clark, Chapin & Bushnell; Gennerick & von Bremen; H. von Lupkin & Co.; Valentine & Bergen; Rafferty & Hosier, and Stoddard, Gilbert & Co. He is a member of the American Bankers' Association, of which he was president in 1909–10, the New York State Bankers' Association, of which he was president in 1903, the New York Chamber of Commerce, the Merchants' Association, the Masonic order, the Royal Arcanum, and the New York Athletic, Hardware and Merchants' clubs of New York city, and the Riding and Driving and Montauk clubs of Brooklyn. He belongs to the Methodist church. He was married, June 10, 1891, to Blanche, daughter of Henry Thorne, of Brooklyn, N. Y., and their children are: Anne R., Alene S., Grace T. and Lewis E. Pierson, Jr.

VANCE, James Nelson, financier and philanthropist, was born in Ohio county, Va., Aug. 1, 1828, son of James and Mary (Waddle) Vance. After a public school education he entered the retail iron business in Wheeling, W. Va., of which he soon became sole proprietor. The business was enlarged in 1861 under the firm name of Dewey, Vance & Co., and a plant was erected in Wheeling for the manufacture of bar iron. It was the initial one of the kind in that part of the country. The business increased so rapidly that a second plant was erected in 1866, and still another six years later at Benwood. In 1875 these foundries were incorporated under the name of the Riverside Iron Works, with Mr. Vance as president. The Riverside Iron Works was at that time the largest and most complete plant of its kind in the country, with a capacity of 10,000 kegs of nails weekly. In 1884 Bessemer soft steel was introduced in the manufacture of nails, which were the first to be so made in the United States. The business was sold to the National Tube Co. in 1899, at which time it was doing an annual business aggregating $6,000,000 and employing over 2,500 men. It was taken into the United States Steel Corporation in 1901. Mr. Vance was a director of the National Tube Co. until its absorption by the latter corporation, when he resigned. Besides his steel interests, he was president of the National Exchange Bank, the Security Trus tCo., the Imperial Glass Co., the Wheeling Bridge Co., and the Franklin Insurance Co., of Wheeling, and was a director of the Fostoria Glass Co., the United States Stamping Works, the State Bank of Elm Grove, the Woodward Iron Works of Birmingham, Ala.; the Wheeling Sheet and Tin Plate Co. and the Federal Trust and Savings Bank of Chicago. Mr. Vance was one of the most generous of contributors to the religious, educational and social welfare of Wheeling. He erected the Vance Memorial Church at Woodlawn, and it was chiefly through his generosity that the Y. M. C. A. building at Wheeling was erected. The Wheeling "Intelligencer" said of him: "A man of unusual business capacity, he accumulated a great fortune which he used wisely and well. In the furtherance of new enterprises appealing to the investing community, he was always active and liberal; in the support of church and charity, he was always generous and often munificent. In his social relations, he was a man of broad and generous sympathies, a character that attracted friends and held them with bonds of loving kindness." He was married, Sept. 15, 1863, to Lillie E., daughter of Samuel McClellan, of Wheeling, and had four children: Henry Edgerton, James Nelson, Jr.; William Mc-

Clellan and Lillie Edgerton, wife of S. W. Harper. He died in Wheeling, W. Va., June 26, 1913.

KITCHIN, Claude, lawyer and congressman, was born in Scotland Neck, N. C., Mar. 24, 1869, son of William H. and Maria F. (Arrington) Kitchin. His father (1837–1901) was a lawyer and planter of North Carolina, and an officer in the Confederate army during the civil war. The son was brought up on his father's plantation, and was educated at Wake Forest College, where he was graduated in 1888. He was admitted to the bar in September, 1890, and in the following year began the practice of his profession in Scotland Neck. He had long been interested in local politics, but he never held office until his election to the 57th congress. He has served in congress by re-election to the present time. In the 64th congress he became chairman of the ways and means committee, which made him the Democratic leader of the house. He was opposed to Pres. Wilson's policy of preparedness, an attitude which caused embarrassment to the Democratic party, because as chairman of the ways and means committee he was expected to take the lead in formulating the laws that would prepare for the necessary expenditures for the army and navy. Mr. Kitchin is a good debater and ready speaker. He was married Nov. 13, 1888, to Kate B., daughter of L. R. Mills of Wake Forest, N. C., and has nine children: Anna, wife of Robert C. Josey, Jr.; Mills, Katherine, Gertrude, Ione, Claude, Jr., Hesta, Pauline Ramsay and Stedman Kitchin.

THAYER, Benjamin Bowditch, mining engineer, was born in San Francisco, Cal., Oct. 20, 1862, son of Benjamin Bowditch and Lucy W (Phipps) Thayer. The first of his family in America was Richard Thayer, who came over from Thornbury, Gloucestershire, England, and was admitted a freeman in Braintree, Mass., in 1640. From him and his wife, Dorothy Mortimer, the line of descent is traced through their son Richard, who married Dorothy Pray; their son Nathaniel, who married Hannah Hayden; their son Nathaniel, who married Sarah Wales; their son Abraham, who married Sarah Hunt; their son Abraham, who married Lydia (Thayer) Thayer; their son Col. Abraham, who married Mary Nash Arnold, and was the grandfather of the subject of this sketch. His father (1828–85) was a druggist and chemist in Boston, was state assayer of California in 1860, and manager of the Guadaloupe quicksilver mine during 1873–84. Benjamin B. Thayer, Jr., was educated at Adams Academy, Quincy, Mass., and at the Lawrence Scientific School, Harvard University, where he was graduated Ph.B. in 1885. Upon leaving college he at once entered the mining field in the employ of the Bi-Metallic Mining Co. of Granite, Mont. Later he transferred his services to the Anaconda Mining Co. of Butte, Mont., and also did some mining in California and New Mexico. He was president of the famous Anaconda mine at Butte from 1908 to 1915, when it was absorbed by the Amalgamated Co., and he is now vice-president of the latter. His technical knowledge, combined with long practical experience and rare executive ability, has given him a national reputation among the mining engineers of the country. And besides this practical ability he possesses an engaging personality that commands the affection and loyalty of the men working under him to an extraordinary degree, traits to which the pre-eminence of Anaconda smelting and Anaconda ore dressing may be attributed. Among his workmen he is popularly called "Big Ben." On a broad foundation of detailed knowledge and skill he has built a solid structure of appreciation for basic facts and a wide outlook. Because of his expert knowledge of explosives he was selected to be a member of the United States navy's advisory board of inventors in 1915. He is one of the leading members of the American Institute of Mining Engineers, of which he was president in 1914–15. He is also a member of the New York Society of Harvard Engineers (president 1911), the Harvard Association of Engineers (president 1912), and he is one of the advisory committee on the conduct and development of mining education at Harvard University. He belongs to the Union League, Harvard, Engineers and Railroad clubs of New York and the Silver Bow Club of Butte, Mont. Mr. Thayer was married Jan. 29, 1890, to Marie C., daughter of Edwin Renouard of St. Louis, Mo., and has three daughters: Cecile Tesson, wife of Douglas Gibbons of New York city, Marie R. and Alice R. Thayer.

SCHENCK, Frederick Brett, banker, was born at Yonkers, N. Y., June 9, 1851, son of Oscar and Cornelia Ann (Brett) Schenck, and a descendant of Johannes Schenck, who came from Middleburg, Island of Zealand, Holland, to New Amsterdam in 1683. The line of descent runs through his son Johannes, who married Marie Lott; through their son Abraham, who married Elsie Vandervoort; their son Henry, who married Hannah Brett; and their son Abraham H., who married Sarah Wiltse and was the grandfather of the subject of this sketch. Frederick B. Schenck was educated in the public schools of Brooklyn, N. Y. In 1865 he entered the office of Saxton, Raymond & Co., stock brokers, with whom he remained for ten years, rising from junior clerk to cashier. In 1875 he engaged in the commercial paper business with James A. Benedict, a connection which continued until his appointment as loan clerk of the Mercantile National Bank in 1881. He was soon after promoted to be assistant cashier and then cashier, as successor to William P. St. John, who had been made president, and upon the resignation of the latter he succeeded to the presidency. In 1907 he became president of the Liberty National Bank, in which capacity he served for almost five years, and at the time of his death he was chairman of its board of directors. Mr. Schenck was also a director of the Bowling Green Trust Co., the Brunswick Terminal and Railway Securities Co., and of the Palisades Trust and Guaranty Co. of Englewood, N. J., to which place he removed in 1897. The work of the Y. M. C. A. was one of Mr. Schenck's chief interests, and he served as president of the Brooklyn branch of that organization for nine years. In 1891 he was elected to the international committee of Y. M. C. A. and a year later became its treasurer. He was a member of the New York Chamber of Commerce, the Union League Club, the Holland Society of New York, the Railroad and Lawyers' clubs, and the Englewood Golf Club. He was twice married; first, Oct. 24, 1877, to Mary Scott, daughter of Junius Gridley, merchant, of New York. She died May 26, 1889, and he was again married June 1, 1893, to Nannie Bostick, daughter of Dr. Henry William de Saussure, of Charleston, S. C. He was survived by one daughter, Dorothy de Saussure Schenck. Mr. Schenck died at his home in Englewood, N. J., May 21, 1913.

BUSSE, Fred Adolph, mayor of Chicago, was born in Chicago, Ill., Mar. 3, 1866, son of Gustav and Caroline (Gross) Busse. His father was a soldier in the civil war and obtained a captain's commission. The son was educated at the public schools and began his business career in his father's hardware store in Chicago. Later he became the proprietor of a coal yard known first as the Northwestern Coal Co., then as the Busse-Reynolds Coal Co., and finally as the Busse Coal Co. Mr. Busse became identified with Republican politics on the north side of Chicago at an early age, and held the offices of clerk of the old town of North Chicago, bailiff in Judge Brentano's court and deputy sheriff, successively. In 1894 he was elected to the state legislature, and he was re-elected two years later. At the expiration of his term he was elected to the state senate, where he was prominently identified with much important legislation, including the establishment of the St. Charles school for boys in Chicago, the creation of the State Pawners' Society to combat usury by money-lenders, the establishment of the Torrens system of land title registration and transfer, the Chicago and Cook county civil service laws, the juvenile court law and the repeal of the franchise-grabbing Allen law. In 1902 Mr. Busse was elected state treasurer of Illinois, and at the expiration of his term he was appointed by Pres. Roosevelt postmaster of the city of Chicago. In 1907 he received the Republican nomination for mayor and was elected by a majority of 13,000 votes, although injuries sustained in a railroad accident prevented him from taking part in the campaign. He was the first mayor under the four-year tenure. The important features of his administration included the passage of the 1907 traction ordinances and the appointment of the famous vice commission of 1910. In advance of the primaries of 1911 he announced that he would not seek re-election, and upon the expiration of his term he retired to private life. Subsequently he became receiver for the Kellogg-Machay Co., and was interested in advanced farming. Mr. Busse possessed a forceful personality and won the affection of a large circle of friends. His career was identified with an important part of Chicago's history, and it was said that he was the best mayor that the city of Chicago ever had. His friends fondly referred to him as the "Burgomaster." He was married Apr. 29, 1908, to Josephine, daughter of Edward Henry Lee, an artist. He died in Chicago, July 10, 1914.

COCKCROFT, James, publisher, was born in New York city, Sept. 2, 1842, son of James and Lucretia M. (Voorhees) Cockcroft, and grandson of Dr. James Cockcroft, one of the most prominent physicians in New York city. He was educated at the Peekskill Academy and subsequently attended the law school of Columbia University. He began business with his uncle, John Voorhees, a publisher of law books, and when the glamour of the growing West drove him to Chicago, Ill., in 1868, he associated himself with James Callaghan in the law publishing firm of Callaghan & Cockcroft. Within a few years the firm became the most prominent in the West, numbering among its publications many law books which still hold an important place in the literature of the bar. The fire of 1871 completely destroyed the property of the firm, and James Cockcroft returned to New York, where he published some important books on his own account. Declining health forced him after a while to give up his business in New York and seek rest and quiet in the little village of Northport, Long Island. There, in 1881, with his friend, Edward Thompson, he organized the Edward Thompson Co., law-book publishers. The magnum opus of the firm is the "American and English Encyclopædia of Law," the first volume of which appeared in 1887. This work is now recognized as a valuable adjunct to every law library. It was conceived and planned by James Cockcroft and carried out by him in the face of difficulties and discouragements that would have dismayed most men. He worked on it as publisher, editor and author, and a large part of the earlier volumes were written by him. "It was in sheer desperation," he said, "that I began work on the first volume. When I think of the failures I experienced in the course of my efforts to get lawyers of note to interest themselves in my plan, I am surprised that I was able to persevere in it myself. Almost every one I talked with was of the opinion that the encyclopædia method was totally unsuited to the science of jurisprudence. In vain I urged the success of that method in dealing with other modern sciences. And when at last I persuaded a few to help me they could not arrange their matter in a manner conformable to my plans. I was fairly driven to do the best I could for myself." Among other publications conceived by him were the "Encyclopædia of Pleading and Practice," "Encyclopædia of Forms and Precedents," "American Railway Reports," "American and English Railroad Cases," "American and English Corporation Cases," "American and English Annotated Cases" and "Federal Statutes Annotated." His last work was editing an edition of Lord Campbell's "Lives of the Chief Justices of England." He was married Nov. 26, 1867, to Alida Theresa, daughter of H. Sidney Ketcham, of Syracuse, N. Y., and had two sons: James Douglas and Arthur Cockcroft. He died at Northport, L. I., Nov. 12, 1911.

WILLARD, Horace Mann, educator, was born at Canterbury, Windham co., Conn., Mar. 24, 1842, son of George Anson and Emerette (Aspenwall) Willard, grandson of Rev. Benjamin and Sally (Conant) Willard, and a descendant of Simon Willard, the founder of the family in America. His parents were both well-known teachers, and determined to give their son every educational advantage. He pursued his studies at the University Grammar School in Providence, R. I., and was graduated at Brown University in 1864. He was immediately elected principal of the Bridgewater (Mass.) Academy and administered the affairs of that institution with signal ability until 1870. As a teacher Dr. Willard made a specialty of the classics, Latin and Greek. From Bridgewater he was called to the head of Colby Academy, New London, N. H., and subsequently he was superintendent of schools at Gloucester, Mass., and at Newton, Mass. In 1876 he resigned his office to take charge of the Vermont Academy at Saxtons River, Vt., a new co-educational school organized through the efforts of the Baptists of the state. He was its first principal and was practically its founder, its early growth and success being due largely to his efforts. Under his principalship it attained a high position among the educational institutions of New England, its pupils being admitted to over twenty of the leading colleges. After thirteen years of devoted labor here, Dr. Willard resigned. He then spent a year in rest, study and travel, and in the following year became principal of Howard Seminary at West Bridgewater, where he remained five years. In 1896 he founded the Quincy Mansion School, a select family school for girls at Wollaston, Mass. The buildings consist of the old historical Quincy mansion, erected by Hon. Josiah Quincy, mayor of Boston, in 1855; Canterbury and Manchester halls, two new well-equipped dormitories. He pro-

vided a healthful, cheerful and attractive school home, enlisting the services of an experienced corps of teachers, numbering fifteen at the time of his death. Throughout his entire educational life he was noted for his eminently Christian influence. Mrs. Mary A. Livermore, in speaking of his work at the Vermont Academy, said: "He has labored under discouragements and indifference that would have driven away a less consecrated man, and I wondered at his patience. All have been carried along by his splendid devotion and enthusiasm, and the compensation has been the growth of the academy and the beautiful development of its students." In 1896 Brown University conferred upon him the honorary degree of Sc.D. and in 1901 he became a trustee of Newton Theological Institution. He was also a director of the Young Men's Christian Association and of the Quincy City Hospital and a member of the National Education Association. Dr. Willard was married at Fall River, Mass, July 11, 1872, to Ruth, daughter of Ashley Sanders, of Manchester, England. He died at Wollaston, Mass., Aug. 24, 1907.

MODJESKI, Ralph, civil engineer, was born in Cracow, Austrian Poland, Jan. 27, 1861, son of Gustave Sinnmayer and Helena (Opid) Modrzejewski. His father was a theatrical director and his mother was the world-famous tragedienne, who on coming to the United States changed her name to Modjeska. Ralph Modjeski was graduated at the head of his class at the Ecole des Ponts et Chaussées, Paris, with the degree of civil engineer in 1885. Coming to the United States in 1885, he became assistant to George S. Morison in the construction of the Union Pacific bridge at Omaha, Neb., and remained with Mr. Morison until 1892, when he engaged in private practice as a civil engineer in Chicago. He has specialized in bridge work, and has become one of the leading engineering authorities on bridges in this country. The first large bridge designed and constructed by him was the double-track-and-highway structure over the Mississippi river at Rock Island, Ill. This was followed by the reconstruction of the Bismarck (N. D.) bridge across the Missouri river and the Thebes (Ill.) bridge across the Mississippi. The latter was built in association with Alfred Noble. After these came the Columbia river and Willamette river bridges for the Spokane, Portland and Seattle railway; the McKinley bridge across the Mississippi at St. Louis, the Columbia river bridge at Celilo, Ore, for the Oregon Trunk railway, and the Broadway bridge across the Williamette for the city of Portland, Ore. During his private practice he has also designed and built a large number of smaller bridges and has been employed as consulting bridge engineer for the Northern Pacific railway and other railroads and corporations. One of his important works outside the field of bridge engineering was the designing and building of a large fireproof warehouse for the ordnance department of the U. S. government at Rock Island, Ill. At the suggestion of the City Club of New York he was selected by that city's bridge department to examine into the plans and structure of the new Manhattan bridge across the East river. He was a member of the board of engineers in the reconstruction of the Quebec bridge, which has the longest span in the world. He is at present engaged in designing the new double-track railway bridge to cross the Mississippi at Memphis, and in the construction of a large concrete arch bridge at Toledo, O. Mr. Modjeski is a member of the American Society of Civil

JAMES COCKCROFT
PUBLISHER

HORACE M. WILLARD
EDUCATOR

RALPH MODJESKI
CIVIL ENGINEER

HENRY PEMBERTON
CHEMIST

Engineers, the Canadian Society of Civil Engineers, the British Institute of Civil Engineers, the American Institute of Consulting Engineers, the Society for the Promotion of Engineering Education, the Franklin Institute of Philadelphia, and the Western Society of Engineers, having been its president. He received the degree of doctor of engineering from the University of Illinois in 1911. He is a member of the Engineers' Club, New York; the Engineers' Union League, and South Shore Country, Cliff Dwellers' and Yacht clubs of Chicago, and the Arlington and Waverly Country clubs of Portland, Ore. He was married in New York city, Dec. 28, 1885, to Felicie, daughter of Felix Benda, of Cracow, Poland, and has three children: Felix Bozenta, Marie Stewart and Charles Emanuel Modjeski.

LEY, Harold Alexander, contractor and philanthropist, was born in Springfield, Mass., May 28, 1874, son of Fred William and Martha (Hallenstein) Ley. His father, a native of Germany, was a musician by profession, and came to the United States in 1848, settling at Springfield, Mass. The son was educated in the public schools of Springfield, and began his business career as errand boy in the employ of a wholesale shoe dealer. A year later, in 1889, he became connected with the actuarial department of the Massachusetts Mutual Life Insurance Co. in Springfield. From there he joined his brother, Fred T. Ley, who was in the contracting business in Springfield, under the name of Fred T. Ley & Co., Inc., and he has been its president since 1898. This company has been engaged in the construction of office buildings, reinforced concrete structures, mills, power houses, flumes, tunnels, dams, bridges, water supplies, reservoirs and similar work. Mr. Ley's chief claim to distinction is the valuable service he has rendered the cause of civilization by furthering the organization of the Life Extension Institute, which is perhaps one of the most unique corporations in the world. Its object is the lengthening of human life for both commercial and philanthropic reasons. It has long been recognized among the medical profession that through the ignorance and neglect of simple and easily applied preventives vast numbers of people meet an untimely death. The Life Extension Institute may be called a practical application of the idea of preventive medicine, which physicians and surgeons have been advocating of late. In the same way that buildings, bridges, machinery, elevators, etc., are regularly inspected to guard against accident, it was the idea of Mr. Ley and his associates to establish and maintain a central institute of national scope devoted to the science of disease prevention, supported by a hygiene reference board of recognized ability in the various fields of health and life conservation. Mr. Ley secured the co-operation of Prof. Irving Fisher, of Yale, and other leading economists and philanthropists, and in 1913 the Life Extension Institute was incorporated by the state of New York with the following officers: Ex-Pres. William H. Taft, chairman of the board of directors; Elmer E. Rittenhouse, president; Dr. Eugene L. Fisk, director of hygiene; Harold A. Ley, vice-president and treasurer, and James D. Lennehan, secretary. The institute is both practical and philanthropic. In order that its benefits to humanity may be continuous, and its existence perpetuated, moderate fees are charged for the service rendered both individuals and organizations. It is not intended to supplant the family physician, but rather to confine its life-saving efforts of the neglected field of prevention only, leaving the question of treatment and cure in the hands of the physician as heretofore. For a small annual fee periodic health examinations of individuals or groups of employees are made to the end that their lives may be prolonged. The movement is ably seconded by the physicians and surgeons of the country. It has been welcomed particularly by the life insurance companies, which recognize that whatever can be done to prolong the life of a policy-holder will be an enormous financial benefit to them, even if the average extension of life be only one year. Inasmuch as insurance companies have some 6,000,000 of the most thrifty and intelligent citizens among their policy-holders in the United States, who may be given the benefits of the institute's service through the co-operation of the companies themselves, an idea will be gained of the enormous benefit to mankind thus possible. As Mr. Ley himself has expressed it, "the whole course of civilization may be changed as the result of the institute's work." Mr. Ley is also treasurer and originator of the Volcanic Research Society, which was formed by Springfield business men to support Frank A. Perret, (q. v.) volcanologist, in his scientific work. Mr. Ley is a director in the Chapin National Bank, Industrial Loan Association and Contractors' Mutual Liability Ins. Co. He is a member of the Nayasset and Winthrop clubs, and Engineers' club of Boston. He was married Feb. 15, 1899, to Anne Lucy, daughter of John C. Kingsley, of Springfield, Mass., and has three daughters: Frances Hubbard, Margaret Kingsley and Elizabeth, and one son, Harold Alexander Ley, Jr.

PEMBERTON, Henry, Jr., chemist, was born in Philadelphia, Pa., Sept. 13, 1855, son of Henry and Caroline Town (Hollingsworth) Pemberton. The first of the family in America was Ralph Pemberton, a native of England, who arrived in Maryland in November, 1682, afterward settling in Bucks county, Pa.; from him and his wife, Margaret Seddon, the line descends through their son Phineas and his wife, Phebe Harrison; their son Israel and his wife, Rachel Read; their son Israel and his wife, Sarah Kirkbridge; their son Joseph and his wife, Ann Galloway; and their son John and his wife, Anna Clifford, who were the grandparents of the subject of this sketch. He was graduated A.M. at the University of Pittsburgh in 1876 and then entered the junior class of the University of Pennsylvania as a special student, subsequently receiving a certificate of proficiency from that institution. He was chemist for the United States Chemical Co. of Philadelphia until 1883, was manager of the Kalion Chemical Co. of Philadelphia during 1883–87, and occupied the same position in the Laramie Chemical Works in 1888. In the taking of the eleventh U. S. census he was special agent of statistics of chemical industry, and was the author of numerous technical papers published in scientific journals. He was also the author of a posthumous volume entitled "Shakepere and Sir Walter Ralegh." He was a member of the Penn Club, the Franklin Institute, the Chemical Society of New York, the Society of Chemical Industry, England, the Numismatic and Antiquarian Society of Pennsylvania, and the Historical, Colonial and Genealogical societies of Pennsylvania, taking a special interest in the work of the latter society. He was married, Mar. 28, 1894, to Susan, daughter of Joseph S. Lovering, Jr., of Philadelphia, and had four children: Joseph, Caroline Hollingsworth, Henry Rawle and Robert Pemberton. He died in Philadelphia, Pa., Oct. 25, 1913. Portrait opposite page 68.

WHITTEMORE, John Howard, financier, was born at Southbury, Conn., Oct. 3, 1837, son of Rev. William Howe and Maria (Clark) Whittemore, and a descendant of Thomas Whittemore, of Hitchins, Herfordshire, England, who was one of the early settlers of Malden, Mass. He was educated at the public schools of Southbury and at Gen. William H. Russell's Military Institute in New Haven. It was intended that he should go to Yale College, but unexpected conditions intervened and at the age of sixteen he entered the office of Elliott F. Shepard and E. D. Morgan, Jr., who were engaged in business in New York under the firm name of Shepard & Morgan. There he remained until the dissolution of the firm in 1857, after which he spent a few months in the private office of Edwin D. Morgan. He was with the firm of E. C. Tuttle & Co., makers of farm tools, of Naugatuck, Conn., until the firm was burned out in 1858, when he formed a partnership with Bronson B. Tuttle, under the firm name of Tuttle & Whittemore, manufacturers of malleable iron. The iron industry in the Naugatuck valley was then in its infancy and gave no promise of the wonderful development that time was to bring it. But John H. Whittemore was endowed with that foresight which is, after all, perhaps the most important essential to successful accomplishment, and marked success justified his enterprise from the very start. In 1870 the firm was reorganized as a joint stock corporation under the name of the Tuttle & Whittemore Co., and ten years later it became the Naugatuck Malleable Iron Co., with John H. Whittemore as president, an office which he held until his resignation in 1900. Under his direction the Naugatuck Malleable Iron Co. became, what it still is, one of the largest and most successful establishments of its kind in the country. He subsequently formed malleable iron companies in Chicago, Indianapolis, Cleveland, Toledo, Bridgeport and New Britain, each of which he served as a director until his death. He was a director of the New York, New Haven and Hartford Railroad Co., Landers, Frary & Clark and the North & Judd Manufacturing Co. of New Britain and the Colonial Trust Co. of Waterbury. Mr. Whittemore was one of the wealthiest, most successful and enterprising business men in Connecticut. Aside from business he was one of the most sincere benefactors the state, and more especially the town of Naugatuck, ever had. Every movement for the betterment of the town received his cordial support; in fact, most of the improvements in Naugatuck owed both their inception and their accomplishment to him. He gave to the town its high school, a graded grammar school and a public library. He spent thousands of dollars in improving the Naugatuck public park, building drinking fountains, and otherwise beautifying the town. The Buckingham building in Waterbury was erected by him at a cost of $350,000 and presented to the city on condition that Waterbury should raise $250,000 for the erection of a hospital—a condition which was fulfilled. The rents from the building are used to maintain the Waterbury Hospital, of which Mr. Whittemore was a director. He was a Republican in politics, and was a member of the constitutional conventions of 1901 and 1902. He was married in Naugatuck, Conn., June 10, 1863, to Julia, daughter of Harris Spencer, of that town, and had four children: Harris, John Howard, Gertrude Buckingham and Julia, of whom Harris and Gertrude Buckingham survive. Harris Whittemore is president of the Naugatuck Malleable Iron Co. Mr. Whittemore died at Naugatuck, May 28, 1910.

FROST, Albert Henry, ornithologist and manufacturer, was born in Portsmouth, N. H., May 26, 1851, son of William and Mary (Bruce) Frost. His first American ancestor was Capt. John Frost, who came to this country from England in the early part of the seventeenth century. Toward the end of the nineteenth century the family settled at Malden, Mass. William Frost, father of our subject, was a native of Newcastle and a seafaring man, who for fifty-five years ran a freight and passenger line between Portsmouth, N. H., and the ports of Spain. His wife was a direct descendant of Robert, the Bruce, King of Scotland. Albert Henry Frost was educated in the public schools of his native town and early in his 'teens entered the employ of a woolen house in Boston, where he worked for several years as an inside and road salesman and gained a valuable commercial experience. In 1874 he went to Cripple Creek, Colo., where he engaged in general merchandising with his brother, George E. Frost. The business was conducted with extraordinary success until 1877, when Albert H. Frost returned East and again entered the woolen trade. In 1880, with Edwin Peterson, he formed the firm of Frost & Peterson, to manufacture veneers of all kinds, and fancy boxes, hair brush backs, and hundreds of articles of that nature. In 1883, with his brother George, he organized Frost's Veneer Seating Co. of Sheboygan, Wis., manufacturers of table tops, panel work and veneers in general. Three years later they also established the Frost Veneer Seating Co. of Newport, Vt., which has become the largest veneer manufacturing firm in the world. Still another concern, the New York Veneer Seating Co. of Jersey City, was launched in 1893. While not a pioneer in the veneer industry, yet through his remarkable business ability, by the adoption of the newest factory methods and by ever meeting the demands of his market with products of excellent design and superior workmanship, Albert H. Frost became the largest and best-known veneer manufacturer in the world. And yet his great business success expressed only part of his life. From his mother's inspiration he gained an absorbing love of the woods and fields, of mountain and valley, of all the wonders of nature and the out-of-doors. And all through his life that love sought and found expression, with the result that at the time of his death he possessed one of the finest and most complete ornithological collections in the world. With Fawn Sleeper of Colorado and Frank M. Chapman of New York he made an extended pilgrimage in search of specimens, and with both of those men, as well as with King Edward VII. of England and Czar Nicholas of Russia, made many exchanges whereby the collection of each was enlarged until Mr. Frost possessed the finest private ornithological collection ever assembled. It contained more than 750 different species of birds of America and over 28,000 eggs, among which were two of the American condor, each worth probably $1,000, and a wild pigeon egg worth $250. He learned to know eggs as few men know them, and he could talk and write equally well about them. Many articles from his pen have appeared in ornithological periodicals, particularly in "Condor," the California ornithological magazine. Mr. Frost was a man of genial and charming personality, ready wit, broad and tolerant attitude, generous hospitality, and unstrained and limitless kindliness. He formed a legion of friends in every state in the Union, and he never knew an

ALBERT H. FROST
ORNITHOLOGIST AND MANUFACTURER

JOHN B. SMITH
ENTOMOLOGIST

GEORGE W. KITTREDGE
CIVIL ENGINEER

JOHN J. LAWLER
BISHOP

enemy. He was a member of Atlanta Lodge of Free and Accepted Masons, and also of the R. A. M., and Cœur de Leon Commandery. He was married June 26, 1883, to Katherine Gardner, daughter of Jacob and Emma Wendell, of Portsmouth, N. H., and left one son, George Lafayette Frost, who succeeded his father as head of the veneer business. Albert H. Frost died Jan. 27, 1912.

SMITH, John Bernhardt, entomologist, was born in New York city, Nov. 21, 1858, son of John and Elizabeth (Scheuerman) Smith. His father, a native of Germany, came to this country in 1853 and settled in New York city, where he pursued his trade as a cabinet maker. The son was educated in the public schools of New York and Brooklyn and was admitted to the New York bar in 1879. For the next five years he practiced law in Brooklyn; but natural history proved more fascinating than the law. "A fly on the wall," he once said, "was more interesting to him than the case in hand." He joined the Brooklyn Entomological Society in 1880 and became editor of the bulletin of the society, a publication which he afterward developed into a periodical known as "Entomologica Americana" and which became a valuable medium for the publication of shorter papers and notes. His work as an entomologist, especially in connection with the study of Coleoptera and Lepidoptera, attracted the attention of C. V. Riley, head of the U. S. Department of Agriculture, through whom he became special agent of the Division of Entomology in 1884. For two years he did field work, devoting himself particularly to the investigation of insects affecting the hop and the cranberry, and gaining his first experience in economic entomology, in which he was eventually to win world-wide fame. He was assistant curator of entomology in the U. S. National Museum during 1886-89 and in that period published a number of valuable papers in systematic entomology, among which may be mentioned: "Monograph of the Sphingidæ of America North of Mexico," "A Preliminary Catalogue of the Arctiidæ of Temperate North America," "A Revision of the Lepidopterous Family Saturniidæ," "Contributions Toward a Monograph of the Family Noctuidæ," "Notes on the Species of Lachnosterna of Temperate North America With Descriptions of New Species." He resigned his post with the National Museum in 1889 to accept the professorship of entomology at Rutgers College and the position of entomologist to the New Jersey Agricultural College Experiment Station at New Brunswick. In 1894 he became state entomologist of New Jersey and in 1902 entomologist to the New Jersey State Agricultural Experiment Station. He held all four positions until his death. His work in those positions was of the very highest importance and gave him a place among the world's greatest economic entomologists. He took a leading part in the work against the San Jose scale in the early days and led the campaign against the numerous insect pests from which the agricultural and horticultural interests of New Jersey suffered so badly. Perhaps he is best known for his splendid crusade against the mosquito—a crusade into which he introduced many original and revolutionary ideas in culicidology. When the work was begun in 1902 little was known about the habits of that insect. "There was no such thing," said Dr. Smith himself, "as a systematic collection and, except for the list in my Catalogue of the Insects of New Jersey, there was no recorded knowledge as

to the number of species to be dealt with. No one was even certain of the names of the species collected, and everything was in a chaotic state." It is a tribute to the remarkable knowledge, ability, and energy of the man that he brought order out of chaos so quickly. In 1903 he secured an appropriation for the work from the state legislature, and after the submission of his final report in 1904 he secured an annual appropriation for the purpose of carrying the recommendations of the report into effect. That report, consisting of 482 printed pages, was a masterpiece. Many of his observations, such as those, for instance, on the inland migration of the salt marsh mosquito, proved a surprise to the old-fashioned students of mosquito life. In the meantime, while he was doing such very valuable economic work, he was acquiring a high reputation as a systematic entomologist. His work in the arrangement and classification of the groups of insects, particularly the lepidoptera, was of the greatest importance. And he showed himself to be perhaps the first authority in the world on the lepidopterous family of the noctuidæ. His "Catalogue of the Lepidopterous Super-family Noctuidæ Found in Boreal America," published in 1893 as Bulletin 44 of the United States National Museum is a fine illustration of his exhaustive knowledge of the subject as well as of his wonderfully painstaking industry. He made several valuable contributions also to the study of insect anatomy, especially upon the structure of the diptera and hemiptera. Many of his conclusions were looked upon as somewhat revolutionary. His "Contribution Toward a Knowledge of the Mouth Parts of the Diptera" (1890), for example, set forth views on the homolgies of these organs which ran contrary to the opinions of the majority of entomologists. But his conclusions in the main have come to be genally accepted by the scientific world. Dr. Smith was a generous contributor to the literature of entomology and his bibliography covers hundreds of titles, a remarkable record of industry for a man of such large and important activities. His three big catalogues of the insects of New Jersey would alone constitute a creditable life-work for any one man. Many of his writings were in a popular vein and designed for the information of the farmer, horticulturist, and layman generally. Such works are his "Economic Entomology" (1896); "Explanation of Terms Used in Entomology" (1906), and "Our Insect Friends and Enemies" (1909). In addition to writing hundreds of systematic papers and practical bulletins in connection with his experiment station work he also delivered numerous lectures before Farmers' Institutes, public schools and scientific institutions. His capacity for work was extraordinary and it continued even in the face of the painful and protracted disease that eventually caused his death. He was a remarkably brave man, a man of unusual strength of will and energy of character. He faced and overcame a mountain of work that would have staggered a man of ordinary mould, with a perpetual cheerfulness and serene confidence that melted difficulties away as the sunshine melts the snow. His aims were high and his purpose earnest, and no difficulties were big enough to prevent their accomplishment. Perhaps no better summary of his life-work could be made than that contained in the memorial address of Dr. Demarest, president of Rutgers College. "Prof. Smith," said Dr. Demarest, "was a man of science emphatically, a searcher into the laws of life, into the life of

God's marvelous creation. . . . By the clearness of his thought and the diligence of his work he became a rare contributor to the world's store of knowledge and achieved high and wide distinction in the world of learning. To his grave he was always a patron of the liberal and useful arts and sciences, and to this college, founded for their promotion, he brought the honor of his achievements and of the tributes he received. And this distinguished, scientific work of his was so practical, so plainly and so promptly a service of men and communities and states and nations." It had not to do with that which is far away or whose fruitfulness for human welfare is remote. It had to do with the seed time and the harvest, with the grain of the fields, and the fruit of the trees, with that whose ingathering means plenty, happiness and hope in the homes of the people. It had to do with the comfort and health and prosperity of his fellow men. So he was in effect and in name a steward of the public good, of talents and powers drafted into the service of the common life. . . ." He was president of the board of health of New Brunswick, and of the New Jersey State Sanitary Association. Most of the leading scientific societies of America carried his name on their rolls of active honorary membership and he held prominent office in many of them. He was president of the Association of Economic Entomologists and the Brooklyn Entomological Society; vice-president and president of the Entomological Society of America and the New Jersey State Sanitary Association; president and treasurer of the New Jersey State Microscopical Society; treasurer of the American Society of Naturalists; secretary of the Biological Society of Washington, D. C.; fellow of the American Association for the Advancement of Science and of the New York Academy of Sciences; honorary member of the Feldman Collecting Social, the Newark Entomological Society and the Ottawa Field Naturalists' Club; corresponding member of the American Entomological Society, Entomological Society of Ontario and New York Entomological Society; member of the American Association of Horticultural Inspectors, Brooklyn Institute, Entomological Society of Washington, National Geographic Society, Society for the Promotion of Agricultural Sciences, Washington Academy of Sciences, New Jersey Science Teachers' Association, Zoological Congress of Entomology and other societies. In 1910 he was elected a member of the council of the International Congress of Entomology at its meeting in Brussels, Belgium. Dr. Smith was married in Albany, N. Y., June 22, 1886, to Marie Henrietta, daughter of Otto von Meske, of Albany, and had three children: John (d. 1889), Hilmar Frederick and Marguerite. He died in New Brunswick, N. J., Mar. 12, 1912.

MARKS, Louis Benedict, consulting engineer, was born in New York city, Jan. 25, 1869, son of David and Leontine (Meyer) Marks. He was educated in the schools of New York city, and was graduated at the College of the City of New York in 1888 with the degree of B.S. From there he went to Cornell University, receiving the degree of M.E. in 1889, and after a post-graduate course there received the degree of M.M.E. in electrical engineering in 1890. He at once became manager for the Washington Carbon Co. at Washington, Pa., and during the three years he held that position made many improvements in electric light carbons, on a number of which patents were secured. In 1893 he took up work in New York city as a consulting electrical and illuminating engineer. For two years his time was principally devoted to the invention and development of the enclosed arc light, the principal features of which are the conservation of the life of the carbons (one pair of carbons lasting over 100 hours, instead of only eight hours as in the open arc), and the improved diffusion and steadiness of the light. Two basic and a number of detail patents were granted to him on this invention. He organized the Marks Enclosed Arc Light Co. to introduce his new inventions, which had come into extensive use in America and Europe, and in 1900 the patents and business were taken over by the General Electric Co. He has designed and developed new methods of illumination and has applied principles of lighting to conserve the eyesight of the public. He is Chairman of the Section on Illumination of the American Museum of Safety. In 1908 he formed a partnership with Julian Woodwell, formerly in the United States government service at Washington, D. C., and the firm acts as consulting engineers in mechanical, electrical, and illuminating engineering, Mr. Marks devoting his attention principally to the subject of illumination, and Mr. Woodwell to the mechanical department. Some of the important projects carried out by the firm have been in connection with the designing, consultation and plans, specifications and supervision of work (mechanical, electrical, lighting equipment) on the following buildings and institutions: The new United States Post Office, Pennsylvania railroad terminal, Chemists' building, and Carnegie branch libraries, all of New York city; the country estate of I. N. Seligman at Irvington, N. Y.; Loeb Convalescent Home at Eastview, N. Y.; Remington, Smith Premier, and Monarch typewriter factories at Ilion and Syracuse, N. Y.; the Edison building at Boston, Mass.; Camp Kobbossee at Kobbossee Lake, Me.; Onondaga county court house at Syracuse, N. Y.; Shelton Mills (Sidney Blumenthal & Co.), at Shelton, Conn.; department store of Younker Bros. at Des Moines, Ia.; Y. M. C. A. building, new National Museum, Library of Congress (new addition), State, War and Navy department buildings, new Army and Navy Club, and the new University Club at Washington, D. C.. Mr. Marks is one of the pioneers in the new science of illuminating engineering and stands among the leading experts in the profession. On Oct. 14, 1905, he issued the first call to form a separate society devoted to the science and art of illumination, which resulted in the formal organization of the Illuminating Engineering Society in February, 1906. He was its first president and has been active in its councils ever since. He is also a member of the American Institute of Electrical Engineers, International Electrical Society of Paris, American Association for the Advancement of Science, New York Electrical Society, and the Cornell University Club of New York. He was chairman of the committee that prepared the "Illumination Primer," issued in 1912 under the ἁuspices of the Illuminating Engineering Society for the purpose of educating the public in the proper use of light, his associates on the committee being Dr. Louis Bell of Boston and J. R. Cravath of Chicago. He delivered a course of lectures at Johns Hopkins University in 1910 on the "Principles and Design of Interior Illumination." Mr. Marks has been a prolific writer on the subject of illumination and allied subjects, and has delivered numerous addresses before scientific societies in the United States and in Europe. He was married in New

York, Mar. 15, 1904, to Sadie, daughter of L. A. Van Praag of New York city, and has three sons: George, Richard and John Marks.

KITTREDGE, George Watson, civil engineer, was born at North Andover, Mass., Dec. 11, 1856, son of Joseph and Henrietta Frances (Watson) Kittredge. He early developed a natural aptitude for engineering problems, and, after a public school education, he entered the Massachusetts Institute of Technology, where he was graduated B.S. in 1877. His first work of importance was the development and improvement of the South Boston Flats (terminals). Three years later he became an employee of the maintenance of way department of the Pittsburg, Cincinnati & St. Louis railway, and for ten years was connected with the Pennsylvania lines west of Pittsburg. In 1886-87 he was also chief engineer of the Louisville Bridge Co. During 1890-91 he was engineer of maintenance of way and assistant chief engineer of the Cleveland, Cincinnati, Chicago & St. Louis railway, and from 1891 to 1896 he was chief engineer of the Cleveland, Cincinnati, Chicago & St. Louis Ry. and of Louisville & Jeffersonville Bridge Co. In 1900, Mr. Kittredge was called East to take the responsible position of chief engineer of the New York Central & Hudson River R.R., and in 1907 succeeded William J. Wilgus, in charge of the construction of the Grand Central terminal. The great importance of the engineering department of a great railroad system covering some 15,000 miles, and extending from the Atlantic seaboard to the Great Lakes, through a region of great agricultural and commercial development, is little realized by the public at large. As chief engineer, Mr. Kittredge had direct supervision of the installation of the electrification system, including the construction of power stations, and the terminal construction and improvements in New York city, involving the erection of the greatest railroad station in the world, an herculean task made much more difficult because there was no interruption to the enormous daily passenger traffic. The chief engineer likewise has supervision of the mechanical department, which pertains to the construction and repair of coaling plants, water stations, bridges and everything connected with the road bed—the construction of new lines, grading, surveying, building new tracks, revising grades, supervising field parties, etc. The greatest monument to his genius will ever be the new Grand Central terminal, erected on the site of the old terminal in the heart of New York city, at an expense of $180,000,000. The surface area has been increased from twenty-three acres to seventy acres by approaching the terminal on two levels, and this improvement required the excavation of 3,000,000 cubic yards of earth and rock. It is a marvel of the engineering world that this feat could have been accomplished without in any way interfering with the incoming and outgoing of over 700 trains per day, carrying some 70,000 passengers. As each new set of tracks was completed a corresponding number of old tracks was torn up, requiring the constant shifting of trains from one set of tracks to another, temporary tracks being used, some perhaps only for a day, then to be removed and put down elsewhere. Another delicate operation was the removal of the old train shed, 600 feet long, with a 200-foot span, containing 1,700 tons of construction iron, 90,000 square feet of corrugated iron, and 60,000 square feet of glass,—which was one of the wonders of the city forty years ago,—with the trains passing in and out daily beneath without ever a bit of the debris falling on the head of a passenger. A novel feature of the new station, which will appeal to the traveling public, is the entire elimination of stairways. The various levels are reached by "ramps" or inclined walks at so slight an angle as to be almost imperceptible. The arrangement provides for the discharge of all express passengers at the upper level, which has forty-two tracks, and all suburban and local passengers at the lower level, which has twenty-two tracks. Each level terminates in a loop, which will greatly facilitate the handling of trains after their passengers are discharged. While in ordinary construction work the architect is the responsible head, in this instance, owing to the peculiar nature of the problems to be solved, the greatest responsibility rested with the constructing engineers, and to these engineers, of whom Mr. Kittredge is chief, belong the credit and glory for the greatest and most magnificent exhibition of engineering skill in the civilized world. For recreation Mr. Kittredge is interested in homing pigeons, and at one time he held the world's record for 1,000-mile flight. He is president of the Westchester District National Federation of Homing Pigeon Fanciers. He is a member of the American Society of Civil Engineers, the American Railway Engineering Association, of which he was president in 1901-1902, and also of the Transportation and Technology clubs. Mr. Kittredge was married Oct. 17, 1888, to Georgia, daughter of George Davis, of Louisville, Ky., and has one son, George Davis Kittredge, and one daughter, Mary Henrietta Kittredge. Portrait opposite, page 71.

LAWLER, John Joseph, third bishop of the Roman Catholic diocese of Lead, S. Dak., was born at Rochester, Minn., Aug. 4, 1862. He was educated at St. Francis' Seminary, Milwaukee, Wis. and the University of Louvain, Belgium, and was ordained priest Dec. 19, 1885. He remained at Louvain about two years thereafter engaged in post-graduate work. He was professor of scripture at the College of St. Thomas at Merriam Park, St. Paul, for one year and then entered upon his work as parish priest, his first charge being St. Luke's Church, which soon became one of the leading parishes of St. Paul. Seven years later he was appointed by Archbishop Ireland, vicar-general and rector of the cathedral. He was consecrated auxiliary bishop of St. Paul on May 19, 1910 being the second native of Minnesota to be made a Catholic bishop, Bishop Keane of Cheyenne, Wyo., being the first. Having won the highest respect of all people regardless of race or creed, his appointment caused rejoicing not alone among his own people, but in every section of the city and throughout the state. He was prominent on the civic and educational activities of St. Paul, and stood for the betterment of social, municipal and industrial conditions. Being a close and constant student himself, he has been tireless in his efforts to ingrain in his people the conviction that higher education is of the upmost importance in the training of their children. He served as chaplain on the staffs of the governors, and for years was vice-president and president of the Associated Charities. On Feb. 5, 1916, he was appointed bishop of Lead, S. Dak., to succeed Bishop Busch. Bishop Lawler speaks the German, French, Flemish and Italian languages. He is a public speaker of remarkable clearness, directness and oratorical power, and he has gained a reputation as a writer and controversialist. He is a man loved and honored, an ecclesiastic revered and respected by all sections of the community in which he dwelt. Portrait opposite page 71.

WHITRIDGE, Frederick Wallingford, lawyer, was born in New Bedford, Mass., Aug. 8, 1852, son of John and Lucia (Bailey) Whitridge. He is a descendant of William Whitridge of Burenden, County Kent, who emigrated to America in 1642. His great-grandfather was William Whitridge of Tiverton, R. I., the son of Thomas Whitridge of Rochester, Mass. William Whitridge was a physician of wide repute who with Pres. Stiles of Yale and Judge Danforth of Boston pursued alchemy for fifty years. His grandfather was William Whitridge of New Bedford, Mass. He was graduated at Amherst College in 1874 and received his A.M. degree from the same institution in 1877. Taking up the study of law at Columbia University, he was graduated in 1878 and was admitted to the bar of the state of New York the following year. Since then he has been in active practice in New York city and is senior member of the law firm of Whitridge, Butler & Rice. Mr. Whitridge was lecturer on administrative law at Columbia University from 1883 to 1888 and lecturer on constitutional and political history during 1888-94. In 1896 he was appointed by Pres. Roosevelt special American ambassador to the marriage of King Alfonso of Spain and Princess Ena of Battenberg. The mission, in view of the recent unpleasantness between the two nations, was one of peculiar difficulty, requiring the utmost delicacy and tact, but Mr. Whitridge acquitted himself in a manner which called forth the highest approbation both of the Spanish people and of his own countrymen, and his finished diplomacy went far towards cementing the cordial relations which now exist between the two nations. In presenting the president's letter to King Alphonso Mr. Whitridge made a neat little speech which was such a departure from the usual formal utterances on similar occasions that it is worth recording. "I esteem myself happy," he said, "to be the bearer of the nation's good-will, especially on the auspicious occasion of your marriage with the charming young Princess from the motherland of my own country. All mankind, we say, sir, loves a lover. But in all the world there are no more sympathetic and sincere well-wishers for long years of happiness and good fortune for yourself and the Princess, than among the American people— standing in this ancient kingdom, before the successor of Ferdinand and Isabella, I am bound to add, youthful American people, whom I have the honor to represent." Mr. Whitridge's polished manners, distinguished bearing and marked personality made a decided impression on the court of Madrid and none of the famous diplomatists present was the recipient of so many attentions both from the King and from Spanish society in general. On his departure from Madrid he was honored by the King with the Grand Cross of the Order of Charles III, being one of the few special envoys who received that much coveted distinction. When the Third Avenue railroad went into ban Mr. Whitridge was appointed receiver and quickly brought what then seemed a hopeless wreck into one of the best and most efficient street railroads in the country. Even before that he had achieved a reputation as a successful reorganizer of railroad and industrial corporations among which were the Reading R. R. Co., the Lake Erie & Western, the St. Louis & San Francisco, and several smaller companies. He was one of the originators of the Civil Service Commission and has always shown an active interest in civic affairs. In addition to his legal and administrative talent Mr. Whitridge has shown decided ability as a writer and has contributed to the leading reviews many notable articles on political and economic subjects. He is a director of the Niagara Development Co., Niagara Falls Power Co., and a number of other corporations, and is a member of the Bar Association of the City of New York, American Fine Arts Society, American Academy of Political and Social Science, New England Society, and the Amherst College Alumni Association. He belongs to the Metropolitan, Knickerbocker, University, Century, Reform, City, Church, Down Town and Automobile Club of America, of which he is president. He was married in Cobham, Kent, England, Dec. 9, 1884, to Lucy, daughter of the English poet, Matthew Arnold. Mrs. Whitridge inherits to a large extent the intellect and culture of her distinguished father. The Whitridges usually spend their summers and autumns in their Highland estate at Balnakeilly, Perthshire, Scotland, where they occupy an old mansion dating back to the days of the Stuarts and overlooking Pitlochry. The estate embraces several thousand acres of wooded land, well stocked with fish and game. It is in the centre of one of the most picturesque districts in the Highlands and is near the famous Pass of Killiecrankie. Personally Mr. Whitridge is a man of picturesque and impressive appearance and distinguished manner. He is endowed with a keen sense of humor, caustic wit and the gift of spontaneous and forceful eloquence, and these qualities, added to his broad culture and wide knowledge of men and affairs, make him a desirable and much sought figure at social functions, both private and public.

BATES, Charles Austin, financier, was born at Indianapolis, Ind., Apr. 18, 1866, son of Charles Austin and Margaret Holmes (Ernsperger) Bates, and a descendant of Clement Bates, a native of England, who came over to the American colonies in 1638 and settled in Plymouth, Mass. Mr. Bates's mother (q. v.) came from a well-known Maryland family. She is a well known writer of fiction, her best stories being "Manitou" (1881); "The Chamber over the Gate" (1886); "The Price of the Ring" (1892); "Shylock's Daughter" (1894), and "Jasper Fairfax" (1897). Charles Austin Bates was educated in the public schools of Indianapolis, and began his business career in a retail bookstore of that city. At the age of twenty he established a printing business in his own name, and for seven years conducted it with marked success and credit to himself. Desiring a larger field for his resourcefulness and abilities, he removed to New York in 1893, and engaged in the advertising business exclusively. He was successful from the outset, and in 1903 the business was incorporated as the Bates Advertising Co. Shortly thereafter he sold out this business, and organizing the Knickerbocker Syndicate, devoted his attention to the promotion and financing of large enterprises. From this was developed the Fidelity Bond and Mortgage Co., incorporated in 1909, with a capital of $1,-000,000, of which he has since been president. Probably the most important industrial enterprise financed by him is the Colorado-Yule Marble Co., organized in 1905, with a capital of $10,-000,000, to quarry and market the largest and most reliable deposit of high-grade white marble known to exist in the world. The quarries are

in Gunnison county, Colo., and are estimated to contain 1,361,500,000 cubic feet of marble. The Colorado-Yule marble is said to be superior to the famous Carrara marble of Italy and the Pentellic and Parian marbles of Greece, which for nearly 1,000 years held the supremacy over all other marbles. A well-equipped marble mill has been erected, the largest single finishing plant in the world, costing, with incidental railroads, power, plant, employees' houses, etc., nearly $4,-000,000, where some 700 skilled artisans are employed at cutting and finishing the marble. The officers are: J. F. Manning, president; Henry J. Utz, vice-president; Dr. William J. Chandler, secretary and treasurer, and Mr. Bates, chairman of the executive committee. The quarries and mill have become the nucleus of an enterprising, modern town called Marble City, containing 1,700 inhabitants at the present writing. The Colorado-Yule marble has already become a factor in building operations, having been used in the construction of the new courthouse in Cleveland, O., courthouses in Omaha, Neb., and Youngstown, O.; the post-office building at Denver, Colo., Colorado State Museum at Denver, the Rio Grande railway station at Salt Lake City, Union Pacific building at Omaha, and the Southern Pacific building at Fort Worth, Tex. Mr. Bates is vice-president of the Crystal River & San Juan railroad, extending from Redstone to Marble, a distance of twelve miles, for the purpose of furnishing communication with the quarries. The company operates seventeen miles of leased road known as the Crystal River railroad. In 1908 he also organized the Rutherford Rubber Co., of which he is president. He has contributed many articles relating to advertising and business to various periodicals and the daily press, and is the author of a notable work entitled "Art and Literature of Business" (1903), in six volumes. He is a member of the New York Athletic Club, the Columbia Yacht Club, and the Fulton Chain Yacht Association. Mr. Bates was married in Chicago, Ill., Sept. 11, 1890, to Belle, daughter of Henry Brandenburg. Portrait opposite page 76.

McALLISTER, Addams Stratton, inventor and editor, was born at Covington, Va., Feb. 24, 1875, son of Abraham Addams and Julia Ellen (Stratton) McAllister. His first paternal American ancestor was Hugh McAllister, a native of Scotland, who settled in Lancaster county, Pennsylvania, about 1732; his wife was Mary Harbison, and from them the line of descent is traced through their son, Hugh McAllister, Jr., who served in the 7th battalion of militia of Cumberland county, Pa., and was captain of a company at Valley Forge and Potter's Fort, and who married Sarah Nelson; through their son, Judge William McAllister, who served in the war of 1812, and who married Sarah Thompson; through their son, Capt. Thompson McAllister, who was a member of the Alleghany light infantry known as the "Alleghany Roughs," and who married Lydia Miller Addams, and through their son, Abraham Addams McAllister, the father of the subject of this sketch. Addams S. McAllister received his preliminary education in the public schools of Covington, and in 1894 entered the Pennsylvania State College, where he received the degree of B.S. in 1898, and subsequently that of E.E. Previous to graduation he spent one summer in the shops of the Covington Machine Co., doing practical mechanical work, and two summers with a civil engineering corps doing local railway and similar

surveying. From July, 1898, to August, 1899, he obtained practical experience in electrical locomotive operation and repair with the Berwind-White Coal Mining Co. at Windbar, Pa., and spent the following year in the factory of the Westinghouse Electric and Manufacturing Co. at East Pittsburgh to acquire information concerning the manufacturing details of direct-current and alternating-current machinery. He took a post-graduate course at Cornell University in electrical engineering, and received the degree of M.M.E. in 1901. In 1905 he received the degree of Ph.D. During 1901-4 he held the positions of assistant and instructor in physics and applied electricity at Cornell and he was acting assistant professor of electrical engineering there in 1904. Since 1905 he has been associate editor of the "Electrical World." He has been professorial lecturer on electrical engineering at the Pennsylvania State College since 1909. Dr. McAllister was the first to expound and formulate the application of the law of conservation in illumination calculations (1911); and he developed the simplified circle diagrams of single-phase and polyphase motors and synchronous motors and the absorption-of-light method of calculating illumination. He received patents for alternating-current machinery in 1903, 1904, 1906 and 1907. Dr. McAllister has lectured on subjects pertaining to his special line of work before the Cornell Electrical Society, the New York Electrical Society, the Columbia University Electrical Society, the Brooklyn Polytechnic Institute Electrical Engineering Society, the Franklin Institute and the Worcester Polytechnic Institute. He is the author of "Alternating-Current Motors" (1906), used as a text-book in many of the leading engineering schools, and of chapters on "Transformers" and "Motors" in the "Standard Handbook for Electrical Engineers." He has also contributed about 100 original articles on engineering subjects to the technical press, the most important of them being: "Complete Commercial Test of Polyphase Induction Motors Using One Wattmeter and One Voltmeter" (1902); "Excitation of Asynchronous Generators by Means of Static Condensance" (1903); "Asynchronous Generators" (1903); "A Convenient and Economical Electrical Method for Determining Mechanical Torque" (1904); "Simple Circular Current Locus of the Induction Motor" (1906); "The Exciting Current of Induction Motors" (1906); "Simple Circle Diagram of the Single-phase Induction Motor" (1906); "Magnetic Field in the Single-phase Induction Motor" (1906); "Circular Current Loci of the Synchronous Motor" (1907); "Absorption of Light Method of Calculating Illumination" (1908); "Bearing of Reflection on Illumination" (1910); "Graphical Solution of Problems Involving Plane Surface Lighting Sources" (1910), and "The Law of Conservation as Applied to Illumination Calculations" (1911). Dr. McAllister is a member of the American Association for the Advancement of Science, the American Electrochemical Society, the National Electric Light Association, the New York Electrical Society, the American Institute of Electrical Engineers, the Society for the Promotion of Engineering Education, the Illuminating Engineering Society, of which he is a director, the Pennsylvania State College Association of New York, of which he has been president since 1911, the New York Southern Society, the "Virginians" of New York, the Virginia Historical Society, the Cornell University Club of New York, the University Club, State College, the Cornell Chapter of the Sigma Xi honor society, the Pennsylvania State College Chapter of the Phi Kappa Phi honor fraternity, and honor member of the Pennsylvania State College Chapter of the Eta Kappa Nu electrical fraternity.

SCHLAPP, Max Gustav, physician, was born at Ft. Madison, Ia., Nov. 4, 1869, son of George and Marie (Depuys) Schlapp, and grandson of George E. Schlapp, who came to America from Germany during the revolutionary troubles of 1848 and settled at Burlington, Ia. His mother, of French-Huguenot parentage, was a native of Munchberg, near Berlin. Dr. Schlapp received his early education in the public schools of Ft. Madison, Ia. He removed to St. Louis, Mo., in his boyhood and was employed for a year in the Sect Wine Co. of Koehler Bros. He subsequently entered the service of P. P. Mast & Co., wholesale dealers in agricultural implements, of Peoria, Ill., and left them to accept a position with George Moore & Co., a branch of Kingman & Co., Peoria. But although the prospects of his success in a commercial career were very promising, he did not find business life particularly adapted to his taste and temperament, and in his search for a more congenial vocation, he became acquainted with Paul Dombrowski, a physician of Peoria, who in addition to his general medical practice, also had a large practice as an oculist. The influence of Dr. Dombrowski determined the final direction of his tastes toward the profession of medicine, and he entered the latter's office as an assistant. He and Dr. Dombrowski made a practice of reading aloud to each other from medical books, discussing the various points that arose as they proceeded, and the doctor was not slow to perceive that the young lad was endowed with an unusual talent for medical science, a talent which he foresaw would lead him, if developed, to distinct eminence in the profession. The elder Schlapp did not look kindly on a professional career for his son, but under the persuasions of Dr. Dombrowski he allowed him to enter the Bellevue Medical School, New York city. From Bellevue young Schlapp went to Cornell University, where he spent two years as a special science student. Subsequently he took the regular medical course at the University of Heidelberg (1893-1894), and then went to the University of Berlin, where he received his degree, summa cum laude, in 1896. Equipped with such an unusually wide and thorough academic training, he turned to a special study of diseases of the nervous system. He studied with Prof. Frederick Jolly, an eminent authority on mental diseases, and for two years was volunteer assistant in the Koenigliche Klinik of the Charite Hospital in Berlin, at the same time pursuing his independent researches in mental and nervous diseases. In 1899 he returned to the United States to enter upon the practice of his profession in New York city, where he became connected with the New York Polyclinic as assistant to Dr. Barnard Sachs. He was appointed an instructor in neuropathology at Cornell University in 1900, and is now assistant professor of neuropathology there. He was also for a time clinical professor of nervous diseases at Fordham University, and consulting physician for nervous diseases in the Fordham Hospital. For ten years Dr. Schlapp was chief of the clinic for nervous and mental diseases in the Presbyterian Hospital, and in 1911 was appointed professor of neuropathology in the Post-Graduate Medical School and Hospital, New York city. He also fills the very important post of psychiatrist to the

Society for the Prevention of Cruelty to Children, in which he has the responsibility of determining the mental condition of the children examined in the children's court. Dr. Schlapp has given much thought and careful study to the sociological influences of mental and nervous diseases, and few, if any, men in this country can speak with more authority on what has become the most vital of present-day questions. He has pointed out in clear and arresting terms the deadly effects of modern industrialism, the grave dangers that lurk behind the watchword of efficiency, the real perils the feminist movement holds for the future of the race. And his views carry a weight that cannot be ignored, because Dr. Schlapp is a scientist of deep knowledge and insight, an absolute authority on those diseases which are the danger signals of our modern civilization, and because he is also an earnest and vigorous thinker, with a mind that cuts below superfluities into the very bedrock of truth. An article from his pen entitled "The Enemy at the Gate," in "The Outlook" of April 6, 1912, was considered by the editors to be of such importance that special attention was drawn to it in a three-column editorial, and it is a typical example not only of his deep knowledge and clear thinking, but also of his courage and ability to voice his views with eloquence, force and precision. Dr. Schlapp has been actively engaged in the field of medical research, and has most convincingly demonstrated the differences in histological structure of the cerebral cortex of the brain, the facts he demonstrated being used as the means of locating the functions of the different cerebral regions. Some of the most important of his papers on these subjects are: "Der Zellenbau der Grosshirnrinde des Affen Macacus Cynomolgus," 1898; "A Case of Ascending Myllomalacia Caused by a Progressing Venous Thrombosis," 1906; "A Case of Syringomyelia with Partial Macrosomia," 1906; "Syringomyelia with Hypertrophy and Atrophy," 1910; "Hysterical Mutism," 1903; "Anomalous General Paralysis," 1903; "Lead Palsey and Trauma," 1903; "Subcortical Tumor," 1903; "The Microscopic Structure of Cortical Areas in Man and Some Mammals," 1902-3, and "A Neuro-epithelioma Developing from a Central Gliosis, after an Operation on the Spinal Cord," 1911; and as co-author with Dr. J. J. Walsh the following: "A Complete Case of Syringomyelia," 1904; "Subcortical Cyst and Fibroma due to Trauma Producing Jacksonian Epilepsy Cured by Operation," 1904, and "Myasthenia Gravis," 1910. He is a man of decided personality, deep insight, rigid determination, conscientious application, scrupulous integrity, and a pure disinterestedness which spares neither time nor effort in the cause of science and humanity. To these characteristics he adds a most genial, cordial and engaging manner, a liberal culture, and a broad and tolerant viewpoint. He is a member of the City Club.

COX, Rowland, soldier and lawyer, was born in Philadelphia, Pa., July 9, 1842, son of John Cooke and Ann Johns (Rowland) Cox, and grandson of Benjamin Cox of English Quaker stock. His father served as lieutenant-colonel in the commissary department of the Federal army during the civil war; and his mother was a daughter of Joseph Galloway Rowland, judge of the supreme court of Delaware. Rowland Cox was prepared for college at home, and completed his education at Princeton University, where he obtained the Alpha medal, the highest prize awarded

MAX G. SCHLAPP
PHYSICIAN

ROWLAND COX
LAWYER

ARCHIBALD COX
LAWYER

CHARLES AUSTIN BATES
FINANCIER

for English composition. At college he became a member of the Zeta Psi fraternity. Before graduating the civil war broke out and he enlisted in the 15th Pennsylvania volunteer cavalry. Shortly afterwards he was appointed assistant adjutant-general, to serve on the staff of Maj.-Gen. J. B. McPherson, and after the death of that officer he was transferred to the staff of Maj.-Gen. Francis P. Blair. When the war was practically over he resigned, and after studying law in the office of Judge Skinner of the Illinois supreme court, he was admitted to the Illinois bar in 1866. Subsequently he removed to New York city, and entered upon a successful and extended practice, being admitted to the supreme court of New York in 1874, and to the U. S. supreme court in 1879. Mr. Cox made a specialty of laws relating to trademarks and copyright. He wrote and compiled Cox's Manual of Trade Marks, a standard work on the subject, and was engaged in a large number of important litigations. Among those which involved new questions of law were: Sawyer v. Horn (1 Fed. Rep. 24), respecting trade-mark on bluing; Anheuser-Busch Brewing Association v. Piza (24 Fed. Rep. 149), the same question being passed upon by the House of Lords in Montgomery v. Thompson, 41 Ch. Div. 33, known as the "Stone Ale Case" some twenty years after; Menendez v. Holt (128 U. S. 514), a leading case; Celluloid Man. Co. v. Cellonite Man. Co. (32 Fed. Rep.); Enoch Morgan's Sons Co. v. Wendover (43 Fed. Rep. 420); Black v. Henry G. Allen Co. (42 Fed. Rep. 618, 56 Fed. Rep. 764), known as the "Britannica Cases," in which the reproduction of the copyrighted articles which constituted a part of the "Encyclopædia Britannica" was restrained; Falk v. Gast Lithographing Co. (48 Fed. Rep. 262); Fischer v. Blank (138 N. Y. 244); Clark Thread Co. v. Armitage (74 Fed. Rep. 936); Untermeyer v. Freund, in the same court; the N. K. Fairbank Co. v. R. W. Bell Manufacturing Co. (77 Fed. Rep.); Royal Baking Powder Co. v. Raymond in the U. S. circuit court of appeals; Johnson & Johnson v. Bower & Black, in the same court. In all of these cases and many others Mr. Cox represented the complainant. They unmistakably indicate a tendency of judicial thought toward the broadest and most philosophical views. Mr. Cox also conducted a case for Oxford University against a New York publishing company, to protect the copyright of the Oxford Bible. This is the only case in which the University of Oxford ever appeared as a litigant in the United States. Mr. Cox was married Oct. 29, 1868, to Fanny Cummins Hill, daughter of Robert Hill of Smyrna, Del., and had three sons: Rowland, Jr., Archibald and Robert Hill Cox. He died at his home in Plainfield, N. J., May 13, 1900.

COX, Archibald, lawyer, was born at Smyrna, Del., Nov. 26, 1874, son of Rowland and Fanny Cummins (Hill) Cox. His father (see above) was also a noted lawyer and the author of "Cox's Manual of Trade Marks." The son removed with his parents to Plainfield, N. J., when very young, and afterwards attended St. Paul's School at Concord, N. H. In 1896 he received the A.B. degree from Harvard University, and three years later the LL.B. degree. Since then Mr. Cox has been actively engaged in the practice of law throughout the country, his work being chiefly concerned to unfair competition in trade, the pure food laws, and the infringements of copyrights, trade marks and patents. In this way he has followed closely in his father's footsteps and

like the latter, numbers among his clients some of the most influential business men in America. Among the more notable cases conducted successfully by him were the following: Royal Baking Powder Co. v. R. T. Royal, wherein the limitations on the right of a man to use his own name were determined by the U. S. court of appeals; in Enoch Morgan's Sons Co. v. Ward, wherein the measure of protection accorded a word trade mark was determined by the U. S. court of appeals; in Ganuet v. Rupert, wherein the legal rights in the titles of periodicals were determined by the U. S. court of appeals; in J. & P. Coats, Ltd., v. John Coats Thread Co., wherein the right of a man to lend his name to a corporation was determined; Heller & Merz Co. v. Shaver, Blake & Co., wherein the right to protection against the misleading use of geographical names was determined by the U. S. court of appeals; Walter Baker & Co., Ltd., v. Puritan Pure Food Co., wherein the measure of protection to be accorded pictorial trade marks was determined; Johnson & Johnson v. Seabury & Johnson, wherein the law relating to misrepresentation collateral to packages was determined by the New Jersey court of errors and appeals; The N. K. Fairbank Co. v. Turner, wherein substitution without oral or written representation was held unlawful, and National Cloak & Suit Co. v. Kaufman, wherein the copyright in trade catalogues was determined. Mr. Cox is a member of the Committee on "Protection of Public Property" of the Merchants Association, having been on that committee since the committee was organized. Mr. Cox was married in Jamaica Plain, Mass., on June 7, 1911, to Frances Bowen Perkins, daughter of the late Edward C. Perkins of New York. Portrait opposite page 76.

IVES, Frederic Eugene, inventor, was born at Litchfield, Conn., Feb. 17, 1856, son of Hubert Leverit and Ellen Amelia (Beach) Ives. He is a descendant of William Ives, a native of London, England, who arrived at Boston in 1635, and settled at New Haven in 1638, the line being traced through William, Joseph, Ebenezer, Lazarus, Lazarus Asa, Leverit and Hubert Leverit Ives. He received a public school education. At the age of eleven his father died, after which he became successively a clerk in a country store, an amateur printer, and an apprentice in the Litchfield "Inquirer" printing office. While serving his apprenticeship he became expert as a job compositor and pressman, and was the editor and publisher of an amateur paper. At this time he first turned his attention to photography, and during 1875-78 was in charge of the photographic laboratory of Cornell University. While in this position he perfected and operated a process for making photo-engraved typographic printing plates from pen drawings, which process was used to illustrate the college papers, "Cocagne" and another, and also brought some orders from far-off cities. There he also invented the first half-tone process which was developed commercially, making by a complicated but beautifully ingenious and scientific procedure blocks identical in character with those used today, but in stereotype instead of copper or zinc etching. He left Cornell in 1878, and removing to Baltimore, Md., established a photo-engraving plant for an illustrated newspaper. In 1879 he established a photo-engraving plant for the Crosscup & West Engraving Co. of Philadelphia, which in 1881 began to manufacture his half-tone plates commercially. The plant was destroyed by fire in 1885. Meanwhile he had conducted experiments for the purpose of accomplishing the results more directly and more simply, and in 1886 he perfected the process by inventing the ruled and sealed crossline or pin-hole glass screen, through which the photographic image is impressed on the sensitized film, giving the same stipple effect as his original ruled or dotted elastic stamp. Although numerous experimenters had previously struggled, with more or less success, with the problem of the type-press reproduction of photographs from nature, his cross-line screen method is the one now universally employed. He was also the first to propose and apply experimentally the three-color half-tone process. His employers advised against taking out patents, and as a result the modern half-tone process is universally used with no pecuniary reward to its inventor. In 1890 Mr. Ives severed his connection with Crosscup & West in order to develop the photochromoscope system of color photography, which brought him medals and other honors from the photographic and scientific societies, but was not a notable commercial success. A triple photograph, made in a special camera at one exposure on one plate, when placed in an optical instrument used like the stereoscope, reproduced the objects with all their colors so perfectly that they appeared to actually stand before the observer's eyes. No method can ever give more perfect results, but the popular demand has always been for color photography on paper, and the general public will accept no substitute. A limited business was done with the invention in England, where Mr. Ives spent some years, in London, and afterwards in Philadelphia, and orders are still occasionally received, but the manufacture was definitely abandoned in 1911. Meanwhile Mr. Ives patented a considerable number of other inventions, mostly relating to color photography, but including a novel binocular microscope, the parallax stereogram and "changing pictures," glass sealed diffraction gratings for use in the spectroscope, the "universal colorimeter," the sensitive tint photometer, etc. The parallax stereogram is a photographic transparency which throws the image into perfect stereoscopic relief by simply holding it squarely in front of the eyes at arm's length. This invention was medalled by the Royal Photographic Society and by the Franklin Institute, and examples can be seen in nearly every university and college physical laboratory, but it is little known to the general public. The glass sealed diffraction gratings are cheap but remarkably perfect transparent replicas of Rowland reflecting gratings, and are in use in college physical and chemical laboratories in all countries. This invention was also medalled by the Franklin Institute. The universal colorimeter is an instrument which matches and measures any color whatever, and gives it numerical expression, so that three numbers, which may be sent by mail, telegraph or cable, will enable another person who has a colorimeter to set the instrument to show them exactly that color, and compare it with any other color. A few of these instruments are in use in testing laboratories and manufactories, but its systematic manufacture and exploitation have been deferred pending the development of a process of color photography on paper and allied inventions which Mr. Ives thinks will prove much more interesting to the general public than anything which he has done in the past. Mr. Ives has received eighteen medals from scientific societies, including the Elliot Cresson medal of the Franklin Institute, the Progress medal of the

Royal Photographic Society, and the Rumford medal of the American Academy of Arts and Sciences. A special gold medal was awarded by the Photographic Society of Philadelphia for work in color photography, and the International Photo-Engravers Association presented him in 1911 with a testimonial and a handsome gold watch inscribed to "Frederic E. Ives, Inventor and Pioneer Photo-Engraver." Mr. Ives is a fellow of the Royal Photographic Society and the Royal Microscopic Society, honorary member of the Philadelphia Photographic Society and the New York Camera Club, member of the Physical Society, the Franklin Institute, the American Microscopical Society, etc. He was married in 1879 to Mary Elizabeth Olmstead, who died in 1904, leaving one son, Dr. Herbert E. Ives, now experimental physicist for the National Electric Lamp Association at Cleveland.

IVES, Herbert Eugene, scientist and inventor, was born in Philadelphia, Pa., July 31, 1882, son of Frederic Eugene and Mary Elizabeth (Olmstead) Ives. His father, Frederick Eugene Ives, is a well-known inventor and pioneer photo-engraver. He was educated in the public schools of Philadelphia, the University College School of London, England, and the Rugby Lower School, Rugby, England. In 1898 he entered the employ of the Ives-Kromskop Co., founded by his father that year in Philadelphia, and remained until 1901, when he entered the University of Pennsylvania. He was graduated B. S. in 1905, and then took a course at Johns Hopkins University, where he was fellow in physics during 1906-08. In the latter year Johns Hopkins conferred upon him the degree of Ph. D. He was laboratory assistant physicist in the Bureau of Standards, Washington, D. C., in 1908-09, and in 1909 was appointed physicist to the National Electric Lamp Association of Cleveland, O. After that concern was made a part of the General Electric Co. in 1912, he became physicist to the United Gas Improvement Co., Philadelphia. Dr. Ives is specializing in physical problems connected with the production, measurement and use of light. His researches have been in connection with the diffraction process of color photography, for which he received the Longstreth medal from the Franklin Institute of Philadelphia in 1906; the Lippmann color photograph, including its application to three-color photography, and the production of special films giving great purity of color rendering; the action of colored light on the photographic plate and its bearing on astronomical photography; color measurements of illuminants and theory of color, and the laws of light production and luminous efficiency. He has made various investigations in photometry, including an exhaustive investigation of the photometry of lights of different color, establishing the reliability and superior advantages of the flicker photometer for such light measurement. He originated and developed the idea of "daylight efficiency" of illuminants, determined by their value when screened to resemble daylight in color; and proposed as the outcome of his studies of photometry and luminous efficiency a rational standard of light, the "watt-lumen," viz., one watt of radiation of maximum luminous efficiency. He has made studies of the firefly by photographic and phosphor-photographic methods, whereby its high efficiency as a light producer was confirmed, and also of the phenomena of phosphorescence, particularly the effect of heat and infra-red radiation therein. He is the inventor of improved

Herbert E. Ives.

WILLIAM BARBOUR

diffraction color photographs (1906); a new type of test object for the measurement of visual acuity and defects of vision (1910); watts-per-candle photometers, for rating incandescent electric lamp on efficiency basis (1912); variable neutral-tint screens (1912), and artificial daylight for color matching (''Ives Daylight Producer,'' 1913). The latter is a powerful incandescent mantle placed immediately beneath a reflector which sends the light downward through a series of delicately-colored screens, resulting in a light equal in every way to sunshine. He has contributed a number of articles to various scientific and technical periodicals in the United States and Europe, the most valuable of which are: ''The Lippmann Color Photograph'' (Astrophysical Journal, 1908); ''Effect of Heat and Infrared upon the Phenomena of Phosphorescence'' (Astrophysical Journal, 1911-12), and ''Studies in the Photometry of Lights of Different Colors'' (Philosophical Magazine, 1912). Dr. Ives is a member of the American Association for the Advancement of Science, the American Physical Society, the Illuminating Engineering Society, of which he was vice-president in 1911-12; the Institute of Electrical Engineers, the American Gas Institute and the Franklin Institute, and is a corresponding member of the London Illuminating Engineering Society. He was married Nov. 14, 1908, to Mabel Agnes, daughter of Charles Louis Lorenz, of Philadelphia, Pa., and has one son, Ronald Lorenz, and one daughter, Barbara Olmstead Ives.

BARBOUR, William, manufacturer, was born in New York city, Sept. 9, 1847, son of Thomas and Sarah Elizabeth (Warren) Barbour. His father was a native of Scotland and his family for many generations was identified with the manufacture of linen thread. John Barbour, the great-grandfather, removed from Paisley, Scotland, to Lisburn, Ireland, in 1768, and, after engaging in flax spinning there, established in 1784 what is now the oldest linen-thread manufacturing establishment in the world. John Barbour had two sons, John and William, and the latter developed the business on a large scale, the works, under the style of William Barbour & Sons, Ltd., covering about twelve acres of land and employing several thousand operatives. William Barbour took his five sons in partnership with him, and two of the sons, Thomas, the father of our subject, and Robert, founded the American branch of the industry. Thomas Barbour, who came to the United States in 1840, began his business career in the service of A. T. Stewart & Co., New York city, in 1849. In 1852 he started on his own account, importing threads and twines, especially the goods manufactured by his father in Ireland. In 1855 he organized the firm of Barbour Bros., taking in partnership with him his brother Robert (1826-92). In 1864 the brothers purchased Passaic Mill No. 2 in Paterson, N. J., and, importing suitable machinery from Ireland, began spinning flax under the firm name of Barbour Bros. In 1865 the Barbour Flax-Spinning Co. was organized with Thomas Barbour as president. The enterprise was eminently successful from the start. The Barbour thread had already attained a world-wide reputation and there was a ready demand for it here. With such an impetus the Barbour Co. speedily developed into one of the leading industries of its class in the world. It included three large mills in Paterson and employed over 250 operatives, while the Barbour family became the heaviest property owners and

taxpayers in Paterson. In 1875 Robert Barbour became president of the company and continued in that position until his death. William Barbour's parents settled in Paterson when he was a child, and there he received his early education. Subsequently he attended the High Street Academy at Newark, N. J., and spent two years in Hanover, Germany, and a year in Tours, France, studying the languages of those countries. His first business engagement was with the house of Howard, Sanger & Co., of New York, and he quickly developed a talent for executive management. From there he went to the business organized by his father—the Barbour Flax-Spinning Co.—and was made secretary, and later vice-president and treasurer. The firm was incorporated as The Barbour Bros. Co. in 1882, with William Barbour president, and he still holds that position. The success that marked his management of the vast industry under his direction naturally attracted the attention of business men connected with other large enterprises, and he has been eagerly sought for influential places in the administration of more corporations than his time would permit him to accept. He is, however, president of the Linen Thread Co., the Algonquin Co., the American Net and Twine Co., the Dunbarton Flax-Spinning Co., the Dundee Water Power and Land Co., the Finlayson Flax-Spinning Co., the Hamilton Trust Co., the Paterson and Ramapo R. R. Co., Passaic Water Co., the U. S. Twine and Net Co., and the W. & J. Knox Net and Twine Co., and is a director of the American Cotton Oil Co., the Automatic Weighing Machine Co., the First National Bank of Paterson, Hanover National Bank, Home Trust Co., Paterson Savings Institution, Pintsch Compressing Co., Safety Car Heating and Lighting Co., the United Shoe Machinery Co. and water companies of New Jersey. He has also been president of the American Protective Tariff League since 1910. The Barbour families in the United States have always been in unswerving affiliation with the Republican party. In 1884 Mr. Barbour was a delegate from New Jersey to the national Republican convention at Chicago which nominated James G. Blaine for the presidency, and has been a delegate to every national convention since that date. In state politics he was a delegate to the convention of 1895 which nominated John W. Griggs for governor, and after Mr. Griggs' election Mr. Barbour was appointed a member of his personal staff with the rank of colonel. Mr. Barbour is a man of liberal views, rising above the prejudices of the hour, eminently just, firm of purpose, and as resolute in pursuit of the right as he sees it as he is earnest and unflinching in maintaining it. He is affable, solicitous for the well-being of those associated with him in business, and a liberal contributor to institutions that are doing good to the community. He is a member of the Union League, Republican Club and Merchants' Association of New York, and the Hamilton Club of Paterson. He was married Nov. 8, 1883, to Julia Adelaide, daughter of John H. Sprague, of New York, and has four sons: Thomas, Robert, vice-president of the Barbour Flax-Spinning Co.; William Warren and Fritz Krupp Barbour

KIMBALL, Francis H., architect, was born at Kennebunk, Me., Sept. 23, 1845, son of Samuel and Hannah H. (Tasker) Kimball; grandson of Caleb and Prudence (Chick) Kimball; great-grandson of Barak and Meribah (Whitten) Kimball; great-great-grandson of Caleb and Beriah (Welsh) Kimball, and great-great-great-grandson of Caleb and Susanna (Cloyes) Kimball. The first of his family in America came over from England about 1660 and settled at Haverhill, Mass. Mr. Kimball attended the public schools of his native town until he was fourteen years of age, when he entered the employ of a relative in Haverhill, Mass., who was a builder, and in the simple structures his employer erected he found his first practical experience in architecture. In the second year of the civil war, at the age of seventeen years, he enlisted in the United States navy and served for sixteen months. In 1867 he entered the architectural office of Louis P. Rogers in Boston, Mass., who soon after formed a partnership with Gridley J. F. Bryant. During his connection with that firm Mr. Kimball was sent to Hartford, Conn., to prepare the working drawings for the Charter Oak Life Insurance Company's building and a business block for the Connecticut Mutual Life Insurance Co. Later, in 1873, he was engaged as supervising architect of Trinity College in Hartford. William Burgees of London, the well-known exponent of French Gothic, was selected as architect of the new Trinity College buildings, and Mr. Kimball was sent to London to familiarize himself with the drawings. For five years he had charge of the erection of such of the buildings as the college authorities decided to build. In 1879 he opened an office in New York city, his first work there being the remodeling of the old Madison Square theatre, in association with Thomas Wisedell, another English architect of Gothic predilections and training. The Casino at Thirty-ninth street and Broadway, was also the creation of this firm; it is one of the best examples of Moorish architecture in this country. He has made a specialty of theatrical architecture, if an architect whose practice has been so varied could be described as a specialist. His authority on the subject of theatres was recognized by his being called upon to prepare those sections of the New York building laws which deal with the special precautions enforced upon the owners of theatres. Other notable examples of his work of this period are the Fifth Avenue and Garrick theatres of New York. In the building of the former he encountered difficulties that led him to adopt a new method of foundation construction, the application of the caisson system, which has revolutionized foundation work. In the extremity of the problem in hand he decided to try a system of cylinders filled with masonry which not only proved of great value in that particular case, but has since been adopted by every leading engineer in the country. The transition of the cylinders to the pneumatic caisson quickly followed, the first practical test being in the foundations of the Manhattan Life building, erected in 1893, and a pioneer in steel construction in New York city. After Mr. Wisedell's death in 1884, Mr. Kimball practiced alone until 1892 when a partnership was formed with George K. Thompson. This marked the beginning of his work on lofty office buildings—"skyscrapers"—the first of which was the Manhattan Life building. Mr. Kimball's versatility is shown by the wide scope and varied character of his work. He has designed many beautiful churches, suburban homes, town and city residences, warehouses, railroad stations and office buildings. Among the most notable of the latter are the Seligman, Brunswick, Trust Company of America, Empire, United States Realty, Trinity and City Investing and Adams Express Co. buildings, all in New York city. Probably the best example of his type of "skyscraper" is the City Investing building, the magnitude and beauty of which has attracted much attention. The entire structure throughout shows character, and the decorations are most pleasing, and there is probably no other building in the country where massiveness, dignity and beauty are more artistically blended. Primarily, Mr. Kimball is an exponent of the Gothic in architecture, but his versatility is the predominant feature of his work. He is a member of the Players' Club, City Lunch Club and Lawyers' Club, and of the New York Chapter of the American Institute of Architects. He was married May 7, 1872, to Jennie G., daughter of Capt. James Wetherell, of North Falmouth, Mass.

NAST, Conde, publisher, was born in New York city, March 26, 1874, son of William and Esther (Benoist) Nast. He was educated in the public schools of St. Louis, Mo., and at Georgetown University, Washington, D. C., where he graduated in 1896. As a further equipment for business, he took the legal course at Washington university, receiving the degree of LL.B. in 1898. In the following year he became advertising manager of "Collier's Weekly," at that time an unimportant publication owned by P. F. Collier. As an advertising expert, and afterwards as publisher, Mr. Nast has contributed several important developments to the field of national advertising. He was the first to demonstrate that a weekly (Collier's), and, later, that business catalogues (The Quarterly and Monthly Style Books, illustrating the Ladies' Home Journal Patterns) could be made large and successful media for national advertising. Still later, recognizing the great advertising opportunity for a fortnightly, he changed "Vogue's" period of issue from weekly to semi-monthly, making it the first periodical in the fortnightly field. Later still, he launched and secured general recognition for the so-called zone system of advertising, by means of which an advertiser is enabled to purchase and use just that portion of the circulation of a national medium which is distributed in the particular territory he desires to reach. So strong was the advertising prejudice against weeklies, at the time Mr. Nast took hold of "Collier's," that the total advertising patronage of that publication was only $5,500 annually. From that point he developed it in less than a decade to an annual total of more than $1,000,000, himself advancing in the meantime from an unimportant position to the general management of the business at a salary of $40,000 a year. Following his demonstration of the advertising value of weeklies, there developed in the weekly field such remarkably successful publications as "The Saturday Evening Post," "Literary Digest," "Life," and the "Outlook," serving the advertiser so effectively that in actual volume of business carried, the weeklies now surpass every other group of magazines. In 1907 he resigned the business management of "Collier's" to devote himself to the development of The Home Pattern Company. The company issued two publications, mere pattern catalogues, which because they published no editorial matter and were given away by dry goods and department stores, had been wholly unable to gain advertising patronage. Mr. Nast's own belief was that even such catalogues as these would command the attention of women because their fashion news was of sufficient interest, and this belief he set about to substitute for the deep-

Condé Nast

rooted prejudice which he found in the mind of advertisers. Within three years he established the Home Pattern Catalogues—the "Quarterly Style Book" and the "Monthly Style Book"—as great advertising mediums. In 1909 Mr. Nast acquired a weekly periodical, "Vogue," and put into effect immediately the belief he had been forming for five years, that for the purpose of most advertisers a semi-monthly is very much preferable to a weekly. This theory, put into practical effect in "Vogue," resulted in a greatly increased circulation and advertising revenue for that publication. Within two years after the change, "Vogue" took the lead of woman's publications in the volume of advertising carried. In 1899, with R. M. McBride, he purchased "House and Garden," and the following year, the two jointly acquired "Travel." In association with Isaac A. Mekeel (q. v.), Mr. Nast organized and financed (1911) the United Publishers Corporation with a capital of $7,500,000, which brought under one management seventeen notable publishing properties, including such widely known and influential publications as the "Iron Age," "Dry Goods Economist," "The Automobile," and "Motor Age." He is a member of the Metropolitan Club, Racquet and Tennis Club, Riding Club, Tuxedo Club, Sleepy Hollow Country Club, City Club, Aero Club of America and the Aeronautical Society. He was married Aug. 20, 1902, to Clarisse, daughter of Charles Coudert, of New York city, and has two children: Coudert and Natica Nast.

BATES, Lindon Wallace, engineer, was born at Marshfield, Vt., Nov. 19, 1858, son of William Wallace and Marie (Cole) Bates, and a descendant of John Bates, who emigrated to the American colonies early in the 17th century and settled at Hempstead, L. I., in 1663. From him the line of descent is traced through his son Joseph, who married Mercy Clement; their son, Benjamin; his son, John, who married Rachel Springer; their son, Thomas, who married Ann ———; their son, Stephen, who married Elizabeth Wallace, and their son, William Wallace, who was Mr. Bates's father. The latter served in the civil war and afterwards was engaged in shipbuilding at Chicago, Ill., where he constructed some of the largest vessels on the lakes. Lindon Bates was educated in the public schools of Chicago. After graduating second in rank at the Central High School in Chicago in 1876, he entered Yale College, but left before graduating to begin his business career. His first employment was with the Chicago, Burlington & Quincy railroad. A year later he went to the Pacific coast, and served with the location and construction forces of the Northern Pacific, the Oregon Railway and Navigation and the Oregon Pacific roads, being employed on the construction of various lines, docks and terminals in Oregon, Washington, Montana and California. Removing to Kansas City, Mo., in 1885, he was engaged in dredging the Kaw river and filling in the land occupied by the present stock yards. At this time he invented an improved dredge which bears his name. An improved form of his dredging machines was used upon the Chicago drainage canal, and in 1894 he built a special dredge, the Beta, for the United States government, in competition with others, to be used on the bars of the lower Mississippi river. The specifications called for a machine that would deliver 1,600 cubic yards of sand per hour, but he far exceeded this specification and constructed one that delivered 7,800 cubic yards an hour, for which he

was awarded a premium of $87,000. This was the first machine designed with the multiple cutter, for which he received patents in the United States and abroad. While traveling abroad in 1896 Mr. Bates submitted proposals for dredging the Schelt river in Belgium with his new machine, and after a full investigation by a commission of Belgian engineers his plans were adopted. He has made several trips abroad, studying the problems of European rivers and harbors and inspecting the methods of draining and deepening them. His travels include every port of prominence in Europe and Africa, as well as in India, Australia, the Philippines, China and Japan. Mr. Bates's fame as an expert on waterways is international, and on several occasions he has been consulted by European governments on important river and harbor improvements. The Russian government commissioned him to report on the deepening of the mouth of the Volga river; the improvement of the harbors of Black sea ports, and the enlargement of the mouth of the river Danube. These reports resulted in an order from the Russian government for a fleet of his dredges, which were built by him in Belgium. They attracted much attention among European engineers; in fact, the interest was so keen that during the trials, which lasted for six weeks, the Belgian government ran excursion trains at reduced rates to accommodate those who wished to observe the dredges at work. During the construction of these Russian dredges Mr. Bates was invited by the government of Queensland, Australia, to examine the harbor of Brisbane, the capital city, and eight other ports, and was awarded the contract for designing the eight harbors and for the regulation of the rivers Brisbane, Mary, Fitzroy, Norman and Albert, and also for dredging the harbors of Port Adelaide and other ports. Subsequently the Bates system of dredging was introduced in India and on the Suez canal, in South Australia, China and Japan. He built a large hydraulic dredge for the Russian government, earning a bonus of $75,000 on capacity test, and also constructed the sea-going dredges Hercules, Samson and Archer for Queensland, Australia, and the Lindon Bates for Calcutta, India. In collaboration with leading engineers of Europe, designated by the governments of Russia, Germany, Austria and Belgium, Mr. Bates prepared an elaborate plan for the improvement of the port of Shanghai, China. One of the most notable contracts Mr. Bates undertook at home was raising the grade of the city of Galveston, Texas, thereby insuring the safety of the city against floods. He is a member of the Western Society of Engineers, the Institute of Naval Architects, the Institution of Civil Engineers of Great Britain, the Civil Engineers of Belgium, the Whitehall and Primrose clubs of London, the Automobile Club of France, and the Yale, Republican, Lawyers' and Union League clubs of New York. He was married Apr. 6, 1881, to Josephine, daughter of William White of Chicago, and had two sons, Lindon Bates, Jr., who lost his life when the Germans sank the Lusitania in the European war in 1915, and Lindell T. Bates. Portrait opposite page 82.

EMERSON, Harrington, efficiency engineer, was born in Trenton, N. J., Aug. 2, 1853, son of Edwin and Mary Louise (Ingham) Emerson, grandson of James and Anne (Weir) Emerson. His grandfather came over to the United States with his widowed mother in 1804, settling in New York city. His father (1823-1908) was a graduate of Princeton College and Theological Seminary; professor of English literature at the University of Troy, N. Y.; he invented a new form of photographic lens, and contributed to the "American Journal of Science" the results of an exhaustive series of investigations in optics and photography. The son received a thorough education in England, France and Germany. In 1872 he entered the Royal Polytechnic at Munich, taking the mechanical engineering course, but was not graduated. After travelling for a year in Italy and Greece, and tutoring his brother, Alfred, he returned to the United States and was appointed head of the modern language department of the University of Nebraska. Shortly after his appointment he was elected registrar of the university and secretary of the faculty and in these positions was active in planning and furthering the modern educational departments of the institution. He left the university in 1882 to engage in banking and real estate operations in the west. From 1885 to 1891 he was engaged in special research work for the Burlington Railroad, such as examining the agricultural possibilities along its newly built lines, making preliminary investigation for irrigation purposes, and similar engineering problems, applying modern scientific methods to new industrial conditions. As the United States representative of a British syndicate investing in America in 1895, he examined minutely many of the industrial plants and mines in Mexico, the United States and Canada, both the finances and operations. In that year also he became interested in Alaska, put into operation some of the first long mail routes in Alaska and down the Yukon, reported on all the known coal deposits of the North American Western coast, and made a report to the United States senate on the Northern submarine cable route to Asia, which has since been largely followed by the war department in laying its Alaskan cables. In 1900 Mr. Emerson moved his headquarters to New York city and took up the work of standard practice and efficiency engineering as applied to industrial plants and transportation enterprises, a new department of engineering for which his long experience in applying scientific methods to new problems had specially fitted him. He has numbered among his clients many of the largest corporations and railroads in North America. Mr. Emerson's theories are that decreasing cost can be made to go hand in hand with increasing wages, that in ordinary operations there is so much loss that its elmination will provide a fund out of which to pay larger dividends and larger wages. He insists that the time and cost of every operation should be standardized before work is begun on it and that every cost statement should consist of two elements: standard cost and preventable waste. He has evolved a number of methods for putting these theories of cost reduction, cost predetermination, waste elimination, and the fair deal into effect on a very large and successful scale. In 1907 he formed the Emerson Co., associating himself with his brother Samuel D. I. Emerson and others. Mr. Emerson was married Feb. 5, 1895, to Mary Crawford, daughter of Nathan Robards Suplee, of Philadelphia, and they have three daughters: Isabel Mary, Margaret Eleanor and Mary Louise Emerson.

BRADLEY, Charles Schenck, engineer and inventor, was born at Victor, Ontario, N. Y., Apr. 12, 1853, son of Alonzo and Sarah (Schenck) Bradley. His first American ancestor was John Foskett, a native of Bristol, England, who came to America in 1648 and resided at Charlestown, Mass. Mr. Bradley's grandfather, Samuel Fos-

kett, of Colerain, Mass., by act of the Massachusetts legislature in 1820, changed his name to Samuel Bradley. Charles S. Bradley was educated in a private school in Rochester, N. Y., and then took a special course in chemistry at the University of Rochester. In 1881 he entered the service of the New York Edison Illuminating Co. as engineer, and the success of this pioneer electric lighting company was due in a great measure to his inventive resources. In 1884 he established a laboratory of his own in Yonkers, N. Y., which became the birthplace of some of the foremost electrical inventions. Here Mr. Bradley devised the method of multipolar windings now so generally used for direct-current machines, the first multipolar machine in this country being constructed by him in 1887. In the following year the first synchronous converter was built by him. The rotary converter is a machine by which an alternating current can be changed to direct, or direct to alternating, and has been for many years indispensable to street railways and large direct-current lighting systems. He has received about ninety patents, over half of which relate to long-distance transmission of power. There are more of Mr. Bradley's inventions involved in the development of the Niagara power stations and uses of electricity from these stations than there are of any other single individual. One of the most important of these is for what is known as the three-phase system of distribution, making it possible to greatly reduce the copper necessary in transmission lines. It may be described as uniting three circuits requiring six wires into a compound circuit of three wires, thus cutting in half the number of wires required. In February, 1892, Mr. Bradley received a patent for the production of aluminum. By this invention the aluminum was produced from its ores by the passage of an electric current, the heat necessary for diffusion being supplied simultaneously by the current which set free the aluminum. It is the first and only method by which aluminum is produced commercially by electricity, inasmuch as the heat was supplied by the current which performed the electrolysis, and did not have to pass through the walls of the containing vessel. Since the Bradley invention, aluminum, which formerly was regarded as one of the precious metals, has become as common as copper and brass, and its price has been reduced from $15.00 to 25 cents per pound. He is also the inventor of the first continuous electric furnace for the production of calcium carbide, for which he received a patent on Jan. 25, 1898, and which is used exclusively by the Union Carbide Co. This consists of a large wheel, on the periphery of which there is a channel in which the electrodes are suspended, the crude material being fed in on the side above the electrodes and the wheel revolving as fast as the carbide is formed at the electrodes, so that a core is formed in the lower half of the circumference within the channel; this core being broken out on the side opposite the electrodes, having had time to cool in transit. Other important inventions of note are two relating to the fixation of atmospheric nitrogen, and constituting the first production of nitrogen compounds from air on a commercial scale, and a wet chemical process for extracting copper from its ores, which does away with the fumes and saves the wastes encountered in previous processes. He was professor of chemistry in the Carnegie Technical School, Pittsburg, Pa., in 1905-6. He is a member

LINDON W. BATES
CIVIL ENGINEER

HARRINGTON EMERSON
EFFICIENCY ENGINEER

CHARLES S. BRADLEY
INVENTOR

HENRY C. JONES
JURIST

of the American Association for the Advancement of Science, the American Institute of Electrical Engineers, the American Electrochemical Society, the Franklin Institute of Philadelphia, Pa., the Mohawk Club of Schenectady, N. Y., and Lawyers' Club, Chemists' Club and Engineers' Club. Mr. Bradley was married Feb. 16, 1876, to Emma, daughter of Nelson Orcutt, of Albany, N. Y., and has two sons, Alonzo B. and Walter E. F. Bradley, and two daughters, Marian O., wife of William J. Baker, of Rochester, N. Y., and Florence, wife of Stewart L. Moore, Jr., of New York city.

SMITH, Marcus Aurelius, U. S. senator, was born near Cynthiana, Ky., Jan. 24, 1852. After attending the public schools he taught in a school at Bourbon, Ky., thus obtaining the means to enter Transylvania University, where he spent three years, but did not graduate. Taking up the study of law, he was graduated at the law department of the University of Kentucky at the head of his class in 1876 He began the practice of his profession in Lexington. He was prosecuting attorney for this city for three years, and then transferred his law business to San Francisco, Cal. In 1881 he removed to Tombstone, Ariz., which has since been his home. He was appointed prosecuting attorney of Tombstone district, also for three years. In 1886 he was elected on the Democratic ticket as territorial delegate to congress, and was re-elected in 1888 and 1890. While in congress he served on the committees of mines and mining and private land claims. He sat in the lower house from the fiftieth to the sixtieth congresses, inclusive, and on March 12, 1912, was elected to the U. S. senate, and was re-elected in November, 1914, for the long term which will expire March, 1921. He is an eloquent speaker and ranks among the ablest lawyers of Arizona.

ALEXANDER, Charles Beatty, lawyer, was born in New York city, Dec. 6, 1849, son of Henry Martyn and Susan Mary (Brown) Alexander, and a descendant of Archibald Alexander, who came to this country from Ireland about 1737 and settled at Nottingham, Pa. From him and his wife, Margaret Parks, the line is traced through their son William and his wife, Agnes Ann Reid; their son Archibald and his wife, Janetta Waddell, and their son Henry Martyn, who was the father of Mr. Alexander. His grandfather, Archibald Alexander (q. v.), was the founder of Princeton Theological Seminary, and his maternal grandfather was Matthew Brown (q. v.), for many years president of Jefferson College. Charles B. Alexander was graduated at Princeton University, of which his father was a trustee, in 1870, and the law school of Columbia University in 1872. He began practice with the firm of Alexander & Green, of which his father and Judge Ashbel Green were senior members, and after their deaths he continued the business in partnership with William W. Green. He was junior counsel for Samuel J. Tilden before the electoral commission when the presidential election was disputed between Tilden and Hayes. Mr. Alexander was admitted to the bar of the United States Supreme Court in 1884, and to the bar of the state of California in 1888. While pursuing a large general practice he has made a specialty of insurance law, and has written a treatise on the New York law of life insurance, which is regarded as an authoritative word on the subject. He has been for many years one of the legal advisers of the Equitable Life Assurance Society, of which he is also a director. He is also a director of the Equitable Trust Co., the International Banking Corporation,

the International Bank and the Mt. Morris Bank. Like his father and grandfather, Mr. Alexander is deeply interested in educational work. His numerous addresses before educational and learned bodies show a particularly clear and thorough comprehension of the true aims of education and the problems which lie in the way of their realization. He was for several years a trustee of Princeton University and of Bellevue Hospital Medical College, and is actively interested in many other educational institutions. In 1913 he was elected a regent of the University of the State of New York. He was a delegate to the Democratic national convention in 1912 which nominated Wilson for the presidency and to the state convention at Syracuse, N. Y., which nominated Gov. Sulzer. He is a member of the Society of the Cincinnati, the Society of Colonial Wars, Sons of the Revolution, Sons of the American Revolution, the bar associations of the city and state of New York, and the Union, University, Riding, Tuxedo, Metropolitan, Army and Navy, Lawyers', and New York Yacht clubs of New York, the Princeton clubs of New York and Philadelphia, the Pacific Union Club of San Francisco, and the Burlingame (Cal.) Country Club. He received the honorary degree of LL.D. from Princeton University in 1895, and from Washington and Jefferson College in 1902. He was married in San Francisco, April 26, 1887, to Harriet, daughter of Charles Crocker, one of the famous pioneers and capitalists of California, and has three daughters: Harriet, Janetta and Mary Crocker Alexander.

JONES, Henry Cox, jurist, was born in Franklin county, Ala., Jan. 23, 1821, son of William Stratton and Ann Harris (Cox) Jones and grandson of Thomas and Prudence (Jones) Jones. His father was a wealthy planter. The son was graduated at La Grange College in 1840 and at the Athens Law School in 1841. A few weeks before attaining his majority he was elected probate judge of Franklin county without being a candidate for the office. Two years later he was elected to the Alabama legislature, and served two terms with distinction. During 1845–53 he practiced his profession at Russellville, and in 1856 removed to Florence, Ala., after having served four years as a member of the state senate. He was a Douglas elector in 1860, and was later elected a union delegate to the secession convention. He vigorously opposed secession, declining to sign the ordinance of secession, and with eleven others had his opposition vote recorded. He was, however, elected a representative from Alabama to the confederate congress, and was the last of the Alabama members of that celebrated body. After the war he resumed his law practice at Florence. In the days of reconstruction he was for five years chairman of the Democratic central committee. In 1874 he was elected state's attorney for the 8th district, an office which he filled for eighteen years and never missed a single court. He was married at Athens, Ala., Oct. 13, 1844, to Martha Louisa, daughter of George Keyes, and niece of Pres. Monroe and had five surviving children: Bertha, wife of Lindsay Melbourne Allen, of Franklin co.; George Presley, Jennie Keyes, wife of William Jones Kernachan, Florence; Martha Bolling, wife of Thomas Sadler Jordan, and Robert Young Jones. He died at Florence, Ala., June 21, 1913. Portrait opposite page 82.

MEKEEL, Isaac A., publisher, was born in Clinton, Ia., Sept. 25, 1870, son of George M. and Maria (Haviland) Mekeel, of Scotch descent. He received a public school education, completed his studies at Friends' Academy at Union Springs, N. Y., and began his business career at the age of twenty in the employ of a printing and publishing firm in St. Louis, Mo. In 1900 he removed to New York to become associated with the Textile Publishing Co., publishers of the Dry Goods Economist, and since then Mr. Mekeel has devoted his time and energies to the upbuilding and development of various important trade journals. By 1912 he had been officer or director in more than thirty financial publishing and business enterprises. In May, 1911, he effected an important merger of trade periodicals into the United Publishers Corporation which took over three groups of trade, technical and class publications, viz.: an iron and steel unit, represented by the publications of the David Williams Co., including "The Iron Age," "Iron Age Hardware," "The Metal Worker" and "The Building Age"; a drygoods and shoe unit, represented by the publications of the Root Securities Co., and including "The Dry Goods Economist," the "Drygoodsman," "The Dry Goods Reporter," "The Boot and Shoe Recorder," and other papers; and an automobile unit, represented by the Class Journal Co., and including "The Automobile," "The Motor Age," "The Commercial Vehicle" and the "Blue Book." Associated with Mr. Mekeel in the formation of this holding company were Charles T. Root, H. M. Swetland, Charles G. Phillips, W. H. Taylor and Conde Nast, all of whom constitute the directors of the new corporation. The older of the above publications are published in New York city (and housed under one roof in the Thirty-ninth Street Building) and the others in Boston, Chicago, St. Louis, Minneapolis and San Francisco. A direct outcome of the merger was a concentration and co-operative arrangement that reduced the operative and publication expenses to a minimum. While thus securing economy, uniformity and permanency of policy the business and editorial management of each periodical is continued on a separate basis as heretofore. Another cogent reason for the merger was the desire on the part of the younger element in the organization to develop the enterprises to still greater possibilities. The United Publishers Corporation is a close corporation capitalized at $7,500,000. All but about five per cent. of its stock is held by those who contributed to the various companies embraced by the merger. Messrs. Mekeel, Nast and H. L. Burrage, president of the Eliot National Bank of Boston, constitute the voting trustees. The successful accomplishment of so difficult an undertaking must be attributed to the energy, executive ability, intelligence and far-sightedness of Mr. Mekeel, whose accomplishments and business acumen have already stamped him as one of America's foremost men of affairs. He was a member of the Lotus Club, Aldine and Engineers clubs of New York. He was married at St. Louis, Mo., Oct. 29, 1896, to Elizabeth M., daughter of John N. Schureman, and has three sons: Haviland Scudder, Jahn Sterling and Ormond Saville Mekeel. He died in Montclair, N. J., Feb. 3, 1913.

CARTY, John Joseph, electrical engineer, was born at Cambridge, Mass., Apr. 14, 1861, son of Henry and Elizabeth (O'Malley) Carty. He received his early education in the schools of his native city. At the time he had finished his preparatory studies for entrance to college he was obliged to abandon his school work indefinitely, because of serious trouble with his eyesight. The telephone having just been invented and being one of the first to appreciate its possibilities, Mr. Carty entered the service of the Bell Telephone Co. in 1879 and has ever since been identified with that company. His first work was in Boston, Mass., and while there he made a number of contributions to the art of telephony which were of much value and have since become a permanent part of the art. Under his direction was installed the first multiple switchboard in Boston, which was at that time the largest ever put into use. For the "express" telephone system, peculiar to that city, he designed and installed a switchboard which was the first metallic circuit multiple board to go into service, the fundamental features of which are in all of the boards of today. In 1887 Mr. Carty took charge of the cable department of the Western Electric Co. in the East, with headquarters in New York city. In this position he studied cable manufacture and laying, and introduced a number of improvements, having charge of all of the important cable-laying projects which were carried on for some time in the East. One of his engineering developments resulted in cutting in half the cost of cable manufacture. He then took charge of the switchboard department of the Western Electric Co. for the East, and under his direction were installed most of the larger switchboards of that period. During this period he made some further improvements in switchboards, which have since become standard practice. He was the first to practically demonstrate how to operate two or more telephone circuits connected directly with a common battery, and about 1888 installed, for the supply of operators' telephones, common battery systems in a number of central offices. In 1889 he entered the service of the Metropolitan Telephone and Telegraph Co., now the New York Telephone Co., for the purpose of organizing all the technical departments, building up its technical staff, and reconstructing the entire plant of the company —converting it from grounded circuits, overhead and series switchboards to metallic circuits placed underground and to bridging switchboards. His achievements in connection with the development of the plant of the New York Telephone Co. has been most successful and far-reaching in its consequences. Based upon his plans and under his direction, there has been constructed a telephone system which, according to the foremost authorities in the world, is without a parallel in its efficiency and scope. His work has been studied and approved by all the technical administrations of Europe and even of Asia, and to a large extent what he has done for the telephone art in the United States has contributed to the pre-eminent standing which the American telephone industry holds in foreign countries. He made an exhaustive investigation into the nature of the disturbances to which telephone lines are subjected, and gave the first public account of his work in a paper entitled, "A New View of Telephone Induction," read before the Electric Club of New York city on Nov. 21, 1889. In this paper he showed the overwhelming preponderance of electrostatic induction as a factor in producing crosstalk, and proved that there is in a telephone line a particular point in the circuit at which, if a telephone is inserted, no cross-talking will be heard. The article gave directions for determining this silent or neutral point, and described original experiments showing how to distinguish between electrostatic and electro-magnetic induction in telephone lines. In March, 1891, Mr. Carty made additional contributions to the knowledge of this subject in a paper before the American Institute of Electrical Engineers, entitled, "Inductive Disturbances in Telephone Circuits." Prior to his work on the subject, the number of telephone stations which could be operated upon one line was greatly restricted because of the impediment offered to the voice currents by the presence of the signalling bells and on account of the inductive disturbances which these bells caused. These conditions made it impracticable to extend the telephone to the rural districts owing to the prohibitive expense involved in providing each customer with a circuit of his own. This problem was exhaustively studied by Mr. Carty with the result that he devised a mechanism known as the "bridging bell" whereby any number of stations that might be required could be placed upon one line without in any way impairing the transmission of speech or introducing disturbing noises. The simplicity and cheapness of the device and the extraordinary success which attended its working resulted in an immediate extension of the telephone into rural districts and the placing of the telephone in the homes of millions of farmers in America and abroad which had formerly been isolated. For this achievement the Franklin Institute of Philadelphia conferred upon him the Edward Longstreth Medal of Merit in 1902. In recognition of his achievements as an engineer and in view of the services which he rendered to the Japanese government in connection with electrical engineering matters, he was decorated by the emperor of Japan with the Order of the Rising Sun in 1909; and with the Imperial Order of the Sacred Treasure in 1912. In China, where a commission investigated the telephone systems of the world, that of New York was selected as the model for Pekin, and as a consequence the first great order for a telephone system in China was given to American manufacturers. Since 1907 Mr. Carty has been chief engineer of the American Telephone and Telegraph Co., in which capacity he is responsible for the standardizing of methods of construction and operation of its plant, which extends into every community of the United States, and which, through its long-distance wires, extends into Canada and Mexico. He is recognized as among the foremost of telephone engineers, and is one of the creators of the profession of which he is a leader. He is a member of the Society for the Promotion of Engineering Education, the Society for the Promotion of Industrial Education, the American Institute of Electrical Engineers, of which he served as president during 1915–16, the New York Electrical Society, of which he was president in 1903-4, and the Society of Arts, and an honorary member of the American Electro-Therapeutic Association, the Telephone Society of Pennsylvania, the Telephone Society of New England and the Telephone Society of New York. He is also a member of the Friendly Sons of St. Patrick, the American-Irish Historical Society, the Baltusrol and Casino clubs of Short Hills, N. J., and the Engineers' and Railroad clubs of New York city. Mr. Carty was married on August 8th, 1891, to Marion Mount, daughter of Joseph Russell, of Dublin, and they have one son, John Russell Carty, now a student at Princeton University.

McKENZIE, William, manufacturer, was born in Glasgow, Scotland, Aug. 22, 1841, son of Joseph and Janet (Mitchell) McKenzie. After a common school education he began his career in the line that became his life work—the bleaching,

dyeing and finishing of cotton fabrics—with the well-known firm of John Leck & Co., of Glasgow. During his apprenticeship he worked in every department of the place becoming familiar with all details and mastering all operations in the process of bleaching. Having married, young McKenzie decided to come to America, and in 1866 he settled in Norwich, Conn., where he became identified with the Norwich Bleachery Works. For nearly eighteen years he remained in charge of its various departments, both in the factory and in the office. In 1884 he transferred his services to the Dunnell Manufacturing Co., a well-known printing works of Pawtucket, R. I., where for twelve months he had charge of the white goods department. Meanwhile he was ambitious to establish a business of his own. At Carlton Hill, N. J., stood an old brick bleachery, noted for years because of the serious losses and even failures of its previous proprietors. The plucky Scotchman felt that here was his opportunity, and forming a partnership with John Ward, manufacturer of gold watch cases, purchased the property and organized the Standard Bleachery in 1885. His intimate knowledge of every detail of the various processes of the work was of great help to him and by the largest kind of personal application the Standard Bleachery became one of the largest in the world for bleaching, dyeing and finishing fine cotton goods. He was the first to introduce into the United States the finishing of French lawns, organdies, long cloths, crepes, Swiss curtains, embroideries, and fancy woven fabrics. The plant now occupies twelve acres, covered with buildings and requires 1,000 employees to handle the weekly output of 3,000,000 yards of cotton goods in a great variety of styles and designs. Mr. McKenzie has not only kept in close touch with every detail of the business, but he has been ever alert to introduce the newest methods, the latest machinery and devices to increase the efficiency of the plant. With this end in view he makes frequent visits abroad to study and learn European methods, and by his inventive ingenuity is frequently able by remodeling a new machine to greatly improve its capacity and usefulness. Beginning with the name of the McKenzie & Ward Standard Bleachery, the business was incorporated in 1896 as the Standard Bleachery Co., and Mr. McKenzie's son, James J. McKenzie, became associated. In 1905 Mr. Ward retired, and in the following year it was incorporated with William McKenzie as president, Kenneth M. McKenzie, vice-president, James J. McKenzie, treasurer, and Bertram D. McKenzie, secretary. Notwithstanding his close application to the management of his business, Mr. McKenzie has ever been interested in civic affairs and has long taken an active part in municipal government. His first political position was as chairman of the Boiling Springs township committee in Bergen county, N. J. While head of this committee he headed the movement to create the borough of East Rutherford, on the accomplishment of which he was made first mayor and served as such for twelve years. He was a member of the Bergen County Republican executive committee for many years, and his services to the party were recognized in 1898 by his election as chairman of the committee. He was also an alternate delegate to the congressional district Republican national convention of 1896, and in 1900 was presidential elector. He took an active part in organizing the Rutherford and East Orange board of trade, was its president for several years, was one of the founders and vice-president of the Rutherford National Bank, and president of the Hobart Trust Co., of Passaic; the Passaic Lumber Co., of Wallington, and the East Rutherford Savings, Loan and Building Association. He was a member of the board of governors of the Passaic Hospital, and was one of the founders of the East Rutherford Free Library, and its president for a number of years. He was a member of St. Andrew's Society of New York, the Union Club of Rutherford, and the Union League of Hackensack. He married twice, first to Helen, daughter of Robert Dick, of Glasgow, Scotland. She died in 1903, leaving four sons: James J., William, Jr., Kenneth M. and Bertram D. McKenzie, and one daughter, Rachel, wife of Harry W. Pierson, of Boston. In 1905 he was married to Margaret D., daughter of Prof. Alexander Balfour Stewart, of Wigtonshire, Scotland. He died at East Rutherford, N. J., Apr. 12, 1914.

BOYD, Andrew Hunter, jurist, was born at Winchester, Va., July 15, 1849, son of Andrew Hunter Holmes and Eleanor F. (Williams) Boyd, grandson of Elisha and Ann (Holmes) Boyd and great-grandson of John and Sarah (Gryfyth) Boyd, natives of England, who settled in Berkeley county, Va., on lands acquired by original grant from Lord Fairfax. Elisha Boyd was colonel of the 4th Virginia regiment in the war of 1812. He was the commonwealth attorney for forty years, was state senator, and was a member of the Virginia Constitutional Convention of 1829–30. Judge Boyd's father was a Presbyterian minister. Our subject was educated at Washington College, Va., and at the University of Virginia. After studying in the law offices of Barton & Boyd at Winchester, Va., he entered the law department of Washington and Lee University and was graduated in 1871. Settling in Cumberland, Md., he began the practice of his profession there and in 1875 was elected state's attorney for Alleghany county. He held that office for four years, after which he devoted himself wholly to his extensive and rapidly growing practice until, in 1893, he was called by the governor to fill the vacancy as chief judge of the 4th Judicial Circuit of Maryland, caused by the promotion to the supreme bench of the United States of Judge Richard H. Alvey. In the fall of that year his appointment was confirmed by election. By virtue of his office as chief judge of a judicial circuit he became, according to the Maryland system, associate judge of the court of appeals of Maryland. Upon the death of James McSherry, chief judge of the court of appeals, in 1907, the governor appointed him to fill the vacancy, and he held those two distinguished offices until the expiration of his fifteen-year term as chief judge of the judicial circuit in 1908. The end of his term came in an off year, and he was appointed by the governor to hold the position until the general election of 1909. In 1909 Judge Boyd, although a Democrat, was re-elected as chief judge of the 4th judicial circuit of Maryland by a majority of 458, though the circuit went Republican on the state ticket by a majority of 2,096. As his term as chief judge of the court of appeals expired automatically at the election, he was reappointed to that office by the governor. Judge Boyd received the degree of LL.D. from Washington College, Md., in 1906, and from the University of Maryland in 1908. His services on the bench were marked by his patience in investigation, profound knowledge of the law, love of justice, independence and a firm adherence to his deliberate opinions of the law. Judge Boyd

was married Dec. 17, 1874, to Elizabeth, daughter of George A. Thruston, of the Allegany county bar, and has two sons: Andrew Hunter and J. Thruston Boyd.

LOOMIS, William Stiles, editor and financier, was born in Munson, Mass., Oct. 7, 1840, son of Elijah W. and Jeannette (Stiles) Loomis. His first American ancestor was Joseph Loomis, a woolen-draper, who came to America from London in the ship Susan and Ellen, settling at Dorchester, Mass., and later at Windsor, Conn., in 1639. Besides his wife, Mary White, he brought with him five sons, all of whom were freemen, and three daughters. The line of descent is traced through Joseph's son, Lieut. Samuel, and his wife, Elizabeth Judd; their son Philip and his wife, Hannah ————; their son Philip and his wife, Mindwell Wilcoxson; their son Philip and his wife, ———— Purchas, and their son Elijah and his wife, Chloe Tyron, who were the grandparents of William Stiles Loomis. He attended the public schools of Holyoke, meanwhile delivering newspapers for a local newsstore. In 1862 he enlisted in company B, of the 46th Mass. regiment, and in 1863 was commissioned second lieutenant by Gov. Andrews. After his father's death, in company with his brother-in-law, Edgar Pomeroy, he carried on his father's grocery business, with the addition of books, stationery and newspapers. With two others, he organized a lecture committee and brought many fine speakers to Holyoke, including Wendell Phillips, John B. Gough, Theodore Tilton and Henry Ward Beecher. He was owner of the "Holyoke Transcript" during 1873-88. Assuming the management and direction of the Holyoke Street Railway Co., he saw it grow from a single horse car line to the present extensive system. He founded Mountain Park, built a trolley road to the top of Mount Tom, which he owned, and was identified with many societies and organizations having for their object municipal welfare and advancement. His devotion to Holyoke is evidenced by his steadfast refusal to permit the railway to pass into the hands of an outside and disinterested company, and the service has always been noted for its excellence. In 1891 the Elmwood line was built, in 1892 the Oakdale line, in 1895 the Springfield and Chicopee Falls lines, in 1896 the South Hadley Center line and in 1897 the Chicopee line and that branch of the Northampton line in Hampden street. In 1888 Mr. Loomis was made treasurer and general manager of the system and from an original capitalization of $25,000 the company rose to a capitalization of $2,000,000. He was president of the Holyoke Railway Co. until his death, was vice-president of the Mount Tom Railroad Co., president and superintendent of the Forestdale Cemetery Association, vice-president of the Holyoke Savings Bank and also the Holyoke Public Library, and one of the founders of the Home for Aged People. The purchase and development of the Forestdale Cemetery was also largely due to him. He was a member of the Masonic fraternity, the G. A. R. and the Loyal Legion. He was married, Oct. 9, 1866, to Augusta R., daughter of S. J. Weston. She died Feb. 4, 1908, and on March 7, 1911, he was married to Harriet L., daughter of John T. Clark. He died at Mount Desert, Me., July 10, 1914.

WILLARD, DeForest, orthopedist, was born in Newington, Hartford co., Conn., Mar. 23, 1846, son of Daniel H. and Sarah Maria (Deming) Willard, and a descendant of the original Puritan ancestor, Major Simon Willard, the founder of Concord, Mass., two of whose descendants, Joseph

William S. Loomis.—

De Forest Willard

and Samuel Willard, were presidents of Harvard College. He entered Yale College in 1863, and from there went to the Medical Department of the University of Pennsylvania, at which he was graduated M.D. in 1867, receiving the degree of Ph.D. three years later on the completion of a course of advanced work in special departments. He early chose surgery as his branch of medical practice, and during the civil war, prior to his graduation, served under the auspices of the U. S. Sanitary Commission at City Point and Petersburg, Va., as acting surgeon. He was demonstrator of anatomy at the University of Pennsylvania from 1867-70; quiz master of surgery and anatomy from 1868-77; demonstrator in surgery, assistant surgeon in Prof. Agnew's clinic, and assistant surgeon in the surgical dispensary of the University Hospital, 1870-77; and attending orthopædic surgeon to the University Hospital during 1889-1910, the chair of orthopædic surgery having been created by the University for Dr. Willard and held by him during that time. Through his exertions, the orthopædic children's ward of the University Hospital was established in 1890, and then enlarged into a department and housed in the Agnew wing. He specialized in orthopedic surgery long before it was recognized as a special branch and was in every sense a pioneer who should rank with Audry, Potts, Stromyer, Mutter and Sayre. He was a member of the American Medical Association; president of the American Orthopædic Association, 1890 and the Philadelphia County Medical Society, 1893-94; vice president of the Medical Alumni Association in 1905, and president in 1907; president of the Medical Board of the Presbyterian Hospital, 1901-07; vice president of the Orthopædic Section of the International Congress, Berlin, 1890; chairman of the orthopædic section of the Philadelphia College of Physicians, 1894; curator of the Philadelphia Pathological Society, 1868-71; pathologist of the Presbyterian Hospital, 1872-81; out-patient surgeon of the Presbyterian Hospital, 1873-76; surgeon to Howard Hospital, 1877-81; organizer and surgeon-in-chief of the Widener Memorial Industrial School for Crippled Children, 1898; consulting surgeon of the Phœnixville Hospital, 1903-10; surgeon of the Presbyterian Hospital, 1876-1910; consulting surgeon of the Atlantic City Hospital, 1901-10; Seashore Children's Hospital, Atlantic City, 1902-10; Germantown Hospital, 1902-10; Jewish Hospital, 1904-10; Municipal Hospital, 1908-10; Home for Incurables, 1881-1910; New Jersey Training School for Feeble-Minded, 1883-1905; and Haddock Memorial, 1901-10; founder of the Midnight Mission, 1868-1910; assistant medical director of the United States Centennial Exhibition, 1876; Mutter lecturer of the Philadelphia College of Physicians, 1893; visiting surgeon of the Lincoln Institute, 1870-73; of the Educational Home, 1873; assistant physician of the Lying-in-Charity, 1872-77; professor of anatomy and physiology at the Wagner Institute of Science, 1870-75; Fellow of the American Orthopædic Association, American Surgical Association, American Medical Association, Philadelphia Academy of Surgery, Philadelphia County Medical Society, Pennsylvania State Medical Society, Philadelphia Pathological Society, Philadelphia Obstetrical Society, and the Lehigh Valley Medical Association. He was on the council of the Philadelphia College of Physicians for twelve years and censor of the Philadelphia County Medical Society for five years. He was a member of the General Alumni Society; Medical Alumni Society (presi-

dent, 1907, and member of its executive committee for twenty years); board of managers of the University Hospital, 1892-1906; board of trustees, Pennsylvania Training School for Feeble-Minded, 1893-97; board of managers, Midnight Mission, 1868-1910; board of managers, Union Benevolent Association, 1883-1903; Academy of Natural Science, 1876-78; New England Society, 1881-1910; Founders and Patriots, Philadelphia, 1906-10; manager of the Young Men's Christian Association, 1875-78; delegate to the International Medical Congress, Berlin, 1890; American Congress of Physicians and Surgeons; Pan-American Medical Congress, 1893; International Medical Congress, Philadelphia, 1876, and the International Medical Congress, Washington, 1888; vice-president of the International Congress of Tuberculosis, Washington, 1908; charter member of the Alpha Mu Pi Omega medical fraternity, and honorary member of the Alpha Omega Alpha fraternity. He was a contributor to the "American Journal of Medical Sciences," "Transactions, American Surgical and Orthopædic Associations," "University Medical Magazine," and other reviews and transactions; among his principal articles were, "Intrathoracic Surgery," "Operative Treatment for Spinal Caries" (1890), "Pneumonectomy and Pneumonotomy" (1891), "Surgery of the Spine) (1893), "Club Foot" (1893), and "Experiments in Nerve Suturing" (1894). He also wrote "Orthopædic Surgery" for Ashhurst's "International Encyclopædia of Surgery"; lectured frequently before learned bodies, and published in connection with Dr. Adler a book on "Anæsthetics" (1901). In 1910, just previous to his death, he published what is considered his greatest book, "Surgery of Childhood." He possessed both judgment and operative skill, to which he added rare inherited culture and marvelous technique. Among his university students he was beloved because of his high ideals, and the two great themes of his addresses to his graduating classes were, "character building" and "faithful service." He received the honorary degree of A.M. from Lafayette College in 1882. He was married, Sept. 13, 1881, to Elizabeth M., daughter of Hon. William A. Porter, and they had one son, Dr. DeForest Porter Willard. Dr. Willard died in Lansdowne, Pa., Oct. 14, 1910.

TAYLOR, David Watson, naval constructor, was born in Louisa county, Va., Mar. 4, 1864, son of Henry and Mary Minor (Watson) Taylor. The first of the family in America was James Taylor, a native of Carlisle, England, and came over in 1652 and settled in New Kent county, Va. From him and his wife, Mary Gregory, the line is traced through their son John and his wife, Catherine Pendleton; their son James and his wife, Ann Pollard; their son John and his wife, Lucy Penn, and their son Henry and his wife, Julia Dunlap Leiper, who were the grandparents of our subject. John Taylor, his great-grandfather, was U. S. senator in the first term of Washington's administration, and another great-grandfather was Thomas Leiper, a member of the first troop of city light horse of Philadelphia, who gave liberally of his private means to government enterprises and to the support of the revolutionary army. He constructed and operated the first railroad in America in 1809-10, was for many years president of the common council of Philadelphia and was a close friend of Thomas Jefferson. David Watson Taylor was educated at Randolph Macon College, and the United States Naval Academy, being graduated in 1885 at the head of a class noted for its brilliant scholars. His record for scholarship at the naval academy has never been equalled before or since. It was 727.07 marks out of a possible maximum of 760, or 95.67%. Later he went to the Royal Naval College, Greenwich, Eng., to study naval construction, and his achievements there, in competition with picked men from all parts of the world, are still unequalled. After his graduation in 1888 he was attached for a time to the bureau of construction and repair, navy department, and later was stationed at Mare Island, Cal. He returned to the bureau of construction and repair as assistant to the chief constructor in 1894, and in 1901 he was promoted to the relative rank of captain. In 1914 he was appointed chief of the bureau of construction and repair of the U. S. navy with the rank of rear admiral. It may be said that Chief Constructor Taylor is responsible for the immense strides in ship design made by the United States navy during the past decade until it has achieved a leading postion among all the navies of the world in the matter of hull design. His researches have resulted in extraordinary improvements in the design of hulls of large naval vessels and a saving of many millions to the nation in the shape of greater speed and efficiency through scientifically determined dimensions. Vessels designed on the basis of Taylor's deductions have practically equalled the speed of vessels of ten years previous on the same horse-power, notwithstanding that the later vessels had nearly doubled the displacement of their forerunners. In terms of mercantile practice, this means that a 9,000-ton cargo boat could be built with only the power necessary to drive an old 5,000-ton boat at the same speed. In 1899 the Washington model basin, the first experimental tank in America, was erected under Chief Constructor Taylor's direction and he has been in charge of it ever since. His experiments there determine the form and dimensions of every ship built for the United States navy. He contributed a paper, "Ship-shaped Stream Forms," to the proceedings of the British Institute of Naval Architects in 1894, which won for him the gold medal awarded to the best original paper, the first time that such a distinction had been conferred upon an American. He has won a world-wide reputation as the foremost designer of large high-power ships. In 1911, at the request of the British government, he was expert witness at the trial of the Olympic-Hawke collision case, and his evidence on the theory of suction between passing vessels was the chief factor in determining the decision of the court in favor of the admiralty and establishing a precedent for all collision cases in British courts. He is vice-president of the Society of Naval and Marine Engineers and a member of the Institute of Naval Architects (British), the Army and Navy and Metropolitan clubs of Washington, the University Club of Philadelphia and the New York Yacht Club. He was married Oct. 26, 1892, to Imogen Maury, daughter of James Maurey Morris, of Louisa county, Va., and has four children: Dorothy Watson, May Coleman, David Watson, Jr., and Imogen Morris Taylor.

CODDINGTON, Wellesley Perry, clergyman, educator and author, was born at Sing Sing, N. Y., Oct. 23, 1840, son of David Cooks and Hannah (Perry) Coddington. His earliest paternal American ancestor was John Coddington, a relative of William Coddington, governor of Rhode Island, who emigrated from England about 1630 and settled in Boston. From him and his wife, Emma, the line of descent is traced through their son John (2d) and his wife, Hannah Gardner; their son Benjamin and his wife, Mary; to their son Jotham and his wife, Mary Millard; to their son Millard and his wife, Phœbe Cock, who were the grandparents of the subject. Wellesley Perry Coddington received his early education at Amenia (N. Y.) Seminary and was graduated at Wesleyan University in 1860. During 1860-2 he was a teacher in mathematics in the Troy Conference Seminary, Poultney, Vt. In 1863 he joined the New York Conference of the Methodist Church and became professor of ancient languages in Amenia Seminary. A few months later he was appointed principal of that institution. The following year he became professor of Greek and acting principal of Cazenovia (N. Y.) Seminary. In 1865 he was elected to the chair of modern languages in Genesee College, Lima, N. Y., and in 1866 became professor of Greek and Latin. He was professor of Greek in Syracuse University in 1871–73 and then succeeded to the chair of Greek, ethics and Christian evidences in that institution. In 1891 he became professor of philosophy and pedagogy, in which capacity he continued until his death. He had supplied some of the most important Presbyterian, Congregational and Methodist pulpits in New York state, and his sermons were always in demand for reproduction in the various religious journals and newspapers. He received and declined several invitations to assume the pastorate of large churches in Chicago, New York and Cleveland. During 1878–79 he traveled and studied in Europe, and it was his custom in later years to travel abroad during the vacation season. He received the degree of A. M. from Wesleyan University in 1866 and that of S. T. D. from Hamilton College in 1880. In 1882 he was elected to a chair in the Garrett Biblical Institute, Evanston, Ill., which he declined. Dr. Coddington was a fine scholar and a brilliant teacher. Greek, Latin, German, ethics, philosophy and pedagogy were all subjects which came within the scope of his unusually broad and versatile mind. He was a diligent and faithful worker and his work left a lasting impression. Among his published writings the best known is a volume of essays entitled "Plain Thoughts on Faith and Life." He was married July 23, 1863, to Louisa Guibord, daughter of Louis Guibord De Bellerose, of Plattsburg, N. Y., and is survived by three children: Herbert Guibord, Gertrude Louise, wife of William C. Stinson, and Winifred. He died in Hamburg, Germany, Aug. 13, 1913.

LUSK, Graham, physiologist, was born in Bridgeport, Conn., Feb. 15, 1866, son of William Thompson and Mary Hartwell (Chittenden) Lusk. The first of his family in America was John Lusk, who with his father came to this country from Scotland in 1702 and settled in Wethersfield, Conn. The line of descent is traced through his son James, who married Love Graham; their son Sylvester, who married Sarah King; their son Sylvester Graham, who married Elizabeth Adams and was the grandfather of Graham Lusk. His father (q. v.) was a prominent obstetrician and his mother was the daughter of Simeon B. Chittenden (q. v.), a merchant and one-time member of congress. The son was educated at Berkeley School, New York city, and was graduated with the degree of Ph.B. at the Columbia University School of Mines in 1887. He earned his Ph.D. from the University of Munich, Germany, in 1891, and on his return became instructor in physiology at Yale University. In 1892 he was advanced to be assistant professor and in 1895 full professor. In 1898 he returned to New York city to accept the chair of physiology in the University and Bellevue Hospital Medical Col-

DAVID W. TAYLOR
NAVAL CONSTRUCTOR

WELLESLEY P. CODDINGTON
EDUCATOR

GRAHAM LUSK
PHYSIOLOGIST

WILLIAM D. BALDWIN
MERCHANT

lege, and in 1909 became professor of Physiology in the Cornell University Medical College. In 1912 he became also the scientific director of the Russell Sage Institute of Pathology, founded by Mrs. Russell Sage and established in Bellevue Hospital. His brilliant investigations have for the most part been confined to the study of metabolism and include papers on such subjects as "On the Metabolism During a Combination of Phosphorus Poisoning and Phlorhizin Diabetes" (1899), "On the Maxim Production of Hippuric Acid in Rabbits" (1900), "On the Formation of Dextrose in Metabolism from the End-Products of a Pancreatic Digest of Meat" (1903), "Metabolism in Phosphorus Poisoning" (1907), and "The Specific Dynamic Action of the Foodstuffs" (1914). He has contributed to the "Journal of Biological Chemistry" a series of twelve important papers on "Animal Calorimetry" (1912–15). Probably his most important work has been in connection with the problem of diabetes, that most insidious disease, concerning the origin of which so little was known. In 1904 he wrote "On the Absence of a Cane-Sugar Inverting Enzyme in the Gastric Juice," and again, in the same year, "Diabetes Mellitus, Report on a Case, Including a New Method of Prognosis," also on "The Influence of Cold and Mechanical Exercise on the Sugar Excretion in Phlorhizin Glycosuria" (1908), "The Production of Sugar from Glumatic Acid Ingested in Phlorhizin Glycosuria" (1908), "Metabolism in Diabetes" (1909), and, more recently, "The Alleged Influence of the Adrenals and the Thyroids upon Diabetic Metabolism" (1913), which he contributed to the proceedings of the International Congress of Medicine. Among his earliest writings was "The Chemistry of the Animal Body," which appeared in the American Text Book of Physiology in 1896, and he is the author of the popular "Elements of the Science of Nutrition" (1906) and "The Fundamental Basis of Nutrition" (1914). Yale University conferred upon him the degree of A.M. in 1896 and that of Sc. D. in 1908. He is corresponding fellow of the Imperial Society of Physicians in Vienna, and a fellow of the Royal Society of Edinburgh, the American Association for the Advancement of Science, the National Academy of Science and a member of the American Society of Biological Chemists (president, 1914). His clubs are the Century, University, American Physiological Society, Society for Experimental Biology and Medicine (president, 1914–15), and the Harvey Society, of which he was the founder and first president. He was married in New York city, Dec. 20, 1899, to Mary W., daughter of Louis C. Tiffany, and had three children: William Thompson, Louise, and Louis Tiffany Lusk.

BALDWIN, William Delavan, president of Otis Elevator Co., was born at Auburn, Cayuga co., N. Y., Sept. 5, 1856, son of Lovewell Hurd and Sarah Jane (Munson) Baldwin. After a public school education he entered the employ of D. M. Osborne & Co., manufacturers of harvesting machines, of Auburn. His rise was rapid. Six years later he was sent to Europe as manager of the European branch of the firm. Resigning in 1882, he became a stockholder and treasurer of the firm of Otis Bros. & Co., manufacturers of elevators whose business now entered upon an era of prosperity and developed rapidly. In 1898 it was reorganized as the Otis Elevator Co., with Mr. Baldwin as its president. The history of the Otis elevator dates back to 1853, when Elisha Graves Otis began building hand-power elevators in a small shop at Yonkers, N. Y., this being the nucleus of the Otis Elevator Co. Later Mr. Otis built steam elevators and then hydraulic elevators, and at the World's Fair Crystal Palace exhibition in New York city showed the first safety device to be applied to elevators. This marked the beginning of elevators as passenger carriers, and since that time the safety appliances have been much improved in order to meet the increasing demand for passenger elevators in our present lofty buildings. In the early nineties, when electricity was fast becoming generally used as the source of power, the electric elevator was developed. The first successful installation of an electric elevator was in the Demarest Building, 335 Fifth avenue, New York city, and it is still in operation. The increasing height of buildings and the speed at which it was necessary for the machines to run compelled the construction of a different type of elevators, and the ingenuity of the experts of the company brought forth the traction elevator, which has enabled builders to erect the towering office buildings of today throughout the country, and at the same time to meet the problem of rapid transportation from the street to the topmost floor. Besides elevators of all types, the Otis Elevator Co. manufactures escalators, which are used in department stores, factories, theaters, railway stations and elevated and subway roads. The Otis Elevator Co. maintains nearly 100 offices throughout the principal countries of the world; in the United States there are fifty-two offices, and Canada, Mexico and South America are well represented. London, England, is headquarters for foreign business, and in all the principal cities of the world may be found branch offices or agents of the company. The largest factory of the company, where the majority of the electric elevators are constructed, is at Yonkers, N. Y., 2,500 persons being employed there in various capacities. There are also factories in Quincy, Ill.; Harrison, N. J.; Buffalo, N. Y., and in France, Germany and Russia. Mr. Baldwin is a director in the Home Insurance Co., National Surety Co., Lincoln Trust Co., Hale & Kilburn Co., Poole Engineering & Machine Co., What Cheer & Hope Mutual Fire Insurance companies, U. S. Life Insurance Co., and a member of the advisory board, United States branch, Employers' Liability Assurance Corporation, Ltd., of London. He is a member of the New York Geographic Society, and the Union League, Lawyers', Engineers, Racquet and Tennis, Calumet, Fulton, New York Athletic, St. Andrews Golf, National Arts and Adirondack League clubs. He was married, Oct. 19, 1881, to Helen Runyon, daughter of Nahum Sullivan, of Montclair, N. J., and has five children: Martin Sullivan, Delavan Munson, Louise, Runyon Sexton and Roland Dennis Baldwin. Portrait opposite p. 88.

PARDEE, Dwight Whitfield, jurist, was born at Bristol, Conn., Feb. 11, 1822, son of Jard Whitfield and Ruth Norton (Upson) Pardee, of Huguenot descent. His first American ancestor was George Pardee, who came when a mere lad to New Haven with the Englishmen who settled that colony. George Pardee married Martha Niles, and the line of descent is traced through their son George and his (second) wife, Mary Denison; their son George and his wife, Sarah Bradley; their son Isaac and his wife, Sarah Leavitt, to their son Leavitt and his wife, Elizabeth Hemingway, who were the grandparents of Judge Pardee. He was graduated at Trinity College in 1840, and studied law at Yale Law School. Trinity College afterward conferred upon him the degree of LL.D. He likewise studied law under the proceptorship of Gov. Toucey, of Connecticut, and began the practice of his profession in Hartford. In 1858 he was the democratic senator from the first district, and was re-elected in 1859. In 1863 he was made a superior court judge and held the position until 1874, when he was advanced to the supreme court bench, continuing there until 1889. He was an influential churchman, and for years had been senior warden of St. John's Protestant Episcopal Church, Hartford, and was most heartily identified with the work and interests of that parish. He was a generous giver towards its charities and was openhanded in alleviating necessity and want. He was a just man, and his decisions on the bench marked him as a singularly clear-headed and impartial thinker. His written opinions, alike for their clarity and their choice literary quality, are among the best on the Connecticut records. His language was quaint and incisive. He possessed great capacity to deal with new questions and combinations of interests. He was a charming and delightful conversationalist on a wide range of subjects and was known and loved for his personal virtues by many to whom his death brought a deep sense of loss. He was married at Hartford, Conn., June 23, 1847, to Henrietta, daughter of Solomon Porter. He died at Hartford, Conn., Oct. 6, 1893.

KENYON, William Squire, jurist and statesman, was born at Elyria, O., June 10, 1869, son of Fergus L. and Hattie A. (Squire) Kenyon. His father, a native of Scotland, was a Congregationalist minister of St. Joseph, Mo., and Iowa City, Ia. Obliged to support himself, the son secured a position in a fence factory, and subsequently taught school. He spent two years at Iowa College, Grinnell, and was graduated at the College of Law of the Iowa State University in 1890 with honors. In that year he was admitted to the bar of Iowa and began the practice of his profession at Fort Dodge. During 1892–96 he was prosecuting attorney of Webster county, with a record of a conviction in every trial. In 1900 he became district judge for the eleventh judicial district, resigning in 1902 because of the small salary. He might have attained the supreme court bench, so excellent was his judicial record, but instead he formed a legal partnership with his father-in-law, John F. Duncombe, in 1904, and upon the latter's death succeeded to the position formerly held by him as local attorney for the Illinois Central Railroad Co. In 1907 he was promoted general counsel of that road, and in 1910 he was appointed assistant to U. S. Attorney-General Wickersham. He instituted the proceedings against the beef trust in Chicago in 1912, and took charge of the examination for the government. He also investigated the harvester trust, supported the action for the Pujo money trust investigation, and sought to dissolve the grocery and the butter and egg trusts. The Sherman Act became a serious affair in his hands and something to be feared by monopolists. In 1911 he was induced to stand for election to serve out the unexpired term of Sen. Jonathan P. Dolliver, and, after a memorable deadlock, was elected on the 67th ballot. He was one of the youngest members of the U. S. senate ever elected, and at once became a dominant factor in the work of that body. In his trust prosecutions he had expressed himself strongly, and advocated a more strict regulation of monopolies. He favors direct elections, tariff revisions downward, an income tax, and a federal corporation tax. He voted against wasteful expenditures in appropriations for federal buildings in minor towns, but sup-

ported the increase in soldiers' pensions. He signed the minority report of the committee on privileges and elections, declaring that Sen. Isaac Stephenson's seat should be vacated, and he opposed Sen. Lorimer in his fight for the retention of his seat. He advocated the passage of a bill providing interstate regulation of liquor traffic, and introduced a measure to prohibit the use of a patent in creating a monopoly, and cancelling the patent whenever it was demonstrated that it was being used for the formation or perpetuation of a combination. The Kenyon bill for amendment of the Sherman anti-trust law favors jail sentences for trust offenders, in order to curb the trusts, and he would "make guilt personal." The Kenyon freight bill passed the senate Aug. 16, 1912. In 1913 he was elected to the senate for the regular term of six years. His religious affiliation is with the Congregationalist church. He was married at Fort Dodge, Ia., May 11, 1893, to Mary, daughter of John F. Dunscombe.

BAILEY, Dudley Perkins, lawyer and author, was born at Cornville, Me., Oct. 24, 1843, son of Dudley Perkins and Hannah Barrows (Cushman) Bailey. His first paternal American ancestor is supposed to have been John Bailey who settled at Salisbury, Mass., in 1635. On the paternal side he was descended from John Alden and Priscilla Mullens. He was educated in the district school and at the Monson, Me., Academy. After teaching school two years he entered Waterville College (now Colby) but left at the end of his junior year; subsequently (in 1877) he received his degree in course as of the class of '67. In 1868 he received the prize offered by the American Free Trade League to undergraduates in American colleges for the best essay on free trade. After leaving college he studied law and was admitted to the bar in 1870. He practised first at Freeport, Me., and in 1872 removed to Everett, Mass., which became his permanent home. He was a member of the school committee; was one of the founders and a trustee of the public library; member of the common council 1893–94 and alderman in 1895. He represented his town for two terms (1886–87) in the Massachusetts legislature and became the second president of the common council. In his profession he enjoyed a large general practice, making a specialty of probate and real estate cases. He was a contributor for fifteen years to the Bankers Magazine and other periodicals, largely along financial lines, and was author of "The Clearing House System"; "History of Banking in Massachusetts"; "The Credit Institutions of Italy"; and "Austrian Paper Money in the Panic of 1873." He also prepared the historical sketches of the town of Everett in Brakes "History of Middlesex County" (1878), besides contributing the chapters relating to clearing houses in Boles "Practical Banking" and the historical sketch on the Boston Clearing House in "The Professional and Industrial History of Suffolk County." He is a director of the Massachusetts Baptist Missionary Society, a member of its finance committee since 1890 and is a trustee of the Newton Theological Institution and Colby College. He is a member of the American Statistical Association; Baptist Social Union; Appalachian Mountain Club; Middlesex Club; Palestine Lodge, F. and A. M.; Beauseant Commandery; Royal Arch Chapter of the Tabernacle of Malder, and the Pine Tree State Club of Everett, of which he was the first president. He was married Mar. 2, 1901, in Geneva, Switzerland, to Mrs. Adelaide P. Potter, daughter of Levi Pierce, of Everett, Mass. Portrait opposite page 91.

DUDLEY P. BAILEY
LAWYER

JANE OSBORN HANNAH
SINGER

AUGUSTIN GATTINGER
PHYSICIAN AND BOTANIST

EDGAR HOLDEN
PHYSICIAN

HANNAH, Jane Osborn, singer, was born at Wilmington, O., July 8, 1876, daughter of Parker Barnard and Rebecca Ann (Randolph) Osborn, and a descendant of Charles Osborn, an orthodox Quaker minister. Early in life she displayed unusual vocal powers, and after a public and high school education in Wilmington she studied music at Chicago under Signor Vittorio Carpi, and three years later became the pupil of Johanna Hess-Burr. She made her debut in Chicago, May 10, 1895, at nineteen years of age, and from that time onward she had a brilliant career as a concert and oratorio singer. While in Chicago she also sang in the choir of St. Paul's Episcopal Church for five years. On Nov. 25, 1907, she was married to Frank Hannah, U. S. Consul at Strassburg, Germany, and also a musician of note. In 1898 Mme. Hannah went abroad to study for grand opera under Mme. Marchesi, Sbriglia, Mme. Rosa Sucher, and others. Her first appearance in grand opera was under the direction of Arthur Nikisch as the leading soprano in the Grand Opera at Leipzig, Germany, an engagement that lasted three years, during which she firmly established her reputation as a soprano of the first rank, appearing in such roles as Santa, Sieglinde, Elsa, Elizabeth, Eva, Donna Anna, Grafin, Madama Butterfly, Mimi, Aida and Desdemona. Her greatest successes were made in the Wagnerian roles, although as Madama Butterfly, a part she created in Leipzig, she won a phenomenal success, being considered one of the best singers of that difficult role in Germany. She was engaged to sing Wagner roles at Covent Garden, London, in the spring of 1906, and sang four times before the king and queen. She also sang "Senta" in Berlin for the emperor and empress of Germany, who personally congratulated her on her splendid voice. She appeared in most of the leading operas in Germany, including Dresden, Hanover, and Munich, and upon leaving Leipzig, she was given such a farewell as had not been surpassed at that theatre in thirty years. After the performance, which was Madama Butterfly, the enthusiastic crowds took the horses from her carriage and dragged it home. She received many flattering offers to remain in Germany, but was anxious to return to her native land. She was engaged to sing at the Metropolitan opera house in New York city in 1909, 1910 and 1911, and in 1912 and 1913 she was a member of the Chicago grand opera company, in both cities, greatly adding to her reputation as a singer of international fame.

GATTINGER, Augustin, physician and botanist, was born in Munich, Bavaria, Feb. 3, 1825, son of August Gattinger, an official of the German government. His preliminary education was obtained in a Latin school and gymnasium of Munich. He entered the University of Munich at a period which proved most disastrous to the German patriots. For a too conspicuous participation in a student celebration of Gen. George Washington's birthday in 1849, the university requested his withdrawal, and the German government allotted him seven days to abdicate the country. He had, however, already completed his course in medicine, and had made great progress in medicinal botany, having had as associate, friend and student companion Ferdinand Arnold, one of Germany's greatest botanists. He sailed from Havre Apr. 24, 1849, and after traversing the South by stage and steamboat finally settled at Cave Spring, Tenn., where he began the practise of medicine, giving his spare time to the study of botany and geology. He removed to Charleston, Tenn., where he continued his practise until 1858, when he accepted a position as resident surgeon at the copper mines at Ducktown, Tenn., a mountainous region possessing a diversity and complication of structure ideal for the pursuit of botanical and geographical work. There he spent six years, 1858-1864, in the saddle traversing the mountains of Tennessee, Georgia and North Carolina. Among unfamiliar modes of life, without access to modern books, and with no information regarding the advance of science, his progress was naturally tedious. In 1864 his advocacy of the Federal cause necessitated his withdrawal from that community, and at Nashville he passed the medical examination and enlisted as an assistant surgeon in the Federal army. After the civil war, he settled in Nashville, and became state librarian in which office he found his long sought opportunity of improving his acquaintance with modern scientific literature. He likewise maintained a correspondence with all prominent American botanists, and his collections, always ably prepared, were much in demand for exchange. He collected the second largest herbarium in the South, it being finally secured by the University of Tennessee in Knoxville. He became prominently identified with the American Association for the Advancement of Science, and as a result of a meeting held by that body in Nashville, he published "Tennessee Flora," a systematic enumeration of 1,708 species, printed at personal expense and gratuitously distributed to the schools of the state. In 1878, he assisted the Commissioner of Agriculture of his state to publish a work on the grasses and forage plants of Tennessee, and in the same year prepared a publication on the trees and shrubs suitable to the local soil and climate. In 1880, he collected for the botanical division of the census specimens of the timbers of the state, and for the mineral division of the census the stones of Tennessee. In 1883, he became an assistant in special work in the office of the Commissioner of Agriculture, collecting minerals and plants for various state and national exhibitions, and in 1894 prepared a publication on the medical plants of the state. He presented his vast botanical library to the University of the South, before his death. The work of half a century of botannical research is concentrated in his last book, "The Flora of Tennessee and a Philosophy of Botany," (1901) he left unfinished a treatise on "Parks and Gardens." He was married in Havre, France, Apr. 24, 1849, to Josephine, daughter of Nicholas Drury and he died in Nashville, Tenn., July 18, 1903, survived by three daughters, Minnie, Penelope, and Augusta Gattinger.

HOLDEN, Edgar, physician, was born at Hingham, Mass., Nov. 3, 1838, son of Asa Hall Holden and Ann Louise (Seymour) Holden. His first American ancestor was Justinian Holden, who was born in England in 1611 and came to Cambridge, Mass., on the ship "Elizabeth" in 1634. His second wife was Mary Rutter and the line of descent appears through their son John and his wife Grace Jennison; their son Peter and his wife Abigail Jones and their son John and his wife Zipporah Hall, grandparents of Edgar Holden. John Holden was one of the original members of the Order of Cincinnati, and his son, Asa H., the father of Edgar, was a manufacturer. Dr. Holden attended the local schools and received his preparatory education at Hingham Academy and at James Hunting's boarding school in Jamaica, L. I. In 1855 he became an assistant teacher in Rev. J. F. Pingry's boarding schools. He was ambitious and industrious and used his spare time to such good account that he was able to enter Princeton College in the sophomore class and was graduated in 1859. That college conferred upon him the degree of A.M. in 1862 and of Ph.D. in 1872. After leaving Princeton, he entered the College of Physicians and Surgeons in New York and was graduated in 1861. The fury of the civil war had begun to rage and wounds, mutilations, and death were summoning all followers of Aesculapius to service. After some service in Kings County Hospital, he passed the Naval examinations and shortly after graduation was commissioned a surgeon in the United States Navy by Pres. Lincoln. He served in this capacity four years, first on the Frigate Minnesota at the battle of Merrimac; then on the Monitor in Hampton Roads; then on the Monitor Passaic in the attack on Fort McAllister and the attack on Charleston. He also served on the Sassacus on blockade duty and at the battle with the Albemarle. He was on shore duty at the Siege of Petersburg. In 1864 he was medical director of the James River Squadron, but was compelled to resign on account of illness. After recovering he was commissioned surgeon in 1865 in the U. S. army and in the U. S. Ward Hospital, his last detail being at the U. S. Ward Hospital in Newark, N. J. Upon leaving the service, he settled in Newark, N. J., and soon became the leading practitioner in that city. About 1867, he was chosen as the medical director of the Mutual Benefit Life Insurance Company, and served as president of its medical board for forty years until his death. Dr. Holden was a man of great culture and refinement and one who had supplemented a broad and liberal education by constant reading and study not only in matters connected with his profession, but also in the whole realm of history and literature. He had a talent for painting and sculpture and his few hours of recreation were largely devoted to work in those arts. As president of the medical board of the Mutual Benefit Life Insurance Company for forty years, he proved himself not only a highly cultured and trained man in the learned profession he adorned, but also an executive of marked and successful administrative ability. Although possessing the poise and dignity of true genius and ability, Dr. Holden always manifested such a sincere affection for those about him and such a personal interest in their welfare and his life was so filled with good works and deeds that he enjoyed the full confidence of every one and was always held in affectionate regard by his friends and business associates and by the community generally in which he lived the greater part of an honorable life. He was a member of the American Medical Association, the American Laryngological Association (Pres.), the American Association of Medical Directors (Pres.), the New Jersey State Medical Society from the Essex Medical District, of the Military Society of the Loyal Legion of the United States and through his grandfather of the Order of the Cincinnati. He was twice married, first in 1861 to Catherine, daughter of Jotham Hedden of East Orange, N. J., and second April 3, 1873, to Helen Stewart, daughter of John Burgess of Orange, N. J. Dr. Holden died at Newark, N. J., July, 1909, survived by his widow, Helen Stewart Holden, and

two sons, Dr. Edgar Holden, Jr., and John Holden, and three daughters, Isabella B. Lowenthal, Elizabeth W. Burnett, and Anna Louise Hunter.

JELLY, George Frederick, physician, was born at Salem, Mass., Jan. 22, 1842, son of William and Sarah (Tay) Jelly. His father was a native of Scotland and came to America when a child, in 1795, settling in Salem, Mass. He was educated in the public schools of Salem and at Brown University, being graduated at the latter in 1864, receiving the degree of A.M. four years later and that of D.Sc. in 1907. Having determined to follow the medical profession he entered the Harvard Medical School, and was graduated M.D. in 1868. After serving as house officer in the Boston City Hospital for a year, he began the practice of his profession in Springfield, Mass. He was appointed assistant physician in the McLean Hospital in 1869, and one year later was made superintendent, a position he held for nine years, when he removed to Boston, Mass. After leaving the Harvard Medical School, he made the subject of insanity a special study, and on removing to Boston, in 1879, began the practice of his specialty of mental diseases. He was appointed examiner for the insane for the city of Boston, a position he continued to fill with much credit for a period of over thirty years. When the state board of insanity was organized in 1898, he was made its first chairman, and was a diligent worker in the cause of the insane, state care of the insane, better methods of hospital organization, more liberal lunacy laws and psychopathic hospitals. Dr. Jelly acted as insanity expert in numerous notable cases, including that of Mrs. Mary Baker Eddy, the head of the Christian Science Church, in 1907, when he gave his opinion after full examination that Mrs. Eddy was competent to manage her own affairs; and that of John W. Hutchinson, the "Bard of High Rock," who was petitioned into court by relatives, on the ground that he was incompetent to care for his own property. In all probability he examined more noted persons and acted in more insanity cases in an official way than any man in Massachusetts. The medical societies throughout the country sought him as a speaker, and his papers on the subject of mental pathology were notable throughout the medical profession. Dr. Jelly's intellectual qualities were of a high order, and his nobility of character was only equalled by his generosity and tenderness of heart. He was a member of the board of consultation of the Massachusetts General Hospital, consulting physician of the New England Hospital for Women, and examining physician of the registration department of the city of Boston. He belonged to a number of societies, among them the American Medical Association, the American Medico-Psychological Association, the New England Society of Psychiatry, the Boston Society of Psychiatry and Neurology, the Suffolk District Medical Society, the Boston Medical Library Association, the American Association for the Advancement of Science, and the Boston Society of Natural History. Dr. Jelly was twice married; first, July 9, 1873, to Ellen A., daughter of Lorenzo Parker of Bath, Me., and after her death in 1894, he was married to Ann Mary, daughter of Lorenzo and Rachael Parker of Bath, Me. He died at Wakefield, Mass., Oct. 24, 1911.

CLARKE, Dumont, banker, was born at Newport, R. I., Oct. 1, 1840, son of Peleg and Caroline (Moore) Clarke. His first American ancestor was

George F. Kelly

Jeremiah Clarke (q. v.) of Aquidneck, R. I., one of the early governors of Rhode Island colony, whose wife was Frances Latham. From them the line of descent is traced through their son Jeremiah Clarke, who married Ann Audley; their son Samuel, who married Hannah Wilcox; their son Audley, who married Sarah Weeden; their son Peleg, who married Mary Gardner; and their son Audley, who married Mary Gardner, and was the grandfather of Dumont Clarke. Dumont Clarke's ancestors were bankers for six generations. His grandfather was founder of the National Bank of Rhode Island. After a private school education, Dumont Clarke removed to New York city, and at an early age obtained a position in the employ of the American Exchange National Bank. He was intelligent, alert, and dutiful, and quickly mastered all the details of the various departments in the institution with which he was intimately associated during the balance of his life. He became cashier of the bank in 1878, vice-president in 1887, and president in 1894, holding the latter position until his death. Under his administration, the American Exchange National Bank developed into one of the largest financial institutions of the city. Mr. Clarke occupied a prominent place in the financial affairs of the metropolis. He sat in all the important councils affecting the policy and conduct of the city's banks; he was president of the Clearing House Association for two years, and enjoyed in a marked degree the confidence and personal esteem of his associates. In the American Bankers' Association, his influence was always potent for sound banking principles, and he had much to do with shaping the official utterances of that body. He was an adviser of many of New York's kings of finance, including J. Pierpont Morgan. His financial interests were diversified. He had an intimate acquaintance with the railroad development in the country, serving as a director of the Delaware & Hudson road, the Long Island railroad, the Norfolk & Southern road and other lines; and his insurance interests led to important official service to the Home Life Insurance Co., the Fidelity and Casualty Co., the Washington Life, and the Lawyers Title Insurance Co. He was one of the prime movers in the reorganization of the Mutual Life Insurance Co., serving as a director until his death. He was also a director or trustee of the United States Mortgage and Trust Co., the United States Safe Deposit Co., Adams Express, Algoma Central and Hudson Bay Railroad, the American Beet Sugar, American Felt, the Audit Co., of New York, Caledonian Insurance Co. of Edinburgh, Commercial Cable Co., Commercial Cable Co. of Cuba, Federal Sugar Refining Co., Lake Superior Corporation, Little Falls & Dolgeville Railway Co., Long Island Consolidated Electrical Companies, the Mackay Companies, Mutual Life Insurance Co. of New York, the New York, Brooklyn, and Manhattan Beach Railroad, the New York Clearing House Building Co., the Orange National Bank, Press Publishing Co., Swift & Co., Vacuum Cleaner Co., and others. A financier of the old school, Mr. Clarke possessed a character the soul of honor, whose integrity was above reproach, and whose manner was modest, gentle, and lovable in all circumstances and under all conditions. At the time of his death, the New York "World" said: "Mr. Clarke was a successful banker who knew how to smile, and who never lost his gift of friendship, a far-sighted financier, who always had time to be courteous and patient and helpful. His was the spirit of the old-fashioned family physician applied to modern finance. Wall Street would be infinitely better, if it had more Dumont Clarkes." He was married May 20, 1869, to Cornelia P., daughter of Com. Frank Ellery of the U. S. navy, and had six children: Lewis L., Stanley, Dumont, Mary, Alice, and Corinne. His eldest son, Lewis L. Clarke, was vice-president of the American Exchange National Bank, and upon succeeding his father in the president's chair, became one of the youngest bank presidents in New York city. Mr. Clarke died at his home at Dumont, N. J., Dec. 26, 1909.

GRANT, Frederick Dent, soldier and U. S. minister, was born in St. Louis, Mo., May 30, 1850, son of Ulysses S. and Julia (Dent) Grant. His father was the eighteenth president of the United States. The early days of our subject were passed in the military posts of Fort Wayne, Mich., Sackett's Harbor, N. Y., and near Jefferson Barracks, Mo., where his father was stationed. After the latter's resignation from the army, the family lived in St. Louis, Mo., and Galena, Ill., and young Grant attended the common schools of the latter town until the outbreak of the civil war. He accompanied the 21st Ill. volunteer infantry, of which his father was colonel, in its march across that state to relieve the troops in northwestern Missouri, then threatened by a Confederate force under Benjamin Harris. When the regiment reached Quincy, Col. Grant sent the boy home, but he rejoined his father at Cairo, after the battle of Belmont and stayed with him until the campaign of Forts Henry and Donelson. At the commencement of the march to Fort Donelson, he was sent to school at Covington, where he remained until the fall of Corinth. In the spring of 1863, he rejoined Gen. Grant at Young's Point, La., and accompanied him in the Vicksburg campaign, where he was for the first time under fire. He was on the same boat with his father during the naval battle of Grand Gulf. In the battle of Port Gibson, he was in action with Powell's battery, being slightly wounded, and later accompanied the 7th Ill. in the advance that drove the enemy from the field. Subsequently he took part in the skirmishes of the Suspension Bridge, Bayou Pierre, and Grindstone Fork, and the battle of Raymond. He was with Tuttle's division in the assault on Jackson and was led by curiosity to enter the city in advance of the Federal troops and before the Confederate force had evacuated the place. In later years, he was accustomed to refer humorously to what he called his single-handed capture of Jackson. After the surrender of the Mississippi capital, he remained with his father until the battle of Champion's Hill and subsequently took part in the charge of Lawler's brigade at Black River bridge, where he was wounded in the leg. He was with his father during the siege of Vicksburg, and after the evacuation of the city was sent North on account of illness. During the whole Vicksburg campaign, he had served unofficially on his father's staff and his conduct, in view of his extreme youth, was remarkably cool and courageous. On recovering from his illness, he joined his father at Nashville, Tenn., and accompanied him to Washington, when the elder Grant was commissioned lieutenant-general by Lincoln. His health would not permit him to take part in the Wilderness campaign, so he attended school at Burlington, N. J., until 1866, when he was appointed at-large to the West Point Military Academy. Upon being graduated in 1871, he waived the usual privilege accorded to graduates of naming the regiments they prefer lest the granting of his request might be attributed to influence. But he was one ot the most expert horsemen that ever attended West Point, and for that reason he was appointed to the cavalry and assigned to the Fourth regiment. After his graduation, he obtained leave of absence and accepted a position as civil engineer on the Union Pacific Railway, in which capacity he assisted in various surveys across the continent and in the construction of part of the Colorado Central road in Clear Creek canon. In the fall of 1871, he went to Europe as aide-de-camp to Gen. Sherman, and on his return, joined his regiment in Texas. During the winter of 1872 and 1873, he commanded the escort of the surveying parties on the Texas Pacific road across the Llano Estacado. In March, 1873, he was appointed to the staff of Gen. Phil Sheridan, with the rank of lieutenant-colonel, and in the same year was with Gen. Stanley on the Yellowstone expedition. In the following year, he was with Custer on the Black Hills expedition. Obtaining a leave of absence in 1877, he accompanied his father on his memorable trip around the world, and after his return, served in the Bannock Indian War of 1878, and on the various expeditions, on one of which he followed Victoria's Apache band for 500 miles into New Mexico. In 1881 he resigned his commission and started in business in New York. During the last days of the life of Gen. U. S. Grant, his son, Fred, was his constant companion and aided in the compilation and preparation of his autobiography. After his father's death, he re-entered business and became identified with a number of important financial interests. In 1888 he was appointed by Pres. Harrison, minister to Austria, where his success in securing the admission of American products and in protecting American citizens from military duty won for him the highest commendation, and on Cleveland's election to the presidency, he was informed that, unless he insisted, his resignation would not be accepted. He did insist, however, and returned to the United States in 1893. In the following year, he became one of the police commissioners of New York under Mayor Strong's reform administration. When the war with Spain began, he became colonel of the 14th N. Y. volunteers, and on May 27, 1898, was appointed brigadier-general of the United States volunteers. He was honorably discharged on April 15, 1899, and on the same day was reappointed brigadier-general of volunteers. During the war, he served for a year in Puerto Rico and after the war, he commanded the military district of San Juan. He commanded the 2nd brigade, 1st division, 8th army corps in the Philippine Islands from April to November, 1899. He commanded the troops that fought the battles of Big Ben and Binancian. In 1899 he was transferred to the 2nd brigade, 2nd division for the advance into Northern Luzon and covered the flanks and rear of MacArthur's division. Later he was detached to invade the provinces of Batan and Zambilles, which he accomplished after a number of heavy skirmishes. In June, 1900, he was assigned to the command of the 5th district, Northern Luzon, and for the following year was engaged in the severe guerilla warfare, which included the battles of Balahad and Ipo and a number of more or less serious skirmishes. On Feb. 18, 1901, he was commissioned a brigadier-general in the reg-

ular army. He was transferred to the command of the 4th separate brigade, Samar and Leyte, in October, 1901, and received the surrender of the last of the insurgents. He was responsible for the subsequent establishment of civil government in those provinces and in this connection showed the diplomacy and constructive states-manship of the highest order and which called for the warm commendation of many of the most prominent men of affairs in the United States. He commanded the department of Texas, 1902-4; the department of the Lakes, in which he had served under Sheridan, July to September, 1904; the department of the East, 1904-8, being promoted to the rank of major-general in February, 1906; the department of the Lakes again, 1908-10; the department of the East, July 25, 1910, to July 1, 1911; and the eastern division, which embraces the department of the East and the department of the Gulf from its establishment on July 1, 1911, until his death. It was inevitable that Gen Grant's career should fall under the shadow of his father's reputation. The elder Grant was one of the big figures of this country's history, ranking with the greatest military leaders of all time. That his son should be subjected to the handicap of a constant comparison is natural enough, and that he stood the comparison so well is perhaps the best compliment that could be paid him. But the comparison was, of course, unfair, for even allowing that Frederick Dent Grant possessed his father's genius, he was never confronted with the same big trial and the same big opportunity. Indian fighting and a war, whose result was a foregone conclusion from the beginning, were the extent of his opportunities, and he acquitted himself as brilliantly as the limitations of those opportunities allowed. It required a big test to bring out the great qualities of his father, a similar test was never applied to the son. That under such a test he would have shown equal powers is quite probable. He was a born soldier, with an innate capacity for leadership and a rare faculty of inspiring confidence and affection in his men. His resemblance to his father was so striking in all other respects, both in character and physique, as to intrude itself inevitably on every description of him. A prominent New York business man said of him several years before his death, "What seems to me the best trait in the man is his honest courage and persistency in facing any kind of circumstances without allowing himself to be disheartened. I have known him over twenty years, and the more I see of him, the better I like him." He was married in Chicago, Ill., Oct. 20, 1874, to Ida M., daughter of Henry Hamilton Honore (q. v.), and had two children: Julia, who married Prince Cantacuzene, of Russia, and Ulysses S. Grant, 3rd, who is a captain in the Corps of Engineers of the U. S. army. Gen. Grant died in New York city, April 12, 1912.

WHITNEY, Andrew, musician and capitalist, was born at Ashby, Mass., Feb. 28, 1826, son of Jonas Prescott and Rebecca (Piper) Whitney. His first American ancestor was John Whitney, who emigrated to America in June, 1635, and settled at Watertown, Mass., and the line of descent is traced through his son, John, who married Ruth Reynolds, their son, Benjamin, who married Abigail Hagar; their son, Ensign David Whitney, who married Rebecca Filebrown; their son, Josiah, who married Sarah Lawrence; and their son Josiah, who married Mary Barrett, and was the grandfather of the subject of this sketch. Whit-

ney's mother was a daughter of Jonathan Piper, of Ashby, and her reputation, as a belle lingers in the memory of her contemporaries, especially as she was the possessor of auburn hair of unusual beauty, a characteristic of her family which was also her legacy to several of her nine children, including Andrew. From his earliest youth, Andrew Wheeler's surroundings led to the development of his unusual and partly inherited musical talent. His father, originally a carpenter, became a manufacturer of organs and a boyhood playmate was his cousin, Myron Whitney (q. v.), the singer and musician. In his boyhood, he obtained the position of janitor of the family church so that on Sundays, he might pump the organ. At the age of fifteen, he was making violins to convert them into spending money, and at eighteen, he built without assistance an organ. It was at this time that his father's organ factory was moved from Ashby to Springfield, Mass., where Andrew became the organist of two churches, and where the Whitney piano-style organs were first introduced. In Springfield, and afterward in Fitchburg, where the organ business was finally removed, he was the leading musician and instructor of the day. He became a partner in his father's business, which thereafter was under the name of J. Whitney & Son. After it was absorbed by the famous organ house of Jacob Estey, Mr. Whitney was enabled to devote more time to his musical career. His singing schools in Ashby and Fitchburg were locally famous, and he had attained more than a local celebrity for his compositions. Among the numbers of the day that had won a considerable reputation were the "Pathfinder's Quickstep," "Gov. Robinson's Polka," and the "Fitchburg Polka." He opened a music store in Fitchburg and built the Whitney Opera House, the initial attempt at a modern theatre, and that there might be no doubt about the service to his townsfolk, Mr. Whitney, during the first three years, managed the house personally. But a man of his ability and indomitable energy was not content to rest merely upon his musical laurels and talents, and by degrees he became the foremost real estate and building operator in the community, his faculty for giving personal supervision over all of his building enterprises being mainly responsible for the fortune that ensued from this line of endeavor. He bought land everywhere in and about Fitchburg and Springfield and built the first steel structure in Springfield, the Auditorium, now Poli's theatre, and the Produce Exchange. He was connected with various banking institutions and railroads, and mainly financed the construction of the Fitchburg and Ashby street railway, of which he was president. His inflexible principle, his mastery of business ethics, his richly endowed character and his venerable and kindly aspect made him greatly esteemed among men, and the works he left behind him combine a practical knowledge and artistic sensibility in keeping with his developed ideas and fortune. In building construction, he never permitted a problem to conquer him and very often his original ideas at first baffled his architects. He adopted for his own the ancient but homely motto, "If at first you don't succeed, try, try again," and his life recorded no failures. He was twice married, first on July 3, 1872, to Didama, daughter of William Hudson, who was the mother of three surviving children, George Andrew, Alice Ethel, and Edith Irene Whitney (Mrs. Gardner Bassett), and second on July 29, 1899, to Jennie, daughter of Thomas Moriarty. Mr. Whitney died at Fitchburg, Mass., May 23, 1912.

KISSEL, Gustav Edward, banker, was born in New York city, Sept. 30, 1854, son of Gustav Hermann and Charlotte A. (Stimson) Kissel. The family was prominent for generations in Heidelberg and Frankfurt a/Main. An uncle of Mr. Kissel's grandmother was a Burgermeister of Frankfurt and one of his cousins held the same position. On his mother's side Mr. Kissel was descended from New England stock and was related to Prof. Frederick Jesup Stimson of Harvard University, Mrs. Frank Bowditch and other prominent New Englanders. His uncle, Benjamin Stimson, was the "S" mentioned in Dana's "Two Years Before the Mast." Gustav Edward Kissel was educated at Prof. Elie Charlier's school, then the leading boys' school in New York city, and subsequently studied in Frankfurt, Germany, and Lausanne, Switzerland. On finishing his studies he entered the office of the late Morris K. Jesup and afterward joined his father in the conduct of the New York branch of Kessler & Co., an old Frankfurt and Manchester drygoods firm, which had been founded by his father in 1837. In 1878, his health broke down and he retired from business for several years, during which he traveled in Europe and studied at the University of Heidelberg. Returning to the United States he entered the service of the Fourth National Bank, and later a private bank in New York. In 1882 he wound up the drygoods business of Kessler & Co. and changed it to that of foreign bankers. Mr. Kissel possessed unusual ability as a banker and under his management the new firm met with striking and rapid success. After another period of retirement because of poor health, he organized with his nephew, G. Herman Kinnicut, the firm of Kissel, Kinnicutt & Co., of which he was a member until his death. He was also a director and a member of the executive committee of the United States Mortgage & Trust Co., and a director of the Morristown Trust Co., Mr. Kissel's business achievements were all the more remarkable in view of the fact that his health made it necessary for him to spend so many years away from his office and that he was never sufficiently robust to devote his full energy to business. Although eminently successful in spite of severe handicaps, business was only a secondary consideration with him. Personally Mr. Kissel was the highest type of the beautifully mannered, well-informed, sagacious gentleman, whose grace and culture were as natural as his courtesy and faith in mankind. Of keen intelligence and wide learning, his companionship was an education and his friendship an inspiration. "Though so well equipped with fit social accomplishments of fashionable life," wrote one of his friends after his death, "his preference was always for the recreations that plead for high companionship in the intellectual world. Books, music and this fine companionship fought in him against overabsorption against the exhaustive methods of modern affairs. I learned to think of him as of the highest class in the business world, as a man of utmost trustworthiness and I have never found reason to think of him as otherwise." He was a thoughtful reader of Plato and the philosophers, a genuine lover of high thinking and of noble mind in the world of culture. And he accumulated as far as he could, the best pictures, notably those that present human life in its merry and glad moods. He loved children also, and throughout his whole life was a thoughtful friend of the child —attentive always to its real want and its true advancement. He was long active in the affairs of the Children's Aid Society and for years presided at the Sunday evening meetings of the Newsboys' Lodging House. Having a hand in many charities, it was never a cold hand that gave out of the purse alone; he gave out of the heart, and would at any time drop a social pleasure for one that would make a pained face shine. With his sympathy for the unfortunate there was a fund of humor which discovered amusing situations in the most unexpected way. George William Curtis, Joseph H. Choate, J. Herbert Morse and other men of the same calibre were among his closest friends and interest in every literary and aesthetic movement of his time was of the keenest. It was through his influence as a member of the American Geographical Society that Mrs. Peary was enabled to obtain sufficient money to bring back her husband from one of his arctic trips. Mr. Kissel was a trustee of the American Museum of Natural History, the Institution for the Blind, and the Children's Aid Society, and was a member of the Union, Century, Knickerbocker, Racquet and Tennis, New York Yacht, Down Town, and City clubs. He was married in December, 1884, to Caroline, daughter of William K. Thorn, and granddaughter of Commodore Vanderbilt, a reigning belle of her day. They had four children: William Thorn, Dorothy, Jeannette, and Louise Kissel. He died in New York city, April 10, 1911.

HUYLER, John S., manufacturer and philanthropist, was born in New York city, June 26, 1846, son of David and Abigail Ann (Deklyn) Huyler. His father was a baker and ice-cream manufacturer, and after a public school education the son began his business career at the age of seventeen years in his father's shop. In 1876 he undertook the manufacture and sale of old-fashioned molasses candy for himself in Eighteenth street, New York, which was the unpretentious beginning of the present large candy business of "Huyler's", with its many branch stores and innumerable selling agents throughout the country. He began by making the candy himself and personally selling it over the counter, and after the business had grown to enormous proportions he continued to give his personal attention to every detail until his death. At that time it consisted of fifty-four branch stores and fourteen factories and its employes numbered 2,000. Far famed as was the name of Huyler for the excellence of his candies, his name is far more worthy of recognition for his life long habit of unostentatious charity and for the benefits he conferred on his fellow men with the fortune his business had brought him. Kind-hearted and generous to a fault, he followed the Scriptures as a rule of life by giving one-tenth of his income to the poor and needy or to some philanthropic or educational movement. For more than a score of years his benefactions exceeded his original tithes, and aggregated throughout his life probably several million dollars. He was interested in all kinds of rescue work and reform movements, and gave liberally to the Anti-Saloon League, St. Christopher's (Orphan) Home, Young Men's Christian Associations, the Jerry McAuley Water Street Mission, and the Hadley Rescue Mission of New York. He was a patron of Syracuse University, of which he was a trustee, Wesleyan University,

Drew Theological Seminary, and various special institutions of learning and reforms organized to meet peculiar needs. He was also active in the work of the Methodist church, being a member of the Calvary Methodist Episcopal Church, president of the Industrial Christian Alliance and of New York City Church Extension and Missionary Society, and through his assistance much of the outdoor work of his church was made possible. He established and maintained fresh air camps for poor mothers and children at Long Branch, N. J., and Becket, Mass. Mr. Huyler carried his love for fair dealing into his business, and many years ago established a pension system for his employes who grew old in service. In fact, his care and consideration of his employes made him beloved by every one of them, and there never was a strike among them in the history of the business. Nor was his pension list confined to his former employes, for a number of other deserving men and women no longer able to earn a living were supported from his purse. Mr. Huyler had the happy faculty of giving himself with his gift; he was not satisfied with mailing a check, but his heart-felt words accompanying it expressed his genuine sympathy and his unbounded love for his fellow man. While his business will perpetuate his name, his real work will live after him in the noble service he rendered for the uplift of humanity. He found his greatest pleasures in making happiness for others and cared nothing for the glitter and sham of society. At the time of his death he was a director of the Bank of the Metropolis, The Chestnut Ridge White Brick Co. and the New York Board of Trade and Transportation, and a member of the New York Chamber of Commerce. He was also a member of the Apawamis Golf Club of Rye, N. Y., the Knollwood Golf Club of White Plains, the American Yacht Club, the Larchmont Yacht Club, and the New York Athletic Club. Mr. Huyler was married about 1868, to Rosa Lee, daughter of Robert Lee of New York city, and had four sons, Frank De Klyn, David, Coulter and John S. Huyler, Jr., and one daughter, Abigail Huyler. He died at Rye, N. Y., Oct. 1, 1910.

GUTHRIE, William Dameron, lawyer, was born in San Francisco, Cal., Feb. 3, 1859, son of George Whitney and Emma (Gosson) Guthrie. The founder of the family came to America from Scotland about 1720, and his father was born at Bainbridge, N. Y., in 1810. Young Guthrie received much of his education abroad, having lived in France nine years and in England three. Upon his return home he attended the New York public schools, but in 1875 was compelled to support himself, and having learned stenography became a clerk in the law office of Blatchford, Seward, Griswold & Da Costa. While there as a stenographer he studied law and attended the Columbia Law School for the term 1879-80, reciting in both the junior and senior classes. He was admitted to the bar in 1880, and in 1884 became a member of the firm of Blatchford, Seward, Griswold & Da Costa. Since then he has been connected with the various law firms of Seward, Da Costa & Guthrie; Seward, Guthrie, Morawetz & Steele; Seward, Guthrie & Steele; Guthrie, Cravath & Henderson, and Guthrie, Bangs & Van Sinderen since 1909. One of his first important cases was the Bankers & Merchants Telegraph Co. vs. the Western Union Telegraph Co., in which he was associated with such legal talent as Robert G. Ingersoll and Roscoe Conkling. Mr. Guthrie has

GUSTAV E. KISSEL
BANKER

JOHN S. HUYLER
MANUFACTURER

WILLIAM D. GUTHRIE
LAWYER

SAMUEL EDWARDS
JURIST

made a specialty of constitutional law, and is recognized as one of the foremost representatives of the American bar. Among the most important cases handled by him during these years were the Income Tax cases, involving the constitutionality of the Income Tax law passed by congress in 1894, when he was associated with Sen. Edmunds, Mr. Seward and Mr. Choate against Atty.-Gen. Olney and James C. Carter before the United States Supreme Court; the Illinois Inheritance Tax cases, the California Irrigation cases, the Lottery cases, the Oleomargarine cases, and the Kansas City Stock Yards rate case, all of which he argued before the United States Supreme Court. Since 1909 he has been professor of constitutional law at Columbia University and a member of the law faculty, and in 1907 he held the Storrs lectureship at Yale. His "Lectures on the Fourteenth Amendment to the Constitution" were published by Little, Brown & Co. in 1898, and he is an authoritative writer on political and legal topics. Mr. Guthrie is a member of the Union, Metropolitan, Union League, Century, Down Town, Catholic, New York Yacht, and other clubs, the American Bar Association, the State Bar Association, the County Bar Association, and the City Bar Association. He received the honorary degree of A.M. from Yale University in 1904. He was married in New York city, May 12, 1889, to Ella E., daughter of George W. Fuller of New York, and has no children. His stepdaughter, Ella, is the wife of Eugene S. Willard of New York city. Mr. Guthrie has a large country place of 350 acres on the north shore of Long Island, where he spends most of his time.

EDWARDS, Samuel, jurist, was born at Glenville, Schenectady co., N. Y., Apr. 24, 1839, son of Samuel Baker and Ruth Louise (Rogers) Edwards, of Irish descent. He attended boarding schools in Schoharie and Washington counties and at the age of nineteen entered Union College, where he was graduated in 1862. Having determined to follow the law, he studied for two and a half years in the office of Stephen L. Magoun, at Hudson, N. Y., and was admitted to the bar in December, 1864. He conducted an office of his own in Hudson, N. Y., until 1875 when he formed a partnership with Robert E. Andrews, a prominent lawyer and able pleader, under the firm name of Andrews and Edwards. The firm became eminent and the partnership continued until Mr. Edwards was appointed by Gov. Hill to a justiceship of the supreme court for the third judicial district in place of Judge Osborn, deceased. His association with Mr. Andrews, who had conducted the largest litigated practice in Columbia county, gave Judge Edwards a grounding in the law that was of great advantage on the bench. In the following November he was elected to the same position and continued in the office until Dec. 31, 1901, a period of fifteen years. During the latter part of his term he served in the appellate division of the supreme court, being elevated to this post by Gov. Roosevelt to succeed Judge D. Cady Herrick. Judge Edwards was notable for his industry and ability, his fidelity to the interests of his clients, his studious habits, and his pure and upright life. His rectitude was unimpeachable. He was a jurist of impartial mind, thoroughly conversant of the law, and his decisions were rarely reversed. By his decisions he acquired a reputation of fairness, sound judgment, insight and knowledge of jurisprudence and the laws of the commonwealth. His opinions were rendered in lucid and logical style. As a writer he was discriminating, concise and forcible, and as a judge he exhibited the modest dignity and attainments of high character which were natural to him and won him high respect. To those who had the good fortune to be his friends he revealed his genial and kindly traits, and the powers of conversation especially in the narration of his travels made him a delightful companion. Though of a serious mind and earnest convictions, he was possessed of a keen sense of humor. Ten years before his death he practically retired and gave himself up to the enjoyment of his books, his friends, his home and foreign travel. He made several extended trips to Europe, Egypt and the Mediterranean, spending long periods in Rome, where his tastes for history and his extensive knowledge of Greek and Latin found a congenial atmosphere. His careful habits of mind and unusual memory gave him the power to quote at length and verbatim what he had read and describe with accuracy and vividness the experiences of his travels and, spiced with a ready humor, made his conversation and reminiscences delightful. Judge Edwards was a member of Hudson Lodge F. & A. M., No. 7, having been raised in 1867. He was a member of the Presbyterian Church, and acted as trustee for many years. He was married Oct. 2, 1867, to Harriet A., daughter of William H. and Katharin Mellen, of Hudson, N. Y. She died July 18, 1891, and on Feb. 1, 1898, he was married to Emma Willard, daughter of Judge Darius Peck. He died at Hudson, N. Y., Feb. 16, 1912. Portrait opposite p. 96.

BATTLE, George Gordon, lawyer, was born near Rocky Mount, Edgecombe co., N. C., Oct. 26, 1868, son of Capt. Turner Westray and Lavinia Bassett (Daniel) Battle, and a descendant of John Battle who came over from Yorkshire, England, in 1659, and settled in what is now Bath county, Va. His father, a graduate of the University of North Carolina, was admitted to the bar, but instead of practicing law, devoted himself to the management of his large plantation. He was captain of a North Carolina regiment during the civil war; his wife was the daughter of Joseph John Daniel (q. v.). The first of his family in North Carolina was Elisha Battle, who removed from Nansemond county, Va., to Edgecombe county, N. C., in 1748. He was a cotton planter, having large holdings of land, and took an active part in public affairs, representing his county in the North Carolina assembly for many years. He was a member of the state constitutional convention which adopted the Federal constitution of 1787. Wheeler, in his "History of North Carolina," says: "He was distinguished for his patriotism and piety, and was an exemplary and consistent member of the Baptist church." His wife was Elizabeth Sumner, and their son, Jacob Battle, who married Elizabeth Edwards, inherited most of his landed estate. Jacob's son, James Smith Battle, married Harriett Westray, and was the grandfather of George Gordon Battle, the subject of this sketch. Mr. Battle's early education was obtained from private tutors and at a preparatory school in Hanover county. After attending the University of North Carolina for a year and a half, he matriculated at the University of Virginia and was graduated M.A. in 1889. He had begun his law studies at the university under Prof. John B. Minor, and after graduating, continued them in the office of his brother, Judge Jacob Battle, at Rocky Mount and at the Columbia University Law School in New York city in 1890. His standing at the law school was so high and he displayed such aptitude in mastering the subtleties of the law that upon the application of District-Attorney Nicoll to Columbia University for an assistant, young Battle was recommended and was promptly appointed assistant district attorney in the department of appeals in 1892. He remained in this position five years, acquiring a varied experience which was to be of great assistance to him in his subsequent work. The last two years of this position were devoted to preparing indictments for the grand jury, and so skillfully were his duties performed that not a single indictment drawn by him was held to be faulty upon demurrer. He also frequently tried cases as assistant district attorney, and argued habeas corpus and extradition proceedings. Mr. Battle resigned from the district attorney's office in 1897 and formed a partnership with Hon. Bartow S. Weeks to engage in the general practice of law in New York. Shortly thereafter H. Snowden Marshall became a member of the firm, which under the name of Weeks, Battle & Marshall, quickly won a foremost place among the eminent legal firms of the metropolis. Subsequent changes in the firm were the withdrawal of Mr. Weeks in 1905 and the addition of Hon. James A. O'Gorman in 1911, the present name being O'Gorman, Battle & Marshall. Mr. Battle has been engaged in many notable civil and criminal litigations. He was one of the counsel for George H. Earle who, as receiver for the Pennsylvania Sugar Refining Co., brought suit against the American Sugar Refining Co. for having prevented the Pennsylvania Co. from engaging in the business of sugar refining in violation of the Sherman act. The litigation was vigorously contested, the Hon. Frank S. Black appearing as trial counsel for the plaintiff, while John G. Johnson of Philadelphia, John G. Milburn of New York, and other eminent counsel appeared for the defense. He has also appeared in a number of notable will contests, such as those of Mrs. Catharine Hunt Tilford and John Wallace. Mr. Battle has taken an active part in local politics, and in 1909 was the candidate of the Democratic party for district attorney of New York county. He is a member of the Protestant Episcopal Church of the Ascension, and vice-president of the People's Forum connected with that church. Some of the more important of the subjects upon which he has lectured either there or at the Fordham University Law School are: "The Duty of an Advocate in Defending a Client Whom He Knows or Has Reasonable Ground to Believe to be Guilty," "The Attitude of the Courts toward Labor Legislation," "A Comparison of the Criminal Procedure of this Country with that of England," and "A Comparison of the Criminal Procedure of this Country with that of France and Germany." In a recent number of the "Editorial Review" he contributed an able article on "How Shall Our Judges Be Selected?" He is a member of the American Bar Association, the New York State Bar Association, the Bar Association of the City of New York, the American Academy of Political and Social Science, the Society for the Encouragement of Labor Legislation, the New York Southern Society, the North Carolina Society of New York, of which he is president, and of The Virginians. He is also a member of the Metropolitan, St. Nicholas, Calumet, Manhattan and Democratic clubs, and of the Oakland Golf Club. He was married Apr. 12, 1898, to Martha, daughter of Dr. George W. Bagby, for many years state librarian of Virginia.

TOWER, William A., financier, was born at Petersham, Mass., Feb. 26, 1825, son of Oren and Harriet (Gleason) Tower, and a descendant of John Tower, son of Robert Tower of Hingham in Norfolk, England, who came to America with a colony led by Rev. Peter Hobart, and settled in what is now Hingham, Mass., in 1637. He was educated in the public schools of his native town, and went to work in a country store in Lancaster, when fifteen years of age. He became a partner in the business in 1845, continuing to carry it on until 1848. After a year in Sterling, Mass., he went into the hay and grain business in Boston, under the firm name of Rice, Tower & Co., which became Tower, Davis & Co., in 1852. In 1855, while on a western business trip, he became acquainted with George Watson, of Chicago, and the two formed a partnership in the banking business under the name of Watson, Tower & Co. The firm prospered until 1860, when Mr. Tower settled permanently in Lexington, still keeping an interest in the hay and grain business. In 1867, he organized the banking house of Tower, Giddings & Co., through which Mr. Tower became well known in Boston. After his death, it was continued by his son under the name of Tower & Underwood. Besides managing this firm, Mr. Tower was a director of the National Bank of the Commonwealth from its establishment in 1871, until it was purchased by the Shawmut Bank and was its president for several years. He was also president of the Concord railroad in New Hampshire during 1870-73, and of the Nashua and Lowell railroad in 1877 and 1878, and was a director of the Manchester and Lawrence railroad, the Equitable Life Insurance Co., the Guarantee Co. of North America, vice-president of the Security and Safe Deposit Co., and trustee of the Boston Five Cent Savings Bank, the Boston Safe Deposit Co., and the New England Trust Co. He was chief marshal of the 100th anniversary of the Battle of Lexington, in 1876. In politics Col. Tower was prominent as a Whig and later as a Republican. He was interested in civic affairs and was a member of the Massachusetts legislature in 1872; later, he was a colonel on Gov. Rice's staff, and in 1882 was a member of the governor's council from the third district. He was married April 29, 1847, to Julia, daughter of Capt. Arthur Davis of Lancaster, Mass., and had two sons, Augustus C. and Richard G. Tower, and two daughters, Charlotte Grey and Ellen M. Tower. He died at his home in Lexington, Mass., Nov. 21, 1904.

RODE, Paul Peter, sixth Roman Catholic bishop of the diocese of Green Bay, Wis., was born in Prussian Poland Sept. 18, 1873, son of Augustine and Christine Rode. With his parents he came to the United States in boyhood and was educated at St. Ignatius and St. Francis colleges, Chicago, Ill. He was ordained priest June 17, 1894, and thereafter served as assistant pastor of St. Adelbert's Church and as pastor of Saint Peter and Paul's and St. Michael's, Chicago, 1896–1908. In the latter year the long agitation of the Catholic Poles for a representative of their race among the hierarchy of the United States culminated in his selection as the first Polish bishop and he was consecrated titular bishop of Barca and auxiliary bishop to the archbishopric of Chicago July 29, 1908. In December of the following year Archbishop Quigley appointed him his vicar-general for the Polish Catholics, who constituted a very large section of the archdiocese. Upon the resignation of Bishop Fox of the diocese of Green Bay, Wis.,

WILLIAM A. TOWER

Bishop Rode was transferred to that see by the pope July 13, 1915. Green Bay has a polyglot Catholic population—English, French, German, Dutch, Polish, Italian—of about 150,000. There are 221 priests, 238 churches, missions and chapels, three colleges (221 students), 111 schools with 18,595 pupils, five orphan asylums with 450 inmates and nine hospitals.

EAMES, William Henry, dental surgeon and editor, was born at Auburn, N. Y., Aug. 23, 1828, son of George and Sarah (Norris) Eames, and a descendant of James Eames, who came from England to America in 1630 and settled at Dedham, Mass. His father, a wagon and carriage manufacturer, was a man of great public spirit, and a dominant factor in the educational, religious and commercial welfare of his section. During the son's early infancy his parents removed to Lee Center, N. Y., where he attended the public schools and the Clinton Academy. After teaching for three years he entered the medical department of the University of Michigan. He became deeply interested in dentistry, but as there was no dental department in the University of Michigan at that time, he went to Cincinnati to attend the Ohio College of Dental Surgery, where he was graduated (D.D.S.) in 1853. He began his professional career at Ann Arbor, forming a partnership with Dr. Henry Porter, built up a considerable practice, and gained a high reputation for skill. In 1857 he removed his practice to Lebanon, Tenn., and when the strife and turmoil of civil war made his stay unpleasant he went to St. Louis, Mo., where his real life-work was begun. He was one of the organizers and charter members of the Missouri State Dental Association, and its fifth president, and for twelve years was recording secretary. Mainly through his individual efforts the early minutes and proceedings of the society, from 1865 to 1883, were compiled and published in booklet form. The meeting for the organization of the Missouri Dental College was held at his house in June, 1866. He was elected the first professor of artificial dentistry, and later professor of the Institute of Dental Sciences, and for twenty-eight years never once missed his lecture hour. After 1875 he was dean of the faculty. He was president of the St. Louis Dental Society in 1868; president of the Mississippi Valley Dental Society during 1873-1874; president National Association Institute of Dental Faculties in 1892, and a member of the American Dental Association, Illinois Dental Society, and Iowa State Dental Society. For several years he was associate editor of the "Missouri Dental Journal," organized in 1869, and during 1887-1890 was editor of "The Archives of Dentistry." His writings contain a vast amount of information of great value to the members of his profession. He was married at Clinton, Mich., Feb. 4, 1855, to Laura M., daughter of Elias Scofield, who survives him, with seven children: Emma, wife of Harry S. Chase, an artist; William S., an architect; Harriet, wife of James P. Williams; Eva; Mary E., wife of Edward E Smith; Capt. Henry E. Eames, U. S. A., and Laura L., wife of Alfred L. Kammerer. He died in St. Louis, Mar. 29, 1894.

FEEHAN, Daniel Francis, second R. C. bishop of Fall River, Mass., was born at Athol, Mass., in 1855. He was graduated at St. Mary's College, Montreal, Can., in 1876, and then entered St. Joseph's Seminary, Troy, N. Y., for his theological course. He was ordained priest there Dec. 20, 1879, and was engaged in parish work in West Brighton and Fitchburg in the diocese of Springfield until 1889, when he was appointed permanent rector of St. Bernard's Church, Fitchburg, Mass. Here he remained until the death of Bishop Stang made a vacancy in the see of Fall River, and he was appointed the successor of that prelate on July 2, 1907, and consecrated on September 19 following. The diocese of Fall River has an interesting, mixed Catholic population of English, French-Canadians, Portuguese, Poles and Italians numbering 165,000. There are 155 priests ministering to them, with ninety-seven churches, stations and missions. The schools number thirty-five, with 13,895 pupils, and there are three orphan asylums with 660 inmates, a home for the aged and a large hospital.

WALSH, David Ignatius, 46th governor of Massachusetts, was born at Leominster, Mass., Nov. 11, 1872, son of James and Bridget (Donnelly) Walsh. He was educated in the public schools of Clinton, Mass., and was graduated at Holy Cross College in 1894, and at Boston University Law School in 1897. He was president and valedictorian of his graduating classes in high school, at college and in the law school. He was admitted to the bar in 1897, and immediately began the practice of his profession with his brother at Fitchburg and Clinton as a member of the firm of Walsh & Walsh. He was elected to the state legislature, lower house, in 1900 and 1901 from the Clinton district, and served in both sessions on the committee on bills in third reading and metropolitan affairs. In the fall of 1901 he was defeated for the state senate by 547 votes, in a district which normally gave a much greater Republican plurality. In 1911 he was unanimously nominated by the Democrats for lieutenant-governor and was defeated at the election by only 4,151 votes. He was renominated in 1912 and elected. He was the unanimous choice of his party for governor of Massachusetts in 1913, and was elected, receiving 183,267 votes, against 127,755 for Charles S. Bird, Progressive, 116,705 for Augustus P. Gardner, Republican, and 20,171 for Eugene N. Foss, Independent. The most important legislation of his administration was a measure providing for the submission to the people of a constitutional amendment giving suffrage to women. The popular vote that followed as a result of this act defeated the measure. In July of his first term a ship canal across Cape Cod was formally opened. He was elected for a second term in 1914. He was a delegate-at-large to the Democratic national convention of 1912, and a member of the committee and sub-committee on platform of that body. He is a member of the Democratic Club of Massachusetts and of the Elks and Knights of Columbus. He is unmarried.

REED, James A., lawyer and senator, was born near Mansfield, Richland co., O., Nov. 9, 1861, son of John A. and Nancy Crawford Reed, of Scotch-Irish descent. His father was a farmer and stock raiser. The son received his education in the public schools of Cedar Rapids, Ia., and at Coe College, Ia. For three years he studied law in the office of Hubbard Clark & Dawley; was admitted to the bar of Iowa in 1885, and began to practice at Cedar Rapids, but two years later removed to Kansas City, Mo., which he made his permanent residence. He quickly attained a foremost position at the Missouri bar, and acquired a reputation as one of the foremost lawyers in the state. Early in his career he became actively interested in local politics. He was appointed county counsellor of Jackson county, Mo., in 1898. Every case against the county was successfully defeated by him, and every opinion of his that was called into question before higher courts was sustained as a correct exposition of the law. In 1898 he was elected prosecuting attorney of Jackson county. Of 287 felony cases tried during his term of two years, he obtained 285 convictions. Upon the urgent demand of the leading citizens of Kansas City, he resigned his office in 1900 to become candidate for mayor. The campaign was a memorable one; although bitterly opposed by the public service corporations, his popularity was such that he was elected by an overwhelming majority, carrying with him the entire Democratic ticket. During his administration as mayor he accomplished much for the good of the city. He compelled the railway company to surrender the recently acquired extension of their franchise for twenty-five years; he instituted universal transfers and increased the assessed valuation of that corporation from $38,000 to $450,000, compelled it to rebuild its entire system and to pay the public eight per cent. of its gross revenues. He reduced the cost of the city electric lighting from $110,000 to $65.00 a year for each light. By the introduction of a competitive telephone company, an inefficient service was greatly improved, and the rate reduced from $96.00 to $60.00 per annum; likewise, the paving monopoly of the city was broken up, with a further reduction of taxes. He held the office of mayor for two terms and then resumed the practice of law, becoming senior member of the firm of Reed & Harvey. He has always been a consistent Democrat from conviction, and in each campaign since 1902 has made at least one hundred speeches in defense of his party's principles. He was a delegate-at-large from Missouri to the national Democratic convention at Denver in 1908. In 1911 he was elected to the U. S. senate, defeating his closest opponent, Hon. David R. Francis, by 30,000 votes for the nomination. He was elected by the state legislature, Jan. 18, 1911, receiving every Democratic vote in both houses. In the senate he served on the commerce, manufactures, Pacific railroads, Philippines, public buildings and grounds, banking and currency, judiciary and railroads committees. Sen. Reed has been a member of the executive committee of the Democratic national committee since 1912. His clubs are: Kansas City Commercial, Kansas City, and Midday, of Kansas City; he is also a member of the Elks, Knights of Pythias, Woodmen and Masonic fraternities. He was married, Aug. 1, 1887, to Lura M. Olmstead, of Cedar Rapids.

UHL, Edwin Fuller, lawyer and diplomat, was born in Rush, Avon county, N. Y., Aug. 14, 1841, son of David M. and Catherine (De Garmo) Uhl. When he was three years old, his parents settled on a farm near Ypsilanti, Mich., and there he worked on the farm and attended the district schools of the neighborhood until he entered the Ypsilanti Union Seminary at the age of thirteen. Later, he was graduated at the University of Michigan in the class of 1862. He was distinguished among his class mates by his sound scholarship and marked oratorical ability. After graduation he entered the law office of Norris & Ninde at Ypsilanti and was admitted to the Michigan bar in 1864. Two years later he formed a partnership with the Hon. Lyman D. Norris, and in 1871, was elected prosecuting attorney of his county. In 1876, he removed to Grand Rapids, and resumed the old partnership of Norris & Uhl, an association which continued for eleven years and was one of the most successful and widely known law firms of Michigan. Mr. Uhl's personal prestige as a lawyer was more than state wide. He was endowed with a hand-

some and commanding personal appearance and long enjoyed the reputation of being one of the most finished speakers that ever pleaded before the bar of Michigan. He was identified with many large and important industrial and financial enterprises, serving as president of the Grand Rapids National Bank for twenty years. He was mayor of Grand Rapids for two terms, 1890-92 and filled the position with conspicuous success. As a staunch Democrat, he was a member of the minority party in Michigan, but it recognized his party services and leadership by unanimously nominating him for the office of U. S. senator in 1894. When Pres. Cleveland was inaugurated in 1893, he tendered Mr. Uhl the position of assistant secretary of war an honor which he declined, but in the following October, the president again asked him to take office, this time as assistant secretary of state, and he accepted. Owing to the illness of the secretary, Walter Q. Gresham, far more responsibility devolved upon Mr. Uhl than ordinarily falls to the assistant secretary, and his services in that office were notable, being for a prolonged period practically the secretary of state. Several very important diplomatic matters were managed by Mr. Uhl, which gave him a country wide reputation, the most conspicuous being the arbitration of the boundary dispute between Brazil and the Argentine Republic. This was a controversy of several centuries standing, that had been the cause of two wars between the two countries, and finally under the treaty of Sept. 7, 1889, it was submitted to the president of the United States for arbitration. The case involved what is known as the "Misiones strip" consisting of about 12,000 square miles, and was one of the most important international arbitrations of the western world. Pres. Cleveland, at the suggestion of Mr. Gresham, turned over the task to Mr. Uhl. and after months of continuous work he made his report to the president. The award to Brazil was signed by Cleveland without the change of a single word, and in appreciation of the services rendered Mr. Uhl was requested to present the award to the representatives of the two countries, which was done on Feb. 6, 1895. The importance of this arbitration was emphasized at the time of Mr. Cleveland's death by Brazil declaring an official mourning of thirty days in his honor, an action almost without precedent. After declining the post of minister to Switzerland, he was nominated in Feb., 1896, ambassador to Germany and the appointment was confirmed by the senate without reference to a committee, the senate's highest compliment. He held the position until June, 1897, and was succeeded by Hon. Andrew D. White. On his return from Germany, Mr. Uhl resumed the practice of law at Grand Rapids and for a time at Chicago, but the last few years of his life were devoted to the building and enjoyment of a beautiful country home, "Waldheim," near Grand Rapids. He was married at Ypsilanti, Mich., May 1, 1865, to Alice, daughter of the Hon. Benjamin Follett of that city, who ably supplemented the life of her husband and won a distinction of her own in Washington and Berlin hardly less notable. They had four children: Lucy Follett, wife of Daniel R. Wood, of San Jose, Cal.; David Edwin; Alice Edwina, wife of Earl D. Babst of New York, and Marshall Mortimer Uhl. He died at his country home near Grand Rapids, Mich., May 17, 1901.

MEYERS, Sidney Stuyvesant, lawyer, was born at New Orleans, La., Jan. 16, 1876, son of Henry

Meyers and Rosalie (Lang) Meyers. His father, who was a native of Bavaria, Germany, came to America in 1852, and was a pioneer in the woolen business in New Orleans, La. The son was graduated at Columbia University in 1895, and at the New York University two years later with the degree of LL.B. Shortly after being admitted to the bar in 1897, he began the practice of his profession and was eminently successful from the beginning. A large portion of his law business has been connected with automobile interests, and he is regarded as an expert in that branch of the law. He is general counsel for the Motor and Accessory Manufacturers, comprising 90 per cent. of the manufacturers of automobile parts and supplies, and representing a capital of $400,000,000, the Rubber Sundries Association composed of the Hodgman Rubber Company, Hood Rubber Company, B. F. Goodrich Company, Seamless Rubber Company, Davold Rubber Company, and others. He was counsel and a member of the Creditors' Committee of the United States Motor Company, and assisted in formulating plans by which it was reorganized in 1912, and in that year he negotiated the sale of the Splitdorf magneto and the organization of the Splitdorf Electrical Company with a capital of $3,500,000 to the Torrington (Conn.) Co. In 1911 Mr. Meyers appeared before the New York state legislature on behalf of twenty-nine of the largest automobile tire manufacturers in opposition to a bill compelling the branding and marking of tires with the date and year of manufacture and successfully argued against the enactment. He was counsel for seven of the largest tire manufacturers in an action brought against them by the Moto-Bloc Import Co., in 1910, for alleged restraint of trade, and he was successful in defending the action before the appellate division of the New York supreme court. In 1913 he represented The Fisk Rubber Company in connection with the increase of its capital stock from four to fifteen million dollars. While studying at Columbia University, Mr. Meyers was a contributor to the college paper, ''Morningside,'' and was the author of the first serial story which appeared in its columns. He has since written a number of articles on legislative and other subjects, and is the author of a number of short plays. He is a member of the American Bar Association.

SHERMAN, Lawrence Yates, U. S. senator, was born in Miami county, O., Nov. 8, 1858, son of Nelson and Maria (Yates) Sherman and grandson of Thomas Sherman. His parents settled on the prairies of Illinois when he was eleven months old, and he grew up on his father's farm, attending the district school during the winter. The early books he read that influenced his later career were Goodrich's ''Pictorial History of the World,'' P. T. Barnum's autobiography, and a book of the statutes of Illinois. His recreation during stormy days when he was unable to work in the field was to attend court proceedings of the local justice of the peace. That and hunting with his father were his principal sources of recreation. He studied at every opportunity and by teaching in local schools earned enough to go to college, paying his way there by teaching and working on neighboring farms. He took the law course at McKendree College, Lebanon, Ill., and was graduated LL.B. in 1882. He was admitted to the bar in Springfield, Ill., and settled at Macomb for the practice of his profession. At the age of twenty-eight years he was elected to the bench as county judge and served four years. In 1897 he was elected to the state legislature, where he served as speaker during

1899–1903. During his earlier days at Springfield, when it was a constant struggle to maintain himself against powerful enemies, he was the joy and delight of all newspaper correspondents. His caustic epigrams and home-striking philippics always meant a news item, and as a coiner of political slang he is singularly gifted. It was Sherman who named the Illinois and Michigan canal ''the tadpole ditch,'' the political game wardens ''the rabbit shepherds,'' and the members of the governor's staff in their resplendent uniforms ''the sunburst colonels,'' and the terms still are familiar. He was an unsuccessful candidate for governor of Illinois in 1904, and in 1905 was elected lieutenant-governor, and for the ensuing four years was president of the state senate. He was nominated to be mayor of Springfield on a law enforcement platform following the Springfield riots of August, 1908, but failed of election. During 1909–13 he was president of the State Board of Administration in control of all the public charities of Illinois. In March, 1913, he was elected U. S. senator to fill the unexpired term of William Lorimer, and in November, 1914, was reelected for the long term expiring in March, 1921. He was married, May 27, 1891, to Ella M., daughter of James L. Crews, of Jasper county, Ill.; she died childless in 1893, and he was married again Mar. 4, 1908, to Estelle, daughter of David Spitler, of Montrose, Ill., who died in 1910, leaving one daughter, Virginia Sherman.

TUTWILER, Julia Strudwick, educator, was born in Tuskaloosa, Ala., in 1835, daughter of Dr. Henry and Julia (Ashe) Tutwiler. Her maternal great-great-grandfather was Samuel Ashe, first president of the committee of public safety of North Carolina, and an uncle, Thomas Ashe (q. v), was senator in the Confederate congress and representative in the U. S. congress. Her father (1807–84) was one of the most distinguished educators in the South. He was the first to take the degree of M.A. at the University of Virginia, the first professor of ancient languages at the University of Alabama, and founder and president of the famous high school for boys at Green Springs, known as the ''Rugby'' of Alabama. He was a classmate of Edgar Allen Poe, a close friend of Thomas Jefferson, and was regarded as one of the finest men of his generation. Under his careful tutelage Miss Tutwiler received her early education. This was supplemented by two years at a private school in Philadelphia, conducted by a Parisian family, and by a year at Vassar College. During part of her time at Vassar she had charge of several French and German classes. After teaching for some time at Greensboro and in her father's school at Green Springs, she entered the Washington and Lee University at Lexington, Va., where she studied Greek and Latin and received a teacher's certificate in those branches. Subsequently she studied and taught for three years in Germany, passing two examinations of the Prussian Board of Education. After her return to the United States she taught for five years at the Tuscaloosa Female Academy, going abroad during one scholastic year to study the schools of Paris. In 1881 she was made co-principal with Dr. Carlos G. Smith of the Livingston Female Academy. The institution was a private one when she entered it, but a year later the state made an appropriation of $2,500 to be used in adding to the academy a training school for teachers. ''This,'' says Miss Tutwiler, ''was the first and only gift which the women of the state had up to that time received from the state or federal treasury.'' A few years later the name of the academy was changed to that of the Alabama Normal College, and Miss Tutwiler was made its first president. Under her guidance the institution grew remarkably in value and prestige, and received several increases in the appropriation from the state. In addition to improving the school she also managed to improve the town of Livingston and its neighbor, Sumter, freeing them from saloons fully twenty-five years before the prohibition movement became a power in Alabama. Having secured opportunity for secondary education for the girls of Alabama, she turned her attention to securing higher education for them, and after several years of persistent effort she succeeded in inducing the University of Alabama to open its doors to women. The first degree ever conferred on a woman in that state was received by Miss Rose Lewthorn, one of Miss Tutwiler's pupils, in 1900, and in the following year another of her girls, Miss Lila MacMahon, received the first degree of M.A. ever conferred in that state upon a woman. Subsequently the trustees of the university erected a building for the women students, which they named the Julia S. Tutwiler Annex. Academic and professional training for women being thus provided, she turned her attention to the needs of the vast majority of girls whose careers would lie in the home or in the industrial world. As a result of her efforts the legislature passed a bill in 1893 providing for the Alabama Girls' Industrial School, afterward named the Alabama Girls' Technical Institute. The school was founded in 1896 and is among the first institutions of its kind in the United States. Practically from the beginning of her career as a teacher Miss Tutwiler has been writing on educational topics. She was the first woman in Alabama ever asked to write a paper for a state educational convention, and her paper was the first ever written in the United States advocating trade schools for women. In 1878 she was selected by the "National Journal of Education" to report the educational features of the Paris Exposition. Her prose writings and poems have appeared in the best magazines in the country, including the "St. Nicholas," "Appleton's Weekly," "The Churchman," the San Francisco "Post" and the London "Christian World." One of her songs, "Alabama," was adopted by the Women's Christian Association of Alabama as their state song, and it was afterward formally accepted by the government as the song of the state. This and some of her other songs, including "Dixie Now" and the "Southern Yankee Doodle," are sung in the public schools of Alabama. For years Miss Tutwiler has labored to bring about reforms in the penal methods of Alabama, and especially to end the barbarous system of contract labor. For twenty-five years she was superintendent of the prison and jail department of the Alabama Women's Christian Temperance Union. Among the specific results of her efforts have been the establishment of the boys' reformatory at Eastlake, Birmingham, known as the Alabama Industrial School; the institution of night schools at the state farm at Speigener and at several convict camps, and a decided amelioration of the contract system. Miss Tutwiler, naturally, has been the recipient of many honors both within and outside her state. In 1893 she was a member of the Congress of Representative Women of the World at Chicago and was one of the judges of liberal arts at the World's Fair, secretary for the state in the International Congress of Charities and Corrections and one of the vice-presidents of the International Congress of Education. A Julia S.

Tutwiler scholarship at the University of Alabama has been founded in her honor by the United Daughters of the Confederacy.

McMAHON, James, bank president, was born in Franklin county, N. Y., Oct. 15, 1831. His education was acquired in Rochester, N. Y., where his parents removed in his boyhood. In 1864 he was appointed deputy grain measurer in New York city, and shortly thereafter with James T. Easton organized the Protective Grain Association, out of which the firm of Easton, McMahon & Co. developed. Having established a line of freight steamers between New York and Philadelphia, the business was reorganized in 1881 and incorporated as the Easton & McMahon Transportation Co., of which Mr. McMahon was president until he retired in 1886. Meanwhile he had become identified with the Emigrant Savings Bank in New York city, was elected a member of the executive committee in 1881, and was elected president in 1892, continuing in that office until his resignation in 1906. Under his direction the institution became one of the best-known savings banks in New York city. Mr. McMahon's public life was conspicuous in the two fields of banking and philanthropy. Although he had never sought public office he was appointed to membership on several important boards in Greater New York. He served at one time on the board of education and took a prominent part in the movement which resulted in the consolidation of Brooklyn with Greater New York in 1898. He served as a director and member of the finance committee of the Equitable Life Insurance Society from 1906 to 1912, director of the National Surety Co., the Produce Exchange Bank, the People's Trust Co., of Brooklyn; the Realty Associates of Brooklyn and other leading financial institutions. He was a trustee of the House of Good Shepherd, a vice-president of the Society for the Prevention of Cruelty to Children, chairman and vice-president of the finance committee of the Irish Emigrant Society and an incorporator and director of the Brooklyn Institute of Arts and Sciences, of which he was a life member. He was thrice married; first, Feb. 19, 1855, to Katherine Augusta Cummiskey, of Rochester, N. Y., who died May 28, 1895; second, June 17, 1896, to Rose Mary Devereaux, who died July 18, 1909, and third, April 7, 1910, to Helena Devereaux, his second wife's sister, receiving a special dispensation from the Pope, permitting the ceremony. A daughter by his first marriage was known as Mother Mary of the Rosary, of the Dominican Order of Corpus Christi, at Hunt's Point, N. Y. The remaining children of the first marriage were: Francis Paul and Joseph Thomas McMahon. The only child by his second wife is Rosemary Devereaux McMahon. Mr. McMahon died at his country home in Smithtown, L. I., Dec. 10, 1913.

MERRILL, Charles Washington, engineer and inventor, was born at Concord, N. H., Dec. 21, 1861, son of Sylvester and Clara Lydia (French) Merrill. He received his preliminary education at the Alameda high school, Alameda, Cal., and was graduated at the college of mines of the University of California in 1891. He began his professional career with Dr. George F. Becker of the U. S. Geological Survey in the Sierra Nevada mountains, and with Alexis Janin, metallurgical engineer in San Francisco and in the field. He was connected with the Standard Consolidated Mining Co. of Bodie, Cal., in 1894, and he was with the Harqua Hala Mining Co. of Arizona in 1895-96, the Montana Mining Co. of Marysville, Mont., in

Jas McMahon

T. E. Stillman

1897-98, and the Homestake Mining Co. of Lead, S. D., during 1890-1906. Since 1906 he has been engaged in independent professional work with offices and laboratories in San Francisco. Since 1910 he has been president of the Western Ore Purchasing Co. of Colorado, and a director of the Union and Caledonia Dredging companies of California. Mr. Merrill has made special study and investigation in the cyanide process, to which he has contributed noteworthy improvements, and he is now engaged in the development and introduction of new metallurgical processes throughout the world, and in the development of other inventions. He has invented a number of metallurgical processes and the apparatus used in carrying on the same. About twenty-five patents concerning these processes have been issued to him in the United States, and in important foreign countries which possess mining industries. Mr. Merrill is endowed with distinctive technical and inventive ability, combined with executive and administrative talent, a rare combination which accounts sufficiently for his great success. He is devoted in an exceptional degree to his home and family, and is fond of travel and outdoor sports. Since 1912 he has been a director of the American Institute of Mining Engineers, and he is a member of the Mining and Metallurgical Society of London, the American Electro-Chemical Society, the Australian Institute of Mining Engineers, the Chemical, Mining and Metallurgical Society of South Africa, the Olympic and Engineers' clubs of San Francisco; the Faculty Club of the University of California, and the Claremont Country and Sequoyah Country clubs of Oakland, Cal. He was married at Alameda, Cal., Feb. 9, 1848, to Clara Scott, daughter of William H. Robinson, and has four children: Betty, Jack, Gregor and Bruce Merrill.

STILLMAN, Thomas Edgar, lawyer, was born in New York city, Mar. 23, 1837, son of Alfred and Elizabeth Ann (Greenough) Stillman. His father was a prominent engineer of New York, one of the founders of the Novelty Iron Works, and with others was instrumental in organizing the first public school society, which afterwards developed into the board of education. He lost his life as the result of a Mississippi river explosion near New Orleans. The son received his education in the public schools of New York, attending the Free Academy, which afterwards became the College of the City of New York, and Alfred Academy (now Alfred University). From these he went to Colgate University at Hamilton, N. Y., being graduated in 1859. At college he stood high in his class, was popular among the students, and was refined in his manner and dress. He studied law in the office of Joseph Mason at Hamilton, and upon his admission to the bar in 1862 at once opened a law office in New York. Shortly afterwards he accepted a position with the firm of Barney, Butler & Parsons, and in 1875 became a member of the firm, which was succeeded by that of Butler, Stillman & Hubbard, his associates being William Allen Butler and Thomas H. Hubbard. The firm enjoyed a large general practice, and its success and high standing in the profession were due largely to Mr. Stillman's energy and ability. Later in his practice Mr. Stillman made a specialty of admiralty law and practice, and attained a foremost position at the admiralty bar. Among the important cases managed by him for the admiralty courts was that of the Scotland, 105 U. S., 24, where the supreme court relieved the owners from a decree for the value of the ship Kate Dyer and her cargo, sunk by collision, and, while holding the Scotland in fault for the collision, granted to her English owners the limitation of liability accorded by our statutes, although the collision occurred on the high seas. By this decision not only were Mr. Stillman's clients relieved from the payment of a large sum decreed, but a new principle was definitely incorporated in the law of this country. Such also were the cases of the Pennsylvania, 19 Wallace, 125, and the Atlas, 93 U. S., 304, where, as in many other cases, the results were in large measure attributable to Mr. Stillman's boldness in laying out the line of attack or defense and to his resourceful aid in conference with his associates. Mr. Stillman's large experience and high repute in corporate litigation and law inclined him naturally to corporate management, which he undertook in 1888 in connection with the interests of the Mark Hopkins estate, the management of which involved considerable labor and responsibility, and resulted in his withdrawal from the active practice of law. In this connection he became a director of the Southern Pacific Co., in which Mark Hopkins had held a quarter interest, and also president of the San Antonio and Aransas Pass Railroad Co., as well as director of the United States National Bank and other minor companies. Mr. Stillman was married Jan. 10, 1865, to Charlotte Elizabeth, daughter of Thomas and Charlotte Greenman, of Mystic, Conn., by whom he had four daughters: Jessie Stillman, wife of William A. Taylor, of New York city; Helen E. Stillman, wife of Dr. William Armstrong, of New York city; Mary E. Stillman, wife of Edward S. Harkness, and Charlotte R. Stillman. Mr. Stillman had a mental tendency to mathematical precision of proof and an apprehension so keen that it sometimes outran the slower processes of logical reasoning. He possessed a warm heart, and was always ready to lend a helping hand to the deserving young, and his high moral sense, exemplary life and fine legal mind proved a source of inspiration and encouragement to many young men who have since made their mark in the legal world. Like his father, Mr. Stillman lost his life as the result of an accident, the collision of his automobile with a wagon. He died at Lisieux, France, Sept. 4, 1906.

NOTMAN, John, lawyer, was born in Brooklyn, N. Y., July 13, 1851, son of Peter and Jane C. (Dunlap) Notman. His father was a native of Edinburgh, Scotland, and came to America about 1845, settling first in Philadelphia, Pa., and later in New York. As president for many years of the Niagara Fire Insurance Co. and also of the New York Board of Fire Underwriters, he was a conspicuous and notable figure in the fire insurance business. The son's early life was spent in Brooklyn, N. Y. He attended the Brooklyn Polytechnic Institute, and after graduating there, the valedictorian of his class, took a course at the Columbia Law School. In 1872, he entered the law office of Barney, Butler & Parsons, of which William Allen Butler was the senior member. He quickly proved himself a valuable addition to the law office, and attracted the attention of Mr. Butler, who remarked "I have at last found some one who can write accurately." In 1875, he became a member of the firm, which was then Butler, Stillman & Hubbard, and when Messrs. Stillman and Hubbard retired in 1896, the name was changed to Butler, Notman, Joline & Mynderse. He made a specialty of insurance law and contracts of indemnity. His chief characteristics were his accuracy, carefulness and thoroughness in the preparation of cases. He was a member o the State Board of Charities; a director of the Commercial Union Assurance Co., the Niagara Fire Insurance Co., and a member of the Association of the Bar of the City of New York, the New York State Bar Association, the Lawyers, Metropolitan, Hamilton and Tuxedo clubs and the Metropolitan Museum of Art. Mr. Notman was married Dec. 27, 1888, to Anna Warren Daniell, who survived him with two daughters. He died in Brooklyn, N. Y., Jan. 6, 1907.

MYNDERSE, Wilhelmus, lawyer, was born at Seneca Falls, N. Y., Nov. 25, 1849, only son of Edward and Lillias (Muir) Mynderse, and grandson of Wilhelmus Mynderse, one of the earliest and most influential citizens of Seneca Falls. His first American ancestor was Myndert Frederickse, a member of a prominent Dutch family, who settled in Albany in 1656. Myndert Frederickse reversed the order of his name, and was the founder of the Mynderse family in America. Wilhelmus Mynderse received his early education at Mount Pleasant Military Academy in Sing Sing, N. Y., and was graduated at Williams College in 1871, where he took a special course in engineering. On returning to Seneca Falls he was engaged for a time as an assistant in the survey of the then projected Pennsylvania and Sodus Bay railroad. He subsequently went to New York, where he became a reporter and finally a special writer on the New York "Sun," and then taking up the study of law, he was graduated at the Columbia Law School in 1875. Upon his admission to the bar he entered the law office of Butler, Stillman & Hubbard. In 1881 he became a member of the firm, and continued in the successive firms of Butler, Notman, Joline & Mynderse and of Butler, Notman & Mynderse. Mr. Mynderse devoted most of his time to the practice of admiralty and shipping law, and achieved prominence and distinction in this specialty. For some years prior to his death he was recognized as the ablest and best equipped admiralty lawyer in New York, and his reputation in that department of the law was as well recognized in Europe as in America, many prominent shipping and underwriting interest in England, Germany and America being among his clients. He represented the United States in 1898 as delegate to the International Maritime Law conference held in London. He was a vestryman of Grace Church (Episcopal), Brooklyn; chancellor and member of the standing committee of the Cathedral of the Incarnation at Garden City; trustee of the Brooklyn Hospital, Church Charity Foundation, Long Island Historical Society, Brooklyn Academy of Music, Franklin Trust Co., National Surety Co., Safe Deposit Co. of New York, Hanover Fire Insurance Co., American and Foreign Marine Insurance Co., Columbia Insurance Co., and a member of the fraternity of the Sigma Phi, the University, Church and Grolier clubs, the Downtown Association and the Hamilton Club, Brooklyn. He took an active and lasting interest in the place of his birth, and a few years before his death presented to it the grounds and library building now bearing his name. He also presented the diocesan house on Remsen street, Brooklyn, to the diocese of Long Island. After the death of his first wife, Miss Mary Swan, of Geneva, N. Y., he was married, Nov. 29, 1887, to Hannah H., daughter of Seabury S. Gould of Seneca Falls, N. Y. He died in Brooklyn, N. Y., Nov. 15, 1906.

GATES, Charles Winslow, fifty-fifth governor of Vermont (1915-   ), was born in Franklin, Vt.,

Jan. 12, 1856, son of Harrison and Loena Rebecca (Shedd) Gates. He is descended from Stephen Gates, a native of Hingham, England, who came over in the ship Diligent in 1638 and settled at Hingham, Mass. Stephen Gates's wife was Ann Hill, and the line of descent is traced through their son Simon, who married Margaret ———; their son Simon, who married Sarah Wood; their son Solomon, who married Mary Clark; their son Paul, who married Zerviah Spooner; their son Paul, Jr., who married Eunice Temple, and their son Harrison, who was the father of the governor. The first Paul Gates was one of the pioneer settlers of Franklin and first town treasurer; the original homestead there is still in possession of the family. Paul Gates, Jr., was commissioned lieutenant and afterward captain in the state militia. Charles W. Gates was educated at Franklin and was graduated at St. Johnsbury Academy in 1880. After teaching school for four years as principal of the Franklin Academy, he purchased a mercantile business at Franklin in 1884, and conducted it successfully, at the same time operating the homestead farm where he resided. He was elected town representative in 1898 for a term of two years, after which he went to the state senate for two years. In 1905 Gov. Bell appointed him state highway commissioner. In this position he made an exhaustive study of the highway work of the state, and took up the work of improving the state roads with a determination to bring about permanent construction and establish a system of maintenance which should be permanent. He labored to create public sentiment throughout the state in favor of better roads, and secured appropriations from the state legislature for road improvements, the result being that Vermont has now 4,000 miles of permanent road and all the highways of the state have been substantially improved. Vermont is now said to have the best gravel roads in New England. He has gained a national reputation as an authority on that subject. His efforts in this direction and the improvements he inaugurated brought about a popular demand for him as the Republican candidate for governor in 1914, and he was elected by a substantial majority at the November election. Gov. Gates was married Apr. 9, 1890, to Mary Elizabeth, daughter of James Hayden of Underhill, Vt., and has one daughter, Edith Rebecca, and two sons, Paul Hayden and Winslow Harrison Gates.

ELLIOTT, Charles Burke, jurist, was born in Morgan county, O., Jan. 6, 1861, son of Edward and Anjaline (Kinsey) Elliott, of English descent. He received his preliminary education at Marietta College, was graduated LL.B. at the University of Iowa in 1881 and for three years was a graduate student at the University of Minnesota, receiving the degree of Ph.D. in 1888. He received the honorary degree of LL.D. from the University of Iowa in 1895, and from Marietta College in 1904. During 1882-83 he was a legal writer in St. Louis for the "Central Law Journal," the "American Law Review," and other publications. After practicing law at Aberdeen, S. D., for a year, he removed to Minneapolis, Minn. He was judge of the municipal court, 1891-94; judge of the district court, fourth judicial district, 1894-95, and associate justice of the supreme court of Minnesota, 1905-09. From the latter date until Feb. 10, 1910, he was associate justice of the supreme court of the Philippine Islands, when he became a member of the U. S. Philippine commission, and secretary of commerce and police in the government of the Philippines, and by virtue of that

JOHN NOTMAN
LAWYER

WILHELMUS MYNDERSE
LAWYER

CHARLES W. GATES
GOVERNOR

CHARLES B. ELLIOTT
JURIST

office was a member of the cabinet of the governor-general of the Philippine Islands. He was head of the department of corporation law, College of Law, University of Minnesota, during 1890-94; lecturer on international law at the same institution, 1890-1909, and professorial lecturer on constitutional law, University of the Philippines, in 1911-12. He is the author of "The Law of Private Corporations" (1893), "The Law of Insurance" (1907), "The United States and the Northeastern Fisheries" (1887), which is in part reprinted in "American History Told by Contemporaries"; "The Law of Municipal Corporations" (1890), "Minnesota Trial Practice" (1900), and "The Philippines, America Overseas" (1915). He also wrote "The Behring Sea Question" (Atlantic Monthly," 1890), "The Legislatures and the Courts" ("Political Science Quarterly," 1890), "The Treaty Making Power Under the Constitution" ("The Forum," June, 1890), "Judicial Control Over Legislative Power in the United States" (printed in Russian in "Journal de Droit Int. et Public," St. Petersburg, 1897), "Review of Legislation in the United States for 1896" ("Jahrbuch der Int.," Berlin, 1897), "The Doctrine of Continuous Voyages" ("The American Journal of International Law" 1907), "An American Chancellor," address before Yale Law School ("American Law Review" 1905), "The Judicial Office," address before Kent College of Law, Chicago, 1905; "International Arbitration," address before Mohonk Conference, 1906; "International Courts," address before South Dakota Bar Association and South Dakota legislature, 1907, and numerous other articles on questions of public law in various magazines and reviews in America and Europe. In 1911 he represented the U. S. government at the ceremonies in Hong Kong in connection with the coronation of King George. He has traveled extensively in Asia and Europe, studying problems of colonization. In 1906 he was vice-president of the International Law Association (London), and he is a member of the American Society of International Law, American Bar Association, Minnesota State Bar Association, Society of Comparative Jurisprudence and Political Economy, Berlin; American Historical Association, and the Phi Beta Kappa, the Alpha Sigma Phi and Delta Chi fraternities. He was married at Muscatine, Ia., May 13, 1884, to Edith, daughter of Charles Coffin Winslow, of Muscatine. They have five children: Charles Winslow, Edwin Eugene, Ethel, Walter A., and Philip C. Elliott.

SAULSBURY, Willard, U. S. senator, was born at Georgetown, Del., Apr. 17, 1861, son of Willard and Annie Milby (Ponder) Saulsbury. The family is of Welsh descent, having settled in Delaware in the seventeenth century. His father was U. S. senator and chancellor of the state of Delaware, and his mother was a daughter of John Ponder and sister of James Ponder, twenty-fifth governor of Delaware. The subject of this sketch was educated in private schools and at the University of Virginia. Having decided to follow his father's profession, he opened a law office in 1882 at Wilmington in association with Victor du Pont, which continued until the latter's death in 1888. He next formed a partnership with James W. Ponder and Charles M. Curtis, and when the latter, who is the present chancellor of Delaware, was elevated to the bench, Mr. Hugh M. Morris was admitted to the firm as his successor. Upon the retirement of Mr. Ponder the firm remained Saulsbury and Morris until Richard A. Rodney was admitted.

Mr. Saulsbury has made a specialty of corporation law. He arranged the consolidation of the Wilmington street railways and electric companies in 1900 and organized the Equitable Guarantee and Trust Co. of Wilmington. He was a director of the latter and also of the Union National Bank until his election to the U. S. senate. Sen. Saulsbury has been interested in local politics as a Democrat for many years. He was chairman of the Democratic county executive committee of his home county, in which two-thirds of all the votes of his state are concentrated, during 1892-98; was chairman of the Democratic state committee during 1900-06, and was a delegate to the Democratic national conventions at Chicago in 1896, St. Louis in 1904 and Baltimore in 1912. In 1906 he was a member of the Democratic national congressional committee. He was elected a member of the Democratic national committee in 1908, and served as a member of its executive committee, was re-elected in 1912 and is still a member thereof. He received all the Democratic votes in the Delaware legislature as the Democratic caucus nominee for U. S. senator in 1899, 1901, 1903, 1905, 1907 and 1911. This period includes the so-called Addicks regime, and probably no man did as much to prevent Addicks going to the United States senate as did Sen. Saulsbury. The period from 1894 to 1904 covers the time of Addicks' greatest activity in state politics, and in this period he opposed him without intermission, exposing many of his methods. In the presidential election of 1912 he advocated the nomination and election of Woodrow Wilson. He was elected to the U. S. senate July 29, 1913, for the term ending Mar. 4, 1919. He is not only one of the foremost lawyers of his state but is a conspicuously able, resolute and potential political leader. It has been largely through his leadership and his constant personal work that the Democratic party has been kept together as a live fighting force in the state of Delaware for the past twenty years. Sen. Saulsbury was president of the Wilmington Club, vice-president of the Wilmington Country Club, president of the Delaware alumni of the University of Virginia, vice-president of the Hope Farm Anti-Tuberculosis Society, and a member of the American Bar Association, the Wilmington Bar Association, of which he was president, the Delaware Historical Society, the Society of the Sons of the American Revolution, the Society of Colonial Wars and the Delta Psi fraternity. In New York city he is a member of the St. Anthony, Manhattan and National Democratic clubs. In Washington, the Metropolitan Club and Chevy Chase Country Club. He was married, Dec. 5, 1893, to May, daughter of Victor du Pont, his former law preceptor and associate.

HAMMOND, John Hays, Jr., inventor, was born in San Francisco, Cal., Apr. 13, 1888, son of John Hays and Natalie (Harris) Hammond. His father (q. v.) is one of the foremost mining and consulting engineers in the United States. He was educated at schools in France, England, South Africa and the United States. He attended the Hill School, Pottstown, Pa., and Lawrenceville, N. J., and was graduated at the Yale Sheffield Scientific School in 1910. His scientific career began at Gloucester, Mass., where he erected one of the most complete experimental laboratories for radio telegraphic research in existence. Since 1911 he has been experimenting on the control of a dirigible boat by wireless. With no large amount of transmitting power and comparatively poor antennæ, he was able to keep a boat of eight tons displacement under complete control at a distance of over a mile. There was a man at the wheel and one at the motors, but by throwing over a switch they both became passengers, and all the work of navigation was done by Mr. Hammond standing at his keys on shore a mile or two away. The steering of the boat was accomplished by using Hertzian wave impulses to control an electric motor mechanically connected with the steering wheel. The apparatus was almost all contained in a long box, in the head of which was a small switchboard, and at the foot of it coils, batteries and mechanims connected with the wireless antennæ slung over the decks from stem to stern. The vessel was maneuvered over a prearranged course in all conditions of sea and weather, and at night lights, automatically controlled by the steering mechanisms, kept the operator on shore acquainted with the boat's position. His experiments were conducted in direct co-operation with the U. S. war department. Improvements in the device now make the vessel under perfect control from the shore at a speed of thirty-three miles an hour—a speed which no battleship can outstrip. A logical development of Mr. Hammond's invention was its application to a torpedo. In 1914 he announced the completion of a radiodynamic torpedo, which is popularly called in the United States coats artillery the "Hammond destroyer." It is a dirigible boat or torpedo which can be steered by wireless in any direction at the rate of fifty miles an hour on the surface, or twenty-seven miles an hour submerged. The wireless control covers a distance of twenty-eight miles, much farther than a ship can be seen; it can even be operated from an aeroplane, and it is so arranged that it cannot be interfered with by adverse wireless waves. The radio system used in the Hammond torpedo control is the only non-interferable radio communication in existence today, and as such is a really selective system of wireless having important military value for signaling. The device has been approved by the U. S. army board of ordnance and fortifications, and by the appropriation committee of the house of representatives, which recommended that Mr. Hammond should receive $750,000 for his patent applications and inventions, and that a radiodynamic torpedo system be installed at Fisher's Island. This invention is one of the most important and far-reaching in the science of warfare that has ever been made. For the first time it has made possible the delivery of a charge of explosive or projectile at a target at sea under constant control from shore, and so valuable is it regarded by army and navy men that arrangements are being made for its purchase and control by the U. S. army. Mr. Hammond has also invented a system of disappearing masts which, with antennæ stretched and guys taut, will spring out of the earth, shoot their energy into the controlling mechanisms on the torpedo or other vessel, and sink into the earth again, all in a few seconds of time; he has developed a system of fire control for automobile torpedoes which is now being tested by the U. S. navy. In 1915 he originated and proposed a plan of coastal patrol by aeroplane equipped by radio. It was endorsed by Pres. Wilson and the secretaries of war and navy. The Areo Club of America obtained $500,000 by private subscription to initiate the system and most of the coast states have adopted it. He also invented a thermite incendiary sheel, which was used in the European war. He has applied for 140 patents in the United States and Europe, covering various inventions and improvements relating to radio telegraphy and telephony and his dynamic (wirelessly controlled)

torpedoes. He was sent by the U. S. government as a delegate to the London Radio Telegraphic Conference in 1912. He is a governor of the Aero Club of America, vice-president of the Society of Aeronautical Engineers, member of the American Institute of Electrical Engineers, American Society of Mechanical Engineers, Coastal Patrol commission, the Institute of Radio Engineers, the Royal Society for the Encouragement of Arts, Manufactures and Commerce of London, the Eastern Yacht Club, Engineers' Club, and the General Committee of the Langley Aero Dynamical Laboratory of the Smithsonian Institute. He is unmarried. Portrait opposite page 107.

HOLCOMB, Marcus Hensey, forty-eighth governor of Connecticut (1915——), was born at New Hartford, Conn., Nov. 28, 1844, son of Carlos and Ada (Bushnell) Holcomb, and a descendant of Thomas Holcomb, a native of England, who came over to the colonies in 1634 and settled at Dorchester, Mass., where he was made a freeman in May, 1634, and later removed to Windsor, Conn. From Thomas Holcomb the line is traced through Joshua, Joshua, Joshua, Caleb, Harvey and Carlos Holcomb, the father of the governor. Carlos Holcomb was a farmer and was elected to a number of public offices. The son, Marcus H. Holcomb, attended the district schools in New Hartford, the private school there and Wesleyan Academy (now Wilbraham Academy) at Wilbraham, Mass. A college course was prevented by ill health. For a time he taught school in New Hartford and vicinity, at the same time pursuing the study of law under Judge Jared B. Foster. He was admitted to the bar in 1871 and in the following year began his practice in Southington, Conn., which has since been his residence. His law business was largely carried on in Hartford, where for a number of years he was associated with Noble E. Pierce under the firm name of Holcomb & Pierce. In 1873 he was elected judge of probate for the probate court of the district of Southington, and he held that office until he became judge of the superior court in 1910. When the borough court of Southington was established in 1905, he was its first judge, and continued in that position until 1909. In 1893 he was elected to the state senate. In 1902 he was a delegate to the state constitutional convention. In 1903, when the state police department was established he was appointed one of five commissioners of state police, and in 1905 he epresented Southington in the general assembly, serving as speaker of the house of representaitves. In 1906 Judge Holcomb was elected attorney-general and held that office until his appointment to the bench of the sperior court. He entered upon his duties as superior court judge Sept. 7, 1910, and continued to serve until his retirement, Nov. 28, 1914, on account of having reached the constitutional age limit. He was elected governor of Connecticut in November, 1914. He is president of the Southington Savings Bank and a director of various manufacturing corporations. During 1893–1908 he was treasurer of the county of Hartford and attorney of said county and he was receiver of the Co-Operative Savings Society of Connecticut when the affairs of that society were liquidated. He is a thirty-second degree Mason. In 1915 Trinity College conferred upon him the honorary degree of LL.D. A member of the First Baptist Church of Southington, he has been superintendent of its Sunday-school since 1890, and he is also chairman of its board of trustees. He was married, Oct. 15, 1872, to Sarah Carpenter, daughter of Deacon Joseph L. Bennett.

JOHN HAYS HAMMOND, JR.
INVENTOR

SAMUEL C. BOOTH
SCIENTIST

MARY A. ALLARD BOOTH
MICROSCOPIST

LeROY PERCY
U. S. SENATOR

BOOTH, Samuel Colton, scientist, was born at Long Meadow, Mass., May 6, 1812, son of David and Margaret (Colton) Booth. The family is of great antiquity and its coat of arms is among the oldest known in England, showing in its device a blood relationship of the family to royalty. The first American ancestor of Samuel Colton Booth was Robert Booth, who came to this country from England in 1644 or 1645, and landed at New Haven, Conn., whence he removed about 1653 to Saco, Me. He was a man of prominence in his community, was a member of the general court at Boston, and held a number of other official positions. From him the line of descent is traced through his son Simon (or Simeon) and his wife, Rebecca Frost; their son Zachariah and his wife, Mary Werriner; their son Joseph and his wife, Sarah Chandler; their son Joseph and his wife, Mary Hale, and their son David and his wife, Margaret Colton. Samuel C. Booth received his education at Amherst Academy and became a prosperous and successful farmer. Having obtained a competence he devoted himself altogether to the study of mineralogy and geology, in which from a very early age he had been deeply interested. He was well known in scientific circles and numbered among his correspondents many famous scientists of the country. For a number of years he devoted himself to the formation of mineralogical and geological collections, industriously procuring new specimens himself and adding to these by purchase and exchange until he possessed large and valuable collections. It is now in the Science Museum of Springfield, Mass., under the title of ''The Samuel Colton Booth Collections.'' Other specimens have gone to make up collections in the schools of Springfield. Mr. Booth was a member of the American Association for the Advancement of Science. He was twice married, in 1833 to Mary Ann Allard, who died leaving one son, David Booth, and in 1840 to Rhoda, daughter of Ebenezer Colton, of Long Meadow, by whom he had two children, one died young and the other was Mary Ann Allard Booth. He died in Long Meadow, Mass., Sept. 23, 1895.

BOOTH, Mary Ann Allard, microscopist, was born at Longmeadow, Mass., Sept. 8, 1843, daughter of Samuel Colton and Rhoda (Colton) Booth. She was educated in the public schools, at Wilbraham, Mass., academy, and elsewhere. Her scientific proclivities were inherited in part from her father, and during years of chronic invalidism she devoted much time to scientific research with the microscope, the study of the seaweeds having first attracted her attention to the study of biology, and acknowledgment is made in many scientific text-books of her assistance in their preparation. At her residence in Springfield, Mass., she has a well-equipped laboratory and large collection of microscopical slides prepared by herself and other expert microscopists at home and abroad. For her work in this department Miss Booth received first honor at the New Orleans Exposition in 1885, and a medal at the St. Louis Exposition in 1904. She is also an expert in photography and photomicrography. She has traveled extensively in the United States, Canada, and Alaska, having crossed the continent no less than a dozen times in as many years. Miss Booth has delivered many lectures illustrated with stereopticon slides which she prepared from her own photomicrographic negatives before scientific societies in such cities as Montreal, Brooklyn, Washington, etc., where they were enthusiastically received and resulted in increased interest in natural science, her great love

for the work and a natural gift for imparting that form of knowledge especially adapting her for the lecture platform. During its whole existence Miss Booth was the editor of ''Practical Microscopy,'' and has been a contributor to many magazines both at home and abroad. When Surgeon General Blue was waging his successful campaign against bubonic plague in San Francisco, Miss Booth made the photomicrographs of the germ-bearing fleas of rats for the stereopticon slides, and since then she has prepared a set of photomicrographs from a collection of Hawaiian Island fleas, and other parasites. She has probably the largest private collection of parasites in this country, many species of which have never been photographed. At the request of the National Museum at Washington she is preparing photomicrographs of the specimens for that institution, to which the collection itself will eventually go. She is a member of the American Microscopical Society, the New York Microscopical Society and the Brooklyn Institute of Arts and Sciences and a fellow of the American Association for the Advancement of Science, and of the Royal Microscopical Society of London, England. Locally she is a member of the Mercy Warren Chapter of the Daughters of the American Revolution, and the Springfield Women's Club, the oldest and largest women's club in the city.

PERCY, Le Roy, U. S. senator, was born in Washington county, Miss., Nov. 9, 1860, son of William Alexander and Nannie Irving (Armstrong) Percy. His father (1834-88) was an officer in the Confederate army in the civil war from Mississippi, having ardently opposed secession, but when it came, raised the first company in Washington county, of which he was captain. The family traces descent from Charles B. Percy, who came over to this country in 1776 from England and settled in Wilkinson county, Miss. His maternal grandfather, Robert Armstrong, was commissioner of Indian affairs under President Jackson. Senator Percy received a thorough education, beginning in the public schools of Greenville and finishing in the University of the South, at Sewanee, Tenn., where he was graduated in 1879. Taking up the study of law in Virginia, he received his degree there in 1881 and then began the practice of law at Greenville, Miss. He has been highly successful in his professional work, having had for years one of the best practices in that state. He is also one of the large successful plantation owners of the Mississippi delta and a partner in a very successful cotton factorage business in Greenville. Although he has always taken a deep interest in politics as a private citizen, he never consented to become a candidate for office until 1910, when he was elected to the United States senate, defeating ex-Governor Vardaman. The main issue of the campaign was the treatment of the negro question, Vardaman contending that the dominating issue in the South should be the agitation by the South for the repeal of the fifteenth and modification of the fourteenth amendment. Senator Percy vigorously opposed the idea that the South should embark on any such crusade. Several years ago he delivered an address before the Mississippi Bar Association which attracted wide attention and was published in the ''Outlook'' on the personal recommendation of President Roosevelt. His term expired March 3, 1913. Senator Percy was married Dec. 9, 1883, to Camille Bourges, daughter of Ernest Bourges, of New Orleans, La., and has one son, William Alexander Percy.

WALKER, William Baker, manufacturer, was born in Cheyenne, Wyo., March 14, 1867, son of Enos and Elizabeth (Shaw) Walker. His father, who was a civil engineer, died in 1875, and the son was obliged to leave school when he was twelve years old. The first money he earned was by capturing prairie dogs and selling them to tourists, and for three years he led the life of a cowboy herding cattle on the plains. In the meantime his mother had established a millinery and dry goods business under the name of E. Walker & Sons. They established a chain of five stores, located at Kearney, Grand Island, Cozad and Gothenburg, Neb., and Cheyenne, Wyo., and were enjoying a large and prosperous business of over half a million a year until the panic of 1893. Mr. Walker left Cheyenne in 1891 and from that time until 1897 resided in Kearney, Neb., where he conducted the Kearney Manufacturing Co. In 1897-98 he was in Denver as manager of a bicycle factory and then removed to Chicago, Ill., where he acted as building broker. He constructed over 300 buildings in the South park section. He went to New York in 1905 to finance the patents of the Gillette Manufacturing Co. Meantime he visited the principal manufacturing centers of the United States and Europe, investigating various industries and searching for some article that could be put to general use and for which there would be a general demand. While in Berlin, Germany, he was introduced to Rheinhold Burger, the famous glass manufacturer, who described an idea that had occurred to him of making a hunting flask with a vacuum lining for the purpose of retaining a uniform temperature. Realizing the possibilities of such a device he at once arranged with Mr. Burger to purchase his patent rights to the idea, and returning home began to develop the first models of the now famous "Thermos" bottle. Shortly afterwards he organized the American Thermos Bottle Co., with a capital of $1,000,000. The first factory was located in Brooklyn, N. Y., but the business was so successful and developed so rapidly that a larger building in New York was taken and in 1912 a model factory was erected at Norwich, Conn., with a capacity of 50,000 bottles per day. The principle of the Thermos bottle is a glass container inside a larger glass bottle, separated by a vacuum, which serves to hold the temperature of the contents for a considerable period, whether it be hot or cold. The company guarantees that coffee or soup, for instance, will retain nearly its original temperature for twenty-four hours, and that cold liquids may be kept as long as eighty hours. The bottles vary in size from a half pint to two quarts and are extensively used by travelers, hunters, fishermen, yachtsmen, hospitals and private families. In 1913 Mr. Walker with W. R. Burrows, engineer for the General Electric Co., perfected a new machine for manufacturing these Thermos bottles automatically, which resulted in a material reduction in cost, so that the Thermos bottle is now within the reach of every housekeeping family. Its chiefest value has been in the preservation of milk in the home, in hospitals and in asylums and it has contributed in no small degree to the reduction of infant mortality. Mr. Walker is also president of the Thermos Bottle Co., Ltd., of Toronto, Canada. He is a member of the Navy League, the Aero Club, the Automobile Club of America and the New York Athletic Club. He was married June 1, 1902, to Mary C., daughter of John Morrison of Cheyenne, Wyo., and has one child, a daughter: Fay Elizabeth Walker.

CONKLIN, Roland Ray, financier, was born in Urbana, Ill., Feb. 1, 1858, son of Joseph Q. and Julia (Hunt) Conklin, of English-Scotch descent. His first American ancestor, John Conklin, settled on the north shore of Long Island in 1640, and it was there, at Huntington, that his father, grandfather and great-grandfather were born, and where he himself resides during a part of each year. He was graduated at the University of Illinois in 1880, and the honorary degree of master of literature was conferred on him by that institution in 1890. Energetic and ambitious, and without any financial assistance from others, he paid his entire expenses through college, and within two years after his graduation was a founder and member of the largest real estate firm in southern Kansas, which was well known in every state west of the Mississippi river. Money was enlisted to build irrigation canals in the arid regions of Colorado and Utah; water-works were established in many of the thriving cities of the West, and electric street railways were built, until the aggregate capital invested in various development enterprises was over $40,000,000. In 1893 the headquarters of the company were removed to New York. In the same year the financial panic occurred, which drove this and many similar investment and mortgage companies of the time into liquidation. A reorganization was effected, however, under the charter of the North American Trust Company, and a general banking business was conducted thereafter. Mr. Conklin was elected vice-president of the corporation in 1896, and in that position contributed largely to its success until June, 1899, when he resigned. In 1898 his company was appointed fiscal agent for the U. S. government in Cuba, being the first American company to begin business in that island after the war with Spain. He then undertook a number of financial operations for the development of Cuba, which have attained a marked success. He was one of the principal organizers and founders of the National Bank of Cuba, the Havana Telephone Co. and the Cuban Telephone Co., and has been instrumental in reorganizing and consolidating a number of sugar companies, and is at present vice-president of the Central Cuba Sugar Co. He is president of the Jucaro and Moron Railway Co., and is now engaged in building the National Railways Co. of Cuba. It is in developing the natural resources of the great West and Cuba that Mr. Conklin has achieved most of his reputation and success, his highest achievement being possibly the system of railways and sugar mills which he is now engaged in combining and building in Cuba. His company now controls and operates two of the oldest railways in Cuba, and with the completion of about three hundred miles of new road and several sugar mills it will open up the richest sugar district in the island, which has heretofore remained practically undeveloped through lack of transportation facilities. Mr. Conklin has spent much time in travel, and made many trips to Europe, and still has found time outside his business interests to indulge his refined literary tastes and bibliophilism, which has resulted in the collection of a most interesting and valuable library. He is a member of the St. Nicholas Club, the Automobile Club of America, the Lotos, City Lunch, Nassau Country Club, Huntington Country Club, Seawanhaka-Corinthian Yacht Club, Huntington Yacht Club, American Club of Havana, and the Havana Country Club. For two years he has been president of the Huntington Association, of Huntington and Cold Spring Harbor, Long Island, organized for the purpose of encouraging good roads and harbor improvements in that vicinity. Mr. Conklin was married in Paris, France, May 4, 1898, to Mary Macfadden, and has three children: Julia Cecilia, Roland Hunt and Rosemary Conklin. While still keeping an active interest in many business enterprises, he spends a good portion of his time in following the peaceful pursuits of farming and country life at Rosemary farm, an estate of several hundred acres at Cold Spring Harbor, near Huntington, Long Island.

BAKER, Henry Albert, specialist in orthodontia and prosthetic treatment of oral deformities, was born at Newport, N. H., Nov. 27, 1848, son of Rufus and Mary Emerson (George) Baker, and a descendant of Thomas Baker, a native of the county of Kent, England, who emigrated to America and settled in Roxbury, Mass. The line of descent is traced through his son John; his son Thomas, who married Sarah Pike; their son Capt. Joseph, who married Hannah Lovewell, daughter of the famous Indian warrior, Capt. John Lovewell; their son Capt. Lovewell, who married Mary Worth; their son Richard, who married Lydia Robinson, and their son Lovell, who married Nancy Lane, and their son Rufus, who married Mary E. George and was the father of Dr. Baker. He matriculated at the medical department of Dartmouth College in 1873, and continued his professional studies at the Boston Dental College, where he was graduated D.D.S. in 1879 and was awarded the first college prize for the excellence of his work in the senior class. Soon after his graduation he was appointed demonstrator in operative dentistry at the Boston Dental College, and in 1880-87 was lecturer on oral deformities. He has also been a special lecturer in the dental department of Tufts College. Dr. Baker is better known as a valuable contributor to the mechanical development of dental science than as a teacher. His first invention was a pneumatic mallet, which he perfected in 1872, and which is probably the best device for condensing gold into the cavities of teeth that has been produced. Five years later he read a paper before the Vermont State Dental Society describing a new invention in artificial dentures for restoring normal features, and in 1881 he invented an appliance for congenital cleft palate, which is universally conceded to be the best known, and which corrects to the greatest degree the imperfections of speech which accompany this deformity. In 1893 he invented the ''Baker anchorage,'' a device for correcting and overcoming protruding and receding jaws. This appliance has given an entirely new aspect to the whole subject of orthodontia. Dr. Baker is author of a chapter on ''Obturators and Artificial Vela'' in the American System of Dentistry, and has written many papers on various professional subjects. He was the founder and vice-president, in 1876, of the Vermont State Dental Society, and is a member of the American Academy of Dental Science, and honorary member of the American Society of Orthodontists, the Vermont State Dental Society, and the New Hampshire State Dental Society. He is very fond of outdoor sports, and is a former president of the Jamaica Plain and Dedham Sportsman's clubs, and at the present time (1916) is a director of the Massachusetts Rifle Association, and holds the record in rifle-shooting on the Columbia target at 200 yards. He is a life member of Woodstock Lodge, Ancient Free and Accepted Masons; a member of the Boston Athletic Association, and of the Highland Club of West Roxbury, where he now resides. Dr.

Baker was married in Woodstock, Vt., Nov. 25, 1874, to Julia M., daughter of F. F. Wills, of Calcutta, India, and has one son, Lawrence Wills Baker. Portrait opposite page 110.

HENRY, Philip Walter, civil engineer, was born at Scranton, Pa., March 24, 1864, son of Eugene Thomas and Emma Elizabeth (Walter) Henry. He is descended from Robert Henry, a native of Scotland, who settled in Chester co., Pa., in 1722, with three sons. One of these, John Henry, had a son William, born in 1729, who was the great-grandfather of Eugene T. Henry. William Henry was a manufacturer of firearms in Lancaster, Pa., and furnished supplies to Indian traders. He accompanied the expedition against Fort Duquesne as armorer of the troops of Braddock and Forbes; was associate justice of the court of common pleas, a member of the assembly and of the council of safety, treasurer of Lancaster county, and member of congress in 1784-85. Philip W. Henry was educated in the public schools of Oxford, N. J. After spending three years in railway surveying he entered the Rensselaer Polytechnic Institute of Troy, N. Y., where he was graduated in 1887, with degree of civil engineer. He then became foreman of the works of the Barber Asphalt Paving Co. at Buffalo, and was made assistant superintendent the following year. In 1889 he became superintendent for the company at St. Joseph, Mo., and Omaha, Neb. He was in turn superintendent in New York (1892), assistant to the president (1894), general manager (1897), and vice-president and general manager (1900). In 1902 he opened an office in New York as consulting engineer. Since that date he has been vice-president of the A. L. Barber Asphalt Co., operating the Bermudez asphalt deposit, Venezuela, and president of the South American Construction Co. (1906-09), which built 125 miles of railroad in Bolivia, from Viacha to Oruro. This was a notable achievement in the engineering world, because all of the road was built at an altitude of 12,000 feet and over. In October, 1908, Mr. Henry was appointed by Gov. Hughes to represent New York state at the first international road congress, called by the French government, and held in Paris, France, at which he delivered an address on ''The Future Road,'' which was favorably commented upon both at home and abroad. Since 1909 he has been president of the Central railroad of Hayti, which owns sixty miles of railroad and a pier, tramways and electric light plant at Port-au-Prince. He is president and director of the Achotla Mines Co., which owns valuable gold and silver mines in Guerrero, Mexico. Operations at this mine were well under way when they were interrupted by the revolution of 1912. Associated with him in this company are José M. Ortiz, of Mexico, and E. O. Holter, of New York. In 1910 he made a railroad reconnoissance in Spain, traveling a distance of 700 miles, studying a proposed railroad from Bilboa to Madrid and thence to Valencia. He is chairman of the board of directors of the Mines Management Co., which was organized by him and Mr. E. O. Holter for the examination and management of mining properties, and of which he was the first president; and since 1911 he has been vice-president of the Eddy-Peruvian Co., which is now making a railroad survey for the Peruvian government, 180 miles in length, from Huancayo to Ayacucho, through a very difficult country. Of recent years he has devoted considerable attention to the development of oil properties, and has made examinations of such properties in Wyoming, Colorado,

California, Texas and Mexico. He is a member of the American Society of Civil Engineers, the American Institute of Consulting Engineers, the Engineers' Club, the Union League Club, the University Club, the Railroad Club and the Century Association of New York, the Sleepy Hollow Country Club, and he is a trustee of the Rensselaer Polytechnic Institute of Troy, N. Y. Besides the paper mentioned above, Mr. Henry is the author of ''Has the United States Repudiated International Arbitration?'' in the ''North American Review'' for December, 1907. He was married Jan. 22, 1906, to Clover, daughter of Charles Epperson Cox of Chicago, Ill., and has one daughter, Clover Eugenia Henry.

BARNARD, Kate, philanthropist, was born at Geneva, Neb., about 1879, daughter of John P. and Rachel (Shiell) Barnard. Her father came to this country with his father when a child and became a lawyer and civil engineer, living successively in Nebraska, Kansas and Oklahoma. He was Irish, a man of unusual qualities of mind and character, and to his training is due much of the practical wisdom which so consistently transfuses his daughter's high idealism. The formation of her character during the malleable and all-important years of childhood was completely in his hands, for her mother died when she was eighteen months old; and that the influence of his teaching and personality upon her life was of incalculable value she has frequently and gratefully testified. Her father had obtained a farm of 160 acres near Oklahoma City when she was about twelve years old, and she was educated at the public school and at the St. Joseph's Academy there. Her father's financial reverses prevented her from going to college, but though the circumstances seemed tragic to her then, it probably had its compensatory advantages. Already she had entertained the desire to be useful in a broader sphere than bounds the ordinary ambition. There had already begun to stir in her heart the deep feelings of sympathy for the down-trodden and suffering. After leaving St. Joseph's Academy, she taught in the public schools for a time, and then, in competition with about 500 applicants, secured the appointment to a position at the St. Louis World's Fair. While representing Oklahoma in this capacity she attended all the conventions which gathered in St. Louis and naturally gave special attention to everything bearing on sociological and humanitarian work. This deepened still further her interest in such work, and returning to Oklahoma she began to devote her efforts to succoring the poor immigrants that were pouring into Oklahoma by the thousand. One appeal alone brought in 10,000 garments. She clothed 400 children, bought them books and sent them to school. As matron of the United Provident Association she began to be a little mother to a considerable proportion of Oklahoma City. During the next three years she took care of 3,000 destitute families and placed 500 children in the city schools. She proved herself a stanch and valuable friend to the workingmen, as well as to their families, obtaining for them many substantial benefits, such as raising the wages of street workers in Oklahoma City from $1.25 to $2.25 a day, and helping to organize the unemployed into the Federal Union, which she affiliated with the American Federation of Labor. These activities made her a political power to be reckoned with, and she used her influence to the best advantage when the new state constitution of Oklahoma was under consideration. On her own initiative she undertook to secure ample provision for the care and

protection of the children. In order to familiarize herself with conditions elsewhere she made a tour of the slums, factories and workshops of the larger cities in the East, and consulted with the members of the National Child Labor Committee and other leading sociologists, and with this first-hand information she entered upon a systematic campaign to create a demand for a child labor plank, a compulsory education plank and a department of charities in the new state constitution. Ambassador Bryce said of Oklahoma's constitution that it was ''the finest document of human liberty written since the Declaration of Independence or the Constitution of Switzerland,'' and no little credit for making it such is due to the activities of a single woman, Miss Barnard. The article in the constitution providing for a department of charities contained references to ''his or her office,'' and it was but a logical outcome of her thorough knowledge of social conditions and her profound interest in the welfare of the people at large that she should be nominated for the office of commissioner of charities. As the Democratic candidate she had the distinction of leading her ticket by 6,000 votes. In Oklahoma City, which went Republican by 900, her majority was 1,500. ''Of course,'' said A. J. McKelway, of the National Child Labor Committee, ''there were other reasons for the victory of the Democrats, but Kate Barnard was several reasons herself. She was thoroughly trusted by the two largest classes of voters, the farmers and the labor union men, and she was the favorite speaker on the Democratic side. Slender, graceful, petite, with dark hair and skin and flashing eyes, and a rapid-fire articulation that was the despair of the reporters, she painted pictures of the wrongs of childhood, of the sufferings of minors without the protection of law, of the needs of the orphans, and of the iniquity of sending juvenile criminals to jails, thrilling her vast audiences with her earnest eloquence.'' Kate Barnard is the first woman in the world to be elected by the people of a whole state to be the head of a state department. That she is eminently capable of performing the duties of her office is proved by her record as head of the department of charities and correction of Oklahoma. It was likewise indicative of her earnestness and sincerity that upon taking office she insisted upon a reduction of her salary, which was originally put at $2,500, to $1,500. In carrying on her work she has displayed executive capacity of a very high order. She has secured legislation embodying the most advanced sociological thought, such as prison laws, prepared by Samuel J. Barrows, ex-president of the International Prison Congress; juvenile court laws, drafted by Judge Ben Lindsey, of Denver, Colo.; child labor and compulsory education laws, by A. J. McKelway, of the National Child Labor Committee; laws for the care and treatment of the insane and feeble-minded, by Alexander Johnson and H. H. Hart. All such unfortunates, including the whole category of weak and suffering humanity, she regards as her protégés. With a motherly heart and an unquenchable ardor she is working for their interests, and what she has accomplished has been so notable as to attract the attention of the leaders of statecraft of the whole world. Miss Barnard's activities are not by any means confined to her own state. Her exposé in 1908 of the atrocious conditions prevailing in the Lansing (Kan.) penitentiary will be long remembered; she inspired the legal battle between Oklahoma and Kansas, which resulted in the breaking of the contract which the latter had with Oklahoma for the care of its 600 prisoners; and

HENRY A. BAKER
DENTIST

PHILIP W. HENRY
CIVIL ENGINEER

KATE BARNARD
PHILANTHROPIST

LOUIS HAUPT
PHYSICIAN

she figured in a big prison reform fight in Arizona in the winter of 1911-12, coming out victorious, as she always does in matters of social reforms. In 1912 she succeeded in restoring $2,000,000 to the Indians and Indian orphans of her state and in prosecuting the men who tried to deprive them of their lands and money. Yet with all her activities she finds time to deliver eloquent addresses before national and international conventions and state and local bodies upon the subject nearest her heart. She made the closing address in the American section of the International Tuberculosis Congress at Washington in 1908, before the Governors' Congress at Richmond, Va., in 1913, and she has frequently delivered addresses before colleges, universities and learned societies.

HAUPT, Louis, physician, was born in New York city, Jan. 7, 1851, son of Christopher and Frances (Ebler) Haupt, both natives of Baden, Germany, who came to the United States in 1848, and settled at New York. The son received his education in the public schools of his native city and in Miami University, Oxford, O. Having decided to follow the medical profession, he entered the Medical College of Louisville, Ky., and later the Medical College of New York University. He was graduated M.D. at the latter in 1877 and engaged in the general practice of medicine in New York city with marked success. Of studious habits and well read in the classics as well as in modern English and German literature, Dr. Haupt has taken a great interest in educational matters. He served for several years as school trustee and since 1902 has been a member of the board of education of New York city, where his ripe knowledge of conditions and extended experience have been of the greatest value for the public schools. He has devoted considerable attention to the development of the playground idea and to physical training and recreation in the public schools. In politics he is a Republican. He is a member of the American Medical Association, the New York State Medical Society, the New York County Medical Society, the German Medical Society of the city of New York, the American Museum of Natural History, the Metropolitan Museum of Art, the American Geographical Society, the New York Botanical Garden, the New York Zoölogical Garden, the Arion Society and German Press Club. Dr. Haupt is visiting physician to St. Francis' Home, a member of the board and treasurer of the German Poliklinik, and president of the Arion Society. Portrait opposite page 110.

SYLVESTER, Allie Lewis, manufacturer, was born in New York city Dec. 17, 1864, son of Lewis and Hester (Fox) Sylvester, and grandson of Seymour Sylvester, a native of Germany, who came to the United States in 1826 and settled in New York city. His father (1834-1907) was a dealer in leaf tobacco in New York. After a public school education the son began his business career in his father's office, the firm at that time being Lewis Sylvester & Son. He was quick to master the details of the business, and as he entered more and more into the management of its affairs, it developed into one of the largest leaf tobacco houses in the United States. His father retired from the firm Dec. 31, 1901. The firm continued under the old name and style until March 1, 1907, when he reorganized it, taking into partnership Maximilian Stern, and its name was changed to Sylvester & Stern. Mr. Sylvester is a man of unusual energy, perseverance and rare executive ability, and he quickly became recognized as one of the most prominent merchants in the United States. In 1909 he was invited by James B. Duke, then president of the American Tobacco Co., to join their forces and accept the management of the leaf department of the American Cigar Co. Two years later he was made vice-president of the company, and in June, 1912, succeeded Percival S. Hill as president of the American Cigar Co., Mr. Hill having withdrawn to become president of the American Tobacco Co., succeeding Mr. Duke. The American Cigar Co. is the largest manufacturer of cigars in the world, and, while it had a very extensive volume of business previously, the same has materially increased under Mr. Sylvester's direction. It now has some forty factories located in different parts of the United States and over twenty factories in the island of Cuba, where Havana cigars are made which are disposed of throughout the world. In addition to their large number of factories they are the largest growers of leaf tobacco, both in Cuba and Porto Rico as well, and also own and operate large packing houses throughout the United States wherever leaf tobacco suitable for the manufacture of cigars is grown, and in the operation of its vast properties it employs in the neighborhood of thirty-seven thousand persons. This business is all directed by Mr. Sylvester from the head office in New York, but a large part of his time is spent in traveling all over the world looking after the interests of this vast corporation. Their interests in Cuba make it necessary for him to be there a considerable part of each year directing the affairs of the companies, which are run independently of their American interests. The officers of the American Cigar Co. are A. L. Sylvester, president; R. E. Christie, R. M. C. Glenn, F. E. Johnson, A. Schneider and N. Weiss, vice-presidents, and G. G. Finch, secretary and treasurer. Mr. Sylvester is thoroughly familiar with every detail of this enormous industry and is recognized in the trade as probably the leading authority on leaf tobacco in the world. Personally he is a man of marked individuality, possessed of an unusual amount of determination and foresight. He seems to have an infinite capacity for hard work, devoting his entire time and services to the advancement and welfare of the business. He takes the deepest kind of interest in his employees, with whom he deals considerately and justly, and enjoys their respect and loyalty to a marked degree. He is regarded as a good judge of men and their capacity, and one of his chief characteristics is acknowledgment of the worth and ability of those with whom he is associated. His genial disposition betokens a kindly nature and a willingness to deal squarely with every man and accord to all the same treatment that he would ask for himself. Mr. Sylvester is also president of H. De Cabanas y Carbajal, the Cuban Land and Leaf Tobacco Co., the Havana-American Co., the Havana Commercial Co., J. S. Murias & Co., Seidenberg & Co., M. Stachelberg & Co., and M. Valle y Ca.; vice-president of the Havana Tobacco Co., the Luis Marx Tobacco Co. and the Porto Rican Leaf Tobacco Co., and chairman of Henry Clay and Bock & Co. and the Havana Cigar and Tobacco Factories, Ltd. He is a member of the Chamber of Commerce of New York and the Merchants' Association.

LESLEY, Robert Whitman, manufacturer, was born in Philadelphia, Pa., July 4, 1853, son of James and Elizabeth (Thomson) Lesley, grandson of James Lesley, who was connected with the State Bank of Pennsylvania and the Union Bank in Philadelphia and was United States Consul at Lyons, France, and great grandson of Peter Lesley, the first of his family in this country, who settled in Philadelphia in the latter part of the eighteenth century. His father (1822-65) was a hardware merchant, later becoming one of the editors of the Philadelphia "Press," and was United States consul at Nice, France, where he died in 1865. His mother was a daughter of Judge Alexander Thomson, a member of congress from Franklin county, Pa. Robert W. Lesley obtained his early education in France and Germany. He was prepared for college at the Langton School in Philadelphia, and entered the University of Pennsylvania in 1867, but left college to go into business. Subsequently (1908) the university graduated him with the degree of A.M. as of the class of 1871, an unusual honor that made him a full alumnus of the university. Mr. Lesley began his business career in the office of the Philadelphia "Ledger" in September, 1868, serving in the business department and later as assistant editor. His natural inclination was for the legal profession, and he began the study of law under Benjamin Harris Brewster, United States attorney-general, and was admitted to the bar in 1879. Because of his prominent connection with the cement industry in recent years his legal career has been forgotten by all but his early associates; nevertheless, up to the time of his withdrawal from practice he represented many leading corporations, including the Pennsylvania Railroad Co. and the Pullman Palace Car Co. Mr. Lesley's interest in the cement industry came about through the firm of Lesley & Trinkle, which, with John W. Trinkle, he organized in 1874 to deal in building materials. Cement of the so-called "Rosendale," or natural, kind had been made extensively in this country for many years previously, but practically all the Portland cement was imported. The late David O. Saylor was then developing the manufacture of that material in this country, and Mr. Lesley, recognizing the importance which the industry would inevitably assume, became associated with him. In 1882, while still practicing law, he became manager of the Cumberland Cement Works. In the following year he established the American Improved Cement Co. in the Lehigh Pennsylvania district. This company was subsequently merged with the Pennsylvania Cement Co. under the title of the American Cement Co., and was later sold to a banking syndicate, when it became the American Cement Co. of New Jersey. It has been for many years one of the largest producers of Portland and natural cements in the country, with works at Egypt and Lesley, Pa., and Norfolk, Va. The use of American Portland cement is now so extensive and so little European cement reaches this country that the difficulties of Mr. Lesley and his associates in the early days of the industry are rather hard to appreciate. American natural cement was used extensively, but when a material of a higher quality was needed the engineer and architect was accustomed to rely on some imported brand which had a good record of serviceability. The first Portland cement made here was a new product, with no record of experience behind it, and those responsible for the security of the foundations of a large office building or a great masonry dam were naturally reluctant to rely on an untried product. Consequently the commercial introduction of American Portland cement was a task of much difficulty, and in carrying it through Mr. Lesley played a most important part, some of his associates in the industry giving him credit for being the leading figure. As the business grew he gradually gave up his law practice and devoted all his time and energies to the development of the business, both in making the merits of American Portland cement known and in enlarging the capacity of his works to meet the growing demand. During that time the output has grown from 3,000 to 84,000,000 barrels of Portland cement per annum, and to his industry, energy and executive ability is largely due the present extent of the cement business. His versatility is well shown in the part he took in developing the process of manufacture. The English material was made from chalk and clay, while the first American cement was made from the peculiar limestones of Lehigh county, Pa., and very little help in the technical details of the process could be obtained from a study of the English methods. Mr. Lesley attacked the problem from the foundation, making a study of chemistry, and pursuing various experiments, resulting in six patents being granted him by the United States government. In this connection he also carried on a number of investigations which settled disputed questions concerning the behavior of cement under various conditions, and he was one of the little group of manufacturers, consumers and experts who brought about the standardization of the specifications for the material, an achievement of the highest technical and industrial importance. It is an indication of his desire to bring about a good realization of the proper uses of the material, as well as his regard for his alma mater, that he donated the Lesley Cement Laboratory to the University of Pennsylvania; this is one of the most complete laboratories of the kind in the country. He was one of the leading organizers of the Association of American Portland Cement Manufacturers in 1902, an organization that has become an important factor in collecting and distributing information regarding the properties and uses of cement. Mr. Lesley was the first president of this association and is a member of its executive committee. In 1904 he established "Cement Age," one of the first trade journals devoted to cement and concrete. In 1912 it was consolidated with "Concrete" of Detroit, and as "Concrete-Cement Age" is now the leading journal in this industry. Mr. Lesley is a director and consulting editor. He is a member of the American Society for Testing Materials (of which he was for ten years vice-president), the International Association for Testing Materials, an associate of the American Society of Civil Engineers, and a manager of the Franklin Institute. He was appointed by President Roosevelt a member of the Government Board on Fuels and Structural Materials. He is a member of the British Society of Chemical Industry, of the American Chemical Society and of the Joint Committee of the Engineering Societies on Concrete and Reinforced Concrete. He is likewise a member of the Engineers' and Railroad clubs of New York, the Racquet, Rittenhouse and Engineers' clubs of Philadelphia, the Livingston Club of Allentown, the Merion Cricket Club of Haverford, the Bryn Mawr Polo Club, the Radnor Hunt Club and the Philadelphia Country Club. He is an enthusiastic golf player, is the president of the Golf Association of Philadelphia, and is the donor of the Lesley Cup, which is played for annually by the Metropolitan, Massachusetts and Pennsylvania Golf associations. Mr. Lesley was married Oct. 23, 1879, to Eulalia, daughter of James M. Willcox of Glen Mills and Philadelphia, Pa., and has one daughter, Mary Eulalia, wife of Richard Berridge of Toomboola, County Galway, Ireland.

PLATT, Isaac Hull, physician, was born in Brooklyn, N. Y., May 18, 1853, son of Frederick Augustus and Augusta Mary (Hull) Platt, of English ancestry. His earliest paternal American ancestor, Richard Platt, of Hertfordshire, England, came to America with his wife, Mary, and four children, settling first at New Haven, Conn., in 1638, and a year later becoming one of the founders of the town of Milford, Conn. The line of descent is traced through his son, Capt. Epenetus Platt, of Huntington, L. I., who married Phœbe Wood, of Halifax. Capt. Platt was imprisoned by Gov. Andros in New York for presenting with others a petition for his fellow-townsmen of the Suffolk Company of Foot, Jan. 9, 1684, and in 1689 was sent in command of the "East End Men" to demand the surrender of the fort at New York. His son Epenetus, also of Huntington, L. I., was a member of the colonial assembly of New York. His son Uriah, of Hempstead, L. I., who married Mary Smith, was a large proprietor of Hempstead, owning a considerable part of Hempstead Plain, including the site of Garden City. His son Epenetus, also of Hempstead, L. I., married Catherine, daughter of William Lawrence and niece of Lady Elizabeth (Lawrence) Carteret, wife of Sir William Carteret, colonial governor of New Jersey. This Epenetus Platt was a surgeon in the Continental army, and lived in White Plains, Westchester co., after the war. His son Epenetus married Mary Simonson, of Hempstead, L. I. He was a practicing physician of New York and White Plains, and died in New York during an epidemic of yellow fever, having gone there to render assistance. His son Epenetus was also a physician of New York city, and married Maria Warner. His son, Frederick Augustus Platt, father of our subject, was cashier of the Corn Exchange Bank of New York from its foundation until 1863. In 1851 he married the daughter of Levi Hull, of the Continental army, and niece of Commodore Isaac Hull and grandniece of Gen. William Hull. Isaac Hull Platt was educated at Adelphi Academy, Brooklyn, and at the Brooklyn Polytechnic Institute. He first turned his attention to the law and was admitted to the New York bar in 1878, but later took up the study of medicine, and was graduated M. D. at the Long Island College Hospital in 1882. After a post-graduate course at the College of Physicians and Surgeons, he served as interne at St. Mary's Hospital, Brooklyn, in 1882-83. He practiced at Lakewood, N. J., for ten years (1886-96), when he was obliged to retire because of ill-health. In 1896 he was elected first vice-president of the American Climatological Association and declined the presidency the following year on account of infirm health. After two years of travel in Europe he settled in New York city, but in 1901 removed to Wallingford, Pa., where he devoted himself to literary labors, chiefly to the study of Shakespeare. Dr. Platt was a frequent contributor to the "Baconia Review." He was the author of "Walt Whitman," in the "Beacon Biographies" series, and of "Bacon Cryptograms in Shakespeare, and Other Studies" (1905). He was a man of brilliant parts, of most versatile accomplishments, and of a rare degree of mental excellence. Whatsoever subject attracted his attention yielded its ultimate secrets to his eager quest. A lawyer before he was twenty-six years of age; an earnest student of the physical sciences; a physician of acknowledged ability before he was thirty; from his youth a man of letters—he possessed a mind of wide range and power. He was a member of the American Academy of Medicine, the Medical Club of Philadelphia, the New York Genealogical Society, the Society of the Cincinnati, Sons of the Revolution, Society of the War of 1812, the Historical Society of Pennsylvania, the Art Club of Philadelphia, and the National Arts and Players' clubs of New York. Dr. Platt was married in Brooklyn, Sept. 2, 1886, to Emma, daughter of Aaron Griffen Haviland, of Westchester county, N. Y., and had three sons, Frederick Epenetus, Haviland Hull and Philip Galpin Platt. He died at his home, "Runnemede," Wallingford, Pa., Aug. 14, 1912.

TOWLE, Harry Freeman, educator, was born at Epsom, N. H., May 20, 1852, son of Benjamin and Eliza (Ham) Towle. His first paternal American ancestor was Philip Towle, of English extraction, who came to America in the first half of the seventeenth century and settled at Hampton, N. H. From him and his wife, Isabella Austin, the line is through their son Joseph and his wife, Mehetabel Hobbs; their son Jonathan and his wife, Anna Norton; their son Jonathan and his wife, Elizabeth Jennis; their son Simeon and his wife, Elizabeth Marden; their son, Benjamin Marden, and his wife, Hannah Sanborn, and their son Benjamin and his wife, Eliza Ham. Simeon Towle fought in the revolutionary war. Harry F. Towle received his early education at the district schools of Epsom and the Pennacook Academy and was graduated at Dartmouth College in 1876. He began teaching school at Wells, Me., and subsequently in the high schools of Hollis and Nashua, N. H. Later he became principal of the high school at Whitman, Mass., whence he went to Yonkers, N. Y., as principal and teacher of mathematics in the grammar school there. Next he became assistant principal and head of the Latin department at the old Central Grammar School, Brooklyn, N. Y. When the Boys' High School was founded in Brooklyn, Mr. Towle became assistant principal and head of the Latin department, and upon its establishment was made principal of the Boys' High School Annex. In 1906 he became principal of the Curtis High School, Staten Island, N. Y., a position which he held until his death. Mr. Towle was for many years one of the most prominent and widely known educators in New York. He was a member of the Schoolmasters' Association and the Brooklyn Principals' Association, and an honorary member of the Alumni Association of Brooklyn Teachers. In collaboration with Paul R. Jenks he was the author of a school edition of "Cæsar's Gallic War" (1903) and of a "Cæsar for Sight Reading" (1912). In 1894 he received the degree of A. M. from Dartmouth College. He was a man of magnetic and attractive personality, with a remarkable faculty of winning affection and for making and keeping friends. He was genial, generous and sympathetic and enjoyed very great popularity both among his professional associates and in the communities in which he lived. He was president of the Dartmouth College Society of New York, a charter member of the University Club, and a member of the Sons of the American Revolution, the New England Society, the Sons of New Hampshire, the Psi Upsilon and the Phi Beta Kappa fraternities, and president of the Brooklyn Teachers' Association, Orion Lodge, F. and A. M., and the first president of the Latin Club. He was married Dec. 23, 1880, to Annie Miller, daughter of John Sproul, of Whitman, Mass., and had one child, Florence

Wilson Towle. He died at New Brighton, Staten Island, N. Y., Dec. 31, 1912.

POTHIER, Aram J., forty-seventh governor of Rhode Island, was born in Quebec, Canada, July 26, 1854, son of Jules and Domitilde (Dallaire) Pothier. He was educated at Nicolet College and in 1870 removed with his parents to Woonsocket, R. I. In 1875 he became a clerk in the Woonsocket Institution for Savings and has ever since been connected with it, since 1909 as its vice-president. He was elected to the Woonsocket school committee in 1885 and two years later was elected to the Rhode Island legislature. During 1889–94 he was city auditor of Woonsocket and in the latter year he was elected mayor of Woonsocket, being re-elected in 1895 and declining a third nomination for the office. He was lieutenant-governor in 1897–98 and declined a renomination. He was elected a member of the state board of education in 1907. In 1908 he became the Republican candidate for governor of Rhode Island and was elected to succeed Hon. James H. Higgins by a vote of 7,270 over that cast for the Democratic candidate. He took office Jan. 1, 1909, and in the following autumn was re-elected by 11,834 plurality over the same opponent, the increased popular vote indicating the success and popularity of his administration. During his incumbency the legislature passed a law limiting the labor of women and children in manufacturing and mechanical establishments to fifty-four hours per week, an important reform in so essentially a manufacturing community as Rhode Island; it also took up the conservation of natural resources, providing for a commission to deal with the question, and a survey of the state's resources, and submitted to the vote of the people a constitutional amendment giving the governor power of veto. Gov. Pothier is a typical man of affairs, the scope of his interests being international. A consequent breadth of view and information, combined with an unusual power of initiative and dignity, rendered him an ideal executive. He was instrumental in introducing a number of industries into Woonsocket and has made the town one of the centres for spinning woolen and worsted yarns by the French and Belgian processes. He is treasurer of the Guerin Spinning Co., the Alsace Worsted Co., the French Worsted Co., the Montrose Woolen Co., and the Rosemont Dyeing Co., all of Woonsocket. He was commissioner from Rhode Island to the Paris International Exposition of 1889 and again to that of 1900.

DRINKER, Henry Sturgis, fifth president of Lehigh University, was born at Hong Kong, China, Nov. 8, 1850, son of Sandwith and Susannah Budd (Shobee) Drinker. His first American ancestor was Philip Drinker, who came to this country from his birthplace, Exeter, England, with his wife Elizabeth and settled at Charlestown, Mass. The line of descent is traced through their son John, also a native of Exeter, England, who accompanied his parents hence in his boyhood, and married Elizabeth———; their son John, who married Ruth Balch; their son Joseph, who married Mary Janney; their son Henry, who married Mary Gottier; their son Henry, who married Elizabeth Sandwith; their son Henry Sandwith, who married Hannah Smith, and their son Sandwith Drinker, the father of the subject of this sketch. Henry Sturgis Drinker was graduated as mining engineer at Lehigh University in 1871. He was colliery clerk for the Lehigh Valley Coal Co. in 1871–72, was with the field corps on the New Jersey extension of the Lehigh Valley Railroad in 1872,

and had charge of the construction of the Musconetcong tunnel on this New Jersey extension during 1872–75, after which he entered the main office of the railroad at Philadelphia. In 1878 he published a work on tunneling. Having studied law and secured admittance to the bar, he became later general solicitor of the Lehigh Valley Railroad Co. He was assistant to Pres. Wilbur and Pres. McLeod at the time of the Reading lease, and served as general solicitor through six successive Lehigh Valley railroad administrations. He edited the revised and enlarged edition of Ball's General Railroad and Telegraph Laws of Pennsylvania, 1884. In 1905 he was elected president of Lehigh University. At this time the university had fifty-two teachers, 685 students and a library of 125,000 volumes. At the present time, 1916, the teaching force numbers seventy-six, the student body 759, and there are 137,000 volumes in the library. During Pres. Drinker's administration Lehigh University has had a marked expansion in its plant, including the erection of two dormitories, a college dining hall, a student club house, a mining engineering laboratory, a testing engineering laboratory, a new gymnasium and field house, and a complete renovation of the athletic field, including the erection of a concrete stadium. During 1912–16 Dr. Drinker was president of the American Forestry Association. He is chairman of the Military Training Camps Association of the U. S., and secretary of the Advisory Committee of University Presidents on the Summer Military Training Camps. He is also vice-president of the American Conservation Congress. The degree of LL.D. was conferred upon him by Lafayette College in 1905, by Franklin and Marshall College in 1910, and by the University of Pennsylvania in 1911. He was married, Dec. 2, 1879, to Aimée Ernesta, daughter of Jean Adolph Beaux, of Philadelphia, Pa., and has four sons and two daughters: Henry Sandwith, James Blathwaite, Cecil Kent, Philip, Aimée Ernesta, and Catherine Shober Drinker.

FIELDER, James Fairman, thirty-ninth governor of New Jersey, was born in Jersey City, N. J., Feb. 26, 1867, son of George B. and Eleanor A. (Brinkerhoff) Fielder. On the paternal side his ancestors were English, and on the maternal side Hollanders, and were among the earliest settlers in the state of New Jersey. On each side the families have been prominent in the religious and political history of the state. His paternal grandfather, a leading citizen of Jersey City, was a member of the assembly from Hudson county in 1871, and his maternal grandfather was for many years a county judge of that county. His father served as register of Hudson county and was a member of the 43d congress. James Fairman Fielder was educated in the public and high schools of Jersey City, at Selleck School, Norwalk, Conn., and was graduated at Columbia University Law School with the degree of LL.B. in 1887. After graduation he entered the office of his uncle, former Sen. William Brinkerhoff, and was admitted to the bar in 1888. He was a member of the assembly from Hudson county in 1903 and 1904, was elected to the senate in 1907, and was re-elected in 1910 by the largest majority ever given to a state senator from his county. In 1913 he was elected president of the senate, and when Gov. Wilson became president of the United States, Sen. Fielder became acting governor according to the state constitution. At the primary election held in September, 1913, James F. Fielder was nominated as a candidate for governor over Frank S. Katzenback by a majority of 45,299. At the regular state

HARRY F. TOWLE
EDUCATOR

ARAM J. POTHIER
GOVERNOR

HENRY S. DRINKER
PRESIDENT LEHIGH UNIVERSITY

JAMES F. FIELDER
GOVERNOR

WILLIAM B. McKINLEY
CONGRESSMAN

JOHN W. WEEKS
U. S. SENATOR

HAMILTON HOLT
EDITOR

HENRY HEIDE
MANUFACTURER

election held on the fourth of the following November he was elected governor over Edward Casper Stokes, Republican and a former governor, by a plurality of 32,886, and was inaugurated Jan. 20, 1914, for a term of three years. Gov. Fielder is a member of St. John's Episcopal Church in Jersey City. He was married, June 4, 1895, to Mabel, daughter of C. Miller, of Norwalk, Conn.

McKINLEY, William Brown, capitalist, philanthropist, was born at Petersburg, Ill., Sept. 5, 1856, son of George and Hannah (Finley) McKinley and grandson of Thomas McKinley, who came from County Donegal, Ireland, in 1801 and settled on a farm near Chillicothe, O. His father was a Presbyterian minister. He attended the University of Illinois but was not graduated. He began his business career in association with an uncle, J. B. McKinley, a dealer in farm mortgages, at Champaign, Ill. Later he became a promoter and builder of electric interurban railroads, eventually becoming president of the Illinois Traction Co., one of the largest systems of its kind in the world. In 1910, because his company was not permitted to use the railroad bridge for his lines, he built a bridge across the Mississippi river at St. Louis at a cost of five million dollars. He is also engaged in building, buying and operating gas plants, electric lighting plants and railroad properties. Living in the heart of the broom corn belt, one of the richest districts of Illinois, he has done much to improve the grade of corn in his section, offering prizes and inducements of various kinds to interest boys and farmers in the natural products. In 1904 he was elected to congress from the nineteenth district of Illinois, serving until 1912, when he was defeated for another term, but in 1914 was again elected. While trustee of the University of Illinois in 1897 he inaugurated a philanthropic plan of loaning money to students of that institution upon no other security than their promissory notes at five per cent. interest. Through his generosity many students were thus helped financially, and scores of graduates aided by him have attained positions of prominence in the business and professional world. In 1912 he offered to the trustees of the University, and they accepted, the outstanding notes of students, aggregating $12,000, to establish a permanent loan fund for worthy students. He believes the success of this plan is an illustration of human honesty deserving wide attention; that most men would rather be honest than dishonest; that nearly all have a code of honor which they cherish, and that an appeal to that code, if rightly made, rarely fails of response. His plan, broadly speaking, is to help deserving students to help themselves. The Young Men's Christian Association and Young Women's Christian Association buildings at the University of Illinois were built through his generosity, and he has given much to charity in other ways. He is a member of the Union League and Hamilton clubs, Chicago, and of the Cosmos Club, Washington, D. C. His favorite pursuits are business and politics, and his dominating personal characteristics are persistency after undertaking a thing, fairness and a desire to always give "the other fellow" a chance.

WEEKS, John Wingate, U. S. senator, was born at Lancaster, N. H., Apr. 11, 1860, son of William Dennis and Mary Helen (Fowler) Weeks. His father was a farmer and probate judge. The first paternal American ancestor of the family was Leonard Weeks, a native of Wells, England, who came to this country in 1656 and settled at Portsmouth, N. H., and the line of descent is traced through his son Joshua, who married Martha Wingate; their son John Wingate, who married Martha Wingate; their son John, who married Mary Brackett, and their son James Brackett, who married Betsy Stanley, and was the senator's grandfather. John Weeks was a captain in the continental forces during the revolution and settled at Lancaster in 1786. His son, John Wingate Weeks, served with distinction in the war of 1812, and was a representative in congress in 1829–33. The subject of this sketch was graduated at the U. S. Naval Academy in 1881. After serving for two years as midshipman in the navy, he resigned and took up the profession of civil engineering. In 1888 he became associated with Henry Hornblower and other partners in the banking and brokerage business in Boston, Mass., under the firm name of Hornblower & Weeks, with which he continued until 1914. During the intervening years he also became identified with a number of national banks and trust companies, and at different times was president of the Newtonville Trust Co., vice-president of the First National Bank of Boston, and a director of many other corporations. He served for ten years in the Massachusetts naval brigade, during the last six years of which he was commander, and he also served during the Spanish war in the volunteer navy as commander of the second division, U. S. auxiliary force on the Atlantic coast. His first prominent appearance in public affairs was in 1899, when he was elected alderman of Newton, Mass. In 1902 he was elected mayor of the city and a year later was elected to the national house of representatives, where he served by re-election until 1912, when the Massachusetts legislature sent him to the senate to succeed Winthrop Murray Crane. In the senate he has served on the committees on banking and currency, coast defenses, conservatism of national resources, forest reservations and the protection of game, Indian depredations, Philippines, post-offices and post-roads, public health and public quarantine and military affairs. As a member of the banking and currency committee he helped formulate the banking and currency act of 1914. Sen. Weeks was chairman of the Massachusetts Republican state convention in 1895 and a member of the board of visitors to the U. S. Naval Academy in 1896. He is vice-president of the American Forestry Association and a member of the Boston Chamber of Commerce, the Sons of the Revolution, Society of the War of 1812, the Society of the Spanish-American War, the Society of the Cincinnati, the Military Order of Foreign Wars, and the University and Exchange clubs of Boston, the Army and Navy, Metropolitan and Chevy Chase clubs of Washington, the Hamilton Club of Chicago and the Country Club of Brookline, Mass. He was married at Haverhill, Mass., Oct. 7, 1885, to Martha, daughter of John G. Sinclair, of Bethlehem, N. H., and has two children: Katherine W., wife of John W. Davidge, and Charles Sinclair Weeks.

HOLT, Hamilton, editor, was born in Brooklyn, N. Y., Aug. 18, 1872, son of George Chandler and Mary Louisa (Bowen) Holt, and a descendant of Nicholas Holt, who came to this country from England in 1635 and settled at Newbury, Mass. From him and his wife Elizabeth the line is then traced through their son Henry and his wife, Sarah Ballard; their son George and his wife, Mary Biebee; their son Nehemiah and his wife, Anna Farnham; their son Nehemiah and his wife, Mary Lamphear; their son Hiram and his wife, Marian Chandler, and their son, George Chandler, father of Hamilton Holt. George Chandler Holt was U. S. district judge of the southern district of New York; he married the daughter of Henry C. Bowen (q. v), founder, editor and proprietor of "The Independent." The son was graduated at Yale University in 1894, and pursued post-graduate work in sociology and economics at Columbia University during 1894–97. In the latter year he became managing editor of "The Independent," continuing thus until 1913, when he became editor and part owner of that publication and has so remained until the present time (1916). Mr. Holt has written and lectured extensively on the peace movement and is associated with many peace organizations and activities. He is one of the founders of the New York Peace Society, and a member of the executive committee of the first American peace congress, held in New York city, May, 1907, and chairman of its press committee. He was a representative from the state of New York to the second American peace congress, held at Chicago, May, 1909, and a member of its committee on resolutions; president of the third American peace congress, held in Baltimore, May, 1911; a member of "Conciliation Internationale," the American Society of International Law and the American Peace Society; a director in the World Peace Foundation, founded by Edwin Ginn, of Boston, director of the Church Peace Union; a founder of the League to Enforce Peace, a trustee of the American-Scandinavian Foundation, and an invited delegate to Albert K. Smiley's Lake Mohonk arbitration conferences. Mr. Holt is also the founder of the Mexico Society of New York, which was formed to promote peace and friendship between Mexico and the United States. In the summer of 1907 he made a special trip to Holland to attend the second Hague conference and to become acquainted with the European leaders of the peace movement. He is the author of "Undistinguished Americans" (1906) and "Commercialism and Journalism" (1909), and is an occasional contributor to reviews, though his writing is chiefly confined to "The Independent." He is a trustee of the American College for Girls at Constantinople; member of the executive committee of the Woman's Trade Union League; member of the American Association for Labor Legislation, National Civic Federation, American Society of International Law, Japan Society of New York, Friends of Russian Freedom, Simplified Spelling Board, Committee of 100, Committee of 107, and the Century, Authors, Liberal, Economic, February, X, and Independent clubs, and the Psi Upsilon college fraternity. In 1906 he was resident at University Settlement. In June, 1909, the emperor of Japan conferred upon him the Order of the Sacred Treasure for the work he did in promoting friendly relations between the United States and Japan, and in 1915 Ursinus College gave him the honorary degree of LL.D. He was married, Feb. 8, 1899, to Alexina Crawford, daughter of Marshall P. Smith, of Baltimore, Md., and their children are: Beatrice, Leila Stuart, John Eliot and George Chandler Holt.

PERRY, Nora, journalist, author, poet, was born at Dudley, Mass., in 1841, daughter of Harvey and Sarah Perry. The family removed to Providence, R. I., while she was a child and her father became a prosperous merchant of that city. Her education was acquired in private schools in Boston and Providence. She early developed a taste for literature and began to write for magazines at the age of eighteen, becoming subsequently Boston correspondent of the Chicago "Tribune," and later of the Providence "Journal." Her earlier serious efforts were for the most part confined to poetry. Of her poems of this period "After the Ball" is well known and was frequently quoted under the title "Maud and Madge." This and other poems were published in a collection in 1875, followed by a second volume four years later. Her other books of poems are "Her Lover's Friend, etc." (1877), and "New Songs and Ballads" (1886). Her first serial story was "Rosalind Newcomb," published in "Harper's Magazine" in 1859. Her other books are "A Book of Love Stories" (1881); "The Tragedy of the Unexpected, and Other Stories" (1880); "For a Woman" (1885) "The Youngest Miss Lorton, and Other Stories" (1888); "A Flock of Girls and Their Friends" (1887); "Brave Girls" (1889); "Legends and Lyrics" (1890); and "Three Little Daughters of the Revolution" (1896). She made a specialty of stories for girls and had the happy gift of inspiring girls to care for big things and to make their lives at once rich and austere. She contributed many beautiful thoughts and phrases to the common stock of public speech, and her writings all abound in wit, humor, pathos and sound sense. She was unmarried and died at Dudley, Mass., May 13, 1896.

LEE, Charles Alfred, physician, was born at Salisbury, Conn., Mar. 3, 1801, son of Samuel and Elizabeth (Brown) Lee. He studied medicine with his brother-in-law, Dr. Luther Ticknor, and was graduated M. D. at the Berkshire Medical College, Pittsfield, Mass., in 1822. He practised his profession in New York city, where he aided in establishing the Northern Dispensary. He held the chair of materia medica and general pathology in the Geneva Medical College, New York, and the last years of his life were devoted chiefly to teaching various principles of medicine in different medical colleges. He wrote extensively on a great variety of medical and scientific subjects, the most important of his books being "Physiology for the Use of Elementary Schools" (1835), which did much to popularize the subject; "Manual of Geology for Schools" (1835). He brought out an edition of William A. Guy's "Principles of Forensic Medicine" in 1845, with extensive and valuable notes and additions, and he edited an American edition of Dr. James Copland's "Dictionary of Practical Medicine." Dr. Lee was married June 28, 1828, to Hester Ann, daughter of John A. Mildeberge, who survived him with three sons. He died in New York, Feb. 13, 1872.

HEIDE, Henry, manufacturer, was born in Obermarsberg, Westphalia, Oct. 24, 1846, son of Burgomaster John and Margaret (Luckey) Heide. In 1866 he came to America to seek his fortune. Not long thereafter he joined a friend who had accompanied him to this country and started a candy business. In 1868 he formed a partnership with Bernard Tieleman, under the firm name of Heide & Tieleman, and opened a candy store in Brooklyn, his partner attending to the retail trade, while he managed the wholesale department. In 1869 they separated, Tieleman continuing the retail business and Mr. Heide the wholesale. In 1874, Herman Blumensaat became his partner under the name of Heide & Blumensaat, and that was the beginning of the present enterprise. Mr. Blumensaat remained only three years, his place being taken by Charles Wirtz. He withdrew three years later and thenceforth the firm name has been "Henry Heide." Under his able management the business continued to expand, and in 1896 he purchased the site of the present factory located at 78-90 Vandam street, which was at once covered by a fireproof building, consisting of nine stories and basement, and this structure was enlarged in 1905. The factory had then a floor space of 200,000 square feet, which, in the year 1911 was further extended, and now has floor space of 350,000 square feet. Mr. Heide has adopted the Diamond H. H. trademark for his confectionery products, and it is recognized by the candy trade as standing for the best quality and finest grade of goods. The sale of Heide's candies extends to all parts of the United States, and into South America, Europe, Africa, Australia, China and Japan. Mr. Heide has taken a prominent interest in the trade organizations connected with his business. He was president of the National Confectioners' Association in 1905 and 1906; also president of the Eastern Confectioners' Association and chairman of the executive committee. He is a member of the National Confectioners' and other kindred associations, of the Board of Trade and Transportation, Merchants' Association and of the chambers of commerce of the state of New York and of the United States. He was a director in the City Trust Co., afterward the Trust Co. of America, and is at present a director in the Greenwich Bank and Emigrant Industrial Savings Bank. He is also president and director of the Iberville Lumber Co., operating in Canada. He belongs to the Liederkranz Society, Arion Society, the Catholic Club and the St. Vincent de Paul Society. He believes in having good assistants, and in treating them well and liberally. The first man he ever employed was on his payroll about forty years up to his death, and many others have been with him for upward of thirty-five years. He was married in 1873 to Mary, daughter of Andrew Jaeger, and had eleven children, of which the following are living: Johanna M., wife of Dr. P. T. Leyendecker; Marie, William F., Julius A., Henry, Bertha, Herman L. and Clara Heide. Portrait opposite page 115.

ELY, Charles Wright, educator, was born in Madison, Conn., Mar. 14, 1839, son of Elias Sanford and Hester Maria (Wright) Ely, and a descendant of Richard Ely, who came to this country from Plymouth, Devonshire, England, between 1660-63, and settled in Boston, whence he removed later to Lyme, Conn. From him and his wife, Joane Phipps, the line is traced through their son Richard and his wife, Mary Marvin; their son Richard and his wife, Phebe Hubbard; their son Robert and his wife, Jerusha Lay, and their son, Simeon Lay, and his wife, Elizabeth Sanford, grandparents of our subject. Robert Ely was a lieutenant in the revolutionary war. Charles W. Ely was educated in the district schools, Lee Academy at Madison, and Guilford (Conn.) Institute, and was graduated at Yale College in 1862. He was a member of the Alpha Delta Phi fraternity. Three years after graduation he received from Yale the degree of A.M. On the outbreak of the civil war he enlisted in the Washburn Rifles, a detachment of the Connecticut volunteers, which formed part of Hancock's corps in the army of the Potomac. He was soon made sergeant, and after the battle of Fredericksburg, in which his regiment lost one-third of its men, he was promoted lieutenant in the Twenty-seventh Connecticut infantry. Having contracted typhoid fever, he was honorably discharged after three months in the army hospitals. During 1863-70 he was a teacher in the Ohio State School for the Deaf at Columbus, O., and was then appointed principal of the Maryland School for the Deaf at Frederick

City, Md. The school was established by the state of Maryland in 1867, and was opened in the old colonial military barracks at Frederick. Mr. William D. Cook was the first principal, and upon his resignation, in 1870, the position was offered to Dr. Ely. From that time until his death he remained at the head of the school, and the organization and development of it into one of the best and most efficient institutions of its kind in the country was almost entirely his work. In the second annual report to the legislature the president of the board of visitors of the school said in part: "It gives the board pleasure to say that Mr. Ely has given unmistakable evidence of his fitness for the delicate, arduous and responsible duties that have devolved upon him as official head of the institution. Having graduated in one of the first universities in the United States, and been an instructor of the deaf and dumb for seven years in one of the most prominent institutions in the country, he combines with a thorough education and large experience that decision of character and forbearance which qualify and eminently fit him for the position which he occupies. The board of visitors, therefore, regard him as a most valuable acquisition to the institution, and congratulate the people of the state and themselves that they were so fortunate as to secure his services." The Maryland School for the Deaf is supported and controlled by the state. Applicants are received to be educated and not for medical treatment. All white deaf mute children, as well as those who, though able to speak, are so deaf as to be unable to receive instruction in ordinary schools, are admitted, board and instruction free. Indigent pupils have state, city or county aid in the matter of clothing. Besides the usual school studies the pupils are taught drawing, shoemaking, cabinetmaking, chair-caning, wood-carving, painting, dressmaking, cooking and housework. The amount of difficult and valuable educational work accomplished by this school can hardly be overestimated, and it owes its efficiency practically altogether to the enlightened and progressive efforts of Dr. Ely during the forty odd years of his principalship. He was one of the most widely known educators of the deaf in the United States, and took a prominent part in conventions of instructors of the deaf. He was chairman of the committee to prepare a uniform course of study for the schools for the deaf, and was a member of the association to promote the teaching of speech to the deaf. In many other activities, too, he played a prominent part, and always took the greatest interest in all public affairs. He was appointed chairman of the board of health of Frederick, Md., when that body was organized in 1886, and he was chairman of the commission for improving the condition of the adult blind of the state of Maryland from 1906 until his death. Dr. Ely was a Christian gentleman of the truest type. He inspired his pupils to noble aims and lofty ideals, and enjoyed the deepest respect of all who had been under his instruction. A former pupil writes: "His moral power inspired others to make life purer, loftier, calmer, brighter. The impression left on those who knew him best will be indestructible—so transparent was his life, so clearly did the true nature of the man show through it. What he taught others to be he was himself. His deep and sweet humanity won him love and reverence everywhere among those whose natures were capable of responding to the highest manifestations of character." Dr. Ely received the degree of L.H.D. from Gallaudet College, Washington, D. C.,

in 1908. He was a member of the G. A. R., the
Loyal Legion and the Sons of the American Revolution. In politics he always adhered to the
Republican party. He was an active member of
the Presbyterian Church, in which he was a senior
elder at the time of his death. He was married at
Elyria, O., Oct. 24, 1867, to Mary Grace, daughter of Solomon Russell Darling, and had five children: Charles Russell, now professor of natural
sciences, Gallaudet College, Washington, D. C.;
Grace Darling, Robert, Mabel Darling and Richard
Grenville Ely. He died in Washington, D. C.,
Oct. 1, 1912.

WHEELER, Thomas Benton, jurist, was born
in Claysville, Marshall co., Ala., June 7, 1840,
son of William Henry Edward and Mary Magruder
(Barton) Wheeler. His grandfather, Benjamin
Wheeler, was a native of Culpepper co., Va., and
served as a regular in Colonel Harrison's regiment
of Virginia artillery. When he was six years of
age, Thomas B. Wheeler's father died, and his
mother and an elder brother, John Gill Wheeler,
went to Hays co., Texas. He had just attained
his majority when the civil war began, and he
enlisted promptly in the Confederate cause, serving
in eastern Texas and Louisiana until the close of
the struggle. He was promoted for efficiency and
gallant conduct, and, although so young, at the
end of the war he had attained to the rank of
captain. After the war he adopted the legal profession, in which he was eminently successful. He
was elected mayor of Austin in 1874, serving during the troublous times of the Coke feud, when an
attempt was made by the radicals to place Texas
again under military rule. This, in common with
other Democrats, he stoutly resisted, and though
his life was constantly in danger, he rendered
great service to the state by his acts of courage
and fearlessness to avert bloodshed. His personal
popularity and genuine abilities as an executive
caused his re-election to the mayoralty for several terms. In 1880 he was elected district judge
for northwest Texas, and served for six years.
He reached the summit of his political career in
1886, when he was chosen lieutenant-governor.
Foreseeing the necessity of another great harbor
besides that of Galveston, to accommodate the
growing resources of the state, he moved to what
has become the city of Aransas Pass, at the
expiration of his term in the state capital, and
participated in the laying out of the town site
and building up this new commercial center. Securing an option on ample territory for a town site,
he organized the Harbor City and Improvement
Co., of which Russell Harrison, son of Pres. Harrison, was made president. Many difficult and unexpected obstacles were encountered and overcome. In 1891 there were three separate and
distinct land and improvement companies: the
Aransas Harbor Improvement Co., the Aransas
Harbor Terminal Railway Co., and the Aransas
Pass Harbor Co., in all of which Gov. Wheeler was
the leading spirit. The U. S. government having
surveyed the Texas coast, and showing that the
Aransas Pass harbor could be converted into a
first-class port at the least expense, Gov. Wheeler,
in 1892, organized the Aransas Pass Harbor and
Improvement Co., and constructed a railroad, now
known as the Old Terminal railway. The state
of Texas will always be indebted to Gov. Wheeler's
indomitable perseverance, pluck and executive ability for the creation of one of her valuable harbors and flourishing cities, and Aransas Pass will
ever remain an enduring monument to his genius,
foresight and energy. While a striving man of

affairs, he was equally deserving of encomiums in
all his private and social relations. His home life
was more than exemplary; he was a life-long member of the Methodist Church South, and for twenty-
two years was superintendent of the Methodist
Sunday-school at Aransas Pass. In the Masonic
order he had attained the degree of Knight Templar. He was twice married, first in 1865, to Kittie Manor, of Manor, Texas, who died in 1881; and
again in 1883, to Ida, daughter of A. W. DeBerry,
by whom he had one daughter, Betty Benton,
wife of R. C. Patterson, and one son, John DeBerry
Wheeler. He died in San Antonio, Texas, Feb.
21, 1913.

ALGER, Philip Rounseville, naval officer,
was born in Boston, Mass., Sept. 29, 1859, son of
William Rounseville and Anne Langdon (Lodge)
Alger. His first American ancestor was Thomas
Alger, who came from England and settled at
Taunton, Mass., about 1665; his wife was Elizabeth Packard, of Bridgewater, and the line of
descent is traced through their son Israel, who
married Patience Hayward; their son Israel, who
married Susanna Snow; their son James, who married Martha Kingman; their son James, who
married Hannah Bassett, and their son Nahum,
who married Catharine Rounseville, and was the
grandfather of the subject of this sketch. His
father, William Rounseville Alger (q. v.), was
a distinguished clergyman of the Unitarian
Church and a writer of much force and remarkable spirituality. Philip Rounseville Alger was
educated at the Boston Latin School, where he
was graduated in 1876. He entered the U.
S. Naval Academy in the same year, and was
graduated four years later at the head of his
class. His first cruise, on the Richmond, took
him to the Pacific station and to China. Returning in 1882, he was ordered to the bureau of ordnance, Washington, D. C., where he entered thus
early in his career upon a path in which he was
to win such marked distinction in later years.
By what seems a remarkable coincidence, in view
of his extraordinary fitness to meet the demands
of the situation, his entrance upon ordnance duty
coincided exactly with the beginning of the "new
navy" of steel ships and built-up guns. Coming
from a cruise in a wooden corvette of the civil
war period, he was called upon at once to bear a
part in the design of guns built up of tempered
steel for ships as strikingly in contrast with the
Richmond as were these guns with the cast-iron
muzzle-loading smoothbores with which that ship
had fought her way past the batteries at New
Orleans and Mobile Bay. The new ships were the
Chicago, Boston and Dolphin, cruisers it is true,
and insignificant to-day, but up-to-date in their
class when designed and more heavily armed than
any other ships of that day which could properly
be compared with them, and, so far as ordnance
was concerned, more nearly allied to the battleship of to-day than to the wooden frigates and
corvettes which had preceded them. A second
tour of duty afloat, this time in the Pensacola on
the European station, during 1885-88, was followed by another assignment to the bureau of
ordnance, and, a year later (November, 1890),
by transfer to the corps of professors of mathematics. With his tenure of duty on shore assured,
Prof. Alger entered now upon a new phase of his
career, and for more than nine years was associated intimately, so far as ordnance was concerned, with every step of the remarkable advance
which in that brief period carried warship design
in the United States from the Chicago and Boston

to the Maine and the Missouri. In 1899 Prof. Alger left the bureau of ordnance under orders to take up the duties of head of the department of mechanics at the U. S. Naval Academy. In 1903 he was induced to accept the position of secretary and treasurer of the Naval Institute, Annapolis, Md., a position which carried with it the editorship of the institute's "Proceedings," and the following year he resumed his connection with the bureau of ordnance by becoming a member of the special board on naval ordnance. This board, created in 1904, was designed to act as an advisory board to the bureau, in connection especially with experimental work in the development and test of ordnance material. In spite of his connection with the U. S. Naval Institute and with the special board, he continued his duties at the Naval Academy until 1907, when the department of mechanics was merged into that of mathematics, and thereafter until his death he was enabled to give his uninterrupted attention to the institute and the special board. The history of the development of naval ordnance in the United States during the last quarter century is a history of the work of Prof. Alger more than of any other one man. He wrote much on subjects connected with ordnance, and two of his books, "Exterior Ballistics" (1904) and "The Elastic Strength of Guns" (1906), have long been recognized as standard works upon the subjects with which they deal. Another book, on "Hydromechanics" (1902), was prepared by request for use at the Naval Academy, and has been a gratifying success as a text-book at other institutions. He had planned and partly outlined a treatise on "Interior Ballistics" which would have been the crowning work of his career. The subject had attracted him for many years, and had so far taken shape that he hoped to push it rapidly to completion. He was also the author of numerous articles on technical subjects, chiefly ordnance, and translated "War on the Sea," by Capt. Gabriel Darrieus, of the French navy (1908). He belonged to the Metropolitan and Army and Navy clubs. He was married Apr. 29, 1891, to Louisa, daughter of Col. J. H. Taylor, of the U. S. army. Their children are: Mary Taylor (married Roy C. Smith, Jr., U. S. navy), Philip Langdon, Montgomery Meigs, Louisa Rodgers and Catherine Rounseville. Prof. Alger died at Annapolis, Md., Feb. 23, 1912.

LORING, Victor Joseph, lawyer, was born in Marlboro, Mass., Jan. 11, 1859, son of Hollis and Laura (Hitchcock) Loring, grandson of Hollis Caleb Loring and great-grandson of Hollis Loring. His maternal grandfather was Winchester Hitchcock, who was a soldier in the revolutionary war, being stationed at West Point when Benedict Arnold attempted to betray the American troops to the British. Mr. Loring's father, Hollis Loring, was both a justice and a merchant. He was prominent in politics and was a friend and colleague of Sumner, Boutwell, Wilson and Garrison, a member of the state legislature and chairman of the committee that drafted the first personal liberty bill in Massachusetts. Victor J. Loring was educated in the public schools of Marlboro and the Boston Latin School. Having determined to follow the law, he entered Boston University Law School and was graduated in 1881 with the degree of LL.B. He was admitted to the Suffolk bar in June, 1881, and later was admitted to practice before the United States circuit and district courts and the United States supreme court. In 1881 he formed a copartnership with his brother, Charles F. Loring, under the firm name of C. F. & V. J. Loring, which was changed in January, 1883, to the present name of Moulton, Loring & Loring, the senior partner being Barron Clinton Moulton. Mr. Loring's practice is almost exclusively confined to life and fire insurance law and corporation law, and in this branch he stands among its leading practitioners. He was the Massachusetts counsel for the Mutual Reserve Fund Life Association of New York and was counsel in the Julia M. Luther estate of New York city, in the famous Ransom will case in Cambridge, and in the case of Alvord vs. Mutual Fire Insurance Co. of New York, which was one of the earliest cases tried in the United States court of appeals, the judgment being rendered by that court in the autumn of 1892. He was admitted to the bar of that court for the purpose of arguing this case, which had been tried at the October term of the United States circuit court in 1892. He has been for several years counsel for the Kidder Press Manufacturing Co. of Boston, and in the celebrated cases of the New York Bank Note Co. against the Kidder Co. and the Hamilton Bank Note Co. of New York, involving the exclusive right to use the presses which print the tickets for the New York and Brooklyn elevated lines, he increased a reputation for ability and skill already established even outside of the legal circles of Boston and Massachusetts. Mr. Loring has been active and influential in Boston and state politics, serving for three years on the Republican city committee and for two years as a member of the state central Republican committee, and during one of those years as one of its executive committee. He was especially active in the election of John Q. A. Brackett for governor; has been a delegate to numerous local and state conventions, and was a member of the committee of twelve that had such wholesome influence upon Boston politics. He managed the municipal campaign that resulted in the election of Homer Rogers and the deposition of John Lee as president of the board of aldermen. Mr. Loring has resided in Wellesley, Mass., since 1900, where he has been prominently identified with public and educational affairs. He has been a member of the school board, and during 1902-8 was counsel for the town of Wellesley in all legal matters and senior counsel in its six years' litigation with the Boston and Worcester Street Railway Co. over its franchises and concerning the building of the new boulevard on the line of the old Boston and Worcester turnpike, involving many intricate questions of law, which went to the highest courts, and even to the legislature, both as to street railways and interurban railways, highway law and land damages. He is a past regent of the Royal Arcanum; was for several years chairman of the committee on laws of the grand council of Massachusetts, and was president of the Royal Arcanum Club of Massachusetts in 1894, 1895 and 1896. He has been very active in the interests of this order, speaking throughout New England and delivering many memorial and other addresses. He is also a member of the Chamber of Commerce, Pilgrim Publicity Association, Exchange Club, Twentieth Century Club, the Boston Art Club, Boston City Club, Braeburn and Economic clubs, for many years was a prominent member of the Union Boat Club, and is a life member of the Y. M. C. A. For the last ten years he has been identified with the movement for the federation of men's church organizations and is now president of the American Federation of Men's Church Organizations. Mr. Loring was married Dec. 9, 1891, to Emilie, daughter of George Melville Baker, author of the celebrated Baker plays, and has two sons: Robert Melville and Selden Melville Loring.

WHITON, Sylvester Gilbert, financier, was born at Westford, Conn., Aug. 8, 1846, son of Ashbel and Jerusha Hodgkins (Fuller) Whiton. His first American ancestor was Thomas Whiton, a native of Hooke Norton, Oxfordshire, England, who came to America in 1635 and settled in Plymouth, Mass. The line of descent is traced through his son James, who married Mary Beal; their son James, who married Abigail ————; their son Joseph, who married Martha Tower; their son Elijah, who married Priscilla Russ; their son Joseph, who married Joanna Chaffee, and their son Stephen, who married Julianna Martin, and was the grandfather of Sylvester G. Whiton. He passed his boyhood upon his father's farm. At the age of sixteen years he went to New York city and entered the employ of Woodruff & Robinson, commission merchants. In 1868 he founded a partnership with James H. Nash, under the name of Nash & Whiton, which continued until 1881, when Timothy L. Woodruff was admitted, and the style was changed to Nash, Whiton & Co. In 1895 Mr. Whiton, Timothy L. Woodruff and others organized the Worcester Salt Co., of which Mr. Whiton was president until his death. He was vice-president of the Merchants' Exchange National Bank, a director of the Union Typewriter Co., the Preferred Accident Life Insurance Co., the West Virginia Paper and Pulp Co. and the Oatka Mining Co. He was a member of the Flatbush Congregational Church, to the building fund of which he subscribed $10,000. He was married three times: first, in Brooklyn, N. Y., Nov. 12, 1867, to Mary V., daughter of Chester Steele Kasson; second, in Brooklyn, N. Y., June 10, 1880, to Mrs. Isabel Taylor Thacher, daughter of George Raymond Atwater, and, third, in Montclair, N. J., Mar. 10, 1892, to Ella French, daughter of Charles Hendrickson Skidmore. He is survived by five daughters and three sons. Mr. Whiton died at his home in Flatbush, Brooklyn, N. Y., Apr. 10, 1910.

SAYRES, Edward Smith, consul, was born at Marcus Hook, Pa., Oct. 5, 1797, son of Caleb Smith and Susan (Richards) Sayres, and grandson of Capt. Matthias Sayres, who was an officer in the revolutionary war. His family trace descent from Thomas Sayres, of Poddington, Bedfordshire, England, who was one of the founders of Southampton, Long Island. His house built in 1640 is still standing. Caleb Smith Sayres (1768-99) was a distinguished physician of Elizabeth, N. J., who is mentioned by Dr. Benjamin Rush as being particularly skillful in the treatment of yellow fever during the epidemic of 1798. He served as surgeon in the 8th battalion, Pennsylvania militia, Lieut.-Col. Vernon commanding; and practiced medicine at Marcus Hook, Chester, and in other parts of Delaware county, Pa. He married a daughter of Jacob and Susanna (Wills) Richards, and was a member of the Presbyterian Church at Westfield. His residence at Marcus Hook, facing the river, is still standing and has a porch extending along its front. He was a justice of the peace for the county, and a pewholder and liberal subscriber to the funds of St. Martin's Church at the Hook. Engraved on his memorial stone are the words: ''In memory of Caleb S. Sayres, Doctor of

Physic, who departed this life, December 3d, in the year of our Lord 1799, in the 32d year of his age.'' His son, Edward Smith Sayres, was educated at the University of Pennsylvania. In early life he went to Brazil as supercargo of his own vessel, the Clio, and afterward engaged in the mercantile business in Philadelphia. He was appointed vice-consul of Brazil, Dec. 3, 1841; vice-consul of Portugal, Mar. 13, 1850; vice-consul of Sweden and Norway, July 10, 1854, and vice-consul of Denmark, May 1, 1862, resident at Philadelphia, Pa. He was appointed by the princess regent of Brazil honorary consul of that empire, with the rank of captain in the Brazilian navy, Feb. 2, 1872, for long and faithful service to the empire; and was at the time of his death dean of the consular corps at Philadelphia, and probably the oldest foreign consul in point of service in the United States. Mr. Sayres was a gentleman of the old school, courteous and dignified. When more than seventy years of age he was erect in bearing, and his step as elastic as a man of fifty. He was widely acquainted with books, possessed a retentive memory, was a good linguist, and was the owner of an extensive library. He was married July 25, 1839, to Jane, daughter of John Humes, of Philadelphia, Pa., and they had two daughters, Emma Stalker (1840-50) and Caroline Augusta Sayres (1843-47), and three sons, Harry, Edward Stalker and Horace, and one daughter, Jennie Humes, surviving. He died in Philadelphia, Pa., Mar. 29, 1877.

SAYRES, Edward Stalker, lawyer, was born in Philadelphia, Pa., July 30, 1850, son of Edward Smith and Jane (Humes) Sayres. He was educated in the Friends' private school of Philadelphia, a private classical academy conducted by Eliphalet Roberts, and the Friends' Central High School. From an early age he had a predilection for the law, and began his legal training under the direction of John Hill Martin. He was admitted to the bar in 1873, and was also admitted to the supreme court of Pennsylvania and the court of claims of Washington, D. C. His practice is confined to the orphans' court, real estate conveyancing and mercantile law. Mr. Sayres is an honorary member of the Law Academy of Philadelphia, and was at one time its recorder. He is a member of the Law Association of Philadelphia, and of the council of the Historical Society of Pennsylvania. He was one of the founders of the Merion Cricket Club, organized in 1865, and has served as its secretary for over forty years. In 1874 he entered company D of the 1st regiment of infantry, Pennsylvania National Guard, and saw active duty at the time of the coal riots in 1875 and the labor riots in 1877, being with his company in the round house at Pittsburgh, and was first lieutenant of his company in 1879-80. He is now a member of the Old Guard of company D and captain and paymaster of the veteran corps of the 1st regiment of infantry of the National Guard of Pennsylvania. He was interested in the organization of the Land Title and Trust Co., and for a brief period was its secretary. He was vice-president of the Merchants' Trust Co. and life member and one of the council of the Mercantile Beneficial Association. He is now a director and counsel for the Delaware Insurance Co. of Philadelphia, and director of the Merchants' Union Trust Co. He was one of the founders, and is a vice-president and recording secretary, of the Genealogical Society of Pennsylvania, and of the National Geographical Society of Washington, D. C. He is secretary of

SYLVESTER G. WHITON
FINANCIER

EDWARD SMITH SAYRES
DIPLOMAT

EDWARD STALKER SAYRES
LAWYER

ELLIOTT W. MAJOR
GOVERNOR

Wm H. Hubbard

the Society of Colonial Wars in the common-wealth of Pennsylvania, was a founder and for some time a member of the council of the Colonial Society of Pennsylvania, is a member of the board of managers of the Pennsylvania Society of the Sons of the Revolution, and has several times served as delegate to the national conventions. He is treasurer of the Society of the War of 1812, and was a delegate to the General Society. For several years he was treasurer-general of the National Commandery of the Military Order of Foreign Wars of the United States, and is now judge advocate of the Pennsylvania Commandery. Mr. Sayres is vice-president of the board of trustees of the Northern Home for Friendless Children and Associated Institute for Soldiers' and Sailors' Orphans, president of the board of managers of the Children's Hospital of Philadelphia, and one of the original members of the Civil Service Reform Association of Pennsylvania. His clubs are the Rittenhouse, Radnor Hunt and Bryn Mawr Polo. He was married first, Dec. 15, 1881, to Caroline Linda Jennings, daughter of S. Weir Lewis of Philadelphia, Pa.; she died Oct. 9, 1882, leaving one daughter, Linda Lewis, wife of Morris Shallcross Phillips, of Pittsburgh, Pa., and on Apr. 3, 1888, he was married to his first wife's first cousin, Mary Victoria, daughter of F. Mortimer Lewis, and sister of Prof. Henry Carvill Lewis, a scientist.

MAJOR, Elliott Woolfolk, twenty-ninth governor of Missouri (1913–17) was born in Lincoln county, Mo., Oct. 20, 1864, son of James Reed and Sarah T. (Woolfolk) Major. He was educated at the public schools and at Watson Seminary; studied law in the office of the Hon. Champ Clark, in Bowling Green, and upon obtaining his majority was admitted to the bar. In 1896 he was elected state senator from the 11th district, composed of the counties of Pike, Lincoln and Audrian, and in 1899 was chosen a member of the commission to revise the statutes. He was attorney-general of Missouri during 1909–12, and in 1912 was elected governor of Missouri on the Democratic ticket. His party resumed complete control of the state with his inauguration. In his message he recommended the creation of a state public service commission, the enactment of a workmen's compensation law, the simplification of court procedure, and municipal and presidential primaries. Upon taking office, Gov. Major at once gave his sanction to many reform measures. An act was passed in March by the legislature to give married women equal rights with husbands in the care of minor children and in the management of their estates, and the state has had the benefit of other enlightened regulations relating to progressive measures. An official state flag of original design, combining the national red, white and blue with the state coat of arms, has been adopted during his term of office. In the spring of 1913 much uneasiness and great discomfort was felt in business circles in Missouri because of the Orr law with its anti-trust features which destroyed the actuarial bureaus of the large insurance companies. A number of these companies, where home offices were in eastern states, suspended business in Missouri rather than comply with the new law. The Merchants' Exchange, the Bankers' Association, the Manufacturers' Club, and the City Club joined in a call for a mass meeting to take up the situation. Nevertheless, Gov. Major declared he would stand by the law, and refused to call a special session of the legislature to relieve a situation which was without precedent. Gov. Major's deep interest is centered in the good roads movement. In April, 1912, an act was passed to provide a system of dragged roads to connect county seats in the state in one general system, and a county highway board appointed. But the most important and picturesque event of his office-holding years was foreshadowed when he issued a proclamation setting aside Aug. 20–21, 1913, as public holidays to be known as "Good Road Days." He asked for a general suspension of business so that every able-bodied man in the rural districts and quarter cities should give their personal aid in improving the highways. Gov. Hodges, of Kansas, joined Gov. Major and, clad in khaki overalls, the two men worked side by side. Nearly 400 miles of new roads were built and old roads improved in those two days, and so successful was the idea that he issued a call to governors in each state of the republic to make this form of "Good Roads Days" nation-wide, and far-spreading results are anticipated from his propaganda. He was candidate for vice-president in 1916. Gov. Major was married, June 14, 1887, to Elizabeth, daughter of Ovid Myers, of Bowling Green, Mo., and has three children: Miacah, wife of John Sanderson, of Mexico, Mo.; Elliott, Jr., and Elizabeth Major. Portrait opposite page 120.

HUBBARD, William Henry, clergyman, was born in Clark county, Ky., April 16, 1851, son of William Henry and Anna Waite (Hinds) Hubbard. He was descended ninth in the direct line from George Hubbard, who came over from England and settled at Watertown, Mass., in 1633. He brought with him an infant son, John, who married Mary Merriam, of Concord, Mass., and the line of descent is traced through their son Isaac, who married Anne Warner; their son John, who married Hannah Cowles; their son Elisha, who married Lucy Stearns; their son John, who married Ruth Dickinson; their son Henry, who married Mercy Warner, and their son William Henry, the father of our subject. William H. Hubbard was graduated at Amherst College in 1871. Having decided to enter the ministry, he went from Amherst to Andover Theological Seminary and a year later to Princeton Theological Seminary, where he was graduated in 1874. His first charge was in Rutland, Mass. This was followed by pastorates at Merrimac, Mass. (seven and one-half years); Concord, Mass. (two years); Holyoke, Mass. (one year); and finally the First Presbyterian Church of Auburn, N. Y., where he served for more than a quarter of a century, placing that church in the front rank of the religious institutions of the state. While of great power as a preacher and endowed fully with that kindness of heart that above all else wins souls to the faith, it was as an important executive of the Presbyterian Church that Dr. Hubbard crowned his long and useful career. He attended many of the synods and other meetings, including the general assemblies, where he always took an active part in the deliberations. During 1896–1909 he was secretary of the general assembly's committee on systematic beneficence. He was moderator of the Cayuga Presbytery, member of the executive committee of the general assembly of the Presbyterian Church, 1908-11, and secretary of the joint executive committee of the executive commission, one of the most important positions in the church. He was editor and publisher of the "Assembly Herald" of the Presbyterian Church (1894–98) and of the "Gospel Message" (1903–05). He was a trustee of the Auburn Theological Seminary and was commissioner of charities at Auburn in the years 1906-07. The degree of D.D. was conferred upon him by Berea College in 1905. He was married Nov. 9, 1886, to Elizabeth Allen, daughter of William Skinner, of Holyoke, Mass., and died in New York city, Jan. 31, 1913.

GRANJON, Henry, third Roman Catholic bishop of Tucson, Ariz., was born at St. Etienne, diocese of Lyons, France, June 15, 1863. His studies were made in the Marist College of St. Chamond and the Sulpician Seminary at Paris, whence he went to Rome and received the doctor's degrees in divinity and canon law and ordination Dec. 17, 1887. In 1890 he emigrated to Arizona and engaged in the work of the missions for seven years. He then took up the organization of the Association for the Propagation of the Faith, and with the Rev. Dr. Magnien, of Baltimore, put it on a substantial basis. When Bishop Bourgade of Tucson was promoted to the archbishopric of Santa Fé in 1899 Dr. Granjon was appointed his successor and consecrated June 17, 1900. The population of the diocese (40,000) is made up mostly of Mexicans and Indians, and Bishop Granjon most successfully met the requirements of the situation. Under his direction (1906–10) the old mission church, San Xavier del Bac, considered the best example of the Spanish mission style north of Mexico, was completely restored. This church and that at Tumacacuri (partly in ruins) are the only two remaining examples of the buildings of the old Spanish missionaries of the seventeenth and eighteenth centuries.

RAMSAY, Francis Munroe, naval officer, was born in the District of Columbia, Apr. 5, 1835, son of George Douglas and Frances Whetcroft (Munroe) Ramsay, and great-grandson of Patrick Ramsay, who came to this country from Scotland and settled at or near Petersburg, Va., about 1750; from him and his wife, Elizabeth Poythress, the line descends through their son Andrew and his wife, Catherine Graham, who were the grandparents of Francis Munroe Ramsay. His father served in the Mexican war, being brevetted major for gallantry at Monterey; he was chief of ordnance of Gen. Taylor's army, and in 1863 was made chief of ordnance in the United States army with the rank of brigadier-general and in March, 1865, was awarded brevet of major-general "for long and faithful service in the army." The son entered the navy as midshipman in 1850, and served on the Pacific station with the Brazilian squadron and at the Washington navy yard until 1862. He was promoted to master and lieutenant in 1858, and lieutenant-commander in 1862, in which year he was assigned to the Mississippi squadron which participated in the expedition up the Yazoo river, destroying the Confederate navy yard in 1863. At the siege of Vicksburg in the same year he commanded a battery of heavy guns mounted on scows in front of the city. During the latter half of the civil war he commanded the third division of the Mississippi squadron in the expedition up the Black river in Louisiana, and was then transferred to the North Atlantic squadron, with which he participated in the engagements before Fort Fisher, N. C., and Fort Anderson and other forts on the Cape Fear river, and was present at the capture of Richmond. For a year after the close of the civil war he was in charge of the department of gunnery at the Naval Academy, and being made commander in 1866, transferred to the Washington navy yard. After serving as chief of staff with the South Atlantic squadron, he returned to the Washington navy yard in 1869 for ordnance duty, and in 1872 was detailed with the bureau of

ordnance, going to London in the same year as naval attaché. In 1874 he commanded the Ossipee, and in 1875 was at the Naval Asylum, Philadelphia. During 1876–78 he served as inspector of ordnance at the New York navy yard, having been promoted to captain in 1877. For three years after 1878 he commanded the torpedo station, and in 1881 he commanded the Trenton, the flagship of the European station. He was detached in the latter part of this year and ordered as superintendent to the Naval Academy, where he remained for five years. Capt. Ramsay was on duty as a member of the naval examining board in 1886, and commanded the Boston in 1887-8. In February of the following year he was detached from the command of the Boston and assumed command of the New York navy yard, the most important shore command in the navy. In March, 1889, he was promoted to commodore, and in October of the same year was detached and appointed chief of the Bureau of Navigation. In 1893 he was reappointed chief of the bureau and was promoted to rear-admiral in April, 1894. He was automatically retired in April, 1897. His last active duty was as a member of the board of awards which selected the medals commemorating the battle of Santiago, and as a member of the court of inquiry which investigated the conduct of Rear-Adm. W. S. Schley during the war with Spain, and particularly in the Santiago campaign and battle. He was a member of the Metropolitan Club, Washington, D. C. (former governor); Columbia Historical Society, Loyal Legion (senior vice-commander, 1892–94; commander 1894–95), and Foreign Wars. He was married, June 9, 1869, at Buenos Ayres, S. A., to Anna Josephine, daughter of Patrick McMahon, a civil engineer of New York city, and is survived by three children: Martin McMahon, George Douglas and Mary Frances Ramsay. Rear Adm. Ramsay died in Washington, D. C., July 19, 1914.

SCHUCHERT, Charles, paleontologist, was born in Cincinnati, O., July 3, 1858, son of Philip and Agatha (Muller) Schuchert. His father was a furniture manufacturer. On completing his studies in the parochial schools he found employment in his father's factory, remaining until 1884, when he became assistant and lithographer to Edward O. Ulrich, the well-known paleontologist in Newport, Ky., with whom he remained for four years (1885–89). During that time he applied himself with more than ordinary zeal to the study of paleontology, of which he soon acquired considerable knowledge. Then for two years he was similarly employed in Albany, N. Y., under James Hall, state geologist of New York. In 1891 he became assistant paleontologist to Newton H. Winchell, state geologist of Minnesota. Anxious to increase his knowledge of that branch of science which he had selected as his life work, he spent part of the years 1892–93 at Yale College, where he was laboratory assistant to Prof. Charles E. Beecher. In 1893 he went to Washington, D. C., as assistant paleontologist to Charles D. Wolcott, of the U. S. geological survey and two years later became assistant curator of the section of paleontology in the U. S. national museum, where he remained eleven years. On the death of Prof. Beecher in 1904 he succeeded his friend and teacher as professor of paleontology in Yale and professor of historical geology in the Sheffield Scientific School, as well as curator of the geological collections in the Peabody museum. His first important work was on Brachiopods, and in 1893 he published a "Classification of the Brachiopoda" and in the same year he contributed an elaborate monograph entitled "The Lower Silurian Brachiopoda of Minnesota" to the third volume of the reports of the geological survey of that state. Later he prepared the chapter on "Brachiopoda" for Zittel and Eastman's "Text Book on Paleontology" (1896). These researches culminated in Bulletin 87, entitled "A Synopsis of American Fossil Brachiopoda Including Bibliography and Synonymy," (1897), prepared for the U. S. geological survey. Meanwhile he devoted much attention to other forms of early life, and in 1904 published in the quarterly issue of the Smithsonian miscellaneous collection the important study entitled "On Siluric and Devonic Cystidea and Camarocrinus." As early as 1896 he became interested in fossil star fishes and from his researches in that fascinating group came his "Revision of Paleozoic Stelleroidea With Special Reference to North American Asteroidea" (1915), as Bulletin 88 of the U. S. National museum. More recently he has devoted himself to American paleogeography, and besides several papers contributed to the "American Geologist" and similar journals, he published in 1910 "Paleogeography of North America," a monograph of nearly 200 pages that appeared in the bulletin of the Geological Society of America. Besides the foregoing he has contributed nearly one hundred smaller papers to various scientific journals and the proceedings of scientific societies. He edited the memorial volume commemorating the centenary of the birth of James D. Dana in 1913 and he is the author of a "Text Book of Historical Geology" (1915). Yale University conferred on him the honorary degree of A.M. in 1904 and the University of New York LL.D. in 1914. He is a member of the American Society of Naturalists, the American Geological Society, the National Academy of Sciences, the American Philosophical Society, the American Academy of Arts and Sciences, and a fellow of the American Association for the Advancement of Science. In 1910 he was made president of the Paleontological Society. He is unmarried.

THAYER, Harry Bates, manufacturer and executive, was born at Northfield, Vt., Aug. 17, 1858, son of James Carey Barrell and Martha Jane (Pratt) Thayer, descendant of John Alden, Governor Brewster and other Pilgrims. Both parents were born in Vermont of stock that came to this country in the earliest days. Of his ancestors some came on the Mayflower, and none is recorded to have come to this country later than 1650. They were hardy people who settled in the towns bordering on the Massachusetts bay and made good citizens, successful merchants and professional men. His first paternal American ancestor was Thomas Thayer, who came to this country from England and was admitted a freeman of Braintree, Mass., in 1647. From him and his wife, Margery Wheeler, Harry Bates Thayer is descended through their son Shadrach and his wife, Deliverance Priest; their son Ephraim and his wife, Sarah Bass; their son Shadrach and his wife, Rachel White; their son Uriah and his wife, Deborah Copeland; their son Samuel White and his wife, Esther French; their son Samuel White and his wife, Ruth Packard; their son James Carey Barrell and his wife, Martha Jane Pratt. Mr. Thayer received his preliminary education at the public schools of Northfield and at Norwich University and was graduated at Dartmouth College in 1879. Subsequently he entered the employ of the Northfield Savings Bank, of which his father was treasurer for many years, and in 1880 he went to the Central Vermont Railroad Co. at Bellows Falls, Vt. In 1881 he became connected with the Western Electric Co. in Chicago, with which his career has been chiefly identified. He was manager of the company in New York in 1884–99, vice-president in 1900-06, vice-president and general manager in 1907-08, and in 1908 was elected president. The Western Electric Co. was incorporated in 1871 as the Western Electric Manufacturing Co., and since then there has been only one change in its corporate form. It is the oldest organization in the United States devoted to the manufacture of electrical apparatus or material. During the first decade of its existence it was engaged chiefly in the manufacture and sale of telegraph apparatus, but with the invention of the telephone it entered largely into the manufacture of telephone apparatus. It has produced most of the telephone apparatus now in use not only in the United States but throughout the world. Since 1881 it has been licensed under the patents owned and controlled by the Bell Telephone System and has been considered as the manufacturing department of that system. As electric light, electric railways and other applications of electricity were developed it entered into the business of distributing supplies in all lines of electrical work and has a very large business outside of its own manufactures. Very early in its history it established relations abroad, and it is interested in manufacturing companies in the large cities of Europe and in Canada, Japan and Australia. Its shops in this country are located in Chicago and it has offices and distributing stations in over thirty other cities. Under normal conditions it employs about 25,000 people. Mr. Thayer was identified with the Western Electric Co. during the greater part of its existence, and not a little of its remarkable growth is due directly to his great administrative ability. In 1909 he was elected vice-president of the American Telephone and Telegraph Co., and until his resignation in 1915 he was also a director of the Bell Telephone Co. of Canada, the Mexican Telegraph and Telephone Co., the Southern Bell Telegraph Co. and the Cumberland Telephone Co. He is a director of the National Bank of Commerce, and a member of the New York Chamber of Commerce, the American Institute of Electrical Engineers, the Society of Mayflower Descendants, the New England Society of New York, the Dartmouth Alumni Association of New York, the Phi Beta Kappa and the D.K.E. societies, the Automobile Club of America, the Union League Club of Chicago, the Engineers, Railroad, Lotos and University clubs, of New York, and the New Canaan (Conn.) Country Club. Mr. Thayer was married at Ransomville, N. Y., Apr. 26, 1887, to Carrie M., daughter of W. H. H. Ransom, and has three children: Dorothy, wife of Floyd C. Noble; Ruth and John Alden Thayer.

THOMPSON, William Boyce, manufacturer and financier, was born at Virginia City, Mont., May 13, 1869, son of William and Anna M. (Boyce) Thompson. His father (1838–1900) was a pioneer settler of Montana, who located, during the gold excitement of 1863, in the famous Alder Gulch, from which $70,000,000 in gold was taken in four years; he was mayor of Butte, Mont., and served for several sessions in the territorial and state legislature. Mr. Thompson's mother was a daughter of Maj. James R. Boyce, also a pioneer of Montana. The son was educated in the public schools of Butte, Phillips-Exeter Academy and Columbia University, School of Mines, class of 1890. He returned to Butte before graduation and became interested in mining, banking and manufacturing. Removing to New York in 1899, he engaged in financial pursuits, and, excepting two years in Boston, Mass. (1902–04), has been in New York ever since. He was the senior member of Thompson, Towle & Co. Having been eminently successful in many business lines of endeavor, he has been a leader in New York business affairs for a number of years. He is a director of the Metropolitan Life Insurance Co., the Chicago, Rock Island and Pacific Co., the Magma Arizona Railroad Co. and the Utah Copper Co., and is president of Inspiration Consolidated Copper Co. He is also interested in a number of western banks. Mr. Thompson's western experience has been of incalculable value to him in forming an accurate estimate of mining securities, and he was among the first to recognize the enormous possibilities of the so-called low-grade porphyry copper properties and took an active interest in their financial development. In 1914 he was elected director of the Federal Reserve Bank of New York, Class B. He was a Taft presidential elector in 1912 and is now chairman of the Twenty-fourth Republican congressional district committee. He is a member of the Union League, Metropolitan, Columbia University, Atlantic Yacht, Sleepy Hollow Country, Recess, City Midday, and Republican clubs, and the Rocky Mountain Club, of which he is vice-president. Mr. Thompson was married Feb. 6, 1895, to Gertrude, daughter of R. O. Hickman, of Helena, Mont., and has one daughter, Margaret Adelaide Thompson.

LUEDEKING, Robert, physician, was born in St. Louis, Mo., Nov. 6, 1853, son of Carl and Elise (Dauber) Luedeking. His father was principal of a school for girls. He passed through the St. Louis High School and studied medicine in the University of Heidelberg, and was graduated M.D. in Strassburg in 1876. After a year of post-graduate work in Vienna he established himself in practice in St. Louis, and became distinguished for original and brilliant work in pathological anatomy. He was lecturer on that subject in the St. Louis Medical College (Washington University), during 1882–92, when he was chosen dean of the college and was thereafter professor of diseases of children. He was dean of the college from 1902 until his death. He was editor of the "St. Louis Medical Review" in 1884–86. Dr. Luedeking was married Oct. 18, 1879, to Elise, daughter of S. W. Biebinger, a banker of St. Louis, who survived him with two daughters. He died in St. Louis, Mo., in 1908.

BROWN, Samuel Peters, ship-builder and banker, was born at North Blue Hill, Me., Dec. 9, 1816, son of Samuel and Ruth (Horton) Brown, and a descendant of one of four immigrants bearing the names of Hugh, Samuel, John and Christopher Brown, who emigrated from England in 1629 and settled in Salem Village, Mass. He was well educated, taught the village school and became the surveyor of that section. His first business venture was the operation of the celebrated Blue Hill granite quarries. Removing to Orland, in 1847, he engaged in the merchandise, ship-building, lumber and ice business on a large scale, building many coastwise vessels and supplying timber for the construction of naval vessels. He owned three plantations in Maryland on the Chesapeake bay; was a partner in the firm of Warren, Brown & Co., operators of the extensive Repentenay lumber mills in Canada; owned a controlling interest in the Alleghany Land, Lumber and Boom Co., which operated in a heavily timbered section called the "Land of Canaan" in West Virginia, and was interested in the Alaska

Commercial Co., operating in Alaska, and secured the lease of the Alaska Seal Islands to that company. In fact, his business operations in lumber, ice and furs was carried on in fourteen states and territories as well as in Canada. He was a member of the Maine house of representatives in 1845–46 and 1858–59, and of the Republican state committee for several years. In 1861 Pres. Lincoln appointed him navy agent at Washington, and through him many millions of dollars' worth of ships, guns and naval war material were purchased during the civil war. He immediately became interested in the reform of the city's administration and through his efforts a number of civic and municipal improvements were inaugurated, including a new school system and a board of health. He served as a member of the levy court, which had jurisdiction over the county of Washington, the section of the District of Columbia outside the cities of Washington and Georgetown, and he founded the residential village of Mount Pleasant, which now comprises a considerable area of the city of Washington, where he built a magnificent home. He was the author of the bill passed in 1871, providing for a territorial form of government for the District of Columbia. The bill repealed the charters of the cities of Washington, Georgetown and the levy court, and provided for a governor, a board of public works, a secretary of the territory and a council of eleven members to be appointed by the president and confirmed by the senate, a legislative assembly of twenty-two members and a delegate to congress to be elected by the voters of the district. He himself was appointed a member of the board of public works, which took complete supervision and control of the streets, sewers, roads and bridges in the district, and immediately formulated a comprehensive plan of improvements, which may be said to be the beginning of the work that has made the capital city of the United States one of the most beautiful in the world. In 1864 he secured the charter of the Metropolitan Street Railroad Co. and was elected its first president and built the road. In 1866 he formed a copartnership with his son, Austin P. Brown, under the firm name of S. P. Brown & Son, for the purpose of carrying on the lumber, coal, building material and contract business with all departments of the government and the public. Within two years the annual volume of the business reached $1,500,000; the firm supplied coal for the entire United States navy, delivering it aboard vessels at Port Richmond, Philadelphia, for shipment to all stations at home and abroad. This business was conducted largely by his son, and Mr. Brown found time to interest himself in other affairs. In 1867 he obtained the charter for the National Safe Deposit Co., of which he was elected the first president. During the civil war he took much interest in caring for the Maine sick and wounded soldiers in the hospitals around Washington. He was married, first, in 1840, to Charlotte Metcalf, daughter of Horatio Mason, of East Orland, Me. She died in 1858, leaving the following children: Austin P., Frank Mason, Helen M., wife of Elias Thomas; Harriet Mason, wife of John M. Morton; Julia Frances, wife of Samuel L. Mattingly; Henry Ward and Chapin Brown. He was married again in 1859 to Harriet, daughter of Isaiah Grendle, of Eastport, Me., by whom he had seven children: Charlotte Metcalf, wife of Frank B. Conger; Samuel Peters, Minnie G., Philip Sheridan, Blanche B., Anna May, wife of Charles W. McDermott, and George G. Brown. He died in Washington, D. C., Feb. 19, 1898.

CRUIKSHANK, John McEliwaine, editor, was born at Carthage, N. Y., June 9, 1865, son of Hugh and Jane (Cruikshank) Cruikshank. His father came from Bailieborough, County Cavan, Ireland, in 1857, and settled at Carthage, N. Y., where he engaged in the hardware business. The son received his early education at the public schools, and was graduated at Cornell in 1892. After his graduation he became a reporter on the Utica (N. Y.) ''Press.'' Subsequently he was engaged respectively on the Watertown ''Standard,'' the New York ''Herald,'' the Brooklyn ''Standard Union'' and the Brooklyn ''Eagle.'' During 1900-6 he was legislative correspondent of the Brooklyn ''Eagle'' in Albany, and became widely known as a writer on political topics. He enjoyed the acquaintance and confidence of a large number of prominent politicians, and he was sent regularly by his paper to state and national conventions, where his grasp of political questions and his close knowledge of the workings of political machinery made his reports of special value. In 1906 he bought out the Carthage ''Republican,'' which he ran alone until 1908, and in partnership with Richard C. Ellsworth until 1910. In the latter year he sold out and became vice-president of a company formed to purchase the Brooklyn ''Times,'' of which he became the editor. Under his management the Brooklyn ''Times'' entered upon a new era of prosperity and developed at a remarkably rapid rate. Although death cut short his career within two years the circulation of the ''Times'' doubled during that short period. ''Mr. Cruikshank,'' said the Watertown ''Times,'' ''was an aggressive newspaper man, with a keen sense of news values. He had the confidence of public men to an exceptional degree and this was a great asset in his career as a newspaper reporter and editor. He was always frank and honest in his talk and came to the point quickly. His judgment was invariably good. He could comprehend a situation accurately and he possessed the faculty of stating a fact directly and in a manner both easily understood and emphatic. The years he spent in Jefferson county when he was editor of the Carthage 'Republican' were during the two Hughes administrations, and Mr. Cruikshank was a stanch upholder of the policies of those administrations. He was a strong and fearless editorial writer and always advocated the best in both political and civic affairs. He was one of the principal movers in the Jefferson County Direct Primary League and was at one time its head. He was more or less closely identified with the political affairs of the county during the period of his editorship of the Carthage paper, and was a delegate to the long-drawn-out congressional convention at Oswego and Pulaski when the three-cornered political fight between Charles L. Knapp of Lewis, Merrick Stowell of Oswego and I. L. Hunt of Adams was waged.'' A resolution of the New York City Publishers' Association on the death of Mr. Cruikshank said in part: ''Mr. Cruikshank's success was due to his native fitness for his profession, supplemented by much hard work and by his high character, as made manifest in his strong sense of obligations both personal and professional, and his unfailing loyalty to his work and to his associates.'' He was married Sept. 6, 1900, to Nora, daughter of John Ross Washburn, of Watertown, N. Y. He died in St. Petersburg, Fla., Dec. 13, 1912. Portrait opposite page 126.

ROBERTS, Steele Foster, jeweler, was born in Pittsburgh, Pa., June 11, 1850, son of John Marks and Elizabeth Porter (Steele) Roberts, and grandson of Joseph H. Roberts, a native of Manchester, England, who came to America with his wife, Sarah Whitaker, in 1830, and settled in Pittsburgh. John Marks Roberts was a well-known jeweler of Pittsburgh, and in 1848 established the firm which afterward became E. P. Roberts & Sons. Steele Foster Roberts received his education at the public schools of Pittsburgh, and at the age of sixteen entered his father's business. The latter died that year and the business was taken over by the young man's uncle, Hon. Thomas H. Steele, who conducted its affairs until 1875. In that year the name of the firm was changed to E. P. Roberts & Sons, the members being Mrs. Elizabeth Porter Roberts, Steele F. Roberts, C. W. Roberts and John M. Roberts, Jr. In 1892 John M. Roberts, Jr., withdrew from the firm and started in business for himself. In 1906 the business was incorporated with Steele F. Roberts as president. Few men in the jewelry trade were as widely known as our subject. His reputation was national, and he exerted a powerful influence in organizing the trade, standardizing its methods, strengthening its credit, and increasing its prestige in the eyes of the public. He organized the Jewelers' 24-Karat Club, of Pittsburgh, and he was a member of the executive committee of the American National Retail Jewelers' Association, both of which he served as president. ''The accession of Mr. Roberts to the ranks of the organized trade,'' said a trade journal at the time of his death, ''inaugurated, in a sense, a new epoch in association history. Previous to that time there were those who claimed that the different associations were but poorly representative of the trade at large, inasmuch as their membership did not comprise the large jewelry houses of high standing. For this reason, the organization leaders regarded with special gratification the accession of Mr. Roberts to their ranks, but they did not then realize to the full the extraordinary enthusiasm, energy, ability and unselfishness of their new acquisition. It is to the credit of the organized trade that these qualities of the deceased jeweler were given prompt recognition in his elevation to the presidency of the National Association, his efficient work in this position entitling him to the honor of a second term, which was appreciatively recorded. It is a trite saying that if you wish to know a man thoroughly you should question his neighbors, and the fact that the members of the Pittsburgh 24-Karat Club elected and re-elected him their president is his neighbors' tribute to his fine character, broad mind and amiable personality. If it be true that his enthusiasm in the cause may have hastened his death, the fact will add still further to the sorrow which his hosts of friends in the trade will feel on hearing the sad news of his sudden passing away.'' In recognition of Mr. Roberts' valuable services to the jewelry trade a Roberts' Memorial Fund of $50,000 has been established to be invested and controlled by the American Retail Jewelers' Association for the advancement of association work and general trade betterment. Mr. Roberts was a director of the Pittsburgh Chamber of Commerce in 1912, a life member of the Western Pennsylvania Exposition Society, and a member of the Credit Men's Association, the Publicity Association and the Pittsburgh Board of Trade. For over thirty years he was a trustee of Christ M. E. Church. He was a governor of the Penwood Club in 1912-13, a member of the Oakmont Golf and Country clubs, and a 32nd degree Mason. He was married April 29, 1880, to Martha Jane,

daughter of Dennis Leonard, of Pittsburgh, Pa.
She died in 1903, leaving a daughter, Jeane Eliza-
beth, and he was married again Sept. 17, 1904, to
Jeanette, daughter of Washington Bartley, of
Pittsburgh. He died in Pittsburgh, Pa., Feb. 6,
1913.

MITCHELL, John, labor leader, was born at
Braidwood, Will co., Ill., Feb. 4, 1870, son of Robert and Martha (Halley) Mitchell. His father,
a native of Dublin, Ireland, emigrated to New
York in 1848, served during the civil war as a
Federal soldier, and afterward settled in Illinois,
where he became a farmer and mine worker. The
son's education was confined to a brief and desul-
tory attendance at a country school prior to the
age of ten years—when he began work on a farm—
and to independent reading and study at night
thereafter. For one year he devoted his evenings
to reading law. His mother died when he was
two years old, and his father when he was six.
He lived with his stepmother until he was ten
years of age, when he left home. At the age of
thirteen he began working in the coal mines at
Braidwood, but soon after, desiring to see something of the world, he started for the West, and
traveled through Colorado, New Mexico, and other
states, and working in the mines of these various
localities. After three years he returned to Illinois,
where he worked in the mines of Spring Valley
until 1890. At the age of sixteen he joined the
Knights of Labor, and early became active in the
local trade union movement, being elected president of the local assembly, Knights of Labor, in
1889. He interested himself in local movements
for the betterment of conditions among the miners, acquired considerable general information upon
matters pertaining to the coal industry, and was
elected delegate to sub-district and state conventions of the United Mine Workers of America,
which he had joined upon its formation in 1890.
In 1896 he was elected secretary-treasurer of the
northern Illinois sub-district of that organization,
a jurisdiction which embraced all the organized
mine workers in the state; and before the end of
the year he was chosen chairman of the legislative
committee and stationed at Springfield, Ill., to
assist in securing the passage of labor legislation.
The most important measures adopted under his
advocacy were the gross weight law and an amendment to the anti-trust law. In 1897 he became a
member of the Illinois state executive board of the
United Mine Workers of America, and when the
general strike of that year was inaugurated he
was appointed a national organizer by the president of the union, M. D. Ratchford. He was
elected national vice-president in January, 1898,
and in September of that year was chosen acting
president, to succeed Ratchford, who had resigned
to become a member of the U. S. Industrial Commission. At the convention held in Pittsburg, January, 1899, he was elected national president, and
was unanimously re-elected annually to that office
for eight years, when, in 1908, on account of his
health, he refused another re-election. During this
period the United Mine Workers of America grew
from a struggling band of 43,000 members to a
strong, prosperous union of 300,000, through whose
influence improvements in wages and working conditions have been secured for the mine workers
of the entire country, organized and unorganized,
and by means of which the hours of labor have
been materially reduced in all the coal-producing
states. Several extensive strikes have been engineered by Mr. Mitchell, the greatest being that
of the anthracite mine workers in 1902, which

closed every mine in the hard-coal fields of Pennsylvania, and nearly produced a national coal
famine before the operators would yield to arbitration. The award of the Anthracite Coal Strike
Commission, appointed by Pres. Roosevelt to arbi-
trate the questions at issue, gave to the mine
workers an advance of ten per cent. in wages, based
on a sliding scale, which has made the actual annual advance about fourteen per cent.; a reduction
in the length of the working day, and numerous
improvements in conditions of employment. The
anthracite miners are still working under the provisions of this award, extended from time to time
by mutual agreement. Mr. Mitchell is a vice-
president of the American Federation of Labor,
having held this position for twelve years; he is
also a delegate from the United Mine Workers of
America to the conventions of the American Federation of Labor. In 1904 Mr. Mitchell represented the miners of America at the International
Mining Congress, held in Paris, afterward making
an investigation of working and living conditions
among the miners in Belgium, France, Germany,
England and Wales, a full report of which he rendered to the convention of the United Mine Workers of America. The National Civic Federation,
in 1900, appointed him one of a committee of three
to draw up plans for a branch for the promotion
of industrial peace through conciliation, mediation
and arbitration, and after these plans had been
formulated he became a member of the division.
Upon the expiration of his term as president of
the United Mine Workers of America he accepted
a position with the National Civic Federation, becoming the active head of the trade agreement
department, with which he had been connected in
an advisory capacity for some years. He was
president of various athletic and political clubs
in his home town up to 1895, but since then his
time has been given up almost entirely to the
interests of labor, which he represents on the executive committees of a number of national and state
organizations for the improvement of industrial
and social conditions. When, in 1906, the Nobel
peace prize was awarded to Pres. Roosevelt, and by
him was contributed to the Foundation for the
Promotion of Industrial Peace, Mr. Mitchell was
appointed to represent labor on the board of trustees of the foundation, being subsequently elected
secretary of the board, in which capacity he is
now serving. He was one of five citizens representing the nation at large, invited to participate
in the conference on conservation held at the
White House in May, 1908. Personally, Mr.
Mitchell has always evinced a strong tendency to
sink his own identity in that of the union; his
career has been notably free from self-seeking;
and despite the peculiarly exposed nature of his
position, there has never been the slightest reflection upon the uprightness and honesty of his character. He is the author of "Organized Labor, Its
Problems, Purposes and Ideals" (1903). He was
married at Spring Valley, Ill., June 1, 1892, to
Catherine, daughter of Henry O'Rourke, of that
place, and has three sons and one daughter.

STOECKHARDT, Carl George, theologian,
was born at Chemnitz, Saxony, Germany, Feb. 17,
1842, son of Adolf Stoeckhardt, professor of
chemistry at Tharandt, Saxony, and author of a
valuable work on chemistry. He was educated at
a private Latin school at Tharandt, and was graduated at the Fuerstenschule at Meissen, Saxony,
in 1862. He then entered the University of Erlangen, and later that of Leipsic, as a divinity
student and pursued his studies in divinity until

JOHN M. CRUIKSHANK
EDITOR

JOHN MITCHELL
LABOR LEADER

CARL G. STOECKHARDT
THEOLOGIAN

WILLIAM A. MARBLE
MANUFACTURER

1866. During 1867-70 he taught at a ladies' boarding-school in his native city. He served in the German-French war as pastor of the German Lutheran Church des Billettes at Paris, France, and later performed pastoral duties at the hospital at Sedan. Returning to Germany, he settled at Erlangen and was enrolled at the university as private tutor in Old and New Testament exegesis, acting at the same time as instructor in religion at the city college. During 1873-76 he was pastor of a Lutheran state church at Planitz, near Zwickau, Saxony, and from 1876-78 was pastor of the Independent Lutheran St. John's Church of that city. In 1878 he accepted a call to Holy Cross Lutheran Church at St. Louis, Mo., and connected himself with the German Evangelical Lutheran Synod of Missouri, Ohio, and other states. Upon the death of Dr. Walther, the founder of the Missouri Synod, in 1887, he was elected to the chair of Old and New Testament exegesis at Concordia Seminary, a position he occupied until his death. He received his D.D. degree in 1903 from the Luther Seminary (Norwegian) at Hamline, Minn. He was one of the foremost theologians of the American Lutheran Church, one of the ablest teachers of Concordia Seminary, a principal figure in the predestinarian controversy which has been waged in the Lutheran church since 1880, and a versatile and impressive speaker and writer. His contributions to the official organ of the Missouri Synod, ''Der Lutheraner,'' to the ''Homiletic Monthly'' and ''Lehre und Wehre,'' the theological monthlies published by the same body, would fill several volumes. Besides these he published a volume of ''Lenten Sermons'' (1885), ''Advent Sermons'' (1886), ''History of the Old and New Testament'' (1896 and 1898) and ''Exposition of Isaiah, chaps. 1-12'' (1895). His ripest studies are found in his latest publications, all of which are commentaries: ''Romans'' (1907), ''Ephesians'' (1910), and ''First Peter'' (1912). Dr. Stoeckhardt's second marriage was on Nov. 28, 1901, to Marie Elisa, daughter of Carl Christian Kohne, of Pittsburgh, Pa. He died without issue in St. Louis, Mo., Jan. 9, 1913.

MARBLE, William Allen, corset manufacturer, was born in Woonsocket, R. I., March 4, 1849, son of Russel and Phœbe (Almy) Marble, grandson of Aaron and Rebecca (Putnam) Marble, and a descendant in the fifth generation of Samuel Marble, the founder of the family in America, who settled in Andover, Mass., in 1648. Both his grandfather, Aaron Marble, and great-grandfather, Enoch Marble, served throughout the revolutionary war. He was graduated at the Moses Brown school, Providence, R. I., and began his business career as a salesman in the linen collar trade. After five years in this work, in 1873 he became identified with the corset business, and for ten years represented the Worcester Corset Co. in New York. In 1884 he associated himself with the firm of Roth & Goldschmidt, manufacturers of corsets, in New York, and after a number of years as salesman on the road became a partner. When, in 1897, the firm was reorganized as the R. & G. Corset Co. Mr. Marble was made vice-president and general manager, a position he still holds. Under his management the firm has become one of the largest manufacturers of corsets in the world. Its factories at South Norwalk, Conn., and the Bush Terminal, Brooklyn, N. Y., employ 1,400 hands. He was elected president of the Corset Manufacturers' Association of the United States in 1912 and 1913. He has been actively identified with the work of the Merchants' Association in New York since its organization in 1897. He was made secretary of the board of directors in 1903, became third vice-president in 1904, second vice-president in 1907, first vice-president in 1911, and upon the resignation of Henry R. Towne, in 1913, succeeded him as president. He was for three years president of the New York State Society of the Sons of the American Revolution, and in 1910 was elected president-general of the National Society of the Sons of the American Revolution. In 1907 he became registrar-general of the Founders and Patriots of America. He is vice-president of the Broadway Association, and is a director and member of the executive committee of the Chamber of Commerce of the United States of America. Mr. Marble was married July 1, 1873, to Catharine Alice, daughter of John Cain, and has one son, William E. Marble. Portrait opposite page 126.

BURRAGE, Robert Lowell, physician, was born in Newark, N. J., June 14, 1857, son of Michael and Matilda (Moore) Burrage. His father, a native of England, was attracted by the many advantages and opportunities for a young man in the new world, and came to America about 1840, settling in Newark, N. J., where he practiced his trade of wood-turning. Robert L. Burrage was educated in the public and high schools of Newark, and having determined to follow the medical profession, took the regular course at the Bellevue Hospital Medical College, New York city, where he was graduated M.D. in 1878. He entered at once upon medical practice in Newark; he displayed exceptional qualities requisite to a successful medical career, and soon acquired a large and lucrative practice. In 1890 he was invited to enter the medical department of the Prudential Insurance Co., of Newark, and from that date until his death he served on the medical staff of that company. He was made an associate medical director in 1898, and ten years later chief medical director. This responsible position involved the supervision of 11,000 branch offices. Dr. Burrage made a special study of tuberculosis, and was the author of a number of pamphlets on that subject, which attracted so much attention that they were printed and distributed by the National Association for the Prevention of Tuberculosis. He was one of the founders and organizers of the Widows' and Orphans' Relief Society and of the Practitioners' Club and was an associate of St. Michael's Hospital. His charity and generosity, though very unostentatious and not very well known to the public, were recognized by those who were in a position to know of them. He was a very close friend of all the Catholic clergymen in Newark and its vicinity, who knew him as a man ever ready to give liberally of his time, money and service to the aid of every worthy cause. He was a member of the American Medical Association and of the Association of Life Insurance Medical Directors, serving on the executive committee of the latter. He was also a member of the Essex Club of Newark, and served on the Essex county auxiliary committee which had in charge the erection of the monument in honor of Pres. Grover Cleveland at Princeton, N. J., in 1910. Dr. Burrage was married April 20, 1882, to Anna Louise, daughter of William L. Pierson, of Newark, N. J. She survived him with one son, Percy Fraser Burrage, who was educated at the Mohegan Lake Military School and Princeton University, and is now connected with the Prudential Insurance Co. Dr. Burrage died in Orange, N. J., Oct. 29, 1911.

KELLOGG, Vernon Lyman, biologist and educator, was born in Emporia, Kan., Dec. 1, 1867, son of Lyman Beecher and Abigail (Homer) Kellogg. He was graduated B.S. at the University of Kansas in 1899, receiving also the degree of M.S. in 1892. Meanwhile he studied entomology at Cornell University during 1891–92, at Leipzig during 1893–94, and again during 1897–98, and later in Paris during 1904–05 and 1908–09. His career as a teacher began in 1890 when he became assistant professor of entomology in the University of Kansas. Three years later he was made an associate professor. In 1894 he transferred his services to Stanford University, becoming an assistant professor, and since 1906 he has been full professor of entomology and lecturer on bionomics. He was an assistant on the Samoan explorations of the U. S. Bureau of Fisheries in 1902, and during part of 1915–16 he served as director of the Belgium relief commission in Brussels. He is a member of the Entomological Society of America, of which he was president in 1915, and of the American Association for the Advancement of Science, of which he has been a fellow since 1901. Prof. Kellogg has been an indefatigable worker in science and a prolific contributor to the current literature of his chosen field. His separate papers, exclusive of those written in collaboration with his students or associates, are more than a hundred in number. Typical of these may be cited the following: "The Histoblasts (Imaginal Buds) of the Wings and Legs of the Giant Crane Fly" (1901), which is one of many contributed to Psyche forming a series of "Studies for Students in Entomology." He also contributed to a similar series "Elementary Studies in Insect Histology" (1903). His papers on "Phagocytosis in the Post-Embryonic Development of the Diptera" (1901); "The Development and Homologies of the Mouth Parts of Insects" (1902); "Poulton and Plate on Evolution" (1909); "Notes on Evolution" (1909), and "Distribution and Species-Forming of Ectoparasites" (1913) appeared in the "American Naturalist." To science he contributed such papers as "Is There Determinate Variation?" (1906; "Variation in Parthenogenetic Insects" (1906); "A Note on Assortative Mating" (1906), and "Ectoparasites of the Monkeys, Apes and Man" (1913). More technical perhaps are his descriptions of "Insects and Spiders of the Galapagos" (Psyche, 1901); "Birds of the High Mountains" (Bulletin of the Sierra Club, 1902); "The Net-Winged Midges of North America" (California Academy of Sciences, 1903); "Regeneration in Larval Legs of Silkworms" ("Journal of Experimental Zoology," 1903); "Insect Bionomics" ("Entomological News," 1907); "Artificial Parthenogenesis in the Silkworm" (Biological Bulletin of Woods Hole, 1907), and "Mallophaga from Birds of the South Atlantic" (Bulletin of the Museum of the Brooklyn Institute, 1914); while "Ernest Haeckel; Darwinist, Monist" (1910) and "Collecting on a Coral Reef" (1912) were scientific papers published in the "Popular Science Monthly." He is the editor and has contributed since 1911 to the "Philosophy of Nature" series. Among his larger works may be mentioned: "Common Injurious Insects of Kansas" (1892); with David Starr Jordan, "Animal Life" (1901); "Elementary Zoology" (1901, 2d ed., 1902); "First Lessons in Zoology" (1903); "American Insects" (1905); with David Starr Jordan and H. Heath, "Animal Studies" (1905); with David Starr Jordan, "Evolution and Animal Life" (1907); "Darwinism To-day: a Discussion of Present-Day Scientific Criticism of Darwinian Selective Theories" (1907); "Insect Stories" (1908); "In and Out of Florence" (1910); "The Animals and Man" (a text book, 1911); "Beyond War" (1912), and "Economic Zoology and Entomology" (with R. W. Doane, 1915).

GREEN, Henrietta [Hetty] Howland (Robinson), financier, was born at New Bedford Mass., Nov. 21, 1834, daughter of Edward Mott and Abby S. (Howland) Robinson, of English-colonial descent. Her father was a leading figure in the shipping and whaling industry in New Bedford, and was well known in financial circles in New York. Before the days of petroleum and transcontinental communication he was an extensive shipper of sperm oil from Alaska to the East. For many generations the family were strict Quakers. Her grandfather, and later her father, suffered from failing eyesight, and it was her lot as a girl to read to them the financial news in the daily papers. In this way she acquired a familiarity with financial affairs. She inherited a frugal disposition and early showed a tendency to use her ample allowance for investment rather than in the frivolous purchases for which it was intended. The death of both her father and an aunt, Miss Sylvia Ann Howland, in 1865, left her in possession of an estate valued at $10,000,000. She had the training and knowledge to handle her heritage to the best advantage, and it increased under her management until she became the wealthiest woman in the United States. Her investments, which were country-wide, were almost invariably in real estate, mortgages, banks and trust companies. They were placed with the idea of helping others and benefiting the community in which they were located. Thus, for example, the dividends on investments in any particular city were always deposited in the banks of that city, though they might have been used elsewhere more profitably to herself. She financed the business of her son, Col. Edward H. G. Green, who built the Texas Midland railroad, and was interested in banking institutions, ranches, mines and real estate in Texas. Mrs. Green was characterized as an extremely human person of simple tastes and kindly impulses, very shrewd, very humorous, very sociable, with a whimsical good-humored disdain of the world's opinions and pretensions. At the time of her death her fortune was said to be approximately $100,000,000. She was married July 11, 1867, to Edward H. Green, a member of the New York firm of Russell Sturgis & Co., and had two children: Edward Howland Robinson and Sylvia Ann, wife of Matthew Astor Wilks of New York. Mr. and Mrs. Green subsequently separated, and he died in 1902. After 1911 her son assisted her in the management of her financial affairs under the name of the Westminster Co. She died in New York, July 3, 1916.

BLUE, Victor, naval officer, was born in Scotland county, N. C., Dec. 6, 1865, son of John Gilchrist and Ann Maria (Evans) Blue, and brother of Rupert Blue. The family is Scotch. The first representative in this country was Malcolm Blue, who had espoused the cause of the Stuarts and after the battle of Culloden fled to escape persecution in 1747, settling at the Longstreet colony on the Cape Fear river, North Carolina; his wife was Sarah Smith, and the line is traced through their son John, who married Mary McKay; their son John, who married Effie Gilchrist, and their son, John Gilchrist Blue, the father of our subject. The second John Blue was a captain in the war of 1812,

Victor Blue was graduated at the United States Naval Academy, Annapolis, Md., in 1887. He was promoted to be assistant engineer in 1889 and transferred to the line as ensign in 1892, becoming lieutenant in 1899, lieutenant-commander in 1905 and commander in 1909. His service was at sea until 1891, when he was on special duty at the Union Iron Works, San Francisco. In 1892 he was transferred to the Norfolk (Va.) navy yard and after another period of sea duty was appointed to the naval academy in 1896. At the outbreak of the Spanish-American war he was assigned to the Suwanee and rendered signal service by conducting an armed boat's crew at the beginning of the war across twenty miles of shoal waters to the Cuban coast, and after defeating a Spanish patrol boat, sent word to Gen. Gomez of the impending relief to the insurgent army. On two other occasions he went ashore and secured accurate information of the location and number of Adm. Cervera's fleet in Santiago harbor. His feat was a hazardous one, for his capture meant certain death. In recognition of these services he was advanced five numbers in rank, in 1901, for "extraordinary heroism." After the war he became staff squadron commander on the Asiatic station; was inspector of equipment at the Cramp shipyards, Philadelphia, in 1901; was on special duty at the Bureau of Ordnance in 1905; was inspector of ordnance, Newport News, Va., 1905–07. As commander of the Yorktown he was appointed chief of staff of the Pacific fleet. He was appointed to special duty on the general board of the navy department in May, 1911, and became chief of the Bureau of Navigation in March, 1913, with the rank of rear-admiral. Adm. Blue is a member of the Army and Navy Club, the Rittenhouse Club, the Chevy Chase Club and the New York Yacht Club. He was married, Oct. 17, 1899, to Eleanor Foote, daughter of John Stuart, of Morristown, N. J., and has two sons: John Stuart and Victor.

BLUE, Rupert, sanitarian, was born in Scotland county, N. C., May 30, 1867, son of John Gilchrist and Annie Maria (Evans) Blue, and brother of Victor Blue of the U. S. navy. He was educated in the University of Virginia and University of Maryland, being graduated M.D. at the latter in 1892 and D.Sc. in 1909. He was commissioned assistant surgeon in the marine hospital service in the following year, after serving an interneship in a marine hospital. Four years later he passed the examination for passed assistant surgeon, and was promoted to full surgeon on May 1, 1909. His first eight years in the service were spent in the usual round of routine duties at various points in the United States. He was in charge of the work of eradicating the bubonic plague in San Francisco, Cal., which had broken out in that port in 1903 and again in 1907–08. He served through the yellow fever epidemic in New Orleans, La., in 1905. At the Jamestown Exposition in 1907 he was made director of sanitation, displaying ability far above the ordinary in organizing and reconciling the various interests represented at the exposition, and making a conspicuous success of its sanitation. In the same year he was detailed to take charge of operations against another outbreak of the plague in San Francisco, Cal., where he remained until 1910. Later he spent some time in Europe studying emigration, preventive medicine and quarantine management, at the London School of Tropical Medicine, and in 1910 he represented the service at the international congress on medicine and hygiene at Buenos Aires, Argentine. In November, 1911, he was detailed as special sanitary adviser to the governor and board of health of Hawaii in carrying out a program for the improvement of sanitary conditions, with a view to minimizing the possibility of yellow fever and plague in that territory after the opening of the Panama canal. While thus engaged he was appointed surgeon-general of the marine hospital service, Jan. 11, 1912, to succeed Dr. Walter Wyman. The marine hospital service is one of the oldest and most peculiarly American of all our national institutions. Its beginning was in an act of congress, July 16, 1798, which put a tax of twenty cents a month on American sailors' wages to provide hospitals for their support and comfort in time of sickness. The first hospital thus erected by the government was at Washington's Point, Norfolk co., Va., in 1800, and three years later a marine hospital was built in Boston. Subsequently others were established in New Orleans, La.; St. Louis, Mo.; San Francisco, Cal.; Staten Island, N. Y.; Chicago, Ill.; Louisville, Ky.; Pittsburgh, Pa., and Ft. Stanton, N. M. At Stapleton, Staten Island, there was established in 1893 a hygienic laboratory, which later was transferred to Washington, D. C., and is now recognized the world over for its excellent contributions to the knowledge of scientific medicine and of public health and sanitation. It is in charge of the foremost medical authorities on public health problems, under whose direction the laboratory makes a practice of assisting state health officers. The public health service licenses all those engaged in interstate traffic in viruses, serums, toxins, etc.; conducts investigations of the hygiene and sanitary arrangements of railroad and sleeping cars; of epidemic diseases and methods of their prevention, supervises relief stations, and controls the quarantine stations at forty-five ports of entry in the United States and eight in Hawaii, Porto Rico and Philippine Islands, as well as of the Canal zone. It also conducts physical examinations of seamen in the various government services, as well as of candidates for entrance, for promotion or for retirement, and medical examinations of emigrants. Persons entitled to medical relief from the public health service are seamen on any registered or licensed vessel of the United States, officers and men of the United States coast guard in the revenue cutter service, the army engineering corps, the life-saving service and even seamen on foreign vessels provided they give security for the payment of the small fees fixed by the department. During the year 1915 over 50,000 patients were treated at the various relief stations of the service. This national health protection, although very little known and its work less completely understood by the public at large, is of more vital importance to the nation than any other of the departments in charge of the United States government. Dr. Blue is peculiarly well fitted to fill the important position of surgeon-general, for continuing the present high standard of the service in personnel and efficiency, and for increasing its prestige and value to the nation at large. He is one of the foremost authorities in the field of preventive medicine and quarantine; he is a man of splendid executive ability, a skillful organizer, an accurate judge of character, and has marked personal characteristics which command great respect and admiration among all who know him. He is a member of the American Medical Association (president 1916), the American Society of Tropical Medicine, the Royal Institute of Public Health, the American Public Health Association, the American Climatological Association, the Association of Military Surgeons of the United States (president 1915), the National Committee for Mental Hygiene, the National Mouth Hygiene Association, the American Association for Labor Legislation, the National Economic League, the College of Surgeons of America, the California Academy of Medicine, the Medical Society of the City and County of San Francisco, and is a fellow of the London Society of Tropical Medicine. His social clubs are the Metropolitan, Chevy Chase, Army and Navy and University, all of Washington, and the Bohemian and Union League of San Francisco. He is unmarried.

WILLARD, James Orville, banker and manufacturer, was born at Charlestown, N. H., July 7, 1814, son of James and Lydia (Willard) Willard. His first American ancestor was Maj. Simon Willard, a native of Horsmonden, County of Kent, England, who came to America in 1634 and settled first at Cambridge, Mass., and subsequently founded Concord, N. H. His wife was Mary Sharpe, and the line is traced through their son Josiah and his wife, Hannah Hosmer; their son Samuel and his wife, Sarah Clarke; their son Joseph and his wife, Susanna Lynde; their son Joseph and his wife, Huldah; their son Francis Willoughby and his wife, Deborah Blood, and their son James and his wife, Lydia Willard. Samuel Willard (q. v.), son of Maj. Simon Willard, was seventh president of Harvard College in 1701-07. James O. Willard acquired a good English education in the public schools and at the Kimble Union Academy, in Plainfield, N. H., whither young Willard's parents had moved before he was a year old. In 1834 he moved to Painesville, O., where he was clerk with the Geanga Iron Co. for three years. In March, 1841, with three others, he rented Buckhorn furnace and in five years the venture paid a profit of $50,000 to the partners. A little later, he purchased the property for $22,500. Pig iron sold then at $60 a ton and the raw material for its manufacture was found in abundance in that part of southern Ohio. The town of Ironton was founded by him and several other iron manufacturers in 1849. In a period of three years what had been a corn and wheat field was transformed into a thriving town of over 2,000 inhabitants. In a statement published in 1852, and signed by James O. Willard, he declared that ''the principal cause of the unexampled prosperity and rapid growth of Ironton is its favorable location and the advantages it possesses for manufacturing purposes, especially of iron. Ten or twelve furnaces will deposit their iron at this place; their owners are building and have built fine, large residences here, making the town their permanent home, and giving it the benefit of their capital, as it may accumulate from their furnace operations. The town contains a large rolling mill, two large foundries, a large machine shop, adapted and designed for the building of locomotives, engines and railroad cars; an axe manufactory, a furniture manufactory and a planing machine. These establishments are all driven by steam power—the Ohio Iron and Coal Co. furnishing the coal and the Iron Railroad Co. dropping it at their doors—at a total cost of $1 per ton. Ironton is the county seat for Lawrence county.'' Subsequently James O. Willard and his associates built a railroad from Ironton to Centre station, of which he was president for several years. The Ohio Iron and Coal Co. was formed about the same time, and by the same men, with 300 acres of Ohio river bottom lands and 4,000 acres of stone coal lands. Mr. Willard was also the founder of the Iron Bank of Ironton, which subsequently became the First National Bank and of which he was the head until his death. He was married in 1839 to Anna Martha, daughter of Uri Seely, of Painesville, O., and had seven children (two died in infancy): Anna, Eugene B. (q. v.), Ella, Abbie and Mary E., wife of Henry Bramble Wilson. He died at Ironton May 19, 1855.

RICH, Jacob, journalist, was born in New York city, Dec. 18, 1832, son of William and Mary (Parks) Rich. His father was a farmer, near Philadelphia, and he was educated in the public and private schools in that city. In 1856 he removed to Dubuque and later to Buchanan county, Ia., where he began the publication of the "Quasqueton Guardian." In 1858 he removed the publication office to Independence, Ia. He was chief clerk of the Iowa general assembly in 1864 and was clerk of the naval committee of the United States senate during 1865–69. In 1870 he purchased a half interest in the "Daily Times," Dubuque, which under his management was greatly enlarged and improved. In 1872–77 he was chairman of the Republican state central committee of Iowa, and in 1874 was appointed pension agent at Dubuque. In 1875 he disposed of his interest in the "Daily Times" and retired from journalism. He was president of the board of trustees of the Carnegie-Stout public library of Dubuque from the date of its establishment until his death. He was an organizer of the Iowa Trust and Savings Bank in 1884 and a director until 1912. His intimate relations with Sen. William B. Allison, of Iowa, and the important part he played in Allison's early political success constitute an important chapter in Mr. Rich's life. He was editor of the Dubuque "Times" when Sen. Allison, then a member of the lower house, made his successful fight for elevation to the senate, and was his most confidential and effective aid in that campaign. When Allison became a candidate for the presidency before the conventions of 1888–96 Mr. Rich was intrusted with the preparation of his claims. He was a sagacious political manager and his judgment of men and of policies was discreet and far-sighted. As a writer he excelled equally in description and in controversy. His methods were painstaking and his style remarkably virile and direct. He polished every sentence with that care the lapidary bestows upon a jewel, and the result was the scintillating product of a brilliant mind. He was married Nov. 27, 1877, to Annie K. Smith, the daughter of Sabin Smith, of Chicago, who survived him. He died in Dubuque, Ia., Sept. 11, 1913.

FISKE, Horace Spencer, editor, author, educator, was born at Dexter, Mich., Nov. 4, 1859, son of Rev. John Billings and Mary (Gregory) Fiske. In the "Fiske Genealogy" (1896), he is tenth in descent from Robert Fiske, the progenitor of the New England family of Fiskes. His father, a native of Waterford, N. Y., was a classmate of Pres. Chester A. Arthur at Union College, and winner of the Phi Beta Kappa prize at that institution; received his theological training at Kalamazoo Seminary and Princeton Theological Seminary, and served for forty-four years in the Congregational ministry, holding pastorates in Massachusetts, Michigan, Iowa, and Missouri, his death taking place at Bear Lake, Mich. Horace Spencer Fiske was graduated at Beloit College (valedictorian) in 1882; received the degree of A.M. from the University of Michigan in 1885; was elected to a fellowship in English, University of Wisconsin, in 1892, and during 1893–94 was a student at Oxford and Cambridge Universities, England, and Trinity College, Dublin. While an under-

RUPERT BLUE
SANITARIAN

JAMES O. WILLARD
MANUFACTURER

JACOB RICH
JOURNALIST

HORACE S. FISKE
EDUCATOR

Alfred H Cowles

graduate he was editor in chief of the Beloit College "Round Table"; gave the Greek oration in his junior year, and represented Wisconsin in the Interstate Oratorical Contest, at Indianapolis. While in England he contributed to the "Oxford Magazine" and "Christ College Magazine." His active professional career was begun as instructor in Latin and civics, Racine (Wis.) High School, during 1882–84. He was instructor in Greek, Latin, and English literature at Beloit College Academy during 1886–87, and during the ensuing six years was professor of political economy and civics at Wisconsin State Normal School. In 1894 he became lecturer on English literature, extension division, University of Chicago, continuing in that capacity until 1912. He was joint editor of "State Readers of Indiana" in 1899; literary editor of "The World Review," Chicago, during 1901–02; assistant recorder, University of Chicago, during 1903–12, and since 1903 has been editor of the "University Record," University of Chicago. He was also associate editor of the "University of Chicago Magazine" from 1908–14, and has been associated with the publication department of the University of Chicago Press since 1912. His literary work covers a wide range, and as poet and critic of fiction he has exhibited marked versatility. He is the author of "The Ballad of Manila Bay and Other Verses" (1900); "Provincial Types in American Fiction" (1903); "Chicago in Picture and Poetry" (1903); contributions in "The Athlete's Garland" (1905); "The Little Book of Sports" (1910); "The Humbler Poets" (1911); "The Praise of Lincoln" (1911); "Poems on the University of Chicago" (1914); also verse and prose in leading magazines and newspapers, including the "Century Magazine," "The Nation," "The Metropolitan," "Harper's Weekly," etc. He is a trustee of the Eagles' Nest Camp Association, Oregon, Ill., an organization of artists and authors; member Michigan Society of Chicago; Cliff Dwellers, Chicago; the Reynolds Club, University of Chicago; and the Phi Beta Kappa fraternity. He was married at Lancaster, N. H., June 22, 1889, to Ida Peck Nettleton, daughter of George Clinton Peck, of Lyndon, Vt.

COWLES, Alfred Hutchinson, metallurgist, was born in Cleveland, O., Dec. 8, 1858, son of Edwin and Elizabeth Caroline (Hutchinson) Cowles. His father (q.v.) was founder, publisher and editor of the Cleveland "Leader," "Evening News" and "Herald." The first of his family in this country was John Cowles, who came over about 1636 and settled in Farmington, Conn., and the line is traced from John through Samuel and Abigail (Stanley) Cowles, Capt. Isaac and Elizabeth (Smith) Cowles, Ezekiel and Martha (Hooker) Cowles, Rev. Giles Hooker and Sally (White) Cowles, and Dr. Edwin Weed and Almira Mills (Foote) Cowles, who were the grandparents of our subject. He spent two years at Ohio State University, studying chemistry and physics, and four years at Cornell University, specializing in science and finishing in 1882. At Cornell he was on the freshman eight-oared crew that won the race with Harvard in 1878; was on the university crew that won at Lake George in 1880; one of the crew that raced at Henley, England, for the famous Stewards' Challenge cup in 1881, and on the Danube in the same year, and was captain of the "varsity" four-oared crew in 1882. His father having invested in ore lands in New Mexico, Mr. Cowles and his brother, Eugene H., became interested in developing that property. The ordinary methods of treating the ore proved unavailing,

and the brothers began to consider the possibilities of an electric furnace to volatilize and catch the zinc in the ore. They designed such a furnace and Alfred Cowles commenced a series of experiments in the pyro-electric reduction of various metallic oxides, which proved to be the most valuable contribution to the science of electro-metallurgy in the nineteenth century. Like so many other inventions of first importance, other minds were at work on the same problem at the same time; namely, Charles S. Bradley in America, and in 1887 Dr. Paul Heroult and Adolphe Minet in France. In the subsequent suits for infringement of patents the evidence was conclusive that the Cowles brothers were the first to use the electric furnace in the production of aluminum, carborundum, silicon, calcium carbide, phosphorous and various alloys. The original Cowles furnace consisted of a cylindrical retort made of stoneware and surrounded by granulated charcoal or other poor conductor of heat; a plate of carbon at one end served as one electrode and a graphite crucible at the other end made the other electrode. Variations in the form and arrangement were made later. Experimenting with their furnaces on different ores as early as 1884, he produced graphite, zinc, aluminum, crystals of rubies and sapphires, silicon carborundum and fused quartz, but his chief efforts were devoted to cheapening and perfecting the process of making aluminum. With a 35 e.h.p. generator that gave the largest amperage current of any generator made up to that time, Messrs. Cowles made 10% aluminum bronze early in 1885 and sold it at 55 cents per pound. The Cowles Electric Smelting and Aluminum Co. was organized with a capital stock of $200,000 (increased to $1,000,000) and in 1886 a water-power plant was completed at Lockport, N. Y., where a new generator, designed by Charles F. Brush, of the Brush Electric Co., was installed. The generator was the largest in the world at the time, and the plant was the first for electric smelting in the world. Announcements of the invention were made to the American Association for the Advancement of Science and the American Institute of Mining Engineers, and following a paper read on Jan. 20, 1886, the Franklin Institute awarded to the Cowles brothers the John Scott legacy medal and the Elliott Cresson medal. A patent for the process of reducing aluminum from alumina was applied for Dec. 24, 1884, by the Cowles brothers and was issued June 9, 1885. In a specific form of the broad invention they had been anticipated in date of application by Charles S. Bradley (q.v.), who had applied for a patent Feb. 23, 1883, which was issued in February, 1892, but they purchased Bradley's application, thus controlling the electric process for manufacturing aluminum commercially. Meanwhile the Pittsburgh Reduction Co. was organized in 1888 by Charles M. Hall and Romaine C. Cole, both of whom had been with the Cowles Co. at their factory at Lockport, and in June, 1889, began the manufacture of aluminum in Pittsburgh and later at Niagara Falls on a large scale. A suit and countersuit followed, by which it was established that the priority of the invention belonged to the Cowles company, and royalties and damages amounting to $1,350,000 were paid by the Aluminum Co. of America, successors to the Pittsburgh Reduction Co. From this valuable invention has developed a number of entirely new industries. It has not only made possible the production of aluminum on a large scale and at a much reduced cost for a great variety of articles, but it has resulted in the great carborundum works at Niagara Falls and in Europe and the graphite business, both developed by E. G. Acheson. The carborundum company after litigation paid the Cowles company over $300,000, an award of the U. S. circuit court of appeals. The calcium carbide industry for acetylene gas was perfected by Thomas Willson and Morehead at Spray, N. C., and later carried on by the Union Carbide Co. of Niagara Falls and Sault Ste. Marie. Its predecessor, the Electro Gas Co., paid the Cowles Co. 12½% of its capital stock for a license during the life of the Cowles patents. The carbon bisulphide industry at Penn Yan, N. Y., was stimulated into existence by the Cowles works. Phosphorus is now made at Niagara Falls by a process originally under license of the Cowles patents. Mr. Cowles was metallurgist of the Cowles Electric Smelting and Aluminum Co. for eight years and then became president. In 1895 the company reorganized as the Electric Smelting and Aluminum Co. He read a paper before the American Electro-chemical Society in 1902 suggesting a new system of units for practical purposes, pointing out that for special subjects like electrolysis, units should be of such convenient dimensions as not to be cumbersome. He found that within human measurement 100 amperes in one sidereal day, as a coincidence, free one c.m. of hydrogen (n.p.t.) in the electrolysis of water and suggested making this a new unit, and as its weight is a kilocrith, he called his electrical quality unit a kilocrith col. He is also president of the Pecos Copper Co. and the Weiller Manufacturing Co. He is a fellow of the American Institute of Electrical Engineers, a founder member of the Mining and Metallurgical Society of America, a member of the U. S. Naval Institute, the American Association for the Advancement of Science, the Franklin Institute and one of the founders and a past vice-president of the American Electrochemical Society. He was married, Oct. 25, 1906, to Helen J., daughter of James Mortimer Wills, of Akron, O.

KNIGHT, Clarence A., lawyer and financier, was born at McHenry, Ill., Oct. 28, 1853, son of John and Sarah Knight. His father was an officer in the Mississippi gunboat service in the civil war, and was killed in the White river expedition in 1862. The son was educated in the public schools and at the state normal school of Illinois. While teaching school he studied law in the office of Spafford, McDaid & Wilson, attorneys of Chicago, and was admitted to the bar in 1874. After the firm of Spafford, McDaid & Wilson was dissolved, Mr. Knight formed a partnership with McDaid in 1875 under the firm name of McDaid & Knight. In 1879 he was appointed assistant city attorney of Chicago, under Julius S. Grinnell. Five years later, upon Grinnell's election as state's attorney, Mayor Harrison appointed Knight city attorney, and he retained the office until the following year, when Mayor Roche tendered to him the position of assistant corporation counsel. He resigned in 1889, and resumed his private practice. During the ten years of his connection with the city law department, a vast amount of municipal legislation and also legislative law-making came under his department. Aside from grants made to quasi public corporations, many measures of immense importance to the people were included. One of these was the act annexing Hyde Park to Chicago. The original act was declared unconstitutional by the Supreme Court. Leading citizens sought to have a new law passed remedying its defects, which would provide not only for the annexation of Hyde Park, but for the absorption of other

suburbs, when in the course of time it was desired to add them to the city. At the request of Joseph Medill, of the "Tribune," Knight prepared an act to cover the case, and it was passed in 1889 by the legislature. It was under the provisions of this law that in June, 1889, Hyde Park, Lake View, Jefferson, the Town of Lake and portions of Cicero were annexed to Chicago. This law has since been thoroughly tested in the courts, and has been declared by the supreme court of Illinois to be constitutional. During his term of office Clarence A. Knight prepared the various acts which the city of Chicago desired to have passed by the legislature of 1889, many of them of great importance. The majority became laws. The franchises of most of the large and successful semi-public corporations operating in Chicago were either granted during the time that Clarence Knight was in office, or in important instances they were added to or otherwise widened. The legal aspect of all of them was scrutinized by him, and he gained in that way an unusually thorough experience in the vexed questions surrounding the scope and meaning of municipal grants. Upon his retirement from office he formed a law partnership with Paul Brown, under the firm name of Knight & Brown, which acquired an extensive practice, largely in corporation, municipal and insurance law. During 1904–6 he was associated with George W. Brown, and after the latter's death Maclay Hoyne became a partner under the firm name of Knight & Hoyne, and on Dec. 1, 1908, the firm was reorganized with James J. Barbour and William A. Adams under the title of Knight, Barbour & Adams. He was general counsel of the Lake Street Elevated railroad, the "Union Loop," "Northwestern Elevated," "Consolidated Traction Co.," and the Suburban Electric surface lines. He represented the Chicago buildings of Charles T. Yerkes, and after the latter's death he represented the estate. Mr. Knight was one of the most brilliant and effective pleaders before the bar. He was the victor in many famous cases, among which may be mentioned that of the Chicago "Inter-Ocean" vs. The Associated Press, in which he represented the plaintiff. He was a member of the Union League, Chicago Athletic and South Shore county clubs, and belonged to the Masonic order, and several other fraternal and social organizations. He was married Oct. 31, 1873, to Adele, daughter of Dr. H. T. Brown, of McHenry county, Ill., and had two children: James H. and Bessie, wife of L. Sherman Aldrich. He died in Chicago, June 21, 1911.

KIMBALL, George Albert, civil engineer, was born in Littleton, Mass., May 14, 1850, son of William and Mary A. (Lawrence) Kimball, and a descendant of Richard Kimball, of Suffolk county, England, who settled in Watertown, in 1634. The line of descent is traced through his son Benjamin, who married Mercy Hazletine; their son Jonathan, who married Lydia Day; their son Benjamin, who married Mary Emerson; their son Jonathan, who married Elizabeth Little, their son Daniel, who married Lucy Dutton; their son James, who married Rachel Hartwell, and was the grandfather of George A. Kimball. Daniel Kimball was a first lieutenant in the revolutionary war. George A. Kimball was educated in the public schools of Littleton and at Appleton Academy, New Ipswich, N. H., where he was prepared for college, but, owing to weakness of the eyes, he abandoned a college career, and in 1869 entered the office of Messrs. Frost Bros., civil engineers, of Somerville, Mass. Beginning as a rodman he had a

Clarence A. Knight.

George A. Kimball

varied and thorough experience in all branches of the engineering profession. He was city engineer of Somerville in 1867-87, and served on the Massachusetts grade crossing commission (1888), and on the Metropolitan sewerage commission (1896–1901). He was also a member of the Somerville board of health (1879-86), the board of aldermen (1888-89), and the Mystic water board (1891-1900). He was at different times consulting engineer for the cities of Brockton, Montpelier (Vt.), New Bedford, Milton, Winthrop, Beverly, Gardner and Arlington on questions of sewerage systems, water works, the abolition of grade crossings, and details of construction work. In 1896 he became consulting engineer for the Boston elevated railway company, and in 1898 chief engineer, a position which he occupied until the close of his life. In 1902 he was sent abroad by the company to study transportation systems in foreign countries, and traveled in England, France, Germany and Austria in pursuit of that purpose. He also traveled in Central America and throughout the United States. Much of the modern transportation system of Greater Boston stands as a tribute to his engineering genius. He designed and built the elevated road from Sullivan Square, Charlestown, to Forest Hills, about seventeen miles of elevated structure; the Cambridge (Main street) subway, about three miles long; the East Cambridge elevated extension, including the concrete bridge over the Charles, and made plans for the Malden and Everett extension, only a portion of which had been erected when he died. With Howard A. Carson, former chief engineer, and Edmund S. Davis, the present chief engineer of the board, he assisted in devising the East Boston and Washington street tunnels. Probably there was no single piece of construction or achievement in which he took more pride than the newly-completed Cambridge (Main street) subway. To this work he gave his closest attention, and it stands to-day a monument to his ability. It is typical of its builder in the thoroughness of its construction and in its convenience and appointment. Mr. Kimball was president of the Boston Society of Civil Engineers, a director of the American Society of Civil Engineers, a member of the Institution of Civil Engineers of London, the New England Street Railway Club, the Winchester Country Club, John Abbott Lodge of Masons, Boston Chamber of Commerce, Royal Arcanum and Knights of Honor. He was a director of the Somerville Co-operative Bank, a trustee of the Symmes Hospital and of Appleton Academy, and a member of the Committee of Twenty-One of Arlington. In connection with his engineering work Mr. Kimball wrote a number of valuable reports, and was author of a life of Edward Frost. His unfailing courtesy, fair dealing and kindness, together with his remarkable self-control under trying conditions, made him hosts of friends and fitted him to carry through the difficult tasks set before him. His sense of humor smoothed over any bitterness between disputants, and his habit of introducing delicate questions by boldly attacking and laying bare the heart of the trouble, and then searching for the redeeming features, always left everybody in pleasant mood. He was a consistent and active member of the Congregational Church, a man of high moral principles, a devoted husband and parent, and a sympathetic and helpful friend. He carried many and great responsibilities, yet never seemed to be burdened. He was married Feb. 29, 1872, to Lizzie Emily,

daughter of Lewis Robbins, of New Ipswich, N. H., and had two sons, Herbert L. and Ernest R., and two daughters, Josephine M., wife of Charles K. Woodridge, of Arlington, and Elizabeth Kimball. He died in Arlington, Mass., Dec. 3, 1912.

JOHNSON, Hiram Warren, twenty-third governor of California, was born at Sacramento, Cal., Sept. 2, 1866, son of Grove Laurence and Annie (De Montfredy) Johnson. His father was a native of Syracuse, N. Y., and went to California for his health, where he practiced law and stood at the head of the bar in northern and central California; he served in the national congress during 1895–97. The son was educated in the public schools of Sacramento and the University of California, but left in his junior year to marry. His first business experience was as a shorthand reporter. Having decided to follow the law, he studied in his father's office while continuing his reportorial work, and after being admitted to the bar in 1888 practiced with his father and brother in Sacramento under the firm name of Johnson & Johnson. In 1902 he and his brother, Albert M. Johnson, removed their headquarters to San Francisco. When describing the uphill road which he, a stranger, had at the outset, he observed characteristically, "I always chop my way in or out." The brothers dissolved partnership in 1904, after which he practiced alone. One of the most prominent cases handled by him was that against George D. Collins, which excited state-wide interest and involved the extradition of Mr. Collins from Canada to California, and resulted in his prosecution and conviction. The attitude which he took immediately against tricksters, gamblers and dishonest officials brought him soon into public notice. Mr. Johnson ably defended Mayor George A. Clark in his refusal to appoint as chief of police a tool of gamblers, and when the mayor was sued for removal by members of the ring, Gov. Johnson made a strong fight in his behalf. In 1906, after the famous graft prosecution was instituted, Mr. Johnson assisted the prosecuting attorney, Francis J. Heney, until 1907, when he resigned to take charge of the fight for the re-election of District-Attorney Langdon. As the fate of graft prosecutions depended on Langdon's election, Mr. Johnson encountered a powerful opposition, but his man was re-elected. Lawyer Heney was shot down in court in November, 1908, while engaged in the prosecution of Boss Ruef, and Johnson was selected to continue the work. He conducted the trial with such vigor and persistence that Ruef was convicted of bribery and sentenced to prison for fourteen years. The reform element in the state, looking for a candidate of militant and unimpeachable character for governor, turned without hesitancy to Mr. Johnson, and he received the nomination. The gubernatorial campaign of 1910 was a memorable one in California. Few political contests have been conducted with more acrimony and unscrupulous methods than were employed against the reform or "Insurgent" candidate, as Johnson was called. He was charged by the press with all kinds of misdemeanors, not the least of which was sheep stealing. Opposed to him were every state official, the Southern Pacific railroad, every public service corporation, the Republican machine, and even his own father. The theme of all his addresses was the motto of the reform party—the banishment of ring government from the state. He toured the state twice, visiting every city, town and hamlet in an automobile and stopping wherever people gathered. The result of the poll showed that he had been elected by a plurality of 22,356. He fulfilled his promise to break the influence of the Southern Pacific railroad. Largely by the force of his own personality he wrote into the state constitution a series of amendments comprising the programme of the initiative, referendum and recall, woman suffrage, employers' liability law and a workman's compensation act. The legislature extended the powers of the railway commission, provided for a public utilities commission, and passed a presidential primary act. He made a sweeping reform in the state government. Appointments were made so as to remove undesirable influence, and in some instances where unworthy incumbents refused to resign upon request, he procured the desired change by act of the legislature. In 1912 he was the candidate for vice-president on the Progressive ticket with Theodore Roosevelt as president. In 1913 the attention of the nation was attracted to Gov. Johnson and the California legislature because of attempts to limit the rights of Japanese in the state. The question in the beginning was an economic one, due to the cheapness of Japanese labor. The legislature of 1909 had attempted to pass various stringent measures prohibiting Japanese ownership of land, segregating Japanese children in schools, and placing other restrictions upon Orientals. Pres. Roosevelt interfered, and as a result of his protest to the governor and the legislature the pending bills were dropped. The legislature of 1913 prepared bills in both houses prohibiting the ownership of land by the Japanese, and a protest by the Japanese government followed. The points at issue as respecting friendly relations between Japan and the United States seemed so important to Pres. Wilson that he telegraphed to Gov. Johnson, suggesting a modification, and later proposed to send Secretary-of-State Bryan to confer with the legislators. Gov. Johnson and the legislature promptly indicated that they would welcome a visit from Bryan. The secretary made four suggestions for possible action on the part of the legislature: (1) to delay immediate action and permit the state department in Washington to frame a new treaty with Japan; (2) to delay immediate action and appoint a legislative commission to investigate alien ownership; (3) to enact a law similar to the Illinois statute which allows all aliens to hold land for six years; (4) to enact a similar law to the federal statute in the District of Columbia, which applies to all aliens. In place of acting upon these suggestions the legislature took up the consideration of a new bill framed by Attorney-General Webb, which passed both houses, its advocates contending that as it specifically guarded treaty rights and also affirmatively conferred rights on all aliens eligible to citizenship, instead of debarring from existing rights those ineligible, it was free from objection or offense. Pres. Wilson requested Gov. Johnson to withhold his signature in order to give the federal government an opportunity to take up the question diplomatically with Japan, but Gov. Johnson signed the bill on the ground that the exigencies of the situation demanded such legislation, that there was nothing in the Webb bill that deprived the Japanese of legal or treaty rights, that it in no way interfered with the existing treaties, and that similar laws had been passed by other states. In 1914 he was re-elected by the Progressive party after one of the most exciting campaigns ever known in the state. Gov. Johnson is a man of strong personality, unshaken honesty, and tireless vigor of mind and body. From early youth he led a life of strenuous and dramatic activity. At the university he was pitcher on the team and editor of the college paper. He is a member of the Native Sons of the Golden West, is a Mason and a Knight Templar. Gov. Johnson was married at Sacramento, Cal., in 1886, to Minnie L., daughter of Archibald McNeal, and they have two sons: Hiram W., Jr., and Archibald M. Johnson.

BALLENGER, Edgar Garrison, physician, was born at Tryon, N. C., Nov. 20, 1877, son of Thomas Theodore and Anna (Garrison) Ballenger. His father was a prominent merchant and planter of North Carolina. He was educated at Furman University, and after graduating at the University of North Carolina in 1897 took up the study of medicine at the University of Maryland, where he received his M.D. degree in 1901. After spending one year at the University of Maryland Hospital, he was appointed surgeon to the Maryland Granite Co. with headquarters at Guilford, Md. In the following year he removed to Atlanta, Ga., established a permanent practice, making a specialty of genito-urinary diseases. Dr. Ballenger has further perfected himself in his special line by studies at the Rudolf Vinchow Hospital in Berlin, and he is rapidly gaining a reputation that will place him in the foremost rank of prominent American physicians. He has been lecturer on genito-urinary diseases in the Atlanta School of Medicine since 1905, and is a member of the staff of the Presbyterian Hospital of Atlanta. He has been editor of the Atlanta "Journal Record of Medicine" since 1905, and is the author of "Genito-Urinary Diseases and Syphilis" (1908). He is president of the Fulton County Medical Society, 1911, and is a member of the American Medical Association, the Southern Medical Association, the Georgia Medical Society, the Sigma Alpha Epsilon and Chi Zeta Chi fraternities, Piedmont Driving Club and the Atlanta Athletic Club. Dr. Ballenger was married Apr. 20, 1904, at Baltimore, Md., to Nora Clarke, daughter of William Gorman of that city, and niece of Sen. Arthur P. Gorman, and has one daughter, Mary Clarke, and one son, Edgar Garrison Ballenger.

CAMPBELL, William Harrison, inventor, was born in New York city Sept. 10, 1846, son of Robert and Margaret (Manning) Campbell. He left home at an early age to seek his fortune, and, entering the United States navy, served in various capacities until he finally became paymaster's clerk. He was for seven years on the United States ship Plymouth and three years on the Franklin. He was twice shipwrecked, and figured in many thrilling adventures on the sea. He retired from the navy in 1872 to accept a position as secretary and general manager of the American Duplex Co. Always of an inventive turn of mind, he perfected the present system of railroad duplex tickets. He took out seventeen patents for various forms of railway tickets and appliances for printing them. He was fond of literature, was a poet of no little ability, and was the author of a number of stories based on his early experiences at sea, which found ready acceptance in the leading magazines. Mr. Campbell was married Feb. 8, 1893, to Eleanor, daughter of Allen G. Betts, of Norwalk, Conn., who survived him, with two daughters: Beatrice L. and Dorothy E. Campbell. He died at his home in Flatbush, Brooklyn, N. Y., Mar. 13, 1906.

DUPONT, Mme. Aime (Etta A. Greer), photographer, was born at North East, Erie co., Pa., daughter of John K. and Elsie Phillips (Custard) Greer. Her father (1817–71) was a native of North East, Pa., where, as a citizen, magistrate, judge, and public officer, he passed a useful and

HIRAM W. JOHNSON
GOVERNOR

EDGAR G. BALLENGER
PHYSICIAN

MME. AIME DUPONT
PHOTOGRAPHER

WILLIAM H. CAMPBELL
INVENTOR

EMERSON C. HARRINGTON
GOVERNOR

LUTHER E. HALL
GOVERNOR

GEORGE F. REINHARDT
PHYSICIAN AND EDUCATOR

CARLOS M. STONE
JURIST

successful life. He was conspicuous during the period before the civil war, when intense political excitement pervaded the whole country, causing a reconstruction of parties. He was associate judge in Erie county for ten years and was a delegate to the memorable convention which first nominated Abraham Lincoln. He was instrumental in founding the Lake Shore Seminary at North East, for which he donated all the land, besides contributing liberally. His home was the abode of hospitality, and he had a most efficient coadjutor in his wife. One of their sons was the late Col. John E. Greer of the United States army, who died in 1907 while in command of the New York Arsenal at Governor's Island, New York. "Battery Greer" in the Philippines was named in his honor. Their daughter, the subject of this sketch, was educated and spent much of her girlhood in Paris, France. It was there that she met, and afterwards married, Aime Dupont, an artist and sculptor. In 1886, because of pecuniary losses, he left Paris for America, and established a photographic studio in New York city, winning immediate recognition and success by his pleasing personality and artistic ability. After his death, in 1900, his wife continued her husband's work under the original name of Aime Dupont. She has one son, Albert R. Greer Dupont.

HARRINGTON, Emerson Columbus, fifty-first governor of Maryland, was born at Madison, Dorchester co., Md., Mar. 26, 1864, son of John E. and Elizabeth (Thompson) Harrington. He was graduated second in his class at St. John's College, Annapolis, in 1884. He was immediately appointed instructor in the preparatory department of that institution and soon after became assistant professor, and then professor of Latin and mathematics. In 1886 he resigned to become principal of the Cambridge (Md.) Academy, which three years later was merged with Cambridge Female Seminary, and he was principal of the dual institution eight years. Meanwhile he studied law under the preceptorship of Daniel M. Henry, Jr., and Gov. Henry Lloyd. In 1897 he passed the state bar examination with the unusual rate of 97 per cent., and at once began the practice of his profession at Cambridge. In 1899 he was elected state's attorney of Dorchester county for the four-year term. In his official capacity he succeeded in putting a stop to the notorious oyster and local option violations, and by convicting two business men for arson he rid Cambridge of a reign of incendiarism, but these activities brought about his defeat, by a narrow margin, for re-election. In 1910 he was appointed insurance commissioner of Maryland, but resigned upon being elected comptroller of Maryland the next year. In 1913 he was re-elected comptroller by 38,000 majority. In this office he inaugurated a complete new system of accounting and established a new fiduciary system for the state. He not only advocated economy in public affairs, but practiced it, having declined to endorse a proposition for the wholesale increase of salaries in his department. In 1915 he was elected governor of Maryland over Ovington E. Weller, his Republican opponent, by a plurality of approximately 3,500. He is a member of the Methodist Protestant Church. He was married at Cambridge, Md., June 23, 1893, to Mary Gertrude, daughter of William T. Johnson, of Cambridge, Md., and has three children: Emerson C., Jr., Mary Virginia and William Johnson Harrington.

HALL, Luther Egbert, 29th governor of Louisiana, was born at Morehouse Parish, near Bastrop, La., Aug. 30, 1869, son of Bolling Cass and Antoinette (Newton) Hall. He was graduated at Washington and Lee University, Lexington, Va., in 1889. He studied law at the law school of Tulane University, New Orleans, where he obtained his LL.B., was admitted to the bar in 1892 and began the practice of his profession at Bastrop, La. In 1898 he was elected to the state senate and two years later was elected district judge. He held the latter office until 1906, when he became judge of the court of appeals, second circuit of Louisiana. In 1910 he was elected associate justice of the supreme court for the term beginning in 1912, but never took office, as he was elected in the meantime governor of the state. During his administration a special election was held to vote for a limited constitutional convention, the chief purpose of the convention being to permit the sale of bonds for refunding the state bonded debt of $11,108,300 due Jan. 1, 1914. The convention having been authorized by popular vote, it met in November and December, 1913, and rewrote and re-enacted the constitution of the state, the chief changes being the bond section and amendments to the acts governing the sewerage and water board of New Orleans. Gov. Hall was married at Brownsville, Tenn., Nov. 23, 1892, to Clara, daughter of John P. Wendel, a teacher and composer of music in that town, and has two children: Clara Wendel and Luther Egbert, Jr.

REINHARDT, George Frederick, physician and educator, was born in Kansas, June 3, 1869, son of John George and Katharine (Trushelm) Reinhardt. He received his preliminary education in the public schools of San Jacinto and elsewhere in southern California, and was graduated at the University of California with the degree of B.S. in 1897 and at the medical department of that institution in 1900. In college he was assistant in physical culture, played on the football team and was football manager and leader in student affairs. He began the practice of his profession at Berkeley, Cal., in 1900, met with unusual success from the beginning, and achieved a reputation as a surgeon. In 1903 he was appointed professor of hygiene at the University of California. He served as president of the California State Board of Medical Examiners and for years was health officer in Berkeley. He spent three different periods of work and study in Europe. In 1906 he prevailed upon the university authorities to carry out the plan which he had for some time been maturing of establishing a co-operative infirmary system, supported by the students. Of this work Dr. Richard Cabot of Harvard said: "No discovery of a new surgical operation or a new microorganism equals in importance the invention of a way to make the whole of medical knowledge more generally available. It is this that Dr. Reinhardt has helped to do by showing that co-operative medical service is not an Utopian dream but a solid fact." Dr. Reinhardt was an intense believer in preventive medicine and had in view a plan to extend this influence all over California. Largely through his efforts the State Hygienic Laboratory was established at the University of California. He was a man of broad vision, combined with executive ability and medical experience. He was a member of the American Medical Association, the California Academy of Medicine, the Phi Delta Theta and Nu Sigma Nu fraternities and the Bohemian Club of San Francisco. He was married at Berkeley, Cal., Dec. 4, 1909, to Aurelia, daughter of William Warner Henry, of Berkeley, and is survived by two children: George Frederick Jr. and Paul Henry Reinhardt. He died at Berkeley, Cal., June 7, 1914.

STONE, Carlos Melville, jurist, was born at Strongsville, O., Mar. 27, 1846, son of Montraville and Mary (Smith) Stone. His first paternal American ancestor was Simon Stone, who came to this country from England in 1635 and settled in Massachusetts. He received his preliminary education at the district school and at Oberlin College. During a vacation from the latter institution, although only seventeen years old, he ran away from home and joined the Federal army, enlisting as a private in the 150th regiment, Ohio volunteer infantry. After serving out his full term of enlistment he was honorably discharged. Having decided to adopt the law as a profession, he entered the law school of the University of Ohio and subsequently attended the Union Law School, Cleveland, where he was graduated in 1869. In the same year he was admitted to the Cleveland bar and began the practice of his profession in that city. Two years later he was elected city prosecutor. He was a member of the firm of Brinsmade & Stone in 1873-76, his partner being Allan Thomas Brinsmade, and in the latter year he joined Edward L. Hessenmuller under the firm name of Stone & Hessenmuller. In the same year he was elected prosecuting attorney of Cuyahoga county for a term of three years and was the only incumbent of that office to hold a third term. On his retirement he again took up private practice as a member of the firm of Stone, Hessenmuller & Gallup. In 1885 he was elected judge of the court of common pleas for Cuyahoga county for a five-year term, and he was re-elected in 1889. He occupied the bench until 1906, making a most creditable judicial record and trying many important cases. His legal learning was broad and comprehensive, and his power of analysis and ability to see the relation of cause and effect made him one of the ablest representatives that had adorned the bench in Ohio. In his private practice he won wide reputation as a corporation lawyer. Extra-professionally, Judge Stone was interested in a number of electric railway projects and was president of the Toledo and Western Railroad Co. As the administrator of criminal law he tempered justice with mercy. His life was at all times an exemplification of honorable, upright manhood and an embodiment of unfaltering devotion to every trust reposed in him. In private life he was an ideal husband and father. Judge Stone was married at Oberlin, O., Dec. 4, 1872, to Jeannette, daughter of Eliphalet Follett, of Ohio, and granddaughter of Eliphalet Follett, of Bennington, Vt., whose name is inscribed upon the monument erected to the memory of the men who fell in the Wyoming massacre. She survives him with two children: Ruth Follett and Katharine Follett. He died in Cleveland, O., Sept. 21, 1908. Portrait opposite page 135.

SIMMONS, Zalmon Gilbert, capitalist and philanthropist, was born at Euphrates, Montgomery co., N. Y., Sept. 10, 1828, son of Ezra and Maria (Gilbert) Simmons, and grandson of Rouse Simmons, who removed from Rhode Island to Montgomery co., N. Y., at the beginning of the nineteenth century. His father was a farmer, who removed to Southport, now Kenosha, Wis., in 1846, and engaged in mercantile pursuits. The son was educated in the public schools and for three winter seasons taught in a district school. Upon attaining his majority he became a clerk in a general store at Kenosha and within six months was placed in charge of the business, which a year later he pur-

chased. He spent twelve years in the mercantile business, and in the meantime his ability had gone out to various other enterprises. In 1856 he paid five hundred dollars for a half interest in the Wisconsin State Telegraph Co., then an almost worthless line between Milwaukee and Madison. He devoted himself assiduously to the development of the telegraph, with the result that lines built or acquired by him throughout Wisconsin, Minnesota, the Dakotas and Canada resulted in the organization of the Northwestern Telegraph Co., of which he was president and general manager. In 1881 he leased that company to the Western Union Telegraph Co., becoming a director in the latter. The Kenosha, Rockford and Rock Island Railway Co., being hopelessly involved, he became its president, carried it through the unstable financial conditions of war times until it finally became a part of the Chicago and Northwestern system. In 1872 he helped organize a company at Kenosha for the manufacture of cheese boxes, and soon afterwards of wire mattresses. Beginning with 1,500 mattresses per annum, it extended its operations, first under the title of the Northwestern Wire Mattress Co., and later as the Simmons Manufacturing Co., which is the largest concern of its kind in the world. He was also identified with the organization of the Scotford Manufacturing Co. and Lane Manufacturing Co., and it was largely through his efforts that Kenosha became a center of the brass industry. For thirty-eight years he was president of the First National Bank of Kenosha. He was the builder of the noted cog road up Pike's Peak, Colorado, to an altitude of 14,000 feet. It was begun in October, 1889, and on June 30, 1891, the first train ascended the mountain. His political affiliation was with the Republican party. In 1865 he was elected to the state legislature, and during 1884-85 was mayor of Kenosha. When he assumed the latter office the city debt was $1,750,000. He refunded the entire debt by a new issue of bonds; labored without compensation, and bore his own expenses in order to get the debt into a manageable condition and in his efforts to float the bonds. His philanthropy was practical. Churches, hospitals and other charities were the constant recipients of his generous aid. He was a contributor to the old Kenosha library, and he provided the splendid new structure in Library Park, which is named the "Gilbert M. Simmons Library" as a memorial to his son. In Library Park he raised to the memory of Kenosha soldiers in the civil war an imposing granite shaft. He built the Simmons gymnasium at Kemper Hall, Kenosha. He was of valuable assistance of Booker T. Washington in the latter's work among Southern negroes, and he showed his friendship for Grand Army men in countless ways. At a national encampment of the Grand Army of the Republic in Denver he was elected an honorary member, a distinction never before bestowed upon a civilian, and at that meeting he presented each veteran with a bronze medal. He was a member of the Chicago and Milwaukee clubs. In early life he was a Methodist, but subsequently joined the Unitarian Church. He was justly known as the "Grand Old Man of Kenosha." He was a man of commanding presence, clear and attractive countenance, a well-set head, erect carriage, all denoting physical and mental strength and activity. His manners were pleasant and engaging; considerate and kind, with a heart full of charity for all and without bitterness of disposition toward any, he gained the respect and confidence of all who came within the sphere of his influence. In all relations of life he was able, conscientious, fearless, incorruptible and patriotic. He left to those who loved him the memory of a stainless character and an example in conduct worthy of imitation in every walk of life. He was married at Kenosha, Wis., Apr. 20, 1850, to Emma E., daughter of Capt. Morris Robeson, a pioneer of Lake county, Ill., and is survived by three children: Minnie J., wife of Arthur F. Towne; Emma Belle, wife of A. H. Lance, and Zalmon G., who succeeded his father as president of the Simmons Manufacturing Co. He died at Kenosha, Wis., Feb. 11, 1910.

NUSSBAUM, Paul Joseph, first Roman Catholic bishop of the diocese of Corpus Christi, Tex., was born in Philadelphia, Pa., in 1870. He attended St. Peter's Parochial School in that city and in early manhood joined the Passionist Order, entering their monastery at Pittsburgh. After the regular course of studies pursued by the members of the order he was ordained priest at St. Michael's Monastery, West Hoboken, N. J., on May 20, 1894. He then taught in the novitiate of his order and later was sent to South America on missionary work in Buenos Aires, and while there became familiar with the Spanish language and customs. In 1903 he was called to Rome and spent several years as one of the assistants to the Passionist General. In 1908 he returned to the United States when the provincial chapter of the province of the Passionist Order elected him to the office of consulter, to which position he was re-elected by the chapter in 1911. He was parish priest at St. Mary's Church, Dunkirk, N. Y., and at St. Michael's, West Hoboken, N. J., and spent five years with the mission band giving missions and retreats throughout the country until he was named first bishop of Corpus Christi. He was consecrated May 20, 1913. Bishop Nussbaum is reputed to be one of the best pulpit orators in the Passionist Order and a linguist familiar with most modern tongues. Corpus Christi, formerly the vicariate of Brownsville, was made a diocese Mar. 23, 1912. It has an area of 22,391 square miles and a Catholic population of 80,000. There are forty-five priests in charge of ninety-seven churches and missions; one college for boys; five academies for girls; twenty-two parish schools, and 2,130 pupils in these institutions; one orphans' school and two hospitals.

LEAMING, Thomas, lawyer, was born in Philadelphia, Pa., May 29, 1858, son of Robert Waln and Julia (Scott) Leaming. His earliest paternal American ancestor was Christopher Leamyeng, who came to this country from England in 1670 and settled at or near Boston, Mass. His wife was Esther Burnett, and the line of descent is traced through their son Thomas and his wife, Hannah Whilldin; their son Thomas and his wife, Elizabeth Leaming; their son Thomas and his wife, Rebecca Fisher, and their son Jeremiah and his wife, Rebecca Waln, who were the grandparents of Thomas Leaming. He was educated in the Episcopal Academy of Philadelphia and the University of Pennsylvania, class of 1879, but was prevented by illness from completing his course. He studied law under Wayne MacVeagh and George Tucker Bispham, and was admitted to the courts of common pleas in 1884, to the supreme court of Pennsylvania in 1887 and to the U. S. supreme court in 1910. As counsel for the Philadelphia Rapid Transit Co. he had charge of the litigation of the passenger railways of the city and made himself the most complete master of the law of negligence. Understanding every question of law which would arise in a suit, he

was able to consider every claim dispassionately and with perfect appreciation of its merits. The Philadelphia Rapid Transit Co. defended an average of two hundred cases in every term of the lower courts, and Mr. Leaming personally revised the preparation of all of them. He spent many summers in Europe, and to his intimate associations with the English bench and bar may be charged his charming and instructive work, "A Philadelphia Lawyer in the London Courts." Scrupulous to a nicety in the ascertainment of facts, zealous in the pursuit of truth and scorning all artifices, he drew his conclusions with relentless logic, and presented his arguments to courts and juries with simplicity, clearness and convincing power. He was a member of the various bar associations, and of the Philadelphia, Philadelphia Country, Rittenhouse, Racquet and Lawyers' clubs, and of the Sons of the Revolution. He was married June 18, 1888, to Josephine Lea (Baker) Brown, widow of Henry Armitt Brown and daughter of John Remigius Baker, of Philadelphia. He died in Philadelphia, Pa., Dec. 14, 1911.

MAXIM, Hiram Percy, inventor, was born in Brooklyn, N. Y., Sept. 2, 1869, son of Sir Hiram S. and Jane (Budden) Maxim. The first of the family in America was Samuel Maxim, a descendant of a French Huguenot family who emigrated from Kent, England, about 1650, and settled in Rochester, Mass., and from him the line of descent is traced through Samuel, who married Elizabeth ————: their son Nathan, who married Martha Chubbock; his son Samuel, who married Saviah Rider; and his son Isaac, who married Harriett Boston Stevens, and was the grandfather of the subject of this sketch. The family was prominent in Colonial history, some of its members being soldiers with Wolfe and Montgomery in Quebec, as well as in the revolutionary war, others, enduring the hardships of the early pioneers, helped to pave the way for the civilization of the northeastern section of New England. Above all, however, they early exhibited that mechanical skill which culminated in the epoch making achievements of the Maxims of to-day. The names of Mr. Maxim's father (q. v.) as well as his uncle, Hudson Maxim (q. v.) are inseparably linked with increased efficiency in modern warfare through the invention of the Maxim gun, smokeless powder and Maximite; and it is a fitting sequel that the new generation represented by the subject of this sketch should round out this record by a discovery of even more far-reaching consequence. He attended the Brooklyn public schools and was graduated at the Massachusetts Institute of Technology in 1886. He was first employed by the Sun Electric Co., of Woburn, Mass., as draughtsman, and then by the Fort Wayne (Ind.) Jenney Electric Co., in a similar capacity. He was also with the Thompson Electric Welding Co., and the American Projectile Co., both of Lynn, Mass. While at the latter his experiments with motor vehicles first took concrete shape. He built a tandem tricycle in 1894 which was purchased by the Pope Manufacturing Co. of Hartford, Conn., and that company engaged Mr. Maxim to further develop it into what became the Columbia motor carriage. Under the auspices of the Electric Vehicle Co., this work was continued by him and the machine proved of practical value. It was put on the market in 1897 as the Columbia phaeton. It had a speed of twelve miles per hour and ran thirty miles on one charge. This model was followed in 1898 by the gasoline tricycle package carriers, which embodied a number of features originated by Mr. Maxim. He designed electric vehicles in many other models, but none of these devices bore Mr. Maxim's name, all being brought out under the trade name "Columbia." During 1901-03 he was with the Westinghouse Electric and Manufacturing Co. of Pittsburg, for which he designed a complete line of electric motor controllers and charging equipment for electric vehicles known as the Westinghouse Vehicle Equipment. In 1906 he became associated with Mr. T. W. Goodridge, late business manager of the Studebaker Automobile Co., under the name of the Maxim-Goodridge Co. The most important field of invention outside of automobiles which has engaged Mr. Maxim's attention is ordnance and firearms, resulting in the production of the Maxim "Silencer." The first suggestion for this device came from the muffler of an automobile, with which Mr. Maxim experimented for some time. In the application of such a device to a gun, however, a new principle had to be utilized. The loud report following the discharge of a gun is the result of the rapid escape of the gases accompanying it. The problem was to interrupt this almost compact mass in its progress and by centrifugal motion dissipate its force before it could escape from the muzzle. This he finally accomplished by a thin steel tub six inches long, attached to the muzzle of a gun and containing twelve little disks separating as many chambers, and penetrated somewhat above the center by a hole slightly larger than the bullet which is expected to pass through. The centre of the disk is pressed back and the outside edge rolled over so as to make a thick ring, hollow on the outside. As the bullet is fired, clearing the holes in the disk without interference, the gases accompanying it are caught by the first disk, and by virtue of its shape are made to rotate rapidly. Being thus diverted from the initial plane and imparted a swirling motion, they pass through openings in the disks from one vortex chamber to the next, each time with diminished volume and velocity. With a part of the gas diverted as each successive chamber is passed, there is practically no gas in the forward plane left to emit from the end of the "Silencer." Thus 97 per cent of the noise is eliminated, so that practically nothing but the impact of the bullet and the cleavage of the air can be heard. The Maxim Silent Firearms Company was formed in 1909 to manufacture and distribute the Silencer. Mr. Maxim is the author of a number of papers and scientific articles published in various periodicals. He is a member of the American Society of Electrical Engineers, Engineers Club of New York, the Automobile Club of Hartford, and the Hartford Golf Club. He was married Dec. 12, 1898, to Josephine, daughter of William T. Hamilton, of Hagerstown, Md., and has one son, Hamilton, and one daughter, Percy Maxim.

SCHOFIELD, William, jurist, was born at Dudley, Mass., Feb. 14, 1857, son of John and Margaret Thompson) Schofield. His father was a native of Ireland. After his graduation at Harvard in 1879 he spent a year in the study of Roman law and subsequently entered the Harvard Law School, where he was graduated in 1883 with the degrees of LL.B. and A.M. During 1883-85 he was private secretary to Justice Horace Gray, and in the meantime (1884) was admitted to the bar. He returned to Harvard Law School as instructor in torts in 1886, and from 1886 to 1892 was in-structor in Roman law at Harvard. In the latter year he formed a law partnership with ex-Mayor Marcellus Coggan, of Malden, Mass., and began a practice which grew to large proportions and won him a high reputation in his profession. In 1898 he was elected to the Massachusetts legislature on the Republican ticket. He served two terms, during which he held important committee appointments and, by reason of his eloquence, ability, personality and grasp of public questions, became the acknowledged leader of the house. In 1903 he was appointed by Gov. Crane a justice of the Massachusetts superior court, and on accepting the appointment he severed all his business connections. His record on the bench was of industry, courage and clear, independent judgment, and he was regarded as a likely candidate for the highest judicial honors. He was elevated to the bench of the U. S. circuit court in June, 1911. Judge Schofield was an eloquent and effective public speaker and was in much demand for commemorative and political gatherings and public banquets. He was the author of many scholarly articles on legal topics. He was a member of the Malden deliberative assembly, and a member of the committee which made a study for a new charter for the city. He was a trustee of the Malden Public Library and the Grand Army Post Associates, first president of the University Club of Malden, and a member of the American Bar Association, the Massachusetts Bar Association, the Harvard Phi Beta Kappa, the Harvard Signet, the Malden Historical Society and the University and Union clubs of Boston. He was married at Rutland, Vt., Dec. 1, 1890, to Ednah May, daughter of Edward R. Green, of Rutland, Vt., and died in Malden, Mass., June 10, 1912.

BARROW, David Crenshaw, twelfth chancellor of the University of Georgia, was born in Oglethorpe county, Ga., Oct. 18, 1852, son of David Crenshaw and Sarah Eliza (Pope) Barrow, and grandson of James and Patience (Crenshaw) Barrow. He was educated at the high school of the University of Georgia and was graduated at the University of Georgia in 1874, receiving the degrees B.S. and C.E. He was employed on the state geological survey from 1874 to 1878. In 1878 he was appointed adjunct professor of mathematics at the University of Georgia, five years later became professor of engineering, and in 1889 was made professor of mathematics. In 1907 he was elected chancellor of the university, a position he still holds. He was a member of the board of educators at Athens, Ga., in 1887–88 and again during 1896–1901. The honorary degree of LL.D. was conferred upon him by Emory College in 1909. He was married, Feb. 5, 1879, to Fannie Ingle, daughter of Asaph K. Childs, of Athens, Ga., and had four children: Susan, wife of S. J. Crowe; Benjamin; Eleanor, wife of H. L. Jewett Williams, and David Francis Barrow.

BOLTWOOD, Bertram Borden, chemist, was born at Amherst, Mass., July 27, 1870, son of Thomas Kast and Matilda (Van Hoesen) Boltwood, grandson of Lucius and Fanny (Haskins) Boltwood, and great-grandson of William Boltwood, the first of the family in America, who came from England. He was educated at the Albany (N. Y.) Academy and at the Sheffield Scientific School of Yale University, being graduated at the latter with the degree of Ph.B. in 1892. He continued his studies at the University of Munich and the University of Leipzig, returning to Yale for his phliosophy degree, which he received in 1897. He was assistant in the chemical laboratory of the

WILLIAM SCHOFIELD

Sheffield Scientific School for two years and in 1894 was made instructor in physical chemistry, a position he held until 1900, when he became assistant professor of physics at Yale University. Prof. Boltwood has made special researches on organic and inorganic chlorids, but he is perhaps best known for his researches on the properties of the new element, radium, with its peculiar emanation qualities. One of the problems upon which many of the leading scientists of the world are now engaged is to estimate the life of radium with the length of time any given quantity of that substance will be disintegrated. Prof. Boltwood has devised a method of his own for arriving at the solution of this problem, which is called radioactive equilibrium. Previously he had announced a new radioactive chemical element, from which he believes the substance of radium is derived. He is a member of the American Chemical Society, the German Chemical Society, the American Physical Society, the Connecticut Academy of Arts and Sciences, the Yale Club of New York and the Graduate Club of New Haven. He is unmarried.

KINLOCH, Robert Alexander, surgeon, was born in Charleston, S. C., Feb. 20, 1826, son of George Kinloch, a native of England, who came to America and became a grain merchant in Charleston, S. C., and married Charlotte Granby, of Philadelphia, Pa. He was graduated at Charleston College in 1845, and three years later received the degree of M.D. from the University of Pennsylvania. He continued his medical studies in Paris, London and Edinburgh. He was practicing in his native city when the civil war broke out, and he enlisted as a surgeon in the Confederate army. He was a member of the medical examining boards at Norfolk, Richmond and Charleston. Subsequently he was inspector of hospitals for South Carolina, Georgia and Florida. In 1866 he was elected to the chair of materia medica in the Medical College of the State of South Carolina, and in 1870 became professor of surgery. Seven years thereafter the chair was divided into two professorships, and he was made professor of clinical surgery and dean of the faculty. Dr. Kinloch's work in surgery was a distinct contribution to the advance of the science. He was the first American to resect the knee joint for chronic diseases, his operation preceding that of Dr. Cross by several months; he was also the first to treat fractures of the lower jaw and other bones by wiring the fragments, and he was the first in any country to perform a laparotomy for gunshot wounds in the abdomen without protrusion of the vicera. He invented several surgical instruments of value, including an improved urethrotome and stricture dilator and a stem pessary. He was one of the most eminent members of his profession in the South. As an operator he was self-reliant and bold, possessing a rare skill in execution and perfect poise in the face of unforeseen emergencies. He was president of the South Carolina Medical Association, South Carolina Training School for Nurses, the Medical Society of South Carolina and the American Medical Association. He was one of the editors of the "Charleston Medical Journal and Review." He was married Nov. 11, 1856 to Elizabeth Caldwell, of Fairfield, S. C., and had four sons and five daughters: George G., Robert H., Edward J., James C., Mary C., Alice B., Elizabeth C., Eva L. and Ida M. Kinloch. Dr. Kinloch died in Charleston, S. C., Dec. 23, 1891.

CORNELL, Oliver Hazard Perry, engineer and inventor, was born at Ithaca, N. Y., Feb. 5, 1842, son of Ezra and Mary Ann (Wood) Cornell, and brother of Alonzo B. Cornell, governor of New York. His father (q. v.) was one of the promoters of the telegraph and founder of Cornell University. O. H. P. Cornell received his early education in the Ithaca schools, and was graduated M.C.E. at Cornell University in 1872. During part of his college course he was instructor in mathematics. In the summer of 1870 he was assistant engineer on the Geneva and Ithaca railroad, now the Lehigh Valley, and in the following spring he left college to assist in the continuation of the road. In 1871 he was appointed chief engineer of the Utica, Ithaca and Elmira railroad, now the Elmira, Cortland and Northern, and in 1875 he established the Emery Agricultural Works at Albany, N. Y. He returned to engineering in 1882, as locating engineer with the Chippewa Valley railroad, and soon afterward was appointed division engineer on construction of the New York, West Shore and Buffalo railroad. In 1889 he was made chief engineer of the projected Cincinnati, Alabama and Atlantic railroad, between Somerset, Ky., and Huntsville, Ala., and two years later he became engineer of the Hemming Gravity Tunnel Co., of New York city, which had obtained franchises for two tunnels between New York and Brooklyn and one between New York and Jersey City. Mr. Cornell had practically finished all the plans for these tunnels and for a complete rapid transit system for New York city when the death of the president and one of the directors resulted in the abandonment of the enterprise. He was chief engineer of the Chesapeake and Western railroad for a time, and was then appointed inspecting enigneer for the Birmingham extension of the Seaboard Air Line, soon after becoming division engineer, with charge of the rebuilding of the old East and West railway in Georgia and Alabama. In 1905, at the head of a corps of engineers, he surveyed the route of the South Bound Railway Co., and this was probably the greatest engineering work of his career. Besides being one of the foremost railroad engineers in the United States, Mr. Cornell was a prolific inventor, and patented many valuable mechanical devices, the most useful being an automatic railway-crossing gate; the coloric cone, a gas-heating apparatus; machinery for making barrels, and a gin cotton picker. He was president of the Albany Agricultural Works, the American Railway Crossing Gate Co., and the Standard Barrel Co., and was connected with a number of other commercial interests. He was married at Dryden, N. Y., Dec. 8, 1861, to Mary Louise, daughter of Nathan Conkling, and his children were: Arthur L. Ella Louise, wife of Arthur Goodspeed; Channing Bristol, Allan, Albert P., Mary F., Edith Hastings, wife of D. Orville Dechert; James H., and Oliver Hazard Perry Cornell Jr. He died at Winston-Salem, Oct. 13, 1911.

HEFFRON, Patrick Richard, second Roman Catholic bishop of Winona, Minn., was born in New York city, June 1, 1860, son of Patrick and Margaret (O'Brien) Heffron. He received his preliminary education in the public schools of New York city, Ripon, Wis., and Mantorville, Minn. After attending a business college and law school in Rochester, Minn., he entered St. Johns College, Collegeville, Minn., and was graduated M.A. in 1878, after which his theological studies were made at the Grand Seminary of Montreal, Can., where he received the degree of D.D. in 1883. Minerva University conferred upon him the degrees of S.T.L. and D.D. in 1889, and Rome University that of D.C.L. in 1910. He was ordained to the priesthood on Dec. 22, 1884. He spent two years on the European continent, mostly in Rome, and upon returning home he succeeded the Rt. Rev. John Shanley, bishop of Fargo, as pastor of the Cathedral of St. Paul, Minn., which charge he held for ten years. In 1896 he became vice-rector of St. Paul Seminary, a corporation for the education of candidates for the Catholic priesthood, and in 1897 he was made president of the seminary, a position he held until 1910. On May 19, 1910, Dr. Heffron was consecrated bishop of Winona, Minn., succeeding Rt. Rev. Joseph B. Cotter. He erected the Cotter School for Boys in 1911 as a monument to his predecessor, and the following year began St. Mary's College for Boys at Winona and St. Teresa's College for Women. In the summer of 1915 a demented priest attempted to shoot him, but the wound, fortunately, was not fatal. The diocese of Winona has a Catholic population of 67,000, with 113 priests, 257 churches, chapels and stations, two colleges, seventeen high schools and academies, thirty-two parish schools with an average attendance of 7,000 pupils, and three hospitals.

ANTHONY, S[ilas] Reed, banker, was born in Boston, Mass., Aug. 5, 1863, son of Nathan and Clara (Reed) Anthony, of Puritan ancestry. Through his father he was a direct descendant of Miles Standish and John Alden, while on his mother's side he was descended from Gov. Thomas Dudley and Maj.-Gen. Daniel Dennison, who married Gov. Dudley's daughter; John Rogers, fifth president of Harvard College; Judge Ellery, of Connecticut, the father of the signer of the Declaration of Independence, and Tristram Coffin. S. Reed Anthony received his preparatory education at Roxbury Latin School. Upon the death of his father in 1881 he secured employment with Kidder, Peabody & Co., with whom he was associated for eleven years. In 1892, in association with W. A. Tucker, he organized the banking house of Tucker, Anthony & Co., which became identified with the development of electric traction and water powers in the middle West, and financed numerous important and successful interurban lines. Mr. Anthony was a member of the New York Stock Exchange and a director of the Boston Consolidated Gas Co., the Commonwealth Trust Co., the Northwestern Power Co. and the Chemical Products Co. He was president and director of the Manchester (N. H.) Street railway; treasurer and director of the Manchester Traction, Light and Power Co.; trustee of the Weeks Real Estate Trust, and treasurer and director of the Mascoma Light and Power Co. He was distinguished for an unusual directness and sanity of judgment and was widely honored for his unswerving loyalty to duty. His broad and generous sympathies won for him a wide circle of friends and found constant expression in unobtrusive acts of charity and kindness. Among his many activities, he was deeply interested in the work of Emmanuel Church, of which he was junior warden, and in the neighborhood work of Emmanuel House on Newcomb street, South End, which was the gift of Mrs. Anthony. He was a trustee of the Roxbury Latin School and vice-president of its alumni association. He was married, June 1, 1887, to Harriet P., daughter of Andrew Gray Weeks, of Boston, and had three children: Andrew Weeks, Ruth and Reed Pierce Anthony. Mr. Anthony died in Boston, Mass., Mar. 10, 1914.

PEABODY, George Foster, financier, was born at Columbus, Ga., July 27, 1852, son of George Henry and Elvira (Canfield) Peabody. The first of the family in America was Francis Peabody, son of John Peabody, a native of England, who came to the colonies in 1635, settling in Massachusetts. The line of descent is traced through his son William, who married Hannah Hale; their son Richard, who married Ruth Kimball; their son Asa, who married Mary Prentice; their son William Henry, who married Ruth Buckley, and their son George Henry, who married Elvira Canfield, and was the father of George Foster Peabody. He is of the same family as George Peabody, the famous banker and philanthropist. He was educated at private schools in Columbus and at the Deer Hill Institute, Danbury, Conn. In 1866 he began his business career with a wholesale drygoods commission firm in New York, and he continued in that line until January, 1880, when he became associated with Spencer Trask, the New York banker. In 1881 he formed a partnership with Mr. Trask under the name of Spencer Trask & Co., which continued until the latter's death. He was especially active in the direction of railroad and electric development and served as director of various industrial companies both in Mexico and the United States, including the General Electric Co. and the Morton Trust Co., of New York. He was also identified as director or officer with the Mexican National Railroad Co., the St. Louis, Alton and Terre Haute Railroad Co. and the New York and Ottawa Co. At one time he was an active committee member of the New York Chamber of Commerce and a member of the New York Stock Exchange. He retired from business in 1906. Mr. Peabody is a close observer of current political and financial affairs and is a forcible public speaker. He was treasurer of the American Free Trade League in 1880, and since 1895 has advocated a single tax on land values, government ownership of railroads and public franchise corporations. He favors the widest freedom in banking, consistent with safety, and advocates better banking facilities for farming regions in the southern and western states. Such reforms, in his opinion, would counteract the evil influences by which farmers are misled into supporting unsound financial schemes. In politics Mr. Peabody is a radical Democrat, and he has been active in national and state civil service reform associations. He is a life member of the Metropolitan Museum of Art, the American Museum of Natural History, the Hamilton Club of Brooklyn, and the Reform Club of New York, and a member of the Long Island Historical Society, the Brooklyn Institute of Arts and Sciences, the Metropolitan, City, National Civic, Tuxedo, National Arts and Lawyers' clubs, the Downtown Association, and the Cosmos Club of Washington. He has been a trustee of the International Committee of the Young Men's Christian Association, Colorado College, Brooklyn Polytechnic Institute, Tuskegee and Hampton institutes, Fort Valley Institute (Georgia), St. Paul School at Lawrenceville (Va.), and the University of Georgia; treasurer of the Southern Education Board; member and treasurer of the General Education Board; member of the finance committee of the American Bible Society, and member of the Southern Society. For fifty years he was an active member of the Brooklyn Young Men's Christian Association, which he terms his alma mater, owing to the fact that, being unable to attend college, he succeeded in obtaining the practical equivalent of college work by the aid of its library and lecture courses. He has long been identified with church, Sunday-school and philanthropic work, having been active in the Episcopal church for thirty years. In 1910 Gov. Hughes appointed him chairman of the New York State Reservation

Commission at Saratoga Springs. Through his well-directed efforts during the time he held that office Saratoga was completely transformed; the misuse of the springs was stopped and their curative waters permitted to flow freely; commodious bathing houses, equipped with all the improved appliances, were built, and the springs were surrounded by a fine park. His retirement from the commission, in 1915, occasioned much regret and many expressions of appreciation of the valuable services he had rendered to Saratoga and the state. Mr. Peabody received the honorary degree of A.M. from Harvard University in 1903, and that of LL.D. from Washington and Lee University in 1903, and also from the University of Georgia in 1906. He is unmarried. Portrait is opposite page 142.

McDONELL, Alexander B., lumber merchant, was born in the Province of Ontario, Canada, Apr. 17, 1840, son of Angus and Marjory McDonell. His father was a native of Scotland, who settled in Glengary county, Ontario, at an early age. Left an orphan in boyhood, he was obliged to make his own way in the world. In 1858 he secured employment in the timber forests on the Ottawa river and the next winter returned to the woods, this time on the Trent river. He had a natural love for the out-of-doors and an inborn knowledge of forestry, hence decided that his future career was in the lumber trade. He followed the business in Saginaw, Mich., Defiance, O., and Minneapolis, Minn., accumulating several thousand dollars, which proved the foundation of his future fortune. In June, 1873, he located permanently at Chippewa Falls, Wis., where he took charge of a lumber camp controlled by Edward Rutledge at South Fork on the Jump river. Later he became superintendent of the Mississippi River Logging Co. Meanwhile he was engaged in various independent efforts, and in 1879 formed a partnership with Thomas Irvine, of St. Paul, Minn., in the purchase of pine timber lands and in logging. His lumber properties covered a wide range. He was one of the early partners of Frederick Weyerhaeuser, who made available the vast lumber supplies of Wisconsin and Minnesota, and who later gave his attention to Western timber. His outside interests were numerous, embracing practically every industry of importance in Chippewa Falls. He was the founder of the Lumberman's National Bank and its president over twenty-five years, and was one of the founders and owners of the Calgary (Ont.) Water Co. He had a fine sense of civic duty and took a keen interest in every movement to enhance the prospects of his adopted city. His political affiliation was with the Democratic party, which made him mayor of Chippewa Falls during 1887–88. Of a philanthropic spirit, he contributed largely to charity, and the McDonell Memorial High School, Chippewa Falls, stands as a monument to his interest in the welfare of others. In 1908 the papal Order of St. Gregory the Great was conferred upon Mr. McDonell, who had previously been made a Knight of St. Sylvester by Pope Pius X. In further recognition of his religious work and of his assistance to Notre Dame parish and the diocese of La Crosse he was honored by the Catholic church with a diploma from the board of governors of the Catholic Church Extension Society which entitled him to a life membership. His practical sagacity and resolute will made him a great force in the community, and Chippewa Falls owes much to his public-spiritedness and generosity. He was a man of matchless courage, positive in his convictions, and was bold in their advocacy. He was married Oct. 17, 1881, to Mary Regina, daughter of Henry O'Neil, of Chippewa Falls; she died in 1892, leaving three children: Alexander Angus, Emily Regina and Donald Henry McDonell. The last two were drowned in 1900. The surviving son, Alexander A. McDonell, is identified with the lumber industry. Mr. McDonell died at Chippewa Falls, Wis., Dec. 17, 1913.

SMITH, Henry Louis, educator, was born at Greensboro, N. C., July 30, 1859, son of Jacob Henry and Mary Kelly (Watson) Smith, grandson of Samuel Runckle and Margaret (Fuller) Smith, and great-grandson of Henry Louis Smith, a native of Germany, who emigrated in the closing years of the eighteenth century and settled in Western Pennsylvania, subsequently moving to Virginia, where he was killed in a battle with the Indians. His mother was a daughter of Judge Egbert R. Watson, of Virginia, whose brother, Judge William Watson, of Mississippi, was a member of the Confederate cabinet. His father was for thirty years pastor of the First Presbyterian Church of Greensboro, N. C. Henry Louis Smith was educated in the public schools of Greensboro and was graduated at Davidson College, N. C., in 1881, winning medals in mathematics, Greek and as essayist. In that year he organized and was principal of Selma (N. C.) Academy. From a modest beginning of twenty-two pupils he built up a school of one hundred and continued as its head until 1886, when he entered the University of Virginia for graduate work in physics and geology. In 1887 he was elected to the chair of physics and geology at Davidson College. He again entered the University of Virginia in 1890 and received the Ph.D. degree in 1891. Meanwhile Davidson College had given him the degree of M.A., and in 1891 he returned there, becoming its vice-president in 1896, and president in 1901. He remained at the head of that historic Presbyterian institution until 1912. When he was called to the presidency, Davidson had but 122 students, but he left it with more than 300. During the same period its area of patronage had doubled; its entrance requirements were raised to fourteen points; the amount of fees collected from students was trebled, and the material equipments of the college more than doubled. The University of North Carolina conferred the degree of LL.D. upon him in 1906. In 1912 he was elected president of Washington and Lee University, and he immediately introduced radical administrative changes and reforms, which attracted wide attention. His policy has been to reduce the attendance by selection and elimination so as to limit the number of students to the teaching capacity of the faculty without regard to dormitory accommodations; he has improved the educational standing of the institution by abolishing assistant instructors and placing the freshmen especially under the ablest and most inspirational of the professional staff, and he has inaugurated a plan of enlarging the official function of the institution so that its scope embraces the training of the whole man, and its typical graduate becomes the ideal citizen, not merely the scholar or investigator. Other radical changes are also under way, and the educational world is watching with interest and approval the progress of the institution under the new policy of Pres. Smith. His remarkable success as a business administrator has brought to him many offers of lucrative positions in the business world, but he considers his life-work in the educational field, in which he is destined to achieve large results. For recreation Dr. Smith is devoting his attention to scientific orcharding, having in cultivation an orchard in Alexander county, N. C., of 4,000 trees, to which he is applying the most modern and scientific methods of cultivation and treatment. He is a member of the American Association for the Advancement of Science, Am. Acad. of Political and Social Science, North Carolina Academy of Science, North Carolina Literary and Historical Association, the North Carolina Teachers' Assembly (president), and the Society for Broader Education, of which he is vice-president. He was for a time interested in the Linden (N. C.) Cotton Mills, of which he was the first president, and is still a director. He has delivered numerous lectures before Chautauqua assemblies, teachers' conventions, Y. M. C. A. and other audiences on various educational, religious and scientific subjects. Dr. Smith was married at Davidson, N. C., Aug. 4, 1896, to Julia Lorraine, daughter of John James Dupuy, of Amherst, Va., and has seven children: J. Henry, Helen Lorraine, Raymond Dupuy, Julia Dupuy, Louise Watson, Opie Norris and Francis Sampson Smith.

RALSTON, Samuel Moffett, twenty-eighth governor of Indiana, was born on a farm near New Cumberland, Tuscarawas co., O., Dec. 1, 1857, son of John and Sarah (Scott) Ralston. His father was a native of Virginia; his mother was of Pennsylvania. In 1865 his father removed with his family to Owen county, Indiana, where he purchased and operated a large stock farm. He lost his property in the panic of 1873, and removed to Fontanet, Ind., where the son spent his boyhood. The latter taught school for seven winters, and attended normal school during the summers, all the while contributing to the support of his parents. He attended the Northern Indiana Normal School at Valparaiso and the Central Indiana Normal School at Danville and was graduated at the latter in 1884. He then began the study of law in Spencer, Ind., was admitted to the bar in 1886, and began the practice of his profession in Lebanon, Ind. He has been associated in the trials of some of the most important cases in the state. He is especially strong in cases involving the rules of equity and the constitutionality of statutes. He has few equals as a cross-examiner and is regarded by many as one of the best criminal lawyers in the state. Withal he is a man of literary taste, and an ardent student of Thomas Jefferson, with whose writings and letters he is very familiar; he is also an enthusiastic advocate of Jeffersonian principles of democracy. In 1912 he was nominated by the Democrats of Indiana for governor without opposition. It was generally conceded that a nomination was equivalent to an election, and the returns showed that he carried eighty-three out of ninety-two counties with a plurality of 109,233. He never held office until inaugurated governor, Jan. 13, 1913. The important legislation of his term included a public utilities commission bill, a bill for industrial and agricultural education, and a graduated inheritance tax law. Gov. Ralston was married, Dec. 30, 1889, to Jennie, daughter of W. R. Cravens of Hendricks county, Ind., and has three children: Emmet Grattan, Julian Craven and Ruth Ralston.

VALUE, Beverly Reid, civil engineer, was born at Montgomery, Ala., Apr. 7, 1863, son of Jesse Rene and Edith (Bailey) Value, and grandson of Victor Value, who came to the United States in 1798 and settled in Philadelphia, Pa. His father was a wholesale dry goods merchant of New Orleans, and his mother was a daughter of Joseph Bailey, of Wilmington, Del. He studied

at the Pingry School of Elizabeth, N. J., and was graduated in the School of Mines, Columbia University, with the degree of E. M. in 1884. In 1885 he was appointed civil engineer on the New York city aqueduct commission, and had charge of section No. 6 on the new Croton aqueduct during 1886-91. He then engaged in contracting at Little Falls, N. J., until 1893, when he was called back to New York as engineer of construction on the Croton dam, a work that lasted seven years. In 1900 he was appointed on the New York rapid transit commission, and was in charge of the third division of tunnel construction until Mar. 1, 1903, when he resigned to accept the position of chief engineer of the erection of a large electric power plant, including the construction of wheel-pits and tail-race tunnel under the Niagara river, at Niagara Falls, N. Y., for the Toronto and Niagara Power Co., subsequently known as the Electrical Development Co. of Ontario, Ltd. His resignation from the New York rapid transit commission was accepted with reluctance, and called forth the highest commendation from Pres. Alexander E. Orr. In 1906-08 Mr. Value was construction engineer of McCall's Ferry Power Co., and in conjunction with Hugh L. Cooper designed and constructed the large hydro-electrical plant at McCall's Ferry, on the Susquehanna river. In 1908 he was made executive engineer of the Empire Engineering Corporation, and since 1910 has been chief engineer and consulting engineer for the H. S. Kerbaugh Co., Inc. Mr. Value is a member of the American Society of Civil Engineers, the American Institute of Mining Engineers, the National Geographic Society, the Psi Upsilon fraternity, the Engineers' Club of New York, the Hartwood (N. Y.) Club, and the Elizabeth Town and Country Club of Elizabeth, N. J. He was married Oct. 26, 1886, to Rebecca Roe, daughter of Charles O. Morris, of Elizabeth, N. J., and has two sons, Mason B. and Morris B. Value, and two daughters, Caroline M. and Betty M. Value.

LUNKENHEIMER, Frederick, manufacturer, was born at Ingelheim on the Rhine, Germany, Oct. 24, 1825. He learned the brass finisher's and brass moulder's trade. At the age of nineteen he came to the United States, and for a few years was employed at his trade in New York city. From there he went to New Orleans, La., where he opened a small shop and engaged in the manufacture of sewing machine needles and other small articles. Finding the climate of New Orleans unsuited to his health, he gave up his business there and embarked for New York on a Mississippi river steamer, but was robbed of all his possessions on the way and was obliged to stop at Cincinnati, O. There he secured employment in the Miles Greenwood factory and rose rapidly to the position of superintendent. In 1862 he resigned this position, and he started in business for himself under the name of the Cincinnati Brass Works. (See Lunken, Edmund H., below). The business was incorporated in 1889 as the Lunkenheimer Co. and was reorganized in 1893 with a paid-up capital of $2,000,000. It is now the largest engineering specialty manufactory in the world. Frederick Lunkenheimer was known in commercial and financial circles as a man of impeccable personal honor as well as of keen business sense, and his credit and influence on that account were both very great. As well through his personal influence as through the large enterprise of which he was the founder he was an important factor in the industrial development of Cincinnati. Apart from his business interests he was prominent in numer-

GEORGE FOSTER PEABODY
FINANCIER

HENRY L. SMITH
PRESIDENT WASHINGTON AND LEE UNIVERSITY

SAMUEL M. RALSTON
GOVERNOR

BEVERLY R. VALUE
CIVIL ENGINEER

FREDERICK LUNKENHEIMER
MANUFACTURER

EDMUND H. LUNKEN
MANUFACTURER

GEORGE STRAWBRIDGE
PHYSICIAN

JOHN ALBEE
AUTHOR

ous connections and took a vigorous part in numerous civic, philanthropic and social activities. He was one of a commission of fifty appointed to investigate the municipal affairs of Cincinnati, and he never lost an opportunity of furthering in any way the welfare of the city. His interest in municipal affairs extended to state and national politics, but keen as that interest was he never would consent to run for public office. He was a member of the German Crematory Association, the German Literary Society and the Masonic fraternity, and was active in the work of the German Evangelical Church. He was married in Cincinnati, O., April 29, 1855, to Louise Henrietta, daughter of Ludolf H. Meyer, a native of Hanover, Germany, and one of the first German Lutheran ministers in Cincinnati. Their children were: Edmund H., Albert Carl (deceased), Ella Louise (deceased), Carl Frederick (deceased), and Clara, wife of Marshal Halstead. Frederick Lunkenheimer died in Cincinnati, O., April 15, 1889.

LUNKEN, Edmund H., manufacturer, was born in Cincinnati, O., June 20, 1861, son of Frederick and Louise H. (Meyer) Lunkenheimer. His father (see above) was the founder and proprietor of the Lunkenheimer Company of Cincinnati. The son was educated in the public schools of his native city, and completed his studies in a military school at Friedrichsdorf, Germany. Returning home at the age of eighteen, he entered the employ of his father's company, where he quickly learned all the details of the business. Inheriting his father's ability and mechanical genius, he originated and improved various parts of machinery and methods for their manufacture before he became of age, and his father secured patents for them. These include an oil cup having a slide top filler which has entirely displaced the old style cup with screw plug filler; a clip gate valve; a lever gate valve; a blow-off valve; a lubricator and similar incidental devices for machines and engines. Being ambitious to become the proprietor of a business of his own, he had perfected arrangements to establish a similar business in the city of Chicago, Ill., and in order that it would in no way conflict with his father's business in Cincinnati, he changed his name by legal process to its present style, "Lunken," and although he did not carry out this intention of going to Chicago, he retained the new name permanently. Shortly after his father's death, in 1889, he acquired a controlling interest in the present business and succeeded to the presidency, a position he holds at the present time. The Lunkenheimer Co. manufactures a full line of engineering specialties, such as brass, iron and steel valves, lubricators, oil cups, etc., and its products are marketed in every country in the world where modern machinery is used. Its factory, which is located at Fairmount, Cincinnati, employs over 1,000 hands. It maintains stores in New York, Chicago, Boston and London, England, and has agents and special representatives in nearly every city in the United States. The expansion and remarkable success of the business in recent years are largely due to the foresight, executive ability and constructive genius of Mr. Lunken. He was married in June, 1887, to Edith I., daughter of William H. Hodgson, of Cincinnati, and has one son, Eshelby F. Lunken, who is the first vice-president of the Lunkenheimer Co.

STRAWBRIDGE, George, physician, was born in Philadelphia, Pa., Oct. 18, 1844, son of George and Jane Van Sise (West) Strawbridge. His great-great-grandfather, John Strawbridge, came from the north of Ireland in 1752 and settled in Maryland, and from him and his wife, Mrs. Miller, the line of descent is traced through their son John and his wife, Hannah Evans; their son John and his wife, Frances Taylor, and their son George, father of Dr. Strawbridge. He received his early education at the Germantown Academy and was graduated at the University of Pennsylvania in 1862. Subsequently he entered the medical department of the university, where he was graduated in 1865. He continued his studies in the universities of Vienna, Berlin, Paris, Heidelberg and Utrecht. He established a private practice in Philadelphia in 1870, specializing in diseases of the eye and ear. He acquired a national reputation for his skill and learning, and patients came to him from all parts of the union. In spite of the exhausting demands of his large practice, Dr. Strawbridge found time and energy to act as lecturer on otology and ophthalmology at the University of Pennsylvania, attending surgeon to Wills hospital, ophthalmologist to the Presbyterian hospital, and surgeon in charge of the Pennsylvania Eye and Ear Dispensary. Though possessed of an unusually robust constitution, the strain of continued overwork eventually proved too much for him, and in 1890 he resigned from Wills hospital and the University of Pennsylvania, but retained his extensive private practice and his work at the Presbyterian hospital and the Eye and Ear Dispensary until shortly before his death. His constant and vivid interest in everything about him was one of his most striking characteristics, and he possessed a rare faculty of making friends easily, and the still rarer faculty of holding them permanently. He was a member of the Geographical Society of Philadelphia and the National Geographical Society of Washington, D. C., and the Union League Club. He was married June 5, 1873, to Alice, daughter of John Welsh, U. S. minister to Great Britain, and had four children: John, Mary Lowber, wife of Joseph Sailer, Welsh and Anne West Strawbridge. He died at Germantown, Pa., June 28, 1914.

ALBEE, John, author, was born at Bellingham, Norfolk co., Mass., Apr. 3, 1833, son of John and Esther (Thayer) Albee, and a descendant of John Albee who came to this country previous to 1640. He was educated at Worcester Academy and was graduated at Phillips Academy, Andover, in 1854. In the same year he entered Harvard University, but was obliged temporarily to relinquish his studies because of ill health and lack of funds. Later he entered Harvard Unitarian Divinity School, and was graduated in 1858. After traveling in Europe for a time he began his career as a teacher and writer. He made some important contributions to "Appleton's Encyclopedia," and contributed prose and verse to various magazines and literary journals. He also delivered courses of lectures on the English language and literature at the Concord School of Philosophy and elsewhere. His published volumes include: "Literary Art" (1881); "Poems" (1883); "History of New Castle, N. H." (1884); "Prose Idylls" (1892); "Life of Henry Dexter, Sculptor" (1898); "Remembrances of Emerson" (1900); "Lake Chocorua" (1910), and "Confessions of Boyhood" (1910). Mr. Albee was a man of high scholarly attainments, but of such a sensitive nature that he was quite unfitted for the struggle in the market place, and lived in retirement all his life, first at New Castle, N. H., and then at Chocorua, N. H., the latter affording congenial surroundings, being a little center of university professors and literary men. He was a founder of the New York Authors Club. Aside from literature, his favorite pursuit was gardening. Mr. Albee was twice married: (1) Sept. 1, 1865, to Harriet, daughter of Michael Ryan, of Boston, Mass.; she died in 1873, leaving two children, Esther Robert and Louise, wife of E. Roscoe Mathews, of New York city; and he was married (2) Mar. 15, 1894, to Helen, daughter of James Rickey, of Minneapolis, Minn. Mr. Albee died in Washington, D. C., Mar. 25, 1915.

FLETCHER, Frank Friday, naval officer, was born in Oskaloosa, Ia., Nov. 23, 1855, son of James Duncan and Nancy Power (Jack) Fletcher, and a descendant of John Fletcher, an Englishman, who was born in Ireland and came to this country in 1728, settling in Adams county, Pa. John Fletcher's son John was the father of Ensign Archibald Fletcher, a volunteer from Bedford county, Pa., in the revolutionary war, and Archibald's son John married a cousin, Rachael Fletcher, and was the grandfather of Frank Friday Fletcher. The name "Friday" was a nickname. Having been born on Friday, his father called him "My little man Friday, and when he went to the naval academy at the age of fourteen, an older brother entered his name on the roster as Frank Friday Fletcher, and it has been thus recorded in the government books ever since. In the navy he is generally referred to as Friday Fletcher. Because of his extreme youth he took five years to complete the course at Annapolis, but he made a brilliant record, and was graduated in the class of 1875. For a single year he was midshipman on the Tuscarora, while surveying a submarine cable route between the United States and Australia. In 1876 he was promoted to be ensign. He served on the Lackawanna in 1877, and on the Constellation during her cruise to the Paris Exposition in 1878. He was next assigned to the Ticonderoga, Com. Shufeldt commanding, which was sent around the world in the interests of commerce and for the purpose of negotiating with the government of Korea a treaty insuring the protection of the lives and property of American citizens. In 1882 he was promoted to be master and in the following year junior lieutenant. He was on duty at the hydrographic office and was sent to the west coast of Central and South America for the telegraphic determination of the longitude of the principal seaports. For three years he served on the Quinnebaug on the European station. A close observer and studiously inclined, Fletcher had been devoting special attention to ordnance, in which branch of the service he was subsequently to become one of the navy's greatest authorities. Aside from the performance of his duties of naval officer, his constructive ability has enabled him to suggest and devise many improvements of value. He was the first to propose the use of range lights at sea to lessen the many collisions, a suggestion that was taken up by the maritime conference held at Washington in 1890 with the result that range lights are now in use by steam vessels all over the world. He solved a number of weighty problems in gunnery to improve the target practice in the navy, and the records show that each ship he commanded, both as commander and captain, made the highest scores in target work, twice winning the trophy pennant; and again as commander-in-chief he introduced improved methods of training which resulted in the battleships making a higher score than had ever been made at sea before. In 1887 he was on duty at the Washington gun factory and the bureau of ordnance, and while there invented improvements in ordnance in connection with rapid

fire guns and mounts, telescopic sights and breech plugs for heavy ordnance, which he patented for the use of the U. S. government. During 1893–96 he commanded the torpedo boat Cushing, with orders to develop the use of torpedoes with the first consignment of sea weapons issued to the navy. He joined the battleship Maine when she was first commissioned in 1896 and was detached from that vessel shortly before she was blown up in Havana harbor. He was on duty at the torpedo station and served on the armor factory board, gun factory board, and was assistant chief of the bureau of ordnance shortly before the Spanish war. Toward the end of that war he was ordered to command the auxiliary gunboad Kanawha and was in charge of affairs at Gibara upon its evacuation by the Spaniards. Surveying work around the Cuban coast occupied him for three years, and during 1901–04 he commanded the torpedo station. He was promoted commander in 1904, captain in 1908 and rear-admiral in 1911. He was chief of staff of the Asiatic fleet in 1905, commanded the U. S. S. Raleigh on the Asiatic station during 1906–07, when he was again ordered to the special ordnance board and the general board of the navy. In 1908 he went to Manila to take command of the battleship Vermont on the voyage of the U. S. fleet around the world. He was a member of the Swift board for the reorganization of the navy department under Sec. Meyer, being selected to serve as aide in that organization. As rear-admiral he successively commanded each of the four battleship divisions of the fleet, being commander-in-chief of the Atlantic fleet in September, 1914. When the Mexican situation became acute in 1914 he was ordered to Vera Cruz, and he had charge of the naval forces on the east coast of Mexico for over a year under rather trying circumstances due to the disturbed conditions of that country. Mexican troops having been accused of insulting the American flag at Tampico, Adm. Mayo demanded a salute of the U. S. flag, and this being refused, Pres. Wilson ordered Fletcher to seize the custom house at Vera Cruz, a step that was fiercely resisted by the Mexicans, resulting in eighteen Americans killed and seventy wounded during the two days' fighting. On. Apr. 22, 1914, the full Atlantic fleet under Adm. Badger arrived at Vera Cruz and 3,000 marines were landed to reenforce the American troops on shore. The Mexican garrison of 1,500 troops withdrew to the interior. American possession was taken of the city, law and order was restored and a temporary government was established. The naval forces withdrew Apr. 30th, turning the city over to the military forces under Brig.-Gen. Frederick Funston. During the period that Adm. Fletcher had supreme charge in Vera Cruz he proved to be familiar with international law and the usages of diplomacy; in the taking of the city and in its administration he displayed executive powers of a high order. Pres. Wilson said of him at that time: "I have tested his discretion; I have tested his temper. I know that he is a man with a touch of statesmanship about him, and he has grown bigger in my eyes each day as I have read his dispatches, for he has sought always to serve the thing he was trying to do in the temper that we all recognize and love to believe is typically American." Adm. Fletcher was married, Feb. 23, 1895, to Susan Hunt, daughter of George R. Stetson, of Washington, D. C., and has two daughters: Sybil and Alice Fletcher. He is a member of the Chevy Chase, Metropolitan and Army and Navy clubs of Washington, and the New York Yacht Club.

MILTON UPDEGRAFF
ASTRONOMER

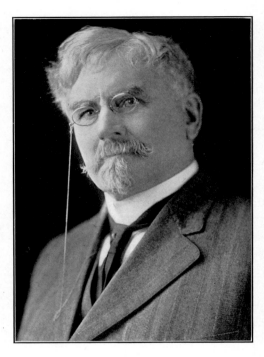

JAMES E. MARTINE
U. S. SENATOR

STUART CLOSE
PHYSICIAN

ROBERT HENRI
ARTIST

UPDEGRAFF, Milton, astronomer, was born at Decorah, Ia., Feb. 20, 1861, son of William Ballinger and Lydia Maria (Shear) Updegraff. His earliest paternal American ancestor was Abraham Op den Graeff (a surname since transformed into Updegraff), who with two brothers, Dirck and Hermann, came from Crefeld on the Rhine in Germany, and settled in Germantown, Pa., Oct. 25, 1683; he was a member of the Pennsylvania Assembly 1689-92, and is mentioned in Whittier's "Pennsylvania Pilgrim" as being a disciple of the Dutch philosopher, Pastorius. From him the line descends through his son Jacob, a pupil of Pastorius, to Nathan Updegraff of Mt. Pleasant, O., who married Cassandra Ballinger and was the grandfather of our subject. At the age of nineteen he entered the freshman class in the State University of Wisconsin, and soon attained distinction for mathematical ability. During his summer vacations he served as an aid on the U. S. coast and geodetic survey in a triangulation of the state of Wisconsin. He was graduated in 1884 with the highest honors, receiving the degrees of B.S. and B.C.E. In 1886 the degree of M.S. was conferred upon him by the University of Wisconsin. After his graduation he was appointed an assistant in Washburn Observatory. He held this position until September, 1887, when he was appointed second astronomer in the National Observatory of the Argentine Republic at Cordoba. He accepted this position for the purpose of observing a list of southern fixed stars proposed by Dr. Auwers, the eminent German astronomer, and spent over two years in Cordoba in accomplishing this and other astronomical work. While in South America he traveled extensively in the mountain districts, crossing the Andes twice and visiting the observatories at Santiago, Chili, and La Plata, near Buenos Ayres. In April, 1890, he returned to the United States and was shortly after appointed director of the observatory of the State University of Missouri, and assistant professor of mathematics. He was subsequently elected professor of astronomy in the same institution. Since June, 1899, he has been professor of mathematics in the U. S. navy. From 1899-1902 he was astronomer at the U. S. naval observatory in Washington, and during 1902-7 he served as instructor at the U. S. naval academy. He was director of the "Nautical Almanac," Washington, 1907-10; was in charge of the six-inch transit circle, U. S. naval observatory, during 1908-10; and was also in charge of the U. S. naval observatory eclipse party at Barnesville and Griffin, Ga., in May, 1900. From January to June, 1914, Prof. Updegraff was in charge of the geodetic and other scientific work connected with a survey of American Samoa Island in the South seas by the navy department, being ordered back to the United States because of sickness. Prof. Updegraff was instrumental in making important improvements in the astronomical apparatus of the naval observatory at Washington. While director of the "Nautical Almanac" office, he revised the "American Ephemeris and Nautical Almanac," which had been published in practically the same form for the past thirty years, and brought that publication up to date. He is a fellow of the American Association for the Advancement of Science; member of the American Astronomical Society; Astronomische Gesellschaft, of Germany; Philosophical Society of Washington; National Institute of Social Sciences; Phi Beta Kappa; Phi Delta Theta; University Club, of Washington, and others. Prof. Updegraff was

married, Sept. 8, 1877, to Alice M., daughter of F. J. Lamb, lawyer, of Madison, Wis. Their children are: Helen, Mabel and Ruth Updegraff.

MARTINE, James Edgar, U. S. senator, was born in New York city, Aug. 25, 1849, son of Daniel and Anna Maria (Neher) Martine. When he was nine years of age his father removed to a farm of 160 acres at Plainfield, N. J., and here the son's early life was spent, attending the public schools. After his father's death in 1863 he assumed the management of Cedar Brook Farm, his father's estate, where the old homestead, built in 1717, is one of the oldest landmarks around Plainfield. He was engaged in practical farming for thirty years, after which part of the property was divided into building lots and sold for residential purposes. Sen. Martine early took an active interest in local politics, and at various times was nominated for assemblyman, state senator and mayor of Plainfield, but failed of election in each instance. He served one term as a member of the common council (1872–74). He was delegate-at-large from the state of New Jersey to the Democratic national convention in Kansas City in 1900 and all subsequent national conventions. He is widely known in his home state as the "farmer orator," an appellation given him on account of his natural gift of eloquence. He was elected to the United States senate in a joint session of the state legislature in January, 1911, following an exciting and notable campaign resulting from the demand that the legislature of New Jersey acquiesce in the choice made in the direct primaries on Sept. 13, 1910. It was the first election of a senator under the direct primary law of New Jersey, and he received 48,458 votes, four times as many as his opponent. He was the first member of the upper house of congress from an eastern state who obtained his election as a result of a direct vote of the people. Sen. Martine is chairman of the committee on industrial expositions and a member of the committees on census, education and labor, national banks, post-offices and post-roads and public buildings and grounds. The committee of which he is chairman is a permanent one. It passed upon the legislation necessary for the expositions of 1915 in California and also the Panama Exposition at Panama. It has recently reported on a bill affecting a Pan-American exposition to be held at San Antonio, Tex., in 1918. Through this committee Sen. Martine has been interested in a permanent exhibit of the resources of the various states to be held in or near Washington, D. C., thus giving a national aspect to the various private local exhibits that have been in vogue throughout the country. He is also interested in legislation affecting post-office and postal matters and labor. He was one of the prime movers in the establishment of the present parcels post system. He was married, Oct. 7, 1905, to Julie Edgar, daughter of Scott Rodman, and grand-daughter of Jacob Lorillard, of New York.

CLOSE, Stuart, physician, was born in Oakfield, Fond du Lac co., Wis., Nov. 24, 1860, son of David and Sophronia (Wells) Close. His first paternal American ancestor was Goodman John Close, a native of Yorkshire, England, who came to this country in 1644 with his wife Elizabeth and family and settled at Stamford, Conn. The line of descent is traced through his son Thomas, who was one of the founders of Greenwich, Conn., and who married Sarah Hardy; their son Reuben; his son Abel, who married Mary McConkey, the daughter of Capt. William McConkey, who operated the ferry which bore his name over the Delaware river, where Washington crossed with his army, Dec. 25, 1776; their son William, who married Frances Blood, and was the grandfather of the subject of this sketch. Stuart Close attended the public schools, and in 1879 engaged in the insurance and collection business in Napa City, and also studied law for one year. Subsequently he studied for two years (1882–83) in the medical department of the University of the Pacific in San Francisco (now the Cooper Medical College). During his vacations in those years he traveled in the South Sea islands, where he devoted considerable time to the study of elephantiasis and tropical fevers. In 1883 he removed to New York city, and took a two years' course at the New York Homeopathic Medical College, where he was graduated in 1885. He also took a post-graduate course under Dr. Phineas Parkhurst Wells and Dr. Bernhardt Fincke in Brooklyn and New York. During 1909–13 Dr. Close was professor of homeopathic philosophy in the New York Homeopathic Medical College. He has been for many years a specialist in applied homeopathic therapeutics and materia medica, dealing especially with chronic and complicated cases. He has delivered many addresses before medical and other societies, and is the author of numerous articles published in medical journals on the philosophy of homeopathy and expository of homeopathic experience and methods. In 1896 he founded the Brooklyn Hahnemannian Union, a homeopathic medical society for scientific discussion, which has met monthly at his residence for eighteen years. He is a member of the International Hahnemannian Association, of which he was president in 1906; the American Institute of Homeopathy, the New York State Homeopathic Medical Society, the Homeopathic Medical Society of the County of Kings, and an honorary member of the Connecticut Homeopathic Medical Society. He also belongs to the Empire State Society of the Sons of the American Revolution, the Long Island Historical Society and the Brooklyn Canoe Club. Dr. Close has long been a student of genealogy, and has devoted a great deal of time to research with special reference to the Close, Wells and McConkey families. He has a large collection of rare books and paintings. He was married in Boston, Mass., April 21, 1885, to Evangeline Leona, daughter of Rev. Valentine A. Lewis, a Presbyterian clergyman. Mrs. Close is a highly accomplished musician, and has more than a local reputation as a chorus leader, pianist, teacher and lecturer on musical topics. Dr. and Mrs. Close have both published poems. They have three children: Mary Lewis, wife of Ralph Kirkman; Elizabeth Stuart and Bernard Wells Close.

HENRI, Robert, artist, was born in Cincinnati, O., June 24, 1865, son of John and Theresa Henri, of French, English and Irish descent. His paternal ancestors came from Kentucky and Virginia. He was educated in the public and private schools of New York city, Cincinnati and Denver. At the age of twenty he began to study art, and in the following year entered the Pennsylvania Academy of Fine Arts, Philadelphia, Pa. Later he continued his studies in Paris, becoming a student of the Académie Julien and of the Ecole des Beaux Arts. Subsequently he went to Spain and Italy, where he studied independently. Returning to America, he held a responsible position as teacher in the Philadelphia School of Design. Meanwhile he established a school in Paris, where young painters wishing to develop their own individuality received needed help which the regulation Parisian schools do not afford. He was a

frequent exhibitor at the Salon of the Champs de Mars, and in 1899 his picture, "La Niège," was purchased from the Salon by the French government for the Luxembourg Gallery. Mr. Henri returned to the United States in 1900 and opened a studio in New York. His picture, "Girl in White," was purchased by the Carnegie Institute, Pittsburgh, for its permanent collection in 1904. Some of his other well-known paintings are: "Young Woman in Black," in the Chicago Art Institute; "Girl with a Fan," in the Pennsylvania Academy of Fine Arts; "The Equestrian," Carnegie Institute; "The Laughing Girl," Brooklyn Museum of Arts and Sciences; "The Girl with Red Hair," which was purchased for the permanent collection of the city of Spartanburg, S. C., 1907; "The Happy Hollander," owned by the Art Association of Texas; "Dancer in Yellow Shawl," in the Columbus Gallery of Fine Arts, Columbus O.; "Spanish Gipsy Girl," owned by the Art Association of New Orleans, La.; "Girl of Toledo, Spain," Carolina Art Association, Charleston; "The Blue Necklace," in the Art Institute of Kansas City, Mo.; "Lillian," in the San Francisco Institute of Art; "The Spanish Gipsy," in the Metropolitan Museum, New York; "Romany Girl," in the National Arts Club, New York; portrait entitled "The Green Cape," which was awarded a silver medal at the Pan-American Exposition in 1901. Mr. Henri was also awarded a silver medal at the Universal Exposition, St. Louis, in 1904; the Norman W. Harris prize of $500 by the Chicago Art Institute in 1905; a gold medal by the Art Club of Philadelphia in 1909; a silver medal by the International Fine Arts Exposition at Buenos Ayres, S. A., in 1910, and the Carlo H. Beck gold medal by the Pennsylvania Academy of Fine Arts, Philadelphia, in 1914. He is a member of the National Academy of Design, the National Institute of Arts and Letters, the Society of American Artists, the National Association of Portrait Painters, the MacDowell Club of New York, the National Arts Club and the Municipal Art Society of New York, and a fellow of the Pennsylvania Academy of Fine Arts. Mr. Henri was an instructor in drawing, portrait painting and composition at the New York School of Art, but severed his connection with that school in 1909 and organized a school of his own. He was one of the group of eight artists who exhibited together and were called the "Group of Eight." The others are George Luks, Ernest Lawson, M. B. Prendergast, Everett Shinn, William J. Glackens, Arthur B. Davies and John Sloan. Mr. Henri has always been a devoted student of the art of painting. He has received inspiration from Velasquez, Hals and Titian, and later he was much influenced by Manet and Whistler. In narrow canvases, like a "Young Woman in Black," the subject fills the space most decoratively, the pose is natural, the tones graduating delicately into one another, and the color of the whole canvas has "quality," a combination of effects that makes the painting rank with what is classical in art. The subjects of his pictures have been people interesting to him from the point of view of human character, the rendering at times low toned, at others in brilliant coloring. Mr. Henri has published "Individuality and Freedom in Art" in the "Craftsman" (1909); "The Exhibition of Independent Artists" in the "Craftsman" (1910), and "Ideal Exhibitions" in "Arts and Decoration" (1914). He was married June 24, 1898, to Linda, daughter of

T. Huston Craige of Philadelphia. She died in 1905, and he was married again in 1908 to Marjorie, daughter of John Organ of New York city. Mrs. Henri is also an artist, having begun her career as a caricaturist when only seventeen years of age. Her series, entitled "Reggie and the Heavenly Twins," ran continuously for three years in the New York "Journal," and a number of other comic series, notably "Just Like a Woman," "Strange What a Difference a Mere Man Makes," and "The Man Haters' Club," captured the popular fancy by their delightful humor. She also contributed caricatures to the New York "World". Portrait opposite page 145.

HANNA, Edward Joseph, third archbishop of the archdiocese of San Francisco, was born at Rochester, N. Y., July 2, 1860, son of Edward and Anne (Clarke) Hanna. After a preparatory course in the local seminary he was sent by Bishop McQuaid to the North American College in Rome. There he attended the classes at the Propaganda, and was one of the favorite pupils of Cardinal Satolli, then professor of dogmatic theology and later the first apostolic delegate to the United States. On July 15, 1886, he made a brilliant display of knowledge and ability in a public theological disputation, which won for him the degree of doctor of theology, and one of the highest scholastic distinctions ever attained by an American student in Rome. He was ordained priest in the Lateran Basilica and remained in Rome as an assistant professor to Archbishop Satolli, whose chair at the Propaganda he filled during that prelate's first visit to the United States. Later he studied at the universities of Cambridge and Munich. After his return to America he was attached to the cathedral of Rochester, and when St. Bernard's Seminary was opened he was appointed to the chair of dogmatic theology, which he filled with special success for nineteen years. In 1890 he went with Bishop McQuaid to Rome and there assisted in obtaining from the Propaganda the authority for St. Bernard's Seminary to confer degrees in philosophy and theology. He was nominated coadjutor archbishop of San Francisco in 1907, but failed to receive the confirmation of Rome on account of a charge of modernism, which was subsequently disproved. On Oct. 12, 1912, Pope Pius X. appointed him titular bishop of Titopolis and auxiliary to Archbishop Riordan, of San Francisco. He was consecrated on December 4 of that year by the apostolic delegate, Archbishop Bonzano, and at once took up with arduous zeal and splendid results the duties of the see that had become too onerous for the failing health of Archbishop Riordan. That prelate died in December, 1914, and Bishop Hanna was made administrator of the diocese. On May 18, 1915, Pope Benedict promoted him to the vacant archbishopric, in which office he was solemnly installed on July 28, in St. Mary's Cathedral, the apostolic delegate, Archbishop Bonzano, again presiding. The archdiocese of San Francisco has a Catholic population of 280,000; 367 priests, 276 churches, seven colleges with 1,973 pupils, forty-six schools with 12,236 pupils, twenty-two girls' academies with 4,704 pupils, six orphan asylums with 1,342 inmates, twelve other institutions and 20,246 young people under Catholic care.

MORLEY, Frank, mathematician and educator, was born in Woodbridge, Suffolk, England, Sept. 9, 1860, son of Joseph R. and Elizabeth (Muskett) Morley. He was graduated at King's College, Cambridge, in 1883, and pursuing higher studies, received his master's degree in 1886. Meanwhile he began his life-work as a teacher, and from 1884 till 1887 served as master in Bath College, England. Coming to the United States in 1887, he accepted an appointment as instructor in Haverford College, where he was professor of mathematics, during 1888–1900. In 1900 he was called to the chair of mathematics in the Johns Hopkins University in succession to the renowned Sylvester and the able Newcomb, a place which he still retains. His original papers have been important and include: "The Value of $S_0\pi^s$ (log. 2 cos. ϕ) $^m\phi^n$d ϕ'' (1901); "Projective Coördinates" (1903); "Orthocentric Properties of the Plane n—line" (1903); "On the Geometry Whose Element is the 3-point of the Plane" (1904); and "On Reflexive Geometry" (1907), all of which have appeared either in the bulletins or the transactions of the American Mathematical Society. More recently he has published "Plane Sections of a Weddle Surface" (1909) in the "American Journal of Mathematics," and "The Contact Conics of the Plane Quintic Curve" (1912) in the circular of the Johns Hopkins University. His larger publications include in joint authorship with Prof. James Harkness, "Elementary Treatise on the Theory of Functions" (1893) and "Introduction to the Theory of Analytic Functions" (1898). He is the editor of the "American Journal of Mathematics" and he is one of the editors of the Bulletin of the American Mathematical Society, of which organization he has been a vice-president. Dr. Morley is a member of the American Philosophical Society, the London Mathematical Society, and the Circolo Matematico di Palermo. The degree of Sc.D. was conferred by his alma mater in 1898. He was married, July 11, 1889, to Lilian Janet Bird, of Hayward's Heath, Sussex, England.

KOUDELKA, Joseph Maria, second Roman Catholic bishop of Superior, Wis., was born in Chlistovo, Bohemia, Austria, Dec. 8, 1852, son of Marcus and Anna (Janoushek) Koudelka. His education was begun in the college at Klattau, Bohemia, and upon coming to the United States in 1868, entered St. Francis' Seminary, Milwaukee. He was adopted by Bishop Gilmour for the diocese of Cleveland, where he was ordained priest Oct. 8, 1875. For thirty-six years following he officiated as a priest of the diocese of Cleveland, being pastor of St. Prokopius and St. Michael's churches. On Feb. 25, 1908, he was consecrated titular bishop of Germanicopolis and auxiliary bishop of Cleveland, and on Sept. 4, 1911, he was transferred to Milwaukee as auxiliary bishop of that see. Bishop Schinner of Superior resigned Jan. 15, 1913, and on Aug. 6 of the same year the pope appointed Bishop Koudelka his successor. At the reception which followed his installation, being an accomplished linguist, he replied to addresses of welcome in eight languages: English, Bohemian, Polish, German, Slovak, Hungarian, Italian and French. In 1882 he prepared a series of readers for Bohemian Catholic parish schools and prayer books for adults and for children, and during 1882–83 he was editor of "Hlas," a leading Bohemian Catholic semi-weekly of St. Louis. He was also the author of a "Short History of the Church for Catholic Schools" in German (1895). The diocese of Superior extends over sixteen counties in the state of Wisconsin, an area of 15,715 square miles. It has a Catholic population of 55,000, including 3,000 Indians. There are ninety priests, 162 churches, chapels and missions, 26 schools with 5,000 pupils, and five hospitals. He was received by the Indians (Chippewas) as one of their chiefs, and they gave him the name of

"Min-werve-gijig," meaning, "He who speaks heavenly."

MANSON, Otis Frederick, physician and surgeon, was born in Richmond, Va., Oct. 10, 1822, son of Otis and Sarah Dews (Ferrill) Manson, grandson of Frederick and Anna (Hemingway) Manson and great-grandson of Frederick Manson, a native of Scotland, who settled in Roxborough, Mass. He studied medicine in the medical department of Hampden-Sidney College, where he was graduated M.D. in 1840 and conducted an extensive practice in Granville county, N. C., until the civil war. At the request of Gov. Vance, Dr. Manson went to Richmond at the beginning of the war and was made surgeon-in-chief of the Moore Hospital for Confederate soldiers there. In 1862 he was commissioned surgeon of the Confederate army and was made medical agent, with the rank of major, by the state of North Carolina to afford relief to its troops in Virginia. Returning to Richmond after the war he became professor of pathology and physiology in the Medical College of Virginia, and after his resignation in 1882 was made professor emeritus. He was associate editor of the "Richmond Clinical Record" in 1871-72. Throughout his life he was a diligent student, an ardent investigator and a voluminous writer. While living in North Carolina he made a thorough study of malarial fevers, and accumulated a large library of both European and American books on the subject. He was the first American writer to describe "Puerperal Malarial Fever," and he was among the first of the leaders who brought the use of quinine sulphate into prominence in the treatment of other diseases than intermittent fever, such as pneumonia, cholera infantum, puerperal fever, etc., for which he advocated its use in large doses. Many of his doctrines and treatments received bitter opposition, but are now generally accepted and practiced by Southern physicians. He was married in 1843 to Mary Ann Spotswood, daughter of Spotswood Burwell, by whom he had six children. She died in 1874, and he was again married in 1881, to Mrs. Helen (Grey) Watson, of Richmond. He died in Richmond, Va., Feb. 1, 1888.

MONAGHAN, John James, third Roman Catholic bishop of the diocese of Wilmington, Del., was born at Sumter, S. C., May 23, 1856. His first studies were made in local schools and for his classics he went to St. Charles College, Ellicott City, Md. After graduating there in 1876 he entered St. Mary's Seminary, Baltimore, for his theological course, and was ordained priest Dec. 19, 1880, by Bishop Lynch in the Pro-Cathedral, Charleston, S. C. He was assistant at St. Joseph's Church in that city for one year, and assistant at St. Patrick's Church until October, 1882, when he was appointed pastor of St. Mary's Church, Greenville, S. C., and the Missions attached, embracing nine counties. After five years of missionary labor, he was transferred in 1887 to the cathedral at Charleston by Bishop Northrop, as pro-rector and chancellor. In 1888 he was appointed assistant to Vicar-General Quigley at St. Patrick's Church, a position he filled for nine years, until his elevation to the See of Wilmington, Del., in 1897, in succession to Bishop Curtis. He was consecrated bishop of Wilmington by Cardinal Gibbons, in the pro-cathedral, Wilmington, May 9, 1897. The diocese of Wilmington embraces the peninsula of Delaware, Maryland and Virginia, and contains an area of 6,211 square miles. At present (1916) it has 38,000 Catholics, with sixty-one priests, fifty-one churches, and numerous chapels and mission stations. Wilmington itself has eleven churches, all equipped with excellent parochial schools, besides the Ursuline Academy for young ladies, and the Salesianum, a high school for boys. There are three religious orders of priests and seven religious communities of sisters, laboring in the diocese.

FORWOOD, William Henry, surgeon general, U. S. A., was born at Brandywine Hundred, Del., Sept. 7, 1838, son of Robert and Rachel Way (Larkin) Forwood. He was educated at the Crozier Academy of Chester, Pa., and was graduated at the medical department of the University of Pennsylvania in 1861. He was at once appointed assistant surgeon in the regular army, and after serving for a few months as executive officer of the Seminary Hospital at Georgetown, D. C., was assigned to active duty in the field, first as surgeon of the 14th infantry, and later as acting medical director of Sykes' division of the 5th corps, army of the Potomac. While surgeon of the 6th cavalry in Stoneman's and Pleasanton's division, he was disabled by wounds received in action. He built the Whitehall General Hospital near Bristol, Pa., with 2,000 beds, and was in command of it to the end of the war. During his active service he took part in numerous engagements, including Yorktown, Gaines' Mills, Malvern Hill, the second Bull Run, South Mountain, Antietam, Gettysburg and Brandywine Station, and throughout the conflict the performance of his duty was attended by conspicuous valor. Promoted to the rank of captain in 1866, he fought alone an epidemic of cholera at Fort Riley which carried off twenty-seven out of fifty-nine cases. In 1870 he devoted a leave of absence to the study of yellow fever at the Philadelphia quarantine station. The next twenty years were spent in frontier duty. He was surgeon and naturalist to the three military exploring expeditions conducted in the north by Gen. Sheridan, and he was attending surgeon on the staff of Gen. Sheridan in Chicago during 1882–86. In 1890 he entered upon a period of duty at the Soldiers' Home near Washington, holding the chair of surgical pathology, and for a time also that of military surgery in the medical department of Georgetown University. When the army medical school was organized in 1893 he became professor of military surgery, and upon the resumption of its sessions after the Spanish-American war he was its president until his promotion to surgeon general. He was chief medical officer of the convalescent camp at Montauk Point during the Spanish-American war, and when the return of the volunteer regiments from Cuba necessitated the establishment of a general hospital at Savannah, Gen. Forwood was selected to make plans and supervise the work of construction. In December, 1898, he became chief surgeon to the department of California—a station then assuming especial importance because of the hostilities in the Philippines. Early in 1901 he returned to Washington as assistant surgeon general with the rank of colonel, having reached that grade in 1897, and a year later succeeded Gen. Sternberg as surgeon general. Gen. Forwood was the author of monographs upon military surgery in Dennis' "System of Surgery" and in Warren & Gould's "International Text Book on Surgery." For a number of years he was editor of the "Military Surgeon," published in Washington in connection with the National Medical Review. The degree of LL.D. was conferred upon him by Georgetown University in 1897. Gen. Forwood was a noted scientist, botanist and mineral-

W. R. Forwood

ogist, and was well known among the scientific men of Europe. It was he who discovered the new mineral sphine, in the Mullen quarries at Bridgewater, Pa. He was a member of the American Medical Association, the Academy of Natural Sciences, Philadelphia, and the American Academy of Medicine, and the Military Order of the Loyal Legion of the United States, the G. A. R., the Cosmos Club of Washington and the Bohemian Club of San Francisco. He was married Sept. 28, 1870, to Mary A. Y., daughter of Antrim Osborne, of Rose Valley, Pa. He died in Washington, D. C., May 11, 1915.

BACON, Albion Fellows, social reformer, was born at Evansville, Ind., April 8, 1865, daughter of Rev. Albion and Mary (Erskine) Fellows. For about ten years after her marriage she was fully occupied with the care of her home and children, and found little time for social work. Then she began, in an humble way, to visit the sick in the hospitals and in their homes. Gradually she interested her friends in the work and organized a Flower Mission and a Men's Circle of Friendly Visitors. Subsequently she helped to organize a Working Girls' Association, of which she later became president. In the course of her charitable work her attention was directed to the squalid and unsanitary conditions in the tenements of Evansville and as there was no one to look after such matters and no existing law to guard against such conditions, she decided to attend to the situation herself. After studying the tenement ordinances of New York, Chicago and Indianapolis, she framed a set of rules governing tenements for insertion in a building ordinance which was about to be introduced in the city council of Evansville. Further investigation convinced her that a state law was needed, and she consequently drafted a bill which, after it had been endorsed by the State Conference of Charities and the Commercial Club of Indianapolis, she succeeded in putting through the Indiana legislature. In the meantime the city ordinance, including her provisions regarding tenements, was passed by the city of Evansville. In order to make these laws effective, she secured the appointment of a building inspector and started a campaign of education in the public press and by lectures. Later she worked, with eventual success, to extend the application of the state housing law, designed only for first-class cities, to all the cities of the state. In the course of this campaign she organized and became secretary of the Indiana Housing Association. She is a director of the National Housing Association, and a member of the District Nurse Circle, the Civic Improvement Society, the State Federation of Women's Clubs, the General Federation of Women's Clubs, and other organizations. Despite the exactions of her civic and philanthropic work, and her household duties, she finds time to write extensively and well, to compose songs, and to draw and paint. With her sister, Annie Fellows Johnston, she is the author of "Songs Ysame" (1897), a book of poems, and she has also written "What Bad Housekeeping Means to the Community," "The Awakening of a State" (1911), and "Beauty for Ashes" (1914). Withal she is very domestic in her tastes and habits, and is known in Evansville as a model wife and mother. She was married in Evansville, Oct. 11, 1888, to Hilary E. Bacon, and has three children.

SHULL, Deloss Carlton, lawyer and banker, was born at Pella, Ia., Mar. 28, 1858, son of Jacob Henry and Martha (Cutler) Shull. His father, a native of Pennsylvania, became a farmer in Iowa; he served throughout the civil war as a private in the 33d Iowa Vol. infantry. The son was educated at Central University (Pella), and Des Moines College, being graduated at the latter in 1881. He was graduated in the first class at the college of law at Drake University, in 1882, and formed a partnership with Congressman John L. Jolly, for the practice of law at Vermilion, S. D., under the firm name of Jolley & Shull. In 1887 he moved to Sioux City, Ia., and was associated first with L. S. Fawcett, and later with O. J. Taylor and W. H. Farnsworth, in the firm of Taylor, Shull & Farnsworth; in 1893 this firm became Shull & Farnsworth; in 1899, Shull, Farnsworth & Sammis, through the acquisition of James U. Sammis; and in 1904, Shull, Farnsworth, Sammis & Stilwill, the new addition being Charles M. Stilwill. In 1913 was organized the present firm of Shull, Gill, Sammis & Stilwill, the second member of the firm being Frank E. Gill, and Deloss Perkins Shull, a son of the subject, and Peter Balkema as associates. He is attorney for the Chicago, Milwaukee and St. Paul Railway Co. He has been connected with much of the important litigation that has been tried in the courts of the district during the past twenty-eight years, and the records bear evidence of his success. Aside from his legal activities he has been a dominant factor in the industrial and financial life of his adopted city; has served as vice-president of the Farmers Loan & Trust Co., National Bank of Commerce, Farmers Trust & Savings Bank, and the Continental National Bank; is president of the Great Western Land Co., New Foundry & Manufacturing Co. and director of Knapp & Spencer Co., and the Guarantee Title & Realty Co., Sioux City. He is a member of the Sioux City Golf and Country, Sioux City Boat, Crucible, and Commercial clubs, Sioux City; and he is a communicant of the Baptist church. His political affiliation is with the Republican party. He finds his chief recreation, aside from studies and research in jurisprudence, in practical farming. He was married: first, at Winterset, Ia., Oct. 16, 1885, to Nettie, daughter of E. G. Perkins, of Winterset, Ia.; she died in 1887; he was married: second, at Sioux City, Ia., Oct. 24, 1889, to Frances E., daughter of Joel Mitzell, of Sioux City. There is one child by the first union: Deloss Perkins, associate member of his father's law firm, and two children by the second union: Henry Carlton and Laurens C. Shull.

McWILLIAMS, Alexander, physician, was born in St. Mary's county, Md. in 1775, of Scotch descent. After receiving his medical degree he entered the navy, in 1802, as assistant surgeon and was present at the burning of the Philadelphia in the war with Tripoli. Columbia College, of the District of Columbia, gave him the honorary degree of M. D. in 1841. He was an incorporator of the Medical Society of the District of Columbia, and served as president of the Medical Association of the District during 1847–50. He was interested in natural science, more especially botany, to which he devoted much attention, even to the neglect of his professional work. During the early years of the medical department of Columbia College he was professor of botany, and subsequently published "The Flora of the District of Columbia." He was one of the "Botanic Club" which published, in 1830, "The Prodromus of the Flora Columbiana." He is said to be the first resident of Washington to build a conservatory, and in it he cultivated many rare plants. During the last of his medical career he was physician to the almshouse in Washington. He died in Washington in 1850.

KENNEDY, John Stewart, financier and philanthropist, was born at Blantyre, near Glasgow, Scotland, Jan. 4, 1830, son of John and Isabel (Stewart) Kennedy. He was educated in the public schools of Glasgow. His father's circumstances made it impossible to expect a college career, and at the age of thirteen the son began his business life as a clerk in a shipping office. Four years later he transferred his services to an iron and coal concern in Glasgow, and in 1850 a London firm in the iron and metal business made him an offer to travel for it in the United States and Canada, and he eagerly accepted the opportunity of broadening his experience and enlarging his prospects for advancement. He came to the United States in June, 1850, and made his headquarters in New York city for two years. He went back to become the manager of the same firm's branch office in Glasgow, and he held that position from August, 1852, until December, 1856, but the institutions and the opportunities of the new world had made a strong impression on the ambitions of the young man, and he determined to return to New York at the first opportunity. That came when he was asked to associate himself with the banking firm of M. K. Jesup & Co., which had been newly started by one who was himself destined to attain a foremost place as a banker and philanthropist. Mr. Kennedy became a member of the firm, the name of which was changed to Jesup, Paton & Co., and shortly thereafter the partners organized the firm of Jesup, Kennedy & Co., with offices in Chicago, Ill., to engage in the railway supply business. He withdrew from this connection July 1, 1867, and after a year of travel and recreation in Europe established the banking house of J. S. Kennedy & Co. He became one of the foremost financiers of the country, and won an enviable reputation for clean and safe methods and a dignified and exalted standard of business ethics. Outside his own firm Mr. Kennedy was identified with many important business organizations. He was appointed by congress one of the incorporators of the Union Pacific railway, and attended the meeting in Chicago when that company was formed. Wall street knew him particularly as one closely associated with James J. Hill in the Northwestern railway development. He was interested in the construction of what is now the Great Northern railway, and was a member of the syndicate that contracted in February, 1881, with the Canadian government to build the Canadian Pacific railway, and after the charter was granted by the Dominion parliament he continued to serve for some time as a director of that company. He retired from active participation in his banking business in 1883, the business being continued by his nephew under the name of J. Kennedy Tod & Co., but he continued to hold the directorships of various railroad interests throughout the country, among which were the Northern Pacific Railway Co., the Chicago, Burlington & Quincy system, the Cleveland & Pittsburgh Railroad Co., the New York, Chicago & St. Louis Railroad Co., and the Pittsburgh, Ft. Wayne & Chicago Railway Co. In 1886 he was appointed by the U. S. circuit court one of the receivers of the Central railroad of New Jersey, and after conducting its affairs for fifteen months the company was placed on a solid foundation. He was a trustee and finance committeeman of the New York Life Insurance Co., and a trustee of the Central Trust Co., the Title Guaranty and Trust Co., the United States Trust Co., the Hudson Trust Co. of New Jersey, and the Manhattan Bank. Widely known as Mr. Kennedy was in the world of finance, he became more widely known in the field of philanthropy. A vein of philanthropic zeal animated and dominated his whole life. He had an overflowing tenderness for those in need; his sympathy was genuine and his hospitality a fine art, and he never lost an opportunity of showing grace and kindness to even slight acquaintances. With him it was no empty honor to be called trustee or officer of an organization; his interest in its welfare was sincere, and he wanted to take a hand in directing it. He gave to all at least a part of his time as well as a part of his money. His oldest and most intimate relation to any charitable institution was to the Presbyterian Hospital, of which he was president continuously for the last twenty-five years of his life. He rarely missed a meeting of the board of managers or of the executive committee, of which he was chairman, and there was no question of hospital policy which did not receive his personal consideration. It was to this hospital that he made, on the occasion of his golden wedding anniversary, in 1908, his largest single gift; namely, $1,000,000. Ten years previously he made almost as large a gift of far-reaching consequences to the charities of New York by erecting the United Charities building on Fourth avenue, which furnishes headquarters for the Charity Organization Society, the Association for Improving the Condition of the Poor, the Children's Aid Society, the New York City Mission and Tract Socity, and many other institutions of equal importance. Mr. Kennedy in his letter of gift to the beneficiary societies said: "It has long seemed to me important that some well-known charitable center should be established in the city of New York in which its various benevolent institutions could have their headquarters, and to which all applicants for aid might apply, with assurance that their needs would be promptly and carefully considered." The building has more than served its purpose, for it has brought together the important charities of New York, not only in locality but in spirit. It has made co-operation between them natural and easy, and it has served as an example to other cities. Nothing impressed Dr. Emil Munsterberg, the director of charities of Berlin, Germany, more during his visit to America than the beneficial effect of this building on social work in New York, and he returned to his native city with the firm purpose of inducing the citizens of Berlin to imitate in this particular the example which New York had set through the generosity of Mr. Kennedy. To the School of Philanthropy of the Charity Organization Society Mr. Kennedy gave $250,000 in 1904, and in 1907 he gave $500,000 to Columbia University. He was president of the board of trustees of Robert College, Constantinople, Turkey, and of the American Bible House in the same city. He was a trustee of Columbia University, vice-president of the Metropolitan Museum of Art, the New York Public Library (having been president of the Lenox Library before its consolidation), and the Society for the Ruptured and Crippled. He was one of the founders of the Provident Loan Society of New York, the well-known and successful philanthropic pawnbroking establishment, serving as its trustee after organization; was a vice-president of the New York Chamber of Commerce, and president of the St. Andrew's Society. His will, under which he left an estate of over $67,000,000, nearly one-half of it for the welfare of the public, indicates the breadth as well as the extent of his philanthropic intentions. With him liberal giving was not merely a pleasure or a pastime, but a solemn duty, and the thought which underlay his large bequests as well as the liberal gifts he made in so many directions before his death, was well expressed by the clause in his will with which he precedes his public legacies as follows: "Having been greatly prospered in the business which I carried on for more than thirty years in this, my adopted country, and being desirous of leaving some expression of my sympathy with its religious, charitable, benevolent and educational institutions, I give and bequeath," etc. Mr. Kennedy was a prominent member and trustee of the Fifth Avenue Presbyterian Church. He found his recreation in various out-door sports. The opening of the trout season always found him at the South Side Sportsman's Club of Long Island, and he never failed to open the salmon season, either at the Restigouche Salmon Club, of which he was president, or at the Cascapedia Club in Canada. He was said to have held the record for the largest number of salmon taken with the fly within a two-week period. Mr. Kennedy was married Oct. 14, 1858, to Emma, daughter of Cornelius Baker of Elizabeth, N. J. He died in New York city, Oct. 30, 1909.

SEGUIN, Edouard, psychologist, neurologist, and philanthropist, was born at Clamecy, department of Nièvre, France, Jan. 20, 1812, son of Dr. O. Seguin. He was descended from a long line of eminent physicians in Burgundy who ranked at the head of their profession, and was himself destined to become the most gifted of his line. He was educated at the college of Auxerre, and at that of St. Louis in Paris. He then commenced the study of medicine, in which he displayed such analytical power and such patience of research that he became a great favorite of Itard and of Esquirol, then the most distinguished psychologists and alienists in Europe, and was associated with them in their investigations. He had imbibed from Itard a great fondness for psychological studies, and while reviewing Itard's apparently fruitless experiments and efforts for the instruction of idiots, his genius led him to the great discoveries which Itard had failed to make—that idiocy was not the result of deficiency or malformation of the brain or nervous system, but simply an arrest of mental development, occurring either before, at, or after birth, induced in a variety of ways and by different causes; that this arrested development could be overcome by appropriate treatment and the idiot restored to society and life, if not to the highest intelligence. This restoration, he believed, could be accomplished by a careful physiological training of all the senses. Accordingly Dr. Seguin decided to step aside from the brilliant career which had opened before him and devote his life to the attempt to rescue from degradation and misery the lowest, most forlorn and abject of God's creatures. The great Esquirol was so delighted with the views of Dr. Seguin that he obtained for him the opportunity to make experiments to prove his theories upon the idiot children of the celebrated Hospice de Bicêtre. Accordingly, in 1839, there appeared in Paris a modest pamphlet entitled "Resumé of What We have Done During Fourteen Months Past—Esquirol and Seguin." Dr. Seguin had now definitely determined on his life work. After six years of experiment, study and labor at his own expense he asked the Academy of Sciences of France to appoint a commission to report upon his methods and work. That commission gave not only its highest commendation to his labors, but declared that previously idiots could not be educated by any means known or practiced, and that Dr. Seguin had solved the problem. His methods

were made known, attention was called to his school, which was visited by teachers and philanthropists of all nations, and schools for the feeble-minded were soon established in England and the countries of the Continent. As a writer, contributing to the best literature of France both in poetry and prose, he attracted great attention. He was a brilliant conversationalist, and one of that coterie of young philosophers including Ledru Rollin, Piere Leroux, Louis Blanc, Michel Chevalier, the elder Flourens, Jean Reynaud, and Victor Hugo. Of this band of brothers, all of whom in after years attained distinction, Edouard Seguin was the youngest, but not, in spite of his modesty, the least brilliant member. In 1850, finding himself in disfavor with the political party in power, Dr. Seguin emigrated to the United States. He aided in the more complete organization of schools for idiots throughout the country, all of which owed their existence, wholly or in part, either to his school at the Hospice des Incurables, or to his treatise, or both. In 1851 he entered upon the general practice of his profession in Cleveland, O., but his heart was too deeply interested for his helpless protegés and in 1854 he went to Syracuse, N. Y., to teach and train idiotic children in the New York state institution. During the following three years he established many new institutions throughout New England, Ohio, Pennsylvania, and the South. In 1857 he revisited France; returned in 1860 to practice medicine at Mt. Vernon, N. Y.; took a special course at the University of the City of New York, where he was graduated in 1861, and removed to New York city in 1863. His thorough knowledge and rare skill, coupled with his pleasant and engaging address, would have won him a large practice in the metropolis, but he preferred to devote his time to the children of the idiot asylum, Randall's Island, and to train teachers for them. Meanwhile he studied the wider application of his "Physiological Method" to the education of children. With the aid of his wife he established a physiological school in New York city for feeble-minded children, the outcome of which was the more pretentious and celebrated Seguin Physiological School at Orange, N. J. This school, for the training of children of arrested mental development and for backward children, is still being conducted by Mrs. Elsie Mead Seguin and has attracted the favorable attention of the American medical world. The school numbers among its consulting physicians many of the best known neurologists, orthopedists, opthalmologists, and aurists in the profession. While the curriculum includes correction of speech defects, kindergarten, primary, intermediate, manual and industrial training, art, piano and voice, domestic science, and medical and educational gymnastics, yet sense and motor training, constituting Dr. Seguin's physiological method, forms the basis of instruction. Dr. Seguin was many times a delegate from the American Medical Association to the International Medical Congress, and was an officer of the latter. Among his more important writings were "Resumé de se que nous avous fait Pendant Quatorze Mois" (with Esquirol); "Conseils à M. O.—sur de l'Education de son Enfant Idiot" (1839); "Thérie et Pratique de l'Education des Idiots," part first (1842), part second (1843); "Hygiène et Education des Idiots" (1843); "Imagés Graduées a l'Usage des Enfants Arriérés et Idiots" (1846); "Traitment Moral, Hygiène, et Education des Idiots, et des autres Enfants Arriérés" (1846); "J. R. Pereire,

Premier Instituteur des Sourds et Muets en France'' (1847); ''Historical Notice of the Origin and Progress of the Treatment of Idiots'' (1852); ''Idiocy and Its Treatment by the Physiological Method,'' revised by the author's son, Dr. E. C. Seguin (1866); ''New Facts and Remarks Concerning Idiocy'' (1870); ''Medical Thermometry'' (1871); ''Prescription and Clinic Records'' (1865-77); ''Mathematical Tables of Vital Signs'' (1865-77); ''Thermometres Physiologiques'' (1873); ''Manual of Thermometry for Mothers, Nurses, Teachers'' (1873); ''Official Report on Education'' (1875); ''International Uniformity in the Practice and Records of Physic'' (1876), and ''Medical Thermometry and Human Temperature'' (1876). Dr. Seguin's first wife died in the early sixties. Their only child was Dr. E. C. Seguin, the well-known neurologist, who died in 1898. On May 26, 1880, he was married in New York city to Elsie M., daughter of Walter J. and Laura C. (Benedict) Mead of Montgomery, N. Y. He died in New York city, Oct. 28, 1880.

PECK, Annie Smith, mountain climber, was born at Providence, R. I., about 1850, daughter of George Batchelor and Ann Power (Smith) Peck, and a descendant of Joseph Peck of Hingham, Norfolk county, England, who came to America in 1638 with his wife, Rebecca Clarke, and settled at Hingham, Mass. The line of descent is traced through his son Joseph Jr.; his son Jathniel, who married Sarah Smith; their son Benjamin, who married Elizabeth Whitaker; their son Solomon, who married Esther Wiswold, and their son Benjamin, who married Sarah Batchelor, and was the grandfather of the subject of this sketch. On the maternal side she is descended from Roger Williams. Her father, a graduate of Brown University, was a member of the Rhode Island bar, but conducted a mercantile business, and at one time served as a member of the city council of Providence and in the state legislature. The daughter was educated at the public schools and in Dr. Stockbridge's School for Young Ladies in her native city. Later she went abroad to study in Germany and in the American School at Athens. She was professor of Latin at Purdue University and at Smith College, and has lectured on classic art, archæology and other subjects before the Chicago Art Institute, the Chautauqua assemblies and elsewhere. She received the degree of A. B. at the University of Michigan in 1878, and A. M. in 1881. Her first experience in mountain climbing was the ascent of Mt. Shasta in 1888. This was followed by the ascent of the Matterhorn in 1895, Popocatepetl and Orizaba in 1897, the last with an altitude approaching 18,500 feet, being the highest point which had then been reached by a woman. In 1900 she ascended the Fünffingerspitze in the Tyrol, Austria, a most hazardous climb, and later the Jungfrau. In 1903, 1904, 1906 and 1908 she made explorations of the Andes to find, if possible, a higher peak than Aconcagua, supposed to be the loftiest on the western hemisphere. In 1904 she attained an altitude of 20,500 feet on Mt. Sorata in Bolivia. She essayed Mt. Huascarán in Peru in 1904 and again in 1906, reaching a height of 18,000 feet, but it was not until Sept. 2, 1908, that she reached the summit, which, according to the latest triangulation, has an altitude of 21,812 feet, 1,500 feet higher than Mt. McKinley. ''Harper's Magazine'' said of this feat: ''The conquering of Mt. Huascarán will stand as one of the most remarkable feats in the history of mountain climbing. That this first ascent has been accomplished by a woman renders it still more wonderful.'' In recognition of this achievement the Peruvian government gave her a gold medal. She wrote an account of this triumph in a book entitled ''A Search for the Apex of America'' (1911), which is an amazingly interesting story of exploration realistically told and replete with exciting experiences. In 1911 Miss Peck made the first ascent of the great mountain Massif Coropuna (21,000 feet) in southern Peru. Through her various explorations she became much interested in the Spanish-American people and in the development of friendly and commercial relations between North and South America. She has delivered many lectures on the subject of mountain climbing, as well as on her travels in Tyrol, Switzerland and South America. She is gifted with a pleasing personality, a fine delivery and a magnetic manner. Miss Peck is a member of the National Geographic Society, the Association of Collegiate Alumnæ, and was in 1900 an official delegate from the United States to the International Congress of Alpinists, held in Paris. She is an original member of the American Alpine Club, an honorary vice-president of the International Peace Forum and honorary member of the Pan-American Trade Association and the Joan of Arc Suffrage League. Portrait opposite p. 153.

DALE, Thomas Nelson, geologist, was born in New York city, Nov. 25, 1845, son of Thomas Nelson and Sarah Patten (Monson) Dale, grandson of Thomas and Cynthia (Lombard) Dale, and great-grandson of Thomas Dale, who was the founder of the family in America. He received his early education at Paris, France, where his father resided during 1850-61. He also attended a private school at Frankfort-on-the-Main in 1856-7, where he studied botany under Dr. J. J. Rein, who took him on his first geological excursion to the mines of Westphalia. In 1860 he made a three months' geological tour in Scandinavia under Dr. K. A. Zittel. In 1861 he returned to the United States and continued his studies at Williston (Mass.) Seminary, and at Northampton with Dr. Josiah Clark. During the following seven years he was employed in his father's manufacturing business, having been debarred by ill health from a college career. In 1870 he studied mathematics at Cambridge, England, and made stratigraphic explorations in the Rhaetic Alps between the lakes of Garda and Idro, the results of which were published privately in 1876, and received commendation from Dr. Zittel and Fr. von Hauer, director of the Austrian geological survey. This led to his first employment by the U. S. geological survey, under Prof. Raphael Pumpelly, at Newport, R. I., in 1880, his duties being the revision and tabulation of the returns from the mines of non-precious minerals for the tenth census. While here he made a private geological study of the south end of Narragansett bay, and published the results in scientific journals. After teaching in Toronto for a year, he was again engaged by the geological survey, with which he has been identified ever since. In 1892 he was appointed geologist, and removed to Massachusetts. His work on the survey consisted chiefly in the geological mapping, with assistants, of some 3,000 square miles of the rock surface between the Green Mountain range and the Hudson river and Lake Champlain, involving a study both of the structure and physiography of the region. Mr. Dale also made a special study of slate, involving visits to the quarries of Maine, Maryland, New York, Pennsylvania, Vermont and Virginia, and com-

ANNIE S. PECK
MOUNTAIN CLIMBER

THOMAS NELSON DALE
GEOLOGIST

FREDERICK WELLHOUSE
AGRICULTURIST

JOHN H. HARPSTER
MISSIONARY

pleted a similar study of the granites of New England and of the marbles of Vermont. In 1877–78 he taught natural science at Drury College and at Vassar College. He was instructor in geology at Williams College during 1893–1901, and from 1897 to 1901 taught botany there also. His chief geological publications are: "The Areal and Structural Geology of Mt. Greylock" (1894), "Structural Details in the Green Mountain Region" (1896); "Geology of the Hudson Valley Between the Hoosic and the Kinderhook" (1904), "Taconic Physiography" (1905), "Slate Deposits and Slate Industry of the United States" (1906), "The Granites of Maine" (1907), "The Granites of Massachusetts, New Hampshire and Rhode Island" (1908), "The Granites of Vermont" (1909) and "The Commercial Marbles of Western Vermont" (1912). He wrote also "Outskirts of Physical Science" (1884), a volume of essays dealing with the relation of Christian faith to scientific pursuits, and "The Master-Key of Life" (1910), an essay on ethics. Mr. Dale's work on geology bears the marks of conscientious care and of a great desire to be accurate and correct. It deals with some of the most puzzling and difficult regions in America, and unravels their stratigraphical relations with marked success. He was married Dec. 22, 1874, to Margaret, daughter of James D. Brown, M.D., of New York city, and has four sons: Norman B., Nelson C., Oswald and Arthur, and two daughters, Sarah N. and Margaret Dale.

WELLHOUSE, Frederick, agriculturist, was born in Chippewa township, Wayne county, O., Nov. 16, 1828, son of William and Hannah (Yohey) Wellhouse. His father was a native of Hanover, Germany, and in 1804 came to America with his parents and settled in Baltimore, Md. Later he moved to Wayne county, O., where he married a daughter of Peter Yohey. Frederick Wellhouse attended school until the age of fifteen. He began farming in 1853 in Christian county, Ill., and in 1859 went to Leavenworth county, Kan., to engage in the growing and sale of young fruit trees. He continued in that line until 1876, when he began planting commercial apple orchards, a work that was destined to make his name famous. He planted 117 acres at Glenwood, Leavenworth co.; 160 acres in Miami, Miami co.; 160 acres in Fairmount, Leavenworth co.; 800 acres in Osage, Osage co.; and 400 acres in Summit, Leavenworth co. The crop of 1890, amounting to 80,000 bushels of apples, sold for over $50,000. It was the most valuable apple crop ever grown by one man in the Middle West and brought to Mr. Wellhouse the title of "The Apple King." By 1913 he had raised twenty-seven crops, aggregating 600,000 bushels. He was a member of the Kansas State Horticultural Society, serving as president ten years. He was a member of the Kansas state legislature in 1865 and again in 1888. During 1861-65 he was captain of company I, 19th regiment Kansas state militia, and took part in the Price raid campaign in 1864. He was married in January, 1848, to Susan, daughter of Daniel Housley, of Ohio, and had four children: Walter, Mary C., wife of Hamilton Moore, of St. Paul, Minn.; Horace M. and Cora, wife of H. Shelby Bullard. He died in Leavenworth, Kan., Jan. 10, 1911.

HARPSTER, John Henry, missionary, was born at Centre Hall, Pa., Apr. 27, 1844, son of George and Frances (Lebker) Harpster. His father was a manufacturer of farm tools. His education was interrupted by the civil war, in which he enlisted before he had attained his seventeenth

year. He was wounded four times at Gettysburg, being carried off the field with a wound which it was believed later caused his death. He was mustered out as captain June 1, 1865, and at once entered an educational institution of the Lutheran Church at Selins Grove, Pa., and later the Evangelical Luthern Theological Seminary at Gettysburg, Pa., where he was graduated in 1871. At that time the India mission of the Lutheran church was in peril of collapse, the civil war having jeopardized the cause of missions, and his heroic spirit was stirred by a call for volunteers to that field. He was ordained for the ministry in Baltimore, Dec. 20, 1871, and sailed for India, Jan. 6, 1872. After four years of strenuous labor to the cause he came home because of ill-health and served congregations at Hays City, Kan.; Trenton, N. J., and Canton, O. He returned twice to India, in 1893, when he remained eight years, and again in 1902, when he was the missionary of the large Bhimawaram district, and, for a time, of the Korukunda district. He was the missionary in charge of Rajahmundry, manager of the printery and book store and director of the entire mission. In 1907 he resigned as the temporary director of the mission—a special title that was then the highest office at the disposal of the Board of Foreigns Missions—but retained the position of chairman of the executive committee. In 1906 he united with the Ministerium of Pennsylvania. The chief monument of his work in Rajahmundry is the Boys' Central School at Luthergiri, the erection of which he carefully superintended. He returned to America in 1909, but continued to devote himself to the cause of foreign missions in the congregations of the general council of his church. He excited interest by his eloquent addresses and untiring efforts; spread information, deepened the sense of American foreign mission obligation, and won the prayers and consecration of those who learned to know him. As a preacher he was calm, persuasive, forceful and eloquent, stirring his hearers to intense feeling and quick action. He was broad in his sympathies, liberal in his gifts to the needy, a good companion and a warm-hearted friend. He was married at Gettysburg, Pa., Aug. 1, 1882, to Julia, daughter of Prof. Michael Jacobs, and died at Mt. Airy, Philadelphia, Pa., Feb. 1, 1911.

MEEK, Channing Frank, capitalist, was born at Mt. Pleasant, Ia., Sept. 26, 1855, son of Aaron and Rhoda (Gardner) Meek, and a descendant of Guy Meek, a native of Wales, who came to the American colonies in 1664 and settled in Maryland. His father (1814–93) was a physician who settled in Iowa in 1854. He matriculated at the medical department of Iowa University, intending to follow the medical profession, but a serious illness compelled him to abandon his studies. He began his very picturesque and varied business career as a messenger boy for the Pacific & Atlantic Telegraph Co. of Davenport, Ia. He at once applied himself to the study of telegraphy, and in 1878 entered the employ of the Rock Island railroad as train master and chief despatcher, remaining until 1881. He was superintendent of the Wabash railroad during 1882–86. When thirty-two years of age he was made general manager of the Denver, Texas & Ft. Worth railroad, and was said to be the youngest general manager of a railroad at that time in America. In this position he built 800 miles of railroad from Denver to Ft. Worth, now a part of the Colorado & Southern system. Before this new line was opened for business, Col. Meek had negotiated a contract with the Southern Pacific road, with which his new road was connected at Ft. Worth, to give it the power to make the through rates from New York to Colorado, and as soon as the new line was ready for business he announced a cut of the first-class rate from $4.40 per hundred to $2.20, and an average reduction of 35 per cent. on other classes of freight. This action precipitated a long and bitter freight rate war, but ultimately the older and stronger roads were compelled to adopt these reduced rates, and they are still in force. From there he accepted the position of general manager of the gulf division of the Union Pacific railroad. In 1890 he became interested in the Colorado Coal and Iron Co., and served as its president for three years, when it was consolidated with the Colorado Fuel Co. under the new name of the Colorado Fuel and Iron Co. Removing to Colorado in 1886, he had a considerable share in the remarkable development of that state's commercial and industrial activities from that time until his death. He developed an extraordinary capacity for the organization and promotion of large corporate interests, an ability first disclosed in the handling of the coal and iron company mentioned above. He was associated with the late Henry D. Perky (q. v.) in the organization of the shredded wheat business, and in 1895 was one of the organizers of the American Biograph Co. In the following year he purchased the street car lines in the city of Mexico, and after reorganizing the system sold them at a considerable advance to a London company. Unquestionably the most important achievment of Col. Meek was the purchase of the white marble deposits in Gunnison county, Colo., in 1904, and the subsequent organization of the Colorado-Yule Marble Co. for the purpose of quarrying and marketing the finest quality of white marble to be found in any part of the world. The marble is even superior to the famous Carrara marble of Italy and the Penetellic and Parian marbles of Greece, which for nearly 1,000 years held the supremacy over all others. Col. Meek constructed a well-equipped marble mill, the largest single finishing plant in the world, costing with incidental railroads, power plant, employés' houses, etc., nearly $4,000,000, and built an electric railroad from the town of Marble to the quarries. The Colorado-Yule quarries and mill have become the nucleus of an enterprising modern town called Marble City, with a population of 1,700 at the present time. To Col. Meek must be given the credit of establishing this flourishing industry, which, beyond all peradventure, promises to be the most important and most valuable as a source of true wealth of any in the state of Colorado. Gov. Shafroth said of him: "Col. Meek was an indefatigable worker and his whole life was devoted to great enterprises. He was trustworthy, reliable and had innumerable friends in all parts of the nation. The United States has lost a good man and one of indomitable energy." In 1885 he was appointed lieutenant-colonel on the staff of Gov. Buren R. Sherman of Iowa. He organized the Grant Club of Des Moines, and was also a member of the Denver Club, the Denver Athletic Club and the Colorado Traffic Club. Col. Meek was married Sept. 25, 1879, to Fannie, daughter of William Melbourne of Xenia, O., and they had one daughter, Helen, and one son, Philip Meek. He died at Marble, Colo., Aug. 14, 1912.

CHISHOLM, Hugh J., financier, was born at Niagara-on-the-Lake, Canada, May 2, 1847, son of Alexander and Mary Margaret (Phelan) Chisholm, of Scotch birth. He acquired his early education in local schools, but at the age of thirteen was thrown upon his own resources by the death of his father. He began his business career as a newsboy on the railroad running between Toronto and Detroit. He was remarkably alert, intelligent, ambitious and industrious, and in a short time had established a railway news business of large proportions. He formed a partnership with his brother under the name of Chisholm Brothers, and by 1867 they had practical control of the newspaper service on trains from Halifax to Chicago and on steamboats of the principal lines of travel in New England, New York and Canada, becoming one of the best-known railway news and publishing enterprises in the country. The Chisholm brothers were the originators of the transportation publishing business, which has to do with the production of railway and tourist guides and souvenirs of travel. Although living in Toronto during the civil war, Hugh Chisholm was a staunch Unionist, and after he removed to Portland, Me., became a citizen of the United States. Meanwhile, having realized the advantages of a more extended education, he took the course in a Toronto business college. In 1865 he sold his business in Canada to his brothers, and in 1872 removed to Portland, Me., which thereafter became his permanent residence. Four years later he bought out his brothers' interests in the New England states and established at Portland a publishing house. It was through his connection with the publishing business that he became interested in the wood pulp industry and the manufacture of paper. As was characteristic of the man, he made an exhaustive study of the subject until he was thoroughly conversant with all its details, with the result not only that he ultimately became the most conspicuous figure in the industry but developed it into one of the most flourishing and important industries in the United States. In 1887 he organized at Livermore Falls, Me., the Otis Falls Pulp Co., and commenced the manufacture of paper. This was followed by the establishment of the Oxford Paper Co. at Rumford Falls. Realizing the enormous power lying dormant in the Androscoggin river, he began acquiring property at Rumford Falls as early as 1883, and in 1890 he organized the Rumford Falls Power Co., which was the nucleus around which grew the city of Rumford Falls. Not only did he conceive and work out the idea of this company, but he even planned the engineering features of it. He arranged to devote a portion of the town to model homes for people of small means, and Strathglass Park was the outcome of this idea, which, oval in shape, with wide streets, flanked with parks and modern brick cottages, has become one of the distinctive features of the town. At the same time he arranged for the establishment of other manufacturing industries. He provided for the erection of a mechanics' institute with the characteristics of a social club and an educational institution along scientific and industrial lines for the benefit of its citizens; and he purchased and extended a small railroad connecting Rumford Falls with the Maine Central railroad system, affording direct communication with the outside world. Thus in a period of twenty-five years his genius and ability created in what was a veritable wilderness in the heart of the state of Maine a model manufacturing town of over 9,000 inhabitants, which will ever stand a permanent memorial to perpetuate his name. Concerning this achievement Judge Putnam of the United States district court of Portland said: "Apparently proper account is not taken publicly of the fact that Hugh J. Chisholm possessed and exercised wonderful mechanical, engineering and constructive genius. . . . It was especially in modern hydraulics, one of the most difficult and perplexing sciences of the day, that he excelled. . . . Indications of it are his masterly share in the building of the dam on the Megalloway river, now about completed, and likewise his enterprise on the Montmorency, little known in the United States, which so attracted the governor-general of Canada when he was at Quebec to meet Lord Roberts that the two called Mr. Chisholm into private conference and luncheon in reference thereto." Mr. Chisholm was the chief organizer, in 1898, of the International Paper Co., consisting of some twenty-five pulp and paper manufacturing plants, located in New York, Vermont, New Hampshire and Maine, of which he was president, 1898-1908, and chairman of the board. The combined factories of the International Paper Co. aggregate some 220,000 horsepower, and produce 1,200 tons of wood pulp, 400 tons of sulphide pulp and 1,700 tons of paper per day. Besides these mills the company owned 1,000,000 acres of spruce woodland in New England and Canada. Like all men of genius, Mr. Chisholm was a dreamer; but, unlike most of them, he was practical as well. In addition to his connection with the enterprises already mentioned, he was president and director of the Portland and Rumford Falls railway, the Rumford Falls and Rangley Lakes railway, the Rumford Falls Realty Co. and the Rumford Lumber Co., and was a director of the Maine Central Railroad Co. "The leading characteristics of Mr. Hugh J. Chisholm," said William De Witt Hyde, president of Bowdoin College, "seem to be a prophetic grasp of future possibilities and indomitable patience, perseverance and energy in developing the means of realizing these possibilities. With all this vision and energy he combined a deep sense of responsibility for the beneficent use of his powers and resources, and a kindly and generous interest in the welfare of those who through their labor became associated with him in his enterprises." "In his early days," said Frederick N. Dow, president of the Casco National Bank of Portland, "he was industrious, energetic and strictly attentive to business, and in these particulars giving promise of progress but few of us who knew him then could have anticipated for him the successful and useful life he led. . . . His career was remarkable then in this country of great successes. Few men of his age, and at that time limited means, would have the foresight, the ability and courage to penetrate a wilderness and arrest a mighty river, as he did the Androscoggin in its unshackled, useless flow toward the sea, and compel it to render service and create wealth for man. . . . Aside from his greatness as a business man, that trait of his character which perhaps impressed one as much as any was his high appreciation of assistance rendered, however slight, and his intense loyalty to his friends. . . . Mr. Chisholm, his life and services may well be cited far and wide as an exemplar and an encouragement for young men everywhere." Mr. Chisholm was a member of the New York Yacht, Metropolitan, Riding and other New York clubs. He was married in Portland, Me., Sept. 5, 1872, to Henrietta, daughter of Dr. Edward Mason of that city, and had one son: Hugh J. Chisholm, Jr. He died in New York, July 8, 1912.

PHELPS, Edmund Joseph, financier, was born at Brecksville, O., Jan. 17, 1845, son of Joseph Edmund and Ursula (Wright) Phelps. His earliest paternal American ancestor was William Phelps, who came from Tewksbury, England, in 1630, and settled at Dorchester, Mass. From him the line of descent is traced through his son Nathaniel and his wife, Elizabeth Copley; their son William and his wife, Abigail Stebbins; their son Ebenezer and his wife, Sarah Taylor; their son Ebenezer and his wife, Phebe Wright, and their son Asahel and his wife, Polly Sears, who were the grandparents of Edmund Joseph Phelps. He received his education in the public schools of Brecksville, at Baldwin University, Berea, O., and at Oberlin (O.) College. For three winters he taught school in Ohio, and during 1866-67 was an instructor in the Northwestern Business College, Aurora, Ill., and teacher of penmanship in the public schools. In 1868 he became a clerk in the banking house of Volintine & Williams, Aurora, Ill., and was promoted teller and cashier. During 1870-78 he engaged in the furniture business in Aurora under the firm name of E. J. Phelps & Co. and then removed to Minneapolis, Minn., and formed the firm of Phelps & Bradstreet, furniture and interior decorations. He sold out in 1883, and with E. A. Merrill organized the Minnesota Loan & Trust Co., of which he was secretary and treasurer, and which was the first trust company in the Northwest. In 1892 he resigned his official position, and became interested in banking, grain elevators and manufacturing. He was at one time or another president of the Moore Carving Machine Co., Belt Line Elevator Co., Minnesota-Cuba Co., and director of the National Bank of Commerce, and since its absorption by the Northwestern National Bank a director in that, but is not now connected actively with either the grain or manufacturing industries. He was first to suggest the celebrated harvest festival of 1891, and he assisted in securing for Minneapolis the Republican National Convention of 1892, being treasurer of the fund. He was an organizer and president, in 1891, of the Minneapolis Business Union, and president of the Minneapolis board of trade during 1884-85, and again in 1898. Although he was always interested in civic and municipal affairs, he never sought an elective office, except that of park board commissioner, a position he has held from 1904 to date. He was president of the board during 1912-13. He is past president (1898) of the Commercial Club, also a member of the Minneapolis, Minikahda and Lafayette clubs. He has always taken an intense interest in business matters and in public affairs, and finds his chief recreation in out-of-door sports. He has ever held a conspicuous place in the business walks of his adopted city, and perhaps has attained even greater recognition in its higher social, intellectual and ethical life. His influence upon industrial, commercial and financial affairs has necessarily been widely felt. He was married at Aurora, Ill., Sept. 16, 1874, to Louisa A., daughter of Charles F. Richardson, a farmer of Naansay, Ill., and has three children: Ruth Shepard, Richardson and Edmund J. Phelps, Jr. Portrait opposite p. 156.

SERGEANT, Henry Clark, inventor, was born at Rochester, N. Y., Nov. 2, 1834, son of Isaac and Ruby (Clark) Sergeant, and a descendant of John Sergeant, a notable missionary to the Indians. His earlier years were spent in Ohio, where he attended the public schools. He took out his first patent when only nineteen years of age for a boiler feed. While employed in a machine shop he designed special machines for making the spokes, hubs and felloes of wagon wheels, and at the age of eighteen he accepted a contract for manufacturing wheel parts in quantity. He was so successful in this venture that in two years he was taken into partnership by a firm manufacturing wagon wheels. In December, 1858, he patented a steam governor for marine engines to prevent their racing to destruction when the propellers were out of water. It was soon after adopted by the United States government for the warships of the period. He also invented gas regulators, steam pumps, steam boilers, brick machines, a fluting machine and water meters. In 1868 he started a machine shop of his own in New York city, building a wide variety of machines and developing many crude ideas into practical working successes. In the early seventies Mr. Sergeant became associated with Simon Ingersoll, who had made some drawings of a rock drill, and, after making of improvements, a patent was issued to Ingersoll and Sergeant as joint inventors. He sold his interest to the Ingersoll Drill Co., and conducted a silver mine in Colorado for a time, but it did not prove a paying one. Having perfected another rock drill with an entirely novel valve motion, in 1886 he formed the Sergeant Drill Co., which began manufacturing the new drill at Bridgeport, Conn. His company was consolidated with the Ingersoll Co. in 1888 as the Ingersoll-Sergeant Drill Co., with Mr. Sergeant as its first president. He labored long to improve the company's machines and to develop new and wider fields for their use. At this time he invented the Sergeant ''Auxiliary'' and ''Arc'' valve, ''Tappet'' rock drills, the Sergeant release rotation for rock drills and the piston inlet valve for air compressors, all of which are in general and successful use to-day. He was also the originator of many new ideas in stone channeling, coal undercutting and allied lines, and was also the inventor of a ticket canceling device, now used extensively on the elevated and subway roads of New York city. It is no exaggeration to say that without the rock drill, which Sergeant did more than any other man to make a success, such enterprises as the Chicago drainage canal, the Niagara power developments, the Croton aqueduct, the New York subway, the Panama canal and the submarine tunnels in New York could not have been commercially possible. He was married Mar. 19, 1860, to Caroline, daughter of Adam Luckhaupt of Columbus, O., and had one son, Charles H. Sergeant, and three daughters, Emma, wife of Paul Philip; Ruby, wife of Paul Q. Oliver, and Ada, wife of Frederick G. Smith. His last years were spent in Westfield, N. J., where he died Jan. 30, 1907.

BYRD, Adam Monroe, lawyer and statesman, was born in Sumpter county, Ala., July 6, 1859, son of John and Elizabeth (Tann) Byrd. His first paternal American ancestor was Col. William Byrd, who settled at Richmond, Va., about 1720. John Byrd, father of Adam M. Byrd, was a private in the Confederate army and died in the service at Clinton, La., in 1863. In 1867 his mother moved to Neshoba county, Mississippi, where young Adam spent the years of his boyhood, his youth, his mature manhood and here the labors of his active life were wrought. He attended the common schools of the county and completed his literary education at Cooper's Institute, Daleville, Miss., and Hiwassee (Tenn.) College. He was graduated at the law department of Cumberland University in 1884, and immediately began the practice of law at Philadelphia, Miss. He met with instant and phenomenal success and he was soon recognized as one of the

leading members of the Mississippi bar. On Dec. 15, 1887, he was married to Margaret, daughter of Capt. Edward Simmons of Decatur, Texas. She died in 1898, survived by two daughters, Annie Kate and Eddie Lee, and on July 26, 1900, he was married to Mary Rutledge, daughter of James Alexander Gulley of Meridian, Miss., by whom he had four children, Lena Elizabeth, Adam Monroe Jr., Mary Rutledge and Joseph Gulley Byrd. When he settled at Philadelphia to begin the practice of his chosen profession the fires of a high and noble ambition burned within his breast. He resolved, while yet a boy, to so live among his fellows that all who saw him as he came and went should know him as a friend of men, and in their innermost thoughts declare the truth, ''There goes a man.'' No man could ask a better friend; no wife had ever a tenderer or more indulgent husband; no son or daughter a fonder or more devoted father. His was a big brain, a big heart, a generous spirit and a lofty soul; and in that undiscovered land whither he has gone, where bigness of heart, generosity of spirit and loftiness of soul are valued at their worth, he rests forever. He early became interested in local politics. In 1887 he was elected county superintendent of education. He represented his county in the lower house of the legislature; represented his district in the state senate; was district attorney of his judicial district; chancellor of his chancery district for two terms, resigning in 1902 to become representative to the 58th congress, 1908-10. He brought to bear upon the duties of his office in congress an unusual insight, acquired by long and accurate study of nations and governments. Possessing a vigorous and aggressive temperament, and equipped with a splendidly developed intellect, he never failed to get a hearing and to make an impression when he spoke on pending questions. His speeches formed a considerable part of the literature of Democracy in campaigns throughout the nation. His knowledge of the tariff was so intimate and accurate that he was regarded as an authority upon that subject within the ranks of his own party. In 1910 he made a speech on the high cost of living and another on the iniquity of the tariff, both of which were immediately adopted as a text for the Democratic campaign. Thousands of copies were sent into doubtful states of the North, and upon their doctrines the Democratic party, that year, secured control of the lower house of congress, and upon the same issues two years later elected a Democratic president, senate and house of representatives. Judge Byrd's speech on the high cost of living was the first ever delivered along that line in the national congress. An eminent Washington writer, at the time, said of him: ''Having digested his subject thoroughly, he asked for an hour's time, during the consideration of an appropriation bill, in which to deliver a speech on the tariff. He was told he could have the time, but the Democrat who controlled the time for his side of the house reminded him that the tariff was a 'dead issue' and that it would be a loss of time to discuss it. Mr. Byrd disagreed with him, however, and proceeded with his speech. . . . It was a regular call to arms against the tariff barons, . . . his colleagues sat spell-bound, charmed at his eloquence, amazed at his logic and the array of facts and figures he presented to prove his case. . . . From that moment Adam Byrd's fame as a great and wise statesman was secure; from that moment every Mississippian sojourning in Washington knew that their beloved state had sent another son to the Federal congress who would bring additional

EDMUND J. PHELPS
FINANCIER

HENRY C. SERGEANT
INVENTOR

ADAM M. BYRD
LAWYER

ISAAC T. MANN
BANKER

JAMES G. WHITE.

glory to their brilliant record. From that moment the Democratic party, which had been sick since 1896, gave signs of returning health; raised its head from the mire; leaped into the open, and started a battle for tariff reform which culminated in victory.'' Judge Byrd was a Shriner, Knight Templar, member of the A. F. A. M., and also a member of the M. E. Church South. He died at Hot Springs, Ark., June 21, 1912.

MANN, Isaac Thomas, banker, merchant and capitalist, was born in Ft. Spring, Greenbrier co., W. Va., July 23, 1863, son of Matthew and Elizabeth (Curry) Mann. His father (1824-1900), who followed farming and grazing for a livelihood, was a man of splendid business acumen, and as president of the Greenbrier Valley Bank of Alderson, W. Va., conducted its affairs prosperously for many years. He was a descendant from William Mann of Kent, England, the brother of Isaac Mann, Bishop of Cork, who came to America in 1735 and settled on a plantation in Alleghany county about eight miles from Covington, Va. William Mann's wife was Jane Hamilton, and the line of descent is traced through their son Thomas, who married Elizabeth Armstrong; their son William Thomas, and his wife, Margaret Alexander, and their son Matthew, the father of our subject. Mr. Mann's great-grandfather, Thomas Mann, was the owner of a large estate in Virginia; he was treacherously killed by Simon Girty (q. v.) and a band of Indians while serving under Gen. Wayne in Ohio. His son, William Thomas Mann, inherited most of his property, and he managed it so successfully that his land holdings were extended over the three counties of Greenbrier, Monroe and Fayette. In the latter county he acquired some 14,000 acres of coal land. Isaac T. Mann, the subject of this sketch, obtained a thorough education under the tutelage of private instructors. He began his business career as teller in his father's bank at Alderson at the age of twenty and in 1889 became cashier of the bank of Bramwell, W. Va. He inherited his father's genius for business and performed his duties with such success that in 1902 he was made vice-president and virtual executive head, a position he still holds. Mr. Mann is also president of the Pocahontas Consolidated Collieries Co., and is identified with banks and various coal and coke companies as director, president or vice-president. Mr. Mann was married Mar. 2, 1899, to Vernie, daughter of Israel Meyers of Bramwell, W. Va., and has one son, William Thomas, and one daughter, Alice Mann. He was a delegate-at-large from West Virginia to the Republican national convention at Chicago in 1908. He is a member of the Metropolitan Club of Washington, the Shenandoah Club, Roanoke Club of Virginia, the White Oak Club of White Oak, Ga., and Chevy Chase and Narrows Island Clubs of Washington, D. C. Portrait opposite p. 156.

WHITE, James Gilbert, engineer and contractor, was born at Milroy, Pa., Aug. 29, 1861, son of John W. and Mary M. (Beaver) White, grandson of William and Kezia (Delaplain) White, and great-grandson of Joseph and Mary (Fullerton) White, the first of his immediate family in America. On his mother's side he is descended from an old Pennsylvania Dutch family, the first members of which came to Pennsylvania early in the history of the colony. His mother was a sister of Gen. James A. Beaver (q. v.), governor of Pennsylvania. Several of his ancestors on both sides took part in the Revolutionary war. James G. White entered the Pennsylvania State College in 1877, and he was graduated there in 1882 as

valedictorian of his class. During his vacations he devoted himself to practical engineering work. In the summer of 1881 he spent some time with a party engaged in surveying northern Pennsylvania, and later worked in the civil engineering department of the Cambria Iron Co. of Johnstown, Pa. After graduation he took a course in civil engineering at the Pennsylvania State College, and subsequently spent a summer on the reconnoissance and location surveys of a steam railroad in central Pennsylvania. In 1883 he entered Lehigh University with the intention of studying mining engineering, but becoming interested in electrical investigations, he decided to adopt electrical engineering as a profession, and went to Cornell University in January, 1884, where he specialized in electrical engineering and physics. He spent the summer of 1884 in the office of the master mechanic of the Cambria Iron Co., working on designs for machinery required in the manufacture of iron and steel. At Cornell he was awarded a fellowship in physics and received the degree Ph. D. in 1885. Subsequently he was instructor of physics in the University of Nebraska, holding that post until 1887, when he became one of the organizers of the Western Engineering Co. This company, of which he was president, did what for those days a large amount of construction work in 1888-90, and built electrical railways in Omaha, Neb.; St. Joseph, Mo., and Salt Lake City, Utah. It also supervised the installation of a hydro-electric generating plant at Kearney, Neb., and in this connection devised a system embodying the three-wire principle with 220 volts on each side, a principle then practically untried. After the company had developed to a considerable extent, it was purchased in 1890 by the Edison United Manufacturing Co., and Mr. White removed to New York, where he took charge of the department of railway installation of the Edison interests. Soon afterwards, on the formation of the Edison General Electric Co., he resigned and started an engineering and contracting business of his own under the title of J. G. White & Co. After a short time he organized the White-Crosby Co. with O. T. Crosby, which, however, was dissolved in 1897. The title of J. G. White & Co. was then resumed, and the company was incorporated under the laws of the state of Connecticut. During these years Mr. White personally supervised the design and construction of a large number of power houses, both steam and water-driven, as well as complete systems of track and overhead construction, bridges, electric light and railway distribution circuits. Of these the Buffalo-Niagara Falls street railway, transmission line from Niagara Falls to Buffalo, Helena Water & Electric Power Co., and the electrical equipment of the Helena & Livingston Smelting and Reduction Co. presented new and interesting problems. The first named, built in 1895, was one of the first high-speed interurban lines in America, and is probably the first to use the four-motor equipment, with series-multiple control, now commonly adopted for interurban service. The transmission line from Niagara Falls to Buffalo is believed to have been the first in America designed to carry on one set of wires as much as 10,000 h. p. Many hundreds of miles of street and interurban railways have been built by J. G. White & Co., as well as many large power plants, steam railroads, harbor improvements and docks, etc., in all parts of the civilized world. The business grew rapidly and soon began to include contracts for engineering works in England and

Australia. To take care of those Mr. White organized in 1900 the firm of J. G. White & Co., Limited, in London, which has carried out a number of important projects, several of them requiring Mr. White's individual attention. Among these may be mentioned a power plant in the interior of western Australia, costing £150,000, and presenting many unusual and novel features. In this case the power had to be generated by steam from water which at different seasons of the year contained from 3 per cent. to 25 per cent. of saline matter. The London company also built many miles of railways in Great Britain and colonies. A building company was subsequently formed by Mr. White in England which has built some of the finest structures there, notably Ritz Hotel, Royal Automobile Club, Selfridge's Stores, and Waldorf Hotel. To promote unified co-operation among the large number of talented engineers who make up the personnel of the White companies, especially when it is remembered that these men are widely distributed, is a matter requiring no small degree of executive ability. To obtain the most far-reaching results in such an organization it is deemed essential that each individual be given the greatest freedom of action comparable with centralized administration. The degree of responsibility which the individual is allowed to accept is limited only by his capacity, but, at the same time, in all important matters decisions are made, not as the result of individual judgment, but after concerted consideration by the engineers best qualified to treat of a given subject. A great unanimity of purpose pervades the personnel of the White organizations; that is apparent even to the casual observer. Mr. White is the source of this cohesive power. It resides in and emanates from him. He is a man of kind, helpful and resourceful personality, of a type to be eminently responsible for the foundation of organized loyalty upon which the reputation of these companies has been built. He is in entire sympathy with all movements which look to the betterment of social conditions and the general uplifting of men, especially those of the younger generation. He is not a perfunctory member of civic and other organizations, but takes an active interest in virtually all of those with which his name is associated. Among electrical engineers he is known as a man of generous impulses, and in no small measure has lent active personal and financial support to important engineering movements. In addition to the above, The J. G. White Management Corporation acts as managers or consulting managers of a large number of public service properties, including the Associated Gas and Electric Co., comprising properties in New York, Pennsylvania and Ohio; Augusta-Aiken Railway and Electric Corporation, Augusta, Ga.; Helena Light and Railway Co., Helena, Mont.; Manila Electric Railroad and Light Corporation, Manila, P. I.; Tri-City Railway and Light Co., Davenport, Rock Island and Moline; Tri-State Railway and Electric Co., Ohio, Pennsylvania and West Virginia; United Light and Railways Co., Illinois, Michigan and Iowa; Southern Utilities Co., owning electric light and power, gas, water works and ice manufacturing plants, etc. Among the properties operated by J. G. White & Co., Limited, are the Manaos Tramway and Light Co., Limited, Manaos, Brazil; the Para Electric Railways and Lighting Co., Para, Brazil; the Cordoba Light and Power Co., Cordoba, Argentine; the Venezuela Light and Power Co., Limited, Caracas, Venezuela; Parana, Argentine; and Merida,

Yucatan. Mr. White is president of J. G. White & Co., Inc., New York; chairman of J. G. White & Co., Limited, and the Municipal & General Securities Co., Limited, London; chairman finance committee of The J. G. White Engineering Corporation; chairman finance committee of The J. G. White Management Corporation; president of the Engineering Securities Corporation; president of the Investors' Securities Corporation; president of the Cardenas-American Sugar Co., etc. He is also a director of many large concerns. Among some of the societies with which he is connected may be mentioned the American Institute of Electrical Engineers; American Society of Civil Engineers; Institute (British) of Electrical Engineers; Pilgrims Society; Society of Sons of Revolution, etc. Some of the more prominent clubs of which he is a member are Engineers Club; University Club; Midday Club; Recess Club; Cornell Club, and New York Athletic Club—all of New York; Maryland Club and Merchants' Club of Baltimore; Sleepy Hollow Country Club; Greenwich Country Club; the Ranelagh Club, London, etc. He was married in Lincoln, Neb., Dec. 15, 1886, to Maud M., daughter of Oscar A. Mullon of that city, and has one son, James Dugald White.

MOORE, William, manufacturer, was born in County Queens, Ireland, March 28, 1827, son of Timothy and Jane (Malloy) Moore. He was endowed with an unusual amount of ambition, determination, pluck and energy, and reading of the greater advantages and opportunities for a young man to be obtained in the new world, he determined to go to the United States. He arrived in New York in 1846, and after investigating the business centers of Rhode Island, Connecticut and Vermont, he finally settled at Cohoes, N. Y., where he became connected with manufacturers of cotton cloth. He became an expert machinist, and in 1859 was given the position of manager of the William Mansfield Mill. By careful management, thrift and enterprise, he had accumulated savings until he was now able to go into business for himself. In 1860 he built a new factory and established the Erie Knitting Mill, which was a success from the outset. Two years later, he also built the famous Granite Mill, which gained the reputation of being one of the largest and finest of its kind in the United States, and in that year he formed a partnership with James Tierney, under the firm name of Moore & Tierney. About this time Mr. Moore established the Manufacturers' National Bank of Cohoes, and served for many years as its first vice-president. Mr. Moore took an active interest in the development and growth of his adopted city. He was alderman of Cohoes during 1880-90. There was probably no other man in the entire history of the place who did more to develop and beautify it. In every way he had the public good close to heart, and was deeply interested in sociological problems and other questions of municipal government. He was particularly successful in his relations with his employés at the mills, and had the reputation of always acting towards them with such absolute fairness that no complaints were ever recorded by any of his working people during his entire lifetime. His employés never cared to join a union while working under him, and none of them ever went out on a strike. He was ever considerate of their welfare and interests, and it is said that he paid higher wages to his employés than the prevailing rates elsewhere. While quiet and retiring in his disposition, Mr. Moore was forceful and determined. The last years of his life were spent in partial retirement, although he retained an interest in his manufacturing plant and kept in touch with his business affairs from his home in Albany. Mr. Moore was married at Montreal, 1880, to Sarah A., daughter of James Tierney and sister of James Tierney, who was associated with him in business. He died at Albany, N. Y., Aug. 15, 1904.

ROBINSON, John Norris, financier, was born at Wilmington, Del., Jan. 8, 1831, son of Robert Randolph (1805-86) and Sarah (Norris) Robinson; grandson of Aquila (1780-1819) and Elizabeth (Tripp) Robinson; great-grandson of Robert (1733-1787) and Ann (Nebeker) Robinson, and great-great-grandson of Robert Robinson (1692-1738), the founder of the family in America, who came to the American colonies from Ireland in 1689 and settled in Wilmington, Del. J. Norris Robinson was educated in the public schools of his native city. When he was eighteen years old his father organized a banking firm in Wilmington under the firm name of R. R. Robinson & Co., the partners being his two sons, John Norris and Robert Emmet Robinson. The brothers possessed unusual foresight, prudence, energy and executive ability, which are the important essentials of successful accomplishment, and marked success justified the new enterprise from the very start. On Jan. 1, 1865, Mr. Robinson went to Philadelphia, Pa., and became a member of the firm of Drexel & Co. This addition to the firm added largely to its prestige, and the house of Drexel & Co. became one of the leading banking institutions of the United States. He was with this firm during the memorable "Black Friday" of 1865, and he was widely commended by the financiers of the day for the able manner in which he handled the company's affairs on that occasion. Mr. Robinson was one of the leading financiers of New York, and possessed an enviable reputation for clean and safe methods and a dignified and exalted standard of business ethics. He was scrupulously and exceptionally honorable in all his business transactions. He had inherited that standard of impeccable honor from his father, and he was careful that it should not be tarnished by any act of the son. He was never in his whole career identified with any deal on which the slightest shade of suspicion could be cast. He never indulged in any questionable or unwarranted speculation, and he never allowed his personal interests to override those of the clients who trusted him in the conduct of their affairs. He was identified with various financial institutions as director. Mr. Robinson was married in 1856 to Mary A., daughter of Edward Moore of Wilmington, Del., and granddaughter of Nathaniel Moore, the manager of a large farm at Trenton and the proprietor of the first ferry across the Delaware. It was this Nathaniel Moore who carried Washington's troops across that river in the memorable retreat from Princeton in 1776. Mr. and Mrs. Robinson had six children: William Moore, Estelle (died in infancy), Mary Estelle, Bertha Norris, John Norris (died in infancy), and Edward Moore Robinson. He died at Torresdale, Pa., Sept. 13, 1878.

BROWN, John Crosby, banker, was born in New York city May 22, 1838, son of James and Eliza Maria (Coe) Brown, and a descendant of Alexander Brown, who came to this country from Ballymena, Ireland, in 1800 and settled in Baltimore. James Brown, his father, was a well-known banker and philanthropist and a member of the firm of Brown Brothers & Co., which has been established for over one hundred years. John Crosby Brown received his early education at the private school of Daniel Bacon, and was graduated at the head of his class at Columbia University in 1859, receiving 11,518 marks out of a possible 11,533. He was awarded the good fellowship prize by his class, and was one of the most brilliant and popular students that ever passed through the university. After graduation he traveled abroad and continued his studies, acquiring, among other things, a knowledge of Egyptian history and antiquities rare at the time. He received his first business training in the Liverpool office of Brown, Shipley & Co., the English branch of Brown Brothers & Co., and in 1862 returned to New York. In 1864 he became a partner in his father's banking house firm, and within a few years was known as one of the most able, far-sighted and trustworthy business men in the country. He had a remarkably keen and sound business judgment, a real capacity for handling large business affairs, but above all he had the peculiar quality which made men give him their unqualified confidence at sight. Besides being senior member in the banking house of Messrs. Brown Brothers & Co., New York, Philadelphia and Boston, and Messrs. Brown, Shipley & Co., London, he was a trustee of the United States Trust Co., the Liverpool and London and Globe Insurance Co., Limited; the Bank of New York, the Bank of Savings, the United States Lloyds, the Ocean Accident and Guarantee Corporation, and the London Guarantee and Accident Corporation, Limited. He was also first vice-president of the United States Trust Co., director of the Liverpool and London and Globe Insurance Co., Limited; the Bank of New York, and the Bangor and Aroostook Railroad Co., and vice-president of the New York Chamber of Commerce. Every movement for the welfare of the city of New York, whether educational, philanthropic or social, claimed a share of his attention. He was for many years a member of the Board of Education, and was a trustee of the Columbia University for twenty-four years. In 1866 he became a member of the board of directors of the Union Theological Seminary, of which his father had been a generous benefactor, and from that time until his death the seminary held an important and increasingly absorbing place among his life's interests. He succeeded William E. Dodge Sr. as vice-president of the board of directors in 1883, and on the death of Charles Butler in 1897 he became president. Much of his time, energy and money was devoted to the work of the seminary, and during the struggle in which it was engaged at the time of the trial of Dr. Briggs for heresy, he was its consistent champion and supporter. To his wisdom and foresight the establishment of the seminary in its new home on Morningside Heights, made possible by the munificent gift of his friend, Mr. D. Willis James, was largely due. He was a trustee of the Presbyterian Hospital and a director of the Union Settlement Association. He was for many years an elder in the Madison Square Presbyterian Church and one of the founders, and for many years superintendent, of the Sunday-school of the Presbyterian church at St. Cloud, Orange Mountain, where he built his summer home. He was keenly interested in civic affairs and actively enrolled on the side of purity and uprightness in the local city government. He was a member of the Committee of Seventy which, in 1894, secured the defeat of Tammany and the election of Mayor Strong. Like William E. Dodge, Morris K. Jesup and others of their kind, he belonged to that little group of men who, during the latter part of the nineteenth century, did so much to lend character to the life of the city and to set the standard for its future development. These men believed that wealth carried responsibilities too serious to be ignored, and in endeavoring to carry out those responsibilities they sought, with noteworthy success, to impress the characteristics of a Christian civilization on the institutions of their time. Mr. Brown's charities were numerous and diversified, but always intelligent and discriminating. Besides his regular contributions to charitable institutions, he gave constantly and spontaneously wherever the need of help was apparent or was brought to his attention. His character was many-sided and well-balanced. Generous and liberal to a degree, he yet had a keen analytical judgment, which weighed and directed and appraised all questions with impartial and almost impersonal accuracy. His sense of justice was as highly developed as was his sense of honor; so that he could be kind and generous without being foolish or prodigal. Firm-willed and independent, he was a natural leader of men, and while his strength and ability won the confidence and respect of those with whom he had dealings, his qualities of heart won their love and loyalty. He was a trustee of the Metropolitan Museum of Art, in which he first became interested through a collection of musical instruments made by Mrs. Brown and bearing his name. Later he became treasurer of the museum, and devoted much time and care to its finances. Mr. Brown received the degree of LL.D. from Williams College in 1907. He was a member of the Century Association, the Metropolitan Club, and the Down Town Association. He was married in New York city Nov. 9, 1864, to Mary E., daughter of Rev. Dr. William Adams, minister of the Madison Square Presbyterian Church, and left six children: Prof. William Adams Brown, D.D., of Union Theological Seminary; Eliza Coe, wife of Prof. Edward Caldwell Moore, D.D., of Harvard University; Mary Magoun Brown, James Crosby Brown of Brown Brothers & Co., Philadelphia; Thatcher Magoun Brown of Brown Brothers & Co., New York, and Amy Brighthurst, wife of Henry Lockwood de Forest of Plainfield, N. J. Mr. Brown died at Brighthurst, N. J., June 25, 1909.

MOLITOR, David Albert, civil engineer, was born in Detroit, Mich., Aug. 16, 1866, son of Edward Philip and Catherine L. (Jung) Molitor. His father emigrated from Stuttgart, Germany, in 1863 and settled at Washington, D. C., where he married in 1865, after serving in the civil war. His paternal grandfather was Joseph Cleander Christian Spensipp von Molitor, who served in the wars of 1813-15 and held the military order of knighthood for bravery in Wurtemberg, Germany. David A. Molitor attended the public schools of Detroit and was graduated at the Smith Academy, St. Louis, Mo., in 1883; at the Washington University, St. Louis, in 1887, and at the George Washington University, Washington, D. C., in 1908. He possesses the two engineering degrees of C. E. and B. C. E. He was resident engineer in 1887-90 on the construction of the German Strategic railway, Weizen-Immendingen, comprising exceptionally difficult engineering work. Afterwards he toured Germany, Austria, Switzerland, Italy and England.

During 1890-92 he was assistant engineer on the Mississippi river cantilever bridge at Memphis, Tenn., having charge of superstructure. He then became assistant engineer of the U. S. government engaged in improvement work on the Great Lakes, in connection with the Sault Ste. Marie canal and channel construction between Chicago, Duluth and Buffalo. During 1898-9 he conducted lines of precise levels along the St. Lawrence river and Lake St. Clair for the U. S. board of engineers on deep waterways. For six years he was engaged in private practice as consulting engineer, his work including paving, sewage disposal, factory management, municipal problems, chemical and bacteriological laboratory, etc., and from September, 1906, to September, 1908, he was designing engineer for the Panama canal on locks and dams, and had special charge of emergency dams. He was professor of civil engineering at Cornell University from September, 1908, until February, 1911, and he then became designing engineer for the engineering firm of Waddell & Harrington, Kansas City, Mo., and also designing engineer for the Toronto harbor commissioners. He possesses a highly artistic temperament and is also an accomplished musician. He is a member of the American Society of Civil Engineers, Detroit Engineering Society, honorary member Cornell Society of Civil Engineers, Society for Promotion of Engineering Education, and many other scientific bodies, clubs and associations. His professional papers and works have covered a diversity of interesting scientific topics, and as an author on engineering subjects his writings have been characterized by broad culture and wide knowledge. They include "Landslides" (1894); "Distortion of a Framed Structure" (1894); "Distortion of Steel Lock Gates"; "Properties of Concrete Under Compressive Stress" (1898); "Municipal Public Improvements" (1897); "Æsthetic Design of Bridges" (1897); "Modern Framed Structures" (Johnson, Bryan and Turneaure); "The Present Status of Engineering Knowledge Respecting Masonry Construction" (1899); "Theory and Practice of Precise Spirit Leveling" (1901); "Hydraulics of Rivers, Weirs and Sluices" (1908); "The Panama Canal, a Lecture" (1910); "Kinetic Theory of Engineering Structures, an Advanced Treatise on Stresses and Deformations" (1911), and "Least Square Adjustments" (1913). He was married in June, 1893, to Clara K., daughter of Frederick Rueping, and has three children: Margaret, Clara and Anita Molitor.

POND, Chester Henry, inventor and capitalist, was born at Medina, O., Mar. 26, 1844, son of Henry Nelson and Mary Jerusha (Castle) Pond. His first American ancestor was Samuel Pond, who emigrated to America early in the seventeenth century and settled in Connecticut, and the line of descent is through Samuel, Philip, Bartholemew, Beriah, Isaac Johnson and Henry Nelson Pond. His maternal grandfather was widely known throughout Central New York as Deacon Samuel Castle, and was a leader of his day in the art of composing and rendering the music of sacred songs. His preliminary education was received in the public schools of York, Brunswick and Oberlin, O. While engaged as a clerk in a mercantile house in Oberlin, O., he became interested in telegraphy and took a course in that science in Cleveland. As illustrating the confidence his manner and bearing inspired in absolute strangers, it is recorded that he obtained both tuition in telegraphy as well as "board and room," to be paid for after he succeeded in se-

JOHN CROSBY BROWN
BANKER

DAVID A. MOLITOR
CIVIL ENGINEER

CHESTER H. POND
INVENTOR

RICHARD W. MICOU
THEOLOGIAN

curing his first salaried appointment. The civil war enlisted him in the U. S. government military telegraph service, in which his skill, judgment and personality soon won for him the mess rank of colonel, though without any military appointment except in the telegraph corps. Returning to Oberlin from the civil war, he renewed his studies. The foundation of the Oberlin Business College, which has since attained high rank in its branch of the educational field, was just being laid, and he was invited to organize a telegraph department, which he did in association with his older brother, Chauncey N. Pond, in the Oberlin Telegraph Institute. It was in those days that he invented a self-adjusting telegraph relay, and also that a suggestion dropped by him to his friend and associate, young Elisha Gray (q. v.), then engaged in an ordinary business capacity in Oberlin, proved a fruitful seed in fertile soil and initiated the inventions which made Gray a shining light in applied electrical science. After 1866 Mr. Pond developed his principal inventions, among which were the union fire alarm system and the self-winding, electric clock, now in general use throughout the country. In 1877 he established an office in New York city to look after the organization and manufacture of the various mechanical devices bearing his patents. He presented a set of his synchronized clock systems to the Oberlin Conservatory and Oberlin College, of which he was a trustee for eleven years. For the last twenty-three years of his life his activities were centered in the town of Moorhead, Miss., which he founded and where he built mills, railroads and schools. The Almeda Gardner Industrial School and other schools and churches, both for white and colored people, were organized by him, and saw and cotton mills with related industries, and a growing settlement of shops, stores and homes was developed. Failures and fires and floods caused heavy losses, but no discouragement. The ''poor white'' and the poorest negro both had a chance here if they would only try. The Yazoo Delta railway was built, making Moorhead a junction business center. Later he projected a more extensive railway enterprise, covering hundreds of miles from Memphis to Pensacola, but did not live to complete it. These transactions brought him into intimacy with such men as Stuyvesant Fish of the Illinois Central, and other railway and money magnates. He was married at York, O., Feb. 14, 1866, to Almeda M., daughter of Reuben Gardner. His wife actively co-operated with him in the development of the town of Moorhead, and was his indispensable assistant in his business, social and benevolent activities, and was besides an inspiration in many of his inventions. He died at Moorhead, Miss., June 11, 1912, survived by his widow and two daughters: Louise Carolyn (Pond) Jewell of New York City, and Alice, wife of M. C. Smith, of Moorhead, Miss.

MICOU, Richard Wilde, clergyman and educator, was born in New Orleans, La., June 12, 1848, son of William Chatfield and Anna (Davenport) Micou. His earliest paternal ancestor in America was Paul Micou, a French Huguenot of Nantes, who emigrated after the revocation of the Edict of Nantes in 1685, and founded Port Micou on the Rappahannock river, Essex county, Va. He was justice of the peace, practicing physician and lawyer—a man of great and acknowledged worth. He married Margaret Le Roy, and the line of descent is through their son John, who married Catherine Walker; their son Richard, who married Anne Boutwell; their son

William, who married Martha Anne Chatfield, and their son William Chatfield Micou, father of our subject, who was a lawyer of prominence in New Orleans and a partner of Judah P. Benjamin. The early education of Richard W. Micou was received at the Tuscaloosa (Ala.) Military Academy. During the civil war he served as a private in the Confederate army. After spending three years in the universities of Georgia and Alabama, he took a course in theology at the University of Erlanger in Bavaria. From there he went to the University of Edinburgh, Scotland, taking the highest honors in the classics under Prof. John Stuart Blackie, the Philologus and Junior Humanity medals, and the prize in English literature. His final course was in the General Theological Seminary, New York city. He received the degrees of M.A. from Trinity College in 1892, and D.D. from Kenyon College in 1898. He was ordained to the diaconate of the Protestant Episcopal church in 1870, and was advanced to the priesthood two years later. While a deacon he was assistant minister in Montgomery, Ala.; he became rector of St. Mary's Church, Franklin, La., in 1872; rector of St. Paul's Church, Kittanning, Pa., in 1874, and in 1877 he accepted the call to the rectorship of the then newly-formed Trinity Church in Waterbury, Conn. While there he was prominently identified with educational work, serving seven years on the board of education and being a member of the committee on text books and teachers during the entire period. He was a fine German scholar and was frequently called upon to minister to the German people, reading for them the baptismal, marriage and death services in their own tongue, and visiting their sick in and out of his own parish. In 1892 he was called to the professorship of Christian Apologetics and Systematic Divinity in the Philadelphia Divinity School of the P. E. Church, going from there in 1898 to fill the same chair at the Virginia Theological Seminary near Alexandria, Va., which position he continued to fill until ill health and desired leisure for publication necessitated a leave of absence in 1912. His literary attainments were of the highest, and his fondness for poetry gave power and beauty to his sermons and lectures. He went to Oxford, England, in 1912 for the purpose of preparing the results of his teaching for publication. A volume on Christian Apologetics will be completed by his widow and son. He kept industriously abreast of the best thought of the world bearing on his specialties, theology and apologetics, and imparted to his students something of his own love of truth. His talents were especially noticeable in the classroom, where he was at his best, making his students at home in the field of theology and giving them fundamental and regulative principles inside of which they could study and think for themselves. He was married in New Orleans, La., May 16, 1872, to Mary, daughter of Granville Price Dunnica of Covington, La. She is the compiler of ''Reflected Lights from Paradise.'' He died at Oxford, England, June 4, 1912. Portrait opposite p. 160.

FAURE, John Peter, merchant and philanthropist, was born in New York city, July 17, 1846, son of John Reauf and Catharine Amelia (Bonesteel) Faure. His great-grandfather, Claude Leon Faure, was a granduncle of President Felix Faure of France, and his grandfather, Jean Pierre Faure, was the first to come to the United States. His father was a dry goods merchant of New York city, a partner of Francis Cottonet & Co., importers of French dry goods, for a time and later of Atherton, Faure & Co. It was natural, therefore, that the son should follow in the footsteps of his father after finishing his education in the grammar schools of Greenwich village, New York, and he began his mercantile career at the age of eighteen as a clerk in the domestic hosiery commission business, which had been established that year by the senior Faure. He applied himself with great zeal to the business, and for a quarter of a century was continuously active in the wholesale knit-goods trade, becoming a figure of power and influence in the wholesale dry goods mart of New York city. He was a director in the Glastonbury Knitting Co., and was secretary of the Wholesale Dry Goods Democratic Club during 1888-92, and a member of the executive committee in 1884. It was for his philanthropies, however, that Mr. Faure was most distinguished. Intensely unselfish and sympathetic, a vein of philanthropic zeal animated his whole life. His principal charitable work was with St. John's Guild of St. John's Chapel, Trinity Church. St. John's Guild was started in 1866, "for the relief of the sick children of the poor of the city of New York without regard to creed, color or nationality," such relief being healthful out-door exercise and outings for the children and their sick mothers by trips down New York harbor in a floating hospital barge and by food and nursing at the Seaside Hospital at New Dorp, Staten Island. In 1874 the guild withdrew from the control of Trinity parish and was incorporated as an independent charity. During the thirty years that Mr. Faure was its secretary, the guild administered to nearly a million and a half mothers and children through its floating hospital and seaside hospital. In 1886 he established salt-water bathing on the floating hospital, beginning with five tubs, and gradually increasing the capacity until there was installed over a hundred tubs of hot and cold spray baths. At the time of his death some 50,000 were accommodated annually, while nurses representing ten nationalities attended at these baths. The floating hospital took rank as one of the foremost charities in New York and its success was due mainly to the indefatigable efforts of Mr. Faure. His genius for working effectively and well gained for him a wide reputation in benevolent circles. He was made secretary of the Committee of Seventy in 1894, and in 1895 was appointed by Mayor Strong to be commissioner of charities and correction. When these two departments were separated in 1896 he became commissioner of public charities. He only served two years, but during that time he erected for the city fifty-six important structures, including the morgue, municipal lodging house, and the dormitory, pavilions and water towers of the county almshouse on Blackwell's Island; he remodeled the ambulance service for the Bellevue and allied hospitals, introducing rubber tires and other improvements of such value that they were adopted in many other cities. He was an expert on hospital administration and trustees of other hospitals often consulted him on questions relating to their institutions. He served as school trustee for eight years, and for fifteen years was a member of the executive committee of the Church Temperance Society, and executive officer of the Church Temperance Legion, with the title of corps commander of the diocese of New York. He was also president of the diocesan council of that body, president of the Industrial Church Alliance, and a member of the executive committee of the New York City Missionary Society of the Protestant

Episcopal Church. He was a member of the New York Wool Club, New York Athletic Club and the City Club. Few men identified with the public life of his day possessed such an attractive personality as was his, and it was that unusual charm of manner which assisted largely in the bountiful success of the myriad of philanthropic enterprises which his brilliant mind conceived and which he fostered with such devoted and unselfish care. He was married in Washington, D. C., Oct. 4, 1888, to Lucie J., daughter of Gen. Charles G. Halpine and Margaret Grace (Milligan) Halpine (q. v.). He died at Ossining, N. Y., June 19, 1912.

HARAHAN, James Theodore, railroad president, was born at Lowell, Mass., Jan. 12, 1841, son of Thomas and Rose (McCurn) Harahan, of Irish and Scotch descent. He was educated in the public schools of Lowell, and at the age of seventeen entered the Boston office of the Boston and Providence railroad as freight clerk. In the following year he joined company G, First Massachusetts infantry, and served in the civil war for three years. After the war he became a conductor on the Nashville and Decatur railroad. In 1870-72 he was head of the Shelby railroad, afterwards the Shelby division of the Louisville and Nashville, and in the latter year became roadmaster of the Nashville and Decatur. He was made superintendent of the Memphis division of the Louisville and Nashville in 1879, and became general superintendent of the road in 1883, and general manager in 1884. In 1885 he became general superintendent of the Pittsburgh division of the Baltimore and Ohio, and in the same year returned to the Louisville and Nashville as assistant general manager, leaving them in 1889 to become assistant general manager of the Lake Shore and Michigan Southern. Next he was general manager of the Chesapeake and Ohio railroad, and soon afterward was made general manager of the Louisville, New Orleans and Texas. He went to the Illinois Central as second vice-president in 1890, and remained in that office until 1906, when he was chosen president. After five years as head of the Illinois Central, he was retired upon a pension in accordance with the rules of the company. He then accepted the presidency of the Memphis Bridge and Terminal Co., which was incorporated for the purpose of building a bridge across the Mississippi river, giving the Chicago, Rock Island and Pacific railroad entrance into Memphis. The outlines of James T. Harahan's career present a remarkable record of a steady and uninterrupted rise from the very bottom to the very top of his chosen profession. The first and most obvious impression they give is the peculiar fitness his experience gave him for the high and responsible position he finally assumed. In the long list of American railroad presidents there is not one who was so thoroughly prepared for his duties, not one who was so completely master of his business. For over forty years he had worked on railroads as brakeman, switchman, section boss, clerk, executive, learning the railroad business in all its details by actual, working contact with those details, and when he finally reached the top he knew all that was to be known about operating a railroad, not by studying the work in report sheets, but by actually doing the work himself. He was not a financier; he was never concerned in any financial deal. Juggling railroad stocks was something he knew nothing about, something he looked upon with justifiable suspicion. It interfered with the proper operation of the road, and the proper operation of the road he looked upon as the main business of the people who owned it. Running a railroad was his specialty. It was a big specialty, and he was master of it in all its aspects. There is no royal road to success, but there are two essentials—knowledge and ability—and Harahan had both. During the long and varied years of his service he made himself master of every job he undertook, and every bit of railroad knowledge his job brought within his ken. He did not jump up the ladder; he stepped on every rung and tested its strength, and when he reached the top he knew what was under him, knew just what it could stand, where it was weak, and where it could be best improved. He had a genius for detail, and not only did he absorb every detail of his work as he went along, but he also kept it in his mind, never allowed himself to forget the dictum of Michelangelo that "trifles make perfection." The captain of a ship is the better for being a good seaman, and the president of a railroad is the better for being a good switchman. This complete and thorough knowledge of his work was the main reason for James T. Harahan's success, the main reason why he was able to do easily most of the remarkable bits of railroading that lie to his credit. Among these may be mentioned the handling of the crowds on the Illinois Central suburban system during the Columbian Exposition, when he was vice-president of the road. So perfectly did he manage the difficult problem of carrying millions of people from the city to the fair grounds that there was never a day when there was a shortage of cars, never a day, either, when there was a wasteful surplus, and during the whole time there was not a single accident. It was a stroke of genius in traffic management, and one possible only to a man with an inexhaustive knowledge of railroading and an unusual talent for organization. It was only on a piece, however, with hundreds of other transportation feats he accomplished during his many years of railroading. He had the promptness, decision and thoroughness that mark the great leader. For example, at ten o'clock on the night of Feb. 26, 1905, he was notified of the big fire in New Orleans. Within seven minutes he had started men and material to New Orleans from the nearest point, and at ten o'clock the next morning the work of rebuilding was under way. Another example of his style of doing things was his standardization of the gauge of the Louisville and Nashville railroad in a single day and without missing a single train. He was emphatically a man who did things, who produced results. And for that reason he was perhaps the most efficient railroad operator this country has seen. Part of his great success, too, was probably due to the fact that he recognized the position of the railroads as servants of the public, and the rights of the public invariably received from him the fullest consideration. When he was general manager of the Louisville and Nashville railroad he issued an order than the full news of all wrecks and other accidents on the road should be given to the public—the first order of the kind ever issued by an American railroad official. And when he was president of the big Illinois Central system he knew most of the people who had dealings with the company, and was always ready to listen to their complaints or suggestions. He was a genial, unassuming and extremely popular man, faithful to his superiors when it was his to serve, and considerate of his employés when it was his to command. At the time of his death, Mr. Harahan

was president of the Memphis Bridge and Terminal Co., and a director of the Central of Georgia railroad, Illinois Central railroad and subsidiary companies, Ocean Steamship Co., Terminal Railroad Association of St. Louis, Harris Trust and Savings Bank of Chicago, and Bank of Commerce and Trust Co. of Memphis. He was a member of the Chicago and South Shore clubs, Chicago; the Pendennis Club of Louisville; the Tennessee Club of Memphis; the Midday Club of St. Louis, and the Boston and Pickwick clubs of New Orleans. He was married in 1866 to Mary Kehoe. She died in March, 1897, and in April, 1899, he was married to Mary, daughter of Capt. W. B. Mallory of Memphis, Tenn. By his first wife he had four children: William J., James T. Jr., Anna Harahan Effingle and Mary Harahan McFarland. He was killed in a railroad wreck near Kinmundy, Ill., Jan. 22, 1912.

BROWN, Archer, merchant, was born in Otsego county, N. Y., Mar. 7, 1851, son of Elijah Huntington and Henrietta E. (Phelps) Brown. The founder of his family in America was John Brown, a native of England, who settled in Plymouth colony before 1635, and the line of descent is traced through his son James, who married Lydia Howland; their son James, who married Margaret Denison; their son Isaac, who married Esther Brown; their son Thomas, who married Hannah Jones; their son Thomas, who married Nancy Frink, and was the grandfather of the subject of this sketch. Archer Brown's father died when he was only six months old, and his mother removed to Flint, Mich., where the son received his preliminary education. He was graduated at the University of Michigan in 1872, and began his career on the staff of the Cincinnati "Gazette," of which he became managing editor within two years. He was also founder of the Cincinnati "Tribune," which was afterwards merged into the "Commercial Gazette." He became identified with William A. Rogers in the iron business in 1881, under the firm name of Rogers, Brown & Co. The business expanded until it handled one-fourth of the raw iron output of the entire United States; branches were established in many cities, and in 1895 Mr. Brown removed to New York city to assume the management of the eastern business of the firm. Mr. Brown had considerable literary ability, which was first developed in his reportorial and editorial work after leaving college. Throughout his life he was a contributor to various newspapers and magazines, writing on the economic aspects of the iron trade as well as on miscellaneous topics. He was an authority on the subject of iron and steel, and it was said of him that "probably no man in the United States was more widely quoted on this subject than he." He was the author of "Top or Bottom—Which?— A Study of the Factors Which Most Contribute to the Success of Young Men" (1903), abounding in sensible advice to young men from the standpoint of a business man. The book was most flatteringly received, and passed through many editions, even being translated into the Japanese and Chinese languages. A prominent and energetic worker for the Young Men's Christian Association, he was one of the most useful men of his times in the development and upbuilding of that institution. He was a member of the Cincinnati branch of the Young Men's Christian Association and of the international committee, and became interested in eastern branches of the association after his removal to New York in

1895. Making his home at East Orange, N. J., he was actively interested in the welfare of that community, and to him was largely due the movement for bettering the municipal and political conditions. He was a member and president of the Citizens Union of East Orange, a member of the Essex Country Club, the Orange Musical Art Society, and the Fine Arts and Lawyers clubs of New York. He was a director of the Whittier Settlement House of Jersey City, and the Oppenheimer Institute of New York. While in every way a successful business man, Mr. Brown rendered valuable service in assistance, inspiration and advice to young men. In this connection Irving Bacheller, the author, said of him: "The tumult of the day was never so great as to deafen him to the appeal of want or the call of friendship; its burden never so heavy as to make him refuse more for the sake of kindness. He had that wonderful apostolic charity which seeketh not her own. He was a great man equipped for the highest service." Mr. Brown was married at Cincinnati, O., June 29, 1880, to Laura Adelaide, daughter of Luke Hitchcock, a minister of the Methodist Episcopal church. They had two sons, Archer Hitchcock and Lowell Huntington; and two daughters, Marjorie Adelaide and Constance Elizabeth Brown. He died at his home in East Orange, N. J., Sept. 23, 1904.

BEACH, Henry Harris Aubrey, surgeon, was born in Middletown, Conn., Dec. 18, 1843, son of Elijah and Lucy S. (Riley) Beach and grandson of Amasa and Polly (Wright) Beach. He was educated in the public schools of Cambridge, Mass., where the family had moved during his childhood. In 1863 he enlisted in the civil war and was assigned to hospital service, with the rank of sergeant of ordnance. Before he was twenty years of age he was placed in charge of the large general army hospital camp at Readville, Mass., and maintained this position throughout the war, having entire supervision of the medical and surgical as well as apothecary departments. After his honorable discharge from this responsible post in 1866, he accepted an appointment as surgical house officer at the Massachusetts General Hospital in Boston, and he saved sufficient money here to take a course at the medical school of Harvard University. He was graduated in 1868 and at once began the practice of his profession in Boston. He rapidly developed surgical skill and soon became surgeon in the Boston Dispensary and subsequently demonstrator of anatomy at the Harvard Medical School. He was finally made a member of the Harvard medical faculty and for fifteen years taught practical anatomy in connection with the lectures of Dr. Oliver Wendell Holmes, with whom he enjoyed a very close personal friendship. Thereafter his teaching was confined to the department of clinical surgery at the Massachusetts General Hospital. He was associated with that institution as surgeon until 1907 and then as consulting surgeon until his death. For two years he was assistant editor of the "Boston Medical and Surgical Journal." His teaching both at the university and in the hospital made him widely known throughout the medical world. Few modern surgeons have contributed more extensively to medical literature in the number and variety of articles, most of which were published in medical and surgical journals both in this country and abroad. As a practitioner Dr. Beach ranked with the leading surgeons of the world. Naturally conscientious and cautious, in operating he obtained good results generally with a large percentage of recoveries. He was worthily characterized as always standing "in the vanguard for everything that was humane, progressive, and wide-reaching in the theoretical, literary and practical sides of his life's work. He was a kind, generous-hearted man who gave freely from his large store of surgical knowledge to help the afflicted." Dr. Beach was married in 1871 to Alice C. Mandell of New Bedford, Mass., who died in 1880. From the overcrowding duties of his professional life he found relaxation in his love for music, and through his study of the great music masters he acquired a comprehensive knowledge which made him a competent critic of the compositions written by his famous wife, Amy Marcy (Cheney) Beach, to whom he was married Dec. 2, 1885. He was a member of the Boylston Medical Society of Harvard (president, 1873-74), the American Medical Association, American Social Science Association, Massachusetts Medical Society, Boston Society for Medical Improvement, Boston Society of Medical Sciences, American Association for the Advancement of Science, Biological Society and the National Geographic Society, and a charter member of the St. Botolph Club of Boston. Dr. Beach died in Boston, Mass., June 28, 1910.

BEACH, Mrs. H. H. A. (Amy Marcy Cheney), pianiste and composer, was born at Henniker, N. H., Sept. 5, 1867, daughter of Charles Abbott and Clara Imogene (Marcy) Cheney, of New England ancestry. Inheriting a love and capacity for music from her mother, who as Miss Marcy was a skilled singer and pianiste, this precocious child at the age of only twelve months was able to sing correctly more than forty tunes. At the age of four years she began composing waltzes, which she wrote out in correct form, although she had received no theoretical instruction. Her memory does not now go back to the time when she could not play the piano. Her studies on the pianoforte were pursued first under her mother and then under eminent instructors, but with the exception of a course in harmony under Prof. Junius W. Hill, at the age of fourteen, she has been self-taught in musical theory and composition. At the age of seven years she made a limited number of public appearances, playing selections of Beethoven, Chopin and others, besides introducing a waltz of her own composing. She was passionately devoted to her music, which made it a most dreadful punishment to be deprived of the daily practice on her beloved piano. At the age of sixteen, this gifted girl made her first appearance as a pianiste in the Boston Music Hall, playing on that occasion Moscheles' G minor concerto, opus 60, with full orchestra. In 1885 she played Chopin's F minor concerto with the Boston Symphony Orchestra under Mr. Gericke, and of Mendelssohn's D minor concerto with Theodore Thomas' orchestra. Since then she has appeared frequently at concerts in other cities, playing with the Boston Symphony Orchestra, and giving recitals, sometimes confined to her own compositions entirely. She was married Dec. 2, 1885, to Dr. H. H. A. Beach, a prominent physician of Boston. In the following year she began a mass in E flat major for quartet, chorus, orchestra and organ, which she completed in three years' time. It was first given by the Handel and Haydn Society Feb. 7, 1892, with the aid of the Boston Symphony Orchestra and a quartet of noted singers, including Mrs. Carl Alves and Campanini. The occasion was considered an important one in the history of music in America, both by reason of the remarkable qualities of the work itself and for the fact

H. H. A. Beach

Mrs H. H. A. Beach

that for the first time in its history the oldest and most conservative musical organization in the country had produced work by a woman. In this the ''Qui tollis,'' ''Thou who takest away the sins of the world,'' is full of grandeur and reverence, while at the credo the music thrills with a very rapture of grief in the cry of ''Crucifixes.'' It is one of the finest examples of Mrs. Beach's dramatic possibilities. In the same year a scena and aria from Schiller's ''Mary Stuart,'' with orchestral accompaniment, was sung by Mrs. Alves at a concert of the New York Symphony Society, directed by Walter Damrosch, and in 1893 a ''Festival Jubilate'' for chorus and orchestra was brought out under Theodore Thomas' direction at the dedication of the Woman's Building at the Columbian Exposition in Chicago. In October, 1896, the Boston Symphony Orchestra, under the direction of Emil Paur, produced her ''Gaelic'' symphony in E minor, opus 32. As a work of form this tone poem may be likened to the proportional lines, outlines, masses, and mouldings, intricate surfaces, or spaces which hold the light and shade of a fine piece of architecture. From the time its harmonies burst forth at the very beginning of the symphony to its final bar, it would be an injustice to the composer, upon a first acquaintance with her work, to offer any technical or academic kind of analysis of its manifold architectural beauties. That there is a uniform bond uniting the four beautiful movements of her work, and a psychological necessity in the symphonic association of its respective entireties, is one of the most masterly achievements that she has accomplished. Beyond this and such other qualities as were unmistakable at its first performance a certain reserve is necessary if we would not lose ourselves in capricious phantasmagoria. While in art and science the creative capacity of woman has arbitrarily been suppressed, and placed at the unjust and humiliating disadvantage of a mere serfdom to man, it is none the less true that in our land of the free her thoughts and feelings, her dearest and most powerful impulses are being permitted to have their full and free play, and that the springtime if not the golden age of their development has at last arrived. Owing to such important testimony in this direction as has been offered by Mrs. H. H. A. Beach, she may quite justly be regarded as an epoch-maker who has broken through old boundaries and presented an enrichment and extension of woman's sphere in art such as has not been surpassed or even equaled by any contemporary of her sex. Summing up her work, the ''Musical Courier'' said: ''Her particular gifts may be found to lie in a spontaneity of inspiration which brings to the subject matter in hand a freshness and originality that stamps each composition an individual masterpiece in its own way.'' All of Mrs. Beach's compositions, 167 in number, include cantatas, anthems, songs and part songs, compositions for piano, a romance for piano and violin, sonata for the same instruments, mass in E flat; ''The Rose of Avontown,'' a cantata for female voices; Gaelic Symphony; ''Festival Jubilate,'' for mixed voices; ''The Minstrel and the King,'' ballad for male voices; ''Sylvania,'' wedding cantata for mixed voices; ''Help Us, O God,'' motet for mixed voices; concerto for piano and orchestra; aria, ''Jephthah's Daughter''; cantatas, ''The Sea-Fairies'' and ''The Chambered Nautilus''; quintet for piano and strings, and Service in A.

DOOLITTLE, Frederick Benjamin, judge, was born at Bovina, Delaware co., N. Y., Dec. 24,

1825, son of William and Polly Ann (Hubble) Doolittle, great-grandson of Abraham and Hepzibah (Tyler) Doolittle, and grandson of Benjamin and Hannah (Kilburn) Doolittle. In 1835 his father removed from New York state to Monroe, Mich., where the son attended school at odd times while assisting to clear up and work the farm. In 1845 he contracted with his father to pay for his ''time,'' obtaining employment in a nearby nursery. By teaching school and practicing frugality he was able within the year to secure a half interest in the nursery, although he was still under legal age. Selling his share in the enterprise he removed to Delhi, Ia., and established the Silver Lake nursery, which became famous not only in the state but throughout the West. This business was the basis of his future success. He invested in choice lands in Easton, Ia., and was soon operating a large number of productive farms, becoming one of the largest land owners in the state. He laid out the town of Delaware in 1860, and succeeded in having it made the junction point of the Illinois Central railroad and the Davenport and St. Paul section, or Calmar branch, as it was known, of the Milwaukee system, when they were being built through the country. The success of the latter was mainly due to the foresight of Mr. Doolittle, for just as the project was being abandoned he immediately organized the Delaware County Construction Co. and built the line. Of this company he became a director and acted as its treasurer for several years. In 1884 he secured control of the Hopkinton Exchange Bank, which became known as the Hopkinton State Bank, and of which he was president until his death. Originally a Whig, he was one of the charter members of the Republican party in this country when it was formed in 1853, but took no active part in political affairs. He was county judge and the first internal revenue collector in his county. With his increasing influence and wealth he was foremost among those who contributed to all worthy objects for the development of the country. He aided liberally in the building of churches, schools, bridges and roads. He was always ready to aid educational objects, and was one of the most generous patrons of Lenox College, Hopkinton, where Doolittle Hall stands on the campus as a permanent testimonial to his interest in education. Judge Doolittle's sturdy honesty and integrity stamped him as a man of the highest character. He had shared with the pioneers in the stress and strain of the hard days, helping his neighbors through all to better things and came to be greatly loved for his fair dealings and justice to all. His success in business, in his real estate undertakings, in his banking enterprise and in his industrial developments made him an honored and respected citizen. Although not a church member he had established for himself a strict code of morals, which he recorded in several small volumes which he published. In ''Thoughts Plucked from Meditation'' (1904) he pointed out the value of creed and character: ''Our characters will be as we build them. Our creeds will be as we adopt them. God does not give us our characters or our creeds. Each individual of necessity builds his own character and may choose his own creed. He may form a creed easy of comprehension. The writer is content with a creed of his own formulating, which consists of only eight syllables, namely: Love and trust God. Love and help man. . . . We cannot divest ourselves of our character. Neither can it be changed, only as we change it by changing our course of action. The spirit with which we meet our experiences in this life determines our character, whether it be good or whether it be bad. The character we develop as we go through life constitutes and is ourselves, our identity as distinguished from others. It cannot be taken possession of by another and substituted as the character of any one else. It is emphatically non-transferable. The character determines our future, both before and after death. No person can avail himself of the merits of another's character. We build our own characters and thereby fix our own destiny.'' Judge Doolittle was married (1) at Dubuque, Ia., Oct. 4, 1851, to Anne, daughter of Thomas Comber of Withyham, England, who died in 1876, leaving six children: Harriet Elizabeth, wife of C. H. Furnam of Delhi; Frederick William, Olie Rosella, wife of C. B. Phelps of Pana, Ill.; John Comber, Nellie Anne, wife of Frank E. Williamson of Hopkinton, and Minnie Augusta, wife of Judge George M. Perry of Texas. He was married again at Delhi, Nov. 25, 1880, to Mrs. Hannah C. Harger. He died in Des Moines, Ia., Nov. 19, 1912.

MASON, Daniel Gregory, musician and author, was born at Brookline, Mass., Nov. 20, 1873, son of Henry and Helen Augusta (Palmer) Mason. His father was a manufacturer of musical instruments, and son of Dr. Lowell Mason (q.v.), the well-known musical educator, and brother of Dr. William Mason (q.v.), the pianist and composer. His mother was the daughter of Asher and Anne (Folsom) Palmer. The family line on the paternal side begins with Robert Mason, born in England about 1590, who came to America in 1630, landing at Salem, Mass., and the line of descent is traced through his son Thomas, who married Margery Partridge; their son Ebenezer, who married Hannah Clark; their son Thomas, who married Mary Arnold; their son Barachias, who married Love Battelle; their son Johnson, who married Caty Hartshorn; and their son Lowell, who married Abigail Gregory, and who was the grandfather of Mr. Mason. Five of these male ancestors in succession lived at Medfield, Mass. Daniel Gregory Mason was educated at Phillips Exeter Academy and at Harvard University (1895), his musical education, begun in childhood, progressing with equal steps under private teachers. After teaching English composition in Harvard College and in Radcliffe College he removed to New York city, and began editing ''Masters in Music,'' a series of monographs issued as a monthly magazine, the first number of which appeared in January, 1903. In 1902 Mr. Mason published ''From Grieg to Brahms'': studies of six composers and their art, undertaking to show ''how each man has brought to his work his own particular temperament and conception of his art, how each has cultivated some special quality of expression or beauty in modern music.'' Dr. Percy Goetschius, the critic, said of it: ''This gifted young author combines most happily the fullest practical insight, as professional musician, into the works of these masters, with the ability of the thoroughbred man of letters to give forcible and fluent expression to his carefully formed opinions of them. This rare combination, to which he adds thoroughly intelligent and impartial judgment, imparts a very peculiar value to his essays.'' Mr. Mason has also written ''Beethoven and His Forerunners'' (1904); ''The Romantic Composers'' (1906); ''The Appreciation of Music'' (with T. W. Surette, 1907); ''A Guide to Music'' (1908); ''The Orchestral Instruments

and What They Do'' (1909); ''A Neglected Sense in Piano Playing'' (1912); and has contributed articles on music to the ''Atlantic Monthly,'' ''Scribner's Magazine,'' ''The Century,'' ''The Outlook,'' and other periodicals. He is recognized as a well-known authority on musical subjects, and has lectured on music at the Harvard Summer School, Chicago University, Columbia University, Brooklyn Institute, and elsewhere. Of his compositions, an ''Elegy'' (1901), for piano, has been played with success by Gabrnowitsch, the Russian pianist, and his violin sonata in C minor has been played by David and Clara Monnes. He is also the composer of other chamber music, various piano pieces and songs. Mr. Mason was married Oct. 8, 1904, to Mary Lord, daughter of Joseph L. Taintor, of South Orange, N. J. Portrait opposite page 167.

MAC EWEN, Walter, artist, was born in Chicago, Ill., Feb. 13, 1860, son of John and Elizabeth (Brannon) MacEwen. His father was a native of Scotland, but resided for some time in Canada, and in 1851 removed to Chicago, Ill., where he became well known as a builder and manufacturer. His mother was a native of Oswego, N. Y. Walter MacEwen was prepared for college at Lake Forest Academy, and in the fall of 1876 entered Northwestern University, Evanston, Ill., but withdrew in the following spring. Having decided upon art as a vocation, he went to Munich, and spent a year in the Royal Academy of Arts in that city. His proficiency was such that at the end of the year he was awarded a silver medal for his work. He was impatient to study painting, but as there was no room for him in the studio of Prof. Dietz, whose instruction he preferred, he began by himself, aided by the friendly criticisms of Frank Duveneck, Frank Currier, David Neal and other American artists residing in Munich. In 1880 he went to Holland, and the somber tones of the Munich school that he had adopted were exchanged for the light and silvery tones of contemporary painters of the Netherlands. In the following year he opened a studio in the village of Hattem, near Zwolle, in the heart of Holland, and nearly every summer since has been spent there. In 1883 he exhibited in the International Exhibition at Munich, and in the same year revisited the United States, taking a collection of some fifty finished works and studies, which were placed on view at the Stevens Art Gallery, Chicago, and the St. Botolph Club, Boston. Since 1885 he has contributed regularly to the Paris Salon, and in 1881 he removed to that city, where he became the friend and pupil of Ferdinand Cormon and Tony Robert Fleury. Among his principal works are ''Returning from Labor'' and ''Judgment of Paris'' (1886), the latter receiving honorable mention at the Salon, and eventually being hung in the Munger collection in the Chicago Institute; ''Ghost Story'' (1888); ''Dutch Children'' (1889), now in the collection of Potter Palmer, Chicago; ''The Absent One on All Souls' Day'' (1890), now in the Museum of Liege, Belgium; ''The Sisters'' (1891), Museum of Magdeburg, Prussia; ''The Witches'' (of Salem, Mass.), 1892; ''The Madeleine'' (1894), collection of James Deering, Chicago; ''Dutch Family'' (1895) and ''Two Friends,'' the former purchased by the Belgian government for the Museum at Brussels; ''Sunday in Holland'' (1895); ''Pieter Van Wint'' (1899), and ''A Study'' (1900). The following honors have been conferred upon him: Second medal, Universal Exposition, Paris, 1889, making

F. B. Doolittle

DANIEL G. MASON
MUSICIAN

WALTER MacEWEN
ARTIST

CHARLES C. BEAMAN
LAWYER

JAMES D. SMITH
BANKER

him "hors concours"; silver medal, London (1890); large gold medal of city of Berlin, given by the emperor in 1891, for his "Portrait of a Lady" and "At the Burgomaster's"; medal (builders), Columbian Exposition, Chicago (1893); medal of honor (grand prize), Universal Exposition, Antwerp (1894); medal of honor, Winter Exhibition, San Francisco (1894); gold medal, Munich (1897); cross of the Legion of Honor (chevalier's cross), (1896). In 1892 MacEwen painted two large canvases, "Music" and "The Textiles," for the corner pavilion of the Liberal Arts Building at the Columbian Exposition, Chicago, and also served on the French advisory committee and jury for that exposition, thereby placing himself out of the competition for awards in 1893. In 1895-96 he painted nine large panels and a number of small ones for the hall of heroes in the Library of Congress, Washington, the subjects being taken from Greek mythology. Mr. MacEwen was married Feb. 8, 1899, to Mary Ward, widow of Robert Graham, and daughter of Gen. John Hobard Ward, all of New York city.

BEAMAN, Charles Cotesworth, lawyer, was born at Houlton, Aroostook co., Me., May 7, 1840, son of Charles Cotesworth and Mary Ann (Stacy) Beaman. His first paternal American ancestor was Gamaliel Beaman, who came to this country from England in 1635, at the age of twelve, and lived at Dorchester, Mass. From Gamaliel Beaman and his wife, Sarah Clark, the line of descent is traced through their son John and his wife, Priscilla Thornton; their son John and his wife, Abigail ————; their son John and his wife, Susanna Holland; their son Joseph and his wife, Hannah Knight; and their son Ephraim and his wife, Rebecca Greenleaf, who were the grandparents of the subject of this sketch. Charles Cotesworth Beaman, Sr. (1799-1883), was a Congregational minister. His son was fitted for college at Smithfield Seminary, Scituate, R. I., and was graduated at Harvard College in 1861, and after serving three years as principal of the Marblehead (Mass.) Academy he entered the Harvard Law School. Because of the depredations of the so-called "Confederate cruisers" the subject of neutrality and the rights of belligerents was much mooted at that time. In the northern states discussion was rife, and feeling ran high regarding the alleged violation of neutrality by Great Britain in respect to such vessels. Young Beaman was much interested in the subject, and at the end of his first year he received a "Bowdoin prize" for an essay on "The Rights and Duties of Belligerent Vessels in Neutral Waters." An article by him on "International Arbitration," which appeared in the "North American Review" in 1866, attracted much attention, and as a result of this, and brilliancy in the law school, Prof. Theophilus Parsons of that school recommended him to Charles Sumner, then U. S. senator from Massachusetts, and chairman of the senate committee on foreign relations. Mr. Beaman accordingly left Harvard in the fall of 1865 to become Senator Sumner's private secretary and also clerk of the senate committee on foreign relations. Before going to Washington he was admitted to the bar of Massachusetts. In 1867 he began the practice of law in New York city, and within a very few years won a position of marked prominence in his profession. He was appointed examiner of claims in the state department in Washington in November, 1871, but resigned in the following January to become solicitor for the United States

before the Arbitration Tribunal at Geneva, Switzerland. Following the decision of the court, his work in the presentation of Alabama claims at Washington involved various new, delicate and important questions of maritime and international law, which he disposed of with consummate skill. In 1871 he had published a book entitled "National and Private Alabama Claims and Their Amicable Settlement," which was pronounced one of the most searching and comprehensive studies of the subject that was ever written. In 1873 Mr. Beaman formed a partnership in New York city with Edward N. Dickerson, one of the ablest patent lawyers in the United States. During this association he was actively engaged in conducting much difficult and important patent litigation in the federal courts, and displayed a complete mastery of that peculiarly specialized branch of his profession. In 1879 he became a member of the law firm of Evarts, Southmayd & Choate. On the retirement of Mr. Southmayd, in 1884, the style of the firm became Evarts, Choate & Beaman, and Mr. Beaman remained a member of it until his death. His work during the twenty-one years he was connected with this firm was very laborious. He was counsel for several railroads and a great number of large financial, commercial and manufacturing firms and corporations, and while his practice was general he was especially learned in maritime and international law. He seldom appeared as an advocate in court, acting rather as counsel and adviser to his clients, whom he invariably served with conscientious fidelity. For many years Mr. Beaman was actively interested in the civic welfare of his city and state, being one of the guiding spirits in the various movements for the abolition of official corruption and the improvement of political conditions, such as the municipal reform campaign in the autumn of 1894, following the disclosures of the Lexow committee, and the reform municipal election campaign of 1897, when Seth Low was first nominated for mayor of New York. In 1900 he was appointed by Gov. Roosevelt on the committee to revise the first charter of Greater New York. In spite of the great pressure of his arduous professional duties, and notwithstanding his failing strength, he devoted much time and energy to this, his last important work, and aided largely in the preparation of the committee's report, which was signed and filed two weeks before his death. Though a well-known member of the best clubs in the city, Mr. Beaman was not a club man. He spent little time in any of them except in performance of his duties as an officer. He was president of the Harvard Club of New York in 1882, president of the New England Society in 1897, and president of the University Club in 1900. To prove humorously that he was a real, all-round New Englander, he would say, "I was born in Maine, fitted for college in Rhode Island, went to college and taught school in Massachusetts, was married in Vermont, have a summer home in New Hampshire, and travel through Connecticut to get there." He had the energy, uprightness, intellectual ability, common sense and sound judgment that distinguish the best New England stock, and in addition he was a most lovable man, with an infinite capacity for making and keeping friends; a warm, tender, generous man, with a cheery nature, a sunny humor and a lively wit. He was devoted to his family— his father and mother, his wife and children. He was always a regular attendant at church, in city and country, and a generous and unfailing contributor to good works. He was a perfect example of the very rare combination of the qualities of lovableness and the qualities of strength. He was married at Windsor, Vt., Aug. 19, 1874, to Hettie Sherman, eldest daughter of William Maxwell Evarts, his associate in business, and had four children: Mary Stacy, Helen Wardner, Margaret and William Evarts Beaman. He died in New York city, Dec. 15, 1900.

SMITH, James Dickinson, banker and broker, was born at Exeter, Rockingham county, N. H., Nov. 24, 1829, son of John and Esther Mary (Woodruff) Smith. He was educated at Wilton (Conn.) Academy, and because of the limited means of his father, who was a clergyman, he had to forego a college education. He began his business career in 1845 as a clerk in a country store at Ridgefield, Conn., where he remained for three years. Removing to New York city, he entered the dry-goods house of Hoyt, Sprague & Smith as clerk and rose to be head cashier. He was a member of the firm of James Low & Co., dry-goods merchants of Louisville, for several years, and in 1867 organized the banking firm of Jameson, Smith & Codding in New York. In 1873 the name was changed to James D. Smith & Co., and as such became recognized as one of the leading financial institutions of that city. Mr. Smith was a member of the New York Stock Exchange, serving as its president in 1886-87, and also for several years a member of the New York Produce Exchange and the Chicago Stock Exchange. He was a director of the Union Pacific, Kansas Pacific, Louisville and Nashville, the New Albany and Chicago railroads, the Panama Railroad, the Pacific Mail Steamship Co., the Atlantic and Pacific Telegraph Co., the Third Avenue Street Railway of New York and other corporations. In addition to his financial interests, Mr. Smith was one of the founders of the Woodlawn Cemetery of New York city, president of the Associated Land Co. of New York and the New England Land Co. of Seattle, Wash. During his last years he resided in Stamford, Conn., where he took an active interest in the welfare of the city and served as its mayor for one term. He was state treasurer of Connecticut, a representative in its legislature and a delegate to several state conventions. In politics he was what was called an "old-line Whig" and later a stanch Republican. He was a member of the New York Yacht Club and commodore from 1881 to 1884, and also vice-commodore of the Brooklyn Yacht Club. He was himself the owner of a fine schooner-rigged yacht, the Viking, 108 feet over all, which twice crossed the Atlantic. He was a member and at one time president of the New York Club, a member of the Union League and Players' clubs and the New England Society of New York city, the New Haven Yacht Club, the Stamford Yacht Club, the Riverside Yacht Club and the Corinthian Yacht Club. Mr. Smith was married Aug. 18, 1857, to Elizabeth Henderson and had two sons and two daughters, only one of whom survived, Helen W., former wife of Homer S. Cummings of Stamford, Conn. He died in Stamford, Sept. 21, 1909. Portrait opposite p. 167.

WALKER, John Baldwin, surgeon, was born in Lodi, N. J., Jan. 16, 1860, son of Rev. Avery Skinner and Rosanna (Baldwin) Walker. He is a descendant of Philip Walker, who came over from England and settled in Rehoboth, Mass., about 1650. Dr. Walker's father was a minister in the Congregational Church. He was prepared for college in Phillips Exeter Academy. After two years at Amherst College he matriculated at Harvard,

and was graduated in 1884 with the degree of A. B. He studied medicine at the Harvard Medical School and after receiving his degree of M. D. in 1888, was house surgeon in the Boston City Hospital for eighteen months. He studied four years at the universities of Vienna, Munich, Heidelberg, Paris and London. Returning to New York in 1893 he was appointed inspector of the New York board of health, holding this position for three years, at the same time serving as instructor in surgery at the New York Post-Graduate Hospital. He then became assistant surgeon in the General Memorial Hospital until 1899. In 1894 he was appointed instructor in surgery at the New York Polyclinic Hospital and assistant surgeon in the Hospital for the Ruptured and Crippled. In 1897 he was appointed instructor of operative surgery at Columbia University. Dr. Walker early became convinced through his surgical work of the need of a large and fully equipped private hospital where special surgical attention and appliances could be provided, and in 1898, with Drs. William T. Bull, Robert F. Weir, Virgil P. Gibney and William M. Polk, he founded the Private Hospital Association, popularly known as "Dr. Bull's Private Hospital." To Dr. Walker's executive ability, as much as to the skill of its staff of eminent surgeons, is due the marked success of this hospital, which has become world-famous for the treatment of surgical cases. In 1899 Dr. Walker was made visiting surgeon to the New York City Hospital, and in 1900 visiting surgeon to Bellevue Hospital. In 1902 he became associate surgeon in the Hospital for the Ruptured and Crippled, and in 1909 he was appointed visiting surgeon. In 1904 he was clinical lecturer on surgery at the College of Physicians and Surgeons; in 1905 he became consulting surgeon to the Manhattan State Hospital, and in 1910 he was made professor of clinical surgery of the College of Physicians and Surgeons. In 1901 he was president of the Harvard Medical Society of New York and councilor of the Harvard Medical Alumni Association; in the same year he became chairman of the surgical section of the New York Academy of Medicine. He is a member of the American Surgical Association, American Medical Association, New York Surgical Society, New York Academy of Medicine, New York State Medical Society, New York County Medical Society, Harvard Medical Society, Therapeutic Club and Physicians' Mutual Aid Association. He is also a member of the New England Society, Sons of the Revolution and the Colonial Wars, and the Brook, Harvard and University clubs. He is the author of numerous surgical monographs on the treatment of cancer and appendicitis. More recently his work and writings have been concerned with the operative treatment of hernia and the modern operative treatment of fractures. He was married June 22, 1910, to Mai Emendorf Hackstaff, granddaughter of Eugene Augustus Hoffman, formerly dean of the General Theological Seminary of New York city.

RICHARDSON, George Francis, lawyer, was born at Tyngsboro, Mass., Dec. 6, 1829, son of Daniel and Hannah (Adams) Richardson. His earliest paternal American ancestor was Ezekiel Richardson, a native of the south of England, who came over with Gov. Winthrop in 1630 and settled at Charlestown, Mass. By a land grant in 1637 he became one of the founders of the town of Woburn, Mass. The line of descent is traced through his son, Josiah, who married Remembrance Underwood; their son, Lieut. Josiah, who married

John B. Walker

GEORGE F. RICHARDSON
LAWYER

JOHN D. LINDSAY
LAWYER

GEORGE H. HALL
ARTIST

WILLIAM S. PORTER
AUTHOR

Mercy Parish; their son, Capt. William, who married Elizabeth Coburn, and their son, Capt. Daniel, who married Sarah Merchant and was the grandfather of the subject of this sketch. On the maternal side George F. Richardson was a direct descendant of the famous Adams family of Massachusetts. His father, his paternal grandfather and great-grandfather were lawyers, and all were natives of Tyngsboro and vicinity. The early education of George F. Richardson was received in the public schools of his native town, and after preparing for college at Phillips Academy, he entered Harvard College and was graduated with the highest honors in 1850. He studied law at the Harvard Law School, being graduated in 1853, taking the first prize of fifty dollars for the best essay. He at once began the practice of his profession in Lowell, Mass. In 1858 he became associated with his brother, Daniel S. Richardson, in a law partnership, succeeding another brother, William A. Richardson, who had accepted the appointment of judge of probate and insolvency of Middlesex county. In politics he was a zealous and leading Republican, as well as an active and strong leader in the Union sentiment in the days preceding the civil war, having already attained considerable prominence as a gifted public speaker and orator. On the day that the Sixth Massachusetts regiment of volunteer infantry was attacked in the streets of Baltimore (April 16, 1861) Mr. Richardson raised the first company of three-year men formed in Massachusetts, which was called the Richardson light infantry. Subsequently the company became the Seventh Massachusetts battery of light artillery and was destined to participate in some of the most notable engagements of the war. By a remarkable coincidence all three of the Richardson brothers were elected president of the common council of the city of Lowell in succession. George Francis Richardson was president in 1862-63. He was in the board of city aldermen in 1864, and in 1867 was elected mayor of Lowell, serving two terms. He was a delegate to the Republican national convention that nominated Gen. Grant for the presidency in 1868 and was a member of the state senate in 1871-73, where he made a brilliant record. He also served four years as a member of the Lowell school board, and was chairman during two years. No man was more active than he in the duties of good citizenship or more alive to the honor, welfare and development of the city. He had a brilliant political career, being gifted with the traits that are essential for success in an executive position, but he preferred the active practice of law to the alluring fields of political preferment or the dignity of the bench. He became one of the most successful and influential lawyers of Middlesex and Essex counties, and he practiced also before all the higher courts, including the supreme court of the United States. In 1903 failing health obliged him to relinquish his services to the most notable clientele in northeastern Massachusetts. He was president of the Prescott National Bank of Lowell, director of the Traders' and Mechanics' Insurance Co. of Massachusetts, president of the Lowell Bleachery Co., of the Stony Brook Railroad Co., the Vermont and Massachusetts Railroad Mechanics' Association and of the Lowell Manufacturing Co. Mr. Richardson was distinctly a man of cultured attainments, a gifted student of literature and a lover of travel and the fine arts. He had one of the best private collections of Shakespeare in America, and his library was rich in all of the English classics. In his defence of Shakespeare against those who attacked the authorship of his plays, Mr. Richardson showed himself a master of literature as well as of forensic composition. He was a delightful host and a most entertaining conversationalist, while his brilliant public addresses were filled with graceful and intellectual culture. His admirable oration upon the occasion of President Grant's visit to Lowell was regarded as a classic and brought much honor to the city. A marked trait of character was his keen sense of honor and his sturdy integrity. He was a member of the Yorick and the Lowell Country clubs and the University Club of Boston. He was married in Lowell, June 8, 1854, to Caroline Augusta, daughter of Ransom Reed, and had one daughter, Marietta, who was the wife of Herbert Jefferson. Mr. Richardson died in Lowell, Mass., March 22, 1912.

LINDSAY, John Douglas, lawyer, was born in New York city, Dec. 31, 1865, son of William F. and Sarah (Vrendenburg) Lindsay. His first American ancestor was Christopher Lindsay, a native of Scotland and grandson of Robert Lindsay of Pitscottie, the chronicler. Christopher Lindsay came over in 1630, settling first at Salem, Mass., and subsequently removing to Lynn, where his sons, John and Eleazer, built a house which remained in the family for seven generations, and where Mr. Lindsay's father was born in 1826. The line of descent from Christopher Lindsay is traced through his son Eleazer, who married Sarah Ally; their son Ralph, who married Sarah Breed; their son Eleazer, who married Lydia Farrington; their son Daniel, who married Deborah Ingalls; and their son John, who married Lucy Nourse and was Mr. Lindsay's grandfather. The subject of this sketch was educated in the public schools of New York, and studied law at the New York University. He was a law clerk in the office of Van Dyke & Van Dyke—later Lord, Van Dyke & Lord—in 1880, and after remaining with them two years entered the district attorney's office as a clerk. He was later put in charge of what was known as the indictment bureau of the office and thus obtained valuable experience in law practice and procedure, which greatly benefited him in the years to come. He was admitted to the New York bar in February, 1887, and in the following June was appointed a deputy assistant district attorney. He became assistant district attorney in 1893 and held that office till January, 1898, when he resigned to become a member of the firm of Nicoll, Anable & Lindsay. In 1907 the firm was changed to Nicoll, Anable, Lindsay & Fuller. For many years Mr. Lindsay has taken a deep interest in the welfare of children. He was elected president of the New York Society for the Prevention of Cruelty to Children on Jan. 1, 1903, a position he still occupies, and two years later became vice-president of the American Humane Association. During the past six years he has served as chairman of the committee on legislation for children of the New York state convention of societies for the prevention of cruelty. He is also a member of the New York Child Welfare Committee. Mr. Lindsay is the author of a number of articles on various subjects contributed to the magazines, the most prominent of which are: ''Extradition in the American Colonies Prior to the Revolution,'' ''History of the Court of Star Chamber,'' and ''An Account of the Boston Massacre.'' He is a member of the American Bar and New York State Bar associations, the Association of the Bar of the City of New York, the American Society of International Law, the American Institute of Criminal Law and Criminology, the American Association for the Advancement of Science, the Society of Medical Jurisprudence, the St. Nicholas Society, the New York Historical Society, the Sons of the Revolution, the Society of Colonial Wars, the Scottish Text Society, and the Manhattan and Calumet clubs of New York, and the Fort Orange Club of Albany. Mr. Lindsay was married in St. Louis, Mo., June 3, 1895, to Stella, daughter of Dr. Elisha Hall Gregory.

HALL, George Henry, artist, was born in Manchester, N. H., Sept. 21, 1825, son of Patten and Parthenia (Coburn) Hall, grandson of John and Mary (Petter) Hall, and a descendant of Thomas and Mary (Dickey) Hall, who came to America in 1718 with a colony from Londonderry, in the north of Ireland, settled on land granted them in New Hampshire, which they named Londonderry, and which was afterward divided into four towns, one of which is Manchester. His father was a ship-timber merchant, who removed with his family to Boston in 1829, where George H. Hall attended the grammar school. At the age of sixteen he began his career as an artist. In 1849 he went to Germany and studied at Dusseldorf Academy, and afterward in Paris and Rome. On his return to America, in 1852, he made New York his permanent residence. He made many trips to Europe, where he found most of his subjects, particularly in Italy and Spain, and also Egypt. The more noted of his paintings are: "The April Shower" (1854); "The Young Lady of Seville and Her Duenna" (1861); "Precious Lading" (1868); "Thursday Fair at Seville" (1869); "The Four Seasons" (1871); "Graziella" (1873); "Roman Fountain" (1874); "A Rug Bazaar at Cairo" (1877), in the Metropolitan Museum; "Luna" and "Nymph of the Blue Grotto" (1886); "Pomegranates and Grapes" and "Ovens at Pompeii" (1887); and "Shakespeare," in the Shakespeare Memorial Gallery in Stratford-on-Avon (1900). Although influenced by the work of Washington Allston, Mr. Hall's style was pre-eminently his own, suggesting the Venetian school of the Renaissance. Color was as fascinating to him as music to its votaries. His fruit compositions are translucent with harmonious color, and the dusky beauty of dark-eyed Italian or Spanish maidens glows upon his canvases, while his studies of scenes in southern Europe are radiant with warmth, light and color. There is nothing American in his work, although the artist was strongly American in his feelings. He slighted no detail, and painted with softness and precision, not for the sake of finish but wholly to embody the beauty of color and form that impressed him in nature. He was painstaking and conscientious, and was unsparing in his efforts to paint his pictures as he thought they ought to be. He did not attempt to follow the cult that arose long after his style was fixed, holding that brushwork was all and detail nothing. Mr. Hall was elected a member of the National Academy in 1868. In his will he left $15,000 to Columbia University. He was unmarried, and died in New York, Feb. 17, 1913. Portrait opposite page 169.

PORTER, William Sydney ("O. Henry"), author, was born at Greensboro, N. C., Sept. 11, 1862, son of Algernon Sydney and Mary Jane Virginia (Swain) Porter, of English extraction. A great-uncle, David L. Swain, was governor of North Carolina. His father was a practicing physician and a man of culture and refinement. His mother dying in his boyhood, he went to live with an aunt, Miss Evelina Porter, who was a school teacher in Greensboro, and who directed his edu-

cation. He was very studious and fond of reading and his literary ability manifested itself at an early age. While working in his uncle's drug store, between the age of sixteen and nineteen, he would entertain the townspeople by reading stories and plays of his own composition and by drawing clever caricatures of the people he met. Because of poor health he was sent to a ranch in Texas, where he lived for two and a half years, and then joined the staff of the Houston (Tex.) "Post." A year later he purchased Brann's "Iconoclast," which he published as a weekly story paper, later changing its name to the "Rolling Stone." As publisher of the "Rolling Stone" he wrote most of the paper and did all the illustrating. Copies of this interesting publication that have been preserved show considerable humor in their composition and a decided talent for caricature in their illustrations. He spent a year or more on a banana plantation in Central America, was employed in a drug store at Austin, Tex., for a time and then went to New Orleans, La., having by this time decided to make literature his life work. He encountered the usual difficulties of the young author in securing acceptance of his stories, and it is said that "The Emancipation of Billy," one of the very best stories he ever wrote, was rejected thirteen times. But whenever a manuscript was returned he would put it in a new wrapper and send it off again to another publisher, and in the end they were all accepted. He never wrote a story that was not accepted sooner or later. As soon as he became known his reputation grew quickly, so that in his later years he was perhaps more in demand than any contemporary writer and magazine editors were glad to take his stories at his own price. Subsequent to 1901, especially after he settled in New York, he contributed voluminously to current periodicals under the pseudonym of "O. Henry." Many of these stories have been republished in book form under the following titles: "Cabbages and Kings" (1905), "The Four Million" (1906), "The Trimmed Lamp" (1907), "The Heart of the West" (1907), "The Voice of the City," "The Gentle Grafter," "Roads of Destiny" and "Let Me Feel Your Pulse" (1910). At the time of his death he was at work on a play entitled "The World and the Door." Since his death a uniform edition of his writings has been issued. They cover a wide variety of subjects and phases of life. They are a broad "comedie humaine" in as real a sense as are the novels of Balzac. His stories of New York and of the West have a distinctly local flavor, but there is not one of them in which the removal of that local flavor would seriously detract from its value as a human document. O. Henry was probably the greatest master of the short story that America has produced with the possible exception of Poe. He has been frequently called the "American Maupassant," but whatever his final place in literature he is too big to pass current as an edition of any one else. The designation is not fair to him; nor is it fair to Maupassant. The two had very little in common. Both, indeed, were masters of short story technique and of terse and poignant expression. Both had the strong dramatic sense and a deep psychological insight, but O. Henry did not possess the intense power and passion of the French master, nor could he sound so strongly the deep notes of tragedy. He was more sane and kindly and had more humor and sympathy. Both O. Henry and Maupassant were clear-seeing realists, but the former saw with a much more cheerful and less jaundiced eye. The two men indeed possessed totally opposite view points. Maupassant lifted the veil from romance and showed the stark reality beneath it; O. Henry lifted the veil from stark reality and showed the romance beneath it. One might say that the brain of Maupassant dictated the Frenchman's stories and the heart of O. Henry the American's. The latter has sympathy, the sympathy which not only understands but feels with the tragic comedy of human life, its humor and its pathos. "Humor," said Hildegarde Hawthorne, in the New York "Times," "was the solvent with which this man worked—Humor and his twin, Pathos, between which lies the very breath of life. His style was perfect and it was the man himself; nervous, picturesque, quick, supple, with easy, inevitable metaphors. His dialogue is extraordinarily vivid—the pathos of the pavement and the plains, the slang of the Rialto and the race-courses, the jargon of the drummer, the argot of the newspapers—all were alike furniture to O. Henry, and familiar he made them each to each; for the American world meets in his pages and grows to know itself better in a handful of his stories than in all the drawing-rooms, playhouses and salons of the three great cities of the continent. Porter was twice married, first, in 1887, to Athol Estis, of Texas, by whom he had one daughter, Margaret Porter, and second, on Nov. 27, 1907, to Sara Lindsay, daughter of Thaddeus Coleman, of Asheville, N. C. He died in New York city, June 5, 1910. Portrait opposite page 169.

BENTON, Guy Potter, twelfth president of the University of Vermont (1911—), was born at Kenton, O., May 26, 1865, son of Daniel Webster and Harriet (Wharton) Benton. He was educated at the Ohio Normal University, Ohio Wesleyan University, Baker University and University of Wooster. During 1890–95 he was superintendent of city schools at Fort Scott, Kan., and in 1895–96 was assistant state superintendent of public instruction for Kansas. In 1896 he was called to the chair of history and sociology in Baker University, and remained there until 1899, when he became president of the Upper Iowa University, at the same time being made a member of the state board of education. In 1902 he was elected the twelfth president of Miami University, which position he held until 1911. In July, 1911, he became president of the University of Vermont. He was M. E. clergyman, lecturer and member of the Ohio conference of college deans, and president, 1903–05; chairman committee from Ohio College Association on an educational policy for Ohio, 1904–05; president Educational Society of Cincinnati Conference M. E. S. Church, 1904–05; president Ohio conference of college presidents and deans, 1906; president Ohio Young Men's Christian Association, 1909–10; secretary National Association of State Universities since 1910. The degree of LL.D. was conferred upon him by Upper Iowa University in 1906 and by the University of Vermont in 1911. He is the author of "The Real College" (1903). He is a member of the Phi Delta Theta, Phi Beta Kappa and Tau Kappa Alpha. The degrees of A.M. and D.D. have been conferred upon him. He has been ordained as a Methodist Episcopal clergyman, and is well known as a lyceum lecturer. He was married at Arcadia, Kan., Sept. 4, 1889, to Dolla Konantz.

LeMOYNE, Francis Julius, physician, was born in Washington, Pa., Sept. 4, 1798, son of Dr. John Julius and Nancy (McCully) LeMoyne. His father left France at the beginning of the French revolution in 1790 and settled at Gallipolis, O., and from there removed to Washington, Pa.

The son was graduated at Washington College in 1815 and received his medical degree at the University of Pennsylvania in 1823. While conducting a general practice he interested himself in education, abolition and other reforms. He was one of the founders of the female seminary at Washington in 1836 and after the civil war he established a normal school for negroes at Memphis, Tenn. Becoming convinced that cremation was the proper and sanitary disposition of the dead, he offered to build a crematory in the Washington cemetery. His offer being declined, he built one on his own ground in 1876, which was the first and only crematory in the United States until 1884. Dr. LeMoyne was married in May, 1823, to Madelain R. Bureau, whose parents were also members of the French colony in Gallipolis, O. He died in Washington, Pa., Oct. 14, 1879. His remains were cremated.

DOWLING, Austin, Roman Catholic bishop of Des Moines, was born in New York city, April 16, 1868, son of Daniel and Mary (Santry) Dowling. His father was a native of Queens county, Ireland, and his mother of England. He obtained his early education in Newport and New York and was graduated at Manhattan College in New York in the class of 1887 and at the Catholic University in Washington, D. C., in 1892. Having prepared for holy orders, he was ordained to the priesthood in 1891 in Providence, R. I. He afterwards filled several pastorates and through the steps of orderly progression advanced in ecclesiastical work until on Apr. 25, 1912, he was created bishop of the diocese of Des Moines, at Providence, R. I. With his removal to the city he took up the study of the conditions of the church in Iowa, and has been active in systematizing and directing its interests and extending the influence of Catholicism in the state.

SCHULER, Anthony Joseph, first Roman Catholic bishop of the diocese of El Paso, Tex., was born at St. Mary, Pa., in 1869, son of Joseph and Albertina Schuler. His father, who was a miner, moved to Colorado in 1876, settling in Georgetown with his wife and six children. He was killed by an accident in a mine when the future bishop was still a boy just old enough to begin to try to support his mother by working as a miner and a clerk. Unable to go to school he studied at night under the direction of his pastor, the subsequent Bishop Matz, of Denver. In January, 1886, young Schuler joined the Jesuit order, entering the novitiate at St. Louis, Mo. After following the usual courses of study and teaching required by the rules of the order, he was ordained to the priesthood in 1901. In 1903 he was appointed president of the Sacred Heart College, Denver, Colo., and held that office for three years, at the end of which returning to St. Louis to make his final studies. He then went back to Denver, and in 1907 was sent to El Paso, Tex., as assistant to the rector of the Church of the Sacred Heart there. Two years later he was made its rector. The new diocese of El Paso was created in April, 1914, to be composed of two counties, El Paso and Culberson, taken from the diocese of Dallas, thirteen counties, Presidio, Jeff Davis, Beeves, Brewster, Terrell, Ector, Andrews and Gaines from the diocese of San Antonio, and Grant, Luna, Dona Ann, Otero, Eddy and a portion of Sierra, New Mexico, from the diocese of Tucson. The Rev. J. J. Brown, S. J., president of the Sacred Heart College, Denver, and superior of the New Mexico-Colorado Mission of the Jesuit order, was appointed first bishop of the diocese. The rules of the order forbid its members to accept any high office or preferment, except at the express command of the Pope, and Father Brown declined the bishopric. It was then given to Father Schuler, and he was consecrated by Archbishop Pitaval in the Denver Cathedral, Oct. 28, 1915. El Paso, the fifth Catholic diocese in Texas, has a Catholic population of about 65,000, with thirty-one priests, 125 churches, missions and stations; thirteen schools and academies with 2,135 pupils and three hospitals. Communities of Sisters of Mercy, Sisters of Charity, Sisters of St. Francis and of Loretto teach the schools and manage the hospitals.

HARRISON, Ross Granville, anatomist, was born in Germantown, Philadelphia, Pa., Jan. 13, 1870, son of Samuel and Katherine (Diggs) Harrison. He was graduated at Johns Hopkins University in 1889 and received the degree of Ph.D. in 1894. His doctorate in medicine was secured at the University of Bonn, Germany, in 1899. In 1894 he became lecturer on morphology in Bryn Mawr College, and two years later, instructor and associate in anatomy in John Hopkins University, a position he held until 1899 when he was advanced to the rank of associate professor. In 1897 he was called to the chair of comparative anatomy at Yale, where he has since remained. The results of his scientific investigations, which are largely on the structure and development of animals, and especially the development of the nervous system, have been recorded in papers on "The Growth and Regeneration of the Tail of the Frog Larva" (1898); "The Occurrence of Tails in Man" (1901); "Ueber die Histogense des Peripheren Nervensystems bei Salmo Salmar" (1901); "Further Experiments on the Development of Peripheral Nerves" (1906); and "The Development of the Peripheral Nerve Fibers in Altered Surroundings" (1910). One of his most important papers was "Observations on the Living, Developing Nerve Fibre" (1907), in which it was shown for the first time that cells would undergo normal differentiation when removed from the body and cultivated in nutrient media. He read a paper, "The Cultivation of Tissues in Extraneous Media as a Method of Morphologic Study," before the American Association of Anatomists in 1911, in which he pointed out that the importance of such experiments rests on the fact that thus the means are afforded of observing the activities of cells and studying the conditions which influence these activities. In addition to his researches as indicated by the titles of the papers mentioned, he has been managing editor of "The Journal of Experimental Zoology" since 1903. He has been a trustee of the Marine Biological Laboratory, Woods Hole, Mass., since 1908. Dr. Harrison was president of the American Association of Anatomists in 1911–13 and the American Society of Naturalists in 1912–13 and is a fellow of the American Association for the Advancement of Science and member of the American Philosophical Society and the National Academy of Sciences.

MICHAEL, Arthur, chemist, was born in Buffalo, N. Y., Aug. 7, 1853, son of John and Clara Michael. After attending private and public schools in Buffalo, he spent the years 1872–74 at the University of Heidelberg, where he came under the influence of the famous Bunsen, then at the zenith of his fame. Hoffman, the great teacher of organic chemistry, was in Berlin, and he attended that university during 1875–78, and then spent a year at the Ecole de Medicine, Paris, where he worked in the laboratory of Wurtz. In 1882 he was called to the chair of chemistry at Tufts College, where he remained for seven years. His wife was not only a chemist herself but a specialist in the study of the application of chemistry to plants, and, after a trip around the world, they settled in Bonchurch, England, where, in a well-equipped laboratory, the two devoted their attention to chemical research in organic chemistry. In 1894 he resumed his chair at Tufts College, remaining there until 1907, when he retired and was made professor emeritus. Five years later he accepted a chair of organic chemistry in Harvard University, where he is still engaged in research work. In his earlier researches Prof. Michael largely devoted his attention to the discovery of synthetic reactions, and among these contributions, may be mentioned the work on enthalylacetic acid, the first synthesis of natural glucosides and new reactions with sodium malonic ester and similar compounds. He then published investigations on the structure of sodium acetoacetic ester and its sodium derivative, which have had considerable influence on the recent development of chemical organic theory, and on the configurations of organic substances, in which he proved that the then universally accepted views of wislicenus were untenable. His researches for the last twenty years, for the most part, have been directed towards the elucidation of various points bearing on the fundamental laws and theory of organic chemistry. A summary of this work is given in the papers entitled, "Some New Laws and Their Application in Organic Chemistry" (19—), "Stereoisomerism and the Law of Entropy" (1908), and "Outline of a Theory of Organic Chemistry Founded on the Law of Entropy" (1910). The results of his investigations have appeared chiefly in the Berichte der Deutschen Chemischen Gesellschaft, Annalen der Chemie and the American Chemical Journal. In recognition of his contributions to chemistry, Tufts College conferred upon him the degrees of Ph.D. in 1890, and LL.D. in 1910, and Clark University gave him the degree of LL.D. in 1909. He is a member of various scientific societies both in the United States and abroad, and in 1889 was elected to the National Academy of Sciences. He finds recreation in travel and in the study of oriental pictorial art and old American silver. He was married June, 1888, to Helen C., daughter of James Abbott, of Philadelphia, Pa.

TICKNOR, Howard Malcom, writer and critic, was born in Boston, Mass., July 4, 1836, son of William Davis and Emeline Staniford (Holt) Ticknor. The founder of his family in America was William Ticknor, who came over from Kent, England, in 1656, married Hannah Stockbridge and settled at Scituate, Mass. From him the line of descent is traced through his son William, who married Lydia Tilden and settled in Connecticut; their son John, who married May Bayley; their son Elisha, who married Deborah Davis and removed to New Hampshire; their son William, who married Betsey Ellis, and their son William Davis Ticknor (q.v.), the father of our subject. The latter was the founder of the well-known book publishing firm of Ticknor & Fields, and was a friend of Nathaniel Hawthorne and most of the great writers of his time. Howard M. Ticknor received his early education at Chauncey Hall School in Boston, and was graduated at Harvard College in 1856. He lived for some time in Italy, studying vocal music and languages and acting as vice-consul in Rome, Naples and Venice, as well as correspondent for a number of English and American newspapers. One of his assignments was reporting the opening of the Suez canal for the New York "Times." He was appointed, with James

Howard M. Ticknor

Russell Lowell, as assistant editor of the "Atlantic Monthly" and edited "Our Young Folks" from the time that magazine was started until 1869. During 1878-87 he was instructor in elocution at Harvard and Brown universities and at a number of preparatory schools. While in Boston he was connected at various times with nearly every newspaper in the city as dramatic and musical critic. "Mr. Ticknor," said a writer, "wrote for many years with vigor and taste on dramatic and musical subjects. His education had been broad and his acquirements were varied. He had a wide knowledge of the literature of several countries; he had lived abroad in an atmosphere of art, of elocution and song; he had heard the most distinguished singers and virtuosi of the opera house and grand concert hall; he had seen the famous tragedians and comedians of forty or more successive years. His critical opinions were therefore something more than the expression of a passing whim or the outburst of one suddenly surprised into admiration or dislike. He believed firmly in canons of art, and his belief was based on a knowledge of accepted rules and approved traditions. At the same time his mind was constantly receptive, and although he would have agreed to the proposition of M. Anatole France that the object of art is beauty, not fixed truth, he would have added that forms and definition of beauty may change with generations. Though his taste was naturally conservative, he was warm in his appreciation of strength and beauty whenever he found it expressed in stage situation or dialogue, or in music by a modern without regard to the nationality of this modern. His articles were written apparently with great care, as though for a review rather than a journal, yet he was an uncommonly rapid writer. His mind was richly stored and even a dull play or a concert of mediocre interest was full of suggestion to him. One thought led quickly to another; there were apt comparisons, pertinent reminiscences, illustrative digressions, so that the article written easily and at one breath, in what Mr. Clement Scott called the red-pepper hour of journalism, when read the next morning, was found to be sound and scholarly, readable and helpful. His criticism was not merely destructive; he would censure a reading, an interpretation that seemed to him unwarrantable or false, and then he would suggest one by which the actor or musician would make a more striking or more legitimate effect. His style had the measured tread, the sonorous cadence, the verbal elegance of the older school of writers who did not believe that literature and journalism were necessarily irreconcilable terms." Mr. Ticknor was a member of the St. Botolph Club of Boston. He was married in Franklin, Mass., Feb. 2, 1864, to Helen Frances, daughter of Simeon Partridge Adams, of Franklin, Mass. He died in San Francisco, Cal., May 13, 1905.

FLOYD, Edward Elbridge, merchant, was born at Charlestown, Mass., Jan. 27, 1834, son of Daniel and Catherine (Poor) Floyd and a descendant of Capt. John Floyd (1636-1701), a planter of Rumney Marsh (now Revere), Mass., and an officer in King Philip's and King William's wars. He attended the old "Training Field School" at Charlestown and expected to go to prepare for the medical profession at Harvard College, but the early death of his father, leaving a large family with small means, forced him to abandon this ambition. At the age of sixteen he entered the employ of Clark, Sweet & Co., dry-goods commission merchants of Boston. His advancement was rapid, and about 1862 he was made a member of the firm, which became known as Clark, Holbrook & Floyd. Associated with him in this firm, at one time or another, were James W. Clark, Edwin W. Holbrook and C. D. Newell. In 1868 the older partners withdrew, and Edward E. Floyd and a younger brother, Charles O. Floyd, succeeded the old firm under the name of Floyd Brothers & Co. This firm was one of the largest wholesale dry-goods commission houses in Boston. It also had a place of business in Chicago, which was the headquarters for the Western trade, and another at New York. Mr. Floyd was the active head of this firm until his death, when its affairs were wound up by his executors. He was frequently in Europe in the interests of the firm, and owing to his reputation for integrity and business ability, was offered many positions of trust and responsibility, few of which he accepted. He was always interested in military affairs and served in the "Washington Home Guard" at Cambridge during the civil war, and later was for nine years in the first corps of cadets, Boston's crack militia organization. Mr. Floyd was a director of the Shoe and Leather National Bank, the Manufacturers' National Bank, the executive committee of the Boston Board of Trade and the Westchester Fire Insurance Co., president of the Iron Railroad Co., the New England Street Railway Co., and president, vice-president and director of the Boston Land Co. He was also a member of the Apollo Club and the Boston Art Club, fellow of the American Geographical Society and a vestryman of St. Paul's Church, Brookline, Mass. He was married Feb. 11, 1858, to Mary J., daughter of Col. Aaron Spaulding, of Greenfield, Mass. She died in 1873 and he was married again at Longwood, Mass., June 6, 1877, to Lisbeth H., daughter of Rufus H. Whitney, of Westboro and Boston, who survive him. His death occurred at York, Me., where he was spending the summer, Aug. 28, 1904. Portrait opposite p. 174.

CAULDWELL, William Al Burtis, merchant, was born in New York city, May 21, 1827, son of Ebenezer and Maria (Al Burtis) Cauldwell, and grandson of Cornelius Cauldwell, a merchant of Birmingham, England, who came to America in 1805 and opened a crockery store in New York city. Ebenezer Cauldwell continued in his father's business and was successful throughout a career of seventy years, during which his name was a synonym for commercial integrity. The son was educated privately and entered Columbia College, but on account of failing health was compelled to forego a college education. After a trip to Europe he entered his father's crockery business and was made a partner upon reaching his majority. Under his management the firm of E. Cauldwell & Son gained the reputation of being the foremost in its line in the United States. Mr. Cauldwell was a man of the strictest integrity, whose upright business principles added to the honor of the firm throughout his whole career. An instance of this high moral integrity is in strange contrast to the methods recently disclosed in the public press of certain importing houses. An invoice of china was received through the custom house and the duties were paid according to the invoice, but upon opening the boxes Mr. Cauldwell found that there were many more goods than the bills called for. He immediately made a memorandum of the unlisted articles and taking it to the custom house paid the additional duties. He retired from active business life in 1880, and thereafter devoted a large portion of his time to religious and benevolent work, principally in connection with the Baptist Church, of which he was a prominent member. It was said of him that no one man, minister or layman, had exercised so large and helpful an influence on Baptist history in New York city as he. The sixteen church edifices, built by the society during his lifetime, were in a large measure the crystallization of his thought, and they remain a most fitting and enduring monument to his memory. In the New York City Mission he was for twenty-two years a leading counselor in all its varied operations, and to its financial management he gave the full benefit of his ripe business judgment and experience. He was for thirteen years superintendent of the Sunday-school of Calvary church; he was a member of the advisory board of the Young Women's Christian Association and the Ladies' Christian Union and was one of the incorporators of the Industrial Christian Alliance. Mr. Cauldwell was a man of varied talents and of literary and poetic taste. He was the author of a number of hymns, the most popular of which are ''Trust,'' ''Mark the Lilies,'' ''Reliance'' and ''Earth is Bound with Icy Chains.'' The versatility of his talents was further shown in his mathematical attainments and his architectural gifts, which were of a high order. He was married Jan. 11, 1855, to Elizabeth, daughter of Samuel Milbank of New York, and they had six children: Charles M., Sophie L., Thomas W., Samuel M., George and Caroline B. Cauldwell. He died in New York city, Mar. 13, 1893.

GOODMAN, William Ernest, merchant and soldier, was born in Montgomery county, Pa., Dec. 10, 1838, son of Henry and Maria (Ernest) Goodman. The first of his family in America was Henry Goodman, a native of Germany, who came over at the beginning of the eighteenth century. His grandson bought ''Speedwell,'' located on the famous Limekiln pike beyond Germantown, Philadelphia, which became the family homestead, and where our subject was born. William Ernest Goodman was educated in the schools of Germantown and was graduated at the Boys' Central High School of Philadelphia in 1859. At the outbreak of the civil war he enlisted as a private in the 19th Penn. Volunteer Infantry; subsequently became second and then first lieutenant in the 28th Penn. Infantry; was transferred to the 147th Penn. Infantry, in which he became a captain, and was honorably mustered out of the service in July, 1865. In that year he was brevetted major of U. S. volunteers for gallant and meritorious service during the campaign in Georgia and the Carolinas, and was awarded the congressional medal of honor for rescuing the colors of an Ohio regiment at the battle of Chancellorsville, in which engagement he advanced his men to the line of Confederate skirmishers, captured many prisoners, and was himself wounded. He was one of six brothers, three others of whom also served with distinction in the civil war, and two in California. After the war Maj. Goodman became a member of the Philadelphia firm of Harrington & Goodman, importers and wholesale dealers in tailors' trimmings. The business was founded in 1855 by Thomas N. Dale, but its greatest growth and development dates from 1867, when it was taken over by Messrs. Henry L. Harrington and Samuel Goodman, general partners, and Lucien P. Porter and Henry Goodman (father of Samuel and Maj. William E. Goodman) as special partners. Under this new organization the business increased rapidly until it became probably the largest in its kind in the United States,

with branches in the principal cities throughout the country. Another member of the firm, Joseph E. Goodman, was admitted in 1880. Maj. Goodman retired from active participation in 1910, although remaining as a special partner up to the time of his death. He was succeeded as an active member of the firm by his son, William E. Goodman Jr. Samuel Goodman retired in 1911, and the present senior member of the firm is Joseph E. Goodman, a brother. Maj. Goodman was a member of the military order of the Loyal Legion, the Grand Army of the Republic, Bachelors' Barge Club of Philadelphia, Huntington Valley Country Club, and the Philadelphia Cricket Club of Wissahickon, of which he was a member of the board of governors. Maj. Goodman possessed a wholesome, vivid personality. His was a nature incapable of doing a wrong act; he had a mind that ever thought the best of his fellow-men, and he was deeply beloved for his singularly open and ingenuous character. He was as brave morally as physically and he scorned anything that was unmanly. His love of out-door sports, of golf and cross-country riding, made him a familiar figure in the beautiful country which had been the scene of his birth and entire life. He was married in Philadelphia Oct. 20, 1870, to Sarah I., daughter of Gen. Abercrombie, a graduate of West Point, who fought gallantly in the Indian and other wars. He died in Chestnut Hill, Philadelphia, Mar. 22, 1912, and is survived by his widow, two daughters, Ernestine Abercrombie and Mrs. Samuel Appleton, and one son, William E. Goodman Jr.

HOTCHKIN, Samuel Fitch, clergyman and author, was born at Sauquoit, N. Y., April 2, 1833, son of Beriah Bishop and Elizabeth Alice (Fitch) Hotchkin and a descendant of John Hotchkin, who came to this country from England about the middle of the seventeenth century and settled at Guilford, Conn. He was educated at Middlebury College, Vt., and was graduated at Trinity College, Hartford, Conn., in 1856 and at the General Theological Seminary, New York city, in 1860. In the latter year he was ordained to the deaconate by Bishop Chase of Ohio, and in 1861 was ordained to the priesthood by Bishop Lee of Delaware. He was rector successively of the Church of the Ascension, Claymont, Del.; Calvary and Grace churches, Brandywine Hundred, Del.; Trinity Church, Red Bank, N. Y.; St. John's Chapel, Little Silver, N. Y., and St. Luke's Memorial Church, Bustleton, Philadelphia, Pa., having been rector of the last named for thirty-one years and rector emeritus three years. He was registrar of the diocese of Pennsylvania for over 20 years. He was a copious writer on historical, topographical and religious subjects, his more important publications being ''Ancient and Modern Germantown'' (1887); ''Gazeteer of Pennsylvania'' (1887); ''Mount Airy and Chestnut Hill'' (1889); ''The York Road, Old and New'' (1892); ''Fox Chase and Bustleton'' (1892); ''The Bristol Pike'' (1893); ''The Mornings of the Bible'' (1893); ''Dark Care Lightened'' (1893); ''The Unseen Christ'' (1896); ''Rural Pennsylvania'' (1897); ''The Living Saviour'' (1898); ''A Splendid Inheritance'' (1898); ''Penn's Greene Country Towne'' (1903), and ''The First Six Bishops of Pennsylvania'' (1911). He also contributed over eleven hundred articles upon general topics to religious and secular papers. Mr. Hotchkin was twice married, at Claymont, Del., June 1, 1869, to Sarah Sully, daughter of John R. Neagle, of Philadelphia, Pa., and in Philadelphia, Pa., May 31, 1899, to Helen Nicholson, daughter of Rev.

EDWARD E. FLOYD
MERCHANT

WILLIAM A. CAULDWELL
MERCHANT

WILLIAM E. GOODMAN
MERCHANT

SAMUEL F. HOTCHKIN
CLERGYMAN

Winfield S. Hutchinson

Edmund Roberts. He died at Bustleton, Philadelphia, Pa., Aug. 1, 1912.

HUTCHINSON, Winfield Scott, lawyer, was born at Buckfield, Me., May. 27, 1845, son of Stephen Drew and Mary (Atkinson) Hutchinson. His first American ancestor was Richard Hutchinson, who came from England and settled in Salem village, now Danvers, Mass., in 1634. His son Joseph married Lydia Burton; their son Richard married Rachel Bance; their son Stephen married Abigail Haskins; their son Rev. Joseph married Rebecca Legro, and their son Stephen married Asneth D. Gilbert, and was the grandfather of the subject of this sketch. Winfield S. Hutchinson received his early education in the village schools of Paris, Me., where his family had moved when he was but two years of age. His preparation for college was obtained at Paris Hill Academy, supplemented by two terms at Hebron (Maine) Academy. He entered Bowdoin College in 1864, a year in advance, and was graduated at that institution with high honors in 1867. While attending school he worked as a farmhand, and when but sixteen years of age he began to teach school. During his entire college course he taught schools through his vacations with marked success and was principal of the high school at Brewer, Me., during his junior and senior year. He continued to teach for three and a half years after leaving college, and then entered the law office of Chandler, Thayer & Hudson of Boston in the fall of 1871. He also attended the Harvard Law School, where he was graduated in 1873. His natural fondness and adaptability for teaching led to his connection with the Boston Evening High School. From the time of his admission to the bar, in 1873, Mr. Hutchinson was most closely associated with Hon. Peleg W. Chandler (q. v.), the head of the firm with whom he had studied law, and this close relationship was maintained up to the time of Mr. Chandler's death. In 1889 Mr. Hutchinson began the practice of law in his own name, devoting himself largely to corporation law and acquiring a large clientele in both Boston and New York. In 1892 he accepted an invitation to become connected with the American Bell Telephone Co. in a professional capacity, and discontinued his general legal practice. He was a director of the American Bell Telephone Co., the Central Union Telegraph Co., and the New England Telephone and Telegraph Co., and was at one period vice-president of the Western Telephone and Telegraph Co. He was the first president of the Unitarian Club of Newton, and a member of the Hunnewell, Newton Golf and Tuesday clubs of Newton and the Boston City Club. He was a member of the Alpha Delta Phi and Phi Beta Kappa fraternities and was a Mason. Mr. Hutchinson was a self-made man, who from small beginnings attained a high position in the legal profession through his ability and intellectual attainments. He had marked personal characteristics which commanded great respect in the community in which he dwelt. He saw something good in everybody and in everything. His nature was essentially optimistic, and to his naturally cheerful and sunny disposition was added a keen sense of humor, but the shafts of his fun needed no healing virtues, for they made no wounds. He was married Jan. 1, 1870, to Adelaide L., daughter of James Berry of Brunswick, Me., and had one son, Harold Hutchinson, a graduate of Harvard and a practicing lawyer. He practiced until his death in 1906. Mr. Hutchinson died suddenly in Boston, Mass., Mar. 20, 1911.

CAMPBELL, Richard Orme, mine operator and capitalist, was born at Milledgeville, Ga., Mar. 22, 1860, son of John Bulow and Virginia (Orme) Campbell. The first of his family in America was John Campbell, a native of Scotland, who, with some twenty-four others, received a grant of land in the province of East Jersey, and came to America in the year 1682. He held a prominent position in the colony from the date of his arrival and served as one of the two members of the Court of Common Rights. He was related to the Duke of Argyle. His wife was Mary, and he had a son named John Campbell, whose wife was also named Mary. Mr. Campbell's paternal grandfather was David Crowell Campbell, the editor and proprietor of the "Federal Union" of Milledgeville, Ga., while his maternal grandfather was Richard McAllister Orme, the founder and editor-in-chief of the "Southern Recorder," a Whig newspaper of the same city, and thus the two men were competitors in business and antagonists in politics, but personally they were friendly and belonged to the same church (Presbyterian). Mr. Campbell's education was received in the schools of Atlanta, Ga., to which his parents removed in 1865. He began his career in the coal business in 1885 as an independent dealer, and later organized the R. O. Campbell Coal Co. For more than a quarter of a century his firm was not only the leader among the concerns of its kind in Atlanta, but one of the largest in the South. He was president of the Campbell Coal and Coke Co. of Isoline, Tenn., and Orme, Tenn.; the Campbell Coal Mining Co. of Westbourne, Tenn., and Eagan, Tenn., and the Westbourne Coal Co. of Westbourne, Tenn. He also held large mining interests throughout Kentucky and Tennessee, and was prominently identified with industrial and commercial institutions in Atlanta outside of the coal trade. In business circles his reputation for fairness and honesty was a byword, while the charm of his personality had endeared him to all who knew him. He was identified with the best interests of Atlanta when that city was in the stages of its sturdiest growth, and it was his lovable temperament that grappled to him the host of friends that assisted in making his own career a success. Energetic, resourceful, public-spirited, he was a personal embodiment of that aggressive and co-operative genius that made Atlanta the Empire City of the South. His commercial vision was broad and prophetic and every step of his career was characterized by intuitive wisdom. With his well-rounded personality he comprised that ideal business man and citizen of whom any community is proud and upon whose initiative and integrity it must depend to attain its destiny. His individual creed was that of cheerfulness and sunshine. He was an omen of hope, of inspiration, of confidence in himself, in his friends, in the people among whom his lines were cast. To these qualities he added a gentle modesty and a kindly consideration, tempering all of his relations, on the business or the social side. He was in his prime and just reaching into the meridian of achievement when his death brought a sense of personal sorrow to all of those who were brought into contact with a nature of singular sweetness and unobtrusiveness. He was a member of the B. P. O. Elks and of various social clubs in his home city and in Knoxville and other centers of the coal trade. He was married Apr. 20, 1892, to Harriet Bunn, daughter of Capt. Frederick Davis and Isoline (Minter) Wimberly, of "Inglehurst,"

Twiggs co., Ga. Capt. Wimberly was a member of the 6th Georgia regiment, Confederate army, during the civil war, and his wife was the daughter of William T. Minter and his wife, Susan A. Bell, the former being at one time president of the Selma and Gulf railroad. He was killed in the civil war at the battle of Selma, Ala., and a monument has been erected on the battlefield to his memory. Mr. Campbell died in Atlanta Aug. 7, 1912, and is survived by his widow, one daughter, Isoline Orme, and one son, Richard Orme Campbell, and two brothers, David Crowell and John Bulow Campbell. Portrait opposite page 179.

RICHARDS, Laura Elizabeth, author, was born in Boston, Mass., Feb. 27, 1850, daughter of Samuel Gridley and Julia (Ward) Howe, both of whose biographies may be found in this Cyclopædia. Notwithstanding the many and exacting activities of Dr. and Mrs. Howe, much of their time was devoted to the care and companionship of their children. ''We were not allowed to disturb my mother's study hours, unless there was some good reason,'' said Mrs. Richards, ''but there came a time in the afternoon that was all our own. Then my mother would sit down at the piano and we would all sing and dance together. First we sang, my mother leading, old German student songs, plantation melodies, 'Dearest May,' and the like, and when we could sing no more, the dancing began, my mother playing the most delightful tunes that ever were. And while we were dancing perhaps the door would open, and father came in to join the merry-making; he might come playing bear, wrapped in his great fur coat, growling terribly. That was wonderful fun, for he was the good-natured bear of the fairy stories, and we could climb all over him, and pull him about, and make him dance with us; only when he was tired he said he had 'a bone in his leg' and we would dance no more. They both read aloud to us a great deal, those dear parents. Both read very beautifully; from them we learned to love Shakespeare and Scott and Dickens; and we never can forget how my father read the Bible, in his deep, melodious voice. They made us read aloud, too, and took great pains to make us finish our words, read clearly and with the right emphasis.'' Laura E. Howe was married in 1871 to Henry Richards, of Boston, Mass., and six years later they settled at Gardiner, Me. From an early age she gave evidence of literary talent, making her début as a writer in the pages of the ''St. Nicholas'' soon after her marriage. Since then she has devoted herself to literature, chiefly stories of New England life, and in that department of literature she has few if any rivals. Her work is distinguished by quaint humor, geniality, and boldness of imagination, to which is added the charm of a pure and finished yet extremely simple style. Although delighting in nonsense she never degenerates into slang and her writings for children must be marked among nursery classics. Besides her juvenile work she also contributed to the ''Atlantic,'' ''Century'' and others of the better-class periodicals, a number of poems, chiefly in the ballad style, which have won considerable reputation and are distinguished for their human and chivalrous spirit, indicating that the daughter of a poet and a philanthropist has inherited her father's courage and love of deeds of high daring, together with her mother's poetic faculty. Her first published book was ''Five Little Mice in a Mouse Trap'' (1880), followed by ''Sketches and Scraps, by Papa and Mamma'' (1881), in collaboration with her husband and

illustrated by him for the amusement of their own children. Her other publications are: ''The Joyous Story of Toto'' (1885), ''Toto's Merry Winter'' (1887), the Hildegarde Books (five vols., 1889-97), ''Captain January'' (1890), ''In My Nursery'' (1890), ''Five-Minute Stories'' (1891), ''When I Was Your Age'' (1893), ''Melody'' (1893), ''Marie'' (1895), the Margaret Books (five vols., 1897-1901), ''Rosin the Beau'' (1898), ''Quicksilver Sue'' (1889), ''Geoffrey Strong'' (1901), ''The Hurdy-Gurdy'' (1902), ''Mrs. Tree'' (1902), ''The Golden Windows'' (1903), ''The Green Satin Gown'' (1903), ''More Five-Minute Stories'' (1903), ''The Merryweathers'' (1904), ''Mrs. Tree's Will'' (1905), ''The Armstrongs'' (1905), ''The Piccolo'' (1906), ''The Silver Crown'' (1906), ''Grandmother'' (1907), ''The Wooing of Calvin Parks'' (1908), ''Life of Florence Nightingale'' (1909), ''A Happy Little Time'' (1910), ''Journals and Letters of Samuel Gridley Howe'' (1910), ''Up to Calvin's'' (1910), ''On Board the Mary Sands'' (1911), ''Two Noble Lives'' (1911), a delightful and historically valuable account of the lives of her parents; ''Miss Jimmy'' (1913), and, in collaboration with Maud Howe Elliott, ''Life and Letters of Julia Ward Howe'' (1914). Much of the work of Mrs. Richards is scattered through magazines and school books and has not yet been collected. Her poems have a distinct musical quality which has attracted the attention of many composers and several of them have been set to music. Her literary efforts, however, have not by any means absorbed all her time and energy. Her influence in the life of her home city has been marked, and she has always been ready to lend a hand to all measures for the advancement of its welfare. Mrs. Richards has often given public readings from her own writings, by request, and still lectures on themes of timely interest. She has six children: Alice Maud, Rosalind, Henry Howe, Julia Ward (wife of Carleton Anderson Shaw), John, and Laura Elizabeth (wife of Charles Wiggins). Portrait opposite p. 177.

AMES, Winthrop, theatrical manager, was born at North Easton, Mass., Nov. 25, 1871, son of Oakes Angier and Catharine (Hobart) Ames. He is a descendant of the well-known Ames family of Massachusetts, the founder of which was William Ames, who settled at Braintree, Mass., in 1638. To this family belonged Fisher Ames, the statesman; Nathaniel Ames, the astronomer; Oliver Ames, the inventor and founder of the well-known Ames shovel works; Oliver Ames, president of the Union Pacific railroad, and Oliver Ames, governor of Massachusetts. Oakes A. Ames succeeded his father, Oakes Ames, as president of the Ames shovel company. The subject of this sketch obtained his preliminary education in private schools in Boston, and was graduated at Harvard University in 1895. While at college he devoted particular attention to the study of literature and the drama, and it is said that one of the most successful extravaganzas presented by the Hasty Pudding Club was ''Proserpina,'' written and produced by him in 1894. He took a post-graduate course in the history of the drama and allied subjects at Harvard during 1896. For three years thereafter (1896-99) he was engaged in editing and publishing the ''Architectural Review'' and ''Masters in Art,'' and other architectural publications in Boston. After spending a year abroad devoted to the study of acting and dramatic production in the best theatres of Germany, France and England, he leased the Castle Square Theatre

LAURA E. RICHARDS
AUTHOR

WINTHROP AMES
THEATRICAL MANAGER

HELEN A. KELLER
BLIND DEAF-MUTE

CARL R. GRIMM
ENGINEER

in Boston in partnership with Lorin F. Deland, who was experienced in practical production. Here he presented a variety of plays with a well-trained stock company for a period of four years. He had ambition, however, to create a theatre from the foundation up, which should be the embodiment of the new ideas he had gathered from his studies abroad, so he bought a plot of ground in Boston, and was about to put his plans into execution when the founders of the New Theatre in New York city persuaded him to assume the management of this new enterprise. The New Theatre was the outcome of a movement started by Clarence W. Mackay, J. Pierpont Morgan, William K. Vanderbilt, Archer Huntington, Otto Kahn and other well-known New Yorkers to raise the standard of the American stage. The New Theatre opened Nov. 6, 1909, with Shakespeare's "Antony and Cleopatra." Mr. Ames was its director, assisted by Lee Shubert as business manager. The enterprise attracted widespread attention, and while the theatre only continued for two years, owing to the state of its finances, its influence was widespread. Following in his footsteps there have been similar movements inaugurated in various other Eastern American cities. Mr. Ames followed this achievement by building at his own expense in New York city another playhouse called the Little Theatre to be used for the production of dramas of a type unsuited to larger theatres. The Little Theatre, whose seating capacity is 300, was opened Mar. 11, 1912, with the production of "The Pigeon," by John Galsworthy. Mr. Ames is a Republican in politics, and belongs to the Unitarian Church. He is a member of the Union Club, Harvard Club, Brook Club, University Club, Players' Club and City Club of New York, the Tavern Club, Tennis and Racquet Club and Union Club of Boston. He was married Sept. 28, 1911, to Lucy, daughter of Frederick T. Fuller of South Walpole, Mass., and grandniece of Margaret Fuller Ossoli.

KELLER, Helen Adams, blind deaf-mute, was born at Tuscumbia, Ala., June 27, 1880, daughter of Arthur H. and Kate (Adams) Keller. She is a second cousin of Gen. Robert E. Lee, and is a descendant of Alexander Moore, one of Lafayette's aides, and of Alexander Spotswood, an early colonial governor of Virginia. Her father was a captain in the Confederate army, and her mother was related to the Adams and Everett families of Massachusetts. She was normal at birth, but at the age of nineteen months she contracted a fever which deprived her of sight and the sense of hearing. When she was seven years old, Miss Anne M. Sullivan, a recent graduate of the Perkins Institution for the Blind, where Dr. Samuel G. Howe (q. v.) had done his great work with Laura Bridgeman, was sent to instruct Miss Keller at her home. The task of finding a method of reaching the intelligence of this untrained, sightless, deaf and consequently speechless child was almost hopeless, and Miss Sullivan's success as a teacher must be considered fully as marvelous as the talent of her pupil, whose education is unquestionably the greatest individual achievement in the history of education. Helen Keller and her teacher lived at the Perkins institution in Boston during part of the years 1888-93. In 1890 Miss Sarah Fuller, of the Horace Mann School for the Deaf in Boston, gave her her first lessons in speech. The method she adopted was to pass the child's hand lightly over her own face as she spoke certain words, so that her pupil

could feel the position and movements of her tongue and lips. Miss Keller was eager to imitate every movement, and in an hour's time had learned six elements of speech. She not only learned to read and talk, but became proficient to an exceptional degree in the ordinary educational curriculum. By 1900 she was sufficiently well informed to enter Radcliffe College, and in four years' time she was graduated A.B. *cum laude.* During all this period Miss Sullivan (now Mrs. John Macy) was her constant and devoted companion. She would translate to Miss Keller, by the manual alphabet, the regular class-room lectures, and the latter would write out as much as she remembered on a typewriter. After leaving college she began to write for the leading periodicals on topics relating to the blind and the deaf. She has contributed articles to the leading magazines, and is the author of "The Story of My Life" (1902), which has been translated into fifteen languages; "Optimism" (1903); "The World I Live In" (1908); "The Song of the Stone Wall" (1910); "Out of the Dark" (1913), which both for literary style and outlook on life are a striking revelation of the results of the modern methods of educating those who have been so handicapped by natural disabilities. It was not until the year 1912 that she undertook to speak in public. In that year she astonished a body of physicians in Boston by talking intelligibly in three languages, and after a course of instruction from Prof. Charles White, a teacher of singing at the New England Conservatory of Music, she began to make addresses before the general public. In recent years she has addressed audiences in public, and is now with Mrs. Macy lecturing in all the principal cities of America. She has taken a keen interest in the education and health of others similarly afflicted. She has served on the Massachusetts commission for the blind, and has been a member of advisory boards of various societies for the blind and deaf.

GRIMM, Carl Robert, consulting engineer, was born in Neuwied, Germany, May 3, 1849, son of Johann Philipp and Clementine (Becklind) Grimm. He was graduated at the Royal Preparatory School at Coblenz, Prussia, in 1869, with the highest honors, entitling him to the privilege of entering any polytechnic school in the empire. Upon the outbreak of the Franco-Prussian war, he enlisted in the German army as a volunteer for one year, during which he participated in five battles. In August, 1871, he entered the Polytechnic School at Aachen (Aix-la-Chapelle), where he studied higher mathematics for two semesters. From there he went to the former Gewerbe Akademie in Berlin, taking a course in steam engineering, and at the same time attending lectures at the University of Berlin. He was employed for two years by the German Empire as engineer in the construction of bridges, during which time he made many laboratory tests of the various construction materials. He was two years with the Schichau machine works at Elbing, Prussia, and in 1881 came to the United States, where he believed he would find larger opportunities for the development of his ideas in engineering. He was connected for many years with prominent bridge firms, principally engaged in designing railroad structures, including the Kinzua viaduct on the Erie railroad, one of the highest railroad bridges. In 1890 he moved to Philadelphia, where for three years he had charge of designing, constructing and inspecting the work on the new city hall tower of that city. After having been engineer of the former Elmira Bridge Co. for four years, he removed to New York city and took charge at various times of important bridge work and also acted as consulting engineer. In the transactions of the American Society of Civil Engineers he published, in 1894, ''The Tower of the New City Hall at Philadelphia, Penna.''; in 1901, ''The Kinzua Viaduct of the Erie Railroad Company''; in 1910, ''The Arch Principle in Engineering and Esthetic Aspects, and Its Applications to Long Spans.'' He is also the author of ''Secondary Stresses in Bridge Trusses'' (1908), of which ''Engineering News'' said: ''This book is a distinct addition to American bridge literature in a field which hitherto has been practically unoccupied. The author has rendered a valuable service to the engineering profession in this country by writing this book, which gives the results of previous investigations and directs attention in an effective manner to the importance of the subject. The book deserves careful study by every engineer who is responsible for the design and maintenance of bridges.'' Mr. Grimm is a member of the American Society of Civil Engineers, American Association for the Advancement of Science, the National Geographic Society, and the Society for the Promotion of Engineering Education. He was married Aug. 28, 1889, at Mt. Vernon, O., to Elizabeth, daughter of James J. McCombs of Ottawa, O.

BRUSH, John Tomlinson, was born at Clintonville, N. Y., June 15, 1845, son of John Tomlinson and Sarah P. (Farar) Brush, and grandson of Eliphalet and Polly (Tomlinson) Brush, of New England ancestry. His grandfather removed from Bennington, Vt., to Hopkinton, St. Lawrence co., N. Y., in 1802. The subject of this sketch was left an orphan at the age of four years, and was brought up by his grandfather at Hopkinton. He began his business career as a clothing merchant in Boston, but in 1863 enlisted for the civil war in the 1st New York artillery. After the war he resumed the clothing business in Troy and Albany, N. Y. In 1873 he became a member of the firm of Owen, Pixley & Co., of Utica, N. Y., but two years later removed to Indianapolis, Ind., where he started a clothing business which he conducted with marked success for many years. In 1901 he bought out his partners and reorganized the business under the name of the When Clothing Co., Incorporated. An eager lover of athletic sports, he early took an interest in the growing game of baseball. With a number of personal acquaintances, he bought the Indianapolis Baseball Club in 1886, of which he finally became president and manager. He sold his interest in 1892, and went to Cincinnati, O., where he became president of the Cincinnati National League Club, and ten years later he purchased the New York National League Club, popularly known as the ''Giants,'' which he owned and directed until his death. John T. Brush will long be remembered as one of the prominent characters of the baseball world. It was generally conceded by business men that he was the most influential figure, in fact the guiding spirit, in the National League, and was more than any other one man responsible for the survival and straightening of the league and for the spirit of cooperation in which it eventually came to work with its rival, the American. Under his control the New York National League became perhaps the most famous and decidedly one of the most successful clubs in baseball and he directed its affairs with remarkable skill, force and judgment, and with an absence of interference in the work of manager and players which was notable in a man of his active mind and dynamic personality. After his death the direction of the New York National League passed by his will into the hands of his son-in-law, Harry N. Hempstead, who had been associated for several years with him in directing the affairs of the club and who was at one with him in all matters of policy. The desire of Mr. Brush that the club remain in the family and the notably close union and agreement that exists between its members insures for its future management the same enlightened and successful spirit that it has enjoyed since it first came under Mr. Brush's control. He possessed a rare faculty for picking men and the rarer faculty of leaving them unhampered to the work for which he chose them. Not only was Mr. Brush a shrewd, astute and forceful business man but he was also one of the cleanest and most sterling sportsman in the country. He did much to free baseball of the many corrupt conditions that threatened to degrade it, and both friends and opponents entertained for him the very highest respect and esteem. All over the country, wherever baseball was played, his name was one to conjure with and his loss to the sport is very real and widely felt. ''His acquaintance in the baseball world was national,'' said the New York ''Sun,'' ''and his death will be regretted by hundreds of players throughout the country who have received little kindnesses at his hands, kindnesses which were none the less welcome because they were bestowed unostentatiously. Mr. Brush always had a hand in his pocket for a player in need, although he was keen to detect fraud of any sort. He was married Oct. 18, 1869, to Margaret A. Ewart, by whom he had one child, Eleanor Gordon, wife of Harry N. Hempstead, of Indianapolis, Ind. Mrs. Brush died in 1888 and he was married again June 6, 1894, to Elsie Boyd, daughter of George W. Lombard, of Baltimore, Md., by whom he had one child, Natalie Lombard. His attachment to his wife was well known. After their marriage he named his estate and residence in Indianapolis Lombardy, in her honor. As a business man, a sportsman, a private citizen John T. Brush was one of the most able, successful, sympathetic and grateful citizens in baseball, and the moral and material value to the sport of his connection with it cannot be overestimated. He was a member of the George H. Thomas Post, 17, G.A.R. He was a 33d degree Mason, Scottish Rite Mason and a charter member and first Illustrious Potentate of the Ancient Arabic Order of the Mystic Shrine. He was a member of the Columbia, County and Commercial clubs, the Board of Trade and the Männerchor Society of Indianapolis and the Lambs and Larchmont clubs of New York. He died at Louisiana, Mo., Nov., 26, 1912.

LUCKE, Charles Edward, mechanical engineer, was born in New York city, June 20, 1876, son of John Franklin and Sarah Frances (McGrury) Lucke. He was educated in the New York public schools, and subsequently took post-graduate work at New York University, receiving in 1908 the degree of M.Sc. He continued his graduate studies at Columbia University, receiving there the degree of Ph.D. in 1902. During the intervening years he took a summer course at Cornell University and spent a considerable time in library study and in private experimental work in a laboratory at his home. Since 1906 he has been professor of mechanical engineering at Columbia University and head of that department. His special line of scientific investigation in connection with engineering and industrial applications has been in thermodynamics, to which field he has contributed in both its pure science and industrial application parts, and is recognized as a leading authority on gas producers, gas and oil engines, fuel, furnaces, combustion, and especially combustion with explosive gaseous mixtures, and mechanical refrigeration. He has taken out a number of patents in these fields, the most important of which is concerned with a new art, based upon some of his early discoveries, concerned with the combustion of mixtures of air and gas or air and oil in correct chemical proportions for perfect combustion.

The various applications of the new methods disclosed in these patents are now being commercialized for both domestic and industrial uses by the Gas and Oil Combustion Co., whose laboratory and office is located at 50 E. Forty-first street, New York city, and which was organized under the laws of the state of Delaware on Apr. 23, 1912. The president of the Gas and Oil Combustion Co. is Dr. Hugo Lieber, who is also president of the Blaugas Co. of America and of Hugo Lieber & Co., manufacturing chemists. Prof. Lucke is vice-president and consulting engineer. This company has acquired control in America of not only the Lucke patents, but also patents by others working in a similar field, and including those of Prof. William Bone of Leeds University, England. Extensive preparations are now being made for the commercial introduction of appliances using this new method of combustion in all the fields of application where heat is required, and there will no doubt be organized a series of manufacturing and contracting companies to carry on this work in each of the respective fields to which it applies.

Prof. Lucke discovered that a gas of any kind, when properly mixed with just so much air as is necessary to burn it, can be supplied through orifices of various forms to a porous layer of refractory matter in which it will burn with very intense heat, producing so-called "surface combustion." In accordance with this action, the solid refractory becomes a glowing incandescent mass, having very high capacity for radiating heat to other bodies and increasing their capacity for absorbing heat to a remarkable degree because of the properties of radiant heat, which are well known from scientific studies of the sun's rays. Such combustion can be carried on at enormously greater rates than in any other way, it being possible to burn ten times as much gas on the square foot of surface in accordance with this method over what could be burned by existing methods. It also minimizes the amount of waste heat carried off in flues, because no excess air is required for the combustion, and such fires can be enclosed in chambers isolated from the atmosphere and may even be submerged, since all air necessary for combustion is previously mixed with the gas before it reaches the incandescent body where it burns. This discovery is applicable specifically to the domestic arts, such as grilling, roasting, toasting, boiling, heating water, warming rooms; to the industries, such as raising steam in boilers by either gas or oil fuel, the carrying on of operations in chemical factories; to the baking and firing of brick, tiling and glass; to the melting of metals in crucible and hearth furnaces and to the extraction of metals from their ores. Prof. Lucke is the author of "Gas Engine Design" (1905); "Power" (1911), and "Engineering Thermodynamics" (1912), and a number of scientific and engineering papers, of which the following is a partial list: "Mean Effective Temperature in Engine Cylinders" (1900); "The Heat Engine Problem" (1901); "Some New

Work on Expansive Mixture" (1902); "Liquid Fuel Combustion" (1902); "Gas Engine Economy" (1905); "Practical Investigation of the Gas Turbine Problem" (1905); "The Gas Turbine Situation" (1906); "Mechanical Engineering" (1907); "Protection of Workmen" (1908); "A Simple Continuous Gas Calorimeter" (1908); "The Value of Gas Power" (1908); "Performance of Ammonia Compression Machines" (1908); "Gasification of Solid Fuel" (1911). He is a member of American Society of Mechanical Engineers, American Institute of Electrical Engineers, American Society of Refrigerating Engineers, American Society of Consulting Engineers, American Association for Advancement of Science, Society of Automobile Engineers, Society for the Promotion of Engineering Education, International Association of Refrigeration and the Engineers' and Chemists' clubs. He was married Mar. 24, 1904, to Ida Marguerite, daughter of Daniel Becker, and has two sons, Charles Edward Jr. and John Becker Lucke. Portrait opposite p. 180.

ALBEE, Fred Houdlett, surgeon, was born at Alna, Me., April 13, 1876, son of F. Huysen and Mary Charlotte (Houdlett) Albee, and a descendant of Obadiah Albee, who came to this country from England in 1640 and settled at Boston, Mass. He was prepared for college at Lincoln Academy and was graduated at Bowdoin College in 1899, and at the Harvard Medical School in 1903. After leaving the latter he became instructor in orthopedic surgery at the College of Physicians and Surgeons, Columbia University, a position which he resigned in 1911. Dr. Albee is assistant professor of orthopedic surgery at Cornell University Medical College, professor of orthopedic surgery at the University of Vermont and adjunct professor of orthopedic surgery at the Post-Graduate Medical School, New York city. He was radiologist to the Hospital for the Ruptured and Crippled during 1906-10, and was clinical assistant at the Hospital for the Ruptured and Crippled (Orthopedic) in 1905-10. At present he is assistant surgeon in charge of the orthopedic service, second surgical division, Bellevue Hospital; chief of orthopedic service, O.P.D., Roosevelt Hospital; visiting physician, Blythedale Hospital, Hawthorne; visiting orthopedic surgeon, chief of clinic, Post-Graduate Hospital, and consulting orthopedic surgeon to the Waterbury, Conn., and the Muhlenberg, Plainfield, N. J. hospitals. Notwithstanding his comparative youth, Dr. Albee is one of the most skillful and highly reputed orthopedic surgeons in the country. He has operated for osteo-arthritis and tuberculosis of the hip and has originated a method of bone transplantation for Pott's disease. He has written extensively on his specialty, among his published papers being "The X-ray in Orthopedic Surgery," "Osteomyetitis," "A New Method for Osteo-Arthritis of the Hip," "Fractures of the Tarsal Bones," "Bone Transplantation for Pott's Disease of the Spine;" "Taylor's Orthopedic Surgery" (co-author), "Epiphyseal Fractures of the Hip—A New Posture in the Treatment," and "A New Method for Treatment of Epiphyseal Fractures of the Upper End of the Humerus." He is a lieutenant in the Medical Reserve Corps, U. S. Army, and is a member of the American Medical Association, New York State Medical Society, New York County Medical Society, New York Academy of Medicine (ex-chairman orthopedic section), American Orthopedic Association, American Röntgen Ray Society, Interurban Orthopedic Club, Harvard Medical Society of New York City (ex-secretary), Washington

Heights Medical Society, Harlem Medical Society, Union County Medical Society (New Jersey), Plainfield Medical Society, Boyleston Medical Society, and Harvard Club of New York city. He was married Feb. 2, 1907, to Louella May, daughter of William E. Berry, of Bryn Mawr, Pa.

HEDSTROM, Oscar Carl, inventor, was born in Smoland, Sweden, Mar. 12, 1871, son of Andrew and Caroline Hedstrom. The family emigrated to America in 1880, settling in Brooklyn, N. Y., where he received a public school education. Possessing an unusual bent for mechanics, young Hedstrom stepped from the class-room to the shop, and became an expert tool-maker in a watch factory. At the age of twenty-four he entered the paths that led to fame and fortune. A devotee to bicycle racing, then in the flood tide of its popularity, he became one of the best riders of his day, at first racing only when it did not interfere with his shop duties. With his marvelous mechanical gift, it was but natural that he should enter upon the design and construction of racing wheels, and his creations were so advanced in lines and so successful in competition that he was commissioned by leading manufacturers to build racing machines for them, which he did. Many of the mounts of the champions of those days were the handiwork of Hedstrom, but bore the name plates of leading makers. When in the late nineties the first motor-paced tandems were brought to this country from France Hedstrom undertook to make a motor tandem after his own ideas, and his production was the most reliable motor tandem in this country, whose performances rapidly enhanced the name and the fame of the builder. Among those who were strongly impressed with Hedstrom's abilities was George M. Hendee, then manufacturing bicycles, and in his day the greatest high wheel champion in American cycling history. Foreseeing a wonderful future for a practical motorcycle for daily use, he commissioned Hedstrom to undertake the construction of such a vehicle, and in January, 1901, he became identified with the Hendee Manufacturing Co., makers of bicycles, of Springfield, Mass., and soon after made the first ''Indian'' motorcycle, the forerunner of the American motorcycle industry. In this machine was instilled all that was known of the gasolene engine art at that time, together with a number of important inventions which since have become accepted standards in the craft. Prominent among these were the Hedstrom motor, Hedstrom carbureter, double grip control, countershaft hanger construction, cushion fork, bayonet locking inlet valve dome, automatic ignition cut-out switch, Hedstrom motor anchorage system, combination tank construction, and compensating sprocket. Assuming at a single bound that leadership of the industry which it never has relinquished, the Indian, under the ever watchful guidance of Hedstrom, has grown until to-day the annual production is 35,000 machines, distributed to world-wide marts, and investing its builders with the enviable prestige of being the largest producers of motorcycles in the world. Perhaps the most signal honor ever bestowed on Hedstrom in token of his motorcycle genius was at the Louisiana Purchase Exposition, St. Louis, Mo., in 1904, when the jury of awards granted him a silver medal and high diploma of merit, the only one granted in the entire motor vehicle section of exhibits. Outwardly reserved and of a retiring disposition, Mr. Hedstrom is a most companionable, whole-souled man. He is a member of the Royal Automobile Club of Great Britain,

the Federation of American Motorcyclists, the Springfield Yacht Club, and the Nayasset Club of Springfield. His pet hobby is motorboat racing, and he won the power boat championship of the Connecticut river for 1912 with his Indian. But his chief devotion is to his family and his home, and he possesses one of the most beautiful country estates at Portland, Conn., affording an entrancing view of that famous stream. He was married to Julia, daughter of Alfred and Helena Anderson, Nov. 14, 1898, and has one daughter, Helen Hedstrom.

HASSLACHER, Jacob Pius Maria, manufacturer, was born at Ems on the Lahn, Germany, July 5, 1852, son of George and Agnes (Schaeffner) Hasslacher. His father was administrator of the government bath, parks and buildings at Ems for many years. The son was educated in the elementary and high schools at Ems, and completed his studies at the Gymnasium at Hadamar, where he was graduated in 1872. After serving the usual term in the Prussian army, during which he became a lieutenant of the reserve, he began his business career at the age of twenty in the service of the German Gold and Silver Refinery in Frankfort-on-the-Main. He was with this concern for six years and was engaged in various other enterprises in Germany as well as in Switzerland. Meanwhile Mr. Roessler had come to the United States, and settling in Brooklyn, N. Y., took up the manufacture of liquid bright gold, a preparation for gold decoration on china, porcelain and glass. Two years later he communicated with Mr. Hasslacher, and the latter came over to form a partnership with Mr. Roessler. The firm name was originally Roessler & Hasslacher, and in 1889 it was incorporated as the Roessler & Hasslacher Chemical Co. The company began with the manufacture of liquid bright gold at its factory in Perth Amboy, N. J. Since then various other chemical products have been added to the business, including the manufacture of acetone from acetate of lime, chloroform from acetone, ceramic colors, oxide of tin, cyanide of potassium and sodium. In 1896 the Niagara Electro Chemical Co. was established as a subsidiary company at Niagara Falls, N. Y., to manufacture metallic sodium and peroxide of sodium under patented processes invented by Hamilton Y. Castner. In 1903 the Perth Amboy Chemical Works was organized for the manufacture of formaldehyde; in 1906 the parent company installed platinum smelting works at Perth Amboy for making platinum sheet, platinum wire, etc.; in 1910 the Enamel Co. of America was established for the manufacture of Leukonin, an antimoniate of soda, which is used in the manufacture of enamel ware, and in the same year the company became interested in the General Bakelite Co., organized by Dr. L. H. Bakeland (q. v.), for the manufacture of an artificial amber called Bakelite. During the past twelve years the manufacture of peroxides has been increased by the company to a large extent, and included under this head now are peroxide of sodium, the peroxides and perborates of other metals, a washing compound known as ''Persil,'' an oxygen washing compound for laundries called ''Boron-O,'' Oxone and ''Trisalyt.'' The company's extensive works at Perth Amboy cover ten acres and employ 350 hands. Besides being president of the Roessler & Hasslacher Chemical Co., Mr. Hasslacher is an officer in the Niagara Electro Chemical Co., the Perth Amboy Chemical Works, the Chlorine Products Co. and the General Bakelite Co. He is a member of the American Asso-

CHARLES E. LUCKE
MECHANICAL ENGINEER

FRED H. ALBEE
SURGEON

OSCAR C. HEDSTROM
INVENTOR

JACOB P. M. HASSLACHER
MANUFACTURER

J. PIERPONT MORGAN, JR.

ciation for the Advancement of Science, American Electrochemical Society, American Chemical Society, American Museum of Natural History, Metropolitan Museum of Art, Chemists' Club, Drug and Chemical Club, New York Zoological Society, National Geographic Society, American Geographical Society, Germanistic Society, Legal Aid Society, New York Athletic Club, Niagara Club of Niagara Falls, N. Y., and National Conservation Association of Washington, D. C. He was married Sept. 28, 1893, to Elizabeth, daughter of Franz Fleck of Perderborn, and has two sons, George and Charles Hasslacher, and four daughters, Agnes, Antoinette, Therese and Emilie Hasslacher.

MORGAN, John Pierpont, Jr., financier, was born at Irvington, N. Y., Sept. 7, 1867, only son of John Pierpont and Frances Louise (Tracey) Morgan, and grandson of Junius Spencer Morgan, founder of the house of J. P. Morgan & Co. He was educated in private schools and at Harvard University, where he was graduated in 1889. He was sent at once to serve an apprenticeship in the English branch of the Morgan firm, as his father had done before him. He started at the bottom and worked as few sons of rich men work, with the result that he was at an early age promoted to responsible positions. His first great achievement was when the United States government asked the Morgans to arrange for the payment to the French Panama Canal Co. of $40,000,000 in gold for the right to take and complete the work at Panama begun and left in ruins by Ferdinand de Lesseps. To the younger Morgan was assigned the task of collecting this great sum, and he did it without causing the least disturbance in the delicate balance of international exchange. Later he was sent to Russia to negotiate an important loan. Returning about the time of the famous panic of May 9, 1901, which resulted from the celebrated contest between the Morgan-Hill and Harriman-Rockefeller interests for control of the Northern Pacific railroad, he assisted his father in restoring normal conditions. Again, in the panic of 1907, when the elder Morgan was the Ararat on which the ark of finance rested, he was his father's most trusted lieutenant. His position in the Morgan firm grew steadily more important and it soon became evident to all familiar with the situation in Wall Street that he was not going to be content with the inheritance of the Morgan wealth unless the control of the vast business of the Morgan firm went with it. When Mr. Morgan, Sr., died in 1913 no doubt remained but that his son was to be his successor in fact as well as in name. Mr. Morgan inherited, together with his father's fortune and position at the head of the house, his indomitable will and a great part of his financial ability. He inherited also his father's distate for publicity, and little was known by the world at large what he was doing in the Morgan offices, but the world of finance was not slow in recognizing his right to the succession. For a few months it appeared, it is true, that the Morgan influence was in peril of being superseded by that of the firm's only peer, Kuhn, Loeb & Co., but the capacity of the younger Morgan and his nine able partners soon restored the status quo ante and their diplomacy destroyed all fear of a contest for supremacy between these two great interests, a contest which might have proved fatal to both, and disastrous to the whole United States. His position in Wall Street remained one of quiet but insistent influence until the outbreak of the European war. From that moment he has been in the first line of international finance. Almost immediately after the opening of hostilities the British government appealed to him to float a loan of $100,000,000 in the United States, but he declined the commission because of the declaration of Pres. Wilson that such a public loan might be construed as unneutral. The administration, however, conceded that a grant of commercial credit to a belligerent nation would not meet with the same objection, and Mr. Morgan thereupon advanced $12,000,000 to Russia. On Jan. 16, 1915, his house was appointed commercial agent of the British government, in the United States, the first appointment of the kind ever made by Great Britain, and all purchases of ammunition and other war supplies in this country for that country thereafter were made through J. P. Morgan & Co. In April, 1915, the administration having still further receded from its position regarding loans to belligerents, Mr. Morgan loaned the French government $50,000,000 on one year 5% notes. In September, 1915, when the heavy purchase of commodities in this country by the allied governments, together with abnormally small American purchases abroad, had depressed sterling exchange to the lowest level in history and was threatening to put an end to the great export trade which had saved the United States from financial collapse, Pres. Wilson gave up his last trench on the loan question. A commission of eminent English and French officials and bankers came to the United States and arranged with Mr. Morgan for a loan of $500,000,000 on five-year 5% bonds, the largest single bond issue ever made here and the first loan of over $50,000,000 by America to Europe. Mr. Morgan formed a syndicate of some 2,200 banks and wealthy individuals who advanced this vast sum to the British government, subsequently offering participation to the American public in the form of bonds. Three-fourths of the entire amount was taken up by the investing public, the remainder being held by the banking syndicate. The success of this transaction was sufficient proof that under the leadership of J. Pierpont Morgan 2d the international influence of the Morgan house was as great as, if not greater than, it was under his father. The amount of money which has passed through this house as commercial agent of the British government cannot be estimated, but ran into the billions. Mr. Morgan's active financial assistance to the allied governments, however, nearly cost him his life. On July 3, 1915, he was shot at his home at Glen Cove, L. I., by a fanatic who had conceived the idea that if he disposed of Mr. Morgan no more ammunition would be shipped to the allies. The culprit committed suicide in jail while awaiting trial and Mr. Morgan, after two or three months' confinement to his house, was back at his desk at 23 Wall street, which he has seldom left except at night and during business visits to England. His purely American activity, besides the flotation of great railroad and industrial corporation security issues, has included the work of director of a large number of corporations and of banks. After the passage by congress of the Clayton act, which forbade "interlocking directorates," he resigned from the boards of the banks with which he was connected, but remained on the boards of many non-banking corporations. These are the Ætna Insurance Co., the International Mercantile Marine Co., the United States Steel Corporation, the Northern Pacific Railway Co., the Pullman Co., the New York and Harlem R. R. Co. and the First Security Co. of the City of New York. He is also a member of the advisory council of the Federal Reserve Board, which is at the head of the banking system of the United States. Mr. Morgan was married, Dec. 11, 1890, to Jane Norton, daughter of Henry Sturgis Grew, of Boston, Mass., and has four children: Junius Spencer, Jane Norton, Frances Tracy and Henry Sturgis Morgan. Mr. Morgan is a member of St. George's Episcopal Church, New York, of which his father was for so many years senior warden. Though Mr. Morgan resembles his father so strikingly in physique, the likeness growing closer as he grows older, and in the trend of his mind and ability in business, he does not seem to have inherited his father's taste for art and for society. He has been criticised for disposing of a portion of the priceless collection of pictures and objects of art which came to him from his father, and he has shown little of that sociability for which his father was distinguished, despite his occasional well-known irascibility. But he is popular among his intimates and is a member of the following clubs: Metropolitan, University, Century, Union, Requet, Harvard, New York Yacht and Tennis of New York, and White's, St. James, and City of London, in London. He is also a member of the New England Society and of the New York Stock Exchange.

HALE, William Bayard, author and editor, was born in Richmond, Ind., Apr. 6, 1869, son of William Hadley and Anna (Bunting) Hale, and a descendant of Samuel Hale, of Cheshire, England, who settled in Chester county, Pa., in 1703. From him and his wife, Mary Bancroft, the line descends through their son Samuel and his wife, Rachel Nichols; their son Samuel and his wife, Ruth Harlan; their son Jacob and his wife, Martha Harvey; and their son Eli and his wife, Ann Hadley, who were grandparents of William Bayard Hale. He studied at Boston and Harvard universities and at the Episcopal Theological Seminary, Cambridge. He was for several years an Episcopal clergyman, holding the rectorates of Our Saviour's, Middleborough, Mass. (where he founded the parish and built the notable Perpendicular Church), and St. Mary's, Ardmore, Pa. He entered journalism in 1900, but retained clerical orders until 1909; was managing editor of the "Cosmopolitan Magazine" in 1900; editor of "Current Literature," 1901; special correspondent for the New York "World," 1902; managing editor of the "Philadelphia Public Ledger" during 1903-07; editor on the staff of the New York "Times" and Paris correspondent of same, 1907-09; editor on the staff of "The World's Work," 1909-13. He has lived much abroad. He is a student of international affairs; has lectured at Oxford on the United States constitution and has advised several governments on political questions. He was special agent of Pres. Wilson in Mexico, 1913-14. Among the decorations conferred upon Mr. Hale by foreign governments are: Officer of the Order of Leopold (Belgium); Knight Commander of the Imperial Order of the Rising Sun (Japan); Grand Cross of the Order of the Liberator (Venezuela). He is the author of "The Making of the American Constitution" (1895); "The New Obedience" (1898); "A Week in the White House with Theodore Roosevelt" (1908); "Woodrow Wilson: The Story of His Life" (1912); and he edited Pres. Wilson's book, "The New Freedom" (1913). He was married Oct. 5, 1909, in London, England, to Olga, daughter of Emil von Unger, and their children are William Harlan and Bayard Hadley Hale.

WHITNEY, Amos, manufacturer, was born at Biddeford, York co., Me., Oct. 8, 1832, son of Aaron and Rebecca (Perkins) Whitney. The Whitney Family is of great antiquity in England.

John Whitney came to America about 1635 and settled at Watertown, Mass., where he was elected town clerk, constable and selectman. His grandson, Jonathan, served in King Philip's war, and the latter's grandson, Levi, was a member of Capt. James Prescott's company, Col. William Prescott's regiment, which marched to Cambridge on the alarm of Apr. 19, 1775, and first lieutenant of Capt. Henry Farwell's company, of the same regiment, at Bunker Hill. Lieut. Levi Whitney served throughout the revolution as an officer in the commissary department and subsequently held a number of public offices in Watertown. Amos Whitney received his education at the public schools of Biddeford and Saccarappa, Me., and Exeter, N. H., where his family lived at different times. At the age of thirteen he was apprenticed to the Essex Machine Co., of Lawrence, Mass., manufacturers of machines for the making of locomotives, cotton products and machinists' tools, and after three years of apprenticeship and another year as journeyman he entered the employ of Samuel Colt's pistol factory, at Hartford, Conn. In 1854 he became a contractor for the Phœnix Iron Works. Soon thereafter a Mr. Conant patented a machine for winding thread, known as a "spooler." The patent was purchased by the Willimantic Linen Co., which invited bids for the manufacture of the machines. Mr. Whitney and Francis A. Pratt, a fellow-employee, secured the contract for the "spoolers." They organized the firm of Pratt & Whitney, and began operations in 1860. In 1863 Monroe Stannard was taken into partnership, and in 1865 the business of the young company had increased to such an extent that Pratt & Whitney were obliged to erect a new four-story building of their own. The business continued to increase steadily year after year, necessitating the erection of many new buildings, until now (1916) it is the largest manufacturing concern in Hartford. In 1869 the company was incorporated with a capital of $350,000. The capital was increased to $400,000 in 1873, $500,000 in 1875, and $2,750,000 at a reorganization in 1893. Originally Mr. Whitney was the superintendent of the factory, having full charge of the production of the machinery and tools, and after the reorganization he continued as general superintendent and vice-president until 1898, when he was made president of the company. In 1902 an arrangement was effected whereby the business was controlled by the Niles-Bement-Pond Co., and at that time Mr. Whitney retired from active service, but continued to serve on the board of directors and is still serving in this capacity at the present date (1916). Following the "spoolers" they brought out a general line of machine tools, including lathes, planers, shapers, milling machines, drilling machines, boring machines, automatic and hand screw machines, profiling machines, etc. As new industries were created the Pratt & Whitney Co. developed machinery suitable for the new conditions, and therefor had much to do with the development of sewing machines, harvesting machinery, electrical apparatus, bicycles, automobiles, etc. They manufacture the special machinery used by makers of small arms in every country in the world. In 1879 they employed William A. Rogers, professor of astronomy at Harvard College, and George M. Bond, a graduate of Stevens Institute of Technology, to conduct experiments with a view to the construction of an apparatus for exact and uniform measurement. The experiments lasted three years. Prof. Rogers obtained reliable transfers of the yard and meter in London

Amos Whitney

and Paris, and in co-operation with the U. S. Coast Survey conducted most minute and exhaustive comparisons between the standard bars prepared by him and the standard "yard" known as bronze No. 11. As a result the company has developed an absolutely reliable set of standards and rescued mechanical science and industry from a vast amount of inconvenience. These experiments cost the company much money without the prospect of any immediate return. In 1888 Pratt & Whitney were selected by the Hotchkiss Ordnance Co., contractors of the U. S. navy department, to make the Hotchkiss revolving cannon and three and six-pound rapid-fire guns, designed for our government by B. B. Hotchkiss on the principle applied to shoulder arms by Christian Sharps. Throughout his business career Amos Whitney kept in close contact with his foremen and employees, and by his educational policy the firm of Pratt & Whitney became a practical technical school for young mechanics. Special attention was given to the young men and apprentices and workmen at the Pratt & Whitney Co. were later found at the head of important institutions throughout the United States, as well as in some foreign countries. Mr. Whitney was married at Hartford, Conn., Sept. 8, 1856, to Laura, daughter of John Johnson, and a descendant of John Johnson who came over with Winthrop, settled at Roxbury, Mass., and was constable of that town and surveyor of all the arms of the colony. There were three children: Nellie Hortense, Nettie Louise and Clarence Edgar Whitney.

CUTTING, R[obert] Fulton, financier, was born in New York city, June —, 1852, son of Fulton and Elise Justine (Bayard) Cutting, grandson of William and Gertrude (Livingston) Cutting and great-grandson of Leonard Cutting, who came from England in 1750 and settled in New York and Hempstead, L. I. He was graduated at Columbia University in 1871, receiving the degree of A.M. from the same institution four years later, and that of LL.D. in 1904. For many years Mr. Cutting has been a leader in many of New York's most advanced and effective movements toward political reform. In 1892 he became president of the Association for Improving the Condition of the Poor, and in this position has performed public services of incalculable benefit. The society is one of the oldest in New York and its sphere a practical one. It does not produce pauperism, but lends assistance here and there in such manner as to render those who are in straightened circumstances self-supporting and self-respecting. Its energies are directed toward having free baths for the people, small parks and houses fit for human families to inhabit. Mr. Cutting participated in the organization and became president of the Citizens' Union, which became an important factor in the political situation in New York city. As chairman of the board of directors of the City and Suburban Homes Co. he has been instrumental in the building of several blocks of model tenements in New York city, which have greatly raised the standard of living. His devotion to the New York Trade School, of which he has been president since 1899, has resulted in the training of thousands of boys in useful and remunerative occupations. He occasionally appears as a lecturer on sociology, one of his notable addresses being "Christianity in Social Life." In religion he is an Episcopalian, and for years has been a vestryman of St. George's Church and also a member of the Church Club. He is a trustee of the American Exchange National Bank, the Mexican Telegraph Co., the Manhattan Warehouse Co., and the Metropolitan Opera House Co., and he is a member of the Chamber of Commerce, the Columbia University Alumni Association, Delta Phi, and the Century, City and Tuxedo clubs. Mr. Cutting has been twice married: (1) in 1871, to Natalie C. P., daughter of Noah H. Schenck, of Brooklyn, N. Y.; (2) Jan. 25, 1883, to Helen, daughter of Charles Suydam, of New York. His children are: Robert Bayard, Helen, Elizabeth M., Fulton, Charles Suydam and Ruth Hunter Cutting.

CUTTING, W[illiam] Bayard, lawyer, was born in New York city, Jan. 12, 1850, son of Fulton and Elise (Justine) Cutting, grandson of William and Gertrude (Livingston) Cutting, and great-grandson of Rev. Leonard Cutting, a clergyman of the Established Church in England, who came to America in 1750, and had parishes at New Brunswick, N. J., and Hempstead and Oyster Bay, Long Island. In 1765 he was a tutor in Kings, afterward Columbia College. His only son, William Cutting, was graduated at that institution in 1793, and became an eminently successful lawyer. He was associated with Robert Fulton (who married his wife's sister, Harriet Livingston) in the latter's experiments in steam navigation, and held the inventor in such esteem that he named his fifth son Fulton after him. Fulton Cutting's son, W. Bayard Cutting, was graduated at Columbia College in 1869 and at the Columbia law school two years later. His forceful character and undoubted legal talents soon brought him into prominence as a corporation lawyer. In 1878 he was elected president of the St. Louis, Alton, and Terre Haute Railroad Co. He took a deep interest in local politics and municipal reform, and during the latter part of his career he devoted more of his time to philanthropic and civic reform movements than to the practice of his profession. During Mayor Strong's administration he was civil service commissioner, and as president of the Improved Dwelling Association he was active in the improvement of living conditions for the poor of New York city. He was a man honored in every walk of life, public and private. He was a trustee of the United States Trust Company; a director of the American Exchange National Bank, the United States Trust Company, the Commercial Union Assurance Company, the City and Suburban Homes Company, the Commercial Union Fire Insurance Company, the Norfolk and Southern Railway Company, the Southern Pacific Railroad Company and the Tropical Land Company of New York. In addition to these activities he was a director of the Metropolitan Opera House Co. and a trustee of Columbia University. He was also a director of the New York Botanical Gardens, the American Museum of Natural History and the Metropolitan Museum of Art. He was a member of the Union, Metropolitan, Century, South Side, Tuxedo, University, City, Delta Phi, Grolier, Church and Jekyll clubs. At the time of his death he was the president of the Union Club. Mr. Cutting was married in 1877 to Olivia, daughter of Bronson Murray, by whom he had three sons: William Bayard Jr., Justine Bayard and Bronson Murray, and one daughter, Olivia Cutting. He died en route from New Mexico to New York, Mar. 1, 1912.

LINDSEY, Benjamin Barr [Ben], jurist and reformer, was born at Jackson, Tenn., Nov. 25, 1869, son of Landy Tunstall and Letitia Anna (Barr) Lindsey. His father was a Confederate cavalryman in the civil war, the ravages of which reduced the family from a condition of ease and comparative affluence to one of poverty. The son was educated in schools at Notre Dame, Ind., and Jackson, Tenn. When he was eighteen years old his father died and he was left as the sole support of his widowed mother and three younger children, then living in Denver, Colo. During the following years he faced a hard, discouraging struggle which would have broken the spirit of nine boys out of ten. From the very cradle he was destined to meet difficulty and opposition at every step of his career. He obtained his education under a handicap; he made his living under a handicap; he won the high position he now holds in spite of powerful opposition, and he carried out the reform work which made him famous in the face of seemingly insurmountable obstacles. Obtaining a position in a real estate office in Denver, at $10 a month, he also sold papers and worked as a janitor after hours. He even found time for study. Soon he was earning $25 a month, but real estate was not to his taste; it had always been his ambition to become a lawyer, not realizing that he did not possess the legal temperament or the taste for the technicalities and subtle sophistries of the law. He was concerned primarily with the ethics of life, with which the profession of law is not primarily concerned. This difference in viewpoint made him an impossible law student at first, and he was so discouraged at his inability to progress in his studies that at one time he actually attempted suicide. Happily, the revolver missed fire, and the reaction from his state of overtension brought him to a more practical frame of mind. He reasoned that if he was to be of service to his fellow-men in any capacity a knowledge of law and legal technique would be of immense aid and he resumed his studies with the tireless energy that is characteristic of him. He organized mock trials, debating societies and ''quiz classes,'' and within a remarkably short time he was a competent and well-posted lawyer. He was given his first case to try at the age of nineteen. He entered upon the regular practice of his profession in 1894, and two years later he formed a partnership with Frederick W. Parks in Denver, Colo. The latter became a member of the Colorado legislature in 1897, and through the promptings of his partner succeeded in having a law passed making the vote of three-fourths of a jury sufficient for a verdict. This was the beginning of Ben Lindsey's connection with reform in court and criminal procedure, a cause in which he has accomplished more than any other man now living. He is a reformer by nature, by training and by observation. He has a profound moral sense tempered by a warm human sympathy, and both qualities have contributed about equally to the direction of his efforts. It was the rebellion of his moral sense against the corruption of machine politics that led him into political life in 1900. He became a delegate to the Democratic convention, chairman of the credentials committee, and a member of the Democratic state executive committee. But he was not put forward for political office. He was ''too radical,'' the party thought. He had too little sympathy with the regnant influence. He was, in fact, too aggressively and uncompromisingly honest. But no combination of influence can keep such a man in obscurity, and when a vacancy occurred in the county court in December, 1900, he was appointed to fill it. His one great weapon of attack in his fight with opposing interests was the public conscience. It was his custom when appeals to authorities failed to call a public hearing before invited citizens—public officials, clergymen, and leading business men—when he would lay bare conditions without reserve and with ample evidence. Naturally he was a thorn in the side of corrupt officialdom. An act was introduced into the legislature practically stripping his court of its efficiency, and when the question of his re-election came up in 1908 he was refused the nomination by both Republican and Democratic parties. But he had reached the public conscience as few men ever do, and in spite of the politicians he was re-elected by a plurality of 15,000. Because the supreme court of Colorado reversed itself in a notable political case in Denver, it has been uncertain for over ten years whether Judge Lindsey's court was a city and county or a state office. The result has been that in the thirteen years he has served on the bench he has had to be appointed three times and elected at general city and county or state elections six times. Twice he was appointed through force of public sentiment by his bitter political enemies, and in each of the six elections (including that of 1912) he led his ticket by large majorities, a tribute of his own people to the success of his labors. His reforms in the city and state laws and particularly laws for minors have been so radical and far-reaching that they are sometimes called the ''New Justice.'' These include a new probate code of great value; an improved registration law; a contributory delinquency law (the first in America); the first master of discipline law in America, conferring on teachers and schools power to settle many cases formerly brought to the juvenile court; a law forbidding charging children under sixteen years of age with crime, and one forbidding putting children in jail; a law giving orphans the right to $2,000 of an estate before creditors can touch it; a law making all men legally responsible for the moral welfare of children with whom they come in contact, and a law applying chancery court powers of probate courts to protect property of children, as well as to protect their moral and physical welfare, a revolution in the old legal procedure. Then he has influenced the opening of public playgrounds and public baths, night schools, a summer camp for children, and a day nursery. But the most radical of all Judge Lindsey's reforms is the juvenile court, the most momentous and far-reaching of recent civic reforms in its bearing on the welfare of children—Judge Lindsey says the children are the state—a movement that has been taken up in other cities, and is rapidly spreading to all civilized parts of the world. An Italian boy was brought before him one day in the city court and sentenced to jail. The agonized cry of the boy's mother touched the heart of the youthful judge. He put the boy on probation, and then personally investigated the conditions surrounding the young culprit's life. He was thus brought to a realization of certain facts recognized by modern penologists, namely, that the limited knowledge and under-development of childhood precludes the idea of responsible criminality; that the burden of responsibility rests on parents and guardians, and that crime is the result of moral weaknesses as well as environment, both of which may be changed by proper treatment, but not by punishment. He saw the necessity of a juvenile court to be conducted solely in the interests of children, and he procured the establishment of such a court, over which he presides, with unlimited chancery court and common law criminal court powers to try youthful lawbreakers as well as adult persons who had ''offended against one of these little ones.'' As criminality is a psychological condition, he treats it psychologically; he appeals to what is best in the child, to his pride in his own powers, and to his crude sense of fair play. The boy is not told that he is bad and must be punished, but rather that he is weak; that he has failed to show himself a man, and it is necessary for him to show his strength to fight the enemy within himself, which, if he play the game fair, he can conquer. If he prove to be too weak to conquer himself, then he must go to the institution at Golden, Colo. He is not sentenced like a criminal; he is led to admit that he ought to go for his own good. He is reasoned with in a way that appeals to his imagination. The whole course of procedure leads the boy naturally and unconsciously to profess his own weaknesses and condemn himself. The most astonishing part of this novel procedure is its effectiveness. If it seems best for a boy to go to the Golden institution, he goes voluntarily without guard, under no surveillance, and without any restraint except his own word. Of 507 boys sent there in the past ten years under no surveillance, only five failed to report at the institution, and even they were reclaimed after a second attempt. A part of this happy result unquestionably should be attributed to Judge Lindsey's personality. He is able to get at the heart of a child in a way that is miraculous. He has addressed thousands of boys in the schools and elsewhere, and they all honor and respect him. He has a way of winning their confidence and holding their friendship and loyalty. Even the unruly boys look upon him as their friend, and appreciate that he is interested in their welfare. In a period of two years some 200 boys visited him voluntarily and made confession of theft and other misdemeanors. He understands boy nature, and he makes boys understand him. In 1902 he brought into existence the Juvenile Association for the Protection and Betterment of Children, which will insure the continuance of his work for generations to come. His ''Children's Court,'' which handles all the juvenile delinquency cases in Denver, has become famous, and is a source of profitable study to jurists and criminologists the world over. He modestly disclaims being the originator of the juvenile court, insisting that it is a growth due to the efforts of many people. But it is generally conceded that he has done more than any other one individual to popularize and advance the idea to which he has also made a number of original contributions, and he may justly be called ''The Father of the Juvenile Court.'' Many other reforms indirectly affecting juvenile delinquency have been effected by him in the course of his investigations. His examination of prison life, for example, disclosed a state of affairs only too common in prisons all over the world. Designed as corrective institutions, he found them actual breeding places of vice. The surroundings, dirt, confinement and criminal associations completed the degradation of those confined there. Entering the prison gates, in many cases merely an accidental offender against the law, the culprit went out again a confirmed criminal, and this condition obtained in practically all prisons in every part of the globe. As sociologists well know, the vast majority of serious criminals are graduates of prisons, and the younger they are when first sentenced, the worse they afterward become. Judge Lindsey found that during a period of five years 1,136 boys and girls had been committed to the prisons of Denver, to associate with hardened criminals of the basest and most degraded sort, and of a practical certainty to become hardened criminals themselves. A very graphic account of these abuses and his methods of rectifying them is recited in his book ''The Beast'' (1906). Aside from their incalculable moral value, Judge Lindsey's reforms have resulted in an enormous financial saving to the city and county. During the first year of its existence the juvenile court saved the county $12,000, and after the union of the county and juvenile courts the saving in six years was $60,000. The method of handling other cases in the juvenile court saved approximately $500,000 in nine years, and in three years $18,000 was saved by dispensing with sinecures. In five years he saved $50,000 in fees for the prosecution of children, and $5,000 for other incidental expenses in the same connection. Between 1901 and 1908 he saved $10,000 on children's cases in the county court. No one has ever done so much to accomplish what Judge Ben Lindsey has done in Denver, and in the matter of child welfare, criminal procedure and social reform he has made that city a model for the emulation of other cities. He realizes that the children of to-day are the mature citizens of to-morrow. ''We must have a city of decent kids,'' is one of his common sayings, and a city of decent kids assuredly means a city of decent men and women. Personally Judge Lindsey is a small, intellectual-looking, magnetic man who gives the impression of extreme keenness and tireless energy. While modest and somewhat shy in manner, he is bold, original and aggressive in thought and action. He is a dreamer and he translates his dreams into reality. Disinterested and generous beyond the ordinary, he cares little for wealth and less for power, except in so far as they may aid in the furtherance of his humanitarian work. The purity of his life and integrity of his character have never been questioned even by his most bitter enemies. But for every enemy made by his uncompromising fight against dishonesty and vice, he has a hundred friends who love and respect him for the splendid qualities of his sterling character. Judge Lindsey was married Dec. 20, 1913, to Henrietta Brevoort, stepdaughter of Dr. F. J. Clippert, of Detroit, Mich.

JOY, Clyde Royal, merchant, was born at Denmark, Ia., June 8, 1867, son of Royal Noah and Rodelia Elizabeth (Epps) Joy. His earliest ancestor in America was Thomas Joy, who emigrated from County Norfolk, England, in 1635 and settled in Boston, Mass., where in 1685 he built the first capitol or state house of Massachusetts. He was married to Joan Gallop and the line of descent is through their son Joseph, an ensign in the American navy, who married Mary Prince; through their son, Joseph, who married Elizabeth (Andrews) Joy; their son, Simon, who married Hannah (Humphreys) Joy; their son Nehemiah, who married Miriam Turner; their son, Nehemiah, a soldier in the Revolutionary war, who married Hannah (—) Joy, and their son, Noah, who married Mercy Ford, and was the grandfather of Clyde Royal Joy. The latter began business life in Keokuk, Ia., in 1884, with S. F. Baker & Son, manufacturers of family remedies and flavoring extracts. He held a clerical position until 1889, when he became manager and a member of the firm, the name being changed to S. F. Baker & Co. The business was founded by Dr. S. F. Baker in 1868, for the sale of home remedies, and began with one or two traveling salesmen. These increased from year to year until now there are nearly 400. The son of the founder, Eugene S. Baker, and grandsons, E. Ross, Jesse E., and Myrle F. Baker, were admitted to partnership at various times, and these, with Mr. Joy, constitute the present personnel of the firm, Dr. S. F. Baker having died in 1898. In addition to the original remedies for home treatment of minor ills, such as coughs, colds, sprains, etc., the firm now manufactures remedies for live stock and poultry, as well as flavoring extracts, ground spices, and talcum powder. Unusual care is given to insure quality and uniformity, and the popularity of the goods with customers is an indication of their merit, the extent of the market supplied embracing the states of Oklahoma, Kansas, Nebraska, North and South Dakota, Iowa, Missouri, Minnesota, Wisconsin and Illinois. The firm employs unique methods in dealing with their customers, numbering 600,000 families or more. No goods are sold wholesale. Salesmen equipped with specially constructed wagons carry their stock with them and trade directly with the customer. New customers, unfamiliar with the goods, are permitted a free trial and may return them without charge in case they do not prove satisfactory. For the manufacture of their products the firm occupies two brick factories in Keokuk with aggregate floor space of more than 50,000 feet, and has fifty employees. A branch office has been established in Sioux Falls, S. D. Mr. Joy is also vice-president of Kellogg-Birge Co., a wholesale grocery house of Keokuk, Ia.; vice-president of the Buffalo (Kan.) Brick Co.; a director of the Keokuk National Bank and president of the Keokuk Industrial Association. He is a member of the Keokuk Club and the Chicago Athletic Association. He has been a trustee of Burlington College, and is now a trustee of Knox College; a director of the Institute and Training School of the Y. M. C. A., located at Chicago; member of the International Committee of the Y. M. C. A., and was chairman of its business committee at the international convention, held at Buffalo, N. Y., in 1904. He is member of various committees of its international committee. He was president of the local Y. M. C. A. at Keokuk (Ia.) from 1896 to 1911, and was a member of the central committee of the Men and Religion Forward Movement in 1910-11; also member of the executive committee and chairman of the business and finance committee of that movement. Mr. Joy was married in Chicago, Ill., Oct. 23, 1890, to Belle, daughter of Gustavus B. Brackett, and has three children, Ralph Brackett, Mildred Anna and Carroll Joy.

LOOMIS, Elisha Scott, mathematician and genealogist, was born near the village of Wadsworth, Medina county, Ohio, Sept. 18, 1852, son of Charles Wilson and Sarah (Oberholtzer) Loomis. He is a descendant in the eighth generation of Joseph Loomis, who was born in Braintree, England, and settled in Windsor, Conn., in 1639. Joseph Loomis was a member of the Windsor troop of horse in King Philip's war. His grandson, Nathaniel, served in the war of the Revolution under Capt. Ebenezer Sheldon and in the French and Indian war, 1757, and was present at Fort William Henry when it surrendered. Charles W. Loomis died Nov. 14, 1864, leaving his widow and a family of seven boys, the eldest being the subject of this sketch, who at the age of thirteen hired out to a farmer, and continued thus working for the next seven years. In 1873 he began teaching school, and by the fall of that year he had earned sufficient funds to enable him to enter Baldwin University, Berea, Ohio, where he was graduated in 1880. He became principal of the Burbank Academy in 1880, and the next year he took charge of the Richfield Central High School, in Summit county, where he remained for four years. In 1885 he was elected to the chair of mathematics in his alma mater. Finding the need of more physical exercise, he took up the study of municipal engineering and became engineer for the village of Berea. In 1888 he received the degree of Ph.D. from Wooster University and fourteen years later that of LL.B. from the Cleveland Law School, in which year he was admitted to the Ohio state bar. He was appointed head of the mathematics department of West High School, Cleveland, Ohio, in 1895, a position he still retains. He was president of the Berea board of education for three years; president of the High School Teachers' Mathematics Club of Cleveland for three years; chairman of the committee on education of the Chamber of Industry, Cleveland, Ohio, one year. Since 1903 he has been a member of the National Educational Association. Prof. Loomis has written extensively and is the author of "Theism: the Result of Completed Investigation" (1888); "The Teaching of Mathematics in High Schools" (1899); "Original Investigation, or How to Attack an Exercise in Geometry" (1901); "Definitions: Their Origin and Function" (1910), and "What Results May We Reasonably Expect in Mathematics of a High School Student and on What Subject-matter Shall We Base Our Expectations?" (1912). He has for many years been making researches into the history of the Loomis family, and is editor of "The Loomis Family in America," a work made necessary by the terms of the charter of the Loomis Institute, which was founded at Windsor, Conn. (1872), for the education of members of the Loomis family. The institute occupies the original site and grounds of the Loomis homestead, which has been in the continuous possession of a Loomis since Joseph Loomis purchased it in 1639. It is supported by an endowment of nearly two millions of dollars, given by Col. John Mason Loomis and his brothers in 1872. Dr. Loomis' work is a marvel of genealogical research and painstaking care in making every item of information easily available, there being fourteen separate indices, in which 32,000 names are classified. He has also completed a "History of the Oberholtzer Family—Descendants of Jacob Oberholtzer, Montgomery County, Pa., 1719." He was married June 17, 1880, to Letitia E. Shire and has two children.

FERULLO, Francesco, musician and composer, was born in Naples, Italy, May 31, 1879, son of Alfonso Carmine and Filomena (Lerro) Ferullo. His father was a merchant in good standing in that city. He early developed an ear for music and showed remarkable precocity in his ability to perform and improvise on various instruments, especially the oboe, one of the most difficult of all the wood winds. Being ambitious to succeed, he studied and practiced diligently while his schoolmates were at play, and at the early age of nine years he entered the San Pietro a Majella Royal Conservatory of Music, studying for seven years there the various forms of music, composition and literature. Upon his graduation in 1898 he obtained the position of first oboe player in the San Carlo Grand Opera Orchestra, one of the best known musical organizations in Europe, and achieved almost instant success. Although thus favorably launched on a promising musical career, he believed there were larger possibilities in the western world, and coming to the United States in 1902, he has made Chicago his permanent residence, taking out naturalization papers in 1908. His first position was as oboist in the Royal Italian Band under the management

CLYDE R. JOY
MERCHANT

ELISHA S. LOOMIS
MATHEMATICIAN

FRANCESCO FERULLO
MUSICIAN

CHARLES WAGNER
MANUFACTURER

of Channing Ellery. Soon afterward he was made assistant director of the organization, and in August, 1904, he became director. He conducted a series of concerts at the Lewis and Clark exposition at Portland, Ore., in 1905, when the citizens of Portland presented him with a silver loving cup, a mark of respect and appreciation that was not duplicated with any other musical organization. Severing his connection in 1906, he organized a company of his own in Chicago under the name of the Ferullo Band. During the first four years of its career it was heard in many cities throughout the country. His repertoire includes the most difficult compositions of Wagner, Saint-Saëns, Tschaikowsky, Massenet, Bizet and Liszt, and in Denver, in 1910, he created a sensation by giving a symphony concert with his band. He was married in Kansas City, Mo., May 16, 1906, to Concetta, daughter of Pasquale Vito Rocco, and they have one daughter, Filomena Ferullo.

CANEVIN, John Francis Regis, fifth Roman Catholic bishop of Pittsburgh, Pa., was born in Westmoreland county, Pa., June 5, 1852. He was educated at St. Vincent's Seminary, Westmoreland county, and was ordained priest June 4, 1879. After serving on various missions he became rector of St. Mary's Church, Pittsburgh. In 1881 he was transferred to the cathedral, where he remained till 1886, when he was named chaplain of St. Paul's Orphan Asylum, the Pennsylvania Reform School, Morganza, and the Western penitentiary. At the end of two years he was recalled to the cathedral and appointed diocesan chancellor. Owing to ill health he was transferred in 1893 to St. Philip's Church, Crafton, Pa., as pastor, and in 1895 recalled to the cathedral as its rector. He was consecrated titular bishop of Sabrata and made coadjutor of Pittsburgh, Feb. 24, 1903, with right of succession to the see. Bishop Phelan died Dec. 20, 1904, and Bishop Canevin succeeded him immediately. The diocese of Pittsburgh has a Catholic population of 500,000, composed of many nationalities, requiring spiritual direction in fourteen languages: English, German, French, Italian, Slovak, Polish, Bohemian, Magyar, Slovenian, Lithuanian, Croatian, Rumanian, Ruthenian and Syrian. To the complex problem involved in this social combination Bishop Canevin applied qualities of administration that evolved the most successful results. He wrote a number of pamphlets and brochures on statistical and other questions in relation to Catholic church topics. The beautiful cathedral of Pittsburgh is another testimonial to his zeal for the material progress of the diocese, which has 418 other churches, chapels and stations, attended by 528 priests. There are three seminaries, three boys' colleges, six girls' academies, 175 parish schools, all having an attendance of 54,379 pupils. Other institutions are four orphan asylums, two industrial schools for boys, eight hospitals, four homes for girls, and a school for deaf mutes.

BAGLEY, George Colt, was born at Stewartstown, Coos co., N. H., Mar. 1, 1851, son of Dudley Selden (1818–1906) and Martha Hopkins (Allis) Bagley. His earliest paternal American ancestor was Samuel Bagley, who came from England in the middle of the seventeenth century and settled at Weymouth, Mass. From him the line of descent is traced through his son Samuel and his wife, Mary Thayer; their son James and his wife, Jane Pierce; their son John and his wife, Esther Pitcher; their son Samuel and his wife, Naomi Curtis; their son Benjamin and his wife, Poly Colt, who were the grandparents of George Colt Bagley. His maternal grandfather was Elisha Allis, of Brookfield, Vt. His father was in the grain elevator business in Wisconsin, and after receiving his education in the public schools of Milwaukee, Wis., he joined his parent and brother in that business in 1876, and has ever since been identified with the elevator and grain commission trade. Since 1885 his headquarters have been in Minneapolis. He is now the chief executive of the George C. Bagley Elevator Co. and also president of the Atlantic Elevator Co. and of the Royal Elevator Co., operating about two hundred elevators in the states of Minnesota, North Dakota, South Dakota and Montana, and terminal elevators in Minneapolis. He is president of the Kellogg Commission Co., of Minneapolis, and the Calcasieu Land and Rice Co., of Vinton, La., and vice-president of the Sabine Canal Co., of the latter town. He is a member of the Minneapolis Chamber of Commerce, Chicago Board of Trade, Duluth Board of Trade, the Society of Colonial Wars, and the Minneapolis, Minikahda and Lafayette clubs, of Minneapolis. He was married at Plymouth, Wis., Nov. 29, 1876, to Cornelia E., daughter of Milan Mead, a farmer of Plymouth, Wis., and has one son, Ralph Colt Bagley.

WAGNER, Charles, manufacturer, was born in Wurtemberg, Germany, Jan. 23, 1837, son of Christian and Johanna (Gunsser) Wagner. His father, grandfather and great-grandfather conducted the same tannery in the town of Balingen and it is but natural that he should have continued in the same business. He received his education in the schools of his native town and at the age of fifteen began to learn his father's tanning business. In 1855 he left Wurtemberg for New York, whence he proceeded by way of Panama to San Francisco. He tried mining for a month in Calaveras county, but not finding it to his taste he settled in Stockton, Cal., and with his brother, Jacob C., started the Pacific Tannery. The tanning business at that time was by no means an easy one, especially for a young man of limited means. The process took at least six or seven months, and it was necessary to buy a few hides, wait until they were tanned and then sell the leather and buy more hides. The principal market was Sacramento, to which the leather had to be hauled by wagon. But Charles Wagner was enterprising and progressive. He studied tanning methods in San Francisco and Santa Cruz, where the best leather in the United States was then made, and equipping himself with the latest machinery, developed the Pacific Tannery into a successful enterprise. In 1865 the firm name became Wagner Bros. In 1869 Jacob C. Wagner retired and Moses Kullman joined, the name being changed to Kullman, Wagner & Co. Herman Kullman became a partner in 1870 and Jacob Salz in 1874, and on the death of Moses Kullman in 1878, his nephew, Charles Hart, inherited half of his share in the firm and thus also was admitted to partnership. The firm was incorporated as the Wagner Leather Co. in 1895, with Charles Wagner as president, and the interests of Herman Kullman, Jacob Salz and Charles Hart were purchased by the Wagner Leather Co. Corporation. The present capacity of the Wagner Leather Co. is 130 heavy cattle hides or 260 sides heavy sole and harness leather per day. This is sold not only on the Pacific coast but through the Middle West, in the Asiatic market and in Australia. Besides the Pacific tannery the Wagner Leather Co. operates an extractor in the bark regions of Humboldt county, California, and tannery and the extractor together give employment to over 200 hands. Charles Wagner was a member of Stockton Lodge,

No. 11, I. O. O. F., and the last surviving charter member of the Stockton Turn-Verein, of which he was a trustee and several times president. He was married at Stockton, Cal., in 1867 to Philipina, daughter of Jacob Simon, of Basenback, Bavaria, and has two children: Edward C., vice-president of the Wagner Leather Co., and Bertha W., wife of George E. Housken, of Stockton, secretary of the corporation. He died in Stockton, Cal., Oct. 17, 1912. Portrait opposite p. 186.

ALTMAN, Benjamin, merchant and philanthropist, was born in New York city, July 12, 1840, son of Philip and Cecelia (————————) Altman. His father was a dry goods merchant and in 1854 founded the business which the son conducted so ably. After a public school education Benjamin Altman entered his father's business in New York, and upon the latter's death continued the business with his brother, Morris Altman, under the firm name of Altman Bros. When Morris Altman died in 1876, Benjamin Altman became sole proprietor, and under the personal supervision of its owner it soon ranked with the older and more famous department stores of New York. In 1906 he moved from Sixth avenue and Nineteenth street to the present site on Fifth avenue. The business became one of the largest of its kind and was admired as a model by his competitors. Early in 1913 Mr. Altman secured the adoption by the New York state legislature of a bill incorporating the Altman Foundation, the purpose of which was to receive and administer funds, and to promote the social, physical and economic welfare of the employees of B. Altman & Co. It also included a system of profit-sharing and provided that the fund may be used for charitable and educational purposes. To the Foundation was given authority to receive and hold absolutely or in trust any property, including the stock of B. Altman & Co. By his will his stock in his dry goods business, estimated to be worth $30,000,000, was left to the Altman Foundation, the income to be applied to the support of such philanthropic and charitable institutions as may be selected by his designees and their successors. His will provided for the continuance of the dry goods house, stipulating, however, that it was to be kept separate from the Foundation it was to support. Mr. Altman was of a retiring nature. Few persons knew him intimately. He was unmarried; for years his business was his sole concern; he seldom traveled, and he had no country home. Without drawing away from his commercial interests, in 1882 he turned to the study of art. He first gave his attention to Chinese porcelains, of which he subsequently acquired the finest collection in the world. In 1888 he took the first vacation he had permitted himself in seventeen years, and at the beginning of the present century his name in both Europe and America came to be mentioned with those of Morgan, Frick, Kahn and Widener as one of the great art collectors of the world. Thereafter he acquired many of the most important treasures of his remarkable collection. He was one of the most fastidious collectors the world has known, and was satisfied with nothing less than perfection. He did not seek to cultivate catholicity of taste, but within the limits he set for them it is indisputable that his collections are incomparable in America and Europe. He made it a practice unhesitatingly to sacrifice a specimen, however great its value, if he could replace it by a finer one. This practice he repeated again and again, until the several rooms containing his art treasures constitute the richest repository of pictures, por-

celains, enamels, textiles and rock crystal in existence. He bequeathed his entire collection, valued at $12,000,000, to the Metropolitan Museum of Art, together with a fund of $150,000 for its care and maintenance—the most valuable gift that institution had ever received. It consists of over fifty pictures of the old masters, including thirteen Rembrandts; some twenty pieces of sculpture, chiefly of the Italian and French schools; about 430 Chinese porcelains, Limoges enamels, including the famous "Rospigliosi Coupe"; Flemish tapestries, rare specimens of jade, rock crystals, etc. Mr. Altman did not court publicity concerning his art purchases; he never printed a list of his treasures, and but few persons enjoyed the privilege of examining them. Yet with careful forethought, wisdom and beneficence he provided that his memory shall be indissolubly linked with the happiness which may accrue to his fellow-beings from the use and enjoyment of his estate. He was a good citizen, and possessed the spirit that for a century and a half has quickened the growth and development of the country. He was a typical American, a worker, a builder of the nobler ideals of life, yet a modest man known to the world only through the work he accomplished. He was naturally of a most retiring and modest disposition; he always avoided attending public gatherings, and never allowed his name to be mentioned in the various philanthropies in which he was interested. Mr. Altman died in New York city, Oct. 7, 1913, survived by two nieces and two nephews.

MEIER, Edward Daniel, engineer, was born in St. Louis, Mo., May 30, 1841, son of Adolphus and Rebecca (Rust) Meier, both natives of Germany, who came to this country in 1837 and settled at St. Louis. After a year of study in Bremen, Germany, he took a special course in the scientific department of Washington University, St. Louis, and finished his education at the Royal Polytechnic College at Hanover, Germany, where he was graduated in 1862. He began practical work as an apprentice at the William Mason Machine Works, manufacturers of locomotives, at Taunton, Mass., but the civil war was in full sway, and the repeated calls to arms were more than the ardent young mechanic could resist. He enlisted in the Thirty-second Pennsylvania militia, known as the Gray Reserves, and served in the Army of the Potomac until the decisive battle of Gettysburg compelled the withdrawal of Lee to Virginia, when the special troops were disbanded and sent home. He re-enlisted in Nim's Second Massachusetts battery. He saw active service in the skirmishes at Opelousas, Cane River, Alexandria and during the Red River campaign in the three days' battle of Sabine Cross Roads. On account of his scientific training, he was detailed to the engineering corps, and was given charge of one section of the fortification of Camp Parapet, extending above New Orleans from the Mississippi river to Lake Pontchartrain. This was followed by a survey of a line of works at Brashaer City, La. He took part in many raids and skirmishes which brought about his promotion as first lieutenant and aide-de-camp on the staff of Gen. J. W. Davidson, commander of the cavalry corps of the division of West Mississippi. While stationed at Natchez, Miss., he received the surrender of Gen. John B. Hood and three members of his staff, May 30, 1865. Upon being mustered out of service at the end of the war, he returned to his professional work, entering the employ of the Rogers Locomotive Works at Paterson, N. J., as finisher and draughtsman. After a year in this position (in 1867) he was

Benjamin Altman

EDWARD D. MEIER
ENGINEER

EDWIN B. CRAGIN
PHYSICIAN

GEORGE H. BOUGHTON
ARTIST

PHILLIPS L. GOLDSBOROUGH
GOVERNOR

made assistant division superintendent on the Kansas Pacific railroad. One experience of Mr. Meier in this capacity well illustrates his resourcefulness, energy and persistence. When a flood of the Republican river swept away the railroad bridge at Fort Riley, Kan., he took up his headquarters in a box car, although the weather was bitterly cold, and obtaining a pontoon bridge from the quartermaster at the fort, placed it in position. The quartermaster's stores, passengers, mail and express matter were thus transported for several weeks. The violence of the flood made it necessary to take up the bridge each night and replace it again in the morning. While with the railroad (1868) he designed, erected and superintended a mill at Junction City, Kan., for planing and turning the soft magnesium limestone obtained from Smoky Hill valley, and later in the course of the year made designs and plans for railroad shops, subsequently built at Moberly, Mo. During his last year in its employ, he was superintendent of the machinery of the Kansas Pacific railroad, but early in 1871 he resigned because of ill health and made a trip to Europe. Here he became interested in the methods employed in the treatment of coal, and made a careful study of the European developments of coal washing and coking. Returning to America, he joined his father and elder brother, John W. Meier, who had organized the Illinois Patent Coke Co. at East St. Louis, Ill. When they had expended over $100,000 and were able to produce coke from the slack of Illinois coal, the panic of 1873 prostrated the business and made its continuance inexpedient. Meantime his father had interested some German capitalists in the iron industry in Missouri, and invested money of his own in organizing the Meier Co. and building two blast furnaces at Bessemer, Ill., near St. Louis. For two years Col. Meier was secretary of the company (1873-74), laying out the railroad, planning and superintending a large part of the mechanical construction. According to his designs, the hot blast stoves were of fire brick, the first stoves of the Whitwell patent that had been used west of the Alleghenies. For nearly three years (1875-77) he was associated with the cotton industry of St. Louis, and as mechanical engineer designed and built machinery for the St. Louis Cotton Factory, and later (1878-84), as manager and secretary of the Peper Cotton Press Co., put up considerable machinery and erected a huge hydraulic press of his own design. Col. Meier's military experience stood him in good stead at the time of the railroad riots in 1877. He organized a battalion of militia to protect the St. Louis water-works, and when the excitement was over the organization still continued and became the Third regiment, national guard of Missouri, with him as lieutenant-colonel. Later it was consolidated with the First regiment, and he was unanimously chosen colonel. He refused the rank of brigadier-general which was tendered him, preferring to keep his own command as ranking colonel. Col. Meier kept himself constantly in touch with the progress of mechanical methods and devices in Europe. In 1885 he became interested in a new German boiler, which seemed to offer peculiar advantages to the trade, and he organized the Heine Safety Water-Tube Boiler Co. for its exploitation, of which he is its president and chief engineer. He has made several important improvements in the boiler which add to its efficiency. He has served as secretary and chairman of the committee on materials of the American Boiler Manufacturers' Association, in which capacity he was instrumental in formulating the first two sets of specifications known as the "uniform American boiler specifications," which were adopted in 1898 as the association's standard and became the authority for the boiler-makers of the country. He also organized the Diesel Motor Co. of America and was its chief engineer until 1909. Col. Meier was at one time president of the American Boiler Manufacturers' Association and also of the Machinery and Metal Trades Association. He was a member of the American Society of Mechanical Engineers, vice-president 1898–1900 and 1910, and president in 1911–12; member of the American Institute of Mining Engineers and the American Society of Naval Engineers, the Grand Army of the Republic, and the Military Order of the Loyal Legion. He was married Oct. 16, 1868, to Clara, daughter of F. W. Giesecke of Braunschweig, Germany; she died in 1870, leaving one son, Edward C. His second wife was Nancy Anderson Runyan of St. Louis, Mo., by whom he had three daughters, Mary Alice, Elizabeth, wife of W. V. Schevill, and Clara, wife of Prof. Ferdinand Schevill, and two sons, Theodore G. and Clement R. D. Meier. He died in New York, Dec. 15, 1914.

CRAGIN, Edwin Bradford, physician, was born at Colchester, Conn., Oct. 23, 1859, son of Edwin Timothy and Ardelia Ellis (Sparrow) Cragin. On the maternal side Dr. Cragin is a descendant of William Bradford, the first governor of Plymouth. His early education was obtained in the Bacon Academy of his native town, and entering Yale College in 1879, was graduated four years later. He studied medicine at the College of Physicians and Surgeons, New York city, receiving his M.D. degree in 1886 and receiving also the first Harsen prize for proficiency in examination. For eighteen months he served on the house staff of the Roosevelt Hospital, after which he began private practice in New York city, making a specialty of gynecology. In July, 1888, he was appointed assistant gynecologist to the out-patient department of Roosevelt Hospital, was made attending gynecologist to the same department in November of that year and assistant gynecologist to the hospital proper in June, 1889. He was assistant surgeon to the New York Cancer Hospital during 1889-93, resigning the position in the latter year on account of pressure of work. In 1895 Dr. Cragin was appointed consulting gynecologist to the New York Infirmary for Women and Children, and in the following year consulting obstetric surgeon to the Maternity Hospital on Blackwell's Island. In December, 1893, he became assistant secretary of the faculty of the College of Physicians and Surgeons and secretary in July, 1895, and three years later was elected to the chair of obstetrics in the college, with the title of lecturer in obstetrics. In 1902 he became professor of obstetrics, and soon after received the appointment of attending physician to the Sloane Maternity Hospital. Dr. Cragin has contributed numerous articles to medical journals, and is the author of "The Essentials of Gynecology" (1910) and a co-author of "The American Text Book of Gynecology." He is a member of the American Gynecological Society, the New York County Medical Society, the New York Obstetrical Society, the Medical Association of Greater New York and the New York Academy of Medicine. He is also a member of the Yale Club of New York city. He was married May 23, 1889, to Mary Randle, daughter of Rev. Samuel G. Willard, of Colchester, Conn., and has two daughters, Miriam W. and Alice G. Cragin, and one son, Edwin Bradford Cragin Jr.

BOUGHTON, George Henry, artist, was born near Norwich, England, Dec. 4, 1833, son of William Boughton. In 1837 he was brought to this country by his parents, who settled in Albany, N. Y. Losing them both shortly after, he was cared for by his brother, a merchant in that city, and was educated at the high school, also taking a course at a commercial academy. His talent for art discovered itself in his earliest boyhood, and after a short experience as a bookkeeper, during which time he made many sketches, he decided to become an artist and began by himself to study painting. This preference meeting with his brother's approval he opened a studio in Albany in 1850, one of his first patrons being the old American Art Union. Through the sale of several pictures, supplemented by the kindness of his brother and many friends, he went abroad to study in 1853. He spent a few months in London and then returned to Albany, subsequently removing to New York city, where he remained for several years. In 1858 he made his first exhibit at the National Academy with "A White Twilight." He painted chiefly landscapes at this period, among them "The Lake of the Dismal Swamp." In 1860 he went to Paris and studied for two years with Edouard Frere. Going to London with the intention of returning home from there, he met friends who advised him to remain and try his fortune in that city. From the first the young artist received encouragement and his pictures, exhibited at the British Institution in 1863 and the Royal Academy in 1864, were immediately successful. He was an annual contributor to the Royal Academy, of which he was made an associate in 1879 and an academician in 1896, and was also frequently represented in American exhibitions. He became a member of the National Academy of Design in 1871. Master of a distinctive style and technique, Mr. Boughton told his story in a naïve way that gave charm to the most trifling episode, and in his more important compositions displayed a knowledge, allied with a faculty for realizing the spirit of his subject, that gave these works a genuine historical value. Many of his pictures, notably those relating to Knickerbocker history, show a delightful sense of humor. He excelled in depicting Puritan life in New England, though he produced some important compositions drawn from Chaucer and other early English poets, besides subjects taken from Brittany and the Netherlands. With a decided fondness for picturesque costumes, his figures were nevertheless painted in an unaffected manner, with a color scheme subdued and harmonious, frequently using a background of winter landscape with fine result. "The Scarlet Letter," "Return of the Mayflower," "Puritans Going to Church" and "Rose Standish" are among his most successful paintings of colonial subjects. Other canvases are: "Passing Into the Shade" (1863), "A Breton Haymaker" (1864), "Wayside Devotion" (1867), "Breton Pastoral" (1869), "Coming from Church," "Cold Without," "Morning Prayer," "Normany Girl in a Shower," "By the Sea" and "Going to Seek His Fortune" (1876), "Canterbury Pilgrims," "A Ruffling Breeze," "Idyl of the Birds" and "The Testy Governor" (1877), "Waning of the Honeymoon" (1878), "The Rose," "Fading Light," "Gypsy Girl," "Tam O'Shanter," "Charity," "Winter in Brabant" (1891), "Council of Peter the Headstrong," "Divided," "Dancing Down the Hay," "Winter Sunrise" and "Love in Winter." Mr. Boughton was the author of "Sketching Rambles

in Holland" (1877), a "Life of Morland" (1895), and various short stories in the Harper and Pall Mall magazines. He was a member of the Athenæum, Reform and Burlington clubs in London, England, and of the Grolier Club, New York city. He was married in 1865 to Katherine Louise, daughter of Dr. Henry Cullen of London, England. Mr. Boughton died at Campden Hill, England, Jan. 19, 1905. Portrait opp. p. 189.

GOLDSBOROUGH, Phillips Lee, fiftieth governor of Maryland (1912–16), was born in Cambridge, Md., Aug. 6, 1865, son of M. Worthington and Nettie M. (Jones) Goldsborough. His father was an officer in the United States navy; he was assistant paymaster in the civil war; promoted to be paymaster in May, 1866, and pay inspector in 1891, and retired from the service in 1896 with the rank of captain. The son was educated in private and public schools of Maryland, and after studying law in the office of Daniel M. Henry, Jr., was admitted to the bar in 1886. He began the practice of his profession in Dorchester county, and acquired a large and lucrative law business. He was elected to the office of state's attorney in 1891 and was re-elected in 1895. Two years later he became comptroller of the treasury of Maryland. In 1902 Pres. Roosevelt appointed him collector of internal revenue for the district of Maryland, and he was reappointed to that office by Roosevelt and again by Taft. He was the unanimous choice of the Republican party for the office of governor in 1911, and was elected in November of that year. During his administration the legislature passed laws continuing the system of good roads throughout the state and appropriating $6,000,000 more for these improvements; providing for a state tax commission to supervise and authorize assessment of property and taxation; granting of extraordinary powers to the state board of health and a large appropriation for its use; creating an advisory board of pardons and parole embodied in a so-called penal reform act; and establishing a liberal workmen's compensation act. Gov. Goldsborough was married, Dec. 14, 1893, to Mary Ellen, daughter of William Showell, of Worcester county, Md., and has two sons: Phillips Lee, Jr., and Brice Worthing Goldsborough. Portrait opposite page 189.

STEWART, Alexander, lumberman, was born in York county, New Brunswick, Canada, Sept. 12, 1829, son of Thomas and Jane (Moody) Stewart. His father came to America from Scotland in 1819 and settled in New Brunswick. He lived in a time and under conditions where self-reliance was the prime requisite and hard work the accepted duty of young and old, and his son Alexander, even during his school days, spent his spare time logging and log-driving in the forests of his native country and on the Merrimac river. At the age of twenty, he went to Blackberry, now Elburn, Ill., and then to a settlement called Big Bull Falls, on the site of what is now Wausau, Wis. There he began his career as a lumberman, engaging in rafting on the Wisconsin and Mississippi rivers in association with his brother John. It was not an age of opportunity, notwithstanding the present-day declamation that so denotes it. Men had to make their opportunities, many times in desperation, not knowing what the end would be, for there were no precedents to guide them, no traveled paths that they could follow. Rugged virility, tireless endurance and unending persistence were the essentials in the men who would wrest success and wealth from the groaning forests and turbulent rivers of the great Northwest, and the man who stood out among his fellows as Alexander Stewart did, had of necessity those qualities. From the beginning the Stewart brothers met with success in their arduous calling and in 1874 they took Walter Alexander into partnership, forming the firm of J. & A. Stewart & Co. The company purchased a mill at Wausau with a capacity of 9,000,000 feet of lumber a year. From year to year the output of the firm grew rapidly until in 1884 it had reached 17,000,000 feet per year. In that year it was reorganized as the Alexander Stewart Lumber Co., with Alexander Stewart as president. Soon afterward the Champaign Lumber Co. was formed, of which he was also president. From this time on, his operations extended rapidly. He became president of the Wausau Boom Co., the Wausau Land and Investment Co., and the Marathon County Bank, and secured interests in the Montreal River Lumber Co., the McCloud River Lumber Co. and the Alexander & Edgar Lumber Co. He was also vice-president of the Greer-Wilkinson Lumber Co. of Indianapolis, Ind., which controlled a wholesale lumber yard at Michigan City, Ind., and some thirty other yards in the same state; was president of the F. H. Gilcrest Lumber Co., which maintained a chain of yards in Nebraska; organized and was president of the Stewart Lumber Co., conducting a chain of yards in Iowa, and the Stewart & Alexander Lumber Co. and the Wisconsin and Arkansas Lumber Co. in Arkansas. In 1904 he was a candidate for congress from the 9th district of Wisconsin and was elected on the Republican ticket by a majority of 7,800 in a normally Democratic district. After serving for three terms he declined a fourth nomination. He served on many important committees, including those on Indian affairs and on manufactures. His virile, vigorous personality, uncompromising honesty and fearless candor commanded the respect of friend and opponent alike, and his keen business sense lent value to his views on any subject that came before the house. While he was a self-educated man, he was a discriminating reader of good books, had a remarkably retentive memory and was widely informed on various subjects, which made him an interesting conversationalist. He was married in Chicago, Ill., March 23, 1858, to Margaret, daughter of John Gray, a native of Scotland, and had three daughters: Margaret, wife of W. O. Lindley, Mary and Helen Stewart. He died in Washington, D. C., May 24, 1912.

WALSH, Thomas Francis, miner and capitalist, was born at Baptist Grange, near Fethard, Tipperary, Ireland, April 2, 1851, son of Thomas and Bridget (Scully) Walsh. His father was a farmer in moderate circumstances. While attending the common schools his interest in geology was awakened by his teacher exhibiting a piece of granite as a rare curiosity in a limestone region, such as Tipperary is. Upon leaving school he was apprenticed to a millwright and in that way acquired practical knowledge in the building of mills which was of great value to him later in his mining operations. He came to the United States in 1865 and followed the carpenter's trade, and in 1872 removed to Colorado at the suggestion of his brother, who had preceded him there and made a start as a builder and contractor. While thus engaged, he studied geology, mineralogy and metallurgy from a practical standpoint and soon found that he had an almost intuitive perception of the values of ore in the rock. The rush to the Black Hills in 1876 carried Mr. Walsh with it, and while working as a builder, he prospected for gold. Before long he discovered with

others a mine that yielded $100,000, and laid the foundation of the brilliant career that soon followed. Returning to Colorado at the time of the Leadville boom, he engaged in a number of successful enterprises. He spent considerable money in experimental smelting, and erected a pyritic smelter at Kokomo, the first in the state, and later another at Silverton. He also prospected scientifically the whole San Juan region, and made a number of investments in gold mines. By 1886 Mr. Walsh had amassed an income of some $15,000 a year, and accordingly he went East to live, but his fortune was lost in the panic of 1893 and he returned to the career of a mining engineer. He believed that there were valuable deposits of gold and silver in the high regions about Ouray, Colo., and though old miners shook their heads, he quietly bought up old claims in 1896, and put men to work prospecting. The reward of his pluck and sagacity was the Camp Bird mine, which was said to be one of the richest gold mines in the world, and for which he refused an offer of $35,000,000. Here he built for his employees a sumptuously equipped hotel, made it over to them at minimum cost, and housed those having families as no miners had ever been housed before. He was one of the first to adopt the eight-hour working day, and did so just after the courts had decided that it could not be enforced. Mr. Walsh owned a magnificent home in the city of Washington, D. C. He visited Europe frequently and entertained in its capitals in the most lavish manner, on one occasion giving a dinner to the King of Belgium, not from love of ostentation, but from pride in his country. He was one of the national commissioners to the Paris Exposition of 1900; and was a member of the American Association for the Advancement of Science, the American Association of Mining Engineers, National Geological Society, American Political Science Association, Washington Academy of Sciences, National Irrigation Association, the American chambers of commerce in Paris and Naples, the New York Chamber of Commerce and the Washington board of trade. He was married in Leadville, Colo., Oct. 7, 1879, to Caroline B., daughter of Stephen Reed, of Darlington, Wis. Three children were born to them. His daughter became the wife of Edward B. McLean, of Cincinnati, O. Mr. Walsh was one of the early advocates of the conservation policy that became a notable feature of Pres. Roosevelt's administration. He took a deep interest especially in the question of irrigating the arid lands of the West, and was a founder and the first president of the National Irrigation Association. He was a man of extraordinary fine parts, generous to a fault, warm-hearted, chivalrous and genial—a typical Western American gentleman. Few self-made men signalized their rise to financial position by gaining such genuine social distinction both at home and abroad as did he. He died in Washington, D. C., survived by his wife and one daughter, Apr. 8, 1910.

MOTTIER, David Myers, botanist and teacher, was born in Patriot, Ind., Sept. 4, 1864, son of John David and Lydia (Myers) Mottier. He was graduated at the University of Indiana in 1891, receiving the degree of A.M. a year later. At once he was appointed to an instructorship in the botanical department of his alma mater, and in 1893 was advanced to the grade of associate professorship. In 1895 he went to Europe and studied at the University of Bonn, where in 1897 he was given the degree of Ph.D., and during 1898 he was at the University of Leipzig and then at the Zoological Station in Naples. On his return to the United States he was made full professor of botany at the University of Indiana, a place he still holds. Among his contributions to his chosen field of investigation are the following: "The Behavior of the Chromosomes in the Spore Mother-Cells of Higher Plants and the Homology of the Pollen and Embryosac Mother-Cells" (1903); "The Development of Heterotypic Chromosomes in Pollen Mother-Cells" (1905); and "Notes on the Sex of Onoclea Struthiopteris" (1910), which appeared in the "Botanical Gazette," also "Fecundation in Plants with Bibliography" (1904). A monograph of 187 pages which he contributed to the publications of the Carnegie Institution of Washington, and "The Development of the Spermatozoid of Chara" (1903); "Some Anomalies in the Female Gametophyte of Pinus" (1908); "Nuclear Phenomena of Sexual Reproduction in Angiosperms" (1910); "The Influence of Certain Environic Factors in the Development of Fern Prothallia" (1912), and "Further Notes on the Seedless Fruits of the Common Persimmon" (1913), which were published in the Trantactions of the Indiana Academy of Sciences. In book form he is the author of "Practical Laboratory Guide for the First Year in Botany" (1902). Prof. Mottier is a member of scientific societies both in this country and abroad, having been in 1907 president of the Indiana Academy of Science, and since 1901 he has been a fellow of the American Association for the Advancement of Science. He is a life member of the Botanical Society of America and member of Phi Beta Kappa and Sigma Xi fraternities.

FITCH, [William] Clyde, dramatist, was born at Elmira, N. Y., May 2, 1865, son of Capt. William Goodwin and Alice Maud (Clarke) Fitch. The family is one of the oldest in America, and is descended from Thomas Fitch, of Bocking, Essex, England, who was married to Anna Pew; and, according to one writer, was a judge. Two of his sons came to America in 1637 and settled in Connecticut, one of them, James, being first pastor of Saybrook and founder of Norwich. Thomas Fitch, fifth of the name in America, was governor of Connecticut from 1754 to 1766. His son, Thomas, was colonel of the Fairfield county militia, was active in sending regiments to the field in 1776-77, and served in the general assembly. Jonathan Fitch was commissary of the continental and state troops of Connecticut during the revolution. Capt. William G. Fitch, father of our subject, was born in Hartford, Conn., Aug. 23, 1833. He was appointed first lieutenant in the Fourth Connecticut Volunteers, May 22, 1861, and served in the civil war until he was retired, Nov. 16, 1863, for disability resulting from sickness and exposure. Clyde Fitch was educated privately and at Amherst College, where he was graduated in 1886. It was his father's intention that he should be an architect, but though the future dramatist had a taste for art he was still more decidedly attracted to amateur theatricals, to marionettes and puppet shows, and to his paper, "The Thunderbolt." During the first few years following his graduation he led an interesting semi-Bohemian, semi-Brummelian existence. He went about the world with a keenly appreciative eye for its humors and foibles, its love and laughter, its tragedy and tears, its yearnings and strivings and its passionate pretences. He saw life as "a delicious comedy," almost a rollicking farce, with many poignant tragedies, undoubtedly, but still, in its broad

aspects, a comedy. And even the poignant tragedies he saw took on a comic aspect when fitted in their real proportions into the panoramic view of life. In one of his plays Fitch made a comedy out of a funeral. When he started life in New York he was situated more fortunately than the majority of literary aspirants. He wrote short stories for magazines, haunted the theaters, bought antiques, dressed in luxurious and recherché fashion, and had an altogether joyous time. That was why he loved children so much and understood them so well, why his home was filled with Della Robbia Bambini, dancing children of Donatello, and smiling angels of Capo di Monte porcelain, why his first book, "The Knighting of the Twins," published in 1891, was one of the best things he ever did. A novel, "A Wave of Life," followed soon after, and although it went through three editions it was not one of his happiest achievements. In the meantime he contributed jokes to "Life" and other humorous papers, wrote verses for magazines, gave subscription Browning readings, and tutored children. He was nothing if not versatile. The production of "Betty's Finish," a one-act comedy of college life, marked the maiden flashing of his dramatic sword. It ran for two months at the Boston Museum, in 1890. About this time Richard Mansfield evinced a special interest in the life and times of Beau Brummel. He was introduced to Fitch, and the result was "Beau Brummel," which was produced at the Madison Square Theater, May 19, 1890. It achieved a triumphant success, ran for over a hundred nights, and remained the most popular play in Mansfield's repertory. The list of his plays, original and adapted, is bewildering. Such amazing and prolific industry is almost unparalleled in the history of play-writing, and the wonder of it is not that there is some that is flimsy and mediocre, but that there is so much of high and lasting value, so much that bears the unmistakable stamp of genius, so much that marks the author as one of the most really notable of modern dramatists. Furthermore, as a technician, America has produced nobody to rival him. His technique is as finished, maintained and clearly cut as Pinero's best. He had a complete knowledge of all the resources of the stage; indeed, he enjoyed a secondary fame as stage manager. Whatever else his dramas lacked, they never lacked theatrical effectiveness; in fact, theatricality was one of his predominant faults, especially in his earlier years, before he had learned to restrain his youthful exuberance and practice the supreme literary and dramatic virtues of condensation and omission. There is no doubt that Fitch left his greatest work undone. He was young when he died. He was unfortunate enough, from one point of view, to win brilliant success too young. He was beset by a wayward and exuberant fancy, an overstock of invention, a too great facility of expression. These qualities accounted for his prodigality; but his very prodigality meant the eventual disappearance of superfluities from his talent, the eventual disclosure of real genius, for of real genius even his early work gave no uncertain hint. No one who has seen or read his two later works, "The Truth" and "The City," can entertain any doubt of his tendency. These two plays have the directness, power and relentless logic of Ibsen. In his later years he was beginning to see life from the point of view of the individual, the point of view which shows moving tragedy and poignant pathos, the difficulty, strife and uncertainty, the tenderness, beauty and

Clyde Fitch

sublimity that life represents to the individual. And there is no doubt that had he lived to the fruition of his rapidly maturing powers he would have given us such a moving drama of real life as the American stage has not yet seen. Altogether, Fitch wrote over fifty plays and adaptations, of which about thirty were marked popular successes, and a considerable number of which were produced abroad. Among the best known of these are "Frederick Le Maitre" (1890); "A Modern Match" (1891), played in England by the Kendals, under the title of "Marriage"; "Pamela's Prodigy" (1891); "His Grace De Grammont" (1892); "April Weather" (1892); "The Masked Ball" (1892), adapted for John Drew; "The Harvest" (1893), afterward elaborated into "The Moth and the Flame" (1898); "Mistress Betty" (1894), for Madame Modjeska; "A Social Swim" (1894), adapted for Marie Wainwright; "Gossip" (1895), for Mrs. Langtry, in collaboration with Leo Dietrichstein; "Bohemia" (1896), adapted from Murger's "Vie de Boheme" "A Superfluous Husband" (1897), with Leo Dietrichstein; "The Cowboy and the Lady" (1899); "Barbara Frietchie" (1899); "Captain Jinks of the Horse Marines" (1901); "The Girl and the Judge" (1901); "The Way of the World" (1901); "The Stubbornness of Geraldine" (1902); "The Girl with the Green Eyes" (1902); "The Bird in the Cage" (1902), from the German; "Her Own Way" (1903); "Glad of It" (1903); "The Frisky Mrs. Johnson" (1904); "Granny" (1904), for Mrs. Gilbert; "A Woman in the Case" (1905), "The Truth" (1906); "The House of Mirth" (1906); "The Straight Road," played by Blanche Walsh in New York in 1907; "Nathan Hale" (1908), for Nat Goodwin, and "The City" (1910). He also wrote short sketches and letters published under the titles "The Smart Set," and "Some Correspondence and Six Conversations," both of which were quite successful. He was unmarried, and died at Chalons-Sur-Marne, France, Sept. 4, 1909.

GUNN, John Edward, sixth Roman Catholic bishop of Natchez, Miss., was born at Five Mile Town, County Tyrone, Ireland, March 15, 1863, son of Edward and Mary (Grew) Gunn. His education was obtained at St. Mary's College, Dundalk, Dublin University, Ireland, and the Gregorian University, Rome, where he was ordained priest Feb. 2, 1890. He then came to the United States and was professor of moral theology at the Catholic University, Washington, D. C., during 1892–98, and pastor at Atlanta, Ga., 1898–1911, where he built a church and college for the Marist Fathers. He was appointed bishop of Natchez June 29, 1911, and consecrated August 29. A number of his addresses and pastorals have been published and widely circulated. Natchez diocese is coextensive with the state of Mississippi and has a Catholic population of 26,000, with fifty-three priests; 180 churches and stations; twenty-seven schools with 4,000 children.

BUMSTEAD, Henry Andrews, physicist, was born in Pekin, Ill., Mar. 12, 1870, son of Dr. Samuel Josiah and Sarah Ellen (Seiwell) Bumstead. From the high school in Decatur, Ill., he entered the Johns Hopkins University, and after his graduation in 1891 served for two years thereafter as assistant in physics. In 1893 he was called to Yale University to serve as instructor in physics at the Sheffield Scientific School and in 1900 was advanced to the rank of assistant professor. Six years later he was given full professorship and made director of the Sloane physical

laboratory. Meanwhile he received the degree of Ph.D. from Yale for his advanced studies. He has made a special study of radio-activity, the Röntgen rays and the theory of the electron. The most important of his papers on these subjects are: "On a Radio-Active Gas in Surface Water" (1903), "The Properties of a Radio-Active Gas Found in the Soil and Water near New Haven," (1904), "Atmospheric Radio-Activity" (1904); "The Heating Effects Produced by Röntgen Rays in Different Metals and Their Relations to the Question of Change in the Atom" (1906); "On the Heating Effects Produced by Röntgen Rays in Lead and Zinc" (1908), and "On the Emission of Electrons by Metals Under the Influence of Alpha Rays (Part 1, 1911; part 2, 1912). He was one of the editors of the two volumes of "The Scientific Papers of J. Willard Gibbs" (1906). He is a member of the American Physical Society, the American Academy of Arts and Sciences, the Connecticut Academy of Arts and Sciences, and since 1910 has been a fellow of the American Association for the Advancement of Science. His brilliant researches in the domain of physics were rewarded in 1913 by his election to the National Academy of Sciences, an honor which is conferred only upon the greatest of American scientists. He was married Aug. 18, 1896, to Luetta Ullrich, daughter of John Ullrich, of Decatur, Ill., and has two children: John Henry and Eleanor Bumstead.

THOMAS, George Clifford, banker and philanthropist, was born in Philadelphia, Pa., Oct. 28, 1839, son of John W. and Sophia K. (Atkinson) Thomas. His father was a prominent merchant and for many years accounting warden of St. Paul's Episcopal Church. The son was educated at the Episcopal Academy, and at an early age assumed the management of his father's financial interests, for which he exhibited a remarkable aptitude. His unusual ability won recognition from Jay Cooke, who invited him to become his confidential secretary, and in one year he was admitted to partnership in the firm. He was one of the active partners during the great financial operations of the national government for the civil war when Jay Cooke & Co. financed the largest and most successful money operations that any government had undertaken at that time. When the firm failed in 1873, Mr. Thomas surrendered every dollar of his fortune for the benefit of his creditors. He now formed a partnership with Joseph M. Shoemaker, under the style of Thomas & Shoemaker. Subsequently Anthony J. Drexel invited him to become a partner in the well-known Drexel house, and from that time until his death Mr. Thomas was a factor in nearly all the large financial transactions of Philadelphia. He was connected with the Reading and Northern Pacific reorganizations, and all the important operations of the Drexel & Morgan firms, before his retirement, ranking for twenty-one years among the first of Philadelphia's international bankers. He retired from active business in 1905 because of ill health. He was a member of the Philadelphia and New York Stock Exchanges; a director in the Farmers & Mechanics National Bank and the Pennsylvania Co. for Insurance on Lives and Granting Annuities; manager of the Philadelphia Savings Fund Society; and an investor in various other financial institutions. As a banker, Mr. Thomas held high standards of personal integrity and business honor. His residence contained a collection of books, pictures, relics and art treasures which was the delight of art lovers of Philadelphia and New York for many years. The library included rare books, autograph letters and documents of priceless value. His copies of the Bible, which embraced almost every rare edition known, included the first complete English Bible, printed by Miles Coverdale in 1535, the Tyndale new Testament, printed at Worms, the first sheets of an issue of the Bible authorized by Thomas Cromwell and printed in Paris, the Ives copy of the Eliot Indian Bible, and the famous Mark Baskett Bible. Among the autographs were the original libretto of Die Meistersinger, in the cramped small writing of Richard Wagner, autographs of all the signers of the Declaration of Independence, originals of Grant's dispatch announcing Lee's surrender, the original Charter of Liberty granted by William Penn to the freemen of the province of Pennsylvania in 1682, famous letters of Lincoln to Gen. Hooker, letters of Washington, of Robert E. Lee surrendering his commission in the U. S. army at the outbreak of the civil war, and autographs of Beethoven, Gluck, Handel, Haydn, Wagner, Jenny Lind, Schubert, and Mozart. His art collection contained Sir Joshua Reynolds' portrait of Lady Gertrude Fitzpatrick as Sylvia, Whistler's portrait of Sir Henry Irving as Philip II of Spain, Millet's ''Laborer's Return,'' Troyon's ''Grazing Scene,'' and canvases of Constable, Rousseau, Corot, Breton, Alma Tadema and Peale. Next to J. Pierpont Morgan Mr. Thomas was probably the greatest benefactor of the Protestant Episcopal Church. For forty-one years he was superintendent of the Sunday-school of the Church of the Holy Apostles in Philadelphia and one of the founders of the Lenten Missionary, offering, was treasurer of the board of missions thirteen years, and for many years was organist both of the church and Sunday-school. He purchased innumerable small houses in the southern part of the city for the charitable purpose of improving the neighborhood of the church and of providing really comfortable homes for the poor at a reasonable price. It was Mr. Thomas' belief that, ''If men who can, do not purchase costly and beautiful things, society will be the worse, in that there will be no premium set upon excellence, and the world's work will degenerate.'' He built the chapel at Twenty-seventh and Wharton streets, and later the Phillips Brooks Memorial Guild House and the group of buildings, at the same location, thus giving the chapel one of the most completely appointed mission foundations in this country. In 1902 he built the Cooper Battalion Hall and Gymnasium, said to be the most perfect edifice of its kind in the country, and a year later he erected what has been pronounced the most successful structure for Sunday-school purposes ever built. In 1905 he gave the sum of $40,000 to build St. Paul's Church at Fifteenth and Porter streets, and in addition he periodically increased the endowment fund of the parish until, at the time of his death it had reached $132,000. He was married, Nov. 26, 1867, to Ada Elizabeth, daughter of J. Barlow Moorhead, ironmaster of Philadelphia, and their children were George C., Jr.; Leonard Moorhead, Sophia Thomas, wife of Walter Schuyler Volkmar, and Bessie Moorhead, deceased. Mr. Thomas died in Philadelphia, Pa., April 21, 1909.

GRAY, Louis Herbert, philologist and editor, was born at Newark, N. J., Apr. 10, 1875, son of Thomas Jefferson and Anna Elizabeth (Earl) Gray. He was graduated at Princeton University in 1896. He was fellow in classics at Princeton, 1896–97; received the degree of A.M. from Columbia in 1898, and that of Ph.D. in 1900, and was a graduate student in Hebrew and Old Irish in 1907–

08, continuing his studies in Celtic at Aberdeen. After being chief cataloger and instructor in Indo-Iranian at Princeton in 1900-02, he was editor of the departments of etymology and the history of modern India on the ''New International Encyclopedia'' 1902-03, for which he also wrote numerous articles on linguistic and Indo-Iranian topics, and was reviser of translations for the ''Jewish Encyclopedia'' in 1904-05. In 1905 he was appointed editor of the departments of Zoroastrianism and primitive religion on the ''Dictionary of Religion and Ethics,'' edited by Dr. James Hastings and published in Edinburgh. In 1913 he was made assistant editor of this encyclopedia, and has since then resided in Aberdeen, Scotland. To this work also he has contributed many articles on primitive Polynesian, American Indian, Hindu, and Zoroastrian religious beliefs. In 1901, and again in 1903, he had charge of the courses in linguistics and Indo-Iranian during the absence of his teacher, Prof. A. V. Williams Jackson, in India and Persia. He has been a member of several international congresses of Orientalists and Americanists. Beginning with the study of the classics, Dr. Gray proceeded to the broader field of comparative linguistics, which is his real centre of scholarly interest, though he has done considerable work in Sanskrit, Avesta, and the religion of ancient Persia. His researches in the latter field prepared the way for wider investigation in comparative religion (especially among the primitive peoples and in India), though the importance of this subject seems to him often overrated. Though a layman, he had long been brought in close contact with theological thought, the result of these studies and of his investigations of non-Christian religions as well as of the methodological problems involved, being to render him distinctly unfavorable both to the theories and the results, in great measure, of the ''critical'' school of theological investigation. He has written upward of forty studies on the languages and religions of ancient Indian and Persia, and on comparative philology for technical periodicals and memorial volumes in America, Europe, and India. He is likewise the author of ''Indo-Iranian Phonology, with Special Reference to the Middle and New Indo-Iranian Languages'' (1902), and translated from the Persian for the first time ''The Hundred Love-Songs of Kamal ad-Din of Isfahan,'' in collaboration with Mrs. Ethel Watts Mumford. In 1913 he published a translation (with a reprint of the rare ''Southern'' text) of the ''Vasavadatta'' of Subandhu, a Sanskrit romance of highly artificial style, written in the latter part of the sixth century, A. D.; and has in preparation an ''Etymological Dictionary of the Sanskrit Language,'' besides being the editor of a projected ''Mythology of All Races,'' the latter to appear in America. He was married June 8, 1905, to Florence Lillian, daughter of George Cooper Ridley, of Brooklyn, N. Y.

MURLIN, Lemuel Herbert, third president of Boston University, was born at Convoy, Mercer co., O., Nov. 16, 1861, son of Rev. Orlando and Esther (Hankins) Murlin. His grandfather migrated from Connecticut to northern Ohio, where his father was a pioneer Methodist minister. At the age of fourteen, the son entered a drug store as clerk and boy of all work. At sixteen he was teaching in the Convoy village school, and later he was called to Fort Wayne (Ind.) College to take charge of the boys' department. By thus teaching and at the same time preaching as pastor of Trinity Methodist Episcopal Church, in Fort

Wayne, he worked his way through the college, and was graduated in 1886. From Fort Wayne he went to De Pauw University, and in the same way was pastor of the Knightsville Methodist Episcopal Church during the four years of his college course. He was graduated at De Pauw in 1891, receiving the degree of S.T.B. from the theological school of that university in 1882. During his college course he spent his vacations in attending lectures on Hebrew and the English Bible by Pres. Harper of Chicago University. In 1891 he was elected to membership in the American Institute of Christian Philosophy, and in that year also he was appointed pastor of the Methodist Episcopal church in Vincennes, Ind. Three years later he was elected president of Baker University, Baldwin, Kan., the oldest college in that state. During the summer of 1895 he engaged in work with the American University Extension Society. He took post-graduate courses at the University of Pennsylvania in 1896, at Clark University in 1897, and at universities in Europe in 1898, serving as acting pastor of the American Church in Berlin, Germany, while on a year's leave of absence from Baker (1909-10). In September, 1911, while still president of Baker University, he was elected president of Boston University. Pres. Murlin received the degrees of S.T.D. from the University of Denver in 1897; D.D. from Cornell College, Ia., in 1897; B.D. from Garrett Biblical Institute in 1899, and LL.D. from De Pauw University in 1909 and from the University of Vermont in 1911. He was a member of the general conference of the Methodist Episcopal church in 1900 and 1904; delegate to the Methodist Ecumenical Conference in London, Eng., in 1901, and to that held at Toronto, Can., in 1911. While in Kansas he was a member of the state text-book commission, and of the special commission to reorganize the educational administration of Kansas. He was also secretary of the Kansas Commission on Rhodes scholarships; served as president of the Kansas Association of College Presidents; was a member of the National Conference on Church Federation, 1906; was state director for Kansas of the Religious Educational Association; and vice-president from Kansas of the North Central Association of Colleges and Secondary Schools. He is a member of the National Educational Association; the Phi Kappa Psi college fraternity; and the University Club, Boston. President Murlin was married Oct. 12, 1893, to Ermina Fallass (Ph.D., De Pauw), preceptress and professor of French and English at Cornell College, Ia., daughter of Henry Fallas, of Lowell, Mich.

KOTZSCHMAR, Hermann, musician, was born in Finsterwalde, Prussia, July 4, 1829. He began to study music under his father, Gottfried Kotzschmar, who was the town musician, and in his teens he was not only a skilled pianist, but was able to play creditably the violin, flute, clarinet and trombone. He spent five years in Dresden studying counterpoint, the piano and organ, and composition, and in 1848 came to America as a member of the Saxonia band. Settling in Portland, Me., he became leader of a theater orchestra and later organist of the First Parish Church of Portland, a position he held until 1898, when he changed to the State Street Church. He was a successful piano teacher and conducted a number of choral societies. Under his baton the Haydn Association of Portland, of which he was conductor during 1869-98, became one of the well-known oratorio societies of the country. His

printed compositions include pieces for the piano, songs, anthems, hymns and carols, and are regarded as a distinct contribution to American church music. His "Te Deum in F" is probably the best of them. He received two honorary degrees of M.A. from Bowdoin College in 1903, and D.Mus. from Eberhardt College in 1905. The great municipal organ in Portland was a gift from Kotzschmar's friend, Cyrus H. K. Curtis, as a tribute to his memory. He was married Dec. 16, 1872, to Mary Ann, daughter of Midian Torrey, and had one daughter, Dorothea, wife of Arthur Sachsse, and had one son, Hermann Kotzschmar, Jr. He died in Portland, Me., Apr. 15, 1908.

MERRITT, Ernest George, physicist, was born in Indianapolis, Ind., Apr. 28, 1865, son of George and Paulina Tate (McClung) Merritt. He entered Purdue University in 1881, but later transferred his studies to Cornell, where he was graduated M.E. in 1886. He spent a year in post-graduate work as fellow in physics, studying especially the efficiency of electric lighting. In 1889 he was made an instructor in physics at Cornell and in 1891 was advanced to an assistant professorship. During 1893-94 he attended lectures at Berlin University. In 1903 he was made full professor of physics, and six years later became dean of the graduate school. He has conducted original researches in the fields of luminescence, conduction in gases, the efficiency of glow lamps, photoelectricity, etc., and the results for the most part have been contributed to the "Physical Review," of which he was an associate editor from 1893 to 1912. His titles include: "On a Method of Photographing the Manometric Flame, with Applications to the Study of the Vowel A" (1894); "On the Absorption of Certain Crystals in the Infrared as Dependent on the Direction of the Plane of Polarization" (1895); "The Trace of the Gyroscopic Pendulum" (1897); "A Vacuum Tube to Illustrate the Slow Diffusion of the Residual Gases in High Vaccua" (1898), and "The Resistance Offered by Iron Wires to Alternating Currents" (1899). With his distinguished colleague, Prof. Edward L. Nichols, he published papers on "The Phosphorescence and Fluorescence of Organic Substances at Low Temperatures"; "A Spectrophotometric Study of Fluorescent Solutions Belonging to Lommel's First Class"; "On Fluorescence Spectra"; "The Influence of Light Upon the Absorption and Electrical Conductivity of Fluorescent Solutions," all of which appeared in the "Physical Review" in 1904 and later under similar auspices appeared "The Luminescence of Sidot Blende" (1905); "The Decay of Phosphorescence in Sidot Blende" (1906); "Further Experiments on the Decay of Phosphorescence in Sidot Blende and Certain Other Substances" (1906); "The Influence of the Red and Infra-red Rays Upon the Photoluminescence of Sidot Blende" (1907); "Note on the Fluorescence of Sodium Vapor" (1907); "The Phenomena of Phosphorescence Considered from the Standpoint of the Dissociation Theory" (1908); "The Spectro-Photometric Study of Certain Cases of Kathado-Luminescence" (1909); "The Distribution of Energy in Fluorescence Spectra" (1911) and "The Fluorescence and Absorption of Certain Uranyl Salts" (1911). This work culminated in a monograph entitled "Studies in Luminescence" (1912), which was published by the Carnegie Institution. He has taken an active interest in the American Association for the Advancement of Science, of which he has been a fellow since 1890, also serving the section in physics as secretary in 1895, and as the presiding officer in 1900 when he delivered a retiring address "On Kathode Rays and Some Related Phenomena" which was published in "Science." He was secretary of the American Physical Society during 1899-1912, and president of the society in 1914-15. In 1914 he was elected a member of the National Academy of Sciences. He was married Apr. 10, 1901, to Bertha A., daughter of Arnold Sutermeister, of Kansas City, Mo., and has five children: Louise, Julia, Virginia, Grace, and Howard Merritt.

HERO, George Alfred, merchant and financier, was born in New Orleans, La., July 28, 1854, son of Andrew and Caroline (Grey) Hero. His father, a native of Sweden, left home when a young man for a trip around the world and arriving at New Orleans in 1837 married there and made it his home. George A. Hero was educated at private schools in New Orleans, and at the age of sixteen entered the employ of a banking firm representing Brown Bros. & Co. of New York, with whom he remained for three years. In 1873 he formed a partnership with C. W. Robinson of Liverpool under the name of Robinson & Hero and engaged in the cotton exporting business until 1886. In 1890 he became associated with Lehman, Stern & Co., Inc., a branch of Lehman Bros., cotton commission merchants and exporters of New York, and was later vice-president. For many years he was one of the most active traders in cotton, being identified with all the notable cotton movements and enjoying an international reputation in the trade. He has been a director of the New Orleans Cotton Exchange since 1900, and he is a member of the New York Cotton Exchange. In association with Pearl White and Maurice Stern, he organized the New Orleans Dry Dock and Ship Building Co., of which he has been vice-president since its organization. He is a director of the Whitney Central Trust and Savings Bank and a director and one of the largest owners of the Southern States Land and Timber Co., owning 1,000,000 acres of land in Florida, which forms part of a 4,000,000 acre area now being reclaimed. Mr. Hero's interest in reclamation began very early in his life, when he was a visitor at his brother's plantation in Assumption Parish, La. At that time he conceived the idea of draining a piece of land containing five square miles which, according to local tradition, had no bottom. He succeeded in his enterprise at a very small cost and to the material advantage of the district. The success of this enterprise led to larger ones. He organized the Orleans-Plaquemines-Jefferson drainage project in 1912, which with a pumping station of 1,000,000,000 gallons capacity per minute, reclaimed 39,000 of the richest acres in the country, the property having 5,000 owners. It increased the value of the land from three dollars to $200 an acre. The forethought, courage and great amount of money involved in this project were keenly appreciated by the people of Louisiana, and Mr. Hero and his associates were the recipients of extraordinary honors. The mayor of New Orleans officially proclaimed Feb. 13, 1915, as "Hero Day." Mr. Hero is a member of the Pickwick, Chess, Checkers and Whist and Country clubs of New Orleans. He was married (1) at New Orleans, La., Apr. 5, 1885, to Fanella Marie, daughter of Charles Olivier; (2) Jan. 6, 1896, to Anna Marie, sister of his first wife, and (3) at New Orleans, La., Aug. 6, 1914, to Angela Emma, daughter of Leon Joubert de Villamarest. He has six children: Alfred Olivier, Numa Charles, Fan-

ella Maria, wife of Walter Castanado; George Alfred, Jr., Alvin Antony and Claire Maire Hero.

FEW, William Preston, president of Trinity College, was born at Greenville, S. C., Dec. 29, 1867, son of Benjamin Franklin and Rachel (Kendrick) Few. His first American ancestor was Richard Few, a native of Lavington, Wiltshire, England, who emigrated in 1681 and settled in Chester county, Pa., the line of descent being traced through Richard's son Isaac and his wife Hannah Stanfield; their son William and his wife Mary Wheeler; their son James and his wife Sarah Howard; their son William and his wife Mary Chastain and their son William and his wife Sallie Ferguson, who were the grandparents of Pres. Few. The first William Few was a colonel in the war of the revolution, and his son James was killed early in that war; William, the grandfather of our subject, served in the war of 1812, and his father was a physician, and was assistant surgeon in the Confederate army. William Preston Few was graduated at Wofford College, S. C., in 1889, and at Harvard College in 1893 with the degree of A.M. He received the degree of Ph.D. from the latter in 1896, and that of LL.D. from both Wofford College and Southwestern University. He began his professional career as professor of English in Trinity College, North Carolina, in 1896, remaining in that capacity until 1910. He was appointed dean in 1902, and president in 1910, a position he still holds. During his administration four important buildings have been added to the college group, and at commencement in June, 1913, gifts amounting to $1,418,000 were announced. Since 1909 Dr. Few has been joint editor of the "South Atlantic Quarterly." He was married at Martinsville, Va., Aug. 17, 1911, to Mary Reamey, daughter of Lyne Starling Thomas, and has two children: William and Lyne Starling Few.

HOY, Philo Romayne, scientist, was born in Ohio in 1816, son of Capt. William Hoy, and a descendant of an old Scotch family named Hawey. He was graduated at the Ohio Medical College, Cincinnati, and after practicing at New Haven, O., six years, removed to Racine, Wis. In this comparatively unknown territory he made a complete collection of flora and fauna, especially of native woods, shells and fossils, specimens of which ultimately went to Racine College at Racine. He was a member of the Entomological Society of France and several scientific societies in the United States, and corresponded with such men as Agassiz, Henry and Kirtland. His name is attached to three or four fossils and four fauna. Dr. Hoy was married to Mary Elizabeth Austin, and had three children: Albert Harris; Jenny Rebecca and Philo Romayne Hoy. He died in Racine, Wis., in 1892.

WINSLOW, Sidney Wilmot, president of the United Shoe Machinery Co., was born in Brewster, Mass., Sept. 20, 1854, son of Freeman and Lucy H. (Rogers) Winslow. On the maternal side he was descended from Thomas Rogers, who came from England on the Mayflower in 1620, and on the paternal side from Kenelm Winslow, who was one of the earliest settlers on Cape Cod. During his boyhood his father moved to Salem, Mass., to establish himself in the shoemaking business, and there the son entered his father's factory to learn to make shoes. During the fourteen years he was thus employed he became impressed with the vital importance of shoe machinery in the development of the boot and shoe industry, and especially with the serious disadvantages under which manufacturers labored because of the multiplicity of companies controlling different machines

for performing different operations in making shoes. He was struck with the economic wastefulness of the various small companies who were striving among themselves for the business of shoe manufacturers, with the resulting loss to both labor and capital. When he first entered his father's shoe factory shoe machinery was in its infancy. The McKay sewing machine for attaching soles to uppers had only recently been introduced, and most of the complicated and expensive machines now in general use had not yet been invented. In early days, as new machines were invented companies were organized to make and introduce them, until there were many small concerns, some of them doing a precarious business. Every manufacturer in fitting out his factory was required to deal with several of them; he could not figure with certainty on his machinery; strikes were frequent among the operatives of one machine or another, so that some of the factories were shut down for a part of every year. The industry was in danger of demoralization. It was the practice of the makers of some but not all machines to employ agents to watch the operation of their machines in factories. Where this was done by several companies it involved wasteful duplication of effort. Where it was not the practice it was found that through the failure of some one company to give prompt attention to the repair of the particular machine which it owned, the machines belonging to other companies were also forced to lie idle, so close is the interdependence of operations in the making of shoes. Mr. Winslow's first venture in shoe machinery was in connection with the Naumkeag buffing machine, invented by his father, who was a man of great inventive talent. He secured a controlling interest in this machine in 1883 and still holds it. Subsequently he was attracted to the hand method lasting machine invented by Jan E. Matzeliger, a shoeworker of Lynn, which was designed to perform a delicate operation that from the beginning of shoe machinery had always been done by hand. Its inventor, after securing the patent, had neither the capital nor the business experience to make it commercially practical, and although others became financially interested, it did not become a commercial success until Mr. Winslow, perceiving its possibilities, associated with himself in 1892 men of organizing capacity and pecuniary resources and put it on a paying basis. In the meantime other lasting machines had come on the market, each adapted especially to make a particular type of shoe. All these various machines were finally gathered into the possession of the Consolidated and McKay Lasting Machine Co., of which Wallace F. Robinson became president and George W. Brown treasurer and general manager, while Mr. Winslow was active in the direction of its affairs. Machines for performing the various other operations in making shoes were still in the hands of separate companies. By degrees the smaller concerns had gone out of business, until in 1899 the making of shoe machinery had centered in the hands of three companies of substantial size, the Consolidated and McKay Lasting Machine Co., the Goodyear Shoe Machinery Co., and the McKay Shoe Machinery Co., each of which respectively made and leased machines adapted to a particular class of operations and not competing with one another. Through the initiative of Mr. Winslow these companies were consolidated under the name of the United Shoe Machinery Co., with a directorate composed principally of leading New England and New York business men. Mr. Winslow

became its president. The United Shoe Machinery Co. has a model manufacturing plant at Beverly, Mass., containing over twenty-one acres of floor space and employing 5,000 hands, where over 300 different machines used in the modern manufacture of shoes are produced. A unique feature of the company's business is the system of leasing their machines instead of selling them outright to shoe manufacturers, although most of the machines can be bought outright if the shoe manufacturer prefers. The leasing system, originated by Gordon McKay shortly after the civil war, was retained and perfected by the present company. By this system a shoe manufacturer pays a small royalty, averaging for two-thirds of the shoes made in the United States only $1\frac{1}{3}$c. per pair, for the use of the many machines required. The company employs a very efficient staff of machinists and inventors, constantly engaged in improving and perfecting various machines, for it is obviously to the company's advantage to keep the very finest machines in the hands of their customers in working order and capable of turning out the largest number of perfect shoes possible. On the other hand, the advantages to the manufacturer are: no capital required to be invested in machinery; the privilege of using always the highest type of perfected machines, and having them kept in repair without expense to him, and the privilege of exchanging them for better machines whenever the company's experts devise or perfect some improvement that would further simplify the process or reduce the cost of manufacturing a shoe. The public is likewise the gainer by this arrangement, because it can purchase a more durable, a more comfortable and a better-looking shoe at a less price than ever before. The United Shoe Machinery Co. is not only one of the greatest and best managed of the world's great industrial corporations, but sociologically it has commanded much attention by its humane, even solicitous, treatment of its army of employees. Welfare work, which is prominent in the conduct of present-day manufacturing enterprises, has been carried as far in the company's factory at Beverly as anywhere in the world. Some of the principal features in this connection are: an emergency hospital with X-ray and other equipment; rest rooms for the women employees; baths, washrooms and lounging quarters for the men; hygienic kitchens and restaurants, where nourishing food, much of it grown in the company's gardens, is served at cost; an attractive clubhouse and extensive grounds, of the country club type, containing a theatre, library, reading-room, sewing-room, bowling-alleys, and, outside, fields for all kinds of athletic sports; and an industrial school for boys. The employees, furthermore, have the opportunity for membership in the United Shoe Machinery Athletic Association, the United Shoe Machinery Band and the Mutual Relief Association, and for participation in the Massachusetts plan of savings bank, life insurance and old age pensions. The wonderful success of this organization must be attributed solely to the remarkable ability of its president, Sidney W. Winslow, who since early boyhood has been interested in the manufacture of shoes, and the officials who are associated with him in the directorate. Mr. Winslow is also the president of the United Shoe Machinery Corporation and the United Shoe Machinery Company of Maine, and treasurer and director of the Naumkeag Buffing Machine Co.; president and director of the Beverly Gas and Electric Co., Danvers Gas Light Co., Newburyport Gas and Electric Co., and director of the

First National Bank, the Old Colony Trust Co., Salem Gas Light Co., and United States Smelting, Refining and Mining Co. He is an indefatigable worker, arriving at his office early and leaving late. He says: "There is always room at the top, and young men can to-day find excellent positions with lucrative salaries if they persevere. The young man who will succeed is the one who will seize the opportunities which circumstances place in his way. Such circumstances will be found only by keeping wide awake to the times and performing one's duties, instead of always being anxious about the time to close one's desk." He is a connoisseur in paintings, his home at Beverly containing many art treasures, and is an enthusiastic chess and tennis player. He is a member of the Commercial, Algonquin and Boston Chess clubs. He was married, in 1877, to Georgiana, daughter of George Buxton of Peabody, Mass., and has four children: Sidney W. Jr., Mrs. Lucy Hill, Mrs. Mabel W. Foster and Edward H. Winslow.

BROWN, George Washington, vice-president United Shoe Machinery Co., was born in Northfield, Vt., Aug. 30, 1841, son of Isaac Washington and Sylvia Elvira (Patridge) Brown. His ancestors were among the earliest of the sturdy pioneers who journeyed, shortly after the revolutionary war, from the settlements in Connecticut to Vermont, conquering its forests and peopling its valleys, the forbears of a race that has served with distinction in the highest councils of the nation and whose representatives have been well to the fore in all branches of intellectual and commercial activity. His great-great-grandfather, Jonathan Brown, was one of the settlers captured by the Indians at the burning of Royalton, Vt., in 1782, and was for a time held captive in Montreal. He was educated in the public schools and the Newbury (Vt.) Seminary, and at the age of eighteen entered the employ of the Vermont Central railroad shops at Northfield. In 1865 he became a member of the firm of Hyde & Brown, grocers, and two years later formed a partnership with a Mr. McGowan under the firm name of McGowan & Brown, dealers in hardware. In 1869 he accepted an offer from the Central Pacific railroad to become auditor of their motive power department, with headquarters in Sacramento, Cal.; but two years later he returned East and entered the employ of the Wheeler & Wilson Co. as salesman. His diligence and unswerving loyalty to his employers carried him rapidly through the different stages of their employment until, in 1876, he was made general manager of their New England business. In 1892 he resigned, to assume his duties as general manager and treasurer of the Consolidated Hand Method Lasting Machine Co., in which for some time he had had a financial interest, and served as its treasurer. This was a most important occasion, not only for Mr. Brown, but for the entire shoe industry as well; for under his management the resources and standing of the company were so developed that it became the prime factor in bringing together the different lasting machine companies, to the great benefit of the shoe-manufacturing world. The new company was known as the "Consolidated McKay Lasting Machine Co." and Mr. Brown was made treasurer and general manager. Under his direction, the important divisions of the shoe-manufacturing industry served by this company were developed and organized as they had never been before. The organization of the United Shoe Machinery Co. in 1899—which subsequent events have proved to be

of the utmost importance in the shoe industry— brought to Mr. Brown the opportunity to furnish to every branch of the trade the highly efficient service and improved machinery that had characterized his management of the enterprises previously mentioned. His policy of securing the best, not only in machines but also in the personnel of those associated with him, speedily resulted in bringing the shoe-machinery industry to a standard before unknown. The measure of success is best shown in the remarkable progress made between the years 1900 and 1905—the census showing that the shoe-manufacturing industry advanced more rapidly during that time than it did in the preceding thirty years. In 1909 Mr. Brown resigned as treasurer and general manager and was made vice-president and chairman of its finance committee. He was married May 5, 1863, to Addie E. Perkins, who died in June, 1900, leaving one son, Edwin P. Brown, well known in the business and financial circles of Boston. Mr. Brown is a patron of art, the frequent additions to his collection showing rare discrimination and judgment; but love of music is one of the predominating features of his character. More than one deserving student has had cause to be thankful for his acquaintance, and friends from every quarter of the globe can recall with pleasure a musical evening spent in his apartments. Socially, few men have such an extensive acquaintance or so large a circle of friends. His travels and active business life have brought him into the closest relations with the most progressive people in the great commercial centers; and his influence has been, and is to-day, a most potent one for progress. Mr. Brown was for many years a member of the old Central Club of Boston. He is a member of the New Algonquin Club of Boston, the Episcopal Club of Massachusetts, Boston Museum of Fine Arts, Boston Press Club, New England Shoe and Leather Association, Boston Boot and Shoe Club, a life member of The Boston Society, Massachusetts Automobile Club, Boston Merchants' Association, Boston Chamber of Commerce, and National Civic Federation, where, as a member of the executive committee for the Welfare Department, he has been in close touch with the great work it is accomplishing, and his interest in all that affects the health and happiness of the army of people employed in the United States Shoe Machinery Co. offices in Boston and factories at Beverly and elsewhere is shown in the many provisions that have been and are constantly being made for their comfort. In 1906 Mr. Brown presented to his native town, Northfield, Vt., a handsome public library as a memorial to his family. Besides his active connection with the United Shoe Machinery Co. and its affiliated companies, he is a director of the First National Bank of Boston— one of the largest institutions of its kind in New England.

COOLIDGE, Louis Arthur, treasurer of the United Shoe Machinery Co., was born at Natick, Mass., Oct. 8, 1861, son of William L. and Sarah I. (Washburn) Coolidge, and eleventh in descent from John Coolidge, one of the original settlers of Watertown, Mass. He was educated in the public schools of his native village and prepared for Harvard at Newton high school, where he was graduated in 1883, *magna cum laude,* with the degree of A.B. Having decided on a business career, he did not go to college, but became a reporter on the Springfield "Republican," and quickly developed abilities that made him a valuable member of the staff. His alertness, energy and business acumen attracted the attention of

Geo. W. Brown.

GRAEME M. HAMMOND
NEUROLOGIST

JOHN G. HIBBEN
PRESIDENT PRINCETON UNIVERSITY

SAMUEL B. McCORMICK
CHANCELLOR UNIVERSITY OF PITTSBURGH

RUFUS P. LINCOLN
PHYSICIAN

Henry Cabot Lodge, then a member of congress, and he was made Lodge's private secretary in 1888. Three years later he resumed his reportorial work as Washington correspondent for various Eastern journals, which included the "New York Record," the "Boston Journal" and "New York Commercial Advertiser," now the "Globe." While in Washington he was also, in succession, editor of the "Congressional Directory" and indexer of the "Congressional Record." He was a personal friend of Pres. Roosevelt, and a member of his famous tennis cabinet. During the Republican national campaign of 1904 Mr. Coolidge was the director of the Republican literary bureau, which supplied facts and arguments for campaign purposes. It was while he was assistant secretary of the treasury in 1908 that his abilities were brought to the attention of the United Shoe Machinery Co., and he was offered the position of treasurer, which he accepted. He is the author of "The Show at Washington," "Kloneke," "The Yukon Country," and "An Old-Fashioned Senator," a biography of the late Sen. Orville H. Platt, of Connecticut; and he contributed to the "Encyclopædia Americana" the article on the Republican party. He is also president of the Innovation Shirt Co., vice-president and director of the American Zinc, Lead and Smelting Co., and treasurer and director of the O. S. Miller Treeing Machine Co., the Security Eyelet Co., the United Awl and Needle Co., the United Fast Color Eyelet Co., the United Shoe Machinery Co. of Canada, the United Shoe Machinery Co. of Mexico, and the United Xpedite Finishing Co. He is a member of the Boston Chamber of Commerce, the Boston City Club, the Alonquin, University, Exchange, St. Botolph, Boston Art, Boston Press and Harvard clubs of Boston, the University and Republican clubs of New York, and the Cumberland Club of Portland, Me. He was married Jan. 2, 1890, to Helen Pickerill, of Washington, D. C., and has three children.

HAMMOND, Graeme Monroe, neurologist, was born in Philadelphia, Pa., Feb. 1, 1858, son of William A. and Helen (Nisbet) Hammond. His father was surgeon-general of the United States army during the civil war. The son was graduated M. D. at the New York University Medical College in 1881. He also studied for three years (1874-77) at the Columbia College School of Mines and received the degree of LL.B. from the New York Law School in 1900. After receiving his medical degree he became an interne at the New York Post-Graduate Medical School and Hospital in 1881 and he has been connected with that institution ever since. He is professor of nervous and mental diseases and is also a director of the hospital. Dr. Hammond has made a specialty of the study of nervous and mental diseases, devoting himself principally to medico-legal work, and has won recognition as a leading authority on insanity cases. He was one of the experts called upon to testify in the murder trial of Harry Thaw. In athletic work and training, he believes, lies the real secret of health, and prescribes more attention to physical development as a prevention and cure of most mental ailments. He is a member of the American Neurological Association; was its secretary and treasurer for twenty-five years and its president in 1911-12. He is also a member of the American Medical Psychological Association, the American Medical Association, the New York Psychiatric Society, the New York Neurological Society and the New York Athletic and Democratic clubs. Dr. Hammond was married

April 27, 1881, to Louise, daughter of Edward Elsworth, of New York city, and has four daughters: Helen, Dorothy, Louise and Clarice Hammond.

HIBBEN, John Grier, president of Princeton University (1912—), was born at Peoria, Ill., April 19, 1861, son of Samuel and Elizabeth (Grier) Hibben. He was graduated at Princeton in 1882 and studied at the Princeton Theological Seminary during 1883-86. Subsequently he took a post-graduate course at the University of Berlin. In 1887 he was ordained to the Presbyterian ministry and became pastor of a church at Chambersburg, Pa. In 1891 he returned to Princeton as instructor in logic. He was instructor in logic and psychology during 1892-94, assistant in Biblical instruction during 1892-97, assistant professor of logic during 1894-1907 and professor of logic during 1907-12. In 1912 he was elected to succeed Woodrow Wilson as president of the university. During his service of over twenty years on the faculty of Princeton, he was engaged in research work in his own special province and contributed many articles to philosophic journals, containing the results of his studies. He is the author of a text-book on "Inductive Logic" (1896), which is much used in colleges and universities, and a text-book on "Logic, Inductive and Deductive" (1905). Three other works, which have brought him forcibly to the attention of students of philosophy on both sides of the Atlantic, are "Problems in Philosophy" (1898); "Hegel's Logic" (1902), and "The Philosophy of Enlightenment" (1909). The last named is one of a series of twelve volumes entitled, "Epochs of Philosophy," of which Prof. Hibben was editor, which constitute a compendious history of philosophy written by members of the faculties in philosophy of colleges and universities in England, Scotland and the United States. He is also the author of a delightful volume entitled "A Defence of Prejudice, and other Essays" (1911). Dr. Hibben is one of the leaders of Idealism in America. He has shown fine judgment and discrimination, remarkable sanity and balance, and a high grade of critical acumen. He has the thorough respect and admiration of all co-workers in his field. The qualities which mark his philosophical writings are characteristic of the man. He is distinguished by good sense and good judgment, he is self-poised and independent, yet moderate in the expression of his views and not only fair and just to others, but courteously considerate of their opinions and feelings. Possessing tact and diplomacy, a gentleman both in his inner being and his outward manifestations, a man of scholarship and high ideals, yet withal a man of the world in the best sense of the term, Prof. Hibben is well qualified for the high office to which he has been elected. Before his elevation to the presidency of Princeton Prof. Hibben was, perhaps, the most popular member of the faculty, and his selection was very gratifying to the student body. He is thoroughly imbued with the spirit and traditions of the college and has a rare faculty of attracting the confidence, affection and respect of younger men. The degree of Ph.D. was conferred on him by Princeton in 1893 and that of LL.D. by Lafayette College in 1907. He was married at Elizabeth, N. J., Nov. 8, 1887, to Jennie, daughter of Henry W. Davidson, and had one daughter, Elizabeth Grier Hibben, who is the wife of Robert Maxwell Scoon.

McCORMICK, Samuel Black, chancellor of the University of Pittsburgh, was born at Irwin, Westmoreland co., Pa., May 6, 1858, son of

James Irwin and Rachel Long (Black) McCormick, grandson of John and Esther (Sowash) McCormick and great-grandson of John McCormick, who came from Cookstown, Ireland, in 1788, and settled at Larimer, Pa. His father, a graduate of Franklin College and Western Reserve Medical College, and at one time county superintendent of schools, was a prominent physician, a classical scholar of considerable reputation, and examining surgeon for pensions. The son was prepared for college by his father and was graduated at Washington and Jefferson College in 1880, receiving the degree of A.M. three years later. After graduation he taught in Canonsburg Academy, and taught Greek for a year in Washington and Jefferson College. While at college he passed the preliminary examinations as a student at law, and was registered with his uncle, Hon. Henry H. McCormick, then U. S. district attorney for the western district of Pennsylvania. He was admitted to the bar in 1882 and a year later removed to Denver, Colo., where he engaged in the practice of law with R. D. Thompson. Having decided to enter the ministry he returned to Allegheny, Pa., in 1887, to pursue his theological studies in the Western Seminary. He was graduated there in 1890 and at once became pastor of the Central Presbyterian Church, Allegheny. During his pastorate at this church he frequently met classes in the theological seminary; was a member of its board of directors; a member of the Freedmen's board and of the Pennsylvania College of Women, and the Sustentation committee of the Synod of Pennsylvania. In 1894 he was called to the First Presbyterian Church, Omaha, Neb. In 1897 he was elected president of Coe College, Cedar Rapids, Ia., and in 1904 he took the chancellorship of the Western University of Pennsylvania, now the University of Pittsburgh. In the work of developing that institution Chancellor McCormick has given full scope to his ability, physical vigor and tireless energy. With unbounded faith in its future he has labored unceasingly to advance its interests, and all his enthusiasm and exceptional powers are devoted without reserve to that end. During his administration a new site has been secured, the endowment has been largely increased and various structures for the use of the university have been erected. He is a trustee of the Carnegie Foundation for the Advancement of Teaching; was a member of the revision committee of the Presbyterian Church, 1901–2; is a member of the College and University Council of Pennsylvania; director of Western Theological Seminary; president of the University Extension Society of Pittsburgh; was president, in 1913, of the College Presidents' Association of Pennsylvania; is a life member of the American Association for the Advancement of Science; member of National Institute of Social Science, and Sons of the American Revolution. He has received the honorary degrees of D.D. from Washington and Jefferson College in 1897, and LL.D. in 1902, and the same degree from William and Mary College in 1913. He was married Sept. 29, 1882, at Carnegie, Pa., to Ida May, daughter of William Steep, of Washington, Pa.; their children are: James Irwin; Gertrude, wife of Lloyd Weir Smith; Samuel Black and Rachel McCormick.

LINCOLN, Rufus Pratt, soldier and physician, was born at Belchertown, Mass., April 27, 1841, son of Rufus S. and Lydia (Baggs) Lincoln, and a descendant of Thomas Lincoln, who came from England to Hingham, Mass., in 1635, removing later to Taunton. He was educated at Williston Seminary, Easthampton; Phillips (Exeter) Academy, and Amherst College. He served in the civil war as captain, major, lieut.-colonel and colonel in the 37th Mass. infantry, under command of Col. Oliver Edwards, and in the last year of the war was assistant inspector-general of the 1st division, 6th army corps, on the staffs of Gen. David A. Russell and Gen. Frank Wheaton. He took part in the battles of Fredericksburg, Salem Heights, Gettysburg, Rappahannock, Wilderness, Spottsylvania, Fisher's Hill, Cedar Creek, Hatcher's Run, Dabney's Mills, Forts Steadman and Wadsworth, Petersburg and Sailor's Creek. He was twice wounded, and was twice breveted for gallantry on the field. At the close of the war he studied medicine at the College of Physicians and Surgeons, New York, and the Harvard Medical School, receiving the degree of M.D. from the latter in 1868. After a term of service in the Massachusetts general hospital he entered upon the practice of medicine in New York city, where for a time he was associated with Dr. William Parker, making a specialty of diseases of the throat, lungs and nose. He had a large practice, his patients coming from all parts of the United States and from South America. During the illness of Emperor Frederick of Germany with cancer of the throat, Dr. Lincoln's advice was sought. He was profoundly versed in the science and theory of his profession, and possessed manual skill and dexterity to an extraordinary degree. He was one of the first physicians to apply the electric cautery to operations on the throat, and one of his most notable operations was the removal by this method of a large tumor from the throat of Gen. Judson Kilpatrick. He was the author of "Laryngeal Phthisis" (1874), "Selected Cases of Disease in the Nasal and Post-Nasal Regions Treated with the Galvano Cautery" (1876), "Naso-Pharyngeal Polypi with Illustrations of Cases" (1879), "On the Results of Treatment of Naso-Pharyngeal Fibromata" (1883), "A Case of Melano-Sarcoma of the Nose, Cured by Galvano-Cauterization" (1885), "The Surgical Uses of Electricity in the Upper Air Passages" (1886), "Recurrent Naso-Pharyngeal Tumor, Cured by Electrolysis, Exhibition of Patient" (1887), "Report of the Evulsion of a Laryngeal Tumor Which Has Returned Twenty-two Years After Its Removal by Laryngotomy" (1890), "The Use of Pyoctanin and Antiseptic in Diseases of the Upper Air Passages" (1891), "The Exanthemata in the Upper Air Passages," "Turbinotomy; Method of Operating" (1897), and "Oro-Pharyngeal Mycosis" (1898). He was a member of the Military Order of the Loyal Legion, the Society of National Arts, the New England Society and the University, Harvard Medical and Mendelssohn clubs. He was married Aug. 20, 1869, to Caroline Carpenter, daughter of Wellington H. Tyler, of New York city, and had three children: Carrie Anna and Rufus Tyler, who died young, and Helen Lincoln. Mr. Lincoln died in New York city Nov. 27, 1900. Portrait opposite page 199.

PITAVAL, John Baptist, fifth Roman Catholic archbishop of Santa Fé, N. M., was born in France, Feb. 10, 1858. His preparatory studies were made in the seminary of Lyons, France, after which he volunteered for the missions in the United States and affiliating himself with the diocese of Denver, crossed the ocean in June, 1881. He remained for a few months at St. Mary's Seminary, Baltimore, Md., and then went to Denver, Colo., where he was ordained priest Dec. 24, 1881. Until 1902 he worked as a missionary in Colorado, and on July 25 of that year was consecrated titular bishop of Sora and auxiliary to Archbishop Bourgade of Santa Fé. The latter prelate died on May 17, 1908, and Bishop Pitaval was first appointed administrator of the diocese and then promoted to the see Jan. 3, 1909. The appointment gave great satisfaction throughout the territory of New Mexico, where he was very popular as a hard-working zealous missionary. The diocese at large is mostly Spanish-American and a number of the quaint old Spanish customs are still retained, though the influx of English-speaking people is steadily making radical changes. The priests, of whom there are eighty-seven, are mainly French, Belgian, German and Italian; the churches, chapels and stations number 470; there are thirty-six schools, with an attendance of 4,200 pupils. The suffrage dioceses are Tucson and Denver.

MILLET, Francis Davis, artist, was born in Mattapoisett, Mass., Nov. 3, 1846, son of Asa and Huldah Allen (Bryan) Millet, and a descendant of Ensign Thomas Millet, who was brought over from England by his parents in 1633 and settled in Dorchester, Mass. The line is through his son, Henry, who married Joyce Chapman; their son, Thomas, who married Mary Greenaway; their son, Thomas, who married Mary Evelith; their son, John, and his wife, Eunice Babson; their son, Thomas, who married Eunice Parsons; and their son, Zebulu, who married Deliverance Rich, and was the artist's grandfather. Frank Millet accompanied his father who was a surgeon in the civil war and became a drummer boy in the Sixtieth Massachusetts regiment; later he was assistant in the surgical corps. After the war he entered Harvard, and was graduated in 1869. He was a brilliant student, a Phi Beta Kappa man, and stood high in his class. He went into newspaper work on leaving college, and was successively reporter on the Boston "Advertiser," city editor of the Boston "Courier," and a member of the staff of the Boston "Saturday Evening Gazette." During his spare time he worked at lithography and drew portraits of his friends. Having decided to devote himself altogether to art, he entered the Royal Academy of Fine Arts at Antwerp in 1871, and for two years he studied under Van Lenius and De Keyser, winning a silver medal of honor in his first year and the gold medal in his second year, a record unprecedented in the history of the academy. In 1873 he was appointed secretary to Charles Francis Adams, commissioner to the Vienna Exposition, and while holding that position continued his art studies, acted as a juror of awards, and reported the exposition for the "Tribune" and "Herald" of New York. Later he traveled through Hungary, Roumania, Greece and Italy, studying art in Rome, Capri and Venice, and deriving his income chiefly from his pen. While in Italy he acted as correspondent of "Le Prescurser," an Antwerp journal, and he always retained his connections with the Boston papers. In 1876 he returned to America, and became assistant to John La Farge on the decorations of Trinity Church, Boston. He had had some experience in painting with a wax medium during his residence in Italy, and he devised the formula used in painting in wax medium which is usually ascribed to La Farge. This association with La Farge was the first opportunity which brought prominently into play Millet's high talents as a mural painter, and some of the best qualities in the mural decorations of Trinity were the

work of his brush. It was at this time that Millet also showed his talent for stained-glass design in a window executed for the Harvard Memorial Hall. Versatility was indeed his marked characteristic, and the facility with which he turned from one line of work to another was extraordinary. Upon the outbreak of the Russo-Turkish war, in 1877, he became correspondent for the New York "Herald," and later succeeded Archibald Forbes as war correspondent for the London "Daily News." Forbes said himself that Millet's ability to secure news, and to devise means of transmitting it, when obtained, was marvelous. For his gallantry under fire and his valuable services to the wounded he received the iron cross from Roumania and the military crosses of St. Anne and Stanislas from Russia, in addition to the war medals of both Russia and Roumania. In 1879 he returned to America, and settled down for a time in Boston, but the year 1881 found him again wandering through Europe, making sketches for "Harper's." By this time he began to show evidence of high literary talent, and was advised by William Dean Howells to abandon painting for literature. While his literary aspirations were not strong enough to win him from his chosen calling, he did write a number of short stories of more than average quality, which were published in a volume entitled "Capillary Crime and Other Stories" (1892). He also wrote "The Danube from the Black Forest to the Black Sea" (1891), an account of a canoe trip down the Danube; "The Expedition to the Philippines" (1800); "A Courier's Ride," and a translation of Tolstoy's "Sebastopol" (1887), besides various magazine articles and chapters contributed to compilations on art. Between 1882 and 1892 he spent much of his time in England, enjoying the association of such men as Sargent, Abbey, Alma Tadema and Alfred Parsons, and exhibited frequently both in Europe and America. In 1892 he was appointed director of decoration of the World's Columbian Exposition in Chicago. As superintendent of decoration he originated the tonal scheme which made it the "White City," and his own decorations—the lunettes in the loggia of the Liberal Arts Building and the ceiling of the grand reception hall of the New York State Building—were the highest achievements in that line in the exposition. Mural painting as a calling by itself was unheard of in this country until Millet organized the work at Chicago and brought together a remarkable group of artists. Following the Chicago exposition he devoted more and more attention to mural paintings, and executed large works for the Baltimore Customs House, the New Bedford Public Library, the State Capitol at St. Paul, Minn., the court house at Newark, the Federal Building at Cleveland, and other public buildings throughout the country. In the meantime he did some easel painting, and rendered important services to art in other ways. He organized the American Federation of Arts for the National Academy of Art, and was one of the incorporators of the American Academy of Art, in Rome, which he served as secretary and director until his death. All this time he wandered at will into every corner of the globe. Not only did he travel unceasingly, but he was a familiar figure at all kinds of functions in the various capitals of the world. He had many remarkable social qualities, was an excellent story teller, and made countless friends in all stations of life everywhere he went. How he managed to crowd so much travel, recreation and social enjoyment into a life filled with important work was a constant source of astonishment to his friends. He had the restless soul of the born adventurer, and once said that if he could choose the manner of his death it would be to live his life to the fullest and then be shot in battle. His life was certainly lived to the fullest, and in essentials the manner of his death was such as he would have wished. He was one of the passengers on the steamer Titanic, which sank in the icy blackness of the mid-Atlantic. It can hardly be claimed that Millet stands among the world's greatest masters, as Whistler or Sargent does, but his work is of a very high order of merit, and his mural paintings are unquestionably among the greatest achievements in decorative art that this country has produced. He did a number of good portraits, and many pictures with Greek and Pompeiian themes, besides a few large canvases, such as "Anthony Van Corlaer, the Trumpeter of New Amsterdam," but the best of his easel pictures are his English genre paintings, of which he turned out a large number. They are excellent in composition, single and sincere in treatment, accurate and carefully finished in detail, precise yet free in drawing, and rich in harmonies and effective coloring. Evidently he had made a very profitable study of Dutch mastery, but he heightened the sky of his color schemes in tune with modern conceptions of color values and beyond everything dreamed of by Reubens or Teniers. Millet's attitude as a painter was a conservatively progressive one, an attitude which does not create art history, but which, nevertheless, makes for sound work. Among the best of his English genre pictures are: "Between Two Fires," "At the Inn," "Rook and Pigeon," "The Black Hat," and "Wandering Thoughts." It is as a mural painter, however, that he ranks highest, not only for the intrinsic value of his work in that kind but also for the influence he exerted on decorative art in America. His masterpiece was, beyond doubt, the decoration for the Baltimore Custom House, "a consummate development," said Sylvester Baxter, "of a unique departure from the conventional traditions, and one of the greatest achievements in decorative art on this continent." Personally he was a man of exceptional character. He was exceedingly genial, considerate and friendly. His friends were legion, and wherever he was known he was as much esteemed as he was loved. He was scholarly, uncommonly talented, capable of doing extraordinarily well almost anything he chose to put a hand to, and democratic—standing on an equal footing with the humble and with self-assumption on a parity with the best of the land. Millet received a medal at the New Orleans Exposition, in 1885, and one from the American Art Association in 1887; he was made chevalier of the Legion of Honor of France in 1900, and received the First-Class Order of the Sacred Treasure from the Japanese government in 1908, an extraordinary distinction in Japan. He was an honorary member of the American Institute of Architects and a member of the National Academy of Design, the American Water Color Society, the Royal Institute of Painters, London. In recognition of his services to the American Academy in Rome, the trustees of that institution have established the Francis Davis Millet Memorial Chair of Fine Arts. He was married in Paris, March 11, 1879, to Elizabeth Greeley Merrill, of Boston, and had three children: Kate, wife of Frank W. Adlard; John Parsons and Lawrence Millet. The date of his death was April 14, 1912.

THOMPSON, Robert Means, capitalist, was born in Corsica, Jefferson co., Pa., Mar. 2, 1849, son of John J. Y. Thompson and Agnes Susan (Kennedy) Thompson, of Scotch descent. He received his early education in the common schools and at the academy of Elder's Ridge, Indiana co., Pa. Unexpectedly, at the age of fifteen, he was appointed midshipman, and with no time for preparation he entered the Naval Academy, then situated at Newport, R. I. He was a member of the famous class of 1868, graduating tenth in his class. His first service at sea was on the Contocook, in the West Indian squadron. Later he served on the U. S. S. Franklin, Richmond and Guard, in the Mediterranean squadron; on the Wauchuset and at the torpedo station at Newport. In 1869 he was commissioned ensign and in 1870 master. In December of that year he resigned to study law, and after being admitted to the bar he entered the law office of his brother, Hon. A. C. Thompson, at Portsmouth. The lessons of thoroughness taught him in the navy left Mr. Thompson dissatisfied with his knowledge of law, and in 1812 he entered the Harvard Law School, where he was graduated in 1874, with the degree of LL.B. He then opened a law office in Boston, and became reporter to the state supreme court, as assistant to John Lathrope, afterward justice of the Massachusetts supreme court, and helped prepare for publication Vols. 115-116 of that court's reports. He was a member of the common council of Boston in 1876 and 1877, and in the latter year was chairman of the Young Republican committee, conducting the campaign in which Thomas Talbot was elected governor over Benjamin F. Butler. While practicing law in Boston Mr. Thompson was retained to investigate the titles to certain mining properties near Sherbrooke, Quebec, Canada, and later he was induced to accept the management of the company organized to work the mines on this property. This company became the Orford Copper Company, which erected smelting and refining works at Bayonne, N. J., and engaged in the smelting and refining of copper. It afterwards became largely interested in the smelting and refining of nickel. Because of his chemical knowledge he took an active part in the technical management of the works, and to him is due the perfecting of the process for the separation of nickel from copper in the ores obtained from the mines near Copper Cliff, in the province of Ontario. When the International Nickel Company was formed, which took over the mines in Canada, it also took over the property of the Orford Copper Company, of which Mr. Thompson was president, and he became chairman of the board of directors of the Nickel company. He is the first president of the Naval Academy Alumni Association of New York, and was the first member of the Naval Academy Athletic Association, for years being looked upon as the patron saint of the U. S. Naval Academy. He was president of the American Olympic committee, which supervised the work of the American athletes at Stockholm, Sweden, at the Fifth Olympiad, in 1912, and the loyal support given him by the officers of the army and navy who formed part of that team did much to secure the splendid moral victory of that team, an achievement as great, if not greater, than their brilliant victories in the games. In a financial way Mr. Thompson has been successful, but he has held and used his wealth as one who acknowledges that its ownership carries with it a duty. He has often said that he hoped to so live

F. D. MILLET

ROBERT M. THOMPSON
CAPITALIST

JOHN B. DRURY
CLERGYMAN AND EDITOR

MME. MARIE W. RAPPOLD-BERGER
SINGER

RICHARD M. PEARCE
PATHOLOGIST

that when he died many would regret him, and none be glad that he was gone. He was president of the Pennsylvania Society of New York in 1911, during which time the William Penn dinner was given by that society in London and the Penn memorial dedicated in the church of All Hallows, Barking. The Emperor of Japan conferred upon him the Order of the Rising Sun of the Second Class, an honor which in Japan was reserved for men of great achievement, such as Marshal Oyama, Admiral Togo and other great leaders in Japan's war with Russia. He has always been a great traveler, being a member of the ''Ends of the Earth Club,'' of New York, whose one requisite for membership is that the candidate shall have circled the globe, and he has visited all the principal cities of the world. Mr. Thompson acquired his title of ''Colonel'' from the fact that during the Spanish-American war he was appointed chief of staff by Gov. Voorhees of New Jersey. He is a member of the American Geographical Society, American Archæological Society, Pennsylvania Society of New York (president, 1911), Naval Architects and Marine Engineers' Society, the Loyal Legion, the University, Army and Navy, Century, Metropolitan, Lawyers', New York Athletic and Players' clubs of New York; the Metropolitan, Army and Navy, Chevy Chase and Riding and Hunt clubs of Washington; the Meadow, Southampton, National Golf Links of America and Shinnecock Golf clubs of Southampton, L. I. He was married, April 30, 1873, to Sarah, daughter of William Channing Gibbs, governor of Rhode Island, and has one daughter, Sarah, wife to Stephen H. P. Pell, of New York.

DRURY, John Benjamin, clergyman and editor, was born at Rhinebeck, N. Y., Aug. 15, 1838, son of Alfred and Maria Ann (Schultz) Drury. His first American ancestor was Nicholas Drury, who came over about 1750, married Catharine Smith, of Long Island, and eventually settled in Albany, N. Y. The line of descent is traced through his son, John, who married Hannah Wilson, of Rhinebeck, and their son, Alfred, father of our subject. John B. Drury was educated at the Rhinebeck Academy, and was graduated at Rutgers College in 1858, and at the New Brunswick Theological Seminary in 1861, Rutgers conferring upon him the degree of A.M., and in 1880 that of D.D. He was ordained for the ministry in 1861 and began his life work in behalf of the Reformed Church, as a missionary in Davenport, Ia., in 1861. In 1864 he became pastor of a church at Ghent, N. Y., where he was successful throughout a period of twenty-three years, and rebuilt the church after it was destroyed by fire in 1868. During that time he held all the ordinary offices in the local Classis and Particular Synod, including the presidency of the Particular Synod of Albany, in 1881. In 1886 he was elected president of the General Synod of the Reformed Church, the highest honor within the gift of that body. In 1887 he became editor of the denominational church newspaper, ''The Christian Intelligencer,'' published in New York city. It was then nearly bankrupt, and through the untiring efforts of Dr. Drury it was rehabilitated and maintained on a paying basis during all the twenty-two years of his connection with it. His share, though, was a labor of love, as he himself never received any financial return. The position, however, brought him into prominence in church circles, and he was regarded as one of the leading men of the denomination. Another honor brought to him was his connection with the Alliance of

Reformed Churches holding the Presbyterian System (called the Pan-Presbyterian Alliance), of whose executive board he was a member from 1887 until his death. He was a delegate to the quadrennial meetings of that body in London in 1888; Toronto, in 1892; Washington, in 1895; and Liverpool, in 1904. During his residence in New Brunswick he was a member of the board of superintendents of the Theological Seminary in that city, and was a trustee of Rutgers College. In theology he was a Liberal Calvinist. He was a member of many organizations, such as Phi Beta Kappa, New Brunswick Historical Society, New York Historical Society, Metropolitan Museum of Art, American Museum of Natural History, the Aldine Club, of New York city, and the American Society of Church History. Dr. Drury's interests ran along three lines, in each of which distinction was achieved. The first was his devotion to the Reformed (Dutch) Church in America; the second was in Rutgers College, of which he was a trustee for many years, and the third had direct result in his published works. Dr. Drury had a lifelong interest in science and scientific study, especially on the philosophical side, and in college won the gold medal awarded for the Suydam Prize in Natural Science. He was the author of ''Truths and Untruths of Evolution'' (1884); ''Historical Sketch of the First Reformed Church of Ghent'' (1876); ''Historical Sketch of the Reformed (Dutch) Church of Rhinebeck, N. Y.'' (1881); an essay on ''Darwinism'' in ''Scribner's Magazine'' in 1875; ''Saratoga of To-day,'' and ''The Catskill Mountains,'' two articles published in ''Outing,'' in 1882, and various addresses, editorials and articles published in numerous church and lay newspapers and magazines. For nearly a quarter of a century Dr. Drury contributed interesting weekly editorials and articles to his own newspaper, ''The Christian Intelligencer.'' His writings were all timely, scholarly and eloquent, lucidly expressed in beautiful language. His editorials were intelligible and forcible, and showed that he discharged his task with a conscientious candor and catholicity of judgment. He was married in Chicago, Ill., Sept. 2, 1869, to Henrietta Wynkoop, daughter of John Mumford Keese, of Rhinebeck, N. Y., and died in New Brunswick, N. J., March 21, 1909, survived by his widow and four children: Alfred, Charlotte Keese, Francis Keese and Henrietta Wynkoop. Portrait opp. p. 206.

RAPPOLD=BERGER, Marie Winterrath, singer, was born in Barmen, Germany, Aug. 17, 1878, daughter of Franz and Mathilde (Winterrath) Finchs. Her father was a well-known sculptor, who brought his family to America two years after the daughter's birth, settling in Brooklyn, N. Y. He was also a fine musician and possessed a good tenor voice, but preferred to follow the art of sculpture. Young Marie inherited from her father a love for music, and having developed a splendid soprano voice while in her teens, she began to study singing in preparation for a professional career. Her teacher for seven years was Oscar Saenger, of New York. She sang in public at an early age with her sister, who carried the alto parts, and her voice aroused admiration wherever it was heard. While singing at the Schiller centennial concert in Brooklyn, N. Y., in 1904, she was heard by Heinrich Conried, director of the Metropolitan Opera House, and was immediately engaged by him to sing in grand opera. Mr. Conried believed that he found in Mme. Rappold the long-sought-for voice suited to the difficult part of Sulamith in ''The Queen of Sheba,'' and he was not mistaken, for at her début in Goldmark's well-known opera, in the following season (November, 1905), she scored an immediate and enthusiastic success. She had previously studied German opera at Bayreuth at Conried's suggestion, and continued her studies under the capable Oscar Saenger, until she had mastered a repertoire consisting of Elsa in "Lohengrin," Elizabeth in "Tannhäuser," Eva in "Meistersinger," Freia in "Rheingold," Inez in "l'Africaine," the title rôles in "Aïda" and "Martha," Helena in "Mephistofele," Marguerite in "Faust," Micaela in "Carmen," Gilda in "Rigoletto," Desdemona in "Othello," and Senta in "The Flying Dutchman." She is the first American singer to gain recognition and immediate success in opera in America without having acquired a European education. She has a high soprano voice that is clear, sweet and dramatic. She made her début in New York on Nov. 18, 1906, at the Metropolitan Opera house, as Sulamith in "The Queen of Sheba," and she has since sung abroad, having been the star for two seasons at La Scala, Milan, at the Paris Opera in 1910 and Bucharest (Roumania), 1910, and again at the Metropolitan Opera House, New York, in 1913. She was first married Jan. 10, 1899, to Dr. Julius C. Rappold, a physician of Brooklyn, N. Y., and after obtaining a divorce, was married July 15, 1913, to Kammersänger Rudolph Berger, a tenor of the Royal Opera of Berlin and Metropolitan Opera House, and has one daughter, Lillian.

PEARCE, Richard Mills, Jr., pathologist, was born in Montreal, Canada, March 3, 1874, son of Richard Mills and Sarah (Smith) Pearce. He received his early education at the public schools of New Haven, Conn., and the Boston Latin School, and was graduated at the Harvard Medical School in 1897. He took a post-graduate course at the University of Leipzig in 1902. He was resident pathologist in the Boston City Hospital for two years. Since then he has held the following positions: Instructor in pathology at Harvard, 1899-1900; assistant pathologist to Carney Hospital (Boston) and Children's Hospital (Boston), 1899-1900; pathologist to St. Elizabeth's Hospital (Boston) and Boston Floating Hospital, 1899-1900; demonstrator of pathology, University of Pennsylvania, 1900-1903; pathologist to Kensington Hospital (Philadelphia), 1902-1903; assistant professor of pathology, University of Pennsylvania, 1903; director of the Bender Laboratory, Albany, N. Y., 1903-08; professor of pathology and bacteriology, Albany Medical School, 1903-1908; director of the Bureau of Pathology of the New York State Department of Health, 1903-08; pathologist to Albany Hospital and Child's Hospital, Albany, 1903-08; member of the advisory council of the New York State Medical Library, 1906-08; pathologist to St. Peter's Hospital, Albany, 1906-08; pathologist to Albany City Free Dispensary, 1907-08; professor of pathology, New York University and Bellevue Hospital Medical School, 1908-10; professor of pathology, University of Pennsylvania, 1910-11; attending pathologist, Philadelphia General Hospital, attending pathologist, University Hospital, Philadelphia, 1910-11; professor of research medicine, University of Pennsylvania in 1910, and lieutenant, Medicine Research Corps, U. S. A., 1911. Notwithstanding his comparative youth, Dr. Pearce has won a foremost place in the medical world, and has shown abilities which will place him among the leading pathologists of the age. His special research work has been on pathology and bacteri-

ology of diphtheria and scarlet fever, leptothricial infections, diseases of the pancreas, nephrolysins, cytolytic immune serum, liver necrosis and experimental arteriosclerosis. He has found time from the exacting duties of his teaching and research work to contribute a large number of important papers to medical literature embodying the results of his researches. He was the author of "Studies from the Bender Hygienic Laboratory (5 vols.) and of chapters in Osler's "Modern Medicine" and Keen's "Surgery." He delivered the Hitchcock lectures at the University of California in 1912, afterward published in the "Popular Science Monthly." Among the societies in which Dr. Pearce holds or has held membership may be mentioned the Massachusetts Medical Society, Boston Medical Library Association, Boston Society of Medical Sciences, Philadelphia Pathological Society (vice-pres. 1912, pres. 1913), Deutsche Pathologische Gesellschaft, Sigma Xi, College of Physicians, Philadelphia; Albany County Medical Society, American Association of Anatomists, Association of American Physicians, Society for Experimental Biology and Medicine, Albany County Medical Association, New York State Medical Association, American Association of Pathologists and Bacteriologists (pres. 1912), American Medical Association, American Association for the Advancement of Science (fellow), International Association of Medical Museums, American Health League, New York Pathological Society (pres. 1910), Harvey Society (lecturer 1909), New York Academy of Medicine, Pennsylvania Society for the Protection of Scientific Research, Society for Normal and Pathological Physiology, Alpha Omega Alpha, American Physiological Society, the Rush Society (pres. 1912-13). He was vice-president of the section on pathology and bacteriology of the International Congress of Tuberculosis in 1908, and served in the U. S. National Committee of the International Congress of Medicine in 1908 and 1912. Dr. Pearce was married in Philadelphia, Pa., Nov. 6, 1902, to May Harper, daughter of Dr. John Herr Musser, of Philadelphia, and has two children.

STOCKTON, Charles Stacy, dental surgeon, was born in Burlington county, N. J., Dec. 17, 1836, son of Stacey and Eliza (Roselle) Stockton, and a descendant of Richard Stockton, who came from England about 1668, and settled in Flushing, Long Island, later removing to New Jersey. He was graduated at Pennington Seminary in 1856. His bent being scientific and mechanical, rather than religious, his preference was for a secular profession, and his choice was dentistry. He entered the office of Dr. George C. Brown, of Mt. Holly, and later of Dr. C. A. Kingsbury, who was one of the founders of the Dental College of Pennsylvania. After two years of study and preparatory work he was fortunate in being able to succeed to the practice of the latter. In 1867 he began a course of advanced study at the Pennsylvania College of Dental Surgery, from which he received a diploma in 1868. He removed from Mt. Holly to Newark, N. J., in 1872, where he practiced for nearly forty years. The great growth in population and wealth of the Oranges finally attracted him, and he settled in East Orange in 1892, while continuing to maintain an office in Newark. Dr. Stockton was one of the notable dental practitioners of New Jersey for a period of fifty-five years. Always progressive, and alert for every advance in the profession, and always conscientious in promulgating whatever he gained through study or experience, he achieved national

Charles S. Stockton

EDWARD L. THORNDIKE
PSYCHOLOGIST

ROBERT KUNITZER
PHYSICIAN

JOHN H. MacCRACKEN
PRESIDENT LAFAYETTE COLLEGE

HENRY N. MacCRACKEN
PRESIDENT VASSAR COLLEGE

distinction through his energy and progressiveness in the cause of American dentistry. Beginning before the days of state dental associations, he was one of the pioneers in the establishment of the New Jersey Dental Association, of which he was first vice-president and later president. He was vice-president of the American Dental Association in 1875, and was an active member of the Alumni Association of the Pennsylvania College of Dental Surgery, and its president for several terms. He was several times a delegate to the district, county and state conventions of the Republican party, and twice served on the board of education in Newark. As a regular communicant of Grace Church, East Orange, he was frequently called upon to represent the church in diocesan conventions. He was a writer of talent and grace of style on topics outside of dentistry, as evidenced by the titles of some of his published addresses and essays. They include: "Dentistry and Something Else," "Culture," "Failures," "The Young Man of To-day," "The Autobiography of a Cent," and "Great Believers." He was married, Sept. 23, 1857, to Martha, daughter of Zoel Smith, who survived him with two children: Mary, wife of Robert W. Elliott; and Dr. Frank O. Stockton. He died at East Orange, N. J., Sept. 9, 1912.

THORNDIKE, Edward Lee, psychologist, was born at Williamsburg, Mass., Aug. 31, 1874, son of Edward R. and Abigail (Ladd) Thorndike. He was graduated at Wesleyan University in 1895, after which he studied at Harvard, where he received the A.M. degree in 1897, and at Columbia, where he received the Ph.D. degree in 1898. For one year he was instructor in education and teaching at the Western Reserve University, after which he resigned to become instructor in genetic psychology at the Teachers' College, Columbia University. In 1901 he was advanced to an adjunct professorship, and in 1904 to a professorship in the same department. Dr. Thorndike's scientific work has been chiefly in applying exact quantitative methods to the study of human nature, behavior and education. The results in detail have concerned the measurement of mental fatigue, memory, the correlation between different abilities or talents, the inheritability of intellect and character, the rate of learning, the conditions of efficient learning, etc. He has also devised scales for measuring school achievement in handwriting, drawing and reading, and has directed the work of students in preparing scales for spelling, English, composition and arithmetic. Among his books and monographs are "The Human Nature Club" (1900); "Mental Fatigue" (1900); "Educational Psychology" (1903, enlarged edition, 1913–14); "Mental and Social Measurements" (1904); "Elements of Psychology" (1905); "Principles of Teaching" (1905); "Measurements of Twins" (1905); "The Elimination of Pupils from School" (1907); "The Teaching Staff of Secondary Schools in the United States" (1909); "A Scale for the Measurement of Achievement in Hand Writing" (1910); "Animal Intelligence" (1911); "The Measurement of Achievement in Drawing" (1913); "A Scale for the Measurement of Achievement in Reading" (1914), and "The Intellectual Status of Children Who Are Public Charges" (1915). Dr. Thorndike is a member of the American Psychological Association, and a fellow of the American Association for the Advancement of Science, and the New York Academy of Sciences. He was married Aug. 29, 1900, to Elizabeth, daughter of John T. Moulton, of

Lynn, Mass., and has one daughter, Elizabeth F. Thorndike, and two sons, Edward M. and Robert Ladd Thorndike.

KUNITZER, Robert, physician, was born in Szegedin, Hungary, Feb. 18, 1865, son of Emanuel and Johanna (Englander) Kunitzer. He was educated at the Gymnasium in Vienna, Austria, and the University of Vienna, where he received his absolutorium in 1888. In 1889 he came to the United States and began the practice of his profession in the city of New York. In the face of innumerable obstacles he made rapid strides to success and achievement, and in a short time he secured a clientele sufficiently large and influential to cause him to be trusted with the upbuilding of an important institution. The Sydenham Hospital was founded more than a decade ago, with its headquarters on the upper east side of New York city, which has since become a crowded center of population. Necessity soon compelled the enlargement of the institution, and at present the Sydenham Hospital occupies nine buildings and maintains eighty beds, besides a dispensary, a training school for nurses, a maternity ward, an X-ray laboratory and a laboratory for research. Mr. Isaac Guggenheim has been the most active supporter of the Sydenham Hospital, and the only conditions he has attached to his generous gifts are that the hospital shall minister to the worthy poor, and that it shall be strictly non-sectarian During all the years of the hospital's existence Dr. Kunitzer has been its head. Being a general practitioner with no personal ends to subserve, he has unselfishly given his time, energy and substance to the constructive work of the institution. In spite of numerous obstacles, untold difficulties and manifold forms of opposition, he has so maintained the hospital that it will remain a tribute to his sturdy leadership and executive ability. In a little more than a score of years his intellectual powers, superadded to his engaging personality, have placed him in the first rank of his profession, and he numbers among his patients some of the best known families of New York and neighboring cities. Dr. Kunitzer is a member of the Medical Society of the City of New York; the American Medical Association; Adelphi Lodge, F. & A. M.; Pinta Lodge, Knights of Pythias; Fortuna Lodge, I. O. O. F.; Humboldt Encampment; Sons of Benjamin, Yorkville Lodge, and Harlem Benevolent Society. He has long been visiting physician and chief of the Sydenham Hospital and Dispensary, and president of the executive board of the medical board. He is professor of the practice of medicine in the New York Medical College; medical examiner for the Denver Hospital for Consumptives, and chief medical examiner for the Empire State Insurance Co. of New York. His clubs are Columbia and Thirteen. Dr. Kunitzer was married in October, 1890, to Cora, daughter of Herman Rossenstraus, of New York, and has one son, Edwin R. Kunitzer.

MacCRACKEN, John Henry, eleventh president of Lafayette College, was born at Rochester, Vt., Sept. 30, 1875, son of Henry Mitchell and Catherine Almira (Hubbard) MacCracken, and a descendant of John MacCracken, who came to this country from the north of Ireland, and settled in Pennsylvania about 1740. From him the line is traced through his son Henry, who married Mary ———— (he was one of the Fair Play Managers of the Susquehanna settlement, and was killed as a ranger in the revolutionary war); their son John, who married Martha Wilson, and their son Rev. John Steele, who married

Eliza Hawkins Dougherty, and was the grand-father of the subject of this sketch. His father (q. v.) was for many years chancellor of New York University, and his brother, Henry Noble Mac-Cracken (below), is now (1916) president of Vassar College. John Henry MacCracken was prepared for college at Lyon's Collegiate School, New York city, and was graduated at New York University in 1894. He won the classical entrance prize, was class president in his senior year, alumni editor of the "University Quarterly," and was appointed valedictorian for highest rank in scholarship. His essay on "The Interstate Commerce Commission" won the James Gordon Bennett prize in economics. Upon graduation he was awarded the Ogden Butler fellowship in philosophy, and spent the year 1894–95 in graduate study at New York University and Union Theological Seminary, and the year 1895–96 in graduate study in Halle, Germany. He received the degree of M.A. from New York University in 1898, and that of Ph.D. with honor from the University of Halle in 1899, his thesis being "The Idealistic Philosophy of Jonathan Edwards." Immediately upon his return he was made president of Westminster College. In 1903 he resigned to become Syndic and professor of politics at New York University, and in this capacity gave courses in the graduate school on municipal government, being one of the first in America to offer courses on city planning, city charters and charter-making, and municipal enterprises. As Syndic of the university he was a member of each of the ten faculties, but had his office at the Washington Square building, and gave special attention to the affairs of the graduate school, the law school and the medical college. He was a member of the University corporation and of its executive committee, and chairman of its standing committee on the University Heights property. He was also vice-president of the University senate. During 1906–15 he was president of the Presbyterian college board, which holds over $1,000,000 of permanent funds and co-operates with some fifty colleges throughout the United States. In 1915 he was elected president of Lafayette College, at Easton, Pa. He is a member of the National Education Association; American Association for the Advancement of Science; National Civic Federation; American Political Science Association; Society for the Promotion of Industrial Education; Society for the Promotion of Engineering Education; fellow of the American Academy of Political and Social Science; member of the National Tax Association; American Civic Association; National Association for the Promotion of Fine Arts, and National Council of Economic Clubs. He is also a member of the Psi Upsilon Club, Phi Beta Kappa Society, Metropolitan, University, City and Bankers clubs, of New York, and a charter member of the American Universities Club, of London. The honorary degree of LL.D. was conferred upon him by Westminster College in 1903, and by New York University, Lehigh University, Pennsylvania College and Rutgers College in 1915. He was married Apr. 20, 1910, to Edith, daughter of the late Frederick A. Constable, of Mamaroneck, N. Y., and has two children: Louise and Constable MacCracken.

MacCRACKEN, Henry Noble, sixth president of Vassar College, Poughkeepsie, N. Y., was born in Toledo, O., Nov. 19, 1880, son of Henry Mitchell and Catherine (Hubbard) MacCracken. He was educated at Lyons Collegiate and Berkeley schools, New York city, and was graduated at the New York University with the degree of B.A. in

1900, receiving the degree of M.A. from the same institution in 1904; during 1904–07 he pursued a post-graduate course at Harvard University, where he received the degree of Ph.B. in the latter year. He received the honorary degree of L.H.D. from New York University in 1915. He began his professional career in 1900 as instructor in English in the Protestant College at Beyrout, Syria, remaining there until 1903. In 1907–08 he was John Harvard fellow, and during 1908–13 assistant professor of English at Yale University. He served as professor of English at Smith College during 1913–15, and in the latter year was elected president of Vassar College to succeed James M. Taylor. His success in teaching students the correct use of English words was considered remarkable. He deplored the ignorance of the English language shown by American college students, and required every student in the English department of the Sheffield Scientific School to possess a dictionary and learn how to use it. He also advocated that students in all universities should study not only their dictionaries, but should memorize the phraseology of many of our laws, and should analyze the messages of presidents to congress. He is the author of "First Year English" (1913); "English Composition in Theory and Practice," part author (1909); and "An Introduction to Shakespeare," part author (1910); and he edited "The Serpent of Division" (1911); "Minor Poems of Lydgate," Part I (1912); "The College Chaucer" (1913); and "The College Shakespeare" (1914). Dr. MacCracken is also a contributor to various magazines on philological topics. In religion he is a Congregationalist. He is a member of the Modern Language Association of America, the American Dialect Society and the Psi Upsilon and Phi Beta Kappa college fraternities. He was married June 12, 1907, to Marjory, daughter of Samuel C. T. Dodd, lawyer, New York city, and has two children: Marjory and Joy MacCracken. Portrait opposite page 205.

O'REILLY, James, second Roman Catholic bishop of the diocese of Fargo, N. D., was born in Ireland in the year 1856 and made his studies at the famous missionary college of All Hallows near Dublin, where he was ordained. Shortly afterward he immigrated to this country and affiliated himself with the diocese of St. Paul, Minn. He served for a time as assistant at Stillwater and at Lake City and was then made pastor of the Church of St. Anthony of Padua, Minneapolis, where he remained for twenty-six years. In that period he built the parish school, made very substantial improvements to the church property and greatly strengthened the parish spiritually and materially. On the death of Bishop Shanley he was appointed his successor and was consecrated bishop of Fargo May 10, 1910. This diocese was originally called Jamestown, but at the request of Bishop Shanley this title was suppressed Apr. 6, 1897, and the name changed to Fargo. It extends for 35,000 square miles, over thirty counties of the state, and has a Catholic population of 70,000. There are 107 priests, 225 churches and stations, twenty-six schools with 2,500 pupils, four hospitals and an orphanage.

MEZES, Sidney Edward, eighth president of the University of Texas (1908–14), was born in Belmont, Cal., Sept. 23, 1863, son of Samuel M. and Juliet (Johnson) Mezes. He was educated at St. Matthew's School, San Mateo, Cal., and at the University of California, being graduated B.S. at the latter in 1884. After spending four years in business, he took a course at Harvard University, being graduated A.B. in 1890, and receiving the degree of Ph.D. three years later. His summers were spent in Germany pursuing post-graduate studies in philosophy at several universities. He taught a year in Bryn Mawr College, and a second at the University of Chicago, and then became adjunct professor of philosophy at the University of Texas in 1894. In 1897 he was made associate professor of the same subject and attained to the full professorship in 1900. This post he retained until his election to the presidency in 1908, combining the duties with that of dean of the college of arts during the last six years of his incumbency. When Dr. Mezes succeeded David F. Houston in the presidency, the university had on its roll 2,574 students and a faculty of 117. He took the work of administration in hand with vigor, his scholarship, as well as his long familiarity with the needs of the institution, fitting him admirably for the task. During his six years' term of office two new lines of work were inaugurated; namely, the department of extension and a bureau of economic geology, both of which received an appreciative patronage. In his administration of the presidency his chief aim was to make the university in appropriate ways helpful to the people of the state at large. In 1914 Dr. Mezes was chosen as the result of a year's search, to be president of the College of the City of New York to succeed John H. Finley, who resigned to become state commissioner of education, and upon his return from a visit to Europe he entered upon the duties of his new office. He is the author of "Ethics: Descriptive and Explanatory" (1901), and in collaboration with Profs. Josiah Royce, G. H. Howison and Joseph Le Conte, "The Conception of God" (1896). As a philosophic thinker, Dr. Mezes is at once original and judicial. He views the subject deliberately in all its aspects, stating his conclusions directly and plainly. At the same time there is a note of freshness in all his work. In his "Ethics" especially he strikes out new ground in treating the subject from the point of view of conscience as developed in the social relations and law. Had his interest not been diverted to the administrative side of college life, it is probable that he would have made even more serious contributions to the study of philosophy. As dean of the college of arts of the University of Texas, Dr. Mezes showed in a marked degree capacity for taking pains, fertility in resource, breadth of sympathy, insight, fairness; as president, he appreciated to the full the position of a state university in the commonwealth. His views are large, his ideals inspiring, but controlling all are a soundness of judgment and a sense of values that make them capable of realization. He is a member of the Texas Academy of Science, and served as its president during 1906–07, and a fellow of the American Association for the Advancement of Science. He was married, Dec. 10, 1896, to Annie O., daughter of A. C. Hunter, of Hunter, Tex.

DENNIS, Louis Munroe, chemist and teacher, was born in Chicago, Ill., May 26, 1863, son of Joseph S. and Faustina (Munroe) Dennis. He was graduated in the scientific department of the University of Michigan in 1885 with the degree of Ph.B., receiving the degree of B.S. a year later. Determining upon chemistry for his life work, he pursued advanced courses in that subject in Munich, Dresden, Aachen, Germany, and in the private laboratory of the great Fresenius in Wiesbaden. On his return to the United States in 1887 he became instructor of chemistry in Cornell University, serving in that capacity two years.

In 1891 he was advanced to the rank of assistant professor and in 1893 was made associate professor of inorganic and analytical chemistry, becoming, on the retirement of the veteran Prof. George C. Caldwell in 1903, head of the department, which place he has since held. Most of his orginal researches have been in inorganic chemistry. The "Investigation of the Rare Earths" has received some attention from him, and he contributed a paper on that subject to the "Year Book of the Carnegie Institution" in 1903. Meanwhile he had added a "Contribution to the Chemistry of the Rare Earths of the Yttrium Group" in 1902, and he investigated "The Atomic Weight of Indium" in 1903, papers on both subjects being contributed to the Journal of the American Chemical Society. He also wrote "The Chemical Nature of the Radium Emanation" in 1907. In joint association with his students he has published papers on "Potassium Perselenate" (1902) and "Hydronitric Acid" (1907), which are typical of the investigations carried on under his direction in the chemical laboratory of Cornell University. He has described methods for "The Determination of Benzene in Illuminating Gas" (1903 and 1908), a subject in which he has been interested ever since his return from Germany, when he translated Hempel's classic "Methods of Gas Analysis." His publications in book form include, in association with Frank W. Clarke, "Chemical Problems in Inorganic Chemistry" (1902); "Laboratory Manual of Elementary Chemistry" (1902); with Theodore Whittlesey a "Manual of Qualitative Analysis" (1902) and "Gas Analysis" (1913). Among his popular writings is one on "The Education of Technical Chemists," which he published in 1905. He is a member of the American Chemical Society and other similar organizations both in the United States and Europe, including the American Association for the Advancement of Science, of which he has been a fellow since 1895. He was married, Aug. 25, 1887, to Minnie Clark, of Grand Rapids, Mich.

WHITMAN, Charles Seymour, forty-fourth governor of New York, was born at Hanover, Conn., Aug. 28, 1868, son of John Seymour and Lillie (Arne) Whitman, and a descendant of John Whitman, who emigrated from Plymouth, England, and settled at Weymouth, Mass., in 1635. His great-grandfather, John P. Whitman, and his grandfather, Seymour Whitman, were among the early benefactors of Williams College. His father, a graduate of Williams College and Union Theological Seminary, was a clergyman, and at the time of his death a member of the American Board of Foreign Missions, the American Bible Society, the American Tract Society and the New York Presbytery. Charles S. Whitman was educated at Amherst College, graduating in 1890, and received the degree of LL.B. in 1894, the degree of A.M. at Williams College in 1904, and the degree of LL.D. from the University of New York and from Amherst College in 1913. During his course in the law school he supported himself by teaching Latin and Greek in Adelphi Academy, Brooklyn, New York, now Adelphi College. He practiced law from 1894 to 1901, when, during the administration of Mayor Low, he was appointed assistant corporation counsel, having charge of the city's legislation in Albany, and later he was legal adviser to the mayor, by whom he was appointed city magistrate. During 1904 and 1906 he was president of the board of magistrates in New York city. During the three years while on this bench he was instrumental in affecting many reforms. He was the originator of the idea of a night court in New York, and he drafted the bill creating such a court, which became a law in 1907, and the first night court in the world was opened in New York city in 1907. The night court has abolished to a large extent the grafting practices of ''professional bondsmen'' who preyed on the unfortunate of both sexes arrested by the police on almost any pretence. Mr. Whitman was taken from the lower bench in 1907 by Gov. Charles E. Hughes, who appointed him judge of the court of general sessions, to fill a vacancy. At the end of his judicial term he resumed his private practice until 1909. In that year he was nominated for the office of district attorney, and, receiving the endorsement of all the anti-Tammany organizations, he was elected, the returns showing that he led his ticket by several thousand ballots. His achievements in what have been called the largest law office in the world have been epoch making. These include the trial and conviction of police lieutenant Charles Becker and the four "gunmen" for the murder of Herman Rosenthal, a New York gambler: the conviction of William J. Cummins and of Joseph B. Reichman, for wrecking the Carnegie Trust Company; of Joseph G. Robin, a banker who stole depositors' money; and of Charles A. Belling, vice-president of the Bronx National Bank. This should also include the conviction of members of the so-called "Poultry Trust," and his vigorous prosecution of violators of the election laws. In his capacity as district attorney, Mr. Whitman was a relentless enemy of the habitually criminal. In 1913 he was nominated by all political parties in New York county to succeed himself as district attorney and was unanimously elected. In 1914 he was elected governor of New York on the Republican ticket by a plurality of 146,000 votes. In religious faith he is a Presbyterian. He is a trustee of the New York Skin and Cancer Hospital, New York Probation Association, Adelphi College, and ex-officio trustee of Cornell University and of Union University. He is a member of the Union League, University Club, Century Association, Republican Club, Sleepy Hollow Club, West Side and City clubs, of the Sons of the Revolution, of the Society of Colonial Wars, and of the Alpha Delta Phi College fraternity. Gov. Whitman was married on Dec. 22, 1908, to Olive Hitchcock, daughter of Oliver N. Hitchcock, of New York, and has one daughter, Olive, and one son, Charles Seymour Whitman, Jr.

KEANE, James John, third R. C. archbishop of Dubuque, Ia., was born at Joliet, Ill., Aug. 26, 1857, son of John and Margaret (O'Connor) Keane. The family moved in his youth to Rochester, Minn., and he was educated at St. John's University, Minneapolis, and at the Seminary of St. Sulpice, Montreal. Here he was ordained priest Dec. 23, 1882, for the diocese of St. Paul. He ministered to his congregation most successfully until Oct. 28, 1902, when he was consecrated bishop of Cheyenne to succeed Bishop Thomas M. Lenihan, who had died on Dec. 15, 1901. In the subsequent development and organization of the church in Wyoming with the growth of the mining and railroad industries, he took a very active and fruitful part. An eloquent and impressive speaker, his services were in constant demand outside his own diocese, and he made several notable tours giving retreats and courses of lectures in various sections of the country. By special invitation he opened the Democratic National Convention in 1908. When his namesake, the Most

Rev. John Joseph Keane, resigned the archbishopric of Dubuque Apr. 3, 1911, the bishop of Cheyenne was elevated to the archiepiscopal dignity, and transferred to Dubuque to fill the vacancy. This diocese has an area of 17,404 square miles in the northeast section of the state, and a Catholic population largely rural of 133,000. There are 246 priests; 280 churches; 112 schools, and 31,000 pupils.

BATES, Onward, civil engineer, was born in St. Charles county, Mo., Feb. 24, 1850, son of Barton and Caroline Matilda (Hatcher) Bates and grandson of Edward Bates, who was attorney-general during Pres. Lincoln's first term. He comes of good English stock, his ancestors having settled in Virginia previous to the revolutionary war. His father (q. v.) was chief justice of the state of Missouri. The son received his preliminary education in the public schools of St. Charles county, and at the age of fifteen entered the service of the Fulton Iron Works, St. Louis, Mo., as an apprentice to the trade of pattern maker. His apprenticeship was soon canceled at the request of Col. C. Shaler Smith, who was building a bridge over the Missouri river at St. Charles, and who employed him in the undertaking first as draftsman and afterward as inspector of the iron work. Subsequently, with the consent of his preceptor, he accepted a position with the contractor for the iron caissons for the piers of the St. Louis bridge and became shop foreman. He laid out all of the iron work for the caissons and served also as principal assistant to the contractor. When this work was finished he attended the Rensselaer Polytechnic Institute, Troy, N. Y., for two years, returning to Col. Smith in 1873 as assistant engineer and inspector on the east approach of the St. Louis bridge. While inspecting this work he was appointed by James B. Eads, who was chief engineer of the St. Louis bridge, as shop inspector for the bridge company, thus serving on the same work in a double capacity. In 1874 Mr. Bates entered the service of the Cincinnati Southern railway as draftsman, and was subsequently promoted inspector of bridges and trestles. Three years later he became inspector of iron bridges with the Chicago, Milwaukee and St. Paul railway, and in that capacity he completed the Kilborn bridge over the Wisconsin river, considered at the time a difficult piece of construction. He then went to Australia for the Edge Moor Iron Company, Wilmington, Del., and there built a bridge over the Shoalhaven river for the New South Wales government; the iron viaducts on the Adelaide and Nairne railway, and a swing bridge for the Adelaide Dock Company. On his return he became president of the Pittsburgh Bridge Co., with which he remained until 1884, when he again served Col. Smith as assistant consulting engineer. During 1887–88 he was engaged in mining in Mexico. In the latter year he re-entered the service of the Chicago, Milwaukee and St. Paul road in charge of their newly-created department of bridges and buildings. He had jurisdiction over one hundred miles of bridging and some 13,000 culverts. His work won merited approval, and he showed a marked ability to organize, design and construct. He left that road in 1901 to become president of the Bates & Rogers Construction Company, Chicago, Ill., and from which he retired from active professional cares in 1907. The University of Wisconsin gave Mr. Bates the honorary degree of C.E. in 1897. He was vice-president of the American Society of Civil Engineers during 1906–7, and president in 1909. He

CHARLES S. WHITMAN
GOVERNOR

ONWARD BATES
CIVIL ENGINEER

JAMES J. KEANE
ARCHBISHOP

MARY GARDEN
SINGER

Andrew J. Shipman

is a past president of the Western Society of Engineers, and a member of the Institution of Civil Engineers of Great Britain, the Engineers', University and City clubs of Chicago, and the Engineers' Club of New York. He is interested in church and philanthropic work, and for many years has been an elder in the Presbyterian Church. He was married June 23, 1892, to Virginia Castleman, daughter of Judge Samuel M. Breckinridge, of St. Louis, Mo.

GARDEN, Mary, singer, was born in Aberdeen, Scotland, Apr. 13, 1877, daughter of Robert Davidson and Mary (Joyce) Garden. Her father came to America with his family in 1881, settling first in Montreal, Canada, and later in Chicago, Ill., and Milwaukee, Wis. He was interested in the bicycle manufacturing business and subsequently was engaged in the sale of the Pierce Arrow automobile in New York city. His daughter Mary displayed unusual talents for music at an early age. She began taking lessons on the violin when she was eight years old. While living in Chicago, at the age of fourteen, she first began singing in drawing-rooms and at small entertainments, exhibiting so much dramatic ability that influential persons became interested in her education for a musical career. She began to study singing under Mme. Robinson-Duff, a local teacher, and in 1897 was sent to Paris, where she became a pupil of M. Fauguere and M. Jules Chevallier. Through the influence of Sibyl Sanderson, the American singer, she became a member of the Opera Comique staff in 1900, and was assigned to learn the title rôle, as understudy to Mlle. Riotton, in Charpentier's "Louise." One day Mlle. Riotton was indisposed and Miss Garden was given the part. It was the opportunity she had long waited for. She completely captivated her audience and made such a profound and instantaneous success that the composer, who was present, insisted that she sing the part regularly thereafter. She continued to sing "Louise" for two hundred nights, during which she firmly established herself in the favor of a large portion of the opera-loving public in Paris. Among the other rôles essayed by her while at the Opera Comique were Marie in "La Marseillaise," Diane in "La Fille du Taberin," Aphrodite in Erlanger's opera of that name; the principal rôle in "L'Ouragan" by Bruneau; Melisande in Debussy's "Pelleas et Melisande," and the chief rôle, Marion, a boy, in Massenet's "Cherubim." The last part was enthusiastically received, as was also that of the title rôle in the same composer's "Thais," which she first sang in Brussels. Her most important successes were in "Louise," "Thais" and "Pelleas and Melisande." After singing in Europe for seven years Miss Garden made her début in the Manhattan Opera House, New York city, in October, 1907, in "Thais." Although the critics were divided as to the quality of her voice, they were unanimous in emphasizing the subtlety, versatility and emotional power of her acting. An unusually handsome and magnetic stage presence added to its effect. During the same season she gave a successful interpretation of the difficult part of Melisande and Richard Strauss' "Salome," which added many cubits to her artistic stature. Her success in New York was such that she was engaged for the following season at the Grand Opera House in Paris. Since 1909 she has appeared each season in New York, winning new laurels each year. Miss Garden has a clear, sweet soprano voice, which is well trained and under perfect control; but the secret of her great popularity is not the voice itself so much as her intelligent use of it in depicting the dominant traits and reflecting the varying moods of the characters she represents. In all her rôles her singing abounds in subtle shaded felicities like a new and strange speech, translating a phrase of the orchestra or vivifying an instrumental suggestion; always her singing is the language of the character. Whatever her part in both outward semblance and in inner suggestion, she gives it sustained and significant illusion. Never does she step without the frame of the picture to become the mere singer addressing her audience with the naked power of song. Portrait opp. p. 208.

SHIPMAN, Andrew Jackson, lawyer, was born at Springvale, Fairfax co., Va., Oct. 15, 1857, son of John James and Priscilla (Carroll) Shipman. His father was a prominent engineer and contractor and was married to the daughter of Bennett Carroll, of Upper Marborough, Md., a lineal descendant of Thomas Carroll, who came to this country with Charles Carroll in 1725 and settled in Maryland. The son received his early education in the Virginia public schools and was graduated at Georgetown College in 1878. He received the degree of A.M. in 1889 and LL.D. in 1911. He edited a newspaper called the "Vienna Times" for two years and in 1882 became assistant manager of the coal mines of W. P. Rend & Co., Hocking Valley, O., and was made superintendent of the mines in 1883. In 1884 he entered the United States customs service in New York and was one of the investigators of the sugar frauds at that port in the following year. He studied law in the law department of the University of the City of New York and was graduated LL.B. in 1886 and admitted to the New York bar. In 1891 he formed a law partnership in New York with Edmund L. Mooney under the title of Mooney & Shipman. The partnership was dissolved in 1895, when Charles Blandy, formerly corporation counsel of New York city, entered the firm and it was reorganized under the title of Blandy, Mooney & Shipman, by which it is still known. Mr. Shipman has been counsel in a number of cases of great importance, making a specialty of those involving the law of religious corporations, of testamentary matters and labor organizations. Among the most notable of these were the St. Stephen's Church cases (1890-1900), involving the right to strike, and the Hopkins will cases (1902-06), involving the cancellation of wills and the powers of surrogates' courts. Outside of his legal practice Mr. Shipman has come into special prominence as a writer on religious and racial topics. He has made a special study of religious and racial conditions in Russia, Austria, Hungary, Galicia, Italy, Palestine, Egypt, Spain and the United States, and his familiarity with many modern European languages and the great bulk of modern European literature, as well as with the people of these countries and the peculiar religious and emigration problems of each, has given to his writings a breadth and importance which place him among the most significant of contemporary writers on religious subjects. He is a special authority on the various branches of the Greek Church, the Orthodox, the Uniate and others, and has written much on this subject. It is rarely that a man holding such a prominent position in his profession is at the same time so eminent as a scholar in another specialized and altogether different field. He is a member of the American Bar Association, the New York State Bar Association, the American Society of International Law, the New York

County Lawyers' Association, the National Geographic Society, the Pan-American Society, the International Peace Society, the American Catholic Historical Society, the American-Irish Historical Society, the Friendly Sons of St. Patrick, the Society of St. John Chrysostom of the Catholic University, the Catholic Club and the Southern Society, besides a number of church and civic organizations. He was vice-president of the Catholic Club and president of the board of managers of the Mohansic State Hospital. He was among the contributors of the Catholic Encyclopedia, and was one of its directors. In 1913 he was elected a member of the board of regents of the University of the State of New York. He was married in New York city, June 28, 1893, to Adair, daughter of George Mooney, of New York. He died without issue in New York city, Oct. 17, 1915.

KELLY, Howard Atwood, physician, was born at Camden, N. J., Feb. 20, 1858, son of Henry Kuhl and Louisa Warner (Hard) Kelly, and a descendant of Thomas Kelly, a linen merchant of Portadown, County Armagh, Ireland, who came to America in the eighteenth century. Dr. Kelly's mother was a daughter of Rev. Anson Hard of Chester, Pa., and a granddaughter of Capt. John Warner of Wilmington, who served in the war of 1812, and also of Michael Hillegas, first treasurer of the United States. His boyhood was spent in Philadelphia and Chester, Pa., where he obtained his early education. He was encouraged to study natural history by Prof. E. D. Cope of Philadelphia, and when he matriculated at the University of Pennsylvania it was his intention to become a naturalist. He was the recipient of the matriculation Latin prize and after being graduated in 1877 took up the medical course as offering him the most direct means of pursuing his studies in natural history. His studies at the university were interrupted because of ill health and he went to a ranch in Colorado to recuperate. He was graduated M.D. in 1882 and spent a year in the Episcopal Hospital, Philadelphia, studying particularly diseases of the eye and skin and gynecology. Upon his return he opened an office near the hospital and soon had a large practice. He began to specialize in medical gynecology and abdominal surgery and is now recognized as one of America's foremost authorities on these subjects as well as on the vermiform appendix and its diseases and myomata of the uterus. His success induced him to start a small hospital on C street, and it grew so rapidly that he opened a larger establishment in Norris Square, which became known as the Kensington Hospital. He was untiring in prosecuting his practice, was ever alert to keep abreast of the times, going each year abroad to study in the leading hospitals of Europe. In 1908 he was appointed to the chair of obstetrics in the University of Pennsylvania, dividing the chair with Dr. Barton C. Hirst. In the following year he received a call from John Hopkins University as professor of gynecology and obstetrics, and in the same year was made professor of gynecology and gynecological surgeon in the Johns Hopkins Hospital. He devoted himself assiduously to his professional duties and wrote voluminously on the subjects of which he was an authority. He is the author of "Operative Gynecology" (1898), "Vermiform Appendix and Its Diseases" (1905), "Water Reed and Yellow Fever" (1906), "Gynecological and Abdominal Surgery" (joint author with Charles P. Noble, 1907-08), "Medical Gynecology" (1908), "Myomata of the Uterus" (1909), a "Cyclo-

pedia of American Medical Biography," published in 1912. Among his contributions to medical journals, which number nearly 350, are "Hysteorrhaphy" (1887), "Note on a Series of New Vesical Specula" (1900), "Removal of Pelvic Inflammatory Masses from the Abdomen After Bisection of the Uterus" (1900), etc. Dr. Kelly received the degree of LL.D. from the University of Aberdeen, Scotland, in 1906, and from Washington and Lee University in 1910. He is an honorary fellow of the Royal College of Surgeons of Edinburgh and of the British, Edinburgh and Glasgow Gynecological and Obstetrical Societies, associated fellow of the Royal Academy of Medicine and corresponding member of Societa Italiana di obstetricia e ginecologia, Rome; Gesellschaft für Geburschülfe and Gynekologie zu Berlin; Gesellschatf für Geburtschülfe und Gynekologie, Leipzig; de la Société de Chirurgie de Paris, K. K.; Gesellschaft Aerzte in Wien; de la Societe d'Obstetrique de Gynecologie et de Paediatrie de Paris. He is a fellow of the American Gynecological Society, American Association of Anatomists; president, 1907, Southern Surgical and Gynecological Association and member of the International Congress of Arts and Sciences, St. Louis, 1904; National Geographical Society and the Washington Academy. Dr. Kelly was married June 27, 1889, to Laetitia, daughter of Dr. Justus Bredow of Berlin and has nine children: Olga, Henry, Esther, Frederic, Howard, Boulton, Margaret, Edmund and Laetitia Kelly.

VAUX, Roberts, penologist, was born in Philadelphia, Pa., Jan. 21, 1786, son of Richard and Ann (Roberts) Vaux, and grandson of George Vaux, of London. His father took the Tory side at the time of the Revolutionary war and was obliged to leave Philadelphia. He visited the West Indies and Europe until after the war, when he returned in 1790 and became a merchant. Roberts Vaux was educated in the William Penn Charter School and Friends' Academy in Philadelphia. At the age of eighteen he entered the counting-room of a Philadelphia merchant, Mr. John Cooke, and upon attaining his majority commenced business on his own account. He was one of the originators of the public school system of Pennsylvania, and for fourteen years held the first presidency of the Board of Controllers of the Public Schools of Philadelphia (1818-31). He was one of the founders of the Blind Asylum, the Asylum for the Deaf and Dumb, the Apprentices' Library, the Philadelphia Saving Fund, the Frankford Asylum for the Insane, was president of the Pennsylvania State Temperance Society, and was one of the earliest and most earnest supporters of the anti-slavery cause. His interest in prison matters was almost lifelong, and as a penologist he acquired his greatest distinction. He was perhaps the first to suggest that the object of imprisonment should be the reformation rather than the punishment of criminals. He was appointed a commissioner in 1821 to devise a plan for the erection of the Eastern Penitentiary and also to draft a code of laws and regulations for its government adapted to the separate system of imprisonment. His plans were, in the main, accepted and became widely known in this country and abroad as the Pennsylvania system of separate confinement and labor. The Eastern Penitentiary was the first to embody these ideas, and as originally constructed it provided for a separate cell for each prisoner, which opened into a small yard for his exclusive use. The ancestors of Roberts Vaux for several generations were members of the Society of Friends, and he re-

Howard A Kelly

mained steadfast throughout life to the society's beliefs and customs. Notwithstanding his various philanthropic and benevolent interests he found time for literary and scientific pursuits, for which it is said he had a strong inclination. He was one of the founders of the Athenæum and the Pennsylvania Historical Society, and was a member of the Franklin Institute, the Philosophical Society of Pennsylvania and the Society for the Amelioration of the Miseries of Public Prisoners, as well as many other literary and scientific organizations at home and abroad. He was married Nov. 30, 1814, to Margaret, daughter of Thomas Wistar, and had two sons, Richard and Thomas Wistar Vaux. He died in Philadelphia, Pa., Jan. 7, 1836.

BOETTGER, Henry William, silk finisher, was born at Altona, near Hamburg, Germany, July 12, 1844, son of Maximillian M. Boettger. He was trained in the textile industry in Germany. Moved by his enterprising spirit to seek a wider field of action, he came to America in 1866, and after a short term of employment in a silk-dyeing factory, formed a partnership with Adolph Hinze and started a silk-finishing business in New York in 1868. The silk trade in America at that period was not very extensive. Black gros-grain imported silk was the principal kind in use, and the new firm was faced with considerable difficulty in getting business in its restricted field. For some time a large part of their business consisted in restoring for importers goods which had been damaged by sea-air and water, but the energy and ability of the partners were the kind that compel success, and before long they were obliged to remove to larger quarters. At that time there were practically no silk mills in Pennsylvania, and most of the goods for finishing came from Hoboken, Jersey Heights, West Hoboken and Paterson, so a three-story factory was erected in Hoboken, N. J., in 1877. The firm of Boettger & Hinze was changed to Boettger, Hinze & Kueppers in 1882, and in 1888 the first two bought out the interest of Mr. Kueppers. Besides a thorough knowledge of the silk industry generally and of the technical details of his own business, Mr. Boettger possessed the remarkable faculty of foreseeing developments in the silk trade and of anticipating them to just the proper extent, and this particular intuition was one of the factors of his continued success. In March, 1891, a "piece dyeing" business was started—an entirely new venture, which was so successful that in 1898 the company built the Piece Dye Works at Lodi, N. J., which is the largest enterprise of its kind in the country. In dyeing, as well as in finishing, Mr. Boettger not only produced the most expert and careful work obtainable, but he was ever experimenting to improve the artistic and economic value of that work. He also possessed an extraordinarily keen judgment of silk in all its aspects and had a rarely dependable judgment as to what was or what was not likely to meet with popular approval. He was one of the first to produce "moire," which is now so much in demand, and many other novelties were also owing to his inventive mind. The interest of Mr. Hinze in the silk finishing plant was purchased by Mr. Boettger in 1895, and in 1903 the business was incorporated as the Henry W. Boettger Silk Finishing Co., with Henry W. Boettger, president; Robert Boettger, vice-president; Theodore Boettger, treasurer, and Henry W. Boettger, Jr., secretary. In 1900 the Boettger Piece Dye Works of Lodi and the Alexander Dye Works of Lodi were consolidated under the name of the United Piece Dye Works of Lodi. In 1912

the Henry W. Boettger Silk Finishing Co., the Charavay & Bodwin Co. and the Zurich Silk Finishing Co. were merged into a new corporation, the Silk Finishing Company of America. Henry W. Boettger was president of this new company until his death and was succeeded in the office by his son, Henry W. Boettger, Jr. He was a member of the Arion Society of New York, the Silk Association of America, the Municipal Art Society, the Museum of Natural History and the New York Zoological Garden. He was married at Union Hill, N. J., May 4, 1870, to Pauline, daughter of Xavier Stopple, of Union Hill, N. J., and had nine children: Maximillian, Martha, Robert, Theodore, Anna, wife of George A. Laughlin, of Wheeling, W. Va., Pauline, wife of Erich Dankelman, an officer in the German army, Henry W., Helen, wife of Harold G. Hesse, of New York, and Matilda, wife of Maxmillian L. Roessel, of Toronto, Canada. Mr. Boettger died in New York, Jan. 20, 1913.

POINDEXTER, Miles, U. S. senator, was born in Memphis, Tenn., Apr. 22, 1868, son of William B. and Josephine Alexander (Anderson) Poindexter. He was educated at Fancy Hill Academy in Virginia, and was graduated in the law department of Washington and Lee University in 1891. He began the practice of his profession in Walla Walla, Wash., and six years later removed his office to Spokane. He was prosecuting attorney for Walla Walla county for one term and assistant prosecuting attorney for Spokane county, holding the latter position when he was elected judge of the superior court of the district in 1904. He continued on the bench until nominated for congress in the newly created 3d district, and was elected in September, 1908. He served in the lower house during the 61st congress. In congress he was classed as an insurgent, siding with those who criticised the policies of Pres. Taft, and being so firmly opposed to some of the Republican measures that he was classed by the regular Republicans as a Democrat. At the primary election for U. S. senator in 1910 he received the largest number of votes, and upon his election by the state legislature in the following January took his seat in the upper house of the national legislature in April, 1911. He was married June 16, 1892, to Elizabeth Gale of Walla Walla, Wash.

RIKER, Andrew Lawrence, electrical and mechanical engineer, was born in New York city, Oct. 22, 1868, son of William J. and Charlotte L. Riker. He came from an old New York family of Dutch descent, his ancestors having settled in the town of Newton, Long Island, in the seventeenth century; he is also a direct descendant of Capt. Lawrence, commander of the U. S. frigate Chesapeake in the fight with the Shannon during the war of 1812. Andrew L. Riker attended Columbia College, studied the law course in that institution, and immediately after entered upon his studies and experimental work in connection with his chosen profession of electrical and mechanical engineer. He was prominent in early days in the electrical development of the country, and the old Riker Electric Motor Co., of which he was president in 1888, was credited with having developed and built the first toothed electric armature. This company also built dynamos and motors of high quality, a number of them being used by other inventors of automobiles in their experimental work. In 1902 Mr. Riker became vice-president and designer of the Locomobile Co. of America, of Bridgeport, Conn., and still (1916) occupies that position. In 1884 he designed and built his first automobile, an electrical tricycle which was successful in every way. In 1895 he had developed and had running satisfactorily a four-wheeled electric motor car. In addition to his work in the manufacture of dynamos and motors, the Riker Electric Motor Co. developed a superior electric vehicle, models of which are still running and giving good service. When Mr. Riker first became associated with the Locomobile Co. he immediately began the design and construction of a gasoline car. His pioneer machine had a sliding gear transmission, steel frame, four-cylinder vertical motor with high-tension ignition, and bronze base, bronze gearcase, and gear-driven electric generator. The construction of the first car was accomplished secretly at Chicopee, Mass., and the appearance of this car in New York city in 1902 created much surprise and favorable comment. He designed Locomobile No. 16, which won the Vanderbilt cup race in 1908. In 1899, at speed trials on Long Island, he established a world's record for electric cars, of one mile in 63 seconds, which he held for ten years. In 1900 he was awarded a medal by the French government for merit in motor-car design. Mr. Riker is a member of the naval advisory board established by the secretary of the navy in 1915. He is chairman of the committee on internal combustion motors, and a member of the committee on aeronautics, including aero motors, and of the committee on transportation, of the same board. He was the first president of the Society of Automobile Engineers; and is a member of the American Society of Mechanical Engineers; American Society of Electric Engineers; Automobile Club of America; Engineers' Club and Aero Club of America. He was married in New York city, Apr. 9, 1890, to Edith, daughter of James R. Whiting, of New York city, and has two daughters and one son: Edith W.; Charlotte L.; and Andrew L. Riker, Jr.

WADE, Levi Clifford, lawyer and railroad president, was born at Allegheny, Pa., Jan. 16, 1843, son of Levi and A. Annie (Rogers) Wade. His first American ancestor Wade came to this country from Denver, near Downham Market, Norfolk, England, in 1632, and the line of descent is traced through his son, Jonathan; his son, Nathaniel; his son, Samuel; his son, Nathaniel; his son, Ebenezer; and his son, Levi. Jonathan Wade was a member of the colonial legislature in 1681-82; the first Nathaniel Wade was a colonel in the colonial service; and Ebenezer Wade served in the patriot army during the revolutionary war. Levi C. Wade was educated in the public schools of Allegheny, at Lewisburg (now Bucknell) University, and Yale College, being graduated with special honors at the latter in 1866. During his college course he took several prizes in debating, declamation and composition, and was one of the editors of the "Yale Literary Magazine." On leaving college he studied Greek and Hebrew exegesis for one year under Dr. H. B. Hackett, and theology for one year under Dr. Alvah Hovey, of Newton, Mass. During 1868-73 he studied law, and upon being admitted to the Suffolk bar entered the law office of J. W. Richardson in Boston. In 1875 he opened an office of his own, and from 1877 to 1880 he was associated with Hon. John Q. A. Brackett, under the firm name of Wade & Brackett. He represented Newton in the Massachusetts legislature, 1876-79, and was speaker of the house during the last year, being the youngest man who ever held that position in the legislature of Massachusetts. After 1880 he devoted himself exclusively to railroad law and management, be-

coming attorney for the Atchison, Topeka and Santa Fé, the Atlantic and Pacific, the Sonora, and the Mexican Central railway companies. He became known as one of the most authoritative and skillful railroad lawyers in the country. He was one of the four original projectors and owners of the railroad lines which later constituted the Mexican Central railroad, of which he was president and general counsel at the time of his death. His services to the Mexican Central Railway Co. are thus summed up in the memorial resolution of the board of directors: "He assumed the position (of president) under circumstances discouraging and disheartening. The railroad was not earning the interest on its first mortgage bonds. The company was heavily in debt, and its credit was gone. Mr. Wade threw himself with all his power and energy into the reorganization of the securities. Upon this he worked incessantly, and succeeded in reorganizing the whole bonded debt. He built the Guadalajara branch, he finished the Tampico branch, and he completed his plans for the improvement of Tampico harbor. And still more, he arranged on a most satisfactory basis for this company a settlement in cash with the government of Mexico for all the subsidy due from the Mexican government to this corporation—in amount over $14,000,000—the last draft having been paid the day before his death. Passing in review his connection with this company, commencing with its organization as its attorney, and later as its president, he met every demand. He mastered and was successful in the details of railroad work, he built branch roads, and he developed and carried to success large schemes of finance. He adapted himself to all these with a quickness and accuracy seldom, if ever, equaled in the history of railroad management." Mr. Wade was also a director of the Atchison, Topeka and Santa Fé, the Sonora, the Atlantic and Pacific, and the Cincinnati, Sandusky and Cleveland railroad companies. He took a large interest in the social, philanthropic and educational activities of his community, was one of the directors of the General Theological Library, and was connected with a number of other public and semi-public institutions. Personally, Mr. Wade was simple in his nature, courteous and gentlemanly in his manners, and easily approached by the humblest person. He showed at all times the fullest integrity and honesty of purpose, and was as magnanimous as he was broad in his conduct of affairs. His whole life was based on religious conviction. He was a man of large attainments and great general knowledge. His mind worked quickly, and he had wonderful power in grasping new subjects and carrying them to a successful issue. He was married at Bath, Me., November 16, 1869, to Margaret, daughter of William Rogers, and had four children: Arthur C., William R, Levi C., Jr., and Robert N. Wade. He died in Newton, Mass., Mar. 21, 1891. Portrait opposite page 213.

MARION, Otis Humphry, surgeon, was born at Burlington, Mass., Jan. 12, 1847, son of Abner and Sarah (Prescott) Marion. Among his ancestors were Gen. Francis Marion (q. v.), a distinguished revolutionary soldier, and Gen. William Prescott of Bunker Hill fame. Otis H. Marion served as a drummer boy in the civil war. He received his early education at Kimball Union Academy and was graduated at Dartmouth College in 1873. During his college years he taught school and was instructor in gymnastics at Dartmouth. He was graduated at the Harvard Medical School in 1876, and after one year as house sur-

LEVI C. WADE
RAILROAD PRESIDENT

OTIS H. MARION
SURGEON

WILLIAM H. TAYLOR
FINANCIER

WOODBRIDGE N. FERRIS
GOVERNOR

geon at the Boston City Hospital he opened an office at Allston Station, Boston, where he built up a large and lucrative practice. In 1883 he joined the 1st regiment, M. V. M., and remained with it until 1897, when he was appointed medical director of the 1st brigade on the staff of Gen. Mathews. In the following year he became major surgeon of the 6th Mass. volunteers, with whom he went into camp near Washington at the beginning of the war with Spain. He was prevented by illness from accompanying the regiment to Porto Rico and after his recovery he resumed his position as medical director on the staff of Gen. Mathews. In May, 1904, he was appointed surgeon-general by Gov. Bates. Gen. Marion was the first to introduce into the militia first aid to the injured, physical training and athletics, and his innovations were attended by very satisfactory results. He was an inspector of schools for the Boston board of health from the time the department was organized and was looked upon as an authority on matters pertaining to school ventilation, heating and sanitary matters generally. For several years he was consulting physician of the Women's Charity Club Hospital. He was an excellent athlete and a crack rifleman and was a member of the famous rifle team which went abroad in 1889 and won every match in which it was entered. Dr. Marion was manager of the medical department of the National Encampment of the G. A. R., held in Boston in 1890; commander of the Old Guard of Massachusetts, and a member of the Sons of the American Revolution, Bunker Hill Association, U.S. Association of Military Surgeons, Emergency and Hygiene Association, Massachusetts Medical Society, Cambridge Medical Society, Massachusetts Benevolent Society and Spanish War Officers' Association. He belonged to the University, Dartmouth and Boston City Hospital clubs of Boston, the Harvard Alumni Association, the Masonic fraternity, Boston Commandery Knight Templars and the Independent Order of Odd Fellows. Dr. Marion was married Dec. 17, 1879, to Carrie Eudora, daughter of James Willis Johnson of Enfield, N. H., and had three children: James Willis Johnson, Philip Prescott and Thalia Marion. He died at his home at Allston Station, Boston, Mass., Nov. 27, 1906.

TAYLOR, William Henry, financier, was born at Paterson, N. J., Sept. 30, 1859, son of William H. and Catharine G. (Deeths) Taylor, and grandson of William H. Taylor, who was a native of Birmingham, England, and came to the United States with his wife, Mary White, and four children and settled at Paterson, N. J. The Taylor family is one of great antiquity, the original name, Taillerfer, having been brought to England by one of the Norman barons who accompanied William the Conqueror. The family has contributed many eminent men in all walks of life and never so far as is known has the name been sullied by an unworthy act. William H. Taylor was educated in the schools of Paterson, N. J., and Allentown, Pa., completing his studies at Dickinson Seminary. He left the latter to enter his father's machinery and supply business as assistant manager, in which capacity he gained a complete knowledge of the business. The firm was originally known as William H. Taylor & Co., and upon the death of his father in 1880 Mr. Taylor assumed entire control. In 1884 he established a branch at Scranton, Pa., the Scranton Supply and Machinery Co., and in 1889 another branch at Hazleton, Pa., the Hazleton Machinery and Supply

Co. Mr. Taylor's prominence in the world of finance kept pace with the growth of his manufacturing business. Becoming interested in coal mining he is now one of the largest individual anthracite operators in the state of Pennsylvania. He is president of the St. Clair Coal Co., for which he acted as councillor in the anthracite strike commission; the Franklin Coal Co. and the Goodwin Car Co. He is also a director of the Coal and Iron National Bank of New York, a member of the New York State Chamber of Commerce and is actively interested in numerous other financial and commercial enterprises. He is a member of the Scranton Club of Scranton, Pa., the National Geographic Society, the American Society of Political and Social Science and the American Institute of Mining Engineers. He is a thirty-second degree Mason (Scottish rite); is a Republican in politics and a member of the Christian Science Church. Mr. Taylor was married June 17, 1886, to Nellie Grace, daughter of Samuel Gunn Barker of Scranton, Pa., and has one daughter, Alice Marion, and two sons, William H. and John D. Higgins Taylor.

FERRIS, Woodbridge Nathan, governor of Michigan, was born at Spencer, Tioga county, N. Y., Jan. 6, 1853, son of John and Stella (Reed) Ferris. His youth was passed upon his father's farm and his early education was received in the neighborhood district school. Subsequently he spent two terms in an academy at Spencer, N. Y.; one term in the Candor Academy, Candor, N. Y., and one year at the Owego (N. Y.) Academy. At the age of sixteen he secured a certificate as teacher in his county. The largest part of his scholastic training was received during 1870-73 at the Oswego (N. Y.) Normal and Training School, and in the fall of 1873 he entered the Medical Department of the University of Michigan, where he remained for one entire course of lectures. He was principal of the Academy at Spencer, N. Y., for one year, and in 1875 he established a business college and academy of his own at Freeport, Ill., which was a success from the start, having in attendance ninety pupils at the end of seven months. In April, 1876, a flattering offer from the president of Rock River University, Dixon, Ill., led him to accept a position there. In the fall of 1877 he organized the Dixon Business College and Academy in partnership with J. L. Hartwell, and this venture also prospered, Mr. Ferris buying Mr. Hartwell's interest in 1878 and continuing the work independently. In the fall of 1879 he became superintendent of the schools of Pittsfield, Ill., but after five years resigned to establish the Ferris Institute at Big Rapids, Mich., of which he is still president. The Ferris Institute has a large attendance from all parts of the country and has enjoyed a constantly increasing reputation for excellent equipment and superior educational facilities. It was originally called the Ferris Industrial School, and opened in 1884 with fifteen pupils in two small rooms, Mr. and Mrs. Ferris being the only teachers. In 1894 it was incorporated with a capital stock of $50,000, and in 1900 the name was changed to the Ferris Institute. In 1904 the school had an attendance of from 700 to 1,200 scholars and its property, situated in nearly the heart of the city, comprising some seventy-five acres, is valued at over $175,000. Sixteen departments are maintained: English, Pharmacy, Commercial, Shorthand, Typewriting, Civil Service, Penmanship, Telegraph, Elocution, Vocal Music, Drawing, Kindergarten, Physical Culture, Professional Preparatory, College Preparatory, and Normal. A large part of Mr. Ferris' time has been devoted to lecturing, and he has spoken in almost every village and city in the state of Michigan. His business capacity was well demonstrated in the planning, construction and conduct of his school, to which he continues to devote the greater part of his time. For years he was a member of the Big Rapids Board of Trade and was one of the founders and is president of the Big Rapids Savings Bank. In 1892 he was the Democratic-Populist candidate for congress from the 11th district of Michigan, and in 1902 was the Democratic candidate for superintendent of public instruction. In both instances he materially reduced the usual Republican majorities. In 1904 he was nominated by the Democratic convention at Grand Rapids for governor. Nothwithstanding the fact that he had the support of the leading newspapers of Michigan and the assistance of thousands of Republicans, his opponent, Fred M. Warner, was elected by 42,877 majority. He was nominated again in 1912 by the Democratic party and was elected by a plurality of nearly 25,000 over Amos S. Musselman, Republican. Gov. Ferris is a public speaker of force and eloquence. His powers are always consecrated to the most ideal aims of citizenship, without the slightest trace of self-seeking. He is a strong advocate of public ownership of public utilities, railways and lighting plants. Gov. Ferris is a member of the Knights of Pythias, the Masonic fraternity, and Modern Woodmen. He was married Dec., 1875, to Helen Frances, daughter of John C. Gillespie, of Fulton, N. Y., and has two sons, Carleton G., a lawyer at Taylorville, Ill., and Phelps Ferris, a teacher in his father's institute. Mrs. Ferris is an unusually able woman, and her tact and energy have been important factors in the success of the institute. For a number of years she taught mathematics.

FOX, Joseph John, fifth Roman Catholic bishop of the diocese of Green Bay, Wis., was born at Green Bay, Aug. 2, 1855, son of Paul and Frances (Bartel) Fox. He was educated at the Cathedral School, Green Bay, whence he went to St. Francis Seminary, Milwaukee, Wis., and for his theological course to the American College in Louvain, Belgium. He was ordained priest June 7, 1879, and returning to the United States, was stationed at New Franken, Wis. Bishop Krautbauer made him his secretary, and during 1883-94 he was rector of the Church of Our Lady of Lourdes at Marinette, Wis. In 1894 he was appointed vicar-general of the diocese and in 1898 was made a domestic prelate by Pope Leo XIII. When Bishop Messmer, of Green Bay, was elevated to the archbishopric of Milwaukee, Mgr. Fox was appointed his successor on May 27, 1904, and was consecrated on July 25. He ruled the see until May, 1914, when ill-health forced him to resign, and he was transferred to the titular see of Gionopolis and made administrator of Green Bay. At the time of his death the Catholics in the diocese numbered 146,765, and there were 221 priests, 248 churches, 108 schools with 18,633 pupils, three colleges, five asylums with 454 inmates, two Indian schools, 296 pupils, 10,732 young people under Catholic care, nine hospitals, one reform school and one infant asylum. Bishop Fox was a life member of the Wisconsin State Historical Society. He died in Chicago, Ill., March 14, 1915.

BUCKHAM, James, author, was born in Burlington, Vt., Nov. 25, 1858, oldest son of Matthew Henry (q.v.) and Elizabeth (Wright) Buckham. His father was the eleventh president of the University of Vermont. His grandfather, James Buck-

ham, Sr., was a Scotch clergyman, who came to the United States early in the eighteenth century, and was for many years actively engaged in the work of the Congregational ministry in New England. James Buckham, the subject of this sketch, graduated (A.B.) from the University of Vermont in 1881 (A.M., 1884), after which he took special courses in English at Johns Hopkins University in 1888 and in religious journalism at Andover Theological Seminary in 1891-92. He entered the field of journalism and for eighteen years was connected with journals in Burlington, Vt., Boston and other cities, finally abandoning newspaper work to devote his entire time to literary pursuits. Mr. Buckham's published volumes include "The Heart of Life," poems (1897); "Where Town and Country Meet," essays (1903); "A Wayside Altar," poems (1905); "Afield with the Seasons," essays (1907); "The Heritage of Life," essays (1907). He was also a frequent contributor to magazines and other periodicals. Mr. Buckham's work is characterized by an intense love of nature in her various moods, by a sane and optimistic outlook upon life, and by a delicate literary style. He was particularly happy in his descriptions of natural phenomena, and his nature studies rendered him not unworthy a place in that small company of American naturalists which includes such names as John Burroughs, John Muir, Bradford Torrey, Charles G. D. Roberts, Seton-Thompson and Mabel Osgood Wright. He was married, Aug. 28, 1895, to Mary, daughter of Hon. Waldo Brigham, of Hyde Park, Vt., and died without issue in Melrose, Mass., Jan. 8, 1908.

CROSS, [Charles] Whitman, geologist, was born in Amherst, Mass., Sept. 1, 1854, son of Rev. Moses Kimball and Maria E. (Mason) Cross. His early studies were made at Waverly high school in Iowa, whence he went to Amherst College and was graduated B.S. in 1875. Choosing geology as his life work, he went abroad and studied at the universities of Göttingen and Leipzig, receiving from the last-named in 1880 the degree of Ph.D. for his studies "Ueber bretonische Gesteine." Returning to the United States, he entered the service of the United States Geological Survey as assistant geologist and eight years later became geologist. He was also in charge of the section of petrology of the survey during 1903-07. Among the many eminent men connected with the U. S. Geological Survey he ranks with the foremost, and as an authority on the Rocky Mountain geology he has no superior. His early researches were in connection with mineralogy and petrology. Among these may be mentioned his joint publication with W. F. Hillebrand entitled "Contributions to the Mineralogy of the Rocky Mountains" (1885), which formed No. 20 of the Bulletin series of the geological survey. He was the author of "Petrography of the Leadville Region" (1887), which formed appendix A to monograph twelve of the survey entitled "Geology and Mining Industry of Leadville, Colo.," by Samuel F. Emmons (1896). His work on the Rocky Mountain region consists of the "Pike's Peak Folio" (1894), which is the first of the series of similar monographs that include "The Telluride Folio" (1899), "The La Plata Folio" (1899), "The Needle Mountains Folio" (1905), "The Rico Folio" (1905), "The Silverton Folio" (1905), and "The Curay Folio" (1907), all of which were prepared under his direction. Two important publications of his earlier period that were issued by the geological survey are the "General Geology of the Cripple Creek District, Colorado" (1895), and "Geology of Silver Cliff and the Rosita Hills, Colorado" (1896). With Joseph P. Iddings, Louis

V. Pirsson and Henry S. Washington he formulated "Authoritative Classification of Igneous Rocks," a complete and original system based on new principles (1903), and also the "Texture of Igneous Rocks" (1906), which was contributed to the "Journal of Geology." The latest of his contributions to science is "Lavas of Hawaii and Their Relations," which was issued as No. 88 of the "Professional Papers" of the survey and gives the results of studies begun in 1902. Dr. Cross is a fellow of the American Association for the Advancement of Science and a member of the National Academy of Sciences, the Geological Society of London and the Geological Society of Washington, of which he was president in 1899. He was married, Nov. 7, 1895, to Virginia, daughter of Moses T. Stevens, of North Andover, Mass., and has one son: Richard Stevens Cross.

NORTON, Edwin, inventor and manufacturer, was born at Rockton, Ill., Mar. 27, 1845, son of Oliver William and Henrietta A. (Willcox) Norton, and descendant of Thomas Norton, who came over from England in 1639 and settled at Guilford, Conn., the line of descent being traced through his son Thomas, who married Elizabeth Mason; their son Samuel, who married Dinah Birdseye; their son David, who married Anne Bronson; their son Oliver, who married Martha Beach, and their son, Oliver William Norton. Edwin Norton was educated in the public schools, served in the civil war, and after clerking in a hardware store in Toledo, O., began, in 1868, the manufacture of tin cans under the name of Norton & Fancher, which subsequently became E. Norton & Co. In 1869 his brother, Oliver Willcox Norton, joined the firm and was its financial and business manager. In 1870 the business was moved to Chicago, Ill., and in 1891 was incorporated under the name of Norton Bros., with Oliver W. Norton president. Meanwhile the Norton Can Co. had been organized with a factory at Whitestone, Long Island; the Norton Tin Plate and Can Co., with a plant in Baltimore, Md.; and the Norton Manufacturing Co., with a plant at Hamilton, Ontario, Canada. In all of these companies Edwin Norton was vice-president. He was one of the organizers of the American Can Co. in 1901, and was its first president, holding the position for about a year. He was of an inventive turn of mind, and obtained over 300 patents for his inventions, which comprised automatic machines for can making, forms of cans, processes for the continuous rolling of sheet metal and the machinery for accomplishing it, automatic furnaces and rolling mills for making thin steel sheets and tin plates, and machines for making hermetically sealed tin cans automatically, and for the preservation of food products in vacuum. He was married Oct. 9, 1876, to Lucy E., daughter of Abiel Akin, and had two sons, Arthur Willcox and Edwin Kenneth Norton, and three daughters, Sylvia (wife of Carle Cotter Conway), Evelyn (wife of C. Linn Seiler) and Henrietta (wife of Dr. Edward Delavan Truesdell). He died in New York city, December 31, 1914.

McCONNELL, Francis John, M. E. bishop, was born in Trinway, O., Aug. 18, 1871, son of Israel H. and Nancy Jane (Chalfant) McConnell, of Scotch-Irish ancestry. He was graduated at Ohio Wesleyan University in 1894 and at Boston University with the degree of S.T.B. in 1897 and Ph.D. in 1899. He entered the ministry of the Methodist Episcopal church in 1894, becoming pastor of a church at West Chelmsford, Mass. His subsequent churches were at Newton Upper Falls,

Mass., 1897–99; Ipswich, Mass., 1899–1902; Cambridge, Mass., 1902–03, and Brookline, Mass., 1903–09. In 1909 he was elected president of De Pauw University, and three years later he was elected bishop of the Methodist Episcopal church. He is the author of "The Diviner Immanence" (1906); "Christmas Sermons" (1909); "Religious Certainty" (1910); "Christian Focus" (1912); "The Increase of Faith" (1912), and "Personal Christianity" (1914). He received the degree of D.D. from Ohio Wesleyan University in 1904, and that of LL.D. from Wesleyan University in 1909, Denver University in 1913 and Ohio Wesleyan University in 1914. He was married Mar. 11, 1897, to Eva Hemans, daughter of William Thomas, a farmer of Scioto county, O., and has three children: Thomas Chalfant, Dorothy Francis and Donald William McConnell.

AITKEN, Robert Ingersoll, sculptor, was born in San Francisco, Cal., May 8, 1878, the son of Charles Hamilton and Katherine Sophia (Higgins) Aitken. His father, a native of Ayr, Scotland, was an engineer, contractor and ship-owner. The son received a public school education and took the full course of instruction in drawing and sculpture at the Mark Hopkins Institute of Art, where he won the Phelan gold medal for sculpture. At the age of nineteen he had set up a studio in San Francisco and entered upon a career that was to win him national fame. One of his first productions was a portrait-bust of Mme. Modjeska as Lady Macbeth, which brought him at once to notice in the upper circles of California society, and he was commissioned to design the monuments to President McKinley at St. Helena, Berkeley, and in Golden Gate Park, San Francisco, which rank among the best works of art ever produced by Western talent. In 1904 he was selected to design the monument to the American navy, which stands in Union square, San Francisco, to commemorate Admiral Dewey's victory at Manila Bay, and in 1905 he completed a statue of Hall McAllister, the California lawyer. Meanwhile he had exhibited in New York city and was ranked by the critics among the foremost contemporary American sculptors. In 1906 he moved his studio to New York, where he was besieged with orders for portrait busts, in which he particularly excelled. Important commissions of the succeeding half-dozen years included busts of Prof. Nathaniel S. Shaler at Harvard University, in the state capitol building of Kentucky and in the Harvard Club, New York, of Augustus Thomas, George Bellows, Willard Metcalf, Senator Edward O. Wolcott, Henry Roger Wolcott, Henry Arthur Jones, President Taft and Bret Harte, and bronze doors for the mausoleums of B. J. Greenhut and John W. Gates. The most notable of his ideal sculptures are "Bacchante" (1908), "The Flame" (1909) and "Fragment" (1909). At the exhibition of the National Academy in 1912 he achieved a triumph with his Michael Angelo, a study of the great sculptor at work upon his figure of "The Day," for the tomb of Lorenzo de Medici. He also exhibited on the same occasion his "Fragment," a study of a delicate feminine type, which won the highest praise from both the press and public. He executed for the Panama-Pacific Exposition at San Francisco four titanic figures representing the elements, Fire, Water, Earth, and Air, which occupied the center of the Court of the Sun and Stars, the great Court of Honor. Mr. Aitken is a member of the Players' Club, the Lambs, the MacDowell Club and the California Society of New York city, and the Bohemian Club of San Francisco. He is an associate of the National Academy of Design and member of the Union Internationale des Beaux Arts et Des Lettres, the French Institute in America, the Municipal Art Society of New York and the Fine Arts Federation. He was first vice-president of the Architectural League of New York city in 1912–13, and is a member of the Council of the National Sculpture Society. He was married in New York city in 1908 to Lolé Louise Ligny of Paris, by whom he had one child, Lolé Francine Aitken.

SEYMOUR, Frederick Henri, author, editor and inventor, was born at Waterbury, Conn., Aug. 1, 1850, son of Frederick Julius and Florentine Marie (Migeon) Seymour. His first paternal American ancestor was Richard Seymour, a native of Berry-Pomeroy, Devonshire, England, who came to America in 1639 and settled at Hartford, Conn. Richard Seymour was a great-grandson of the Duke of Somerset, Lord Protector of England and uncle of Edward VI. His name appears on the Settlers' monument at Hartford, and his Bible, bearing on its cover the family coat of arms, is in the museum of the Connecticut Historical Society, Hartford. From him the line of descent is traced through his son Capt. Richard, who married Hannah Woodruff; their son Ebenezer, who married Abigail Hollister; their son Richard, who married Mary Hickox; their son Samuel, who married Mehitable Dayton, and their son Samuel, who married Lura Taylor and was the grandfather of Frederick H. Seymour. When the younger Migeon emigrated to America in 1828 he bore letters of recommendation from Gen. Lafayette to Mayor Howe, of New York, and others. Henri Migeon devised a successful process for refinishing woolen cloth, which netted him a large fortune. He purchased the estate of Gov. Wolcott at Litchfield, Conn., where he brought up his family of one son and six daughters. His sons-in-law, all poor boys, subsequently became men of prominence and large estate. Frederick Julius Seymour (1825-89) in early manhood was placed in charge of one of the rolling mills of the Waterbury Brass Co. The production of sheet brass was then in its infancy, and he studied the subject so thoroughly that he became a widely-recognized authority on the working of brass, copper and zinc and their alloys. He was the inventor of a number of machines for working these metals, and the originator of many processes and improvements in the alloys. He took part in the organization and development of the Waterbury Brass Co., of Waterbury, Conn.; the Coe Brass Co., the Turner & Seymour Manufacturing Co. and the Union Hardware Co., of Torrington, Conn., and other metal industries. The son received his early education at the Bassett School, Waterbury, and the celebrated Gunnery School, Washington, Conn. He afterwards took private instruction in various branches, and a finishing course in art and medicine in France. In 1871 he went to Detroit, Mich., and joined the editorial staff of the "Tribune." He also became associated with the Detroit "Journal," edited "Dollars and Sense," the official organ of the Detroit Business University; was editor of the culture department of the "Sunday News-Tribune," and was a constant contributor to magazines. Among the short stories which he contributed to the magazines was a series of "Foggarty Papers," written in Irish dialect and full of Irish humor. He wrote "Fire Protection and Prevention," which was subsequently published in the "British Fire In-surance Encyclopædia." He was also author of a quaint oriental work entitled "Yutzo," "Ye Wisdom of Confucius," "Son" (negro dialect and philosophy), "Dennis Foggarty" (Irish philosophy), and he took a French romance of the time of Charlemagne and converted it into an English novel entitled "Maugis, Ye Sorcerer." He was for ten years secretary of the Detroit fire commission, relinquishing the position to organize the Detroit Copper and Brass Rolling Mills. He invented the well-known Acme monkey-wrench, which was patented Feb. 27, 1883, and took the place of the old wooden-handled wrench invented by Charles Monekey (from whose name was corrupted "monkey-wrench"). The Acme wrench was composed of only four pieces, which simplified its manufacture and reduced its cost. It is still sold by the Whitman & Barnes Manufacturing Co., of Akron, O. In 1886 he invented a pipe-wrench attachment for his monkey-wrench, and on July 2, 1895, received a patent for a cash register, one of the first moderate-priced of the modern cash registers, which was sold for many years by the Seymour Cash Register Co., of Detroit. Mr. Seymour possessed an unusually charming personality. His countenance was prepossessing, his manner winning and his temperament lively and entertaining. He had a happy, jovial disposition and his reservoir of humorous anecdotes and witticisms seemed inexhaustible. Broad-minded and generous, he was an admirable combination of the inventive genius, the scholarly student, the desirable citizen and the worthy friend. He was a member of the Numismatic and Antiquarian Society, Philadelphia; American Numismatic Association, Theosophical Society, with headquarters at Madras, India; Detroit Association of Science, Detroit Microscopic Society and the October Club, Detroit. He was married, first, in 1878, to Sarah, daughter of Col. Balantyne C. Hanna, of Detroit, and second, in 1904, to Grace, daughter of Whitson G. Baldwin, of Colcester, Ont., Canada, who survives him, with one son, Frederick Migeon Seymour. He died in Detroit, Mich., July 28, 1913.

MONTGOMERY, Thomas Harrison, Jr., scientist, was born in New York city, Mar. 5, 1873, son of Thomas Harrison and Anna (Morton) Montgomery, and a descendant of William Montgomery, who came to this country from Scotland in 1692 and settled at Eglinton, near Allentown, N. J. His father was for many years president of the American Fire Insurance Co. of Philadelphia. The family is descended from the Montgomerys of Eglinton, an ancient and noble Norman family famous in Scottish annals. He was descended from a line of distinguished physicians and scientists. His grandfather, Dr. Samuel George Morton (q.v.), was one of the founders of the modern science of anthropology and craniology, and was president of the Academy of Natural Sciences of Philadelphia, 1849-51. Prof. Montgomery received his early education in Westchester, Pa., where at twelve years of age he began to make a systematic study of the birds in that vicinity. Later he attended the Episcopal Academy in Philadelphia, the University of Pennsylvania, and the University of Berlin, receiving the degree of Ph.D. at the latter in 1894. Soon after his return to America the University of Pennsylvania assigned him a room in the Wistar Institute for research work, and during the next four years he fully justified this recognition of his abilities by issuing a series of brilliant monographs on some of the most difficult problems of zoology

FREDERICK H. SEYMOUR
AUTHOR AND INVENTOR

THOMAS H. MONTGOMERY
SCIENTIST

ARTHUR V. MEIGS
PHYSICIAN

WILLIAM W. GORDON
SOLDIER AND MERCHANT

and embryology. He later studied in the laboratory of Alexander Agassiz at Newport, the U. S. Fish Commission at Woods Hole, Mass.; the marine laboratory of the University of Pennsylvania at Sea Isle City, N. J., and the Marine Biological Laboratory at Woods Hole. He was lecturer and assistant professor in zoology at the University of Pennsylvania, 1897-1903; professor of biology and director of the museum in the Wagner Free Institute of Science, 1898-1903, and professor of zoology in the University of Texas, 1903-08, after which he returned to the University of Pennsylvania as professor of zoology. Prof. Montgomery's zoological researches have given him a high place among American scientists. His studies of cellular structure and sex determination are of the very highest importance. "It would be impossible," said a resolution of the American Society of Zoologists, "to write a text-book upon the rôle of the chromosomes in the determination of sex without referring to his crucial labors in this field." He was the author of "Analysis of Racial Descent in Animals" (1906), and of over eighty monographs on the habits of spiders, on the nucleolus, and on spermatogenesis. In the latter field a discovery of really epoch-making importance was his observation of the conjugation of separate chromosomes in preparation for the maturation divisions, and his clearly reasoned conclusion that one chromosome of each pair is of paternal and the other of maternal origin. Another discovery of distinct importance was that in certain hemiptera an odd number of chromosomes may be present in the divisions of the spermatocytes, but he just missed the discovery that this phenomenon is associated with the determination of sex, though, after this discovery was made by McClung, Stevens and Wilson, his later work did much to confirm it. His discrimination of the different kinds of chromosomes and his terminology for these has been widely accepted, and now forms part of the science of cytology. A minute adopted by the faculties of the University of Pennsylvania says of him: "He was essentially a scholar and teacher, and for the greater part of his short life his energies and interests were largely absorbed in his professional work; but he was much more; he was a man of the most sterling integrity, carrying into all the relations of life the sincerity, candor and faithfulness to truth which made him great in the realm of science. By his strength of character and pleasing personality he exerted a deep influence upon all who knew him, and by the extent and value of his scientific work he has made a distinct and lasting contribution to the science of zoology. He was a member of the American Society of Zoologists (president 1910), American Association for the Advancement of Science, American Society of Naturalists, American Philsophical Society, Academy of Natural Science of Philadelphia, and the Texas Academy of Science. He was married in 1901 to Priscilla Braislin, daughter of John Braislin, of Crosswicks, N. J., and had three sons: Thomas, Hugh and Raymond Braislin Montgomery. He died in Philadelphia, Pa., Mar. 19, 1912.

MEIGS, Arthur Vincent, physician, was born in Philadelphia, Pa., Nov. 1, 1850, son of John Forsyth and Ann Wilcocks (Ingersoll) Meigs, and grandson of Charles D. Meigs. Both his father and grandfather were practicing physicians in Philadelphia. He was of the eighth generation in direct descent from Vincent Meigs, who came to America from England prior to 1640 and settled in Massachusetts. Dr. Meigs received his early education at the Classical Institute of John W. Faires, Philadelphia, and was graduated in the medical department of the University of Pennsylvania in 1871. He began practicing in Philadelphia, and was soon recognized as one of the leading physicians of that city. He was physician to the Children's Hospital and to the Pennsylvania Hospital, president of the Philadelphia College of Physicians and Surgeons (1904-07), honorary member of the Association of American Physicians and member of the American Philosophical Society. Dr. Meigs was the author of the monographs "Milk Analysis and Infant Feeding" (1885); "The Origin of Disease" (1899) and "A Study of Human Blood Vessels in Health and Disease" (1907). He also published in various medical journals about sixty scientific articles on medical subjects, including: "Milk Analysis," Philadelphia "Medical Times" (July 1, 1882); "Proof That Human Milk Contains Only About One Per Cent. of Casein, With Remarks Upon Infant Feeding," proceedings of the Philadelphia County Medical Society (December, 1883); "A Study of the Arteries and Veins in Bright's Disease," transactions of the College of Physicians of Philadelphia (June 6, 1886); "Chronic Endarteritis and Its Clinical and Pathological Effects (Chronic Bright's Disease)," transactions of the College of Physicians of Philadelphia, third series, Vol. XI (1889); "A Study of the Paths of Secondary Degeneration in a Case of Injury of the Cervical Spine," "American Journal of Medical Sciences" (1890); "The Microscopical Anatomy of the Human Heart, Showing the Existence of Capillaries Within the Muscular Fibers," "American Journal of the Medical Sciences" (June, 1891), and "The Quantitative Analysis of Human and of Cow's Milk," by Arthur V. Meigs and Howard L. Marsh, the "Medical Record" (Dec. 30, 1911). Notwithstanding an extensive medical practice, Dr. Meigs found time for much scientific research, of which the most valuable, perhaps, was that on milk analysis and infant feeding. He did much to establish the fact, now generally recognized, that human milk is decidedly poorer in protein and richer in sugar than cow's milk. Dr. Meigs was a man of unusually gentle and sympathetic nature, but these qualities were to some extent held in abeyance by his strong desire never to express more than he really felt. His scientific views were formed under a steady determination to think for himself and not to be influenced by the dicta of "authority," and he was entirely fearless in expressing his opinions, however overwhelming might be the majority against him. He was married, Oct. 16, 1878, to Mary Roberts, daughter of Edward Browning, of Philadelphia, and had three children: Edward Browning, John Forsyth and Arthur Ingersoll Meigs. Dr. Meigs died in Philadelphia, Pa., Jan. 1, 1912.

GORDON, William Washington, soldier, merchant and banker, was born in Savannah, Ga., Oct. 14, 1834, son of William Washington and Sarah Anderson (Stites) Gordon, grandson of Ambrose and Elizabeth (Mead) Gordon, and great-grandson of Jonathan Rhea Gordon, of Monmouth county, New Jersey. His father was the first Georgian to graduate at the U. S. Military Academy, West Point, N. Y.; he was a distinguished lawyer of the South, was mayor of Savannah, and built the first railroad in Georgia, the Georgia Central, of which he was the first president. The preliminary education of William Washington Gordon was received at Russell's Preparatory School, New Haven, Conn., after which he entered Yale College, and was graduated in 1854. In that year he accepted a clerical position in the office of Tison & Mackay, cotton dealers of Savannah, Ga., and in 1856 became a partner, the name of the firm becoming Tison & Gordon. On the death of the senior partner, W. H. Tison, in 1878, it was changed to W. W. Gordon & Co. The firm made a specialty of handling Sea Island and Upland cotton, and Gen. Gordon was identified with the business for more than fifty-eight years. At the outbreak of the civil war he was commissioned second lieutenant in the Georgia hussars, which was subsequently attached to Gen. J. E. B. Stuart's cavalry brigade. Besides other exploits, he participated in the famous ride around Gen. McClellan's army. Later he served as captain and inspector in Mercer's brigade of infantry; also as captain and adjutant in Anderson's brigade of Wheeler's division of cavalry. He was wounded at Lovejoy Station, Georgia, and was placed upon the roll of honor for gallantry at Frederick City, Maryland. After the civil war he served in the Georgia cavalry, attaining the rank of colonel, and four times was in command of troops for riot duty. In the Spanish-American war he served as brigadier-general in command of the second brigade, first division, seventh army corps, U. S. V. He was appointed by Pres. McKinley a member of the Porto Rican evacuation commission, serving with Gen. Brooke and Adm. Schley from August to October, 1898. Gen. Gordon became a member of the Savannah Benevolent Association in 1866. He remained in Savannah during the yellow fever epidemic of 1876, and gave his services day and night during this trying period to the care of the sick. In 1890 he was elected president of the association. He was president of the Savannah Cotton Exchange, 1876-79, and during 1894-98 was vice-president of the Merchants' National Bank of Savannah. In 1884-90 he was a member of the Georgia house of representatives. Gen. Gordon was a man of decided and attractive personality, large and benevolent purpose, and really useful accomplishment, who won and retained, during his long and busy career, a high and honored place in the nation. The loftiest principles, not merely of integrity, but of honor, governed him in all of his transactions. He was a delightful raconteur, who in a congenial party could bring out the merits of an appropriate story with a copiousness and a vivacity which fascinated, and he possessed a keen sense of humor—humor of good-natured variety that made no wounds because of his kindly, considerate and sympathetic nature. His personal attainment was very great, for he added to a singular symmetry and elevation of character an unusual intellectual culture. His literary taste was unfailing, and his reading thorough and extensive. He was essentially a gentleman of the old Southern school who believed in humility, courtesy and goodness, and he inspired much affection from all with whom he came in contact. He was married in Chicago, Dec. 21, 1857, to Eleanor Lytle, only daughter of Col. John H. Kinzie, by whom he had five children: Eleanor, wife of Wayne Parker of West Orange, N. J.; Juliette, wife of William Mackay Low of London, England; William Washington, a lawyer of Savannah; Mabel, wife of Hon. Rowland Leigh of London, England, and George Arthur Gordon, a cotton merchant of Savannah and member of the firm of Gordon & Co. Gen. Gordon died at White Sulphur Springs, W. Va., Sept. 11, 1912.

HAMMER, William Joseph, consulting electrical engineer, was born at Cressona, Schuylkill co., Pa., Feb. 26, 1858, son of William Alexander and Martha A. (Beck) Hammer; grandson of Joseph and Phoebe (Huntzinger) Hammer; great-grandson of John and Elizabeth (Helwig) Hammer, and great-great-grandson of George Frederick Hammer, who came from the Rhine provinces of Germany in 1763 and settled in Hamburg, Pa. His early education was received in private and public schools at Newark, N. J., and was supplemented by lectures abroad. He became an assistant to Edward Weston of the Weston Malleable Nickel Co., Newark, N. J., in 1878, and in the following year entered the employ of Thomas A. Edison in his laboratory at Menlo Park, N. J. In common with Mr. Edison's other associates he assisted in the experiments on the telephone, phonograph, electric railway, ore separating and other inventions being developed at the laboratory, devoting his attention, however, particularly to the incandescent electric lamp. He had charge of the experimental tests and records of the Edison lamps and subsequently became electrician of the first incandescent electric lamp factory at Menlo Park, N. J. In 1881 he became chief engineer of the English Edison Co. and assisted in the installation of the Holborn viaduct central electric light station in London. This plant contained three "Jumbo" steam dynamos, and operated 3,000 incandescent lamps, and on Jan. 12, 1882, Mr. Hammer personally closed the switch which started the operation of the first central station ever constructed for incandescent electric lighting, the New York Edison station in Pearl street not being started until Sept. 4 of that year. While in London he also installed a large isolated lighting plant at the Crystal Palace Electrical Exposition. At this time he designed and built the first electric sign ever made; it was erected over the organ in the Crystal Palace concert hall, and spelt the name "Edison" in electric lights. The efficiency of his work in England brought him offers of the posts of chief engineer from both the French and German Edison companies, and he accepted that of the latter company, the Deutsche Edison Gesellschaft, now known as the Allegemeine Elektricitaets Gesellschaft. He had entire charge of the organization of the working force, and laid out and supervised all the installations of the company until the fall of 1884, when he returned to America. While in Berlin, he invented the automatic motor-driven flashing electric sign. He constructed a sign which flashed the name "Edison" letter by letter and as a whole, being placed on the Edison pavilion at the Health Exhibition in Berlin in 1883, and upon its principle all flashing signs of to-day are founded. Returning to the United States, he was put in charge of the Edison exhibits, some eight in number, at the International Electrical Exposition held under the auspices of the Franklin Institute in Philadelphia in 1884. Mr. Hammer became confidential assistant to Edward H. Johnson, president of the parent Edison Co. in 1884, and later became an incorporator, trustee and the first secretary of the Sprague Electric Railway and Motor Co. Shortly thereafter he was appointed chief inspector of central stations of the parent Edison Co., making electrical, mechanical and financial reports upon the various stations throughout the United States for over two years (1884-86), and was next sent to Boston as general manager and chief engineer of the Boston Edison Electric Illuminating Co. In one year's time he changed

WILLIAM H. PECK

this plant from a losing investment to one paying twelve per cent. on its capitalization. Acting as a contractor for the company, he installed in Boston the company's elaborate underground system of conductors, and by the installation of ninety-two Sprague electric motors made this the first plant for the electric transmission of power worthy of the name established anywhere in the world. Later he took up special expert work for the parent Edison Electric Light Co. in New York, and, in 1888, he was placed in charge of the installation of the 8,000-light plant of the Ponce de Leon Hotel at St. Augustine, Fla., which at that time was the largest isolated incandescent lighting plant ever constructed. In 1888 he was appointed consulting electrical engineer to the Cincinnati Centennial Exposition, and devised and constructed the elaborate electrical effects as an attraction to the exposition. He was next appointed Mr. Edison's sole representative at the Paris Exposition of 1889, at which time he had upward of $100,000 placed at his disposal and a corps of forty-five assistants. Returning to the United States in 1890, he opened an office in New York city as a consulting electrical engineer, which office he still maintains. Much of Mr. Hammer's professional work has been in connection with tests, investigations and reports upon electrical properties and inventions, and acting as an expert in electric lighting, telephone, storage battery, aeronautical and other patent cases, accident cases, etc. He has done considerable original work in the laboratory in connection with selenium, radium, X-rays, wireless, phosphorescence, fluorescence, etc., and has had a dozen or more patents issued to him here and abroad upon his inventions. He is a life member and a fellow of the American Institute of Electrical Engineers and a member of the New York Electrical Society, fellow of the American Association for the Advancement of Science; ten years president of the National Conference on Standard Electrical Rules, which organization prepared and promulgated the "National Electric Code" now in use throughout the United States; was for two years president of the Franklin Experimental Club; member of the Franklin Institute, the Agassiz Natural History Society (one of the chapters of which was named in his honor), and the Aeronautical Society. He was awarded both the John Scott legacy medal and premium in 1902 and the Elliot Cresson gold medal in 1906 by the Franklin Institute, the former for his telephone relay and long-distance sound experiments, and the latter for his historical collection of incandescent electric lamps. This very complete collection, upon which Mr. Hammer has worked upward of thirty-four years, is practically a "History of an Art," and this is the only art in which such a record has been made showing for the first time the complete development of the incandescent electric lamp from its initial stages to date. Its historical importance and value were attested by the award of the "Grand Prize" at the St. Louis Exposition of 1904 and a special silver medal at the International Electrical Exposition, at the Crystal Palace, London, England, in 1882. Mr. Hammer was chairman of the jury upon telegraphy, telephony and wireless at the St. Louis Exposition of 1904, and also a member of the "Departmental" jury, and was on the committee appointed to organize the International Electrical Congress at St. Louis, 1904. He is the author of "Radium and Other Radio-active Substances" (1903), and articles on radium and radio-activity in the Encyclopædia Americana.

Mr. Hammer was married Jan. 3, 1894, to Alice Maude, daughter of Thomas H. White, of Cleveland, O., and has one child, Mabel White Hammer.

MILLIGAN, John, jurist and legislator, was born at Bohemia Manor, Cecil co., Md., Dec. 10, 1795, son of Robert and Sarah C. (Jones) Milligan, and great-great-grandson of Col. Cantwell, who had a grant of 5,000 acres in Delaware from his Britannic majesty. He was also descended from the great Quaker martyr, Mary Dyer. After receiving an academic education he entered Princeton College, but only remained three years. He took up the study of law under James A. Bayard, Sr., and was admitted to practice in New Castle county, Delaware, in 1818. Here he pursued his profession for several years and acquired an extensive and successful business, but subsequently retired to a country seat near Wilmington. In 1831 he was sent to the United States congress as a Federalist, and served for six years. In 1839 he was appointed by Gov. Comegys to be associate judge of the supreme court of New Castle county, Del., and he served on the bench until 1857, when he resigned. Meanwhile he had been offered a place in President Fillmore's cabinet, but on account of failing health he was obliged to decline. His opinions delivered from the bench were marked by great research, logical reasoning, clear statement of legal principles and a careful examination of the facts of each case. A ripe scholar, a strong, ready and graceful speaker, and an expert parliamentarian, he possessed a magnetic personality that irresistibly attracted and firmly held the attention of his listeners. Judge Milligan was married in February, 1820, to Martha M., daughter of Judge Moses Levy, of Philadelphia, and had five children: Robert, Mary, George, Katherine and Martha E. Milligan. He died at his residence in Philadelphia, Apr. 20, 1875. Portrait opp. p. 220.

PECK, William Henry, author and educator, was born in Augusta, Ga., Sept. 30, 1830, son of Samuel Hopkins and Sarah (Holems) Peck. His earliest paternal American ancestor was Deacon Paul Peck, a native of Essex, England, who came to America in 1635 and settled in Hartford, Conn. His wife was Mary Hart, and the line is traced through their son Deacon Paul and his wife, Abigail Collier; their son Deacon Samuel and his wife, Thankful Winchel; their son Deacon Samuel and his wife, Ruth Hopkins, and their son Samuel H. and his wife, Dolly Upson, who were the grandparents of William Henry Peck. He was educated at Prof. French's boarding-school for boys, New Haven; at the Military Institute of Kentucky, at Georgetown, and at Harvard College, where he was graduated in 1853. He was principal of a public school in New Orleans in 1854, and two years later accepted the professorship of history in the University of Louisiana. Deciding to make literature his life work, he went to New York city in 1859, and was engaged by Robert Bonner, of the New York "Ledger," to write exclusively for that newspaper. But the civil war changed his plans, and in 1861 he returned to Georgia and established in Atlanta a literary quarto, entitled "The Georgia Weekly," which, however, did not long survive. In 1862 he became president of the Masonic Female College, Greenville, Ga., and while occupying this position he revived the "Weekly," which was noted throughout the South for its brilliant and strong editorials and graphic accounts of all war events. In 1864–65 he was professor of languages in the Le Vert Female College, Tarlberton, Ga. Prof. Peck was a prolific writer, being the author of some hundred or more novels, besides a large list of shorter tales and romances contributed to periodicals. His earlier writings were mostly war romances, and, while they brought him fame in the South, were not remunerative. Accordingly, he returned to New York in 1868, and Robert Bonner renewed a previous contract to pay him $5,000 for each story he should write. His writings are principally historical novels, and are the result of much laborious study and historical research. The best known of his books are: "The Renegade" (1859), "The Conspirators of New Orleans" (1865), "The Phantom" (1866), "The Confederate Flag on the Ocean" (1866), "Maids and Matrons of Virginia" (1867), "The McDonald, or the Ashes of the Southern Homes" (1868), "The Diamond Merchant" (1869), "The Miller of Marseilles" (1870), "The Executioner of Venice" (1871), "The Stonecutter of Lisborn" (1871), "Luke Hammond the Miser" (1871), "Locksmith of Lyons" (1872), "Iron Robert, or the Armorer of Rouen" (1872), "A Romance of Joan of Arc" (1873), "Icholine Lochran, a Romance of Cornwallis' Capture" (1877), "The Towel of Gold, or The Maiden of Seville," "A Romance of Pedro the Cruel" (1875), "Irene, or The King's Last Dream," a romance of the dying hours of Charles VII. of France (1876); "Red Butler, or The Warrior of Lake Champlain" (1870), and "Wild Redburn, an Indian Tale" (1877). His works were not only thrilling in plot, but noted for their quick incidents and short duration of time in novels of great length. Each was unlike the other, except in vigor, clearness, and a certain graphic power peculiar to his pen. Mr. Peck was a Knight Templar, and a member of the American Association for the Advancement of Science. He was a lover of nature, and during his last years lived on an orange grove in Florida. He was married in New Orleans, La., Oct. 20, 1854, to Monica Blake, daughter of Bernard Kenny, of Menlough Castle, Galway, Ireland; she died in 1891. His children were: Samuel Henry Peck, of Grand Rapids, Mich.; Bertha, wife of Harold E. Trower, of Capri, Italy; Myrtis, wife of Charles G. Matthews, of Charleston, S. C.; Byrnina, wife of Edward P. Porcher, Indian River, Fla., and Daisy, wife of Delos A. Blodgett, Grand Rapids, Mich. He died at Jacksonville, Fla., Feb. 4, 1892.

LAMBIE, Frank Dalton, inventor and capitalist, was born at South Tamworth, N. H., July 15, 1865, son of Edward Lawrence and Johanna F. (Mason) Lambie. His father, a native of Virginia, was a lieutenant in the Confederate army. His maternal grandfather, Larkin D. Mason, was judge of probate of Carroll county, N. H., and an active worker in the Republican party, and his great-grandfather, Jeremiah Mason, was a lieutenant-colonel in the revolution. The boyhood of Frank D. Lambie was spent on his grandfather's farm in New Hampshire. At the age of sixteen he began work in a grocery store in Boston. In 1883 he became a traveling salesman for Field, Thayer & Co., one of the largest wholesale shoe houses in New England. In 1894 he engaged in the shoe business with George Baxter under the firm name of Lambie & Baxter, but four years later purchased the interest of his partner, and continued alone until his retirement in 1899. After a year abroad he settled in Montclair, N. J., and devoted his attention to real estate, a business he has since continued with marked success. Through his acquaintance with Thomas A. Edison he became interested in concrete houses in 1908. From the time Mr. Edison made his remarkable announcement regarding the possibilities of con-

crete houses and the alleged revolution that would be ushered in by the proposed system of moulds, Mr. Lambie devoted much time and money to perfecting methods for their construction. Taking up the problem where Mr. Edison left off, he invented a novel system of steel forms or moulds, the basic patent for which was granted him Sept. 17, 1912. He has also obtained twenty-seven other patents in Canada and abroad. The Lambie steel moulds are made of sheet steel about one-eighth of an inch thick, braced around the edges with angle iron, and with holes properly placed, so that they can be conveniently bound together. All the ornamental work is run in galvanized iron moulds. The stairs are cast in one solid piece, and the window sills are made a part of the walls. The roof may be flat or peaked, as individual taste prefers. The first house built by this method, in May, 1911, was finished in thirty days by five laborers and a foreman. The time consumed in building the second house was reduced one-half by the use of more men and a larger mixer and conveyer, and it is now possible with the Lambie invention to build a concrete bungalow of one story in one working day. Mr. Lambie has reduced the human labor required to a minimum, almost 90 per cent. of the work being done by the special machines; consequently the cost of one of his houses is correspondingly reduced. By this invention the all-concrete house is practical in every detail, being moderate in cost, fireproof, dampproof, dust- and vermin-proof, and satisfactory to the housewife. He organized the American Building Corporation in New York in 1912 to introduce this method of house-building, and in 1913 established the Lambie Patents, Ltd., of Toronto, Canada. He has already built several hundred concrete houses for large manufacturing industries whose employees are numerous. Mr. Lambie is vice-president of the Anglo-American Distributing Co., engaged in shipping typewriters to foreign countries. He was married at Des Moines, Ia., Apr. 27, 1898, to Addie R., daughter of Peter Rattray, and has five children: Catherine, Phyllis, Dalton, Harriet and June Lambie.

TOWNSEND, Charles Elroy, United States senator, was born in Concord, Jackson co., Mich., Aug. 15, 1856, son of James W. and Eunice S. (Parmeter) Townsend, of Scotch-English ancestry. Both his grandfathers, Isaac Townsend and Jesse Parmeter, removed from New York state to Michigan in 1834, both families settling in the township of Concord. He was educated at the public schools of Jackson, and was a student in the literary department of the University of Michigan in 1877-78. Taking up the study of law, he was admitted to the bar in 1895 and began the practice of his profession in Jackson. He was register of deeds of Jackson county during 1886-96. Early in his career he began to take an interest in local politics. He was a delegate to the Republican national convention of 1888 and was a member of the state central committee during 1896-1902. Having become a factor in the political affairs of his state, he was nominated for and elected to the 58th congress, and was re-elected to the succeeding congresses up to and including the 61st. In congress he was the instigator of the fights for Federal regulation of railroads, for a revision of the railroad rates and for a revision of the house rules, and was known as the "original insurgent." He had the gratification of seeing many of his views eventually enacted as administration measures. He was always active in promoting his views, and, possessing a pleasing de-

FRANK D. LAMBIE
INVENTOR

CHARLES E. TOWNSEND
U. S. SENATOR

WILLIAM H. PATTERSON
BOAT BUILDER

JOHN MILLIGAN
CONGRESSMAN

livery and considerable power in debate, with the knack of presenting his arguments in an attractive, convincing way, he quickly secured the support necessary for the success of his measures. At the senatorial primaries held throughout the state, Sept. 7, 1910, he received a majority of 41,000 votes over U. S. Sen. Julius Cæsar Burrows, and Jan. 18, 1911, he was chosen to succeed the latter for the term 1911-17. In his campaign he helped to elect a progressive Republican governor for the state. Sen. Townsend, though strongly Republican, is also quite independent in his attitude in regard to party policies, and is thus considered one of the strong members of the party in the state. He was married, Sept. 1, 1880, to Rena, daughter of Joseph Paddock, of Concord, Mich.

PATTERSON, William Henry, yacht builder, was born at St. John, New Brunswick, Canada, Dec. 29, 1854, son of Robert J. and Anne (White) Patterson. Although born in Canada, it was only during a temporary visit of his parents, and the greater part of his life has been spent in New York city and Brooklyn. He was educated at Goodwin's Academy, St. Johns, N. B. When about twenty years of age he began to learn the ship-joiner and cabinet-maker's trade, and gained most of his experience by working with his father, who was a shipbuilder. He was employed twelve years with John J. Mumm, yacht builder, and five years with H. C. Wintringham, designer, and after thoroughly mastering the business, in 1895, he engaged in business for himself. In his shops in Brooklyn, N. Y., he employs as many as 130 men at a time. He has gained a splendid reputation for the high quality of his work, for his dependableness in the fulfilling of contracts and for giving the best material and workmanship possible. Among the yachts designed or equipped by Mr. Patterson are: The Aphrodite, belonging to Col. Paine; Electra, Juanita, Wadina, Eleanor, Aloha and the Virginia, while his lists of patrons include such distinguished names as Henry Clay Pierce, owner of the yacht Yacona; Arthur Curtiss James, of the Aloha; Daniel G. Reid, of the yacht Rheclai, and William B. Leeds, of the Noma. Mr. Patterson was elected president of the Logan Republican Club of Kings County for 1906-07. He was a delegate to the local conventions of his party, including one which nominated Mayor Low in 1901, and he was a delegate to the convention that nominated Congressman Bennet in 1909. He has been a delegate to the city conventions for seven years consecutively. He is a charter member of the 12th assembly district of the Republican Club of the 22d ward, and is patriotic and loyal to a high degree, considering his political activity as a duty each and every American owes to his country without thought of reward, financial or otherwise. All his life he has been active in church work and is a member of All Saints' Episcopal Church, of which he is a vestryman. As a Mason he is member of St. John's Lodge No. 1, F. and A. M., the oldest Masonic lodge in New York state, taking his obligation on the same Bible that George Washington used when he pledged his vows to the fraternity. For social recreation he is an attendant of the Logan Club, for some years has been a member of its executive committee and for three years served the latter as chairman. Mr. Patterson was married Mar. 23, 1886, to Nancy Anderson, daughter of Robert Crozier, a prominent dry goods merchant of St. John, N. B., and has six children: Hamilton Byron, Beatrice Shirley, Helen Louisa, Kenneth LeRoy, Audrey Girard and Alva Lillian Patterson.

MEEKER, Charles Augustus, dental surgeon, was born in Troy, N. Y., July 13, 1846, son of John Dodd and Eliza Ann (Meeker) Meeker. His earliest paternal American ancestor was William Meeker, a native of England, who emigrated in 1630 and settled in Massachusetts, later removing to New Haven, Conn. From him the line of descent is traced to Josiah Meeker and his wife, Sarah Preston; to their son Elias O. and his wife, Nancy Dodd, who were the grandparents of the subject, and were also pioneers in the settling of Troy. His maternal grandfather was Eliakim Meeker, a distant cousin of the direct line. His father (1818-72) was a manufacturer of leather goods. The only child, Charles Augustus Meeker, was thrown upon his own resources at a very early age. He was educated in the public schools of Troy and the Newark (N. J.) Academy, after which he entered the dental office of Dr. Atkinson as an office boy. In 1871 he established a dental office in Broad street. Subsequently he attended the Baltimore College of Dental Surgery, and was graduated in 1884. He opened his office in his home in Fulton street, Newark, where he continued to practice until his death. He had splendid executive ability and was regarded as one of the greatest organizers in his adopted state. He organized the State Dental Society of New Jersey in 1870, was its secretary for thirty-six years and president for one year. He organized the Central Dental Association of Northern New Jersey, of which he was treasurer for thirty years, and was the principal organizer of the National Association of Dental Examiners, serving as secretary and treasurer for fourteen years. He was organizer and founder of the American Academy of Dental Surgery, and obtained a college charter for that institution in 1884. He was active in promulgating and having passed the state dental law of New Jersey. He was the founder of the Newark Free Dental Clinic, and he secured the enactment of the necessary legislation to establish free dental clinics throughout the state. He organized the Home Dramatic Club, Newark, and the Interstate Dental Fraternity of the United States and Canada, which now thrives in the West and South. He was the organizer, founder, editor and owner of "The Dental Scrap Book," a social dental journal established in 1908. For eight years he was state prosecutor of illegal dental practitioners. He was a member of the American Dental Association, the Odontological Society of Manhattan, the American Academy of Dental Surgery and the New York Institute of Stomatology. In these various positions devotion to duty, personal responsibility, uprightness, sterling integrity and unquestioned loyalty were the characteristics of his manly nature which nerved him on to fill his true niche in the record of human progress. He was unostentatiously generous. His mission in life was to do good. His acts of kindness and charity, if known, would fill a volume. His thirst was not for fame nor gold, but good deeds. He left no riches, but he did leave a heritage that gold could never buy—a stainless reputation and a deathless name. His heart was a guest chamber reserved for all who sought the hospitality of his friendship. His nature was susceptible of great enjoyment. He loved all nature and all art, but he loved his friends best, and his friendships were deep, strong and fervent. He was married in New York city, Apr. 30, 1868, to Mary Elizabeth, daughter of Edward Van Beuren, a manufacturer of New York. He died in Newark, N. J., Sept. 8, 1913.

FERNALD, Bert Manfred, forty-first governor of Maine, was born at West Poland, Me., Apr. 3, 1858, son of James H. and Betsy Small (Libby) Fernald. His first American ancestor emigrated to this country from France and settled at Kittery, Me. He was educated at the town school of Poland and at Hebron Academy, and engaged in business at Poland in 1888 with C. L. and H. A. Keene. F. D. True was taken into the firm in 1892, and the Fernald, Keene & True Co. was formed, of which Mr. Fernald is manager. The firm established a canning factory in 1888 with a capacity of 6,000 cases. It operates six canneries located at Poland, Oxford, Cornish, Bryant Pond, Turner and Lisbon in the state of Maine, and puts up sweet corn exclusively under the Poland and Alice Rose labels. The combined factories produce 100,000 cases or 250,000 cans per day. They employ 1,000 hands, and do a gross annual business of $400,000. Gov. Fernald is also president of the Poland Telegraph Co. and director of the Poland Dairy Co. and the Fidelity Trust Co. He was for several years superintendent of schools at Poland, was a member of the state legislature in 1897 and state senator during 1899–1901. In 1908 he was elected governor of Maine for the term 1909–11, and has discharged the duties of his office in a way to set forth the approbation of every unbiased citizen of the state. In answer to the charges brought against his administration, for electioneering purposes, by his political enemies he said in effect: "I stand ready to answer every charge that may be made against my administration. I challenge any Democrat or any one else to show anything in that administration which has not been honest and aboveboard and which has not been done for the interests of the people of Maine." The Republican party expressed its entire confidence in Gov. Fernald by unanimously indorsing him as its candidate for governor in 1910. One of his associates has said of him: "The need of the hour in Maine is a leader who stands for wise and progressive statesmanship, who believes in the conservation of our great natural resources, who stands for honest and economical administration of public affairs, who commands the confidence and love of the people. All these qualifications Mr. Fernald possesses in an eminent degree. Trained in the school of experience, tried in public life for many years, he has shown himself competent to discharge every duty and to meet every demand of the public service with ability and honor." During his administration of the office a new state house was built at Augusta entirely within the appropriation made by the state, and a conservation commission was established for preserving the forests and waterways, this being the first of the kind in the state. In 1915 Gov. Fernald was a candidate for U. S. senator. He as married at Poland, Me., in 1877, to Annie A., daughter of Orrin S. Keene, of that town, and has two children: James Henley and Millie Hutchinson Fernald.

PRENDERGAST, Edmond Francis, third Roman Catholic archbishop of Philadelphia, was born at Clonmel, County Tipperary, Ireland, May 3, 1843, of a family that gave many of its members to the service of the Church. His brother, Rev. Dr. Peter J. Prendergast, was rector of the Epiphany Church, New York; another, Rev. Francis Prendergast, ministered at Dungarvan, County Waterford, Ireland; two of his sisters became nuns and three uncles were priests. At the invitation of one of the latter, Rev. Francis Carew, of Carbondale, Pa., the future archbishop entered the Philadelphia seminary in 1859, and fol-

lowing his theological course there, he was ordained to the priesthood Nov. 17, 1865. After serving at St. Paul's, Philadelphia, at the mission at Susquehanna Station, at Bristol, and at Allentown, Father Prendergast, in February, 1874, was appointed rector of St. Malachy's, Philadelphia, where he labored for thirty-seven years. He remodeled the church and built a rectory and a school building. In 1879 he was made vicar-general of the diocese, and on Dec. 3, 1896, the Pope appointed him titular bishop of Scillio and auxiliary bishop of Philadelphia. His consecration took place in the cathedral, Archbishop Ryan officiating, on Feb. 24, 1897. He retained the rectorship of St. Malachy's, which he again remodeled in 1900, making it practically a new building. For fifteen years the multiplied activities of the episcopal office, owing to the growing infirmities of Archbishop Ryan, kept him busily occupied. Notable among his accomplishments was, as chairman of the diocesan building committee, the promotion of the construction of the Catholic Protectory for Boys, the Archbishop Ryan Memorial Library, attached to the seminary, the new Catholic Home for Girls, the Catholic Girls' High School and St. Edmond Hall, an addition to the diocesan seminary of St. Charles Borromeo. On Feb. 11, 1911, Archbishop Ryan died and Bishop Prendergast became the administrator of the see. Three months later, May 27, the Pope elevated him to the vacant archbishopric and he was solemnly enthroned in the cathedral on July 26, 1911. Six months after, on January 31, 1912, the Pallium was conferred on him, Cardinal Gibbons, Cardinal Farley, fourteen bishops and a host of prelates and priests attending the ceremony. In the five years following he made a remarkable record of diocesan progress in the establishment of new parishes, schools and institutions. In 1912 the Missionary Sisters of the Sacred Heart were introduced into the diocese, a building for Italian immigrants was opened and also a chapel for Spanish-Americans. In 1913 St. Francis' Country Home for Convalescents was opened, St. Edmond Hall, at the Overbrook Seminary, was dedicated and the Don Bosco Institute was inaugurated by the Salesian Fathers and in 1914 the Catholic Home for Dependent Children was established. The movement for the support of the foreign missions of the Church, under his inspiration and encouragement, was advanced to an annual contribution from the archdiocese of more than $50,000. On Nov. 17, 1915, a three-days' celebration of the sacerdotal golden jubilee of Archbishop Prendergast — which was happily synchronous with the fiftieth anniversary of the dedication of the cathedral—began with an imposing ceremony in the cathedral, at which the Apostolic Delegate, two American cardinals, several archbishops, a score of bishops, hundreds of prelates and priests and a multitude of the laity were present. This ceremony was followed by a banquet and public parade in the evening, in which 50,000 participated. He also received an autograph letter of congratulation from Pope Benedict XV, in which the Pontiff said: "We on our part would not have this day pass without an expression of our congratulations. All the more so because, holding you in great esteem, we consider it of the utmost importance to bestow on you an evidence of our fatherly love. First we wish to thank God for having preserved to this day you who deserve so well of His Church. For we know with what great diligence you have discharged the duties of the good shepherd, with what great devotion you have al-

ARCHBISHOP PRENDERGAST

George McClellan
M.D.

ways revered this Apostolic See, and how solicitous you have been that others should do likewise. Furthermore, amid many works of manifold beneficence, the restoration and the building of churches, the enlargement and complete equipment of the seminary, the founding of a splendid hospital are conspicuous features of your episcopal administration which will be lasting monuments of your generosity and zeal for religion. Equally patent to all is the fact that your lively interest has done much to aid the wonderful growth of the Holy Name Society, that society which, founded for the purpose of suppressing the use of words insulting to the Divine Majesty, has been of inestimable value in defending and cherishing everything connected with religion. Notwithstanding this varied activity, you have found time to promote a cause which should be dear to the heart of every good man, the propagation of the Catholic faith, for if, as we learn, your diocese has shown great generosity in this matter, it is certainly because of your encouragement and favor.'' In 1915 the statistics of the archdiocese of Philadelphia showed these figures: Catholic population, 700,000; priests, 674; churches, chapels and stations, 415; colleges, three; religious orders of women twenty-four; members 3,153; schools 154, pupils 77,934; orphan asylums fourteen, inmates 3,677; hospitals, five; industrial schools, homes, protectories, fourteen. The suffragan sees of Philadelphia are: Altoona, Erie, Harrisburg, Pittsburgh, and Scranton.

JOHNSTONE, Arthur Weir, physician, was born at Paint Lick, near Danville, Ky., July 15, 1853, son of Rev. Alexander Johnstone, a Presbyterian clergyman. He was graduated at Center College, Danville, in 1872, and after a brief service with a corps of United States engineers working on the Mississippi river, he studied medicine at Tulane University and the University of New York, receiving the degree of M.D. at the latter in 1876. For the purpose of specializing in gynecology he took a special course under Dr. Lawson Tait, of Birmingham, England, and upon his return to Danville opened a private hospital. In 1889 he removed to Cincinnati, O. Here, for a short time, he was professional partner of Dr. Thaddeus Reamy and established another private hospital near Mt. Auburn. He was the author of a number of valuable papers on the subject of gynecology. He was married in 1897 to Ethel, daughter of Maj. William H. Chamberlin, of the United States Army, and died in Cincinnati, O., Sept. 14, 1905.

McCLELLAN, George, surgeon and author, was born in Philadelphia, Pa., Oct. 29, 1849, son of Dr. John Hill Brinton and Maria (Eldredge) McClellan, grandson of James and Eunice (Eldredge) McClellan, great-grandson of Samuel and Rachel (Abbe) McClellan and great-great-grandson of William McClellan, who came from Scotland in 1718 and settled near Worcester, Mass. His father was one of the most noted surgeons of his day, and his uncle was Gen. George B. McClellan (q. v.), the famous Union officer in the civil war. Dr. George McClellan began his education in Philadelphia at Dr. Short's school, entered the department of arts at the University of Pennsylvania in 1865 and left there in his senior year in order to matriculate at the Jefferson Medical College, where he was graduated M.D. in 1870. He at once began the practice of his profession, devoting himself especially to surgery. In 1872 he studied at the famous hospitals in Paris, Berlin, Vienna, London and Edinburgh. He was a pupil of Prof. Hyrtl in Vienna and determined to follow the

latter's method of teaching, which he later adopted in the Pennsylvania School of Anatomy and Surgery, established by him in 1881, and where he taught both anatomy and surgery for twelve years. Upon his return he was successively elected surgeon to the Howard Hospital, the Philadelphia General Hospital and the St. Joseph's Hospital. In 1875 he became a fellow of the College of Physicians. In 1890 he was elected professor of anatomy for art at the Pennsylvania Academy of the Fine Arts, where he continued to develop his talent for free-hand drawing in illustration of his lectures on anatomy, and in 1906 he became professor of applied anatomy at the Jefferson Medical College. He held both professorships until the time of his death. His work on ''Regional Anatomy'' (1891), an innovation in scientific illustrating, was illustrated by a remarkable series of photographs from his own dissections, colored from nature by himself. Anatomists up to that time had supplied their works with artists' drawings. Although these were beautifully executed and carefully compared with actual dissection, they never could be quite free from diagrammatic features. Dr. McClellan conceived the idea of employing photography to eliminate as far as possible this diagrammatic element. He therefore made a study of photography with the same care and earnestness which characterized all his undertakings. In the course of his studies of photography he obtained results with other than scientific subjects, which are beautiful examples of artistic effect and photographic knowledge. Among these, his photographs of moving birds and horses portray many important facts regarding the position of animals in motion. The large number of dissections personally executed by him, and requiring years in accomplishment, were then photographed with all the knowledge acquired in his thorough study of this subject. Only one who has dissected can appreciate what a task this was. His accurate knowledge of anatomy and skill in photography caused him to discard hundreds of failures before he obtained the results which make his ''Regional Anatomy'' unique in the field of anatomical writing. This book was translated into French, and passed through five editions in the United States and two in Paris. In Dr. McClellan's lectures on anatomy, as the scheme gradually unfolded, the listener felt himself taking each step with the lecturer. No instructor ever more completely held the interest of his pupils, as was evidenced by the stillness of the listening classes. In the Academy of Fine Arts lectures, art was always the keynote. In his medical lectures, detail and accuracy were the dominant features. In both he made use of the living model on which to point out anatomical landmarks, supplementing this in his medical lectures with demonstration. In 1901 he published ''Anatomy in Relation to Art,'' also original in its method of illustration, as the skeleton was at first depicted in the position required for each figure, then, as covered with flesh, it was represented in the nude, and finally as clothed with the appropriate drapery. He was the author of ''Anatomy of Children'' in Keating's ''Encyclopædia of the Diseases of Children.'' Chief among his scientific papers are ''A Study of the Effect of Shock,'' ''Repair of Wounds,'' ''Treatment of Carbuncle by Sponge Dressing and Pressure'' and ''Uses of the Antiseptic Sponge Dressing in Amputations of the Joints,'' and a number of papers on various subjects. Besides occupying the chairs of anatomy at the Academy of Fine Arts and at Jefferson Medical College, he was lecturer on descriptive and regional anatomy at the Pennsylvania School of Anatomy and Surgery. He was a member of the Association of American Anatomists, the Academy of Natural Sciences, the Academy of Surgery, the Medical Club of Philadelphia, the University Club, the Contemporary Club, and vice-president of the Phelobiblion Club. Dr. McClellan was married, June 25, 1873, to Harriet, daughter of Robert Harford and Caroline (Fleeming) Hare, of Philadelphia. He died in Philadelphia, Pa., Mar. 29, 1913.

HARTLEY, Frank, surgeon, was born in Washington, D. C., June 10, 1856, son of John Fairfield and Mary D. (King) Hartley. His father was a lawyer, and for many years assistant secretary of the U. S. treasury; his grandfather was Samuel Hartley, who, during the war of 1812, held a letter of marque from the U. S. government, and a commission as lieutenant in the navy. Dr. Hartley attended the Emerson Institute in Washington, and was graduated at Princeton College in 1877. He studied medicine at the College of Physicians and Surgeons, New York city, receiving his medical degree in 1880. For two years he was interne at Bellevue Hospital, and then took special courses at Heidelberg, Vienna and Berlin universities. Returning to New York, in 1884, he was appointed assistant demonstrator of anatomy at the College of Physicians and Surgeons, and four years later became demonstrator. Meantime, in 1886, he became visiting surgeon to Bellevue Hospital, and assistant visiting surgeon to Roosevelt Hospital, holding the former position for four years and the latter for thirteen. In 1890 he was appointed attending surgeon to New York Hospital, and in 1893 consulting surgeon to the New York Skin and Cancer Hospital. He was also instructor in operative surgery on the cadaver at the College of Physicians and Surgeons in 1888–1900, and then clinical professor of surgery. In the same year he became consulting surgeon to the French Hospital, New York, Nyack Hospital, Nyack, N. Y., and St. Joseph's Hospital, Paterson, N. J. In his private practice Dr. Hartley made a specialty of surgery and diseases of the brain, in which he attained great distinction. He was associated with Dr. Henry B. Sands in practice, and was the latter's assistant at Roosevelt Hospital. Dr. Hartley wrote many monographs on surgical subjects. Among his papers are "Congenital Deformities of the Neck," "Early Operation in Appendicitis," "Thyroidectomy," "The Operative Treatment of Club-foot," and "Abdominal Echinoccus and Laminectomy." His most memorable contribution to literature was on the subject of the intracranial method of operation for the relief of trigeminal neuralgia. His bi-section of the ganglion of the fifth cranial nerve marked the first successful cure of neuralgia, and the operation is now known as the Hartley-Krause method, Dr. Hartley having been an independent discoverer simultaneously with Dr. Krause, of Altona, Germany. He was a member of the New York Pathological Society, New York Surgical Society, New York Clinical Society, and the New York Medical and Surgical Society, American Medical, American Gastro-Enterological and American Urological societies, as well as the University, New York Athletic and Princeton clubs, and the Southern Society. He was an enthusiastic lover of all forms of athletic sport. He was married, Aug. 1, 1897, to Emma Allyce Parker, daughter of George Burton, of

Norfolk, Eng., who survived him. Princeton conferred upon him the degree of LL.D. in 1909. He died in New York city, June 19, 1913.

O'DONAGHUE, Denis, fifth Roman Catholic bishop of the diocese of Louisville, Ky., was born in Davies county, Ind., Nov. 30, 1848. He was educated at St. Meinrad's College, Indiana, and at the Sulpician Seminary, Montreal, Can., where he made his theological studies preparatory to his ordination Sept. 6, 1874. He was appointed rector of St. Patrick's Church, Indianapolis, Ind., in 1884, vicar-general of the diocese in 1899 and consecrated auxiliary bishop of Indianapolis and titular bishop of Pomario Apr. 25, 1900. When Bishop McCloskey of Louisville, Ky., died, Sept. 17, 1909, Bishop O'Donaghue was transferred to fill the vacancy in that see on Feb. 7, 1910.

SCHOOLHOUSE, Charles, merchant, was born in Hessen Cassel, Germany, Jan. 20, 1832, son of Jacob and Theresa (Lorgé) Schoolhouse. He was left an orphan at an early age and came to the United States in 1847 to seek his fortune. He made the acquaintance in New York of a man who advanced him a small capital, with which he obtained an outfit, and started out to sell goods from house to house in central New York state. His success was such that in 1856 he was able to open a small drygoods store in Greenwich, Washington co., N. Y. He also prospered in this enterprise, and in 1875 settled in New York city, where he engaged in the manufacture of clothing, forming a partnership with Julius Oppenheimer, under the firm name of Schoolhouse, Oppenheimer & Co. In 1878 the business was sold out, and two years later he became a partner in the firm of L. H. Rice & Co., manufacturers of shirts, but retired from that in 1883. He then acquired an interest in the firm of Newwitter, Strassburg & Co., importers and jobbers of silks and ribbons. He become interested in this firm on account of the association of his son Lewis with it, and, although the latter withdrew in the following year, the elder Schoolhouse continued a member of Newwitter, Strassburg & Co. until 1887, when he became a partner in his son's firm, which had been established in 1885 as Schoolhouse & Hydeman. The name was now changed to Charles Schoolhouse & Son, and it grew to be one of the largest and most important firms specializing in ribbons, silk and velvet in the United States. Mr. Schoolhouse retired Nov. 30, 1911. He was married in New York, July 22, 1856, to Fanny, daughter of Joseph Nussbaum, who died in 1888, leaving three children: Sarah, wife of Isaac Hydeman; Lewis, and Tillie, wife of Solomon Cahn, of New York. Mr. Schoolhouse died in New York, May 7, 1913.

SCHOOLHOUSE, Lewis, merchant, was born in New York city, Jan. 19, 1862, son of Charles (above) and Fanny (Nussbaum) Schoolhouse. He was educated in the district schools at Greenwich, Washington co., N. Y., and in a grammar school in New York city, to which his parents had removed in 1875. In 1877 he entered the employ of Newwitter, Strassburg & Co., dealers in silks and ribbons. His father acquired an interest in the business because of the son's connection with it, and became a partner in the firm in 1883. However, Lewis Schoolhouse left the employ of the company the following year, and with his brother-in-law, Isaac Hydeman, organized a similar business under the name of Schoolhouse & Hydeman. Mr. Hydeman died in 1887, and the business was conducted by Mr. Schoolhouse alone until in 1890 his father joined him as a partner, and the name of the firm was changed to Charles Schoolhouse &

Son. Lewis Schoolhouse has from the beginning been the active and managing head of the house, which is one of the most important in the ribbon, silk and velvet trade, which specializes in the novelty business. The company is an importer and converter, contracting with silk mills at home and abroad for their product and converting the same into novelty ideas and current shades. Ever since the establishment of the business in 1885 Mr. Lewis Schoolhouse has controlled its affairs, and, aside from his brother-in-law and father, he has had no partners, although a working interest was given by him to six old employees of the firm. The company employs 125 hands, and in addition has twenty-four traveling salesmen. Mr. Schoolhouse is a member of the Merchants' Association and the Fairview Country Club. He is a member of no social organization, spending most of his spare time at his camp on Upper Twin Lake on Dunderberg Mountain, near Central Valley, N. Y. He is unmarried.

MERSHON, Ralph Davenport, engineer, was born in Zanesville, O., July 14, 1868, son of Ralph Smith and Mary (Jones) Mershon. After a public school education he began his engineering career at the age of seventeen, as a member of an engineering corps engaged in railway location and construction. He was graduated M. E. at the Ohio State University in 1890. He was employed by the Westinghouse Electrial and Manufacturing Company of Pittsburgh during 1891-1900 in both practical and experimental work. For that company he designed the transformers which received an award at the World's Columbian Exposition at Chicago in 1893. In 1893-95 he had charge of the extension of the transmission plant of the Telluride (Colo.) Power Transmission Company, which was a single phase alternating current transmission, employing single phase synchronous motors, and in 1896-97 he conducted an investigation of the phenomena which occur between conductors at high voltages. This investigation was carried out on a transmission line at Telluride, about two and one-half miles long, and was the first in which quantitative measures were obtained of the ionization and other atmospheric losses occurring between conductors at high voltages. He devised original methods and special apparatus for this investigation by means of which quantitative measurements were made up to 72,000 volts. Securing leave of absence from the Westinghouse Company in 1897–98, he served as chief engineer of the Colorado Electric Power Company during the designing and installation of their transmission plant, which generates current by steam at Canon City, Colo., and transmits power at 25,000 volts to Cripple Creek, twenty-five miles away. In 1900 Mr. Mershon resigned from the Westinghouse company to engage in private practice as a consulting electrical and mechanical engineer in New York city. Some of the more important pieces of engineering work accomplished by him since entering practice as a consulting engineer are the reconstruction and enlargement of the water wheel, generating, transforming and transmitting equipment of the Montreal and St. Lawrence Light and Power Company (now a part of the Montreal Light, Heat and Power Company), transmitting 20,000 horse-power at 25,000 volts to Montreal, a distance of seventeen miles; the design and supervision of the transmission plant of the Shawinigan Water and Power Company, transmitting power at 50,000 volts, a distance of eighty-five miles, to the city of Montreal; the design and installation of the sub-station equipments of the Montreal Street

Railway Company, having an aggregate capacity of about 12,000 horse-power, for utilizing the power transmitted to Montreal from various hydraulic plants; the design and supervision of the transmission plant of the Niagara, Lockport and Ontario Power Company for transmitting power at 60,000 volts from Niagara Falls to various points in New York state. The last mentioned is the largest transmission plant which has ever been undertaken in point of capacity, and is one of the most important in point of distance of transmission. Its present capacity is 60,000 horse-power, and it is laid out for an increase to 180,000 horse-power. Mr. Mershon is the inventor of the six-phase rotary converter, covering the transformation of current from three phase to six phase by means of three transformers and feeding the six-phase current into the rotary converter, resulting in a much larger output than in the case of the quarter-phase and three-phase rotaries previously used; the compounded rotary converter, using an artificial reactance in series with the alternating current side of the rotary converter, a system of lightning protection for electrical apparatus, especially applicable to high voltage circuits, and a system of protection against the possibility of fire in the case of installations of oil-insulated transformers. He also invented a compensating voltmeter, enabling the indication at any point of a transmission system of the voltage at any other point without the use of pressure wires. This device takes account of the resistance, reactance, leakage and capacity current of the transmission line and of the power factor of the load, and for it Mr. Mershon received from the Franklin Institute of Philadelphia the John Scott medal and premium. He is the author of a number of technical papers giving the results of the experiments and investigations. Mr. Mershon is a member of the American Institute of Electrical Engineers (president in 1912–13), the American Society of Mechanical Engineers, the American Society of Civil Engineers, the American Institute of Consulting Engineers, the American Electrochemical Society, the Franklin Institute of Philadelphia, the Canadian Society of Civil Engineers, the Institution of Electrical Engineers (British), and the Inventors' Guild (president in 1910), and a fellow of the American Association for the Advancement of Science. He is a member of the University, Engineers' and Railroad clubs of New York, and the St. James Club, of Montreal. Portrait opposite page 226.

KELLEY, Alfred, lawyer, was born at Middlefield, Conn., Nov. 7, 1789, son of Daniel and Jemima (Stow) Kelley, grandson of Daniel and Abigail (Reynolds) Kelley, and great-grandson of Joseph and Lydia (Caulkins) Kelley, early settlers of Norwich, Conn. The family removed to Lowville, N. Y., in 1798, and there Daniel Kelley became first judge of Lewis county, was county treasurer, county clerk, and one of the incorporators of Lowville Academy. The son was graduated at Fairfield Academy in 1807. After studying law in the office of Judge Jonas Platt, of the supreme court of New York, in 1810, he removed to Cleveland, O., was admitted to the Ohio bar, and on the same day (his twenty-first birthday) was appointed prosecuting attorney, an office he held by successive appointments until 1822. He was an advocate of unusual power, and his practice was as large and lucrative as that of any attorney in northern Ohio. In June, 1814, he was elected first "president" of the village of Cleveland, and in the same year was elected a member of the Ohio house of representatives. Although the youngest representative in the legislature, he was one of the most prominent and influential members of that body. He was the author of the first legislative bill, either in this country or Europe, to abolish imprisonment for debt (1818), but it failed then to become a law. During the legislature of 1822–23 he endeavored to have all fictions in the action of ejectment abolished, one of the first steps towards simplifying legal proceedings and preparing the way for our present practice. Among the important matters with which he dealt was the claim of the older states of the Union to public lands for school purposes. After submitting a committee report, of which he was the author, the claim was no longer urged. He continued at intervals a member of the legislature until 1823, when he was appointed state canal commissioner and threw himself with enthusiasm into the proposition to construct a waterway which would do for Ohio what the Erie canal had done for the state of New York. After the project was finally authorized by the legislature he was recognized as its responsible head, and during its construction every part of the work came under his supervision. The canal was practically completed in 1832 and was in successful operation by 1834. In 1830 he removed to Columbus, O., where he resided during the remainder of his life. He was again a member of the legislature in 1836, and introduced a bill providing for the appointment of a state school commissioner, which resulted in the establishment of the school system as a part of the state government. In 1840 he was appointed state fund commissioner. When in 1841–42 a formidable party arose in the legislature and state, which advocated the non-payment of the maturing interest of the state debt and the repudiation of the debt itself, he went to New York, where he raised nearly $250,000 on his own personal security, by which the interest was paid at maturity and the state of Ohio saved from repudiation. He was a member of the state senate in 1844–45 and originated the bill to organize the State Bank of Ohio and other banking companies, thus forming the basis of the national banking law afterward passed. At the end of his senatorial term he was elected president of the Columbus and Xenia Railroad Co., and in 1840 he accepted the presidency of the Cleveland, Columbus and Cincinnati railroad. Three years later he was chosen president of the Cleveland, Painesville and Ashtabula Railroad Co., afterward absorbed by the Lake Shore and Michigan Southern. Mr. Kelley closed his public career as a member from Columbus of the state senate in 1857. He was the first president of the Commercial Bank of Lake Erie, the first bank in Cleveland, organized in 1816. Few persons have left behind them more numerous and enduring monuments of patient and useful labor. He despised cant and hypocrisy, his love of order was great, and he carried his habits of punctuality even into social life. He was married, Aug. 25, 1817, to Mary Seymour, daughter of Maj. Melancthon Woolsey Welles, of Lowville, N. Y., and had eleven children: Maria, Jane, Charlotte, Edward, Adelaide, Henry, Helen, Frank, Annie, Alfred and Katherine. He died in Columbus, O., Dec, 2, 1859.

KELLEY, Hermon Alfred, lawyer, was born on Kelley's Island, O., May 15, 1859, son of Alfred Stow and Hannah (Farr) Kelley. His first paternal American ancestor was Joseph Kelley, who came from England in the early part of the eighteenth century and settled at Norwich, Conn. From Joseph Kelley and his wife, Lydia Caulkins, the line of descent is traced through their son Daniel and his wife, Abigail Reynolds; their son Daniel and his wife, Jemima Stow, to their son

Datus and his wife, Sara Dean, who were the grandparents of Hermon Alfred Kelley. Daniel (third) was one of the pioneers of Cleveland, whither he removed in 1810, and was elected second president of Cleveland village in 1816 to succeed his son Alfred (q.v.), who was first president. His maternal grandfather was Aurelius Farr, of Rockport, O., a descendant of Stephen Farr, of Acton, Mass. His father was trustee of the Cleveland Museum of Art. Hermon A. Kelley was graduated at Buchtel College, Akron, now the University of Akron, in 1879, receiving the degrees B.S., A.B., and A.M. from that institution. Subsequently he entered the Law School of Harvard University, where he was graduated in 1882, and later took a post-graduate course at the University of Göttingen. In 1897 the University of Akron gave him the honorary degree of LL.D. He began the practice of his profession in the office of Don M. Dickinson, Detroit, in 1884, but removed to Cleveland in the following year and formed a partnership with Arthur A. Stearns under the firm name of Stearns & Kelley. In 1891–93 he was first assistant corporation counsel of the city of Cleveland. Later he became associated with James H. Hoyt and Alton C. Dustin in the firm of Hoyt, Dustin & Kelley. By the addition to the partnership of Homer H. McKeehan and Horace Andrews the firm subsequently became Hoyt, Dustin, Kelley, McKeehan & Andrews. Since 1895 Mr. Kelley has specialized in admiralty law. Active in the promotion and building of the Cleveland Museum of Art, he is a member of the $1,200,000 building committee which began the construction of the museum in 1912. A considerable part of these funds came from the bequest of Horace Kelley, a cousin. He is trustee, president and treasurer of the Horace Kelley Art Foundation and trustee, secretary and member of the executive committee of the Cleveland Museum of Art. He is also a trustee of Buchtel College and is a member of the Union, Country, University, Euclid, Mayfield Country, and Chagrin Valley Hunt clubs, of Cleveland, and of the Twaalfskill Club, Kingston, N. Y. He finds his chief recreation in his well-appointed library of 6,000 volumes. He was married in Cleveland, O., Sept. 3, 1899, to Florence Alice, daughter of Maj. Frederick A. Kendall, of the U. S. army, and a descendant of the famous Hutchinson family of singers. There are two surviving children: Alfred Kendall and Hayward Kendall.

McCLURE, Charles Franklin, capitalist, was born at Raymond, N. H., Mar. 23, 1828, the son of John N. and Mary (Brown) McClure, and a descendant of David McClure, who came from Scotland or the north of Ireland and settled at Charmingfare (now Candia), N. H., in 1740. From him and his wife, Martha Glenn, the line descends through their daughter Elizabeth and her husband, Alexander McClure, a nephew of David McClure, and a soldier in the war of the revolution, to their son Alexander and his wife, Sarah Nay, who were the grandparents of Charles Franklin McClure. His father, a farmer, subsequently became a merchant of Cambridge, Mass., to which city he had removed from Raymond, N. H. The son was graduated at the Cambridge High School, but ill health prevented his entering Harvard College, as he had hoped to do. In the attempt to regain his health he sailed for California in March, 1849, by way of the Isthmus of Panama, arriving in San Francisco the following June. Here he successfully conducted a general supply store for outfitting miners, but at the end of a

RALPH D. MERSHON
ENGINEER

ALFRED KELLEY
LAWYER

HERMON A. KELLEY
LAWYER

CHARLES F. McCLURE
CAPITALIST

JOHN M. HALL

year returned to Boston and was married. After a number of years in the dry-goods business with his brother John he went to Virginia City, Nev., where he was associated with the first mining venture of the place. Subsequently he bought a mill to handle the ore which he purchased in large quantities at the Comstock mines. During this period he was also interested in the grain importing business in San Francisco. On his return to Boston, in 1864, he was sent to Nova Scotia by some Boston capitalists to report upon the merits of a gold mine in the Renfrew district. His visit induced him to report favorably on the property, and thus began his career as a mining operator in the Provinces. This property, upon which the Ophir Co. was organized, and of which he was manager and a principal owner, was bought in 1865; it paid expenses from the start, and during 1865–69 produced 15,839 ounces of gold. In "The Gold Fields of Nova Scotia" (1868) the following statement gives some idea of the position held by him in the Provinces: "Next to the actual discoverers of gold there is no one who deserves more the thanks of the Nova Scotian public than Mr. Charles F. McClure, a capitalist of Boston, for his exertions to sustain and redeem the character of the Nova Scotian gold mines. As one of the first owners of gold-mining property in the province Mr. McClure, by his example, invited investments on the part of his countrymen, and when, afterward, swindling operators on the New York and Boston exchanges did their utmost to depreciate the mines and every cent of United States capital was recommended to be withdrawn, he stepped forward as their champion and revived public confidence by investing still more largely himself." In the latter part of the eighties he relinquished his interests in Canada and retired from active business cares. Thereafter, until his death, he resided either in Boston or Cambridge, and also had a country residence on Gerrish Island, near Kittery Point, Me. In 1870 he accompanied the Boston Board of Trade on its transcontinental trip to San Francisco by the first through train to cross from the Atlantic to the Pacific direct. While a dry-goods merchant of Boston he served as an alderman in the city council of Cambridge. He was a member of the Boston Art Club and of the New England Association of California Pioneers. Fond of nature and out-of-door life, one of his favorite pursuits was farming. His chief characteristics were persistency, business integrity and determination. He was a man of superior courage, positive in his convictions and bold in their advocacy. Having once determined his course of action, nothing could swerve him from it. Of genial nature and affable manner, he also possessed a ready appreciation of humor which made him a most entertaining companion. He was married May 19, 1852, to Joan Elizabeth, daughter of Sherburne Blake, a farmer and manufacturer of Raymond, N. H. There are five children: Mary Louise, wife of S. Ellery Jennison; Elizabeth Blake, wife of Edward V. Bird; Arabelle Hersey; Ethel Malvina, wife of of Dr. Edward C. Briggs; and Charles Freeman Williams McClure, professor of zoology, Princeton University. Mr. McClure died in Boston, Mass., Jan. 17, 1914.

McCLURE, Charles Freeman Williams, biologist, was born in Cambridge, Mass., Mar. 6, 1865, son of Charles Franklin and Joan Elizabeth (Blake) McClure. He was educated in the public schools of Boston and Cambridge, continuing his studies in Exeter, N. H., and was graduated at Prince-

ton University in 1888. He at once became a fellow in biology at his alma mater, and a year later began a post-graduate course in the New York College of Physicians and Surgeons (1890–91). In 1891 he was appointed instructor in biology at Princeton, and held that position until 1895, when he was promoted to be assistant professor of biology, and in 1901 became professor of comparative anatomy, a position he holds at the present time. He made several trips to Europe for further studies in his special science, going to Berlin in 1892, to Kiel in 1897 and to Wurzburg in 1897. His special line of research work has been on the nerve cells of mollusca, primitive vertebrate brain, and the development of the lymphatic system. Prof. McClure was a member of the Peary relief expedition of 1899, sent out by Princeton University. He is a member of the American Society of Naturalists, the American Zoological Society, the Association of American Anatomists, of which he was vice-president in 1910, the American Philosophical Society, the National Geographic Society, Anatomische Gesellschaft, the University Club of New York, and the Ivy and Nassau clubs of Princeton. He received the degree of A.M. from Princeton in 1892, and Sc.D. from Columbia University in 1908. Prof. McClure is unmarried.

HALL, John Manning, jurist and railroad president, was born at Willimantic, Conn., Oct. 16, 1841, son of Horace and Elizabeth (Manning) Hall, grandson of Dixon Hall, and great-grandson of George Hall, who came here from England and settled on the Isle of Aquidneck, Rhode Island, where for twenty years he was a judge in the district of which Newport is now a part. He was educated at Dr. Fitch's Academy, South Windham, Conn.; at Williston Academy, and was graduated with honors at Yale College in 1866. He studied law at the Columbia Law School and in the office of Robert Bonner, New York city. In 1870 he was admitted to the bar of both New York and Connecticut, opening a law office in Windham and subsequently in Willimantic, where he also entered the field of politics. He was elected to the state legislature in 1871 and again in 1881, serving throughout the following year as a speaker of the assembly. In 1889 he was elected state senator from the 17th district, becoming president pro tem. of the senate, chairman of the committee on judiciary, and head of numerous other committees and commissions. In the same year he was appointed to the superior court of Connecticut, resigning in 1893 to accept the vice-presidency of the New York, New Haven and Hartford Railroad. He was made president of the road in 1899, and held that office until 1903, when he became general counsel, a position which, in view of the road's vast expansion and extension of territory by both traffic agreements and consolidation, involved close attention and endless labor. With his constructive mind Judge Hall was a genius for work, and his enthusiastic spirit and buoyant imagination never permitted that work to become irksome. Those were lifelong characteristics which easily permitted him to win his way to the trust and affections of men. The results accomplished by him at the bar, in the legislature, on the bench and in a corporate advisory capacity demonstrated that he possessed the qualities of true greatness. His fine intellect and convincing powers of conversation permitted him to bring an immense range of knowledge to bear in an orderly, persistent way on a multitude of onerous tasks. The power that came to him was used with a fine sense of sympathy for human needs and with a full measure of common sense which endeared him to those about him. He was a member of the Union League, Transportation and Yale clubs, of New York; the Union League, Republican, Country and Graduates, of New Haven; the Union, of Boston, and of the State Bar Association of Connecticut from its organization. He was married, 1870, to Julia W., daughter of Silas Loomer, of Willimantic, Conn., and had one son, John L. Hall, a lawyer of Boston, and two daughters, Florence Hall Day and Helen Hall Owsley. He died in New Haven, Conn., Jan. 27, 1905.

TELLER, Henry Moore, statesman, was born in Granger, Allegany co., N. Y., May 23, 1830, son of John and Charlotte (Moore) Teller. He was descended from Wilhelm Teller, a native of Holland, who came to America in 1639 and settled upon a tract of land at Fort Orange (Albany), N. Y., as trustee of the king of Holland. His wife was Mary Douchen (or Dusen), and the line is traced through their son Wilhelm, his son Wilhelm, his son William, his son Isaac, who married Rebecca Remsen; their son Remsen, who married Catherine McDonald, and was the grandfather of Henry Moore Teller. Isaac Teller was a physician of New York city who died while in active service as a surgeon in the continental army during the revolutionary war, and John Teller was a farmer in comfortable circumstances who moved to Girard, Erie co., Pa., in 1852, and ten years later to Morrison, Ill. Henry M. Teller passed his early years upon his father's farm. After teaching school he studied law in the office of Judge Martin Grover, at Angelica, N. Y., and was admitted to the bar in 1858. He began the practice of his profession in Morrison, Ill., but in 1861 removed to Colorado and settled in Central City, then one of the principal mining towns of the territory, where he resided until near the close of his life. His exceptional abilities as a lawyer soon brought him into prominence, and gained for him a numerous and profitable clientele. Three years later, his brother Willard, also a lawyer, arrived in Central City, and the firm of H. M. & W. Teller was formed, which continued until the death of Willard Teller in 1905. From the day he entered Colorado Mr. Teller was recognized as its leading attorney, and for many years his firm was employed on one side or the other of every important piece of litigation, first in the territory and afterward in the state. Mining and irrigation law were his specialties. He was the originator and promoter of the Colorado Central railroad, now merged in the Colorado and Southern. He framed and presented its charter to the territorial legislature in 1865, and as president of the company during its first five years placed the road upon a sound financial basis. At the time of the Indian troubles, in 1863, he was appointed major-general of militia by Gov. John Evans and served for three years. Originally a Democrat, he joined the Republican party soon after its organization, but when the financial question became paramount, some thirty years afterward, and his party refused to continue to stand for bimetalism, he forsook its standard and followed his convictions back into the ranks of the Democracy. He declined to become a candidate for office until the admission of Colorado into the Union in 1876, when he was chosen United States senator. His was the short term, ending Mar. 4, 1877, and he was re-elected for the full term, closing Mar. 4, 1883. He was not, however, permitted to complete this term, for in April, 1882, he was appointed as secretary of the interior in Pres. Arthur's cabinet. He administered the af-

fairs of the interior department most efficiently for the three years of Arthur's administration, and then resumed his seat in the senate, to which he had been again elected in January, 1885, this time to succeed Nathaniel P. Hill. He was re-elected in 1891, 1897 and 1903, after which he refused to be a candidate again. He held the almost unprecedented record of having received six elections to the United States senate. Mr. Teller served successively as chairman of the committees on civil service and retrenchment, pensions, mines and mining, patents, privileges and elections, five civilized tribes of Indians, claims and private land claims. For many years he served simultaneously on the committees on finance, rules and the judiciary, three of the six leading committees of the senate. He was on the committee on public lands during the greater part of his senatorial service, and in that capacity did much toward shaping the land laws of the country as he did toward setting the pace for their enforcement while secretary of the interior. Probably the most notable constructive legislation of which he was the author was his amendment to the house joint resolution of April, 1898, authorizing the president to take steps to stop the war being waged by Spain in Cuba. As passed by the house the measure had provided merely for intervention by this government to bring about a cessation of hostilities and to establish a stable government in that island. Mr. Teller's amendment was a disavowal of "any disposition or intention to exercise jurisdiction or control over the island except for its purification," and the expression of a determination, when this was accomplished, to leave the government and control of the island to the people thereof. It was adopted by the senate and ultimately accepted by the house, and to its controlling influence must be attributed the splendidly magnanimous course of this country toward Cuba after the Spanish-American war. Senator Teller was an especially close student of the financial history of the world, and his investigations along monetary lines, even more than the interest of his state in silver, led him to accept bimetalism as the correct system of finance. He gave much attention to the framing of the banking laws of the country, and because of his recognized mastery of the intricacies of finance he was chosen by the senate as a member of the monetary commission toward the close of his senatorial career. The tariff received close scrutiny at the hands of Mr. Teller, and while never an extremist in that respect, he always leaned toward protection, even after he became a Democrat. He was one of the great men of the nation, always fair and just in his judgments, and no taint ever touched his good name. As a statesman he measured up to the highest standards of wisdom, patriotism and devotion to the common weal. He labored not alone for his own state, but for all the states of the Union. Gifted with a marvelous intuition concerning the motives of men, he clearly previsioned the effects of proposed laws and enactments upon the welfare of the people and of the country which he loved. He was sagacious in council; cool, calm and skillful in debate; cheerfully tolerant of the opinions of others, slow to criticise or censure—indeed, a master of men because he had mastered himself. His habits were simple, and he cared little for public applause. The touchstone of his life, by which he tested every question of public and private morality, was, "Is it right?" No suspicion ever rested upon his integrity, nor upon his official acts. His religious affiliations were with the Methodist Episco-

HENRY M. TELLER

pal Church. He was made a Knight Templar in 1863, was elected grand commander in Colorado in 1876, an active member of the supreme council in 1882 and grand prior of the supreme council in 1913. The degree of LL.D. was conferred upon him by Alfred University in 1886, the University of Colorado in 1903 and the University of Denver in 1909. He was married, June 7, 1862, to Harriet M., daughter of Packard Bruce, of Cuba, N. Y., and had three children: Emma A., who married Dr. George Edward Tyler, of Denver, Colo.; Harrison John and Henry Bruce Teller. Senator Teller died in Denver, Colo., Feb. 23, 1914.

RIGGS, Elisha Francis, banker and philanthropist, was born at "Corn Riggs" (now part of the U. S. Soldiers' Home), near Washington, D. C., Oct. 2, 1851, son of George Washington and Janet Madeleine Cecilia (Shedden) Riggs. His earliest known paternal American ancestor was John Riggs, whose forebears are supposed to have come from Fareham, Hampshire, England, and who lived in Anne Arundel county, Md., early in the eighteenth century. His wife was Mary Davis, and from them the line of descent is traced through their son Samuel and his wife, Amelia Dorsey, to their son Elisha and his wife, Alice Lawrason, who were the grandparents of Elisha Francis Riggs. Elisha Riggs was a successful merchant in Georgetown, D. C., in Baltimore and later in New York city, and was a partner of George Peabody. George Washington Riggs, educated at the celebrated Round Hill School, Mass., and at Yale, was a partner of W. H. Corcoran in the Washington banking firm of Corcoran & Riggs in 1840-48. The firm rendered essential aid to the government by taking several very large loans during the war. George W. Riggs was the head of the firm of Riggs & Co., bankers, from 1854 until his death in 1881, and throughout his life was active in civic and charitable affairs in Washington. E. Francis Riggs received his education at Gonzaga College, Washington, D. C., and at St. Mary's College, Oscott, England. He began his business career in the counting house of Riggs & Co. in 1871; became a partner five years later, and upon the death of his father became the head of the firm, remaining in that capacity until 1896, when he retired from active business cares, with an international reputation as a banker. Upon his retirement, Riggs & Co. became the Riggs National Bank. For years he was treasurer of the National Savings and Trust Co., of which he was vice-president from 1897 until his death, and he was also for some years a director of the National Metropolitan Bank. He held numerous public positions of honor and responsibility, including membership on the board of directors of the Garfield Memorial Hospital and on the finance committee of the Catholic University of America. He was treasurer of the Mount Vernon Ladies' Association in 1881-1910. In 1889 he presented to Georgetown College the Riggs Memorial Library, in memory of his father and of his brother, Thomas Lawrason Riggs. An annex was also presented by him a few years before his death. A member of the Roman Catholic church, he always took an active part in its affairs. He was particularly interested in St. Vincent's Orphan Asylum, and he aided financially and otherwise in the reform of church music ordered by Pope Pius X in 1903, especially at St. Paul's Church, Washington, from which his funeral took place. The Riggs Memorial Maternity Hospital, dedicated in 1912, was presented by his

widow to Georgetown University in Mr. Riggs' memory. He was a charter member of the Columbia Historical Society and a member of the Metropolitan and Alibi clubs, Washington, and of the Society of the Colonial Wars, through his descent from Nicholas Greenberry (1627-1697) and Henry Ridgely, member of the assembly of Maryland in 1692. Aside from his charitable and religious activities his favorite pursuits were traveling and reading, and, after 1900, the care of his country place, "Fareham," in the Pequot section of New London, Conn. He was married in New York, Feb. 19, 1879, to Medora, daughter of James S. Thayer. There are two surviving children: Elisha Francis, Jr., a lieutenant in the U. S. army, and Thomas Lawrason. He died at "Fareham," New London, Conn., July 6, 1910.

REED, Elizabeth Armstrong, author, was born at Winthrop, Me., May 16, 1842, daughter of Alvin and Sylvia (Sylvester Morrell) Armstrong, of an old English family. She received the best education that the times afforded. Her father and mother were both prominent educators, and her training was largely conducted by private tutors. She had married at the age of eighteen, and the union was a singularly harmonious and happy one. She and her husband worked and studied together and he was in close sympathy with her literary activities. Her first serious production was "The Bible Triumphant" (1866), which has passed through several editions and has been translated into the Hindu tongue. This was followed by "Earnest Words," published first in London and later in Boston. She is also the author of "Hindu Literature; or, The Ancient Books of India" (1891); "Persian Literature, Ancient and Modern" (1893); "Primitive Buddhism, Its Origin and Teachings" (1896). The first two are fascinating volumes representing the history, poetry and romance of Indian and Persian literature. Her literary style is clear and attractive. Her Oriental writings indicate a high order of scholarship and have received the indorsement of the most eminent European scholars who specialized along these lines. Mrs. Reed is the first woman author whose writings have been accepted by the Philosophical Society of Great Britain, of which she has been a member for many years. She became, on the recommendation of Prof. A. H. Sayre, of Oxford University, a member of the Royal Asiatic Society, the Victoria Institute and the Woman's Press Association, of which she was president for four terms. Her literary labors have extended to editorial work on the Course of Universal Literature, published in 1896 by the University Association, and she has also contributed articles on India and Persia to the Encyclopædia Americana and the Biblical Encyclopædia. She was married in 1860 to Rev. Hiram von Reed, and had two sons, Earl Hiram and Dr. Charles B. Reed, and one daughter, Myrtle, who married James Sidney McCullough, and as "Myrtle Reed" became well known as an author.

McCULLOUGH, Myrtle Reed, (Myrtle Reed) author, was born in Chicago, Ill., Sept. 27, 1874, daughter of Hiram V. and Elizabeth (Armstrong) Reed. Her mother (above) enjoyed an extensive reputation for her researches in and publications on Persian and Hindu literature. At an early age Myrtle Reed began to write tender verses and exceptionally good prose. While at the West Division High School, Chicago, she served as the editor of the school paper, and soon after her graduation published her first volume, "Love Letters of a Musician" (1899), which was followed shortly by "Later Love Letters" and "The Spinster Book," publications that surprised her friends not only by their unusual promise but by their actual merit. Thereafter, once each year, she gave to the world a book which, in its own way, was sweet, clean and soul-nourishing, and almost unrivaled in its capacity to sell. Her volume, "The Book of Clever Beasts," won from Theodore Roosevelt a warmly appreciative letter. Mrs. McCullough was possessed of a most engaging personality. She was hospitable to a fault, had a gentle, quaint, original humor, and was fond of all sorts of simple gayety. All the year round she worked steadily, though not always actually writing. Sometimes she left her home and took refuge in some quiet place where she was not known, until she had accomplished her new literary creation. She did all her work herself, seldom having a stenographer even to transcribe the final version of the stories over which she toiled with such intense and arduous concentration. "Lavender and Old Lace" was thrice rewritten before satisfying both author and publisher. She loved her work devotedly and had a high conception of her vocation. Sentiment of the tenderest and purest kind was the keynote of her writing, and into her stories she threw all the energy of a strong, sweet, wholesome nature. When asked which she considered her best book, she replied: "I trust I have it yet to write. I am never satisfied with anything I do, after the first glow of ecstasy that comes with creation is over." In her stories appears an unvarying appreciation of all the finer lights and shadows of love—the fire and dew commingled in life's rarest and most rapturous experiences. Her optimism was dauntless, her humor unfailing; while she brought into being many characters that are widely known and loved. Included in the list of Mrs. McCullough's publications are the following: "Love Letters of a Musician" (1899); "Later Love Letters" (1900); "The Spinster Book" (1901); "Lavender and Old Lace" (1902); "Shadow of Victory" (1903); "Pickaback Songs" (1903); "The Master's Violin" (1904); "Sign of the Jack-o-Lantern" (1905); "Spinner in the Sun" (1906); "Love Affairs of Literary Men" (1907); "Flower of the Dusk" (1908); "Old Rose and Silver" (1909); "Master of the Vineyard" (1910); "Sonnets to a Lover" (1910); "Weaver of Dreams" (1911); "Year Book" (1911); "White Shield" (1912); "Happy Women" (1913); "Threads of Gray and Gold" (1913). Myrtle Reed was married Oct. 22, 1906, to James Sidney McCullough. She died in Chicago, Ill., Aug. 17, 1911.

MOREHEAD, John Henry, eighteenth governor of Nebraska, was born in Lucas county, Ia., Dec. 3, 1861, son of Andrew and Frances (Cooper) Morehead. He was educated in the public schools and when twenty-two years of age removed to Nebraska, where he taught school two years, afterward entering a mercantile business. Finally he turned to banking and for more than twenty years has been successful in this field. During 1896–98 he was treasurer of his county; was mayor of Falls City in 1900; district delegate to the Democratic national convention in Denver in 1908; state senator and president pro tem. of that body in 1911, and became lieutenant-governor in 1911 by reason of the death of the incumbent. In 1912 he was elected governor of Nebraska, and he was re-elected in 1914 by the largest majority given a governor in his state in twenty years. In public life he has steadfastly refused to accept anything but the

salary of the office, although by custom many other expenses incident to the position have been paid heretofore by the state. He has not cared to battle for his views on public questions, even as expressed in his messages to the legislature, and has interfered but little with the legislative end of the state government. In favor of economy of administration, he yet refused to vote appropriation items, preferring to let the legislature stand sponsor for such measures. A Democrat in politics, Gov. Morehead represents the conservatives of his party but has been a moderate. Although not able to cement the affairs within his party, he has won to his cause in each election most of the conservative Republicans. He has been a steady critic of the present direct primary law, but has left the remedy to others. Rather than any considerable increase in navy and army, he is an advocate of rural paving and construction of railroads and wagon roads. He is a member of the Masonic Order and of the Elks. He was married, Feb. 14, 1885, to Minnie Weisenreider, of Aspinwall, Neb.

BURTON, Oliver Milton, manufacturer and inventor, was born at Geneva, Ill., Mar. 18, 1877, son of John and Elizabeth Lucy (Long) Burton, and grandson of John and Catherine (Drayton) Burton. His grandfather was a native of Melford, England, and after his marriage, in 1829, came to the United States, settling in Chicago, Ill., where he died in 1852. Mr. Burton's mother was also of English descent. He was educated in the public schools and at a business college in Chicago. He began his business career in 1895 in association with his father, founding the J. Burton Co., for the manufacture of cotton felts for the bedding, furniture, automobile, carriage and other industries. Four years later he was made secretary and treasurer of the company, and in 1907 became president and treasurer. In 1913 the name of the firm was changed to Oliver M. Burton Co., its present title. Besides the manufacture of felts it deals in cotton linters, bleachers of linters, converters of ticking, and imports Kapok or silk floss. In its mills, in Chicago, Ill., and Brooklyn, N. Y., it employs on an average 375 hands. It is the largest manufacturer of felts in the United States. In 1908 Mr. Burton founded the Dixie Cotton Felt Mattress Co., of which he is president and treasurer. This company is one of the largest manufacturers of cotton and felt mattresses in the United States. Mr. Burton is sole proprietor of the Dixie "Notuft" compartment mattress, which his firm manufactures, and also a life-raft (mattress), made with his company's Kapok; an inner strap mattress, which is reinforced within so that it cannot widen out; a spring mattress, containing a cushioned spring center; and dissectible box springs, so arranged that the cover can be removed for cleaning purposes. He is a member of the Edgewater Golf Club, the South Shore Country Club, the Chicago Athletic Association, and finds his principal recreation in golf and out-door sports. He is also a member of the Association of Commerce of Chicago and the Chicago Credit Men's Association. He was married Oct. 20, 1909, to Anne, daughter of Robert Tathan, a leading lawyer of Chicago.

GARDNER, Obadiah, U. S. senator, was born near Port Huron, Mich., Sept. 13, 1852, son of John and Mary (Strevils) Gardner. His first paternal American ancestor was John S. Gardner, who came from England and settled at Hingham, Mass., in 1617. From him the line of descent is raced through his son Thomas and his wife Abigail Ellis; their son Obadiah and his wife Lois;

MYRTLE REED McCULLOUGH
AUTHOR

JOHN H. MOREHEAD
GOVERNOR

OLIVER M. BURTON
MANUFACTURER

OBADIAH GARDNER
U. S. SENATOR

their son ———— and his wife Jeannette; their son Obadiah and his wife Julia Daniels Marnier, who were the grandparents of Senator Gardner. Young Obadiah lost his father when he was twenty months old and lived with his mother and grandfather until the age of twelve, when, on account of poor health, he went to Maine. There he attended the district schools, as he had also done in Michigan, and went to work for himself at fifteen in lumber camps, lime quarries and shipyards, thus acquiring money enough to pay his own way through Eastman Business College at Poughkeepsie, N. Y., and Coburn Classical Institute, Waterville, Me. Subsequently he worked as clerk in a country store, and finally, in 1872, he saved enough to go to farming near the city of Rockland, Me. In 1875 he purchased a farm near Pleasant Valley and soon became known nationally as a prominent member of the Grange. He made his farm and his "blue-ribbon" prize-winning herd of Jersey cattle noted throughout the East, his other stock being also prize-winners at the fairs. About this time he also became interested in the lumber and lime business. He became a member of the city government of Rockland in 1876 and a member of the Maine state board of agriculture in 1880. Later he was made chairman of the executive committee of the state Grange and continued in this office for eight years. He was master of the state Grange in 1897–1907, during which period the membership gained 35,540, making 60,000 active members. For four years he was overseer of the national Grange, and in the voting for the national mastership he received the votes of the states that represented two-thirds of the members of the order. Under the ordinary rules of election and representation this vote would have placed him at the head of that order, but, according to the rules of the national Grange, each state cast two votes. In 1908, against the protests of the Democratic politicians, the rural delegates to the state convention named him as their candidate for governor, and he was unanimously nominated. He stumped the state, attacking the railroad and corporation policies of the Republican administration, and at the election he polled the largest vote ever received by a Democratic candidate for governor of Maine up to that time on a straight party ticket, coming within 7,000 of winning. He would have been the logical candidate in 1910 but, through the attention he had called to the existing inequalities on the question of taxing the state's wild lands, he had incurred the opposition of William R. Pattangall, later attorney-general, and several of the other self-constituted leaders of the Democratic party in Maine. Regardless, however, of this opposition of the organization, he was only defeated by a small majority by his opponent, Frederick W. Plaisted. Indeed, without Mr. Gardner's support, Mr. Plaisted would surely have been defeated; but the former came loyally to the support of the party's candidate. On the meeting of the legislature, Mr. Gardner was a candidate for U. S. senator, but was again opposed by the same organization, headed by Mr. Pattangall, who favored Chas. F. Johnson. He was, however, appointed chairman of the state board of assessors for a term of six years, accepting the post as a favor to Gov. Plaisted. Then, on the death of Senator Frye, he was appointed by the governor, Sept. 22, 1911, to fill the term of the latter, expiring Mar. 4, 1913. He was a candidate to succeed himself and was defeated for re-election by one vote. Among his most notable achievements while in the senate was his advocacy of the postal express, and it was the influence of the farmers exerted and crystalized through him that did much to secure the liberal parcel post laws. He was from the first one of the strongest and most aggressive supporters of Governor Woodrow Wilson for the presidency, and largely through his efforts Maine went Democratic. He had strong support from representative men all over the United States for secretary of agriculture under the Wilson administration. On Oct. 1, 1913, he was appointed by the president a member of the international joint commission, an international court created in 1910 by treaty between the United States and Great Britain to control the use, diversion and obstruction of the boundary waters between the United States and Canada. The commission has large judicial powers for the settlement of all controversies between the two governments and the people of both in the use of these waters. Their decision is final. After one year's service as a member, Senator Gardner was unanimously elected chairman of the U. S. section of the commission, a position of responsibility and honor which he now holds (1916.) He is a Universalist and an Odd Fellow. Senator Gardner was married at Rockland, Me., Dec. 15, 1875, to Corinna A., daughter of Charles Sherer, and has two children: Nina A., wife of C. S. Beverage, and Albert Kinsman Gardner.

GLYNN, Martin H., fortieth governor of New York, was born at Kinderhook, N. Y., Sept. 27, 1871, son of Martin and Anne (Scanlon) Glynn. He was educated in the public schools and at St. John's College, Fordham, N. Y., where he was graduated with honor in 1894. Joining the staff of the "Albany Times-Union," he later became managing editor of that publication, and eventually acquired control of it. Notwithstanding his journalistic duties, he found time to engage in the study of law, and was admitted to the bar in 1897. He represented the 20th New York district in congress during 1899–1901, being one of the youngest members that ever served in the national house. He attracted the attention of Pres. McKinley and, although he was of another political faith, received from the chief executive a position on the Louisiana Purchase Exposition commission, subsequently becoming vice-president of that body. In 1906 he was the nominee of both the Democratic party and Independence League for state controller, was elected, and continued in that office for two years. While controller he obtained a reputation as a foe to graft and as a persistent reformer of abuses. He was a consistent champion of the barge canal and highway improvements and conducted, during his tenure of office, two of the greatest bond sales in the history of the state, selling $5,000,000 of highway improvement bonds at rates that netted the state a premium of $348,000, and $5,000,000 of barge canal improvement bonds that brought in a large premium. When he retired from office he left the state treasury in a highly improved condition. Mr. Glynn was elected lieutenant-governor of New York in November, 1912, and assumed the office of governor, Aug. 14, 1913, after impeachment proceedings had been instituted against Gov. William Sulzer (q. v.). He recommended to the legislature the Massachusetts form of ballot, the direct primary law abolishing state conventions, and the workingmen's compensation law, measures that passed both houses by an almost unanimous vote. He continued the investigations of the state departments begun by Gov. Sulzer, such as the state architect's office, the executive department, the department of highways, the banking department, department of prisons, etc., in nearly all of which conditions of corruption or mismanagement were found. He also recommended an early convention for the revision of the state constitution, advocating a short ballot. Such a convention was held two years later. During his administration provisions were made for revising the state banking law, for creating a bureau of employment in the department of labor, for providing a factory for the boys' reformatory at Elmira to manufacture bricks for state roads, and inaugurating camps for prisoners to work on country roads; for a co-operating bureau for farmers and for an agricultural land bank to furnish the farmers with short time loans. This land bank, based on the French and German systems, is the first of the kind to be established in the United States. On the whole, Gov. Glynn's administration was a notable one, quite as much for the reforms and economies that he advocated as for the new legislation. During his term he reduced the expenses of the state twenty-five per cent. In 1914 he was again a candidate for the governorship on the Democratic ticket, but was defeated by the Republican candidate, Charles S. Whitman. Gov. Glynn is characterized as a man of stability, sense, culture, solid attainments and sterling honesty. As a public speaker he arouses enthusiasm by his telling presentation of his views. He was married Jan. 2, 1901, to Mary C. E., daughter of P. B. Magrane, of Lynn, Mass., a woman of high intellectual and social attainments, interested in charitable work, a linguist, well read, well educated, but of an unassuming and retiring disposition.

COLLIER, Price, author and historian, was born in Davenport, Ia., May 25, 1860, son of Robert Laird and Mary (Price) Collier, and a descendant of Robert Collier, a native of England, who emigrated in 1675 and settled in Somerset county, Md. He held, under the lord proprietary of Maryland, land called "Collier's good success," near Nanticoke river, in what was then (1675) Somerset county, now Wicomico county. From 1675 to 1799, when George Collier was born, there seem to be no records in the possession of the family, which nevertheless had been living in Maryland during that interval. George Collier, a descendant of Robert Collier, married Martha Dashiel; their son, Levin Dashiel, married Alice Dashiel, and they were the grandparents of Price Collier. On the distaff side his grandfather was Hiram Price, one of the most notable public men of Iowa. The mother of Price Collier was widely famed for her charm and virtues, and after her death a chapel was erected in Chicago in honor of her memory. His father (q. v.) (1837–90) was a distinguished Unitarian minister, and at various times served churches in Chicago, Boston, and Birmingham, England. At the age of twelve Price Collier was put to school in Geneva, Switzerland, and during the succeeding five years lived there and in England. At the age of seventeen he prepared for Harvard College at the Joshua Kendall School, Cambridge, Mass. A serious illness prevented his entering college at this time, and he went to Germany, where he became a student at Leipzig University. In 1879 he returned to America and entered the Divinity School of Harvard University, where he was graduated (B.D.) in 1882. He immediately entered the ministry and became pastor of the old First Parish Church (Unitarian) at Hingham, Mass. In 1888 he was called to the Church of the Saviour in Brooklyn, N. Y. In 1891 he resigned this pastorate and left the ministry permanently. He at once became

well known as an author, his works attracting unusual attention. As early as 1891 he published a volume of essays (E. P. Dutton & Co.), which was followed by "Mr. Picket Pin and His Friends" (Dutton. 1893). For nearly two years (1893) he acted as foreign editor of the "Forum" while living in England and was a frequent contributor to American and English periodicals. He then wrote his essays or studies of the characteristics of different nationalities, his first being "America and the Americans from the French Point of View" (Scribners, 1896). This volume created a sensation when it appeared, especially as some mystery was attached to the authorship of it, since Mr. Collier had withheld his name from the title page, although it had frequently been rumored that the work was from his pen. The book showed keen insight, the possession of rare critical qualities, and a thorough knowledge of American life and character. In it he was especially severe on so-called fashionable society, and particularly on Newport life and foibles, despite the fact that he himself had a recognized position in the smart world of New York. He also wrote a volume of verse, was the joint author of "A Parish for Two" (1903), and in 1905 completed a volume on "Driving" in Macmillan's Sporting Library. He next turned his attention to a study of the English people, and the result was his "England and the English from an American Point of View" (1909), followed by "The West in the East from an American Point of View" (1911), and in 1913 "Germany and the Germans from an American Point of View." During the war with Spain he served in the United States navy as signal officer and adjutant of the battalion, with the rank of ensign, on board the U. S. S. Prairie. He was fond of all out-of-door sports, and especially of shooting. He had a country place at Tuxedo Park, N. Y., and was a member of the Harvard, Metropolitan, Tuxedo, Army and Navy, New York Yacht, City, Midday and National Arts clubs of New York, and of various learned and historical societies. Mr. Collier's writings abounded in vigor, fire and vivacity. They were at once genuinely interesting and strikingly elegant, and free from mystery, vagueness and jargon, embodying the spirit of a man of the world who was incomparably better informed than the mass of his congeners. He analyzed with agreeable frankness the characteristics of his fellow-men, even those who sat in high places, and as an unmasker of political and social humbug he was unsurpassed. His personal attainments were very great, and he added to a singular symmetry and elevation of character an unusual intellectual culture. His literary taste was unfailing and his reading thorough and extensive. His influence over others was far-reaching, and he inspired much affection from all with whom he came in contact. He was married in New York city, Aug. 8, 1893, to Mrs. Katherine (Delano) Robbins, daughter of Warren Delano, and a member of a distinguished New York family of Newburgh-on-Hudson. She survives him, with two children: Katharine and Sara Collier. Mr. Collier died on the Island of Funen, Baltic sea, Nov. 3, 1913.

DOHERTY, Henry, manufacturer, was born in Macclesfield, England, Feb. 6, 1850, son of Henry and Jane (Yarwood) Doherty. He learned the weavers' trade, and came to this country when eighteen years of age, following his father, who had preceded him by several years. He soon became superintendent of the Phillip Mackay mill

Price Collier

in Paterson, and later purchased an interest in the plant. After occupying that position for a number of years he entered into partnership with Joseph Wadsworth in 1879. Until 1895 the firm of Doherty & Wadsworth was housed in the Arkwright mill in Paterson. The building was burned in that year, and a large mill was erected at Beach and Essex streets. In 1901 Mr. Doherty established an individual plant in the Hall mill on Fulton street, beginning to make plain silk goods, and was the first manufacturer to produce this kind of fabric upon a large scale in Paterson. His business prospered, and in 1903 he also utilized the old Hamil & Booth mill on Ward street, and in 1905 opened still another branch in the Congdon mill on Van Houten street. About the same time he leased a floor in the Granite mill on Grand street, where he opened a throwing plant. In December, 1908, the manufacture of plain goods

IN MEMORY OF
HENRY DOHERTY SR.
BORN 1850   DIED 1915

FOUNDER OF THE
HENRY DOHERTY SILK CO.

ERECTED BY THE EMPLOYEES
AS AN EXPRESSION
OF THEIR HIGH ESTEEM FOR HIM
1915

had expanded to such proportions that it was deemed best to incorporate the business; the Henry Doherty Silk Co. was organized, and in 1909 the large mill at Lakeview was built. All the branches of the business were consolidated there with the exception of the throwing plant, which is still operated in the Hall mill as a branch of the business at Lakeview. The total business aggregates about $3,000,000 annually, and nearly 1,000 operatives are employed, when running to full capacity. In 1892 Mr. Doherty was a candidate for congress on the Republican ticket, his sole venture into the political field. For many years he was a leading figure in the industrial world, and was an authority on all matters relating to the silk trade, of which his knowledge was complete. He was known as the "optimist of the silk industry," and the stimulus of his cheerful spirit infected even his operatives. He

was a close student of conditions and was endowed with a keen and reliable judgment. His paper on "Strikes and the Remedy," presented before the Paterson board of trade, commanded wide attention, and helped to solve real difficulties. By the gift of $1,000 he founded the Workmen's Institute of Paterson, and in many other ways evinced sincere interest in the welfare of the laboring people. He was responsible for the introduction of the linotype machine in the newspaper offices of Paterson, and was a member of the Hamilton Club of that city. Mr. Doherty was a man of gentle, sensitive and modest disposition, attractive personality, and magnanimous temperament, strong in character, strictly honorable in all his dealings, and broad, democratic and progressive in his views. He had, to an exceptional degree, the faculty of winning the esteem and affection of all who were brought into contact with him. A memorial tablet at the main entrance to his mills, subscribed for by his employees, was unveiled May 15, 1915. He was thrice married; (1), to Annie Hough, of Paterson, N. J.; (2), in 1898, to Mrs. Sarah Books, also of Paterson; (3), in 1904, to Mrs. Cornelia R. Liggett, of Philadelphia, Pa. He was survived by four children by his first wife: William, Harriet, wife of Paul G. Schoonmaker, Henry, Jr., and Raymond Doherty. Mr. Doherty died in Los Angeles, Cal., Feb. 1, 1915.

INGALLS, Melville Ezra, railroad president, was born in Harrison county, Sept. 6, 1842, son of Ezra T. and Louisa (Maybury) Ingalls and a descendant of Edmund Ingalls, the founder of the famliy in America, who came over from Lincolnshire, England, in 1628 and settled in Salem, Mass. He received his education at the common schools, at North Bridgeton (Maine) Academy and at Bowdoin College. Leaving the latter before finishing his course he studied law at the Harvard Law School, where he was graduated in 1863. In the following year he began the practice of his profession in Boston and conducted a large and successful business until 1870. During that time he was prominent in politics, serving on the city council of Boston, of which he was president, and also serving a term in the Massachusetts senate. In 1870 he commenced his railroad career as president of the Cincinnati, Indianapolis and LaFayette Railroad Co., with headquarters at Cincinnati, O. He was appointed receiver of the company in 1871, and continued in that capacity until 1873, when the road was reorganized and he was elected president. He resigned on Jan. 1, 1905, to become chairman of the board, which office he held until he retired from active business in November, 1912. Under his management what was known as the old "Big Four," viz., Cincinnati, Indianapolis, St. Louis and Chicago railway, successor to the Indianapolis, Cincinnati and LaFayette railway, was consolidated with the Cleveland, Cincinnati, Chicago and Indianapolis railway, which also owned the Indianapolis and St. Louis railway. That company in turn acquired the Cincinnati, Wabash and Michigan railway, the Cairo, Vincennes and Columbus, and the Peoria and Eastern railroad, all of which are now included in the system known as the Cleveland, Cincinnati, Chicago and St. Louis railway, commonly termed the "Big Four." Between 1889 and 1891 this system grew from 400 to 2,200 miles. Mr. Ingalls succeeded the late Collis P. Huntington as president and director of the Chesapeake and Ohio railway in 1888 and served in that capacity until 1899. His record with the Chesapeake and Ohio equals if it does not exceed his splendid achievement with the Big Four. The former, when he first took hold of it, was in poor physical condition, with gross earnings of between three and four million dollars a year. When he retired, the gross earnings were more than one million dollars per month, the physical condition of the property compared favorably with that of any other road in the country, and he had the enviable reputation of having placed the C. and O. upon a dividend-paying basis before he resigned. Under his management branch lines were built and traffic developed; the property was supplied with first-class passenger equipment and its passenger business was built up hand in hand with the freight traffic. Mr. Ingalls also served as president of the Kentucky Central Railroad Co. (now a part of the Louisville and Nashville railroad), from January, 1881, to October, 1883, and upon the reorganization of the C. N. O. and T. P. Railway Co., he served it as a director for some five or six years, resigning in 1912. He went into every detail of railroading thoroughly, and it was his custom to have the heads of all of the departments report directly to him, conducting his railroad practically without vice-presidents. He was always ready to learn and was always accessible to the humblest employee of the company. In the early days when the mileage of the systems under his management was smaller he knew most of the employees from section men up. In the railroad world Mr. Ingalls was best known for his constructive ability, which nowhere showed to better advantage than in his efforts to solve the problem of railway rates. He was among the first to recognize the dangers of unrestricted competition and of the resulting chaotic conditions. He was one of the originators of the Central Freight Association, which had charge of the traffic relations of railroads west of the Alleghanies and east of the Mississippi river, and he originated the well-known Joint Traffic Association, which had for its object the elimination of rebating and the regulation of rates. The scheme here developed was later followed in the formation of the Trans-Missouri Association, which the supreme court later declared illegal, thus forcing the abandonment of the scheme. The resulting demoralization of the railway rate situation forced most radical changes in the laws affecting carriers and the organization of the Interstate Commerce Commission. When Mr. Ingalls retired from the active management of the Big Four railway he became interested in banking and, with his associates, purchased control in what was known as the Merchants' National Bank of Cincinnati, which he built up until it was the second largest national bank in the city. In 1913 the bank was purchased by the First National of Cincinnati, of which Mr. Ingalls was elected a director. His interests in Cincinnati extended far beyond his business connections, though he never sought public office except in 1903, when he ran for the office of mayor on a reform ticket. At that time, although defeated, he shook the hold of the "gang" on the city government and made its subsequent overthrow possible. During the many years of his residence in Cincinnati there was hardly any movement for civic betterment in which he did not take a prominent part. One of the many projects most intimately connected with his name was the development of the Cincinnati park system, for which he was largely in-

strumental in obtaining the necessary legislation. He served as president of the Cincinnati exposition in 1880 and as director thereafter; was one of the founders of the Cincinnati Art Musuem, of which he was president until his death, and also helped to found the Cincinnati Training School. Among his other activities, not purely of a business nature, may be mentioned the development of Virginia Hot Springs, which was due almost entirely to him. Mr. Ingalls was a stanch Democrat and gave his support to the party throughout his life with the exception of one year, when he felt that his duty and interests warranted his support of William McKinley for president. He was founder and first president of the Cincinnati Country Club, a founder and for several years president of the Queen City Club of Cincinnati, and a member of the Metropolitan clubs of New York and Washington, D. C. Physically he was an exceptionally fine specimen of manhood and his devotion to outdoor exercise kept him always in good condition. His social attainments were marked and he was one of the best after-dinner speakers in the country. He was married at Gray, Me., July, 1867, to Abbie M., daughter of Thomas Stimson, and had six children: Melville E., Jr.; George H., Albert S., Fay, Louise, wife of Alfred Barnard, and Gladys Ingalls. He died at Hot Springs, Va., on July 11, 1914.

DUFFY, James Albert, first Roman Catholic bishop of the diocese of Kearney, Neb., was born in St. Paul, Minn., Sept. 13, 1873. Left an orphan at an early age, he was placed in the Boys' Orphan Asylum at Minneapolis, remaining in this institution until he entered St. Thomas' College, St. Paul. He was graduated at St. Thomas' in 1893 and then began his studies for the priesthood at St. Thomas' Seminary. He was one of the first to enter the St. Paul Seminary when it was opened for students the following year. Archbishop Ireland ordained him to the priesthood there on May 27, 1899, and he was the first alumnus of that institution to be promoted to the episcopate. After his ordination he was assistant pastor at the Immaculate Conception Church, Minneapolis, and three years later pastor of St. Ann's, Le Sueur, but owing to ill health he had to resign this charge and went to Cheyenne, Wyo., to recuperate and work under Bishop Keane, who made him pastor of his cathedral and chancellor of the diocese. The diocese of Kearney was created on March 8, 1912, to include a territory of 38,000 square miles of the western portion of the state of Nebraska, north of the Platte river, and formerly included in the diocese of Omaha. The Catholic population numbers about 12,000, ministered to by twenty-nine priests located at great distances from each other in parishes covering over 1,000 square miles of territory; some of them more than 3,000 square miles. There are ninety-seven churches, stations and chapels; two parish schools with 283 pupils and thirty Sisters teaching. Father Duffy was appointed bishop of the new see on Jan. 25, 1913, and was consecrated by Archbishop Keane, of Dubuque, in St. Mary's Cathedral, Cheyenne, on April 16 of the same year, Bishop Dowling, of Des Moines, preaching the sermon, and Bishop Scannell, of Omaha, and Bishop McGovern, of Cheyenne, being the co-consecrators.

KNIGHT, Henry Martyn, physician, was born at Stafford, Conn., Aug. 11, 1827, son of Rev. Joseph and Ruby (Hyde) Knight. He was descended from Richard Knight, born in Newport, R. I., where his English ancestors settled early

in the seventeenth century, and whose wife was Sarah Rogers, the line of descent being through their son David and his wife, Sarah (Spencer) Backus; their son Benjamin and his wife, Hannah Jewett; their son Benjamin, Jr., and his wife, Mary Adams; their son Asher and his wife, Martha Clarke, and their son, Rev. Joseph Knight, who was the father of Henry Martyn Knight. He was educated under his father, who was a graduate of Brown University, and attended Williston Seminary. He studied medicine at the Berkshire Medical Institute, where he was graduated with the degree of M. D. in 1849. He began the practice of his profession at Stafford Springs, Conn., but two years later removed to Salisbury. He made a specialty of nervous diseases and early in his career became interested in the feeble-minded, arousing public interest in their behalf, establishing institutions for their care and training, and working with great heartiness and sympathy on the lines followed by his friends, the elder Seguin and Dr. Harvey Wilbur. In 1855 he was appointed by the state of Connecticut upon a commission to study the conditions and claims of this class of unfortunates. The knowledge acquired in this service so impressed him with the necessity of definite and sustained effort on their behalf that following the defeat in the Connecticut senate (by one vote) of a bill providing for a state institution for the special care and education of the feeble-minded and epileptic, he began such treatment as a part of his private practice in Salisbury. The Connecticut School for Imbeciles was incorporated in 1861, and although conducted as a private institution, it received occasional aid from the state. It became known far and wide for its efficiency and its home-like atmosphere, in which the patients were always known as ''children,'' never ''cases.'' A man of boundless energy, strong in his convictions, resolute in action, and with the rarest personal charm, the enthusiasm with which Dr. Knight devoted himself to the cause of these most helpless members of the human family revolutionized public sentiment toward them whenever and wherever he had an opportunity to present their claims. He was well known and constantly consulted by men of his own specialty in other lands, and at home other states turned to him for both precept and example in their foundation work. In 1879 he spent the summer in Minnesota, assisting by personal direction and advice the creation of the Minnesota Institution for the Feeble-Minded, which is to-day one of the leading institutions of the kind. He was a fellow of the Conn. Medical Society, an honorary member of the medical societies of the states of New York and California. He was medical visitor to the Retreat for the Insane at Hartford, and was the author of ''Hallucinations of Childhood'' (1870). He was married in October, 1850, to Mary Fitch, daughter of Darius Phelps, of Norfolk, Conn., and had two sons, Robert Phelps and George Henry Knight. He died in Fernandina, Fla., Jan. 22, 1880.

KNIGHT, George Henry, physician, was born at Lakeville, Conn., Nov. 24, 1855, son of Dr. Henry Martyn and Mary Fitch (Phelps) Knight. He was educated at the Hopkins Grammar School, New Haven; Williston Seminary, Easthampton, Mass., and Yale College, class of 1877, but left the latter before graduating to begin the study of medicine at the College of Physicians and Surgeons in New York. In 1898 Yale conferred upon him the honorary degree of A.M. and enrolled him

as a regular graduate of his class. In 1879 he was graduated M.D. In that same year the state of Minnesota had enlisted the services of Dr. Henry M. Knight in establishing an experimental institution for the feeble-minded at Faribault, and Dr. George Knight was offered the superintendency. Within a year the legislature voted to make the experiment a permanent addition to its charitable work, and appropriated liberally for the rapidly growing institution at each session during the six years of his service as superintendent. After the death of his father, Dr. Knight took charge of the institution at Lakeville in 1885, where he remained uninterruptedly until his death. He made the study of epilepsy a specialty and obtained results which speedily gave him an international reputation. He was a constant participant in the discussions of the National Conference of Charities and Corrections, and served for years as a member of its executive committee. He was a member of the American Medical Association and various local societies. In 1890 he attended the International Medical Congress in Berlin as the representative of the state of Connecticut. In his later years he became deeply interested in the treatment of tuberculosis and in the problems of eugenics. He advocated the segregation of the feeble-minded and obtained the passage of a law in his own state which makes the marriage of the feeble-minded and of the epileptic a crime. But his greatest genius was manifested in the sane, efficient and helpful management of the affairs under his direction. For years the Lakeville institution had the record of costing less per capita than any other state institution, while it maintained the highest percentage of health of any similar institution in the country. For the last six years or his life Dr. Knight was of service to the Connecticut legislature as the chairman of the committees on public health and safety, humane institutions and appropriations, and influenced important legislation for the betterment of existing conditions in charitable and reformatory work, such as compulsory vaccination, public sanitation, meat inspection, the establishment of a colony for epileptics and a reformatory for boys and, in particular, the acceptance of responsibility by the state for its tubercular poor. He served also on the State Board of Pardons until his death. In addition to his professional duties, he was identified with every public enterprise which served the township or village, and contributed generously to every good cause. Like his father before him, he was greatly beloved and held in universal respect. A man of vigor and decision, he was singularly tolerant, open-minded and friendly. His neighbors, no less than his state, trusted him and sought his judgment. He personified the sterling New England virtues of uprightness, thoughtful generosity, devotedness to duty and capacity for service. He was married, Sept. 16, 1879, to Katherine M., daughter of John Brannon of Cambridge, Mass., and had one daughter, Gertrude Marguerite Knight. He died at Lakeville, Conn., Oct. 4, 1912.

McDONALD, Hunter, civil engineer, was born at Winchester, Va., June 12, 1860, son of Angus William and Cornelia (Peake) McDonald. His earliest paternal American ancestor was Angus McDonald, a native of Scotland, who fled to Virginia after the battle of Culloden, in which he was engaged, and became a merchant and planter; his wife was Anna Thompson, and from them the line of descent is traced through their son Angus and his wife, Ann Linton Lane, who were the grandparents of Hunter McDonald.

Angus McDonald, the settler, engaged in the Indian wars under Governor Dinwiddie; commanded the Wapatonica expedition in Dunmore's war of 1775, and was commissioned lieutenant-colonel in the Colonial army in 1777. His son Angus was captain in the 12th regiment U. S. infantry during the war of 1812. Mr. McDonald's father was graduated at the U. S. Military Academy in 1817; served in garrisons at Mobile and New Orleans until 1819, and then became the agent and inspector of the Missouri Company, spending many years among the Indians on the headwaters of the Missouri river. In 1858 he was sent to England as commissioner to define the boundary line between Maryland and Virginia. At the outbreak of the civil war he organized and became colonel of the regiment in the Confederate army, which was the nucleus of Ashby's Virginia cavalry. He was the inventor and patentee of the railroad track tank, and during 1852–58 made studies in air brakes as applied to railroad trains. Hunter McDonald was educated by his mother until the age of eleven, after which he attended schools at Lexington, Va., until 1873; the Louisville Rugby School, Louisville, Ky., until 1878, and Washington and Lee University until 1879. In the latter year he began his professional career in the engineering department of the Louisville and Nashville Railroad, and near the close of the same year was appointed assistant engineer and payroll clerk of the Nashville, Chattanooga and St. Louis Railway. He was engaged in maintenance of way and construction work until 1889, when, in addition to these duties, he was made division superintendent of the Huntsville division of that road. In 1891 he became resident engineer for the Western and Atlantic Railroad, leased by the Nashville, Chattanooga and St. Louis Railway from the state of Georgia. In 1892 he was appointed chief engineer of the Nashville, Chattanooga and St. Louis Railway. In 1900 that road created a real estate department and he was made real estate agent in addition to his other duties. He is still the road's chief engineer. He was president of the American Railway Engineering and Maintenance of Way Association during 1904–5. In 1889 he assisted in organizing the Engineering Association of the South, of which he subsequently became president. He was elected president of the American Society of Civil Engineers in 1914, and is a member of the National Geographic Society and the Franklin Institute. He became a member of the Advisory Board for Testing Fuels and Structural Materials, created by President Roosevelt, which assisted in the establishment of the present Bureau of Standards. In 1905–06 he organized the Wholesale Merchants' Warehouse Company, of Nashville, which constructed the Cummins Station building in that city, and of which he is general manager. He was the second president of the Nashville Golf and Country Club; is past-president of the Old Oak Club, and member of the Hermitage, Commercial and Rotary clubs, of Nashville. Mr. McDonald was married at Columbia, Tenn., Feb. 8, 1893, to Mary Eloise, daughter of Richard Cross Gordon, of Maury county, Tenn. He has one son: Hunter McDonald, Jr.

VINCENT, George Edgar, president of the University of Minnesota (1911——), was born at Rockford, Ill., Mar. 21, 1864, son of John Heyl (q.v.) and Elizabeth (Dusenbury) Vincent. His father was one of the founders of the Chautauqua Institution, and bishop of the Methodist Episcopal Church. The son attended Pingrey's Academy, Elizabeth, N. J., and was graduated at Yale College in 1885. In 1885-6 he was engaged in newspaper work in New York city. After a journey through Europe and the Orient, in 1886-7, he became literary editor of the Chautauqua press. Since 1888 he has served as vice-president of the Chautauqua system, and he has been principal of instruction since 1898 and president of the Chautauqua Institution since 1907. During 1892-1911 he was a member of the faculty of the University of Chicago. He was fellow in sociology during 1892-4, assistant in 1894-5, instructor in 1895-6, assistant professor during 1896-1900, associate professor during 1900-4, professor during 1904-11, dean of the junior colleges during 1900-7 and dean of the faculties of arts, literature and science during 1907-11. In 1911 he became president of the University of Minnesota. The university, regarded as one of the great educational institutions of the Northwest, now has a total registration of 737 students and comprises a college of science, literature and the arts, a college of engineering and mechanical arts, a college of agriculture, a law school, a medical school, a college of dentistry, a college of pharmacy, a school of chemistry, a school of mines and a college of education. Dr. Vincent is the author of "An Introduction to the Study of Society," with Albion Woodbury Small (1895), and "Social Mind and Education" (1896). The degree of Ph.D. was conferred upon him by the University of Chicago in 1896 and that of LL.D. by the University of Chicago and Yale University in 1911 and by the University of Michigan in 1913. He is a member of the University clubs of New York and Chicago and of various social clubs in Minneapolis and St. Paul. He was married Jan. 8, 1890, to Louise, daughter of Henry W. Palmer, an attorney of Wilkes-Barre, Pa., and their children are: Isabel, wife of Paul W. Harper, John Henry and Elizabeth Vincent.

GODDARD, Henry Herbert, psychologist, was born at Vassalboro, Me., Aug. 14, 1866, son of Henry C. and Sarah (Winslow) Goddard. His earliest paternal American ancestor was William Goddard, who came from England in 1665 and settled at Watertown, Mass. His wife was Elizabeth Miles, and from them the line of descent is traced through their son Joseph and his wife, Deborah Treadwell; their son James and his wife, Mary Woodward; their son James, to his son Israel, who was the grandfather of Henry Herbert Goddard. His maternal grandfather was Elijah Winslow, a direct descendant of Edward Winslow, governor of the Plymouth colony. He received his preliminary education at the Moses Brown School, Providence, R. I., and was graduated at Haverford College in 1887. He received the degree of A. M. from that institution in 1889 after one year of graduate work, and that of Ph.D. from Clark University in 1899 after three years' residence. He spent 1906-7 studying in German universities. In 1899 he began his professional career as professor of psychology at the Pennsylvania State Normal School, West Chester, Pa., remaining in that chair until 1906, when he became psychologist and director of the research laboratory of the Training School, Vineland, N. J., an institution devoted to the care, training and scientific study of "those whose minds have not developed normally." The institution was organized in 1888 under the auspices of an association known as the New Jersey Home for Education and Care of Feeble-Minded Children. The objects of the school were primarily to furnish asylum for mentally defective children, to give them such mental and manual training as

HUNTER McDONALD
CIVIL ENGINEER

GEORGE E. VINCENT
PRESIDENT UNIVERSITY OF MINNESOTA

HENRY H. GODDARD
PSYCHOLOGIST

MORDECAI T. ENDICOTT
CIVIL ENGINEER

James L. Houghteling

they were capable of receiving and to make them as comfortable and happy throughout life as possible. The humanitarian motives which led to the organization of this school found expression in 1906 in the organization of a research laboratory in connection with the Training School, where accurate, comprehensive, scientific study of feeble-mindedness gives promise of invaluable revelations as to the cause of these defects, their amelioration and the methods of prevention. It is proposed to carry on this research work, which has been highly systematized, until the cause of feeble-mindedness is known, until its prevention is understood and until all that can be learned from special cases of mental development has been found out. The result of investigations running throughout six years was partly set forth by Mr. Goddard in a volume entitled "The Kallikak Family" (1912), and was more fully recorded in "Feeble-Mindedness: Its Causes and Consequences" (1914), "School Training of Defective Children" (1914) and "The Criminal Imbecile" (1915). He has devoted his entire time since 1906 to studies into the causes and consequences of feeble-mindedness. He is a member of the American Association for the Advancement of Science, the American Psychological Association, the American Health League, the American Association for the Study of the Feeble-minded (president 1914–15) and the Phi Beta Kappa and Sigma Xi fraternities. He finds his chief recreation in mountain climbing and has made the Matterhorn, Jungfrau, Mont Blanc, and Finsteraarhorn, as well as other peaks in Switzerland, Colorado and the Canadian Rockies. He was married at Winthrop, Me., Aug. 7, 1889, to Emma Florence, daughter of Cyrus Robbins.

DREISER, Theodore, author and journalist, was born in Terre Haute, Ind., Aug. 27, 1871, son of John Paul and Sarah (Schanab) Dreiser. He was educated in the schools of Warsaw, Ind., and the State University of Indiana. In 1892 he entered journalism and for a time was connected with the Chicago "Daily Globe." He then became dramatic editor of the St. Louis "Globe-Democrat" and later traveling correspondent for the St. Louis "Republic." (1893–94). From 1895–97 he edited a literary and musical magaine entitled "Every Month," subsequently engaging in special work for "Harper's," "McClure's," "Scribner's," "Cosmopolitan" and "Munsey's" magazines. He edited "Smith's Magazine" (1905–06), and the following year served as editor of the "Broadway Magazine." In 1907 he became editor-in-chief of the Butterick publications, including the "Delineator," "Designer," "New Idea" and the English "Delineator," continuing in this position until 1910. Mr. Dreiser's published volumes are: "Sister Carrie" (1900); "Jennie Gerhardt" (1911); "The Financier" (1912); "A Traveler at Forty" (1913); "The Titan" (1914) and "The 'Genius'" (1915). He also contributes both prose and verse to the magazines. His stories are written with great care and are remarkable for the analytic qualities which they display as well as for the impression which they convey of the unique and forceful personality of their author. Mr. Dreiser organized the National Child Rescue Campaign in November, 1907. He was a member of the American Social Science Association and of the Salmagundi and Economic clubs. He was married in Washington, D. C., Dec. 28, 1898, to Sarah Osborne, daughter of A. H. White, of St. Louis.

ENDICOTT, Mordecai Thomas, civil engineer and naval officer, was born at May's Landing, N. J., Nov. 26, 1844, son of Thomas Doughty and Ann (Pennington) Endicott. His first paternal American ancestor was the famous John Endicott (q.v.), a native of Dorchester, England, who came over in 1628, settled at Salem, Mass., and was first governor of the Massachusetts Bay Colony. From him the line of descent is traced through his son Zerabbabel, his son Joseph, his son John and his wife, Mary Coslin; their son Benjamin, and his son William and his wife, Hanna Smith, who were the grandparents of Mordecai Thomas Endicott. His father, a native of New Jersey, was a sea captain and vessel owner. Adm. Endicott received his preliminary education privately and at the parochial school of the Presbyterian church at May's Landing, and was graduated at the Rennselaer Polytechnic Institute, Troy, N. Y., in 1868, with the degree of C.E. In the latter year he began his professional career as an assistant to Richard P. Rothwell, a civil and mining engineer of Wilkes-Barre, Pa. He entered the corps of civil engineers of the U. S. navy in 1872, and until 1889 was an engineer officer of various navy yards. Subsequently he was consulting engineer of the bureau of yards and docks of the navy department, and in 1889 he became chief of the bureau, in which capacity he served until 1898. In 1896 he was appointed a member of the Nicaragua Canal Commission and in 1905 he became a member of the Panama Canal Commission. He was placed upon the retired list in 1906. He was a member of the Franklin Institute, honorary member of the Washington Society of Engineers, and president of the American Society of Civil Engineers in 1911. He is a member of the Cosmos and the Army and Navy clubs, Washington, and of the Engineers' Club, New York city. Adm. Endicott was married at Dresden, O., May 29, 1872, to Elizabeth, daughter of George Adams, a farmer and flour mill owner of Dresden, O., and has seven daughters: Maud, Anna, Grace, Elizabeth, Edith, May and Louise Endicott. Portrait opposite page 236.

HOUGHTELING, James Lawrence, capitalist and philanthropist, was born in Chicago, Ill., Nov. 29, 1855, son of William De Zeng and Marcia Elizabeth (Stockbridge) Houghteling. His earliest paternal American ancestor was Jan Willemsen Hoog'eyling, a native of Loosdrecht, Holland, who emigrated in 1661 and settled at Kingston, N. Y. Through him and his wife, Barbara Jans, the line of descent is traced to their son, William Jans, and his wife, Amantje Samuels; their son Philipus and his wife, Jannetje Roosa; their son Wilhelmus (now spelled Hoogteling) and his wife, Blandina Kierstede; their son Abraham and his wife, Catherina Hasbereck; their son Jacobus (now spelled Hooghteling) and his wife, Ernestine F. A. J. De Zeng, who were the grandparents of the subject. All of them were good citizens and highly respected in the community, the ancestors on the distaff side as well as the direct belonging to the most distinguished Dutch stock of the New World. The maternal grandparents of the subject were John and Eliza (Russell) Stockbridge, of Bath, Me., the former a practicing physician. The father (1819–98) of our subject, first of the line to spell the name Houghteling, was a manufacturer, and a man noted for his sterling honesty and public spirit. James Lawrence Houghteling received his preliminary education in the public schools of Chicago. He was graduated at Yale University in 1876. The following year he began his business career in Chicago as an employee of the Menominee River Lumber Co., becoming secretary of that concern in 1879, and in 1882 treasurer of the Mackinaw Lumber Co., the Black River Lumber Co. and the Lumberman's Mining Co. In 1885 he became a member of the important Chicago banking house of Peabody, Houghteling & Co., his partner being his father-in-law, Francis Bolles Peabody. He was also an officer and director in sundry other commercial, industrial and lumber companies. He was particularly active in the Episcopal Church, also in non-partisan movements in Chicago and throughout the country, and one of the founders of the Municipal Voters' League. He was a founder of the Brotherhood of St. Andrew. On St. Andrew's Day, 1883, twelve young men, with the approval of their rector, Rev. W. H. Vibbert, D.D., and under the leadership of Mr. Houghteling, who was the teacher of the parish Bible class, agreed to follow the example set by St. Andrew in bringing St. Peter into a personal acquaintance with the Messiah. To guide their efforts they adopted two rules: To pray daily for the spread of Christ's kingdom among young men; and to make an earnest effort each week to bring at least one young man within the hearing of the Gospel. Their efforts were so successful that information about the work spread from place to place and similar guilds were formed in several dioceses. In 1886 thirty-five of these scattered parochial guilds united in a general organization known as the Brotherhood of St. Andrew in the Protestant Episcopal Church in the United States. There are now in the United States 1,511 parochial branches, or chapters, with a total membership of about 20,000 men. There are now National Brotherhoods in Canada, England, Scotland, Australia, the West Indies and other countries of the Anglican communion. Mr. Houghteling was president of the Brotherhood of St. Andrew during 1887–99, president of the Chicago Young Men's Christian Association during 1881–84, and member of the Commercial, Union League and University clubs, of Chicago, also the Onwentsia and other golf and country clubs of that city and its environs. He was a righteous man who lived in accordance with the noblest and purest standards of religion. To that firm foundation of righteousness was added the qualities that indicate the great business man, the loyal, devoted, kindly, generous and modest friend of all who came within his influence. He had come to be regarded as something much more than manufacturer and capitalist and useful, high-minded citizen. He was regarded almost as the visible embodiment of the life of the community in which he pursued his career. His great heart responded to every appeal made to his generous nature, and responded in whole-hearted devotion to ideals that were never dimmed nor tarnished. He was married in Chicago, Ill., Sept. 20, 1879, to Lucretia Ten Broeck, daughter of Francis B. Peabody, of Chicago. His six surviving children are: Francis S., James L., Jr., Harriot, William, Leila and Margaret Stuyvesant. James Lawrence Houghteling died at his country home, in Winnetka, Ill., July 28, 1910.

WHARTON, John Austin, lawyer and soldier, was born in Texas, July 5, 1829, son of William H. Wharton. His father and uncle were both prominent in the Texas revolution against Mexico. He was graduated at the University of South Carolina in 1850 and, after studying law with Harris & Jack in Galveston, practised his profession with Clinton Terry at Brazoria, and with James Masterson at Houston. He was elected district attorney in 1859, and was a delegate to the convention that passed the ordinance of secession in 1861. Upon the outbreak of the civil war he became a captain in Terry's Texas Rangers, and when Col. Terry fell at Woodsonville, Ky., Wharton was elected colonel. He was wounded at Shiloh, April 6, 1862, and again when Forrest captured Murfreesboro, Tenn., July 13, 1862. For distinguished services during Bragg's invasion of Kentucky in 1862 he was made brigadier-general. His services through the campaign that culminated in the battle of Murfreesboro, and before and during the battle of Chickamauga, brought him the rank of major-general and his selection to command the cavalry of the Trans-Mississippi department. Gen. Wharton was married Feb. 25, 1851, to Penelope, daughter of David Johnson, governor of South Carolina. In a personal difficulty with an officer of his command he was killed at Houston, Tex., Apr. 6, 1865.

KEENE, James Robert, financier, was born in London, England, Apr. 25, 1832, son of James and Cecelia Jeanetta (Gaughenlaugh) Keene. His father, who was of North of Ireland ancestry, was a merchant. The son was educated in a private school in Lincolnshire, and afterward in Dublin, in the home of a friend of his father, an old professor of Trinity College, and throughout his life was a pronounced advocate of the benefits of a classical education. Financial reverses overtook his father, and in 1850 the family came to America and settled in San Francisco, Cal. Young Keene was employed at different times at caring for horses, in freighting, milling, mining and school teaching. Following the discovery of the Comstock Lode he went to Virginia City, Nev., where he soon accumulated a small fortune by judicious speculation. Returning to San Francisco he owned and edited the San Francisco "Examiner" for two years and studied and practiced law. He began to speculate in the Mining Exchange, operating in Nevada mining stocks, which were the active feature of that market. He did well for a time, but when one of the Comstock mines failed at the lower levels confidence fled, prices sank, and business depression brought disaster to nearly all stock dealers in that market. Mr. Keene's fortune was swept away with that of others, and not until nearly two years later, when the market had recovered, was he able to resume his operations. His reputation as a sagacious speculator was already established. Among the men who were impressed by his talent was Cornelius N. Felton (q. v.), then one of the most powerful stock operators on the Pacific coast. Mr. Felton commissioned young Keene to handle his business, and, when Felton became the assistant treasurer of the United States, he sold his seat on the exchange to Mr. Keene, who soon revealed himself as the most skillful and masterly member of that organization, and was elected its president. His remarkable bear campaign against the inflated stock of the Bonanza mines netted him $3,000,000. He organized the syndicate to protect the depositors of the Bank of California when that institution failed, and was one of the four contributors to the guarantee fund of $8,000,000 that saved the bank. His daring and astuteness in speculation made for him a record of brilliant success that has not been equaled on the San Francisco exchange. In 1877 he started for the East with the purpose of visiting Europe, but found the New York stock market too attractive to resist, and he postponed his holiday indefinitely. No man in the New York market ever demonstrated a more notable mastery of tactics, an ampler outlook or a more balanced judgment than Mr. Keene. In the financial struggles of Wall street has appeared no abler strategist. Many of the greatest movements in New York's financial history were intrusted to him. Subsequent to 1884 he was involved in large financial operations with J. Pierpont Morgan, John W. Gates, the Standard Oil Co. and the United States Steel Co., and he is known to have had charge of a number of important pooling arrangements, including Sugar, National Cordage, Third Avenue railroad, Brooklyn Rapid Transit, Tobacco, Metropolitan Street Railway and Hocking. When in a campaign extending over two years, from 1895 to 1897, Mr. Keene created a market for sugar stocks it was regarded as a work which even more signally exhibited his unusual ability than the initial market which he opened for United States Steel in 1901. With like surpassing generalship he managed the early upward movements in Amalgamated Copper in 1905. An achievement still more noteworthy, in celerity, silence and completeness, was the startling *coup* by which was secured the control of the Northern Pacific railway. Mr. Keene was one of the most successful of American turfmen, and his breeding farm at Castleton, near Lexington, Ky., was famous throughout the world. The great Sysonby headed his stable, and among his other horses were such celebrated winners as Domino, Voter, Ballot, Colin, Superman, Delhi, Conroy, Hornpipe, Celt, Maskette, Sweep and Peter Pan. For many years he was prominently represented in most of the great races of England and France, winning with his horse Foxhall the Grand Prix at Paris in 1881, and the Cesarewitch and Cambridge stakes at Newmarket; he also won the English Oaks in 1901 with his filly Cap and Bells. Every year, from 1905 to 1909, his name headed the list of winners, and in 1907 his winnings aggregated $500,000, thereby eclipsing the record previously held by the Duke of Portland. He won the Futurity and the Brooklyn handicap five times each. He was one of the cleanest sportsmen on the American turf and did more than any of his contemporaries to uphold the reputation of the sport in America. It is safe to say that if all American horsemen had been of the same type as James R. Keene, horse-racing would never have declined to the point it has now reached in this country. In 1893 he began to agitate the subject of reform in racing matters by advocating the establishment of a central authority for the government of racing. He made a thorough study of the English racing system, which embodied the experience and views of the ablest English horsemen for 150 years, and he urged the adoption of that system in the United States. The result was the establishment of the Jockey Club, of which Mr. Keene was vice-president; he was also one of the working members of its board of stewards, and through his wide acquaintance with racing rules and practices exerted a strong and healthful influence on turf methods. Mr. Keene's philanthropies were very numerous, but he never wished his charities to be discussed nor, if possible, known; he strove to conceal his benevolence, which was as quick as it was deep and spontaneous. He was widely read in science, art, literature and economics and made the best thought of the age a part of his own mental equipment. His word he held sacred, and a promise once given was scrupulously performed. He was married in San Francisco, Cal., in 1860, to Sara Jay, daughter of Col. Leroy Daingerfield, of Virginia, and a sister of Judge William P. Daingerfield, of the United States circuit court of California. There were two children: Foxhall Parker and Jessica Harwar,

wife of Talbot J. Taylor. He died in New York city, Jan. 3, 1913.

BROWN, Samuel Queen, oil operator, was born at Pleasantville, Venango co., Pa., Sept. 19, 1835, son of John and Mary (Queen) Brown. His father was a pioneer settler in Pennsylvania, having removed from New York city and located at Pleasantville in 1833. He was prepared for a clerical course at Alleghany College, Meadville, Pa., but was obliged to leave at the close of the freshman year because of failing health. Subsequently he took the course at Duff's Commercial College, Pittsburgh, Pa., and then joined his father at Pleasantville in the management of a country store which had now grown to a business of large proportions. In 1859, shortly after the discovery of petroleum in Pennsylvania, he formed a partnership with one of his neighbors and obtained control of the Buchanan farm at the mouth of Cherry Run in Rouseville, Pa. The partners were joined by Henry R. Rouse, of Enterprise, who had already taken an interest with W. H. Abbott and others of Titusville. This firm completed the second well to find oil. Messrs. Brown and Mitchell kicked down a "spring pole" well, the third on Oil Creek, that pumped ten barrels a day from the first sand, but being drilled to the third sand later produced 300 barrels a day for a long period. After the death of Mr. Rouse, the management of the property vested principally in Mr. Brown. When nearly a hundred wells had been drilled by themselves and sub-leases, Mr. Brown put both farms into the Buchanan Farms Oil Co., with a capital stock of $4,000,000, realizing $1,000,000 from his share. He at once established a broker's office in Philadelphia, and the following year opened another office in New York, where he dealt extensively in oil stocks, traveling by night from one city to the other, and giving alternate days to each office. While in the brokerage business he obtained a charter for the Farmers' railroad, from Oil City to Shaffer in Pennsylvania, and in 1862 secured a charter for a pipe line from Tarr farm to Oil City. Along with his other activities at this time Mr. Brown and his two brothers opened a store at Oil City and in 1866 he became a partner in a large mercantile house in New York, continuing the Pleasantville store as a wholesale and retail branch. When oil was discovered near Pleasantville, he took an active part in the development of the territory, including several hundred acres of his own lands. He opened a bank in Pleasantville which later became the Pleasantville Banking Co., of which he was president. In 1872, following the agitation against the South Improvement Co., he was elected a trustee of the Petroleum Producers' Agency, and later a member of the business committee of that organization. He was an active operator in the Enterprise district, assisting at the same time in organizing the Seaboard Pipe Line, and in 1878 he was a leader in the organization of the Tide-Water Pipe Line Co., Ltd. He took charge of the financial management of the Chester (Pa.) Oil Co., a tide water refinery with headquarters in Philadelphia. In 1889 the line was extended to Bayonne, N. J., with headquarters in New York. He was a manager of that company from 1886 to his death, and president during 1893–1908. He was elected president of the Tide Water Oil Co. when it was organized in 1888 and continued in that office until May, 1908, when he was elected chairman of the board of directors and remained so until his death. He was also a director of the Associated Producers Co. during 1894-1908, and was its president from 1903-1908. In all of these companies Mr. Brown was a strong factor in their success and his executive ability was shown by the phenomenal success of the Tide Water companies during the fifteen years he was the chief executive. He was married July 11, 1865, to Nancy, daughter of John Lamb of Pleasantville, Pa., and had four children: Louise, wife of James D. Voorhees; Dickson Queen, Florence and Margery Brown. He received in 1871 the honorary degree A. M. from Princeton University. He represented the petroleum interests on the Second Geological Survey Commission of the State of Pennsylvania. He was a Republican in politics and a member of the Union League Club, New York city, and various other clubs. He gave generously to the churches where he resided, not only to the Presbyterian, to which he belonged, but to all other denominations. He was a man who furthered every enterprise designed to secure the welfare of his neighbors and his fellow men and he was noted among his business associates for his steadfast integrity. He died in New York, Oct. 5, 1909.

MAY, Frederick John, physician and surgeon, was born in Washington, D. C., May 19, 1812, son of Dr. Frederick May (q. v.). He was educated at Columbian College, Washington, D. C., being graduated A. B. in 1831 and M. D. in 1834, and after a period in the leading hospitals of London and Paris he opened an office in Washington for the practice of his profession. He was professor of anatomy and physiology at Columbian College during 1839–41 when he was transferred to the chair of principles and practice of surgery. Resigning in 1858, he was appointed to the chair of surgery in the Shelby Medical College, Nashville, Tenn. He was one of the first surgeons in America to amputate with success at the hip joint, and the first in Nashville to perform ovariotomy. He resided in New York city for a number of years after the civil war, and then removed to Washington. In 1884 he was elected surgeon on the consulting staff of Garfield Memorial Hospital, Washington. He died in that city May 2, 1891.

JEMISON, Mary, Indian captive, was born on the Atlantic ocean while her parents, who were probably natives of Ireland, were emigrating to America in the winter of 1742-43. Her father took a farm on the western border of Pennsylvania and was enjoying the fruits of prosperity until the outbreak of the French and Indian war. The family was taken captive by the Indians, and all but Mary and a brother were killed. Her captors, Shawnee Indians, gave her to a tribe of the Seneca nation, who treated her with fond kindness and made her life as happy as possible. She married a Delaware Indian, whom she described as a "noble man." After his death she married an Indian named Hiokatoo. She became reconciled to her Indian life and refused opportunities when they came to return to people of her own race. The Indians held her in profound respect and in 1797 granted to her by deed a large tract of the choicest land in the Genesee valley, comprising nearly 18,000 acres, known as the Gardeau reservation. Here she lived in seclusion until the white settlers became too numerous, when she sold her property and resided in Buffalo with her married daughter and five grandchildren. Besides this daughter, who married a George Shongo, she had a son by her first marriage, Thomas Jemison. The facts of her extraordinary life were first obtained from her and published by James E. Seaver in 1824. Subsequently Mrs. Asher Wright, who with her husband labored for years among the Indians of western New York, gathered much additional information about Mary Jemison, from which she drew this conclusion: "From all I have learned of her from those who were for years contemporary with her, she possessed great fortitude and self-control; was cautious and prudent in all her conduct; had a kind and tender heart; was hospitable, generous and faithful in all her duties as a wife and mother." A statue by Bush-Brown, entitled "The White Woman," was erected by William Pryor Letchworth near her grave in Letchworth Park, N. Y., in 1910. She died in Buffalo, N. Y., in September, 1833.

KEYT, Alonzo Thrasher, physician, was born at Higginsport, O., Jan. 10, 1827, son of Nathan and Mary (Thrasher) Keyt. His father was of Dutch descent, and his mother came from a Quaker family descended from Edward Penn, of Pennsylvania. In his youth the family removed to Moscow, O., and after an academic education he began the study of medicine and received his M. D. degree at the Ohio Medical College in 1848. He began practicing in Cincinnati, O. In 1873 Dr. Keyt's attention was attracted to the consideration of the graphic method in the portrayal of the movements of the circulation. He first experimented with M. Mavy's spring instrument, but it did not take long to discover that the spring did not furnish all the undulations of the blood-column to the slide. To elucidate the problems of the circulation, a double instrument was required—one that would take two tracings, the heart and an artery, or two arteries, the one above the other, upon the slide, with a chronographic trace below, so that the time could be recorded and the difference in time between the two tracings computed. Such a mechanism Dr. Keyt devised, a cardiograph and sphygmograph combined, which he termed the compound sphymograph. This invention has stood the test of time, and is today the best adapted for its purpose. A scheme was arranged, by means of which lesions of the miral and aortic cardiac orifices were represented and their relations to pulse-wave velocity. The developments were recorded by the compound sphygmograph, and the results secured have been confirmed by graphic tracings of clinical cases. These experimental researches formed the basis of a series of articles in the "Journal of the American Medical Association" for 1883, and their results were published in "Sphygmography and Cardiography" (1887), which is an enduring monument to his industry and genius. To him is due the discovery that abnormal delay of the pulse-wave follows upon mitral regurgitation. Dr. Keyt was married Oct. 10, 1848, to Susannah D. Hamlin, by whom he had seven children. He died in Cincinnati, O., Nov. 9, 1885.

ROBINSON, Edward Arlington, poet, was born at Head Tide, Me., Dec. 22, 1869, son of Edward and Mary E. (Palmer) Robinson, of New England ancestry. His father was a shipwright and carpenter of literary tastes and studious habits, of whom it was said that he spent twelve hours a day at work in the shipyard and then went home and read the classics until midnight. The son showed plainly the inheritance of this literary taste, with the difference that he displayed also the creative instinct which his father lacked. His parents had moved to Gardiner, Me., while he was still a child, and he received his education at the public schools there. In 1891-93 he took a two-years' special literary course at Harvard University and subsequently became secretary to Pres. Charles S. Eliot. He held that post for only a few months, though he remained in Cambridge for the next three years, absorbing its literary atmosphere and cultivating still more the esoteric quality which has always been apparent in his work. In 1896 he published privately his first book, containing two poems, "The Torrent" and "The Night Before," and in the following year he published a collection of about fifty short poems, under the title of "The Children of the Night." They confirmed the impression of those who knew him that he was a poet of originality and sincerity of thought and expression, but a poet for the discriminating few rather than the many. "The Children of the Night" won the praise of the cognoscenti, even of such a meticulous authority as Edmund Clarence Stedman, who proclaimed its author "a new poet of an individual cast of thought." In 1900 Mr. Robinson settled in New York. Two years later appeared his "Captain Craig, a Book of Poems," which was followed in 1910 by "The Town Down the River." Although the former went through two editions it was not until 1905 that Mr. Robinson was made known to the public at large, when Theodore Roosevelt in "The Outlook" proclaimed him the foremost American poet of this era. His publishers, alive to the commercial possibilities of such an announcement, republished "The Children of the Night" and sold several editions, while its author retired still farther from the public gaze. For three years he held a place in the New York Custom House by appointment of Pres. Roosevelt, and since then he has lived in retirement in New Hampshire. His "The Man Against the Sky" appeared in 1916. The fundamental characteristic of Mr. Robinson as a poet is his intense and sincere interest in the vital problems of every-day life. In a limited sense only is he a dreamer. He is not nebulous nor mystic, neither is he romantic nor sentimental. He is very representative of his race, or rather of the Anglo-Saxon race. His point of view is the Anglo-Saxon point of view. He looks at life squarely and practically; he does not wrap it in the rosy cloud of poetic idealism nor in the gloomy pall of decadent pessimism. To him life is real, earnest and serious, and he interprets it that way. His view and his interpretation are quite comprehensive to any one, but the manner of his interpretation is still too exquisite for the general public. He is ranked by some of his warmest admirers as second among the present-day American poets to the late William Vaughan Moody. Probably neither of these is as yet understood by the people. He has been described by his critics as a true optimist, a true realist and a master of style.

STEWART, Samuel Vernon, sixth governor of Montana, was born in Monroe county, Pa., Aug. 2, 1872, son of John W. and Maria A. (Carle) Stewart. When eleven years of age he removed with his parents to Coffey county, Kan., and located near the town of Waverly. He lived the life of the average farm boy, devoting his time between the seasons of active work on the farm to the laying of the foundation of an education. Desiring greater advantages than the rural schools could afford him, he entered the Kansas Normal School at Fort Scott, and after remaining there one year, spent two years in the State Normal School at Emporia. He then entered the law department of the Kansas University at Lawrence, where he was graduated in 1898, and subsequently began the practice of his profession at Virginia City, Mont. He has been prominent in the activities of the Democratic party in Montana since his arrival in that state. In 1904 he was elected county

attorney of Madison county, and occupied that office for two terms. He was chosen chairman of the state central committee in 1910, which position he filled until he entered the campaign that resulted in his election as governor of Montana in 1912 for the term ending Dec. 31, 1916. He is affiliated with a number of fraternal organizations, stands high in all of the Masonic bodies, having held the state presidency of the Eagles, and is identified with the Elks and Modern Woodmen of America. Gov. Stewart was married April 27, 1905, to Stella D., daughter of William R. Baker, of Booneville, Mo. They have three daughters: Emily, Marjorie and Leah Stewart. Portrait opposite page 242.

COMSTOCK, Anthony, reformer, was born at New Canaan, Fairfield co., Conn., Mar. 7, 1844, son of Thomas A. and Polly Ann (Lockwood) Comstock and a descendant of Christopher Comstock, one of the founders of Norwalk, Conn., in 1640. After attending the academy in New Canaan and the high school in New Britain, he obtained employment as a clerk in a country store. When his brother, Samuel Comstock, who had enlisted in the 17th Connecticut regiment for the civil war, lost his life at the battle of Gettysburg, Anthony volunteered to take his place in the regiment, and he served in the department of the South under Gen. Gilmore until the war closed. In 1872, while employed as a salesman in New York, his attention was directed to the baneful effects of gambling, lotteries and obscene literature upon young men and was moved to take some action against the evil. Through an appeal to the Young Men's Christian Association, Morris K. Jesup heard of his plan and agreed to help him. Jesup formed a committee to supervise his work, and in 1872 the New York Society for the Suppression of Vice was chartered, with Morris K. Jesup president and Anthony Comstock secretary. The object of the society was the enforcement of the national and state laws for suppressing obscene literature, licentious pictures and indecent advertisements, and its support has ever been by voluntary contributions. In March, 1873, owing chiefly to his personal efforts, congress enacted a law closing the mails to obscene and indecent matter of all kinds, and he was appointed a special post-office inspector, and was reappointed each year thereafter until his death. He also fathered many national and state laws against such evils as lotteries and "green-goods" circulars. Armed thus by legal authority, he began, almost singlehanded, a lifelong crusade that has undoubtedly had considerable effect in raising the moral standard of the nation. He destroyed more than fifty tons of obscene books, four million objectionable pictures and seventeen thousand photographic negatives for printing such pictures, and he caused the arraignment of some four thousand persons, of whom twenty-five hundred either pleaded guilty or were convicted. Year after year he met with the bitterest opposition, misrepresentation, and even personal assaults, and had great difficulty in preventing the repeal of the laws under which he worked. His excessive zeal for his work at times caused errors of judgment, as in the case of Paul Chabas' nude painting, "September Morn." By threatening to arrest an art dealer who had the original painting on exhibition, the public's attention was drawn to an innocent and beautiful work of art, and it was copied and parodied from one end of the nation to the other. Mr. Comstock was the author of "Frauds Exposed" (1880); "Traps for the Young" (1883); "Gambling Outrages"

(1887); "Morals vs. Art" (1889). He was married Jan. 25, 1872, to Margaret, daughter of John Hamilton, of Brooklyn, N. Y., and had one daughter, Adele Comstock. He died in Summit, N. J., Sept. 21, 1915.

SCOVELL, Melville Amasa, scientist and educator, was born at Belvidere, N. J., Feb. 26, 1855, son of Nathan S. and Hannah (Aller) Scovell. His earliest paternal American ancestor was John Scovell, who came from the south of England prior to 1672 and settled at Farmington, Conn.; his wife was Sarah Barnes, and from them the line of descent is traced through their son Benjamin; his son Nathan and his wife, Elizabeth Gates; their son Nathan and his wife, Ruth Harris, to their son Nathan and his wife, Hannah Black, who were the grandparents of Melville Amasa Scovell. He was a descendant of several early settlers of Plymouth, Connecticut and Rhode Island. He received his preliminary education in the public and high schools of Champaign, Ill., and was graduated at the University of Illinois in 1875 with the degree of B.S. He remained with the university for seven years after graduation, being successively instructor in chemistry, assistant professor, and later professor of agricultural chemistry. He received from that institution the degree of M.S. in 1877 and Ph.D. in 1906. While at the university he gave considerable study to the production of sugar from sorghum, working out (with Prof. H. A. Weber) a method for obtaining sugar from this plant in quantities which at prevailing prices was thought profitable. During 1883-4 he was superintendent of the Kansas Sugar Works, Sterling, Kan., and in 1885 was special agent for the U. S. department of agriculture in the erection of diffusion batteries for extracting sugar from sorghum and sugar cane in Kansas and Louisiana. Also in 1885 he was elected director of the newly established Kentucky Agricultural Experiment Station, where he enjoyed a continuous period of service for twenty-seven years. The equipment of that station was provided in large measure from its earnings. At the time of his death the revenue reached $200,000. For many years, by economy, he managed to save from these earnings funds needed for building up the physical equipment. With the reorganization of the state university, in 1910, he accepted the additional task of directing the college of agriculture. He was prominently identified with the leading national movements for agricultural advancement. As one of the leading members of the Association of American Agricultural Colleges he supervised the tests of dairy cows at the World's Columbian Exposition. He was an expert in dairy cattle and was much in demand as a judge at fairs. He was selected to establish the famous herd of Jersey cattle at Elmendorf Farm, Kentucky. He was a member of the U. S. food standards committee, a fellow of the American Association for the Advancement of Science, and a member of the Society for the Promotion of Agricultural Science, the American Chemical Society, the Society of Chemical Industry, London; the International Congress of Applied Chemists; past president of the American Association of Official Agricultural Chemists and a member of its committee on food standards; a member of the American Academy of Political and Social Science; past secretary, treasurer and president of the American Association of Agricultural College and Experiment Stations; past secretary of the Mississippi Valley Cane Growers' Association; a director of the American Jersey Cattle Club; past president of the Lexington (Ky.) Park

Commission; member of the Kentucky State Board of Agriculture; director of the Kentucky State Fair Association; a member of the National Dairy Association, the American Poultry Association, the National Pure Food and Dairy Association, the American Breeders' Association, the Kentucky Grange; president of the Lake Ellerslie Fishing Club; member of the Lexington Country Club and the Phi Delta Theta and Alpha Zeta fraternities. His published contributions and papers include more than two hundred titles, many of which may be found in the bulletins of the Kentucky Agricultural Experiment Station. He was married at Monticello, Ill., Sept. 8, 1880, to Nancy, daughter of Hon. Chester P. Davis, of Monticello. He died near Lexington, Ky., Aug. 15, 1912.

PORTER, Gene Stratton, author and illustrator, was born on a farm in Wabash county, Ind., in 1868, the daughter of Mark and Mary (Shallenbarger) Stratton. Her first paternal American ancestor was Mark Stratton who came from England in 1700 and lived in New York, where he married the famous beauty, Ann Hancock, and later settled on Stratton Island, afterward corrupted to Staten, according to family tradition. From Mark Stratton the line is traced through his son Daniel and the latter's wife Mary Sharp; and their son Joseph and his wife Elizabeth Perrigo, who were the grandparents of the author. Her mother was of Dutch extraction, and like all Dutch women had a passionate love of flowers which the daughter inherited. The daughter, in fact, loved all living things, and very early roamed in the woods, watched the birds, fed butterflies, made pets of the squirrels and rabbits, collected wild flowers, and as she grew older she gathered arrow points and goose quills for sale in Fort Wayne. Such schooling as she had was from private sources. Marriage, a home of her own, and a child filled the author's hands for a time. In her spare time she mastered photography, and began to write "nature studies sugar coated with fiction." Her stories were accepted by "Recreation," "Outing," "The World's Work" and "Country Life," and in 1903 appeared her first book, "The Song of the Cardinal," which she herself illustrated with the most complete series of photographic studies from life ever made of a pair of birds. It is the love story of a pair of birds and has probably done more for the protection of birds than any other one book ever published. It was followed by "Freckles" (1904), a book of natural history with a slender love story running through it; "What I Have Done With Birds" (1907); a book of ornithology and bird photography, also illustrated by the author; "At the Foot of the Rainbow" (1907); "A Girl of the Limberlost" (1909); "Birds of the Bible" (1909); a valuable contribution to bird science and to the literature of the Bible; "Music of the Wild" (1910), "The Harvester" (1911); "Moths of the Limberlost" (1912); "Laddie" (1913), and "Michael O'Halloran" (1915)—all have gained wide audiences and a circulation of more than 3,000,000 copies. Behind her nature books there lie always the exact knowledge of the scientist, the enthusiasm of the nature lover and the imaginative feeling of the author who sees with a poet's eyes, and all her books possess the qualities that make for great popularity. The gradual disappearance of the Limberlost Swamp under the encroachments of business, caused Mrs. Porter's removal some time ago to the head of the swamp in Noble county, Indiana, where a new cabin was built and where she makes her home. Love of nature and

SAMUEL V. STEWART
GOVERNOR

ANTHONY COMSTOCK
REFORMER

MRS. GENE STRATTON PORTER
AUTHOR

MELVILLE A. SCOVELL
SCIENTIST

Edward Mann

persistence in the pursuit of an idea are her leading characteristics, while her favorite diversion is growing wild flowers. She is a member of the National Geographic and Audubon societies, and is vice-president of the woman's branch of the Chicago Press Club. She was married April 22, 1886, to Charles Darwin Porter, son of Dr. John Pomeroy Porter, of Decatur, Ind., surgeon U. S. A., and they have one daughter, Jeanette, wife of G. Blaine Monroe.

WISNER, Edward, known as the "Father of Reclamation," was born at Athens, Mich., Feb. 27, 1860, son of Jehiel and Harriette (Deming) Wisner. He received a grammar school education, and during the early part of his career taught school at Newton, Mich. For two years he was principal of a school at Tekonsha, and later he engaged in banking and in newspaper work at Athens and Saugatuck, Mich. He was especially devoted to newspaper work, but failing health compelled him to abandon it and his banking business in 1888 and go South. Settling in Franklin parish, northern Louisiana, he began to deal in land, timber and cotton, and established a bank at Delhi as a side issue. He purchased 5,000 acres of Louisiana land and founded the town in Franklin parish below Winnsboro which bears his name. His bank was affected in the panic of 1893, and in an endeavor to protect the interests of his depositors he lost every dollar he had acquired. Noting the value of timber lands he secured options upon successive tracts and induced friends and investors in the North to purchase and profit. His fondness for geology had already led him to investigate the wet lands of Louisiana, and he became convinced that the combination of the humus of the delta of the lower river with the continuous deposit of silt which the Mississippi had seized in sweeping by the farm states of the upper valley offered the most fertile lands in the world. A study of reclamation, as accomplished in Holland, Denmark and other countries, convinced him that redemption could also be achieved here at a cost much less than Europe had paid and far below the price of irrigating poorer lands in the West. At the time he began his operations in the wet fields of southern Louisiana the prairie or swamp lands were considered worthless. However, in spite of discouragement from various sources, he acquired in a brief period about 1,350,000 acres scattered over Terrebonne, Lafourche, Jefferson, St. Charles, St. John, Plaquemines, St. Bernard and other parishes. Some of this land he purchased for as little as twelve-and-one-half cents an acre; several years later the price of similar land had risen to twenty dollars. Mr. Wisner began active operations in land reclamation in 1902, organizing the Louisiana Meadows Co., of which he was president, and as the head of that organization he perfected measures that brought into use thousands of acres of wet land now occupied by families from the North and West. He did not wait for the completion of one project before he began another, and, despite all obstacles, delivered a vast empire to the plow, brought farmers to the land, guided them to success, and derived a profit that paid in some degree for his splendid creative leadership. Though Mr. Wisner modestly disclaimed originality in the conviction that the wet lands could be easily converted into farms, he was the first man who initiated the work on a scale of magnitude that promises to double the cultivable area of the state. Largely as a result of his foresight, energy and ability, it is now evident that a vast acreage, which was for years regarded as practically waste land,

will be brought under profitable cultivation. As the author of various admirable and convincing articles in favor of the development of the country surrounding New Orleans, he was an undoubted factor in stimulating the movement to make that city a great truck and fruit-growing region. He was married June 17, 1885, to Mary J., daughter of Holland Rowe, of Athens, Mich., and had two children: Harriett Rowena, wife of Harry Peneguey, and Clarissa Elizabeth Wisner. Mr. Wisner died in New Orleans, La., Mar. 8, 1915.

ALTHOFF, Henry, second Roman Catholic bishop of the diocese of Belleville, Ill., was born at Aviston, Ill., Aug. 30, 1873. His classical and philosophical studies were made at Teutopolis, Ill., and at St. Francis Solanus' College, Quincy, Ill., whence he passed to the University of Innsbruck, Austria, for his theological course. Here he was ordained priest on July 26, 1902, by the Prince Bishop Simon Aichner. Returning to his native diocese he served for a time as assistant priest at St. Henry's Church, East St. Louis; pastor at Damiansville, Ill., and in 1908 was given charge of St. Barbara's Church, Okaville, Ill. He remained there for five years until named as the successor of Bishop John Janssen, of Belleville, who died in 1913. Bishop Althoff was consecrated by Archbishop Quigley in the cathedral, Belleville, on Feb. 24, 1914. The Catholic population of the diocese of Belleville is 71,500, and to assist him he has 127 priests officiating in 147 churches and chapels. There are eighty-three high schools, academies and parish schools with 10,320 pupils; one orphan asylum with 193 inmates; eleven hospitals and four homes for the aged. The diocese covers an area of 11,678 square miles in that part of Illinois south of St. Clair, Clinton, Marion, Clay, Richland and Lawrence counties.

DORAN, Thomas Francis, titular bishop of Halicarnassus and auxiliary bishop of the Roman Catholic diocese of Providence, R. I., was born in Barrington, R. I., Oct. 4, 1856, son of James and Catherine (Nolan) Doran. After attending the schools of his native town he went to Mount St. Mary's College, Emmetsburg, Md., and was graduated there with the class of 1876. He returned to the seminary of the same institution for his theological course and was on its completion ordained priest in St. Charles' Church, Woonsocket, R. I., on July 4, 1880, by Bishop Hendricken. All his sacerdotal life he was prominently identified with the activities of the church in the state of Rhode Island as a member of many of the corporations controlling the charitable and educational institutions of the diocese of Providence. He was pastor of St. Joseph's Church in that city for fifteen years and was vicar-general of the diocese for more than twenty years when he was made auxiliary bishop. Previously Pope Pius X had honored him with the dignity of Domestic Prelate and Prothonotary Apostolic. He was consecrated bishop in Sts. Peter and Paul's Cathedral, Providence, by Bishop Harkins, on Apr. 27, 1915, and died in Providence, Jan. 3, 1916.

MILES, Manly, scientist, was born at Homer, Cortland co., N. Y., July 20, 1826, son of Manly and Mary (Cushman) Miles. His father was a soldier in the revolutionary war and a lineal descendant of Miles Standish. He was brought up on his father's farm in Flint, Mich., improving every opportunity to read and study. His neighbors came to know him as "the boy with a book," and he had the reputation of never failing to accomplish anything he undertook. He was graduated M. D. at Rush Medical College in 1850, and practised his profession at Flint until 1859, when he was appointed assistant state geologist. A year later he became professor of animal physiology and zoology in the Michigan State Agricultural College at Lansing. In 1864 the duties of acting superintendent of the farm were added to his chair, while a year later he was made professor of animal physiology, practical agriculture and farm superintendent, being the first professor of practical agriculture in the United States. In all agricultural subjects he was far in advance of his day. In 1875 he resigned to accept the chair of agriculture in the Illinois State University. He held the same position at the Massachusetts Agricultural College, Amherst, from 1880 until 1886, when he returned to Lansing and devoted his last years to study and authorship. He was an authority among both professors and students on birds, beasts, reptiles, insects and stones of the field. He discovered two new shells, and two others were named after him by Lea. In teaching agriculture he aroused such enthusiasm among the students that they regarded it a favor to work with him in the fields. He contributed numerous articles to the "American Agriculturalist," "Popular Science Monthly" and other scientific journals, and was the author of "Stock Breeding," "Experiments with Indian Corn," "Silos and Ensilage" and "Land Drainage." He was a fellow of the American Association for the Advancement of Science and the Royal Microscopical Society and a member of the Michigan State Medical Society and the Buffalo Society of Natural Science. He was married Feb. 15, 1851, to Mary E. Dodge, of Lansing, and died at Lansing, Mich., Feb. 15, 1898.

SPRAGUE, Otho S. A., merchant and philanthropist, was born at East Randolph, Vt., May 13, 1839, son of Ziba and Caroline (Arnold) Sprague. His earliest American ancestor was Ralph Sprague, who, with two brothers, Richard and William, emigrated from Upway, Dorsetshire, England, in 1629, and settled in what is now called Charlestown, Mass. Ralph Sprague soon became a man of influence and affluence in the Massachusetts colony, and was a member of the first jury impaneled in that colony, Sept. 28, 1630. He was selectman and deputy to the general court. He was a charter member (1638) of the celebrated Ancient and Honorable Artillery Co. of Boston. He married Joan Warren, and the line of descent is through their son John, through his son Edward, through his son William, through his son Jonathan, who married Mary Townsend; through their son Edward, who married Annette Corliss, to the father of the subject. His preliminary education was received in the district school of East Randolph, Vt., after which he entered the Kimball Union Academy at Meriden, N. H. On leaving school he entered the general store of H. Holden, East Randolph, as a clerk, and in 1860 purchased an interest in the store, the firm being H. Holden & Co. At the outbreak of the civil war he enlisted as orderly sergeant in company G, 8th Vermont regiment of volunteers, and went to New Orleans, La., in the corps of Gen. Benjamin F. Butler, but after a short service was compelled to resign on account of a severe illness. As soon as his health would permit he went to Chicago, Ill., joining his brother, A. A. Sprague, and Ezra J. Warner in establishing the firm of Sprague, Warner & Co., which has grown to be the largest wholesale enterprise in the United States. He was a director in the Pullman Palace Car Co., Elgin National Watch Co. and the Southern California Railway Co. He was one of the Greek commissioners at the World's

Columbia Exposition in Chicago, for which service he received from the King of Greece the cross of an officer of the Royal Order of the Saviour. He was a member of the Chicago, Commercial, Union League and Chicago Literary clubs of Chicago. He went to California in 1894, broken in health, and remained there until his death. In Pasadena, Cal., he built and furnished a hospital as a memorial to his wife. He was not only a man of unusual business ability, but a great reader and of fine literary tastes. His private library in Chicago was one of the largest and finest in the city, and no man who had lived in Chicago had a greater number of friends. From a fund he had placed in the hands of his brother, A. A. Sprague, there was incorporated in Chicago in 1911 the Otho S. A. Sprague Memorial Institute, its purpose being for the investigation and prevention of disease and the relief of human suffering. It was organized under the provisions of the will of the benefactor, and had as members of the corporation and first board of directors Martin A. Ryerson, Charles L. Hutchinson, A. C. Bartlett, Byron L. Smith, Albert A. Sprague, Dr. Frank Billings, John P. Wilson and Albert A. Sprague 2d. The directors elected Dr. H. Gideon Wells, of the University of Chicago, to direct the medical research work for which the institution was founded, and its work will be done in co-operation with the University of Chicago, the Rush Medical College, the Presbyterian Hospital of Chicago and the Children's Memorial Hospital of Chicago. He was married at Malone, N. Y., on July 15, 1871, to Lucia E., daughter of Ebenezer and Elvira (Tucker) Atwood. She died in Chicago, Ill., Sept. 25, 1901. He died in Pasadena, Cal., Feb. 20, 1909, and is survived by four children: Mary, who became the wife of Prof. A. C. Miller, of the University of California; Albert A. 2d, a member of the firm of Sprague, Warner & Co., Chicago; Nancy A. and Lucy, dean of women and professor in the University of California.

WARNER, Ezra Joseph, merchant, was born in Middlebury, Vt., Mar. 8, 1841, son of Joseph and Jane(Meech) Warner, and the offspring of two lines of ancestry honored in the annals of New England. His line of descent is traced from Joseph Warner, born at Walpole, N. H., early in the eighteenth century, and through the latter's son Joseph, merchant and magistrate of Sudbury, Vt., who died while serving in the Vermont legislature. He married Asenath Little of Springfield, Vt., whose family was prominently identified with the history of that commonwealth from before the revolution, and they were the grandparents of the subject of this sketch. His father, Joseph Warner III, was a prosperous banker, and a delegate for Vermont to the Republican national convention which nominated Lincoln for the presidency in 1860. His mother, Jane Meech, was the daughter of Judge Ezra Meech of Shelburn, Vt., the largest land holder in New England. Ezra Joseph Warner prepared for college at Meriden, N. H., and was graduated at Middlebury College, Vermont, in 1861, as valedictorian of his class. His intention was to become a professor of classics, but that same year, at his father's request, he went to Wisconsin to examine some property owned by his father, and while there engaged in the study of law. In 1862 he visited Chicago, was deeply impressed with the commercial energy and enterprise of that growing city, and entered into an engagement with the firm of Sprague & Stetson. So satisfactory was his business experience that he abandoned all thought of

O. S. A. Sprague

practicing law and purchased the interest of Mr. Stetson, becoming a partner of Albert A. Sprague. The ensuing year Otho S. A. Sprague (above) became a member of the firm, which has continued under the name of Sprague, Warner & Co. until to-day, and is at present (1916) the largest wholesale grocery house in the United States. To Mr. Warner was intrusted the management of the finances of the concern, which he conducted with notable discretion and ability until his death. It was said of him by his fellow merchants that he exhibited the financial instincts of a banker, combined with the judicial temperament which affords the highest qualifications for the bench. In his character there were marked and worthy traits. One of them was poise, which he acquired by means of self-directed and prolonged effort. He was tender-hearted, sensitive to adverse criticism, and shrank from hostile controversy, but he ever held himself in calm and fine restraint, baffling his adversaries by his very serenity. Another trait was his courtesy. He invariably observed the manners of refined and gentle society, and was noted for his marvelous ability to withhold the inconsiderate word. With him secrets were sacred; he never betrayed a confidence. He was a diligent reader of great books. Deeply interested in the cause of education, he assisted in the development of Lake Forest College, of which he was a trustee for many years, serving with absolute fidelity as a member of its important executive committee. He gave the Eliza Remsen cottage to the Academy of Lake Forest College as a memorial of Mrs. Warner's sister. At Middlebury College, his alma mater, he erected the science building known as "Warner Hall," his father having been treasurer of the college. Mr. Warner was essentially domestic, finding in his home the social pleasures which some men seek at the club. He was genial but never effusive, firm in his convictions, but never offensive in expressing them. Of retiring disposition, he sought to evade no duty which was justly his. His religious affiliation was with the Presbyterian Church, in which he held office as trustee and was always asked to bear responsibility when matters of vital importance were under discussion. His interest in the world-wide kingdom of Christ was revealed in his personal support of a missionary at Hainan, China, which he continued to the time of his death. He was married Nov. 25, 1861, to Jane, daughter of William H. Remsen of Cornwall, Vt., and had five children: Frank, Maud (Mrs. A. A. McCormick); Ezra Joseph, Jr. (vice-president, secretary and director of Sprague, Warner & Co.); Ethel (Mrs. J. L. Mothershead, Jr.), and Harold Warner. Mr. Warner died in Chicago, Ill., Sept. 9, 1910.

STONE, George Frederick, merchant and statistician, was born in Newburyport, Mass., Apr. 24, 1836, eldest son of Jacob and Eliza (Atkins) Stone. He came of New England stock, his first American ancestor of the name being Elias Stone, who came to this country about 1640. The line of descent is traced through Elias Stone, Jr.; John Stone, Jacob Stone and Jacob Stone, Jr. George F. Stone, the subject of this sketch, was educated in private and public schools of Newburyport, and at Dummer Academy, Byfield, Mass. He entered business life early in Boston and became in time a member of the firm of Gardner, Stone & Co., commission merchants, the senior partner being an ex-governor of the state. For two years, 1872-73, Mr. Stone was president of the Corn Exchange of Boston, known as the Boston Commercial Exchange, now the Chamber of Commerce. His residence was in Melrose, a suburb of Boston, where he held various public offices. At the age of forty years he went to Chicago, Ill., to represent his house, and soon after the business was transferred to that city. After the dissolution of the firm he became, in 1884, secretary of the Chicago Board of Trade, holding this position with ever-increasing power and efficiency until his death. He had his residence in Evanston. Mr. Stone was consul for Guatemala, Nicaragua and Honduras for several years. During the Columbian Exposition in 1893 he served as general commissioner and vice-president in the congress of boards of trade. He was a member of the commission instrumental in organizing the congress of arbitration and peace, and was a member of the world's congress auxiliary on water commerce. He was a fellow of the Royal Statistical Society of London and a member of the National Board of Trade, also a member of the Loyal Legion by inheritance from two brothers who fell in the civil war. Mr. Stone was a member of the Masonic fraternity and of Illinois commandery, Knights Templar, and he was also member and past grand master of Odd Fellows. During his twenty-eight years as secretary to the Chicago Board of Trade he became an authority on statistical matters connected with the grain trade of the city and of the country in general. His official annual repors were models of well-digested and comprehensive information. As the years passed by, his mind became the repository of all that was to be known of the commercial laws, rules and customs which governed the enormous daily transactions of the board. He was a speaker of fervor and ability, and a writer of singular lucidity, brilliancy and attractiveness in a field of dry facts. More than a collator and imparter of facts, he has been styled a "poet-statistician." He possessed an effective literary style full of vital optimism, vigorous but kindly. His statistical knowledge, extensive and accurate, was a wealth of fact and detail ever at ready command. Gentle, considerate, courageous, firm, enthusiastic, he possessed a poet's vision and sympathy, and an integrity moral and intellectual. Mr. Stone had a peculiar charm in conversation and was ready with classical allusions and apt stories. His was an inspiring personality. With him originated the now familiar phrase, used by Pres. McKinley, "Commerce follows the flag." Mr. Stone was married in 1861 to Julia S. Spaulding, of Newburyport, Mass., daughter of the Rev. Ephraim Spaulding, who had been one of the early missionaries to the Sandwich Islands. Mr. Stone is survived by his wife and by a daughter, Eliza Atkins Stone. He died at his home, in Evanston, Ill., June 21, 1912. Portrait opp. p. 246.

PENDLETON, Edmund, author, was born in Cincinnati, O., June 22, 1843, son of Nathaniel Greene and Anne (James) Pendleton. His first American ancestor was Philip Pendleton, who came from Norwich, England, in 1672, and settled in Virginia. The line of descent is traced through his son Philip, who married Elizabeth Hart; their son Henry, who married Mary Taylor; their son Nathaniel, who married Susan Bard and was the grandfather of the subject of this sketch. The first Nathaniel Pendleton was chief magistrate of Culpeper county, Va., and his name appears as the head of the protest to King George III. against the Stamp act. Edmund Pendleton was educated by private tutors. At the outbreak of the civil war he became 2nd lieutenant in Company E, of the 4th New York artillery, serving during 1863-64 as aide-de-camp on the staff of Gen. Edmund de Russy. After his discharge the greater part of his life was spent in traveling, outdoor sports, and the numerous other affairs to which a gentleman of the so-called ''leisure class'' usually turns his attention. He was the author of several striking novels; ''A Conventional Bohemian'' (1886), ''A Virginia Inheritance'' (1888), ''One Woman's Way'' (1890), and ''A Complication in Hearts'' (1902). His book evoked praise from critics and the reading public throughout the country. They are described as being of strong dramatic power, always spirited in character sketching, vigorous in narrative, and picturesque in description. Mr. Pendleton was a member of the Society of Colonial Wars, the Sons of the American Revolution, and the Society of the War of 1812. He was president of the Cincinnati Exposition of Arts and Industries during 1875-79 and the Cincinnati musical festivals during 1880-82. The latter half of his life he passed the summers at Bar Harbor, Me., and the winters in Florida until he purchased Montpelier Manor near Laurel, Md. He was a member of the Union Club (New York), Metropolitan, Chevy Chase (Washington), Rittenhouse (Philadelphia), and Queen City (Cincinnati) clubs. He was married twice. His second wife, Margaret, daughter of Capt. A. Riviere Hetzel, U. S. A., survives him. He died in Washington, D. C., Mar. 14,1910.

MERRILL, James Cushing, surgeon and ornithologist, was born at Cambridge, Mass., Mar. 26, 1853, son of James Cushing and Jane Hyslop (Hammond) Merrll. His grandfather, James Cushing Merrill (1784–1853), was a prominent jurist of Boston, Mass., and his father (1822-69) was a well-known lawyer of Cambridge, Mass. He was educated in private schools in Cambridge and Boston. He began the study of medicine in Germany and obtained his degree of M.D. at the medical department of the University of Pennsylvania in 1874. In 1875 he became assistant surgeon in the U. S. army, his first assignment being to the St. Louis (Mo.) barracks. He was stationed subsequently at most of the posts in the West and Southwest until 1897. During 1891-94 he had charge of all medical supplies and medical property of the army in the surgeon-general's office in Washington. In 1894 he was made full surgeon in the army. After serving two years at Fort Sherman, Ida., in 1897 he was appointed librarian to the surgeon-general's office, and held that position when he died. A lifelong student of natural history, Maj. Merrill paid particular attention to ornithology and entomology. He collected birds, birds' nests and eggs, and insects, particularly beetles, but he made no systematic collection of his own, giving freely specimens to other collectors and to museums. Most of his nests and eggs went to the National Museum, Washington. While at Fort Brown, Tex., in 1874 he obtained specimens of twelve species and subspecies of birds that up to that time were unknown north of Mexico. Species of goatsucker, horned lark and song sparrow have been named in his honor. He was the author of ''Notes on Texan Birds'' (1876), a paper dealing with birds and animals he found at Fort Brown; ''Notes on the Birds of Fort Klamath, Ore.'' (1883); ''Notes on the Birds of Fort Sherman, Ida.'' (1897); a paper ''On the Habits of the Rocky Mountain Goat'' (1880), and ''A Silver Tip Family'' (1897). In 1898 he published a memoir in the nature of a tribute to Maj. Charles Emile Bendire. Maj. Merrill was a fellow of the American Ornithological Union and a member of the National Ornithological Society, the Biological Society of

Washington, the Washington Academy of Sciences, Association of Medical Libraries, Association of Military Surgeons, the Society of Colonial Wars, the Boone and Crockett Club, the Cosmos Club of Washington, the Devil's Island Shooting Club in Currituck Sound and the Tourelle Fishing Club of Canada. He was also a corresponding member of the Linnæan Society of New York and the Boston Society of Natural History. He was noted for his quick intelligence, sound judgment and high ideals, and was self-reliant, unselfish and devoted to duty. He spoke French and German fluently and was able to read and translate Latin, Italian, Spanish, Portuguese, Dutch, Danish, Swedish and Russian. He was married Nov. 16, 1892, to Mary Pitt, daughter of Dr. Thomas B. Chase, of Annapolis, Md., and died in Washington D. C., Oct. 27, 1902.

DE NAVARRO, José Francisco, financier, was born at St. Sebastian, Spain, April 21, 1823. After graduating at the Spanish Royal Naval Academy in 1838 he left Spain for Cuba and shortly afterward came to the United States. He taught for a while in the Jesuit College at Baltimore, Md., and subsequently entered the employ of the shipping firm of Kirkland, Chase & Co. Returning to Cuba in 1841 he became identified with a number of commercial ventures, and in 1844 established the firm of Casanova & De Navarro, which did a large general warehouse and shipping business, and of which he remained a member until 1855, when he returned to New York and organized the banking firm of Mora, De Navarro & Co. As a member of this firm he organized the Brazilian Steamship Co., which operated the first steamship line between the United States and Brazil. In 1858 he founded the Commercial Warehouse Co.; in the following year he was one of the organizers of the Equitable Life Assurance Co., and in 1870 of the Edison Electric Light Co. and later the Ingersoll Rock Drill Co., which he controlled. Foreseeing the inevitable vogue of the apartment house in New York, he organized, in 1882, the Central Park Apartment Co., and at a cost of $6,000,000 built the Navarro Apartments, which were made from altogether original designs. The Navarro, on Central Park West, was the first apartment house in New York city, and was the pioneer model on which the modern apartment house was copied. In 1889 he founded the Atlas Portland Cement Co., of which he was the first president. This was his last important achievement, though he continued for many years to hold a conspicuous place in the business world. José F. De Navarro was a remarkable and in many ways a unique man. During his whole active career his interests centered chiefly in the creation and development of new and productive enterprises, many of which are landmarks in the history of American industry. Any one of the organizations for which he was wholly or partly responsible would be an achievement sufficiently creditable to give him a place in America's business annals. He was as distinguished for his character as for his business genius, and few of his contemporaries bore such a wide reputation for honor and probity. He was generously philanthropic in an unpretentious way and took a special interest in the religious and charitable activities of the Catholic Church, being one of the original contributors to the building of St. Patrick's Cathedral, New York. He was married May 28, 1857, to Ellen A., daughter of John Hudson Dykers, first president of the Harlem River railroad, and senior member of the banking

GEORGE F. STONE
STATISTICIAN

EDMUND PENDLETON
AUTHOR

JAMES C. MERRILL
ORNITHOLOGIST

JOSE F. DE NAVARRO
FINANCIER

Charles S. Dean

house of Dykers, Alstyne & Co., and had four children: John Dykers, Antonio, Alfonso and and José Francisco De Navarro. He died in New York city, Feb. 3, 1909.

GUNTER, Archibald Clavering, author, was born in Liverpool, England, Oct. 25, 1847, son of Henry and Elizabeth Agnes (Sharpless) Gunter. In 1852 he was brought to New York by his parents who soon after took him to California. After five years he returned to Europe on the death of his father, and was partly educated there. He completed his education in the School of Mines, University of California, and began his professional career in that state as a junior engineer on the Central Pacific railway, which was at that time in process of construction. Afterward he devoted his attention entirely to mines and metallurgy, acting as superintendent of the McKay mines of Utah and chemist in the California assay office. During 1874-77 he was a stockbroker in San Francisco. His first literary effort was a drama which he composed for the students of his college society. Later he wrote a number of plays, his first, ''Cuba,'' being produced at the California Theater in 1873. In 1879 he removed to New York, determined to make literature his profession. He devoted his attention primarily to playwriting, his drama, ''Two Nights in Rome,'' being produced at the Union Square Theater, New York, in 1881. ''The Soul of an Actress,'' ''Fresh, the American,'' ''Courage,'' ''After the Opera,'' ''Prince Karl,'' and ''The Deacon's Daughter'' followed in the next few years. In 1884 Mr. Gunter wrote his first novel, ''Mr. Barnes of New York,'' and published it himself in 1887 through the Home Publishing Company, which he organized for that purpose, after his book had been rejected by a number of New York publishers. In 1881 he published ''Mr. Potter of Texas,'' which had the largest first edition sale of any novel at that time—61,242 copies. His other books, all of which he published himself, are: ''Miss Nobody of Nowhere,'' ''Miss Dividends,'' ''Florida Enchantment,'' ''Baron Montez,'' ''A Princess of Paris,'' ''The King's Stockbroker,'' ''The First of the English,'' ''The Ladies' Juggernaut,'' ''Jack Curzon,'' ''Billy Hamilton,'' ''Bob Covington,'' ''Lost American,'' ''Don Balasco of Key West'' and ''M. S. Bradford Special.'' Mr. Gunter was married Nov. 8, 1886, to Esther Lisbeth, daughter of Col. John G. Burns, of Maine, who survived him. He died in New York city, Feb. 26, 1907.

DEAN, Charles Leroy, legislator and business man, was born at Ashford, Conn., May 29, 1844, son of John Sayles and Hannah Minowa (Knowlton) Dean. After attending the public schools he entered the employ of the Westford (Conn.) Glass Co., and upon reaching his majority he became a member of the firm of E. A. Buck & Co., glass manufacturers. In 1871 he went to Boston and organized the firm of Dean, Foster & Co., dealers in glassware, of which he was the senior member until his death. The business was prosperous from the start and grew to be one of the substantial business institutions of Boston. Mr. Dean had long played a prominent part in politics, and during 1879-80 he was senior aide, with the rank of colonel, on the staff of Gov. Andrew of Connecticut; while the two following years he was a member of the state legislature. Becoming a resident of Malden, Mass., he was elected a member of the common council (1892), a member of the board of aldermen (1895), a representative in the state legislature, and mayor

(1898). He served in that office until 1904, when he was elected to the state senate. Few men of modern Massachusetts were so well known in both the business and political world, or so highly respected in private circles, as Senator Dean, known as the ''Grand old man of Malden.'' His hearty handshake was celebrated, while his wit, kindness and good-fellowship won him friends wherever he turned. At the time of his death he was president and founder of the First National Bank of Stafford Springs, Conn.; president of the Malden Trust Co.; director of the Malden Co-operative Bank; trustee and member of the finance committee of Malden Hospital; member of the building commission of the Malden Y. M. C. A. building; trustee and member of investment committee, Boston Five Cents Savings Bank, and trustee of the Center Methodist Church of Malden. He was director of the Anchor Garter Co., Malden City Lumber Co., and George P. Cox Last Co.. In public life he always served on committees relative to financial matters. In the Malden government he was accorded a place on the finance committee and at the state house was always on ways and means. Besides being president of post 40, Grand Army of the Republic associates, Mr. Dean was a member of the Middlesex Club, Republican Club of Massachusetts, Boston Methodist Social Union, the Massachusetts Mayor's Club and Malden and Kernwood Clubs. He was married at Willington, Conn., July 28, 1869, to Juliette H., daughter of John and Oliva Preston Fuller, of Stafford Springs, Conn., and had one son, John Knowlton Dean. He died in Malden, July 29, 1909.

CORBETT, Timothy, first bishop of the Roman Catholic diocese of Crookston, Minn., was born in Mendota, Minn., July 10, 1858. After attending a parish school in Minneapolis, Minn., to which city his parents had removed, he was sent by his pastor to the college of Meximieux, France, in 1876 for his classical course and then made his theology at the Sulpician seminaries at Montreal and Brighton, Mass. He was ordained priest June 12, 1886, and returning to the diocese of St. Paul worked in several parishes there until the diocese of Duluth was established in 1889, and his boyhood pastor and patron, Rev. Dr. McGoldrick, was made its bishop. He became pastor of its cathedral and was so acting when the diocese of Crookstown was created, March 21, 1910, to include 16,598 square miles in thirteen counties of the state. He was consecrated May 19, 1910. The diocese of Crookstown has a Catholic population of 23,000, with thirty-six priests, eighty-two churches, chapels and stations.

MICHENER, Ezra, physician and botanist, was born in London Grove township, Chester co., Pa., Nov. 24, 1794, son of Mordecai and Alice (Dunn) Michener. He was brought up on his father's farm with little opportunities for education, but he early displayed a fondness for plants which was manifest throughout his life. He studied medicine at the University of Pennsylvania, at the same time attending lectures on botany by Dr. William P. C. Barton. He was graduated M. D. in 1817 and began to practise at the place of his birth. On the grounds about his house were planted many rare trees; he collected an extensive herbarium of Hysterophyta, and he made a collection of the mammalia, birds and reptiles of Chester county, now in the possession of Swarthmore College. He corresponded with many of the eminent scientists of his day, and Agassiz said of him ''that he did not belong exclusively to Chester county, Pennsylvania, or America, but to the whole scientific world." He wrote "Conchologia Cestrica" in collaboration with Dr. William D. Hortman, and assisted Barton in writing "Florula Testrica." He was married in 1819 to Sarah Spencer, who bore him seven children, and after her death he was married in 1844 to Mary S. Walton. He died at his home in Chester county, Pa., July 23, 1857.

RIORDAN, Patrick William, second R. C. archbishop of San Francisco, was born at Chatham, New Brunswick, Canada, Aug. 27, 1841, son of Matthew and Mary (Dunne) Riordan. His father came from Kinsale, county Cork, Ireland, about 1830, and settled at Chatham, New Brunswick. The son received his preliminary education at the University of St. Mary's of the Lake, Chicago, and was graduated at the University of Notre Dame, Indiana, in 1858. He was then sent to Rome. The first year in Rome was spent in the College of the Propaganda, but on the opening of the American college he entered that institution as one of its first students. At the close of his second year his health was so greatly impaired that he was sent to the College of the Holy Ghost, Paris, and later to the American College, Louvain, where he received the degree of licentiate in theology in 1866. He was ordained priest by Cardinal Stercks in Malines in 1865 and on his return home in 1866 was appointed professor of ecclesiastical history and canon law in the University of St. Mary's of the Lake, and later professor of dogmatic theology. At the closing of the university in 1868 he was appointed pastor of St. Mary's Church, Woodstock, Ill., and later that year, pastor of St. Mary's Church, Joliet, which position he retained until 1871, when he assumed the rectorship of St. James' Church, Chicago. On Sept. 16, 1883, he was consecrated titular archbishop of Cabesa, and coadjutor with the right of succession to Archbishop Alemany of San Francisco. He arrived in San Francisco in the following November, and after taking part with his superior in 1884 in the 3d plenary council of Baltimore, succeeded to the archbishopric on the resignation of Archbishop Alemany, Dec. 28, 1884. The first distinctive feature of his régime was the successful effort to bring the priesthood and laity in closer touch with each other. A marked evidence of this was in the subdivision of parishes as fast as circumstances would permit. He likewise provided churches and schools for every nationality in his diocese. He erected the Cathedral of St. Mary and the archiepiscopal residence, and under his energetic exertions great progress was made in reviving religion among the old Spanish population as well as among the numerous classes of Catholics immigrating to California. Conversions to the faith were numerous during his episcopate. The Diocesan Seminary, his crowning work, was the embodiment of his long thought out plans for supplying a pious and learned clergy for the future, and it began the most important chapter in the history of the church on the Pacific coast. In the great disaster of 1906, when his province suffered a total loss of many million dollars, he at once perfected a complete temporary organization and inaugurated the open-air mass as well as the tent meetings in which automobiles served as portable pulpits. While studiously avoiding anything which might be interpreted as politics, he always took a fearless, open stand on all questions and never faltered in denouncing wrong and suggesting its remedy. In 1900 he was successful in removing the California taxation upon houses of worship, a service of benefit to all religious denominations. Another important achievement was

his settlement of the Pious Fund, a famous case that had attracted the attention of the civilized world to San Francisco. His administration was crowded with big undertakings, in which he was uniformly successful. Friends among the laity came to his aid in these projects with princely sums, and the results in building alone have been extraordinary. He exercised more territorial jurisdiction than any civil governor and will be numbered among the great in the ecclesiastical annals of his church. Archbishop Riordan was a democratic, tolerant, extremely lovable man, a brilliant conversationalist, an eloquent orator and an eminent scholar. He died in San Francisco, Cal., Dec. 27, 1914.

WEHRLE, Vincent, first Roman Catholic bishop of the diocese of Bismarck, N. D., was born in Berg, Switzerland, Dec. 19, 1855, son of John Baptist and Elisabeth (Hafner) Wehrle. His studies were made at the diocesan seminary of St. Gall and at the famous college of the Abbey of Einsiedeln. He joined the Benedictine order in 1875 and after the usual theological course he was ordained April 23, 1882. Coming to the United States immediately after his ordination, he was stationed in Arkansas and Indiana until 1887, when he was sent to Yankton, S. D., to work among the Indians. When St. Gall's Priory was established in 1893 at Devil's Lake he was appointed prior and in 1893 Bishop Shanley gave him charge of the mission work of his diocese west of the Missouri. The monastery of the order at Richardton having been erected into an abbey he was consecrated its abbot Nov. 24, 1903, and the erection of the diocese of Bismarck to cover an area of 35,998 square miles of the state, March 21, 1910, was followed by his appointment to be its first bishop. He was consecrated May 19, 1910. The diocese has a Catholic population both white and Indian of about 34,000, with sixty-nine priests and 128 churches and missions.

KELLAR, Frances Alice, sociologist, was born in Columbus, O., Oct. 20, 1873, daughter of Daniel and Mary (Sprau) Kellar. She was graduated at the Cornell Law School, New York, in 1897. During 1898–1904 she did undergraduate and graduate work at the University of Chicago, and in 1901 she studied at the New York Summer School of Philanthropy. In the meantime she had made a study of Southern prisons and printed a report upon her investigations. The College Settlement of New York city gave her a fellowship in 1902, and under the auspices of the Woman's Municipal League she began an investigation of employment agencies. The results of her researches and those of eight other investigators were published in book form under the title "Out of Work" (1904) and created a profound impression. Associations in New York, New Jersey and Pennsylvania formed an Inter-Municipal Research Committee with which Miss Kellar worked for four years, planning and superintending investigations in several cities and working for legislation to remedy existing conditions. One important outcome of her efforts was the enactment of the New York city law of 1906 governing employment agencies. Her work has brought her intimately in touch with the nefarious and profitable business of exploiting immigrants, and she began to stir up official action in that direction. After the Probation Commission to which Gov. Higgins appointed her had finished its work and had been succeeded by a permanent commission, Gov. Hughes appointed her a member of the Commission on Immigration, formed in 1908. Miss Kellar became secretary of the commission. In accordance

+ Patrick William Jordan
Archbishop of San Francisco
California.

with its report, transmitted to the legislature in 1909, a Bureau of Industries and Immigration was established, with Miss Kellar as chief investigator. She held this office until 1913, accomplishing many important reforms. With the object of extending the sphere of her influence in this direction, she resigned in 1913 to become managing director of the legislative committee of the North American Civic League for Immigrants, a committee engaged in investigating the possibilities of governmental action in all matters pertaining to the transportation, employment, education, naturalization and standard of living of immigrants. In the same year she became chairman of the National Progressive Service of the newly formed Progressive party. She is also secretary of the National Conference of Immigration, Land and Labor Officials, and a member of the Commission on Urban Conditions Among Negroes and the New York Research Council. She is the author of "Experimental Sociology" (1902), "Out of Work" (1904) and "Education of Women by Athletics" (1909).

BRINCKERHOFF, Elbert Adrain, merchant and banker, was born at Jamaica, L. I., Nov. 29, 1838, son of John N. and Mary (Adrain) Brinckerhoff. His maternal grandfather was Robert Adrain, LL.D. (q.v.), a noted mathematician. His father was the principal of the Union Hall Academy at Jamaica, L. I., during 1837–65. Union Hall Academy furnished his preliminary education and he was about to enter college when he was offered the opportunity of a voyage around the world on a clipper ship, which he accepted. Upon reaching San Francisco he decided to stay in California, and entering a commercial house, became identified with the affairs of San Francisco. He was an active member of the second "Vigilance Committee" and was largely instrumental in establishing law and order in California during those years. In 1858 he became cashier of the Wells, Fargo & Co. bank and express office at Shasta and a year later was made head of the cashier's department in San Francisco. He was the first messenger on the route between San Francisco and Sacramento, conveying all the treasure and mail passing to the seaboard from the northern mines. He carried the first packet of the noted Pony Express to Sacramento. Returning to New York in 1860, he entered the office of the American Express Company at Albany, but soon resigned and took a clerical position with Fox & Polhemus, leading commission merchants and manufacturers of cotton duck. He entered the firm, the name of which was changed to Brinckerhoff, Turner & Co. It was later reorganized as J. Spencer Turner Co., with Mr. Brinckerhoff treasurer. He was for thirty-six years a director in the Merchants National Bank and from 1894 its vice-president. He was also a director of the Harriman National Bank, Barrett, Nephews & Co., the Consolidated Cotton Duck Co., and the International Cotton Mills Corporation. He was a member of the St. Nicholas and Holland societies and of the Down Town and Rockaway Hunt clubs. Mr. Brinckerhoff made his home in Englewood, N. J., in 1865, and the pride which he took in the city and the active interest which he displayed in promoting its welfare resulted in his being twice elected mayor. In later years he was a Presbyterian, but his religious and philanthropic activities were not confined by creed. He was treasurer of the Presbyterian Hospital and was one of its most generous supporters; he was also vice-president of the American Bible Society and a member of many other institutions devoted to charity and the advancement of the Christian faith. As a business man his judgment was sound and his experience varied; hence his services were much sought on important directorates. His business friends, as well as the citizens of Englewood, esteemed him, not only for the integrity of his character, but for the deep religious spirit which ordered his daily speech and conduct. He was thoughtful and painstaking in every relation of life—in commercial affairs, in service to his church, and in the charitable and philanthropic causes which occupied an important part of his time. His interesting and varied conversation was marked by a cheerful humor, the kindly outgrowth of a wide experience. His youth was brave and generous, and his after life was rounded by the virtues that go to make a useful and honorable man. He gave generously and unostentatiously, bestowing his benefactions, not to be seen of the eyes of men, but to comfort sorrow and relieve distress. He was married in April, 1869, to Emily A., daughter of Washington R. Vermilye, of New York, and their children were: Emily, wife of Frederick S. Duncan, of New York; Mary E., wife of James D. Armstrong, of St. Paul; Elbert Adrain, Jr.; Elizabeth, wife of W. B. Chapin, of Englewood, N. J.; Margaret, wife of H. LeRoy Pitkin; Helen, wife of Frank B. Probst, and Janet, wife of Clarence D. Kerr. He died at Englewood, N. J., Mar. 23, 1913.

ALEXANDER, James Waddell, president of the Equitable Life Assurance Society, was born in Princeton, N. J., July 19, 1839, son of Rev. James Waddell and Elizabeth (Cabell) Alexander, and grandson of Prof. Archibald Alexander, an eminent theologian and one of the founders of the Princeton Theological Seminary. The family combines scholastic talents and commercial instincts to an unusual degree, his five uncles being men of high distinction: William Cowper Alexander, who was president of the New Jersey state senate, a delegate to the peace congress at Washington and first president of the Equitable Life Assurance Society; Dr. Joseph Addison Alexander, a professor at the Princeton Seminary and one of the most learned scholars and linguists of America; Rev. Dr. Samuel Davis Alexander, pastor of the Phillips Memorial Church in New York city; Dr. Archibald Alexander, a distinguished physician at Princeton; and Henry Martyn Alexander, the head of the law firm of Alexander & Green. The subject of this sketch began his education in New York city and in 1860 was graduated at Princeton University, receiving the degree of M.A. three years later. After a course of preparatory study he was admitted to the bar and became a member of the firm of Cummins, Alexander & Green. He gave up the practice of law in 1866 to take the position of secretary of the Equitable Life Assurance Society. At that time Henry Baldwin Hyde was vice-president. The latter had been cashier of the Mutual Life Insurance Co., and founded the Equitable Life Assurance Co., in 1859, with our subject's uncle as president and Mr. Hyde vice-president. At the close of the first year the society's insurance in force amounted to $1,144,000, the surplus to $96,154, and not a death claim had been presented. On Dec. 31, 1898, the insurance in force amounted to $987,000,000; the income exceeded $50,000,000; the assets were $258,309,298; the surplus was $22,821,074; the total liabilities, $201,058,809, and the total disbursements, $32,753,952. During the forty years of his connection with it the society paid $307,000,000 in insurance, and at the close of that period it held $265,000,000 for its policy holders, this unparalleled result being the work of Mr. Hyde. In 1871 Mr. Alexander was elected second vice-president, and three years later, first vice-president. Upon the death of Henry B. Hyde in 1899 he succeeded to the presidency. Both as the nephew of the first president of the Equitable and by reason of his vast experience and ability in insurance matters, he seemed peculiarly fitted for this post of responsibility. His temperament was even, his judgment quick and unerring, and though decisive, he displayed infinite tact in dealing with people as well as vexatious questions. Dr. Charles C. Bombaugh, writing of Mr. Alexander in the Baltimore "Underwriter," said: "We hear a great deal nowadays of the scholar in politics, but here is the scholar in the field of insurance, showing in his daily walk the compatibility between the refining influences of an honored position in the republic of letters and the weighty responsibilities of an office which demands business capability of the highest order." Mr. Alexander was president of the Equitable Life Assurance Society until 1906. That year were passed the Armstrong Bills, reorganizing and remodeling the whole system of life insurance in New York state. The committee of investigation had discovered a terrible mismanagement and officials were charged with misusing the policy holders' money. More than 5,000,000 policy holders were paying half a billion dollars a year in premiums and only about one-third of this was ever paid out in one year. The vast "capital stock" had been used by the managers of the companies for their own aggrandizement. When Thomas F. Ryan secured control of the Equitable Life Assurance Society by purchasing for $2,000,000 the 502 shares held by James H. Hyde, son of Henry B. Hyde, he called upon Grover Cleveland, Morgan J. O'Brien and George Westinghouse to act as trustees and straighten out its affairs. Mr. Cleveland drew up a new charter and Mr. Ryan, having quietly secured control of the Equitable Trust Co., the Mercantile Trust Co., the Bank of Commerce and the other subsidiary companies controlled by the old managers, transferred his stock to the policy holders. Suits for the restoration of more than $10,000,000 were brought against the officers. Some fled to Europe, some were indicted for forgery and perjury, and other paid out of their private purses certain sums they had received. Mr. Alexander was married Nov. 24, 1862, to Elizabeth Beasley, daughter of Chancellor Benjamin Williamson of New Jersey, and has two sons, Henry Martyn, Jr., and Frederick Beasley, and one daughter, Elizabeth, wife of John W. Alexander, the artist. He died at Tuxedo Park, N. Y., Sept. 21, 1915.

CUNNINGHAM, John Francis, first Roman Catholic bishop of the diocese of Concordia, Kan., was born in Irremore, County Kerry, Ireland, July, 1842, son of John and Catherine (Fitzgerald) Cunningham. His classical studies were begun in Ireland, and after coming to the United States in 1860 he studied theology at St. Francis Seminary, Milwaukee, Wis., and was ordained a priest for the diocese of Leavenworth, Aug. 8, 1865. During the succeeding years he was a successful pastor at Fort Scott, Laramie and Topeka, and in 1876 toured the country soliciting funds for the benefit of the Kansas sufferers by the economic troubles of that period. He was made vicar-general of the diocese June 1, 1881, and rector of the cathedral. He was serving in that office when he was made Bishop of Concordia and consecrated Sept. 21, 1898. Concordia was created a diocese Aug. 2, 1887, out of the territory formerly included in the area of Leavenworth, and has 33,000 Catholics,

ninety-six priests, 115 churches, thirty-eight schools with 5,000 pupils. Bishop Cunningham built the new cathedral in 1902.

BROKAW, Isaac Vail, merchant and philanthropist, was born at Metuchen, N. J., Nov. 27, 1835, son of Simeon and Prudence (Vail) Brokaw, of French Huguenot ancestry. The first of his family in America was Bourgeon Broucard, who with his wife, Catherine Le Fèbre, came from the south of France in 1675 and settled on Long Island. Bourgeon Broucard, with a few others, established the first French Protestant church in New York. Isaac V. Brokaw received his early education at a boarding school in New Brunswick, N. J. Deciding at an early age to enter upon a business career in New York city, he found employment as a clerk in the well-known house of Wilson G. Hunt & Co., probably the leading cloth importers at that time. He applied himself diligently to the study of textiles until he became an expert in judging and handling woolens. Realizing that the opportunity for advancement in such a large establishment was remote, he determined to organize a similar business on his own account and in 1856 formed a partnership with George Dunham under the firm name of Dunham & Brokaw. The enterprise was a success from the beginning. Mr. Dunham retired in 1861 and Mr. Brokaw carried on the business under his own name until 1866, when he admitted to partnership his brother, William Vail Brokaw, and the name of the firm became Brokaw Bros., which has continued uninterruptedly to this day. It was incorporated in 1895 with Isaac V. Brokaw, president; William V. Brokaw, vice-president; John Hill Armstrong, treasurer, and John R. Thorpe, secretary. Two years later his son, Howard C. Brokaw, entered the firm, subsequently succeeding to the head of the business. At the fiftieth anniversary of the business in 1906 the employees of the firm presented Isaac V. Brokaw with a loving cup as a token of their esteem and appreciation. For years the house of Brokaw Bros. has been recognized as one of the best managed and most successful in the entire country, due as much to the ability and enterprise of its members as to their unwearying vigilance in matters of detail and to the high quality of the goods which they sold. For many years Mr. Brokaw's name was synonymous with high purpose and altruistic achievement. He was largely interested in religious and philanthropic affairs, and was liberal in his donations to various public institutions. He gave generously for the establishment of the French Protestant Church in New York, was the founder of the Bethany Day Nursery, built the Bethany Memorial Chapel and gave the Brokaw Memorial to Princeton University in memory of his son Frederick, who lost his life in 1891 while attempting to save the life of another. In politics Mr. Brokaw was a stanch Republican. He was a member of the Union League Club and of the Huguenot Society of America, and for many years served as an officer in the late Rev. Dr. Howard Crosby's church. He was married, Nov. 14, 1865, to Eloise Elvira, daughter of Joseph Tuttle Gould, of Newark, N. J. There were seven children: Irving, Elvira, wife of William B. McNair; Howard Crosby and George Tuttle Brokaw. Mr. Brokaw died at his summer home at Elberon, N. J., Sept. 29, 1913.

POST, George Browne, architect, was born in New York city, Dec. 15, 1837, son of Joel Browne and Abby Mauran (Church) Post. The first of the family in America was Lieut. Richard Post, son of Arthur Post, of Maidstone, Kent, England.

Isaac V Brokaw

The date of his arrival in the colonies is not known. He lived for a time in Lynn, Mass., and then removed to Southampton, Long Island. From this Richard Post the line of descent is traced through his son John, who married Mary ———; their son Richard, who married Phoebe ———; their son Richard, who married Mary Willis; their son Jotham, who married Winifred Wright, and their son Joel, who married Elizabeth Browne, and was the grandfather of George B. Post, the architect. George B. Post was educated at Churchill's Military School at Sing Sing, N. Y., and was graduated C.E. at the Scientific School of New York University in 1858. For two years he studied architecture in the office of Richard M. Hunt, a man whose name will remain famous in the annals of the profession not only for his own noble work, but for the influence he exerted upon his art and the many noted leaders of architecture who were his pupils. Mr. Post began his professional career in New York city in 1860 in partnership with a fellow student, Charles D. Gambrill, but it was soon after dissolved by the outbreak of the civil war. He volunteered his services and was made captain of the 22d regiment, New York volunteers. He was present at the battle of Fredericksburg as a volunteer aide on the staff of Gen. Burnside, and after the war he was promoted to be major, and later to lieutenant-colonel and colonel of the 22d regiment. Resuming his practice in New York, he soon developed an extensive business and won recognition as an architect of exceptional abilities. He was a pioneer in the use of wrought iron and steel construction; having been brought up as a civil engineer, he was able to exercise a strong direction over the new combination. The first use of iron construction in New York, if not in the country, was in the Produce Exchange building, erected by him in 1881. He was the designer of a long list of notable buildings in New York and elsewhere in the United States, among them the New York Cotton Exchange, New York Stock Exchange, College of the City of New York, the building formerly occupied by the New York "Times" on Park Row, the Pulitzer Building, the building of the Equitable Life Assurance Society that was burned in 1912, Chickering Hall, the Western Union Telegraph Co.'s office, the New York Hospital, the Long Island Historical Society, the Post Building, of which he was secretary and trustee, and the St. Paul Building. Some of his most important designs in other cities were the Prudential and Mutual Benefit Life Insurance companies, Newark, N. J.; Bank of Pittsburgh, Troy (N. Y.) Savings Bank, Erie County Savings Bank, Buffalo; Williamson Building, Cleveland, O.; Commercial Trust Building, Jersey City, N. J.; Montreal Stock Exchange, Montreal, Canada; the Wisconsin capitol building at Madison and the Cleveland Trust Co. Building, Cleveland, O. Among the New York residences designed by him are those of Cornelius Vanderbilt and Collis P. Huntington. He was the architect of the Manufacturers and Arts building at the Chicago Columbian Exposition in 1893, which was the largest building of its kind ever erected, and may be mentioned as typical of Post's general style of work. In 1904 he was appointed a member of the board of commissioners to the St. Louis Exposition by the governor of New York. His practice was in his own name until 1905, when his sons, William S. and J. Otis Post, became associated in the business and the firm of George B. Post & Sons was organized. He served on the tenement house commission, appointed by the New York legislature and known as the Gilder commission. He was made a member of the expert committee to appoint a sculptor and select a design for the Lafayette monument in the Louvre in Paris. In 1906 he was appointed collaborator of the United States forest service, and that same year by appointment of Pres. Roosevelt became a member of the national advisory board on fuel and structural materials, serving by reappointment through the three following years. Mr. Post occupied a position of singular prominence among the great architects of the modern world, and it is generally admitted that no other individual has done so much to beautify and adorn the metropolis of the United States as he. He was a delegate to the World's Congress of Architects in London in 1906. He was a member of the committee of patronage of the seventh and eighth International Congresses of Architects in 1906 and 1907, and was a member of the permanent committee of that body from 1908 until his death. He was also an honorary corresponding member of the Royal Institute of British Architects in 1907. He was decorated Chevalier de la Légion d'Honneur, France, in 1901, and in 1910 the gold medal of the American Institute of Architects, the highest gift within the bestowal of that body, was awarded him in the presence of a distinguished company, presented by Pres. Taft, in Washington. At that time Pres. Taft congratulated the venerable architect, saying he was glad that the latter had lived "to see his profession develop to such a height in this country and to feel that so much of it had been due to his efforts." In 1907 he was elected an associate of the National Academy of Design, and the following year an academician. In 1908 Columbia University conferred on him the honorary degree of LL.D. He was president of the American Institute of Architects (1896-99), also president of its New York chapter (1904), president of the Architectural League of New York (1893-97), a charter member of the National Arts Club (president 1898-1905) and member of the National Institute of Arts and Letters, the American Academy of Arts and Letters, the New York Academy of Sciences, Fine Arts Federation of New York (president in 1898), American Society of Civil Engineers, New York Chamber of Commerce, Archæological Institute of America, National Society of Craftsmen, Municipal Art Society (director 1901-09), Province of Quebec Association of Architects, National Sculpture Society, National Academy of Design, American Geographical Society, National Geographic Society, Public Art League, Metropolitan Museum of Art, New Jersey State Chamber of Commerce and Century Association. Mr. Post was also a member of the Century, Union, Lawyers' (charter member) and Seawanhaka Yacht clubs of New York, Comos Club of Washington and Duquesne Club of Pittsburgh. The following summary of the personality of Mr. Post is taken from the resolutions passed by the Architectural League at the time of his death: "It was characteristic of Mr. Post either as an officer of the various architectural societies or as a member of any of their committees, that he was always ready at any personal sacrifice, or at any cost of time or labor, to give his best efforts to the interests of his profession, to which he devoted his whole life. Mr. Post was a man of great personal force and physical vigor and was endowed with a constructive imagination and with courage to carry out his ideas, qualities which made him a pioneer in a period when new structural problems and new materials were being developed from day to day. No man has contributed more to the solution of the architectural problems of his generation. The great works which he has left behind him are of inestimable value to the art of building. In his private character Mr. Post earned the warm regard and devotion of the members of his profession. His enthusiasm and active interest in all matters pertaining to the practice of architecture up to the very last day of his life have furnished a brilliant example and endeared his memory to the whole artistic fraternity.'' He was married, Oct. 14, 1863, to Alice M., daughter of William W. Stone, a prominent merchant of New York. They had five children: George B., Jr.; William S., A. Wright, James Otis and Alice W., wife of Arthur Turnbull. Mr. Post died at his summer home in Bernardsville, N. J., Nov. 28, 1913.

POTTER, Frances Squire, educator, was born at Elmira, N. Y., Nov. 12, 1867, daughter of Truman Squire, who was a surgeon of local fame, and a poet and idealist as well. She was educated, during 1883-87, at Elmira Female College, where her vivid and gifted scholarship carried off the honors in mathematics and natural history. During this period she sang in the operettas she composed, acted in the plays she wrote, and was fond of outdoor sports, being the most expert tennis player in school and among the women of the city. The death of her father threw her upon her own resources, and until her marriage she taught French in the college, gave violin and singing lessons and tutored. After a wedding trip to Europe, Egypt and the Orient she settled in Minneapolis, Minn. In 1899 domestic circumstances made it necessary for her to take a position as teacher in the East Side High School of Minneapolis. In the following year she was transferred to the English department of the University of Minnesota, where she remained ten years, becoming full professor. ''The Ballingtons,'' her first novel (1904), received wide attention as ''the best presentation in modern fiction of the economic dependence of women.'' It was an economic manifesto in disguise, and from this point on her interest in the economic problem underlying all social struggles began to lure her out of the university into the wider arena of public life. The year of 1904-05 was spent abroad, chiefly in England, where she engaged in research work at Cambridge University and where she first became interested in the woman's suffragist movement. On her resumption of university life she made her first speech for woman suffrage before the Minnesota legislature, and from that time till she resigned her professorship, in 1909, to become corresponding secretary of the National American Woman Suffrage Association, she was active in suffrage affairs in her state. She was a national lecturer of the Women's Trade Union League, department editor of ''Life and Labor'' and chairman of the department of literature and library extension in the General Federation of Women's Clubs. Until her death she bent her unrivaled eloquence, ripe scholarship, brilliant pen and wide experience of life to the cause of the workers of the world. As a member of many organizations for public service she was continually urged to speak in all parts of the country, but her services as lecturer were chiefly restricted to the University Lecturers' Association, an international organization to which she was the first American woman to be elected, and to the Brooklyn Institute, New York. Life in the placid College of Arts and Sciences in the University of Minnesota felt a new impulse when she first entered the lecture room. Before a week had passed the class had experienced a mental resurrection, and the end of a year saw two lecture rooms made into one to accommodate the enormous classes which flocked to hear her. A wonderful teacher, she made the past live again in splendor and heroic meaning for her students. To her the study of literature was the study of life. Nothing short of the love she inspired wherever she went can measure her influence and achievement. She was married at Elmira, N. Y., Dec. 10, 1891, to Winfield Scott Potter and left three children: Agnes Squire, Mark Louis and Truman Squire Potter. She died in Chicago, Ill., Mar. 25, 1914.

WALSH, Louis Sebastian, fourth Roman Catholic bishop of Portland, Me., was born at Salem, Mass., Jan. 22, 1858, son of Patrick and Hanorah (Foley) Walsh. His parents were among the Irish pilgrims of 1849 who settled in Salem, Mass., where they resided to the end of their lives. The son received his education in the Old St. Mary's Parish School and in the public schools of Salem. After graduating at the high school, in 1876, he spent a year at the Holy Cross College of Worcester, Mass. Then he devoted two years to the study of philosophy at the Grand Seminary at Montreal, Canada. His theological studies were pursued at St. Sulpice Seminary in Paris for three years, after which he took the post-graduate course in canon law at the Papal Seminary in Rome, and at the same time took a course in theology at the Dominican School of the Minerva, also in Rome, Italy. He received the degrees of licentiate in canon law and theology at Rome in 1883. Before his return to America he was ordained to the priesthood at St. John Lateran Cathedral in Rome, Dec. 23, 1882. After so thorough an equipment for the ministry it is not surprising that the young clergyman made rapid progress in his chosen career. He was assistant in St. Joseph's Church in the west end section of Boston for one year, during 1883-84. Upon the opening of St. John's Seminary at Brighton, Mass., in 1884, Bishop Walsh was appointed a director and professor of church history, canon law and liturgy, and for thirteen years was intimately associated with his superiors, Father John B. Hogan and Father Charles B. Rex, in the administration of the affairs of the institution. During his ministry in Boston Bishop Walsh was actively identified with various educational movements connected with the Catholic Church, and he has long been recognized as an authority on such matters. He was one of the founders of the New England Catholic Historical Society in 1900, and an active promoter of the Catholic Educational Association of America, in 1903. The latter is an organization that brings Catholic educators of all departments and of all sections into annual meeting for conference on matters relating to the efficiency of Catholic educational work. It has now 1,200 members. He was elected the first president of the school department of the association, and continued in that office by unanimous re-election until his elevation to the bishopric. A man of deep learning, scholarly attainments, endowed with the ability of thought and expression, dignified bearing and oratorical powers, he was often called upon to officiate as master of ceremonies or as preacher at various church functions, such as the laying of corner-stones of new edifices, dedications, consecrations, ordinations ,etc. In 1906 he was appointed bishop of the diocese of Portland, Me., and was formally consecrated in the Cathedral of the Immaculate Conception. Portland, Oct. 18, 1906, Rt. Rev. Matthew Harkins, bishop of Rhode Island, officiating. Bishop Walsh is the author of a "History of the Catholic Church in Old St. Mary's and the Immaculate Conception Parishes in Salem, Mass.''

GROSSCUP, Peter Stenger, jurist, was born at Ashland, O., Feb. 15, 1852, son of Benjamin and Susannah (Bowermaster) Grosscup, grandson of Paul and Rebecca (Shearer) Grosscup, of Holland extraction, and great-grandson of Paul Grosscup, a member of the Pennsylvania colonial assembly; of the convention that framed the first Pennsylvania constitution, and of the first Pennsylvania legislature, and he was a captain in the war of the revolution. He was graduated at Wittenberg College in 1872, with the degrees A. B. and A. M., and at the Boston Law School in 1874, with the degree of LL.B. Knox College conferred upon him the honorary degree of LL.D. in 1896. He began the practice of his profession at Ashland in 1874 as the associate of Judge William Osborn. He was city solicitor during 1874–78, and Republican candidate for congress in 1876. Removing to Chicago, Ill., in 1883 he entered the law firm headed by Leonard Swett, a former law partner of Abraham Lincoln, and the best known lawyer at that time in the West. In 1892 Pres. Harrison appointed him U. S. district judge for the Northern District of Illinois, and in 1898 Pres. McKinley appointed him U. S. circuit judge of the seventh district (Illinois, Indiana and Wisconsin). Since 1905 he has been presiding judge of the circuit court of appeals. Soon after going on the bench Judge Grosscup attracted the attention of the country by issuing an injunction, in 1893, enjoining Eugene Debs and others from interfering with interstate commerce or the transmission of the mails. This was the origin of the phrase "Government by injunction" so frequently used. When his injunction against the Debs rioters in 1894 was disregarded he saved the city of Chicago from mob violence by calling upon the president for federal troops. Then summoning a grand jury he delivered to them a charge that gave him instant national reputation. This charge is preserved in the "Federal Reporter," and is regarded as a model of classic, forceful and apt English, as well as a courageous judicial act. The indictment and arrests that followed were the beginning of the end of mob violence. Other cases decided by him that have attracted wide attention are the whiskey trust cases, the railroad case, the interstate commerce cases, the telegraph, beef trust, railway injunction, and the Chicago traction cases. As presiding judge of the circuit court of appeals he wrote the decision of that court reversing the decision of the lower court which fined the Standard Oil Company $29,240,000. ''Yet Peter Stenger Grosscup,'' asserted the New York "Tribune" at the time, ''is one of the most outspoken and determined enemies of corporation abuses on or off the bench." He has shown his power to go directly to the core of a controversy, to eliminate the unessential things, and to build up argument in language so attractive that it holds attention, and so clear that it reaches the commonest intelligence. He has delivered many addresses on questions of the day, one at Indianapolis in 1896, which had a circulation of more than 100,000 copies, and one at Galesburg, Ill., in 1894, that was widely commented on in connection with the railroad strike of 1894, and one before the University of Nebraska touching upon the problem of the corporation in American life. He has never been what is

called a ''trust buster''; has never been the enemy of the corporation or incorporated property; has never advocated destructive methods, nor even regulation to the extent that "regulation" would interfere with the freedom of individual initiative and energy. He has no leaning toward socialism, nor paternalism, but is an earnest individualist. He is a member of the Chicago, Athletic, University, Union, Union League, and Illinois clubs. He was married at Loudenville, O., Dec. 14, 1885, to Virginia, daughter of A. A. Taylor, an extensive flour manufacturer of Loudenville; she died in 1899, leaving one daughter: Kathryn, wife of Frank Leslie Moon.

BAARE, Frederick, manufacturer, was born at Minden, Prussia, June 19, 1823, son of Frederick August and Charlotte (Buring) Baare. He was educated in the local gymnasium and served his required time in the army, retiring as an officer in the Landwehr. For nine years he found employment at Coblentz and Cologne as a clerk and commercial traveler, being connected with two houses prominent in the chemical and dyestuff line, and in 1850 he started on his own account in the coal trade in the Boehum (Westphalia) district. In 1852 he came to America and settled in New York city, where he formed a partnership with his brother-in-law, J. Gross Garelly, under the firm name of J. Gross Garelly & Co., importers and manufacturers of ladies' dress and mantilla trimmings. His partner withdrew from the firm in 1854 and he then associated himself with G. Warren Geer, with whom he continued the business as Baare & Geer. Two years later his former partner re-entered the firm, retaining his residence in Paris. The style of the house was then changed to Garelly, Baare & Geer, Paris, and Baare, Geer & Co., New York. Silk ribbons, silk linings, gros grains and velvets were added to the dress trimmings in the manufacturing as well as importing lines. The factories were in New York, Schoharie, N. Y., and Union Hill, N. J. In 1864 the firm was dissolved by mutual consent, and Mr. Baare devoted himself entirely to broad silk power loom weaving, with a salesroom in New York. In 1870 he removed to Paterson, N. J., where, with members of the firm of John Ryle & Co., the Baare Manufacturing Co. was organized, and broad silk power loom weaving alone was followed in the upper Murray Mill. Upon the change of John Ryle & Co. into the Pioneer Silk Co., he continued in business independently at South Paterson, where he brought his methods of weaving and his machinery to that modern perfection which became recognized and was adopted gradually by the trade, and is now in general use at Paterson. He participated in the Philadelphia Centennial Exhibition in 1876, and in 1877 sold out to the Sauquoit Silk Co., Philadelphia, with which he remained as superintendent for one year, introducing broad silk weaving successfully in that city. Returning to Paterson, he found the trade suffering from want of help in soft silk winding, and started a winding shop in the old Van Houten Market. He retired from the silk business in 1883. He was a conspicuous figure in the German-American Alliance, and as chairman of the forestry committee of that body he assisted in the preparation of a huge petition to congress. He wrote interesting and instructive articles relating to the silk industry for German and English publications; was an acknowledged authority on the history of the silk industry, its growth and development, and as a citizen was highly esteemed and respected. He was a charming conversationalist on a wide range of subjects, and was known and loved for his personal virtues. In 1886 removed to Wilkes-Barre, Pa., and in 1902 to Hazelton, Pa., where he died Mar. 19, 1910.

GOFF, John William, jurist, was born in county Wexford, Ireland, Jan. 1, 1848. Both his parents died when he was about nine years old, and he then lived with an uncle until he was fourteen. He learned telegraphy, and was in the government service in both England and Scotland. Coming to America when fifteen years of age, he settled in New York city, where he obtained a position as telegraph operator and later as clerk in the dry goods stores of Arnold, Constable & Co. and A. T. Stewart & Co. He attended the public evening school, took a course of instruction at Cooper Union, and studied law in the office of Samuel J. Courtney, U. S. district attorney. He supported himself by working in a telegraph office at night and by working for newspapers. At that time he was an ardent member of the Irish Land League, and in 1874 he organized an expedition which, after a number of adventures, succeeding in rescuing John Boyle O'Reilly and other agitators who had been transported to Australia. He was admitted to the bar in 1876 and at once began the practice of his profession with Francis W. Pollock as a law partner. This co-partnership continued until 1894, when Mr. Goff was elected recorder of New York city. He was appointed assistant district attorney under John R. Fellows, in January, 1888, and served for three years. In 1890 he was nominated by the Republicans for district attorney to succeed Col. Fellows, and was defeated by De-Lancy Nicoll (q. v.), a Tammany candidate. In the history of the bar of New York city, Justice Goff's name will be prominent as the counsel for the celebrated Lexow committee, appointed by the state senate to investigate the conditions and workings of the police department of New York city. The investigation began in the spring of 1894, and during its progress Mr. Goff so impressed his personality on the people of the city that he was placed in nomination by the party opposed to him politically, and was triumphantly elected recorder of the city in November to succeed Recorder Smythe, who had held the office continuously for fifteen years. He received the largest vote accorded to any candidate on the elected ticket. Judge Goff had previously served as counsel for the New York Law Association in the investigation and prosecution of election frauds in New York. In 1907 he became justice of the supreme court of New York, 1st district, for the term ending in 1920, and in 1912 was appointed by Gov. Dix as special judge to conduct the trials of the men indicted in connection with the police graft and Rosenthal murder cases; and it was generally noted that a jurist better fitted for this particular task could hardly have been selected. One of Justice Goff's chief characteristics is a disposition to disregard minor technicalities in the admission of testimony when a strict adherence to the letter of the law of evidence would defeat the ends of justice. In person he is of middle height, slender, erect, white-haired and white-bearded, with piercing blue eyes in which appear the compelling force and dignity of the man. He is at once gentle and austere. He was married May 26, 1881, to Catherine O'Keefe of New York, and their children are: John W., Jr., and Innisfail Goff.

STEVENSON, J[oseph] Ross, theologian, was born at Ligonier, Westmoreland co., Pa., March 1, 1866, son of Ross and Martha Ann (Harbison) Stevenson. His father was born in Ireland in 1814, emigrated to the United States in 1838, and had charge of churches at Connellsville, Johnstown, Ligonier and Corsica, Pennsylvania. The son was educated in the old Jefferson Academy at Canonsburgh, Pa., and the Washington and Jefferson College where he was graduated in 1886. From the same college he subsequently received the degrees of A.M. (1894) and D.D (1897), and the degree of LL.D. was conferred by Ursinus College in 1908, and Lafayette in 1915. He studied theology at McCormick Seminary, Chicago, and after his graduation in 1889, went to Germany for special courses in the universities of Berlin and Halle. His first pastorate was in the Presbyterian church at Sedalia, Mo. He was professor of church history in the McCormick Seminary, during 1894–1902, and then accepted a call to the Fifth Avenue Presbyterian church, New York city. From there he went to the Brown Memorial church in Baltimore, and in 1914 he became president of Princeton Theological Seminary the successor of Francis L. Patton. In 1915 he was elected moderator of the General Assembly. He is a member of the Presbyterian church in the U. S. A., the International Committee of the Y. M. C. A., the Student Volunteer Movement for Missions, Board of Missionary preparation, and of kindred organizations. On May 16, 1899, he was married at Indianapolis, Ind., to Florence Day, daughter of Thomas C. Day, of that place, and has three sons, William Edwards, Donald Day and Theodore Dwight Stevenson.

COMEGYS, Benjamin Bartis, banker and author, was born at Dover, Del., May 9, 1819, son of Cornelius Parsons and Ruhamah (Marim) Comegys, and a descendant of Cornelius Comegys, who emigrated from Holland in 1651 and settled on the eastern shore of Maryland. His maternal grandfather was John Marim, a lieutenant in the war of the revolution. His father (q. v.) was governor of Delaware during 1838–41 and an older brother, Joseph Parsons Comegys, was U. S. senator and chief justice of Delaware. Benjamin Comegys was debarred from the privileges of a college education, but he was a life-long student, and much of his literary taste and the trend of his studies were inspired in early life while under the pastoral care of the celebrated divine, Rev. John Todd. He began business in the employ of a dry goods firm in Philadelphia, and later transferred his services to the Philadelphia Bank, where he was in turn clerk, cashier, vice-president and president. He was a member of the Philadelphia Clearing House Committee and for many years chairman of that body, director and vice-president of the Philadelphia Trust Safe Deposit Insurance Co., manager of the Western Savings Fund, and director of the City Trusts. Outside of his business life he was especially interested in the religious and moral education of youth. For a quarter of a century he was a monthly speaker in the chapel of Girard College, whose eccentric founder had decreed that no minister of any religious body was to be permitted within its walls. In the course of his long life he had gathered a library of more than 3,000 volumes of general literature, especially rich in theology, poetry, fiction, art and architecture, and editions of favorite authors that he extra illustrated. He was manager of the American Sunday School Union, manager of the House of Refuge, trustee of the Jefferson Medical College, delegate to the Pan-Presbyterian Council in Edinburgh, member of the Philadelphia Board of Education, and a director of the Pennsylvania Railroad Co. In 1895 Jefferson Medical College gave him the honorary degree of LL.D. He was the author of

FREDERICK BAARE
MANUFACTURER

JOHN W. GOFF
JUDGE

J. ROSS STEVENSON
THEOLOGIAN

BENJAMIN B. COMEGYS
BANKER

FRANCIS P. KINNICUTT

"Talks With Boys and Girls, or Wisdom Better Than Gold"; "Beginning Life"; "How to Get On"; "Old Stories With New Lessons"; "Girard College Addresses"; "Turn Over a New Leaf"; "A Tour Round My Library and Other Papers"; "A Primer of Ethics"; "A Manual for the Chapel of Girard College"; "A Manual for the Chapel of the House of Refuge"; "An Order of Worship, With Forms of Prayer for Divine Service"; "Public Worship—Partly Responsive"; "Household Worship"; "Prayers for the Chapel and Family"; "Thirteen Weeks of Prayer for the Family"; "Scriptural Prayer Book for Church Services"; "A Presbyterian Prayer Book," and "Last Words for My Young Hearers and Readers." Mr. Comegys was distinctly a man of letters. Whenever he touched a literary or historical theme his whole being seemed to undergo a transformation. Data and details, facts and traditions, poetry and prose, came tumbling in headlong but not disorderly array. He excelled in phrase making, and his quotations were apt and novel. He was married May 20, 1847, to Sarah Porter, daughter to Col. James Boyd of Philadelphia, and had one son, Benjamin B. Comegys, Jr., who died in 1884, and three daughters, Clara, Mary Elizabeth and Amy Comegys, who survived him. He died at his home in Philadelphia, Pa., Mar. 29, 1900.

McKEEN, James, physician, was born in Beverly, Mass., Nov. 27, 1797, son of Joseph McKeen, the first president of Bowdoin College. He was graduated at Bowdoin in 1817 and obtained his medical degree at the Harvard Medical School in 1820, after which he began the practice of his profession at Topsham, near Brunswick, Me. He was professor of obstetrics in the Medical School of Maine for fourteen years; was one of the founders and incorporators of the Maine Medical Society, afterward the Maine Medical Association. He was a life-long student of medicine and during a serious yellow fever epidemic in New York city he braved the terrors of a stage coach journey and the risks of contagion to satisfy his medical curiosity to study the symptoms of the disease. He acquired a large and lucrative practice, and was said to be one of the ablest physicians who ever practiced in the state of Maine. He died in Topsham, Me., Nov. 28, 1873.

KINNICUTT, Francis Parker, physician, was born in Worcester, Mass., July 13, 1846, son of Francis Harrison and Elizabeth (Waldo) Kinnicutt, of New England ancestry on both sides. The first of the family in America was Roger Kennicott, a member of the Kennicott family of Totnes, Devonshire, England, who came to this country in 1661 and settled at Malden, Mass., whence he removed to Warren, R. I., in 1666. From him and his wife, Joanna Sheperdson, the line of descent is traced through their son John and his wife, Elizabeth Luther; their son John and his wife, Hannah Gohren; their son Shubull and his wife, Elizabeth Burr, and their son Thomas and his wife, Amey Whitman, who were the grandparents of Dr. Francis P. Kinnicutt. His mother was descended from Capt. James Parker, the first proprietor of Groton, Mass., in 1660. The subject of this sketch received his early education privately and was graduated at Harvard College in 1868, receiving the degree of A.M. in 1869. After his graduation at Harvard he attended the College of Physicians and Surgeons, now the medical department of Columbia University, where he was graduated in 1871. For eighteen months he was a member of the resident staff of Bellevue Hospital. On the conclusion of his services in the hospital he went abroad and continued his studies at the hospitals of Vienna and London and the University of Heidelberg. In 1893 Dr. Kinnicutt was appointed professor of clinical medicine in the College of Physicians and Surgeons, and held that chair until his death. Besides his post at Columbia he held many important professional positions. He was a physician to St. Luke's, the Presbyterian and the Cancer hospitals, and consulting physician to the Hospital for the Ruptured and Crippled, the Women's Hospital, the Babies' Hospital and the Minturn Hospital for Contagious Diseases, and was a member of the advisory board of the New York Board of Health. He also served as a member of the advisory board of the port officer of the state of New York, and as trustee of the General Memorial Hospital. Dr. Kinnicutt was a director of the Brearly School, Ltd., and the Children's Aid Society, and a member of the Association of American Physicians, of which he was president in 1906-7; the American Medical Association, the New York Academy of Medicine, the Practitioners' Society, the American Museum of Natural History, the Century Association, and the Harvard, City and University clubs. With Dr. N. B. Potter he was editor of the English translation of Sahli's "Clinical Diagnosis" (1905) and he was the author of many medical papers. Dr. Kinnicutt was married, Nov. 19, 1874, to Eleonora, daughter of Gustav Hermann Kissel, of Frankfort, Germany, and later of New York city, and left two sons: Francis H. and G. Hermann Kinnicutt. He died in New York city, May 2, 1913.

LIVERMORE, Abiel Abbot, author and educator, was born at Wilton, N. H., Oct. 30, 1811, son of Jonathan and Abigail (Abbot) Livermore, and a descendant of John Livermore, who came from Thurloe, Suffolk, England, in the seventeenth century, and was a freeman of Watertown, Mass., in 1642. He received his preliminary education at Chelmsford (Mass.) and Phillips Exeter Academies; was graduated at Harvard College in 1833, and at Harvard Divinity School in 1836. Harvard gave him the D.D. degree in 1888. He was ordained pastor of the Unitarian Church, Keene, N. H., in 1836, where he remained for fourteen years. He was pastor of the Unitarian Church, Cincinnati, during 1850-6, and at Yonkers, N. Y., during 1856-63. In 1862 he was elected president of the Meadville Theological School, Meadville, Pa., and remained at the head of that institution until 1890. During the period of his pastorate at Yonkers he was editor of the "Christian Inquirer," New York. The Meadville Theological School was founded in 1844 to educate without distinction of sect students wishing to prepare themselves for the Christian ministry. Unitarians and the Christian Baptists have supplied the majority of the students, and about one-third of the ministers of the Unitarian Church have been educated there. Dr. Livermore was the author of "The Four Gospels," with a commentary (1841); "The Acts of the Apostles," with a commentary (1844); "Christian Hymns" (1845); "Lectures to Young Men on Their Moral Dangers and Duties" (1864); "The War with Mexico Reviewed" (1850); "The Marriage Offering," prose and poetry (1852); "Discourses" (1854); "The Epistle of Paul to the Romans," with a commentary and revised translation and introductory essays (1854); "The Epistles of Paul to the Corinthians, Galatians, Ephesians, Philippians, Colossians, Thessalonians, Timothy, Titus, and Philemon" (1881); "The Epistle to the Hebrews, the Epistles of James, Peter, John and Jude, and the Revelation of John the Divine" (1881); "Anti-Tobacco" (1883); "History of the Town of Wilton, N. H." with a genealogical register (1888), and various lectures and sermons in pamphlet. He edited Priestley's "Corruptions of Christianity." As an author and commentator, a lucid style gave effective expression to his thorough scholarship. His preaching was notably persuasive and devout, and was marked by an unusual sweetness and spirituality of tone. Dr. Livermore was married (1) at Windham, Mass., May 17, 1838, to Elizabeth Dorcas, daughter of Jacob Abbot, of Windham; (2) at Meadville, Pa., June 18, 1883, to (Mrs.) Mary A. Moore, widow of A. A. Moore and daughter of William Keating. of Searsmont, Me. He died at Wilton, N. H., Nov. 28, 1892.

COUCH, Joseph James, inventor, was born in Newburyport, Mass., March 24, 1828, son of Rev. Paul and Harriet (Tyler) Couch, and grandson of John and Clarina (Heard) Couch, of Welsh descent. His father was a Congregational clergyman. He married a daughter of James Tyler, of Griswold, Conn. His maternal great-grandfather was Ebenezer Penderson, a native of England, who settled in Connecticut shortly before the Revolutionary war. He was a man of strong character, and because of his love for the land of his birth, as well as for the country of his adoption, refused to take up arms on either side during the struggle for independence. As a result of this neutral attitude, he was persecuted and lodged in jail and his property confiscated. The subject of this sketch received a thorough classical education. After a public school education, the son went to Brooklyn, N. Y., and was employed in perfecting machinery and developing mechanical inventions. To Mr. Couch belongs the credit of inventing the famous rock drill. Unfortunately, he did not obtain a patent, and it was developed and perfected by others. His device, which was the forerunner of the rock drill of Messrs. Rand, Sergeant, Ingersoll, etc., was used chiefly in the boring of the Hoosac tunnel in Massachusetts. He also invented a thread controller for sewing machines, which has been utilized very generally. He was in the employ of the United States custom house of the port of New York for over forty-seven years. Mr. Couch was a Mason, having become a member of Joppa Lodge, No. 201, in Brooklyn shortly after taking up his residence in that city. He was a past grand master and the first and only one to be made a life member of his lodge (1885). He was married June 29, 1862, to Mary, daughter of Philip Anthony, of Brooklyn, N. Y. He died in Brooklyn, N. Y., Feb. 10, 1909.

CARROLL, William Simpson, lawyer, banker and diplomat, was born in Mercer county, Pa., April 7, 1838, son of William and Barbara (Ghost) Carroll. He was the seventh William in direct lineal descent from Sir William Carroll, whose father, Daniel Carroll, was born in Ireland in 1570, and later married the granddaughter of the Duke of Argyle. He was educated at Allegheny College, Meadville, Pa., and after teaching for several years he studied law and opened a law office at Franklin, Pa., shortly after the discovery of oil in that region. Wisely profiting by the unusual opportunities for investment which abounded on every hand he amassed a fortune. During 1873-93 he traveled extensively throughout Europe and in the West, chiefly for health and pleasure, but occasionally in connection with his law practice. On his return he settled in Baltimore, Md., where he was president of the People's Bank for eight years and was also treasurer of the Chesa-

peake Gas Co. A personal friend of Pres. Cleveland, in 1893 he was appointed consul-general to Dresden, Saxony. The consulate post at Dresden is one of the most important in the diplomatic service, as Saxony ranks next to Prussia in the German Empire. Mr. Carroll had formed many friendships there on previous visits, and he was accorded the most flattering reception on his return to the U. S. consulate. His wife's personal attractiveness and tact aided her husband's earnest and intelligent efforts to represent his country worthily, and the Carrolls were soon acknowledged favorites at the Court of Saxony. At the expiration of his term he devoted another year to travel and on his return to America made Washington, D. C., his home. He had a personality, a range of culture and a strength of character that endeared him to a large circle of friends in the very highest walks of life. He was a member of the Metropolitan and other leading clubs of Washington and he was chairman of the board of trustees of the Church of the Covenant. He was twice married, first in 1864, to Nannie Rose, by whom he had four children: May, Norman, Rose and Grace Carroll, and on Nov. 15, 1905, to Maud Clifton, daughter of Wm. M. Bremer, who bore him two children, William S. and Maud Carroll, who with their mother and sister Grace survive them. He died in Washington, D. C., Jan. 15, 1911.

PADDOCK, George Laban, soldier and lawyer, was born at Augusta, Ga., where his parents were temporarily residing, Oct. 8, 1832, son of George Hussey and Rebecca (Bolles) Paddock, of old New England stock. He received his early education at private schools in New York city, and was graduated at the Harvard Law School in 1859. He practiced law at Princeton, Ill., until the outbreak of the civil war when he became first lieutenant, company I, 12th Illinois Infantry, U. S. V. He took part in the capture of Forts Henry and Donelson, at Shiloh, and in the campaign against Corinth. In the engagement at Fort Donelson Lieut. Paddock was acting as aide to Gen. John A. McArthur, and when the latter was wounded in the foot he dismounted under a heavy shower of shot and shell and cut off the general's boot, escaping without a wound. Resuming the practice of law at Princeton, Ill., he remained there until 1868, when he removed to Chicago, Ill., and built up a business which placed him among the foremost lawyers of the Cook county bar. He was especially successful in insurance and real estate law, and was esteemed as a lawyer who upheld in his practice the highest and most dignified standards of his profession. "Maj. Paddock," said the memorial of the Loyal Legion, "was loved and respected by his legal brothers for his sterling character, which was never sullied by any unprofessional act or thought, and for his bravery and devotion to duty. He was an earnest Christian, tolerant and liberal in his views regarding all worthy and honest beliefs in every form of religion. He was an earnest reader, interested in all matters of public import, and an agreeable conversationalist with a rare humor in his social and home life." Maj. Paddock was an Original Companion of the first class, military order of the Loyal Legion, and became junior vice-commander in 1889, senior vice-commander in 1890 and commander in 1891. He was married in October, 1862, to Caroline M., daughter of Judge John A. Bolles, of Boston, Mass., who survived him with five children: Charles A., George A., Caroline, Margaret and Evelyn, wife of Arthur Bowen. He died at Wilmette, Ill., Sept. 11, 1910.

ABIEL A. LIVERMORE
CLERGYMAN AND EDUCATOR

JOSEPH J. COUCH
INVENTOR

WILLIAM S. CARROLL
DIPLOMAT

GEORGE L. PADDOCK
LAWYER

H. H. SINCLAIR

HARRIS, William Laurel, artist, was born in New York city, Feb. 18, 1870, son of Henry Earl and Julia (Gillingham) Harris. Orphaned at the age of four years, he was brought up by his paternal grandmother at Windsor, Vt. He began at the early age of six years to plan decorations for the old church at Windsor, and it was a serious disappointment for him to find that his rough, child-like sketches were not understood by his elders. A number of artists visited Windsor each summer, and young Harris made the acquaintance of Thomas W. Dewing, Augustus Saint Gaudens, John W. Alexander and others, from whom he gained inspiration and enthusiasm as well as instruction. He began the serious study of art in Boston at the age of sixteen years, and after a term in the Art Students' League of New York, went to Paris in 1889, drawing and painting under Lefebvre, Doucet and Constant at the old Academy Julian. Subsequently he entered the Ecole National des Beaux Arts, studying art under Gerôme, and the principles of decorative design and its relation to architecture under Galland. He spent six years at the Beaux Arts, and while there became a leader among the French students, received the first prize of the atelier, and was elected massier of the Gerôme studio. He made many excursions to cathedral towns in the provinces while abroad and studied church decoration and stained glass, in which he was destined to excel. Returning to the United States in 1896 he was engaged for almost a year on decorative work at the Congressional Library in Washington, D. C., and then became assistant to Francis Lathrop in the decoration of St. Bartholomew's Church, New York city. In 1908 he again went abroad to visit the cathedral towns of France and make further color studies of the marvelous windows of other days, after which he began making stained glass windows on his own account. His first exhibition at the Architectural League was in 1899. His chief mural decoration is ''The Crucifixion,'' in the Paulist Church, New York city. Mr. Harris was elected a member of the Architectural League in 1898 and became vice-president in 1902. He is also a member and secretary of the National Society of Mural Painters, a director of the Artists' Aid Society, and president of the Municipal Art Society, and a member of the Catholic Club, the National Arts Club, and the MacDowell Club of New York.

SINCLAIR, Henry Harbinson, hydro-electrical engineer, was born in Brooklyn, N. Y., Dec. 22, 1858. He received his preliminary education in the public schools and academies of Brooklyn and at the age of fifteen went to sea for three years. Upon his return he entered Cornell University, but subsequently engaged in the shipping business in New York, following which he studied marine law at Columbia University and practiced in New York. Later he was obliged, because of impaired health, to go to Redlands, Cal. There he organized in 1892 the Redlands Electric Light and Power Co., of which he became president and general manager. Power for this enterprise was developed from the comparatively small stream in Mill Creek Canyon. Mr. Sinclair and his colleagues were convinced by a consulting engineer that they would find themselves hampered by obsolete apparatus unless they developed a plant capable of transmitting to any reasonable distance a new form of electrical energy—the three-phase. However, it required much negotiation with electrical manufacturers before one consented to construct the plant, which is still furnishing power.

This plant was the scene of new and knotty problems, especially that of operating three-phase generators in parallel. Here were used successfully the first three-phase generators, three-phase synchronous motor, and three-phase induction motor ever manufactured. In 1896 Mr. Sinclair, as an organizer of the Southern California Power Co., undertook the development of power in Santa Ana Canyon, near Redlands, and its transmission to Los Angeles, eighty miles away, at 33,000 volts. The voltage and distance proposed were twice as great as in any long-distance line then existing or contemplated and foremost electrical authorities discouraged the project. Both technically and financially the undertaking was one of immense difficulty. However, he succeeded in obtaining capital and starting the work. During construction the company's property was purchased by the Edison Electric Co., Los Angeles, and the entire system became a success under his management. During this period, likewise under his direction, the Mill Creek plant, with 1,960 feet head, was built. This was for many years the highest head in the world. During 1901-07 the Edison Electric Co. continued its policy of hydro-electric development by constructing on Kern river a 20,000-kw. plant. The plant had the best concrete-lined power tunnel then existing and had also the first pressure tunnel of importance. Its 120-mile transmission to Los Angeles at 75,000 volts on steel towers was also a step in advance. During this time Mr. Sinclair was vice-president and general manager of the Edison Electric Co. of Los Angeles. Under his active supervision the company installed on its system the first oil-break switches, revolving field generators, 12,000-volt generators, high potential measuring instruments, steel towers and steam turbines ever taken west of Chicago. Upon the completion of the Kern river plant he maintained an office as consulting engineer in Los Angeles until 1909, when he went to San Francisco to assume the management of the construction department of the Great Western Power Co., which position he occupied two years. During that time the company carried on the construction of two mammoth dams and developed an extensive power market. After severing his San Francisco connection he returned to Los Angeles, where he remained until 1914. During this period and under his management the industrial city of Torrance was built. Mr. Sinclair was a member of the American Institute of Electrical Engineers, the Bohemian Club, San Francisco, and the California Club, Los Angeles. He was well known and popular as a yachtsman, having made long cruises in his schooner yacht Lurline, and with her won two races from California to Honolulu. He was a man of very charming personality and was endowed with a character that combined to an unusual degree strength, pride, courage, humility, patience, humor, unselfishness and generosity. Mr. Sinclair was married in Brooklyn, N. Y., Jan. 4, 1882, to Agnes, daughter of Levi Rowley, of that city, who survives him with two children: Marjorie Rowley and Arthur Wells. He died at Pasadena, Cal., Sept. 1, 1914.

CLARKE, George W., governor of Iowa, was born in Shelby county, Ind., Oct. 24, 1852, son of John and Eliza Clarke. His parents moved to Davis county, Ia., in 1856, and there he lived and worked on a farm until manhood, pursuing his studies and for a while teaching school. Later he entered Oskaloosa College, where he was graduated in 1877. He was graduated at the law department of the state university in 1878 and immediately began the practice of his profession at Adel, Dallas co., Ia., where he has since resided. He was elected on the Republican ticket to the state house of representatives in the twenty-eighth, twenty-ninth, thirtieth and thirty-first general assemblies and was speaker during the last two sessions. In 1908 he was elected lieutenant-governor, and he was re-elected in 1910. He was elected governor in 1912. In his inauguration address (Jan. 16, 1913) he recommended a workman's compensation act and a public utilities bill; legislation for good roads, for improvement in rural schools, greater activity in the interest of the public health and reform in the management of penitentiaries and of court procedure and methods of taxation; the introduction of what is known as "the blue sky law"; the purchase of additional grounds surrounding the capitol building to meet the future needs of the state, and an act for arbitrating disputes and preventing strikes. All these suggestions for progressive legislation, except those relating to public utilities and county management, have since been enacted into laws, together with other legislation of great public value. With Governor Clarke's approval the sum of $10,000 was appropriated by the legislature for the purpose of sending the war veterans of the state to take part in the semi-centenary celebration at Gettysburg in July, 1913. He accompanied the men to Pennsylvania on that occasion and represented Iowa officially at the anniversary exercises. Gov. Clarke was re-elected for a second term in 1914. He was married at Adel, Ia., June 25, 1878, to Arletta, daughter of Benjamin Greene, of that town, and has four children: Frederick G., Charles F., Portia and Frances A. Clarke.

HARDING, Alfred, second P. E. bishop of Washington, and 240th in succession in the American episcopate, was born at Lisburn, Ireland, Aug. 15, 1852, son of Richard and Mary (Ferguson) Harding. He was educated at Pyper's Academy, Belfast, and at public schools in Dublin. In 1867 he came to the United States, and after several years in business entered Trinity College, Hartford, Conn., where he was graduated as valedictorian in 1879. In 1882 he received the degree of M.A., having pursued post-graduate studies in preparation for the ministry at the Berkely Divinity School, Middletown, Conn., where he was graduated in 1882. He was ordained a deacon of the Protestant Episcopal Church and served his diaconate in Trinity Church, Geneva, N. Y., in 1882-83. In 1883 he was ordained priest and became assistant at St. Paul's Church, Baltimore, Md. Four years later he was called as rector to St. Paul's Church, Washington, D. C., which charge he continued to hold for twenty-two years. He was one of the founders of the Episcopal diocese of Washington and secretary of the standing committee from the beginning. He also represented the diocese in four general conventions and was a canon of the Cathedral of St. Peter and St. Paul. On Jan. 25, 1909, he was consecrated second bishop of Washington to succeed Rt. Rev. Henry Y. Satterlee. At the time of his accession the diocese consisted of one hundred churches with 18,381 communicants. Bishop Harding received the degrees of D.D. from Trinity College in 1902 and LL.D. from George Washington University in 1909. He is a member of the Alpha Delta Phi fraternity and of the Alpha Phi Club of New York and Cosmos Club of Washington. He was married in New York, June 9, 1887, to Justine Butler Prindle, a talented musician and linguist and step-daughter of Dr. John Hancock

Douglas. They have three children: Alfred, Charlotte G. and Paul C. Harding. Portrait opp. p. 259.

BROWN, William Perry, cotton merchant and capitalist, was born at Caledonia, Miss., Nov. 14, 1860, son of John Cherry and Margaret (Dowdle) Brown, of Scotch ancestry. He received his preliminary education at private schools near the family plantation and finished his education at night schools. His business career began at the age of fourteen when he secured employment in a general merchandise store in Columbus, Miss. In a few years he had a store of his own, and in addition to merchandise he dealt in cotton. Later he moved to Ruston, La., and soon built up a large spot cotton business in north Louisiana. In a few years he moved to New Orleans, became a member of both the New Orleans and New York Cotton Exchanges and entered the export business. He was a close student of cotton statistics and became convinced that the southern farmer was selling his cotton crop year after year far below its intrinsic value. He was one of the first men who realized the certainty of an enormous increase in the consumption of cotton, and he decided to use his energy, intellect and business ability towards obtaining for the South the true value of its principal crop. His first attempt was in 1900, when he was one of the leaders of a movement that advanced the price of cotton from five cents a pound to over twelve cents per pound, the highest price that it had reached for many years. In 1903 he formed a bull party in association with Frank B. Hayne, H. De L. Vincent, T. J. Majors, E. G. Scales and C. C. Cordill, and succeeded in wresting from the New York bears the power to control the price of the cotton crop of the South. In 1909-10 occurred the next and most famous of the cotton campaigns, when a group composed mostly of southern operators, Mr. Brown being one of the leaders, had the bears at their mercy and pressed them so hard that, according to a leading cotton expert, "they had to call in the assistance of the United States government to indict the operators of the campaign for doing what President Wilson and the whole country is striving to do now—to put up the price of cotton." Apart from his cotton operations, Mr. Brown was prominent in many other large financial enterprises. He was one of the leaders in organizing the Hibernia National Bank and Union National Bank, of New Orleans, into the Hibernia Bank and Trust Co., one of the largest banking institutions in the southern states, and helped organize the D. H. Holmes Co., Ltd., the largest department store in the South, besides many other large enterprises that helped materially the city of New Orleans. In Mr. Brown's younger days he took a great interest in military affairs. While a resident of Columbus, Miss., he organized and became captain of a military company known as the Brown Cadets. He was a member of the Boston Club and Pickwick Club, and a member of the carnival organizations of New Orleans. He was married in New Orleans, La., Dec. 27, 1894, to Marguerite, daughter of Judge George H. Braughn, and had six children: Edward, Perry, Frank, Phillip, Mildred and Marguerite Brown. He died in New Orleans, Oct. 5, 1914.

KING, John, physician, was born in New York City, Jan. 1, 1813, son of Harmon and Margaret (LaPorte) King. His father was an officer in the New York custom house, and his mother was a daughter of the Marquis LaPorte, who came to America from France with Lafayette to aid the

ALFRED HARDING
BISHOP

JOHN KING
PHYSICIAN

GEORGE W. CRILE
SURGEON

CHARLES S. HOWE
EDUCATOR

colonists in their struggle for independence. His parents gave him a liberal education intending that he should enter mercantile life, and at the age of nineteen he was proficient in five languages. He was graduated at the Reformed Medical College of New York in 1838 and thereafter devoted many years to practical work as a botanist, pharmachologist and chemist. When twenty-two years of age he delivered a course of lectures in the Mechanic's Institute, New York, on magnetism and its relation to the earth, to geology, to astronomy, and to physiology, which were enthusiastically received and which were repeated before the New Bedford (Mass.) Lyceum. He studied the remedies employed in domestic medication and searched the fields and forests for untried drugs. He discovered and introduced podophyllin (1835), and also macrotin irisin independently of William S. Merrill, and he introduced into medical practice hydrastis and sanguinaria. Abhorring heroic medication, with great faith in vegetable remedies, he became one of the founders of the Eclectic School of Medicine. He practised medicine in Sharpsburg, Ky., during 1846–49, and then removed to Memphis, Tenn., to occupy the chair of materia medica in the Memphis Institute. He resigned in 1851 to take the chair of obstetrics in the Eclectic Medical Institute, Cincinnati, O., where he taught for forty years. He was a life-long reader and student and kept in touch with the French, German and American literature of medicine. It was his interest in Virchow's work which prompted his "Manual of Practical Microscopy" (1859). His most important book was "American Dispensatory" (1855), which passed through eight editions and was recently revised by John Uri Lloyd and Harvey W. Felter. He also wrote "Obstetrics" (1855); "Gynecology" (1855); "Chronic Diseases" (1856); "Women, Their Diseases and Treatment" (1858); "The Microscopist's Companion" (1859) and "The American Family Physician" (1860). Dr. King possessed a remarkable personality, greatly admired by his friends and students for his equipoise of character, his tremendously active mind, his universal philanthropy. He was twice married; first to Charlotte D., daughter of Russell Armington of Lansingburg, N. Y.; she died in 1847 leaving six children, and his second wife was Mary, daughter of John Rudman and widow of Stephen Henderson Platt of New York city. He died at his residence, North Bend, O., June 19, 1893.

HOWE, Charles Sumner, educator and scientist, was born at Nashua, N. H., Sept. 29, 1858, son of William R. and Susan D. (Woods) Howe. In his early infancy his parents removed to Boston, where he received his preliminary education in the public schools, and subsequently prepared for college at the high school of Franklin, Mass. He was graduated at the Massachusetts Agricultural College in 1878 and spent a year in post-graduate study there, taking up mathematics and physics. Afterward he did a year of graduate study in the same subjects at Johns Hopkins University. He began his professional career as principal of the Longmeadow High School, Longmeadow, Mass., in 1879, and from the latter part of that year until 1881 was principal of a preparatory academy at Albuquerque, N. Mex., under the charge of Colorado College, Colorado Springs, Colo. In 1883 he became professor of mathematics and astronomy at Buchtel College, Akron, O., continuing in that capacity for six years, when he was called to the chair of mathematics and physics in the Case School of Applied Science, Cleveland. He has been president of that institution since 1902. Dr.

Howe has been actively identified with numerous educational societies, among them the National Educational Association, North Central Association of Colleges and Preparatory Schools, College Entrance Examination Board, Ohio Association of Teachers of Mathematics and Science (first president), Society for the Promotion of Engineering Education (life member of the council and past president), Society for the Promotion of Industrial Education (first chairman of the Ohio section) and the Cleveland Educational Commission. He has been chairman of the advisory committee of the Cleveland High School of Commerce, chairman of the committee on the simplification of engineering degrees (Society for the Promotion of Engineering Education), member of the committee on the teaching of mathematics to engineering students, appointed by the American Society for the Advancement of Science; chairman of the section on technical schools of the international committee on the teaching of mathematics, member of the committee of ten on the relation of industrial education to the public school system, appointed by the Society for the Promotion of Industrial Education, and member of the council from the section of education, American Association for the Advancement of Science. He was president of the Cleveland Chamber of Commerce, the Cleveland University Club, and the Cleveland Engineering Society, and is a member of the Merchants' Marine League, the first White House conference on the conservation of the natural resources of the United States, the national committee on city planning and the National Civic Federation. He is a fellow of the American Association for the Advancement of Science, in which he has been vice-president of the section of engineering, secretary of the section of mathematics, secretary of the council and general secretary. He is also a fellow of the Royal Astronomical Society, an honorary member of the University Club, Washington, D. C., and a member of the American Mathematical Society, the American Astronomical and Astrophysical Society and the University and Rowfant clubs of Cleveland. He received the degrees of B.S. from Boston University in 1878, Ph.D. from Wooster College in 1887, D.Sc. (Hon.) from the Armour Institute of Technology in 1905, LL.D. (Hon.) from Mt. Union College in 1911 and LL.D. from Oberlin College in 1911. He was married at Amherst, Mass., May 22, 1882, to Abbie A., daughter of Geo. W. Waite, of North Amherst, Mass., and has three children: William C., Erle W. and Francis E. Howe.

CRILE, George W., surgeon, was born at Chili, Ohio, Nov. 11, 1864, son of Michael and Margaret (Deeds) Crile. He was graduated A.B. at the Ohio Northern University in 1884 and M.D. at the University of Wooster in 1887, receiving the degree of A.M. from the latter in 1888. Subsequently he began the practice of medicine in Cleveland, Ohio, and in 1893, 1895 and 1897 he went abroad for research and study. In 1901 he received Ph.D. from Hiram College. Dr. Crile became a lecturer and demonstrator of histology in the medical department of Wooster University in 1889, professor of physiology there in 1890, and professor of the principles and practice of surgery in 1893, retaining the last position until 1900. During 1900–11 he was professor of clinical surgery in Western Reserve University, and then became professor of surgery. He also served on the surgical staffs of the Cleveland General, St. Alexis, City, Lutheran, and Lakeside hospitals. While conducting a general practice, Dr. Crile has made a specialty of surgery of the respiratory system, and the study of traumatic shock in surgical operations. His discovery of a method of preventing traumatic shock, which he calls anoci-association, marks a step in the advance of operative surgery second in importance only to the discovery of anesthetics. In essence his theory is very simple. By way of making it clearer, it may be explained that what we call pain is a shock to the brain conveyed by the nerves from the part affected. The effort to meet this shock results in an expenditure of energy varying in amount with the intensity and duration of the pain, as we may see from the exhaustion of persons under severe or continued suffering. Violent emotions, such as fear, produce similar effects. By repeated careful experiments Dr. Crile established that under the influence of chloroform, ether, and, to a less extent, nitrous oxide, though the trauma in operation causes no conscious shock to the subject, it causes a subconscious shock, resulting in an expenditure of energy perhaps as great as if there were no anesthesia. He also found by clinical observation that there was a decided expenditure of energy due to fear before operation. These are facts of profound importance, gravely affecting the mortality in major operations. Indeed, in these days of perfected surgical technic, they are probably the main factors in post-operation mortality. Dr. Crile's method of dealing with these factors consists in the elimination of fear by psychic suggestion or the administration of narcotics for some days preceding operation, and by blocking with cocaine the nerve channels between the region of operation and the brain. The region of operation may in this way be shut off from the brain for a week if necessary. A full treatment of his discovery and a discussion of the surgical technic is given by Dr. Crile in his book, "Anoci-Association" (1914), written in collaboration with Dr. William E. Lower. He has also worked out a successful technic for blood transfusion, which has been very widely used, and he has initiated various innovations in surgical practice in other directions. At the annual meeting of the Medical Society of the State of New York in 1914, Dr. Crile advanced a theory of what he called the kinetic system. This system is composed of a chain of five organs in the body and is the only system that has as its primary purpose the transformation of potential or latent energy into heat and motion. The organs of the system are the brain, the sprarenals, the liver, the muscles and the thyroid. Deficiency in one of the organs of the kinetic chain causes alike loss of heat, loss of muscular and emotional action, of mental power and of the power of combating infection. They are all vital links in the chain. It is Dr. Crile's idea that, with knowledge of the kinetic system, men in present day life, by intelligent control of the system at the brain link, may conserve the whole system and keep each link of the chain strong. In addition to his book on "Anoci-Association," he is the author of the following books and monographs: "Surgical Shock" (1897); "Surgery of the Respiratory System" (1900); "Certain Problems Relating to Surgical Operations" (1901); "On the Blood Pressure in Surgery" (1903); "Hemorrhage and Transfusion" (1909); "The Origin and Nature of the Emotions" (1915); "A Mechanistic View of War and Peace" (1915), and "Man and Adaptive Mechanism" (1916). Dr. Crile won the Alvarenga prize at the College of Physicians and Surgeons of Philadelphia in 1901. He is a fellow of the American Association for the Advancement of Science, honorary fellow of the Royal College of Surgeons (London), and member of the Association of American Pathologists and Bacteriologists, the American Medical Association, the Society of Clinical Surgery, the Society of Experimental Biology and Medicine and the American Physiological Society. He was married Feb. 7, 1900, to Grace, daughter of John H. McBride, of Cleveland.

SHAW, John William, Roman Catholic bishop of San Antonio, Tex., was born at Mobile, Ala., Dec. 12, 1863, son of Patrick and Elizabeth (Smith) Shaw, natives of Ireland. He received his preliminary education at the Academy of the Brothers of the Sacred Heart, Mobile, and at St. Finian's Seminary, Navan, County Meath, Ireland, where he made his classics. Later he studied philosophy and theology at the American College, Rome, Italy, and was ordained to the priesthood May 26, 1888. Returning to Mobile in that year he exercised the ministry at the cathedral in that city, and in the following year he was appointed assistant at St. Peter's Church, Montgomery, Ala. In 1891 he returned to the Mobile cathedral, where he remained in charge until his consecration as bishop of Castabala, with the right of succession to Rt. Rev. John A. Forest, then bishop of San Antonio. He was consecrated in 1910 by the Most Rev. J. H. Blenk, archbishop of New Orleans, and in the same year, owing to the illness of the bishop of San Antonio, was appointed administrator of the diocese. He succeeded the late Bishop Forest in 1911. The see of San Antonio has a Catholic population of 140,000, with 141 priests, 225 churches, seventy schools and 10,000 pupils.

HASKELL, Jonathan Amory, merchant, was born in New York city, July 7, 1861, son of Samuel and Mary Frances (Amory) Haskell, and a descendant of Roger Haskell (q. v.), the founder of the family in America, who, with his two brothers, William and Mark Haskell, emigrated to the New England colonies in 1637 and settled at Beverly, Mass. Many of his descendants followed the sea for a livelihood. Roger Haskell's second wife was Elizabeth Hardy, and the line of descent is traced through their son Roger, who married Hanah Woodbury; their son Samuel, who married ——————————; their son Nathaniel, who married Peggy Frissell, and their son Samuel Haskell, who was the grandfather of our subject. Samuel Haskell was a member of the firm of Carnes & Haskell, importers of drugs and chemicals of New York. The son was educated at the military institute at Sing Sing, N. Y., and began his business career in the office of A. & L. Neilson in New York city. Four years later (in 1883) he became associated with the Rochester and Pittsburg Coal and Iron Co., with headquarters at New York. He served in the various departments of the business, acquiring a full knowledge of all its details, and then was made general manager and treasurer of the company. During 1890-92 he was general manager of the Helvetia mines at Helvetia, Pa., resigning this position to become president of the Repauno Chemical Co. of Wilmington, Del. In 1895 he became financially interested in the Laflin & Rand Powder Co., one of the oldest and largest producers of gunpowder in the United States, and served as its president from 1895 until 1912, when it was taken over by the du Pont Powder Co. Mr. Haskell is now vice-president and director of the E. I. du Pont de Nemours Powder Co. He is a member of the New York Historical Society, the Metropolitan Club, the New York Riding and Driving Club and the Down Town Association. Mr. Haskell was married Dec. 9, 1891, to Margaret Moore. daughter of John Lawrence Riker (q. v.), of New York, and they have one son, Amory Lawrence Haskell, and two daughters, Mary Riker and Margaret Riker Haskell.

MINER, Thomas, physician, was born at Westfield, Middletown, Conn., Oct. 15, 1777, son of a Congregational minister. He was graduated at Yale College in 1796. After teaching school for three years he took up the study of law, but discontinued it because of ill health, and began the study of medicine in 1802, practising that profession at Middletown, Conn. He was one of the most learned physicians of his day, being also proficient in the French, Italian, Spanish and German languages, although his career was blighted by poor health. He was one of the first to investigate cerebrospinal meningitis, and he wrote an admirable account of an epidemic of that disease in Middletown in 1823. He also published with Dr. Tully "Essays on Fevers and Other Medical Subjects" (1823). He was president of the Connecticut State Medical Society for three years. His wife was Phebe, daughter of Samuel Mather, and he died in Worcester, Mass., Apr. 23, 1841.

LAWRENCE, Jason Valentine O'Brien, physician, was born in New Orleans, La., in 1791. He was educated at the University of Pennsylvania, receiving his medical degree there in 1815. He began the practice of medicine in New Orleans with his step-father, Dr. Flood, but abandoned a promising career to return to Philadelphia for further scientific studies. To accommodate private pupils, a number of Philadelphia physicians had opened private dissecting rooms during the first half of the nineteenth century. In 1820 Dr. Lawrence opened such a school, but it differed from the others in that it was more systematically organized and was also open to the public. He delivered lectures on anatomy and surgery which were distinguished for the ease and perspicuity of their style. The school continued for many years after Dr Lawrence's death and became known as the Philadelphia School of Anatomy. Dr. Lawrence was assistant to Dr. William Gibson, and later to Dr. William E. Horner of the University of Pennsylvania. He was an enthusiastic member of the Academy of Medicine, which was established in 1821 "for the development of scientific medicine." With other members of the academy he conducted an elaborate study of the action of veins as absorbents. He performed several hundred experiments with living animals, and the results, showing that the veins as well as the lymphatics served as absorbents, were published in the "Philadelphia Journal of Medical and Physical Science." He died in Philadelphia, Pa., in 1823.

THROOP, Benjamin Henry, capitalist, was born at Oxford, Chenango co., N. Y., Nov. 9, 1811, son of Daniel and Mary (Gagere) Throop. A legendary account of his ancestry, brought down from generation to generation, affirms that Adrian Scrope, one of the regicide judges who condemned King Charles I., escaping to America, changed his name to Throop in 1668. Both his father and his grandfather, Benjamin Throop, served in the revolutionary war. The subject of this sketch was left fatherless at twelve years of age. He was educated in the old Oxford Academy, and studied medicine first under Dr. Perez Packer and then at the Fairfield Medical College, where he was graduated M.D. in 1832. He opened an office for the practice of medicine in Honesdale, Pa., practised in Oswego, N. Y., and New York city, and then settled in Providence, Pa. He became associated in business with George

W. and Selden Scranton and Sanford Grant, who established the first iron works in the city of Scranton, under the name of Scranton & Grant. Having married a sister-in-law of Mr. Grant, Dr. Throop made Scranton his permanent home. He was one of the pioneers in the settlement of the town; opened the first drug store, was prominent in the establishment of the first postoffice during the administration of Pres. Pierce and served as first postmaster during 1853–57, and was one of the originators of the Scranton Gas and Water Co., whose charter he framed. Meanwhile his medical practice, which was very exacting and laborious, spread over a large territory. In 1853 and 1854 he engaged extensively in the purchase and sale of coal lands, selling many valuable properties, and assisted in the organization of a number of mining companies. He purchased a large quantity of land in and about Scranton, which increased in value when the Delaware, Lackawanna & Western railroad was built through the town. He made additions to Hyde Park, Providence and Dunmore, laid out the village of Priceburg, and founded the town of Throop. Upon the outbreak of the civil war Dr. Throop was appointed surgeon of the 8th Pennsylvania infantry and so thoroughly did he enforce the laws of hygiene that the regiment did not lose a man by disease while away from home. At Harpers Ferry he was attacked with a fever, and was incapacitated for further service. On account of his growing business interests he withdrew from the practice of medicine after the war, but for many years continued an active participant in the affairs of the community in which he dwelt. In 1872 he was appointed trustee of the Danville Insane Asylum, a position he held until his death. He founded the Lackawanna Hospital, which for a long time he maintained at his own expense, and which he was instrumental in having endowed by the state of Pennsylvania, and for many years he was surgeon for the Delaware, Lackawanna & Western railway and the Delaware & Hudson Land Co. railway. He was president of the Scranton City Bank and the Scranton Illuminating, Heat and Power Co. He was one of the leaders in establishing the first lodge of the I. O. O. F. in Scranton, and donated a medical library of 200 volumes to the Lackawanna Medical Society. He was the author of numerous histories and reminiscences, the most important of which is "A Half Century in Scranton" (1895). Dr. Throop was married Jan. 19, 1842, to Harriet F., daughter of Justin McKinney of Ellington, Conn., and had one son, George S. Throop, also a physician, and one daughter, Mary Throop, wife of Horace B. Phelps. He died in Scranton, Pa., June 26, 1897.

GRANT, Percy Stickney, clergyman, was born in Boston, Mass., May 13, 1860, son of Stephen Mason and Annie (Stickney) Grant, and descendant of John Grant, who emigrated to Massachusetts in 1700. He was educated in the public schools of Boston, at Roxbury Latin School, and at Harvard University, where he was graduated in 1883. His theological studies were pursued at the Episcopal Theological School, Cambridge, Mass., where he took the degree of B.D. in 1886, and he received in the same year, the degree of M.A. from Harvard. Ordained deacon in 1886 and priest in 1887, after serving as curate at the Church of the Ascension, Fall River, he became rector of St. Mark's, Fall River, in 1887, where he remained till 1893. For three years he also served as rector of Christ Church, Swansea. Mr. Grant founded the Young Men's Christian Association and other philanthropic institutions of Fall River, and in

1890-93 was a member of the school committee of that city. In 1893 he removed to New York city to become rector of the Church of the Ascension. This church was founded in 1827 by Manton Eastburn, later bishop of Massachusetts, who in that year became rector of the French Church of the Holy Spirit in Pine Street, uniting with that congregation a number of friends and forming a new parish. The church of the Ascension was admitted into the union with the diocesan convention in October of that year. In 1829 a new church, situated on Canal Street east of Broadway, was consecrated, and here the congregation worshiped till June 30, 1839, when the building was burned. A temporary home was found in the chapel of the University of New York, and on March 19, 1840, the cornerstone of the present edifice was laid by Bishop Onderdonk. At that time Fifth Avenue, hardly more than a name, ended at Twenty-third Street, and the church stood in the midst of open meadows. In March, 1843, Dr. Eastburn was succeeded by Gregory Thurston Bedell, and during his incumbency the church of the Ascension was conspicuous in members and wealth, the locality in which it is situated having become the fashionable part of the city. On Dec. 29, 1859, Dr. John Cotton Smith took charge of the parish, and upon his death in 1882, Dr. E. Winchester Donald became rector. During his rectorship the church was beautified and altered and the parish house was built. In the spring of 1893 Dr. Donald succeeded Phillips Brooks as rector of Trinity Church, Boston, and on Sept. 30th Mr. Grant assumed the duties he had laid down, having previously made it a condition of acceptance that the pews should be free. Under him the debt has been greatly decreased, an endowment fund has been created, more than $500,000 have been contributed for all purposes, and the work of the church, which is institutional, has been broadened in every direction. In 1899 Mr. Grant was appointed honorary secretary to the committee "on the relation of the Protestant Episcopal Church to our new possessions," and in that capacity accompanied Rt. Rev. Henry C. Potter, D.D., visiting Honolulu, Japan, China, the Philippines, India and other countries. In 1907-8 he was preacher to Harvard University. He is a trustee of Berea College and of Manassas Colored Industrial School, a director of the American Society for the Prevention of Cruelty to Animals, and a member of the Century, City, New York Athletic and Authors' clubs. He is the author of "Land Questions in the Philippines," "Church Missions in Asia," "Marriage and Divorce," "Monologues of Robert Browning," "Ad Matrem and Other Poems," "The Search of Balisarius," "Observations in Asia" and "Socialism and Christianity." Hobart College conferred upon him the degree of S.T.D.

CARROLL, John Patrick, second Roman Catholic bishop of the diocese of Helena, Mont., was born in Dubuque, Ia., Feb. 22, 1864. He was graduated at St. Joseph's College in June, 1883, and entered the grand seminary, Montreal, Canada, for his theological course shortly after. He finished in six years with the doctor's degree and was ordained priest July 7, 1889. In Dubuque he subsequently joined the faculty of his alma mater and became its president. He never held a pastorate, all his priestly career being devoted to teaching. On the death of Bishop Brondel, of Helena, Nov. 3, 1903, Dr. Carroll was appointed his successor and was consecrated Dec. 21, 1904. The diocese covers 51,922 square miles in the western section of Montana and has 243 churches, stations and chapels with eighty priests, thirty-one schools and 6,700 pupils.

CUTLER, S[amuel] Newton, merchant, was born at East Boston, Mass., Jan. 25, 1855, son of Samuel and Sarah Jane (Bennett) Cutler, and descended from John Cutler who came over from England in 1637 and settled at Hingham, Mass. From him the line of descent is traced through his son Samuel, who married Sarah Church; their son Ebenezer, who married Mary Marsh; their son Ebenezer, who married Mary Stockwell; their son Jonathan, who married Elizabeth Holman; their son Jonathan, who married Lydia Waldron, and their son Samuel, who married Ruth Phillips, and who was the grandfather of the subject of this sketch. He was graduated at Harvard College in 1877 with the degree of A.B. cum laude. During his college course he won several prizes for scholarship, and was a member of the Phi Beta Kappa society. After a brief period in teaching and in traveling throughout the West, he became associated with his father's firm, Messrs. Hill & Cutler, dealers in cotton and wool stock in Boston, Mass. He was quick to grasp the details of the business, and passing rapidly through the various departments, was admitted to the firm in 1892, since which he has been closely identified with its management. The firm of Hill & Cutler is one of the best known exporting houses in New England, doing a business of $500,000 to $750,000 per annum throughout the entire United States and Europe. He was a member of the Somerville board of education during 1886—1903, being chairman of the board for the last three years and in 1903 was elected to the state legislature, serving two terms, during which he was a member of the committees on education, taxation and labor. He was also actively interested in improving and equipping the textile schools of Massachusetts. Mr. Cutler is a member of the Baptist Church and a life member of the Harvard Chapter of the Phi Beta Kappa Society, the Harvard Union, the Bostonian Society of Boston, the New England Historic Genealogical Society, the Somerville Historical Society and the Plymouth Society of Plymouth, Mass. He is also a member of the National Geographic Society, the Republican Club of Massachusetts, the Boston Baptist Social Union, of which he was first vice-president for the year 1908—09, the Vermont Association of Boston, the Harvard Club of Somerville, the Mystic Valley Harvard Club, and the Excelsior Council of the Royal Arcanum. He is a trustee of the Somerville Savings Bank, the Somerville Hospital and the New England Baptist Hospital. He was married Nov. 9, 1882, to Ella Francis, daughter of Hiram Newell Stearns of Somerville.

AMES, Louis Annin, merchant, was born on the island of St. Helena, S. C., Sept. 5, 1866, son of Jacob Meech and Phebe (Annin) Ames, and a descendant of William Ames, a native of England, who came to America in 1629 and settled at Preston, Conn. His father was a merchant, and his mother was a daughter of Alexander Annin, a well-known ship-chandler of New York. Mr. Ames was educated in the public schools of Jersey City, and began his business career in 1888 with the firm of Annin & Co., flag makers. The business was organized in 1847 by Edward J. and Benjamin F. Annin, sons of Alexander Annin, who continued the flag department of their father's ship-chandlery business. Beginning in a small way, the business has grown until it is now the largest of its kind in the country. Annin & Co.'s flags have

S. Newton Cutler

LOUIS ANNIN AMES
MERCHANT

ELEANOR GATES
AUTHOR

BENJAMIN C. TILGHMAN
INVENTOR

SARAH J. McNUTT
PHYSICIAN

been furnished for innumerable festivals, celebrations and occasions of state, and have been purchased by the United States government for both the army and navy. Edward J. Annin retired from the business in 1869, another brother, John, taking his place, and when Benjamin F. Annin died in 1896 the subject of this sketch was admitted to the firm. John Annin died in 1909, and in the following year the firm was incorporated as Annin & Co., with Louis Annin Ames as president. While still occupying the original site on Fulton street, the business has grown to a capacity of four buildings and two factories. Mr. Ames is also president of the Ira Brown Co. and the Old Glory Realty Co. He has long been interested in civic and patriotic affairs. He is president of the Empire State Society of the Sons of the American Revolution, councillor of the New York Society of the Order of the Founders and Patriots of America, secretary-general of the general order of the Founders and Patriots of America, secretary of the American Flag Association, a member of the United States Navy League, Washington Continental Guards, Sons of the Revolution, Society of Colonial Wars, the Laity League of Social Service, life member of the New York Historical Society, and an associate of the John A. Dix Post of the Grand Army of the Republic. For many years Mr. Ames has taken a deep interest in religious movements. He was at one time president of the Universalist Club of New York city and the Sunday School Institution of New York state; since 1909 he has been president of the Laymen's League, and is now (1916) president of the New York State Convention of Universalists, and a director of the Universalist General Convention. During 1900-05 he was president of the national society of the Young People's Christian Union. Mr. Ames is a director in the American Institute of Civics, was one of the vice-presidents of the Hudson-Fulton Commission, and for three years has been a member of the executive board of the New York City Safe and Sane Fourth of July Committee. He is a member of the Merchants' Association, the American Scenic and Historic Preservation Society, the Fulton Club, the Twilight Club, the Cosmos Club and the Motor Boat Club of America. He was married Jan. 20, 1909, to Abby Whitney, daughter of Joseph Crowell, of New York city, and has two daughters: Edith and Jean Ames.

GATES, Eleanor, author and playwright, was born at Shakopee, Minn., Sept. 26, 1875, daughter of William Cummings and Margaret Ann (Archer) Gates, and a descendant of Sir Thomas Gates, of Gates Manor, Essex, England, who was granted the Atlantic coast half of the colony of Virginia by King George the Third, and came to this country in the early part of the seventeenth century. His son, Stephen Gates, settled in Massachusetts about 1657, and from him and his wife, Anna Hill, the line is traced through their son Simon and his wife, Margaret Brown; their son Amos and his wife, Hannah Oldham; their son Amos and his wife, Mary Trowbridge; their son John and his wife, Eunice Winch; their son Leonard and his wife, Lucretia Mack, and their son William Cummings Gates. Miss Gates' father was a rancher, and her childhood was spent in the clear, open envinronment of a Dakota farm, where, she says, "I herded cattle with my brothers for six years." Her higher education was obtained at Stanford University and the University of California. She taught school for four terms in Shasta county, Cal., and was engaged in news-

paper work for five years, serving successively on the staffs of the "Examiner," the "Call" and the "Chronicle" of San Francisco, and the "Enquirer" of Oakland, Cal. In the meantime she had begun to contribute to "Scribner's," the "Century," the "Book Lover's Magazine," the "Saturday Evening Post" and other periodicals. Her first book was "The Biography of a Prairie Girl" (1902), followed by the "Plow Woman" (1906); "Cupid, the Cow-Punch" (1907); "Good Night" (1907); "The Justice of Gideon" (1911), and "The Poor Little Rich Girl" (1912). These were stories of merit and gave her a fairly satisfactory place among contemporary writers. They brought into the hot-house atmosphere of our literature something of the clean, stimulating freshness of the prairies—a point of view which, though not original, was sufficiently rare to be novel. Her talent is not altogether of the straightforward type, nor is it altogether of the whimsical type. She combines a lively and poetic fancy and a certain dreamy tenderness with a very clear realization of actualities and a keen insight into social conditions. Her "Poor Little Rich Girl" is a combination of fairy tale and social satire, to which there is hardly a parallel in American literature. She afterwards dramatized the story, and under the same title it was first performed in New York, in February, 1913. It was said to be the best child's play since "Little Lord Fauntleroy." Miss Gates is a member of the Prytanean Society of the University of California and the Society of American Dramatists and Composers. She was married at Merced, Cal., Jan. 26, 1901, to Richard Walton Tully, a playwright and author, and was divorced in 1915.

TILGHMAN, Benjamin Chew, inventor, was born in Philadelphia, Pa., Oct. 26, 1821, third child of Benjamin and Anna Maria (McMurtrie) Tilghman. He was descended from Richard Tilghman, a surgeon in the British navy under Admiral Blake, who, having signed the petition that justice be done to one Charles Stuart, was flouted as a regicide by the Royalists, and just before Charles II. came to the throne emigrated to Lord Baltimore's colony in Maryland, where he obtained lands on Charles river and built a manor house. His descendants have been prominent at the bar and as jurists for several generations. Benjamin C. Tilghman was educated at Bristol College, and later the University of Pennsylvania, where he was graduated in 1839. Maintaining the legal traditions of his family, he studied law, and was admitted to the bar, but never practiced his profession. In all his work of research he associated with him his younger brother, Richard Albert Tilghman, to whom he was devotedly attached. They journeyed through Europe together, visiting laboratories, chemical works, factories and mills. On his return Benjamin perfected the production of steel shot of extraordinary hardness, for use in sawing, polishing and grinding stone, and under a ring drill, for driving wells in prospecting for mines, quarries and veins of oil. When the civil war broke out he promptly enlisted as captain in the 26th regiment, U. S. volunteers. In the field he speedily earned promotion to a lieutenant-colonelcy and then to a colonelcy. In the battle of Chancellorsville he was severely wounded in the thigh and upon his partial recovery was given the command of a colored regiment. At the close of the war he was a general by brevet, in command of a brigade in Florida. Shortly after this he discovered a process for the chemical production of paper from wood fiber. In 1871 he invented the sand blast, devising an apparatus which in economy has never been surpassed. The sand blast is employed for removing scale from forgings and castings; for depolishing glass, china, porcelain and other brittle substances; for producing cameo effects in glass of different hue; for labeling bottles used by chemists and druggists; for scouring the outside of bank safes; for smoothing the armor plates of warships; for incising marble, limestone or granite with letters and ornaments; for removing dirt and discolorations from buildings of brick and stone; for cleansing tubes, tanks and boilers from rust and scale; for refacing wheels of emery and corundum; for granulating celluloid films for cameras; for bringing into relief the grains of wood; for perfecting the joints in reservoirs, boilers and tanks; for preparing steel rails and girders for welding; for finishing files and rasps as first manufactured or in restoring their points after wear; for exposing cracks in the teeth of cutters of milling machines, and for taking off the layers of paint successively laid upon a ship. Gen. Tilghman also designed a torpedo to be propelled rocket-fashion by a slow-burning powder, but it was not a success. The establishment which he founded, and where his scientific library remains, still continues in Philadelphia. He was unmarried and died in Philadelphia, Pa., July 3, 1901.

McNUTT, Sarah Jane, physician, was born at Warrensburg, Warren co., N. Y., twin daughter of James and Adaline (Waite) McNutt. The MacNaughts occupied the estates of Kilquhanite in Galloway, Scotland, since 1400. The last proprietor of the name, John MacNaught, started for America with his four sons in the beginning of the eighteenth century, but he died on the way at Londonderry, Ireland. In 1718 his second son, William MacNaught, joined a company of Scotch-Irish Presbyterians, who established a colony at Londonderry (now Manchester), N. H. He married Jean Galbreath, and the line of descent is traced through their son William, who married Sarah Elkin James; their son, Elijah Allen, who married Susanna Mudgett, and their son James, who was Dr. McNutt's father. She received a thorough classical education, graduating at the Albany Normal College and attending the Emma Willard School at Troy, after which she took a special course in languages. After teaching a few years she decided to become a physician, and entering the Woman's Medical College of the New York Infirmary was graduated M.D. in 1877. She was instructor in gynecology at the Woman's Medical College for a number of years; later became consultant to the same department in the dispensary, and was five years assistant to the chair of general surgery, during which she was also college instructor of surgery. She gradually made a specialty of diseases of women and children and achieved a reputation as one of the foremost authorities on these branches of medicine. When the New York Post-Graduate Hospital was organized she became instructor and lecturer on the diseases of children. At that time there was not in all New York a single ward in any hospital devoted exclusively to children under two years of age. Realizing this need Dr. McNutt founded the babies' wards at the Post-Graduate Hospital and gave bedside instruction in children's diseases that could not be obtained elsewhere. She was the first to establish by research the fact that infantile paralysis following difficult labor was due to meningeal hemorrhage, which resulted

from injury to the brain during birth, and her paper on this subject, "Double Infantile Hemiplegia," she presented to the American Neurological Society upon her admission to that body in 1884. The paper was published in 1885 in the "American Journal of Medical Science," and extracts from it have been quoted frequently by both American and European authorities. Out of the babies' wards grew the Babies' Hospital, which was opened in 1888 with Dr. McNutt and her sister, Dr. Julia G. McNutt, its attending physicians. Dr. McNutt was one of the attending physicians and surgeons in the gynecological department of the New York Infirmary, and was clinican in the dispensary for a number of years. In 1888 she resigned from the faculty of the New York Post-Graduate Medical School to devote all her time to the practice of gynecology and special surgery. She was one of the incorporators of the Post-Graduate Training School for Nurses founded by her sister, Dr. Julia G. McNutt. In her medical practice Dr. Sarah McNutt is resourceful, enthusiastic and untiring, deeply absorbed in her work and in the progress of medicine and surgery in general. No mention of her career would be complete without reference to her work in the New York morgue. The idea of utilizing the material at the morgue for instruction in the pathological conditions of children was original with her, and thus her classes at the New York Post-Graduate Medical School had practical experience in all the operations performed on children, while she found here an excellent opportunity to perfect herself in gynecological surgery and abdominal work. She is a member of the New York Academy of Medicine, Medical Society of the County of New York, the State and American Medical Associations, New York Pathological Society, Woman's Medical Society, the Woman's State Medical Society, the Schenectady County Medical Society, American Society of Sanitary and Moral Prophylaxis, and first woman member of the American Neurological Society. She is the author of "Therapeutics of Children's Diseases" (1884); "Acute Diffuse Nephritis Following Intestinal Catarrh" (1884); "Report of a Case of Entire Destruction of Left Lung with Small Remains of Right Lung" (1884); "Report of a Case of Croupous Pneumonia in an Infant" (1884); "Intra-cranial Hemorrhage in Children" (1885); "Apoplexia Neonatorium" (1885); "Seven Cases of Spastic Hemiplegia" (1885); "Double Infantile Hemilegia" (1884-85); "A Rare Case of Meningocele" (1887); "Infant Feeding" (1888); "A Case of Retention Cyst of the Vagina" (1888); "A Case of Multiple Tumors of Cerebrum in a Child" (1888); "A Summer's Work in the Babies' Hospital" (1889); "Pachymeningitis Internae Hemorrhagicae" (1889); "Epithelioma Ovarii" (1890); "Hygiene of Childhood" (1890); "Dress" (1890); "Some European Notes, Medical and Otherwise" (1897); "Non-Operative Gynecology" (1905); "A Year's Progress in Medicine" (1905); "Old Age and Its Postponement" (1906); "Results of Research Work on Yellow Fever and Direct Transfusion of Blood" (1909), and "Present Day Benefits of Research Work" (1910). Portrait opposite page 263.

LOCKE, John, scientist, was born at Lempster, N. H., Feb. 19, 1792, son of Samuel Barron and Hannah (Pussell) Locke. He early developed a mechanical bent and a love for reading. He studied medicine at Yale College and was graduated M. D. in 1818, but his practice was not successful, and he abandoned it for a teacher's profession. He became assistant professor in a female academy at Windsor, Vt., and later established schools for girls in Lexington, Ky. (1821), and Cincinnati, O. (1822). His method of instruction was largely conversational and his schools were popular. In 1835 he was elected professor of chemistry in the Medical College of Ohio, and in 1854 became principal of an academy at Lebanon, O. Dr. Locke invented a number of scientific instruments, among them the thermoscopic galvenometer, designed so that its indications may be seen on the lecture table, and at the same time so delicate in its operation as to show extremely small changes in temperature; a microscopic compass; a gravity escapement for regulator clocks (1844); a spirit level for engineers, and the electric chronograph, or magnetic clock (1849), which Lieut. Maury of the National Drugatory characterized as "the most important discovery in astronomy." He had a most accurate knowledge of geology, and in 1838 made a geological survey of Ohio. He was also associated with David Dale Owen in the survey of the mineral lands of the Northwest for the United States government, during which his familiarity with electricity and magnetism was very helpful in indicating the depth and course of ore. He was the author of "The Outlines of Botany" (1829), an English grammar and textbook on botany. Dr. Locke was married in Cincinnati, O., Oct. 25, 1825, to Mary Morris, of Newark, N. J. He died in Cincinnati, O., July 10, 1856.

LONGWORTH, Langdon Rives, physician, was born in Cincinnati, O., Dec. 25, 1846, son of Joseph and Anna Maria (Rives) Longworth. He was named for his uncle, Dr. Langdon Rives, who was for many years professor of obstetrics in the Medical College of Ohio. He was graduated at Harvard College in 1867. After spending two years in Europe he took up the study of medicine and was graduated at the College of Physicians and Surgeons, New York city, in 1873. He studied another year abroad and then became assistant demonstrator at the Medical College of Ohio. Later he was made professor. He specialized in surgery and dermatology, and although he acquired an extensive practice, he abandoned it for the more congenial scientific investigation. He developed the process of photography of microscopic preparation; devised a new instrument for injecting and invented the electric candle for his demonstrations in anatomy, for which a patent was granted May 1, 1878, and just before his death he completed the construction of an electric lantern, by the means of which he could throw images of solid bodies upon the screen, thus enabling him to perform dissections of organs before large classes. He was unmarried and died in Cincinnati, O., Jan. 14, 1879.

HAMLIN, Charles Sumner, financier, was born in Boston, Mass., Aug. 30, 1861, son of Edward Sumner and Anna Gertrude (Conroy) Hamlin, and descended from James Hamlin, first of the family in America. James Hamlin settled in Barnstable on Cape Cod in 1639. His son Eleazer served in Capt. Gorham's company in King Philips' war. Eleazer's grandson of the same name served as major in the revolutionary war. At the close of the war he moved to Harvard, Mass., where his homestead remains standing at the present time. The line of descent is continued through his son Asia, and the latter's son, Nathan Sumner Hamlin, who was the grandfather of Charles S. Hamlin. Hannibal Hamlin, vice-president of the United States, and Dr. Cyrus Hamlin, of Lexington, Mass.,

were of the same stock, and closely related to Mr. Hamlin. The latter was fitted for college at the Roxbury Latin School, and was graduated at Harvard University in 1883. Choosing the legal profession, he entered the Harvard Law School and was graduated A.M. in 1886. He immediately began the practice of law in Boston and continued it up to the time of his appointment, in 1893, to be assistant secretary of the U. S. treasury. The change of tariff policy during his term of office, substituting ad valorem schedules for specific, opened greater opportunities to those disposed to defraud the revenues, and to these undervaluation abuses Mr. Hamlin devoted himself untiringly. He changed the entire accounting system of the treasury, serving on the commission appointed by congress to arrange for a new system. He devoted much attention to the question of the seal fisheries of Behring Sea while in office, making a trip to Alaska in 1894, and laboring to procure more adequate protection for the seal herd than is afforded by the regulations adopted by the Paris tribunal. He also devoted much time to the consular service, and his constant aim was to increase the efficiency of our representatives abroad by simplifying and systematizing their duties in connection with the customs service. He resigned his secretaryship in April, 1897. The next day he was offered by Pres. McKinley the position of commissioner of the United States, to serve with Hon. John W. Foster, in negotiating a satisfactory settlement of the fur seal controversy between the United States, Great Britain, Japan and Russia. He accepted the position, and while his colleague, Mr. Foster, went to Russia he went to Japan to confer with the government of that country. A treaty between the United States, Russia and Japan relating to the fur seal fisheries of Behring Sea was entered into at this convention, and signed by Mr. Hamlin and his colleague in the name of the United States in 1897. Following this he was delegated to a similar convention between Great Britain and the United States of which Mr. Hamlin was presiding officer. He now returned to the practice of law in Boston, Mass., and distinguished himself in various lines of civic activity. He was a member of the executive committee of the Civic Federation of New England; was a delegate to the International Arbitration convention which met in New York in 1907. In politics Mr. Hamlin is a Democrat. He was a delegate to the Democratic national convention in St. Louis in 1904. In 1912 he was made vice-president of the Woodrow Wilson College Men's League and also president of the Woodrow Wilson League of Massachusetts. In 1913 Pres. Wilson appointed him assistant secretary of the treasury and in 1914 governor of the Federal Reserve Board, which was created in that year as a currency reform measure. The purpose of the board is to supervise the finances of the nation as a whole, somewhat in the same way as the Interstate Commerce Commission supervises the railroads. Its original members were the following: the secretary of the treasury, chairman; Charles S. Hamlin, governor; Paul M. Warburg, of New York; W. P. G. Harding, Adolph C. Miller, Frederick A. Delano, vice-governor, and John Skelton Williams. Mr. Hamlin has always championed ultra-progressive measures. He advocates the income tax, the popular election of U. S. senators, direct primaries and the initiative and referendum. He is a member of the American Bar Association, the Boston Bar Association, the Massachusetts and New York Reform clubs, Civil Service League, University Club of New York, Union, Somerset and Tavern clubs of Boston, and the Metropolitan and Cosmos clubs of Washington. His dominant personal characteristic is his love for order and passion for details. He has compiled an index digest of the interstate commerce laws and of the Federal Reserve act, and he has written a number of pamphlets on statistics and financial matters. He was married June 4, 1898, to Huybertie Lansing, daughter of John V. L. Pruyn, of Albany, where the Pruyns, who are of Dutch descent, have been settled for more than two centuries.

BRADY, James Henry, 8th governor of Idaho, (1909–11) was born in Indiana county, Pa., June 12, 1862, son of John and Catherine (Lee) Brady of Scotch-Irish and German stock. He is a descendant of Hugh Brady, the first American ancestor, who married Hannah McCormick, and the line of descent is through their son James, who married Rebecca Young, and their son James Young, who married Sarah Ricketts, and was Gov. Brady's grandfather. Two sons of the emigrant Hugh Brady, Capt. Samuel Brady and Gen. Hugh Brady, distinguished themselves as soldiers, the former as an Indian fighter, whose name became a household word for bravery and resourcefulness in Western Pennsylvania in early years, and the latter as a colonel in the war of 1812. Gov. Brady was brought up on the farm which his father had purchased in Johnson county, Kan., within twenty miles of Kansas City, Mo., attended the public schools of the district and the Leavenworth Normal College. He taught school for three years after receiving his diploma, fitting himself in the meantime for the practice of law. After editing a semi-weekly newspaper for two years he engaged in the real estate business in St. Louis, Mo., Chicago, Ill., and Houston, Tex., and in 1895 settled in Idaho where he became identified with the upbuilding of the Snake River Valley which included the construction of the Idaho canal, the Marysville canal and the Fort Hall Indian Reservation canal. He became interested in the electric development of the water power in southeastern Idaho, and he is president and principal owner of the Idaho Consolidated Power Co., at American Falls, which owns and controls one of the largest power plants in the state. He was a delegate to the Republican national convention of 1900; chairman of the Idaho delegation to the Republican national convention of 1908, and a member of the delegation from that convention to notify William H. Taft of his nomination at Cincinnati, O.; vice-president of the national irrigation congress, 1896–98, and a member of its executive committee 1900–04. As chairman of the Republican state central committee of Idaho in 1904 and 1906, he was the leader of the party in the state, which nominated him by acclamation to be governor. He was elected Nov. 3, 1908. Gov. Brady was a strong adherent of the direct primary and the local option bills, and was largely instrumental in their enactment into law. The former provides for the expression of the people's choice for U. S. senator. Among other legislation enacted during his administration were an amendment of the law regulating the period of employment in underground mines, an employer's liability law, and a law prohibiting wholesale liquor dealers being interested in places doing retail business. Provision was made for the protection and care of orphans and of homeless, neglected or abused children; and for the indeterminate sentence of persons convicted of felonies, except treason and murder in the first degree. Gov. Brady contributed both time and money to almost every movement which has had for its purpose the betterment of the

state. His most striking characteristics, besides his keen foresight and great executive ability, are a truly inspiring activity and genuine public spirit. He is a member of the Pocatello Commercial Club; Boise Commercial Club; Salt Lake City Commercial Club; Rocky Mountain Club of New York; president of the Western Development Association; president Idaho Children's Home Finding and Aid Society; honorary vice-president Panama-Pacific Exposition; chairman advisory board National Council Women Voters; honorary member Grand Army Republic, Department of Idaho, and honorary member Kansas Historical Society. He is a member of the Woodmen of the World, an Odd Fellow, a Mason, an Elk, an Eagle and a member of the Congregational Church. He is a widower and has two sons: James Robb and Silas Edward Brady, the former of whom is editor and publisher of a newspaper at Caney, Kan., and the latter in the jewelry business at El Reno, Okla.

FRENCH, William Merchant Richardson, director of the Art Institute, Chicago, Ill., was born at Exeter, N. H., Oct. 1, 1843, son of Henry Flagg and Anne (Richardson) French, and brother of Daniel C. French, the sculptor. His father was a noted lawyer in New Hampshire and later in Massachusetts. His grandfather, Daniel French, was at one time attorney-general of New Hampshire, and his maternal grandfather, William Merchant Richardson, was chief justice of that state. Mr. French was educated at Phillips Exeter Academy, and was graduated at Harvard College in 1864. During the civil war he served in a massachusetts regiment until illness compelled him to retire. He practiced engineering and landscape gardening in 1865–67, and subsequently settled in Chicago, where his numerous professional writings for journals and societies soon attracted wide notice. In 1874 he began to develop his natural taste for art pursuits, wrote art reviews, delivered lectures, and in 1878 became secretary of the Chicago Academy of Design. A new society was organized in 1879 under the name or the Chicago Academy of Fine Arts, which, three years later, was changed to the Art Institute of Chicago. Mr. French had charge of the school and museum from the beginning, at first holding the title of secretary and subsequently that of director. Despite his duties at the institute, he acquired a national reputation as a lecturer and art critic. He appeared in most of the larger cities of this country, illustrating with the crayon a series of six lectures entitled "The Wit and Wisdom of the Crayon," "Smiles and Tears; or, The Expression of the Emotions," "An Hour With the Caricaturists," "Conventional Art in Pictures and Decoration," "A Knack of Drawing, Natural or Acquired?" "National Character and National Art." He was also a lecturer in the university extension courses of the University of Chicago. As a lecturer he united superior artistic ability with fine literary taste and ready wit, and for more than twenty years was one of the most popular men on the American platform. Mr. French saw the Chicago Art Institute, of which he was director for thirty-five years, grow from little more than an intangible idea to its present position among the leading art museums of the country. A beautiful building of Bedford limestone was erected on the lake front at Adams street in 1891 and was opened in 1893. Its permanent collections consist of valuable acquisitions in all departments of painting, sculpture and the decorative arts, valued at over $1,500,000, and its art school has a large and efficient faculty. A man of unusual refinement and scholarship, an

JAMES H. BRADY
GOVERNOR

CHARLES S. HAMLIN
FINANCIER

WILLIAM M. R. FRENCH
ART DIRECTOR

GEORGE W. MARTIN
AUTHOR AND EDITOR

Bowdoin S. Parker.

orator of singular ability, a famous lecturer and writer, an artist of enviable gift, he was above all a Christian gentleman whose genial, kindly influence penetrated every part of the great institution which he guided. Mr. French was one of the founders and a charter member of the American Association of Museums, and its president during 1907-08. He was superintendent of the Sunday-school of St. Paul's Evangelical Church of Longwood and Beverly Hills for eighteen years, a charter member of the Chicago Literary Club (president 1912-13), at one time vice-president of the National Prisoners' Aid Society and president of the Central Howard Association at the time of his death. He was married (1) Sept. 9, 1879, to Sarah M., daughter of Owen Lovejoy, of Princeton, Ill.; (2) Mar. 27, 1890, to Alice, daughter of Henry T. Helm, of Chicago. Two children were born of the latter union: Henry Helm and Prentiss French. Mr. French died in Chicago, Ill., June 3, 1914.

MARTIN, George Washington, author and editor, was born at Hollidaysburg, Pa., June 30, 1841, son of David and Mary (Howell) Martin. His father, a native of County Antrim, Ireland, came to America in 1819 and settled first in Indiana county, Pa., and later in Douglas county, Kan. George Washington was educated in the public schools of Pennsylvania until the age of fourteen, when he became a printer's apprentice in the office of the Hollidaysburg "Register"; worked for two years on the "Union" and "Kansas National Democrat," Lecompton, Kan., and concluded his five years' apprenticeship in a book office in Philadelphia. In 1861 he established the "Union," Junction City, Kan.; was a postmaster there for a period, register of the land office, and assistant assessor of internal revenue. President Andrew Johnson removed him as register of the land office, but he was reappointed by President Grant in 1869, serving until 1871. He was elected state printer by the legislature in 1873, and was thrice re-elected, holding the office for eight years. He was grand master of the Kansas Odd Fellows in 1872-72, and represented the state in the grand lodge of the United States in 1875-76. He represented Geary county in the legislature in 1883-84, and during that period was also mayor of Junction City. In 1888 he removed to Kansas City, Kan., and became editor of the "Gazette." In the Republican state convention of 1894 he received 122 votes for governor of Kansas, although he was not seriously a candidate for the nomination. In 1899 he was elected secretary of the Kansas State Historical Society, of which he was a founder, and he retained that position until a few weeks before his death. Many of his articles and addresses were published in the volumes of "Kansas Historical Collections," which he edited. His "Owl Club Letter" is celebrated in Kansas, and considered an unusual and effective temperance lecture. Mr. Martin was married (1) at Junction City, Kan., Dec. 20, 1863, to Lydia, daughter of Allen Coulson; (2) at Topeka, Kan., Oct. 10, 1901, to (Mrs.) Josephine Morgan, widow of Major William S. Blakely. He left three children, Lincoln, Amelia, wife of Napoleon Bonaparte Burge, and Charles Coulson Martin. He died at Topeka, Kan., Mar. 27, 1914. Portrait opposite page 266.

PARKER, Bowdoin Strong, lawyer, was born at Conway, Mass., Aug. 10, 1841, son of Alonzo and Caroline (Gunn) Parker, of New England ancestry. His father (1814-92) was a well-known architect and builder, who probably designed and constructed more churches in the state of Massachusetts than any other one person. Possessed of an inventive mind, he devised a number of labor-saving tools and machines, and later established a large manufacturing business to produce and market them. After his graduation at the Greenfield high school, the son entered the employ of Pettibone & Dodge, wholesale hardware merchants of New York, where he was completing his apprenticeship when the civil war broke out. He volunteered his services in the 52nd Massachusetts infantry and served under Gen. Banks in the department of the Gulf and the investment of Port Hudson, La., being wounded in the second general assault. After the war he was commissioned in the Massachusetts state militia, and held the rank of first lieutenant, captain, adjutant, judge advocate, assistant adjutant general with the rank of lieutenant-colonel and chief of staff of the first brigade. He was retired in 1897 with the rank of colonel. In 1866 he became connected with his father's manufacturing business, the Greenfield Tool Co., of which he was treasurer and manager after the latter's retirement in 1874. He inherited from his father a practical and inventive mind which found expression in a number of useful inventions. The first drop-forged or machine-made shoes for oxen were forged under one of his patents and started a new industry. He was in active management for fifteen years. During this period he was more or less prominent in civic affairs, being an officer in the fire department, a trustee of the library association, and chairman of the board of assessors of taxes. Meanwhile he determined to study law and taking the law course in Boston University, was graduated with the degree of LL.B. in 1876. While continuing his manufacturing business he gradually acquired a general law practice. He was admitted to the Suffolk bar in 1875, to the U. S. district and circuit courts in 1878, and later to the U. S. circuit court of appeals and the U. S. supreme court. He gradually made a specialty of patent and trade mark litigation in the United States courts, and was recognized as a reliable authority in that department of practice, but with the consolidation of all lines of business, those branches of law largely decreased, and his practice again became general. In 1881 he removed to Boston. In 1889, 1890 and 1891 he was elected a member of the Boston common council and was a member of the state house of representatives in 1892 and 1893, serving on the judiciary committee. In 1910 he was appointed collector of taxes for Boston and Suffolk county. He was married June 25, 1867, to Katharine Helen, daughter of John Eagen, of New York city. She died in 1899, leaving one daughter, Helen Caroline, wife of Dr. Charles W. McConnel of Boston. As a Mason he belongs to its several organizations and has filled the highest offices in them. He is a permanent member of the Grand Commandery of Knights Templars of Massachusetts and Rhode Island; and past vice-president of the Massachusetts and Rhode Island Association of Knights Templars Commanders, and member of the order of Nobles of the Mystic Shrine. Among civic societies, his membership has included the Middlesex, Beacon, Shawmut, Bostonian and Winthrop Yacht Clubs and the National Geographic Society of Washington.

WOODWARD, James Thomas, banker, was born in Anne Arundel county, near Annapolis, Md., Sept. 27, 1837, son of Henry Williams and Mary E. (Webb) Woodward. The family was a noted one in colonial and revolutionary times and derives descent from William Woodward of London, England, who settled in Anne Arundel county, Md., in 1695. James T. Woodward was educated at the local schools and in Baltimore, and after a brief mercantile experience in that city removed to New York, where he entered the importing house of Ross, Campbell & Co. There his sound judgment and business aptitude soon led to his admission to the firm and gave him a permanent reputation in commercial circles. In 1873 he became a director in the Hanover National Bank, and in 1877 was elected president. Under him the deposits increased from $6,000,000 when he took charge to $45,000,000 in 1910 and $75,000,000 at the time of his death. It is rated among the most substantial in New York city, paying sixteen per cent. on its stock with a large reserve fund, and its brilliant record is recognized as largely due to Mr. Woodward's business genius and unremitting industry. On all questions of financial policy his opinion was considered sound and trustworthy, the result of broad experience and deep thinking, and he was frequently consulted regarding bond sales by the U. S. treasury and on other important public matters. In 1898 he was elected president of the New York Clearing House Association, a position which afforded his financial genius new scope and influence, and afforded one of the highest tributes to his integrity, balanced judgment and executive ability. In politics Mr. Woodward was an old-line Democrat. Grover Cleveland was his close personal friend, and he was a delegate to the national convention in Chicago which nominated Mr. Cleveland for the presidency in 1884. Mr. Woodward's circle of friends was large and his friendships were strong and enduring. In his later years he contributed extensively to charitable institutions. He was a trustee of the New York Hospital, and of St. John's College, Annapolis, and to the latter institution gave an athletic field, a handsome library and a physical laboratory building called Woodward Hall. In 1909 the college conferred on him the honorary degree of LL.D., Justice Harlan, of the U. S. supreme court, presenting the certificate. Mr. Woodward was a member of the Society of Colonial Wars, the Union, Knickerbocker, Metropolitan, Tuxedo and Riding clubs, of New York, and was a vestryman of St. Thomas' Episcopal Church. He was unmarried. He died in New York city, Apr. 10, 1910.

WHEELER, Edward Jewitt, author and editor, was born in Cleveland, O., Mar. 11, 1859, son of Alfred and Lydia Priscilla (Curtis) Wheeler. His father was a minister of the Methodist Episcopal church. The founder of the family in America was Thomas Wheeler, a native of Kent, England, who settled at Concord, Mass., in 1635, and the line of descent is traced through his son John, through three generations of the name of Joseph, through the third Joseph's son Zalmon, who married Hannah Butler, and through their son Salmon, who married Gillen Chipman, and was the grandfather of Mr. Wheeler. After a preliminary education in the public schools of Meadville and Erie, Pa., and Warren, O., he entered the Ohio Wesleyan University, where he was graduated in 1879, valedictorian of his class. His literary career began as an assistant editor of the Pittsburg "Christian Advocate," with which he was connected for three years. Meanwhile he contributed short stories and poems to "The Independent," New York "Evening Post," "St. Nicholas," "Christian Union," "Youth's Companion," etc. In 1883 he entered the employ of Messrs. Funk & Wagnalls Co. as literary editor of their publications, and in the following year he published "Stories in Rhyme for Holiday Time." When "The Voice" (later "The New Voice") was started in that year he became its managing editor, and continued as such until 1899. In 1895 he

was made editor of "The Literary Digest," published by the Funk & Wagnalls Co., and during 1894–1904 he was a director of that company. In 1905 he became editor of "Current Literature," changing its name in 1913 to "Current Opinion." In 1913 he became president of the Current Literature Publishing Co. and in 1915 became also literary advisor to the Funk & Wagnalls Co. During 1884-96 Mr. Wheeler was a prominent member of the Prohibition party, and for a number of years was secretary of the New York state committee. He made many speeches in support of the cause, and published "The Evolution of a Crank" (1885) and "Prohibition: the Principle, the Policy, and the Party" (1888), besides many shorter articles and leaflets. During 1897-99 he was president of the board of the Westerleigh (Staten Island) Collegiate Institute, and was for several years president of the Westerleigh Building and Loan Association. He is a member of the Players, National Arts and Economic clubs and is president of the Poetry Society of America. He was married Nov. 23, 1887, to Jennie L., daughter of Ferguson Fleming, of Nashville, Tenn., and has one son, Edward Curtis Wheeler.

HARRISON, Edwin, capitalist and philanthropist, was born at Washington, Ark., Jan. 29, 1836, son of James and Maria Louisa (Prewitt) Harrison, grandson of John and Elizabeth (McClanahan) Harrison, and great-grandson of James Harrison, who came from the north of Ireland in 1740 and settled in Pennsylvania. The latter married Jane Carlyle, and served in the Chester county (Pa.) militia in the revolutionary war. His father, a pioneer of St. Louis, became owner of the famous Iron Mountain property, and in association with Pierre Chouteau and Felix Valle organized the Iron Mountain Company; he inspired the organization of the Iron Mountain Railway, and was its managing director; was a director of the Missouri Pacific Railway Company, and as a member of the celebrated firm of Chouteau, Harrison & Valle built the extensive rolling mills in North St. Louis. The son received his preliminary education at a French school at Ste. Genevieve, Mo.; a Jesuit college at Namur, Belgium, and at Wyman's School, St. Louis. He was graduated at the Lawrence Scientific School of Harvard University in 1856. He was a pupil and close friend of Asa Gray, the botanist, and during 1856-58 was a special student under the elder Agassiz in geology and paleontology, a training that qualified him for the position of assistant state geologist, to which he was appointed in 1859. In 1871 he became a member of the board of managers of the geological survey. During 1860–62 he went several times to Santa Fe, N. Mex., having established himself as a merchant in that city. Returning to St. Louis in 1865 he entered upon an active business career, becoming head of the firm of E. Harrison & Co., manufacturers of pig iron. In 1870 he was elected president of the Iron Mountain Co. and of the Chouteau, Harrison & Valle Iron Co., owners of the Laclede Rolling Mills. About this period he was one of the organizers and the first president of the St. Louis Smelting and Refining Co., and of its branch, the Harrison Reduction Co., located on the site of the present city of Leadville, Col. He superintended the erection of these works in 1877, and it was the enterprise which gave birth to the town of Leadville. He was likewise president of the Harrison Wire Works, a St. Louis company now out of existence. He was engaged in many mining enter-

EDWIN HARRISON

prises, and from their inception was identified with the Hope and Granite Mountain mines of Montana. He was widely known as a mining expert of ability and followed that vocation for a number of years. He served as president of the Society for the Prevention of Cruelty to Animals, St. Luke's Hospital Association, Mercantile Library Association, St Louis Academy of Science, Missouri Historical Society, as director of Washington University, Manual Training School and the St. Louis Fair Association. In politics he was a Democrat. He was a Mason and member of the Legion of Honor. Six feet four inches in height, tall and straight, with a courtly grace and dignity that were habitual, his presence lent distinction to any company, and he always made a lasting impression upon those he met for the first time. He was married at Glasgow, Mo., Nov. 13, 1873, to Laura Elizabeth, daughter of John Yelverton Sterne, a farmer. She survived him, with three children: James, chief engineer Kimlock Telephone Co.; Louise and Edwin Sterne. He died in St. Louis, Mo., May 13, 1905.

SCHINNER, Augustine Francis, first Roman Catholic bishop of Superior, Wis., was born in Milwaukee, Wis., May 1, 1863, son of Michael and Mary (Koenig) Schinner. He studied for the priesthood at St. Francis' Seminary, near Milwaukee, and was ordained priest there in 1886 by Archbishop Heiss. He was pastor at Richfield, Wis., in 1886-87 and during 1887-93 served as a professor at St. Francis' Seminary. In 1893 he became secretary to Archbishop Katzer and chancellor and vicar-general of the archdiocese of Milwaukee. On the subdivision of the archdiocese of Milwaukee he was appointed first bishop of Superior and consecrated July 25, 1905. He resigned this charge on January 15, 1913, and was appointed first bishop of Spokane on March 18, 1914, and formally installed in the see on June 18 of that year. Spokane was created a diocese Dec. 17, 1913, to include Okanogan, Ferry, Stevens, Pend Oreille, Douglas, Grant, Lincoln, Spokane, Adams, Whitman, Benton, Franklin, Walla Walla, Columbia, Garfield and Asotin counties in the state of Washington, an area of 32,980 square miles. It is a suffragan of the Metropolitan of Oregon City and has a Catholic population of 23,700. There are sixty-one priests; seventy-two churches; four colleges and academies; ten parish schools; five academies for girls; two Indian schools and an attendance for all of 2,610 pupils; three training schools for nurses; four hospitals and one House of the Good Shepherd.

STROMBERG, Alfred, electrical engineer, inventor and manufacturer, was born near Stockholm, Sweden, Mar. 9, 1861, son of Andrew and Louisa Stromberg. His father was a manufacturer of threshing machines. He was educated in the Stockholm schools, and at the age of fourteen entered the great Ericsson electrical establishment, thus becoming connected with the telephone industry from its earliest days. For five years he was engaged in telephone construction work throughout Norway, Denmark and his native country. In 1884 he came to America and obtained employment in the repair department of the Bell Telephone Co., Chicago, where he remained five years, and effected certain improvements in apparatus, notably in the automatic hook switch, which were regarded as meritorious. In 1889 he became superintendent in charge of the burglar alarm system of the Chicago Electric Protective Co. There he took out a number of patents relating to the business, and it

was largely due to his efforts that the company was successful. In 1893 the first of the fundamental Bell telephone patents expired, and he was one of the earliest to recognize the enormous possibilities of the independent or competing telephone industry. He was employed by the Western Telephone Construction Co., Chicago, one of the first independent manufacturers, and in 1896, associated with Androv Carlson, a fellow employee, organized the Stromberg-Carlson Telephone Manufacturing Co., of which he was made president. From the beginning the business of the company was highly prosperous. It was at first based on the inventions and practical ideas of the two partners, but as the business developed a staff of electrical designers was employed. The growth of the company was due mainly to his tireless energy and the genius he displayed in the manufacturing and design of telephone systems. The company was capitalized for fifty thousand dollars, but in 1902 the business was sold to a group of Rochester (N. Y.) capitalists for three-quarters of a million dollars. The new owners retained his services for some years, but he gradually withdrew from the business and returned to Chicago. There he organized, in 1907, the Stromberg Electric Co. for the manufacture of electric time stamps, and he also was largely instrumental in the organization of the Stromberg Motor Devices Co. (manufacturers of carburetors and automobile accessories), of which he was likewise president. He was a member of the Union League Club, Chicago; a 32d degree Mason, and a Knight Templar. Possessed of a magnetic personality, he attained great popularity among men in the independent telephone trade. In his business relations he was shrewd, a close observer of commercial ethics, and not without a vein of mysticism, which did not affect, however, his great common sense in all the practical relations of life. His rugged, genial character, simple tastes, retiring nature, broad human sympathy and quiet democracy won for him high place in the esteem of his fellow men. He died in Chicago, Ill., Mar. 8, 1913.

RANGER, Henry Ward, artist, was born at Geneseo, N. Y., Jan. 16, 1858, son of Ward Valencourt and Martha Ranger, of New England ancestry. His father was for many years a professor in Syracuse University and was employed in several government scientific expeditions, notably that of the transit of Venus expedition to Pekin, China. Henry W. Ranger was educated at the public schools of Geneseo and at Syracuse University. Subsequently he studied art for some years in Europe. He is largely self-taught, and his professional success is the result chiefly of hard work. The manner in which he fitted himself for his life-work shows his character in this regard. He did not sit at the feet of some master and follow his leading blindly, but frequented the art museums and worked over his own canvas until he had made it into a true copy of the original. He is now recognized, not as a copyist, but as one who has created a style of his own and worthy to be copied; and his influence upon the young men of his profession has been wholesome and healthy. Mr. Ranger resided many years in Europe, and has traveled extensively all over the world. Although perhaps clinging somewhat to the conventional and traditional in his paintings, he is a powerful portrayer of nature and excels in landscape work. His paintings impress the critic as the work of an expert technician, skilful in composition and possessing a strong and vigorous touch. His work is reminiscent of Rousseau and Dupré. The most important of his paintings are: "A Group of Oaks," in the Fine Arts Academy, Buffalo, N. Y.; "Entrance to the Harbor," "Connecticut Woods," "The Cornfield," "Bradbury's Mill Pond No. 2," in the National Art Gallery, Washington, "Sheep Pasture," in the Pennsylvania Academy of Philadelphia, "Spring Woods," in the Brooklyn (N. Y.) Institute Art Museum, "The Top of the Hill," in the Corcoran Art Gallery, Washington, "An East River Idyl," in the Carnegie Institute, Pittsburg, and "Landscape," in the Toronto Museum of Art. He is also represented in various foreign art collections. Mr. Ranger was awarded a bronze medal at the Paris exposition of 1900; a silver medal at the Pan-American exposition, Buffalo, N. Y., in 1901, a gold medal at the Charleston exposition in 1902, and a gold medal by the American Art Society of Philadelphia in 1907. He is an associate of the National Academy of Design, and a member of the American Water Color Society, the National Arts Club and the Lotos Club of New York. He was married in New York, in 1884, to Helen E. Jennings, of New England and South Carolina ancestry.

BROWNELL, William Crary, editor and author, was born in New York city, Aug. 30, 1851, son of Isaac Wilbour and Lucia Emilie (Brown) Brownell. He is related to Thomas Church Brownell, former bishop of the Protestant Episcopal church and founder of Trinity College, Hartford, and Henry Howard Brownell, the poet. He was educated at Choules Institute, Newport, R. I., and at Amherst College, being graduated at the latter in 1871. During 1871-79 he was on the editorial staff of the New York "World," and during 1879-81 on the staff of the "Nation," of New York. The years 1881-84 were spent in Europe, mainly in France, and upon his return he became connected with the Philadelphia "Press." Since 1888 he has been a literary adviser of the publishers, Charles Scribner's Sons. In the following year appeared his "French Traits—An Essay in Comparative Criticism," a book dealing with the morals and manners, the social and art instincts and the psychology of a people greatly misunderstood by Britons and Americans, and comparing and contrasting them with his own countrymen, of whom the book is secondarily also a portrayal. Of this work Russell Sturgis, the art critic, wrote: "The book is one of the finest pieces of careful discrimination which the language contains. It is little to say that nowhere in English, among books that one handles or hears of, or that influence the thought of many students, is subtlety of criticism carried further." Following this he wrote "French Art, Classic and Contemporary Painting and Sculpture" (1892) which is a splendid example of art criticism undertaken in the way of comparing thought, sentiment, observation of humanity and of the external world as expressed in the graphic and plastic representation of objects ˜ud of humanity, with a similar observation expressed in words. Mr. Brownell's remaining volumes are concerned with English and American literature. They are published in the form of a series entitled "Victorian Prose Masters" (1901) and include critical studies of Thackeray, Carlyle, George Eliot, Matthew Arnold, Ruskin and George Meredith. A. T. Quiller-Couch, the English novelist and critic, reviewing this series said: "When Mr. W. C. Brownell, an American critic, addressing an American audience, has the modesty and courage to speak of 'England, and its literary dependency, ourselves,' an Englishman

must take pleasure in replying, with at least equal truth, that in criticism, at any rate, it needs but a very few professors of Mr. Brownell's calibre to redress the balance." "American Prose Masters" appeared in 1909, and treated of Cooper, Hawthorne, Emerson, Poe, Lowell and Henry James, showing the same characteristics of careful analysis and fine discrimination as its predecessors. He is also the author of "Newport" (1896), "Criticism" (1914) and numerous articles contributed since 1875 to "The Galaxy," "Art Journal," "Magazine of Art," "Scribner's," "Century," and "Atlant' Monthly." Mr. Brownell received the honorary degree of L.H.D. from Amherst College in 1896, and that of Litt. D. from Columbia University in 1910. He is a member of the American Academy of Arts and Letters. He was married Jan. 3, 1878, to Virginia S., daughter of Daniel Thomas Swinburne, of Newport, R. I.

CLAXTON, Philander Priestley, U. S. commissioner of education, was born in Bedford county, near Shelbyville, Tenn., Sept. 28, 1862, son of Joshua Calvin and Anne Eliabeth (Jones) Claxton. The family came originally from England to Virginia, whence they moved through North Carolina to Tennessee in the first quarter of the nineteenth century, settling first in East Tennessee near Knoxville, and later in Bedford county, Middle Tennessee. James Claxton, grandfather of Philander P. Claxton, fought with Andrew Jackson in the war of 1812. Philander P. Claxton received his early education at the public schools of Bedford county and the Turrentine Academy, near Poplin's Crossroads, Bedford county, and was graduated at the University of Tennessee in 1882. Practically all his life since his graduation from college has been spent in teaching and educational work. He began teaching in the city of Goldsboro, N. C., in 1882, and, in 1883–84, was superintendent of schools at Kinston, N. C. In 1884–85 he studied at Johns Hopkins University, and, in 1885-86, he studied education and school systems in Germany. He was superintendent of schools at Wilson, N. C., in 1886–87, and at Asheville, N. C., during 1887–93. In the latter year he was appointed professor of pedagogy and German at the North Carolina State Normal and Industrial College, and in 1896 became professor of pedagogy and director of the practice and observation school at the same institution. In 1902 he was appointed professor of education, and in 1906 professor of secondary education and inspector of high schools at the University of Tennessee. He was appointed U. S. commissioner of education in 1911. Dr. Claxton was editor of the "North Carolina Journal of Education" in 1897–1901, and of the "Atlantic Educational Journal" in 1901–03. He is a member of the Southern Educational Board and was chief of its bureau of investigation and information in 1902–03, was superintendent of the Summer School of the South during 1902–11, and is a member of the National Education Council and the Southern Educational Association, a director of the Playground Association of America, chairman of the executive committee of the National Story Tellers' League and the American School Peace League, and a member of the National Society for the Scientific Study of Education, the American Association for the Advancement of Science, the Rockefeller Sanitary Commission, and the Cosmos Club of Washington, D. C. He is author of "From the Land of Stories," joint author with M. W. Haliburton of an edition of "Grimm's Fairy Tales," and has published sev-

HENRY W. RANGER
ARTIST

WILLIAM C. BROWNELL
EDITOR AND AUTHOR

PHILANDER P. CLAXTON
COMMISSIONER OF EDUCATION

RALZEMOND A. PARKER
LAWYER

eral pamphlets and articles on subjects pertaining to education. Dr. Claxton was married (1) at Wilson, N. C., December, 1885, to Varina Staunton, daughter of William Moore, of Goldsboro, N. C.; (2) at Tarboro, N. C., September, 1894, to Anne Eliabeth, daughter of Joseph Porter, of Tarboro, N. C.; (3) at Nashville, Tenn., April, 1912, to Mary Hannah, daughter of George S. Johnson, of Nashville. There are four children: Claire, Helen, Calvin Porter and Eliabeth.

PARKER, Ralzemond Allen, soldier, lawyer, was born in Genesee township, Genesee co., Mich., Feb. 17, 1843, son of Asher Bull and Harriet Newell (Castle) Parker, and a descendant of William Parker, who came from England and in 1639 joined Thomas Hooker in the settlement of Hartford, Conn. From him the line of descent is traced through his son John, who became a resident of New Haven; his son John, who became a resident of Wallingford, and married Hannah Bassett; their son Joseph; their son Andrew and his wife, Suanna Blakeslee; their son Ezra, of North Adams, Mass., and Oneida county, N. Y., was ordnance sergeant in the war of the revolution, served with Arnold at Quebec during 1775–1776, and at Saratoga in 1777, and married Elizabeth Perry; their son, William M., born in Oneida county, N. Y., was a Michigan pioneer, who settled at Royal Oak, married Lydia Bull, and was the grandfather of Ralzemond A. Parker. Our subject was graduated (LL.B.) at the Law School of the University of Michigan, in 1872. In the summer of 1862 he enlisted as a private in company E (Normal Company), 17th regiment, Michigan volunteer infantry, which was known as the Stonewall regiment, and was attached to the 1st brigade, 1st division, 9th army corps. He participated in many of the actions, engagements and battles of that command, notably South Mountain and Antietam. During 1867–1869 he was deputy county clerk of Oakland county, Mich. In 1872 he removed to Detroit and engaged in the general practice of his profession, but since 1890 he has made a specialty of patent and corporation law, and has handled many celebrated cases. The most notable of them was the Selden patent (automobile) case, involving the validity of a patent issued to George B. Selden, of Rochester, N. Y., in 1895, covering the combination with a road locomotive of a so-called "liquid hydrocarbon gas engine of the compression type." Mr. Selden had been selling licenses under this patent to automobile manufacturers, and these licensees organized an association known as the "Licensed Association of Automobile Manufacturers," which association undertook the prosecute infringers of the Selden patent, paying the expenses of such infringing suits under a proviso that in case a court of final resort should determine that the patent was invalid the licenses should lapse and the association be dissolved. It brought a suit in October, 1903, against the Ford Motor Co. of Detroit, the O. J. Gude Co. of New York, one of the Ford's customers, and John Wanamaker & Co., its sales agent in New York, as well as against several foreign automobile manufacturers. The case hinged on the question of the originality of the Selden engine. After two years had been consumed in taking testimony, the United State circuit court in September, 1909, affirmed the validity of the patent, holding that the Ford Co. and the others were infringers. Mr. Parker took an appeal to the United States court of appeals, which reversed the lower court, and that decision was final. Other notable cases with which Mr. Parker was identified

were that of Frederick Stearns Co. vs. Russell (85 Federal reporter), involving the question whether the transfer of an old device to a new use was invention; and the case oi Torrants & Armes Lumber Co. vs. Rogers (112 U. S.), involving the validity of reissues. In 1882 he became a member of the firm of Parker & Burton, his partner being Charles F. Burton, which relationship terminated by Mr. Burton's death in October, 1912. He has since practiced alone. He has long been lecturer on patent law and trademarks in the Detroit College of Law. For years he has been active in the affairs of the Grand Army of the Republic, local, state and national; is a member of the staff of the state organization and (1914) judge advocate of the department of Michigan. He was president of the Microscopical Society of Detroit and the Detroit Associated Charities; is president of the Patent Law Association of Detroit and a member of the Chamber of Commerce of the U. S. A., Detroit Board of Commerce, American Bar Association, Michigan State Bar Association, Bar Association of the City of Detroit, and of the Detroit Automobile and Michigan clubs, Detroit, and the Engineers' and Automobile clubs of America, New York city. He finds his chief recreation in motoring. He was married Sept. 24, 1869, to Sarah E., daughter of Flemon Drake, of Oakland county, Mich. They have three surviving children: Mina L., now Mrs. Edward Boshert, Mt. Vernon, N. Y.; Grace E., a librarian, of Detroit, and Ralzemond D., assistant professor of electrical engineering, University of Michigan, and now in the service of the American Telephone and Telegraph Co., New York city. Portrait opposite page 270.

ROOT, Joseph Cullen, capitalist and the founder of the Modern Woodmen of America, was born at Chester, Mass., Dec. 3, 1844, son of Aurelius Clark and Eliza (Abbott) Root, and a descendant of John Roote, who came from Badby, Northamptonshire, England, in 1637 and settled at Farmington, Conn., on land which is still in possession of the family. His wife was Ann Russell, and from them the line descends through their son Thomas, his son John, his son Elisha, his son Joseph, and his son Joseph A., who married Alphia Clark and was the grandfather of Joseph Cullen Joseph, and his son Joseph A., who married Alphia Clark and was the grandfather of Joseph Cullen Root. Among his other ancestors were Jonathan Clark, a member of Gen. Washington's staff in the revolutionary war, and Col. Mattoon, an officer in Gen. Lafayette's army in America. His maternal grandfather was Joseph Abbott, a descendant of John S. C. Abbott, the historian. His father was a prominent business man and once mayor of Lyons, Ia. Joseph Cullen Root was educated at Cornell College, Mt. Vernon, Ia.; Northern Illinois College, Fulton, Ill., and was graduated at Eastman Business College, Poughkeepsie, N. Y., in 1865. At the age of sixteen he was given full charge of a book and jewelry store owned temporarily by his father. After his graduation he became manager of two flouring mills and a grain elevator at Lyons, Ia. Three years later, in partnership with O. Ogden, of Elmira, N. Y., he leased the elevator and one of the mills, both of which they subsequently sold. During the next four years he was revenue collector of the second Iowa district; engaged incidentally in the real estate and insurance business; studied law and was admitted to the Clinton county bar. In 1862 he was one of the founders of the Young Men's Association Library of Lyons, which now owns 10,000 volumes. He was elected to the Lyons board of aldermen, and following in the footsteps of his father, was elected and served two terms as mayor. Subsequently he declined the congressional nomination, but accepted the nomination for the state legislature, and was duly elected. He was appointed by the governor of Iowa as an expert in the investigation of the transactions of state officers, the reports of which made 2,000 closely printed pages. In 1877 he organized the Northwestern Bell Telephone Co. and established the second telephone exchange in the United States at Clinton, Ia., embracing lines in Clinton county, Ia., and Whiteside and Carroll counties, Ill. He was one of the originators and first grand treasurer of the Iowa Legion of Honor, and was president of the V. A. S. beneficiary order of Iowa during its four most successful years. In 1882 he founded the Modern Woodmen of America; was elected head consul, and annually re-elected until 1890, when he declined further honors. During this period 65,000 members had been enrolled. By its charter and laws the order was confined to nine of the west central states. In 1890 he decided to make it international in its scope. In that year at Omaha he organized the Sovereign Camp, Woodmen of the World, of which he became the sovereign commander, continuing thus until his death. He was a 33d degree Mason and a Shriner, was actively identified with the Odd Fellows, Knights of Pythias, Ancient Order of United Workmen and other organizations; was a governor of the Ak-Sar-Ben, the most pretentious and progressive of the Omaha organizations, and in 1908 became president of the Associated Fraternities of America. He was a director of the Corn Exchange National Bank and the Lion Bonding Co. His benevolence was proverbial, and he left a rare heritage to the millions of recipients of the bounties of Woodcraft which he successfully evolved and promoted. He was married Sept. 23, 1868, to Louise M., daughter of William Inslee of Lyons, Ia., and had two children, Harry J. and Alanson Inslee Root. Mr. Root died at Hendersonville, N. C., Dec. 24, 1913.

BUSCH, Joseph Francis, fourth Roman Catholic bishop of the diocese of St. Cloud, Minn., was born at Red Wing, Minn., April 18, 1866, brother of Rev. William Busch, professor of Church history in the St. Paul, Minn., Seminary, and Rev. F. X. Busch, a Jesuit. His father was among the pioneers of that section of the state. After his preparatory studies here the future bishop completed his theological course at Innsbruck, Austria, where he was ordained priest on July 28, 1889. He spent the following year at the Catholic University, Washington, D. C., and on his return to St. Paul he was made secretary to Archbishop Ireland. He served as assistant pastor at the cathedral and at St. Mary's Church, St. Paul, and as pastor at South St. Paul, at Le Sueur, and at St. Lawrence's parish, Minneapolis. He was head of the Diocesan Mission Band from its organization in 1902 until he was appointed bishop of Lead, S. D., in 1910. On May 19 of that year he was one of six bishops consecrated by Archbishop Ireland. Some time after taking up his residence in Lead, he tried to secure for the miners who constituted a large portion of the population there some amelioration of industrial conditions, especially the abolition of work on Sunday, and an opportunity for them to practise their religion. The miners were worked on Sunday and practically all business in the town went on as usual. The Homestake Company, which owned the mines and controlled the community, refused to meet the bishop's suggestions in this direction, and he appealed in a protest to the public opinion of the country to back him in his effort for Sunday observance. The mining corporation resented the movement. Opposition meetings were organized in Lead and their promoters forwarded complaints against the bishop to the Apostolic Delegate at Washington. The delegate refused to approve their action, severely rebuked the instigators of the opposition movement and upheld Bishop Busch in his efforts to reform conditions in Lead. The controversy precipitated became so acute that Bishop Busch left Lead in 1913 and took up his residence at Rapid City as a protest against his treatment and the social disorder in the former city. Here he remained until he was appointed to the see of St. Cloud, Minn., Mar. 19, 1915, made vacant by the resignation of Bishop James Trobec. St. Cloud is a diocese of 12,251 square miles, with a Catholic population of 65,500 ministered to by 145 priests, with 135 churches and chapels. There is a university, a college, three academies for girls and twenty-five parish schools, all having an attendance of 5,240 pupils. Besides these there are 5,760 pupils in other schools in Catholic settlements in charge of Sisters or lay teachers. Other institutions are four hospitals, one orphan asylum and one home for the aged.

HOLLIS, Henry French, U. S. senator, was born in Concord, N. H., Aug. 30, 1869, son of Abijah and Harriette Van Meter (French) Hollis, being a descendant on both sides of early Massachusetts families. His maternal grandfather, Henry F. French, was assistant secretary of the treasury during 1876–85. He was graduated at the Concord high school in 1886, and after engaging in railroad engineering work in the West for a year and a half resumed his studies, and was graduated at Harvard University in 1892 magna cum laude. During the last two years of his regular college course he also took up the study of law, so that after a few months further study in the office of Harry G. Sargent, of Concord, he was admitted to the New Hampshire bar in 1893. He immediately commenced the practice of law in partnership with his preceptor, Mr. Sargent, and Edward C. Niles. Later he was associated for six years with Att'y-Gen. Edwin G. Eastman, and afterwards with Judge James W. Remick, Alexander and Robert C. Murchie, and Robert Jackson, the firm becoming one of the prominent law organizations of the state. He has always been an earnest member of the Democratic party, and entered into active political life in 1900, when he became the Democratic candidate for congress in a district that was hopelessly Republican. Two years later he was his party's candidate for governor of the state, and his stumping canvass was one of the most brilliant ever conducted in New Hampshire, resulting in a big reduction in the Republican majority, and, two years later, in an increased vote. Although his legal work grew in volume and importance, his inclination towards political life continued strong, and early in 1912 he announced his candidacy for the United States senate. A hotly contested campaign followed, which was characterized as "the most strenuous contest for such position in the state within the memory of living men," and which resulted in his election by the legislature on the forty-second ballot. He was the first Democratic senator to be elected from the state of New Hampshire since 1852. His term will expire Mar. 3, 1919. He was enthusiastically welcomed by his Democratic associates on his entrance to the senate, and he almost immediately gained a standing in their ranks such as had never been accorded a newly chosen senator. He was assigned to the committees on banking and currency, immigration, District of Columbia, woman suffrage and enrolled bills, of which he is chairman. He is a regent of the Smithsonian institution. He was married June 14, 1893, to Grace Bruerton, daughter of Edwin E. Fisher, of Norwood, Mass., and has one son, Henry French Hollis, Jr., and one daughter, Anne Richardson Hollis.

TOWER, William Lawrence, zoologist and educator, was born in Halifax, Mass., Dec. 22, 1872, son of Lorenzo Augustus and Mary Sheldon (Thompson) Tower. He studied at the Lawrence Scientific School during 1893–96, and at the graduate school of Harvard University during 1898–1900, and received the degree of B.S. from the University of Chicago in 1902. While working for his degree he laid the foundations for a career as teacher of science by serving as assistant entomologist in the Massachusetts Department of Agriculture (1893), as assistant in zoology at Harvard (1894–96), as instructor in the Central High School in Akron, Ohio (1897), and again as assistant in Harvard (1898–1900). In 1900 he became professor of zoology and physiology in Antioch College, but a year later resigned to accept an appointment as assistant in embryology in the University of Chicago, with which institution he has since remained, reaching in 1901 the rank of associate professor. Among his more important publications are: "The Development of Colors and Color Patterns of Coleoptera with Observations Upon the Development of Color in Other Orders of Insects," which he contributed to the publications of the University of Chicago in 1903. Subsequently the Carnegie Institution of Washington published his "Experimental Investigations of the Production and Preservation of New Character Races and Species in Insects" (1905) and a second part (1907), and "An Investigation of Evolution in Chrysomelid Beetles of the Genus Leptmotarsa" (1906). He has also contributed to the Biological bulletin, published at Woods Hole, Mass., his "Observations on the Changes in Hypodermis and Cuticula of Coleoptera During Ecdysis" (1906), and "The Determination of Dominance and the Modification of Behavior in Alternative (Mendelian) Inheritance by Conditions Surrounding or Incident Upon the Germ Cells at Fertilization," with Bibliography (two papers, 1910). Prof. Tower is a member of the American Society of Zoologists, the American Society of Naturalists, and since 1909 has been a fellow of the American Association for the Advancement of Science, as well as a number of the well-known Quadrangle Club of Chicago.

O'NEAL, Emmet, thirty-first governor of Alabama (1911–15), was born in Florence, Ala., Sept. 23, 1853, son of Edward A. and Olivia (Moore) O'Neal. His father (q.v.) was also governor of Alabama. The son was educated at the University of Mississippi (one year); was graduated at the University of Alabama in 1873, and after being admitted to the bar in 1875, began the practice of law at Florence, Ala. He early became interested in local politics. He was presidential elector in 1888, was elector at large in 1892 and 1908, and was appointed United States attorney for the northern district of Alabama in 1893, serving for a term of four years. He was a member of the Democratic state executive committee, and of the constitutional convention for the state at large in 1901. He was a delegate to the Democratic national convention in 1904. In 1910 he was elected governor of his state by the local option party opposed to prohibition. At a meeting of the legislature in January, 1911, a measure was introduced providing for local option in Alabama, and Gov. O'Neal signed the bill in the following month. This bill made the county the unit in voting on the liquor question and in pursuance of this bill the local option elections were held in Montgomery, Mobile and Birmingham during the following summer, resulting in the defeat of prohibition in those cities, where it had been in effect since 1909, and throughout the year other counties defeated the prohibition movement. During his term the legislature created a state court of appeals to relieve the state supreme court, and other acts were passed creating a state highway commission, a measure for enforcing better sanitary conditions in hotels and restaurants, a bank department of the state, and various measures providing for the adoption of a commission form of government in municipalities. At the conference of governors held in September, 1911, Gov. O'Neal attacked the initiative, referendum and recall, his speech drawing forth a strong reply from Gov. Woodrow Wilson, of New Jersey. The paper he read at the governor's conference at Denver in 1913 entitled "Distrust of States Legislatures: The Cause and Remedy" attracted national attention, was republished in the North American Review and was used as a text-book at the University of Wisconsin. He is recognized as the South's chief exponent of states' rights, especially in regard to the intervention of the Federal government in the regulation of railroads. He conducted negotiations with the New York bankers in the fall of 1911 to raise a fund of $50,-000,000 to enable the Southern farmer to secure advances or loans on his cotton crop, so as to market it gradually and prevent a disastrous decline in prices. He was president of the Alabama Bar Association in 1909-10 and was a member of the general council of the American Bar Association in 1911. He was a delegate-at-large to the national Democratic convention of 1912 and chairman of the Alabama delegation. He was married July 21, 1881, to Elizabeth Kirkman, of Florence, Ala. Portrait opposite page 274.

HOLMES, John Haynes, clergyman, was born in Philadelphia, Pa., Nov. 29, 1879, son of Marcus Morton and Alice Fanny (Haynes) Holmes, and a descendant of John Holmes, who came over from England to Plymouth, Mass., in 1630. He was graduated at Harvard University *summa cum laude* in 1902, and at the Harvard Divinity School with the degree of S.T.B. in 1904. In the same year he was ordained to the Unitarian ministry and installed at the Third Religious Society in Dorcester, Mass. In February, 1907, he became associate pastor of the Church of the Messiah, New York, with Robert Collyer, and succeeded to the full pastorate upon Dr. Collyer's death in 1912. He is an eloquent and inspiring public speaker, a man of great learning and forceful and attractive personality. His interest in social reforms, which began at college, was stimulated by a study of the Unitarian leaders, Wendell Phillips, William Lloyd Garrison and Theodore Parker. He caught not only the fire and enthusiasm of these reformers, but their fearlessness as well. The latter trait is perhaps the most conspicuous of his whole career. He went to New York at a time when the spirit of greed dominated the great corporations, which in turn dominated the great political parties. He was most outspoken in his criticisms of this among other wrongs, despite the fact that in his congregation were men of great influence in the financial world. He believed that the church should be a leader in improving social conditions, and out of this belief came his first book, "The Revolutionary Function of the Modern Church" (1912). His own church, located in a downtown section of New York, has become under his leadership a center for social service in many lines. Besides the above-mentioned book he is the author of "Marriage and Divorce" (1913); "Is Death the End?" (1915), and many tracts, addresses and magazine articles on religious and sociological subjects. He is the editor of the Unitarian periodicals "Unity" (Chicago) and "The Unitarian Advance" (New York), and in 1914 edited Robert Collyer's "Clear Grit." Mr. Holmes was president of the Unitarian Fellowship for Social Justice during 1908–11, and is president of the Free Religions Association of America; vice-president of the Middle States Unitarian Conference; chairman of the General Unitarian Conference, and trustee of Flower Hospital and Medical College, New York. He is an accomplished pianist, and is very fond of walking and reading. He is a member of the City Club of New York, and of the Phi Beta Kappa and Delta Upsilon college fraternities. He was married June 27, 1904, to Madeleine Hosmer, daughter of Edwin H. Baker, of Brooklyn, N. Y., and their children are: Roger Wellington and Frances Adria Holmes.

SHEPPARD, Morris, U. S. senator, was born in Wheatville, Tex., May 28, 1875, son of John Levi and Alice (Eddins) Sheppard. His father, a native of Alabama, was a prominent lawyer and judge of Texas and served in the national congress in 1899–1902. The son was graduated at the University of Texas in 1895, and was graduated in law two years later, after which he spent a year at Yale University and received the degree of LL.M. in 1898, at the same time winning the Wayland prize for debate and delivering the master's oration at the Yale Law School commencement. He began the practice of his profession at Pittsburg, Tex., as a member of the firm of Sheppard, Jones & Sheppard. He removed to Texarkana, Tex., in 1899, which has become his permanent home. Early in his career he became interested in politics. In October, 1902, he was elected to the 57th congress to fill the unexpired term of his father, who had died, and he was elected thereafter to the 58th, 59th, 60th, 61st and 62nd congresses. As chairman of the committee on public buildings he undertook to rehabilitate the antiquated system by which federal structures were erected throughout the country. The committee had charge of planning the new departmental buildings in Washington, which cost many millions of dollars, and he also favored the erection of a suitable permanent fireproof building for the preservation of the archives of the government. At the Democratic primaries of July, 1912, he was nominated for U. S. senator to succeed Joseph W. Bailey, and was elected by the state legislature in the following January. At that time he was elected not only for the unexpired term of Sen. Bailey, who had resigned, but also for the following term beginning March, 1913, and expiring Mar. 3, 1919. He is a member of the committees on Agriculture and Forestry, Commerce, Irrigation, Military Affairs, Census, Transportation Routes, and Expenditures in Department of Agriculture, being chairman of the last. Sen. Sheppard is an active member of the Woodmen of the World, the second largest fraternal insurance order in the United States, and has

been sovereign banker or national treasurer since 1899. He is a man of scholarly attainments and gifted with rare elocutionary and oratorical talent. His voice has a silvery ring; he has a vocabulary of great range, with an easy and confident manner of speech, and is said to be the peer of any orator in the national legislature. He is called upon frequently to deliver orations on patriotic occasions. It was stated that his speech in defence of keeping upon the coinage of the United States the symbolic inscription, "In God We Trust," was an epic prose poem. A collection of his addresses was published under the title "Fraternal and Other Addresses" in 1910. Sen. Sheppard was married, Dec. 1, 1909, to Lucile, daughter of Noah P. Sanderson, a lumber dealer and cottonseed oil merchant of Texarkana, and has two daughters: Janet and Susan Sheppard.

SELLERS, Matthew Bacon, scientist, was born in Baltimore, Md., Mar. 29, 1869, son of Matthew Bacon and Annie (Lewis) Sellers, and grandson of Matthew Sellers. His paternal ancestors were Quakers, the family originally settling in Pennsylvania shortly after the founder, William Penn, went there. He was educated by private tutors and in private schools in Baltimore, studying one year in Goetingen, Germany, and Evreux, France. On his return he entered the Harvard Law School, and was graduated LL.B. in 1892. Early in his life he displayed a decided taste for mechanics and the sciences, and to his extensive general education he now added a special course in science at the Lawrence Scientific School and Drexel Institute. He is one of the pioneer students of aerodynamics. In 1903 he began the determination of lift and drift of arched surfaces, devising for this purpose a "wind tunnel" for measuring the dynamic air pressure on bodies. Some of the results of his studies were embodied in a paper read before the Aeronautical congress of St. Louis in 1904, and in an article which appeared in the "Scientific American Supplement" in November, 1908. After many experiments with models, and his "wind tunnel," he invented a novel flying machine which has a number of original features that are likely to make it a popular one for general use. It may be called a quadruplane, with the planes arranged like steps. The operator is on a line with the lowest plane, and the center of gravity being lower than in the biplane the machine is more stable. He made his first successful flight in December, 1908. It was only 110 pounds in weight and carried an eighthorse-power engine, with which he attained a speed of about twenty-one miles per hour, the machine being especially designed for slow flying. It is small enough to be enclosed in the ordinary carriage house. With a maximum of safety and a minimum of cost it will no doubt contribute largely to the popularity of aviation as a sport. Mr. Sellers has written a number of papers on the science of aeronautics which have been published chiefly in "Aeronautics," of which he was for four years technical editor, and in 1915 he was appointed a member of the Naval Consulting Board. He is a director of the Aeronautical Society of America, and of the American Society of Aeronautic Engineers, and a member of the Aero Club of America, the Harvard Club of New York and the Harvard and University clubs of Baltimore.

COX, James M., forty-sixth governor of Ohio (1913–15), was born on a farm near Jacksonburg, Butler co., O., Mar. 31, 1870, son of Gilbert and Eliza (Andrew) Cox, of Scotch descent. He obtained his education in the public and high schools

EMMET O'NEAL
GOVERNOR

JOHN HAYNES HOLMES
CLERGYMAN

MORRIS SHEPPARD
U. S. SENATOR

MATTHEW B. SELLERS
SCIENTIST

JAMES M. COX
GOVERNOR

ARTHUR CAPPER
GOVERNOR

EDWIN L. SHUMAN
EDITOR

COLE L. BLEASE
GOVERNOR

of Butler county. He taught school for a time, and was employed in a printing shop as "printer's devil." He became a reporter on a local newspaper, subsequently joining the staff of the Cincinnati "Inquirer." For a time he was private secretary to Paul J. Sorg (q.v.), and then returned to his newspaper work, and has been identified with that profession ever since. In 1898 he acquired a controlling interest in the Dayton "Daily News." Later he purchased the Springfield "Daily News," and has since conducted them both as owner and publisher, the two papers comprising what is known as the News League of Ohio. In 1908 he was elected to the 61st congress on the Democratic ticket, and in 1910 to the 62d. He was inaugurated governor in January, 1913. On the same day he sent a message to the legislature recommending a constitutional amendment providing for the direct election of senators, which was subsequently adopted. During his administration various cities in the state adopted the commission form of government, and the legislature passed an unusual number of important measures. These included an act compelling lobbyists to file a statement of disbursements with the secretary of state and obtain a certificate, a measure providing that in civil actions the jury may render a verdict upon the concurrence of three-fourths of its number, and acts providing for indeterminate sentences for all felonies, except treason and murder in the first degree, limiting the hours of labor, establishing an agricultural commission, and putting into effect the Torrens land title system, a mothers' pension act, a workmen's compensation law, a corrupt practices act and an act providing for a system of primary election for members of congress, state, county and municipal officers and delegates to national and state conventions. He called two special sessions of the legislature in 1914 for the purpose of supplementing the work done in the regular session of the previous year, and their most important enactments were: reorganizing the agricultural interests of the state now under the control of an agricultural commission provided for at the previous session, and reorganizing the common school system. He was characterized as the "reform governor," because so many reforms were inaugurated at his instigation.

CAPPER, Arthur, nineteenth governor of Kansas (1915–), was born in Garnett, Kans., July 14, 1865, son of Herbert and Isabella (Mc-Grew) Capper. His father was a native of England. During his school days the son learned the practical side of the printing business, and in 1884 secured a position as a typesetter on the "Daily Capital," at Topeka, Kans., of which he is now owner and publisher. Later he became a reporter on the same paper, and then its city editor. He was employed for a time on the New York "Tribune," and as Washington, D. C., correspondent for the "Daily Capital." He began business for himself in 1893 by the purchase of the "North Topeka Mail"; later he bought and combined with the "Mail" a paper known as the "Kansas Breeze," under the name of the "Farmers Mail and Breeze," which has a weekly circulation of 125,000. Mr. Capper is also owner and publisher of the "Topeka Daily Capital," the "Capper's Weekly," the "Missouri Valley Farmer," the "Nebraska Farm Journal," the "Missouri Ruralist," the "Oklahoma Farmer," "The Household" and "Poultry Culture." These publications go into a million American homes, and the influence of Mr. Capper's high ideals and sterling character

is felt in no small way in homes now nourishing into manhood and womanhood citizens of to-morrow. The Capper building, which is devoted entirely to the publishing business, is one of the finest and most attractive buildings in Topeka. While Mr. Capper has achieved remarkable success in his newspaper business, he gives freely of his time and ability in aiding public enterprises. He is a director of the Topeka Provident Association for the Relief of the Poor, the Prudential Trust Co., the Farmers National Bank, the Topeka Young Men's Christian Association and a member of the executive committee of the Young Men's Christian Association; vice-president of the Kansas State Historical Society, and president of the Kansas State Good Roads Association. From 1909 to 1913 he was president of the board of regents of the Kansas State Agricultural College, and he was also president of the Kansas State Editorial Association in 1913. In November, 1914, he was elected governor of Kansas, being the first native-born Kansan to attain the office. During his administration laws were passed creating a state department of education; imposing inheritance taxes; making owners of premises where liquors are sold liable for damages caused by intoxicated persons who obtain liquor on such premises, such damages to be a lien on the premises as soon as suit is filed; creating an industrial welfare commission; forbidding banks to engage in trade or commerce or to invest in the stock of other banks or corporations or to loan money on or purchase their own shares, unless to prevent loss on debts previously contracted; prohibiting the sale of merchandise, goods and chattels in bulk in fraud of creditors. By nature Gov. Capper is extremely democratic in ideals and in actions. He is a member of the Benevolent and Protective Order of Elks, the Independent Order of Odd Fellows, the Fraternity of Modern Woodmen of America, and the Topeka, Country and Commercial clubs. Gov. Capper was married Dec. 1, 1892, to Florence, daughter of ex-Gov. Samuel J. Crawford.

SHUMAN, Edwin Llewellyn, author and editor, was born in Manor township, Lancaster co., Pa., Dec. 13, 1863, son of William Colhozeh and Rebecca Catharine (Fertig) Shuman. His earliest paternal American ancestor was George Shuman, who came from Würtemberg, Germany, in 1760 and settled in Lancaster county, Pa. George Shuman's wife was a Manning, and from them the line of descent is traced through their son Jacob and his wife, Margaret Wissler, who were the grandparents of Edwin Llewellyn Shuman. Edwin L. Shuman received his preliminary education in the public schools and was graduated at Northwestern University, Evanston, Ill., with the degree Ph.B. in 1887. He received the degree Ph.M. from that institution in 1890. In 1880 he began his newspaper career as printer and proofreader's assistant on the Chicago "Evening Journal," under his uncle, Andrew Shuman, editor of that paper and lieutenant-governor of Illinois. After his graduation from college he was editor of the Evanston "Press" in 1889–91 and subsequently he was for three years a reporter and editorial writer on the Chicago "Evening Journal." In 1895–1901 he was literary editor and editorial writer on the Chicago "Tribune," and during the ensuing twelve years, until 1913, was literary editor of the Chicago "Record-Herald." Since 1913 he has been assistant general manager of "The Associated Sunday Magazines," New York city. With a fellow-student of Northwestern

University, R. O. Vandercook, he founded the University Press Co. in 1887 and was its president and also was editor of the Evanston ''Press'' in 1887–90. He is author of ''Steps into Journalism'' (1894), ''Practical Journalism'' (1903), ''How to Judge a Book'' (1910), and, in collaboration with Mrs. Shuman, of the ''Rainy Day Scrap Book'' (1910) and the ''Animal Rainy Day Scrap Book'' (1913). During 1909–13 he was a member of the board of managers of the Evanston Public Library. He is a member of the Players' Club, New York city, and of the Phi Beta Kappa and Sigma Chi fraternities. His favorite pursuits include foreign travel and the study of European languages and ornithology, but he finds his chief recreation in books. He spent the year 1891 in the wilds of the Alaskan peninsula and in 1913 he wrote a series of ''Literary Zigzags in Europe'' for the Chicago ''Record-Herald.'' He was married at Evanston, Ill., Dec. 25, 1895, to Emma, daughter of James S. Thompson.

BLEASE, Coleman Livingston, governor of South Carolina (1911–15), was born in Newberry county, S. C., Oct. 8, 1868, son of Henry Horatio and Mary A. (Livingston) Blease, and grandson of Thomas Wainwright Blease, who came from Liverpool, England, and settled in Edgefield county, S. C. One of his uncles, Basil Manly Blease, was the first volunteer from Newberry county in the civil war, rose to the rank of captain in the Confederate service and was wounded at Cold Harbor. Four uncles on his mother's side also fought in the Confederate ranks. His father owned a hotel and livery stable at Newberry Courthouse, and served as magistrate of that town for several years. The son was educated at Newberry College and was graduated in law at Georgetown University in 1889. In that year he was admitted to practice before the supreme court of the District of Columbia and the courts of South Carolina. Since then he has practiced law at Newberry, first in partnership with his brother under the title of Blease & Blease, and later as senior member of the firm of Blease & Dominick. He served for some time as city attorney of Newberry, and for years he has been known as one of the ablest criminal lawyers in his state. His professional eminence, however, has been overshadowed by his meteoric political career. As early as 1888 he was a candidate for the legislature, but did not receive a nomination. He was elected to the house of representatives in 1890 and 1892, and served as chairman of the committee on privileges and elections and as a member of the state board of canvassers, besides being chosen speaker *pro tem.* on several occasions. In 1898 he was military secretary to Gov. Ellerbe, and in the same year was returned to the house of representatives, where he served as chairman of the committee on military and was an ex officio member of the board of visitors of the Military Academy of South Carolina. He was defeated for lieutenant-governor in 1900 and 1902. In 1904 he was elected to the state senate, where he served as president *pro tem.* He was an unsuccessful candidate for governor in 1906 and again in 1908, but in the next year was elected mayor of Newberry. He was elected governor of South Carolina in 1910 and was re-elected in 1912. During his two terms as governor he attained nation-wide prominence—in fact, nation-wide notoriety. He exercised the pardoning power of the executive to an extent hitherto unknown in the history of the union, granting pardons or paroles to about 2,000 convicts; he vetoed more legislative measures than any other governor South Carolina ever had; he fought the constitutional

right of the supreme court of the state to designate special circuit judges; he entered into a dispute with the war department concerning the administration and status of the national guard of South Carolina, and just before the end of his second term he disbanded the guard; he was loud in his championship of state's rights against what he considered the increasing encroachments of federal authority, and openly justified the lynching of negroes for a certain offence. These features of his administrative policy, added to his very frank and vigorous expression of his personal opinions and his equally frank and vigorous condemnation of those who differed with him, aroused much unfavorable criticism both within and outside his state. On the other hand, his administration had notable and substantial merits which his rather flamboyant eccentricities obscured in the eyes of his critics. It was notable for its economy, both in the governor's office and in the conduct of affairs generally, for an earnest effort on the part of the executive to ease the burden of taxation, and for a marked increase in the amount of taxable property and invested capital in South Carolina. Many other measures for the checking of extravagance and waste, for the better administration of the state finances, and for the promotion of education and public health were vigorously advocated by him but made no headway in the legislature. The establishment of the State Medical College at Charleston, the abolition of the state hosiery mill located in the penitentiary, and the establishment of the state cotton warehouse system were achievements in his administration of which he was especially proud. After his second term he retired to the practice of law at Columbia. He has served as chairman of the Newberry county Democratic committee, was for eighteen years a member of the state Democratic executive committee and has represented Newberry county in practically every state Democratic convention since he entered politics. He was a presidential elector on the Bryan ticket in 1896 and 1900. Mr. Blease is a trustee of the University of South Carolina, the South Carolina Military Academy and the Winthrop Normal and Industrial College of South Carolina; past grand master and past grand representative, I. O. O. F.; great representative and past great sachem, Improved Order of Red Men; past chancellor, Knights of Pythias, and a member of the B. P. O. E. He was married, Feb. 8, 1890, to Lillie B. Summers, of Anderson county, S. C. Portrait opposite page 275.

HARVEY, Edwin Bayard, physician and surgeon, was born at Deerfield, N. H., Apr. 4, 1834, son of Ebenezer and Rozella (Winslow) Harvey. He was educated in the public schools, the Pembroke (N. H.) Military Institute, the Northfield (N. H.) Academy and Wesleyan University, being graduated at the last in 1859. He taught school for a time and then studied medicine at the Harvard Medical School, where he was graduated in 1866. At Westboro, Mass., where he established his practice, he soon attained a leading position, not only as a physician, but in all public affairs. He was a member of the school board for eighteen years; was superintendent of schools, chairman of the board of trustees of the public library, trustee of the Westboro Savings Bank, and for six years trustee of the Massachusetts Reform School, Westboro. He was elected to the Massachusetts house of representatives in 1884, and to the state senate in 1894. He was the author of the bill creating a state board of registration and engineered it through the legislature for

Edwin B Harvey

enactment. At the personal request of Gov. Greenhalge he resigned from the senate in 1895 to serve as secretary, a post in which he continued for eighteen years, giving his entire time to the duties and requirements of the office, and doing much towards raising the standard of legal fitness to those seeking a license to practice medicine in that state. During his régime from thirty to forty per cent. of applicants failed to pass the rigid examinations, whereas in some states from three to five per cent. represented the failure to pass. He also originated, introduced and carried through the legislature the bill for supplying free text-books to the pupils of the public schools of the state, and he drafted many other laws now appearing on the statute books. His advice often was sought by members of the different legislatures upon questions pertaining to public health matters, and because of his help many pernicious bills were defeated. In 1872 he visited the leading hospitals of Europe. He was a member of the American Medical Association, American Academy of Medicine, president of the Massachusetts Medical Society during 1898-1900, and councilor of the society for thirty years. He was a Master Mason and a member of the Evangelical Church of Westboro. Dr. Harvey was a clear thinker, a close reasoner, having intellectual attainments of a high order. Honest, earnest, fearless, with high ideals, well versed in medico-legal matters, familiar with the machinery of legislation, as well as with the basic principles of government, he was indeed a useful member of the community, and loyal to every interest with which he was associated. He was married at Concord, N. H., July 30, 1860, to Abby K., daughter of Eldad Tenney, who survives him. He died at Westboro, Mass., Sept. 28, 1913.

COFFINBERRY, Henry D., ship-builder and financier, was born at Maumee City, O., Oct. 14, 1841, son of Judge James McClure and Anna Maria Gleason Coffinberry. He was educated at the public and high schools of Cleveland, O. At the outbreak of the civil war he enlisted in the U. S. navy as a common seaman, and upon the recommendation of Commanders Pennock and Phelps was promoted master's mate. On the first call for duty he reported to the commander of the iron-clad Louisville, upon which he served until the close of the war, being promoted first to ensign, and later to acting master and executive officer of the Louisville, and finally to commander of the ship. In 1865 he put the Louisville out of commission and assumed command of the U. S. steamer Fairy, but preferring private life, he resigned in 1866, and was honorably discharged, with the personal thanks of Admiral Porter and of the naval department. He then became a partner with Messrs. Leavitt & Crane, and founded the first carriage and axle manufactory in Cleveland, O. Subsequently he purchased a fourth interest in a small machine shop, doing business under the firm name of Robert Wallace & Co. The firm afterward bought the controlling interest in the Globe Iron Works, and Mr. Coffinberry became its financial manager. The business was successful, and not long after was able to purchase a half interest in the Cleveland Dry Dock Co., of which Mr. Coffinberry also took financial charge. The company began to build wooden vessels, and soon acquired a reputation for honesty and good workmanship which secured a large and profitable business. Realizing the superiority of steel and iron vessels for fresh-water navigation, Mr. Coffinberry induced his partners to establish a plant in Cleveland, and it was

subsequently incorporated as the Globe Ship Building Co., of which Mr. Coffinberry was president and financial manager. In January, 1887, in connection with Mr. Wallace and several wealthy ship-owners, he purchased the plant of the old Cuyahoga Steam Furnace Co., adding largely to the realty and greatly increasing its capacity for general machinery and foundry work, adding a boiler shop and iron ship-building yard capable of constructing four of the largest class of iron ships per annum. This company was organized and incorporated as the Cleveland Ship Building Co., with Mr. Coffinberry as president and financial manager. They next turned their attention to the erection of a gigantic dry dock, known as the Ship Owner's dry dock, and purchased a controlling interest in the shipyard of William Radcliff. Mr. Coffinberry was a pioneer in the metal ship-building of the Great Lakes, and to his courage, persistence, energy and farsightedness, more than to any other man, is due the credit of making Cleveland the Clyde of fresh-water ship-building in America. At all times he displayed strenuous force and will power in meeting the difficult problems that had to be solved. In 1893 he retired from active business. He was appointed to serve an unexpired term as city treasurer, was elected to the same office by an unusual majority, and declined re-election. He was a member of the Loyal Legion, the first board of fire commissioners of Cleveland, and the Committee of Safety; a director of the First National Bank, the People's Savings and Loan Association, and various other companies. He was married in 1875 to Harriet Duane, daughter of Gen. George W. Morgan (q.v.), of Mt. Vernon, O., and had two children: Nadine Morgan and Maria Duane Coffinberry. He died in Cleveland, O., Jan. 17, 1912.

DODGE, Arthur Murray, capitalist and philanthropist, was born in New York city, Oct. 29, 1852, son of William Earle and Melissa (Phelps) Dodge, and a descendant of William Dodge, who came to this country from England in 1629 and settled at Salem, Mass. His father was the head of the firm of Phelps, Dodge & Co., one of the first directors of the Erie railroad, sometime president of the New York Chamber of Commerce and a founder of the Union League. He was one of the most prominent financiers of his time and left a supreme and lasting reputation as a philanthropist. His sister, Elizabeth C. Dodge, was the mother of Edmund Clarence Stedman, the poet, and was herself a poet of considerable reputation. Arthur M. Dodge received his early education in private schools and was graduated at Yale College in 1874. After his graduation he traveled in Europe for about a year, and upon his return he went into the lumber business, with which his father was identified on a large scale. The latter had acquired extensive timber holdings in northwestern Pennsylvania as early as 1836 and to these he gradually added large tracts in Canada, Michigan, Wisconsin, Georgia and elsewhere. So much had the elder Dodge done to develop the timber lands of the South that the state of Georgia named Dodge county in his honor. These Canadian lumber interests were inherited by Arthur Dodge, and the conservation and development of them furnished the chief activities of his business career. Under his management the properties increased materially in value and his manner of handling them stamped him as a business man of real capacity. With his father's business acumen he inherited, too, his father's high standard of business ethics, and he held a high and widespread reputation for clean and upright methods. He He was interested in a large number of charitable institutions, especially the Charity Organization of New York, of which he was one of the originators and first treasurer. Like all really charitable men he was reticent, even sensitive about his benevolence, and the amount of good he wrought during his lifetime cannot be even vaguely estimated. Until the end of his days Mr. Dodge maintained a deeply affectionate interest in Yale College, and he showed his interest in many practical ways. He was largely instrumental in securing a new gymnasium for the university and he was for many years an active officer of the Yale Alumni Association. His social interests were wide and he was for many years a prominent social figure in circles that were more select than conspicuous. He was a member of the council of the University Club, and he belonged also to the Union, Riding, Rockaway Hunt, New York Yacht, Seawanhaka, Corinthian, and University Athletic clubs. Among his intimates he was known as a man of sterling character, broad and sincere enthusiasm, and warm, genial temperament. He was married Oct. 6, 1875, to Josephine Marshall, daughter of Marshall Jewell (q. v), and had six children, Marshall Jewell, Murray Witherbee, Arthur Douglass, Pliny Jewell, Geoffrey, and Percival Dodge. He died at Weatogue, Simsburg township, Conn., Oct. 16, 1896.

LONG, Franklin Bidwell, architect, was born at South Bainbridge (now Afton), Chenango co., N.Y., March 3, 1842, son of Lewis and Eliza Juliette (Bidwell) Long, and a descendant of John Long, who settled in Vermont. He was educated in the common schools of South Bainbridge and Woodstock, Ill., and then went into business, trying his hand at a number of different enterprises. While carpentering in Chicago he became interested in architecture, and entered the office of J. C. Cochrane as student and draughtsman. A year later he formed a partnership with a fellow student, under the firm name of Long & Ackeman, and met with considerable success. Failing health, however, compelled him to dissolve the partnership in 1869 and remove to Minneapolis, Minn. He opened an office, and practiced his profession until his death, winning a reputation throughout the Northwest as one of the leading architects of the country. For a time he was in partnership with R. S. Alden, and after Alden's death became associated with C. F. Haglin, of New York, under the firm name of Long & Haglin. Later he formed a partnership with Fred Kees, of Baltimore, Md., under the firm name of Long & Kees, and after the dissolution of that partnership he formed the firm of Long, Lamoreaux & Long. Mr. Long was the designer of many of the largest and most handsome buildings in Minneapolis, including the court house and city hall, the Hotel Radisson, the Lumber Exchange, the Masonic Temple, the Kasota block, Andrus building, Dyckman hotel, the Palace and Plymouth buildings and the Security Bank building. He was a man of originality and inventive ingenuity. The equalizing chain, used on many elevators, was his idea, and in his architectural work he was continually creating novelties in design and in methods of construction. He was also the designer of a number of racing yachts. He was a member of the Minnetonka Yacht Club and Minneapolis Automobile Club, and the American Automobile Association, and was a Mason. Mr. Long was married at Binghamton, N. Y., Jan. 7, 1869, to Gertrude C., daughter of John Fisher Landers, of Afton, N. Y., who was a grandson of Matthew Long. They had two children: Louis Landers, a member of the firm of Long, Lamoreaux & Long; and Jessie, wife of Thomas S. McLaughlin, of Minneapolis, Minn. He died in Minneapolis, Minn., Aug. 21, 1912.

COPE, Walter Burton, jurist, was born in Sacramento, Cal., Oct. 22, 1861, son of Warner Walton and Martha Ann (Neel) Cope. His father (q.v.) was chief justice of the supreme court of California, and left a shining name among the brilliant ones of the first two generations of the California bench and bar. He was educated at Brewer's Academy, in San Mateo, and was graduated at the University of California in 1883. Inheriting his father's legal and judicial temperament, he determined to follow the law, and took a three-year course at Hastings Law School at San Francisco, which granted him his legal diploma in 1886. Soon after he joined Judge Charles Fernald and John J. Boyce in a law partnership in Santa Barbara, and became so popular as a highly efficient and successful practitioner that while still in his twenties he was elected district attorney, in the face of the usual overwhelming Republican majority. His prestige and popularity steadily increased, until in 1890 he was elevated to the bench of the superior court of Santa Barbara county and was re-elected in 1896 for a second term of six years. He resigned from the bench in 1897 to resume the active practice of his profession, and removed to San Francisco, where he entered the firm of Morrison, Foerster & Cope, which later became Morrison, Cope & Brobeck. Although he passed away in his prime, his life being undoubtedly cut short by his indefatigable zeal for his profession, the career of Judge Cope was a singularly full and successful one. He was held in high esteem for his legal attainments as well as his personal character, and was twice elected president of the San Francisco Bar Association, the highest mark of favor which the profession can bestow. He was a member of the board of trustees of Hastings College of Law, and served one term as president of the Alumni Association of the University of California. He was a member of the Pacific Union, University of California, Southern, Olympic and Commonwealth clubs. He was also a member of Santa Barbara Parlor, N. S. G. W., and a Mason of high rank. He seems to have combined the rare qualities of a learned judge, a successful advocate and a ripe scholar. His mind was stored with the best in English literature, his one pastime away from his profession being the study of the English masters. At his death the San Francisco Bar Association said: "His nature was singularly gentle and winning and deeply imbued with those rarer graces and sentiments which distinguished the scholar and the gentleman. He possessed, indeed, that charm of personality which makes it easy to inspire warm friendships, but over and beyond this personal magnetism his character had that solid basis of sincerity, kindliness and integrity which enlisted and retained the enduring esteem of all who came to know him well.'' Judge Cope was married Feb. 11, 1904, to Asenath, daughter of Hon. Chancellor Hartson, of Napa, Cal., who survived him with two children: Hartson and Anne Burnell Cope. He died in San Francisco, Cal., Dec. 4, 1909.

STARRETT, Theodore, builder and engineer, was born at Lawrence, Kan., Jan. 21, 1865, son of Rev. William Aiken and Helen (Ekin) Starrett. His father was a clergyman of the Presbyterian church, and his mother was a well-known educator, conducting a classical school for girls

ARTHUR M. DODGE
CAPITALIST

FRANKLIN B. LONG
ARCHITECT

WALTER B. COPE
JURIST

THEODORE STARRETT
BUILDER

Thos. P. Anshutz.

in Chicago. She was the author of "Future of Educated Women" (1880); "Letters to a Daughter" (1882); "Letters to Elder Daughters" (1883); "Gyppie, an Obituary" (1884); "After College, What?" (1885); "Letters to a Little Girl" (1886); "The Future of Our Daughters and Other Educational Essays" (1909). She is also an occasional contributor to the leading magazines on educational topics. The son was educated in the public schools of his native place and at the University of Kansas. He completed his studies at Lake Forest University, class of 1884, but did not graduate. He began his business career in the employ of Burnham & Root, the well-known architectural firm of Chicago, and pioneers in the construction of the modern skyscraper. Here he served a long apprenticeship and became familiar with all the details of building construction. Three years later he went into business for himself and built many buildings in Chicago, Cleveland, Toledo and Milwaukee. In 1897 he formed a partnership with Henry S. Thompson under the firm name of the Thompson-Starrett Co., of which the subject of this sketch was president for eight years, after which he resigned and continued the work under his own name. The Thompson-Starrett Company is one of the best known of the building corporations in the United States. It has built many of the most important buildings in the principal cities East and West, among which may be mentioned the Gimbel, Maiden Lane and Woolworth buildings, the New York Municipal building, Hotel McAlpin and the new Equitable Life Assurance Society's building, all of New York city; the Continental and Commercial Bank buildings and the Field Museum, of Chicago, Ill.; the Hotel Arlington in Washington, D. C.; the Union Central Life Insurance Company's building in Cincinnati, O.; in fact, there are over 150 of these modern fireproof office buildings that stand in the principal cities of the country as monuments to his energy and ability. Mr. Starrett has made a long study of the engineering problems connected with the erection of tall buildings, and as a leading expert on the subject he is frequently consulted on important building problems. He is the author of a number of articles contributed to the magazines and press of the country on matters relating to his specialty. The most valuable of these have been collected and published in two books entitled "Light on Dark Places" (1904) and "Skyscraper Building" (1905), which are regarded as valuable contributions to the literature of the subject. Mr. Starrett is married and has two sons, Robert and Theodore Starrett.

ANSHUTZ, Thomas Pollock, artist and art instructor, was born at Newport, Ky., Oct. 5, 1851, son of Jacob and Abigail Jane (Pollock) Anshutz, and grandson of Johann Peter Anshutz, of Jagerthal, Alsace, Germany, who came to America with his family in 1818 and settled in the Ohio Valley. His mother was of New England ancestry and a descendant in the direct line from Thomas Kent, founder of Gloucester, Mass., and the father of Rev. Elisha Kent, whose daughter, Abigail Kent, was Thomas Anshutz's maternal ancestor. Our subject was educated in the schools of Newport, Ky., and in Cincinnati, O. He developed a natural aptitude for drawing, and in 1872 he was sent to the National Academy of Design in New York. He continued his studies in the Pennsylvania Academy of the Fine Arts, Philadelphia, under Thomas Eakins, and in 1881 he was made assistant in-structor there. Prof. Anshutz was an instructor of unusual ability. He exerted a wide influence throughout the art world, and more recently the productions of his brush have added to his fame as an artist of merit. His own work was remarkable for its versatility and range, for he painted with equal facility landscape, portrait and still-life studies in crayon, pastel, water-color and oil. He was free from eccentricity and cant, and belonged to no one school of art. When asked what class of subjects or mediums of expression he preferred he replied that it was immaterial what style was used when one was learning to paint. This answer, so characteristic of the man, touches the secret of his success and pre-eminence as a teacher of art. He was an absolute master of the subject, and was thorough in everything he did. He sought to train the individual in the way he found his nature inclined, developing tendencies as they appeared. He strove to develop the ability and enlarge the possibilities that he found in every student, and he was suggestive and stimulating rather than assertive or assentient. He was decidedly original in his teaching and took novel methods to illustrate his remarks. The quality of his teaching is shown by the fact that in the Philadelphia exhibition of 1908, which was national in its scope, over 100 of the exhibitors were formerly his pupils. In addition to his work at the Philadelphia academy, Prof. Anshutz lectured at the New York Art School and the Maryland Institute. His own pictures possess a wondrous power of truth and sincerity, although perhaps lacking the highest romantic imagination, but they are always perfect in draughtmanship and are pleasing in their color effects. Although a master of both oils and water-colors, he was unrivaled in pastel. "The Tanagra," a lady standing before a Tanagra figurine upon a pedestal, is perhaps the best known of his works. It won the Lippincott prize of $300 in 1909, and was purchased by his pupils for a gift to the academy. His work as an artist was recognized by honorable mention at the Art Club exhibition in 1901, and by a silver medal at the St. Louis exposition in 1904. In 1909 he received the gold medal of honor at the Academy of Fine Arts, and in 1910 he won the gold medal offered to the artists of the world in the South American exposition at Buenos Aires. Some of his other notable canvases are: "Incense Burner" and "A Rose" in oil, and "The Iris," "Burnt Orange," "Study in Scarlet" and "A Bird" in pastel, and many portraits owned by private individuals. He was a life-long member of the Sketch Club of Philadelphia, and served as its president several years prior to his death. He was also a member of the Water-Color clubs of Philadelphia and New York, and an associate member of the National Academy of Design and of "L'Union Internationale des Beaux Arts and des Lettres." In person he was tall, slender and graceful and had a remarkable eye, clear blue, kindly and true. He was most precise in his speech and was gravely reticent in manner. Although undemonstrative and reserved he was companionable and won the unbounded respect, love and admiration of his many pupils, who affectionately referred to him as "Tommy" Anshutz. He gave his life to the furtherance of art, and although he devoted the best of himself for a small salary, he accomplished more through the work of his students, if not by his own brush. He was married at Wheeling, W. Va., Sept. 1, 1892, to Effie Shriver, daughter of William Hoge Russell, of Gettysburg and Bedford, Pa., and is survived by one son, Edward Russell Anshutz. Prof. Anshutz died at his Fort Washington country home near Philadelphia, Pa., June 16, 1912.

ABBEY, Edwin Austin, artist, was born in Philadelphia, Pa., April 1, 1852, son of William Maxwell and Margery Ann (Kipel) Abbey. He was educated at the Randolph school and Dr. Gregory's school in Philadelphia, and studied drawing under Isaac L. Williams of the Pennsylvania Academy. For three months of the year 1868 he studied penmanship at the writing school of Richard S. Dickson, and meanwhile contributed picture puzzles to Oliver Optic's ''Our Boys and Girls'' under the pseudonym of ''Yorick.'' His first definite employment as an artist was with the firm of Van Ingen & Snyder, wood engravers of Philadelphia, his work being almost exclusively commercial and news illustrations. Recognizing his unusual talent, Van Ingen & Snyder sent him to the antique and life classes of the Academy of Fine Arts, and his subsequent artistic development was rapid. He also studied with Prof. Christian Schussèle at the Pennsylvania Academy and began to turn his attention to historical compositions—a field of endeavor which he was destined to make peculiarly his own. From the beginning, history and historical associations exercised a very strong fascination for him, and he made extensive and exhaustive researches in history and costume with a painstaking thoroughness that only a fervid enthusiasm for the subject could inspire. In 1871 he went to New York and was appointed to the art department of Harper & Bro., with whom he remained for twenty years and for whom he did his best pen-and-ink work. It was as a pen-and-ink artist that he first attracted the attention of both the American and the English public, and though his highest and most permanent fame must rest rather on his color work than on his work in black-and-white, his pen drawings hold a high place among contemporary productions of this kind, and have not often been surpassed in delicacy and finish. Abbey went to England in 1878 with the very congenial commission from Harpers' to illustrate Herrick's poems. He found the country of Herrick as congenial as the commission, and, except for occasional visits to America, he remained a resident of England until his death. His illustrations of an edition of '' Dickens's Stories'' (1876) were the first book illustrations from his pen to come into public notice. They were followed by ''Herrick's Poems'' (1882), ''She Stoops to Conquer'' (1887), ''The Good-Natured Man'' and ''Old Songs'' (1889), ''The Tragedies of Shakespeare'' and ''The Comedies of Shakespeare'' (1896). The last-named illustrations—132 pictures—were exhibited by invitation at the Salon of the Société Nationale des Beaux-Arts, Paris, in 1896. In 1885 appeared a book of ''Sketches and Rambles in Holland,'' composed of drawings by Abbey and his friend, George Henry Boughton, the results of a walking tour in Holland. Abbey's ''A Milkmaid,'' in black-and-white, was exhibited at the Royal Academy, London, in the same year. In the meantime he had done an amount of good work in water-color, pastel and oil, and as time went on he devoted himself more and more to the one medium—first more particularly to water-color and later more particularly to oil. His more important water-colors of this period were ''Rustics Dancing in a Barn,'' ''The Widower,'' (1883), ''The Bible Reading'' (1884), ''The Old Song'' (1885), ''The March Past'' (1887), ''An Attention'' (1893-4-5) and

''Quiet Conscience'' (1896). Many brilliant pastels are included in his work for the same period, e. g., ''Good Friday Morning'' (1895) and the pastel sketches from Goldsmith's plays. The remarks of Henry James apropos of the latter are generally true of all Abbey's work. ''Mr. Abbey,'' he said, ''has evidently the tenderest affection for just the old house and the old things, the old faces and voices, the whole irrevocable scene, which the genial hand of Goldsmith has passed over to him, and there is no inquiry about them that he is not in a position to answer. He is intimate with the buttons of coats and the buckles of shoes; he knows not only exactly what his people wore, but exactly how they wore it, and how they felt when they had it on . . . His drawing is the drawing of direct, immediate, solicitous study of the particular case, without tricks or affectations or any sort of cheap subterfuge, and nothing can exceed the charm of its delicacy, accuracy and elegance, its variety and freedom, and clear, frank solution of difficulties.'' Abbey's first oil picture, ''A May-day Morning,'' appeared at the Royal Academy exhibition in 1890, and it was followed in 1894 by ''Fiammetta's Song,'' a work of rare excellence, which procured his election as an associate. Next came ''Richard, Duke of Gloucester, and Lady Anne'' (1896); ''King Lear, Act 1, Scene 1,'' and ''Hamlet'' (1897); ''The Bridge'' (1898), which procured his election as an academician; ''Who Is Sylvia, What Is She . . . ?'' and ''O, Mistress Mine, Where Are You Roaming?'' (1899) (now in the Walker Art Gallery, Liverpool); ''The Lute Player''; ''The Trial of Queen Katherine'' (collection of Senator W. A. Clarke); ''The Penance of Eleanor, Duchess of Gloucester'' (1900); ''Crusaders Sighting Jerusalem'' (1901); ''Pot-Pourri'' (1903); ''A Measure'' and a decoration, a triple panel reredos for the Holy Trinity Church, Paris (1904); ''Columbus in the New World'' (1906), a composition that attracted much attention, owing to the striking novelty of its decorative scheme; ''The Camp of the Army at Valley Forge, February, 1778,'' and the great upright decoration, '' Penn's Treaty with the Indians''—both for the Pennsylvania state capitol at Harrisburg; ''The Poet,'' one of the few of his paintings exhibited at the New Gallery, London; ''A Pavone'' (1897), painted for Whitelaw Reid; ''Fair Is My Love'' (1906), in the Corporation Gallery at Preston, Lancashire, and the official picture of ''The Coronation of Edward VII,'' at Buckingham Palace. The last-named is an enormous canvas, fifteen by nine feet, and containing 120 actual portraits. Notable beyond doubt as were the easel pictures of Edwin A. Abbey, it was in his mural paintings that he achieved the finest expression of his essentially picturesque art. His most famous, most exquisite, and, probably, his greatest work in that line, is the splendid frieze, the ''Quest of the Holy Grail,'' in the Boston Public Library. Abbey was engaged on that work from 1890 to 1891. Most of it was done at Broadway, Worcestershire, that famous retreat of artists, founded by Frank Millet, where John S. Sargent was engaged at the same time on his famous ''Pageant of Religion'' for what is now the Sargent gallery of the Boston Public Library. Hardly second to the Grail pictures in interest and importance are the ''Apotheosis of Pennsylvania'' and the ''Flight of the Hours,'' two of a series of large panels for the Pennsylvania state capitol at Harrisburg. Of the former a noted academician said that no other living painter in England could have approached it in mastery of decorative art. Among Abbey's other designs is a mural panel representing the reconciliation of two city companies, the Skinners and the Merchant Taylors, in 1484, painted for the Royal Exchange, London, in 1904. He made the designs for Sir Henry Irving's contemplated production of Richard II in 1898, a project which was abandoned, and he superintended the decoration of the peers' corridor of the Houses of Parliament which was completed in 1910. "Abbey's artistic and intellectual merits," said M. H. Spielman, F. S. A., in the English "Dictionary of National Biography," "which his personal charm and sympathetic and generous temperament enhanced, were widely acknowledged. He rapidly became the leading force in the English and American art of the day and founder of a school. Steeped in mediæval and seventeenth and eighteenth century art and literature, he captivated the public by the charm, dignity and dramatic ability which he brought to the rendering of his subjects. At the same time his artistic qualities, alike as to color, draughtsmanship, composition and invention, appealed on technical grounds to his fellow-artists, whether his mediums were oil, water-color, pen-and-ink or pastel." Abbey was one of the incorporators of the American Academy in Rome and one of the original members of the American Academy of Arts and Letters. He was a chevalier of the Légion d'Honneur, an honorary member of the Royal Bavarian Academy and the Madrid Society of Artists, an honorary associate of the Royal Institute of British Architects, a corresponding member of the Institut de France and the Société Nationale des Beaux-Arts, and a member of the American Water Color Society, the Royal Institute of Painters in Water Color (resigned 1893), and the American Academy of Design. Yale University conferred upon him the honorary degree of M. A. and the University of Pennsylvania that of LL.D., and he was awarded medals at the expositions of Munich (1883), Paris (1889), Chicago (1893), Philadelphia (1897), and Vienna (1898). By his will he left his residence, Chelsea Lodge, London, to the Royal Academy as a residence for its president. To the Royal Academy he also left the furnishings of Chelsea Lodge and the library at Morgan Hall, and he created a trust fund of $30,000 for the maintenance of Chelsea Lodge. Original drawings, 133 in number, illustrating the comedies of Shakespeare, were left to the Metropolitan Museum of Art, New York, with several paintings and the original color designs made to illustrate the Shakespeare tragedies, while to the Boston Art Museum was bequeathed his original drawings to illustrate Goldsmith's "Deserted Village," and to the National Gallery of British Art his painting, "The Crusaders Sighting Jerusalem." The residuary estate was left conditionally to create the Mead-Abbey fund, to be used in the purchase of the best works of art from the annual exhibition of the Royal Academy, "such works of art so purchased to be forwarded at the expense of said fund to the Corcoran Gallery at Washington, to be the property of the United States of America." Mr. Abbey was married Apr. 22, 1890, to Mary Gertrude, daughter of Frederick Mead, of New York. He died in London, Eng., Aug. 1, 1911.

ROGERS, Robert Cameron, editor and poet, was born in Buffalo, N. Y., Jan. 7, 1862, son of Sherman Skinner and Christina (Davenport) Rogers. His first American ancestor was Thomas Rogers, one of the passengers of the Mayflower in 1620. From him the line of descent is traced through his son Joseph, his son John, his son Nathaniel, his son Jabez, his son Samuel, his son Gustavus Adolphus Rogers, who was the grandfather of the subject of this sketch. Sherman S. Rogers (q. v.) was one of the most prominent lawyers in Buffalo, of the firm of Rogers, Bowen & Rogers, and for many years played an important part in New York public life. The son was graduated at Yale in 1883. He spent about a year in his father's law office, but his distaste for the legal profession was strong, and he finally turned from law to literature, for which he had from his earliest youth shown a decided aptitude. He had a special facility for writing verse, and even his youthful effusions were imbued with a fine depth and delicacy of feeling. Many poems and stories of merit came from his pen in the years immediately following his graduation, and showed a rapidly broadening and ripening talent. His technique was always remarkably good, and even his least successful efforts show a rythmical finish and a well-balanced choice of words which redeemed them from the mediocre. In 1898 he settled at Santa Barbara, Cal., and in 1901 purchased control of "The Morning Press," which, under his direction, grew to be one of the most influential and best edited newspapers in the State of California. Rogers' activity in politics stopped short at public office, for which he had no desire and which he steadily refused. The only public office he ever held was the honorary one of state commissioner for the Panama Exposition. He took a prominent part in business and social as well as in civic affairs. He was one of the founders and for several years vice-president of the Central Bank; he was at various times a director of the Chamber of Commerce, Santa Barbara Club, Santa Barbara Country Club and the Santa Barbara Polo Club. Above all things, however, Robert C. Rogers was a poet, and it is as a poet that he must chiefly be considered. His work in other lines has been surpassed by thousands of his contemporaries, his work as a poet has been equaled by few. It is, in a way, rather unjust to his reputation that he should be known so exclusively by his "Rosary," beginning,

"The hours I've spent with thee, dear heart, Are as a string of pearls to me."

It is without doubt a little masterpiece, but he has written many other poems, especially his songs of the sea and mountains and prairie, which appear much nobler, stronger and more vital—such songs as "A Ballad of Dead Campfires," and the "Steersman's Song." The bulk of his poetry has been published in three collections, entitled, "The Wind in the Clearing and Other Poems (1895), "For the King and Other Poems" (1900), and "The Rosary and Other Poems (1906), the latter being a collection from the two earlier volumes. Among them are fresh, breezy, stimulating songs of the open, carrying in their lilting lines the strong tang of the sea, the clean, sweet breath of the mountain wind, the pungent odor of the camp-fire smoke. Some of them touch a deep, philosophic and serious note. Of these the best example is "Eulogy," which was written for the Santa Barbara Elks' Lodge of Sorrow, and has since been adopted as part of the ritual of the order. He wrote the dedication ode for the Buffalo Pan-American Exposition, and also the following fiction: "Will o' the Wasp: a Sea Yarn of '12" (1896) and "Old Dorset: The Chronicles of a New York Country-Side" (1897). Mr. Rogers traveled very widely, both in America and Europe, went twice around the world, and crossed the Atlantic more than twenty times. He was a member of the Century and University clubs of New York, the Saturn Club of Buffalo, the Yondotega Club of Detroit, the Authors' Club of London, England, and the Society of Mayflower Descendants. He was married July 21, 1898, to Beatrice, daughter of Judge Charles Fernald, a pioneer of Santa Barbara, Cal., and had three sons: Sherman S., Robert Cameron and Alan Stewart Rogers. He died at Santa Barbara, April 20, 1912.

KING, Edward, banker, was born in Weehawken, N. J., July 30, 1833, son of James Gore and Sarah Rogers (Gracie) King, and a descendant of John King, who came over from England, and settled in Boston, Mass., in 1702. His father (q. v.) was a president of the New York chamber of commerce, and a son of Rufus King (q. v.). He was educated under the famous Prof. Anthon of Columbia College and in a private French school in New York, and after two years' study abroad entered Harvard College, where he was graduated in 1853. He spent several months at the military academy at West Point, taking a private course in engineering with a view to a scientific career, but the death of his father in 1853 changed his plans, and he determined to make banking his occupation. He at once became identified with his father's banking business, later acquiring an interest therein, and continued in its active management until 1861. In that year he became a member of the New York Stock Exchange, of which he was president in 1872–73. Subsequently he was a member of the firm of James Robb, King & Co., and was president of the Union Trust Co. of New York from 1873 until his death. Assuming the latter position at a time when the company was in a weakened financial condition on account of the financial panic of 1873, he devoted all his energy and ability to its reorganization, placing it on such a sound business basis that during the thirty-five years he was at its head the Union Trust Co. was a synonym for careful, conservative management, and was regarded as one of the strongest institutions of its kind. His last and perhaps most important public service was as chairman of the Committee of Associated Trust Company Presidents appointed to restore public confidence, and to aid some of the more oppressed institutions during the financial crisis of 1907. Mr. King was a member of the Metropolitan Museum of Art, the American Museum of Natural History, the New York Historical Society, the National Academy of Design, the St. Nicholas Society (president 1896–97), the Harvard Club (president 1890–95), the University Club, the Century Association, the Riding and Ardsley clubs. He was twice married, first, Oct. 20, 1858, to Isabella Ramsay, daughter of Rupert J. Cochrane; she died in 1873, leaving five children: Isabella Clarke; Alice Bayard, wife of Herman Le Roy Edgar; James Gore; Elizabeth Gracie, wife of Alpheus Sumner Hardy, and Rupert Cochrane King. His second marriage was May 26, 1885, to Elizabeth, daughter of William Fisher, of Philadelphia, by whom he had one son, Edward King, Jr. He died in New York Nov. 18, 1908. Portrait opposite page 283.

VEEDER, Curtis Hussey, mechanical engineer and inventor, was born at Alleghany, Pa., Jan. 31, 1862, son of Herman and Hanna (Adair) Veeder, and a descendant of Simon Volkertse Veeder, who came from Holland in 1654 and settled in Schenectady, N. Y., in 1662. From Simon V. Veeder the line descends through his son Johannes and the latter's wife, Susanna; their son, Mindert and his wife, Elizabeth Doruv; their son Johannes and his wife, Lena (Magdelena) Vrooman; their son Pieter Vrooman and his wife, Jannetje (Jane); their son Johannes and his wife, Rebecca Van Petten, who were the grandparents of Curtis Hussey Veeder. Our subject's mechanical ability was inherited from this grandfather, an engineer who built a portion of the Erie Canal and the railroads from Newburyport to Boston, Mass., and from Boston to Providence, R. I. His father was a mining engineer and manage. or iron mines and oil refineries in Pennsylvania. The son was graduated at Lehigh University in 1886 with the degree of M.E. His natural bent for mechanics was developed at an early age. After reading an account of the high wheel bicycle in 1879, he constructed one of his own which attracted no little attention; he devised an original bicycle saddle, made of flexible leather stretched over a steel frame, the patent for which, dated Apr. 5, 1881, he sold to the Pope Manufacturing Co. He also devoted some attention to manufacturing ball bearings for bicycles. In 1886 he became chief draftsman in the Calumet & Hecla Mining Co., Michigan, where he remained until 1889. He then entered the electrical business in the Boston office of the Thompson-Houston Co., later going to the drafting department of the company's plant in Lynn, Mass., where he designed an electric hoist and an electric magnetic clutch. In 1893 he prepared plans for the construction of a power plant at Washington, D. C., and in September of the following year became assistant to the superintendent of the Hartford Cycle Co. In 1895 he invented a cyclometer for bicycles and for its manufacturing Co. organized the Veeder Manufacturing Co. in association with David J. Post and others. The Veeder Manufacturing Co. erected a new plant in 1897; their present office building was constructed in 1906, and in 1912 they doubled the capacity of the factory building, which now turns out about 100,000 Veeder cyclometers per annum. Among his other inventions are an automatic die casting machine (1896), designed originally to expedite the manufacture of his cyclometers and adaptable to making small parts for any mechanical devices; and a tachometer (1901), or speed indicator, using the principle of a centrifugal pump to force a colored liquid in the tube varying approximately as the square of the speed of the pump. The device has been applied to electrical machinery and to automobiles, and is recognized as the standard speed measure. The company also manufactures counters for use on various machines, odometers for measuring distance travelled by automobiles, and a large number of castings of small parts for machines, like voting machines, cash registers, etc., for other companies. The factory has 25,000 square feet of floor space and employs about 250 hands. Altogether, Mr. Veeder has received sixty-eight United States and fifty foreign patents, and the Veeder Manufacturing Co., of which he is president, is well known in every civilized country on the globe. He is a member of the American Society of Mechanical Engineers; Franklin Institute; American Association for the Advancement of Science; American Geographic Society; National Geographic Society, and the Hartford Society of the Archeological Institute of America. He is also a mem-

Robert Cameron Rogers

EDWARD KING
BANKER

CURTIS H. VEEDER
INVENTOR AND MANUFACTURER

ALICE BROWN
AUTHOR

MAYER SULZBERGER
JURIST

ber of the Lehigh Alumni Association; Lehigh Club of New York; American Forestry Association (life); American Civic Association; National Municipal League; Municipal Art Society of Hartford; Young Men's Christian Association; Hartford Board of Trade; Get Together Club; Twentieth Century Club; Lake Champlain Association; League of American Wheelman (life); Laurentides Fish and Game Club; Auto, Hartford, University, Hartford Golf, and Rotary clubs of Hartford; and the Aero Club of America. He was married Sept. 19, 1908, to Louise G., daughter of John Stutz of Luzerne, Switzerland, and has two children: Josephine Adair and Dorothy Irwin Veeder.

LYNCH, Joseph Patrick, third Roman Catholic bishop of Dallas, Tex., was born at St. Joseph's Mich., Nov. 16, 1872, son of John V. and Veronica (Bothan) Lynch. On graduating at St. Charles' College, Maryland, in 1891, he went to St. Mary's Seminary, Baltimore, for his theological course, which he finished at Kenrick Seminary, St. Louis, where he was ordained priest June 9, 1900. In the course of pastorates at Weatherford, Hanley and Dallas he proved himself a successful executive and church builder. He was made vicar-general of the diocese June 19, 1910, and on the death of Bishop Dunne, Aug. 5, 1910, became its administrator. He was shortly after appointed the successor of that prelate and consecrated July 12, 1911. Dallas extends over an area of 98,266 square miles in north Texas, with a Catholic population of 33,000, having eighty-eight priests, 168 churches, fifty-one schools with 6,000 pupils.

BROWN, Alice, author, was born at Hampton Falls, N. H., Dec. 5, 1857, daughter of Levi and Elizabeth (Lucas) Brown. She was educated at the Robinson Female Seminary, Exeter, N. H., and after being graduated in 1876, taught school for a time in New Hampshire, and later in Boston, Mass. For a number of years she was on the staff of "Youth's Companion." Her first literary work consisted of short stories of New England rural life, the field with which she has been mainly identified ever since. These stories, published in the leading magazines, attracted favorable attention because of their excellence in characterization and the unobtrusive but charming quality of the author's style. She proved that the well-worked New England field was substantially limitless in variety, for her types impressed even New Englanders as original, while they yet bore all the marks of familiar acquaintance. Her first volume was a novel under the title "Strafford by the Sea," and this was followed by "Fools of Nature (1887); "Meadow Grass" (1895); "Robert Louis Stevenson—A Study," with Louise Imogen Guiney (q.v.) (1895); "By Oak and Thorn," a book of travel in rural England (1896); "Life of Mercy Otis Warren" (1896); "The Road to Castaly," poems (1896); "The Day of His Youth," a story (1897); "Tiverton Tales," stories (1899); "King's End" (1901); "Margaret Warrener" (1901); "The Mannerings" (1903); "The Merry Links" (1903); "High Noon" (1904); "Paradise" (1905); "The Country Road" (1906); "The Court of Love" (1906); "Rose MacLeod" (1908); "The Story of Thyrza" (1909); "Country Neighbors," stories (1910); "John Winterbourne's Family" (1910); "The One-Footed Fairy" (1911); "The Secret of the Clan" (1912); "My Love and I" (1912); "Vanishing Points," stories (1913); Robin Hood's Barn" (1913), and "Joint Owners in Spain" (1914). It was not until Miss Brown's place in literature had become distinctive that she ventured upon a novel, and her long stories have, without exception, contributed to raise her to a high rank among American authors. Her style is lucid and simple, and her art so perfect as to conceal its own artistic nature. Much of this admirable quality may be due to that which makes her work so appealing to the less critical reader—her clear-sighted vision of her subject. It is not a highly developed people, with complex emotions and conflicting impulses, from among whom she takes her characters. The very simplicity of the rural New Englander demands the sympathetic student and historian a method of portrayal that shall be of the same atmosphere, and this she has attained after making the most searching study of her subjects. What she sees she expresses, and she sees with marvelous clarity. In 1914 Miss Brown won a prize of $10,000, offered by Winthrop Ames (q.v.), for her play entitled "Children of Earth." There were more than 1,600 competitors, and the play was Miss Brown's essay in that direction.

SULZBERGER, Mayer, jurist, was born at Heidelsheim, Baden, Germany, June 22, 1843, son of Abraham and Sophia (Einstein) Sulzberger. His father, a teacher and minister of Heidelsheim, came to America as a result of the revolution of 1848, and settling in Philadelphia, became known for his philanthropic activities. The son was educated at the Central High School, Philadelphia, and studied law in the office of Moses A. Dropsie, lawyer and founder of Dropsie College for Hebrew and Cognate Learning. He was admitted to the bar in 1865, and for over thirty years was one of the leaders of the Philadelphia bar. In 1895 he was elected judge in the court of common pleas No. 2, on the Republican nomination, and was re-elected in 1905 on both Republican and Democratic tickets. By this time he had acquired a unique reputation for the incisiveness, independence and sound learning of his judgments, which have mostly been affirmed in the court of appeals and have, not infrequently, established new lines of judicial precedent. The honorary degree of LL.D. was conferred upon him by Jefferson College in 1896 and by Temple University in 1916. In addition to his professional work Mr. Sulzberger has devoted himself to the interests of the Jewish community, of which he is considered one of the leaders in America. He was appointed by Baron de Hirsch one of the charter trustees of the fund established by him in 1900, and when a representative body of American Jews was established in 1906 as the American Jewish Committee, he was its first president, in which capacity he delivered an appeal to the senate in Washington on the Jewish passport question, which was regarded as having a decisive effect in determining the senatorial vote advocating the denunciation of the treaty of commerce with Russia. He is a trustee and one of the founders of the Jewish Theological Seminary of America, the Dropsie College for Hebrew and Cognate Learning, the American Jewish Historical Society and Gratz College, Philadelphia. He is also vice-president of the Jewish Hospital of Philadelphia and the Young Men's Hebrew Association, and indeed may be regarded as the recognized lay head of the Jewish community of that city. Mr. Sulzberger is an ardent collector of books, and his library is one of the largest and best selected private libraries in America, being specially distinguished for its collections of English poetry, history, Orientalia, philology, and Jewish history and literature. He presented a large number of Hebrew incunabula and Hebrew printed works and manuscripts to the Jewish Theological Seminary of America, in recognition of which and of other services to Jewish learning he was granted the degree of Doctor of Hebrew Literature by that body. Mr. Sulzberger is a charter member of the Jewish Publication Society of America, founded in 1882, and from the inception of that body has acted as chairman of its publication committee, being regarded as chief inspirer of its long series of publications. He is resident lecturer on Jewish law at Dropsie College, and in that connection has published a series of works on Hebrew legal antiquities, including "The Am ha-Aretz, the Ancient Hebrew Parliament" (1909), "The Policy of the Ancient Hebrews" (1912) and "The Ancient Hebrew Law of Homicide" (1915). In the general community he is regarded as one of the leaders of the Republican party in Pennsylvania, and was offered the ambassadorship to Turkey on two occasions, by Pres. Harrison and by Pres. Taft. He is a member of the American Philosophical Society, American Oriental Society, the Law Association of Philadelphia, the Phi Beta Kappa fraternity, the Jewish Historical Society of England (corresponding member), the Triplets, Union League, of Philadelphia, and the Mercantile and Oriental clubs.

HEYWARD, Duncan Clinch, fifty-ninth governor of South Carolina (1903–07), was born in Richland county, S. C., June 24, 1864, son of Barnwell and Catherine Maria (Clinch) Heyward, and grandson of Duncan L. Clinch, soldier and congressman. He was educated at Cheltenham (Pa.) Academy and Washington and Lee University, 1882–85, but was not graduated. He conducted a flourishing rice plantation in South Carolina for many years. In 1903 he was a candidate for governor of his state, and was elected with a majority of 31,817 votes in the face of a strong opposition led by Sen. Tillman. He was re-elected in 1905 with 51,907 votes. Gov. Heyward is president of the Standard Warehouse Co. and the Columbia Savings Bank and Trust Co. In 1913 he was appointed collector of internal revenue for the South Carolina district.

DAMON, William Emerson, author and naturalist, was born at Windsor, Vt., Nov. 15, 1838, son of Luther and Betsy (Thayer) Damon. His first American ancestor was John Damon, a native of Berkshire, England, and came to this country in 1631 and settled in Reading, Mass. The line descends through John Damon's son Joseph, his son Joseph, his son Jabez and his son Aaron Damon, grandfather of our subject. He was educated at the district school of Windsor and the Kimball Union Academy, Meriden, N. H. He remained in Windsor for several years, obtaining a valuable training in commercial life, and at the same time developing his inherent genius for natural science. He conducted a mercantile business in Galena, Ill., for one year and in 1860 became associated with P. T. Barnum in New York. Barnum was at that time gathering scientific collections from all parts of the world for his museum and found in Mr. Damon a most ardent helper in this work. In 1862 Mr. Damon and Prof. Albert S. Bickmore, an assistant of Prof. Agassiz, of Harvard, conducted a scientific expedition to Bermuda, and succeeded in bringing back over 600 living specimens of tropical fish. On his return he became associated with Tiffany & Co., the New York jewelers, and for over forty years was part owner of the business and also superintendent of the credit department. But while thus engaged he did not give up his scientific activities. He was one of the founders and original directors of the New York aquarium, and his advice and assistance contributed in no

small degree to its success and present popularity. Mr. Damon was the author of "Ocean Wonders" (1879), and in scientific circles he was a recognized authority in his specialty. He was a remarkable man who combined in the highest degree the qualities of commercial success and of rare scientific attainment. He was married at Windsor, Vt., Feb. 14, 1865, to Alma C. Otis, daughter of Timothy Bradford Otis. He was a member of the Mycological and the Naturalist clubs of New York, the New York Scientific Alliance, the Microscopical, the Zoological, and the New England societies of New York, and the Royal Microscopical Society of London. He died at Windsor, Vt., Dec. 1, 1911, and is survived by his widow.

HITCHCOCK, Gilbert Monell, U. S. senator, was born in Omaha, Neb., Sept. 18, 1859, son of Phineas W. and Annie (Monell) Hitchcock. His father was one of the pioneers of Omaha, a successful business man prominently identified with its growth and development. The son was educated in the public schools of Omaha, and at Baden-Baden, Germany. Having decided to follow the law, he took the regular course at the University of Michigan, and was graduated in 1881. He practised his profession in Omaha for four years, and then established the Omaha "Evening World," of which he is still the proprietor. He introduced methods of his own, which were remarkably successful, and in 1889 he took over the Omaha "Morning Herald," combining the papers under the new name of "World-Herald." In politics he is a Democrat, and in his papers he was a frank exponent of policies which were then called radical and sometimes populistic, but which were really progressive and in advance of the times. He also advocated the municipal ownership of public utilities and the management of street and state railroads by a railroad commission similar to the Interstate Commerce Commission. His paper grew in circulation and popularity, and is to-day one of the leading and influential newspapers of the middle west. In 1904 he was elected on the Democratic ticket to the national congress. He was defeated at the next election, but two years later was re-elected and served for two terms, in the 60th and 61st congresses. While in congress he introduced the resolution which brought about the Ballinger-Pinchot investigation, which resulted in uncovering a remarkable condition of affairs in the Interior department. In 1910 he was nominated for United States senator, and was elected to serve for the long term, expiring March, 1917. Sen. Hitchcock was married Aug. 30, 1883, to Jessie, daughter of Lorenzo Crounse, governor of Nebraska in 1893–95.

WARMAN, Cy, author, was born at Greenup, Ill., June 22, 1855, son of John 22, 1855, son of John and Nancy (Askew) Warman. Wilson Warman claimed to be the first white child born in Browns county, Indiana. His father served in the Mexican war as a member of the 4th Indiana Volunteers and was given a grant of land near Greenup, Cumberland co., Ill., for gallant and meritorious services in the war. The son was in the employ of the Denver & Rio Grande railway at Salada, Colo., as a fireman and locomotive engineer until sciatic rheumatism compelled him to abandon railroading. He then started the "Western Railway Journal" in Denver, but it failed; subsequently he established the "Daily Chronicle," at Creed, Colo., which also suspended when the Sherman law ruined the silver camp. While at Creed the New York "Sun" began to buy his verses, and in an editorial introduced him to the world as "The

Poet of the Rockies," saying, "Here is a new poet with but one equal in all the west," and, through the efforts and assistance of Mr. Dana and the "Sun," he was able to enter the magazines of America and some in England almost immediately after this introduction. He began to utilize his railroad experiences in literary production, and soon was recognized as a leading writer of fiction in a new field. One of his railroad stories, "A Thousand Miles in a Night," related his experience in riding on a locomotive from New York to Chicago, and was published in "McClure's Magazine." Mr. Warman traveled two years in Europe and the Orient, spent two years in Washington, and visited the Klondike, about which he wrote a book entitled, "A Pleasure Trip to a Busy Country." His published volumes are: "Tales of An Engineer" (1895), "The Express Messenger" (1897), "Frontier Stories" (1898), "The Story of the Railroad" (1898), "The White Mail" (1899), "Snow On the Headlight" (1899), "Short Rails" (1900), "The Last Spike" (1906), "Weiga of Temagami" (1898). He was a member of the Chicago Press Club, the Royal Roosters, the Indiana Society of Chicago, and was at one time president of the American Press Humorists. He married (first) Ida Blanche Hays, of St. Jacobs, Ill., who died in 1887, and (second), May 17, 1892, Myrthle Marie Jones, the original of Mr. Warman's well-known song, "Sweet Marie." Mr. Warman died in Chicago, Ill., Apr. 7, 1914.

HERRON, William Christie, capitalist and philanthropist, was born in Cincinnati, O., Sept. 1, 1843, son of Joseph and Cordelia (Weeks) Herron, and grandson of John and Rebecca (Clarke) Herron. John Herron was a native of Ireland of English descent; having purchased lands in Pennsylvania, he emigrated in 1790, and settled in Lancaster county. The name was originally spelt "Heron," and originated from a Scotch clan which adopted the plumes of the white heron for a crest. Other members of the family after coming to America added a second "r" to the name, so as to avoid confusion with the families of Hern and Hearne, and John Heron likewise adopted the changed spelling. Joseph Herron was a prominent educator of Cincinnati, and founder of Herron Seminary, where the son obtained his education. At the outbreak of the civil war the latter enlisted in the United States navy, serving until its close. He began his business career with the hardware firm of Howell, Gano & Co. Subsequently he became a member of the hardware firm of Green & Herron, of Dayton, O., and then became associated with the pig-iron firm of Rogers, Brown & Co., of his native city, with whom he was identified until 1901. In that year he retired from active business and devoted the rest of his life to travel and to intellectual and philanthropic pursuits. He was vice-president and director of the American National Bank, and a director of the Fifth-Third National Bank, the American Rolling Mill Co. of Middletown, O., and of the Hanging Rock Iron Co. He was vice-president of the Young Men's Christian Association of Cincinnati; a trustee of the Children's Home, the Christ Hospital and the Elizabeth Gamble Deaconess Association; director of the Cincinnati Associated Charities; manager of the Freedman's Aid Society, and a commissioner of the Twentieth Century Thankoffering of the Methodist Episcopal church. He was a dominant factor in the affairs of these institutions, and was likewise active in religious welfare work. He was president of the board of trustees of the Avondale Methodist Episcopal Church, and through his church activities became interested in the affairs of the Methodist Book Concern, of which he was a member of the Book Committee. Having experienced the horrors of war he became an apostle of peace, serving as president of the Cincinnati branch of the Universal Peace Society and on the executive committee of the first peace congress held in New York city, besides attending a number of the annual peace conferences at Lake Mohonk. Mr. Herron was greatly beloved in his community for his peculiar gifts of mind and heart. He was married first in Cincinnati, O., in 1873, to Laura, daughter of George B. Winchell, a manufacturer of Cincinnati; and second in Cincinnati, O., June 16, 1886, to Anna, daughter of Phineas C. Fish of Oneonta, N. Y. Mrs. Herron is a member of the Cincinnati Woman's Club and an ex-president of the club, and active in the affairs of the Woman's Home Missionary Society of the Methodist church. There are two children by the first union, George Winchell and Mason P. Herron. Mr. Herron died in Cincinnati, O., May 21, 1909.

COHAN, George Michael, actor and playwright, was born in Providence, R. I., July 4, 1878, son of Jerry J. and Helen Frances (Costigan) Cohan. His father was also an actor from whom the son inherited his genius for stage work. As a small boy he played second violin in one of the theaters of Providence, and made his professional debut on the stage of Keith's Theatre in Boston, at the age of nine, his act consisting of a violin solo and musical imitations which he extracted from various kitchen utensils with the aid of his violin bow. Stage dancing was also one of his accomplishments. In 1890 he was featured as the boy in the mirth-provoking play, "Peck's Bad Boy," his father, mother and sister, Josephine, appearing in the same piece. The young man advanced rapidly in his profession, and early gave evidence of the remarkable ability with which he was later to achieve a foremost place on the American stage. With his father, mother and sister, known as "The Four Cohans," he played the entire season at Shea's Music Hall in Buffalo, N. Y., in 1891–92, and the act was so successful that it was followed by tours with Gus Williams, Charles A. Loder, Weber & Fields' "Vesta Tilley" Company, and the Harry Williams' All Star Vaudeville Company. Meanwhile young Cohan was doing very creditable work as an author and playwright. When only fifteen years of age he began writing songs which became popular all over the United States. His first original sketch was called, "The Professor's Wife," which had a successful run on the vaudeville stage. This was followed by "Money to Burn," another big hit, and "The Governor's Son." The latter was originally written as a one-act sketch and afterward lengthened into a three-act play, which was given at the Savoy Theatre, New York city. in 1899–1900, with the four Cohans in the cast. It was followed by "Running for Office" (1902), and "Little Johnny Jones" (1904), both of which had successful runs in New York city and on the road. In 1902 he became associated with Sam H. Harris, and thereafter the firm of Cohan & Harris managed the plays he wrote. These were, "George Washington, Jr." (1905); "45 Minutes from Broadway" (1906), which is said to have yielded over a million dollars in profits and royalties; "50 Miles from Boston" (1906); "Talk of New York" (1907); "The Yankee Prince" (1908); "The American Idea" (1908); "The Man Who Owns Broadway" (1909); "Get-Rich-Quick Wallingford" (1910); "The Little Millionaire" (1911). In the fall of 1911 he returned to the stage in "The Little Millionaire," which was brought out at the New Cohan Theatre in New York, and also under his own management. In the season of 1912–13 he appeared for the first time as a light comedian in straight comedy, playing the title role in his own play, "Broadway Jones." It was described as the best of its kind, and the consensus of opinion of the critics was that Mr. Cohan had reached a higher rung in the ladder of fame than ever before. His next achievements were his dramatization of "Seven Keys to Bald-pate," by Biggers, and "The Miracle Man," by Packard, following by his first "Revue" entitled, "Hello Broadway." In 1915 he wrote "Hit-the-Trail-Holliday," and in 1916 another "Revue" which surpassed his first. As an originator of mirth, music and good cheer Mr. Cohan probably has no equal on the American stage to-day. Seemingly at will this clever young Irish-American turns out a successful play, a fascinating song number, dramatizes a book or evolves a rapid-fire farce, always with the sure touch of genius that marks the student who has acquired his knowledge of the stage and its technique at first hand, and therefore presents his work with the secure feeling of certain approval. No writer since the days of Hoyt has been so successful in transferring humanly interesting character studies to the stage and depicting them with the naturalness to be found in real life. As a theatrical manager he is not only the director of his theatre, the Cohan, at Broadway and Forty-Third street, New York, which was opened in 1910, but the firm of Cohan & Harris is manager of the Astor theatre at Forty-fifth street and Broadway, the Bronx Opera House in upper New York, and the George M. Cohan Grand Opera House Chicago. He was married in 1899 to Ethel Levy and had one daughter, Georgette. He was divorced in 1906, and was again married June 29, 1907, to Agnes, daughter of John Nolan, of Brookline, Mass. There were three children by this marriage: Mary Agnes, Helen Frances and George Michael Harris Cohan.

ROACH, John Baker, ship-builder and manufacturer, was born in New York City, Dec. 7, 1839, son of John and Emeline (Johnson) Roach. His father (q.v.) was one of the leading ship-builders of the United States. The son was educated in the public schools of New York and at the Ashland Collegiate Institute, Green co., N. Y. In 1867 his father purchased the Morgan Iron Works in New York, and with his son as partner formed the firm of John Roach & Son. In 1871 the firm purchased the plant of Reaney, Son & Archbold, at Chester, Pa., and John B. Roach, though but thirty-two years of age, was placed in charge. This shipyard was developed by John Roach & Son under the name of the Delaware River Iron Ship Building and Engine Works, and at times employed more than 2,000 hands. For many years John B. Roach gave the business the closest and most persistent attention. The first vessel contracted for was the City of San Antonia for C. M. H. Mallory & Co., of New York, and in the same year (1872) the Pacific Mail Steamship Co. contracted for two large iron vessels, with compound or double expansion engines, which were the first ships equipped with such engines in America. They also built vessels for the Pacific Mail, Mallory, Old Dominion, Alexandre, Ocean Steamship Co. of Savannah, Cromwell, Ward, Old Colony, Oregon Navigation Co., Brazil Mail and other steamship lines followed in rapid succession. In 1883 John

Roach & Son obtained the contracts for the new steel cruisers Chicago, Boston, Atlanta and Dolphin, the first vessels of the new navy, the contract price being $2,440,000. The Priscilla, Puritan, Plymouth and Pilgrim, which his company built for the Fall River Line, were in their day the finest steamboats in the world. In the reorganization following his father's death John B. Roach became president of the Ship Building Corporation of Chester, and vice-president of the Morgan Iron Works of New York. He was a member of the Union League of Philadelphia, the Engineers' Club of New York, the New York Chamber of Commerce, the Penn Club of Chester, the board of managers of the Chester Hospital, and a director in the Seaboard Steel Casting Co., the Chester National Bank, and the Cambridge Trust Co. He was married Dec. 12, 1861, to Mary Caroline, daughter of David Wallace of Staatsburg, N. Y., and had eleven children, four of whom survive: Emeline Wallace, wife of William C. Sproul of Chester, Pa.; Mary Garretta, wife of Geo. Forbes of Baltimore; John and William McPherson Roach. He died in Chester, June 16, 1908.

BURR, Willard, Jr., composer, was born at Ravenna, O., Jan. 7, 1852, son of Willard and Sarah Almira (Burr) Burr, and a descendant of Benjamin Burr, who came from England in 1630 and was one of the original settlers and proprietors of Hartford in 1635. From Benjamin Burr the line is traced through Samuel, Samuel, John, John, Reuben and Salmon Burr, the grandfather. Willard Burr, Sr., was a Congregational minister and was settled over various churches in Ohio. Willard Burr, Jr., was graduated at Oberlin College in 1876 and at the Oberlin Conservatory of Music in 1877. For two years he taught music in New Hampshire, at the same time studying at Cambridge with J. K. Paine. In 1879 Oberlin College conferred upon him the degree of A.M. Later he studied in the fugue, counterpoint and composition in Europe under August Haupt, and on his return settled in Boston. He taught music, sang in church choirs, gave concerts and pursued the work of composition. In an address on "Musical Art Creation in America and the Relation of Music Teachers Thereto," delivered before the Music Teachers' National Association at Cleveland, O., in 1884, he advocated the creation and encouragement of an American school of composition. His ideals were high and his work effective for the creation and building up of an American school of musical art, and the results have been important and far-reaching. He was the originator of the movement for an international copyright law to place American compositions on an equal basis with foreign. He was a member of the Manuscript Society of New York, the Euterpe and Apollo clubs of Boston, and a constitutional member of the American College of Musicians. His compositions are numerous and are noted for their originality, strong thematic treatment and scholarly style. They have been performed many times in public and have received favorable notices from the press. Among them may be mentioned: Andante and Scherzo for string orchestra; trio for pianoforte, violin and 'cello; String Quartette No. 2, in C minor; String Quartette No. 3, in F major; Sonata for pianoforte and violin, in B flat minor; "The Wreck of the Hesperus," a dramatic ballad with orchestral and pianoforte accompaniment; "Dove Song," with violin obligato; three anthems: "The Lord Is Thy Keeper," "God Is My Rock" and "I Will Lift Up Mine Eyes"; nine songs: "Song of the Four Seasons," "Song of the Arab,"

GEORGE M. COHAN
ACTOR

JOHN B. ROACH
SHIPBUILDER

WILLARD BURR
COMPOSER

WALTER B. CANNON
PHYSIOLOGIST

"O Spirit of the Summer Time," "Sleighing Song," "O Evergreen Isle," "My Life Barque Floats to Music," " 'Tis Home Where'er the Heart Is," "Es Blücht Ein Blümchen Irgendwo" and "Under the Daisies"; Oberlin College Alumni song; male chorus with tenor solo, "The Ship and the Sunshine"; three "Aeolian Fantasies" for the pianoforte: "By the Fireside," "In the Forest" and "On the Sea"; three pianoforte pieces op. 24: "Barcarolle," "Romanza" and "Melody"; four street lyrics, op. 27: "A Harp Serenade," "Umbrellas to Mend," "Old Rags" and "Pie Apple"; seven idyls for pianoforte: "From Shore to Shore," "Cradle Song," "Merrimen," "Love's Mystery," "Bridal March," "Duetto," "Memory" and "Scotch Fantasie on the 'Sweet Bye and Bye' "; three concert nocturnes, three etudes, "Grand Fantasie and Fugue in E Minor," and many other vocal, pianoforte and chamber music compositions. Mr. Burr was married at Franklin, N. H., July 1, 1879, to Hattie A., daughter of John Plummer Colby and widow of Frank H. Aiken. He died in Boston, Mass., May 8, 1915.

CANNON, Walter Bradford, physiologist, was born in Prairie du Chien, Wis., Oct. 19, 1871, son of Colbert Hanchett and Wilma (Denio) Cannon, and grandson of Lucius Cannon, who was a member of the Wisconsin legislature. He was graduated at Harvard College in 1896, and received his A.M. degree in 1897. He studied medicine at the Harvard Medical School, and received the degree of M.D. in 1900. He was instructor in zoology at Harvard College during 1899–1900, and instructor in physiology at the Harvard Medical School during 1900–02. In the latter year he became assistant professor of physiology at the medical school, a position he held until 1906, when he was chosen for the George Higginson professorship. Dr. Cannon has made a special study of the alimentary canal and the motions of the digestive tract, beginning his researches while a student at the medical school with the use of the then newly discovered x-rays. He was the first to utilize insoluable bismuth salts for making obvious with the x-rays the motions of the alimentary canal (January, 1897), a method that is now in general use in the medical world in the diagnosis of disease of the esophagus, stomach and intestines. His various reports on these researches were collected in book form and published as the first of a series of International Medical Monographs under the title, "The Mechanical Factors of Digestion," (1912). Early in his studies of the alimentary canal he was struck by the cessation of all digestive activities in the presence of emotional disturbances. He instituted a series of researches and studies on this phase of the subject, which revealed a group of remarkable alterations in the bodily economy under the stress of great emotion—responses nicely adapted to the individual's welfare and preservation when great feats of strength and endurance are demanded. The results of these investigations have been embodied in a volume, "Bodily Changes in Pain, Hunger, Fear and Rage" (1915). These in turn led logically to an investigation of the activities of the glands of internal secretion by the use of their electrical manifestations. He is also the author of, "A Laboratory Course in Physiology" (1911). While in the medical school Dr. Cannon wrote a paper, "The Case System of Teaching Systematic Medicine," in which he criticised the educational methods in medicine, and suggested that the study of case records by the students and the active use of their judgment on these records would be preferable to the com-

mon practice of taking lecture notes. The outcome of this paper has been the publication of a series of case books in medicine, surgery, obstetrics, neurology, gynecology, etc., which are being used for teaching purposes. He is a member of the Boston Society of Medical Sciences (president, 1908), the Massachusetts Medical Society, the American Medical Association, the American Association for the Advancement of Science, the American Physiological Society, the Society for Experimental Biology and Medicine, the American Philosophical Society, the American Psychological Association, the American Academy of Arts and Sciences, the Association of American Physicians and the National Academy of Sciences, and an honorary member of the New York Röntgen Society, and the American Röntgen Ray Society. He was married June 25, 1901, to Cornelia, daughter of Henry Clay James of St. Paul, Minn., and has five children: Bradford, Wilma, Linda, Marian and Helen Cameron. Portrait opposite page 286.

STERLING, Thomas, U. S. senator, was born on a farm near Amanda, Fairfield co., O., Feb. 21, 1851, son of Charles and Anna (Kessler) Sterling; grandson of Thomas H. and Mabala (Reed) Sterling, and great-grandson of William Sterling, a native of northern Maryland, and of Scotch-Irish descent. When he was four years old his father removed to a farm in McLean county, Ill., and here he was educated in the district school, later attending the Illinois Wesleyan University at Bloomington, where he was graduated in 1875. He was superintendent of schools at Bement for two years, when having determined to follow the legal profession he studied law at Springfield and was admitted to the bar in 1878. He began practice in Springfield in partnership with Joseph M. Grout, the firm name being Sterling & Grout. He was city attorney of Springfield during 1880–81. In the following year he removed to Spink county, South Dakota, and made that his permanent residence. He also served as district attorney of Spink county (1886–88). He was a member of the constitutional conventions of 1883 and 1889, and was elected a senator to the first state legislature in 1889, in which he was chairman of the judiciary committee. Meanwhile his law practice had be · growing, and during the following ten years he devoted his entire time to professional work. In 1901 he was appointed dean of the College of Law of the state university at Vermilion, S. Dak., and held that position for ten years. In 1913 he was elected to the United States senate to succeed Robert J. Gamble, his term expiring in March, 1919. In the senate he is keenly interested in both administrative and legislative action on foreign affairs and has devoted special attention to tarif and trust legislation, and because of conditions in his own state, to laws relating to the disposal of public lands. He has served on the committees on Public Lands, Pensions, Mines and Mining, District of Columbia, Civil Service and Retrenchment, Immigration and Post Office and Post Roads. Sen. Sterling was twice married: first, Oct. 17, 1877, to Anna Dunn, of Bement, Ill., who died in 1881, leaving one son, Cloyd Dunn Sterling, a lawyer; and, second, May 1, 1883, to Mrs. Emma R. Thayer.

MacCALLUM, William George, pathologist and educator, was born in Dunnville, Ontario, Canada, Apr. 18, 1874, son of Dr. George Alexander and Florence (Eakins) MacCallum. His father was medical superintendent of the London Hospital for the Insane. He was graduated at the University of Toronto in 1894, and then studied medicine at the Johns Hopkins University, receiving his M.D. degree in 1897. For a year after graduating he served as resident house officer, becoming assistant resident pathologist in 1898 in the Johns Hopkins Hospital, and then by successive promotions was advanced until 1908, when he received the appointment to the chair of pathological physiology, with the lectureship on forensic medicine in the medical department of Johns Hopkins University. In 1909 he was called to the chair of pathology in the medical department of Columbia University, which place he still holds. Since New York became his home, he has also held the important office of pathologist to the Presbyterian Hospital. Dr. MacCallum is a member of many scientific societies both in this country and abroad, including the American Medical Association and the International Association of Medical Museums, of which he was president in 1908, and since 1910 he has been a fellow of the American Association for the Advancement of Science. In 1908–09 he delivered the Harvey lectures on "Fever," which with an extensive bibliography were published in Philadelphia in 1910. In addition to the various duties of his profession as well as those of his teaching, he has found time to enrich the literature of pathology by numerous studies on the special subjects of malaria, the lymphatics, the pathological physiology of the circulation, the organs of internal secretion and trematode parasites. He has contributed the following papers to the Johns Hopkins Hospital Bulletin: "On the Mechanism of Granular Materials from the Peritoneum" (1903); "The Relations Between the Lymphatics and the Connective Tissue" (1903); a series of several papers on "The Teaching of the Pathological Physiology" (1908); "On the Relation of the Islands of Langerhans to Glycosuria" (1909), and "The Changes in the Circulation in Aortic Insufficiency" (1911). He has published in the "Journal of the American Medical Association" "Regenerative Changes in Cirrhosis of the Liver" (1904); "The Internal Secretion of the Pancreas" (1911), and "The Function of the Parathyroid Glands" (1912). Among his other papers may be mentioned: "On a Cause on the Pathological Physiology of the Circulation" (1906) "Inflammation in Tissues Separated from Connection with the Central Nervous System" (1910), and "The Seat of Action in Tetany After Parathyroidectomy" (1911). The subject of tetany is one to which in recent years he has devoted some attention, and in association with his students he has published "On the Relation of Tetany to the Parathyroid Glands and to Calcium Metabolism" (1909), and "Further Experimental Studies in Tetany" (1913), which have appeared in the Journal of Experimental Medicine. He is unmarried.

MacCALLUM, John Bruce, physician, was born in Dunnville, Ontario, Canada, June 8, 1876, son of Dr. George Alexander MacCallum, and brother of William G. MacCallum. He was graduated at Toronto University in 1896, and from there went to Baltimore to study medicine at the Johns Hopkins Medical School, where he received his M.D. degree in 1900. While a student he conducted some original investigations in anatomy, the most important being on the architecture of the ventricles of the heart. At this early period of his career he began to show symptons of tuberculosis to which he later succumbed. He was assistant in anatomy at Johns Hopkins University for one year, taught anatomy for a short time at the Denver (Colo.) Medical School, where he went for the benefit of his health, and then removed to California, where he became assistant professor of physiology at the University of California under Prof. Jacques Loeb. Although handicapped by disease he conducted many valuable experiments, continuing his researches to the very last, testing the effects of various drugs on jelly fish because he could no longer control a rabbit, and dictating the results to his mother. Throughout his brief but brilliant career he bore himself with fortitude and cheerfulness that was characteristic of the author Stevenson. His scientific papers were published in the "American Journal of Anatomy," the "Johns Hopkins Hospital Reports," the "Journal of Experimental Medicine," and a University of California publication. He died unmarried in Berkeley, Cal., Feb. —, 1906.

PORTER, William Townsend, physiologist, was born in Plymouth, O., Sept. 24, 1862, son of Dr. Frank Gibson and Martha (Townsend) Porter. He was graduated at high school in St. Louis, Mo., in 1879, and studied medicine in the St. Louis Medical College of Washington University, receiving his M.D. degree in 1885. He pursued post graduate studies in the universities in Kiel, Breslau and Berlin, Germany. On his return to the United States he became resident physician in the St. Louis City Hospital, being for some time in charge of the medical and surgical work of that institution. In 1887 he was appointed professor of physiology in the St. Louis Medical College, which chair he held until 1893, when he resigned to accept a call to an assistant professorship of physiology in the Harvard Medical School. Since 1906 he has been professor of comparative physiology there. Prof. Porter, although actively engaged in teaching, has also found time to publish the results of many of his investigations and descriptions of the appliances devised by him in the prosecution of his work. Among his papers, most of which have been contributed to the Proceedings of the American Physiological Society, which are published in the "American Journal of Physiology," of which he was the editor until 1915, are the following: "Respiration Scheme" (1904); "The Condition of the Vasoconstrictor Neurons on Shock" (1904); "Studies in the Physiology of Muscle" (1906); "The Effect of Uniform Afferent Impulses Upon the Blood Pressure at Different Levels" (1907); "The Relation of Afferent Impulses to the Vasomotor Centers" (1910), and "A Method for the Study of the Vasomotor Nerves of the Heart and Other Organs" (1912). For facilitating his research work he has devised an improved kymograph, a muscle warmer, and an electrometer for the stage of the microscope. More recently his publications have been in collaboration with his associates, and include special developments of his particular studies, such as "The State of the Vasomotor Apparatus in Pneumonia" (1914). His larger works include "An Introduction to Physiology" (1901), of which a second edition of 587 pages appeared in 1906; "Physiology at Harvard" (1902), of which the fifth edition was published in 1906, and his Harvey Lectures on "Vasomotor Relations" (1908). In recognition of his high attainments he received the degree of LL.D. from the University of Maryland in 1907. He is a member of the Massachusetts Medical Association, the American Medical Association, the Society for Experimental Biology, and the American Physiological Association, and in 1901 he was elected a fellow of the American Association for the Advancement of Science.

BUNCE, William Gedney, landscape painter, was born at Hartford, Conn., Sept. 19, 1840, son of James Marvin and Elizabeth Huntington (Chester) Bunce. His first American ancestor was Thomas Bunce, who came to this country from the county of Kent, England, at an undetermined date and was one of the first settlers of Hartford, Conn. From this Thomas Bunce and his wife, Sarah ————, the line is traced through their son John and his wife, Mary Barnard; their son John, and his wife, Abigail Sanford; their son, John and his wife, Anne Bunce; their son John and his wife Susanne Kilbourn; their son Russell and his wife, Lucinda Marvin; their son, James M. Bunce, father of the artist. Gedney Bunce studied art at Cooper Union and under William Hart in New York and subsequently under Andreas Achenback and P. J. Clays in Brussels, Belgium. For twelve years he lived continuously in Europe, sending his first pictures to America for exhibition in 1871. From the beginning he showed impressionistic tendencies modified by a desire for definite effects which has kept him from the ranks of the very moderns. The clash of two rather irreconcilable styles has resplted in a manner and charm decidedly his own, and an entire absence of the brutal strength and scientific verism which seems to be the aim of present-day art. The predominating quality of his painting is a gentle, sensuous charm, a misty dreaminess as of one who looks at life through the sun-tinted haze of a summer morning. For forty years he lived in Venice, studying the dreamy, vaporous atmosphere and moving colorful life which lend such glamour to that city, and so well did he transfer that glamour to his canvases that he has become known as the painter of Venice. His pictures of Venice are numerous. Naturally he has used the same subjects over and over again—the white towers and marble façades, the colored sails, the gondolas and harbor buoys—all that is physically characteristic of Venice. But each picture is different; each catches one of the myriad atmospheric moods which make Venice the perpetual delight of the dreamer. His Venice is not the conventional one, but it is the real one. He has gone beneath the mere prettiness of Venice and painted the misty, languorous soul of it. Among the best of his Venetian pictures are "Sunset, San Georgio, Venice" (National Gallery, Washington, D. C.); "Early Morning View in Venice"; "Morning View in Venice" (Metropolitan Museum, New York); "Venetian Boats," 1881; "Venice, Bit of Harbor"; "Sun, Sails and Sea"; "Venice, Day in May"; "Venetian Day"; "Venetian Night" and "Among the Sails." He has a studio in Hartford, Conn., and has painted a number of characteristic New England landscapes, among which may be mentioned "Watch Hill, Rhode Island," and "Nantucket Hillside, New England." He has exhibited frequently in Paris, Rome, Munich, London and New York, and was awarded a bronze medal at the Paris Exposition in 1900; a silver medal at the Pan-American Exposition, Buffalo, in 1901; a silver medal at the Charleston Exposition in 1902 and a silver medal at the St. Louis Exposition in 1904. One of his pictures of Venice was bought by the French government. Mr. Bunce is a member of the National Academy of Design, the National Institute of Arts and Letters, and the Players' and Lotus clubs of New York. He is unmarried.

REA, Samuel, president of the Pennsylvania railroad, was born at Hollidaysburg, Pa., Sept. 21, 1855, son of James D. and Ruth B. (Moore) Rea, grandson of John and Elizabeth (Culbertson) Rea, and great-grandson of Samuel Rea, who came from the north of Ireland about 1754-55 and settled in Pennsylvania. His grandfather was an officer in the revolutionary war and in the war of 1812, and a representative in congress during 1803-11 and 1813-15. Upon the death of his father Samuel Rea obtained employment in a general store. In 1871 he entered the employ of the Pennsylvania railroad as chainman and rodman, but during the financial panic of 1873 all engineering work was stopped, and for about a year he acted as a clerk for the Hollidaysburg Iron and Nail Co. In the spring of 1875 he was attached to an engineering corps of the Pennsylvania railroad stationed at Connellsville, Pa., and for two years was assistant engineer on the chain suspension bridge over the Monongahela river at Pittsburgh. He was assistant engineer of the Pittsburgh and Lake Erie railroad during its construction, 1877-79. Returning to the Pennsylvania system after its completion, in 1879, he became assistant engineer in charge of building the Pittsburgh, Virginia and Charleston railway, an important line in the Pennsylvania system. From 1879 to 1883 he had charge of surveys in the coke regions of the state and in reconstructing the Western Pennsylvania railroad into a low grade freight line, after which he was appointed principal assistant engineer to Vice-President J. N. DuBarry, at Philadelphia, serving five years. In 1888 he was made assistant to the second vice-president of the road, but in the following year he resigned this office to become vice-president of the Maryland Central railway and chief engineer of the Baltimore Belt railroad, which was the connecting tunnel through Baltimore, Md., for the Baltimore and Ohio railroad. In 1892 he was chosen assistant to the president of the Pennsylvania railroad, and on the day of his appointment left for London, England, to make a thorough examination and report on the underground electric railways, both constructed and proposed. After the death of Vice-President DuBarry, in 1892, Mr. Rea was given charge of general engineering construction work then in progress, the acquisition of right of way and real estate in that connection, the promotion of all new lines or branches, and the financial and corporate work incident thereto. In 1897 he was appointed first assistant to the president of the Pennsylvania Railroad Co., and following the election of A. J. Cassatt as president was elected fourth vice-president. In 1905 he became third vice-president, and in 1909 second vice-president. In addition to his former duties he was placed in charge of the engineering and accounting departments. In 1911 he was elected first vice-president, and when the practice of designating the vice-presidents numerically was discontinued a year later, he became vice-president. On the resignation of James McCrea, Jan. 1, 1913, he was elected president. He is also president of the Pennsylvania Co., Northern Central railway, Philadelphia, Baltimore and Washington railroad, West Jersey and Seashore railroad, and Pittsburgh, Cincinnati, Chicago and St. Louis railway companies, and also a director of the Pennsylvania Railroad Co., and many other railroad corporations in the Pennsylvania system east and west of Pittsburgh. For many years he was interested in the project to bridge the Hudson river from Hoboken to New York and thus establish in the metropolis a terminus for the railroads using ferries from the New Jersey side. He was one of the incorporators of the North River Bridge Co., chartered by an act of congress to build that bridge. When finally the Pennsylvania railroad determined to build its own extension into New York by tunneling the Hudson river, Mr. Rea was given direct charge of that important engineering enterprise, and carried it out to a successful conclusion at a cost of $100,000,000. In recognition of his achievement, the University of Pennsylvania conferred on him the degree of Sc.D. in 1910. A continuation of this project was the construction of the New York Connecting railroad jointly by the Pennsylvania and the New York, New Haven and Hartford railroads, designed to form a through route for railroad transportation between the southern, western and the New England states. Mr. Rea is president of the New York Connecting Railroad Co., and has charge of its construction. Its chief feature will be the East river (New York) bridge, an erect arch of about 1,000 feet span and aggregating, with its viaduct approaches, about three miles in length and costing about $20,000,000. Mr. Rea initiated the many consolidations and acquisitions of subsidiary companies which have been carried out by the Pennsylvania railroad in the last twenty years, so as to simplify the accounting and operating features, and, by unification of these companies, have the parent company do the necessary financing for the entire system, instead of having these various small companies issuing and selling their own securities. He is the author of ''The Railways Terminating in London'' (1888). He is a member of the American Society of Civil Engineers, Institution of Civil Engineers, London; Society of Naval Architects and Marine Engineers, New York Chamber of Commerce, Pennsylvania Scotch-Irish Society, Pennsylvania Society of Sons of Revolution, Society of War of 1812, Pennsylvania Society of New York, Fairmount Park Art Association, Pennsylvania Academy of Fine Arts, Metropolitan Museum of Art (New York), American Academy of Political and Social Science, American Railway Guild, University (of Pennsylvania) Museum, Society of Arts (London), the Philadelphia, Engineers', Rittenhouse and Automobile clubs, of Philadelphia; Merion Cricket Club of Haverford, Union, Lawyers', Century Association and Economic clubs of New York; Sleepy Hollow Country Club, Metropolitan Club of Washington, and the Royal Auto Club of London. Mr. Rea was married at Pittsburgh (1879) to Mary M., daughter of George Black, of Pittsburgh, Pa. Of this union have been born one son, George Black Rea, who died in 1908, and one daughter. Mr. Rea's varied railroad experience of over forty years has stamped him as one of the foremost constructive minds, giving him a chief place among the few who have displayed real genius for organization and achievement, yet he has ever retained his simple tastes and quiet demeanor, and has practiced a benevolence devoid of ostentation. The European estimate of his attainments was expressed in the London ''Statist'' at the time of his selection to the presidency of the Pennsylvania Railroad Co., as follows: ''To find a successor worthy of the chair of Mr. McCrea, Mr. Cassatt and former presidents was not an easy task, but the choice of Mr. Samuel Rea was universally approved. Mr. Rea has for many years been one of the most valued of the officers upon whose judgment and suggestions Mr. Frank Thomson, Mr. Cassatt and Mr. McCrea have relied for advice and assistance in carrying out their respective policies. They have all spoken in no unstinted terms of the great value of the services

rendered to them by Mr. Rea and of the soundness of his judgment. We venture to think that no better appointment could have been made, for not only has Mr. Rea's long service and experience made him acquainted with all the physical and traffic problems of the road, but he possesses what may be termed railroad statesmanship in a high degree. The relations of the company to the employees in the matter of wages and labor, the relations of the company to the public in the matter of rates and facilities, the relations of the company to the Interstate Commerce Commission and to the lawmakers in the matter of governmental control, the relations of the various railroads to each other, and, last but not least, the relations of the Pennsylvania to the trend of the economic current which in the past has brought about railway systems of increasing importance, have, as we are personally aware, all been carefully studied by Mr. Rea. In brief, realizing as we do the importance of the human element in the conduct of great undertakings, and the extent to which the prosperity of corporations, great or small, depend upon the ability and judgment of those responsible for their management, we consider that the Pennsylvania railroad has been specially fortunate in having possessed Mr. James McCrea as president, and we look forward to its future in confident expectation that it will continue to grow increasingly strong under the presidency of Mr. Samuel Rea.'' Portrait opposite page 292.

HILL, Percival Smith, merchant, was born in Philadelphia, Pa., Apr. 5, 1862, son of George W. and Sarah (White) Hill, and grandson of John Hill, a native of Sussex, England, who came to the United States in the early part of the nineteenth century and settled in Bucks county, Pa. His father, a native of Bucks county, Pa., conducted an extensive carpet business in Philadelphia, from which he retired to assume the presidency of the American Life Insurance Co. of that city. Subsequently he was president of the Seventh National Bank. Percival S. Hill received his early education in Rugby Academy, Philadelphia, where he was graduated in 1876. He spent two years at the University of Pennsylvania and two years at Harvard. Upon the death of his brother, George R. Hill, in 1880, circumstances forced him to buy out the firm of Hart & Hill, jobbers of cotton and woolen goods, which he had carried on under his own name for two years. In 1882 he became a member of the firm of Boyd, White & Co., carpet jobbers and retailers in Philadelphia, with which he was connected until 1894, when he sold his interest to John Wanamaker. Two years previously (1892) he was made manager of the sales department of the Blackwell Durham Tobacco Co., manufacturers of Bull Durham tobacco, with a branch office in Philadelphia. Through Mr. Hill's efforts the business was widely extended, and the sales increased enormously. He subsequently acquired a proprietary interest in the company in association with Julian S. Carr (q. v.). In 1898 he became president of the Durham Tobacco Co., of Durham, N. C. In the same year the Union Tobacco Co. was organized in opposition to the American Tobacco Co., and the Blackwell company was taken over by the former. The Union Tobacco Co. had an option on Liggett & Myers Co., of St. Louis, which they failed to exercise, and when Bernard M. Baruch bought that concern and turned it over to the American Tobacco Co., the Union company was absorbed by the American Tobacco Co. The Union Tobacco Co.'s operations extended over a period of only ninety days. In 1900, upon the death of Josiah Brown, Mr. Hill was appointed secretary of the American Tobacco Co., and in the following year was elected one of its vice-presidents. In 1909 he became president of two of the important subsidiary companies, namely, the American Cigar Co. and the Havana Tobacco Co., which handled the Cuban branch of the business. When James B. Duke (q. v.) resigned as president of the American Tobacco Co., in March, 1912, and assumed control of the British-American Tobacco Co., Mr. Hill succeeded him as president of the American Tobacco Co. On July 10, 1907, the United States filed a petition in the southern district of New York to dissolve the American Tobacco Co. as an illegal combination. Decision was rendered, Nov. 7, 1908, in favor of the government, except as to individual defendants and certain foreign and other corporations. An appeal taken by both sides was argued and submitted to the supreme court, where a sweeping decision was rendered, May 29, 1911, sustaining the government on every point. In 1912 Mr. Hill made a detailed announcement as to the manner in which the American Tobacco Co. was to be dissolved under the ruling and order of the United States supreme court. The initial movement, he said, was to distribute among the stockholders $100,000,000 in securities, producing an annual income of more than $9,000,000. These securities were selected by the court itself, and took from the American Tobacco Co. those elements that had excited comment and criticism and which were said to have given the American Tobacco Co. power over other manufacturers, such as the control of or connection with the licorice business, the tinfoil business, the United Cigar Stores Co., the foreign alliance with the Imperial Tobacco Co., Limited, and British-American Co., Limited; all relations with the R. J. Reynolds Co. and the American Snuff Co. The next step was the disintegration of the very factories, brands and businesses that had been owned outright by the American Tobacco Co. In recognition of the possibility of a feigned and not a real competition, in view especially of the common stock-holding, the decree of the court not only provided for a disintegration, but it entered continuing injunctions which provided that none of the companies shall directly or indirectly co-operate in control or management of a corporation or in fixing the prices. Mr. Hill is also president and director of the H. de Cabanas Y. Carbajal, the Havana Commercial Co. and the Havana Tobacco Co.; director of the American Cigar Co. (chairman), the Cuban Land and Leaf Tobacco Co. and the Havana-American Co. He is a member of the Union League and Racquet clubs of Philadelphia, the Metropolitan Club of New York, and the Greenwich, the Baltusrol and Sleepy Hollow Country clubs. He was married, Apr. 3, 1882, to Cassie, daughter of John Milnes, a well-known coal merchant of Philadelphia, and has one son, George Washington Hill, and two daughters: Gertrude and Catherine Hill.

GREEN, Adolphus Williamson, president of the National Biscuit Co., was born in Boston, Mass., Jan. 14, 1843, son of John Henry and Jane (Ryan) Green. He was educated in the public schools of Boston, the Boston Latin School, graduating in 1859, and Harvard University, where he received his bachelor's degree in 1863. After serving as principal of the high school at Groton, Mass., for one year, he went to the Mercantile Library, New York city, as assistant librarian, and in 1867 he was advanced to the position of librarian, an office he held for two years. In 1869 he became associated with the law firm of Evarts, Southmayd & Choate, and after studying law in the office of these well-known lawyers he was admitted to the bar in 1873. He began the practice of his profession in Chicago, Ill. His natural business ability and legal attainments soon won for him a high standing at the Chicago bar. He was attorney for the village of Hyde Park during 1882-84, and later became attorney for the South Park commissioners, also serving in the same capacity for the Chicago Board of Trade. In 1884 he formed a partnership with Hon. William C. Goudy (q. v.) under the firm name of Goudy & Green. Later he was senior member of Green, Willits & Robbins, and still later formed another firm, Green, Peters & Babst. Mr. Green made a specialty of corporation law, and through his legal connections became interested in the organization of the American Biscuit Co. in 1890. He also helped to organize the United States Baking Co., and when these companies were purchased by the National Biscuit Co. in 1898 he became director and general counsel of the latter. As he became more and more identified with the business affairs of the National Biscuit Co. he gradually relinquished his law business and devoted his whole attention to its affairs. In order to get the largest benefit from his services, the position of chairman of the board of directors was made for him. In 1905 he was elected chief executive of the company in fact as well as in name, and he is still its president. He was quick to see that the old method of selling crackers in bulk, either in boxes or barrels, was not only crude but wasteful and unstable, and he devised the plan of selling crackers in packages or cartons, an idea that was revolutionary to the business, and one that was destined to mark a new era in the history of the industry. Accordingly, the National Biscuit Co., in January, 1899, put upon the market its now celebrated package of soda crackers under the trade-name of "Uneeda Biscuit." The packages are made of paper by machinery, and are so nearly air-tight that they keep the contents absolutely fresh, untouched by human hands, and uncontaminated by the surroundings of its journey from the bakery to the table of the consumer. Two factories were built and equipped with special machinery designed to carry out this idea, one in New York and one in Chicago, duplicates in every particular as to size, arrangement, equipment and operation. The process of manufacturing the Uneeda Biscuit in the factories of the National Biscuit Co. is as follows: The flour, yeast and water are mixed by huge mixing machines in a special mixing-room on the top floor. The dough, after being allowed to rise, is rolled out by huge rollers on to a moving endless band or apron made of canvas about thirty inches wide, which carries it, now only one-thirty-second of an inch in thickness, under a series of stamps, which cut out the crackers, and letter and perforate them in rows of six. Continuing on the canvas apron, they are carried in the direction of the ovens. The National Biscuit Co. was one of the first to locate its ovens on the top floor, where a double row of large windows on all four sides afford ample ventilation. Each oven consists of a large brick inclosure, about ten feet wide, the fires for which are tended and regulated from the floor below. In each furnace is a huge wheel, at the circumference of which hangs a series of parallel trays or platforms of metal at regular intervals, so suspended as to always hang in a horizontal position, like the cages of a huge Ferris wheel. The stamped-out dough is now transferred to the oven by means of peels or flat wooden paddles in the hands of employees. With his peel the attendant deftly scoops up about a dozen rows of the stamped dough and transfers them to the iron platform in the oven. Four men are required at each oven to do this work. When each has deposited his peelful of unbaked crackers, the wheel begins to revolve and the tray starts on its downward journey around the oven. The details of the operation are so nicely adjusted that one revolution of the wheel is sufficient to bake the crackers. The freshly-baked crackers are removed from the platform by the same hands to make way for the next lot of cracker dough. Each of the trays holds about thirty-six dozen crackers, and the magnitude of the company's output may be judged from the fact that there are twelve of such ovens on the same floor of the Uneeda Biscuit factory in New York, and a duplicate factory is turning out the same quantity daily in Chicago. The crackers, still warm from the oven, are carried to another floor by conveyers and deposited on moving tables, to be placed in their paper boxes. The paper box, or container, with its paraffin paper lining, is folded by machinery, and by an ingenious arrangement is locked at the side, all at one operation. The boxes are carried by an endless belt to the cracker tables, where they are packed and inspected by girls, this being the first and only time the crackers are touched by human hands. Continuing on their journey, the cartons are inclosed in a label and the In-er-seal trade-mark affixed at the ends, also by machinery, and carried to still another floor, where they are wrapped in dozen lots ready for the wholesaler. "In-er-seal" is the trade-name given to all of the company's goods that are packed in cartons, and the two factories thus described are used to manufacture "Uneedas" exclusively. In themselves they represent an industry of enormous proportions, employing about 1,000 people, but there are thirty or more other factories in different sections of the United States where every variety of plain and fancy cracker is made and packed in cartons and also in bulk (chiefly in tins) to supply the enormous demand of the company's business. That the National Biscuit Co. is now one of the biggest industries in the United States is largely due to the genius and enterprise of Mr. Green. His ability has not only demonstrated the success of a single article, but it has placed the National Biscuit Co. in the front rank of industrial corporations. He was married July 3, 1879, to Esther, daughter of Charles Walsh, of Chicago, Ill., and has one son, John Russell, and five daughters: Jane, wife of Orville B. Carrott; Mary; Margaret, wife of Ensign Bushrod B. Howard, U. S. N.; Elizabeth and Josephine Green. Portrait opposite page 293.

HODGES, George Hartshorn, nineteenth governor of Kansas, was born in Richland county, Wis., Feb. 6, 1866, son of William W. and Lydia A. Hodges. His father, who was a school teacher, removed to Johnson county, Kan., in 1869, and shortly afterward died. The son attended the district schools, and at the age of twenty obtained a position in a lumber yard at Olathe, of which he soon became assistant manager. In 1889 he established a lumber business of his own at Olathe, and subsequently formed a partnership with his brother, Frank Hodges. The firm now operates ten lumber yards and does an annual business of about $400,000. From early life George H. Hodges took an active interest in civic and municipal affairs. He was first a member of the Olathe city council, and in 1904 was elected to the state senate on the Democratic ticket, being the first Democratic senator ever elected from his district. He was re-elected by a greatly increased majority in 1908. During his eight years of service in the senate he was in the forefront of every fight for the enactment of progressive measures, and the soundness and practicability of the many reform laws enacted during that period are largely due to the wisdom of his counsel and his uncompromising attitude in support of progressive principles. He was chairman of the committee that wrote the public utilities bill, and his support made possible its enactment in 1911. He introduced and secured the passage of the reciprocal demurrage bill, coal-weighing bill, express companies' excise tax, and was joint author of the bill simplifying the Australian ballot law, and introduced the first measure that provided for Kansas voters the Massachusetts form of ballot. He was joint author of the anti-pass law; prepared the bill and secured its passage, reducing freight rates on grain and grain products; assisted in passing the bank guaranty, anti-lobby, child labor and railroad employee protection bills, and brought about the primary election law. He introduced the initial measure providing for the state publication of text-books, and their distribution at actual cost; also bills requiring reports of factory accidents to the state inspector; requiring a better bond under the laborers' lien law, and supported the workman's compensation and employers' liability laws. In 1910 he was a candidate for governor of Kansas, and although failing of election reduced the Republican majority to 16,000. Two years later he was elected to the office by an official majority of twenty-nine, overturning a Republican majority of 75,000. The ascendency of the Democratic party in Kansas dates from the William A. Harris convention of 1906. Gov. Hodges was temporary chairman of that convention which nominated Sen. Harris for governor. He appointed the resolutions committee that drafted the first platform, whose dominant plank was the strict enforcement of the prohibition law. From a weak and disorganized minority, the Democracy of Kansas thereafter predominated in the state, and it was the dying request of Sen. Harris that Hodges assume the leadership and carry on the work which he had begun. Once in power the Democrats did not hesitate to carry out the programme, and the legislature of 1913 placed upon the statute books more progressive laws than Kansas ever before had. It removed the judiciary from politics, placed state institutions under single boards, repealed the inheritance tax, and provided additional state revenues by enacting a corporation tax law; enacted the Massachusetts ballot law, white slave and divorce proctor laws, provided the small debtors' court, abolished fees for county officers, ratified the amendment for the direct election of U. S. senators, enlarged appropriations for irrigation and educational purposes, and placed private charitable institutions under state control. The most progressive enactment was the divorcing of the state educational institutions from politics and political boards and placing them under a non-political commission who give their entire time to the management of these most vital institutions. It provided for state publication of state school text-books and their distribution to the students at actual cost. In line with Gov. Hodges' promise of a business administration is his advocacy of a small, one-house legislature

ADOLPHUS W. GREEN
MERCHANT

GEORGE H. HODGES
GOVERNOR

WILLIAM J. KENNY
R. C. BISHOP

FLORENCE MACKUBIN
ARTIST

which shall be non-political, the state to be governed by a commission, similar to the commission rule now used by over 300 cities. He believes that the American system of law making, founded on the English parliament, is antiquated and inefficient, that no reason now exists for it, and that such a system, with its biennial session, where hurried action is taken on important measures and hundreds of meritorious bills are permitted to die on the calendar because of lack of time for discussion, does not make for efficiency. Gov. Hodges is a Knights Templar, Knights of Pythias, a thirty-third degree Mason and a member of I. O. O. F. He was married at Olathe, Kan., March 8, 1899, to Ora May, daughter of Arnold Murray, and has two children: Georgia Ferree and Murray H. Hodges.

KENNY, William John, R. C. bishop, was born at Delhi, N. Y., Oct. 9, 1853, son of John and Ann (McDonough) Kenny. He was educated at St. Bonaventure College, Allegany, N. Y., and ordained to the priesthood at St. Augustine, Fla., Jan. 15, 1879. Subsequently he was stationed at Jacksonville and Palatka, Fla., until his appointment in 1904 as pastor of the Church of the Immaculate Conception, Jacksonville, where he remained until 1902. He was appointed vicar-general of the diocese of St. Augustine in 1889 and continued in that office until the death of Bishop Moore in 1901, when he was named administrator of the diocese. Thoroughly familiar with all the affairs of the diocese of St. Augustine, he was well qualified to fill the vacant bishopric to which he was appointed. The whole of his priestly career was spent in this diocese and he devoted himself unreservedly to its interests. He was untiring in his devotion to his cosmopolitan flock of 40,000, which included 16,000 Cubans, 10,000 Italians, 4,000 Spaniards and a variety of other nationalities. At the time of his death the diocese contained forty-six priests, 152 churches, two colleges and twelve academies with 4,146 pupils, and one asylum with forty-five inmates. He died in Baltimore, Md., Oct. 23, 1913.

MACKUBIN, Florence, artist, was born in Florence, Italy, May 19, 1861, daughter of Charles Nicholas and Ellen Marietta (Fay) Mackubin. She is descended from many distinguished colonial ancestors. Her father, son of George Mackubin, treasurer of Maryland, 1823-43, was born in Annapolis, Md., in 1821, and became a lawyer, banker and a member of the state legislature in St. Paul, Minn. Miss Mackubin was born while her parents were spending a year abroad, and after her father's death, in 1863, her mother returned to Europe, where the children were educated. She first studied drawing in Florence, Italy, and entering the Protestant school of Les Ruches at Fontainebleau, where she made rapid progress under her master, M. Lainé, of Barbizon. In 1889 she began the serious study of art at the Künstlerinen Verein, Munich, with Prof. Herterrich, and going to Paris in 1890 she studied painting in oil with Louis Deschamps, in pastel with Julius Rolshoven, and in 1893 miniature painting with Mlle. Jeanne Devina. Miss Mackubin is distinctively a portrait painter, and it is by her miniatures that she has won the most material recognition. During a period of twelve years she received 360 orders for these "portraits in little," and she has painted many society women in New York city, Boston, St. Louis, Washington and Baltimore, and in England. Her miniatures have appeared in most of the important exhibitions since 1893

in America and abroad, and she was awarded a bronze medal and a diploma of honorable mention at the Tennessee Centennial Exposition in 1897. Among her best portraits (pastels and miniatures) may be mentioned those of Mrs. Thomas F. Bayard, Mary E. Wilkins, Mrs. Charles J. Bonaparte, Mrs. Horace Gray, Miss Louisa Loring, Mrs. Henry Oothout and Mrs. Horace Du Val, and in England the Marchioness of Bath, the Lady Algernon Percy, Lady Drury and many other distinguished women. While in Paris she exhibited at the Salon de Femmes Peintres, at the Royal Academy, London; at the Art Gallery, Manchester, England, and after 1887 she was a constant exhibitor in oils and pastels at the National Academy of Design, the Pennsylvania Academy, New York Water Color Club, etc. Her first large oil painting, "A Florentine Cobbler," was shown at the Union League Club, New York city, in 1887, and was purchased by her uncle, Sigourney W. Fay. "A Portrait Study in Yellow" (1892), for which her sister posed, was one of fifty-eight pastels accepted out of many hundreds sent in to the art department of the Columbian Exposition, at which she also exhibited "The Mandolin Player" (1890) and "Sans Famille" (1891) in oil. In 1901 she was commissioned by the board of public works of Maryland to copy a portrait of Henrietta Maria, consort of Charles I. of England (after whom Maryland was named), to hang in the state house. This copy was made after the famous Van Dyck in Warwick Castle, England. She has also painted portraits of Govs. Lloyd, Winder, Ridgely, Swann and Lowndes to be hung in the executive chamber in the Maryland state house. The first and second Barons Baltimore were painted after the originals belonging to their descendant, Sir Wm. Eden, at Windleston Hall, and were purchased by the Baltimore Club (1908); a portrait of Prof. Basil Gildersleeve for the University of Virginia (1910); a miniature of Cardinal Gibbons exhibited in the Paris Salon (1909) was purchased for the Walters Gallery in 1910; a portrait in oils of Prof. Marshall Elliott for the Johns Hopkins University in 1912, and a portrait of Sir Wm. Van Horne of Montreal in 1913. Miss Mackubin's present summer home and studio is Oriole Cottage, St. Andrews-on-the-Sea, Canada. Miss Mackubin is a member of the Colonial Dames, the Daughters of the American Revolution, the Colonial Lords of Manors, former vice-president of the Baltimore Water Color Club, member of the Baltimore Country Club, and the York Club of New York. Her tastes are literary as well as artistic, and she has written several historical papers which have been read before the clubs to which she belongs and letters on social or political matters for the newspapers in Baltimore and New York. Her oldest sister, Ellen Mackubin, is the author of "The King of the Town" (1898), and many stories published in the "Century Magazine," "Atlantic Monthly," "Youth's Companion," and other periodicals.

STRINGER, Arthur (J. Arbuthnott), author, was born in London, Ont., Can., Feb. 26, 1874, son of Hugh Arbuthnott and Sarah (Delmage) Stringer. His father was an inventor and manufacturer. He was educated at the London (Ont.) Collegiate Institute, the Toronto University, and the University of Oxford, England. He at once entered the field of journalism as a member of the editorial staff of the Montreal "Herald" and afterward joining the staff of the American Press Association in New York, with which he was connected during 1898–1901. He was literary editor of the magazine "Success" in 1903–04. He has devoted considerable time to Shakespearean research and to studies in Shakespeare, and is a frequent contributor to various magazines. He is the author of "Watchers of Twilight" (1897); "Pauline and Other Poems" (1898); "Epigrams" (1899); "A Study in King Lear" (1901); "The Loom of Destiny" (1901); "The Silver Poppy" (1902); "Lonely O'Malley" (1903); "Hephæstus and Other Poems" (1905); "The Wire Tappers" (1906); "Phantom Wires" (1907); "The Occasional Offender" (1907); "The Woman in the Rain" (1907); "The Gun-Runner" (1910); "Irish Poems" (1912); "The Shadow" (1913); "Open Water" (1914); "The Hand of Peril" (1915), and "The Prairie Wife" (1915), his strongest work in fiction. "The Loom of Destiny," which first appeared serially in "Ainslee's Magazine," is a book of stories about children, chiefly the ragged urchins of the New York slums, and is unique in its sympathetic treatment of this particular type of childhood. In its literary skill, "The Wire Tappers" seems to foreshadow that the Balzac of the future will concern himself mainly with the miracles of science, his hero being some thaumaturgist of the laboratory, some modern Prometheus like Berthelot, Marconi or Edison. "Phantom Wires," a continuation of "The Wire Tappers," deals with electricity and telepathy, and belongs to that class of books in which things happen, and happen promptly. Mr. Stringer, outside his literary work, is the owner of a fruit farm on the Canadian shores of Lake Erie, and also has a ranch in Alberta, of which he is justly proud. This however, has not prevented him from being an extensive traveler in Europe, his favorite pursuits embracing ranching, fruit-growing, and camping and canoeing in Canada.

HARTNESS, James, mechanical engineer, inventor and manufacturer, was born at Schenectady, N. Y., Sept. 3, 1861, son of John Williams and Ursilla (Jackson) Hartness, grandson of James and Anne E. (Farnham) Hartness, and great grandson of John Hartness, who came from County Monahan, Ireland, in the eighteenth century and settled at Albany, N. Y. His father was a machine shop foreman. He was educated in the public schools, and began working in a machine shop at the age of sixteen years. Since 1889 he has been successively superintendent, manager and president of the Jones & Lamson Machine Co., of Springfield, Vt., manufacturers of the Hartness flat turret lathe, automatic screw cutting dies and the Fay automatic lathe. He is also a director in the Jones & Lamson Power Co., Fellows Gear Shaper Co., and Bryant Chucking Grinder Co., all of Springfield, Vt., and is consulting engineer of the Fitchburg Machine Co., Fitchburg, Mass. Inventor and patentee of more than eighty American patents, his inventions include the turret equatorial telescope, the Loswing lathe, and the flat turret lathe. He is also a designer and builder of machinery. He is the author of "Machine Building for Profit," "Flat Turret Lathe Manual," and "Human Factor in Works Management." The University of Vermont conferred on him the honorary degree of M.E. in 1910, and Yale that of M.A. in 1914. He was president (1914) of the American Society of Mechanical Engineers; is fellow of the American Association for the Advancement of Science; and member of the Institution of Mechanical Engineers (British); Royal Society for the Encouragement of Arts, London;

Astronomical Society of America; Verein Deutscher Ingenieure; and Boston Chamber of Commerce. He is vice-president of the Western New England Chamber of Commerce, and holds membership in the following clubs: Engineers'. Machinery and Aero, of New York City; New Bedford Yacht Club, New Bedford, Mass., and the Royal Society Club, London. He is a member of the board of education of the state of Vermont. To him the community at large is indebted for improvements of fundamental importance in the production of accurate machinery of every kind, and his numerous inventions have gained for him the highest admiration among mechanical engineers of all countries. He was married May 13, 1885, to Leña Sandford, daughter of Frederick L. Pond, a druggist of Winsted, Conn. They have two children: Anna Jackson, wife of William H. Beardslee, a physician at Springfield, Mass., and Helen Edith, wife of Ralph E. Flanders, manager of Jones & Lamson Machine Co., Springfield, Vt.

O'CONNELL, William Henry, cardinal, was born at Lowell, Mass., Dec. 8, 1859. He received his early education in the local schools and at St. Charles College, Ellicott City, Md. Later he attended the Jesuit College at Boston, Mass., where he was graduated A.B. in 1881. At school he was distinguished as a diligent student, and while an undergraduate at Boston received the award of a scholarship at the North American College at Rome, Italy. This institution, founded and maintained by bishops of the United States and working in intimate touch with the fountain head of the church of Rome, trains ecclesiastics of the highest type of scholarship and devotion. Here O'Connell studied theology during 1881–84 and was ordained priest by Cardinal Parocci, the vicar of Rome, June 8, 1884. He remained at the college as prefect until 1886. Returning to the United States, Father O'Connell was occupied with parish work at Medford and at Boston, Mass., for nine years. In 1895 he was appointed rector or president of the North American College at Rome, the first important step in his career of continued advancement, for the prelate selected for this position is always chosen because of superior qualities of both mind and heart. Under his incumbency, which continued for five years, the seminary prospered exceedingly, enlarging its buildings and adding to its enrollment. During this period Father O'Connell became very well known to the ecclesiastical authorities at Rome and especially to Pope Leo XIII. On June 9, 1897, he was made a domestic prelate. In 1901 he was made bishop of Portland, Me. He was appointed Apr. 22, and consecrated in the Church of St. John Lateran on May 19. On his arrival in the United States he was installed in the cathedral at Portland, July 4, 1901. His administration of his diocese proved that the choice had been an excellent one, fully justifying the high estimate of him held by his friends at Rome. In January, 1905, he was honored with the title of assistant at the pontifical throne. The most notable event in his career, while bishop of Portland, was his mission as special apostolic delegate to Japan, where he was sent in 1905 by Pope Pius X. to arrange for the appointment of a vicar apostolic to that country and to secure better opportunities there for the spread of Roman Catholicism. He obtained valuable concessions that made it possible for the Jesuit Fathers to start a university in Tokio and for the Ladies of the Sacred Heart there to open a school for girls. Upon his return to Rome from this embassy he was warmly commended for the success of his efforts by the pope, who, on Jan. 26, 1906, named him titular archbishop of Tomi, and coadjutor at Boston, Mass., with rights of succession, to Archbishop Williams, his title being archbishop of Constance. Returning to America he was canonically installed in Holy Cross Cathedral, Boston, in March, 1906. Upon the death of Archbishop Williams he succeeded to the metropolitan see of Boston, Aug. 3, 1907. Here he was given ample scope for his powers as an administrator and as an originator of many educational and charitable enterprises. The city of Boston, with its environs, had become a great Roman Catholic center and in his archdiocese were nearly 1,000,000 people. During the four years after his elevation to the miter he organized over forty new parishes in Boston alone, fostering parish life in every aspect. Deeply interested, as ever, in education, especially in that of the clergy, he became the patron of every mode of intellectual development. Under his government there was a wonderful unification of interests in the diocese, and this drawing together of all forces became the main purpose of his work. A typical example of thoroughly practical methods was illustrated in his organization of the Guild of St. Luke of Boston and the Association of Roman Catholic Physicians. This represents a power for good in the community and fulfills a function in professional life the value of which can scarcely be estimated. Of his addresses the first notable one was delivered in Boston while he was still bishop of Portland, his theme being a comparison between the Latin and Teutonic races. A vigorous pastoral against modernism, issued when he became archbishop, and the address he delivered in 1908 on the one hundredth anniversary of the founding of his see are also particularly noteworthy compositions. On Nov. 27, 1911, Archbishop O'Connell was elevated to the cardinalate. On that occasion eighteen new cardinals received the red biretta, including two other prelates from America, Monsignor Falconio, of Washington, and Archbishop Farley, of New York. The ceremony was epoch-marking, for it represented the official entrance of America into the comity of the old Catholic powers. Cardinal O'Connell belongs to that type of zealous ecclesiastic whom Pius X. delighted to honor, and his investiture was considered a crushing defeat for modernism in the United States. At the same time his elevation was received with generous satisfaction because it was a recognition of the numbers and the fidelity of the Roman Catholic church in New England. In no country has that church prospered as in the United States, and while the influence of his eminence of Boston would seem to have been local, yet it has always been effective, wholesome and protective of the church's interests and its elevation among men. Curial by taining, he is curial in ruling, a teacher of sound doctrine in the church. In his personal career Cardinal O'Connell has demonstrated his tremendous energy and untiring capacity for work, combined with spiritual power, intellectual capacity and abundance of human sympathies. He is a linguist and musician, a forcible writer and an eloquent orator. His administrative ability, as he has shown, is of a high order, and he is well fitted to be the champion of the church militant and a prince of that church. Among other honors bestowed upon him, he received, in 1905, from the Mikado, the grand cordon of the sacred treasure of Japan in recognition of his service as apostolic delegate.

LONGYEAR, John Munro, capitalist, was born at Lansing, Mich., Apr. 15, 1850, son of John Wesley and Harriet (Munro) Longyear. His first known American ancestor was Jacob Langjahr who came to this country from Germany and after living for a time in New York city, settled at Shandaken, Ulster co., about 1750. He married Maria Cox and the line of descent is traced through their son, John, who translated the name Longyear, and married Annatje Winne; and their son, Peter, who married Jerusha Stevens, and was the grandfather of John M. Longyear. His father (1820–75) was a lawyer, congressman and later judge of the United States district court for eastern Michigan. The son was educated in the preparatory departments of Olivet (Mich.) College, the Georgetown (D. C.) College and the Cazenovia (N. Y.) Seminary. He was forced by ill health to abandon a college course. During 1871–78 he was employed as lumber inspector, and then became land agent for the Lake Superior Ship Canal Railway and Iron Co. in 1878, later known as the Keweenaw Land Association, Ltd. He published the first private maps of the Menominee and Gogebic iron ranges and was actively connected with the development of those districts. His timber and mineral interests multiplied rapidly and among others he acquired a large holding in the Mesaba iron range (Minn.). He took an important part in the negotiations of the so-called "Hill lease" whereby in 1906 enormous iron ore bodies controlled by the Great Northern Railroad, the Northern Pacific Railroad and Mr. Longyear and associates were leased to the United States Steel Corporation. This deal is said to have involved the largest amount of any single commercial transaction in history. During an excursion to Spitzbergen (No Man's Land) in 1901 Mr. Longyear learned of coal deposits there and after fully investigating them two years later, he organized the Arctic Coal Co. to develop and operate these coal deposits. He has succeeded in placing this proposition on a successful commercial basis, and as there are several seams and thousands of miles of coal formation he has added another and entirely new field to be developed by American enterprise. The quality of the coal corresponds most nearly to the American "Pocahontas," and the market is largely found in Norway. Mr. Longyear formerly resided in Marquette, Mich., of which he was mayor for two successive terms (1890–91). He had built there one of the largest and most beautiful stone residences in the middle Northwest and when he decided to remove to the East, with his customary disregard of precedent, he had the building removed, stone by stone, and transported to Brookline, Mass., where it was re-erected on the summit of Fisher hill in 1906. Mr. Longyear also maintains an estate of several thousand acres near Marquette, Mich., where he conducts experimental work in forestry and game raising, besides breeding a fine strain of Holstein cattle. He is president of the Marquette National Bank and of the Arctic Coal Co. (an American corporation) and a director of the Quincy Mining Co. and the International Trust Co. of Boston; president of the Longyear Mesaba Land and Iron Co., chairman of the board of directors of the Gogebic and Ontonagon Land Co.; the Michigan Iron and Land Co.; the Porcupine Land Association, Ltd.; and the Albany Pool, Ltd. Agent of the Keweenaw Land Association, Ltd.; Gogebic Land Co.; Kimberly Iron Co. of Michigan; Newport Land Co., and a joint owner in the Ayer and Longyear, Davenport and Longyear and the Sparrow and Longyear properties, these companies controlling in all over

1,000,000 acres of agricultural, mineral and timber land. He has taken an active part in public
affairs and was one of the leading spirits in the
organization of the Michigan Taxpayers Association, has been a member of the board of control
of the Michigan College of Mines since 1892 and
is also a member of the Lake Superior Mining Institute. He is a member of the United States
Geographical Society, the American Historical Association, American Civic Alliance, American Forestry Association and the Society for the Promotion of Engineering Education. In politics he is
a Republican and during its existence was a member of the Michigan Republican Club and is now
a member of the Republican Club of Massachusetts. He has been president since its organization
of the Huron Mountain Club, is a member of the
Marquette and Detroit clubs (Mich.), the Twentieth Century Club of Boston and the Brookline
Country Club. He was married at Battle Creek,
Mich., Jan. 4, 1879, to Mary Hawley, daughter of
Samuel Peck Beecher, and has five children, Abby
Beecher, wife of Alton True Roberts, Helen Mc-
Graw, Judith Folger, John Munro, Jr., and Robert
Dudley Longyear.

GLASS, Joseph Sarsfield, second Roman Catholic bishop of Salt Lake, Utah, was born in Bushnell, Ill., Mar. 13, 1874, son of James and Mary
Edith (Kelly) Glass. After finishing his collegiate course at St. Mary's, Perryville, Mo., he
became a Lazarist, entering the novitiate of the
Congregation of the Mission for his theological
studies. He was ordained priest at the Los
Angeles, Cal., church of his community, Aug. 15,
1897, and then went to Rome for higher studies,
taking the degree of D.D. at the Minerva University in 1899. On returning to the United States
in the same year he was made professor of theology at St. Mary's Seminary, Perryville, Mo., and
in June, 1901, he became president of St. Vincent's
College and pastor of its church at Los Angeles,
Cal. Here he remained until 1915. The death
of Bishop Scanlon, May 10, 1915, left a vacancy
in the diocese of Salt Lake, which Dr. Glass was
named by the Pope to fill, and he was consecrated
Aug. 24, 1915. The Salt Lake diocese includes the
whole State of Utah and eight counties of Nevada,
an area of 82,190 square miles in the first and
71,578 in the second. It has a Catholic population of 14,000; twenty-seven priests; and seventy-
two churches.

PHYFE, William Henry Pinkney, author,
was born in New York city, June 13, 1855, son of
James Duncan and Julia Matilda (Pinkney)
Phyfe, and grandson of Duncan Phyfe, who came
over from Scotland with his parents in 1783 and
settled in Albany, N. Y.; he was a cabinet maker,
and the originator of the celebrated Duncan Phyfe
furniture. He was educated at the Charlier's
School in New York and Columbia University, class
of 1879, but did not graduate, owing to weak
eyes. He continued his studies, however, with
private tutors, going far beyond the college course.
He never engaged in business pursuits, save for
the care of his property, and spent much time in
travel at home and abroad. He was author of
"How Should I Pronounce?" (1885); "The
School Pronouncer" (1888); "7,000 Words Often
Mispronounced" (1892); "5,000 Words Often
Misspelled" (1901); "5,000 Facts and Fancies"
(1902); "10,000 Words Often Mispronounced"
(1903); "The Test Pronouncer" (1904); "Napoleon, the Return from St. Helena" (1907), and of
various magazine articles published in educational
journals, works of fiction, etc. He was a member

of the American Spelling Reform Association,
American Philological Association, and of the
Century Club, New York. Fond of home and fam-
ily, he was most domestic in his tastes, and a
great student. He was married in New York city,
Feb. 17, 1909, to Edith T., daughter of Jared
Weed Bell, of New York city; she survives him,
with two children: Henry Pinkney, Jr., and
Churchill Bell Phyfe. He died in New York city,
Mar. 7, 1915.

SHELDON, Theodore, lawyer, was born in
Plainfield, N. J., June 24, 1853, son of George and
Martha (Lyman) Sheldon. His forefathers for
six generations lived in Northampton, Mass., on
the land originally purchased from the Indians in
1654, and through him the property has passed to
his son. Mr. Sheldon was graduated at Princeton
College in 1875, and two years later at the Columbia Law School. He joined his brother, Henry I.
Sheldon, who was practicing law in Chicago, and
under the firm name of Sheldon & Sheldon he remained associated in practice with his brother
until his death. For twenty-five years he was general counsel of the Scottish-American Mortgage
Co. of Chicago, and for ten years was general
solicitor of the St. Louis and Omaha railroad. He
was one of the most able property lawyers in
this country. His work as a lawyer, however,
was overshadowed by his achievement in introducing and establishing in the United States the Torrens system of land registration. This system was
devised in its present general form by Robert R.
Torrens, and first promulgated in the form of law
in South Australia in 1857. From there it spread
throughout Australasia, and was adopted by England in 1862, Ireland in 1865 and British Columbia
in 1871. While in England in 1883 Mr. Sheldon
made a study of the various systems of land transfer in vogue in Great Britain and her colonies,
and resolved to introduce a similar system here.
For eight years he worked zealously with tongue
and pen, by argument and exhortation, and finally,
in 1891, Gov. Fifer appointed a commission, of
which Mr. Sheldon was a member, to investigate
the subject. A bill to adopt the Torrens system
failed narrowly in the Illinois legislature of 1893,
and the reform was established by the successive
acts of 1895 and 1897. The constitutionality of
the act of 1897 was upheld by the supreme court in
the case of the People vs. Simon. Two years later
the system was put into operation in Cook county,
and a department was established with Theodore
Sheldon at its head. Briefly stated, the system is
as follows: The unit of registration is the county,
and generally the registrar of deeds or similar
officer is the recorder. The operation of the system is confined to estates in fee simple absolute.
There is a judicial proceeding which is heard in
the local court having equity jurisdiction. The
"suit" is analogous to one to quiet title. The
facts are prepared for the court (based upon the
petition or other pleadings) by officials generally
known as examiners of title, who, in some states,
are required to be lawyers. The complaint or
petition must set forth the names and addresses
of all persons interested, jurisdiction over whom
is obtained by service of summons, either personally or by publication, and the allegations of the
complaint may be traversed by any defendant. In
addition to the usual forms of service, the summons must be posted upon the property. If there
be a contest, a hearing is had in the usual form
and in due course a decree is entered by the court
directing (or denying) registration of the title
subject to whatever incumbrance may have been

THEODORE SHELDON

BENJAMIN F. KEITH
THEATRE PROPRIETOR

JAMES H. HAWLEY
GOVERNOR

WILLIAM T. SABINE
BISHOP

JOHN CHAMBERS
CLERGYMAN

found existent, and a certificate and duplicate is thereupon issued by the registrar. The decree, after a varying period, becomes absolute and conclusive. The title so registered is indefeasible, except by private parties for fraud, for varying periods and under varying conditions; and is indefeasible as to boundaries except in certain states and where adjacent property owners are involved. It is defeasible as to unrecorded leases not required by law to be recorded, and in actions by the state or Federal government, as for eminent domain, taxes, etc. The system, with local modifications of the foregoing, has been adopted by Ohio, Massachusetts, New York, California, Minnesota, Oregon, Colorado, Washington, Hawaii and the Philippine islands, while in other states preliminary legislative or other action has been taken toward the same end. "By his friends and associates," says a writer in the "Memorials of the Chicago Bar Association," "Theodore Sheldon is remembered as a sound thinker, a real property lawyer of the first class, a generous adversary, and a man of great charity in his judgments of his fellow-men. He will be most remembered, however, by his long years of work as a pioneer and champion to introduce and establish the Torrens system of land registration." He was a member of the University, Chicago Golf and Chicago Athletic clubs, and was the author of "The Torrens System." He was married July 8th, 1881, to Mary, daughter of Henry Strong, of Lake Geneva, Wis., and had three children: Theodore, Edward (the playwright), and Mary Sheldon. He died in Chicago, Ill., May 25, 1905.

KEITH, Benjamin Franklin, theater proprietor, was born at Hillsboro Bridge, N. H., Jan. 26, 1846, son of Samuel C. and Rhoda S. (Gerould) Keith, of Scotch descent. He began his struggle with the world at the early age of seven on a western Massachusetts farm, where he remained until he was eighteen, meanwhile acquiring his education in the district school and the village academy. When he was seventeen years old he attended a country circus and, coming to it fresh from the secluded farm, was greatly impressed thereby. At length the time came when his farm life ended, and he found himself insensibly drawn toward the entertainment business. He was first connected with Bunnell's Museum in New York, next with Barnum, and later with Doris and Forepaugh. Meanwhile, he added to his experience by taking small shows on the road, on three consecutive occasions returning home with his finances completely exhausted. His real career as a showman began in 1883, when in company with Col. William Austin he opened a popular-price show in a hall in Boston. Mr. Keith said: "My only attraction was Baby Alice, a midget that at the age of three months weighed but one and one-half pounds, but I installed a small stage in the rear of our room and secured several acts from the variety theaters, with the understanding that all vulgar or suggestive language was to be cut out of every act." Soon an upstairs room was added, and from time to time, as the business increased, additional space was secured, until finally he could seat 400 persons in the lower auditorium, while the room above was used for the exhibition of curiosities. It is worthy of note that during this early period, and in the limited space then available, he succeeded in introducing to delighted audiences many of the foremost vaudeville artists of the day. Mrs. Tom Thumb held her daily levees in these contracted quarters for a series of weeks, and it was in this hall that Mr.

Fred Kyle, famous for his unique dog, cat, baby and bird shows in Horticultural Hall, duplicated his successes while connected with Mr. Keith for the period of about one year, adding to them a beauty show, which was the most successful of all. In May, 1884, Mr. Keith was joined by George H. Batcheller of Providence, R. I., having previously purchased the interest of a Mr. Gardner, with whom he had been associated for about thirteen months. He now realized that some radical departure from existing methods must be made, if any marked financial success was to be achieved. He believed that if a performance was begun at a stated hour and was continued without intermission through the day and evening, there would be no waiting by patrons, but each person would be sure of finding something interesting going on upon the stage. His idea resulted in the continuous performance entertainment, which was inaugurated on July 6, 1883, and marked a new era in the amusement world. The plan proved an immediate success, and his theater became so popular that before long he was obliged to secure the Bijou Theater adjoining. Mr. Batcheller withdrew, and thereafter Mr. Keith was the sole proprietor of the "Gaiety and Bijou," as the combined house was called. With the courage and enterprise that were characteristic of the man, he began to establish similar entertainments in other cities. In Providence he opened the Gaiety Museum in 1887, in Philadelphia the Bijou Theater in 1899, and in New York the Union Square Theatre in 1893. At the present time Keith's Theaters are to be found in all of the principal cities throughout the East and West. In 1906 the United Booking Offices was incorporated, of which Mr. Keith was president, to control and manage his numerous theaters. It was probably the greatest consolidation of money and power in the entertainment world, and ranks with the most important of America's industrial combinations. Its weekly payroll exceeds $500,000. The star players who have appeared in the Keith theaters include Sarah Bernhardt, Mrs. Langtry, Neil Burgess, Lillian Russell, Lew Dockstader, Nat Goodwin, Yvette Guilbert, Julian Eltinge, Olga Nethersole, Weber and Fields, Ethel Barrymore, Eddie Foy, David Bispham, Marie Tempest, Bessie Abbott, Robert Mantell, David Warfield, Joseph Jefferson 2d, Isadora Duncan, Eva Tanguay and Cecilia Loftus Carmencita. Mr. Keith was twice married; first, in 1873, to Mary Catherine, daughter of Thomas Branley, of Providence, R. I. She died in 1910, leaving one son, Andrew Paul Keith, who succeeded as head of his father's theatrical business; and he was married again Oct. 29, 1913, to Ethel Bird, daughter of Plympton B. Chase, of Akron, O., and later, Washington, D. C. Mr. Keith traveled extensively both abroad and in his native country, and was well versed in national affairs throughout the world. He was a patron of art and music, and contributed liberally to the support of such institutions in his home city designed to encourage the education of the masses in art and music. He died at Palm Beach, Fla., Mar. 26, 1914.

HAWLEY, James Henry, tenth governor of Idaho, was born in Dubuque, Ia., Jan. 17, 1847, son of Thomas and Annie (Carr) Hawley, and grandson of William Hawley, who came to this country from England in 1811 and settled in Brooklyn, N. Y. After a public school education James H. Hawley went to California in 1861. Stirred by the gold excitement prevalent at that time, in April, 1862, he journeyed into what is now northern Idaho, and engaged in mining. In

1864 he began a course of study at the City College, San Francisco, at the same time studying law in the office of Sharpstein & Hastings. While engaged in mining operations in Idaho he was elected a member of the lower house of the legislature of Idaho Territory in 1870, and in February of the following year was admitted to the bar of the supreme court of the state. In 1874-75 he was a member of the upper house of the Idaho legislature, and during 1879–83 was district-attorney of the second district of Idaho. For the past thirty-five years he has been identified with most of the important criminal cases of the state. In the troubles in the Cœur d'Alenes in 1899-1901, Mr. Hawley and W. E. Borah, now a U. S. senator, were specially employed as attorneys for the state. He had entire charge of the case growing out of the Steunenberg murder in 1896, being assisted in the trials of Haywood and Pettibone by Mr. Borah (q.v.). In addition to having participated in most of the important criminal cases of Idaho, he has been extensively engaged in civil practice, especially in cases affecting the irrigation, mining and power interests of the state. In 1904 he was elected mayor of Boise City. He introduced many public improvements, built a thorough sewer system, established an effective fire department, graded and paved many of the streets, and established an extensive parking, paving and sidewalk system. In 1910 he ran for governor of Idaho upon the Democratic ticket, and although the state was Republican by a majority of many thousands, he was elected over Hon. James H. Brady. He was the first Democrat ever elected to a state office upon a straight Democratic ticket in Idaho. He ran again for governor in 1912, but was defeated by a small majority. Gov. Hawley was prominently mentioned for secretary of the interior in Pres. Wilson's cabinet, and was very strongly urged for that position by most of the people of Idaho and many others in the Northwest. On leaving the office of governor he resumed the practice of law at Boise as head of the firm of Hawley, Puckett & Hawley. He was married July 4, 1875, to Mary E., daughter of William Bullock, of Quartzburg, Ida. Their children are: Edgar T., Jesse B., Emma, wife of Reilley Atkinson, of Boise; Elizabeth, wife of E. W. Tucker, of Boise; James H. and Harry R. Hawley.

SABINE, William Tufnell, bishop of the Reformed Episcopal Church, was born in New York city, Oct. 16, 1838, son of Gustavus A. and Julia Hannah (Tufnell) Sabine. His father, a native of Dorset, England, was a ship's surgeon who settled in New York in 1837 and soon took rank as one of its most eminent physicians. The son attended Thayer School, was graduated at Columbia College in 1859 and at the General Theological Seminary in 1862. In that year he received the degree of M.A. from Columbia and New York University gave him his D.D. degree in 1890. He was ordained deacon in the Church of the Transfiguration, New York, in 1862, and priest in the Church of the Ascension, New York, in 1863. In 1862 he was appointed assistant to the Rev. Stephen H. Tyng. Upon being ordained presbyter in 1863 he was called to the Church of the Covenant, Philadelphia, and in 1865 he was called to the Church of the Atonement, New York, where he labored with more than unusual success for nine years. He resigned his ministry in the Protestant Episcopal Church in 1874 to identify himself with the then new movement of the Reformed Episcopal Church. A few months later, upon the death of Bishop Cummins, he was called

to take the latter's place at the First Reformed Episcopal Church, and remained there until ill-health compelled him to retire in 1907. The congregation thereupon unanimously elected him rector emeritus. Meanwhile, in 1902, Dr. Sabine was consecrated bishop of the New York and Philadelphia synods of the Reformed Episcopal Church. Then began an even wider ministry, and the bishop's visits to the several parishes were eagerly anticipated, and never failed to be a source of blessing. Several times he tried to resign that office, but the synod would never accept his resignation, being determined that he should retain the honor until the end, and he therefore held the office until his death. Bishop Sabine was enthusiastically active in many lines of endeavor related to church and reform work. He was prominently connected with the National Temperance Society, was president of the trustees of the Theological Seminary of the Reformed Episcopal Church, vice-president of the Evangelical Alliance, manager of the American Tract Society and president of the incorporated company publishing the "Episcopal Recorder", the organ in America of his church. His character was as strong as it was tender, and as loved as it was both. Its key-note was loyalty—loyalty to what he believed to be the truth, and loyalty to his friends. All other claims seemed as nothing to this. He was a warrior of no small courage in both defense and attack, and yet through it all there broke a kindly humor which prevented his most pungent utterances from wounding. As a preacher he was clear, concise, fearless and passionate in his proclamation of the Gospel. His voice was one of the most thrilling, flexible, melodious that ever vibrated through an assembly, and his discourse was crisp, emphatic and powerful. In his sermons he was ready and forcible, and when he dealt in criticism the edge of his sword was mercilessly whetted against pretension and vanity. The inflection of his voice, the flash of his eye, the poise of his head, the action of his hand, all lent their special emphasis to his words. As a bishop he was interested in and helpful to all the churches committed to his care. He assisted his friends in every way within his power, and he loved those to whom he gave his confidence with a love as rare as it was beautiful. He left to his church and to his family a great heritage, and the influence of his godly life will be an inspiration to many. He was married in New York city, Oct. 6, 1868, to Maria Theresa, daughter of Philip Schieffelin, of New York city, and niece of Samuel B. Schieffelin. She died, Feb. 19, 1892, survived by nine children: Edith Schieffelin, wife of O. Faulkland Lewis, secretary of the New York Prison Association; Elizabeth Haines, William Tufnell, Philip Schieffelin, Alice Winifred, Gustavus Arthur, Julia Hannah Tufnell, Samuel Schieffelin and Mary Theresa Sabine. He died in New York city, Aug. 11, 1913. Portrait opposite page 297.

CHAMBERS, John, clergyman, was born at Stewartstown, County Tyrone, Ireland, Sept. 19, 1797, son of William and Mary (Smythe) Chambers. His father, who was one of the United Irishmen and a follower of the famous Wolf Tone, was imprisoned by the British authorities, but managed to escape to America shortly before the rebellion of 1798. He settled in Jefferson county, O., and the son took his share in the hard pioneer work of clearing the forest and tilling the virgin land. He learned to read and write at home, and at the age of fifteen was sent to Baltimore, Md., to be educated. He joined the Presbyterian Church and studied for the ministry in the classical academy of the Rev. James Gray. He was licensed to preach in 1824 and the following year was called to the pastorate of the Margaret Duncan (Associate Reformed) Church of Philadelphia, Pa. At the regular meeting of the First Presbytery of Philadelphia in the autumn of the same year his call was rejected because he refused to subscribe to the confession of faith, and the congregation of the Margaret Duncan Church consequently declared themselves independent and kept Chambers as their minister. Failing to win the recognition of the conservative presbyteries he turned to the Congregational Church and, in December, 1825, was ordained at a special meeting of the Association of Congregational Ministers of the western district of New Haven county. He did not, however, become a Congregationalist, and he continued to govern his church according to Presbyterian form, though he always retained his belief in Congregational ordination. In 1840 he organized the Youth's Temperance Society in connection with his church, which proved an excellent breeding-ground of temperance champions and prohibition recruits. He was indefatigable in his condemnation of the liquor evil and he was generally known as the "war horse" of the temperance cause. He was equally energetic in the enforcement of rigid Sunday-keeping and in the promotion of evangelical work, and he trained and inspired many young men who successfully carried out his teachings, young men who, like John Wanamaker, attained more than local repute and influence. He had a special power of appealing to young men and developing the best that was in them, and it is more in what he inspired others to do than in what he did himself that his long pastorate was so productive. He was a magnetic, forceful, sincere and persuasive preacher, whose personality might be described, as his teaching has been, as "the quiescence of turbulence." Though extreme to the verge of intolerance on ethical questions he was marvelously tolerant in religious matters. He had decided views on theology and dogma, and he expressed them with the dynamic vigor that was characteristic of him; but he freely allowed to other men the right to hold opposite views and express them as freely. He was tolerant enough finally to set aside his own pride and convictions in favor of the future interests of his church, and to re-enter the Presbyterian Church of Philadelphia. This he did in 1874, and in that year the First Independent Church of Philadelphia ceased to exist and became the Chambers Presbyterian Church. Over six feet high, in superb health and vigor, always invitingly clean in person, he reinforced every day the teaching of good fathers and mothers who strove to lead their sons to noble manhood. He was three times married: (1) Mar. 14, 1826, to Helen, daughter of Francis Dean McHenry, of Baltimore, Md., by whom he had two children, John Mason Duncan and Helen Frances, wife of James Hackett; (2) Sept. 30, 1834, to Martha, daughter of Alexander Henry and widow of Silas L. Weir, both of Philadelphia; (3) to Matilda, daughter of Peter Ellmaker, of Philadelphia, and widow of Dr. Stewart. He died in Philadelphia, Sept. 22, 1875. Portrait opp, p. 297.

PEARSON, Raymond A., educator, was born at Evansville, Ind., Apr. 9, 1873, son of Leonard and Lucy (Jones) Pearson. His father was a native of Byfield, Mass., where his family was one of the earliest settlers from England. His early life was spent in Missouri, Iowa and New York state, and he received his preliminary education in the public schools and high school of Ithaca, N. Y. He was graduated at Cornell University in 1894 with the degree of B.S. in agriculture. He conducted a milk business in Philadelphia for one year and then was appointed assistant chief of the dairy division of the U. S. department of agriculture. During 1902-03 he was general manager of the Walker-Gordon Laboratory Company, New York and Philadelphia. In 1904 he became professor of dairy industry and head of department at Cornell University, remaining in that capacity for years. During 1908-12 he was commissioner of agriculture for the state of New York. In 1912 he was appointed president of the Iowa State College of Agriculture and Mechanic Arts, Ames, Ia. In 1899 he received the degree of M.S.A. from Cornell University, and in 1910 was awarded the degree of LL.D. by Alfred University. He received a gold medal as collaborator from the Paris Exposition. He is the author of numerous papers, bulletins and reports published by the state and national governments and in agricultural and college journals. He is a member of the Sigma Xi and the Phi Kappa Phi fraternities. He is a member of the Society for the Promotion of Engineering Education; the American Academy of Political and Social Science, and fellow of the American Association for the Advancement of Science. He is unmarried.

WALLACE, Charles William, philologist, was born at Hopkins, Mo., Feb. 6, 1865, son of Judge Thomas Dickey and Olive (McEwen) Wallace of Scotch extraction. He is descended from Thomas Wallace and his wife Jean, who emigrated from Coleraine, in county Antrim, Ireland, and settled in Londonderry, N. H., in 1726, and later in Bedford, N. H.; the line being traced through Thomas' son William who married Ann Scobey; and their son Adam and his wife Martha McClure who were the grandparents of the subject of this sketch. Prof. Wallace was graduated with first honors at the Western Normal College, Shenandoah, Ia., in 1885, and at the University of Nebraska in 1898. He attended the University of Nebraska graduate school during 1900-02, the University of Chicago during the summers of 1902-03-04; and German universities during 1904-06, receiving the degree of Ph.D., magna cum laude, at the University of Freiberg in 1906. During 1886-94 he was professor of Latin and English at the Western Normal College, and at the Fremont (Neb.) Normal School in 1894-1905. He was assistant in Latin at the University of Nebraska in 1896-97, and in the latter year founded the preparatory school to the University of Nebraska (now Lincoln Academy), of which he was principal until 1900. He was assistant instructor in English literature and languages in the University of Nebraska in 1901-03; instructor, 1903-04; adjunct professor, 1904-05; assistant professor, 1905-07; associate professor, 1907-10; and professor of English dramatic literature since 1910. Prof. Wallace was extensively engaged in special research work on Shakespeare and the Tudor-Stuart drama in European archives during the summers of 1904-09, and continuously since then, 1909-16, during extended leave of absence, on behalf of the University of Nebraska. With his wife as his principal assistant, he examined over five million original records, discovered many documents on Shakespeare, his associates, predecessors and successors, and published several that created wide interest in Europe and America. The complete collection of records, the most extensive ever made on Shakespeare and the early English drama, is soon to be published. His

discoveries have given a world-wide impetus to a
fresh study of Shakespeare and the drama on the
historical side, and brought honor to American
scholarship. His published works include: "Lyrics
for Leisure Moments" (1892); "The Children of
the Chapel at Blackfriars, 1597–1603" (1908);
"Three London Theatres of Shakespeare's Time"
(1909); "Shakespeare and His London Associates"
(1910); "The Evolution of the English Drama
Up to Shakespeare" (1912); "The First London
Theatre" (1913), and the following papers: "New
Shakespeare Documents," (University of Nebraska
Studies, 1905); "Shakespeare in London" (London "Times," Oct. 2 and 4, 1909); "Shakespeare
as a Man Among Men" ("Harper's Magazine,"
1910); "On Shakespeare, the Globe and Blackfriars" ("Century Magazine," 1910); "Ben Johnson and the Swan Theatre" ("Englische Studien,"
1911), and "New Light on Shakespeare" (London
"Times," Apr. 30 and May 2, 1914). He is a
founder and fellow of the London Society of
Genealogists, an honorary life member of the New
York Shakespeare Society, and member of the
Phi Beta Kappa. He was married June 14, 1893,
to Hulda A., daughter of Nils B. Berggren of
Wahoo, Neb. Mrs. Wallace has been an invaluable assistant in the department of English
literature at the University of Nebraska, and a
devoted helper of her husband in Shakespearean
research.

KIMBARK, Seneca D., merchant and manufacturer, was born at Venice, Cayuga co., N. Y.,
Mar. 4, 1832, son of Adam C. and Sarah (Masten)
Kimbark, both natives of Ulster county, New
York, and of English extraction. His family removed to Livingston county, New York, and he
was educated in the district schools and at the
academies of Genesee and Canandaigua. The expense of his more advanced courses he met by
teaching in the country schools. Removing to
Chicago in 1852, he became connected with the
firm of E. G. Hall & Co. He was soon made
junior partner, and in 1860, the name was changed
to Hall, Kimbark & Co. In 1873 his brothers,
George M. and Daniel A. Kimbark, joined the
firm, and the style was changed to Kimbark Bros.
& Co. The Kimbark store was lost in the fire of
1871, but a temporary building, 400 by 100 feet,
was immediately constructed on the lake front,
the building permit for which was the first issued
after the disaster. In 1876 Seneca D. Kimbark
became sole owner of the business, which, under
his management, became the largest iron and steel
concern in the West. He owed his success primarily to keen business acumen, to a thorough
grasp of details and to a strongly developed executive ability. To these qualities he added enterprise, perseverance and a painstaking industry.
His long business career of more than fifty years
was unsullied by a single stain on his good name
and was dignified by the admiration and respect
of his associates and contemporaries. In 1904 he
retired from active business. He always took a
deep interest in all measures for the public welfare, and particularly for the people of Chicago.
With Chauncey T. Bowen and James H. Rees he
formed the commission appointed by the governor
of the state of Illinois to locate the south park
system in the city of Chicago, and in his study
of the question he showed a complete realization
of the needs of the people of Chicago, both then
and in the years to come. The result of the deliberations of the commission was the selection
of Washington and Jackson parks and the boulevard now known as the Midway. To Mr. Kimbark

also was chiefly due the preservation of Grant Park,
bordering on the lake, to the people of Chicago.
He was an ardent supporter of the Democratic
party until the repeal of the Missouri compromise,
when his warm abolitionist sympathies led him to
join the newly-formed Republican party. During
the civil war he was a generous contributor to the
war fund, and until his death he remained a stanch
Republican, heartily supporting every progressive,
public-spirited movement in the party and just as
heartily combating every tendency to conservatism
and party privilege. For many years he was a
prominent member of the Union League Club of
Chicago and took an especially active part in its
efforts for the improvement of municipal government. He was also a member of the Chicago,
Washington Park and Calumet clubs. He was
married in Chicago, Ill., Sept. 25, 1856, to Elizabeth, daughter of Hon. Peter Pruyne, at one time
a colleague of Stephen A. Douglas in the Illinois
senate. There were four children: Charles A.,
Walter, Marie Rebecca and Grace, wife of F. J.
Howell. Mr. Kimbark died in Chicago, Ill., Aug.
13, 1912.

FOSTER, William Trufant, educator, was
born in Boston, Mass., Jan. 18, 1879, son of William Henry and Sarah (Trufant) Foster. He was
graduated at Harvard University in 1901, and
after a post graduate course in English literature,
received the degree of A.M. in 1904. He was instructor in English in Bates College for two years.
In 1905 he became professor of English and argumentation in Bowdoin College and later professor of education. While at Bowdoin he was also
chairman of the board of proctors, chairman of the
committee on relations with secondary schools, and
a member of the administrative committee. He
was lecturer in the principles of education at
Harvard University in the summer of 1909 and
then went to New York to become fellow in education at the Teachers' College of Columbia University (1909–10). Soon after he had been made
lecturer in educational administration at Columbia
in 1910, he was elected president of the newly
organized Reed College, at Portland, Ore. He received the degree of Ph. D. from Columbia University, in education and sociology, in 1911, and LL.D.
from Colorado College in 1913. Pres. Foster is
the author of "Argumentation and Debating"
(1908), "Administration of the College Curriculum" (1910), "Essentials of Exposition and
Argument" (1911), and several articles on college
administration in Monroe's "Cyclopedia of Education." Among his contributions to periodicals
are: "Dangers of the Small College," "Concentration and Distribution of Studies," "College
Course in Public Speaking and Intercollegiate Debating," all contributed to the "Nation";
"Scholarship and Athletics and College Studies
and Success in Life," contributed to "Science";
"Should the School Diploma Admit to College?"
"Education"; "The American College on Trial,"
"Arts Subjects in the A.B. Course," "The Elec-
tive System in Public High Schools," printed in
the "School Review"; "The Gentleman's Grade"
and "On the Teaching of English," in the "Ed-
ucational Review"; "Scientific Distribution of
College Credits," in "Popular Science Monthly";
"Impressions of One Hundred Colleges," in New
York "Evening Post"; "Debating in Secondary
Schools," in "New England Association, Leaflet
58"; "The Spelling of College Students," in
"American Journal of Educational Psychology";
"Uniformity in College Requirements," in "Na-
tion." He is a member of Phi Delta Kappa, Amer-

ican Association for the Advancement of Science, National Society of College Teachers of Education and American Peace Society. He was married Dec. 25, 1905, to Bessie Lucile, daughter of Ernest Wesley Russell, of Lewiston, Me., and has three children: Russell Trufant, Le Baron Russell and Faith. Reed College, of which he was first president, was founded by the bequest of Mr. and Mrs. Simeon G. Reed. The character of the new institution was decided with the aid of Ex-President Eliot of Harvard University and the General Education Board, Dr. Wallace Buttrick, the secretary of the board, having made two trips to Oregon for the purpose of studying the needs of Portland and the Northwest. After an independent study of the numerous types of schools and the institutions of higher education already established in the Northwest, the trustees decided to found a college of liberal arts and sciences, an institution requiring for admission the completion of a satisfactory four-years course of secondary grade, or the equivalent, and offering courses of approximately four years leading to the bachelor's degree. The Ladd Estate Co., donated forty acres of land for a campus, comprising part of Crystal Springs Farm, about four miles from the centre of Portland, on the east side of Williamette river. To this property was added the purchase of forty-six acres east and north of the original gift. The building of a college or university from the very foundations upon an open field with $3,000,000 for endowment is a most unusual undertaking. Pres. Foster visited institutions of higher learning in all parts of the country. On Sept. 18, 1911, the first class of fifty students of both sexes assembled for the opening exercises in a temporary building constructed in Portland for the purpose. The faculty for the first year consisted of Bernard Capen Ewer, assistant professor of philosophy; William Trufant Foster, president; Frank Loxley Griffin, professor of mathematics; Hudson Bridge Hastings, professor of mechanical drawing and surveying; Jasper Jacob Stahl, instructor in modern languages, and Arthur Evans Wood, instructor in social sciences.

SULLIVAN, Patrick Francis, street railway president, was born in Cork, Ireland, Mar. 16, 1856, son of Dennis Sullivan, with whom he came to America in 1873, settling in Lowell, Mass. He found employment with the Lowell Manufacturing Co., but at no time neglected his education. He attended night schools, was tutored privately, and finally took a course at the Lowell Commercial College, where he followed a natural inclination for mathematics and accounting. In 1883 he became chief clerk to the Lowell Board of Assessors. After serving three years in that capacity, he resigned because he wished to study law, and securing a civil service appointment, was assigned to the law division of the United States Pension Bureau at Washington. His duties there were so competently and intelligently performed that he was offered a promotion, but because of family reasons resigned and returned to Lowell, where he associated himself with his brother, the publisher of the "Lowell Daily News." About this time a committee from the Lowell Horse railroad and the Lowell and Dracut Street railway offered him the position of joint secretary. He reluctantly accepted, took hold earnestly, and was soon interested in the then pending problem of electrification. The two roads were consolidated in 1891, and he became general manager. He went abroad to study continental railway systems, and upon his return handled his own problems with

renewed confidence. In 1899 seventy-one street railway companies of Massachusetts were consolidated. The needs of the public as well as the requirements of the railways demanded this, but it meant the virtual disappearance of many of the old-time managers. Mr. Sullivan was selected as president of these enormous and diverse interests, which gave him opportunity for success that has culminated in the final consolidation of the eastern Massachusetts railway interests under the title of the Bay State Co., of which he likewise became president and director. He is also president and director of the Boston and Revere Electric Co., Newport and Fall River Electric Co., general manager Massachusetts Electric Co., director Nashua, N. H., Street Railway Co., Dorchester Mutual Fire Insurance Co., Old Colony Trust Co., Union National Bank, Lowell; director and member executive committee, Massachusetts Employers' Insurance Association, and trustee Central Savings Bank, Lowell. He is a member of the Algonquin, Exchange and Economic clubs, of Boston; the Vesper, Country and Yorick clubs, of Lowell, and the American Academy of Political and Social Science. He was married in 1887, at Lowell, Mass., and has five children, three sons and two daughters.

CARREL, Alexis, surgeon and physiologist, was born at Sainte Foy, Lyons, France, June 28, 1873, son of Alexis Carrel, a silk merchant, and his wife, Anne Ricard. He was graduated at the University of Lyons, B.L. in 1890, receiving the degree of B.S. the following year. He served as interne in the Lyons Hospital and took his M.D. degree at the university in 1900. While still pursuing his medical studies he published a monograph on "Cancerous Goitre" ("Le Goitre Cancereux," 1900), which is a careful study of an affection usually considered quite rare, but which an examination of some eighty-three cases shows to be relatively frequent. This initial contribution to medical literature was much more than the conventional thesis of the graduate in medicine, and will hold a place in recent medical literature. Early in his career he began the original research and experimentation work that he is now engaged in. After serving as prosecuteur a la faculté de medicine at the University of Lyons for two years he went to Canada, and in 1905 he joined the staff of the physiological department of the University of Chicago, under Dr. G. N. Stewart. With Dr. C. G. Guthrie he continued his experiments, which were destined to bring his name prominently before the world. His first important contribution to the science of surgery was a successful method of suturing of blood vessels, whereby veins and arteries may be so cleverly united that the point of union when healed is hardly discernible. For centuries surgeons had sought to find a way to cut arteries or veins and then cause them to unite again. They sometimes succeeded, but oftener failed. Dr. Carrel's method is to bring the ends of an artery together and catch them with a needle that is put through three times in such a manner as to form a small triangle; then each corner of this small triangle is gently pulled so that the little tube of the artery or vein is drawn into a triangular shape. While the ends are thus held in place by an assistant, the surgeon takes the ends or flaps that thus lie flat on the three sides of the triangle and sews them together with a whip stitch, as a seamstress does when she wishes to join two pieces of cloth with the least possible seam or ridge. Because it is so rapid and simple the Carrel method has practically superseded all the

older sutures. ''Anastomosis and Transplantation of Blood Vessels'' and ''Transplantation of
Veins and Organs'' were Dr. Carrel's first announcement of a new and most important field of
research in modern surgery. He describes one of
his operations of this kind as follows: ''In 1905
I succeeded with Guthrie in transplanting segments of jugular veins into the carotid artery
and found that the vein quickly undergoes
structural changes, consisting chiefly of the thick-
ening of its wall. Stick and Makkas confirmed
these results. Watts succeeded also in transplanting segments of jugular on the carotid. I obtained excellent results in the transplantation of
the vena cava into the aorta, operations which had
been attempted by Goyanes in Spain. From all these
experiments it is possible to know the anatomic
evolution of a piece of vein transplanted on an
artery. . . . These experiments show that a vein
can adapt itself to the arterial functions. But it
seems that the transplantation of veins on arteries
is less safe than the transplantation of arteries on
arteries.'' Dr. Carrel presents this account of the
transplanting of the thyroid glands: ''In 1905 I
succeeded, with Guthrie, in extirpating and replant-
ing the thyroid gland with reversal of circulation.
Eleven days after the operation the wound was
opened and the circulation of the gland was found
going on. The animal is still alive.'' An article,
which appeared in ''The American Journal of the
Medical Sciences'' for 1906, by Drs. Carrel and
Guthrie was on ''Amputation of the Thigh and
Its Replantation,'' showing the possibility of having the whole series of structures in the leg grow
together after complete separation. This idea was
not entirely new, but it was so far in advance of
anything that had been thought possible before as
to prove startling. Dr. Carrel said: ''I received
a human leg from a New York hospital. I removed some of the arteries and put them in a dog,
which easily survived the operation and remained
healthy. I opened the dog later and found that
it was doing beautifully. The important thing is
whether tissue from animals can be used in man.
That the restored circulation is adequate is demonstrated by the absence of gangrene or other symptoms attributed to this factor, both in the case of
a hind leg replanted on a dog, and also by both
fore and hind legs transplanted from dogs to dogs
of other breeds. In addition, dogs' heads have
been temporarily transplanted with partial preservation of cerebral and bulbar function. Since
there has been found no evidence of serious de-
rangement of metabolism (tissue change) in dogs'
thighs up to twenty-two days after transplantation, nor in a dog's foreleg in six days after transplantation, and since there are no physiologic or
other reasons known why such tissues as those
found in the limb may not live and again function
under such conditions, it seems justifiable to con-
clude that it is possible to transplant such a member with surgical success.'' In 1905 he was able
to remove the heart from a dog, and after more
than an hour transfer it to the throat of a larger
dog, graft it into the coronary circulation, and
make it beat again. After a year in Chicago, Dr.
Carrel received a call to the Rockefeller Institute
of Research in New York city, where his most remarkable experiments have been conducted. In
1907 he announced that it was possible to preserve
portions of veins and arteries in such a condition
by cold storage that the ordinary death changes
did not occur in them, and that they could be
grafted on to arteries or veins successfully. He
transplanted successfully on a dog a human artery

which had been preserved for twenty-four days in
cold storage. In 1910 he described the successful
replantation of kidneys and also the transplantation
of kidneys from one animal to another. Both kidneys were successfully transplanted, and the animals not only survived, but functioned normally
and remained healthy for some time. The ''Cultivation in Vitro of Thyroid'' appeared in 1911, and
was a demonstration of the growth of the cells of
various organs when placed upon proper nutritive
media in glass or other vessels. Thus portions of
thyroid placed on plasma of an animal corresponding to that from which the organ had been removed actually grew new cells and new tissue was
formed. In the spring of 1912 it was announced
that he had succeeded in keeping the heart tissue
of a chicken alive for a period of 104 days after
its removal from the body. At a meeting of the
American Medical Association, in June, 1912, Dr.
Carrel read a paper entitled, ''Preservation of
Tissues and Its Application to Surgery,'' in which
he declared: ''If it were possible to transplant immediately after death the tissues and organs which
compose the body into other identical organisms,
no elemental death would occur; all the constituent parts of the body would continue to live.''
In an article in the ''Journal of Experimental
Medicine'' for September, 1913, entitled ''Contributions to the Study of the Mechanism of the
Growth of Connective Tissue,'' he says: ''In
previous articles it has been shown that connective
tissue cells can be preserved permanently in vitro
(glass jars) in a condition of active life. Strains
of these cells have now been proliferating rapidly
outside of the organism for more than sixteen
months. In the course of experiment it was observed that a constant relation existed between the
rate of growth and the composition of the medium.
This fact indicated that certain cell phenomena of
the higher animals, such as multiplication, growth
and senility, might now be investigated profitably.
The results of the experiments lead one to assume
that in a culture of tissue progressive diminution
of the tissue's rate of growth and its ultimate
death are probably brought about by similar modifications of the medium. It was this supposition
which enabled me to prolong indefinitely the life
of connective tissue in vitro. It was found that
by washing the tissues of a culture in Ringer solution and placing them in a new medium the rate
of growth did not diminish and death failed to
occur. . . The experiments indicate that the growing tissues modify their medium; but the nature
of the modification has not yet been determined.''
In January, 1913, Dr. Carrel startled the scientific
world by announcing that he had devised a method
of causing tissues to grow in vitro at many times
their normal rate. If tissue were artificially ac-
tivated at ten times their normal rate and the
principle were actually applied in surgical practice,
a wound would heal in twenty-four hours and a
broken leg would mend in a few days. The experiment was tried in the case of a dog. Pulp of the
thyroid gland applied to the wounds promoted
healing at an increased rate. These experiments
led to the discovery that connective tissue cells
can be kept in a condition of active life outside
of the organism for more than two years. On Oct.
22, 1912, Dr. Carrel was awarded the Nobel prize
for medicine, and in the same year Columbia University conferred upon him the degree of Sc.D.
His scientific work was interrupted by the
European war, at the oubreak of which he
entered the French army medical service with
the rank of medicine-major. Dr. Carrel's

work has not been due to flashes of genius or brilliant ideas that luckily worked out into scientific demonstrations. He is an indefatigable worker, but personally far from the kind of a man so often portrayed as the tpyical scientific investigator. He is interested in literature, sociology and philosophy, and in certain phases of psychology. The influence of the mind on the body, and the remarkable cures of physical disorders that sometimes follow strong influence exerted upon the mind, have had special attraction for him. He is a fellow of the American Surgical Association, and of the American Philosophical Society; a member of the American Society of Physiology, and of the Society of Clinical Surgery, and an associate member of the American Medical Association. He was married in 1913 to Anne de la Motte, Marquise de la Mairie.

GAVIN, Michael Freebern, physician and surgeon, was born in Roscommon, Ireland, May 12, 1844, son of John Gavin, a carriage manufacturer. He came to America in 1857, and was educated in the old Boston grammar school, the private school of William J. Adams in Boston, and the Harvard Medical School. He was graduated M.D. in 1864 after which he was house surgeon in the Boston City Hospital for one year. During the last month of the civil war he was assistant surgeon in the 57th Mass. Vol. infantry. He continued his medical studies abroad after the war; first in the hospitals of Paris and then in the Royal College of Physicians and Surgeons, Dublin, Ireland, from which he received diplomas as fellow in surgery and fellow in medicine with high honors. He began the practice of his profession in South Boston in 1867 and at the same time became visiting surgeon in the out-patient department of Boston City Hospital, of which he was trustee during 1879–85, visiting surgeon during 1886–96, senior visiting surgeon during 1897–1906 and consulting surgeon from 1906 until his death. He was continuously on the staff at St. Elizabeth's Hospital, surgeon and consulting surgeon, and trustee from 1871 to 1910, and he was surgeon and consulting surgeon at Carney Hospital from 1880 until his death. During 1888–91 he was professor of clinical surgery at the Boston Polyclinic. At these and at other hospitals he performed many noteworthy and original operations. He was a recognized authority on the treatment of burns, and he compiled valuable statistics on suicide that attracted widespread attention. He was a skillful diagnostician and during the last of his career did much consultation work. He contributed numerous articles on medicine and surgery to various medical and scientific magazines. Dr. Gavin was a trustee of the Union Institution for Savings, and a director of the Mattapan Deposit & Trust Co. He was a fellow of the Royal College of Surgeons of Ireland and the Massachusetts Medical Society, member of the British Medical Association, American Medical Association, Boston Society for Medical Improvement, and Boston Society of Medical Observation, and a member of the Papyrus Club and the Boston Athletic Association. He was a profound reader and literary student, and took pleasure in collecting a large library. He possessed an intuitive knowledge of human nature and his dominating personal characteristics were his kindness, thoughtfulness and a remarkable solicitude for the comfort and welfare of his patients. It is said that he treated each case as though it were one of his immediate family. His attitude to his patients was that of a father and it was his custom frequently to call unexpectedly at night to inquire about a case. He was married in New York city, Nov. 22, 1876, to Ellen Theresa, daughter of Patrick Doherty, a real estate operator and owner, of New York city. She survives him with two children: Basil and Hilda Theresa Gavin. He died in South Boston, Mass., May 20, 1915.

SHUSTER, William Morgan, lawyer, financial and legislative expert, was born in Washington, D. C., Feb. 23, 1877, son of William Morgan and Caroline (von Tagen) Shuster. After graduating at the Central High School of Washington in 1893, where he was president of his class, he took a partial course at the Columbian College and Law School, now George Washington University, and was admitted to the Washington bar in 1910. Meanwhile he had been appointed assistant secretary to the evacuation commission, having charge of the arrangements for the evacuation of Cuba by the Spanish government and troops, and upon the termination of these duties he was appointed to the Cuban customs service, then under the American government. In a period of three years he was successively chief of statistics, chief appraiser and deputy collector, and special deputy collector of customs for Cuba. He performed his duties so satisfactorily that, in 1901, he was appointed collector of customs for the Philippine Islands, where he revised the new Philippine tariff laws and reorganized the entire Philippine customs service. He was also entrusted with the enforcement of all immigration, navigation and registration laws in those islands. In 1906 Pres. Roosevelt appointed him secretary of public instruction in the Philippines as well as member of the Philippine Commission, which was then the sole legislative body of the Islands. He had executive control of the Bureau of Education, employing nearly 8,000 American and Filipino teachers, the entire prison system, the Bureau of Supply, the Bureau of Printing and the Philippine Medical School. In 1907 he was made chairman of the code committee, which codified and compiled the American legislation for the Islands, covering a period of nearly ten years. In fact, he had charge of making and revising a number of different tariff laws in Cuba also, and he is considered an expert in the framing, execution and interpretation of customs and other revenue legislation. After three years of hard and effective work on the Philippine Commission he returned to the practice of law in the United States. About this time, Persia finding herself bankrupt, appealed to Pres. Taft to recommend someone to take charge of her exchequer, and Mr. Shuster was suggested. On Feb. 2, 1911, he was appointed financial adviser and treasurer general of the Persian empire, and in the following June the national council adopted a measure investing him with direct, effective control of all the financial and fiscal operations of the Persian government, including the collection of all receipts, control of all government expenditures, and the power to establish whatever departments and appoint such assistants as he considered necessary. The reforms he instituted began to interfere with certain Russian and English interests, and, in consequence, the plans of the Nationalist government were combated at every turn. Those same interests were averse to having the tottering empire placed on a sound financial and consequently independent basis. So great was the apprehension that one time an armed Russian force moved on Teheran for the apparent purpose of ejecting Shuster and his American associates. The inevitable destruction of the Nationalists followed in December of that year (1911) and Mr. Shuster was forced to resign. Returning to Washington, he resumed his law practice in partnership with Clement L. Bouve. In 1915 he became business manager of the Century Co. in New York city. He is the author of "The Strangling of Persia" (1913) and magazine articles dealing with international politics and policies. He is a member of the bar of the Supreme Court of the United States, the United States Court of Custom Appeals, of the Supreme Court, and the Court of Appeals of the District of Columbia (to be dictated). He is an honorary member of the Army and Navy Club, Manila, P. I.; honorary vice-president of the United Engineers' Association, Manila; life member of the National Geographic Society of the United States; member of the Washington Board of Trade, Bar Association of the District of Columbia, Pan-American Society of the United States, the Cosmos Club, Washington, D. C., and of The Recess, City Midday and Press clubs, of New York city. He was married, Apr. 20, 1904, to Pearl Berthé, daughter of Col. Henry C. Trigg, a banker of Glasgow, Ky., and has two children: Caroline Trigg and Litie McElroy Shuster.

LEE, Margaret, author, was born in New York city, Nov. 27, 1840, daughter of Joseph and Mary Georgina Lee, both natives of Dublin, Ireland. She was educated under private tutors and in the public schools. During 1861–63 she wrote a story simply for the pleasure of writing it, and when, in 1865, the New York "Herald" offered a prize of $1,000 for a distinctly American novel, she submitted hers in competition. It won the prize and was published in the Sunday edition of the "Herald" under the title of "Arnold's Choice." Her second novel, "Dr. Wilmer's Love," was published in 1868. It was followed by "In Bonds of Wedlock" (1877); "Lorimer and Wife" (1881); "Marriage" (1882); "Lizzie Adriance" (1882); "Divorce' (1882); "Since I Saw Your Face" (1883); "The Missing Marriage Certificate" (1883); "The Story of a Story" (1883); "A Brighton Night" (1884); "A Brooklyn Bachelor" (1886); "One Touch of Nature" (1892); "This Man and This Woman" (1894); "Romance of the Russells" (1896; "The Master Chivalry" (1900); "The Tongue of a Woman" (1902); "Separation" (1902); "A Broken Engagement" (1904); "The D'Estimanvilles" (1905); "Lovers and Shekels" (1906); "Gallatin" (1913); "The Blot on the Board" (1913), and "The Wanderer" (1913). "Divorce" was a plea for uniform divorce laws in the United States, and, at the time of writing it, Miss Lee was unaware of the fact that a divorce reform league was in contemplation by the people of New England. In 1888, having seen a copy of William E. Gladstone's letter to the league, she sent him a copy of her book, and received in return a request to allow the republication of the work in England. Copyright arrangements with Miss Lee's American publishers were made by Mr. Gladstone himself, and "Divorce" was issued in London as "Faithful and Unfaithful," a title of his own origination. In the "Nineteenth Century Magazine" for February, 1899, Gladstone wrote an exhaustive review, from which we quote the following: "It is with great gallantry, as well as with great ability, that Margaret Lee has ventured to come back in the ranks on what must be taken nowadays as the unpopular side, and has indicated her belief in a certain old-fashioned doctrine that the path of suffering may not be the path of duty only, but likewise the path of glory and of triumph for our race." Miss Lee was greatly interested in securing the perpetual copyright law, and to this object devoted much time for several years. She was a member of the Writers' Club of Brooklyn and the Society of American Authors. She died in Brooklyn, N. Y., Dec. 24, 1914.

MOSHER, Eliza Maria, physician, was born near Cayuga Lake, N. Y., Oct. 2, 1846, youngest daughter of Augustus and Maria (Sutton) Mosher, and a direct descendant of Hugh Mosher, who was the first of the family to come to the American colonies. Her paternal grandfather, Allen Mosher, settled in Cayuga county, and her maternal, Abraham Sutton, in Madison county, N. Y., when those portions of the state were yet a wilderness; both became large landowners, and throughout their lives were men of great influence in the localities in which they lived. Both parents were members of the Society of Friends. Her preliminary education was received at the Friends Academy, Union Springs, N. Y., and under private tutors. She began the study of medicine in Boston in 1869 under the direction of Dr. Lucy E. Sewall. In 1871 she entered the medical department of the University of Michigan, arranging for herself a graded course of three years instead of the two required in all medical schools at that time. At the beginning of her second year she was asked to serve as assistant to the demonstrator of anatomy and to conduct a quiz for the women's class, which she did, giving up the year mainly to anatomy, and allowing herself a fourth year of study before graduation. The third year of her course was spent in clinical study in New York city and attendance upon lecturers at the Woman's College of the New York Infirmary. After graduating at the University of Michigan in 1875, she began the practice of medicine in Poughkeepsie, N. Y. Her ability was so pronounced that when the Massachusetts State Reformatory Prison for Women was established at Sherborn in 1877, Dr. Mosher was urged to become its resident physician, and although out of the direction of her ambition, she accepted the position. This was the first prison in the world conducted exclusively by women, and in the building up and management of its hospital and maternity department she displayed unusual ability as an organizer and executive. She withdrew after completing the organization of the prison hospital, leaving her work in the able hands of Dr. Lucy M. Hall—with whom she afterwards associated for many years. As a further preparation for the private practice of medicine, she spent a year studying in London and Paris. A serious crisis in the management of the reformatory prison led Gov. Long, of Massachusetts, to urge upon Dr. Mosher the superintendency of the prison. Very reluctantly she postponed her medical work and bent her energies toward its reorganization. She introduced a system of grading and marking, and a probation department for second offenders, as well as many other improvements which made her superintendency a signal success. After three years she resigned to take up the practice of medicine in Brooklyn, N. Y. Almost immediately she was invited to reorganize the medical work at Vassar College. Unwilling to give up the Brooklyn field, she accepted the position of resident physician and professor of hygiene upon half time, sharing it with her associate, Dr. Hall until she resigned in 1886 to devote her entire attention to medicine. In 1896 she was offered the position of woman's dean and superintendent of physical education at the University of Michigan, as well as a full pro-

John Cadwalader

fessorship in hygiene in the department of literature, science and the arts, and again left the occupation of her choice, and for six years devoted herself to the needs of her alma mater. After having firmly established the work for women which she had undertaken there, she once more resumed her practice in Brooklyn (1902). While conducting a general practice of medicine, Dr. Mosher has made an exhaustive study of the normal poise of the human body and established certain facts relative to the influence of habits of posture upon its symmetry and health, the most important of which is that upon the position of the pelvis depends the shape of the body. She may well be called a ''pioneer in the campaign of physical education.'' She has lectured extensively on hygiene and other topics relating to physical welfare, and is the author of ''The Health of Criminal Women'' (1882), ''Prison Discipline'' (1883), ''A Critical Study of the Biceps Cruris Muscle and Its Relation to Diseases In and Around the Knee Joint'' (1891), ''The Influence of Habits of Posture Upon the Symmetry and Health of the Body'' (1892), ''Habitual Postures of School Children'' (1892), ''Habits of Posture a Cause of Deformity and Displacement of the Uterus'' (1893), and ''Vacation Letters to My Girls'' (1911), and she is one of the editors of the ''Woman's Medical Journal.'' She devised a ''Posture Model,'' made up of the human vertebræ so articulated that it can be easily placed in the various natural positions for demonstrative purposes; a ''Pelvic Obliquimetre''; school desk with a book-rest adjustment for reading and a hygiene school chair; also a kindergarten chair bearing her name. Dr. Mosher is a member of the Kings County Medical Society, the Brooklyn Pathological Society, the American Medical Association, the American Public Health Association, the American Association for the Advancement of Physical Education, the Women's Medical Association of New York City, the Women's Press Club of New York, the Medical Society of the State of New York and the Brooklyn Woman's Club.

CADWALADER, John, jurist, was born in Philadelphia, Pa., Apr. 1, 1805, son of Thomas and Mary (Biddle) Cadwalader. His father, only son of Gen. John Cadwalader of the Revolution, held a commission as major-general of volunteers in the war of 1812, and his mother was the daughter of Col. Clement Biddle, quartermaster-general of the revolutionary army and Washington's personal friend. The son was graduated at the University of Pennsylvania in 1821, studied law under Horace Binney, was admitted to the bar in 1825 when still a minor, and in 1830 became solicitor for the bank of the United States. He early acquired an extensive practice in the law of real property and of commercial relations. His father's management of the estates held by the family of William Penn induced in him a careful study of the laws of title and descent, and his connection with the bank of the United States opened up another wide field. He soon obtained a large practice, and his office became a school of law where many of Philadelphia's most prominent advocates began their careers. In 1854 he was elected to congress on the Democratic ticket, and in his speeches always upheld constitutional principles against the passions of the Anti-Slavery party. Four years later he was appointed judge of the U. S. district court for the eastern district of Pennsylvania by Pres. Buchanan, and served on that bench until his death. His judicial services included the civil war and reconstruction periods, the most critical in our history. His decision in the case of the Gen. Parkill was the first to sustain the right to condemn as prize vessels belonging to citizens of the Confederate states, and was finally accepted as sound by the U. S. supreme court. Judge Cadwalader, though a consistent Democrat, recognized the conditions created by the war and sustained the federal authority in all proper exercise of its powers, securing the respect and confidence of all parties. He was one of the few judges of his time who followed the English practice of expediting justice by rendering oral decisions, which he would do even in important cases whenever they were governed by well-established principles. Cases, however, which involved somewhat new principles, or as he preferred to view them, new applications of old principles, would receive at his hands the fullest consideration, and decisions were rendered which were in fact treatises. This might be said of Winter vs. Ludlow on the law of equitable assignments and appropriation in favor of creditors; of Keene vs. Wheatley on the law of copyright and literary property, and of Camblos vs. Philadelphia and Reading Railroad Company on the common law duty of common carriers against discrimination in rates. His administration of the bankruptcy law after the Jay Cooke failure and the panic of 1873 showed him to possess great familiarity with the business methods and a practical knowledge of affairs very unusual in one whose tastes were rather of the closet than of the market-place. His most important decisions, excluding those in bankruptcy, were published in ''Cadwalader's Cases'' (1907). As a lawyer, learning and common sense were combined in him to an unusual degree, and although rated the most learned man in the profession, his learning did not unfit him to deal promptly and aptly with the practical affairs of life. The purity and gentleness of his character, as testified to by those members of the bar who best knew him, are strong proof of the high standards of the bench in the days when the judicial recall was still undreamed of. He received the honorary degree of LL.D. from the University of Pennsylvania in 1870. On his tablet in the U. S. district courtroom in Philadelphia is inscribed this motto: ''Pace ac bello Inter Cives et Inter Gentes Salva Justitia Patria Salva Jus Dixit.'' He was twice married: (1) in 1828 to Mary, daughter of Horace Binney; she died in 1831, leaving two daughters: Elizabeth, wife of Lieut. George Harrison Hare, and Mary, wife of William Henry Rawle of Philadelphia; (2) in 1833 to Henrietta Maria, daughter of Charles Nicoll Bancker, of Philadelphia, by whom he had four children: Frances, Anne, wife of Rev. Henry J. Rowland; Charles Evert and John Cadwalader. Judge Cadwalader died in Philadelphia, Pa., Jan. 26, 1879.

CADWALADER, John, lawyer, was born in Philadelphia, Pa., June 27, 1843, son of John Cadwalader (above) and his wife, Henrietta Maria Bancker. He was graduated at the University of Pennsylvania in 1862, receiving the degree A.M. in 1865, and the honorary degree of LL.D. in 1912, and is now a trustee of the University. He began the study of law in the office of Hon. Peter McCall and completed it with William Henry Rawle, at the same time attending the law lectures in the law department of the University of Pennsylvania. He was admitted to the bar in 1864, and acquired an extensive practice, his professional work being largely connected with estates and proceedings arising in the orphans court. At an early age he served on the board of examiners for admissions to the bar, and for many years was the jury commissioner of the United States court. With Chief Justice Sharswood and Chief Justice Mitchell, he served on a commission to complete the publication of the early laws of the commonwealth. Active in local politics as a Democrat, he was at various times candidate for the city council, the state legislature and the United States congress, and was a delegate to the state and national conventions. In 1885 Pres. Cleveland appointed him collector of the port of Philadelphia. He was president of the Trust Company of North America, and is now president of the Baltimore and Philadelphia Steamboat Co. He is a member of the American Philosophical Society, the Pennsylvania Historical Society, vice-president of the Academy of Natural Sciences and president-general of the Society of the War of 1812 since the office was created. He is also president of the Pennsylvania Institution for the Instruction of the Blind, and belongs to the Rittenhouse, University, Art, Penn and Philadelphia Country clubs of Philadelphia, and the Metropolitan Club of Washington. Mr. Cadwalader was married, April 17, 1866, to Mary Helen, daughter of Joshua Francis Fisher, of Philadelphia, and has two daughters: Sophia and Mary Helen, and two sons, John, Jr., and Thomas Francis Cadwalader.

BAACKES, Frank, vice-president of the American Steel and Wire Co., was born at St. Toenis, Prussia, Mar. 9, 1863, son of Godfrey and Franziska (Maassen) Baackes. He laid the foundation of his successes in the wire nail mills of Oberbilk-Dusseldorf. In 1879 he came to the United States and entered the service of the H. P. Nail Co. mills at Cleveland, O. He was quick to master the details of the work assigned to him, and in two years had shown such complete knowledge of the business that he was appointed superintendent. He left the Cleveland company in January, 1884, to supervise the erection of the Hartman Steel Company's wire plant at Beaver Falls, Pa. In 1885 he invented the standard wire nail, which attained great favor, and resulted in his organizing the Salem Wire Nail Co., capitalized at $200,000, of which he was general manager and a principal stockholder. The success of the Salem company was so great, and so powerful was it in controlling the business of the country for twelve years, that it was one of the first to be taken over by the American Steel and Wire Co. of Illinois in 1897, and Mr. Baackes was retained as general manager of the latter. A year later the corporation was merged into the American Steel and Wire Co. of New Jersey, of which he was first general superintendent, and in 1900 general sales manager. In 1905 he was elected vice-president. He is a man with a great capacity for work, of tireless energy, and with such an intuitive faculty that he judges men at sight for their proper business capacity and when so placed gets the greatest amount of work possible from them. He has been a great reader, and has found time from his strenuous activities to acquire a great fund of general information and a broad culture, which fittingly crowns his practical ability. Aside from his large and well-selected library, his recreation is mostly taken at his country place in Vilas county, Wis., which he maintains in almost primitive wildness. He is also a director of the Columbia Wire Co. and the American Mining Co., and a member of the following clubs: Union League, Chicago Athletic, South Shore, Chicago Automobile, Midday, New York, Engineers, Lawyers, Railway, Hardware and Germania. Mr. Baackes was twice married: first to Catherine O'Rourke of Cleveland,

O., and to them was born one son, Godfrey D. Baackes. The second marriage was to Mamie E. Lutz. To this union two sons were born, Frank, Jr., and Karl Baackes.

WILLIAMS, Talcott, journalist and educator, was born at Abeih, Turkey, July 20, 1849, son of William Frederic and Sarah Amelia (Pond) Williams. His father was a missionary of the American Board. He prepared for college at Phillips Academy (Andover) and was graduated at Amherst in 1873. While in college he was one of the editors of the ''Amherst Student,'' and after graduation he became a space reporter on the New York ''World.'' As a reward for having secured an interview with Harry Hill on the career of John C. Heenan, he was placed on the regular city staff. He was Albany correspondent of the ''World'' in 1875 and 1876 and after serving as night editor and editorial writer was sent as correspondent to Washington. He was Washington correspondent of the New York ''Sun'' and San Francisco ''Chronicle'' during 1876-79. In 1879 he went to the Springfield ''Republican'' as editorial writer, and in 1881 he became associate editor of the Philadelphia ''Press,'' with which he was connected for thirty-one years, during three of them being managing editor. In March, 1912, Mr. Williams was appointed director of the School of Journalism, founded by Joseph Pulitzer, with an endowment of $2,000,000 to be administered in accordance with an agreement with Columbia University. A trained newspaper man, possessing a broad education and wide information, a copious writer and felicitous speaker and a natural born instructor, he is well qualified to be the director of this pioneer school of journalism. In addition to his newspaper work he has written extensively on art and the drama, and for twenty-five years he contributed monthly reviews of new books for the ''Book News.'' He made two trips to Morocco, to collect anthropological material for the Smithsonian Institute and the Archæological Museum of the University of Pennsylvania, and was for many years a member of the committee on Babylonian research of the latter. Dr. Williams is a trustee of Amherst College, and Constantinople College for Girls. He was associate editor of the new International Cyclopedia, 1914-16. The degree of LL.D. was conferred upon him by the University of Pennsylvania in 1895, Hobart College in 1899, Western Reserve University in 1909, University of Pittsburgh in 1912, and Franklin and Marshall College in 1915; the degree of L.H.D. by Amherst College in 1896, and Western Reserve in 1909, and that of Litt. D. by the University of Rochester in 1902 and Brown University in 1915; a member of the executive committee of the League to Enforce Peace, and of the National Civic Federation on the part of the public manager of the Archæological Museum of the University of Pennsylvania, the Free Hospital for Poor Consumptives, and the White Haven Sanatorium; vice-president of the Pennsylvania Society for the Prevention of Tuberculosis, the Pennsylvania Society for the Prevention of Social Diseases and the Armstrong Association, the City History Club of New York; the American Philosophical Society, the American Academy of Political and Social Science, the American Statistical Society, the American Oriental Society and the Washington Academy of Sciences. For two years he was president of the Alpha Delta Phi graduate chapter and fraternity, and he is a member of the Amherst Alumni Association, the University and Contemporary clubs of Phila-

TALCOTT WILLIAMS
JOURNALIST

IGNAZ A. PILAT
LANDSCAPE GARDENER

CARL F. PILAT
LANDSCAPE ARCHITECT

ROBERT L. MacCAMERON
ARTIST

delphia, and the University and Alpha Delta Phi clubs of New York. He was a member of the Clover Club of Philadelphia for twenty years. He was married May 28, 1879, to Sophia Wells Boyce, of Albion, N. Y.

PILAT, Ignaz Anton, landscape gardener, was born at Aschach, Austria, June 27, 1820. He was originally intended for the ministry and obtained the necessary technical schooling for that profession, but early developing an intense love for gardening he began to prepare himself for that vocation at the botanical gardens in Vienna and Schönbrunn. He showed himself such an ardent pupil and such a highly gifted and tasteful landscape gardener that he quickly received public recognition and honor. His first important work was the laying out of the grounds of Prince Metternich in Vienna. He was connected with the imperial botanical gardens in Schönbrunn from 1843 to 1848, when, because of political troubles, he left Austria and came to the United States. After remaining in New York a short time he went to Dalton, Ga., where his services were sought in laying out the grounds of Alexander H. Stephens, Thomas Metcalf and others. He returned to Vienna in 1852 and was appointed director of the botanical gardens there. While thus engaged he wrote a treatise on botany that became a textbook in schools. He returned to the United States at the call of the New York park commissioners about 1856 and was appointed chief landscape gardener of Central Park, New York, occupying that position during the remainder of his life. He became a naturalized citizen soon after. He planned, superintended and directed the work on the park from its commencement up to the time of his last illness, and to him more than to any other man is due the credit of the park as it appears to-day. He planned and effected improvements on the Battery, City Hall Park, Mount Morris Park and several other parks and places under the department of public parks. He worked in a professional capacity for such persons as William Cullen Bryant, Cyrus W. Field, William E. Dodge, Fernando Wood, Moses D. Hoge (for whom he designed the monument to Rev. Dr. William J. Hoge in Hollywood Cemetery), H. Cummings, W. S. Gurnee, Gov. Sprague, of Rhode Island, and Morris K. Jesup. So interested was he in his profession and so unwearying in his labors that, although his salary was sadly insufficient to meet the needs of his large family, he thought less of pecuniary rewards than of the fact that he was the first official appointee as landscape gardener of Central Park. He was married, July 3, 1859, to Clara Louise, daughter of Anton F. Rittler, M.D., of New York city, and his children were: William C., Herman F., Emma Louise, wife of Alfred L. Holihan; Victor, Oliver Ignaz and Clara Marie, wife of William H. King. He died in New York, Sept. 17, 1870.

PILAT, Carl Francis, landscape architect and engineer, was born at Ossining, N. Y., Aug. 19, 1876, son of Carl Francis and Anna (Enzinger) Pilat. His father, a native of Vienna, Austria, came to America in 1848, settled at Dalton, Ga., and subsequently lived at Ossining, N. Y. He was a noted teacher and naturalist; his uncle, Ignatz A. Pilat, was a noted landscape architect of New York city. Carl F. Pilat was educated in the public and high schools of Ossining, and at Mt. Pleasant Military Academy. He spent two years in New York University and two years at Cornell, being graduated at the latter in 1900 with the degree of B.S. in agriculture. In 1898 he be-

came associated as a landscape architect with Warren H. Manning, in Boston. After graduating at Cornell he spent a year in travel and study in England, Germany, France and Italy. During a portion of this period he was connected with the celebrated botanical gardens in Berlin. Upon his return, in 1901, he became assistant landscape architect in the office of Charles W. Leavitt, Jr., New York city, remaining in that capacity until 1906. He then organized the firm of Hinchman, Pilat & Tooker, architects and landscape engineers, his partners being Frederick B. Hinchman and Frank W. Tooker. In 1910 the firm became Hinchman & Pilat, architects and landscape engineers. His work included designing the industrial villages of Felton and Woodfred in Cuba for the Spanish-American Iron Co.; the Orange Playground, Orange, N. J.; private estates—Spencer Trask, Lake George; Edward M. Shepard, also at Lake George; Cleveland H. and Grace Hoagland Dodge, Riverdale, N. Y.; Theodore N. Vail (Vail Memorial Park), at Parsippany, N. J. In June, 1913, he was appointed landscape architect to the park board of New York city. In this connection he redesigned Union Square, and designed Isham, Gaynor, Silver Lake and Telewana parks. Mr. Pilat is a fellow of the American Society of Landscape Architects, member of the American Civic Association, and a governor of the Phi Gamma Delta Club, West Forty-fourth street, New York city; also a member of the Glenwood Country Club, and City Club of New York.

MacCAMERON, Robert Lee, artist, was born in Chicago, Ill., Jan. 14, 1866, son of Thomas and Hattie (Cameron) McConnell. Early in his career he legally adopted the name of MacCameron. On the paternal side he was descended from a family in the north of Ireland, his great-grandfather having come to this country three generations before. His paternal grandmother was related to Robert E. Lee of Virginia. When Robert was one year old his parents removed to Necadah, Wis., where the father became a member of the state legislature. At the age of fourteen the son had developed a fine physique, and earned a man's wages as a lumberjack in the Wisconsin forests. His artistic talents were early apparent, and while still a youth he went to Chicago and subsequently to New York to earn a livelihood as an illustrator. In 1888 he went to London and secured employment on a juvenile publication entitled "The Boys' Own." Later he studied at the Beaux Arts, Paris, under the famous masters, Gerome, Whistler and Raphael Collin. His rise in the world of art was slow but sure, and his reputation as a portrait painter became firmly established on both sides of the Atlantic. He is represented in the Metropolitan Museum of Art, New York; Corcoran Art Gallery, Washington, D. C.; Memorial Art Gallery, Philadelphia, Pa.; and the Musée de Luxembourg, Paris. His pictures in the Metropolitan Museum of Art are a portrait of the French sculptor, Auguste Rodin, and "The Daughter's Return." His most celebrated portraits are of Pres. McKinley, Justice Harlan, of the U. S. supreme court; Archbishop Ryan, Maud Adams, Auguste Rodin, Pres. Taft, the Duke and Duchess of Rutland, and Mme. Melba. He also excelled as a painter of the poor, depicting with rare fidelity their misery and squalor. In such works as the "Group of Friends" and the "People of the Abyss," the latter representing a quintet of outcasts on a Thames Embankment bench, he displays a sympathetic touch that lifts its canvases to the loftiest pinnacle of art. Among his best-known works, other than portraits, are "Les Habitues," "The Daughter's Return," "Don Quixote," and "The Absinthe Drinkers," a canvas showing types of the underworld, and which appeared in the Paris Salon. In 1912 he received the ribbon of a Chevalier of the Legion of Honor, awarded by the French government. He was a member of the Societé des Artists Française (Paris), the International Society of Painters and Sculptors, the Paris Society of American Painters, the Institute Français aux Etats Unis, the National Academy of Design, New York, and the National Association of Portrait Painters. He was a Royal Knight of La Mancha, and received distinguished honors from art circles all over the world. He was awarded honorable mention in the Paris Salon in 1904, in 1906 he received the medal of the third class, in 1908 the medal of the second class, and then followed his decoration in the year of his death. In addition to the soundness of his technique, he possessed the faculty of painting portraits from the psychological point of view as well as from the picturesque. Any portrait he produced was a work of art, and as such would claim attention whether the beholder knew the subject or not. Mr. MacCameron was characterized by perfect mental equipoise and a magnetic personality and talent marvelously combined. His sympathy with all classes of his fellow-men was quick and strong, while he was idolized by the models who sat for his pictures of the poor. The accompanying portrait is a copy of a painting by himself. He was married July 31, 1902, to Louise, daughter of John Van Voorhis, a distinguished lawyer of Rochester and a descendant of old Dutch settlers of New York. The yhad two children: Robert Francis and Marguerite MacCameron. He died in New York city, Dec. 29, 1912.

ZUKOR, Adolph, theatrical producer, was born in Hungary, Jan. 7, 1873, son of Jacob and Hannah (Lieberman) Zukor. He came to America in 1888, and after learning the fur business with A. A. Frankel in New York city, he started a fur business of his own in Chicago, in 1892, in partnership with Max Schosberg. Schosberg withdrew two years later, and in 1897 he formed a partnership with Morris Kohn and continued in that business until 1904. Meanwhile he had invested in a penny arcade in New York city, and the venture proved so profitable that he decided to go into the amusement business on a larger scale. In 1906 he became associated with William A. Brady in a show called "Hale's Touring Cars," and henceforth he devoted himself altogether to the moving picture and vaudeville business. He was one of the first to perceive the extent of the public's interest in educational moving pictures, and the featuring of educational pictures has since been an important part of his policy. With Marcus Loew, a personal friend, he leased the Grand Street Theater, New York, and turned it into a moving picture house. This was the first time in New York that a legitimate theater had been used for that purpose, and the venture excited much comment. It was an unqualified business success, and within six months the partners sold their lease at a profit of $100,000. Assuredly the moving picture form of entertainment had come to stay, and it was time to take it seriously. Mr. Zukor now organized the Famous Players Film Co., and securing the coöperation of Daniel Frohman, one of the most noted of living managers, produced a long list of high-class plays, such as Sarah Bernhardt in the

part of Queen Elizabeth, James K. Hackett in "The Prisoner of Zenda," James O'Neill in "Count of Monte Cristo," Lillie Langtry in "His Neighbor's Wife," Mrs. Fiske in "Tess of the D'Ubervilles," the Belasco original all-star cast in "A Good Little Devil," "The Silver King," "The Masquerader," "Saints and Sinners," and "The Dancing Girl," by Sir Henry Arthur Jones; "The Eternal City," by Hall Caine; "Madama Butterfly," "Madame X," "The County Chairman," "Peter Pan," "Trilby," "Secret Service," "Held by the Enemy," "Sherlock Holmes," "The Thief," "The Sign of the Cross," "Zaza," "Mistress Nell," "Jim, the Penman," "Everywoman" and Monsieur Beaucaire." In addition to the activities of the various studios of the Famous Players Film Co., situated in New York city, Los Angeles and London, Mr. Zukor effected an alliance with Charles Frohman and Henry W. Savage, two of the most prominent theatrical producers in the world, whereby he secured for film purposes the long list of dramatic successes controlled by these managers. Mr. Zukor is president of the Famous Players Film Co., and treasurer of the Marcus Loew Theatrical Enterprises, and he is without doubt one of the most prominent and vital figures in the theatrical world of to-day. He was married Jan. 10, 1897, to Lottie, daughter of Herman Kauffman, of Chicago, Ill., and has two children: Eugene J. and Mildred Zukor.

HAIGHT, George W., lawyer, was born at Cuba, N. Y., in 1842, son of Gen. Samuel S. and Maria W. (Cheeseman) Haight. His first American ancestor was Simon Hoyt, a native of England, who emigrated before 1630 and settled at Charlestown, Mass. The line of descent is traced through his son John and his wife Mary, their son John and his wife Elizabeth, their son Jonathan, of Rye, New York, who used the name Haight, and his wife, Susanna Theall, and their son Stephen and his wife, Margaret Cooke, who were the grandparents of the subject. Gen. Samuel Haight was an officer in the war of 1812, and afterward practiced law at Cuba, N. Y. A notable incident of his legal career was when he appeared in the celebrated Church murder case at Angelica as opposing counsel to his eldest son, Fletcher M. Haight (q. v.), also a lawyer, and who later became a judge in southern California. The preliminary education of George W. Haight was received at the Model School for Boys, Lima, N. Y., and at Alfred University, where he spent one year. After serving two years as principal of the Normal and Scientific Institute at Sharon, Wis., he returned to the University of Rochester, where he had previously studied, and graduated in 1874. He went to San Francisco, Cal., and began the study of law in the office of Haight & Taylor, of which Gov. Henry H. Haight (q. v.) was senior partner, and was admitted to the bar. Upon the death of Gov. Haight he formed a partnership with the surviving member of the firm, Edward Robeson Taylor, who was afterward mayor of San Francisco. He succeeded his nephew, Gov. Haight, as counsel for the Protestant Orphan Asylum of San Francisco, the most largely endowed charitable organization there, and continued in that capacity for thirty years. Meanwhile he had made extensive investments in real estate, and in 1893 the partnership was dissolved so as to give him greater freedom for his personal affairs. He owned a two and one-quarter acre home in Berkeley and also 1,000 acres near Richmond, Cal. In 1906 he formed a partnership with his son, Samuel

C. Haight, under the name of Haight & Haight, with offices in Berkeley. He was a member of the Theta Delta Chi fraternity and the first president of the Pacific Coast Graduates' Association of that society. As a lawyer he was keen, astute and resourceful. He possessed a magnetic personality which made his influence over others great. He had deep respect for the ethics of his profession, and he early gained a reputation for his remarkable success and ability in persuading clients, or prospective clients, to settle their differences outside of the courts. Naturally this advice and his steadfast refusal to profit personally at the expense of others inspired much admiration from all with whom he came in contact. He was an absolute authority on the complicated Spanish land grant laws of California, and in his ability to unravel the intricacies of such cases he was without a peer. His salient characteristics were modest self-effacement, heartful loving-kindness, remarkable foresight, calm, courageous judgment, sereneness of manner and of soul, and absolute surrender at the call of duty. His fairness, his considerateness, his sturdy and courteous manner never forsook him, and made him a man to lean upon and to carry human burdens. An incident of his mental power was the memorizing after he was sixty years of age of Arnold's "Light of the World," which required an hour and forty-five minutes without interruption to recite. He was always a busy man, yet he found time to give generous support and hard work to innumerable good causes. He took part in many reform movements for the better government of San Francisco, and his life was an admirable example to every citizen because of his patriotic labors for the welfare of the municipality, for his breadth of interests and for his disinterested devotion to worthy public causes. He was married at Batavia, N. Y., Sept. 27, 1881, to Mary Ellen, daughter of David Haydn Setchel. For many years Mrs. Haight was notable as a talented English reader and for her able participation in educational and club activities. She survives him, with one son, Samuel Chase Haight. He died at Berkeley, Cal., Sept. 23, 1913.

KOZLOWSKI, Edward, auxiliary bishop of the Roman Catholic archdiocese of Milwaukee, Wis., was born at Tarnow, Galicia, Austrian Poland, Nov. 11, 1860. In his youth he served in the Austrian army and pursued his classical studies in his native land. Coming to the United States at the age of twenty-five, he entered St. Francis' Seminary, Milwaukee, Wis., for his theological course and was ordained priest on June 29, 1887, by Bishop Richter, of Grand Rapids, Mich. He spoke English, French and German as well as Polish, and during his ministry attained quite a reputation as an energetic, tactful priest, a careful financier and a successful church builder. He was pastor at Midland and Manistee, Mich., until 1890, when he was put in charge of the church at Bay City. In the movement for Polish representation among the hierarchy of the United States he was one of the leaders, and on Oct. 13, 1913, he was appointed auxiliary bishop of Milwaukee. He was consecrated in St. John's Cathedral on Jan. 14, 1914, being the second Polish priest to be appointed to a bishopric in the United States. He had just begun to develop the details of this office when death cut short his career. He died in Milwaukee, Wis., Aug. 7, 1915.

MEACHAM, Franklin Adams, physician, was born in Cumberland Gap, Rock Castle county, Ky., Oct. 28, 1862, son of Dr. Franklin and Sarah (Adams) Meacham. His father was a U. S. army surgeon, who served through the civil war as medical director of the army of the Cumberland. On his mother's side he was descended from Henry Adams, who landed in Boston, Mass., in 1630 from Devonshire, England, with eight sons. He was prepared for college at Phillips Academy, Andover, Mass., and was graduated at Yale University in 1887. After receiving his degree of M. D. from the medical department of the University of Virginia in 1889, he located in Salt Lake City, Utah, where he quickly secured a large general practice. He was appointed associate surgeon to the Holy Cross hospital of that city, and on June 30, 1890, was appointed city physician and a member of the board of health of Salt Lake City, being the first gentile that ever held that office in that city. He served four years as U. S. examining surgeon for pensions. His most important work was as chief house inspector in the Philippine Islands, where his heroic efforts in fighting unsanitary conditions won high praise. He went to Manila, P. I., in 1900 as chief of the House Department and when Asiatic cholera broke out in 1902, he at once took energetic measures for eradicating the plague and for removing the source of the evil by the extermination of rats, the fungus treatment for the extermination of locusts and the virus inoculation for plague prevention. Dr. Meacham was an able demonstrator and was endowed with the faculty, as valuable as it was unusual, to discharge disagreeable duties in such a way as to win not only the respect but the regard of those most injuriously affected. He sacrificed his life in the discharge of his duty, dying in Manila, Apr. 14, 1902.

KIDDER, Jerome Henry, surgeon and scientist, was born in Baltimore county, Md., Oct. 26, 1842, son of Camillus and Mary (Herrick) Kidder. He was graduated at Harvard College in 1862. He was appointed a medical cadet during the civil war, and the study of medicine, begun at that time, was continued at the University of Maryland, where he received his medical degree in 1866. He was commissioned assistant surgeon in the U. S. navy and was promoted to past assistant surgeon in 1871 and to surgeon in 1876. Resigning his commission in 1884, he became especially interested in chemical and physical research. He was a member of the United States government's party sent out to observe the transit of Venus at Kerguelen Island in 1874, and the results of his researches in natural history were published in the bulletins of the National Museum in 1875—76. He resigned his position in the navy in 1884 and was appointed chemist to the Fish Commission. Dr. Kidder was a contributor to the National Medical Dictionary, compiled by Dr. John S. Billings, and he wrote many other valuable reports and papers on medical, sanitary and scientific subjects. He was married at Constantinople, Sept. 18, 1878, to Anne Mary, daughter of Horace Maynard of Tennessee, and had three children: Anne Maynard, wife of Prof. Edwin Bidwell Wilson, the mathematician; Henry Maynard, and Dorothy Laura, wife of Lawrasor Riggs of New York. He died suddenly from pneumonia Apr. 8, 1889.

SHAFTER, Oscar Lovell, jurist, was born in Athens, Vt., Oct. 19, 1812, son of William Rufus and Mary (Lovell) Shafter. His grandfather, James Shafter, fought with the revolutionists at Bunker Hill, Bennington, Saratoga and in other engagements, and was a member of the Vermont legislature for twenty-five years. His father was a farmer and merchant, county judge, legislator and member of the constitutional convention of his state in 1836. Oscar L. Shafter was educated at

Wilbraham, Mass., Academy and at the Wesleyan University, where he was graduated in 1834. Afterward he studied law at the Harvard Law School under Judge Story, and was graduated in 1836. He began practice at Wilmington, Vt., and rapidly rose to the front rank of the bar of his native state. He took an active part in politics, and on one occasion was the abolitionist candidate for governor, and on another for United States senator. Through the influence of Trenor W. Park, a brother attorney who had gone West during the gold excitement of 1849, Mr. Shafter received an offer of $10,000 a year from the law firm of Halleck, Peachy, Billings & Park in San Francisco, and went to California, in 1854, without taking his family. One year later he joined with Gen. Williams and Mr. Park in organizing the firm of C. H. S. Williams, Shafter & Park. The offices of the new firm were noted for efficiency of organization remarkable in that early day. Besides employing a bookkeeper and cashier, and having their own notary, the various phases of legal work were assigned to departments, each under a competent head. Under the partnership agreement each member of the firm retained for himself the practice of clients previously acquired, and, besides handsome personal fees from this source, the end of the first year showed that the firm had realized $110,000 above expenses. His practice continued with remarkable success for several years. He successfully conducted the suit of Bensley-Perkins & Co. vs. Mountain Lake Water Co., involving property valued at $1,500,000, and continued for years as attorney for the Bensley Water Co., the pioneer water company of the San Francisco section. He was also attorney for the "Evening Bulletin." Some of his notable cases related to the determination of titles in connection with large Spanish land grants of the state, the intimate knowledge thus gained giving him excellent advantages for acquiring considerable areas for himself. He was one of the first to introduce the successful policy of tenant farming, committing to the responsibility of each various designated portions of a 60,000-acre rancho near Point Reyes. In this he displayed the same capacity for efficient business organization that he had in connection with his professional practice. He was distinguished as a lawyer "of massive intellectual strength and unequaled forensic power in debate." During the activities of the vigilantes in California his influence was sturdily on the side of law and order regardless of his personal sympathies, and his resolute moral character stands out in history among the very few who were not caught in the whirlpool of moral irresponsibility which claimed so many even among the strongest men. A letter written to his father in the East before his family had yet joined him expressed this attitude as follows: "My family attachments have if possible a greater ascendency than ever in my isolation, and the great law of conscience is in my thought more fully than even at home." He was among the first group of judges to be elected following the amendment to the state constitution providing for separate elections and increasing to ten years the term of office of supreme court judges. He began his term of office as associate justice in January, 1864, but resigned in 1867 because of ill health. This marked his retirement from both professional and judicial life, and he went abroad in the hope of regaining his failing strength. The decisions of the supreme court during his service are contained in Vols. 24 to 34, inclusive, California Reports. Of the 900 decisions handed down during this period he wrote 140, and his conclusions were rarely questioned. The honorary degree of LL.D. was conferred upon him by the College of California. Judge Shafter's professional activities, together with his intense loyalty to every tie and responsibility of his family, absorbed his life. His brief hours of leisure were spent in the indulgence of his great conversational powers in his own home, his instant command of a remarkably wide range of poetry, romance and history entertaining alike family and friends. His language was elegant in its simplicity and he had a great sense of humor, which frequently illuminated his logic with a sudden flash of light. His fatherhood in its fullest sense was exemplary and his application of principles in guiding the mental development of his children was prophetic of the best educational methods widely adopted many years later. He was remarkably genial in his social relations; he loved the society of young men, to talk with them, counsel them, encourage them in their plans and studies. Exact in his business, he was yet bounteous in his benefactions. He gave without ostentation, but liberally and continuously. It was said of him that his "life was a daily record and teacher of faithfulness, of wisdom, of patience, of courtesy, of gravity and mirthfulness, of singular tenderness, of modest benevolence and parental love. From himself, from his earnest soul, his ceaseless labor and reverence for wisdom beyond himself he was most honored." He was married at Wilmington, Vt., in 1840, to Sarah Riddell, and had seven daughters and one son. Judge Shafter died at Florence, Italy, Jan. 23, 1873.

BYLLESBY, Henry Marison, electrical engineer, was born at Pittsburgh, Pa., Feb. 16, 1859, son of Rev. De Witt Clinton and Sarah (Matthews) Byllesby, and grandson of Langdon and Mary (Salade) Byllesby. He was educated in the public schools of Pittsburgh and at Lehigh University, but did not graduate. He began his professional career in the employ of the Corliss engine works of Robert Wetherill & Co., of Chester, Pa., and the Edison Electric Light Co. He made all of the drawings and many of the designs for the first central station in New York city, this being one of the first two electric central stations to be built. Subsequently he had charge of the Edison Company's operations in Canada, and served as representative of that company at different points in the United States. During 1885-90 Mr. Byllesby was first vice-president and general manager of the Westinghouse Electric & Manufacturing Co., of Pittsburgh, and also managing director of the Westinghouse Electric Co. of London, England. He was at one time first vice-president of the Electric Vehicle Co. of New York city; vice-president of the Washington Light and Traction Co., Washington, D. C., and first vice-president of the General Electric Co. at Portland, Ore., having organized the last in 1892, and being largely instrumental in financing the company and constructing the plant. He resigned in 1902 to organize an engineering business of his own in Chicago, Ill., under the firm name of H. M. Byllesby & Co., operators of public utility companies, and of which he is president. The company has branch offices in New York city and Tacoma, Wash. He is also an officer and director of the Mobile (Ala.) Electric Co., the Fort Smith (Ark.) Light and Traction Co., the Oklahoma Gas and Electric Co., Oklahoma City, Okla., the Enid (Okla.) Electric and Gas Co., the Muskogee (Okla.) Gas and Electric Co., the Ottumwa (Ia.) Railway and Light Co., the San

Adolph Zukor

Diego (Cal.) Consolidated Gas and Electric Co., the Tacoma (Wash.) Gas Co., the Northern Idaho and Montana Power Co., and a director of the Chicago, Milwaukee and Puget Sound Railway Co., and the Bellingham and Northern Railway Co., the Public Service Co. of London, England, and the Public Utilities Corporation of Boston, Mass. Mr. Byllesby was active in the introduction of the alternating system of electric current at the time when the prevailing use of electricity was by means of low-tension, continuous current, and he has taken out some forty-five patents on various electric distribution systems and electrical apparatus using the alternating current. He was chairman of the executive board of the Civic Federation of Chicago for two years, and at the present time is a member of the executive committee and treasurer of that organization. He is a member of the National Electric Light Association, American Society of Civil Engineers, American Society of Mechanical Engineers, American Society of Electrical Engineers, Western Society of Civil Engineers, and the National Civic Federation. He is also a director of the Chicago Grand Opera Co. and a member of the Chicago, Union League, Midday, University, and the Glenview clubs of Chicago, the Metropolitan, Lawyers, Railway, and Recess clubs of New York city, the Minnesota Club of St. Paul, Minn.; the Minneapolis Club of Minneapolis, Minn.; the Arlington Club of Portland, Ore.; the Pendennis Club of Louisville, Ky.; the Lake Geneva, Wis., Country Club and the Lake Geneva, Wis., Yacht Club. He was married, June 15, 1882, to Margaret Stearns, daughter of Henry P. Baldwin, of Roselle, N. J.

PENFIELD, Frederic Courtland, author and diplomat, was born at East Hadden, Conn., Apr. 23, 1855, son of Daniel and Sophia (Young) Penfield. He was educated in Russell's Military School at New Haven, Conn., and completed his studies in Germany. He selected journalism for his vocation, and spent five years on the reportorial and editorial staff of the Hartford "Courant," but his newspaper career was terminated by his appointment as vice-consul-general in London, England, in 1885. He accordingly took up seriously the study of diplomacy, and since that period has been recognized as an authority on the subject. Upon the election of Pres. Harrison he retired from the London post, and became a writer on topics of world politics and international relations. When Pres. Cleveland returned to Washington Mr. Penfield served the administration for a time as an adviser on the diplomatic and consular service, always advocating especial fitness rather than political influence in filling positions. In 1893 he was appointed United States minister to Argentine, but before the appointment was published he was named for diplomatic agent and consul-general to Egypt with the rank of minister resident. While serving at the Egyptian capital he won the close friendship of Khedive Abbas, became a potential influence in the public life of Cairo, and administered the affairs of his office with marked success. Following his retirement in 1897 he traveled extensively throughout the Far East and in Africa. In 1913 Pres. Wilson appointed him to be ambassador to Austria-Hungary, and as a reward for a masterly treatise on the political control of the White Nile he was awarded the gold medal by the French Academy. When the United States was debating the rival projects for an isthmian canal, Mr. Penfield conducted a vigorous propaganda in favor of the Panama route, and advocated in strongest terms the justice of dealing fairly with the French people. When finally our government contracted with the old French Panama Co. to purchase its rights, franchises and property, in recognition of Mr. Penfield's services, the French government decorated him with the cross of the Legion of Honor (1904). Previously he had been awarded the decoration of the Palmes Academique. On retiring from office in Egypt, the Ottoman government gave him the grand cross of the Order of the Medjidieh, and the Khedive of Egypt made him grand commander of the Osmanieh. Other honors that have been conferred upon him are the Takova cross from Servia, and the grand cross of St. Gregory the Great, conferred on him by Pope Pius X. in 1911 in acknowledgment of his generous support of Catholic educational and charitable institutions, he being the first American to receive the highest class of this order. Mr. Penfield's work as an author may be said to have begun with his connection with the Hartford "Courant." He has written "Present Day Egypt" (1899) and "East of Suez" (1907), which are standard authorities on their subjects, and many scholarly articles on various economical and international subjects of importance; he contributed to the "North American Review," the "Forum," the "Century Magazine," "Saturday Evening Post," the "Review of Reviews," etc. Mr. Penfield is a member of the Authors' Club, the New York Yacht Club, the Manhattan Club and the Century Club of New York, and the Metropolitan Club of Washington, D. C., and is a fellow of the Royal Geographical Society, England. He was twice married, first in April, 1892, to Katharine Alberta McMurdo, daughter of Albert Wells of Palmyra, N. Y. She died in 1905, and on Feb. 26, 1908, he was married to Anne, daughter of William Weightman (q.v.), of Philadelphia, Pa., and widow of Robert J. C. Walker. Mrs. Penfield is an accomplished linguist, and a patron of art, music and literature. Her gifts to Catholic institutions and charities have been munificent, and she has frequently been honored by the Pope. The honorary degree of L.L.D. was conferred upon him in 1914 by Hobart College an dthe Catholic University of Washington, D. C. Portrait opposite page 312.

STEWARDSON, Langdon Cheves, clergyman, fourteenth president of Hobart College (1903-13), was born in Marietta, Ga., Nov. 10, 1850, son of Dr. Thomas and Hannah (Hollingsworth) Stewardson. He was graduated at Kenyon College in 1873. He studied theology at an Episcopal school in Philadelphia, Pa., and took courses in philosophy, psychology and pedagogy at the universities of Leipzig, Tubingen and Berlin for three years, after which he was ordained priest of the Protestant Episcopal church in 1878. His first pastorate was the Church of the Reconciliation at Webster, Mass., and in 1889 he received a call to St. Mark's Church, Worcester, Mass. In 1898 he was appointed professor of philosophy at Lehigh University, and held this chair for five years, when in 1903 he was elected president of Hobart College to succeed Robert E. Jones. During the ten years he was president, Hobart's endowment grew from $600,000 to $1,200,000; the special student system was abolished, and with the addition of new laboratory buildings it enlarged its scientific curriculum, enabling it to confer the degree of B.Sc. Many of the old college buildings were remodeled and important new ones added, such as the Medbery dormitories, a gymnasium building with swimming pool, Smith Hall, containing the biological and psychological laboratories, and other buildings of the William Smith College for Women, made possible by the gift of $490,000 from William Smith, of Geneva, N. Y. The faculty was strengthened and made adequate to carry the students satisfactorily on the liberal degree of A.B. or the scientific degree of B.Sc. Pres. Stewardson held office ten years, when he was succeeded by Lyman P. Powell.

POWELL, Lyman Pierson, fifteenth president of Hobart College, was born at Farmington, Del., Sept. 21, 1866, son of James Ben Ralston and Mary Anna (Redden) Powell, and grandson of George and Mary (Hall) Powell, of Welsh ancestry. He spent one year at Dickinson College and was graduated at Johns Hopkins University in 1890. He took post-graduate courses in history, jurisprudence and economics at Johns Hopkins, the University of Wisconsin and the University of Pennsylvania, and was graduated at the Philadelphia Divinity School in 1897. Ordained to the ministry of the Protestant Episcopal church, his first appointment was at Ambler, Pa., a small parish which he found worshipping in a chapel, but which he left in a church erected at a cost of nearly $250,000. From Ambler he went to the Church of St. John at Lansdowne, Pa., where he remained for five years and built a stone church which is a model of semi-rural architecture. In 1904 he was called to St. John's Church, Northampton, Mass., and while there came in close contact with the problems of college education at both Smith and Amherst colleges. He became a regular contributor to the "Daily Hampshire Gazette" and was in demand as a speaker. His study of educational problems led to a series of articles in which he defended the position of colleges upon the subject of religion. His interest in psychotherapy led to an experiment locally adapted to the special needs of his parish, an account of which he published in book form. In 1912 Dr. Powell became professor of business ethics at New York University, and at the close of his first year there was called to be president of Hobart College and William Smith College, at Geneva, N. Y. Following a year's interregnum, when Dean William P. Durfee served as acting president, he was inaugurated and at once took charge. His administration began very auspiciously, following the ten years' expansion and development of Pres. Stewardson's administration. Hobart College has attained a high standard of scholarship, and has been pointed out as the best example of the efficient small college. In a series of competitions among several American colleges, covering a term of years, three-fourths of all the honors fell to Hobart. The attendance for the season 1913–14 passed the hundred mark, and it is now (1915–16) 140 at Hobart and 108 at William Smith. Pres. Powell received the honorary degrees of D.D. from Dickinson College in 1913 and LL.D. from Rochester University in the same year. He is an occasional contributor to such magazines as the "Review of Reviews," the "Atlantic Monthly," the "Outlook," "Good Housekeeping," the "Chautauquan" and "Harper's Weekly," and is the author of: "The History of Education in Delaware" (1893); "Family Prayers" (1905); "Christian Science—A Critical Estimate" (1907); "The Art of Natural Sleep" (1908); "The Emmanuel Movement in a New England Town" (1909); "Heavenly Heretics" (1910), and "Religion in Colleges and Universities" (1912). He has also edited: "Historic Towns of New England" (1898); "Historic Towns of the Middle States" (1899); "Historic Towns of the Southern States" (1900); "Historic

Towns of the West" (1901); "Current Religious Literature" (1902), and "The Devotional Series," 3 vols. (1905–07). He is a member of the American Academy of Political Science and the National Civic Federation. He was married, June 20, 1899, to Gertrude, daughter of Dr. Francis Wilson, of Jenkintown, Pa. Mrs. Powell, a graduate of Wellesley, was for a number of years teacher of history in the girls' seminary at Troy, N. Y., and has been active in college affairs and social life. They have two sons: Talcott Williams and Francis Wilson Powell.

BOYNTON, George W., soldier of fortune, was born in New York city May 1, 1842. The name "George W. Boynton" was assumed. He inherited from his father, who was a distinguished New York surgeon, a comfortable fortune which was safely invested for his benefit. He ran away from home at nineteen years of age and enlisted in the civil war in a troop of cavalry. He served under Gen. Grant along the lower Mississippi, and was present at the battles of Pittsburg Landing and Shiloh, in the latter engagement receiving a saber cut in the cheek. Resigning from the army, he engaged in blockade running for a year and then formed a partnership with "Jim" Fisk in the operation of a distillery in Brooklyn, with which they made $350,000 in less than two years. In 1868 he conceived the idea of aiding the Cuban insurgents by furnishing them with arms, ammunition and other supplies, and then began a series of adventures as a filibuster, Fisk being still his partner in the financial part. At the outbreak of the Franco-Prussian war he disposed of several cargoes of war materials to the French, on each occasion nearly losing his ship and his life. About this time the Spanish government engaged in quelling an insurrection in the Philippines, and Don Carlos seized the opportunity to attempt to overthrow the ruling house. Capt. Boynton opened a negotiations with the pretender, and sold him a cargo of rifles. He also chartered several ships in British ports, bought large cargoes of war supplies, and ran the blockade successfully. He never received payment from Don Carlos, who even planned Capt. Boynton's death to avoid collection of the debt. What he regarded as his most exciting adventure was an expedition against Chinese pirates in the China Sea, which he conducted in 1874–75. With three vessels and twenty-five men he made war on the numerous Chinese and Malay pirates for two years, capturing numerous junks, killing scores of their crews. And it was all for sheer love of excitement and adventure, for the prospect of financial reward was always subordinate, and in this instance he divided the loot among his men. In 1876, when trouble arose in the Balkans, he took sides with the Servians and Montenegrins against the Turks. He also sold munitions of war to the Russians, and was present at the siege of Plevna. He next sought adventure in the Orient, taking part in any disturbance he could find in China and visiting Japan. He now went to the gold diggings of Australia. A revolution breaking out in Chile, he hastened there and identified himself with the party opposing the government. He next visited Central America, seeking a fortune in that field of revolution. Then he saw an opportunity for excitement in attempting the escape of Arabi Pasha, who had led a rebellion in Egypt against the British in 1881, and had been sentenced to life imprisonment in Ceylon, but he had scarcely completed his arrangements for this adventure when Arabi Pasha was released. When trouble broke out in

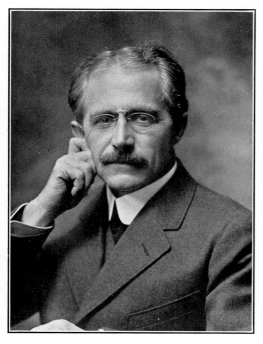

LYMAN P. POWELL
PRESIDENT HOBART COLLEGE

GEORGE W. BOYNTON
ADVENTURER

JAMES G. WHITE
EDUCATOR

FREDERIC C. PENFIELD
DIPLOMAT

Charles D. Nash

Venezuela, Capt. Boynton went there to assist in the overthrow of Pres. Castro. During the last struggle of the Cubans for independence he was again blockade-running, when he was captured by the Spaniards and sentenced to be shot at sunrise. His negro attendant informed the British officers in the vicinity that Boynton was a Mason, and they effected his escape before the time set for the execution. Capt. Boynton ran the blockade at Rio Janeiro during the revolt in Brazil in 1893. Having thus figured in scores of hair-breadth escapes in nearly every country where trouble had occurred, he was made the hero of a novel, "Soldiers of Fortune," by Richard Harding Davis, a bid for immortality which Capt. Boynton greatly resented. He evinced much fondness for Venezuela and Valparaiso, and was appointed resident director of the Oronoco Corporation in New York city. He was a type of adventurer often met with in fiction and rarely in real life. He was a tall, bronzed, athletic, broad-shouldered man with a constitution of iron and nerves of steel, utterly fearless, supremely selfish and cheerfully arrogant. The story of his life is told in "The Wark Maker," by Horace Smith. He died in New York Jan. 19, 1911.

WHITE, James Garrard, educator, was born at Harrodsburg, Ky., Oct. 16, 1846, son of Henry Hall and Nannie (Garrard) White, and a descendant of Elder John White, a native of Messing, England, who emigrated in 1632 and settled in Cambridge, Mass. James Garrard White was educated by his father until the age of twelve, when he entered the academy of Kentucky University, where his father was professor of mathematics. Impaired health necessitated his retirement to the country in his senior year, and he contemplated entering commercial life when his health would permit. In 1868, however, he was selected as a tutor in mathematics and Latin and assigned to duty in the Agricultural and Mechanical College, then one of the colleges of Kentucky University. During the forty-five years that he was connected with state college and university he held the following offices: instructor of mathematics, 1868–69; adjunct professor of mathematics, 1869–72; secretary of the faculty, 1870–78; professor of mathematics and astronomy, 1877–1913; dean of the College of Arts and Science, 1892–1909; business agent, 1893–1900; vice-president, 1909–13; acting president, 1910–11, and dean of men, 1911–13. Prof. White made the supervision of the state university interests his life work, and it is difficult to properly estimate the part for wholesome good that he played in the history of the institution. He was a lifelong member of the Christian Church, in which he was a deacon and Sunday-school teacher. There was no more kindlier or benign influence in educational affairs in Kentucky than that exerted by Prof. White, and there never was a teacher in his community that set before his students a higher standard of gentleness, patience and Christian charity. The present high standing of the Kentucky State University is due in a great measure to his ability and loyal devotion. He assumed the heaviest burdens of any member of the faculty pertaining to student welfare. In 1887 the university conferred upon him the degree of M.A. He was married at Harrodsburg, Ky., Aug. 11, 1869, to Elizabeth A., daughter of Frederick Ripperdan, of Danville, Ky., who survived him, with two daughters: Clara Warland and Martha Ripperdan, wife of George F. Blessing, of Swarthmore College. He died at Lexington, Ky., July 18, 1913. Portrait opposite page 312.

SMALLEY, Frank, educator, was born at Towanda, Pa., Dec. 10, 1846, son of Isaac and Sarah (Compton) Smalley. He was educated at the Susquehannah Collegiate Institute, Towanda, and at Northwestern University, Evanston, Ill., and was graduated at Syracuse University in 1874. The degree of A.M. was conferred on him on examination in geology in 1876. He was instructor in geology, zoology and botany at Syracuse University in 1874–77 and was then transferred to the department of Latin. He was adjunct professor of Latin in 1877–81, and since that time has been professor of the Latin language and literature. He has been professor of the theory and practice of teaching Latin in the Teachers' College since 1906. He was registrar of the university during 1894–1900; was acting dean of the College of Liberal Arts from September, 1900, to January, 1901, and since the latter date has been dean of the college. He was acting chancellor of the university in the summer of 1903 and during the college year 1908–09. Prof. Smalley has edited "Alumni Record and General Catalogue of Syracuse University, 1835–99" (1899), Vol. II (1904) and Vol. III (1912); and has also published "Latin Analysis" (1879); "Latin Verse" (1884) "Lucretius: Philosopher and Poet" (1880); "Latin Etymology" (1882); "Introduction and Notes to the Fifth Book of Cicero's Tusculan Disputations" (1892); "Brief Selections to Illustrate Roman Literature" (1894); Libretto, "Plauti Trinummus" (1895); "Syllabus of Lectures in Roman History" (1895); "Status of Classical Studies in Secondary Schools" (1899), and also Latin hymns, translations, etc. Prof. Smalley is a member of the American Institute of Archæology, the Classical Association of the Atlantic States, the New York State Classical Teachers' Association, of which he was president during 1907–10, and a member of the managing committee of the American School of Classical Studies at Rome. He received the degree of LL.D. from Colgate and Union colleges in 1909. He was married Sept. 7, 1876, to Jennie, daughter of Abram Mather, of Rushville, N. Y., and has one son: Frank Mather Smalley.

NASH, Charles Dexter, merchant, was born at Abington, Plymouth co., Mass., Dec. 4, 1843, son of Eleazar Dexter and Annie Reed (Hunt) Nash. His earliest paternal American ancestor was James Nash, a native of England, who emigrated in 1628 and settled at Weymouth, Mass. Through him the line of descent is traced to his son Jacob, his son James and his wife, Experience Petty; their son James and his wife, Mary Pratt; their son James and his wife, Tamar Bates; their son James and his wife, Sarah Brown, and their son James and his wife, Mary Otis Churchill, who were the grandparents of the subject. James Nash, settler, was thrice representative to the general court, as was his son Jacob, who was also a lieutenant in the Weymouth militia. James, of the third generation, was an ensign in the British service in the French and Indian war, and he was the first town treasurer of Abington. Charles Dexter Nash was educated in the public schools and at Payson Commercial College, Boston, and began his business career as a telegraph operator and clerk in the drug store of a relative in his native town. In July, 1862, he enlisted as a private in company C, 38th regiment, Massachusetts volunteer infantry; was promoted corporal, was with Gen. Banks at Port Hudson, Gen. Sheridan in the Shenandoah valley and participated in all the engagements and battles of the 19th army corps. In 1866 he re-entered the drug business at Fitchburg, Mass., and subsequently engaged independently in the drug and jewelry business at South Abington, now Whitman, Mass. There he entered actively and enthusiastically into all town matters, and was soon the acknowledged leader in every civic, municipal, political and commercial undertaking, as well as in all social affairs. At one time, when Whitman joined with Plymouth to prevent the removal of the courthouse to Brockton, Mr. Nash was put forward to lead their representation, and appearing in Boston he prevailed over an array of able lawyers retained to plead the opposing claims. He introduced the telephone, projected the street railway system, was active in the formation of the savings bank and the Whitman Co-operative Bank, founded in 1886 the Whitman Unitarian Church and became a trustee, was president of the Plymouth and Bay conference of Unitarian churches; was for years water, park and road commissioner, and as a member of the school committee introduced many reforms. He was the Democratic candidate for secretary of state in Massachusetts and enjoyed a state-wide reputation as a public speaker. For years he sang in the quartette of the Whitman church, and was likewise a member of the Owl Quartette, of Whitman. He retired from the drug business in 1901 and went to Chicago for a brief period. Later he became clerk in the office of the secretary of the commonwealth of Massachusetts, and subsequently superintendent of the Soldiers' Home. He was commander of Whitman Post, G. A. R., and junior vice, senior vice-commander and commander (1887) of the department of Massachusetts. He was a member of Puritan lodge of Masons, Massasoit lodge, Knights of Honor and Whitman lodge, N. E. O. P. He was a man of matchless courage. Positive in his convictions he was bold in their advocacy. His course of action, once determined upon, and supported by an approving conscience, no fear of popular disfavor or personal discomfiture could swerve him from his fixed purpose. No matter what the emergency, he was always equal to it. He was married at Abington, Mass., June 7, 1868, to Abbie Louise, daughter of Sylvanus Cushing, 2d, of Abington, who survives him, with three children: Marie Wales, wife of Herbert E. Stevens, U.S.N.; Ethel Sawyer, wife of Herbert R. Brunton, D.D.S., and Grace Copeland, wife of Hugh Heaton, M.D. He died at Whitman, Mass., Aug. 5, 1913.

BARTON, Clara (Clarissa Harlowe), humanitarian, was born at North Oxford, Worcester co., Mass., Dec. 25, 1821, daughter of Capt. Stephen and Sarah (Stone) Bartin, and a descendant of Edward Barton, the first of the family in this country, who came over from England in 1640 and settled first at Salem, Mass., later removing to Portsmouth, N. H., and finally to Cape Porpoise, Me. Her grandfather was Dr. Stephen Barton, who was not successful as a physician because his "generosity forbade him to present his bills to patients." He left a diary giving a full account of the early history of the Barton family, and making clear the remarkable versatility of the man. He could shoe an ox, shingle a barn, keep a store, prescribe for the sick or make a coffin. Her father fought side by side with William Henry Harrison and Richard M. Johnson in the campaign against the Indians of 1793–96 in Michigan, Indiana and Ohio; he was a prosperous farmer and leader in public affairs, and gave his children the best possible education. He was a lover of horses and

one of the first in Worcester county to introduce blooded stock. When a little girl, Clara Barton's brother David taught her to ride bareback on the swift-footed colts of the pasture, broken only to halter and bit. She was a very precocious child, spelling and reading at the age of three, and much of her early book knowledge was also acquired at home under the tutelage of her older brothers and sisters. In addition to regular school work she took private lessons in philosophy, chemistry and Latin. At sixteen she commenced teaching, and later she established at Bordentown, N. J., a free public school, one of the first in the state. At the close of her work at Bordentown, Miss Barton went to Washington to recuperate her never robust health, and to indulge herself in congenial literary pursuits. While there she was appointed by the commissioner of patents, without solicitation on her part, to the first independent clerkship ever held by a woman under our government. She overcame the opposition and antagonism that the appointment aroused by her tact, faithfulness and remarkable executive ability. After the election of Pres. Buchanan, she was deposed, and a large part of her salary withheld, because of her Republican and anti-slavery sentiments. The following three years were spent in the study of art, belles-lettres and languages, and shortly after Lincoln's election she was recalled to the patent office. When the civil war began she refused to draw her salary from an already overtaxed treasury, and, resigning her position, devoted herself to the work of nursing wounded soldiers. Her skill as a nurse had been demonstrated years before, when as a child eleven years of age, alone and unaided, she nursed her brother David through a serious illness resulting from a fall. For two years she said she only left his bedside for half a day. The long confinement and continuous care seriously impaired her own health, but the experience brought out the gift that was in her and was prophetic of things to come. The first wounded soldiers to receive her attention were the men of the Sixth Mass. volunteers, injured in the Baltimore attack of Apr. 19, 1861. She saw at once the great need of woman's help in nursing, feeding and caring for the sick and wounded, and consecrated herself to this task. Women never had been permitted in hospitals, camps or on battlefields, and both military and civil officials declined her services. But in her own unequaled manner she succeeded in gaining their confidence, and finally made her way to the front. Supplies sent to her care poured into Washington from her own and other states and were forwarded at her own expense. Her wonderful work, under the most distressing conditions, in a short time gained her the name of "Angel of the Battlefield." By her quiet self-reliance and prompt decision she obtained such complete recognition that camp and hospital supplies, a corps of assistants and military trains were placed at her disposal. She was always calm, cheerful, well poised and philosophical, but strict and firm in maintaining authority. She never engaged in hospital service. From the beginning her labors were on the battlefield with the wounded and dying. During the four years of the war she endured the exposures and rigors of a soldier's life in action, side by side with the field surgeons and on the hardest fought fields. Always under fire in severe battles, her clothing pierced with bullets and torn by shot, she was exposed at all times, but was never wounded. She was present on sixteen battlefields, among them Cedar Mountain, Second Bull Run, Chantilly, Antietam, Falmouth, old

Clara Barton.

JOHN P. METTAUER

Fredericsburg, the siege of Charleston, the Wilderness, Spotsylvania, the Mine, and the sieges of Petersburg and Richmond. She knew no North nor South, but bestowed her care indiscriminately on the blue and the gray. When the war ended Miss Barton's fame had become national, and her presence was demanded for the lecture platform. She became one of the most highly paid speakers of the day, and from her profits of three winters' tours she laid aside $25,000, which she used in her later work. While visiting Geneva, Switzerland, in 1869, the international committee of the Red Cross called to confer with her, and thus she became acquainted for the first time with the purpose of that organization. Ten years before, Jean Heuri Dunant had written a book describing the horrors of Solferino, and headed a movement for relief from such conditions. In 1864 a convention had been held in Geneva at which almost every civilized nation was represented except the United States. Ten articles of agreement were adopted, known as ''The Treaty of Geneva for the Relief of Sick and Wounded Soldiers,'' providing that all wounded or sick soldiers, the surgeons and nurses attending them, and all hospital and other supplies shall be held neutral in time of war, and shall not be captured by either army. Additional articles were drafted later to include the navy. To this document twelve governments affixed their official signatures, Aug. 22, 1864. In compliment to Switzerland, the Swiss flag, with colors reversed, was adopted for a distinguishing badge of that organization, and thus originated the ''Red Cross,'' which has become the insignia of the greatest humanitarian movement the world has known. Miss Barton was in Berne when war was declared between France and Germany in 1870. She immediately tendered her services, under the Red Cross of Geneva, and was present during nearly all the battles of the war. Her royal highness the Grand Duchess of Baden invited her to aid in establishing the Badine Hospitals; she was present at Hagenau, Metz, Belfor, Woerth and Moutbelard; on the fall of Strasbourg she entered the city with the Germans, organized remunerative labor for impoverished women, and clothed over 30,000 people. She was present during the siege of Paris and the Commune, remaining there two months to distribute money and clothing, and extended succor to the poor of every besieged city of France. When she returned to America she had pledged herself to European nations to devote the rest of her life to introducing and forwarding the institution of the Red Cross in America. The years immediately following were those of invalidism. In 1877 she was well enough to present to Pres. Hayes suggestions and letters from Monsieur Gustav Moynier, president of the International Committee, but it was not until 1882, under the administration of Pres. Arthur, that the treaty was signed. At Miss Barton's suggestion the scope of the Red Cross work in America was extended to aid in any great national calamity, a modification that has become known as the American amendment, and has distinguished the United States as the ''Good Samaritan of Nations.'' After its incorporation she was made president of the American Association of the Red Cross. The list of calamities which brought aid from the Red Cross includes the forest fires in Michigan in 1881; the floods of the Mississippi and Ohio rivers in 1882; the Louisiana cyclone in 1883; and other Ohio river floods in 1884; the Charleston earthquakes in 1886; the Texas famine in 1886; Florida yellow fever epidemic in 1887; the Johnstown disaster in 1889; the hurricane and tidal wave in Galveston, Texas, in 1900, and the San Francisco earthquake in 1906. Twice the Red Cross has carried relief to Russia's famine victims and was present to aid Armenia after the massacres. Miss Barton was present in the camps of the reconcentrados in Cuba during the Spanish-American war, and after the destruction of Cervera's fleet she entered the harbor of Havana in command of the relief ship, the transport Clinton, for which the whole American navy made way. Never before in history of warfare was there a triumphal entry such as this. To insure immediate action in any emergency, Miss Barton placed $3,000 of her own money at the disposal of the committee to meet a sudden demand. She also organized the First Aid Department of the Red Cross Association, whose object is to form classes of instruction in first aid methods. She resigned the presidency in 1905, and soon after the old organization was dissolved and a new one, the American National Red Cross, was incorporated. Her last years were passed at Glen Echo, Md., where she built, as a veritable Red Cross museum, a unique house fashioned after the temporary Red Cross relief work structures, where she stored in fireproof vaults the records and other data relating to the Red Cross Association. On its walls may be seen the numerous diplomas and testimonials presented to her by various rulers of Europe and the German war veterans, the Red Cross of Austria, the sultan of Turkey, the prince of Armenia, the Cartes of Spain, the Portuguese Red Cross, and the governor and legislature of Texas. In cabinets were many jewels and decorations and innumerable medals from potentates and societies, including the Iron Cross of Prussia from Emperor William I. and Empress Augusta. Miss Barton was the only honorary member of the National Woman's Relief Corps. She was a strong advocate of woman suffrage, and attended all the national conventions. In spite of her ability as a speaker, she dreaded this form of publicity, for she was by nature timid and sensitive. In performance of her duties in camp and on battlefield, she was a great commander, but she never asked for favor and aid because she was a woman. Gentleness, moral courage, energy, diplomacy, fidelity to trust and unwavering integrity were her chief characteristics. She had two rules of action—unconcern for what cannot be helped, and control under pressure. A career such as hers teaches that the wealth of human life is not in what it gets, but what it gives, and biographical history has no more eloquent record of self-sacrifice, courage and devoted service to humanity than that of this brave, tender and true woman. Miss Barton represented the United States at international conferences of the Red Cross at Geneva (1884), Carlsruhe (1887), Rome (1890), Vienna (1897), and Russia (1902). She was the author of ''History of the Red Cross'' (1882, published by the U. S. government), ''America's Relief Expedition to Asia Minor'' (1896), ''History of the Red Cross in Peace and War'' (1898), ''A History of the Red Cross'' (1904), ''Story of My Childhood'' (1907), and numerous pamphlets and reports. Her gift for versification showed itself when she was a mere child. Of her poems composed at maturity the most noteworthy are: ''A Christmas Carol'' (1893), and ''Marmora'' (1896). She died at Glen Echo, Md., April 12, 1912.

METTAUER, John Peter, surgeon, was born in Prince Edward county, Va., in 1787, the son of Francis Joseph and Elizabeth (Gaulding) Mett-

auer. His father, who was also a surgeon, came
to this country with Lafayette, and after the revolutionary war was persuaded by prominent citizens
to remain here. The son was graduated at Hampden-Sidney College in 1806 and received his medical instruction at the University of Pennsylvania
under such men as Rush, Shippan, Wistar and
Physick. He received his M. D. degree in 1809 and
built up an extensive practice in his native state.
From 1848 until its discontinuance in 1860 he was
professor of various departments of medicine in
the medical department of Randolph-Macon College. Of the many able men that Virginia has
given to the medical profession, Dr. Mettauer was
unquestionably the most remarkable. His marvelous
surgical skill and ingenuity gained for him such a
reputation that despite the fact of his working in
an obscure country village, patients flocked to him
from all parts of the country and even from
abroad. He performed almost, if not every, operation known to the science, and it is said that he
did over 800 operations for cataract and 400 for
versical calculus, and in the last week of his life,
in his eighty-eighth year, he operated successfully
for cateract, for stone and for excision of the
breast. To him belongs the priority of the cure of
vesico-vaginal fistula, his first successful operation
occurring in August, 1838, and preceding Dr. Hayward's by nearly a year, and Dr. Sims' by ten
years. In this operation he used a concoidal spec-
ulum, curved scissors and lead wire sutures. He
was a strong advocate of lead wire as a suture material in all plastic work. He was the first surgeon in Virginia, and one of the first in America,
to operate successfully for cleft palate (1827).
During the whole of his professional life he was
a constant contributor to medical journals, and his
writings appeared in almost every medical journal
published in this country. The most notable of
his papers was one entitled "The Continued Fever
of Middle Virginia from 1816 to 1829," which
shows that he recognized typhoid as a distinct disease and was familiar with its characteristic lesions.
In other papers he advocated new methods of
treatment and new uses of remedies, often showing that he was far ahead of his time in his views
and practice. In 1837 he organized a number of
his private pupils into a school known as Mettauer's Medical Institute, which, in 1848, became the
medical department of Randolph-Mason College.
He was an ingenious mechanic and many of the
surgical instruments that he used were made by
himself or by workmen under his direction. He is
described as tall, well-formed and robust, with a
high forehead and piercing black eyes overshadowed by heavy brows. A peculiar characteristic was his aversion to the removal of his hat
which was always of the style shown in his portrait. He wore his hat on all occasions, even at
meals and when called upon to testify in court, and
it is said that he left directions that he should be
buried with the hat on. "He is credited," said the
"American Journal of American Sciences" after
his death, "with more improvements in operations
and inventions of instruments to date than any
other man." "Facile princeps of the medical and
surgical profession of the world" was the opinion
of him expressed by Dr. Mutter, of Philadelphia,
in 1845. Dr. Mettauer was four times married:
to a Miss Woodward of Norfolk, a Miss Carter of
Prince Edward county, a Miss Mansfield of a northern state, and to Miss Dyson of Norfolk. He left
three sons: John Peter, Jr., Francis Joseph and
Archer Mettauer, all practising physicians, and
three daughters. He died at his home in Virginia
in November, 1875.

SMITH, William, nurseryman and philanthropist, was born near Canterbury, Kent county,
England, Sept. 2, 1818. His brother, Edward
Smith, had settled at Geneva, N. Y., in 1837, and
established a truck-gardening business. William
and another brother, John, joined him in 1842.
William Smith entered the employ of Isaac
Hildreth, the proprietor of a small nursery, and
after acquiring a good working knowledge of
the business organized with his brothers a similar
undertaking, known as the Geneva Nursery. The
business grew to be one of the greatest in the
country, comprising nearly one thousand acres.
William Smith was an energetic, persistent worker,
possessed keen commercial acumen and foresight,
and was a man of the highest order of honor and
integrity. Kind-hearted, public-spirited and progressive, he was actively identified with many enterprises which added to the growth, development
and wealth of Geneva. He was also one of the
organizers and president of the Standard Optical
Co. and a director of the First National Bank.
He was interested in science to such a degree that
he maintained at his personal expense an observatory which he built near his home, the William
Smith Astronomical Observatory, and engaged Dr.
W. R. Brooks (q. v.) to conduct it. He gave a
million dollars to Hobart College, Geneva, to found
the William Smith College for Women, which was
built in 1906. He died unmarried, in Geneva,
N. Y., Feb 6, 1912.

SCHREMBS, Joseph, R. C. bishop of To-
ledo, was born at Wuzelhofen, near Ratisbon,
Bavaria, Mar. 12, 1866, son of George and Mary
(Gess) Schrembs. His father was the village
blacksmith and young Joseph was one of a family
of sixteen. At the age of four he entered the
Catholic communal school at Raisbon, joined the
Cathedral choir, and began to serve mass in the
Church of St. Ehrhardt. In 1876 he entered the
Progymnasium. His older brother, Rudesind, had
emigrated to America some years before and entered the Benedictine order, so that America had
been for some time the Eldorado of Joseph's
dreams and the goal of his youthful ambitions.
He followed his brother in 1877 and he managed
to secure admission to St. Vincent's Arch-Abbey,
in Pennsylvania, where he completed, with marked
success, the classical course at the age of sixteen,
when most boys are just beginning the rudiments
of Latin. He left college at this time and went
to Louisville, Ky., where he taught for two years
in St. Martin's parochial school, then in charge
of the Franciscan Fathers. At the age of eighteen
he resolved to resume his studies for the priesthood. Bishop Henry Joseph Richter accepted him
as a student of the diocese of Grand Rapids, Mich.,
and ordered him to make his philosophical and
theological studies in the Montreal Grand Seminary. Early in the spring of 1889, owing to
failing health, he was ordered to Grand Rapids
by his bishop. He had already been ordained sub-
deacon at Trinity and promoted to the deaconate
in the fall of 1888. He was ordained to the
priesthood June 29, 1889, and was appointed assistant at St. Mary's, Saginaw, July 12, 1889.
Subsequently he was transferred to St. Mary's,
West Bay City, as assistant, and there he preached
weekly in French and English. In 1896 he became pastor of that church, and raised $10,000 to
pay off the French portion of the congregation,
the heighth of the A. P. A. movement his lectures
which then started a church for themselves. At
in Bay City set forth the true Catholic
standard and attitude toward their fellow-citizens

so clearly as to completely banish all prejudice and bigotry; and he built a new school in Bay City. In 1900 he was transferred to St. Mary's, Grand Rapids, where for years the principal language spoken in the pulpit was German, yet his ability and eloquence became known to all the people of the city. He had more influence in city affairs than any other one man in the city, and he was instrumental in bringing about flood protection, pure water, extension of the park system and many other reforms. He built a splendid convent for the sisters in Grand Rapids and also the imposing pastoral residence, while he beautified the church with splendid and costly treasures. Chiefly through his efforts two Catholic high schools for both sexes were established, thus inaugurating a movement which is sweeping the country. He likewise shared in founding St. Joseph's Preparatory Seminary. The bishop sent him to represent the diocese at the Federation of Catholic Societies, the Catholic educational convention and other national conventions. Every good cause found in him a powerful exponent and advocate, and he was highly esteemed by non-Catholics and loved by Catholics. In January, 1911, he was made auxiliary bishop of Grand Rapids and in the following August he was appointed first bishop of Toledo, having previously been appointed vicar-general of the diocese of Grand Rapids, and created a domestic prelate of his holiness. Although he went to the new see of Toledo practically as a stranger, still he did not go there as an unknown quantity. He has attained national eminence as an orator; he has a deep and clear knowledge of ecclesiastical law, having carried several cases through all the courts of appeal; he is a brilliant conversationalist, and the magnetism of his personality draws toward him hosts of friends from every rank and walk of life. He is the soul of cheerfulness and radiates sunshine wherever he goes. On the day of his consecration as bishop the Rev. Michael J. Gallagher, chancellor of the diocese of Grand Rapids, said: "By his elevation to the episcopate the center of ecclesiastical gravity in the United States has swung to the province of Cincinnati, and in the years to come the voice of Bishop Schrembs will be heard, eloquently, potently, dominatingly, in the counsels of the church of America."

HEALY, George Peter Alexander, artist, was born in Boston, Mass., July 15, 1813, son of William and Mary (Hicks) Healy. His father, born in Ireland, was a sailor, who, after numerous adventurous experiences as commander of a merchant vessel, settled in Boston in 1812. The son attended the public schools, and at the age of sixteen began to copy all the prints he could find and make likenesses of all who would sit to him. His first success was a copy of the canvas of Guido Reni's "Ecce Homo," which a Catholic priest purchased for ten dollars and placed in his church. Some time before this the boy and his work came to the notice of Miss Stuart, daughter of Gilbert Stuart, the painter, who encouraged him in many ways, and lent him the Guido Reni which he had copied. She also induced Sully to look at his work; and Sully, recognizing young Healy's talent, advised him to make painting his profession. Seven years later they met in London, where Healy was engaged on a portrait of Audubon, and after looking in silence at it, Sully said: "Mr. Healy, you have no reason to regret having followed my advice." In 1831 he opened a studio in Boston, but lacked sitters, and was unable to pay his rent,

until his landlord came to his rescue by ordering portraits of two members of his family, which were exhibited and attracted some attention. Seeing a very charming portrait of a lady by Sully, Healy had but one desire, that of painting a woman's portrait, but knew not where to find a sitter. At the suggestion of a friend whose portrait he was painting, he called on Mrs. Harrison Gray Otis, the queen of fashion in Boston society. Mrs. Otis, amused at the audacity of the young painter, consented to sit to him. His success was such that from that time sitters came to him. In spite of his success and great natural facility, his one object was to study abroad. In 1834 he went to Paris and entered the atelier of the eminent French painter, Baron Gros. Here he formed a close friendship with Thomas Couture, one of the glories of France, which continued until Couture's death. Healy worked much in the Louvre gallery; one day, as he was copying Corregio's beautiful "Marriage of St. Catherine," two English persons, husband and wife, stopped and, with some courteous words of appreciation, passed on. Several months later, when Healy had undertaken a journey to Italy, principally on foot, for economical reasons, he met this English couple at the inn of the Mont Cenis Pass. Sir Arthur and Lady Faulkner recognized the young American student, invited him to sit at their table, and finally offered him a seat in their traveling carriage, so as to visit Italy together. This was the beginning of a warm friendship. On his return to Paris he took up his studies with renewed ardor. His most successful portrait, at that time, was that of Gen. Cass, then minister to France. After eighteen months of ceaseless study, he went to London. During his three years' residence in that city he had as sitters Sir Arthur and Lady Faulkner, the Duke of Sussex, uncle to Queen Victoria; Lady Agnes Buller, twin sister of the Duke of Northumberland; Lord and Lady Waldegrave, Audubon, and Prescott, then minister to England. In the summer of 1839 he was recalled to France, where he painted the portraits of Marshal Soult and Louis Philippe; the latter commissioned him to make a copy of Stuart's Washington, besides portraits of many American statesmen, including those of Jackson, Clay, John Quincy Adams and Webster. About this time he executed his two large pictures, "Webster Replying to Hayne" and "Franklin Before Louis XVI."; the latter won a gold medal at the Universal exhibition (1855). The revolution of 1848 deprived him of his royal patron and ended his fortune in France. He had frequently returned to this country and had painted many people of note. Upon the warm invitation of William B. Ogden, of Chicago, he sailed for America and went to that city, where he painted an almost incredible number of portraits. Early in 1861 he visited Charleston, S. C., where he had painted the portrait of Gen. Beauregard, and was a witness of the bombardment of Fort Sumter. At Washington he had sittings from Pres. Lincoln, Gens. Grant, Sherman and McClellan, Adm. Porter and many other celebrities. At the close of the war he conceived the idea of a picture to be called "The Peacemakers," which was carried out some years later. It represented Lincoln, Grant, Sherman and Porter, who all sat to Healy for these portraits. This conference took place on board the River-Queen, where the possibilities of peace were discussed. The picture was burned in 1892, when the Calumet Club, of Chicago, was destroyed. In 1867 Healy returned to Europe and spent several years in Rome, where he painted Longfellow, Pope

Pius IX., the Princess Oldenberg, then affianced to the Duke of Weimar; the Princess (afterwards queen) of Roumania, Liszt, and others. Returning to Paris, Gambetta, Pres. Thiers, de Lesseps, and Jules Simon sat to him. In 1877, at the request of E. B. Washburne, he went to Berlin and painted a portrait of Bismarck. In 1892 he returned to Chicago, where he remained until his death. He was married in the Church of St. Pancras, London, in July, 1839, to Louisa Phipps, and the following children survived: George, Agnes, wife of Tiburee de Mare, the engraver; Emily, Mary, wife of Charles Bigot of Paris, France; Edith, wife of Lysander Hill of Chicago; Maria, and Kathleen, wife of Howard Basly of Chicago. A most delightfully written biography of Healy, with some of his letters, was published by his daughter Mary (Mme. Bigot). Mr. Healy died in Chicago, Ill., June 24, 1894.

McCANN, James, physician, was born in Allegheny county, Pa., Apr. 12, 1837, son of Thomas and Sarah (Wilson) McCann, of Scotch-Irish descent. He began the study of medicine at the University of Pennsylvania and while there enlisted in the Federal army for the civil war. He participated in the battle of Gettysburg. Returning to the University of Pennsylvania, he was graduated M. D. in 1864 and began to practice medicine in Pittsburgh, Pa. He was one of the organizers of the Western Pennsylvania Medical College, now the medical department of the University of Pittsburgh, and was professor of the principles and practice of surgery until his death. He was a member of the American Surgical Association, and of the county, state and national societies. He was married in 1862 to Sarah Boyd and had nine children. His wife died in 1883, and he was married again in 1889 to Martha Scott, who bore him one daughter. He received the degree of LL.D. from Heidelberg College, Ohio, and died in Pittsburgh, Pa., July 13, 1893.

BAXTER, Nathaniel Jr., soldier and manufacturer, was born in Columbia, Tenn., Nov. 4, 1844, son of Nathaniel and Mary V. (Jones) Baxter, grandson of Jeremiah and Katharine (Hardridge) Baxter, great-grandson of John and Margaret (Balthrope) Baxter and great-great-grandson of Jeremiah Baxter, a native of England, who emigrated in the early eighteenth century and settled in Maryland, later removing to Virginia and subsequently in North Carolina. When Nathaniel Baxter, Jr., was still a youth his father moved to Nashville, Tenn., and located on a farm, the site of which has since become Glendale Park. He was educated in private schools, and at the age of fifteen joined the Confederate army, being assigned to Freeman's battery of Tennessee artillery. He was soon promoted to a lieutenancy, and when Capt. Freeman fell in battle he succeeded to the command of the company, which position he held until the close of the war. For two years he served under Gen. Nathan B. Forrest. He was in the battles of Fishing Creek, Shiloh, Missionary Ridge, Chickamauga, Knoxville, Franklin, Atlanta and Savannah. The unique but distinguished honor of having been "first in the charge and last in the retreat," of having fired the first and last gun that shook the field of Chickamauga, belongs to him and his company. He was twice wounded, once seriously in an engagement at Macon, Ga., following the battle of Atlanta. He participated in the assault at Johnsonville, which resulted in the burning of the Federal gunboats, and was captured at the battle of Franklin, Tenn. For six months he was imprisoned at Fort Delaware, after

which he joined Johnson's army and surrendered with him at Hillsboro, N. C. Returning to Nashville at the close of the war, he studied law and was admitted to the bar. With his father and brother, Edmund Baxter, he formed a partnership and begun the practice of his profession in that city. In 1871 he was appointed clerk and master of the chancery court of Davidson county, holding this office until 1877, when he was elected president of the First National Bank of Nashville. He was also clerk of the supreme court of Tennessee for six years. He had long recognized the potentialities in the iron district of Tennessee and Alabama and was one of the pioneers who undertook to develop the iron and steel industries which to-day make the Birmingham district second only to that of Pittsburgh. In 1892 he resigned the presidency of the bank to become president of the Tennessee Coal, Iron and Railroad Co., one of the largest and most important industrial corporations in the country. The wonderful industrial growth of the South to-day is in no small measure due to Nathaniel Baxter's untiring efforts to establish the iron and coal industry on a firm foundation. In 1902 he retired to his farm, near Nashville. He was elected to the state senate in 1911 and became speaker, and was re-elected in 1912, and was the acknowledged leader of his party not only in Davidson county, but throughout the state. He was a member of McKendree Methodist Church and served on the board of trustees of Vanderbilt University. Col. Baxter was a soldier who had earned the right to be called one, a statesman, a philanthropist, a worthy citizen, a Christian gentleman and a true and loyal friend. A fine example of that rapidly disappearing type of the Southerner who redeemed the South from the desolation of the reconstruction period, and who laid the foundation for the wonderful development of which the present generation is the inheritor, is to be found in his life. Of sterling honesty and rare personal charm, it is as the master-builder and master-restorer that Nathaniel Baxter, Jr., will appeal to the historian of his state and section. He was married in Memphis, Tenn., in December, 1868, to Laura Sharpe, daughter of James F. Lavender, who survived him, with two children: Mannie B., wife of Robert F. Jackson, of Nashville, and Lollie L., wife of Robert F. Maddox, of Atlanta, Ga. He died in Nashville, Tenn., Sept. 29, 1913.

GAILLARD, David Du Bose, military engineer, was born in "Spring Hill," Fulton P. O., Sumter co., S. C., Sept. 4, 1859, son of Samuel Isaac and Susan Richardson (Du Bose) Gaillard. His first paternal American ancestor was Pierre Gaillard, a Huguenot, who after the revocation of the Edict of Nantes emigrated to America in 1686 and settled in the Santee country of South Carolina. From him and his wife, Elizabeth Le Clair, the line of descent is traced through their son Theodore and his wife, Lydia Peyre; their son Peter and his wife, Elizabeth Porcher, and their son David and his wife, Louisa Caroline du Bose, who were the grandparents of David Du Bose Gaillard. Peter Gaillard was an officer in Francis Marion's brigade during the war of the revolution, and a collateral ancestor, John Gaillard, was U. S. senator. An ancestor on the maternal side was Gen. Richard Richardson, who served in the Cherokee wars; was a member of the Provincial congress and of the legislative council of 1775, and reached the rank of brigadier-general during the revolution. During the civil war Col. Gaillard's father and six uncles gave their service to their state, the former as sergeant-major in Hampton's Legion. David Du Bose Gaillard was educated in

GEORGE P. A. HEALY
ARTIST

JAMES McCANN
PHYSICIAN

NATHANIEL BAXTER, JR.
SOLDIER AND MANUFACTURER

DAVID D. GAILLARD
MILITARY ENGINEER

WILLIAM C. GOUINLOCK

private schools in South Carolina and, entering the U. S. Military Academy, West Point, was graduated in 1884, fifth in a class of thirty-one. He was immediately promoted second lieutenant in the corps of engineers and attached to the battalion at Willets Point, N. Y. He was graduated in the Engineer School of Application at that place in 1887, being also made first lieutenant in that year. His first engineering work was in surveys and harbor improvements at St. Augustine, Tampa and elsewhere in Florida. In 1891 he was appointed a member of the International Boundary Commission between the United States and Mexico, and upon the completion of that work in 1896 was given special duty at Fort Monroe, Va. In 1895 he was sent to Washington and placed in charge of the aqueduct work, being also a member of the board of officers which decided upon the completion of the Washington tunnel. During this period he was promoted to captain, and for a brief period was engaged on the survey of the Portland channel, in Alaska. In 1898 he was detailed as engineer officer on the staff of Maj.-Gen. James F. Wade and was stationed at Chickamauga Park. In June of that year he was appointed colonel of the Third regiment, U. S. volunteer engineers. He then served at Jefferson Barracks, Mo.; Lexington, Ky., and Macon, Ga., until the Spanish-American war. He was sent to Cienfuegos, Cuba, in 1899. A battalion under his command so effectively cleaned up that city that during the American occupation there was no fever, and Gen. John C. Bates pronounced his engineers the best regiment, volunteer or regular, he had ever seen. After being honorably mustered out of the volunteer service, he was assistant to the engineer commissioner of the District of Columbia, and later had charge of river and harbor improvements on Lake Superior. When the general staff of the army was established in 1903, Gaillard, then a captain, was one of the engineer officers chosen, and he served almost uninterruptedly as a member of that corps until he was ordered to Panama. In 1904 he was promoted to major and became assistant to the chief of staff of the Northern division at St. Louis, and was subsequently ordered on duty at the Army War College, Washington. In 1906 he was made chief of the military information division of the Army of Cuban Pacification at Havana. When Pres. Roosevelt decided to assume the responsibility of building the Panama canal as a public enterprise, Lieut.-Col. Gaillard was one of three army officers recommended to him as qualified to carry out the undertaking. He was appointed on the Isthmian Canal Commission; was elected a director of the Panama railroad, and, under the chief engineer, Col. Goethals, was made supervising engineer in charge of the Department of Excavation and Dredging. From July, 1898, to 1908 he was in charge of the central division, from Gatun to Pedro Miguel, and from that period was one of the greatest, although not the most conspicuous, figures in the making of the canal. His special task was the onerous one of digging the vast Culebra cut, the one thing on which the success of all the rest depended. The task included almost literally the moving of a mountain and placing it thirty miles away, to be set up anew as Gatun dam. The Culebra cut runs through the backbone of the American continent. It is nine miles long, and the only place on the Isthmus which presented a continuous problem of dry digging. The excavatio nhere was almost entirely done by steam shovels, and is generally regarded as the most trying and probably the most difficult be-

cause of the problems, new to engineering science, which were constantly presented. At Cucuracha and its vicinity the earth and the rocks, finding a part of their foundations removed, would slide into the excavation, seeking a new foothold. Col. Gaillard had almost unsurmountable difficulties to overcome because of this tendency. As a member of the commission he had a voice in civil administration matters as well as in the general conduct of affairs. In April, 1909, he was made a lieutenant-colonel, and at the time of his death a bill was pending in congress promoting him to the rank of colonel in recognition of his distinguished service on the Isthmus. After he died congress awarded him the unusual honor of passing a joint resolution of appreciation of his services and regret at his death. Col. Gaillard has given the world an admirable example of self-abnegation and absolute devotion to duty. Unremitting toil, nervous strain and exposure to the intense tropical heat broke his health, and while the news of the successful flooding of the waterway was being greeted with applause by millions of his countrymen, this army engineer who had pierced the backbone of the continent, and whose name will be associated with the names of Goethals and Gorgas as the conquerors of the Isthmus, was on his deathbed in a state of unconsciousness. He was the author of "Wave Action in Relation to Engineering Structures," and of various articles relating to the canal published in the technical and scientific press. He was a member of the National Geographic Society, the Huguenot Society of South Carolina, the Officers' Club, Fort Monroe, Va., and the Army and Navy Club, Washington. He was married at Winnsboro, S. C., Oct. 6, 1887, to Katherine Ross, daughter of Henry Campbell Davis, of Columbia, S. C., who survives him with one son, David Saint Pierre Gaillard, an electrical engineer, a graduate of the Massachusetts Institute of Technology. Col. Gaillard died at Johns Hopkins Hospital, Baltimore, Md., Dec. 5, 1913.

GOUINLOCK, William Chalk, physician and manufacturer, was born at Tuckersmith, Harpurhey, Ontario, Canada, Dec. 31, 1844, son of George and Hannah (Chalk) Gouinlock. The family came originally from the environs of a lake in Scotland, the banks of which were covered with daisies, hence the name Gowan—daisy, and loch—lake, which has been changed into the present spelling. Dr. Gouinlock was educated, at Goderich (Ont.) Grammar School and at Upper Canada College, Toronto, and was graduated M.D. at the College of Physicians and Surgeons, New York city, in 1864. In the following year he was placed in charge of the medical department of Blackwell's Island, New York. Upon the death of his maternal grandfather he returned to Harpurhey to take over the latter's practice. Subsequently he took a special course at the University of Toronto, and was graduated there in 1869. While in Ontario he became interested in the salt industry at Seaforth, also conducting a sawmill and lumber and barrel business in connection with the salt works. He was one of the first to establish the salt industry in western New York, having organized a successful business at Warsaw under his own name in 1883. The salt deposits being too far beneath the surface for mining, he drilled wells about 1,400 feet, through which fresh water was poured to the salt deposits. This dissolved the salt and the saturated brine was pumped from the well, purified, and the water evaporated by direct coal firing. The pans, made of steel, were 100 by 20 feet and 12 inches deep, with sloping sides, **from**

which the salt was raked when dry, and stored in bins to be seasoned for a week or ten days, and then packed in barrels for shipment as common salt. The Guinlock establishment was one of the first and also one of the most successful salt plants in the field. In 1886 he formed a partnership with State Senator L. Hayden Humphrey, under the name of Guinlock & Humphrey, for the construction of another salt plant on the Erie railroad at Warsaw, N. Y. Both of these plants had a capacity of about sixty tons of salt per day. In 1887 he removed to Hutchison, Kan., and there built and put in operation the first salt plant west of the Mississippi river, but he sold the business two years later and returning to Warsaw purchased his partner's interest in the second plant. In 1898 he sold out to the National Salt Co. Subsequently he became interested in the Warsaw Button Co., the Oatka Hosiery Co., the American Electrolytic Co., manufacturers of caustic soda at Warsaw, N. Y., and the Warsaw-Wilkinson Co., manufacturers of ensilage cutters and general structural steel bridges. He experimented at Rock Glen with a new process for making caustic soda, and he subsequently organized the Rock Glen Salt Co., took over the Bidwell bean thresher property at Batavia, N. Y., in 1911, and reorganized it as the Batavia Machine Co. He was president of all these companies save the Warsaw Button Co. He was president of the village of Warsaw during 1900-3, and was also president of the board of education. Dr. Gouinlock was a man possessed of remarkable versatility of talents, and he combined personal culture and intellectual tastes with sound business judgment. He was married in Toronto, Canada, Mar. 24, 1879, to Margaret Gilchrist, daughter of James Strachan of Toronto. She died in 1906, leaving nine children: Margery, wife of Murlin Smallwood; William, Mary, Agnes, wife of Barber Conable; Jane, wife of J. Harry Van Arsdale; Harold, Johanna, Dorothy and Edward Gouinlock. He died at Warsaw, N. Y., Aug. 30, 1914.

AYER, Frederick, financier, was born at Ledyard, Conn., Dec. 8, 1822, son of Frederick and Persis (Cook) Ayer, and a descendant of John Ayer, who came from England and settled at Haverhill, Mass., in 1632, going from there to Saybrook, Conn., early in the eighteenth century. His father was a commissioned officer in the war of 1812. He was educated in the public schools of Ledyard, and afterwards attended a private academy in Baldwinsville, N. Y. His first employment was as a clerk in a general store at Baldwinsville. Later he went to Syracuse, N. Y., and managed another store belonging to his employer. In 1844 he formed a partnership with Hon. Dennis McCarthy, under the firm name of McCarthy & Ayer, which continued about eleven years. In 1855 he joined his brother, Dr. James C. Ayer, in Lowell, Mass., in the manufacture of proprietary medicines, under the name of J. C. Ayer & Co. The business was incorporated in 1877 as the J. C. Ayer Co., of which Frederick Ayer was treasurer until 1893, when the accumulation of other interests compelled him to retire. In 1871, with his brother James C., Mr. Ayer purchased a controlling interest in the stock of the Tremont Mills and Suffolk Manufacturing Co. of Lowell, and effected a consolidation of the two companies under the name of the Tremont and Suffolk Mills. In June, 1885, he purchased the entire property of the Washington Mills at Lawrence, Mass., and reorganized the corporation, retaining the name of the Washington Mills

Co., of which he was treasurer. In 1899 he was one of the organizers of the American Woolen Co., of which he was president until 1905, when he was succeeded by his son-in-law, William M. Wood. Mr. Ayer was one of the founders and president of the Lowell and Andover railroad. At different times he has been connected with the Old Lowell National Bank, Merchants' National Bank, Central Savings Bank, and was one of the organizers of the New England Telephone and Telegraph Co. He was also one of the organizers and for several years the treasurer of the Lake Superior Ship Canal Railway and Iron Co., and was one of its directors until it was merged into the Keweenaw Association. He is director of the United States Mining Co., the Columbian National Life Insurance Co., the American Woolen Co., the International Trust Co., The J. C. Ayer Co., Tremont and Suffolk Mills, Boston Elevated Railroad Co., and the Lowell and Andover Railroad Co. Mr. Ayer has been unostentatious in his benefactions, but the public charities are few in which he has not joined. He is a member of the Algonquin Club, the Beacon Society, and the Country Club of Boston. He was married in 1858 to Cornelia, daughter of Charles A. Wheaton of Syracuse, N. Y., and they had two sons, James C. and Charles F. Ayer, and two daughters, Ellen W. and Louise R. Ayer. His first wife died in 1878, and he was married again in 1884 to Ellen B. Banning of St. Paul, Minn., and the children of this marriage are: Beatrice B., M. Katharine and Frederick Ayer, Jr.

WOOD, William M., manufacturer, was born at Edgartown, Martha's Vineyard, Mass., June 18, 1858, son of William Jason and Amelia Christine (Madison) Wood. His ancestors were prominent in the colony of whalers and seamen who have made the coast of Massachusetts famous in nautical song and story. His father abandoned the sea on account of delicate health and retired to New Bedford, Mass., where the son was brought up. He supplemented his public school education by spare-time study of Latin, French, German and the higher mathematics. Indeed the habit of study never deserted him, and in spite of the exacting demands of his business career he is a man of varied knowledge and scholarly tastes. During his vacations from school he worked as cashboy in the store of George M. Eddy, an old New Bedford Quaker of high character and standing. His first independent business venture, undertaken when he was still quite a child, showed a precocious spirit of enterprise. One day in New Bedford he noticed an auction sale of apples and bought in a barrel for one dollar. These he brought home in a borrowed wheelbarrow and sold by the peck to the neighbors at a profit of about one hundred per cent. The next day he bought two barrels, and he was in a fair way to become a very prosperous young person when the local grocer got wind of the scheme and bought up all the apples on sale at a price that effectually barred all other speculators. This was an early and very effective lesson to the boy in the meaning of business competition. It is to be assumed that he did not think very much about it. He did not in fact have very much time to think. His father died when he was twelve years old and the main support of the family fell upon his boyish shoulders. New Bedford was at that time beginning to devote some attention to the textile arts and contained a cotton factory, the Wamsutta Mills, which was a pioneer in the manufacture of the finer cotton fabrics. Here young Wood obtained a position. After three years in the counting-room he was transferred to the manufacturing department, where he spent three more years and made himself familiar with the technical details of the industry. After six months in a banker's and broker's office in Philadelphia, he accepted a position in the banking house of J. A. Beauvais & Co., of New Bedford. The variety and scope of the enterprises controlled by Mr. Beauvais provided a very valuable experience for young Wood. He kept the books of the famous shipping firm of James B. Wood & Co., assisted his employer in organizing a national bank and was in other ways brought into close touch with affairs of magnitude and importance. When Otis N. Pierce was appointed treasurer of the reorganized Border City Mills, of Fall River, Mass., William Wood became his assistant and paymaster, a position he held for six years. In 1885 the Washington Mills, of Lawrence, Mass., passed into the hands of Frederick Ayer, of Lowell, who invited Thomas Sampson, a prominent manufacturer of Rhode Island, to become his agent. Sampson persuaded young Wood to abandon the idea of a cotton mill of his own and take over the management of the cotton manufacturing department of the Washington Mills. It was suddenly decided, however, to devote the plant entirely to the production of worsted goods, and Mr. Wood became assistant to the manager. The plant was henceforth devoted to the manufacture of woolen worsted goods and soon after Mr. Wood was made manager. The concern had for some time been working under a heavy debt, which was generally looked upon as a fatal handicap to its success. The situation involved an unusually difficult problem in mill finance, but he handled it so efficiently that the Washington Mills were not only placed on a firm financial footing but became one of the most flourishing and profitable textile concerns in the country. In 1899 he organized a number of New England woolen mills into the American Woolen Co. Associated with him in the organization were Frederick Ayer, of Lowell; Charles Fletcher, of Providence; James Phillips, Jr., of Fitchburg, and Charles R. Flint and A. D. Juillard, of New York. Frederick Ayer was made first president and Mr. Wood treasurer, but he soon succeeded Mr. Ayer as president. The American Woolen Co. is now the largest single organization in the wool manufacturing industry of the world. It is capitalized at $60,000,000 and owns forty mills, including the Assabet Mill, at Maynard, Mass., and the Wood Mill, at Lawrence, Mass., which are the largest carded woolen paltn and the largest worsted manufacturing establishment, respectively, in the world. Its output reaches an approximate gross value of $50,000,000 a year. The American Woolen Co. is not only the conception and creation of William Wood, but it is, as it now stands, an incontrovertible testimony to his unique genius for management. In spite of difficulties familiar to every student of the woolen industry the American Woolen Co. has been consistently and increasingly successful. It has paid a regular annual dividend of seven per cent. on the preferred stock and has accumulated a surplus of over $8,000,000. It experienced a serious strike among its operatives at Lawrence in 1912, instigated by a new labor organization called Independent Workers of the World, despite the fact that the mills embody the most advanced ideas and inventions for manufacturing textile goods and for the welfare of the employees. Its welfare provisions are said to have no equal in the country and it had voluntarily advanced wages four times during the last ten years, paying the highest rate of wage in the country. The strike lasted two months. Besides being president and director of the American Woolen Co., Mr. Wood is president and director of the National and Providence Worsted Mills, Providence, R. I., and the Southern Illinois Coal and Coke Co., of Chicago, and director of the Merchants' National Bank, the Pierce Manufacturing Co. and Pierce Bros., Ltd., New Bedford; the Rhode Island Insurance Co., Providence, and the Washington Mills and Nyanza Mills, of Lawrence. He is vice-president of the Home Market Club and the National Association of Wool Manufacturers and a trustee of the Lowell Textile School. Mr. Wood was married in 1888 to Ellen, daughter of Frederick Ayer, and has four children: William M., Jr.; Cornelius Ayer, Rosalind and Irene Wood.

DONOVAN, Cornelius, civil engineer, was born in Ann Arbor, Mich., Oct. 12, 1850, son of Patrick and Catharine (O'Hara) Donovan. He was graduated at the University of Michigan, civil engineering department, in 1872. After working on railroad construction for two years, he became assistant engineer in the corps of engineers of the United States army. For many years he has been identified with government work on the improvement of the mouth of the Mississippi river. This project may be said to have begun at the time James B. Eads (q. v.) undertook to clear the mouth of the river by building jetties several miles out and thus allowing the force of the current to sweep through and clear out a considerable amount of the sand and mud obstructing the channel. Upon the expiration of the contracts for this work made with Mr. Eads and his heirs, the United States government placed the completion of the project in the hands of its army engineers. The Mississippi and its tributaries, draining as it does a large section of the United States, deposits annually an enormous quantity of sand and mud at the mouth of the river, the accumulation of which has divided the mouth of the river into three principal outlets extending far into the Gulf of Mexico. The government engineers have undertaken the prodigious task of dredging these shallow outlets and maintaining deep water channels for the benefit of the nation's navigation. Mr. Donovan has had direct charge of the work of deepening the South and Southwest passes, two of the three principal outlets. His task has consisted of building huge jetties of stone and concrete and dredging the main channels to secure a mean depth of thirty-five feet. Mr. Donovan has made it his lifework, and has performed the many arduous duties with ability, faithfulness and zeal. For twenty-five years he lived at the mouth of South Pass over 100 miles below the city of New Orleans, but since 1903 he has been stationed at New Orleans. He is a member of the American Society of Civil Engineers; the Country Club, Yacht Club, Opera Club, Chess, Checkers and Whist Club of New Orleans, and of the Michigan Gamma Chapter Tau Beta Society. He is unmarried.

BETHELL, Union Noble, vice-president American Telephone and Telegraph Co., was born at Newburgh, Ind., Sept. 12, 1859, son of Union and Eva (Parrett) Bethell. The first of his family in America was Samson Bethell, a native of England, who, at an early date, settled in South Carolina and married Mary Cantrell. From them the line of descent is traced through their son Cloud, who married Rachel Floyd, and was the grandfather of U. N. Bethell. Mr. Bethell's father (Union Bethell, b. 1826, d. 1907) was a prominent merchant in Indiana. The son was educated in the public schools and at Hanover College, being graduated at the latter in 1879 and later receiving the degree of A.M. In 1885 he was graduated from the Columbian Law School, and in the same year was admitted to the bar of the District of Columbia. Mr. Bethell's connection with the telephone service began in 1889, when he removed to New York and became secretary and treasurer of the New York and New Jersey Telephone Company, with headquarters in Brooklyn. In 1893 he was made general manager of the New York Telephone Co., and in 1901 became president of the Chesapeake and Potomac Telephone Co., operating in Washington, Baltimore and surrounding territories. A few years later he was made president of the company operating in Philadelphia and eastern Pennsylvania. Successively he assumed the management of the several Bell telephone companies operating throughout the states of New York, New Jersey and Pennsylvania. These various companies, with Mr. Bethell as president of each, were grouped into one operating unit in 1909, covering the territory from Washington on the south to Pittsburgh on the west, New York on the east and the Canadian border on the north, and comprising about 125,000 square miles. The New York Telephone Co., of which he is still the president, consists of over 1,500,000 telephone stations with a plant investment of $200,000,000, and employing nearly 35,000 people. In 1910 Mr. Bethell became senior vice-president of the American Telephone and Telegraph Co., of which Theodore N. Vail is the head. In recognition of his work in adapting the telephone to conditions in Japan the Mikado conferred upon him the Order of the Rising Sun in 1909. He is president of the First National Bank of Montclair, president of the Board of Education, and president of the Playground commission. He is a member of the Lotos, Railroad, Bankers, and Economic clubs of New York, Japan Society, Telephone Society of New York, American Institute of Electrical Engineers, New York Electrical Society, and the Upper Montclair Country Club. He was married Dec. 5, 1893, to Donna I. Brink, and has three sons, Richard Sargent, Francis Cutler and John Warren Bethell.

FARNSWORTH, Frederick Eugene, banker, was born in Detroit, Mich., Dec. 2, 1852, son of Leander Lewis and Frances (Higgins) Farnsworth. His first American ancestor was Matthias Farnsworth, born in 1612 in or near Farnworth, Lancastershire, England, who came to America about 1649 and settled at Lynn, Mass. From him the line of descent is traced through Matthias Jr., Ebenezer, Matthias, Ebenezer, Harbour, Ebenezer, Leander, father of the subject of this biography. His father (b. 1821) was one of the pioneer settlers of Detroit, in 1836; he embarked in the shoe business in 1848, first as Lyon & Farnsworth and subsequently in his own name. His mother, a native of Utica, N. Y., was the daughter of Sylvester W. Higgins, a civil engineer, who was one of the California ''forty-niners'' and occupied various official positions in Detroit and Michigan. The son received a public school education, and began his business career in his father's shoe store. Owing to the latter's impaired health, the entire management of the business devolved on the young man, who conducted it successfully and built up a trade that at the time of his retirement in 1883 was the largest boot and shoe business in Detroit. In 1883 he was general secretary and executive

officer of the Art Loan Association, which gave the largest art loan exhibit ever held in this country, and from this undertaking was organized the Detroit Museum of Art, of which he was one of the forty incorporators and its first secretary. For ten years he was secretary of the famous Michigan Republican Club, renowned for its annual banquets and for its influence in political affairs, and during 1891-97 he was city assessor. His banking experience began on his retirement from the city office when he became cashier of the Union National Bank. Although its assets were good, the bank had not paid dividends for several years, but his administration of its affairs was so satisfactory that soon after he took office he had the institution upon a dividend-paying basis. He was likewise active in a number of public enterprises in Detroit, serving as a member or general secretary of various citizens' committees which had charge of national reunions, annual meetings and conventions and similar celebrations. He was assistant treasurer of the Detroit fair and exposition which was held in that city in 1889. In 1876 he identified himself with the state national guard, and served in various capacities. He was a member of the staff of Gov. Luce, with the rank of colonel, and was also a member and treasurer of the state military board, which had entire control of the military funds of the state of Michigan, the purchase of supplies, uniforms and equipments, and a hospital fund for soldiers of the civil war. He was for many years re-elected secretary of the Michigan Bankers' Association, and also secretary and treasurer of the Bankers' Club of Detroit. In 1902, through his instrumentality and suggestion, the organization of secretaries of state bankers' associations was established, whose object was to meet annually and exchange ideas regarding modern association work, and he was its secretary from its inception until 1911. When in 1899 the conference of clearing houses of the United States was organized through the efforts of the Michigan Bankers' Association, Mr. Farnsworth was elected executive officer. The object of this conference, which was composed of representatives of the clearing houses of the United States, was to meet annually at the time of the conventions of the American Bankers' Associations and discuss matters appertaining directly to clearing house work, exchange charges, Par points, and kindred subjects. The outcome of these conferences was the organization of a Clearing House Section of the American Bankers' Association in 1906, of which Col. Farnsworth was elected vice-president and secretary. At the annual convention of the American Bankers' Association in 1907 he was elected secretary of that organization, and removed to New York city to take up the duties of the position. Since then he has been unanimously re-elected each year, and, through a change in the constitution, he has been given the title of general secretary. The association, during his incumbency, has increased in power and influence, and its membership now numbers 15,000 banks, representing $16,000,000,-000 of assets. Many new departments have been inaugurated, and the association has been placed on a firm and progressive basis. With his executive and business experience, Col. Farnsworth's life has been broadened by his interest in art, literature, music and travel. He has traveled extensively throughout the United States, some portions of Canada, the West Indies, Great Britain and Europe. Personally he is characterized as easy in manner, affable and agreeable;

MARTIN KALBFLEISCH
CHEMIST

OWEN BRAINARD
CIVIL ENGINEER

WILLIAM R. BOGGS
SOLDIER

WILLIAM H. RUSSELL
LAWYER

always courteous under all circumstances; cool and collected and capable in great emergencies. He was married Dec. 2, 1891, to Henrietta Bloomfield, daughter of John J. Clarkson, of Jackson, Mich., and has two sons: Frederick Clarkson and Clarkson Lewis Farnsworth.

KALBFLEISCH, Martin, chemist, was born in Flushing, Netherlands, Feb. 8, 1804, son of John and Petronella (Van Pollja) Kalbfleisch. When he was twelve years of age he sailed to the island of Sumatra, but finding that the Asiatic cholera was epidemic there he returned with his ship to Antwerp. Thence he journeyed to Havre, France, where he spent four years in commercial pursuits. In 1826 he came to the United States. He secured employment in New York city in various lines until 1835, when he began to manufacture colors in Harlem, New York. Subsequently he moved to Brooklyn, New York, and the enterprise continued to grow until the works covered many acres of ground. Mr. Kalbfleisch was a clear thinker, possessed of a well-balanced judgment and of proved business ability. Upon settling in Brooklyn he organized a school so that his and his neighbors' children might have the advantage of a good education, and for a considerable period paid the teacher's salary himself. In politics he was an indefatigable worker in the Democratic party. He was elected supervisor of the old town of Bushwick in 1851, became an alderman of Brooklyn in 1855 and was elected mayor in 1861. War measures required most of his time, and the Federal cause had no more stanch advocate nor the national government a more single-hearted adherent. In 1862 he went to congress and in 1867 he again became mayor of Brooklyn. He held office for four years and proved himself as safe and efficient an administrator of civic affairs as he had during the trying years of his previous term. In 1868 he retired from active business in favor of his sons, who then organized the firm of Martin Kalbfleisch's Sons, which became the largest of its kind in the United States. Besides the Bushwick Chemical Works in Brooklyn, the sons operated chemical works in Bayonne, N. J.; the Buffalo Works in Buffalo, N. Y., and the Baltimore Acetate Works in Baltimore. Mr. Kalbfleisch was married, first, in 1825, to Elizabeth West; second, in 1850, to Matilda Bartlett Higgens. He had eleven children: Elizabeth W., wife of Robert Robinson; Frederick W., Helen M., wife of Rodney Thursby; Edward L. G., Charles H., Isabella G., wife of James E. Weaver; Albert M., Franklin H., John and George Kalbfleisch and Josephine M. L., wife of Robert S. Fleet. He died in Brooklyn, Feb. 12, 1873.

BRAINARD, Owen, civil engineer, was born at Haddam, Conn., Mar. 10, 1865, son of Hubert and Cynthia V. (Brainerd) Brainard, and a descendant of Daniel Brainard, who came from Essex county, England, in 1652 and settled at Haddam. Three generations of the ancestors on his father's side were members of the state legislature, and the family was always identified with the town and county government. He was educated in the public school of Haddam, and began his professional career with Carrere & Hastings, architects of New York, with whom he is still associated. In 1892 Mr. Brainard removed to New York city and began his work as structural engineer, being at that time chief engineer for the firm of Carrere & Hastings, and was identified with that firm's work, including the New York Public Library building; First Church of Christ Scientist, New York; H. M. Flagler residence, Palm Beach; Blair & Co. build-

ing, New York; Goldwin Smith hall in Cornell University, Richmond Borough Hall, Staten Island ferry, congressional office buildings, Washington, D. C.; Yale bi-centennial memorial building, New Haven; New Theater, New York; E. H. Harriman residence, city hall, Portland, Me.; office buildings in Toronto and Montreal, Canada, and alterations on the United States Capitol. Mr. Brainard became a partner of Carrere & Hastings in 1901, continuing as such until 1904, since which time he has acted as consulting engineer for this firm in connection with all of the architectural work, and has carried on an independent practice as consulting engineer on various structures. In 1907 he designed and supervised the construction of subways at the Capitol in Washington. In 1908 he became consulting engineer for the county of Cuyahoga, in charge of the $4,000,000 courthouse building in Cleveland, O. He was also the consulting engineer of the Cathedral of St. Paul at St. Paul, Minn., and the Pro-Cathedral in Minneapolis. Mr. Brainard is the consulting engineer for the United States Steel Corporation in charge of the development and construction of the industrial town of Ojibway, Ontario. He is a member of the American Society of Civil Engineers, the American Society for Testing Materials, the International Society of Testing Materials, the New York chapter of the American Institute of Architects, the Architectural League of New York, the Engineers' Club, the Apawamis Country Club and the Aldine Club. He was married Mar. 10, 1909, to Jean Sawyer.

BOGGS, William Robertson, soldier, was born in Augusta, Ga., Mar. 18, 1829, son of Archibald and Mary Ann (Robertson) Boggs. Several of his ancestors fought in the revolution and in the war of 1812. He received his preliminary education at the Augusta Academy and was graduated at the United States Military Academy at West Point in 1853, standing five in his class in scholarship and third in the academy in conduct. After his graduation he served in the topographical bureau and on the Pacific railroad survey until 1854, when he was transferred to the Watervliet arsenal at Troy, N. Y. In 1856 he was appointed first lieutenant and in the following year he was transferred to the arsenal at Baton Rouge, La. He was appointed inspector of ordnance at Point Isabel, Tex., in 1859, and later to a similar position in the arsenal at Pittsburgh, Pa. Upon the outbreak of the civil war he enlisted and was commissioned a colonel by Gov. Brown. He took part in perfecting the defenses at Charleston, Pensacola and Savannah, and in 1862 was on staff duty with Gen. Kirby Smith during the invasion of Kentucky. For his services in this campaign he was made a brigadier-general by the Confederate congress. In 1863 he was appointed chief of staff to Gen. Kirby Smith in the Trans-Mississippi department, where he served until the close of hostilities. After the war he engaged in engineering and architecture and for five years was professor of mechanics at the Virginia Polytechnic Institute. Gen. Boggs was married in Troy, N. Y., Dec. 19, 1855, to Mary Sophia, daughter of Col. John Symington, U. S. A., and had six children: William Robertson, Elizabeth McCaw, Archibald, John Symington, Edith Allston and Henry Patterson Boggs. He died at Winston-Salem, N. C., Sept. 15, 1911.

RUSSELL, William Hepburn, lawyer, was born at Hannibal, Mo., May 17, 1857, son of Daniel L. Russell, a Baptist clergyman of English descent. He was educated in the public schools of Hannibal and under the tutelage of his mother, who was a teacher of high standing before her marriage. At the age of seventeen he became a reporter on the Hannibal "Daily Courier," and so quickly did he comprehend the nature of his duties and carry them out that he was promoted to be managing editor. Later he transferred his services to the Hannibal "Morning Journal," becoming proprietor and editor-in-chief, as well as of the "Daily Clipper-Herald," which the former absorbed. During 1880-84 he was correspondent of the Associated Press, and also acted as special correspondent of the New York "Sun," Chicago "Times" and St. Louis "Republic." Mr. Russell had always a leaning toward the legal profession, and, having determined to take up the practice of law, began systematic study in the office of William C. Foreman and later with George W. Easley, of Hannibal. He was admitted to the Missouri bar in 1882, and since that date has been in active practice. Almost immediately he was elected to the office of city attorney, and at the expiration of his term was re-elected. In November, 1884, he was appointed one of the attorneys of the Louisville, New Albany and Chicago railway, with headquarters first at Lafayette, Ind., and later at Frankfort in the same state. At Frankfort he became a member of the law firm of Bayless & Russell, still continuing to serve as attorney for the railroad. Removing to Chattanooga, Tenn., in 1889, he was appointed general counsel for the East Tennessee Land Co, of which Gen. Clinton B. Fisk was then president. Upon its failure he became counsel for the bondholders in connection with the reorganization, and he served as president of the reorganized company, the Harriman Land Co. In 1890, with Gen. Fisk, I. K. Funk, A. W. Wagnalls, James B. Hobbs, Fred Gates and A. A. Hopkins, Mr. Russell established the town of Harriman, Tenn., and with Col. Geo. W. Easley drew the charter for the new town, incorporating a feature for the absolute prohibition of the sale of intoxicants in the city limits. This was one of the earliest efforts at local option, and its success can be estimated by the growth of Harriman from a population of 791 in 1890 to 5,000 in 1910, with two banks, ten churches and some twenty industries. In 1894 Mr. Russell removed to New York city, and forming a partnership with William Beverly Winslow of Carrollton, Ky., conducted a general law business, the partnership continuing until 1906. Mr. Russell was of counsel in the case of Tift vs. Southern Railway Co. (206 United States reports), involving and establishing the right of the Interstate Commerce Commission and the Federal courts to determine the reasonableness of railway freight rates, and the case of Hayward, receiver, against Lesson and Hopewell, reported in 176 Massachusetts 310, which is probably the leading case in the United States holding directors and promoters of a corporation liable to the receiver of the corporation for the full market price of stock secretly appropriated by them without payment therefor in connection with the organization of the corporate enterprise. He has also been of counsel for the directors of the Anglo-American Savings and Loan Association of New York in the multiplicity of suits brought against them by stockholders in that unfortunate company, and has succeeded in the courts of the state up to this time in establishing the proposition that directors, guilty merely of carelessness and neglect in the discharge of their functions as directors, cannot be held guilty of intentional deceit so as to make them liable to stockholders for investments in the corporate stock. He contributed to

the "American and English Encyclopædia of Law" the articles on "Comparative Negligence," "Contributory Negligence," "Implied Warranties" and "Railroad Crossings." He is joint author with his former partner, William Beverly Winslow, of "Russell and Winslow's Syllabus-Digest of the United States Supreme Court Reports," and he has also contributed many articles on legal subjects to various periodicals. Although a Democrat in politics, in 1902, Mr. Russell was appointed commissioner of accounts of New York city by Mayor Low, having joined in the fusion movement which resulted in the latter's election in that year. In 1904 he resigned from this office and again became an active worker in the regular Democratic organization, believing that Mr. Low should not be re-elected mayor of the Democratic city of New York, and the fusionists refusing to consider the nomination of an independent Democrat to succeed Low. Mr. Russell was a presidential elector from the state of Tennessee in 1892, when Grover Cleveland was elected president for the second term, and he has represented his party as a delegate to state conventions and elsewhere, achieving fame as an orator of convincing power. He is a member of the American Bar Association, the International Law Association, the Missouri Society, of which he was elected president in 1910; the Southern Society and the Tennessee Society, the American Economic Association, the National Geographic Society, the Benevolent and Protective Order of Elks and the Knights of Pythias. He is a member of the Manhattan, Hardware and New York clubs, and is a trustee of the latter. Mr. Russell was married June 23, 1880, to Mary Gushert, of Hannibal, Mo., and they have one son, Todd Russell, and five daughters, Mary G., Anne V., Ruth A., Judith Shakespeare and Rowena Russell.

LETCHWORTH, William Pryor, manufacturer and philanthropist, was born in Brownville, N. Y., May 26, 1823, son of Josiah and Ann (Hance) Letchworth. The family was of ancient English stock, originating probably in Saxon times. The first of the name in America was John Letchworth, of London, and a member of the Society of Friends. John Letchworth emigrated to America in 1766 and settled at Philadelphia, Pa., whither, three years later, he brought from England his wife and children; his younger son, William, was the grandfather of the subject of this sketch. His father, Josiah Letchworth, was active in social work, was greatly interested in schools, spoke frequently for temperance and against slavery, and became a man of note in Auburn, N. Y., where his last years were spent. William Pryor Letchworth was educated in the public schools, and when fifteen years old became a clerk with the firm of Hayden & Holmes, manufacturers and dealers in saddlery hardware at Auburn, N. Y. In 1848 he entered into partnership with Pratt & Co., hardware merchants of Buffalo, N. Y., and soon after a new firm was organized under the name of Pratt & Letchworth, whose business of importing or manufacturing every variety of saddlery and carriage hardware and trunk trimmings was separate from that of Pratt & Co. In 1856 the firm began the manufacture of malleaable iron at Black Rock, in the establishment of which Mr. Letchworth's brother Josiah took part. In 1873 Mr. Letchworth withdrew from all business connections and devoted his remaining years to philanthropic work. He was commissioner and later president of the New York Board of Charities, and the first work that he undertook was that of correcting abuses in

Josiah Letchworth

the Erie county poorhouse, as affecting the care of the dependent children and the insane. In a memorandum, found among his papers after his death, he says: "I regard the child-saving work as the most effective means of upbuilding society, of reducing the volume of pauperism and crime, and of lessening the burden of taxation." He went abroad in 1880 to study the European methods of caring for delinquent children and insane, and upon his return, devoted his attention to modes of dealing with juvenile delinquency. He advocated a rational classification of offences and offenders among the young, and believed that every boy should be instructed in some useful trade or occupation, preferably by the Russian system of technical training. He was also active in improving the conditions of the insane departments of the poorhouses in the various counties of the state. He resigned from the state board of charities in 1896 to give more time to his private affairs, but later he interested himself in the victims of epilepsy. He was president of the National Association for the Study of Epilepsy and the Care and Treatment of Epileptics. In May, 1909, the New York legislature passed an act establishing Letchworth Village in Rockland county for the custodial care of epileptics of unsound mind, and for other feeble-minded persons requiring custodial care, and a documentary history of the founding at Sonyea of the first colony for epileptics in the state of New York was compiled by him in his last years. He was founder and president of the Buffalo Historical Society and also of the Buffalo Fine Arts Academy. Mr. Letchworth was the owner of the beautiful estate, "Glen Iris," in the Genesee valley, at the falls of the Genesee river, and in succeeding years developed it with fond and unceasing assiduity. During the half-century and more of his personal care of it, he planted more than 10,000 trees so that Glen Iris now possesses a greater variety of flora than any other equal area in the State. In 1906 he conveyed the entire property of over 1,000 acres to the state of New York, to be used as a park reservation under the control and jurisdiction of the American Scenic and Historic Preservation Society, and it is now called "Letchworth Park." In 1893 he received the degree of LL.D. from the University of the State of New York. Mr. Letchworth's life was one of singular beauty and of noble motive and purpose in all its activities. One of the mildest, most gentle-mannered of men—Quaker bred, and realizing in his whole character the ideals of that culture of the quiet spirit—he was capable, nevertheless, at need, of an iron determination in what he undertook to do, and a persistence which never tired, never yielded to discouragement and rarely suffered defeat. His enjoyments were of the sweeter and quieter sort. The lovelier sides of nature, the finer things of art, the generous exhibitions of humanity appealed to him most. Besides numerous pamphlets and reports, he was the author of "The Insane in Foreign Countries" (1889); "Care and Treatment of Epileptics" (1899); "Transactions of the National Association for the Study of Epilepsy at the First Annual Meeting, Held in Washington, D. C." (1901), and "A Narrative of the Life of Mary Jemison, De-he-wa-mis, the White Woman of the Genesee" [edited] (1877, 1898, 1910). He was also the author of "Aston Hall" and "The Burial of a Broken Heart," two serial tales contributed to "The Home Monthly" under the pseudonym of "Saxa Hilda." Mr. Letchworth was unmarried and died at Glen Iris, N. Y., Dec. 1, 1910.

LETCHWORTH, Josiah, manufacturer and capitalist, was born at Sherwood, Cayuga co., N. Y., May 1, 1836, son of Josiah and Ann (Hance) Letchworth. His preliminary education was received in the public schools of that city, and subsequently he attended the academy at Auburn. He began his business career as an employee in a manufacturing and mercantile house in Auburn, but at the age of twenty left Auburn for Buffalo to join the firm of Pratt & Letchworth, founded in 1848 by his brother, William Pryor Letchworth, and in which he soon became a partner. The Buffalo Malleable Iron Works, Buffalo Steel Foundry, Buffalo Saddlery Hardware Factory and Hame Works were among the enterprises established and controlled by the Pratt & Letchworth Co. Since 1893 he had been comparatively active in the firm only in a supervisory and financial manner, devoting much of his time to the leisure which his advanced years required, but he retained the treasurership of the firm until his death, and had visited his office within a few days of that event. He was an officer and active member of the First Presbyterian Church and prominently connected with the board of managers of the Buffalo General Hospital, the Buffalo Bible Society and many other organizations of a similar character. Josiah Letchworth was one of the most distinguished of the older citizens of his adopted city and one of the strong factors in its developed business life. He was respected both for his character and his business ability, and it may be justly said that his influence went far toward making Buffalo the Queen City of the Lakes. During the years of a busy life he found much time for travel, for extensive reading and study and for the cultivation of his tastes in art and literature. His personal attainment was very great, for he added to a singular symmetry and elevation of character an unusual intellectual culture. His literary taste was unfailing and his reading thorough and extensive. He was essentially a gentleman of the old school who believed in humility, courtesy and goodness, and who was altogether averse to ostentation and self-assertion. His influence over others was great and he inspired much affection from all with whom he came in contact. In his death the family lost a guide and a guardian, the church an example and the community a benefactor. With years he grew in strength of resolve, in wealth of culture, in beauty of style, in purity of character and in beneficence of influence. He was keenly susceptible to the charms and fascinations of social life, and peculiarly attracted by the adornments of scholarship and the delights of culture. Clear-visioned, prudent, fearless and strong, he was also rich in exquisite sensibilities. Open to all things beautiful and lovely in nature and in art, he was likewise the recipient of invisible supplies of spiritual support. He was a member of the Buffalo Society of Artists, Buffalo Natural Sciences, Buffalo Historical Society, Bible Society and Buffalo General Hospital. He was married (first) in Buffalo, N. Y., 1865, to Mary Rachel, daughter of Judge John B. Skinner, of Buffalo; he was married (second) at Le Roy, N. Y., 1874, to Katharine, daughter of Freeman M. Edson, who survives him, with three children by the second union: Pierre Edson, of Covina, Cal.; Mabel Rachel, now Mrs. Charles R. Wilson, of Buffalo, and Geoffrey Josiah, of Buffalo. He died at his country home, Glenwood Beach, Lake Owasco, N. Y., June 30, 1913.

DUNNE, Edmund Michael, second Roman Catholic bishop of Peoria, Ill., was born in Chicago, Ill., Feb. 2, 1864, son of Maurice and Catherine (Walsh) Dunne. He was educated at St. Ignatius' College, Chicago, the American College, Louvain, Belgium, and the Gregorian University, Rome. He was ordained priest June 24, 1887, and after serving as assistant at St. Columkille's Church, Chicago, founded in 1898, and most successfully administered for seven years the Parish of the Guardian Angel, one of the largest Italian congregations in the city. During 1905–09 he held the office of chancellor of the diocese. He was consecrated bishop of Peoria, Sept. 1, 1909. The diocese covers a cross section of the state of 18,554 square miles and has 109,000 Catholics, 228 priests, twenty-three churches, eighty-nine schools and 15,000 pupils.

KINCANNON, Andrew Armstrong, chancellor University of Mississippi, was born in Noxubee county, Miss., Aug. 2, 1859, son of James and Araminta (Connor) Kincannon, and a descendant of James Kincannon, who came to this country from Scotland about 1720, and settled in Virginia. One of his ancestors, another James Kincannon, was captain of a Virginia company in the revolutionary war and fought at Kings Mountain. His father held several county and federal offices. He was educated at the University of Mississippi and the Normal University, Ohio. In 1882 he became principal of the graded school at Verona, Miss. He was appointed assistant professor of engineering at the Mississippi Agricultural and Mechanical College in 1884, and in 1887 was made superintendent of city schools at Meridian, Miss. In 1896 he was elected state superintendent of schools, the only elective office he ever consented to run for, and in 1898 was made president of the Mississippi Industrial College at Columbus. The latter is a state institution for the education of young women, and the work of Prof. Kincannon as its president attracted national attention. The chancellorship of the state university was declined by him in 1906, but the trustees so earnestly urged him to reconsider that he consented to accept it in 1907. Prof. Kincannon is one of the most prominent and capable educators in the South. He has held every office in his profession in Mississippi and has had many tempting offers of high positions in other states. He is not, however, very desirous of outside honors and prefers to devote himself to the educational interests of his native Mississippi. He is a director of the Southern and National Education Association, and has written a large number of official reports that have been highly praised by critics of such work. He was married at Meridian, Miss., Dec. 20, 1888, to Mary George, daughter of William R. Barksdale, of Nevada, Miss., and has five children: Franklin, Mary George, Andrew A., Jr., Patti Cothron and Elizabeth Kincannon.

ANDREW, Abram Piatt, Jr., economist, was born in La Porte, Ind., Feb. 12, 1873, son of Abram Piatt and Helen Merrill Andrew. He is descended from James Andrew, probably from Scotland, who was a resident of Raritan, N. J., in 1732, and whose wife was Catherine Livingston, and the line descends through their son John, who whostudied at Princeton, served as surgeon in the Revolutionary War and who married Rachel Chamberlain; their son John, who married Catherine Piatt, a descendant of French Huguenots who settled in New Jersey early in the eighteenth century; and their son, Abram Piatt, who married Viola Armstrong, daughter of John Armstrong, of Irish descent, commander in the Revolutionary army and at one time treasurer of the Northwest Territory. This Abram Piatt Andrew, grandfather of our subject, moved to Indiana in 1818, and for certain government contracting work was paid in land grants, the city of La Porte standing to-day as a monument to his foresight and constructive ability. His son, Abram Piatt Andrew, was commander of the 21st Indiana battery in the civil war, and is a man of wide influence. His son was educated ʃt the Lawrenceville (N. J.) school, at Princeton University (1893) and at Harvard University (1895–97), receiving the degree of A.M. and Ph.D. from the latter in 1900. He also studied at the universities of Halle, Berlin and Paris in 1898–99. In 1900 he was made instructor in the department of economics at Harvard University and three years later he became assistant professor of economics, a position he occupied until 1909. While at Harvard he served as assistant editor of the "Quarterly Journal of Economics." He was also for several years a member of the athletic committee, and was particularly active in the affairs of the Cercle Français, an organization devoted to the propagation of interest in French literature. Through this association he was honored in 1906 by the minister of public instruction in France with the title of "Officier d'Académie." Dr. Andrew predicted the panic of 1907 in the New York "Journal of Commerce" of Jan. 1, 1907. In 1908, when the National Monetary Commission was organized to devise a plan of permanent relief from such financial collapses as had afflicted the United States during the preceding year, Dr. Andrew was engaged to assist the commission in its researches, and, having been granted two years' leave of absence from Harvard University, he visited London, Berlin, Paris and other important financial centers of Europe to collect information concerning foreign banking systems. Upon his return he edited the commission's publications, which comprise more than a score of volumes and constitute the most comprehensive library dealing with the world's banking that has ever been published. He also had a large share in framing the bill and report of the National Monetary Commission. In August, 1909, Pres. Taft appointed him director of the mint, and during the year of his administration the organization of the several mints and assay offices was radically overhauled and the number of employees reduced by more than 530 from a total of 1,300, thereby accomplishing an annual saving of more than $320,000. In June of the following year he became first assistant secretary of the treasury, resigning in July, 1912, on account of differences with Secretary MacVeagh. Dr. Andrew's writings have covered many phases of financial questions. Among those which have attracted wide attention were his arraignment of the policies of Secretary Shaw in his "The Treasury and the Banks under Secretary Shaw" and his "The United States Treasury and the Money Market," issued at the time of the retirement of the former secretary of the treasury in 1907, both of which were pleas for an absolute divorce of the treasury from "the Street." Several of his studies concern the currency questions of Oriental countries, notably "Currency Problems of the Last Decade in British India" in the "Quarterly Journal of Economics" for August, 1901, and "The End of the Mexican Dollar" in the same journal in May, 1904. Other articles treat of different aspects of panics, such as "The Influence of the Crops upon Business," "Hoarding in the Panic of 1907" and "Substitutes for Cash in the Crisis of 1907" in the "Quarterly Journal of Economics," the latter describing more than 200 substitutes for money used at that

A. Piatt Andrew

time, "The Influence of Credit on the Value of Money" in the proceedings of the American Economic Association for 1904 and "The Crux of the Currency Question" in the "Yale Review" for July, 1913. During 1910–12 Dr. Andrew was treasurer of the American Red Cross, and he was a delegate to the ninth international conference of the Red Cross in 1912. He is a member of the Harvard (New York), Harvard (Boston), Metropolitan, Chevy Chase and Cosmos (Washington) clubs. He is unmarried.

MAIN, Charles Thomas, mill engineer and architect, was born at Marblehead, Mass., Feb. 16, 1856, son of Thomas and Cordelia (Reed) Main. On the distaff side he is descended from the Rev. George Phillips, a native of Boxted, Essex, England, who emigrated, with Winthrop and Saltonstall, in 1630 and settled at Salem, Mass. His father was a machinist and engineer in Marblehead. He was educated in the public schools of Marblehead and by private tutors. He was graduated at the Massachusetts Institute of Technology in 1876 with the degree of S.B., and remained for three years at that institution as an assistant instructor. In 1879 he was draughtsman for the Manchester Mills, Manchester, N. H., and then went to the Lower Pacific Mills, Lawrence, Mass., as engineer in charge of the reorganization of the plant, becoming assistant superintendent and superintendent. Since 1892 he has been engaged in general engineering practice in Boston, being associated in his professional work with Frank P. Sheldon, in Providence, R. I. In 1893 he removed to Boston and formed a partnership with Francis W. Dean, which continued until 1907. He designed a large number of steam and water power plants, including those of the Lynn Gas and Electric Co., Washington Mills, American Woolen Co., Columbian Rope Co., Wood Worsted Mills, Ayer Mills, Pacific Mills, Troy Blanket Mills, Pennman Manufacturing Co., the Marblehead Electric Light Station, Lynn Gas and Electric Co., Beverly Gas and Electric Co., Newburyport Gas and Electric Co., the L. S. Starrett Co., of Athol, Mass.; the Hochanum Mills, of Rockville, Conn.; the Warrenton Woolen Mills, Torrington, Conn.; Yale & Towne Manufacturing Co., Stamford, Conn.; Bigelow Carpet Co., Lowell and Clinton, Mass.; United States Worsted Co., Lawrence, Mass.; S. Slater & Sons, Webster, Mass.; Great Falls Water Power and Townsite Co., Great Falls, Mont.; Nashua Manufacturing Co., Nashua, N. H.; Smith & Dove Manufacturing Co., Andover, Mass.; Tyer Rubber Co., Andover, Mass.; Ludlow Manufacturing Associates, Ludlow, Mass.; Dwight Manufacturing Co., Chicopee, Mass., and many others. He has been in consultation concerning the plants of many public service corporations. He was consulting engineer for the Rockingham development, Pee Dee river; Puyallup development, near Seattle, Wash.; Taylor's Falls development, near Minneapolis, Minn.; Goat Rock development, in the Chattahoochee river; Guanagnato Electric Co., Mexico. He made reports on proposed developments of the Platte river, Neb.; Housatonic river, Conn.; Kinderhook and Valatie creeks, N. Y.; Flat river, Mich.; Ashuelot river, N. H.; Susquehanna river, Md.; Arros river, Mexico; Mississippi river at Otsego, Chattahoochee river at Columbus, Ga., and of powers near Seattle, Omaha and in Montana. He is an expert on the valuation of properties using steam and water power as well as on the subjects of rental, tax, insurance, condemnation, sale and purchase figures. While a resident of Lawrence, Mass., he served as alderman, a member of the school committee and trustee of the public library, and he was a member of the water board of Winchester, Mass., during 1895–1906. In 1905 he was elected a term member of the corporation of the Massachusetts Institute of Technology and was re-elected in 1913. He is a member of the American Society of Mechanical Engineers, American Society of Civil Engineers, Boston Society of Civil Engineers (past president) and National Cotton Manufacturers' Association, and of the Exchange, Engineers' and the Technology clubs, Boston, and the Calumet Club, Winchester, Mass. In 1887 he invented a receiver pressure regulator for compound engines which has been widely used. His published papers cover the subjects of steam power, water power, mill construction and valuation of industrial properties. Mr. Main was married at Somerville, Mass., Nov. 14, 1883, to Elizabeth, daughter of John Appleton, of Marblehead, and has three children: Charles R., Alice A. and Theodore Main.

BURDEN, Isaac Townsend, manufacturer, was born in Troy, N. Y., Feb. 21, 1838, second son of Henry and Helen (McQuet) Burden, and brother of James Abercrombie Burden (q.v.). His father (Vol. II, p. 333) was the proprietor of the well-known iron works of Henry Burden & Son at Troy, N. Y., and the inventor of a machine for making spikes and a horseshoe-making machine, by means of which he amassed a fortune. I. Townsend Burden received a public school education, and completed his studies at a private academy in New Haven, Conn. At the age of nineteen he entered his father's iron manufacturing business at Troy. Ten years after his father's death (1881), the firm was reorganized under the name of the Burden Iron Co., with which Mr. Burden was identified until his death. Mr. Burden's business interests were not limited to the Burden Iron Co. He was at one time president of the Port Huron Iron Co.; he was also one of the organizers of the Knickerbocker Trust Co. of New York, in which he held a large interest, and at the time of his death was a trustee of the Lake Champlain and Moriah Railroad Co. He was married in 1871 to Evelyn Byrd, daughter of William A. Moale, of Baltimore, Md., and had two sons: William Moale and Isaac Townsend Burden, Jr., and one daughter, Gwendolyn, wife of David Dows. For many years Mr. Burden had a summer home at Newport, R. I., having purchased the former residence of Hon. Levi P. Morton in Bellevue avenue. Here he and his family were the center of Newport's most thoughtful and brilliant society, and his personal attainments and wide popularity won for him a large circle of friends. He was foremost in the organization and management of Bailey's Beach at Newport, and was its president until his death. Of simple tastes and quiet demeanor, Mr. Burden possessed a strong personality which impressed itself upon his entire community. He was a man of clear intellect, pure tastes and personal refinement and grace, attributes which were as natural to him as his courtesy and faith in mankind. While exclusive in bearing, he was profoundly democratic, modest, unassuming, kind-hearted and sincere. He died in New York city, Apr. 23, 1913.

CRAM, Ralph Adams, architect, was born at Hampton Falls, Rockingham co., N. H., Dec. 16, 1863, son of William Augustine and Sarah Elizabeth (Blake) Cram. His father was a Unitarian minister and a descendant of John Cram, a native of Newcastle-on-Tyne, England, who came to America in 1635 and settled in Brookline, Mass.

Subsequently he was one of the founders of Exeter, N. H., with John Wheelwright. The line of descent is traced through John Cram's son Benjamin, who married Argentine Cromwell; their son John; his son Jonathan, who married Elizabeth Heath; their son Nehemiah, who married Hannah Philbrick; their son Jonathan, who married Rhoda Tilton; their son Joseph, who married Sally Sanborn and was the architect's grandfather. The American family comes from the house of Von Cramm, which is one of the most ancient of the noble families of Germany, their nobility antedating royal or imperial grants. All the earlier male members of the family belonged to the Knights of St. John and the Teutonic Order of Knighthood, and took part in several crusades. During the reign of Henry VIII. Hans Von Cramm emigrated to England "with his wife and men at arms," entered the military service of Cardinal Woolsey, then titular Bishop of Durham, and was granted a large estate for his services in fighting against the Scots. Ralph Adams Cram was educated chiefly at the Exeter (N. H.) high school and the Westford (Mass.) academy. After studying architecture in the offices of Rotch & Tilden, of Boston, and acting for two years as art critic on the staff of the Boston Transcript, he associated himself with Charles Francis Wentworth in 1889 for the practice of his profession under the firm name of Cram & Wentworth. In 1892 Bertram G. Goodhue was admitted as partner, and the style became Cram, Wentworth & Goodhue, continuing as such until the death of Mr. Wentworth, when it was changed to Cram, Goodhue & Ferguson. His firm has built many churches and public buildings throughout the United States. Mr. Cram worked particularly for the improvement of ecclesiastical architecture and towards the acceptance and development of gothic as a logical style in place of classic of any type, and has begun construction of a large college for women, Sweet Briar Institute, in Amherst county, Virgina, the completed scheme comprising about twenty buildings. In 1903 his firm submitted designs in competition with ten other especially invited architects for the rebuilding of the U. S. Military Academy at West Point, the government appropriation being $5,500,-000. As a result of the competition, the design submitted by his firm received the unanimous vote of the jury, and they were appointed architects. This work involved many buildings, varying in size from the riding-hall, costing $700,000; the post headquarters, costing $400,000, and the chapel, costing $300,000, down to the houses for married officers, and minor buildings, barracks, cadet headquarters, storehouses, cavalry and artillery barracks and stables, etc. The scheme embraced the transformation of the entire group of buildings, preserving those that were still available for use, replacing the old ones and adding new structures. Among the churches built by his firm may be mentioned All Saints' Ashmont, Mass.; All Saints', Brookline, Mass.; St. Stephen's, Cohasset, Mass.; Emmanuel Church, Cleveland, O.; St. Mark's Church, Toledo, O.; St. Andrew's Church, Detroit, Mich.; St. Mary's, Walkerville, Ont., and Calvary Church, Pittsburgh, Pa., and among the public libraries are those in Fall River, Mass.; Pawtucket, R. I., and Nashua, N. H. He designed St. Thomas' Church in New York, one of the most important in the United States. His latest work is the graduate collegt group of Princeton University. Mr. Cram is a fellow of the American Institute of Architects and of the Royal Geographical Society of London, and of the Puritan Club, Boston. He has published the "Decadent," "Black Spirits and White," "Church Building," "Impressions of Japanese Architecture and the Allied Arts," "The Ruined Abbeys of Great Britain," and has contributed numerous essays and poems to the periodical press. Mr. Cram was married at New Bedford, Mass., Sept. 20, 1900, to Elizabeth Carrington Read, daughter of Capt. Carrington Read, C. S. A., and Mary Carrington Johnson, and has two children: Mary Carrington and Ralph Wentworth Cram.

CAMPBELL, Henry Munroe, lawyer, was born in Detroit, Mich., Apr. 18, 1854, son of James V. and Cornelia (Hotchkiss) Campbell, and a descendant in the fifth generation of Duncan Campbell, an officer of a Highland regiment, who came to this country and settled on the Hudson river about 1750. From Duncan Campbell the line descends through his son Thomas to the latter's son Henry Munroe and his wife, Lois Bushnell, who were the grandparents of the subject of this sketch. James V. Campbell was one of the judges of the supreme court of Michigan from 1857 until his death in 1890, and was pre-eminently influential in establishing and determining the system of jurisprudence now prevailing in the state of Michigan. His wife was a daughter of Chauncey Hotchkiss, one of the builders of the Erie canal. Henry M. Campbell received his preparatory education in the public schools of Detroit, and was graduated (Ph.B.) at the University of Michigan in 1876, and at the law department of that institution in 1878. He at once began the practice of his profession in partnership with Henry Russel, now general counsel for the Michigan Central Railroad Co., and continued this relation until 1912, when the firm of Campbell, Bulkley & Ledyard was organized, of which Mr. Campbell is senior member, and with which Mr. Russel is associated as counsel. In 1880 he was appointed master in chancery of the U. S. circuit court, and occupied that office until the circuit was abolished, Jan. 1, 1912. Mr. Campbell is one of the leading lawyers of the state of Michigan, and is recognized as an authority on corporation law. He is general counsel for numerous important financial and industrial houses of Detroit, and for various prominent eastern interests as well. He has always maintained his association with the University of Michigan, is counsel for the board of regents, and when the literary fraternity, Phi Beta Kappa, was organized at the university, he was made one of the members from the class of 1876. Mr. Campbell is closely identified with many of the business interests of Detroit; he is a director of the People's State Bank; vice-president of Parke, Davis & Co.; general counsel for the receivers of the Père Marquette railroad; director of Cass Farm Co., River Rouge Improvement Co., Chestnut Ridge Improvement Co., Union Trust Building Co., Union Trust Co and Woodlawn Cemetery. He has always been an unswerving adherent of the Republican party, his work for which in the state has been of marked value. In 1908 he was elected a delegate to the state constitutional convention by the largest vote cast for any candidate in the city of Detroit and in Wayne county. He was one of the leaders of the convention, served on various important committees, and was chairman of the committee on the legislative department. In 1911 he was appointed by the U. S. circuit court of appeals for the sixth circuit a member of the committee to revise the rules of equity practice in the federal courts. He is a member of the American Bar Association, Michigan Bar Association,

RALPH A. CRAM
ARCHITECT

HENRY M. CAMPBELL
LAWYER

THOMAS WILLIAMS
LAWYER

GEORGE H. POWERS
PHYSICIAN AND SURGEON

Detroit Bar Association, the Yondotega, Detroit (president 1897–1900), Country, University, Detroit Boat, Witenagemote and Prismatic clubs, all of Detroit, and the Huron Mountain Club. He was an original member of the Michigan Naval Brigade, and was president of the Detroit Naval Reserves during the Spanish-American war. His favorite recreations are shooting, fishing and golf. Mr. Campbell is the author of various essays and studies of constitutional questions and theories of government, and has written numerous leading articles challenging the expediency and legality of the initiative, referendum and other forms of so-called direct legislation and political action. He has been a life-long member of the Episcopal church and for many years a vestryman of Christ Church, Detroit. He was married, Nov. 22, 1881, to Caroline B., daughter of James Burtenshaw, a merchant of Detroit, and has two children: Henry Munroe, Jr., and Douglas, both following the profession of law.

WILLIAMS, Thomas, lawyer and congressman, was born at Greensburg, Pa., Aug. 28, 1806, son of Robert and Agnes (Singer) Williams; grandson of Robert Williams, who was commissioned lieutenant in the revolutionary war and who married Jane Meek, and great-grandson of Robert Williams, of Welsh descent, who came to America in the first part of the eighteenth century, purchasing property in Charlestown, Cecil co., Md. He attended Greensburg Academy and was graduated at Dickinson College in 1825, after which he began the study of law under Judge Richard Coulter, then a member of congress from Greensburg, and Judge John Kennedy, of Pittsburgh. He soon distinguished himself as an advocate and rose rapidly to a high place in his chosen profession. The events which brought him into public life were those connected with the great upheaval against Pres. Jackson on account of his attitude toward the United States Bank in 1832. The Whig movement of 1834 began with him as one of its first managers and its ablest leader in advocating its principles. Soon he became the rising leader of the Whigs and the editor of their newspaper organ, "The Advocate." On July 4, 1835, he delivered his first notable oration at a Whig meeting. Scarcely, therefore, was he fairly launched in his professional career when he was called to supply a vacancy for the Pittsburgh district in the state senate, to which he was elected in 1838. His first appearance in that legislative body was on the occasion of the public disturbance of the Capitol which resulted in what has since been known as the "buckshot war." In his place in the state senate he at once participated actively in the debates of that body, and his reputation as a speaker soon became coextensive with the state itself. He was re-elected in the following year, served with his usual activity, while outside he took a leading part in the exciting canvass which resulted in electing William Henry Harrison to the presidency. On the sudden death of the president he was unanimously delegated by the two houses of the legislature to deliver a funeral eulogy, passages from which, because of their unusual eloquence, became subjects of school declamations throughout the country. Retiring from the senate he resumed his law practice, and soon achieved a leading position at the bar of the state, holding aloof from politics for many years. However, at the inauguration of the Republican party he became a delegate-at-large to the Philadelphia convention of 1856, by which he was appointed a member of the national committee for his own state, and he participated actively in the canvass which followed in several of the adjoining states as well as his own. He was one of the original organizers of the Republican party, having been aroused by the repeal of the Missouri compromise. Subsequently he wrote the call for the Chicago convention which nominated Lincoln for the presidency, and was actively engaged in the great and decisive campaign which elected him. In that same election he himself became a member of the lower house of the Pennsylvania legislature, and was especially active in urging the state government to stand by the Union and prepare for war. In 1862 he was elected to congress. At the time of the impeachment of Andrew Johnson he was a member of the house judiciary committee, and was appointed as one of the managers to prosecute the impeachment proceedings before the United States senate. He never fully recovered from the effects of the labor and responsibility incident to the impeachment trial. He was re-elected to the 39th and 40th congresses, and served also on the committees on coinage and weights and measures, distinguishing himself as a representative by the authorship and defence of some of the most important measures presented to the house, and held the reputation of being one of the strongest lawyers of the body. His speech as a manager in the Johnson trial was pronounced by the best judges as equal to anything delivered on that or any other like occasion in the history of the country. During the 40th congress he was an efficient supporter of the policy of the party for the reconstruction of the southern states. His war, waged for years before he entered congress, against municipal subscription to railways produced an amendment to the constitution. He was an untiring student, and his learning was extensive and varied. Apart from his profound and exact knowledge of law, he was a keen and appreciative scholar, well versed in general literature and an accomplished linguist. He was married, May 5, 1831, to Sarah D., daughter of Dr. William Reynolds, of Wilmington, Del., and had eleven children, three of whom survive him: Margaret D., Sarah D. and Mary C. Williams. He died in Allegheny City, Pa., June 6, 1872.

POWERS, George Herman, physician and surgeon, was born in Boston, Mass., June 13, 1840, son of Herman and Caroline Hayward (Carter) Powers. His first American ancestor was Walter Power, who emigrated early in the seventeenth century and settled in Middlesex county, Mass. His wife was Trial Shepard, and the line of descent is traced through their son William and his wife, Rebecca ————; their son Thomas and his wife, Elizabeth Littleton; their son Jeremiah and his wife, Hannah Fiske; their son Aaron and his wife, Olive Osborne; their son Benjamin and his wife, Rhoda Cannon, and their son Herman, who was the father of Dr. Powers. After attending the public schools of Chelsea he was graduated at Harvard College in 1861 and at the Harvard Medical School in 1865. Among his preceptors at Harvard were Asa Gray and Oliver Wendell Holmes. He directed the glee club during his four years of academic life, and was organist of the Park Street Church, Boston. His education was continued at the Boston City Hospital as house officer, receiving there his first training in opthalmology. Responding to the call of troops for the civil war, he enlisted as assistant surgeon in the 60th Mass. volunteer infantry. After the war he began practice in San Francisco, Cal. He became professor of opthalmology, otology, rhinology and laryngology in the medical department of the University of California. He was opthalmologist and otologist at St. Luke's, St. Mary's and the Children's hospitals, and was chief consulting surgeon in these specialties for the Southern Pacific Railroad Hospital Association. His contributions to medical literature were numerous, among his later writings being "A Rare Anomaly of the Lateral Sigmoidal Sinus." He was the originator of the bifocal lens which bears his name, an ingenious combination of reading and distance lenses. Always possessed of rare judgment, his surgical work was ever painstaking and successful, and from the earliest years of his practice his technique in the cataract operation was his particular hobby, and it gave him a prominent place among the foremost opthalmologists of America. The blind who received sight by his skill and care and the recipients of his devoted kindness still thrill at the memory of his good deeds. He brought this skill, and the tireless devotion of the accomplished surgeon, to minister alike to rich and poor. For twenty years he served as organist of St. Paul's Church, San Rafael, Cal., and for many years was treasurer of St. Luke's Church, San Francisco, and a vestryman of that church until his death. He was a member of the G. A. R., Loyal Legion, and the Bohemian, University, Pacific Union and Loring clubs, of San Francisco. His musical ability made him conspicuous in the entertainments of the Bohemian Club dramatic circle, and he was always a favorite in amateur musical circles in his adopted city. He was also a member of the American Medical Association, and of various local medical societies. He was married in Sacramento, Cal., July 30, 1871, to Cornelia Janet, daughter of Russell Chapman, of New Haven, Conn., who survives him, with four children: Katharine, wife of Edward R. Chapman, of Detroit; George Herman, Jr., a practicing physician, of Boston; Allan Raymond, a practicing physician, of Rio Vista, Cal., and Ruth Powers, of Detroit. He died in Detroit, Mich., May 4, 1913.

BAEKELAND, Leo Hendrik, chemist, was born in Ghent, Belgium, Nov. 14, 1863, son of Karel Lodewyk and Rosalia (Merchie) Baekeland. He was educated in the Athenæum of Ghent, attending at the same time the free evening lectures of the Ghent technical school. After a three-years' chemistry course at the latter he was graduated with honors in 1880, barely seventeen years old. Soon after this he received an offer as assistant chemist at the state agricultural station, but being ambitious for a higher degree of proficiency, he declined, and in the same year matriculated at the University of Ghent, being the youngest student there. He prepared himself for a medical career; his chief interest, however, was centered in the branches of chemistry and the natural sciences, for which he had early displayed peculiar aptitude and to the study of which he now devoted himself with ardor. In 1882 he obtained the degree of bachelor of sciences "summa cum laude." The salaried government position of laboratory assistant in chemistry being offered by his professors, he accepted and abandoned the study of medicine for that of natural science. In 1884 he received the degree of doctor of natural sciences with a special diploma in chemistry, again passing both examinations "summa cum laude." He was appointed assistant professor of chemistry in the University of Ghent and professor of chemistry and physics at the Government Normal School for Sciences—then located at Bruges. The latter appointment was due to the recommendations of Eugene Stas, well known by his classical work

on the revision of atomic weights. Stas also presented Baekeland's earliest publications of original scientific research before the Academie des Sciences de Belgique. In 1887 Baekeland was proclaimed laureate in chemistry of the four Belgian universities for original research work on chemical dissociation. The prize included a subsidy for travel and study, and this enabled him to visit the higher institutions of learning in Germany, England and Scotland. Resigning his position as professor in the normal school, he was raised to the rank of associate professor of chemistry at the University of Ghent. About this time he became interested in the then recently invented photographic dry-plate, having been an enthusiastic amateur photographer from his boyhood. He also began to acquire some reputation as an industrial chemist, and was frequently consulted by several important dry-plate manufacturers in Ghent. In 1888 he patented a dry-plate which could be developed in a tray of water. The importance of this invention has since been eliminated by the greatly simplified developing methods. He was married in Ghent, on Aug. 8, 1889, to Celine, daughter of his chief professor, Theodore Swarts, dean of the faculty of sciences at the University of Ghent, and immediately afterwards, during his vacation and as the last stage of the traveling scholarship he had won two years before, he visited the United States on a government mission, to report about the institutions of higher education here. He had scarcely arrived in this country when he was called in consultation by A. & H. T. Anthony & Co., of New York, on some chemical problems connected with the manufacture of bromide papers and photographic films. The result was that a well-paying position was offered him, and having become an enthusiastic admirer of this republic and its institutions, he resigned his position at the University of Ghent. In 1891 he left the service of Anthony & Co. and established himself as a consulting chemist in New York city. Soon after he started several lines of chemical research, which quickly exhausted his little supply of cash. In association with his friend, Leonard Jacobi, he established the Nepera Chemical Co. at Nepera Park, Yonkers, in 1893, to manufacture a new photographic paper, "Velox," invented by him ten years before. This new paper made photographic printing entirely independent of daylight, but its merits were slow to be recognized. It was very exceptional to find photographers who believed in the practical possibilities of the process, and the greatest opposition was encountered from experts and professional photographers who predicted failure. But by sheer stubborn introduction work and an educational campaign, carried on under very discouraging conditions, the advantages of the new process began to be appreciated, at first slowly, then quite rapidly, and after three years the demand for the paper had increased to such an extent that the manufacturing plant had to be enlarged several acres in dimension, and miles of "Velox" paper were manufactured and sold every day. Since then the process has become accepted all over the world. Many kinds of paper are now manufactured here and abroad, all based on the same principle. In 1899 the business was sold to the Eastman Kodak Co., and Dr. Baekeland was able to retire from active business and devote his life to study and research in his private laboratory at Yonkers, N. Y. Since 1905 he has been chemical counsel for the Hooker Electrochemical Co., manufacturers of caustic soda and chloride of lime, and took an active part in the development

Henry T. Eddy.

of the Townsend electrolytic cell, the patents of which they own. One of his later inventions, Bakelite, should be specially mentioned. This is a material resembling both amber and the best Chinese lacquer, which he succeeded in producing by the synthesis of carbolic acid and formaldehyde. Its chemical name is oxybenzylmethyleng-lycolanhydride. It is used for the most varied purposes, not only for the manufacture of jewelry and fancy goods, but to a much larger extent as an insulating material for the manufacture of electrical machinery; also for the impregnation of wood, moulded articles which heretofore were made of hard rubber, such as billiard balls, fountain pens, phonograph records, buttons, umbrella handles, telephone receivers, cigar holders, pipe stems, and similar plastics. It has the advantage over hard rubber and amber of being considerably cheaper and easier to work. But its main characteristic is its unusual strength, resistance to heat, solvents and chemicals. He sold his patents in America to the General Bakelite Company, of which he is the president, and in Europe to the Bakelite Gesellschaft, of Berlin. Bakelite is now being used in ever-increasing quantities here and abroad. Dr. Baekeland is past president of the American Institute of Chemical Engineers; past president of the Chemists' Club of New York (1904); past president of the American Electrochemical Society (1909); past vice-president of the Society of Chemical Industry of London (1905); past vice-president of the American Chemical Society (1910); past chairman of the New York Section of the latter society (1909); member of the University Club of New York; Cosmos Club of Washington; Inventors' Guild (president); government delegate to the Seventh International Congress of Applied Chemistry in London (1909); member of the executive committee and president of Section V-b (Plastics), of the Eighth International Congress of Applied Chemistry, Washington and New York (1912). He was awarded the Nichols medal by the American Chemical Society in 1909, the John Scott medal by the Franklin Institute in 1910, the Willard Gibbs medal in 1913, the Chandler medal in 1914 and the Perkins medal in 1916. In 1915 he was made a member of the advisory board of inventors and scientists to assist the U. S. navy. The most important of his papers on original chemical research are: "Oxidation of Hydrochloric Acid Under the Influence of Light," "Dissociation of Nitrate of Lead," "A Practical Method for the Quantitative Determination of Silver in Photographic Paper," "A Method for Determining the Relative Permanency of Photographic Prints," "On the Toning Action of a Mixture of Thiosulphate of Sodium and Alum," "Photoretrogression, or the Disappearance of the Latent Photographic Image," "On the Influence of Hygrometric Conditions of the Atmosphere in the Manufacture of Photographic Paper," "The Electrolytic Action of Metal Particles in Sensitized Papers," "Centrifugal Bromide of Silver for Bromide Emulsions," "The Synthesis, Constitution and Uses of Bakelite," and "Fusible, Soluble, Resinous Condensation Products of Phenols and Formaldehyde." He was married Aug. 8, 1889, to Celine, daughter of Prof. Theodore Swarts, of the University of Ghent, and has two children: George Washington and Nina Baekeland.

EDDY, Henry Turner, mathematician and educator, was born at Stoughton, Mass., June 9, 1844, eldest son of Henry and Sarah Hayward (Torrey) Eddy. His earliest American ancestor was his great-great-grandfather, Charles Eddy, who settled in Glastonbury, Conn., not later than 1737 and died there in 1771. From this Charles Eddy and his second wife, Hannah Loveland, the line descends through their son Charles and his wife, Hannah Kelsey; their son Thomas and his first wife, Abi Lewis, who were the grandparents of the subject of this sketch. His father was a clergyman of the Congregational Church, and later a physician and inventor. At Yale College young Eddy excelled in mathematics, receiving a first prize at every competition, and the senior gold medal at his graduation in 1867. He continued his education by entering the engineering course of the Sheffield Scientific School of New Haven, where he received the degree of Ph.B. in 1868. He was instructor in mathematics and Latin at the University of Tennessee, Knoxville, during its reorganization in 1868–69, following the civil war. During 1869-73 he was assistant professor in mathematics and civil engineering at Cornell University, where he received the graduate degree of C.E. in 1870, and in 1872 the first degree of Ph.D. conferred by that university. He was adjunct professor of mathematics at Princeton University during the year 1873-74, when, upon the organization of the new university at Cincinnati, he was elected its first professor to fill the chair of mathematics, astronomy, and civil engineering. The course in civil engineering was established at his suggestion; and as the institution was without a president during a large part of his sixteen years' residence there, many of the duties of that office devolved upon him as dean of the academic faculty. In 1890 he declined the presidency to accept that of Rose Polytechnic Institute, Terre Haute, Ind., where he became established in 1891. During 1879-80, on leave of absence, he studied mathematical physics at the Physikalische Institute and the University of Berlin, and at the Sorbonne and the Collège de France, Paris. He became professor of engineering and mechanics at the University of Minnesota, Minneapolis, in 1894, and in 1906 he was made dean of the graduate school of that institution; the following year he was also put in charge of the department of mathematics and mechanics in the college of engineering. In June, 1912, he was retired from the university with the title of professor and dean emeritus, with an allowance from the Carnegie Foundation for the Advancement of Teaching, and is now (1916) engaged in practice as a consulting engineer, and in the publication of his researches in the theory of reinforced concrete flat slabs. Dr. Eddy is a member of the American Philosophical Society, the American Mathematical Society, the American Physical Society, and fellow of the American Association for the Advancement of Science, of which he was vice-president in 1884 for section A. (mathematics and astronomy); he was one of the founders of the Society for the Promotion of Engineering Education and was its president in 1896-97; affiliate of the American Society of Mechanical Engineers; member and secretary of the section for applied mathematics at the International Congress of Arts and Sciences, St. Louis, 1904; member of the honorary societies of Phi Beta Kappa and Sigma Xi. He is author of "Analytical Geometry" (1874), "Researches in Graphical Statics" (1878), "Thermodynamics" (1879); "Neue Constructionen aus der Graphischen Statik" (1880); "Maximum Stresses Under Concrete Loads" (1890), "Theory of Reinforced Concrete Floor Slabs" (1913), co-author with C. A. P. Turner, "Concrete

Steel Construction'' (1914), and many papers in mathematical and technical journals. He has also contributed important papers to the transactions of the American Society of Civil Engineers, the American Society of Mechanical Engineers and the American Institute of Electrical Engineers. Many of the graphical methods originated by him were later introduced into technical literature and engineering textbooks. He has delivered lectures on the physical constitution and condition of the various colored stars, the kinetic theory of gases, the theory and action of the steam turbine, the theory and application of the gyroscope to the monorail car, and other subjects of a scientific nature. He received the degree of LL.D. from Centre College, Kentucky, in 1892, and the honorary degree of Sc.D. from Yale University in 1912. Dr. Eddy was married at New Haven, Conn., Jan. 4, 1870, to Sebella Elizabeth, daughter of Rev. Horace Addison Taylor, a clergyman of the Congregational Church. Their children are: Ruth Elizabeth (married Charles F. Keyes, of Minneapolis), Horace Taylor, Esther Mabel (married Clive Hastings, of Atchison, Kan.), Beatrice Emogene, and Helen Frances, wife of Jenness B. Frear.

JAMES, Ollie M., U. S. senator, was born in Crittenden county, Ky., July 27, 1871, son of L. H. and Elizabeth James. He received a public and academic school education. After serving one year as a page in the Kentucky legislature (1887), he began the study of law in his father's law office and was admitted to the bar in 1891. He acquired a large and lucrative practice of both civil and criminal law. He was one of the attorneys for Gov. Goebel (q. v.) in his celebrated contest for governor of the state of Kentucky. His interest in politics began as a schoolboy when he perused the pages of the congressional records, learning some of the speeches by heart and delivering them before his class when his turn came to declaim. He was a delegate to the Democratic national convention at Chicago in 1896, and a delegate-at-large ot the Democratic national conventions at St. Louis in 1904, and in 1908 at Denver, Colo., serving as chairman of the Kentucky delegation at all three conventions. At St. Louis in 1904 he made one of the speeches seconding the nomination of William J. Bryan for president. He was also delegate-at-large to the Baltimore convention in 1912 and delivered the address notifying Woodrow Wilson of his nomination for the presidency. He was chairman of the state convention of Kentucky in 1900 which sent delegates to the national convention at Kansas City. He was elected to national congress in 1902, serving in the 58th, 59th, 60th, 61st and 62d congresses. In July, 1911, he was elected to the U. S. senate by the Democratic party in a state-wide primary and was ratified by the Kentucky legislature in January, 1912, for the term of six years beginning Mar. 4, 1913. Sen. James is a striking figure in the national house, being six feet six inches in height, well built, with massive, square shoulders, and weighing 275 pounds. He possesses oratorical abilities of a high order, being compared to Robert G. Ingersoll in the manner of diction and felicitous phrase, and to William J. Bryan in his manner of voice. He is one of the best orators in both houses of congress. He was married Dec. 2, 1903, to Ruth, daughter of Henry A. Thomas, a Methodist clergyman of Marion, Ky.

COTTER, Joseph B., first bishop of the Roman Catholic diocese of Winona, Minn., was born in Liverpool, England, Nov. 19, 1844, son of Lawrence P. and Anne Mary (Perrin) Cotter. The family came to America in 1850 and located in Cleveland, O., whence, in 1855, they moved to St. Paul, Minn. His primary studies were made in the local schools and he then went to St. Vincent's College, Beatty, Pa. He was ordained priest in St. Paul by Bishop Grace, May 23, 1871, and shortly after was made pastor of St. Thomas' Church, Winona. Here his ministrations extended over the six adjoining counties, a rich agricultural section of the southern part of the state which with the building of railroads developed so rapidly that in 1889 it was formed into a diocese with Winona as the see city and Father Colter as the first bishop. His consecration took place in the Cathedral, St. Paul, Dec. 27, 1889, and during his administration of nearly twenty years the resources and material fabric of the diocese were doubled to meet the requirements of the equally increased congregations. He was an ardent temperance advocate and served for several terms as president of the Catholic Total Abstinence Union of America. Under its auspices he lectured in the leading cities of the country and secured more than 60,000 pledges of total abstinence. He died of Bright's disease at Winona, on June 28, 1909.

GROSE, George Richmond, president of De Pauw University, was born in Nicholas co., W. Va., July 14, 1869, son of Andrew Dixon and Mary Estaline (Harrah) Grose. His father was a farmer. He received his preliminary education in the public schools, in which he became a teacher for two years. He was graduated at Ohio Wesleyan University in 1894, and at Boston University in 1896 with the degree of S. T.B. From Ohio Wesleyan University he received the degree of A.M. in 1896, and that of D.D. in 1908. He was licensed to preach at the age of seventeen, and in 1896 joined the New England Conference. He was pastor of the following charges: Cherry Valley Methodist Episcopal Church, Mass., 1896-97; First M. E. Church, Jamaica Plain, Mass., 1897-1900; First M. E. Church, Newton, Mass., 1900-05; First M. E. Church, Lynn, Mass., 1905-08, and Grace M. E. Church, Baltimore, Md., 1908-13. In 1912 he was elected president of De Pauw University, Greencastle, Ind., and was inaugurated Apr. 23, 1913. During the first three years of his administration of the college $300,000 was added to the permanent endowment of the institution, a new building costing $125,000 was erected, and a department of Home Economics was added. Six professors and instructors have been added to the faculty, and there has been a steady growth in the number of students enrolled. He is the author of "The Outlook for Religion" (1913), and "Religion and the Mind" (1915), and is a contributor to "The Methodist Review" and "The Bible Magazine." In college he was president of the Y. M. C. A., and he is a member of the Twentieth Century, and Itinerants clubs, Boston; the Twentieth Century and Eclectic clubs, Baltimore, and of the Sigma Alpha Epsilon fraternity. He was married June 28, 1894, to Lucy, daughter of Samuel M. Dickerson, of Cadiz, O., and has five children: Mary Frances, Wilbur Dickerson, Helen, Virginia and William Edwin Grose.

HUSTING, Paul Oscar, U. S. senator, was born at Fond du Lac, Wis., Apr. 25, 1866, son of John Pierre and Mary Magdalene (Juneau) Husting, and grandson of L. Solomon Juneau (q.v.), one of the pioneers of the Northwest country, who married Josette Vieux, daughter of Jacques Vieux, whose wife was a daughter of Ah-na-pe-wah, a chief of the Menomonee tribe of Indians. John Pierre Husting, father of the senator, was a native of Lingten, Luxemburg, and coming to America in 1855, settled at Theresa, Dodge co., Wis. Paul O. Husting received his preliminary education in the public schools, and studied law at the law school of the University of Wisconsin. He was admitted to the Wisconsin bar in 1895, and in that year began the practice of his profession at Mayville, Dodge co. From 1897 to 1910 he was a member of the firm of Lamoreux & Husting, and since the latter year his firm has been Husting & Brother. During 1902–06 he served as district attorney of Dodge county, and he was a member of the Wisconsin state senate during 1906–15. Since Mar. 4, 1915, he has been a member of the U. S. senate. He has been especially active in sustaining the rights of the people to hunt and fish in navigable waters, and in the conservation of their rights in natural resources of state. As a lawyer in general practice he participated in litigation in all of the federal and state courts in Wisconsin. He is unmarried.

BREWER, Earl Le Roy, thirty-sixth governor of Mississippi (1912–16), was born on a farm near Vaiden, Carroll co., Miss., Aug. 11, 1869, son of Ratcliff Rodney and Mary Elizabeth (McEachern) Brewer, grandson of Le Roy Brewer, and great-grandson of Le Roy Brewer, a schoolteacher in Dublin, Ireland, who came to this country in 1780 and settled in Georgia. He was educated in the public schools of Mississippi, and was graduated in the law department of the University of Mississippi in 1892. He immediately began the practice of his profession in Water Valley, Miss., forming a partnership with Julian C. Wilson, which continued until 1901. He was state senator during 1895–99, being the youngest member of that body, and in 1902 he was appointed district attorney of the newly-created eleventh judicial district of Mississippi, serving until August, 1906, when he resigned to enter the race for governor of Mississippi. He was defeated, and then resumed the practice of law at Clarksdale, Miss. In November, 1911, he was elected governor, without opposition, and was inaugurated in the following January. His first year in office witnessed many reforms inaugurated and progressive laws passed in the legislature. One of these called for an appropriation for the maintenance and support, and provided the necessary equipment for the indigent Confederate soldiers, sailors, their wives and widows at Beauvoir, the Confederate Soldiers' Home. Another appropriated $5,000 for the benefit of the Confederate Veterans' Hospital Annex at Vicksburg. Gov. Brewer has also shown his deep interest in the King's Daughters Hospital and Training School at Gulfport. He is a member and ex-officio president of the board of trustees of the University of Mississippi, the Agricultural and Mechanical College, and the Industrial Institute and the Alcorn Agricultural and Mechanical College. Under his regime an act has been passed by the legislature abolishing and prohibiting Greek letter fraternities and sororities, and all secret orders among students in the State University and in all other education institutions supported in whole or in part by the state. This is a radical measure, but one which has been taken under advisement by educators and legislators in different parts of the country, and the stand thus taken by Gov. Brewer will undoubtedly be followed elsewhere. Another no less unusual legislative measure supported by him was an act prohibiting hotels, restaurants, cafés, dining-cars, railroad companies and sleeping-car companies from allowing gratuities or "tips" to be given to employes.

Employes themselves and persons giving the "tips" are also prohibited from, and held responsible and liable to punishment for disregarding the law. In 1913 Gov. Brewer displayed his sense of mercy and justice when he pardoned an escaped prisoner who had been at large and leading an honest life since 1888, declaring that the ends of justice had been served. The Mississippi Centennial Exposition Co., with a capital of $500,000, was chartered by the legislature in 1913 to celebrate the centennial anniversary of the state's admission into the Union of the United States of America in 1917, and the governor was authorized to call upon congress for suitable aid and to invite foreign countries to participate in the celebration, as well as each of the states and territories of the United States. During his administration the legislature also passed an act providing for an inspection system of state banks and a tax on banks to provide a fund for paying depositors of failed banks. The state of Mississippi had hitherto lived under the appointive judicial system, but beginning with Gov. Brewer's administration district and supreme court judges and chancellors were elected by popular vote. Another constitutional amendment at this time provided for the initiative and referendum. He is a member of the Knights of Honor, Knights of Pythias, Masonic Lodge, the Woodmen of the World, the Benevolent and Protective Order of Elks, and formerly belonged to the Grange Farmers' Alliance. Gov. Brewer was married in 1897, to Minnie Marion Block, daughter of Adrian Block, a merchant of Water Valley, Miss., and has three daughters: Minnie, Earlene and Claudia Brewer.

STUART, Henry Carter, governor of Virginia, was born at Wytheville, Va., Jan. 18, 1855, son of William Alexander and Mary Taylor (Carter) Stuart, and a descendant of Archibald Stuart, who fled from Scotland because of political uprisings, in which he had taken a leading part, and settled in Virginia in 1726. Archibald Stuart married Jeanet Brown, and the line is traced through their son Alexander and his second wife, Mary Moore Paxton; their son Alexander and his wife, Nancy Dabney, and their son Archibald and his wife, Elizabeth I. Pannill, who were the grandparents of Henry Carter Stuart. Archibald Stuart (4) was the representative of Virginia in congress for a number of years. Another distinguished member of the family was Gen. J. E. B. Stuart, the Confederate cavalryman. Gov. Stuart was graduated at Emory and Henry College in 1874, with the degree of A.B., subsequently taking the law course at the University of Virginia. Instead of practising his profession, he engaged in farming, first as the manager of a large estate, and later as its owner. Having come of a long line of planters, he turned to this occupation with an especial aptitude, and was soon known as one of the most progressive farmers of his state. By degrees his interests expanded, to include cattle raising and the ownership of large coal lands and iron mines, in both of which he is now an extensive holder of valuable properties. He is president and treasurer of the Stuart Land & Cattle Co. of Virginia, and president of the Buckhorn Iron & Improvement Co., and the First National Bank of Lebanon, Va. He gained public notice in connection with civic and political questions when still a young man, and since then has frequently taken an active interest in public affairs. He was a delegate to the National Democratic Convention of 1892, and in 1902 was a member of the Virginia Constitutional Convention. He served on the Virginia state corporation commission, which is entrusted with supervision over corporations operating in Virginia, from 1903 to 1908. In November, 1913, he was elected governor of Virginia for the term of 1914–18, and brought to the duties of that office an unusual equipment in character, experience and ability. During his administration the state legislature enacted a statewide prohibition law, which was voted on by the citizens of the state Sept. 22, 1914, and went into effect Nov. 1, 1916. He is a member of the Westmoreland and Commonwealth clubs of Richmond; the Shenandoah Club of Roanoke; the Society of the Sons of the American Revolution; the O. B. K. fraternity, and other organizations. He was married Feb. 26, 1896, to Margaret Bruce, daughter of Charles D. Carter, of Saltville, Va., and they have one daughter, Mary Stuart.

OSBORNE, Thomas Burr, chemist, was born in New Haven, Conn., Aug. 5, 1859, son of Arthur D. and Frances Louisa (Blake) Osborne. He was graduated at Yale College in 1881, and then devoting himself to special studies in chemistry, he continued at Yale, receiving in 1885 the degree of Ph.D. In 1886 he accepted the appointment of research chemist to the Connecticut Agricultural Experiment Station and in 1904 that of research associate to the Carnegie Institution of Washington, both of which offices he still holds. Of his earlier investigations the following were published in the "American Chemical Journal": "The Separation of Zinc and Nickel" (1884) and "On Paraform-nitr-anilide" (1886). An important study on "The Determination of Phosphoric Acid in Fertilizers by the 'Citrate Method'" (1890) was taken up in association with Prof. Samuel W. Johnson, the results of which appeared in the report of the experiment station for 1889. After studying the methods of mechanical soil analysis for two years, Dr. Osborne devoted himself to the study of the chemistry of the vegetable proteins, which became his life work, and the results of his researches are included in more than one hundred published papers. Among these may be cited the following: "The Proteids or Albuminoids of the Oat Kernel" (1891–92); "Proteids of the Flax Seed" (1892); "The Proteids of the Kidney Bean" (1894); "The Proteids of the Rye Kernel" (1895); "The Proteids of Barley" (1895); "The Chemical Nature of Diastase" (1895); "Egg Albumin" (1899); and "The Protein Constituents of Egg White" (1900), all of which were contributed to the Journal of the American Chemical Society. Among his more recent papers are a series on the hydrolysis of various proteins, notably "Hydrolysis of Hordein" (1907); "Hydrolysis of the Proteins of Maize, Zea Mays" (1908); and "Hydrolysis of Crystallized Albumin from Hen's Egg" (1909), which were published in the "American Journal of Physiology." He contributed an article on the "Preparation of Vegetable Proteins" to the Handbuch der biochemischen Arbeitsmethoden (1909); a review of the "Knowledge of the Vegetable Proteins" to the Ergebnisse der Physiologie (1910), and a chapter on the "Chemistry of the Vegetable Proteins" to the Biochemisches Handlexikon (1910). To the publications of the Carnegie Institution of Washington he has contributed "The Proteins of the Wheat Kernel" (1907), a volume of 119 pages, and in collaboration with Lafayette B. Mendel of Yale, "Feeding Experiments with Isolated Food Substances" (1911), a work containing 191 pages. He is also the author in book form of "The Vegetable Proteins" (1909), and of "The Chemistry of the Proteins," which he de-

livered in New York as one of the Harvey Lectures. His more recent publications have been chiefly in collaboration with Prof. Mendel and concern the relative nutritive value of various proteins which had been the subject of his earlier investigations. These have appeared during the last six years in the "American Journal of Biological Chemistry" and Hoppe-Seyler's "Zeitschrift für physiologische Chemie." Dr. Osborne is an associate editor of the "Journal of Biological Chemistry," and he is a member of chemical societies both in the United States and abroad, including the American Society of Biological Chemists, of which he was president in 1910. In recognition of his many valuable contributions to science, Yale University conferred upon him the honorary degree of Sc.D. in 1910, and in the same year he was elected to membership in the National Academy of Sciences, to the biographical memoirs of which he contributed in 1911 an appreciative sketch of his life-long friend and senior colleague, Samuel W. Johnson. He is an honorary member of the London Chemical Society, and a fellow of the American Academy of Arts and Sciences. He was married June 23, 1886, to Elizabeth Annah, daughter of Prof. Samuel W. Johnson, of New Haven, Conn.

PERRET, Frank Alvord, inventor and volcanologist, was born in Hartford, Conn., Aug. 2, 1867, son of Charles and Mary Elizabeth (Alvord) Perret. His father, a native of Switzerland, was an importer of Swiss watches, and at the time of his death (1916) had lived in this country for more than sixty years. The son was educated at the Brooklyn Polytechnic Institute, and began his scientific career as assistant in Edison's East Side laboratory. In 1886 he organized the firm of Barrett & Perret in Brooklyn to manufacture medical batteries, and Mr. Perret busied himself with electric motors. He invented two-pole motors, and a multi-polar low speed motor and dynamo, with carbon brushes and self-oiling bearings, that could be run by a novice, and was subsequently combined with the Stine-Smith coal mining machine used extensively to undercut soft coal in mines, and patented in 1886. He saw a great field for electric motors, and his motor with laminated magnets the first to be extensively manufactured. At the age of nineteen he assisted in organizing the Elektron Manufacturing Co. in Brooklyn, which was afterward removed to Springfield, Mass., and devoted to the manufacture of the Perret electric motors and dynamos. He invented the "counter electromotive force" principle of electric elevator control, which is now in general use. In 1896 he designed and constructed an automobile to carry five persons, using the electric storage battery as motive power, and subsequently he invented a light weight storage battery for this purpose. His health having broken down, he went to Naples, Italy, in 1904, for a rest, and while there became much interested in Mt. Vesuvius and the Royal Vesuvian observatory. He was appointed honorary assistant to the director, Prof. R. V. Matteucci, and has made Italy his headquarters for what has become his life's work, conducting a series of close range studies and direct observations of volcanic and earthquake phenomena of the greatest scientific value, often in the midst of the greatest danger, the work being financially supported principally by the Volcanic Research Society, of Springfield, Mass. The Science Museum of Springfield contains a unique collection of volcanic materials collected by him. After four years of observation he was able to

EARL L. BREWER
GOVERNOR

THOMAS B. OSBORNE
CHEMIST

HENRY C. STUART
GOVERNOR

FRANK A. PERRET
VOLCANOLOGIST

William Rotch

forecast and determine with scientific accuracy the time and duration of eruptions of the largest volcanoes of the world. An instance of this is found in the eruption of Stromboli in 1907, the heaviest that had occurred in many years. On the island were 4,000 people in fear for their lives. The government, having sent warships to the spot, consulted Mr. Perret as to the necessity of removing the inhabitants, and he announced that the culmination of the eruption was passed and that, although there would be a revival at a certain date, it would be less severe and not dangerous. The subsequent action of the volcano confirmed his opinion in every respect. In February, 1908, he predicted the eruption of Mt. Etna that occurred three months later, and also an event for December of that year, which proved to be the Messina earthquake. The Italian government, in recognition of what he has accomplished, conferred upon him knighthood with the cross of Official Cavalier of the Crown of Italy. He visited the eruption at Teneriffe in 1909, lived through the eruption of Etna in 1910, and as director of the Hawaiian Expedition of the Massachusetts Institute of Technology, lived at the crater of Kilauea through the summer of 1911. He witnessed the great eruptions of Stromboli in 1912 and 1915, and that of Sakurashima (Japan) in 1914. He is the first student of volcanoes to depend exclusively upon precise personal observation of actual volcanic activity, and he has been fortunate in being a spectator of nearly all the accessible great eruptions of the past decade. He is also first to make a serious attempt to predict eruptions through the indications of earth sounds and tremors given by the dictograph and other modern apparatus. His collection of some thousands of photographs of volcanic phenomena is unique, and has received highest awards at expositions in Florence and Rome. He was a founder-member of the department of electricity of the Brooklyn Institute of Arts and Sciences, and is a member of the Société Astronomique de France, the Accademia dei Zelanti, of Acireale, Sicily, and honorary inspector of the evening schools of the Naples Chamber of Commerce. Mr. Perret is the author of various scientific papers published in the "American Journal of Science" and the "Bulletin of the Brooklyn Institute of Arts and Sciences." He is volcanologist of the Carnegie Geophysical Laboratory, of Washington, D. C. In politics he is a Republican, and in religion a communicant of the Protestant Episcopal church. He is unmarried.

ROTCH, William, civil engineer and capitalist, was born at New Bedford, Mass., July 22, 1844, son of William J. and Emily (Morgan) Rotch. His earliest paternal American ancestor was William Rotch, a native of Salisbury, England, who emigrated at the close of the seventeenth century and settled in Massachusetts. From him the line of descent is traced through his son Joseph and his wife, Love Macy, to their son William, who was the great-great-grandfather of William Rotch. Joseph Rotch founded New Bedford in 1765 and established the whale fishery there. His son William was considered the first citizen of the New Bedford of his day; owned the ship Bedford, which first displayed the American flag in British waters after the war of the revolution, and with his brother Francis owned the ship Dartmouth, from which the British tea was thrown overboard in Boston harbor in 1773, the Dartmouth having been chartered to the East India Co. of England. Mr. Rotch's father, a graduate of Harvard College and marshal of his class,

was the second mayor of New Bedford, served as representative to the Massachusetts general court and was identified with almost every industrial and financial institution of New Bedford. After graduating at Harvard in 1865, the son entered the Ecole Centrale des Arts et Manufactures, Paris, graduating in 1869 ninth in a class of 225, and receiving the degree of Ingénieur Civil. He began his professional career in 1871 as assistant engineer of the Fall River (Mass.) water works, in course of construction, and was chief engineer from 1874 until the completion of the works in 1880. Thereafter he became consulting engineer and purchasing agent of the Mexican Central Railway Co., the Sonora Railway Co. of Mexico, Atlantic and Pacific Railroad Co. and the California Southern Railroad Co.—the last-named two now forming the western portion of the "Santa Fé System"—and was engineer of other railroads in Ohio, Massachusetts, etc. During 1880-1900 he was a director of the Mexican Central Railway Co., the Atchison, Topeka and Santa Fé Railway Co. and others. During 1886-94 he was president of the Tremont Electric Lighting Co. and the Consolidated Electric Manufacturing Co., and a director of its successor, the Walker Co., which installed the complete electric plant in the Waldorf-Astoria Hotel, New York, then the finest electric lighting plant in America. In 1881 he was appointed by Gov. Long engineer of the commission which finally established the boundary line between Massachusetts and Rhode Island, which had been in dispute for over 250 years. He is president of the Railroad Wharf and Storage Co., State Wharf and Storage Co., Terrible-Dunderberg Mining and Powder Co., vice-president Bonanza Development Co., treasurer Broadway Storage Co., Nonquitt Real Estate Trust, Rotch Traveling Scholarship for Architects, and director of the Adams Nervine Asylum and of the Infants' Hospital. In 1870 he was elected first president of the Union for Good Works, still the leading philanthropic institution of New Bedford. He is president of the Alliance Française of Boston and Cambridge, member of the American Society of Civil Engineers, the Association des anciens élèves de l'Ecole Centrale of Paris, the Bostonian Society, the Society of Colonial Wars, the Somerset and Harvard clubs of Boston and of the Nonquitt Golf Club and Wamsutta Club of New Bedford.

THOMPSON, J[ames] Walter, advertising, was born in Pittsfield, Mass., Oct. 28, 1847, son of Alonzo D. and Cornelia (Roosevelt) Thompson. His boyhood was spent in Ohio, where he was educated in the public schools. He removed to New York city in the early sixties and, when twenty years of age, secured a position as bookkeeper and general assistant in a small advertising agency. Soon afterwards he became a solicitor for the agency, and eventually purchased the business of his employer, whose successor he became. Mr. Thompson was a pioneer in the development of magazine advertising. He was one of the first to appreciate its vast possibilities as an economic and efficient method of distributing the merchandise of the world, and it was largely through his early efforts that advertising in magazines became recognized as a great merchandising tool in modern business methods. In 1868 most of the magazines were literary ventures, some of which, like "Harper's Monthly," refused outside advertising on any terms. He conceived the idea that if he could unite the magazines in an advertising propaganda the advantages to both advertisers and publishers would be enormous; that all of the principal magazines, presented collectively as a unit, would be a factor which would demand the attention of the largest advertiser. His task was twofold: to persuade publishers that a substantial revenue might be derived from this little cultivated field and to convince possible advertisers that their interests would be served by magazine advertising. A remarkably successful advertisement of one of his clients in "Godey's Ladies' Book" and "Peterson's Magazine" gave him his start. With the tangible results of that "ad" he demonstrated the soundness of his views and soon afterwards became the sole advertising representative of thirty magazines. Merchants learned that the price of one insertion in the magazines secured a thirty-day presentation of their announcements in the homes of the people, and that in no other way could they so quickly and economically build up a nation-wide business, while the publishers discovered that these back pages were a hitherto unworked gold mine. The revenue thus obtained enabled them to improve the quality of their product; to use better paper, type and illustrations; to adopt the newly-invented half-tone process of illustration, later on to make use of color plates. More money could be paid to authors and higher class artists could be employed. Ten and fifteen cent magazines, with circulations above the half-million mark, furnishing entertainment and instruction to millions, were made possible by the income derived from their advertising pages. And these carefully and often artistically prepared pages, in the modern magazine, are to many readers no less entertaining and instructive than the body of the magazine itself. It is estimated that fully $600,000,000 is expended annually in all kinds of advertising in the United States. The J. Walter Thompson Co., of which Mr. Thompson is president, is one of the largest as well as oldest advertising agencies in the United States. It operates fully-equipped branch offices in Boston, Chicago, Detroit, Cincinnati and Toronto, Canada, and maintains an office in London. Through its Spanish department it covers Latin-America, being in close touch with all the prominent newspapers and periodicals in the West Indies, Central and South America. It has correspondents in every important city of Europe and is recognized as an authority in every branch of advertising. Mr. Thompson was married in 1877 to Margaret R., daughter of James Bogle, a portrait painter and member of the National Academy of Design. They have one son, Walter Roosevelt Thompson. Mr. Thompson has many interests aside from the J. Walter Thompson Co. He is a member of the New York Chamber of Commerce, the New York Yacht Club, the Players' and many other clubs. For many years he made yachting his recreation, having owned a boat of some kind from his eighth to his sixty-fourth year. The portrait accompanying this article, in the costume of the New York Yacht Club, is from the only photograph available of the few which he has ever had taken.

TRACY, Howard Crosby, lawyer, was born at Westborough, Mass., Aug. 1, 1866, son of Jeremiah Evarts (1835) and Martha Sherman (Greene) Tracy. His earliest paternal American ancestor was Stephen Tracy, presumably a native of Great Yarmouth, England, who came over in 1623 and settled in Plymouth, Mass. From him the line of descent is traced through his son John and his wife, Mary Prince; their son Stephen and

his wife, Deborah Bingham; their son Thomas and his wife, Elizabeth Warner; their son Joseph and his wife, Ruth Carter, and their son, Ebenezer Carter, and his wife, Martha Sherman Evarts, who were the grandparents of Howard Crosby Tracy. His maternal grandfather was the Rev. David Greene, of Roxbury, Mass., who was one of the first secretaries of the American Board of Commissioners for Foreign Missions. His father is a lawyer who retired from active practice in 1907, having been formerly a member of the firm of Evarts, Choate & Beaman. He was graduated A.B. at Yale University in 1887 and at the law school of Columbia University in 1889 with the degree of LL.B., *cum laude*. In the latter year he began his professional career in the office of the celebrated law firm of Evarts, Choate & Beaman, New York city, and remained in that office as a clerk until 1893, when he became a member of the firm of Tracy & Lane, with Wolcott G. Lane as his partner. This partnership continued until 1902, after which he practiced independently for a brief period, and then entered the employ of the Lawyers' Title Insurance and Trust Co. With Philip S. Dean and Francis J. McBarron, he organized the firm of Dean, Tracy & McBarron in 1913. His legal practice has been chiefly in connection with real estate matters, the examination of titles, foreclosure and partition suits, accountings, management of estates, and acting as one of the counsel of the Lawyers' Title Insurance and Trust Co. He served several years as a member of the Republican city committee of Plainfield, N. J. He is a member of the Association of the Bar of the City of New York. His residence is at Plainfield, N. J., where he indulges his favorite pursuits of gardening and fruit growing. He was married in St. Paul, Minn., June 24, 1893, to Minerva Bingham, daughter of Eastburn E. Lamson, of Salt Lake City, Utah. Portrait opposite page 337.

BLAVATSKY, Helena Petrovna Hahn, theosophist, was born at Ekaterinoslav, Russia, July 31, 1831, daughter of Col. Hahn von Rothernstern Hahn, who was of a noble family originally hailing from Mecklenburg; her mother was a daughter of the Russian statesman, Andrew Fadeef, and of the Princess Helena Dolgorouky. She was thus a descendant of Rurik and a member of the highest Russian aristocracy, the Dolgoroukys being a considerably older and nobler family than the Romanoffs themselves. Her mother, who had some renown in Russia as a novelist, died while Helena was still a child, and the greater part of her childhood was spent at Saratoff on the Volga, at the castle of her grandfather, who was governor of the province. At the age of fourteen she visited Paris and London with her father, and three years later was married to Gen. Nicephore Blavatsky, vicegovernor of Erivan in the Caucasus. Within a few weeks, however, she found that life with Gen. Blavatsky was impossible, and she left him. She was but a girl of seventeen; he was over sixty. The following years were spent in traveling, during which she visited all parts of Europe, Egypt, India, and both North and South America. In 1848, while in Egypt, she met an old Copt with whom she studied the ancient teachings of that country; she met him again several times during her travels, and spent some time with him at Boulak in 1871. It is said that she fought under Garibaldi in the wars of Italian liberation, and that she was wounded at Mentana. After the death of her father Mme. Blavatsky came to the United States in 1873, was naturalized and supported herself in New York

HOWARD C. TRACY
LAWYER

MME. HELENA BLAVATSKY
THEOSOPHIST

WILLIAM Q. JUDGE
THEOSOPHIST

KATHERINE W. TINGLEY
THEOSOPHIST

city by her writings, which attracted considerable attention. With Col. Henry S. Olcott and William Q. Judge she founded the Theosophical Society in September, 1875, the objects of which were: (1) To be the nucleus of the universal brotherhood without distinction of race, creed, caste, sex or color; (2) to study oriental and other religions, philosophies, science and art; (3) to indicate the importance of this inquiry; and (4) to investigate the hidden mysteries of nature and the latent powers of man. Col. Olcott was the first president and Mme. Blavatsky, although holding officially only the position of corresponding secretary, was regarded as teacher and inspirer of the whole society. A stir in the literary world was created by the publication of her first theosophical book, "Isis Unveiled" (1877), in which almost all the literatures of the world are laid under contribution for the sake of introducing the ideas of theosophy to the western world. Briefly, the book undertakes to prove the existence of a secret wisdom, preserved by sages in all lands, which is the root from which all the world religions have sprung. Throughout her life she devoted her immense learning and the titanic force of her nature to ethical and moral ends; she elucidated and examined the world religions in order to prove the essential unity of all religions and of man, and thus to remove one of the most potent causes of strife and human separation. She founded "The Theosophist" magazine, for a time dwelt at Madras, India, and after 1884 in London, where she was largely engaged in literary work, writing and publishing "The Secret Doctrine" (1888); "The Key to Theosophy" (1889); "The Theosophical Glossary" (1892); translating fragments from the Thibetan "Book of Golden Precepts" under the name of "The Voice of the Silence" (1889); editing and writing for her magazine "Lucifer" and contributing to other theosophical magazines both in French and English; also in teaching the body of disciples that grew up around her and in holding receptions for the public. She labored under great physical suffering towards the end, and some who worked with her during her latter years declare that her life was shortened by the bitter persecutions she received from her enemies. She died in London, May 8, 1891.

JUDGE, William Quan, theosophist, was born in Dublin, Ireland, Apr. 13, 1851, son of Frederic H. and Alice M. (Quan) Judge. At an early age he began an earnest study of books on religion and mysticism, devoting himself particularly to the mystical books of the Bible. He came to America in 1864, settling in New York city, where he entered the law office of Delafield Smith. He became naturalized upon reaching his majority, was admitted to the bar a month later and practiced successfully for many years, specializing in commercial law. In 1874 he met Mme. Blavatsky through Col. Henry S. Olcott, and in the following years joined with these in the founding of the Theosophical Society, of which he was elected counsel. In 1878, when Mme. Blavatsky and Pres. Olcott went abroad, the burden of conducting the affairs of the society and extending its work in America fell on his shoulders, for though Gen. Abner Doubleday had been made president pro tem., he recognized the talents and devotion of the young lawyer and gladly coöperated with him. For several years he continued a quiet and almost unsupported struggle to advance the cause of theosophy, devoting his energies to his legal work by day and studying and writing on theosophy and holding theosophical meetings by night. Gradually

he won support, mainly among solid business men in New York and elsewhere; larger offices were taken, and the Aryan Theosophical Society was formed in New York with a large and influential membership. Branches sprang up throughout the country wherever he was able to lecture himself or to organize meetings and lectures. In 1886 he founded "The Path," the official publication of the Theosophical Society in America, which he edited until his death. His theosophical work took him on several journeys to Europe and India, and on one of these visits to his native Ireland he formed a theosophical society in that country. In 1888 Mr. Judge suggested to Mme. Blavatsky that she should establish an inner group of students, to be open only to the most earnest among the members, who should pledge themselves to work for human brotherhood and upliftment and self-purification on sane lines. At her request he organized such a body, drew up its rules, and was the teacher in it under her. He now gave up his law practice and devoted himself entirely to the work of the Theosophical Society, touring the country and lecturing in many cities on the subject. In 1895 he was elected president of the American society for life. Members of the parent society in other parts of the world took similar action and the society was thus freed from certain elements that imperiled its existence as a working organization for the upliftment of humanity. Meanwhile the persecution that he endured had had its effect on the health of Mr. Judge. His constitution, undermined by recurring attacks of chagres fever and weakened by the struggle he had maintained in protecting the society from becoming dogmatic and a tool in the hands of ambitious self-seekers, at last gave way under the strain. He passed away on Mar. 21, 1896, leaving the charge of the theosophical movement to Katherine Tingley, the present leader, who for several years, although known only to a few of the members, had been his constant counsellor and supporter. His chief literary monument is "The Path," edited and largely written by him during the last ten years of his life. He also wrote "Echoes from the Orient" (1890); "Letters That Have Helped Me" (1891), and "An Epitome of Theosophy" (1893), and numerous pamphlets and mystical stories, many of the latter dealing with ancient life in Ireland. His writings are marked by simplicity, in some cases by great beauty of style, and above all by the light they shed on the inner nature of man. He was married in 1876 to Ella M., daughter of Joseph Smith, of Brooklyn, N. Y. He died in New York city, Mar. 21, 1896.

TINGLEY, Katherine Westcott, theosophist, was born at Newburyport, Mass., July 6, 1852, daughter of James P. and Susan (Chase) Westcott, and a descendant of Stukely Westcott, one of the founders of Providence, R. I., and a close friend of Roger Williams. The trend of her nature from her earliest years was toward helping others and was particularly shown while living in a Southern city during the civil war. One night, unknown to any of her family, she stole out with her nurse, and later was found giving food to the Federal troops and Confederate prisoners bivouacked in the city and binding up the wounds of stragglers who had fallen exhausted on the pavement. After her marriage in 1889 to Philo B. Tingley, of Philadelphia, she continued philanthropic work along the same lines in New York, ministering to prisoners and unfortunates, establishing an emergency relief organization for the striking cloak makers in 1892, founding the "Do Good Mission" on the East

Side and establishing unsectarian Sunday-schools and classes for parents. While she was engaged in this work William Q. Judge, of the Theosophical Society, sought her out and interested her in the society's activities, and when Judge died in 1896 she became his successor. Upon assuming the leadership of the theosophical movement she announced her intention of establishing a city at Point Loma, Cal., which would be an educational center as well as the headquarters of theosophy for the whole world. One of her first acts was to found the School of Antiquity, and she instituted a theosophical crusade around the world, visiting most of the European countries, as well as Egypt, India, Ceylon, Australia and New Zealand. Many new centres of the Theosophical Society were formed and the membership trebled in that year. In Athens she cared for hundreds of Armenian refugees who were encamped outside the city, and in India she organized extensive relief work for the sufferers from famine. Returning to the United States in 1897, she formed the International Brotherhood League. At its annual convention in 1898 this league was reorganized, adopting the constitution of the Universal Brotherhood and the name being changed to the Universal Brotherhood and Theosophical Society. Its object primarily is to teach brotherhood, demonstrate that it is a fact in nature, and make it a living power in the life of humanity; secondly, to study ancient and modern religion, science, philosophy and art, and to investigate the laws of nature and the divine powers in man. By this action Mme. Tingley was accepted by the whole society as leader and official head for life, with power to appoint her successor. The society is unsectarian and non-political, and the services of its officers are gratuitous. In 1897 Mme. Tingley founded "The New Century," a theosophical weekly, afterward enlarged into the "Theosophical Path," with a world-wide circulation. In 1900 the headquarters of the theosophical movement was transferred from New York to Point Loma, Cal., where she erected a number of beautiful buildings, including the Raja Yoga Academy, the Aryan Memorial Temple (dedicated 1915 as the Temple of Peace), the international headquarters building, the Greek theatre (the first open-air Greek theatre in the United States) and the Aryan Theosophical Press. Soon afterward she established Raja Yoga schools in Cuba at Santiago, Pinar del Rio and Santa Clara. In 1897 she founded the Isis League of Music and Drama, the study of both of which forms an important feature of the Raja Yoga system of education. "Raja Yoga" is a Sanskrit term meaning "royal union," and signifies in its application to true education, the balance of all the faculties, physical, mental and moral. That is the fundamental idea of the Raja Yoga system—the development of character and emphasis of individual responsibility. The college was opened in 1900. It now has fifty-six teachers and professors and over 300 students, and degrees are conferred in arts and literature. In 1906 Mme. Tingley founded the Woman's International Theosophical League (unsectarian-humanitarian) and in 1911 the Men's International Theosophical League of Humanity, the purpose of both being "to promote a higher life and education for both men and women; to demonstrate the spirit of universal brotherhood and purity as the mainspring of true living, and to create a truer coöperation between men and women in the home, in civic and national life, and as members of the same human family in pursuit of the highest ideals for the upbuilding of the human race." A zealous worker for peace, she founded the Parliament of Peace and Universal Brotherhood in 1913, the first public sessions of which were on the island of Visingsö, Lake Vettern, Sweden, in that year. Soon after the European war began, Mme. Tingley proposed that all the neutral countries unite in an effort for peace, urging upon Pres. Wilson to take the initial step. The Parliament of Peace and Universal Brotherhood under her direction held public sessions at Point Loma and San Diego in 1915, and during the Panama-California Exposition in San Diego she lectured on peace almost every Sunday evening in the Isis Theater. She was one of the speakers at the International Conference of Women Workers to promote Permanent Peace at the International Panama-Pacific Exposition in San Francisco. In addition to the "Theosophical Path" and "El Sendero Teosofico," theosophical magazines are published under her direction in England, Sweden, Holland and Germany. As a lecturer she is recognized as one of the most brilliant orators of the day, having power possessed by few to inspire the mind and touch the heart. Over twenty-five nationalities are represented among the students at the Raja Yoga College and the international theosophical headquarters at Point Loma. Every child as well as every grown student that has come under her influence has been taught the principles of the highest patriotism, the loftiest morality and the purest life.

MONTGOMERY, John Joseph, scientist and inventor, was born at Yuba City, Cal., Feb. 15, 1858, son of Zachariah and Ellen (Evoy) Montgomery. His father was assistant attorney-general under Cleveland and his cousin was the Most Rev. Archbishop George Montgomery of California. His preparatory schooling was received at Santa Clara (Cal.) College, and he was graduated at St. Ignatius College, San Francisco, Cal., in 1879, his classmates including Hon. Francis C. Cleary, Hon. James D. Phelan, afterward mayor of San Francisco, and Rev. Richard H. Bell, well known for his researches in the field of wireless telegraphy. His inventive genius was early developed. After completing his college course his family removed to San Diego, Cal., where he conducted experiments in aeronautics, which had interested him since early youth. To test his theories in regard to aerodynamics he visited the sea coast and watched the flight and habits of sea birds, and studied the relation between weight and wing surface. Thus he evolved the idea of the parabolic curve in aeroplane wings. While a student at St. Ignatius College it was his good fortune to participate in the experimental electric work of Father Neri, the Jesuit scientist, then attracting universal attention. After the Franco-Prussian war the famous "Alliance Machine," used to furnish light for the defensive work during the siege of Paris, and which was called the parent of the dynamo, was sent to San Francisco. Father Neri devised a scheme of strengthening the magnets by means of a current from a storage battery. When Montgomery fitted up his first laboratory in San Diego he reproduced the "Alliance Machine" plus the Neri improvements, resulting in a modern dynamo of great power, but he did not patent it. Of his patented inventions the best known are the electric rectifier, which has proven a highly economical means of recharging storage batteries and changing electricity from an alternating to a direct current, and the telautoprint, by which the characters of the Morse telegraph alphabet are transmitted and recorded by a typewriter. But his name will be chiefly remembered for his contribution to the science of aeronautics. After giving much time and thought to the study of equilibrium, in 1884, he constructed an aeroplane on the model of the seagull and with it descended from a height of 300 feet. Successful gliding machines followed. In 1893 he went to Chicago and participated in the discussions of the Aeronautical Congress, of which Octave Chanute was then president, and his mastery of the subjects gained him admission to membership in the congress. In 1894 he became professor of applied sciences at Mt. St. Joseph's College, Humboldt county, Cal., and later held a similar chair in the University of Santa Clara, Cal. At both places he continued his studies of aerodynamics. In 1903 he constructed a successful aeroplane which, as he described it, "consists of two winged surfaces parabolic from point to rear edge, a flat tail, and a vertical fin or keel." After learning of its operation Alexander Graham Bell declared "all subsequent attempts in aviation must begin with the Montgomery machine." His first flights in this aeroplane took place on Mar. 16, 18 and 20, 1904, in the Santa Cruz Mountains, Cal., and were entirely independent of the knowledge of what the Wright brothers were doing in the East. Prince Hugo Deitrickstein of Austria, honorary president of the corporation for the furtherance of aerial navigation, and Brig.-Gen. Leopold Schleyer of the Imperial army, wrote informing Prof. Montgomery that the Austrian government after an investigation covering a period of years had decided that he should be placed as the master of aero navigation before Otto Lilienthal, to whom the honor had been given for a quarter of a century. In 1905, in the Santa Clara valley, an aeronaut, Daniel Maloney, descended 4,000 feet from a balloon with one of Montgomery's improved gliders, performing steering and diving movements scarcely excelled by the modern volplanes of the day, and terminating the flight upon a selected spot. These experiments are of peculiar interest in that they made possible the granting of United States patents on aeroplane devices. Up to the time of the successful demonstration of the Montgomery machine all flying machines were classed in the same category as perpetual motion devices, and patents were withheld on the ground that they were manifestly inoperative. A remarkable fact in connection with the activity and inventive genius of Montgomery is that he was at no time in touch with others in the world who were giving serious attention to aeronautical problems, he having but a vague and superficial knowledge of contemporary investigations at home and abroad. He is thus to be regarded as a pioneer in the art of flying, if not the actual father of aviation in America. While conducting experiments in a motorless aeroplane at Evergreen, near San Jose, Cal., he sustained injuries which resulted in his death. He possessed a theoretical and practical engineering ability of the rarest order, and his contributions to aeronautics were of unquestioned value to the scientific world. His contributions to aeronautic literature included, "New Principles of Aerial Flight" (1905); "The Aeroplane, a Scientific Study" (1906); "Some Early Gliding Experiments in America" (1909); "Soaring Flight"; and "Principles Involved in the Formation of Wing Surfaces and Soaring Flight" (1908). He was a man of delightful personality, simple and unassuming, and deserves an honorable place in public memory for his nobility of character and his devotion to the primal virtues on which all stable society rests. Prof. Montgomery was mar-

ried June 30, 1910, in San Francisco, Cal., to Regina F., daughter of Patrick Cleary, a pioneer merchant of San Francisco. He died at Evergreen, Cal., Oct. 31, 1911.

FOSS, Eugene Noble, forty-fifth governor of Massachusetts, was born at West Berkshire, Vt., Sept. 24, 1858, son of George Edmund and Marcia Cordelia (Noble) Foss. When he was nine years of age his parents removed to St. Albans, Vt., where he attended the public schools and St. Albans Academy. He matriculated at the University of Vermont in 1877, but left college at the end of his sophomore year to read law with his uncle. His impatient desire to be self-supporting led him to abandon his law studies and become a traveling salesman for the St. Albans Manufacturing Co., of which his father was manager, and for which he sold a patent lumber dryer with remarkable success. Later he took up other goods, among them the products of Benjamin F. Sturtevant of Boston. In 1882 he was placed in charge of the manufacturing department of the B. F. Sturtevant Co., and two years later became treasurer and general manager of the firm. Under his direction the business developed rapidly, until it became the largest concern of its kind in the world, sending its products into every corner of the globe. In 1901 he consolidated a number of independent manufacturing firms into the Becker-Brainerd Milling Machine Co., of which he became president and which produces the largest line of selling machinery in the world. His political career was the outcome of his interest in reciprocity. He was an advocate of reciprocity with Canada and he made this a prime article of his political faith. In the spring of 1906 he made a trip abroad in the interest of reciprocity and was received with great cordiality in England, France and Germany. Through a sense of loyalty he remained in the Republican ranks as long as he conscientiously could; but after the adoption of the Payne-Aldrich tariff bill he left the party in the fall of 1909 and accepted the Democratic nomination for lieutenant-governor of Massachusetts. He stood squarely on the issue of a downward revision of the tariff and for reciprocity with Canada, and reduced the Republican majority of 96,000 to a little over 8,000. In the following spring he was elected to congress from the 14th Massachusetts district, turning a Republican majority of 14,250 into a Democratic majority of 5,640 in a total vote of 24,320. In the same year (1910) he was nominated for governor on the Democratic ticket and, in face of powerful opposition, was elected by a plurality of 36,000 in a state which a year before had gone Republican by 110,000. He was re-elected in 1911 and again in 1912, but the fourth time was defeated by David I. Walsh. Gov. Foss's record as chief executive of Massachusetts removed him from local politics and placed him prominently before the eyes of the nation. The highest good of all the people was his principal aim. During his administration the legislature passed a presidential primary bill—a minimum wage law, and acts restricting the hours of work for women and miners and providing for mothers' pensions. Broadly active in religious, educational and charitable work, he has served as trustee of the University of Vermont, Newton Theological Institution, Colby College, Hebron Academy, Vermont Academy, Boston Baptist Hospital, Moody School at Northfield, and many other similar institutions. He is a trustee of the Boston Young Men's Christian Association, and a director of the Robert B. Brigham Hospital corporation. Besides

B. F. Sturtevant Co. and the Becker Milling Machine Co., mentioned above, he is president of the Maverick Mills, vice-president of the Massachusetts Real Estate Exchange, and director of the East Boston Land Co.; and was formerly an officer or director of the American Loan & Trust Co., American Pneumatic Service Co., Bridgewater Water Co., Brooklyn Heights Railroad Co., Brooklyn Rapid Transit Co., Chicago Junction Railway & Union Stock Yards Co., Hyde Park National Bank, Manhattan Railway Co., Massachusetts Electric Co., Mead-Morrisson Manufacturing Co., and United States Smelting, Refining & Mining Co. He is a director of the Boston Merchants Association and a member of the Boston Chamber of Commerce, New England Shoe & Leather Association, Beacon Society, and the New Algonquin, Boston Art, Exchange, Jamaica, Highland and other clubs. He was married June 12, 1884, to Lilla, daughter of Benjamin F. Sturtevant, his former employer and business associate.

EMMET, William Le Roy, engineer and inventor, was born at Pelham, N. Y., July 10, 1859, son of William Jenkins and Julia Colt (Pierson) Emmet; grandson of Robert and Rosina (Hubley) Emmet, and great-grandson of Thomas Addis Emmet (q. v.), the first of the family in America. The latter was the distinguished Irish patriot and leader in the Society of United Irishmen in 1798, and an elder brother of the ideal patriot of the Irish race, Robert Emmet, who was executed in Dublin in 1803. He came to America in 1804, and soon became a leader of the New York bar. His son Robert was a prominent lawyer and judge in New York city. William Le Roy Emmet was educated at schools in Canada, New York and Maryland, and subsequently entered the United States Naval Academy, where he was graduated in 1881. He served as a cadet midshipman until 1883 at Annapolis and on board U. S. S. Essex, and re-entered the navy as junior lieutenant in 1898, serving as navigator on the U. S. S. Justin during the period of the Spanish war. His principal civil employment has been with the Sprague Electric Railway and Motor Co. and the General Electric Co. He has achieved fame as an electrical engineer and as an inventor, and has obtained many patents for inventions in electricity, mechanics and thermo-dynamics, most of which have been incidental to his undertakings as an engineer. His most important electric work has been in the development of the general use of alternating currents and in the invention and design of machinery to further the practical application of alternating currents, while his most important mechanical work has been in connection with the development and introduction of the steam turbine. He designed and directed the development of the Curtis turbine by the General Electric Co., a very large work, every detail of which was radically new, and which was carried on with a rapidity almost unprecedented in such undertakings. He designed the machinery for the first ships driven by electric motors, and he was the first serious promoter of electric ship propulsion, conducting a series of experiments with the United States collier Jupiter which are destined to be epoch-making in the history of marine transportation. He is the inventor of several types of transformers, including an air-blast type which has been extensively used; of several type of insulation for alternators, and of other details of the design of alternators which have met with general acceptance. He is the original inventor of the oil switch, a device which is now almost universally used in large electrical

work. In 1907 when large alternating current uses were in rapid course of development, there were no safe and satisfactory means of current opening. Very small circuits and fuses had been opened under oil, but the possibilities were unknown. After experimentally investigating the possibilities at Brooklyn and Niagara Falls, the heaviest circuits then existing, he was the first to design and first to use switches of this type. The varnished cambric cable, which is widely used, is also an Emmet invention. He is the inventor of the verticle shaft steam turbine, of which a very large number have been built, and many details of turbine design in general use are to his credit. Mr. Emmet was responsible for most of the later and most successful and largest electric work of the Niagara Falls Power Co., also for the design and introduction of the Curtis steam turbine for electric uses. His achievements have been as a pioneer of new methods rather than as an inventor, and much of his most original and most useful work could not be effectively patented nor perhaps even classified as invention. Mr. Emmet is the author of "Alternating Current Wiring and Distribution" (1894). He is a member of the American Philosophical Society, American Institute of Electrical Engineers, American Society of Mechanical Engineers and the Society of the Naval Architects and Marine Engineers. He is also a member of the University and Engineers clubs of New York, of the Mohawk Golf, the Tobique, Salmon, Mohawk and Schenectady Boat clubs. He received the degree of D.Sc. from Union College in 1910. He is unmarried.

EMMET, Lydia Field, artist, was born at New Rochelle, N. Y., Jan. 23, 1866, daughter of William Jenkins and Julia Colt (Pierson) Emmet and sister of William Leroy Emmet, above. She was educated privately and began her art studies upon leaving school. Ever since she was fifteen she has been more or less actively engaged in art, illustrating, designing, teaching and painting portraits. She studied at the Art Students' League and at the Academie Julien, Paris, under Bourguereau and Fleury, also with Collin and Frederick MacMonnies. One of the decorative panels of the Women's Building at the Columbian Exposition in Chicago in 1893 was her work and the Cullom geographical medal presented to Robert E. Peary at the meeting of the American Geographical Society in 1897 was designed by her. Among her paintings are: "Dorothy" (1898), "Playmates" (1909), which took the Clarke prize at the National Academy of Design, and "Olivia" (1911). Since 1895 her career has been entirely devoted to portrait painting, her subject being pictures of children. Miss Emmet received a bronze medal at the Columbian Exposition in Chicago in 1893, a bronze medal at the Atlanta Exposition in 1895, a silver medal at the Louisiana Purchase Exposition in St. Louis in 1904 and an honorable mention at the Pan-American Exposition in Buffalo in 1901 and the International Exhibition at Pittsburgh in 1912. She also received the Shaw prize from the Society of American Artists for the "Boy in White" in 1906, the Proctor prize from the National Academy of Design for "The Sisters" in 1907, and the Clarke prize from the National Academy of Design for "Playmates" in 1909. She is a member of the National Association of Portrait Painters, the Art Students' League, the New York Municipal Art Society, the Metropolitan Museum of Art, the New York Water Color Club, the Connecticut Academy of Fine Arts, the New York Zoological Society, and the Amer-

EUGENE N. FOSS
GOVERNOR

WILLIAM L. EMMET
ENGINEER

LYDIA F. EMMET
ARTIST

ERNEST LISTER
GOVERNOR

Carrie Chapman Catt

ican Museum of Natural History. In 1909 she was elected an associate of the National Academy of Design and in 1912 a National Academician. She is a member of the Women's Political Union, and is an advocate of woman suffrage.

LISTER, Ernest, sixth governor of Washington (1913——), was born in Halifax, England, June 15, 1870, son of Jeremiah Hartley and Ellen (Hey) Lister. His parents came to the United States when he was fourteen years old, and located at Tacoma, Wash. He was educated in the public schools of Tacoma and the Tacoma Business College, after which he entered the employ of an iron foundry conducted by an uncle. After a brief period in the real estate and insurance business he established the Lister Construction Co. in Tacoma, and engaged in the contracting business on a large scale, particularly in the paving of highways. In 1910 he organized the Lister Manufacturing Co. at Tacoma for manufacturing porch columns and other finished wood products, of which he is president and general manager. Early in his career he became interested in local politics. He was elected city councilman of Tacoma in 1894, and took a prominent part in the Fusion campaign two years later, which resulted in the election of Gov. Rogers. The latter appointed him chairman of the state board of control, which operates the dozen or more penal and eleemosynary institutions of the state of Washington. He held this office six years. He was one of the framers of the new charter of the city of Tacoma providing for the commission form of government. He was elected governor of the state on the Democratic ticket in 1912 on a platform of efficiency and economy in the administration of public affairs. He was inaugurated Jan. 15, 1913, for a four-year term. During the first two years of his administration the forty-five departments and institutions under his control were successfully operated, and over $450,000 of the moneys that had been appropriated by the legislature for maintenance and operation of those departments during the biennium was turned back into the state treasury unexpended. Gov. Lister, as a practical road builder in private life, has devoted much attention as governor to the construction and proper maintenance of an adequate system of state highways. He has stood vigorously against the issuance of bonds for road construction, and insisted on a policy of paying for roads as they are built. Under his administration the total bonded indebtedness of the state of Washington has been reduced to less than $300,000, and there is at the present time sufficient money in the general fund of the state, aside from the current needs of the state, to retire this indebtedness whenever legislative sanction for so doing is given. Besides his business interest mentioned above, he is a director of the Scandinavian-American Bank of Tacoma. He is a Mason and a member of the Methodist church. Gov. Lister was married Feb. 28, 1893, to Alma Thornton. Portrait opp. p. 340.

CATT, Carrie Lane (Chapman), suffragist, was born at Ripon, Wis., Jan. 9, 1859, daughter of Lucius and Maria (Clinton) Lane. When she was seven years of age, her parents, who were natives of Potsdam, N. Y., removed from Wisconsin to Charles City, Ia., where she received her preparatory education. She entered the Iowa State College and was graduated at the head of her class in 1880, having paid her own way through college by teaching. She was then appointed principal of the high school in Mason City, Ia., at the same time beginning the study of law. She became superintendent of all the schools in

Mason City, and continued in this office until her marriage, in 1884, with Leo Chapman, editor of the "Mason City Republican." With her husband she became joint owner and editor of the paper, and she also gave lecture courses on general subjects throughout the state. Because of the failure of Mr. Chapman's health, they sold the paper at the end of the year and removed to San Francisco, Cal., where Mr. Chapman died in 1886. Mrs. Chapman remained in that city for a year, engaged in newspaper work, and was the first woman reporter in San Francisco. She early became interested in the working women and resolved to devote her life to their welfare, especially their rights as wage-earners; to do so effectually she determined to espouse the cause of equal suffrage, in which she had been a strong believer since her girlhood. She made her first suffrage speech in 1887, and for two years thereafter served as state organizer of suffrage clubs in Iowa. Since then she has visited every state and territory in the Union, working without salary and speaking before innumerable women's clubs and meetings upon her special theme. Her energy and enthusiasm led to her election as chairman of the organization committee, and in 1900 as president of the National Women's Suffrage Association, in succession to Susan B. Anthony, who had headed the organization for eighteen years. In 1893, when the constitutional amendment giving the ballot to women in Colorado was submitted to the voters, she went there, organized the movement in its favor and spoke daily in its support. In 1895 she equipped organizers in Idaho for the agitation of suffrage there, and continued the work until that state also adopted the measure in 1897. She aided the movement which secured the inclusion of a clause in the Louisiana revised constitution giving taxpaying women the right to vote on all questions submitted to the taxpayers. In 1895 she visited state, county and local suffrage clubs in Colorado, Idaho, South Dakota, Kansas, Iowa, California, Montana and New Hampshire, advocating woman suffrage. She addressed constitutional conventions and legislative bodies in Maine, Massachusetts, Rhode Island, Montana, Louisiana and Great Britain, Norway, Sweden, Denmark, Holland, Saxony, Bohemia, Prussia and Hungary. In 1902 Mrs. Catt organized the International Women's Suffrage Alliance, composed of national woman suffrage associations comprising twenty-six nations, and two years later she resigned as president of the National Women's Suffrage Association to become president of the Alliance. The countries already affiliated include Australia, Austria, Belgium, Bohemia, Bulgaria, Canada, China, Denmark, Germany, Finland, France, Galicia, Great Britain, Hungary, Iceland, Italy, the Netherlands, Norway, Portugal, Russia, Sweden, Switzerland, Servia, South Africa and the United States. To arouse world-wide interest in the movement, Mrs. Catt started, Apr. 6, 1911, on a tour around the world—the most remarkable effort ever made for the suffrage cause. Her address at the congress in Stockholm that year was translated into twenty-four tongues and distributed in every country as the accepted plea for woman suffrage. She organized a Union Suffrage Association in South Africa; she then proceeded to Cairo and formed a suffrage committee of English, Egyptian and native women; thence to Ceylon and India, visiting Bombay and other cities, where she found Mohammedan, Hindu, Parsee and Buddhist women exercising the franchise. From Rangoon she went to Hongkong and into China; then returned home by way of San Francisco, Cal. In December, 1915, she was elected president of the National American Woman Suffrage Association, succeeding Dr. Anna Howard Shaw, retired. In her appeals from the platform Mrs. Catt speaks extemporaneously in an easy, confidential and convincing manner. Her voice is clear, musical and ringing. She is withal a model housekeeper. She can cook her own meals, make her own dresses, trim her own hats, and is an enthusiastic gardener and cultivator of flowers. Her second marriage was to George W. Catt (q. v.), president of the Atlantic, Gulf and Pacific Co., engineers and contractors, who died in October, 1905.

FLETCHER, Henry Prather, diplomat, was born at Green Castle, Pa., Apr. 10, 1873, son of Lewis Henry and Martha Ellen (Rowe) Fletcher. He was educated at Ziegler's Private School and at the Chambersburg (Pa.) Academy. He studied law for four years under the preceptorship of Hon. D. Watson Rowe, was admitted to the bar in 1894, and after practicing by himself for two years, became a member of the law firm of Rowe & Fletcher, which continued until 1898. During 1891–98 he served as official reporter of the 39th judicial district of Pennsylvania. At the outbreak of the Spanish-American war he enlisted as a private in troop K, 1st U. S. cavalry volunteers (rough riders) and served through the Cuban campaign. After peace was concluded he re-enlisted in the regular army and from 1899 to 1901 served in the Philippine Islands as first lieutenant and battalion adjutant of the 40th U. S. volunteer infantry. In May, 1902, he entered the diplomatic service as second secretary of the American legation at Havana, Cuba. From Havana he was sent for the first time to China as second secretary of the legation, Edwin H. Conger being at that time U. S. minister at Peking. Two years later he became first secretary of the legation to Portugal, but in 1907 was returned to China as first secretary of the legation, serving under the distinguished diplomat, W. W. Rockhill. In the spring of 1907 he was appointed chargé d'affaires, in which capacity he represented the United States in China until Apr. 15, 1905, and from June 1, 1909, until Apr. 2, 1910. It was during this period that he secured for the first time an agreement whereby the United States was to participate in a joint loan with European powers for financing railroad construction work. Later Pres. Wilson withdrew the active support of our government from the international deal. In 1910 he was appointed envoy extraordinary and minister plenipotentiary to Chile. In October, 1914, he became American ambassador to that country, serving thus until December, 1915, when he was appointed American ambassador to Mexico. His mission in Chile was eminently successful in winning the good-will of and establishing cordial relations with the Chilean people to a degree never attained before. In all the posts that he has filled Mr. Fletcher has made an admirable record. For the difficult position in such a capital as Mexico City, a better selection could not have been made. It is the usual custom in the diplomatic service that the first representative of a foreign country to present his letters of credence becomes thereby "Doyen," or dean, of the diplomatic corps, sitting as chairman in their meetings and representing them in their collective functions. In the regular order of events the American ambassador held this position with the reconstituted Mexico under Pres. Venustiano Carranza, and as such he acted as counselor to the Mexican government. In politics he is a Republican and his re-

ligious affiliation is with the Presbyterian church. Mr. Fletcher is a member of the American Society of International Law and of the Metropolitan and Chevy Chase clubs of Washington, and the Army and Navy Club of New York. He is unmarried.

FELT, Joseph Pollard, manufacturer, was born in Mason Village, N. H., Aug. 8, 1850, son of Aaron and Sarah Pierce (Stevens) Felt, and a descendant of George Felt, who came from England to this country with Gov. John Endicott and settled in Charlestown, Mass., prior to 1633, and subsequently was one of the pioneer settlers of North Yarmouth. From him and his wife, Elizabeth Wilkinson, the line is traced through their son Moses and his wife, Lydia Felt; their son Aaron and his wife, Mary Wyatt; their son Aaron, a selectman, and his wife, Tabitha Upton, and their son David, a soldier in the revolutionary war, and his wife Susan Pollard, who were the grandparents of Joseph P. Felt. Three of his ancestors, Aaron, Peter Samuel and Joseph Felt fought in the revolutionary war. Joseph P. Felt was educated in the public school at Caledonia Center, Wis., and at the high school in Coldwater, Mich., where his father was engaged in the lumber business. In 1868 he went to New York city to learn electrotyping in the establishment of his brother-in-law, Henry W. Lovejoy, and ten years thereafter he organized the firm of Joseph P. Felt & Co., electrotypers, in New York, which obtained a high reputation throughout the country for the superiority of their work over that of their competitors. Mr. Felt was of an ingenious turn of mind, and invented for his own use many improved devices for the process of electrotyping which were never patented. He built several of such machines for the electrotyping department of the government printing office, Washington, some of which are still in use. These improvements are now being used by many foundries throughout the country. He was devoted to his business, was an indefatigable worker, and achieved a fortune, though he began his career as a poor boy with no other capital than his own hands and brains. He was fond of travel, and journeyed much at home and abroad, but his chief pleasure in later years was his country home at Oscawana Lake in Putnam county, N. Y. His leading characteristics were courage, patience, dogged perseverance and cheerfulness; he was very sympathetic and possessed a marked fondness for animals. He was a member of the 7th regiment, N. G. N. Y., and won many prizes for accuracy in shooting, notably the 7th regiment veteran's trophy, which became his property by his having won it three times in succession. His clubs were the Long Island Auto and the Alta of Salt Lake City; he was a thirty-second degree Mason, a member of the New England Society of Brooklyn, the Oscawana Lake Association, and a number of business associations. He was thrice married: (first) in Brooklyn, N. Y., Aug. 19, 1871, to Alice, daughter of George Webster, a merchant of Jersey City, N. J.; of this union three children survive: George Aaron, a contractor; Henry William, a partner in his father's business; and Alice Webster, wife of Albert John Rabing. Mrs. Felt died in 1880, and he was again married June 22, 1882, to Betsey Eleanor Webster, sister of his first wife; she died in 1889, and his third marriage was at Salt Lake City, Feb. 6, 1894, to Anna Irene, daughter of Horatio Jones Hewitt, of New York city, who survives him. He was killed by a fall from the porch roof of his country home in Putnam county, N. Y., Nov. 16, 1913.

BULLITT, William Christian, lawyer, political reformer and philanthropist, was born in Philadelphia, Pa., June 18, 1856, son of John Christian and Therese Caldwell (Langhorne) Bullitt, and a descendant of Benjamin Bullitt, who came from the Province of Languedoc, France, and settled at Port Tobacco, Maryland, in 1685. From him the line descends through his son Benjamin and the later's wife, Elizabeth Harrison; their son Cuthbert and his wife, Helen Scott; their son Alexander Scott and his wife, Priscilla Christian; their son William Christian and his wife, Mildred Ann Fry, who were the grandparents of William C. Bullitt. His father, one of the leaders of the Philadelphia bar, was president of the commission which drafted the Bullitt law, creating the present city charter. The son was educated at the classical school of Dr. J. W. Faires, and was graduated at the University of Pennsylvania in 1876. He studied law at the University of Virginia, and after his admission to the bar in 1878 began practice in the office of his father. In 1882 he was elected to the state legislature, and introduced the Bullitt bill that had been prepared by his father, and although it was not passed until the session following his retirement, his activities in behalf of the measure brought him conspicuously before the public. For a quarter of a century, 1885-1909, he was closely identified with the executive department of the Norfolk and Western Railroad Co. His first connection with that company was as assistant to the president. He was vice-president during 1887-1893, and thereafter, until his resignation, was general manager. In 1898 he joined the firm of Castner & Curran, which then became Castner, Curran & Bullitt, miners and shippers of high grade steam coals, and was vice-president of the company at the time of his death. The firm has extensive mines in the Pocahontas coal field in West Virginia. Mr. Bullitt was also president of the Pocahontas Coal Co., and a director of the Dunbar Furnace Co., and of the Virginia Coal and Iron Co. Originally a Democrat, when there was a break in the national Democratic ranks in 1896, he supported the so-called gold Democrats, and with the election of McKinley became an independent Republican. He took an enthusiastic part in all political reform movements, was chairman of the reform party in Philadelphia, and was a member of the committee of seventy. In 1912 impaired health necessitated his almost complete retirement, and in 1910 he resigned from the directorates of the Fourth Street National Bank, of Philadelphia, and the company that owns the Bullitt building. He was a member of the Philadelphia, Philadelphia Country, Rittenhouse, City, Southern and St. Anthony clubs of Philadelphia, and of the University Club of New York. His death was considered a grave affliction in business walks of Philadelphia, and was felt even more in its higher social, intellectual and ethical life. Many general philanthropic and educational activities profited during his lifetime through his lavish generosity, and there never was a truer, more loyal, more helpful friend. His influence upon the industrial and commercial life of the community was necessarily felt. He was a man of extraordinary acumen, inflexible will, resistless energy, exact method and irreproachable honesty. His counsel was courted and his advice sought by many a business or financial institution among whose directors his name never appeared. He was married in January, 1886, to Emily M., daughter of Henry B. Tatham, of Philadelphia, who died in October of the same year, leaving one son, John C. Bullitt, 3d; he then married in Baltimore, Md., June 4, 1889, Louisa G., daughter of Orville Horwitz, of Baltimore, who survives him, with two children: William C., Jr., and Orville H. Bullitt. He died in Philadelphia, Pa., Mar. 22, 1914.

CHILTON, William Edwin, U. S. senator, was born in Kanawha county, W. Va., Mar. 17, 1858, son of William Edwin and Mary Elizabeth (Wilson) Chilton, grandson of Blackwell Chilton, who came to the United States from Ireland and settled in Virginia, where he was interested in large land grants with Albert Gallatin and Savory de Valconlon, a French refugee. The family is of English ancestry on both sides. At the time of the civil war the Chiltons allied their fortunes with the Confederate cause, and at the close of hostilities found themselves in greatly reduced circumstances. The senator's father died soon after the war, and the son's preliminary education was obtained from private tutors. He attended Shelton College, but was not graduated. At the age of seventeen he taught a district school, in the meantime studying law. He was admitted to the bar upon reaching his majority, and at once began his practice in Charleston, W. Va., in partnership with John E. Kenna (q. v.), U. S. senator, under the firm name of Kenna & Chilton. He materially assisted Sen. Kenna in all the latter's political contests, and at this period served as prosecuting attorney of Kanawha county for one term. In 1897 he joined with his brother and ex-Gov. William A. MacCorkle in establishing the firm of Chilton, MacCorkle & Chilton, which became one of the most influential legal organizations in the state. Besides conducting a very large legal practice, he was president of the Charleston Interurban Street Railway. Early in his career he became actively interested in local politics, and it is said that he has done more for the Democracy of West Virginia than any other individual in that state. He was chairman of the Democratic state executive committee in 1892, conducting an active campaign for Grover Cleveland and for his subsequent law associate for governor. Upon the election of Gov. MacCorkle he appointed Mr. Chilton secretary of state. In 1894 West Virginia went Republican, and since then he has devoted his energies to the task of winning it back to his party, which he succeeded in accomplishing in 1910. In the next year he was elected to the United States senate. In the senate he is a member of the committees on the Judiciary, Naval Affairs, Mines and Mining and Printing and the census committee. He was married, Dec. 19, 1892, to Mary Louise Tarr, of Wellsburg, W. Va., and has two sons, William E., Jr., and Joseph E., and two daughters, Eleanor C. and Elizabeth L. Chilton. He is a member of the Manhattan Club of New York city, and belongs to the Masonic fraternity and the Benevolent and Protective Order of Elks. Sen. Chilton is a forceful and ready public speaker, with an affable and attractive personality which has won a large circle of friends and made him one of the most popular men in public life. Since 1912 he has fathered a claim of the state of West Virginia against the federal government amounting to millions of dollars arising from the covenant contained in the grant of the Northwest territory by Virginia made in 1784. He has taken a prominent part in the debates in the senate on the tariff, the repeal of the Panama tolls bill, the Clayton bill, the river and harbor improvement legislation, and the water-power bill. He is unmarried.

BIGELOW, Maurice Alpheus, biologist, educator, was born in Union county, O., Dec. 8, 1872, son of Alpheus Russell and Hattie (Parthemore) Bigelow, grandson of Eliphas and Miriam (McCloud) Bigelow, great-grandson of Alpheus and Melinda (Converse) Bigelow, and a descendant of John Bigelow, who emigrated from England about 1639 and settled in Massachusetts. His father was a farmer and manufacturer. He was graduated at Ohio Wesleyan University in 1894 with the degree of B.S., at Northwestern University in 1896 with the degree of M.S., and at Harvard University in 1901 with the degree of Ph.D. He began his professional career in 1894 as instructor in biology at Ohio Wesleyan University. He was fellow and assistant in zoölogy at Northwestern University during 1895–96, and instructor of zoölogy at that instruction during 1896–98. He then went to Harvard as a graduate student and as assistant in zoölogy to Radcliffe College for one year, after which he became instructor in biology at Teachers College of Columbia University, New York. He was appointed adjunct professor in 1903, and since 1907 has been professor and head of the department of biology at that institution: Since 1912 he has been director of the School of Household Arts in Teachers College. He is the co-author of "Teaching of Biology" (1903); "Applied Biology" (1911); "Introduction to Biology" (1913). His principal research work has been along the lines of animal embryology, and includes the embryology of lower Crustacea, especially Cirripedia, and comparative studies of the early development of some lower Crustacea. In this connection he is the author of "Early Development of Lepas," published by Harvard University (1901), and of various shorter papers. He was the founder of "The Nature-Study Review" in 1905 and edited it for five years. He is a fellow of the American Association for the Advancement of Science, and was secretary of the section of zoölogy, 1907–12; member American Society of Zoölogists, American Society of Naturalists, and of the American Nature-Study Society, of which he was secretary in 1908–10. He was married in Chicago, Ill., June 14, 1900, to Anna, daughter of Pierre Neiglick.

HUIDEKOPER, Frederic Wolters, railway president, was born at Pomona Hall, Meadville, Pa., Sept. 12, 1840, son of Edgar and Frances (Shippen) Huidekoper, and grandson of Harm Jan Huidekoper (1776–1854), who emigrated to the United States from Holland in 1796. He received his early education under private tutors, and was graduated at Harvard College in 1862. He received the degree of A. M. in 1871. In 1863 he served as a captain in the 58th Penn. volunteer militia, and participated in the operations along the Ohio river resulting in the capture of Gen. Morgan, whose prisoners he conducted to Columbus, O. During 1862-77 he was chiefly engaged as the executor of his father's estate and in closing up the affairs of The Holland Land Co. of Pennsylvania, which had become merged into the Huidekoper family. In 1875 he was elected chairman of the reorganization committee of the Chicago, Danville and Vincennes Railroad Co. which, like many other roads, had gone into the hands of receivers in consequence of the panic of 1873. Under his able direction the company was rehabilitated as the Chicago and Eastern Illinois railroad, and he was elected its first president Aug. 30, 1877. While in that position he built, in association with J. B. Brown, the Chicago and Western Indiana railroad from Hammond, Ind., and Dolton, Ill., into Chicago. In 1881 he also be-

came president of the Evansville and Terre Haute railroad, but at the end of that year he was obliged to resign the presidency of both roads owing to ill health. Notwithstanding the terrible strikes of 1877 and the almost hopeless condition of the Chicago, Danville and Vincennes railroad when he took charge, Mr. Huidekoper succeeded in evolving order out of chaos, and the policy which he dictated during his presidency of the Chicago and Eastern Illinois railroad has been continued to the present time and has resulted in making this road, now part of the St. Louis and San Francisco system, one of the most prosperous of the smaller lines in the middle West. The results obtained during his régime are considered in the railway world to be among the most remarkable achievements in rehabilitating a bankrupt company. He was offered the presidency of the Canadian Pacific Railway Co., but accepted instead in 1885 the first-vice-presidency of the Richmond and Danville railroad system (now the Southern railway), over which he was given absolute control, although, at his suggestion, a Southern man was retained as the president. In 1885 he also became the first vice-president of the Richmond and West Point Terminal Railway and Warehouse Company, and president of the Virginia Midland Railway Co. On May 25, 1886, he had the entire main line of the Richmond and Danville, south of Danville, changed between sunrise and sunset from five feet to the standard gauge of four feet eight and one-half inches, and so admirably was the work carried out that the through trains between New York and New Orleans were delayed only two hours. It was at Mr. Huidekoper's suggestion that the Pennsylvania railroad put on the "Congressional Limited" on Jan. 16, 1886. The headquarters of the Richmond and Danville railroad were then in Richmond, Va., but it was Mr. Huidekoper's opinion that they should be in Washington, both because it was the northern terminus of the road and because of its closer connection with the industrial centers of the North. Accordingly he moved the general offices to Washington in 1886, despite the strong opposition of the governor of Virginia and others, but the wisdom of his action time has amply justified. At the close of the year 1886 he severed his connection with the Richmond and Danville system, and a few months later became president of the Virginia, Tennessee and Carolina Steel and Iron Co., now the Interstate Coal and Iron Co. During 1889-91 he was the president and chairman of the reorganization committee, and from 1889 to 1893, receiver of the Pittsburgh, Shenango and Lake Erie railroad, now the Bessemer and Lake Erie. He was president of the South Atlantic and Ohio railroad in 1890-91 and built that part of the road which runs from the Clinch river through the natural tunnel, the mountains and Big Stone Gap, Va., to a junction with the Louisville and Nashville railroad. In the meantime the Richmond and Danville system had become involved in financial difficulties and on June 15, 1892, he and Reuben Foster were made receivers for the road and its affiliated lines, including the Georgia Pacific, the Charlotte, Columbia and Augusta, the Columbia and Greenville and the Western North Carolina railroads. Thirteen months later Samuel Spencer, representing J. P. Morgan & Co., was made a co-receiver as the result of a new plan formulated in consequence of information supplied by Mr. Huidekoper and Mr. Foster. The final outcome of the subsequent reorganization of the Richmond and Danville system in 1895 was the consolidation of that and several other lines into the Southern railway, which is now the chief railroad system of the South. On April 25, 1896, Mr. Huidekoper became the president of the Chicago, Peoria and St. Louis railroad, and within two years he had effected the needed reorganization. He then resigned the presidency and, together with Gen. Charles Miller, president of the Galena-Signal Oil Co., bought out The Disston Land Co., which owned 1,598,000 acres of land covering several counties in southern central Florida. The company was reorganized as The United Land Co., of which Mr. Huidekoper was the president and half-owner from 1901 until his death. He was an incorporator and director in a number of companies, and was also a member of the executive committee of the Pennsylvania Water Works Association. He owned a large amount of real estate in West Washington and was one of the principal factors in the development of that section of the city. In 1894 he was admitted to the bar of Crawford county, Pa., but he never engaged in active practice, although during the whole course of his business career he showed a remarkably ready and comprehensive knowledge of the law and would undoubtedly have made a distinguished reputation for himself as a lawyer had he chosen to follow this profession. Mr. Huidekoper's career in the railroad world is probably unique, for he began as the president of a road and never occupied any position subordinate to that of first vice-president, in which case he was vested with absolute power. He was a man of conspicuous natural ability, energy and resource. His judgment was clear and sound, and his grasp of large affairs was masterly and comprehensive. He possessed to a remarkable degree the faculty of extracting order out of business chaos, and as a reorganizer of bankrupt railways he has had few peers in this or any other country. His absolute fidelity to duty and his scrupulous integrity won him the esteem and implicit confidence of financiers all over the country, and his mere report on the affairs of a railroad or a new railway project was sufficient to insure whatever capital was needed. There were indeed few, if any, men in his position whose word alone carried such weight in financial circles. He possessed a charming personality, an unusually distinguished appearance and the graceful, courtly manners of a gentleman of the old school. He was a member of the Metropolitan, Chevy Chase and Country clubs of Washington, and the University and Harvard clubs of New York; the Hereditary Order of Descendants of Colonial Governors; the Society of Colonial Wars in the District of Columbia (deputy governor, 1899-1900; governor, 1900-1901, and gentleman of the council, 1901-1907); and the District of Columbia Society, Sons of the Revolution (vice-president, 1904-1905, and president from 1905 until his death). He was also a member of the Meade Post, G. A. R., and for forty-four years was a trustee of the Meadville Theological School, founded by his grandfather in 1844. Mr. Huidekoper was married at Meadville, Pa., Jan. 22, 1867, to Virginia, daughter of Fitz-James and Elizabeth Anna (Johns) Christie, of Erie, Pa, and had three children: Gracie (d. July 6, 1872), Frederic Louis and Reginald Shippen. He died in Washington, D. C., April 29, 1908.

GORRIE, John, physician and inventor, was born in Charleston, S. C., Oct. 3, 1803. Of his parentage and early history nothing is definitely known, though he was supposed to be of Spanish extraction. Dr. Gorrie was educated in the schools of Charleston, S. C., and, having prepared for entrance to a medical college, he was sent to New York, where he was graduated M. D. in 1825. He began the practice of his profession at Apalachicola, Fla., in 1833, at that time one of the principal cotton ports on the gulf, and was soon recognized as the leading physician of the city. He became treasurer of Apalachicola, was postmaster for four years, a member of the city council, and intendent (mayor) for one year. During this time he contributed to the "Lancet" and the "Southern Quarterly Review" a number of articles on science, medicine and refrigeration. In the course of his practice he conceived the idea of cooling the air in sick rooms and hospitals for fever patients. His ideas were so advanced for those times that he feared they would be rejected by the press, hence he wrote "On the Prevention of Malarial Diseases" under the nom de plume of "Jennier." From this period he virtually abandoned his practice and devoted his entire attention to the subject of cooling air. Having accomplished this end, he next experimented in the production of ice by artificial means. In 1850 he built a small working-model ice machine with which he made ice, and obtained a patent May 6, 1851. "Chambers' Encyclopædia" gives no account of an ice machine prior to the one perfected by Mr. Seebee, of Lambeth, and the one shown at the London exhibition in 1862 by Carre & Co., a French firm, when, in fact, the first machine invented for the manufacture of ice was publicly exhibited by Dr. Gorrie in 1850. In describing his machine, Dr. Gorrie said: "My invention consits in taking advantage of the natural law to convert water into ice artificially by absorbing its heat of liquefaction with expanding air. To obtain this effect in the most advantageous manner, it is necessary to compress atmospheric air into a reservoir by means of a force pump to one-eighth, one-tenth, or other convenient and suitable proportion of its ordinary volume. The power thus consumed in condensing air is to a considerable extent recovered, at the same time that the desired frigorific effect is produced by allowing the air with its expansive force upon the piston of an engine, which by a connection with a beam or other contrivance common to both helps to work the condensing pump. This engine is constructed and arranged in the manner of a high-pressure steam engine, having cutoffs and working the steam expansively. When the air, cooled by its expansion, escapes from the engine, it is made to pass round a vessel containing the water to be converted into ice, or through a pipe for effecting refrigeration otherwise, the air while expanding in the engine being supplied with an uncongealable liquid, whose heat it will absorb, and which can in turn be used to absorb heat from water to be congealed." He did not profit by his invention, although the principle of the process discovered by him underlies the entire fabric of the great ice-making and cold storage industry of the present day. The Florida legislature, in 1911, provided for the erection of a marble statue of Dr. Gorrie in Statuary Hall, Washington, D. C. He was married in Apalachicola in May, 1838, to Mrs. Caroline F. Beeman (nee Myick), and had two children: John, Jr., and Sarah Gorrie. He died in Apalachicola, Fla., June 16, 1854. Portrait opposite page 347.

JARVIS, Samuel Miller, capitalist, was born in McDonough county, Ill., Jan. 21, 1853, son of James and Permelia J. (Miller) Jarvis. While teaching school he studied law at Winfield, Kan., and was admitted to the bar in 1873. He began his practice with Hon. A. J. Pyburn at Winfield. He quickly became imbued with the spirit of the growing West and realized that what that growing country needed most was additional capital for agricultural development. With Roland R. Conklin, he organized in 1878 the Jarvis-Conklin Mortgage Trust Co., at Kansas City, Mo. This company became the agent for capitalists and large financial corporations, both at home and abroad, for whom it purchased municipal bonds and made loans on real estate mortgages aggregating many millions of dollars. He made a specialty of agriculture, and became recognized as an authority on land values and irrigation projects. He also organized the Farmers' and Drovers' Bank at Kingman, Kan., of which he was president, and the Bank of Columbus, Columbus, Kan., of which he was vice-president. He was an incorporator of the Montpelier Street Railway Co., and an organizer and president of the Land Title and Guarantee Co., of Kansas City. In 1894 he removed to New York, and with a number of associates organized the North American Trust Co., of which he was first president. At the time of the Spanish-American war Mr. Jarvis was among the first to realize the opportunity for exploiting the wonderful natural wealth and resources of the island of Cuba. Immediately after the fall of San Diego, in July, 1898, Pres. McKinley offered the North American Trust Co. the position of fiscal agent of the U. S. government in Cuba, and thereafter, during the American occupation, that company furnished the currency for disbursement to the army and for public improvements in Cuba. He disposed of his interests in the North American Trust Co. in 1900, and shortly thereafter organized the National Bank of Cuba, which planned the withdrawal of the trust company, and became the depository for funds of the United States and Cuban governments. It has twenty-five branches throughout the island, and its total assets exceed $38,000,000. Mr. Jarvis was also identified with the Cuban Telephone Co. and the National Bank of Santo Domingo. He was a member of the New York Chamber of Commerce, Chamber of Commerce of Westchester County and Southern Society, Japan Society, Missouri Society, Kansas Society, Mexico Society, Pan-American Society, Automobile Club of America, Larchmont Yacht Club, Country Club of Havana, the American Museum of Natural History, the Metropolitan Museum of Art, the Lawyers' Club of New York, and Pilgrims' Club of London. He died in New York city, Dec. 26, 1913.

MEERSCHAERT, Theophile, first bishop of the Roman Catholic diocese of Oklahoma, was born at Russignies, Belgium, Aug. 24, 1847. He was educated at the College of Audenarde and the University of Louvain, where he was ordained priest Dec. 23, 1871. He came to the United States in the following year and became affiliated with the diocese of Natchez, where he labored until 1889. During that period he distinguished himself in two yellow fever epidemics, in the first of which he was himself stricken by the disease. He acted as administrator of the diocese and twice was appointed its vicar-general. When the Vicariate Apostolic of the Indian Territory was formed May 29, 1891, he was put in charge and consecrated titular bishop of Sidymorum Sept. 8, 1891. His work there was of the pioneer order, with no railroad facilities and with primitive accommodations. He kept pace with the developments of new settlements and growth by immigration and such progress was made that the vicariate was erected into the diocese of Oklahoma, co-

extensive with the formation of the state Aug. 23, 1905, of which he was named its first bishop. There are about 40,000 Catholics within its boundaries, with ninety-five priests; 142 churches and stations, forty-eight schools with 5,000 pupils.

SYMONDS, Joseph White, lawyer, was born at Raymond, Me., Sept. 2, 1840, son of Joseph and Isabella (Jordan) Symonds. His descent is from John Symonds, afterward of Salem, Mass., who took the freeman's oath in Boston, March, 1638, with Samuel Symonds, afterward of Ipswich, and deputy governor of Massachusetts. He was graduated at Bowdoin College in 1860, studied law in the offices of Samuel Fessenden and of Edward Fox, afterward judge of the U. S. district court for Maine, and was admitted to the bar in 1863. He practiced alone in Portland until 1869 when he associated himself with Charles F. Libby, under the firm name of Symonds & Libby. This partnership continued until 1872 when Mr. Symonds was appointed to the superior bench of the state. In 1878 he was appointed to the supreme bench, and he held that position until 1884, when he resigned. Since then he has practised law in Portland as senior member of Symonds, Snow & Cook, and Symonds, Snow, Cook & Hutchinson, respectively. During his long professional career, Judge Symonds has handled with success a large number of important cases, and for years he has been recognized as the leader of the Maine bar. Joined to an exceptional legal scholarship and a thorough grasp of the principles of equity he is endowed with a quick, logical mind, a clear, well-poised judgment, a ready wit and a remarkable facility of expression. The integrity of his character has been one of his strongest assets both at the bar and on the bench. His decisions on the bench were models of clear, incisive and logical exposition. As an author he is one of the most distinguished in Maine, and he has often been called upon to make addresses to political conventions and before the alumni of Bowdoin College, the Maine Historical Society, the Rhode Island Historical Society, the state bars of Maine and New Hampshire, the national convention of the Psi U Society, and other bodies. Bowdoin College conferred upon him the degrees of M.A. in 1863, and LL.D. in 1894. His elder brother was William Law Symonds (1833–62), a graduate of Bowdoin, and a Unitarian minister who won a high reputation as a writer. He wrote a number of articles for the "Atlantic Monthly," one of which was described by James Russell Lowell as the best essay ever contributed to that publication. He wrote many cyclopedia articles on philosophical, historical and biographical subjects. Among them were some of the weightiest articles in Appleton's new "American Cyclopedia," including those on English literature, history and philosophy. Judge Symonds was for many years an overseer of Bowdoin College, and is a member of the Maine Historical Society and the Cumberland and Fraternity clubs. He was married in New York city, May 13, 1884, to Mary Campbell, daughter of Carlos D. Stuart, of Huntington, N. Y., and has one son, Stuart Oakley Symonds, a lawyer in Portland.

SCUDDER, Janet, sculptor, was born at Terre Haute, Ind., Oct. 27, 1874, daughter of William H. and Mary (Sparks) Scudder. Her father was a merchant. She is descended from Thomas Scudder, of London, who, with his wife Mary, came over in 1635 and settled in Salem, Mass.; through Benjamin and Sarah Scudder, Jacob and Abia (Rowe) Scudder, Lemuel and Elizabeth (Longstreet) Scudder, Richard and Jane (Norton) Scud-

Joseph W. Symonds.

JANET SCUDDER
SCULPTOR

GEORGE HITCHCOCK
ARTIST

BRYAN CALLAGHAN
LAWYER AND JURIST

PHOEBE COUZINS
LAWYER

der and John and Anna B. (Hollingshead) Scudder, who were her grandparents. She was educated at the high school in Terre Haute. She began the study of sculpture at the Cincinnati Art Academy under Louis T. Rebisso, and continued it at the Chicago Art Institute for three years under Lorado Taft, and in the academies of Vitti and Colarossi in Paris, becoming finally the pupil of Frederick MacMonnies. While studying in Chicago Miss Scudder received orders for some figures for the Columbia Exposition, one for the Illinois building and one for the Indiana building, and she executed them so satisfactorily that she was awarded a bronze medal. In 1901 eight of her portrait bas-reliefs were acquired by the state for the Luxembourg Museum in Paris. She exhibited a bronze sun-dial at the Louisiana Purchase Exposition in 1904, for which she received a bronze medal. Her most important works of sculpture are a seal for the Bar Association of New York city; a cinerary monument for Daniel Mather Walbridge, Woodlawn cemetery, New York; bronze fountain for the Archbold cottage at Bar Harbor, Me.; a marble sun-dial for Mrs. Warner Leeds on Long Island; a fountain for the public school building, Richmond, Ind.; a marble memorial tablet to Bishop Hare, of South Dakota, in the chapel of All Saints' School, Sioux Falls, S. Dak.; a fountain, entitled "The Fish Girl," for Alex. M. Hudnut, Princeton, N. J.; a fountain for Robert Bacon, Esq., formerly U. S. ambassador to France; a fountain for John D. Rockefeller, Esq., for Pocantico Hills, N. Y.; a bronze, "The Frog Fountain," and a collection of silver portrait bas-reliefs were acquired by the Metropolitan Museum of Art in New York city in 1906. She is also represented in the Congressional Library at Washington, D. C., and the Indianapolis Museum of Fine Arts. Miss Scudder is a member of the National Sculptors' Society, the National Arts Club of New York and the Colonial Dames. She has exhibited at the National Academy, the Architectural League and elsewhere, and in 1913 gave an exhibition of her principal works in New York. Miss Scudder is attaining a foremost place among American sculptors. Her modeling, highly poetical in its conception, is delicately composed and indicates ability of a high order. Her best talent is shown in her numerous fountains, designs in which a type of ebulliently healthy, even sporty, childhood is studied in different attitudes with extraordinary spirit and with a very sound technique. Her chubby, elastic, joyous urchins are conceived in precisely the vein that is most appropriate to lovely gardens, and she has a rare gift for so composing her designs that each one looks well from any point of view.

HITCHCOCK, George, artist, was born at Providence, R. I., Sept. 29, 1850, son of Charles and Olivia George (Cowell) Hitchcock, and a descendant of Matthias Hitchcock, who came over from England and settled in New Haven, Conn., in 1635. The line of descent is traced from Matthias Hitchcock through his son Nathaniel, who married Elisabeth Moss; through their son Nathaniel, who married Rebecca Morris; their son Benjamin, who married Abigail Olds Ward; their son Benjamin, who married Mary Johnson, and their son Samuel Johnson Hitchcock, who married Laura Coan, and was the grandfather of the artist. Samuel Johnson Hitchcock was the founder and first dean of the Yale Law School. His maternal grandfather, Benjamin Cowell, was judge of the court of common pleas in Rhode Island, and the author of "Spirit of '76," which gives a complete list of those who served in the colonial and revolutionary wars from Rhode Island. His father (1823-58) was also an artist, and from him the son undoubtedly inherited his talent for painting. The latter was educated at Brown University and Harvard Law School, graduating A.B. at the former in 1872, and LL.B. at the latter in 1874. He studied art under Boulanger and Lefebvre, in Paris, and also at the Dusseldorf Academy in 1882, after which he opened a studio in Paris, where he resided permanently. The best of his paintings are: "Tulip Culture" (1887); "A Holland Morning" (1887); "The Annunciation" (1888); "Maternity" (1889); "The Holy Mother" (1891); "Hagar and Ishmael" (1894); "St. George" (1896); "Magnificent" (1896); "St. Genevieve" (1898); "Dutch Bride" (1899); "The Birth of Venus" (1901); "Calypso" (1903). For the first picture he ever exhibited in Paris he received honorable mention (1887), and he has received gold medals from almost all the great art exhibitions in Europe, a gold medal at the Paris exposition of 1889, and at the World's Fair, Chicago, Ill., 1893. His pictures are hung in the Dresden Art Gallery; the Imperial collection, Vienna; the Municipal Museum, Alkmaar, Holland; the Chicago Art Institute; the Rhode Island School of Design; the Providence Art Museum; the Telfair Gallery, Savannah; the John Herron Art Institute, Indianapolis; the St. Louis Museum of Art; the Minneapolis Art Institute, and the Allbright Gallery, Buffalo. Mr. Hitchcock was a corresponding member of the Paris Society of American Painters, an officer of the Franz Joseph Order of Austria, the Munich Secession and the Vienna Academy of Arts; a member of the Sons of the American Revolution, and an Associate National Academician. He divided his time between Paris and Egmond, north Holland, and with his friends and pupils established a distinct school of art. He wrote a series of papers on art subjects for various magazines, the best of which was on Sandro Botticelli, published in "Scribner's." In 1876 he competed in the first champion athletic meeting ever held in the United States, and won the hurdle championship and was second in the broad jump. Mr. Hitchcock was married, first, in July, 1881, to Henrietta Walker, daughter of Henry Richardson, of New York; and second, in 1905, to Cecil, daughter of J. A. B. Jay, of Litley Court, Hereford, England. He died at Egmond, Holland, Aug. 2, 1913.

CALLAGHAN, Bryan, lawyer and jurist, was born in San Antonio, Texas, Apr. 6, 1852, son of Bryan and Conception (Ramon) Callaghan. His father, a native of Cork, Ireland, emigrated in 1839 and settled in west Texas. His mother was a native of San Antonio, Texas. He was educated at St. Mary's School, San Antonio, and the Lycee de Montpelier, Montpelier, France. Upon his return he entered the employ of a mail carrier, who held valuable government contracts, and during this period he participated in many stirring adventures on the Texas plains, including exciting engagements with bands of Indians bent upon the robbery of the mail-coaches. Ambitious for a professional career, he entered the University of Virginia law school in 1872 and was graduated in 1874 with the degree of L.B. He began the practice of his profession in San Antonio and was in El Paso for a brief period. He was elected alderman of San Antonio in 1879, but resigned with four other members in a successful effort to avoid the state's demand for tax levy in support of the Mexico and Gulf railroad project, a line that never was built from San Antonio. During 1883-85 he was city recorder. He was elected mayor of San Antonio in 1885 and was re-elected in 1887, 1889, 1891. He was defeated in 1895, but instead was elected judge of the Bexar county court and was re-elected in the following year. In 1897 he was again elected mayor. Defeated in 1899, seven years later, he was returned to the executive position and was re-elected in 1907, 1909 and 1911, thus serving as mayor of his native city for a period of eighteen years. No man in San Antonio's history has filled so conspicuous a place in the public mind as Bryan Callaghan. Almost every enterprise that contributed to making that city the metropolis of Texas had its inception in his fertile brain. He was pre-eminently the father of modern San Antonio, and his service to the city was inspired alone by high and generous motives. The new city hall, the courthouse, the paved plazas, the splendid park system and many improvements of lesser note are all eloquent reminders of his industrious efforts. He possessed rare traits of character and was a man "four square to all the winds that blow." Like every commanding figure, he had zealous supporters and earnest opponents, but those who differed with him were as ready as his warmest friends to concede to him the possession of a stainless honesty and extraordinarily powerful elements of leadership. He was deliberate in action, firm in conviction, and ever ready to accept responsibility for what he did. He was married in 1879 to Adele, daughter of Francis Guilbeau of San Antonio, and had four sons and three daughters: James, Bryan, Charles, Alfred; Conception, wife of Theodore Muegge, of San Antonio; Rosaria and Marie Callaghan. He died in San Antonio, Texas, July 8, 1913.

HELLIER, Charles Edward, lawyer and capitalist, was born in Bangor, Me., July 8, 1864, son of Walter Schermerhorn and Eunice Blanchard (Bixby) Hellier, and grandson of John Hellier, a native of Devonshire, England, who settled in Bangor, Me., in 1824. His maternal grandparents were Rufus and Betsy (Weston) Bixby, and on the distaff side are many distinguished Puritan ancestors, among them Joseph Bixby, of Ipswich and Boxford, who emigrated from Suffolk in 1637; John Daggett, who, in 1630, accompanied Gov. Winthrop to America in the ship Arabella, settled at Watertown and Martha's Vineyard, was a member of Sir Richard Saltonstall's company in the war of the revolution, and became the progenitor of the various Daggett or Doggett families of New England, and John Weston, a native of Buckinghamshire, who emigrated in 1644 and settled at Reading, Mass. The Daggetts, Westons and Bixbys were all well-known Puritan families in the seventeenth century, and their descendants were persons much respected in the several communities in which they lived. Joseph Weston, a great-grandfather of the subject, served as a volunteer in Arnold's expedition against Quebec in the war of the revolution, and died from the effects of the hardships endured by him on that occasion. The father of our subject was a merchant and manufacturer of Bangor, who was distinguished alike for his firm integrity of character, devotion to his family and application to business. As a boy Charles E. Hellier was almost equally fond of reading and of outdoor sports, and a fortunate youthful inclination toward the perusal of the English classics and works on biography proved helpful in preparing him for certain phases of his life-

work. He received his preliminary education at the Bangor high school, and was graduated at Yale University in 1886. He matriculated at the University of Berlin in the winter semester of 1886-87, and after taking a course in law at the Boston University received the degree of LL.B. in 1890. In the same year he was admitted to the Massachusetts bar and shortly thereafter became associated in practice in Boston with Robert M. Morse, one of the most eminent lawyers of New England. He had scarcely entered upon his legal career when he became interested in the development of the Elkhorn Coal and Coke Company, known since 1902 as the Big Sandy Company, of Pike county, Ky., of which he is president. He was chiefly responsible for the construction of a hundred-mile extension of the Chesapeake and Ohio railroad from Whitehouse, Ky., the line passing through a hitherto isolated district rich both in timber and mineral resources, the site of the famous Elk Horn coal fields, probably the most valuable in the world. Other important commercial concerns with which he has been identified are the Metropolitan Coal Company, which was organized by him in 1898, and the Massachusetts Breweries Company, which he formed in 1902. He is also general counsel for the Union Twist Drill Co. and the L. S. Starrett Co. of Athol, Mass.; the S. W. Card Manufacturing Co. of Mansfield, Mass.; Butterfield & Co., of Derby Line, Vt.; the Baush Machine Tool Co., the Quigley Furnace and Foundry Co. and the Package Machinery Co. of Springfield, Mass.; the Rivett Lathe and Grinder Co. of Boston, Mass.; the Mitchell Coke Co. and the Allegheny Coke Co. His political affiliations have been with the Republican party, and while he has ever been alive to the duties of citizenship and taken an interest in municipal matters he has never held any political office nor sought to do so. He is a member of the Natural History Society of Massachusetts, the Massachusetts Horticultural Society, the University Club, of New York; University and Engineers clubs, of Boston; Graduates' Club, of New Haven, and the Beverly Yacht Club, of Beverly, Mass. He is also a member of the Congregational church. He was married July 8, 1886, to Mary Lavinia, daughter of George Harmon, of New Haven, Conn., and had four children: Mary Louise, Walter Harmon, Edward Whittier and John.

COUZINS, Phoebe, lawyer, was born in St. Louis, Mo., in 1845, of French Huguenot ancestry. Her father was U. S. marshal under Pres. Cleveland's administration. She assisted her mother, who was among the first to offer her services as volunteer aid to the Sanitary Commission in the civil war in ministering to the sick and wounded soldiers, and from her own observations concluded that woman, vested with political powers, would be as potent to prevent war as, devoid of such powers, she was to lessen its horrors. In 1869 her ideas took form in the Woman's Franchise Organization, and that same year she applied for admission to the Law School of the Washington University of St. Louis, and was admitted by unanimous vote. This university was the first in the United States to open its law school to women, and both its faculty and trustees were in complete sympathy with the movement for advanced education for women. Miss Couzins was graduated in 1871, and was soon after admitted to the bar, being the first woman to become a professional lawyer in this country. She did not practice extensively, but was among the few who presented their cases when Gen. Butler was chairman of the judiciary committee of congress at Washington. She took the lecture platform in 1876 as an advocate of woman's suffrage, achieving a brilliant record in this field. At the time her father was U. S. marshal in Missouri he appointed his daughter a deputy, and when his health failed she discharged the duties of marshal. She wore a badge, attended courts, and, in addition to the discharge of office routine, actively engaged in apprehending counterfeiters and other violators of law. She was probably the first woman ever clothed with such authority. She was commissioner for Missouri on the national board of Charities and Correction, and was a woman commissioner for Missouri on the World's Fair board of directors. She was one of the best posted women in the country on politics and was the author of several standard works. Toward the close of her life repeated disappointments, poverty, and the infirmities of age wore away her physical strength, and she died in St. Louis, Mo., Dec. 7, 1915. Portrait opp. p. 347.

ANDERSON, Larz, diplomat, was born in Paris, France, Aug. 15, 1866, son of Nicholas Longworth and Elizabeth (Kilgour) Anderson, grandson of Larz and Catherine (Longworth) Anderson and great-grandson of Richard Clough Anderson, a colonel in the Virginia line in the revolution and aide-de-camp to Lafayette. In the same family were Gen. Robert Anderson, of Fort Sumter fame; Col. Charles Anderson, governor of Ohio, and Richard Anderson, member of congress and first diplomatic representative to the Central American states. Mr. Anderson's father, a graduate of Harvard, was colonel of the 6th Ohio regiment in the civil war, and breveted brigadier and major-general at the age of twenty-seven. His paternal grandmother was the daughter of Nicholas Longworth, of Cincinnati, O., the philanthropist and first millionaire of the West. The subject of this sketch attended schools at home and abroad and after graduating at Phillips Exeter Academy in 1884 he entered Harvard with highest honors and was graduated in 1888, cum laude. He subsequently spent two years in travel around the world, after which he entered the Harvard Law School. He was appointed by Pres. Harrison in 1891 second secretary of the legation in London under Robert T. Lincoln, and he remained second secretary when the mission was advanced to an embassy, and Thomas F. Bayard was appointed ambassador. In 1894 he was promoted by Pres. Cleveland to be first secretary of the embassy at Rome. There on several occasions in the temporary absence of the ambassador, Wayne MacVeagh, he acted as chargé d'affaires, and in that capacity handled successfully some delicate diplomatic situations arising out of the lynching of Italians in the United States. In 1897 he resigned in order to return home to be married, but remained on for some time under the new ambassador, William F. Draper, who was a close personal friend. Upon the outbreak of the war with Spain he volunteered for service and was commissioned captain and assistant adjutant-general of volunteers at Camp Alger, being assigned to the staff of Gen. George W. Davis as acting adjutant-general of the second division of the 2d army corps. When peace was concluded he made a trip to Ceylon and India, and in 1910 was a member of Secretary of War Dickinson's party on an official visit to the Philippines. As they passed through Japan they were royally entertained by the emperor and empress, and later in Peking he was received with the special embassy at the foot of the dragon throne by the prince regent on behalf of the infant emperor. When not traveling Capt. Anderson made his winter home in Washington, and with Mrs. Anderson has been prominent in the social life of the capital. In 1911 he was appointed envoy extraordinary and minister plenipotentiary to Belgium, where he was most cordially and kindly received. He had previously met King Albert when as prince the latter had visited the United States. As minister he settled several questions of long standing, especially with regard to discrimination against American oils, in a manner satisfactory to both governments. In November, 1912, Mr. Anderson was promoted to be ambassador extraordinary and minister plenipotentiary to Japan, where he was able to be of particular service because of his previous visits to that country, during which he had made many friends. During his mission to Japan there was an uninterrupted continuance of happy relations between the two nations. With the change of administration in 1913 he resigned, being the first of the American diplomatic corps to retire after having passed through in order all the grades of his time in the diplomatic service. He is a member of the Society of the Cincinnati, the Military Order of the Loyal Legion and the Order of the Spanish-American War. He is a commander in the Order of Sts. Maurice and Lazarre, and a grand officer of the Order of the Crown of Italy. His winter home is in Washington and his summer home is in Brookline, near Boston. He was married at Boston, Mass., June 10, 1897, to Isabel, daughter of Com. George H. Perkins (q. v.).

LORING, George Bailey, publicist, agriculturist and diplomat, was born at North Andover, Mass., son of Bailey and Sally Pickman (Osgood) Loring, and a descendant of Caleb Loring, a native of England, who early came to the American colonies and settled at Hull, Mass. He was educated at Franklin Academy and Harvard College, being graduated at the latter in 1838. He received his M.D. degree from the Harvard School of Medicine in 1842, and in the following year was appointed surgeon to the Marine Hospital at Chelsea, Mass., where he served for seven years. In 1849 he was appointed a commissioner to revise the U. S. marine hospital system and introduced many much-needed reforms. Pres. Pierce appointed him postmaster of Salem, Mass., in 1853, and he served throughout that administration until 1857. Abandoning the practice of medicine, he divided his time between politics and practical and scientific agriculture. He contributed to the agricultural and scientific journals, and became well known as a speaker and lecturer before historical and agricultural bodies and at expositions and fairs, in every way promoting the interests of advanced agricultural knowledge. In 1864 he established the New England Agricultural Society, and served as its president until his death. He was a member of the legislature in 1866-67; was a delegate to the national Republican conventions of 1868, 1872 and 1876; chairman of the state Republican committee during 1869-76; U. S. commissioner to the Philadelphia Centennial Exposition in 1876, and president of the Massachusetts state senate during 1873-77. He was elected to the 45th national congress and re-elected to the 46th congress, and in 1881 was appointed U. S. commissioner of agriculture. In this capacity he formulated laws for the preservation of our forests, made investigations for the stamping out of tuberculosis and pneumonia in cattle, had a number of large artesian wells dug for the reclamation of arid lands, introduced many improvements in agricultural science throughout the United States, began the irrigation of arid western lands, and was active in promoting agricultural and horticultural conventions and expositions throughout the country. In 1889 Pres. Harrison appointed him U. S. minister to Portugal, where he remained but one year. He was the author of "Classical Culture" (1866); "Eulogy on Louis Agassiz" (1873); "The Cobden Club and the American Farmer" (1880; "The Farmyard Club of Jotham," a sketch of New England life and farming (1876), and "A Year in Portugal" (1890). His services to the government in behalf of advanced agriculture alone would have fully engaged the lifetime energies of any ordinary man. The energy and talent of Dr. Loring were of a quality far above the ordinary. He was an unusual man with an unusual grasp of affairs and an unusual executive capacity. He was married in 1851 to Mary T. Pickman, and had one daughter, Sally, wife of Theodore F. Dwight. He was married again in 1880 to Mrs. Anna S. Hildreth, widow of Charles H. Hildreth, of New York city, and the daughter of Isaac Townsend Smith, who was one of the founders of the Union League Club of New York city and the financial agent and consul-general of the King of Siam in New York city. Although a score and a half of years the junior of her husband, Mrs. Loring took the deepest interest in his achievements. Mrs. Loring is a woman of more than ordinary intellectual attainments, and her home in Washington during the life of her husband was the center of refined and cultivated taste where she entertained a thoughtful and brilliant society. Her salon there was a social center and became celebrated all over the world. Her guests were senators, congressmen, presidents, diplomats and distinguished people from all over Europe and America, who lived in or were visiting the capital. These were invited to the Saturday evening receptions she held throughout four administrations, until she went with her husband to the court of Lisbon. Those receptions more nearly approached the French salons of the eighteenth century than any others held in the capital before or since. The active social régime of Mrs. Loring was greatly appreciated by the great men of the day. In "The Letters of Mrs. James G. Blaine," edited by Mrs. Truxtun Beale, is mentioned "Mrs. Loring's reception where came all the people one would like to meet." Dr. Loring died at Salem, Mass., Sept. 21, 1891. Portrait opposite p. 351.

CHANDLER, Peleg Whitman, lawyer and author, was born at New Gloucester, Cumberland co., Me., Apr. 12, 1816, son of Peleg and Esther (Parsons) Chandler. His first American ancestor was Edmund Chaundelor, who emigrated from England and settled at Duxbury, Mass., in 1632, and the line of descent is traced through Joseph, Joseph, Phillipp, Peleg, Peleg, Peleg, and Peleg Whitman Chandler. The spelling of the name was changed from Chaundelor to Chandler about 1700. His father was a law partner of Albert W. Paine, of Bangor, Me. Peleg W. Chandler attended the Bangor Seminary, and was graduated at Bowdoin College in 1834. He studied law in his father's office in Bangor, in the office of his kinsman, Theophilus Parsons, in Boston, and at the Harvard Law School, Cambridge, Mass., being admitted to the bar in 1837. He acquired an extensive general practice that lasted over fifty years, and he was rated one of the best lawyers in New England. Early in his career he became associated with the "Daily Advertiser," as a reporter of law cases in the higher courts, and for many years afterward he was identified with that paper, frequently contributing to its editorial columns. In 1838 he established the "Law Reporter," the first successful law magazine published in the United States. Subsequently he sold it to Stephen H. Phillips. In 1848 he published the first volume of his "American Criminal Trials," which was soon followed by a second volume. The books were written in an untechnical, popular style, which attracted many readers, and an edition was brought out in London. Mr. Chandler was elected to the common council in Boston, in 1843, serving as its president in 1844 and 1845, when he declined re-election. He was twice a member of the state house of representatives, during 1844-46 and 1862-63, and was the successor of John Pickering as city solicitor in 1846, holding the office until he resigned in 1853. During his administration he prepared and published a volume containing the ordinances of the city of Boston and the digest of the laws relating thereto, most of the ordinances being redrawn by himself. After his retirement from the city solicitorship he was appointed to revise the city charter and subsequent laws affecting it. In 1849, while a U. S. commissioner of bankruptcy, he published a useful work on the "Bankruptcy Laws of the United States and the Outline of the System, with Rules and Forms in Massachusetts." In 1850 he was a member of Gov. Emory Washburn's council, and was foremost among the citizens who planned and advocated the "Back Bay Improvement." The act of 1859, providing for the establishment of the public garden, was drawn by him. At his own expense, and under his earnest leadership, the attempts to sell the public garden, then marsh land, and cut it up into house lots, was defeated; but he was not satisfied until he had secured a law and carried through a referendum and had a vote of the people of Boston to forever dedicate to public use the beautiful garden adjoining the Boston common. Mr. Chandler prided himself on this service to the public more than any other act in his life. In 1860 he was presidential elector at the first election of Abraham Lincoln. At the time of his death he was one of the oldest members of the Massachusetts Historical Society. He prepared a memoir of Gov. Andrew for the society, and this, subsequently enlarged, was published in a separate volume. Another work from his pen was a striking essay, published anonymously, on the "Authenticity of the Gospels," which has passed through several editions. For nearly twenty years he was a member of the board of trustees of Bowdoin College, and this institution conferred upon him the degree of LL.D. in 1867. As a counsellor, Mr. Chandler was eminent for chamber advice, and before he was afflicted by deafness he was one of the foremost of jury lawyers. Judge E. Rockwood Hoar said of him: "He was thoroughly a public-spirited man, and a public man from the time he began life in this community; and his influence never ceased until the fifty-two years during which he was a member of the bar were terminated by death. In every public position that he filled he learned all about the duties that appertained to that position, and understood them thoroughly thenceforth and forever. When he was chosen a member of the legislature, and became a member of the governor's counsel, he learned the whole system and plan of the government of the commonwealth of Massachusetts, and from that day until the day of his death nobody

GEORGE B. LORING
AGRICULTURIST

PELEG W. CHANDLER
LAWYER

STEPHEN A. NORTHWAY
CONGRESSMAN

JULIAN C. EDGERLY
EDITOR

Austin Stickney

ever gave more counsel to those who administered the affairs of state than he." He was married in 1837, at Brunswick, Me., to Martha Ann Bush, daughter of Prof. Parker Cleaveland, of Bowdoin College, and had four children: Ellen Maria, Horace Parker, Parker Cleaveland and Arthur Whitman Chandler. He died in Boston, Mass., May 28, 1889.

NORTHWAY, Stephen Asa, lawyer and congressman, was born at Christian Hollow, Onondaga co., N. Y., June 19, 1833, son of Orange and Marie (Graff) Northway, grandson of Zenas and Rhoda (Finney) Northway, of English descent. Zenas Northway served in the revolutionary war in Capt. Adam Bailey's company of the Massachusetts line. Stephen A. Northway removed with his parents in early childhood to Ashtabula county, O., where he attended the district school and Kingsville Academy, pursuing his more advanced studies at the Orwell Academy under the celebrated Jacob Tuckerman. In 1858 he began the study of law with Messrs. Chaffee & Woodbury, of Jefferson, O. He was admitted to the bar in the following year and, opening an office at Jefferson, he was soon after elected prosecuting attorney of Ashtabula county. His powers of mind and untiring devotion to his business caused him to rise rapidly in public esteem, and he soon became one of the leading attorneys of northern Ohio. He was re-elected to the office of prosecuting attorney in 1863, and resigned in 1865 to accept the Republican nomination for representative in the Ohio legislature, in which he served for two years. During 1867-80 he devoted himself to his law practice, taking no part in politics, except to further campaign work for the Republican party. He was elected to congress from the 19th congressional district by a plurality of 7,800 votes in 1892. In 1894 he was returned by 15,000 votes and two years later was again returned by an overwhelming majority, serving until his death. Stephen A. Northway was intellectual in his tastes and devoted much of his leisure time to reading and study. He was an unusually fine speaker, never wandering from his subject into vain declamation, but pursuing it closely in pure and classic language, soothing always the feelings of his adversaries by civilities and softness of expression. In his social life he was genial and gentle, thoughtful of others, warm-hearted and very sympathetic, with a vein of humor which made him a very enjoyable companion. He was passionately fond of his home and made every effort to make it a happy one. He was a thirty-third degree Mason and a Knight Templar. He was married Jan. 1, 1862, to Lydia Ann, daughter of Anson Dodge, of Lenox, O., and had one daughter, Clara Laura, wife of James P. Burns, of Los Angeles, Cal., and a son, Bruce Orange, who died in infancy. He died in Jefferson, O., Sept. 8, 1898. Portrait opp. p. 350.

EDGERLY, Julian Campbell, editor, was born at North Haverhill, N. H., Apr. 22, 1865, son of Andrew Jackson and Sarah (Carr) Edgerly, and a descendant of Thomas Edgerly, a native of England, who took the oath of fidelity June 21, 1669, in the Province of New Hampshire, and was admitted a freeman June 25, 1672. His wife was Rebecca Ault, widow of Henry Halloway, and the line of descent is through their son John, who married Elizabeth Rawlings (or Rollins); their son Zachariah, who was married twice, first to Johanna Drew, second to Susanna Taylor; their son Samuel, who married Lydia Shepherd Johnson; their son Samuel Johnson, who married Elizabeth Bickford, and was the grandfather of Julian

Campbell Edgerly. He was educated in the public schools of his native town, and fitted for college at Haverhill Academy. While a student at Tufts College he was associate editor of the college paper and a correspondent of the Boston "Globe." After graduating at Tufts College in 1888, he became a member of the regular staff of the "Globe," remaining with that paper five years. In 1891, with his wife, who had been the head of the department of Delsarte in the Boston School of Oratory, he founded the Boston College of Oratory. This enterprise was abandoned when Mrs. Edgerly died, and after spending some time in life insurance work Mr. Edgerly returned to the newspaper field, taking a place on the news staff of the Boston "Herald." From the "Herald" he went to New York city, where he joined the staff of the New York "Journal," remaining there until 1904, when he returned to Boston to assume an editorial position with the newly-founded "Boston American." In the spring of 1907 he returned to the Boston "Herald," remaining there until 1909, when he went back to his former place with the Boston "American." He left the "American" in 1910 to go to the Boston "Journal," after which he became connected with the advertising firm of Wood, Putnam & Wood. In 1912 failing health compelled his retirement from active work. As a man, his calm dignity and unfailing courtesy won him esteem and affection everywhere. He possessed an unerring judgment of news, and was noted for his constant serenity in the midst of the most strenuous circumstances incident to his calling. In the newspaper offices where he worked he is remembered as a man of kindly disposition, whose thoughtfulness and consideration for those around him were unfailing. His efficiency as a newspaper man was undisputed, while his splendid strength and indomitable courage triumphed over obstacles that would have dismayed another. He was a member of the Boston Press Club, the Zeta Psi Fraternity and of the Pilgrim Publicity Association. He was a trustee of the First Methodist Episcopal Church of Medford, Mass. Mr. Edgerly was married twice; first in 1891 to Clara Tileston Power, and second, July 13, 1900, to Mrs. Eleanor Joslin Geisinger, daughter of William F. Joslin, of Westville, N. H., by whom he had three children: Julian Joslin, Ruth and Sarah. He died in Westville, June 25, 1913. Portrait opposite p. 350.

STICKNEY, Austin, educator and scholar, was born in Cambridge, Mass., Nov. 25, 1831, son of William and Lucy (Burgess) Stickney. He traces descent from William Stickney, a native of Frampton, Lincolnshire, England, who emigrated in 1638, and settled in Rowley, Mass.; through his son Samuel, who married Julian Swan; their son William, who married Anna Hazeltine; their son William, who married Anne Whiting; their son William, who married Abigail Walker, and their son William, who married Sarah Gibson, and was grandfather of our subject. For four generations the family remained in the neighborhood of Rowley, living successively at Rowley, Bradford and Billerica. Samuel Stickney was delegate from Bradford at the council which met in Boston May 9, 1689, for the formation of a new government after the rebellion against Gov. Andros. Deacon William Stickney was representative from Billerica to the three provincial congresses of Salem, Cambridge and Watertown. It was before him (and others) that the depositions relating to the battle of Lexington were taken down on Apr. 23 and 25, 1775, and sent to England in one of the "Hon.

Richard Derby's fast-sailing ships," reaching there eleven days before Gen. Gage's report. Deacon Stickney's house is still standing at Billerica, now Groveland, a part of Lowell, Mass. William Stickney, son of Deacon William, fought at the battle of Lexington in his cousin, Jonathan Stickney's, company, and at the close of the war, about 1784, removed to Grafton, Vt. William Stickney (1799-1850), Austin Stickney's father, was a merchant of Boston, and his son's preliminary education was received chiefly at the Roxbury and Boston Latin schools. He was graduated at Harvard in 1852, and entered the law school, but was obliged to leave two years later on account of broken health. In 1858 he had sufficiently recovered to accept the chair of Latin at Trinity College, Hartford, Conn. This position he held until 1864, and again during the winter of 1870-71, sometimes teaching Greek also. After marrying he lived abroad for sixteen years, excepting 1870-71, when he resumed his professorship at Trinity College. In 1879 he settled in New York city. Besides his work at Trinity College, he edited for school use: "De Natura Deorum," "De Officiis," "De Senectute" and "De Amicitia," and the romance poem, "Daude de Pradas," which was published in Florence. His literary taste was unfailing and his reading thorough and extensive, embracing, besides that of his own tongue, the languages he also spoke fluently. Of Dante he made an exhaustive study, and he was well versed in old French. He was also a great lover of music and played skillfully on the violin. As an educator, he was remarkable for the thoroughness and lucidity of his teaching and for his sympathetic insight, both into the minds of his pupils and the subject in hand, which he never failed to make a living and inspiring reality. Mr. Stickney was a member of the Century Club of New York, the Church Club of New York, the Société pour l'encouragement des études grecques of Paris, the American Philological Association, the American Folk-Lore Society and the Archæological Institute of America. He was married July 7, 1863, to Harriet Champion, daughter of Henry Champion Trumbull, of Hartford, Conn., and great-great-granddaughter of Gov. Jonathan Trumbull (q. v.). They had two sons and two daughters: Lucy Madeleine, wife of William Williams Mathewson; Eliza Trumbull, Joseph Trumbull, author of "Poems of Trumbull Stickney" (1905) and instructor in Greek at Harvard at the time of his death in 1904, and Henry Austin Stickney, practicing lawyer in New York city. In 1894 Mr. Stickney went abroad again and died in Paris, France, Nov. 30, 1896.

PAGE, Samuel Davis, lawyer and banker, was born in Philadelphia, Pa., Sept. 22, 1840, son of Dr. William Byrd and Celestine Anna (Davis) Page. His first American ancestor was John Page (1627-92), the first of the name in Virginia and a member of the colonial council of that colony in the time of William and Mary. The line of descent is traced through John's son Matthew, who married Mary Mann; their son Mann, who married Judith Carter; their son Robert, who married Sarah Walker; their son John, who married Maria H. Byrd, and their son William Byrd, who married Evelyn Byrd Nelson, and who was the grandfather of Samuel Davis Page. His father (1817-77) was a distinguished member of the medical profession, and for many years professor of surgery in the Pennsylvania Medical College in Philadelphia. His education was acquired in the Gregory Latin School and in Dr. Williams' Classical School, and

he was graduated at Yale College with honor in 1859, before he was nineteen years old. He was a member of the Delta Kappa Epsilon and of Phi Beta Kappa, was commodore of the Yale navy, and trained the first Yale crew that ever won a victory over the Harvard crew. After his graduation he studied law in the law office of Hon. Peter McCall, one of the leaders of the Philadelphia bar, and also attended the law schools of the University of Pennsylvania and Harvard College. He was admitted to the bar in 1864, and since then has practiced his profession without interruption, except for seasons of travel and the demands of public office. As an advocate Mr. Page stands deservedly high, and few attorneys of Philadelphia or elsewhere have enjoyed to such a full extent the confidence and trust of the community at large. Twenty-five years after his admission to the bar, he organized the law firm of Page & Allinson, with Edward P. Allinson. In 1890 Boies Penrose became a member, and to the firm of Page, Allinson & Penrose Mr. Page's son, Howard Wurts Page, was admitted in 1891. After Mr. Allison's death and the withdrawal of Sen. Penrose in 1901, it became Page & Page, comprising Mr. Page and his son. Always interested in local politics, he entered the city council in 1877, resigning in 1883 to accept the office of city controller, to which he had been appointed by Gov. Pattison. While in the city council he took part in every important movement for better government during that period, and served on many general and special committees. He was active in the investigation and reorganization of the tax office, and formulated and secured the adoption of the act known as "The pay-as-you-go act." He figured prominently in the investigation of the old gas trust which led finally to its abolition, and labored in behalf of the new charter for the city of Philadelphia, known as the Bullitt bill. He served as city controller in 1883-84 and was assistant United States treasurer for two years under Cleveland and two years under Harrison. Mr. Page was president of the Quaker City National Bank during 1890-92, and is still a director of that institution. He has been a director of the Merchants' Trust Co. since its incorporation in 1890, and in 1891 he was a member of the commission appointed by Gov. Pattison to investigate the accounts of the city treasurer with the Keystone National Bank. Of Mr. Page's personal characteristics, a leading journalist wrote: "His standards of duty are lofty, his methods clean and manly. He employs the truth, though the telling of it creates enmities. He knows no master except his own conscience. He has sought to perform his whole duty, as a citizen and as a public servant, according to the soul-inspiration which dominated the actions and eventualities of the life which was not his, but God's. Never, in all my experience, have I been associated with a man whose conceptions of duty are purer, whose heart possesses less of guile, whose pulse-beats are more completely adjusted to the higher attributes which go to make up the ideal gentleman." Mr. Page is the governor of the Pennsylvania Society of Colonial Governors, president of the Colonial Society and deputy governor-general of the General Society of Colonial Wars and lieutenant-governor of the Society of Colonial Wars in the Commonwealth of Pennsylvania. He is a member of the historical societies of Pennsylvania and Virginia, the Law Association of Philadelphia, the American and Pennsylvania bar associations, the Yale Alumni Association of Pennsylvania, the Phi

Beta Kappa Society, and was president of the Alumni Association of the Delta Kappa Epsilon fraternity. His clubs are: The Rittenhouse, University, Lawyers', Democratic and Harvard. Mr. Page was married Sept. 25, 1861, to Isabella Graham, daughter of William Wurts, of Philadelphia. Mrs. Page died Mar. 23, 1867, leaving three children: Howard Wurts, Ethel Nelson and William Byrd Page.

BROWN, John Sidney, merchant, was born in Ashtabula county, O., June 10, 1833, son of Reuben and Betsey (Hill) Brown. His ancestors emigrated from England in the early part of the sixteenth century and located at Southampton, Mass., whence they moved subsequently to East Kingston, N. H. Moses Brown, grandfather of J. Sidney Brown, fought in the revolutionary war. Betsey Hill was descended from Gen. Robert Sedgwick, who, with the younger Winthrop, in 1643, established the first iron works in America. She was a cousin of the Rev. Horace Bushnell, of Hartford, Conn., for whom Bushnell Park is named. She was also a cousin of Hon. James Campbell, chief justice of Michigan, who was at the head of the law department of Ann Arbor University. Her brother, Gen. Charles W. Hill, was adjutant-general of Ohio in 1861-63, and aided largely in raising the quota of troops in Ohio during the civil war. J. Sidney Brown attended the district schools when work on the farm was not pressing, and before his majority studied a few years in Conneaut Academy. In 1858 he joined his brother, Junius F. Brown, at Atchison, Kan., in the manufacture of lumber. At the outbreak of the civil war a decrease in the demand for lumber induced the firm to utilize their many teams by loading a wagon-train with merchandise and sending it across the plains to Denver. J. Sidney Brown made two such trips across the plains to Denver in 1861, each a weary trip of forty days, attended with many difficulties and serious dangers. In 1862, his third trip, his mule-train was attacked and destroyed in the night by Indians, who were, however, finally routed after a stiff fight. Impressed by the prospects of Denver, Brown decided to settle there permanently. The ensuing years were marked by difficulties and reverses, but his indomitable pluck, energy and perseverance enabled him to finally overcome all and to use them as stepping stones to a brilliant success. He started in the grocery business, but in the following year the entire stock was burned. He and his partner, Alvin B. Daniels, bought out the firm of Carter & Co. and of Wilder Jenks & Co. In 1868 Daniels retired from the firm, and the business went on under the name of J. S. Brown until 1870, when the new firm of J. S. Brown & Bro. was incorporated, with his brother, Junius F. Brown, as partner. The business continued under this arrangement until succeeded by the J. S. Brown & Bro. Mercantile Co., in the year 1893. After having been engaged in business as partners for over forty years J. F. Brown withdrew in 1900. J. Sidney still continued at the head of the old establishment, of which he has been president since its organization. It is now owned by J. Sidney Brown & Sons. Mr. Brown has been in the same line of business longer than any other man in Denver. He is a member of the Colorado Commandery of Knights Templar. J. Sidney Brown was one of the most conspicuous financial figures in Colorado and one of the most influential factors in building up the city of Denver. He assisted in organizing the City National Bank, of which he was for several years president; founded banks at Alamosa and Durango, Colo., and was a member of the banking house of Daniels, Brown & Co., of Del Norte, known as the Bank of San Juan, and at one time rated the strongest financial institution in the West. He was one of the original promoters and largest stockholder of the Denver and New Orleans railroad, afterward consolidated with the Union Pacific and Gulf railroad, and was its vice-president for several years and trustee for all its stocks and bonds. He was one of the promoters and a stockholder in the Denver Pacific and was largely instrumental in building the South Park railroad, the first road into Denver. When the road was sold to Jay Gould in the early eighties, he received as trustee for the stockholders a check for $2,250,000. He was an original promoter of the Denver Tramway Co., the Telephone Co., the Denver Steam Heating Plant and the Denver, Utah and Pacific railroad, now owned by the Burlington. He was also vice-president of the Colorado Milling and Elevator Co., and built the first grain elevator and roller flour mill in the state. "Cheerfulness, generosity and optimism," said the Denver "Times," "combined with resourcefulness and gigantic purpose—the latter a quality which gave him rank among the state's foremost builders—were his characteristics, and they remained indelibly written in his character up to the moment of his death." "J. Sidney Brown," said the Denver "News," "was lavish in gifts of money to his children, generous to charities, and to such public institutions as the Denver University, Y. M. C. A., etc. He was a home-loving man, caring absolutely nothing for club life. He was genial, smiling, lovable, and at once progressive and conservative. He delighted in reviving memories of the early days of the West, and was an excellent story-teller. He was a man of strict moral character. He never took a drink in his life and had not smoked a cigar since 1888. He was interested in the First Congregational Church and always contributed generously to its support." Mr. Brown was married May 7, 1868, to Irene, daughter of Capt. Richard Sopris, one time mayor of Denver. She died in 1881, leaving five children: Frederick S., vice-president and manager of the J. S. Brown & Bro. Mercantile Co.; Elizabeth, wife of A. B. Inglis; Edward N., Katherine, wife of N. A. Johansen, and William K. Brown, secretary of the Brown corporation. He was married for the second time Aug. 15, 1882, to Adele, daughter of John Overton, of Dane, Wis. Mrs. Brown is a cousin of Sen. Henry M. Keller and the late Sen. Jerome B. Chaffee, of Colorado; is a Daughter of the Revolution, and is very prominent in social and patriotic circles in Denver. There were six children of his second marriage: John Sidney, Jr., Ben Overton, Carroll Teller, Sedgewick Bushnell, Alice, wife of Samuel Martin, and Irene L. Brown. He died in Denver, Colo., Jan. 15, 1913.

WILBUR, Ray Lyman, physician and third president of Leland Stanford Junior University, was born at Boonesboro, Ia., Apr. 13, 1875, son of Dwight Locke and Edna Maria (Lyman) Wilbur, and grandson of Ezra Wilbur who was a native of Connecticut and a New England sea captain, and after serving in the war of 1812 settled at Unadilla Forks, N. Y. He married Lois Ray. He was descended from the English Wildbore family, a representative of which emigrated to New England in the early part of the seventeenth century. On the maternal side Dr. Wilbur is descended from Richard Lyman, of Kent, England, who came to America and first settled in Charleston, Mass.

He was one of the party of immigrants which went from Massachusetts to Connecticut in 1635 and established a settlement in Hartford. From this Richard Lyman the line is traced through John, Moses, Elias and Joel Lyman, the latter being the maternal grandfather of our subject. Dr. Wilbur's father was a graduate of the law school of the University of Michigan and a veteran of the civil war. He practiced law in Iowa, North Dakota and California, becoming president of the Chamber of Commerce of Riverside in the latter state. Ray Lyman Wilbur was educated in the schools of Riverside and was graduated at the Leland Stanford Jr. University in 1896, receiving the degree of A.M. in the following year. He studied medicine in Cooper Medical College and received his medical degree in 1899. He began his professional career as instructor in physiology at his alma mater and for two years (1898-1900) was a lecturer and demonstrator in physiology at the Cooper Medical College. He was assistant professor of physiology at Stanford until 1903, when he went to Europe to pursue special studies. He also conducted a private practice at Palo Alto until 1909, when he became professor of medicine at the university there. In the latter year Stanford University organized a medical school of high standard upon the basis furnished by the gift to the university of the endowment funds of Cooper Medical College, Lane Hospital and Lane Medical Library. After another trip through Europe for further studies in surgery and medicine Dr. Wilbur became executive head of its medical school. He was made its dean in 1913. This medical school requires three years of university work for admission, and is one of the first institutions in this country to place its professors in the clinical branches upon a full-paid academic basis and to require a year of actual hospital work before the degree of Doctor of Medicine is granted. The university owns and controls its own teaching hospital and has a large out-patient department, with about 80,000 visits annually. After a nation-wide search the trustees of Leland Stanford university in 1915 elected him president of that institution to succeed John Casper Branner, resigned. Dr. Wilbur is a member of the Academy of Medicine (president 1912-13) and the California Academy of Medicine; a fellow of the American Medical Association, the American Association for the Advancement of Science; associate member of the Association of American Physicians and a member of the Phi Beta Kappa fraternity, University and Commonwealth clubs of San Francisco. He is the author of scientific papers on acidosis, urobilin, action of drugs on the heart beat, as well as of a number of articles on clinical medicine. He is esteemed and respected by his medical associates for his professional knowledge and unquestioned ability and his absolute conscientiousness in the performance of his duties. His professional career has been peculiarly signalized by an intense interest in his work and marked conservatism in his opinions. He was married Dec. 5, 1898, to Marguerite, daughter of Charles E. Blake, of San Francisco, Cal., and has five children: Jessica Foster, Blake Colburn, Dwight Locke, Lois Proctor and Ray Lyman. Portrait opp. p. 355.

MELTZER, Samuel James, physician, was born in Troupe, in western Russia, March 22, 1851, son of Simon and Taube (Kowars) Meltzer. He attended school in his native town and at Koenigsburg, Prussia, and was graduated at the University of Berlin in 1882 with the degree of M.D. He came to New York in 1883 and opened an office for the practice of his profession. He early acquired distinction as a profound physiologist, and upon the opening of the Rockefeller Institute for Medical Research in 1906 he was called to the head of the department of physiology and pharmacology. One of the first important announcements made from his new position was the discovery of the anesthetic properties of sulphate of magnesium and that the new anesthetic was a powerful remedy for tetanus (lockjaw). Intra-spinal injection of magnesium sulphate for lock-jaw is a treatment now in use all over the world when all other remedies, including anti-tetanus serum, have failed. Dr. Meltzer is also the originator of intratracheal insufflation (the introduction of air through the windpipe to the lungs), a method of artificial respiration which has resulted in great saving of life. This method is the simplest for all thoracic surgery, and permits free access to the heart and lungs without any danger. Before the discovery of this method by Meltzer the dangers in chest surgery were extremely great; it required the most costly apparatus, and the surgeon was obliged to work with the utmost haste to guard against the collapse of the patient's lungs. By intratracheal insufflation there is no probability of the lungs collapsing, and haste is unnecessary. This method of intratracheal insufflation led to the discovery of pharyngeal insufflation, which is artificial respiration designed for the use of laymen in the cases of accident by electric shock, drowning, coal-gas poisoning, etc. Its discovery was due to the appointment of a commission to study the effects of electric shock, and possible resuscitation from it, in the hope of lessening the number of casualties in the industrial world. The commission consisted of such well-known scientists as Prof. W. B. Cannon, of Harvard (chairman); Dr. George W. Crile, of Cleveland; Dr. Yandell Henderson, of Yale; Dr. E. A. Spitzka, Jefferson Medical College, Philadelphia; Dr. A. E. Kenney, of Harvard; W. C. L. Eglin, National Electric Light Association; Dr. E. Thompson, of the General Electric Co.; W. D. Weaver, editor of the "Electrical World," and Dr. Meltzer. Meltzer's earlier method of intratracheal insufflation naturally pointed to him as the man. Within a few months he devised a simple and ample means of artificial respiration by pharyngeal insufflation (the rhythmical forcing of air to the lungs through the channels of the mouth and pharynx), a successful method readily available in emergency cases in all kinds of industrial plants. The apparatus can be packed into a hand-bag. Briefly, it consists of a properly shaped tube, made of metal (the pharyngeal tube), to be forced through the mouth into the pharynx, and so shaped as to prevent the escape of air through the mouth. This is connected by tubing with the insufflation apparatus proper—*i.e.*, a small foot bellows (or, if experts or physicians are at hand. an oxygen tank to be used in alternation with the foot bellows). The flow of air is controlled by a respiratory valve conveniently placed on the connecting tube, and which is worked rhythmically back and forth by the operator's thumb, inserted in a ring handle. By one movement of the thumb the air is admitted, by the next the respired air is ejected. A safety valve of very simple design is attached to the tube so that the air in the lungs is kept at the same pressure as the outside atmosphere, thus permitting the chest to be opened wide without any danger of collapse. The fresh air enters the lungs through the tube, and the vitiated air leaves through the narrow space between the tube and

RAY L. WILBUR
PRESIDENT STANFORD UNIVERSITY

SAMUEL J. MELTZER
PHYSICIAN

JOHN N. NORTON
AUTHOR

CHARLES W. RAE
NAVAL OFFICER

the walls of the windpipe. The patient does not breathe at all; in place of the usual respiratory movements the operator simply pumps air into the lungs, which can remain distended five or six hours. As a practical result the surgeon now has access to the body's last unexplored field. Dr. Meltzer received the degree of LL.D. from the University of Maryland in 1906, and from St. Andrew's, Scotland, in 1912. He is a fellow the American Associaton for the Advancement of Science, New York Academy of Sciences, New York Academy of Medicine; a member of the Association of American Physicians, the American Physiological Society (president), American Pharmacological Society, Association of American Pathologists, American Society of Naturalists, Society for Experimental Biology and Medicine, American Gastro Enterological Association; president Association for the Advancement of Clinical Research (1909); president the Harvey Society; member of the National Academy of Sciences and of the German Imperial Academy of Natural Sciences; chairman section of physiology, International Congress of Arts and Sciences, St. Louis, 1904. He is the author of nearly two hundred articles and monographs, as well as of many lectures and addresses. Dr. Meltzer was married in June, 1876, to Olga S., daughter of Girshe Lewitt, and has two children: Clara Meltzer Auer, M.D., and Victor Meltzer, M.D.

NORTON, John Nicholas, clergyman and author, was born at Waterloo, N. Y., in 1820, son of George Hatley and Maria (Gault) Norton. He received his preliminary education in public and private schools and was graduated at Hobart College in 1842, and at the General Theological Seminary, New York, in 1845. He was ordained deacon of the P. E. Church in Geneva, July 20, 1845, and was advanced to the priesthood a year later. He was assistant minister of St. Luke's Church, Rochester, N. Y., in 1845. He became rector of Ascension Church, Frankfort, Ky., in 1846, and while in that city spent part of his time as professor in Dr. Lloyd's English School. He also taught in the Kentucky Military Institute. He was very zealous, founding several churches in the central part of Kentucky, and a church for colored people in Louisville. In 1870 he was called to Louisville as associate rector of Christ Church, and remained there until his death. He received the degree of D.D. from Hobart College in 1862. He was a member of the standing committee of the diocese of Kentucky, and for nine years was a deputy to the general convention and trustee of the Theological Seminary of Kentucky. He was a fluent and interesting writer. His publications, numbering nearly forty volumes, include: "The Boy Trained to the Ministry" (1854), "Full Proof of the Ministry" (1855), "Rockford Parish" (1856), "Lives of Bishop White and Others" (1857), "Short Sermons" (1858), "Life of George Washington" (1860), "Life of Benjamin Franklin" (1861), "The King's Ferry Boat" (1876), "Life of Bishop Berkeley" (1862), "Life of Archbishop Cranmer" (1863), "Life of Laud" (1864), "Milk and Honey" (sermon for children, 1870), "Warning and Teaching" (sermons, 1878), and "Old Paths" (sermons, 1880). Dr. Norton was distinguished for his tact and magnetism and also for his humor, some of which often crept into his sermons. He was greatly loved, and especially so by the poor people of Louisville. As a preacher he was clear and direct. He knew just what he wanted to say, said it and stopped. The simplest of the congregation could remember all there was

in the sermon; he never failed to interest both old and young. He was heard to say that twenty minutes was long enough for a good sermon and too long for a bad one, and what he preached he practiced. His life for nearly forty years was spent in doing good, and many were the testimonies of both old and young that his labor was not in vain. He was married, in 1855, to Mary Louisa, daughter of George W. Sutton, a prominent citizen of Lexington, Ky., who survived him with one daughter, Juliet M., wife of Paul Evarts Johnson, of Washington, D. C. He died in Louisville, Ky., Jan. 18, 1881. Portrait opposite p. 354.

RAE, Charles Whiteside, naval officer, was born at Hartford, Conn., June 30, 1847, son of Luzerne and Martha (Whiteside) Rae. His preliminary education was received at Champlain Academy, N. Y., and he was graduated at Rensselaer Polytechnic Institute in 1866. Enlisting in the United States navy as an acting assistant engineer, he took a two-years' course of instruction at the United States Naval Academy, Annapolis, and was graduated in 1868. After a period of sea service he was placed in charge of the work of establishing a line of levels across the isthmus of Tehuantepec, Mexico (in 1870), and subsequently was attached to the original Nicaragua canal and survey expedition. For several years thereafter he was instructor at the naval academy, and after a period of sea service with the European, South Atlantic and North Atlantic squadrons, in 1893 he became head of the department of steam engineering at the naval academy. During the Spanish-American war Admiral Rae was chief engineer of the battleship Iowa, participating in the bombardment of San Juan and the battle of Santiago. He was advanced three numbers for "eminent and conspicuous conduct" during the battle of Santiago, and was awarded a medal of honor for distinguished service in the Cuban campaign. After the war he was in charge of the installation of new machinery at the Yuerba Buena naval station, and was inspector of machinery at the Newport News Shipbuilding and Dry Dock Co. He was then assigned to the bureau of steam engineering, Washington, and in 1903 was appointed engineer-in-chief of the United States navy and chief of the bureau of steam engineering, with the rank of rear-admiral, a position he filled until his death. He was president of the American Society of Naval Engineers, vice-president of the Society of Naval Architects and Marine Engineers, member of the Washington Society of Engineers, the National Geographic Society, the Metropolitan and Alibi clubs of Washington, and the Engineers' Club of New York. In 1906 he received the degree of Sc.D. from the University of Pennsylvania. Admiral Rae was a capable and efficient officer whose influence will long be felt for good in the navy. Courteous and dignified in manner and bearing, he was a man of charming personality, and one who inspired affection from all with whom he came in contact. He was married Jan. 9, 1890, to Rebecca Gilman Dodge, of Washington, who survived him. He died in Washington, D. C., May 13, 1908. Portrait opposite page 354.

SHAW. Thomas, inventor and scientist, was born in Philadelphia, Pa., Apr. 5, 1838, son of James and Catherine (Snyder) Shaw. His earliest paternal American ancestor was John Shaw, a native of England, who settled in Pennsylvania previous to 1694, and whose descendants were closely associated with the settlement of the city of Philadelphia and the state of Pennsylvania. James

Shaw, grandson of the settler, and great-great-grandfather of Thomas Shaw, was a soldier of the war of the revolution, as were his eight sons. James Shaw, father of the inventor, was a Philadelphia merchant, while his mother possessed considerable inventive ingenuity, her home being filled with original devices of her own handiwork. Thomas Shaw early displayed decided mechanical genius, at the age of eight years constructing models of machinery in wood. At the age of ten he built a retort, and from the molten glass of old bottles made various useful objects. In his boyhood he invented the rotary shears, a recording reel for winding yarns and a mowing machine with a vibrating knife, which was afterward perfected by Obed Hussey. His first patent was for a gas-meter, dated Apr. 12, 1858, and on Dec. 14, 1858, he patented a gas stove, the first stove having an oven attached. He received in all 187 patents. In 1859 patents were granted him on a gas heating device for college use, on glass moulds and sewing machines. His unique attachments for the latter are in use on most of the improved machines of to-day. On May 29, 1860, a patent was granted him for a method of burning ignitable fluids. This was the germ of the idea that has made possible the burning of oil fuel on steam vessels. It was intended principally for ocean steamships, and was the first test of the character made in the world. A second patent was obtained on the invention June 2, 1863. The most notable of his inventions are: The Verona lock-nut washer, commonly known as the spring pawl washer, patented Apr. 28, 1868, which is used chiefly between the nut and the fish-plate in bolting rails together; a self-cocking pistol, patented Dec. 24, 1861; a sewing machine attachment; methods of armor plating; quartz crushers; steam boiler feeder, patented July 31, 1860; the mercury steam gauge, still the standard the world over, which was patented Feb. 24, 1863; hydraulic gauge; force pumps; low water detectors and indicators; the noiseless steam exhaust, patented May 18, 1869, which muffles the sound of escaping steam, and which is now used universally on all locomotives and steamships; faucet grinders, a floating crane, steam whistles, a process of generating carbonic oxide, a method of shotting metals, which for years was a valued secret process; a power hammer, patented Feb. 27, 1866, now in universal use; a method for burning hydrocarbon, patented May 20, 1860; an artillery forge, pile drivers, a paddle wheel ice-cutter, a device for detaching boats at sea, which was granted a medal at the Philadelphia Centennial Exposition; air chamber feeders; submarine observatories; pile sawing machines; a water cartridge; a fire alarm system; a cooling process for fruit cars; a miner's safety lamp; methods for purifying mine air and water; signaling tubes for mines, and an apparatus for testing and recording mine gases. This last, known as the Shaw gas tester, was his greatest contribution to science. It has been in general use since 1889, and has been instrumental in saving thousands of lives. It is now the official standard in Pennsylvania and Ohio and has the official indorsement of the United Mine Workers of America. The instrument is sensitive to the change of 1/1000 part or 1/10 of 1 per cent. of explosive gas in air, and has the power of weighing and measuring noxious and explosive gases. Thomas Shaw became superintendent of the Butcher Steel Works in 1858. Here, with William B. Butcher, he invented a method of casting car wheels and tires, and supervised the rolling of the first steel tires

ever made in America; and here also he devised the bolster and semi-elliptic spring, now in universal use under passenger cars. When, in 1871, that plant was reorganized as the Midvale Steel Co., he was retained as superintendent, but resigned to go into the manufacture of his own inventions in association with J. Howard Mitchell and Philip S. Justice. Capt. Eads consulted with him regarding the foundations for the Eads Mississippi bridge at St. Louis, and he had also confidential relations with William Weightman, Franklin B. Gowan, president of the Philadelphia and Reading Railway Co., and other noted men of his day. His gunpowder pile-driving apparatus was awarded the medal of honor of the American Institute and the Scott legacy medal from the Franklin Institute. His compound propeller pump had a capacity of 200,000 pounds of water per minute, and was used in all districts where floods were prevalent. At various times during his career Mr. Shaw received flattering offers of engineering positions from the French, British, Russian and Japanese governments. Shawmont avenue, in Philadelphia, and the beautiful suburb of Shawmont in Philadelphia were named in his honor. For twenty-five years Mr. Shaw was a member of the committee on science and arts of the Franklin Institute of Philadelphia, and he was the recipient of the Elliot Cresson gold medal from the institute for his system of testing mine gases and signals in mines. The name of Thomas Shaw should be enrolled among America's most notable inventors. He was a man of extraordinary genius and mechanical ability, whose many contributions to science are remarkable for the diversity of their character, as well as for their practical utility and value. He was married in 1859 to Matilda Miller, daughter of John Garber, of Philadelphia, and had three children, of whom only one survives, Cora, wife of Joseph R. Wilson, of Philadelphia. He died in Philadelphia, Pa., Jan. 19, 1901.

HASBROUCK, Henry Cornelius, soldier, was born in Newburgh, N. Y., Oct. 26, 1839, son of William Cornelius and Mary Elizabeth (Roe) Hasbrouck. His earliest paternal American ancestor was Abraham Hasbroucq, of French Huguenot descent, who emigrated from England in the seventeenth century and settled at New Paltz, N. Y. His wife was Maria Deyo, and the line of descent is through their eldest son, Joseph, and his wife, Elsie Schoonmaker; their son Benjamin and his wife, Elidia Schoonmaker, and their son Cornelius Benjamin and his wife, Janet Kelso, the grandparents of the subject. The following is from the manuscript of Col. Abraham Hasbroucq, settler and patentee: "In the year 1677 Abraham Hasbroucq and his associates, to the number of twelve, obtained a patent of the then governor (of New York), named Edmund Andross, under his Royal Highness, James, Duke of York, and called it by the name of New Paltz, and it bears the name to this day." The Hudson river was the eastern boundary of this patent, Lake Mohonk the western, and it extended south nearly to Newburgh. Joseph Hasbrouck was an Indian commissioner. The Hon. Wm. Cornelius Hasbrouck, some time speaker of the house at Albany, was a lawyer. Henry Cornelius Hasbrouck was graduated at West Point in 1861 at the beginning of the civil war, and was promoted in the army as second lieutenant, 4th artillery. A week later he became first lieutenant and participated in the Manassas campaign of the civil war, being engaged in the battle of Bull Run. For gallant and meritorious services at Blackwater Bridge, Va., he was breveted captain in 1862; was in the defence of Washington and the operations about Suffolk, Va., and in September, 1863, being on sick leave, went to the U. S. Military Academy as assistant professor of natural and experimental philosophy. At this time he suggested the idea of a battle monument and contributed the first money for the monument dedicated June 15, 1864. He returned to the front in February, 1865, and took part in the operations before Richmond. He declined to be breveted major for his services during the siege of Petersburg. While a captain in the 4th artillery he took part in the famous Modoc expedition of 1873, being in command during the action of Sorass Lake, Cal., and near Van Bremer's ranch in May, 1873. He was breveted major for gallant services in routing Captain Jack of the Modocs at Sorass Lake. He was on the expedition against the Nevada Indians in 1875, and was in the field until 1878. He was commandant of cadets at West Point during 1882-88 and in the latter year he was a member of the commission to prepare a system of tactics for the army. In 1896 he was promoted lieutenant-colonel and in 1898 became a brigadier-general of volunteers. At the outbreak of the war with Spain, Gen. Hasbrouck was placed in command of the third brigade, second division, 7th army corps, and served at Jacksonville, Savannah and Marionao, Cuba. He was in command of the department of Pinar del Rio, Cuba, in March and April, 1899. He was promoted colonel, 7th artillery, in February, 1899, and on Dec. 1, 1902, was appointed a brigadier and was placed on the retired list Jan. 5, 1903. Our country affords no higher type of man and the army no better type of soldier than Gen. Hasbrouck. He was absolutely free from guile and from every form of smallness, and his extreme modesty diminished somewhat his otherwise positive character to those who knew him but slightly. After retirement his life was spent mainly at Newburgh at the family homestead where he was born and reared. He was a member of the Military Order of the Loyal Legion, the St. Nicholas Society, Holland Society, University Club of New York and the Army and Navy Club of New York. He was married in 1882 to Laetitia Viele, daughter of Edward Stevens Warren, of Buffalo, by whom he is survived. He died at Newburgh, N. Y., Dec. 17, 1910.

SEVERANCE, Louis Henry, capitalist and philanthropist, was born in Cleveland, O., Aug. 1, 1838, son of Solomon Lewis (1812-38) and Mary H. (Long) Severance, and a descendant of John Severance, a native of England, who came to this country and settled in Boston in 1637. His wife was Abigail Kimball, and from them the line of descent is traced through their son John; his son Joseph, who married Anna Kellogg; their son Jonathan, who married Thankful Stebbins; their son Solomon, who married Hannah Hoyt, and their son Robert Bruce, who married Diana Long, and was the grandfather of the subject of this sketch. Louis Severance's father, who died two weeks before the birth of his son, was a merchant. His mother, who died at the age of eighty-six, was prominent in the Presbyterian Church, and one of the founders of the Protestant Orphan Asylum, and also of the Lakeside Hospital, in Cleveland. Louis Henry Severance received his early education in the public schools of Cleveland, and at the age of eighteen entered the Commercial Bank, where he remained until 1864, except the time

passed in the hundred-day service of the national guards, who went to the defence of Washington in 1863. In 1864 he removed with his family to Titusville, Pa., where for ten years he was engaged in the oil business. Returning to Cleveland, he became cashier and treasurer of the Standard Oil Co., a position which he retained until 1896, when he retired from active business affairs. While a resident of Titusville he became an elder in the Presbyterian church, and upon his return to Cleveland he identified himself with the Woodland Avenue Presbyterian Church, becoming superintendent in the Sunday-school and an elder in the church, to which he gave unremitting and devoted personal service and financial support. He was deeply interested in the mission work of the Presbyterian Church and in general Christian education. This interest manifested itself in great benefactions to the Christian educational institutions of this country and to those in foreign lands, and to the erection of hospitals and training schools in distant parts of the world. In an extended journey around the world in 1907-08 he made a thorough study of the various forms of Christian activity in mission lands, which were of assistance to him as a member of the Presbyterian board of foreign missions. Mr. Severance seemed to be largely dominated by the thought that in the training of young men to enter the Christian ministry the church would be furnished with the motive power necessary to its usefulness and highest success, hence he turned his attention to the subject of Christian education. The first college to receive his particular attention was Oberlin, of which he became a trustee, and for which he erected and endowed the Severance Chemical Laboratory, besides giving the college material assistance in other ways. He also became interested in Western Reserve University, of which he was a trustee, assisting in erecting there the Harkness memorial chapel in memory of his wife, and aiding the institution in a number of its departments. By his contributions to Wooster University after a disastrous fire he made possible its re-establishment and by his active interest and large gifts he furthered its development into a well-equipped and endowed institution. His benefactions extended to a large number of other colleges, among them being Occidental, Marysville, Bellevue, Park, Huron, Greenville and Tusculum, Whitworth, Idaho and Dubuque Seminary. While numerous institutions were the beneficiaries of his generosity, he seemed to feel especially obligated to those affiliated with the Presbyterian Church. Shortly after his return from his journey around the world he was elected a member of the Presbyterian board of foreign missions, and thereafter devoted a large part of his time to the work of the board. The extent of his sympathy with Christian effort to evangelize the world is further indicated by the fact that he was a member of the Presbyterian college board, assistant moderator of the Presbyterian general assembly and president of the board of trustees of Nanking University (China). He was interested in the work of the Y. M. C. A. and the Y. W. C. A., and did much for the support of this work, not only in this country, but also in Manchuria, Japan and other portions of the Orient. So intense was his belief that aggressive Christian work was of the utmost importance, and so great was his desire to aid the missionary cause, that, in addition to his regular support of the boards, he purchased at various mission stations numerous tracts of land, erected many buildings, residences and hospitals, aside from the hospital and medical college at Seoul, Korea. The religious life of Louis Henry Severance was his real life. The Kingdom of God, in himself and in others, predominated in every thought and purpose. All values were determined by Divine standards. In a thousand ways his religious earnestness found expression. His catholic and unfailing interest in humanity led him to engage in benefactions that have few, if any, parallels in the line of individual activity for the uplift of mankind. In the Orient these enterprises are of vast importance in carrying the message of enlightenment and right living to countless thousands. He gave not only of his wealth but contributed liberally from his personal resources of business acumen and skill for organization, and no man may say to what extent his broad generosity has been instrumental in moulding the lives of others into forms of usefulness that would not have been attainable without his intelligent helpfulness. Mr. Severance was a member of the Union, Country, Euclid and Mayfield clubs of Cleveland, and of the Union League Club of New York. He was twice married: first, Aug. 13, 1862, to Fannie B., daughter of Jonas Benedict, of Norwalk, O.; Mrs. Severance died Aug. 1, 1874, and he was married, second, Sept. 19, 1894, to Florence, daughter of Stephen Harkness, of Cleveland, O. There were four children of the first union: John L., Elisabeth S., wife of Dudley P. Allen, M.D.; Annie Belle (deceased) and Robert B. Severance (deceased). He died in Cleveland, O., June 25, 1913.

RUSSELL, Charles Wells, lawyer and diplomat, was born at Wheeling, W. Va., March 16, 1856, son of Charles Wells and Margaret Wilson (Moore) Russell. His father (1824-67) was chief counsel of the Baltimore and Ohio railroad, and was a prominent member of the Confederate congress, and his maternal grandfather was Henry Moore, a member of the celebrated firm of Neill, Moore & Co., which owned a stage line between Washington, D. C., and Columbus, O., and was president of the Wheeling and Belmont Bridge Co. Charles W. Russell was a student at Georgetown University, from which he received the degree of LL.B. in 1883 and that of LL.M. in 1884. He entered the department of justice, Washington, in 1886, and argued many French spoliation cases. During 1893-95 he was legal adviser of the Dockery joint congressional commission, and for the next six years was engaged in general legal, including supreme court, work. During January and December, 1897-98, he investigated and reported on reconcentrado starvation and military situation in Cuba, and from August to October of the latter year acted as legal adviser of the Porto Rican evacuation commission. In 1901 he argued the Maine explosion cases before the Spanish claims commission. In 1902 he became special assistant to the attorney-general, in charge of insular and territorial appointments, continuing in that capacity until 1905, when he was appointed assistant United States attorney-general. In 1902 Att'y-Gen. Knox sent him to Paris to investigate the title to the Panama canal, and he returned to Paris in 1904 to effect a transfer of the title and property of the Panama canal to the United States, and the payment of $40,000,000 in gold to France, for which he arranged with J. Pierpont Morgan in Paris. In the same year he was sent to Panama as legal adviser to the United States government in the canal zone. Subsequently he revisited Cuba to prepare the case of Countess O'Reilly against Gen. John R. Brooks concerning

her Havana slaughter-house monopoly. Later, at the instance of the Italian and Austrian governments, the attorney-general sent him to the southern states to investigate charges of peonage, and he prosecuted numerous peonage cases. During 1906-09 he sued several thousand persons of Muscogee, I. T., for illegally obtaining Indian lands. In 1909 he was appointed United States minister to Persia during Pres. Taft's administration. Mr. Russell is the author of "Cuba Libre" (1897), a play; a novel, "Lays of the Season" (1909) and "The Secret Place and Other Poems" (1911). He was married (first) in Washington, D. C., Feb. 19, 1879, to Lucy Floyd, a daughter of Alfred D. Mosby, of Virginia. She died in 1884, and he was married (second) at Lynchburg, Va., Oct. 5, 1885, to her sister, Lelia J. Mosby. By the first union there is one surviving son, John Mosby Russell, and by the second union, a daughter, Lucy V. Russell. Portrait opposite p. 359.

COPELAND, Royal Samuel, physician, was born at Dexter, Mich., Nov. 7, 1868, son of Roscoe Pulaski and Frances Jane (Holmes) Copeland. His first American ancestor was Lawrence Copeland, who came from England and settled in Plymouth, Mass., in 1650. He married Lydia Townsend in 1651, and the line of descent is traced through their son William, who married Mary Bass, granddaughter of John Alden of colonial fame; through their son Samuel, who married Mary ————; their son Samuel, who married Mary Owen; their son Samuel, a soldier of the revolution, who married Emma Parker, and their son Royal, who married Alice Davis, and who was the grandfather of the subject of this sketch. Dr. Copeland early developed an inclination for medicine and surgery, in which he was encouraged by his family physician, who acted as his preceptor. He was educated in the Michigan State Normal College and the University of Michigan, being graduated M.D. in 1889. He was house surgeon in the University of Michigan hospital (homeopathic) one year and then took post-graduate courses in medical study in England, France, Germany, Austria, Switzerland and Belgium, and, returning home, commenced the practice of his profession in Bay City, Mich. Lawrence University conferred upon him the degree of A.M. in 1897. In 1895 he was appointed professor of ophthalmology and otology at the University of Michigan (homeopathic department), and retained this position until 1908. In addition to his surgical work, Dr. Copeland took an active interest in civic, educational and religious affairs in Ann Arbor. He was a member of the national board of control of the Epworth League, three times elected to membership in the general conference of the Methodist Episcopal church, president of the Michigan Epworth League, mayor of Ann Arbor in 1901-03, member and president of the board of education of Ann Arbor during 1903-08, member of tuberculosis commission of Michigan and trustee of State Tuberculosis Sanitarium and president of Ann Arbor board of park commissioners. He is the author of "Refraction," "Diseases of the Ear," "The Scientific Reasonableness of Homeopathy," and of numerous magazine articles on various professional topics, especially relating to the operative surgery of the eye, and foreign travel. Dr. Copeland is a typical representative of what industry, perseverance and the ability to acquire friends can accomplish. His first friendship with his family physician developed in him the desire for medical research, and he attributes a great portion of his success to the influence ex-

CHARLES W. RUSSELL
DIPLOMAT

ROYAL S. COPELAND
PHYSICIAN

IRVING A. FINCH
MANUFACTURER

ARTHUR FARWELL
MUSICIAN

erted by the friends he has acquired throughout his life. In 1908 he was appointed dean of the New York Homeopathic Medical College and director of Flower Hospital, and his work resulted in an increased efficiency of the curriculum of the former and a much greater usefulness of the latter. In 1910 he was appointed a member of the ambulance board of the city of New York by Mayor Gaynor. He is a member and former president of the Saginaw Valley Medical Society, secretary, vice-president and president, respectively, of the Michigan Homeopathic Society, president of the American Ophthalmological, Otological and Laryngological Society, president of the American Institute of Homeopathy and delegate to the World's Homeopathic Congress in London, England, in 1896. He is a governor of the Michigan Society of New York and president of the University of Michigan Club. His college fraternities are Delta Kappa Epsilon and Alpha Sigma (medical). Dr. Copeland was married July 15, 1908, to Frances, daughter of Major Spalding, of Ann Arbor, Mich.

FINCH, Irving A., manufacturer, was born at Windham, N. Y., Aug. 4, 1836, son of Selah P. and Sarah (Hubbard) Finch. His father was a manufacturer of machinery in Scranton, Pa. The son was educated in the public schools, and after studying law for two years decided upon a business career, and entering his father's manufacturing firm served an apprenticeship in the various departments until he had mastered all the details. The company made a specialty of heavy coal machinery and enjoyed a large and extensive business. It was originally known as A. P. Finch & Co., but after his father's death Mr. Irving A. Finch became the proprietor, and the name was changed to I. A. Finch & Co. It was incorporated in 1892. Under his able management it was developed to extensive proportions and ranked among the largest of its kind in the United States. He steadfastly refused all offers of amalgamation with other concerns, and continued to carry on his business successfully and independently despite strong pressure which was brought to bear by various rivals that had merged their interests. Mr. Finch inherited from his father an active, mechanical mind. He was the inventor of a hoisting engine and various devices which he manufactured in his business. He was characterized as being liberal, just, cautious and persevering. He resembled Edmund Burke in his passionate love of principle and in his proud hatred of shifts and compromises, and his best efforts were always directed to producing goods of the highest standard. He was a director of the Traders' National Bank, and a member of the Engineers' Club of New York and the Scranton Club. He was married Sept. 29, 1863, to Hannah S. Bump, and had two sons, Edward and William Irving, and one daughter, Florence G. Finch. Irving A. Finch died in New York city, June 28, 1904.

FARWELL, Arthur, composer, was born at St. Paul, Minn., Apr. 23, 1872, son of George Lyman and Sara Gardner (Wyer) Farwell, and a descendant of Henry Farwell, the founder of the family in America. His mother came from an old New England family, her mother having been first cousin to Ralph Waldo Emerson. Arthur Farwell was educated at Baldwin Seminary, St. Paul, Minn., and at the Massachusetts Institute of Technology, Boston, Mass., where he was graduated B.S. in the department of electrical engineering in 1893. Although thoroughly equipped in a congenial and enlarging profession, his passion for music caused him to seek honors in the field of composition. After studying in Boston with Homer Norris, he spent the years 1897-99 in Germany and France, with such masters as Egelbert Humperdinck, Hans Pfitzner and Alexandre Guilmant. After his return to the United States he became lecturer on the history of music at Cornell University, holding this position for two years. During this time, besides composing a "Cornell" overture, he began his study of the songs of the American Indians, and he has wrought many of the themes derived from this source into rare and beautiful compositions that form a particularly individual contribution to the music of to-day. In 1901 Mr. Farwell founded in Newton Center, Mass., the now famous Wa-Wan Press for the double purpose of issuing American compositions having a definite bearing on modern musical art, and the various folksongs of America, and of affording a ready and sympathetic means for encouraging struggling American composers. This concern inaugurated and led for eleven years the radical movement for American musical progress, and the development of national resource in musical composition. A number of the composers whom it first brought to notice are now among the recognized leaders of American music. During 1903 Mr. Farwell made many trips across the country, playing his own compositions, preaching the gospel of American music, and making further studies in Indian and other American folk-music. The summer and fall of 1904 he devoted to an intimate study of the songs of the southwestern Indians and Spanish Californians. Among his compositions of this period may be mentioned "American Indian Melodies," a group of harmonized Indian themes, mostly Omaha; "Dawn" (for pianoforte, and for orchestra), a romantic composition developed from the Omaha melody, "The Old Man's Love Song"; "Ichibuzzhi," a development of two Indian melodies based on the Omaha legend of the hero, Ichibuzzhi; "The Domain of Hurakan" (for pianoforte, and for orchestra), a development of two Indian themes, Pawnee and Vancouver, in the spirit of creation myths; "Folksongs of the South and West"; "Navajo War Dance"; "Impressions of the Wa-Wan Ceremony," a pianoforte suite based on the ceremony from which the Wa-Wan Press derived its name. Among compositions not based on Indian themes were the songs, "A Ruined Garden," "Drake's Drum," "The Sea of Sunset," "Love's Secret," and "Symbolistic Study," for piano. In 1905 Mr. Farwell began the organization of the American Music Society, which eventually had "centers" in most of the principal cities of the United States. He was called to the editorial staff of "Musical America" in New York in 1909, which position he still holds. In 1910 he was made supervisor of municipal concerts in the parks and recreation piers of New York city, which position he also still retains. In this capacity he has instituted many progressive reforms in public music. His duties in New York compelled him to relinquish the Wa-Wan Press, which was sold to the publishing house of G. Schirmer in 1912. His later compositions have not dealt with Indian themes, and include a song, "The Farewell"; "Hymn to Liberty," sung at City Hall, New York, July 4, 1911; "Tone Poem for Voice and Orchestra," on a poem by George Sterling; "Mountain Vision," for orchestra with piano; incidental music for Louis N. Parker's pageant drama, "Joseph and His Brethren," and music for the Pageants of Meriden, N. H., and Darien, Conn. (1913).

McCULLOCH, Edgar Allen, jurist, was born at Trenton, Tenn., Aug. 21, 1861, son of Philip Doddridge and Lucy Virginia (Burrow) McCulloch. His first American ancestor was Alexander McCulloch. who emigrated from Scotland to North Carolina in the early part of the eighteenth century and settled near Halifax. He was councillor of the province, and during the revolution was an ardent supporter of the continental cause, though too old to participate in the war. His wife was Sarah Hill, and from them the line of descent is traced through his son Benjamin and his wife Sarah, and their son, Benjamin, and his wife Sarah Ann Caswell, who were the grandparents of our subject. His father was a physician. After studying law privately, the son went to Arkansas in 1893, and was admitted to the bar in July of that year. He at once entered upon the practice of his profession at Marianna, Ark. During his more than twenty years' practice he gained a wide experience in all branches of the law, and was recognized as among the foremost leaders of the bar of the state. In 1904 he was elected associate justice of the state and supreme court, and on Feb. 1, 1909, he was appointed chief justice to succeed Hon. Joseph M. Hill. In the many important cases which have come before him, Judge McCulloch has displayed both learning and keen judgment, and his opinions have been impartial and fair throughout. He possesses judicial poise, the capacity for rapid and thorough work, and a happy style which make him one of the strongest men on a state bench in the United States. Judge McCulloch has taken an active part in the Masonic fraternity, having served as grand master of the Arkansas Grand Lodge of Masons (1908–09). He was also grand commander of Knights Templars during 1900–02. He was married at Trenton, Tenn., Nov. 30, 1887, to Hattie Louise, daughter of John Hassell, and has four sons: Hugh, Edgar H., Ben and Richard B. McCulloch.

SPERRY, Thomas Alexander, founder of mercantile premium advertising, was born in Knoxville, Tenn., July 6, 1864, son of Jacob Austin and Susan Butler (Langley) Sperry. His first paternal American ancestor was Peter Sperry, who, with his wife, Elizabeth Wolf, emigrated to America in 1738 and settled at Winchester, Va. His son, Peter, Jr., was the grandfather of our subject. At the outbreak of the civil war, Jacob Austin Sperry was editor and owner of the Knoxville (Tenn.) "Daily Register." He espoused the Southern cause so stanchly as to excite fierce protest from the North, with the result that when Gen. Burnside captured Knoxville the presses of the "Register" were confiscated. Escaping to Atlanta he joined the Confederate army, but was afterward captured and imprisoned until the close of the war. His son, Thomas Alexander, was reared on the farm of his uncle at Centreville, and when seventeen years old began his business career with a mercantile firm at Bridgeport, Conn. In 1897, while a traveling salesman for the Howard Cutlery Co., he conceived the idea of the "trading stamp" to be used as a means of increasing a merchant's business. Stamps of about the size of postage stamps are furnished to merchants and by them are given to the customers in proportion to the size of the purchase, and when a sufficient number has been collected, they are redeemed or exchanged by the customer for some household article selected from a stock. The merit of the idea, coupled with the vigor and ingenuity with which Mr. Sperry promoted it, brought almost instant success, and seeking a larger field in New York city, he incorporated the Sperry & Hutchinson Co. in 1900. The Sperry & Hutchinson Co. furnishes its green trading stamps at a certain price per thousand to merchants, who give them to their customers at the rate of one for each ten-cent purchase. The customers paste them in trading stamp books provided by the company for that purpose. A book when filled contains 990 stamps and may be redeemed at any of the hundreds of supply stores maintained by the Sperry & Hutchinson Co. throughout the United States, whose stock consists principally of such household furnishings as furniture, glassware, silverware, jewelry, leather goods, rugs, etc. The green trading stamps soon become known in every city in the United States as an attractive method of increasing sales and discouraging the habit of buying on credit. The stamp gives the merchant a means of offering a discount for cash on a sale as small as ten cents. A constantly enlarging demand for the stamps was increased by the co-operation of various stores in different lines of business, enabling the merchant to retain the patronage of an increasing percentage of his customers. The business of the Sperry & Hutchinson Co. grew to enormous proportions and millions of dollars' worth of the premium goods are distributed annually in exchange for their stamps. In addition to his trading stamp enterprise, Mr. Sperry became interested in the development of a stock farm at Cranford, N. J., along the Rahway river, which he named "Osceola Farm," after the old family plantation in Winchester, Va. Here he devoted a portion of his time to the breeding of pure-blooded, pedigreed horses and cows. He was a man of large affairs and sterling character. He was president of the Cranford Trust Co. and a director of the Bronx National Bank of New York. He was a member of the Azure Lodge, F. and A. M., of Cranford; the Baltusrol and Cranford Golf clubs, the Essex County Country Club, the New York Athletic Club, the Michigan Society of New York and the Sons of the Revolution. He was married at Centreville, Mich., Jan. 1, 1891, to Kate, daughter of John Stewart Major, whose ancestors were among the early settlers of the Mohawk valley, New York. He died in New York city, Sept. 2, 1913, leaving a widow and four children: Katherine, Thomas A., Jr.; Stewart Major and Marjorie Sperry.

CALDWELL, George Brinton, president of the Sperry & Hutchinson Co., was born in Dunkirk, N. Y., Aug. 24, 1863, son of Charles Melville Caldwell and Mary Ann (Kelner) Caldwell. On his father's side his ancestors were Scotch-Irish, and on his mother's English and German. His early life was spent on his father's farm. He was educated in the public schools of Ionia and Greenville, Mich., and took courses in business practice at Sweenberg's Business College at Grand Rapids. After teaching for about one year, he secured a position as accountant in an insurance agency at Greenville, Mich., and in 1884 became bookkeeper for the City National Bank of that city. Four years later he removed to Grand Rapids, Mich., and was made chief accountant and financial man of the lumber firm of Tucker, Hoops & Co., a position he held until he was appointed state accountant for Michigan in 1890. During 1891–93 he served as secretary of the state board of equalization, in which position he inaugurated the uniform system of accounting for the state institutions that is now in use. In May, 1893, Mr. Caldwell was appointed national bank examiner for the state of Michigan and the northern part of Indiana, and held that

Thomas A. Sperry

GEORGE B. CALDWELL

office for six years, resigning in 1899 to become assistant cashier and credit man of the Merchants' National Bank of Indianapolis, Ind. The next change in his business career was in 1902, when he gave up commercial banking to enter the investment department of the American Trust and Savings Bank of Chicago. He held that position until 1910, when the bank was absorbed by the Continental and Commercial National Bank under the new name of the Continental and Commercial Trust and Savings Bank, of which Mr. Caldwell was vice-president. He resigned from this office in 1915 to become president of the Sperry & Hutchinson Co. in New York city. This company was organized by Thomas A. Sperry (above) in 1900 to exploit a system of profit-sharing by the use of trading stamps. The Sperry & Hutchinson Co. has lately adopted the Hamilton coupon in addition to the green trading stamp, the coupons being put in the original packages by the manufacturer. Both the Sperry & Hutchinson green trading stamp and the Hamilton coupon are made interchangeable on the basis of two stamps for one coupon, and the system has grown to be not only the most complete in the country but probably the greatest selling agency ever devised, being handled by 30,000 merchants and manufacturers and having over 10,000,000 stamps and coupon collectors in the United States. Mr. Caldwell brought to the new enterprise a broad financial experience, and a reputation as one of the most able bankers in the country. He holds a recognized place among the leading financiers and business men of America, and under his direction the Sperry & Hutchinson Co. has entered upon a new era of prosperity and progress. He is a director of the Commercial National Bank of St. Joseph, Mich., the State Bank of Oak Park, Ill., the United Light and Railways Co. of Chicago, the Chicago, Anamosa and Northern Railway, the Chattanooga Gas Co., and the Grand Rapids, Grand Haven and Muskegon Railway Co. He was actively interested in the organization in 1912 of the Investment Bankers' Association, which embraces in its membership leading investment bankers of the country, for purposes of mutual aid and co-operation on lines similar to the American Bankers' Association, and was its first president. He is a member of the Union League, the Midday Club and the Oak Park Club of Chicago; the Michigan Society of Chicago; the Indiana Society of Chicago; the Athletic, Lotus and Aldine clubs of New York, and the Baltusrol Golf and Wykagyl Country clubs. He was married Oct. 15, 1886, to Lucy S., daughter of Benjamin S. Patrick of Ionia, Mich., and has one daughter, Helen Marie Caldwell. Mr. Caldwell is a man of rare executive ability, who by the force of his own enterprise and intelligence has attained an eminent place among the leaders of American commerce. The dominating traits of his character are his faith, determination, integrity and powers of application and perseverance.

HUBERT, Philip Gengembre, architect, was born in Paris, France, Aug. 30, 1830, son of Charles Colomb and Marianne (Farey) Gengembre. Because of the difficulty they met with in the pronunciation of their surname in this country, he and his brother added the name of their English grandmother, Hubert, some years after coming to America. His father was an architect and civil engineer and was constructing the grand canals of the Seine when his work was interrupted by the revolution of 1830, in which he was wounded and financially ruined. He decided to come to America with the expectation of finding a wider

field in his profession and the family settled in Cincinnati, O., in 1849, where young Philip first studied architecture under his father. Mons. Gengembre, however, was disappointed in the amount of architectural work then in demand in Cincinnati, and in order to eke out the family expenses the son had recourse to his pen. His mother being an English woman, he had always been familiar with that language and wrote English fluently. He created quite a stir by his contributions to the newspapers and magazines of that day. He also formed classes in French, and was so successful as a teacher, introducing original methods of his own, that he was appointed, when only twenty-three, professor of French, Spanish and history in Girard College, Philadelphia. In 1860 he removed to Boston, Mass. Where his success, both as a teacher and as a writer, was so great that he refused an assistant professorship at Harvard rather than give up his classes, some of which numbered 500 pupils. At the same time he was winning such a place for himself as a magazine contributor of both short and serial stories that there is no doubt but that had he continued in this line he would have been known to-day as a writer instead of as an architect. All his literary

CENTRAL PARK APARTMENT BUILDINGS

work was published under various pen-names. Few of his friends knew that he was a playwright and that the "Philip Hamilton" who figured on the programs as co-author of "The Witch," which enjoyed a prosperous run in the 90's of over two years, was Mr. Hubert. Even when his play received enthusiastic praise from the leading New York critics, he maintained his incognito. Notwithstanding his facility with his pen he disliked writing as a profession, and, when still in his twenties, he invented the first self-fastening button, which was sold outright for $120,000. He now turned to his chosen study of architecture. After some time spent abroad, he began his career as an architect in New York in 1870, forming a partnership with James L. Pirsson, under the firm name of Hubert & Pirsson. The former St. Luke's Home building and the Church of the Beloved Disciple adjoining were the first large buildings erected by this firm. But although the designer of many public buildings and beautiful homes, it is as the pioneer architect of the modern apartment houses that Mr. Hubert is best known. Foreseeing that the narrow shape of New York city would soon make the problem of providing space for homes for the rapidly increasing population a serious one, he solved this difficulty by building skyward. At first people were afraid to live above the fifth story in the air, but the many advantages soon became apparent, and the upper stories were more in demand than the lower. He was the architect of the Navarro apartments on Seventh avenue, New York, which at the time of their erection, in 1882, were the largest apartment houses in the world, and still hold their place in the front rank for solid grandeur and for the spaciousness and delightful arrangement. Mr. Hubert held a patent for the "Duplex" and "Triplex" style of apartments, and the subway court for delivery wagons, and many other features adding to the comfort and elegance of the apartment house home were originated by him. In The Sevillia, on Fifty-eighth street, he introduced a number of new features, including the first use of stone floors throughout an apartment building. He also originated, in 1880, the co-operative apartment house, in which the apartments are owned individually by the stockholders. They were known as "The Hubert Home Clubs," and the first one— erected by a club of artists—was "The Rembrandt" on West Fifty-seventh street. This proved so successful that he built many others, among the most imposing of which are "The Chelsea," on West Twenty-third street; "The Hawthorne," and "The Hubert," both on Fifty-ninth street; No. 80 Madison avenue and No. 121 Madison avenue. The old Lyceum Theater on Fourth avenue was originally built by Mr. Hubert as a co-operative club theater, intended for the use of the members in the evening for amateur theatricals, and in the daytime as a home for a dramatic school. It was the beginning of the Lyceum School, which under the management of Franklin H. Sargent developed into the present Academy of Dramatic Arts. He was the inventor of the method of storing furniture and goods in fireproof vans which are transferred directly to the compartments provided for them in the storage houses and remain there undisturbed until sent for, thus doing away with the damage from several handlings and risk of theft. He retired from active practice in 1893. Although such an ardent advocate for shortening the laboring hours of the working people, Mr. Hubert himself worked incessantly early and late, and at eighty-one years of age was superintending the making of models for new inventions in his shops in Los Angeles, Cal., from morning to late afternoon, often doing with his own hands what his workmen failed to execute. His chief interest was devising contrivances to facilitate domestic work, that he might in this way ease the burden of the overtaxed housewife. He died in Los Angeles, Cal., Nov. 15, 1911.

POWERS, James Knox, educator, was born at Lauderdale county, Ala., Aug. 15, 1851, son of William and Rosanna (Reeder) Powers, of Irish descent. He was educated at Wesleyan University, which, after the war, became the Alabama State Normal School, and was graduated at the University of Alabama in 1873, his average in the senior year being 99.5, the highest grade ever made in that institution. He was subsequently given the honorary degree of LL.D. by that institution. In 1873 he became professor of mathematics at the Alabama State Normal School, and in 1888 was elected president of that institution, a position he retained until 1897, when he became president of the University of Alabama. In 1901 he relinquished that position to become Southern representative of the B. F. Johnston Publishing Co., of Richmond, Va. In 1911 he returned to Florence, Ala., to resume the presidency of the Alabama State Normal School, and continued to fill that position until his death. He was one of the leaders in the organization of the Alabama Educational Association and was conspicuous in its councils, serving as chairman of the executive committee and as president. He was likewise an organizer of the Southern Educational Association, and was a member of the National Educational Association. He was president of the Association of Southern Colleges and Preparatory Schools, and a member of the National Geographical Society. He was the author of numerous addresses and papers on educational subjects, and co-author of a series of elementary and practical arithmetics (Colaw, Duke & Powers). During 1886-88 he was grand dictator of the Knights of Honor of Alabama. Under the able administration of Dr. Powers the Alabama State Normal School reached as high a degree of proficiency and attendance as any similar institution in the South. To his friends and acquaintances he was ever sunny, genial and good-natured. His nature was one that responded to the best in man and in nature. He was a fine type of Christian gentleman, with all the chivalry and honor of the true Southerner. Always with his face towards the right and progress, he was a power in educational matters in his native state, and no one exhibited a greater influence along the line of stable progress than he. Dr. Powers was keenly susceptible to the charms and fascinations of social life, and peculiarly attracted by the adornments of scholarship and the delights of culture, yet he deferred all social enjoyments and intellectual luxuries to what he considered the stern and imperative demands of duty. He was married Jan. 31, 1879, to Loula, daughter of Calvin A. Reynolds, of Giles county, Tenn., who survives him, with five children: Loulie, Mrs. Pearl Powers Moody, Elizabeth, Anne and James Knox Powers, Jr. He died at Florence, Ala., Aug. 15, 1913.

LAEMMLE, Carl, manufacturer and financier, was born at Laupheim, Germany, Jan. 17, 1867, son of Julius Baruch and Rebekka (Laemmle) Laemmle. He received a general and business education in Germany, and came to this country with a friend in 1884. He was first employed in a drug store in New York, then entered a department store in Chicago, and subsequently worked for a short time on a farm in South Dakota. Returning to Chicago, he obtained a position with the firm of Butler Brothers, with whom he remained for several years, and later he was employed successively as a bookkeeper in the wholesale jewelry firm of L. Heller & Co., clerk in the stock yards for Nelson Morris & Co., and clerk with the wholesale jewelry firm of Otto Young & Co. In 1894 he went to Oshkosh, Wis., as bookkeeper for a retail clothing company, known as the Continental, and four years later became manager of the store. He remained with this company for eleven and a half years, and, though not admitted to partnership, he received a share of the net profits. In 1906 he embarked in the moving picture business. He first opened a small theater in Milwaukee avenue, Chicago, and, a few months later, he started a film exchange. In January, 1907, this business was incorporated as the Laemmle Film Service. In September of the following year he began to establish film exchange offices in other cities, and within a short time had branches in Minneapolis, Omaha, Evansville, Ind.; Memphis, Tenn.; Salt Lake City, Portland, Ore.; Winnipeg, Montreal and Des Moines, Ia. By this time the moving picture business was beginning to follow the tendency toward monopolistic combination; and a trust in this, as in every other case, spelled ruin to independent manufacturers and a large reduction of the profits of the dependent exhibitors.

The capital behind the companies, forming what is now recognized as the moving picture trust, was enormous, and it looked for a long time as if an absolute monopoly was inevitable. That such a monopoly does not in effect exist is due chiefly to Mr. Laemmle and to the brilliant, resolute fight he has made against heavy odds. He saw the necessity of fighting the growing power of the trust by establishing a factory that would turn out pictures as good as, or better than, any produced by the combination. This was more difficult of accomplishment than would appear on the surface. Opposed to Mr. Laemmle was almost unlimited financial resources, and the varied influence, talent and ingenuity that such resources can always command. On his side were only his own courage, grit and ability and a belief in the justice and feasibility of his plan which was shared by few even of those who would profit most from its success. Being warned that if he built such a factory his successful exchange business would be ruined at once, he proceeded to make his exchange business independent of the trust by negotiating for a regular supply of the best films, both at home and abroad, after which he built a factory and organized the Imp Films Co., of which he became president. The extent of his achievement may be judged from the fact that, when he started to make films in competition with the trust, there were less than 1,000 independent moving picture exhibitors in the United States; there are now (1916) over 7,000. Meanwhile Mr. Laemmle was also making some of the biggest and best productions that had ever been put on the screen. During a lawsuit over the Gaumont camera he transferred his entire organization to Cuba, where he made many remarkable and original pictures. He secured the film, "Roosevelt in Africa," and also "Crusaders, or Jerusalem Delivered." It is characteristic of Carl Laemmle and of the high standard of his methods and ideals that he was the only man engaged in the latter deal who made nothing out of it, though it fattened the pocketbooks of thousands of independent exhibitors. He has taken more satisfaction in the fight for its own sake and in the success of the principle for which he was fighting than in the personal profit he has derived from it. He takes a peculiar pleasure in meeting and overcoming difficulties, in meeting ingenious plots with more ingenious counterplots, in giving shape to the countless original ideas that swarm through his brain; and he takes a particularly intense pride in the quality of his films and in the welcome given to them by the public. In 1912 Mr. Laemmle brought about an amalgamation of the leading independent film manufacturing companies making the "Imp," "Rex," "101-Bison," "Nestor," "Powers," "Gem," "Animated Weekly," "Crystal," "Frontier" and "American-Eclair" films, the new concern being known as the Universal Film Manufacturing Co., of which Mr. Laemmle is president. The new company established a ranch near Los Angeles, Cal., where moving pictures are produced in the open air the year 'round. The population of the ranch grew to such proportions that in 1913 it was incorporated as a city, known as Universal City, with its mayor, chief of police and city officials, all chosen from the employees of the Universal Film Manufacturing Co. It is the first city in the world whose population is made up entirely of moving picture actors, directors and experts in the various lines of the film business. Mr. Laemmle also supervised the building of a world-wide organization for the marketing of his company's products. He was married Aug. 28, 1898, to Recha, daughter of Loeb Stern, and has two children, Rosabelle and Julius Laemmle.

MORGENTHAU, Henry, lawyer, financier and diplomat, was born in Mannheim, Germany, Apr. 26, 1856, son of Lazarus and Babette (Guggenheim) Morgenthau. He came to America with his parents in 1865, and settling in New York city attended the public schools and the city college, and was graduated at the Columbia Law School in 1877. From then until 1899 he practiced law, making a specialty of real estate. In 1899 he organized and became president of the Central Realty Bond and Trust Co. which was merged with the Lawyers' Title and Insurance Trust Co. in 1905, and he was vice-president of the latter for three years; he is at present a director and a member of the executive committee. He was one of the original organizers of the United States Realty Co., the George A. Fuller Co., and, with Albert Flake and Robert E. Dowling, the Alliance Realty Co., which built the Broad Exchange building. He was chairman of the finance committee of the Democratic party in 1912, and after Woodrow Wilson's election to the presidency was appointed U. S. ambassador to Turkey. Although without previous experience in the diplomatic service, he displayed unusual ability as a diplomat. With rare intelligence, executive ability and skill in the handling of men, he quickly won the confidence, respect and friendship of all the officials with whom he came in contact, and so impressed the Turkish government that he was invited to join the Turkish cabinet. When Turkey entered the European war the interests of eight different nations were placed in his hands. He rendered valuable service in helping the refugees to leave Constantinople and by interceding on innumerable occasions for enemy aliens in distress in Turkey. Perhaps his greatest service was in persuading the Turkish government to permit the American colleges to continue their work after the capitulations has been abrogated. He not only secured the consent of Enver Pasha, but to afford better protection he established his summer embassy in one of the buildings of Robert College. The House of Commons in England and the Chamber of Deputies in France placed their thanks to Mr. Morgenthau upon their public records, and the official papers of the various belligerent nations, dealing with the situation in Constantinople, made his diplomatic services part of the history of the war. Upon his return to the United States in the spring of 1916, just before he resigned the office, he was received with open arms, and Americans from all parts of the country sent their thanks for personal services in saving the lives of friends and relatives. He is a director and a member of the executive committee of the Underwood Typewriter Co.; a director of the Lawyers' Mortgage Co., Columbia Bank, Herald Square Realty Co., and some twenty other realty companies. He is also a member of the Chamber of Commerce, and trustee of the Mt. Sinai Hospital, the Solomon Loeb Memorial Hospital and the United Hebrew Charity building; member of the Bureau of Municipal Research and the National Conference on City Planning; being on the committee on congestion of population two years previous; on the executive committee of Economic Club, and chairman of the industrial committee of the Merchants' Association. He is a liberal patron of music, having been the principal backer of the Conreid Metropolitan Opera Co., and is a director of the New York Oratorio Society.

He was married in New York, May 10, 1883, to Josephine, daughter of Samuel and Helen Sykes, and has four children: Helen, wife of Mortimer J. Fox, of New York; Alma, wife of Maurice Wertheim, of New York; Henry, Jr., and Ruth Morgenthau.

BREWER, John Hyatt, organist and composer, was born in Brooklyn, N. Y., Jan. 18, 1856, son of William and Anna Eliza (Neil) Brewer, and grandson of John Brewer, who came to this country from Gloucester, England, in 1847, and settled in New York. He began his musical career at eight years of age as a soprano in the choir of St. John's Episcopal Church, Brooklyn. Two years later he became solo soprano in Zion Church, New York city, whose organist, Dr. H. E. Cutler, was closely identified with the permanent introduction of vested choirs in that city. Subsequently he sang in Trinity Chapel, New York, and after a year returned to St. John's, Brooklyn. Meanwhile he had pursued the study of piano and organ, and when about fifteen years old (1871) he secured the position of organist of City Park Chapel. From there he went to the Church of the Messiah in 1873, and four years later to the Clinton Avenue Congregational Church; thence in 1881 to the Lafayette Avenue Presbyterian Church, where he still remains (1914). Under Mr. Brewer's direction the musical services of the church have become notable. In addition to a competent quartette of soloists, he has a well-trained chorus of about thirty-five voices, which has made possible the rendering of selections from oratorios as well as standard sacred cantatas. In 1900 a choral society, composed of young people of the church, was organized under Mr. Brewer's direction and continued for several years. He was a charter member of the Apollo Club (Dudley Buck, conductor), organized in 1877, and its only accompanist from that time, and upon the retirement of Dudley Buck, in 1903, he was elected conductor. He is director of the Flatbush Glee Club; was for eight years musical director of the Cæcilia Ladies' Vocal Society, and was for seven years professor of vocal music in Adelphi College, and since 1901 secretary of the department of music of the Brooklyn Institute of Arts and Sciences, of which he is also a fellow. He has been identified with many organizations for the promotion of music in general, particularly the State Music Teachers' Association; the Manuscript Society, and the American Guild of Organists, of which he is a co-founder and fellow, and of which he served as warden for three years (1905-8). He is not only a teacher of the voice, piano and organ, but is the composer of numerous cantatas, anthems, choruses, vocal and instrumental solos and chamber music, all of which are characterized by remarkable grace of movement and felicity of expression. Mr. Brewer's musical education has been wholly American, his teachers having been Dr. William H. Walter, Dr. H. E. Cutler, W. E. G. Evans and James Marlin Wilder, voice; Rafael Navarro, piano and harmony; W. A. M. Diller, V. W. Caulfield and S. B. Whitely, organ, and Dudley Buck, organ, counterpoint, fugue, composition and orchestration. Among his compositions are: "Bedouin Love Song" (prize, Madrigal Club, Chicago), "Evening Star," "O Jesus, Thou Art Standing"; for men's voices, "Birth of Love," "Lord of the Dunderberg" (prize, Schubert Club), "Break, Break, Break," "Hymn to Apollo"; for women's voices, the cantatas, "Twilight Pictures," "Hesperus," "Herald of Spring," "Sea and Moon";

sacred solos, "God's Acre," "Angel's Easter Song," "Angel's Christmas Song," "Suffer Little Children"; sacred duets, "O Love Divine," "The Lord Is My Leader"; secular solos, "Rockabye, Dearie," "Rockaby Lady from Hushaby Street," "Because It's You," "There's Ever a Song"; for organ, "Canzonetta," "Springtime Sketch," "Autumn Sketch," "Romanza." In addition, Mr. Brewer has written fifty children's songs set to Mother Goose and other nursery rhymes, suites for orchestra and string quartette, violin and violoncello solos with piano accompaniments, and harp solos with organ accompaniments. He has published a book of school songs entitled "Songs of the Year," original and compiled, and six bound volumes containing more than 150 of his compositions. Four of Mr. Brewer's compositions have been awarded prizes: the Mason and Hamlin prize in 1890; the A. A. Low prize in 1895; the Schubert Glee Club prize in 1905, and the W. W. Kimball prize in 1905. He was married June 27, 1888, to Emma Amelia, daughter of Isaac Chauncey Thayer, of Brooklyn, N. Y.

PARKER, Robert Meade, manufacturer and railroad man, was born at Newark, N. J., Sept. 19, 1864, son of Cortlandt (q.v.) and Elizabeth (Stites) Parker. His first paternal American ancestor was Elisha Parker, who came to this country, probably from the county of Kent, England, in 1640, and settled at Barnstable, Mass. Elisha Parker moved from Massachusetts to New Jersey in 1667, and was one of the original settlers of Woodbridge and later of Perth Amboy in that state. From him and his wife, Elizabeth Hinckly, the line of descent is traced through their son, Elisha 2d, who married Hannah Rolfe; through their son, Col. John Parker, who married Jennet Johnston; their son James, who married Gertrude Skinner; their son, James 2d, who married Penelope Butler, and who was the grandfather of the subject of this sketch. On the paternal side, Robert Meade Parker is connected with the Van Cortlandt, Schuyler, Johnston and Skinner families of New York and New Jersey, and the Butler family of Philadelphia, while his maternal ancestry includes the Chaunceys, Goodriches, Elys, Worthingtons and Cookes of Connecticut, and the Waynes and Cliffords of Georgia. His grandfather, James Parker, served in the New Jersey legislature and in the national congress, and was a member of the constitutional convention of New Jersey in 1846. Robert Meade Parker received his early education at St. Paul's School, Concord, N. H., and at Phillips Exeter Academy, and was graduated at Princeton University in 1885. He entered the employ of the Erie railroad, first as clerk in the office of the president in 1890 he was appointed division freight agent; in 1896, assistant general freight agent, and in 1902, general freight agent. In 1905 he became traffic manager for the American Sugar Refining Co., which office he still retains. In June, 1906, he became president of the Brooklyn Cooperage Co., and he is also president of the Pennsylvania Stave Co., the Butler County Railroad Co. and the Great Western Land Co., and is a director of the Ansco Co. and the Pacific Coast Co. Though the management of the Brooklyn Cooperage Co. is his most important concern, Mr. Parker still takes a strong interest in transportation matters, and he is regarded as one of the best informed authorities on freight problems in the country. He served in the Essex Troop of New Jersey during 1890-98, and on the outbreak of the Spanish-

HENRY MORGENTHAU
DIPLOMAT

JOHN H. BREWER
MUSICIAN

ROBERT M. PARKER
MANUFACTURER

HAROLD V. MAGONIGLE
ARCHITECT

American war was appointed first lieutenant and battalion adjutant of the 12th infantry, N. Y. V. Soon afterward he was promoted captain and regimental quartermaster. He had complete charge of the field equipment for the war, and until the declaration of peace he served with the regiment at Peekskill, Chickamauga Park, Ga., and in Kentucky. Subsequently he joined the 12th regiment, New York National Guard, and from 1900 until his resignation in 1908 was captain of company A of the regiment. Mr. Parker is a member of Holland Lodge, F. and A. M., New York; the University, Union, Brook, New York Yacht, Midday and Riding clubs of New York, and the Essex Club of Newark, N. J.

MAGONIGLE, Harold Van Buren, architect, was born at Bergen Heights, N. J., Oct. 17, 1867, son of John Henry and Katherine Celestine (Devlin) Magonigle, and grandson of John Magonigle, a native of Greenock-on-the-Clyde, Scotland, who emigrated to America in 17—, and married Elizabeth Van Buren, a cousin of Pres. Van Buren. His father was for many years a prominent theatrical manager in New York city; he built and managed Booth's Theater, was treasurer for Messrs. Booth and Barrett and was superintendent of the Players' Club in New York city during 1888-1908. Mr. Magonigle's mother was a daughter of Charles Devlin, the Irish poet, and sister of Mary Devlin, the first wife of Edwin Booth. He was educated in the public schools and began the study of his profession at the age of fourteen with Van & Radford, architects of New York. He subsequently entered the offices of Charles C. Haight and McKim, Mead & White. When twenty-one years of age he won the gold medal of the Architectural League. In 1891 he entered the office of Rotch & Tilden, Boston, to qualify for the Rotch scholarship in architecture, and received that in 1894. He traveled and studied in Europe for two years and in 1896 re-entered the office of McKim, Mead & White in New York. In the spring of 1897 he formed a partnership with Evarts Tracey, and two years later became the managing assistant for Messrs. Schickel & Ditmars. In 1901 a partnership was formed with Henry W. Wilkinson, but was dissolved in 1903, and he is now practicing alone. Mr. Magonigle designed the national monument in New York in memory of the seamen who perished in the Maine (1900), the Cornell Alumni Hall at Ithaca, N. Y. (1901), the Gates avenue courthouse, Brooklyn, N. Y. (1901), and the Fulton-Hudson memorial in New York in 1910. The firemen's memorial in New York was awarded him without competition. His most important competition was for the national McKinley memorial, erected in Canton, O., in 1907, his plans being chosen in competition with nine other architects and firms of the leading cities of the country. This mausoleum cost over $500,000. During the Spanish-American war Mr. Magonigle was battalion adjutant of the 109th regiment, New York national guard, serving until the regiment was mustered out. He is a member of the Architectural League of New York, the Grolier Club, the Players' Club, the Salmagundi Club, the New York Press Club, the Boston Architectural Club, the Cosmos Club of Washington, D. C.; the Canton and Canton Country clubs of Canton, O.; the City Club of Auburn, N. Y., and the Essex County Country Club. He is a fellow and director of the American Institute of Architects and one of the twenty-five members of the Digressionists of New York. He was president of the Alumni Association of the American Academy in Rome, of

which he was the first beneficiary, and is also the oldest alumnus. He was married Apr. 24, 1900, to Edith Marion, daughter of John Day, of New York. Portrait opposite p. 364.

WHITMAN, John Lorin, penologist, was born at Sterling, Whiteside co., Ill., July 23, 1862, son of Platt L. and Helen M. (Quick) Whitman, and grandson of Lorin M. Whitman. He was educated at the public schools and at Edwards' Seminary, Sterling, Ill. At the age of eighteen he started in business for himself at Tampico as a house-painter and paper-hanger, and four years later he engaged in the manufacture of farming implements. In 1890 he was appointed guard in the Cook county jail, and from the very first he entered upon the work in the spirit of one who had at last found his vocation. Some idea of his peculiar methods may be gathered from the words of a prisoner who had served a sentence in Cook county jail: "As a jail guard he was a revelation. He spoke to prisoners in kindness, in sympathy, and placed himself on the same plane with them and aimed to make them as comfortable as their unhappy lots in life permitted. Other guards were gruff, and at times were brutal. He was pleasant, spoke sympathetically and was always anxious to satisfy." The strong influence he had over the prisoners attracted the attention of the jailer, who took him into his office to assist in the jail management. A year and a half later he was appointed assistant jail clerk, soon afterward chief clerk and in 1895 he was made jailer. In his instructions to his guards when he took office he said: "Always keep in mind that kindness is the key to all human hearts, and sympathy the password to good fellowship. Men imprisoned here are human and are entitled to every consideration they can consistently receive at our hands. Never strike a blow, never abuse an inmate; rather give him a kind word, a little sympathy, and the necessity for harsh treatment will vanish. Get the men to believe that you are their friends, and that you are here merely to do a plain duty as kindly as it can be done." These words are the key to Mr. Whitman's whole theory of penal government. Correctional rather than repressive discipline, or, as he puts it, "expressive rather than repressive measures," should, he thinks, be the aim of those in charge of criminals, and in this view he is joined by the most advanced modern penologists. In spite of general skepticism as to the feasibility of his views, he has applied them in the Cook county jail with remarkably successful results. One of the fruits of his administration there was the formation of the John L. Whitman Moral Improvement Association, perhaps the most unique association of its kind in existence. Its object, as its name implies, is to promote the manhood and womanhood of its members, to create among them a larger fund of self-respect and joy, so that they may by and by return to the world with stronger wills and nobler ideals. In 1907 Mr. Whitman was appointed superintendent of the House of Correction, Chicago, which has a daily average of 1,850 inmates, and in 1910 he was appointed by the mayor to serve on the vice commission of that city. He is the author of a number of writings on the treatment of criminals, among them, "Tamers of Men" (1903), "Perfecting the Work of Correction" (1908) and "Correctional Discipline" (1912). Mr. Whitman is a member of the National Union, Modern Woodmen of America, the Central Howard Association, the Chicago Men's Alliance, the Knights of Pythias, the Association of Commerce and the Illinois, Hamilton and City clubs of Chicago. He was married Nov. 14, 1880, to Anna M., daughter of Thomas Glennon, of Woodstock, Ill.

RICE, John V., Jr., engineer and inventor, was born in Wilmington, Del., June 1, 1871, son of John V. and Sarah (Lowe) Rice. The Rice family, which comes from the ancient family of Ap-Rhys, of South Wales, and the Maguires, of Ennis Killen, Ireland, settled in the lower part of Delaware in colonial days. Mr. Rice's great-uncle, Gen. J. O. Bradford, was the first paymaster-general of our navy, and when the United States fleet made its tour of the world he was on Admiral Farragut's staff; he was also with Com. Perry at the opening of the ports of Japan. Mr. Rice's father, who was a graduate of Union College, was a member of the bar of Delaware and Pennsylvania, having removed to Chester, Pa., when the boy was about three years old. At the age of eleven the son was sent to the Bordentown Military Institute and subsequently was placed under the tutorage of his uncle, Col. James H. Rice, to study the classics. But the boy's mind was absorbed in constructing mechanical devices, and after attempting the dry study of law refused an aliment foreign to its development at that period. Blackstone was abandoned for the Morse code and he began his mechanical training by entering the employ of the Chester Foundry and Machine Co. He was an apt student and willing worker. Some three months later an order came from the navy department demanding that the well-known brotherhood engine be made reversible. Young Rice's creative mind seized the opportunity thus presented, and to the great surprise of the management offered a design of a single eccentric valve gear for reversing engines that made even the head draughtsman look to his laurels. The invention was accepted by the company. He was fifteen years old when this patent was taken out, and since then it has been universally adopted. But this was not his first experience in inventions. At the age of eight he had constructed a clever device for mixing and grinding India ink. His next invention, a triple cylinder gas and steam engine, was produced at the age of seventeen and duly patented. His preparation for his work was purely practical—he had no instruction such as the schools give in free hand drawing, even not having had a drawing lesson in his life. And yet his mastery of that subject and of the mathematical calculations necessary to evolve a perfectly constructed engine shows an intuitive insight in the subject for which the word genius alone is a synonym. When the patent congress held its centennial celebration at Washington two years later, young Rice, full of enthusiasm for his chosen work, decided to attend it. Then occurred his first acquaintance with Richard J. Gatling, inventor of rapid-firing guns. A friendship sprung up between the two which lasted up to the time of Dr. Gatling's death. Mr. Rice remained with the Chester foundry until 1902, when he organized the Taylor-Rice Engineering Co. of Wilmington, Del., of which he was vice-president. This concern was engaged in manufacturing tools of precision, Rice steam engines and it also had a large contract for building air drills, wherein time was the essence of the contract under forfeiture. While waiting for accessories which were necessary for operating and testing these drills a considerable sum was forfeited. Mr. Rice then conceived the idea of inventing a gasoline rock drill which would do away with all the supplemental material necessary to operate an air drill. These patents were duly applied for. The

company attempting to seize this invention on the ground that all of his inventions were the property of the company, several years of litigation followed and the inventor was absorbed in defending his rights. The lack of financial resources at this period increased his hardships, but brought out a characteristic not often seen in inventors as a class—an indomitable determination not to be swallowed up by the commercial spirit, and his success in this particular was as brilliant as it was unusual. This invention, antedating as it did the development of the automobile and the demand for gas engines, was little appreciated by financial interests, and Rice was unable to obtain proper assistance to exploit it immediately. Five years elapsed before he successfully defeated his opponents in the highest courts and sustained his rights as the inventor of the only portable rock drill in the world. Then eminent financial and mining interests, represented by Harris Hammond, son of John Hays Hammond, identified themselves with it and are materially contributing to its development. Since 1902 Mr. Rice has been engaged in the manufacture of the well-known Rice gas engine, which resulted in the formation of the Rice Gas Engine Co. of Bordentown, N. J. His latest invention is a double acting or mono-cycle gas engine which overcomes many difficulties existing in the two-cycle gas engine, making it flexible as a steam engine and which promises to revolutionize the present gas engine practice. It is applicable to all forms of gas engines, including marine automobiles and stationary work. Mr. Rice's work covers nearly a hundred inventions, some of which were not patented but were applied immediately by the various companies in which he was engaged. In November, 1910, Mr. Rice with Mr. Harris Hammond jointly purchased the historic Bonaparte Park of Bordentown, N. J., which was at one time the residence of Joseph Bonaparte, elder brother of Napoleon and ex-king of Spain and Italy.

MOWBRAY-CLARKE, John Frederick, artist, was born in Jamaica, West Indies, Aug. 4, 1869, son of Myrry Mowbray-Clarke, a physician, and Margaret Ann Hawkins, his wife. His mother was the daughter of a physician, and was very talented as draughtsman, singer and linguist. The subject of this sketch was brought up by a great-aunt, Harriet Hawkins, and educated at a private school at Clifton, near Bristol, in the county of Gloucester, England. At the age of seventeen he was apprenticed to a chemist, with whose family he spent three years, and then went to London, where, while assistant to a doctor, he managed to find time to study art at the Lambeth School of Art. As a student he was successful, and in his final year at Lambeth won the annual competition for sculpture between all the schools of London. Two or three years afterwards he came to America and worked in the studio of Massey Rhind for about one year. His time till the year 1907 was then spent in making statuettes, portraits and memorials. He was married in 1907 to Mary Helena Bothwell Horgan, of Scotch and Irish parentage and teacher of art history. In 1912 he was invited to join a group of artists in founding an association for the encouragement of individuality in art—The Association of American Painters and Sculptors. He was one of three selected to form its constitution, and in 1913, before the opening of the first exhibition, was elected its vice-president, to replace Gutzon Borglum, who resigned. Some of his works that have attracted interest are "The Parasites," "Antiquities," "The Tree," "Whither," and "Spring." The memorials to Bowles Colgate and Leonard Lewisohn and numerous medals are also to be numbered among his successful works to this time. Portrait opposite page 368.

LONG, Robert Alexander, lumberman, was born near Shelbyville, Ky., Dec. 17, 1850, son of Samuel N. and Margaret K. (White) Long. His mother was a cousin of U. S. Senator Blackburn and of Gov. Luke Blackburn, of Kentucky. His education was received in the public schools and at a private school in Shelbyville. Anxious to share in the greater opportunities offered by the rapid development of the middle West, he went to Kansas City, Mo., at the age of twenty-two, and after two small business ventures, which were not to his liking, invested his whole capital (less than $1,000) in the retail lumber business at Columbus, Kan., under the firm name of R. A. Long & Co. The venture prospered far beyond his expectations, and following the policy of using his profits in the lumber business, he was able, within a decade—through his capital and the excellent credit which his policy had established—to extend his retail lumber business to some thirty towns in Kansas and Missouri. In 1884 the Long-Bell Lumber Co., in which he has ever been the dominating factor, was incorporated, with a capital of $300,000, the new corporation including the wholesale lumber business in its activities, and entering in 1891 into the manufacture of lumber. In the latter year the headquarters were removed to Kansas City, already the great lumber center of the southwest. Mr. Long's interests have continued to expand until at this time the aggregate investments of the Long-Bell Lumber Co. and its allied companies amount to approximately $31,000,000, consisting of some 350,000 acres of virgin yellow pine timber in Louisiana, Texas and Arkansas, and ten modern manufacturing plants, the annual output of which is from 25,000 to 30,000 car-loads of lumber. In addition, the companies now operate eighty-six retail lumber yards in Kansas, Oklahoma and Texas. He built and personally owns the R. A. Long Building, a fourteen-story office building, the first steel frame structure of consequence in Kansas City. He is a leading authority in the lumber world, and was one of the organizers of the Missouri and Kansas Association of Lumber Dealers, of which he was later director. He is also actively identified with the National Lumber Manufacturers' Association and numerous other organizations of lumbermen, before which he has delivered a number of addresses. On behalf of the lumbermen he responded to the address of welcome extended them by Pres. Francis of the Louisiana Purchase Exposition in St. Louis in 1904, and with James J. Hill, Andrew Carnegie and many others addressed the first conservation congress, called by Pres. Roosevelt to Washington in 1908. Since an early age Mr. Long has been an active member of the Christian Church, his Kansas City membership being with the largest congregation of that denomination in the country, the Independence Boulevard Christian Church, and devotes much time to it and to personal charitable and philanthropic work. Through the church and its affiliations, through the Y. M. C. A., Y. W. C. A. and other organizations, he has given generously of his time and wealth toward the physical, moral and spiritual uplifting of humanity throughout the United States, India, Japan and the Philippines. He has been president of the American Christian Missionary Society, the Brotherhood of Disciples of Christ, and

an officer in many other connections of the church. He purchased the "Christian Evangelist," a religious periodical, which he presented to the Christian Church, and in addition gave several hundred thousand dollars toward the erection of a non-sectarian hospital in Kansas City, to be under the control of the National Benevolent Association of the Christian Church. He was married Dec. 16, 1875, at Columbus, Kan., to Ella, daughter of George Wilson, and has two daughters: Sallie America, wife of Lieut.-Commander Hayne Ellis, U. S. N., and Loula Long.

ALBERTSON, Ralph, social economist, was born at Jamesport, Suffolk co., N. Y., Oct. 21, 1866, son of Richard and Sarepta Young (Aldrich) Albertson, and a descendant of Peter Albertson, who came from Holland and settled at New Amsterdam in its early days. His father (1827–1907) was a man of unusual versatility. He was a farmer and mechanic, taught school, was major in the 16th N. Y. volunteers, clerk in the war department (1861–66), a music master, temperance lecturer, and held numerous town and county offices. Ralph Albertson was educated at Greenport (N. Y.) Academy and at Oberlin College and Theological Seminary. Before going to Oberlin he learned the trade of cabinet maket, serving three years' apprenticeship, and afterward taught an ungraded country school. He was ordained to the Congregational ministry in 1890, and was pastor at Penfield, O., for two years, and at Springfield, O., during 1892–95, where he built one of the first "institutional" churches in the country. He took a leading part in the organization and management of the Christian Commonwealth, which was a communistic society established in Muscogee county, near Columbus, Ga., in 1896. About 1,000 acres of farm land were secured; its membership grew from about forty-five in the beginning to 300. While chiefly engaged in farming, the members also operated a saw-mill, a cotton-mill, a printing-press and a laundry, and maintained a school and library for its members. It was incorporated Nov. 14, 1899, and the following was adopted as a part of its constitution: "The Christian Commonwealth is a society whose purpose is to obey the teachings of Jesus Christ in all matters of life and labor and in the use of property. The society is incorporated to establish a community of people on a co-operative basis with the purpose of demonstrating to the world the practicability and desirability of Christian co-operation as the best method of earning a livelihood and developing nobility of character and promoting all the ends of a true Christian civilization." Shortly thereafter disagreements arose among its members, typhoid fever broke out, and finally, a dissatisfied member having applied for a receivership, its affairs were wound up. Mr. Albertson was editor of the "Social Gospel," 1897-1901; the "American Co-operator," Lewiston, Me., 1902–04; "Equity," Philadelphia, 1906–07, and a member of the staff of the "Arena." He is the author of "The Social Incarnation" (1897), "Little Jeremiads" (1902), "Little Preachments" (1903), "The Religion of a Citizen" (1905) and "Fellowship Songs" (1907). As collaborator and literary executor of the late Frank Parsons he published "The Railroads, the Trusts and the People" (1908), "Choosing a Vocation" (1910) and "Legal Doctrine and Social Progress" (1911). In 1907 he became superintendent for the large specialty store of William Filene's Sons' Co., of Boston. He organized and was president of the "Twentieth Century Magazine" from 1909–12 and of the Co-operative Publishing Co., publishers of the "Boston Common," during 1910–12. From 1910 to 1912 he was general manager of the William S. Butler & Co. department store in Boston, and in 1913 he became general manager of the Home Pattern Co., of New York city. In social and civic work he has been officially connected with the National Direct Legislation League, the National Public Ownership League, the School City League, the Single Tax League, the Co-operative Association of America, the Co-workers Fraternity Co., the Equal Suffrage League of Boston, and similar local educational and civic enterprises. He is a member of the Boston City and Economic clubs, the Boston Chamber of Commerce, the American Academy of Political and Social Science, and the Liberal Club, of New York. In 1898, with E. T. Keyes, George D. Herron and others of Chicago, he organized the Right Relationship League. He was twice married; first, Aug. 6, 1886, to Irene, daughter of Henry W. Mulford, of Greenport, N. Y., and, second, May 8, 1904, to Hazel, daughter of Ernest W. Hammond, of Corry, Pa. His children are: Phyllis, Sarepta Fay, Christine Mulford, Jean, Wyatt, Rachel and Miriam Albertson.

ANDERSON, Joseph Gaudentius, Roman Catholic auxiliary bishop of Boston, Mass., and titular bishop of Myrina, was born in Boston, Mass., Sept. 30, 1865, son of John J. and Ellen (McVay) Anderson. His studies were made at Boston College and at the Brighton Seminary, after which he was ordained priest May 20, 1892. Social betterment work interested him and he served as state prison chaplain during 1894-1904, and head of the Diocesan Board of Catholic Charities during 1903-1908. He was appointed pastor of St. Paul's Church, Dorchester, Mass., Jan. 1, 1908; vicar-general Jan. 14, 1909; prothonotary apostolic April 9, 1909, and auxiliary bishop of Boston the same year, and consecrated bishop of Myrina July 25.

READING, Pearson B., pioneer and soldier, was born in New Jersey, Nov. 26, 1816. Shortly before coming of age he went to Mississippi and engaged in general merchandising in Vicksburg. In 1843, in company with twenty-five others, he crossed the plains to the Pacific coast by the way of Fort Boise, Snake river, Sacramento valley and the upper Sacramento or Pitt river—a country that had never previously been visited by white men. In the following year he received a grant of land in Shasta county, Cal., and soon after entered the service of Gen. Sutter at Sutter's Fort. In 1845 he was left in sole charge of the post while Sutter marched with all his forces to assist Micheltoreno in quelling the insurrection headed by Castro and Alvarado. Subsequently he engaged in hunting and trapping throughout the northern part of California, southern Oregon and western Nevada. In all these dangerous expeditions his intelligence, bravery and imposing personal appearance exercised over the hostile Indians a commanding influence that not only protected him and his party from attack, but also secured their friendly aid in all his undertakings. When it became probable that war would be declared against Mexico, he enlisted under Fremont, and upon the organization of the California battalion by Comr. Stockton was appointed paymaster, with rank of major. He served until the close of the war and then returned to his ranch in Shasta county. With Samuel J. Hensley and Jacob R. Snyder he engaged in a mercantile business in Sacramento in 1849. In 1850 he fitted out an expedition to explore the bay in which he supposed the Trinity and Klammath rivers must empty. The bark Josephine, in which the party sailed, was driven out of her course and was compelled to return. Following out his idea, others subsequently discovered the bay and named it after the celebrated traveler, Humboldt. In 1851 he was the Whig candidate for governor of California, failing in election only by a few votes. His last years were devoted exclusively to agriculture, with a view of developing the interests of the state. He was a charter member of the Society of California Pioneers. He was married in Washington, D. C., in 1856, to Fanny Washington. He died at Rancho Buenaventura, Cal., May 29, 1868.

INTEMANN, Ernest August George, merchant, was born at Eversen, Hanover, Germany, Oct. 25, 1848, youngest son of Claus Hinrich and Anna Margaretha (née Ficken) Intemann. Orphaned when ten years old, he came to America in May, 1861, and attended school in New York city for two years. In 1863 he entered the confectionery trade as an apprentice, and in 1869 started in that business on his own account. In 1886 he was called upon to take charge of the business of the United Confectioners' Association, engaged in the confectioners supply business. It is now the United Confectioner Supply Co., and Mr. Intemann is president; Frederick Lange, vice-president; J. Henry Cordes, treasurer, and Ernest A. G. Intemann, Jr., secretary. In 1900 he organized the Confectioners' Manufacturing Co. to manufacture hygienic ice, of which he is also the president. He is chairman of the Allied Underwriters at New York and Chicago Lloyds, doing an insurance business in a conservative manner. For many years he conducted a manufacturing and retail confectionery business at 51 and 53 Sixth avenue, New York, until he was made president of the corporation with which he is now connected. Aside from his manufacturing and business interests he is closely identified with several benevolent organizations. He is of high standing with the Free Masons, among which he has held offices of trust, and in recognition of his services he was made an honorary member of a number of lodges working in the German language in Manhattan, Brooklyn and Richmond boroughs, New York city. He is a member of St. John's Evangelical Lutheran Church, president of its board of trustees; United Brothers' Lodge No. 356, F. & A. M.; General Society of Mechanics and Tradesmen of the City of New York; Confectioners' and Ice Cream Manufacturers' Protective Association, and Fritz Reuter Home for the Aged. He was married Sept. 7, 1869, to Catharine Margaretha, daughter of Johann Christoph Lange, of Ahausen, Hanover, Germany, and they had four sons, Ernest A. G., Jr.; Charles L. H., Alfred C. and Frederick W. Intemann, and four daughters, Mary M., wife of William F. Hoops; Carrie W., wife of William J. Lohrman; Agnes H., wife of Herman Asendorf, and Flora D., wife of J. Frederick Lange, Jr. His first wife died in 1911, and he was married again in November, 1912, to Anna Sophia, widow of William Schierenbeck, daughter of Henry Heeve, of Jersey City Heights, N. J.

FISK, Everett Olin, educator, was born in Marlborough, Mass., Aug. 1, 1850, son of Franklin and Chloe Catherine (Stone) Fisk. His earliest paternal American ancestor was Nathan Fisk, a native of England, who emigrated in 1642 and settled at Watertown, Mass. From him and his wife Susanna the line of descent is traced through

RALPH ALBERTSON
SOCIAL ECONOMIST

PEARSON B. READING
SOLDIER AND PIONEER

ERNEST A. G. INTEMANN
MERCHANT

JOHN F. MOWBRAY-CLARKE
ARTIST

Everett O. Fisk

their son Nathaniel, who married Mrs. Mary (Warren) Child; their son Nathaniel, who married Hannah Adams; their son Moses, who married Mehetabel Broad; their son Moses, who married Rebecca Clark; their son Moses, who married Sibella Jennison, and who was the grandfather of the subject of this sketch. Moses 2d fought at the battle of Bunker Hill, and in subsequent years was a member of the Massachusetts general assembly. His father (1836-96) was a Methodist Episcopal clergyman, especially noted for his sense of kindly humor, his self-poise and wise judgment. The preliminary education of Everett O. Fisk was received in the district schools. In 1869 he was graduated at the Wesleyan Academy, Wilbraham, Mass. However, he was not satisfied with the education already gained and longed ardently for college training. By dint of teaching winter schools, tutoring and hard work during vacations he was enabled to take a four-years' course at Wesleyan University, Middletown, Conn., at which institution he received his B. A. degree in 1873 and that of M. A. in 1876. Immediately upon graduation he accepted a position as principal and superintendent of schools at Wallingford, Conn., and the following year he was principal of the high school at Enfield, Conn., but the state of his health forced him to relinquish that vocation in favor of a business career. Accordingly, in 1875, and for the decade succeeding his experiences in the schoolroom, he was the New England agent of the important school-book publishing house of Ginn & Co., with headquarters at Boston, Mass. His duties required him to make frequent trips throughout his territory, and thus he obtained a knowledge of educational men and institutions which stood him in excellent stead when he subsequently organized his own business. He has since continued to travel widely, both at home and abroad. In 1884 he established the Fisk Teachers' Agency, which has grown to be the largest of its kind in the world. In the thirty years of its existence it has filled nearly 40,000 positions of all grades, from the college presidency to the kindergarten. Important institutions in every one of the United States have been served through its means, including nearly all academies of high grade, over 500 colleges and universities, and many thousands of public schools, as well as throughout Canada, Mexico, the West Indies, South America, Europe, Asia and Africa. Mr. Fisk is a member and trustee of the First Methodist Episcopal Church of Boston and during 1881-97 was its treasurer. He is president of the Preachers' Aid Society of the New England conference; member of the Wesleyan Association, and a trustee of the Wesleyan building, in Boston. He was a member of the general conference of the Methodist Episcopal Church in 1892; president of the Boston Missionary Society of that church during 1894-96; the New England Conference Missionary Society during 1893-95, and the Boston Methodist Social Union in 1895. He is a trustee of the New England Home for Little Wanderers in Boston and chairman of the executive committee; vice-president of the Massachusetts Peace Society; member of the National Geographic Society, the National Municipal League, Roxbury Historical Society, New England Methodist Historical Society; and the Twentieth Century, Massachusetts and Boston City clubs, of Boston. In spite of the active life he has led, Mr. Fisk has always been a reading man; works on history, sociology, economics and literature having been most helpful to him, his favorite

authors being Dickens, George Eliot, Sir Walter Scott and Thackeray. His advice to those desirous of meeting success, and derived from his own personal experience, is: "Be of good courage; study attentively the best class of biographies; do one's best at all times, and never worry." Once he had launched upon a business career the mental and vital energy of Mr. Fisk made it impossible for him to be subordinated in his surroundings. In his many undertakings he acted with conviction, and he chose his native country and the world as his field in carrying out the activities of his fertile brain. His moral as well as his intellectual endowments are of a high order. The loftiest principles, not merely of integrity, but of honor, govern him in all of his transactions. He is keenly susceptible to the charms and fascinations of social life, and peculiarly attracted by the adornments of scholarship and the delights of culture. He was married at Wilbraham, Mass., Sept. 12, 1882, to Helen Chase, daughter of Francis Asbury Steele. She died Aug. 31, 1901, leaving one daughter, Harriet Storer Fisk, a graduate of the Boston University and a teacher of English language and literature at Wyoming Seminary, Kingston, Pa.

MARSHALL, Edwin Jessop, financier, and ranch owner, was born in Baltimore, Md., Mar. 18, 1860, son of Henry Vincent and Amanda C. (Jessop) Marshall. He comes from a long line of distinguished ancestors, to which belonged in America Humphrey Marshall, the botanist, and John Marshall, first chief justice of the United States supreme court. The earliest American ancestor was Abraham Marshall, a native of Gratton, Derbyshire, England, who came to America in 1682 and settled at Chester, Pa. From him the line of descent is traced through his son John, who married Hannah Caldwell; their son Abraham, who married Alice Pennock; their son Abraham, who married Ann Roberts, and their son H. Vincent Marshall, the father of our subject. The Abraham Marshall who lived at the time of the revolution organized a company and joined Gen. Braddock on the Brandywine river. But the protests of the Society of Friends, to which he belonged, decided him to resign after a time. Abraham Marshall, the grandfather of our subject, was a lawyer. In order to settle an estate for which he was attorney, he rode on horseback from Philadelphia to Illinois, and as a fee received a large tract of land in Illinois. He became one of the leading figures in the new country, and Marshall county was named after him. During the war between Texas and Mexico he joined the Texans with a company of men and fought in the famous battle of San Jacinto. He was intrusted by Gen. Houston with the charge of Santa Ana, the Mexican general, who was taken prisoner. A few weeks later Capt. Marshall, in the delirium of fever, wandered into the desert and was never seen nor heard of again. Notwithstanding their Quaker faith, there was a very strong adventurous strain in the Marshall family. George Marshall, a grand-uncle of our subject, lived an adventurous life in the service of Spain, married the daughter of the captain-general of Cuba, and died a romantic death in his prime. Others of the family had similarly adventurous lives. The old Marshall farm, with the original Marshall homestead, a two-story house of stone, is still in the possession of a member of the family, and among the interesting documents preserved there is the deed to the farm, signed by William Penn. Chester county,

Pa., has been the home of many prominent Marshalls and Sharplesses, with whom they were closely intermarried, for over two hundred years. Mr. Marshall's father was a chemist, who at one time was associated with the chemical manufacturing house of Sharp & Dohm, of Baltimore. The son was educated in the public schools of Baltimore and Illinois, and received an appointment to West Point from Pres. Grant, but the Quaker traditions of the family interfered with his ambitions and he ran away from home at the age of sixteen to seek his own fortune. He secured a clerkship in a railroad office in St. Louis; was employed on a passenger steamer on the Great Lakes, and after serving as Pullman palace car conductor, running out of St. Louis, became private secretary to the general manager of the Gulf, Colorado and Santa Fé road, and subsequently assistant master of transportation of the same road, all before he attained his majority. He then invested his savings in a farm near Lampasas, Tex., and became associated with a partner in raising sheep. He made a scientific study of raising live stock, and became recognized as an authority both on the various breeds of cattle and the best methods of breeding them. Meanwhile he became cashier of the First National Bank of Lampasas, and was that institution's president for twelve years. In 1900 the great oil field was discovered at Beaumont, Tex. At the invitation of an old business associate he made an examination after the field was well opened up, and was induced to invest in oil lands. Together they formed the famous Hogg-Swayne syndicate, consisting of Marshall, Campbell, Hogg and two others, and purchased a tract of fifteen acres. About half of this tract was sold within a few weeks at a net profit of over $300,000. Subsequently Mr. Marshall interested John W. Gates, of New York, and others in the Texas Company, which he and his associates had formed, and which is now the second largest oil company in the world. In 1904 he made arrangements to close out his oil interests, and removed to Los Angeles, Cal., to accept the vice-presidency of the Southwestern National Bank. Shortly after settling in the state of California he acquired title to a large ranch of 42,000 acres in Santa Barbara county, known as the Rancho de Jesus Maria on which he established a herd of between 4,000 and 5,000 thoroughbred Hereford cattle. In 1905 he bought the Rancho Santa Ana del Chino, located between Pomona, Riverside and Corona, Cal., consisting of 46,000 acres. Part of this property has been divided up into small farms which have been sold, and what a few years ago was a large waste of unproductive land has been transformed into valuable farms under irrigation, producing a great diversity of products, such as deciduous fruits, alfalfa, cereals, orange and walnut groves and sugar-beets. The property supports a flourishing town of 2,000 inhabitants, containing a high school, banks and a newspaper. Mr. Marshall is likewise the principal owner of what is probably the largest ranch in the world, the "Palomas" in Mexico, consisting of some 2,000,-000 acres. With 15,000 acres under cultivation in the Santa Barbara ranch, 20,000 acres in the Chino ranch, and 6,000 acres in Mexico, Mr. Marshall is, in all probability, the largest operator of farm property in the United States. He is president of the Chino Land and Water Co., Sinaloa Land and Water Co., Palomas Land and Cattle Co., Grand Canyon Cattle Co., and Jesus Maria Rancho; vice-president of Torrance, Marshall & Co., of Los Angeles, one of the strongest bond houses in the United States; director of the Los Angeles Trust Co., First National Bank of Los Angeles, Pacific Mutual Life Insurance Co., Home Telephone and Telegraph Co. of Los Angeles, Home Telephone Co. of San Francisco, and over thirty other corporations. In addition, he is part owner of the Central, Security, Title Insurance and Commercial buildings, four of the largest office blocks in Los Angeles. He is a member of the California, Jonathan, Los Angeles Athletic, Los Angeles Country, Pasadena Country, and Bolsa Chica Gun clubs, of Los Angeles, and the Bohemian Club of San Francisco. He was married June 7, 1892, to Sally, daughter of Marcus McLemore, of Galveston, Tex., and has one son, Marcus McLemore Marshall.

LINSLEY, John Hatch, physician, was born in Windsor, Vt., May 29, 1859, son of Daniel C. and Patty (Patch) Linsley. He was educated in the public schools and was graduated in medicine at the University of Vermont in 1880. He practised first in Burlington, Vt., and in 1888 removed to New York city, where he was professor of pathology in the Post-Graduate Medical School. He was one of the earliest students of the new science of bacteriology, and spent some time in Berlin, Germany, in 1890, under Prof. Koch. When Koch's famous discovery of tuberculin was announced, Dr. Linsley was sent by the Post-Graduate Medical School to secure what information he could in regard to the new serum, and he brought back to the United States the first bottle of tuberculin used here. In 1891 he returned to Burlington, and was made professor of histology, pathology, and bacteriology at the University of Vermont. Dr. Linsley was the originator of the Vermont State Laboratory of Hygiene. In 1897 he proposed to the State Board of Health to give to the people of Vermont, especially the physicians, an object lesson in the use of the laboratory for preventing disease, and an arrangement was made by which Dr. Linsley agreed to examine specimens from practitioners of the State of suspected cases of diphtheria and typhoid fever. The experiment was so successful that he proposed to the state legislature the establishment of a state hygienic laboratory; the result was the present state laboratory of hygiene, organized in 1898, which is one of the most completely equipped of its kind in this country. As its first director, Dr. Linsley did his last and most valuable work. He was married in July, 1880, to Nettie, daughter of Harmon A. Ray, of Burlington, and was survived by one son, Daniel Ray, and one daughter, Patty Hatch Linsley. He died in Burlington, Vt., Feb. 17, 1901.

MORRIS, John Baptist, third Roman Catholic bishop of Little Rock, Ark., was born at Hendersonville, Sumner co., Tenn., June 29, 1866. His classical course was made at St. Mary's College, St. Mary, Ky., and his theological studies at the North American College, Rome, where he was ordained priest at the Lateran Basilica June 11, 1892. Returning to the United States, he was appointed assistant of the cathedral in Nashville, Tenn. On Aug. 4, 1894, Bishop Byrne made him chancellor of the diocese, on June 11, 1900, its vicar-general, and on Dec. 5, 1905, the pope promoted him to the dignity of domestic prelate. He became bishop of Armonica, a coadjutor bishop of Little Rock, Jan. 11, 1906. Bishop Fitzgerald of Little Rock died on Feb. 21, 1907, and Mgr. Morris was consecrated as his successor June 11, 1908. Under his direction the first diocesan synod was held in Little Rock Feb. 16, 1909; the first normal school for

Catholic teachers started June 11, 1909; Little Rock College was opened, St. Joseph's Orphan Asylum inaugurated in 1908, and St. John's Seminary was established in 1911.

BANCROFT, Samuel, capitalist, publisher and manufacturer, was born at Rockford, Del., Jan. 21, 1840, son of Joseph and Sarah (Poole) Bancroft, of same family as George Bancroft, the historian. His father, a native of Manchester, England, came to America during his early manhood, settled in Delaware, and founded cotton mills at Rockford, Del., in 1831. The son was educated at private schools in Wilmington, and began his business career at the age of sixteen in the cotton mills of his father at Rockford. He was employed in every department and became thoroughly grounded in the business. In 1860 he was given sole charge of the bleaching and finishing departments which were at that time added to the Rockford plant. With his elder brother, William, he was admitted to partnership in 1865, the name being changed to Joseph Bancroft & Sons. In 1889 it was incorporated as the Joseph Bancroft & Sons Co., and Samuel Bancroft was president until his death. He was the dominating factor in the affairs of the company, the business under his guidance evolving into one of the two or three largest manufacturing concerns in the country. In addition to his textile interests, Mr. Bancroft was a director of the Wilmington Trust Co., director, vice-president, president, and from 1910, chairman, of the Huntingdon and Broad Top Mountain Railroad and Coal Co. in Pennsylvania. He also served on the directorate of the Delaware, the Baltimore, Chesapeake and Atlantic and the Maryland, Delaware and Virginia Railroad companies, and in spite of these many interests found time to aid in many local civic matters, also in state affairs. In 1866 he was elected to the Delaware house of representatives; he was defeated for a second term. He subsequently left the Republican party, and thereafter never voted for its candidates for president or congress, his views differing most radically from the policy of that party in relation to the tariff and other public questions, especially regarding the constitutionally reserved rights of the states and the question of legal tender. In 1872 he became interested in the Every Evening Printing Co., and later the controlling owner of the newspaper, "Every Evening." As such he frequently caused to be published in its columns articles strongly advocating sound Democratic doctrine and denouncing unfailingly the wave of political corruption which bade fair to engulf the state of Delaware. His upright stand for civic righteousness was most positive, and not only through his newspaper, but personally, he gave freely of his time and means for the real welfare of the community. He was especially interested in the city's park system, serving as a member of the board of park commissioners several terms, during which he joined with his brother, William P., in a gift of much valuable land to the city for park purposes. In 1907 he was a dominant factor in the erection of a memorial statue in Rockford Park to Thomas F. Bayard. For more than twenty year he was a trustee of the Wilmington Homeopathic Hospital, and he was a trustee since its inception and member of the advisory board of Delaware Industrial School for Girls. He took a keen and helpful interest in these as well as in many other charitable institutions in the city and state. Deeply interested in fine arts, he possessed perhaps the finest private collection of paintings in this country by the English pre-Raphaelites, and his many valuable paintings by other artists also attest his interest in and love for art. He was an original member of the Wilmington Society of Fine Arts. Endowed with a most retentive memory, his constant reading and wide experience made him an exceedingly entertaining and instructive companion, for his mind became a perfect storehouse of knowledge. He was a member of the Chamber of Commerce and Metropolitan Museum of New York, the Franklin Institute of Philadelphia, the Society of Colonial Wars, Historical Society of Pennsylvania, Historical Society of Delaware, and of the Masonic lodge and chapter. His club affiliations included membership in the New York, Lambs, Century Association, Grolier, Players', Manhattan, and National Arts, New York city; Union League, Philobiblon, and Pen and Pencil, Philadelphia; Caxton, Chicago; Maryland, Baltimore; Wilmington, Wilmington Country, and Wilmington Whist, Wilmington; Arundel, London, and the Brazenose, Manchester, England. Like his ancestors he was a member of the Society of Friends, and was connected with the Wilmington Monthly Meeting of Friends. He was a man of sterling character, frank almost to bluntness, fearless in the right, loyal, kind-hearted and charitable. He was married, June 8, 1865, to Mary Askew, daughter of Samuel and Susanna (Robinson) Richardson, of Delaware, who survives him, with two children: Elizabeth R., wife of John Blymer Bird. of Wilmington, and Joseph Bancroft, vice-president and treasurer of Joseph Bancroft & Sons Co. He died at Wilmington, Del., Apr. 22, 1915.

MARTIN, George, physician and botanist, was born near Claymont, Delaware co., Pa., in 1826. He was educated in a Friends' school and at the University of Pennsylvania, where he took his M. D. degree in 1847. He practised in Concordville, Del., until the civil war, when he volunteered his services in the military hospitals in Chester, and after the war settled in West Chester. He was a fellow of the College of Physicians of Philadelphia. The later years of his life were devoted to the study of botany, especially mycology, and only a few days before his death he completed "A Synopsis of the North American Species of Septoria." He was in close touch with the leading botanists of the day, and contributed a number of interesting papers to the "Journal of Mycology." Dr. Martin died in West Chester, Pa., Oct. 28, 1886.

ADAMS, George William, journalist, was born in Lagrange county, Ind., in 1838, son of Chauncey and Catherine (Browne) Adams. His parents removed to Washington, D. C., while he was a boy, and there he obtained his early education. He took up the study of patent law, but the legal profession proved distasteful to him, and he abandoned it for that of journalism, for which he was by nature, taste and acquirements much better fitted. He was first a reporter on the staff of the Washington "States and Union," one of his fellow reporters being Henry Watterson, of the Louisville "Courier-Journal." He was successful in this new profession, and it was not long before he became Washington correspondent of such dailies as the New York "World," the St. Louis "Republic," the Cincinnati "Enquirer," the Philadelphia "Bulletin," the Boston "Herald," the New Orleans "Picayune" and the Baltimore "Sun." He represented the New York "World" in Washington from the day of its first issue for over twenty years. In his capacity as correspondent he attended the national conventions of the various political parties for years, thus forming the acquaintance of many leading statesmen of the United States, by whom he was always esteemed for his intelligence, enterprise and integrity. In 1867 he acquired an interest in the Washington "Evening Star," and twelve years later he gave up all other work to devote his entire attention to that paper. Thereafter the history of the Washington "Star" (of which he became president) was the history of Mr. Adams, and the great success it achieved was entirely due to his scholarship, foresight, executive ability and broad business views. In his editorials he exhibited a mastery of the subject and treated it with scholarly and philosophical tone, supplemented by picturesque descriptions full of life and color. He had a genuine vein of wit and much dexterity in phrase-making. Mr. Adams was married Dec. 22, 1868, to Jane L., daughter of Col. J. M. Barclay, clerk of the United States house of representatives, who survives him, with two daughters: Grace Barclay, wife of Beale R. Howard, and Mary B. Adams. He died in Washington, Oct. 10, 1886.

EMERSON, Victor Hugo, inventor, was born at Forest, O., Jan. 27, 1866, son of George Edward and Elvira (Shanks) Emerson, and a descendant of Edward Emerson, a native of Durham, England, who came to the colonies in 1635 and settled at Ipswich, Mass. His father was the inventor of the present time clock stamp system. He was educated in the public schools of San Francisco, Cal., where his father was located as general manager of the Southern Pacific railroad. He began his business career in the employ of the Lehigh Valley Railroad Co. at Flemington, N. J., and for four years was engaged in the installation of wireless telegraphy outfits. His interest in the development of talking machines began in 1888, and he has secured about twenty patents covering the phonograph field. Mr. Emerson was one of the organizers of the United States Phonograph Co. in 1894, and served as its president for four years. When it was absorbed by the National Phonograph Co. he became manager of the New York laboratory and recording department of the American Graphophone Co., and it is in this capacity that some of his best work has been done. All of the records of the American Graphophone Co. have been made under his direction, and he is recognized as the foremost authority in this department of the phonograph business. Mr. Emerson was married at Flemington, N. J., in 1888 to Kittie, daughter of William Rockefellow, and has three children: Victor Hugo, Jr.; Adelbert Tewksberry and Edna Elvira Emerson.

HALSEY, Charles Day, banker and broker, was born in New York city, Sept. 20, 1865, son of Silas Condit and Fannie L. (Day) Halsey, and a descendant of Samuel Halsey, a native of England, who came over to the American colonies in 1640 and settled at Hampden, Long Island, where the family became well established. His mother was the daughter of Charles Day, a prominent manufacturer of Newark, N. J. The son received a thorough education in the Freehold Institute of Freehold, N. J., and at Princeton University, being graduated at the latter in 1886 with the degree of C.E. His first professional engagement was in the service of the Pennsylvania railroad of New Jersey, being connected with their engineering department for eight years. In 1894 he withdrew and, removing to New York city, formed the Wall street firm of Toller & Halsey, to engage in a general private banking and stock brokerage business. Seven years later, in 1901, the firm was changed to C. D. Halsey & Co., his associates being

Gerald V. Hollins and John E. Daily. Mr. Halsey was successful from the outset, and is now the head of a well-established business that is destined to be one of the important financial concerns of the metropolis. In addition to his brokerage business Mr. Halsey is president of the Gilchrist Manufacturing Co. and the Sub-Surface Torpedo Co. He is a member of the Union League Club, the University Club, the Racquet and Tennis Club and the Princeton Club of New York. He was married in 1895 to Effie Grubb, the daughter of Gen. E. Burd Grubb (q. v.), and has two sons: Cortlandt Van Rensselaer and Charles Day, Jr., and one daughter, Lillie Van Rensselaer Halsey.

JEFFERIS, William Walter, mineralogist, was born at West Chester, Chester co., Pa., Jan. 12, 1820, son of Horatio Townsend and Hannah (Paul) Jefferis, of English descent. His father was for many years cashier of the Bank of Chester County, which afterwards became the National Bank of Chester County. The son was educated at the West Chester Academy, and after his graduation entered the service of the same bank with which his father was connected, becoming second teller in 1843. He subsequently became cashier, a position he held with credit until his resignation in June, 1883. His interest in mineralogy began in boyhood, and for seventy years he was a zealous collector of mineral specimens. He spent lavishly of his means in the pursuit of his hobby, and accumulated a collection which was pronounced one of the finest and most valuable of its kind in the world. In its entirety it contained over 12,000 catalogued specimens, not including the many valuable cut gems, a large number of microscopic mounted specimens, and about 3,500 rare specimens, each not over 1½ inches in size, in some 150 boxes, similar to the original Smithsonian collection. The collection possessed an asteriated ruby corundum, color deep blood red, so far as known the finest and largest specimen ever found; a beryl crystal weighing fifty-one pounds; a collection of brucite in a great variety of crystalline forms, from Lancaster county; a crystal of clinochlore, found in the Serpentine quarry at Birmingham, Chester county; a perfect specimen of barite, weighing thirty-four pounds, from Cumberland, England, and some remarkably brilliant crystals of stibnite, both single and in groups, from Japan, and diaspore from Chester county. Mr. Jefferis was the discoverer of aquacreptite, eupllyllite, Jefferisite, first found in a quarry a few miles south of West Chester; emerald nickel-zaratite, melanosiderite and roseite. He also contributed largely to the growth of the science by the assistance he rendered others. Dana drew extensively from his notes and specimens for his "Systems of Mineralogy," while Dr. F. A. Genth acknowledged his indebtedness to Mr. Jefferis in the preface of his "Mineralogy of Pennsylvania." Removing to Philadelphia in 1883, he became curator of the William S. Vaux collection, to which he devoted all his spare time for fifteen years. In 1878 he was made emeritus professor of mineralogy of the State Normal School of West Chester. His collection of minerals is now in the Carnegie Museum, Pittsburgh, Pa. He was a member of the American Association for the Advancement of Science, the Academy of Natural Sciences of Philadelphia, the American Philosophical Society, the Department of Archæology of the University of Pennsylvania, the Buffalo Society of Natural History and the New York Mineralogical Club. Mr. Jefferis was three times married; first, July 22, 1844, to Elmira, daughter of Dr. James B. Cherrington. Their

GEORGE W. ADAMS
JOURNALIST

VICTOR H. EMERSON
INVENTOR

CHARLES D. HALSEY
BANKER

WILLIAM W. JEFFERIS
MINERALOGIST

children were: Emma C., wife of John Bogart, the engineer, of New York; Alonzo, William Alger and Elsie J., wife of Ellis B. Noyes, a naval engineer. His second marriage was on Dec. 13, 1882, to Marea Jackson, daughter of Dr. Foster Flagg, of Philadelphia, and widow of Thomas Wood, and third, Dec. 14, 1898, to Mrs. Anna Elmore, widow of Dr. C. A. Elmore, of Fort Edward, N. Y. Mr. Jefferies died at his home in New York city, Feb. 23, 1906.

LOEWE, Dietrich Eduard, manufacturer, was born at Greste, Lippe Detmold, Germany, June 21, 1852, son of Adolph and Charlotte (Schalk) Loewe. While attending school winters he spent his summers at work on his father's farm until in 1870 he came to America. He secured employment at Middletown, N. Y., where a railroad was in process of construction. In the ensuing winter he found work on Long Island, and the following summer was employed as shipping clerk by a wholesale grocery firm in New York city. Removing to Danbury, Conn., he learned the hatter's trade. He became foreman of a Danbury hat factory in 1876, and three years later engaged in business for himself under the firm name of D. E. Loewe & Co., makers of fur hats for youths. His firm attracted widespread attention from a legal controversy with the labor unions, which resulted in a test case, involving many years of litigation. The hatters' union undertook to force Mr. Loewe to adopt the closed shop. Other hat factories in Danbury were being unionized, and in the winter of 1900–01 a labor leader suggested that he adopt the principle of the closed shop. Mr. Loewe replied that he had built up a business amounting to $500,000 annually in a quality of hat that was not manufactured anywhere by union labor or by any other firm in Danbury, and if compelled to unionize and thus substitute full pay journeymen for boys at part of the work, he could not compete with non-union firms; moreover, he refused to cancel his contract with his many faithful and capable employees, declaring that his factory would not be unionized, and that he would adopt every lawful measure to protect his rights. The union then ordered his men out, and by threats of physical violence and social ostracism drove all but eight employees from the Loewe factory, while throughout the entire country union agents effected a boycott of the Loewe hats. A short time previously a Massachusetts court had declared that a boycott was illegal, so Mr. Loewe published for a week in the "Danbury News," and sent to every member of the union a warning that that member would be held individually responsible for the illegal actions of the union. With his fellow manufacturers he organized the American Anti-Boycott Association, to finance the enforcement of the law against boycotts, and in 1903 suits were brought in the superior court of Fairfield county and in the U. S. district court against the 200 United Hatters of North America in Danbury, Bethel and South Norwalk, and real estate, property and bank accounts of members to the amount of $200,000 were attached. The officers of the American Federation of Labor were named as defendants, but their counsel claiming that the suits had no standing in the courts, the boycott was pushed with renewed energy, particularly in California, where it involved one of Mr. Loewe's largest customers. However, when Mr. Loewe's ruin seemed imminent, he suddenly appeared in California and applied for a temporary restraining order in the U. S.

court of that district. The injunction was not only granted but made permanent, and the boycott ceased. In February, 1908, the suits were heard in the U. S. supreme court, and a decision was rendered declaring the United Hatters and the American Federation of Labor guilty of a boycott that was "illegal and in restraint of interstate trade," establishing the principle that "labor unions and their officers are personally liable for damage inflicted by boycott, and the victim may sue and recover three-fold the loss actually sustained." After a six-months trial in the U. S. circuit court of appeals, before Judge James P. Platt, Mr. Loewe obtained a judgment of $225,-000. The case has become one of the most famous in the annals of American law, as well as in the history of labor unions, for it established on the highest legal authority, the illegality of the boycott, and the responsibility of those who use the boycott for the injury of another. It is entirely due to the fearlessness, pluck and perseverance on the part of Mr. Loewe that the issue was pushed to final decision. When he announced that he was going to fight for the principle of the open shop, he stood alone against a great trade union which had an uninterrupted record of successes in compelling manufacturers to unionize their factories and was backed by the Federation of Labor with all its forces. Mr. Loewe was assistant chief of the Danbury fire department in 1880, town assessor in 1884–85, member of the state legislature 1887–88 and the city council in 1889–90, and alderman in 1891. In politics he is a Republican. He was married, June 21, 1877, to Christina, daughter of Christian Heinzelman, of Danbury, Conn., and has six children: Charlotte Christina, Mathias Christian, Ernest Edward, Dietrich Carl Frank, Melaine Caroline and August Percival Loewe.

WILDE, William Allan, publisher, was born at Acton, Mass., July 11, 1827, son of Joseph and Sarah (Conant) Wilde, and a descendant of John Wild, who was a resident of Braintree, Mass., prior to 1690, the line being through his son William, and his wife, Ruth Hersey; their son William, and his wife, Deborah Allen; and their son Benjamin, and his wife, Sylvia Thayer, the grandparents of William Allan Wilde. He was educated at the academies of Pepperill and Groton. After teaching school for ten years he became New England agent for Ivison, Blakeman, Taylor & Co., of New York, school book publishers. From early life he had taken an interest in Sunday-school work and in the international lessons. In 1865 he established the publishing firm of W. A. Wilde & Co., which became one of the largest publishers of Sunday-school and miscellaneous juvenile works in the world, with a branch in Chicago, Ill., and agencies in London and Melbourne. Their most important publications have been "Peloubet's Select Notes," which has been running for over forty years and has a world-wide distribution; "Peloubet's Graded Quarterlies" and the "Teachers' Quarterlies." A resident of Malden, Mass., he was foremost in every movement for the betterment of the city. He was superintendent of schools in Malden 1873-74, for several years chairman of the board of water commissioners, member of the state legislature in 1887-88, chairman of the state board of prison commissioners during 1889-94 and trustee of the Malden hospital and Malden public library. In 1890 he presented to his native town a memorial library building and grounds, with over 4,000 volumes and a number of valuable works of art. He was a member of the Malden Historical Society, the Malden

Club and of Converse lodge of Masons, of the Royal Arch Chapter, of Beauseant Commandery, K. T., and of the Knights of Honor, as well as first regent of Mystic Shrine Council, R. A. He was an honorary member of Hiram G. Berry post, G. A. R. He was a man of culture and extensive reading. He was married three times, first to Lois A. Mace, second to Lydia Jane Gilbert Bride and third on Jan. 15, 1867, to Celestia Dona, daughter of Dr. Peter Livingston Hoyt, of Wentworth, N. H. The three surviving children were William Eugene, Allan Hoyt and Alice Elisabeth (Mrs. Wylie C. Burns). Mr. Wilde died in Malden, Mass., Dec. 2, 1902.

GRISWOLD, Chester, manufacturer, was born in Troy, N. Y., Sept. 10, 1844, son of John Augustus and Elizabeth (Hart) Griswold. The founder of the family in America was Edward Griswold of Kenilworth, England, who came to America in 1639, and was one of the founders of Windsor, Conn., and the line of descent is traced through his son, George; his son, Daniel; his son, Simeon, who married Anne Hutchison; their son, Chester, who married Abbey Moulton, and their son, John Augustus, the father of the subject of this sketch. The latter was associated with Messrs. Charles F. Bushnell and John W. Winslow in the iron business; was the builder of Ericsson's Monitor in 1861 and seven other vessels of the same type for the U. S. navy. Chester Griswold was educated in private schools and at an early age became associated with his father in the iron business. In 1869 he was made a member of the firm of John A. Griswold & Co., the other partners, besides his father and himself, being Messrs. Erastus Corning Sr. and Jr. This firm secured possession of the rolling mill of the Troy Vulcan Co., located on the south side of the Poestenkill in 1846. Some years later the company erected a rail mill on the north side of the Poestenkill and engaged in the rolling of steel rails for railroad purposes. They bought the United States patent rights for the Bessemer process of making steel, and it is important to record that this firm of John A. Griswold & Co. was the first to manufacture steel rails in America. In 1875 the Albany and Rensselaer Iron and Steel Co. was organized by the consolidation of Erastus Corning & Co. and John A. Griswold & Co., Chester Griswold becoming its vice-president. Subsequently this company was succeeded by the Troy Steel and Iron Co. with Chester Griswold as president, and it was again changed to the Troy Steel Co. While a resident of Troy Mr. Griswold was also president of the Crown Point Iron Co., and was interested in the Fort Edward Blast Furnace, the Rensselaer Iron Works, the Columbia Furnace, and the Bessemer Steel Co. He was also a trustee of the Troy Savings Bank; a member of the Troy Club and held the rank of major on the staff of Maj.-Gen. Joseph B. Carr and was on the staffs of Govs. Fenton and Dix. In 1870 he removed to New York city, and at once became a factor in business affairs, as well as a leader in social affairs and an active club man. He enjoyed the friendship of the foremost men in the world of commerce and finance. He was a member of the Union, Metropolitan, Down Town, Racquet, Riding and South Side clubs and the New York Yacht Club. He was also a member of the Sons of the Revolution. He was married April 14, 1868, to Grace, daughter of Le Grand B. Cannon (q. v.), and had two sons: Chester and Le Grand Canon Griswold. He died in New York City, Jan. 23, 1902.

SPALDING, Franklin Spencer, first Protestant Episcopal bishop of Utah and 222nd in succession in the American episcopate, was born at Erie, Pa., Mar. 13, 1865, son of Rt. Rev. John Franklin and Lavina Deborah (Spencer) Spalding. His earliest American ancestor was Edward Spalding, who settled at Braintree, Mass., in 1630. His father (q. v.) was the first Protestant Episcopal bishop of Colorado. Before his elevation to the episcopate he had been some time rector of St. Paul's, Erie. The son, Franklin Spalding, was educated at the public schools of Erie, Pa., and at Jarvis Hall, Denver. He was graduated at Princeton University in 1887, and at the General Theological Seminary, New York city, in 1891. He was ordained deacon in St. John's Cathedral, Denver, Colo., in 1891, by his father, Bishop J. F. Spalding, and was elevated to the priesthood in 1892. He was rector of All Saints' Church, Denver, 1891-92, and was in charge of Jarvis Hall and St. Luke's, Montclair, Colo., during 1892-96. He had the distinctive happiness to succeed in the sometime charge of his father when he became rector of St. Paul's Church, Erie, Pa., and where he ministered for nine years, until 1904. In the latter year he was elected in Boston, Mass., by the house of bishops, bishop of Salt Lake (the third bishop of the district and the 222nd in succession in the American episcopate). He was consecrated, Dec. 14, 1904, in St. Paul's Church, Erie, Pa., by Bishops Tuttle, Whitaker, Scarborough, Whitehead, Walker, Talbot and Vincent. In October, 1907, the title of the see was changed and he became first bishop of Utah. Bishop Spalding received the degree of S.T.D. from the General Theological Seminary in 1891. He is a member of the University Club of Salt Lake City and is unmarried.

MILLS, Harriet May, lecturer and reformer, was born in Syracuse, N. Y., Aug. 9, 1857, daughter of Charles de Berard and Harriet Anne (Smith) Mills. Her earliest paternal ancestor in America was Simeon Mills, who emigrated from England in 1630 and settled at Salem, Mass., removing in 1635 to Windsor, Conn. His grandson Elkanah, a captain in the war of the revolution, settled at Litchfield, Oneida co., N. Y., and the line of descent is through his son Abiram (grandfather of Harriet May Mills), who married Grace, daughter of Charles Joseph de Berard, member of a distinguished south of France family. Joseph de Berard came to America in 1789 with one of the French fleets sent to assist the American colonists in their struggle for liberty. After the war of the revolution he settled in Connecticut, married Polly Johnson, of Branford, and then removed to New Hartford, N. Y. Charles de Berard Mills (1821-1900) was a writer, scholar and lecturer, a social reformer and philanthropist. He was educated for the ministry and took an active part in the anti-slavery agitation. His intimate acquaintance with Oriental thought and life was demonstrated in his several volumes, "Buddha and Buddhism," "Gems of the Orient" and "Tree of Mythology." Miss Mills was graduated at Cornell University in 1879 in the course of literature. Her childhood home was a center for lecturers and workers in reform and literary lines, and there she met such men as Wendell Phillips, Ralph Waldo Emerson, A. Bronson Alcott, and such women as Susan B. Anthony, Lucy Stone, Elizabeth Cady Stanton and Ednah D. Cheney. The impressions made by their personalities were deepened by education and travel. After leaving college she organized one of the first and largest clubs in

WILLIAM A. WILDE
PUBLISHER

CHESTER GRISWOLD
MANUFACTURER

HARRIET MAY MILLS
REFORMER

CLIFFORD S. WALTON
LAWYER

REBECCA W. LUKENS

the country for the study of Robert Browning, and for years has been a successful Browning speaker. She first became an advocate of equal suffrage in 1892, and in 1894 took an active part in the constitutional campaign in New York state, holding meetings and organizing societies in many counties and speaking in company with Susan B. Anthony and the Rev. Anna H. Shaw. In 1896 she traversed California in behalf of the proposed amendment to enfranchise women, enthusiastic receptions from large audiences testifying to her success. In New York state few public workers for the suffrage cause are better known than she. During 1892-96 she served as recording secretary and lecturer of the New York State Woman Suffrage Association, and during 1896-1902 was organizer and lecturer for that association. She became its vice-president in 1902 and president in 1910. She is a member of the National Suffrage Association, the Syracuse Suffrage Society, the Farmers' Grange of New York state, the Women's University Club of New York city, the Association of Collegiate Alumnæ, College Equal Suffrage League and many other literary and charitable societies. She is interested in sociological questions and in societies of constructive philanthropy, including the George Junior Republic. Her principal lecture subjects are "The Oriental Woman," a study of social conditions in Northern Africa; "The Power of the Ballot," "A Modern Discovery"—the progress of women toward self-knowledge and self-development; "Democracy and Its Results," "Robert Browning and His Philosophy" and "A Winter in the Sahara Desert." She is a bright, effervescent, enthusiastic speaker, presenting her arguments with force and grace and unanswerable logic and producing effect also by a keen wit and brilliant sarcasm. The cause of suffrage owes many of its converts to the able pleadings of Miss Mills for political equality.

WALTON, Clifford Stevens, lawyer, author, was born at Chardon, O., Mar. 2, 1861, son of Andrew J. and Caroline (Griswold) Walton. He was educated at the Michigan Agricultural College, the United States Military Academy, West Point and at the National Law School, Washington, D. C. After graduating at the latter he was admitted to the Washington bar. He began his professional career as principal examiner in the United States patent office, and subsequently served two years in the United States land office. He then began the practice of law in Washington, and from the beginning met with unusual success. He was a gifted and fluent author, writing "The Civil Law in Spain and Spanish-America" (1900) and "Leges Commerciales y Maritimas de la Commercia Latina" (1908), in six volumes, the largest and most complete work on international, commercial and maritime law ever published in this or any foreign country. A licentiate in Spanish law, and an expert on civil and international law matters, he spent years in collecting data for this work in Madrid, Havana, Mexico City, Portugal and Brazil. In it he worked out a commercial and maritime code for the United States on the lines of the Spanish codes, which was in advance of the work gradually being done by the commissioners of the various states and territories on uniform legislation. This maritime code, besides containing the laws of the various countries of the western hemisphere, including the Portuguese-Brazilian and the French-Haytian codes, is annotated with respect to the decisions of European high courts, as well as those of international maritime con-

gresses and continental codes. The work was considered of such importance that it was printed by the United States state department and the bureau of American republics for the use of the diplomatic and consular officers, and the United States navy department placed it on board of all its vessels for the use of naval officers. It clears up many controverted points and misunderstandings between the United States and foreign countries, and has done much to encourage peace and promote trade relations. At the outbreak of the war with Spain he was appointed major and paymaster on the staff of Maj.-Gen. Brooke. He served in Porto Rico with Gen. Brooke, and in Cuba on the staff of Gen. Ludlow, becoming the chief paymaster of Havana, and had charge of all the custom-house funds. Because of his knowledge of Spanish, he was given the task of revising the Spanish codes for the use of the military authorities. Maj. Walton was a member of both the European and American international law associations and of many foreign societies, also of the Chevy Chase, University, Army and Navy clubs of Washington. He stood in the front rank of jurist consults and publicists, and was frequently called into various courts as an expert on matters pertaining to international law. He was one of the most brilliant members of the Washington bar. His salient characteristics were modest self-effacement, heartful loving kindness, clear vision, deliberate judgment and sereneness of manner. His fairness, his considerateness, his courtesy, his calm judgment never forsook him. He was kindly and broad in his views of the faults of others, and so above those faults himself. He was married in Washington, D. C., Apr. 9, 1890, to Annie G., daughter of Col. Wheelock G. Veazey, judge of the Vermont supreme court, who survives him. He died in Washington, May 15, 1912. Portrait opposite p. 374.

LUKENS, Rebecca Webb, iron manufacturer, was born in Pennsylvania, Jan. 6, 1794, daughter of Isaac Pennock, the founder of the Lukens Iron & Steel Co. Isaac Pennock was reared a farmer, but in 1780 erected the Federal Slitting Mill at what is now called Rokeby, on Buck Run, Chester co., Pa. This was the beginning of the present mammoth manufactory which has remained in the possession of his descendants for one hundred years. Upon the death of Isaac Pennock the manufacturing plant passed into the hands of his son-in-law, Dr. Charles W. Lukens, who conducted the business until the close of his life in 1825. Dr. Lukens was one of the most notable and successful of the early iron makers. Besides the slitting of rods and the rolling of plates, he also engaged in the manufacture of nails. At Dr. Lukens' request his widow, Rebecca W., assumed the direction of affairs after his death. She contended with enormous difficulties, but was equal to all emergencies. Railroads had not yet been built and the coal used was hauled by wagon from Columbia, thirty-five miles away, while the finished product of the mills was similarly transported to Philadelphia or Wilmington, Del. Surmounting obstacles almost insuperable, Mrs. Lukens, who was the first woman to engage in this industry, carried on the business with unusual success. Although employing a superintendent, she maintained a general oversight of the manufacturing and exercised entire control of the finances and the commercial department. In fact, her talent in handling the commercial end of her business was extraordinary, and she built it up to a far greater extent than either Pennock or her husband had done. She left the property to her heirs in a highly prosperous condition, and in recognition of her ability the name of the Brandywine Mills was changed to the Lukens Mills. The boiler plates made by her were so famous that George Stephenson used them in the construction of his early locomotives. Mrs. Lukens' daughter, Isabella Pennock, was born in the old residence, which still stands south of the present office building, and in 1848 married Dr. Charles Huston, who soon after became manager of the plant. Mrs. Lukens died in Coatesville, Oct. 12, 1854.

HUSTON, Charles, physician and manufacturer, was born in Philadelphia, Pa., in 1822, son of Robert Mendenhall and Hannah (West) Huston. He graduated at the University of Pennsylvania in 1840 and at the Jefferson Medical College in 1843, after which he spent eighteen months in special study in Europe. On his return he began the practice of his profession in Philadelphia. In 1850 he entered the iron business as a member of the Brandywine Iron Works, of Coatesville, Pa. The Brandywine Iron Works was established in 1780 by Isaac Pennock, one of the pioneer iron makers in this country, who built the "Federal Slitting Mill" at Rokeby, Chester co., Pa. Here charcoal slabs were heated in an open charcoal fire, rolled out into plates and then slit into rods for general blacksmith use, the slabs being obtained from charcoal iron bloomeries with which the neighboring valleys were dotted. Notwithstanding the many difficulties that confronted him, Pennock met with decided success and in 1810 he purchased another mill at what is now Coatesville, which was variously known as the Brandywine Mill, Brandywine Iron Works and the Brandywine Rolling Mill. Dr. Charles Lukens, Pennock's son-in-law, came into possession of the property in 1816 and continued the business. Dr. Lukens was one of the most notable and successful of the old iron makers. The first boiler plates were rolled by him between 1816 and 1825. Besides the slitting of rods and the rolling of plates he also engaged in the manufacture of nails, as is evidenced by documents extant showing his purchase of the exclusive rights and privileges in several nail-making machines. The making of rolled boiler plates was first undertaken about 1820. "The original plates," says the "Iron Age," "were made in the old mill from single charcoal iron blooms, being made in old-fashioned forge fires, which were quite numerous in the neighborhood. These bloms were reheated over an ordinary grate fire, the exact type of which is not now known, and were then rolled into plates or sheets. The plates were not sheared, being at that period shipped rough, the shearings at a later date being cut into nails. The plate rolls at that time, as near as known, were about about 16 inches in diameter and from three to four feet long between the housings. These were driven by an over-shot water-wheel directly connected with the roll train and without a fly-wheel. Many times when it seemed probable that the mill would stall, the workmen would rush for the water-wheel, climb upon its rim and by their united weight help to complete the "pass" through the rolls, thus preventing a "sticker," which invariably meant fire-cracked and later broken rolls. With this crude mill sheets were rolled as thin as No. 28 gauge, in packs of three. Owing to the constant increase in business, which necessitated more power, the over-shot wheel was afterward supplanted by a breast wheel so geared that it would convey more power to the rolls, and, in addition, a fly-wheel was introduced, geared to high speed for the storage of

power. This permitted the use of larger rolls, which were changed to 21 inches in diameter and 66 inches long. A reverberatory furnace was later installed, enabling the scrap from the plate shearings to be worked up. When Dr. Lukens died in 1825 he was succeeded at his special request by his widow, Rebecca W. Lukens. She was the first woman to engage in the iron industry and she was rated among the most able and successful manufacturers in the business. Her talent in handling the commercial end of her business was extraordinary and she built it up to a far greater extent than either Pennock or her husband had done. After twenty-two years of remarkably successful management, Mrs. Lukens died and was succeeded by her sons-in-law, Abram Gibbons and Dr. Charles Huston, the name of the mill being changed on her death from "Brandywine" to "Lukens." On the retirement of Abram Gibbons in 1855 the supreme management of the business devolved on Dr Huston and he remained at the head until his death. The history of the concern under Dr. Huston is one of continuous and increasing prosperity. In 1870 a modern steam plate mill was erected near the old water power mill. The new mill was of the two-high type in which chilled rolls 28 inches in diameter and 84 inches long were used. The old mill was changed into a puddling to prepare stock for the new. "In 1890," to quote the "Iron Age," "there was erected a three-high mill with chilled rolls 34 inches in diameter by 120 inches long, weighing 18 tons each. At the time of Charles Huston's death it was the largest mill of its kind in the United States." Dr. Huston was not only a business man of remarkable ability, initiative and executive capacity but he was also one of the most noted authorities on iron and steel in the country. In 1877 he was chairman of the committee sent to Washington by the boiler-plate manufacturers at the request of the treasury department to advise with the board of steamboat inspectors in framing a proper standard of tests, and his recommendations were adopted practically without change and his advice was constantly sought by government officials, steam boiler inspectors, insurance companies and municipalities. In 1878-9 he contributed a number of articles upon the behavior of iron and steel under varying conditions of heat and stress to the "Journal" of the Franklin Institute, and several years later these articles figured prominently on the same subject undertaken by foreign engineers. Dr. Huston was married in 1848 to Isabella Pennock, daughter of Dr. Charles and Rebecca W. Lukens, and had two sons, Abraham F. Huston, president of the Lukens Iron and Steel Co., and Charles L., vice-president of the same company, and four daughters. He died at Coatesville, Pa., January, 1897.

HUSTON, Abraham Francis, manufacturer, was born at Coatesville, Pa., July 7, 1852, son of Charles and Isabella Pennock (Lukens) Huston. He received his early education under private tutors and at the Taylor Academy, Coatesville, and was graduated at Haverford College in 1872. After graduation he entered the employ of the Lukens Iron Works, of which his father was the head, and, beginning at the bottom, acquired a thorough knowledge of all the details of the business. His father retired from active management about 1882 and since then Abraham F. Huston has been practically the head of the firm. The business was incorporated as the Lukens Iron and Steel Company in 1890, and in 1897 Mr. Huston became the president, an office which he still (1916) holds. The growth of the business since

1882 has been remarkable, and to-day the Lukens Iron and Steel Co. stands as one of the largest single independent iron and steel companies in the country and one that has never lent itself to stock market exploitation. The great expansion in the business of the company which has taken place under the leadership of Mr. Huston began in 1890 with the installation of a new three-high mill with chilled rolls 34 inches in diameter, 120 inches long, weighing 18 tons each. This was the largest mill of its kind which had up to that time been erected in the United States. It was driven by a large Corliss engine and was equipped with automatic hydraulic lifting tables and modern cooling tables with mechanical transfer to the hydraulic or steam shears. Various improvements were added from time to time, including a set of straightening rolls placed so as to take and level the plates as they came from the mill. In 1899 there was added a 48-inch universal mill with a capacity for making plates with rolled edges from 8 to 48 inches wide and over 100 feet long. A new open-hearth steel plant with six 50-ton furnaces was added in the same year. This plant practically doubled the steel-making capacity of the company. In 1902 an immense slabbing mill, one of the largest and best in the country, was installed, and in the following year there was added another mill with rolls 140 inches long and capable of rolling plates up to 136 inches wide. The latter mill is the largest in the Lukens plant, and at the time of its installation had a capacity for rolling greater widths of plates than any other mill in the United States. The auxiliary equipment of the mill consists of three continuous furnaces and two pit furnaces with four pits each, two hydraulic shears capable of shearing plates 2¼ inches thick, four large steam shears, and powerful electric cranes to handle the raw and finished product. All the finishing mills in the plant are equipped with straightening rolls for flattening the rolled plates as soon as they leave the mill and while still hot. The first steel rolled by the Lukens company as a regular business was made in 1880. The first open-hearth furnaces were built in 1891 and the company now has fifteen in operation, most of them 60 tons' capacity each per hearth. The present plant covers an area of over 200 acres, comprising twelve large buildings, as follows: a 140-inch plate mill, a 48-inch universal mill, two open-hearth plants, one containing six 40-ton furnaces and the other nine 60-ton furnaces; a 34-inch slabbing mill, three large boiler houses, a 22-inch puddle-mill, an 84-inch plate mill, a 112-inch plate mill, a machine-flanging shop and a roll turning shop. The products of the works include all kinds of boiler, ship and tank plate and flat structural steel for building purposes, bridges, etc., and flanged work, much of which is covered by the company's own patents; also trolley poles formed from steel plates. To the large property of the company has recently been added a beautiful office building built of brick and stone in the colonial style of architecture. The building is practically fire-proof, with steel and concrete floors upon which rests the floor proper. The building is lighted by gas and electricity, the latter from the company's own plant, and heated by the vapor system, regulated by thermostats. . . . An idea of the growth of the business under the direction of Mr. Huston may be gained from the fact when he took charge in 1881 the total output of the mills was 2,135 tons; in 1890 it was 14,390 tons; in 1900, 64,700 tons, and, in 1910, 226,550 tons. During the same period the number of employees has increased from a dozen to over 2,000, and the wages paid them have multiplied sixty-five times and amount now to considerably over $1,000,000 per annum. The product of the plant includes all kinds of boiler and flat structural steel for building purposes, bridges, ships, etc.; flanged work, much of which is covered by the company's own patents, and a large variety of steel plate products. There are branch offices in Philadelphia, New York, New Orleans, Boston, Baltimore and selling agencies in Chicago, Cleveland, Louisville, Los Angeles and San Francisco. It was incorporated in 1890 as the Lukens Iron and Steel Co. and the present officers are A. F. Huston, president; Charles L. Huston, vice-president; Joseph Humpton, secretary and treasurer. In addition to his connection with the Lukens Iron and Steel Co. Mr. Huston is president of the Jacobs-Shupert U. S. Fire Box Co. and the Coatesville Trust Co.; a director of the Pennsylvania Sugar Co., of Philadelphia, and the Wilmington and Northern branch of the Philadelphia and Reading railway. He was president of the American Steel Manufacturers' Association in 1902. He is president of the Coatesville Hospital, a director of Haverford College and Bryn Mawr College, and a member of the Merion Cricket and St. David Golf clubs. Mr. Lukens has traveled widely and is a man of keen observation and varied attainments. Mr. Huston was married Jan. 17, 1889, to Alice, daughter of Manlove H. Calley, of Delaware, by whom he had four children. She died in 1906 and he was married again in October, 1907, to Alfie Frances Sly.

HUSTON, Charles Lukens, manufacturer, was born at Coatesville, Pa., July 8, 1856, son of Dr. Charles and Isabella Pennock (Lukens) Huston, and brother of Abraham F. Huston. He began his education under private tutors, and graduated at Haverford College in 1875. After a brief course in a Philadelphia business college he began his active career in the Lukens Co.'s works, laboring in turn in every department and becoming proficient in all the operations of each. In 1880 he entered the firm of Huston & Penrose Co., and at the time of his father's partial retirement in 1881 shared with his brother the management of the company's operations. In the latter year, also, Mr. Penrose died and the style of the firm then became Charles Huston & Sons. After the incorporation of the Lukens Iron and Steel Co. in 1895, he was chosen second vice-president, having been before then and since general manager of the works. On the death of his father in 1897, he was made first vice-president. He is well known as a mechanical engineer and takes care of the practical part of the business, while his brother is chiefly concerned with the conduct of its financial and general affairs. The phenomenal growth of the enterprise, beginning in 1890, is largely attributed to Mr. Huston's skill, energy and executive ability. Mr. Huston has given personal attention to various movements for improving the welfare of the people in the company's employ. Many of the unskilled workmen are secured from the Inasmuch and Galilee missions in Philadelphia, and the old Lukens homestead, adjoining the mill, was fitted up with all modern conveniences and meeting-rooms, reading-room and shower baths especially for the use of the men from these missions. For several years he has been conducting a large Bible school in one of the company's buildings, in which work he is assisted by his wife. An attractive feature of this school is the "Lukens Band" of thirty-three pieces, the instruments and uniforms for which were contributed by him. In fact, Mr. Huston is well known for his great public spirit and the fostering of various philanthropic enterprises. He has served as director of the poor of Chester county, and for a number of years he supported at his own expense a private hospital for the benefit of the sick and injured of the borough, and when a new hospital was organized as a public institution he was made president of its board of trustees. He is interested in the work of the Y. M. C. A. both at home and throughout his state, and in 1902 was elected president of the state association. To him was chiefly due the organization of the Y. M. C. A. in Coatesville in 1891; he has been its president from that time. Mr. Huston was president of the Belmont Iron Works of Philadelphia from its organization until 1908, and is still one of the directors. He is also a director of the Allegheny Ore and Iron Co. and the Philadelphia Mortgage and Trust Co., and is a member of the American Society of Mechanical Engineers and the American Institute of Mining Engineers. He was married, July 23, 1895, to Annie, daughter of Maj. James T. Stewart, of Savannah, Ga., and they had two sons, James Stewart and Charles Lukens, Jr., and two daughters, Mary and Ruth Huston.

NORRIS, Frank, author, was born in Chicago, Ill., Mar. 5, 1870, son of Benjamin Franklin and Gertrude G. (Doggett) Norris. His father (1836–1901) founded the wholesale jewelry house of B. F. Norris & Co., later Norris, Allister & Ball, of Chicago. Frank Norris went with his parents to San Francisco, Cal., in 1884. He attended a boys' school at Belmont, Cal., and after studying art in the Julian Academy in Paris for two years entered the University of California in 1890. His first book, "Yvernelle," a three-canto poem of medieval France, was published in 1891. In 1894–95 he pursued a course in literature at Harvard University, after which the San Francisco "Chronicle," Chicago "Inter-Ocean" and "Harper's Weekly" sent him to Johannesburg, South Africa. During the plans for the Jameson raid he rode as a courier for John Hays Hammond and his allies, but for this was not imprisoned on the failure of the raid, although he was ordered out of the Transvaal by the Boer government. In 1896 and 1897 he was connected with the San Francisco "Wave." He was sent by the Doubleday, McClure Co., of New York, to Cuba as a war correspondent in 1898, his articles appearing in the "Century Magazine," and in the same year he published his first novel, "Moran of the Lady Letty," a story of adventure, in which he demonstrated his ability to draw characters, to create an atmosphere and to hold the reader's interest without interruption. This was followed by "McTeague (1899, "Blix" (1899) and "A Man's Woman" (1900). The Washington "Times" said of him: "Since Bret Harte no one has ever written of California life with the vigor and accuracy of Frank Norris, and the best of it is he is not in the least like Bret Harte, or very much like anyone but himself." Mr. Norris now planned a trilogy of novels, narrating consecutively "the epic of the wheat." The first of the series was "The Octopus" (1901), dealing with an incident known in California as the "Mussel Slough Affair," which was based mainly on fact. Its theme was the monopolistic oppression of the grain-grower in California by the railroads. The story ends with one of the most striking and dramatic illustrations of "poetic justice" in literature, the oppressor's vain struggle for life in a whirlpool of wheat in the hold of a wheat schooner. The second story of his trilogy is "The Pit," and appeared posthumously in 1902. His short stories and essays were subsequently collected and published in separate volumes entitled "A Deal in White" and "The Responsibilities of the Novelist," respectively. The interest in his work was so keen that a demand for his earlier work in the San Francisco "Wave" (all the files of which were destroyed in the fire of 1906) induced a publisher to bring out in 1909 a book of short stories hitherto unpublished in book form, entitled "The Third Circle." Another novel, "Vandover and the Brute," was published posthumously in 1914. Mr. Norris was married in New York city, Feb. 12, 1899, to Jeanette Williamson Black, of San Francisco, who survived him, with one daughter, Jeanette Williamson Norris. He died in San Francisco, Oct. 25, 1902. Portrait opposite page 379.

McGOVERN, Patrick Alphonsus, fourth Roman Catholic bishop of Cheyenne, Wyo., was born in Omaha, Neb., Oct. 14, 1872, son of Patrick and Alice McGearty McGovern. He was educated at Creighton University, and at Mt. St. Mary's Theological Seminary, Cincinnati, O. He was ordained priest Aug. 18, 1895, and officiated as rector of St. Philomen's Church from 1898 to 1907, and St. Peter's, Omaha, during 1907-12. Civic affairs received from him active attention, and he served as a member of the board of charities of Omaha. He was consecrated bishop of Cheyenne Apr. 11, 1912. The diocese takes in the whole state of Wyoming and is mostly missionary territory, which improved under his administration. The Catholic population of the diocese of Cheyenne is now 13,000, with twenty priests and ninety-one churches, chapels and stations.

STARIHA, John N., first Roman Catholic bishop of Lead, S. D., was born in the Province of Krain, Carniola, Austria, May 12, 1845. He was educated and ordained in his native land, and, coming to the United States, became a priest of the diocese of St. Paul, Minn., where for many years he was pastor of the Church of St. Francis de Sales. When the diocese of Lead was formed on Aug. 6, 1902, out of that part of South Dakota west of the Missouri river, he was appointed its first bishop and consecrated Oct. 28, 1902. The opening of the Rosebud reservation to settlers and railway enterprise attracted many settlers to South Dakota, and under Bishop Stariha's zealous activity new parishes were established, churches built in the new settlements and missions and schools located among the Indians. The territory of the new diocese extended over 41,750 square miles and had a scattered Catholic population of about 6,000, including the Catholic tribes of the Sioux reservations. In 1915 this had increased to 15,000 (8,500 whites and 6,500 Indians). Bishop Stariha, worn out by his missionary labors, resigned the see Mar. 9, 1909, was made titular bishop of Antipatride and died at Laibach, Austria, Nov. 28, 1915.

WING, Daniel Gould, banker, was born at Davenport, Ia., Sept. 10, 1868, son of George and Mary Elizabeth (Gould) Wing. He was educated in the public school of Devenport, and began his banking career at the early age of seventeen, as messenger in State National Bank of Lincoln, Neb. He was quick to grasp the various details of the business, and was advanced rapidly, becoming assistant cashier in 1884. In 1890 he was appointed cashier of the American Exchange National Bank of Lincoln. He was treasurer and auditor of the Republican national committee in Chicago, Ill., during the campaign of 1896, and in

FRANK NORRIS
AUTHOR

DANIEL G. WING
BANKER

HENRY C. PETTIT
LAWYER

ALVAH F. WHITMAN
PHYSICIAN

the following year Pres. McKinley appointed him national bank examiner. After an examination of the affairs of the Broadway and the Globe National banks of Boston, Mass., in 1899, both institutions closed their doors, and the comptroller of the currency appointed Mr. Wing receiver. He promptly took charge of the affairs of both institutions, and succeeded in paying the depositors of both banks in full, and a dividend to the shareholders of the Globe National. He displayed such executive ability, and so complete a knowledge of banking matters, that the board of directors of the Massachusetts National Bank at once elected him vice-president. When its president, John W. Weeks, resigned, in January, 1903, he was unanimously elected to that office. Under Mr. Wing's management the bank continued its successful growth, and during the six months following his election to the presidency its deposits increased over $1,000,000. In June, 1903, the Massachusetts National Bank was consolidated with the First National Bank. As its name indicates, the First National Bank of Boston was the first bank in that city organized under U. S. laws. It occupied the building at 17 State street thirty-two years, until 1902, when it was sold to the Ames estate, and upon its consolidation with the Massachusetts National removed to the building of the latter. In April, 1904, a further consolidation was made with the National Bank of Redemption, whose deposits then amounted to $35,000,000. In 1908 it took possession of its new building at Federal, Franklin and Congress streets, Boston, one of the most stately and most imposing bank edifices in New England. The first year in the new building was one of phenomenal growth. Its deposits increased nearly $20,000,000; it attained the rank of second largest bank in Boston and New England, and twelfth on the list of 6,900 national banks of the United States. In 1914 its capital was $3,000,000, surplus $5,800,000, and its deposits $60,000,000. Mr. Wing is a member of the Boston Clearing House Association, the Algonquin and Exchange clubs of Boston, the Newton Club of Newton, and since 1904 he has been a trustee of Boston University. He was married Jan. 23, 1902, to Josephine, daughter of George and Eliza (Baldwin) Cable, of Davenport, Ia., and has one daughter: Katherine.

PETTIT, Henry Corbin, lawyer, was born at Wabash, Ind., Nov. 20, 1863, son of John Upfold and Julia (Brenton) Pettit. His first American ancestor was John Pettit, an English gentleman, who emigrated early in the eighteenth century and settled in Connecticut, and the line of descent is traced through their son Jonathan and his wife, Agnes Riddell, and their son George and his wife, Jane Upfold, who were the grandparents of the subject. Hon. John Upfold Pettit (1820-81) was born at Fabius, N. Y., and after graduating at Union College in 1839 practiced law in Wabash, Ind. In 1850 he was appointed consul at Maranham, Brazil, serving also as vice-consul, which gave him supervision of ten other consulates in northern Brazil. He served in the national congress during 1854-60, and was elected from Miami and Wabash counties to the Indiana legislature in 1864, being re-elected in 1866 and serving as speaker. He was chosen colonel of the 75th Ind. Vol. infantry for the civil war, but ill-health obliged him to resign his commission before seeing active service. At the time of his death he was judge of the circuit court. His son, Henry Corbin Pettit, received his preliminary education in the public schools of Wabash, and was graduated at the United States Naval Academy in 1883. He then studied law in

the office of Cowgill & Shively, Wabash; was admitted to the bar in 1886, and in 1887 became a member of his preceptors' law firm. At the same time he was admitted to the supreme and appellate courts, and to the United States court in Indianapolis. In 1887 he was elected a member of the Wabash city council, and in 1888 became mayor, serving for two years as the youngest executive the city ever had. In 1894 he was elected to the Indiana general assembly, and was re-elected in 1896 and chosen speaker. He was a member of the Morton monument commission in 1899 and a member of the board of visitors to the United States Naval Academy. In 1901 Pres. McKinley appointed him United States marshal for the district of Indiana, and, being reappointed by Pres. Roosevelt, he served continually until May, 1911, meanwhile retaining his residence and law office at Wabash. He subsequently formed a partnership with Thomas L. Stitt, under the firm name of Pettit & Stitt. He was a charter member of Wabash Lodge, Knights of Pythias, and St. Anastasia Mesnil Lodge of Odd Fellows. He was also a member of the Wabash County Bar Association, of the Semper Idem Club of Wabash and Columbia Club of Indianapolis. Endowed with a clear and active mind, tirelessly industrious, persistent and indefatigable in the discharge of every duty, unswerving in his devotion to what he believed to be right, kind and considerate to all with whom he was associated, broad-minded and generous, the world is the better for his having lived in it. In his personal relations he was unfalteringly loyal, and he was pre-eminently faithful to every trust. His fidelity, whether in his political, professional or private life, was proverbial. He courted and enjoyed the felicities of the family circle, and it was in his home that he found his greatest happiness. He was married at Wabash, Ind., Oct. 3, 1888, to Eva, daughter of William Simpson Stitt, of Wabash, who survives him, with one child, Mary Pettit. He died at Wabash, Ind., July 26, 1913.

WHITMAN, Alvah F., physician and surgeon, was born at Galway, Saratoga co., N. Y., Nov. 29, 1831, son of William and Melissa (Green) Whitman. When a child his family removed to Brunswick, Ill. In 1845 a typhoid epidemic swept the new settlement, and the death of his father left him at the age of fourteen the head of a family of five. The family subsequently removed to Sun Prairie, Wis., where he was educated in the public schools. In 1851 he entered the University of Wisconsin, but the failure of a business project necessitated the abandonment of a college career. He then joined a party that surveyed the right of way for the old Milwaukee and La Crosse railway from Beaver Dam to Portage. Later he surveyed the town site of Hampton, Ia., where he exchanged his transit for real estate and subsequently devoted his time to teaching and farming until 1862, when he began the study of medicine in the office of Dr. H. L. Butterfield, of Waupun, Wis. In 1865 he was graduated at the University of Michigan Medical School, and practiced his profession at Charles City, Ia., and Spring Valley, Minn. In 1874 he took post-graduate courses at the Women's, Bellevue, Presbyterian and Charity hospitals, New York city. In 1883 he removed to St. Paul, where he continued his practice until his death. From 1896 he was necrologist of the Ramsey County Medical Society. His religious affiliation was with the Congregational Church. His piety was unostentatious, but steadfast, and he was first in charity and benevolence. Dr. Whitman was never too busy to lend a helping hand to a neighbor in distress, or a struggling young student puzzled in his studies. The close of each day witnessed some act of kindness to those about him. He was eminently a utilitarian so far as doing good to his fellow-men was concerned. He was married Oct. 2, 1865, to Matilda, daughter of Russel Smith, of Charles City. He died in St. Paul, Minn., Apr. 20, 1913.

McDOWELL, Alexander, banker, was born at Franklin, Pa., Mar. 4, 1845, son of Parker and Lavinia (Titus) McDowell. His father (1805-60) was a lumber merchant and his maternal grandfather was Jonathan Titus, founder of Titusville, Pa. He was educated in the public schools and at Franklin Academy. In 1862 he enlisted in company A, 121st Penn. Vol. infantry, and was subsequently breveted major of the 21st U. S. Vol. reserve corps in acknowledgment of gallant conduct. He was wounded at the battle of the Wilderness. He began his business career as part owner of the Venango ''Citizen'' in 1865, remaining with that newspaper until 1869. In the following year he became a partner in the banking house of James Bleakley Sons & Co., Sharon, Pa., and two years later acquired control of the banking house of Alexander McDowell, which he managed for thirty-five years. In 1907 this institution became the McDowell National Bank, of which he was president until his death. He was elected to the Fifty-third congress as congressman-at-large from Pennsylvania in 1893, and in the next congress he was chosen clerk of the house of representatives, serving in that capacity sixteen years. For forty years he was a school director and was also treasurer of Sharon, Pa., and during 1886-1913 of the Protective Home Circle. Mr. McDowell added to a singular symmetry and elevation of character an unusual intellectual culture. He was essentially a gentleman of the old school who believed in humility, courtesy and goodness. His influence over others was great, and he inspired much affection from all with whom he came in contact. He was married Sept. 17, 1867, to Clara, daughter of James Bleakley, a banker and oil operator, of Franklin. She survives him, with six children: James Parker, Lizzie, wife of Edward Buchholz; Willis, of U. S. N.; Mary B., Clara, wife of Glenn Carley, and Harry B. McDowell, cashier of the McDowell National Bank. He died at Sharon, Pa., Sept. 30, 1913.

WHITE, John Barber, lumberman, was born in Chautauqua county, N. Y., Dec. 8, 1847, son of John and Rebekah (Barber) White. His first American ancestor was John White, of South Petherton, Somerset, England, who came to America in 1638, and settled in Salem, now Wenham, Mass. From him and his wife, Joan West, the line is traced through their son Josiah and his wife, Mary Rice; their son Josiah and his wife, Abigail Whitcomb; their son Josiah and his wife, Deborah House; their son Luke and his wife, Eunice White, hereinafter named, and their son John and his wife, Rebekah Barber. Members of the family have held a position of independence and honor, both in England and America, for several centuries, and many have rendered valuable public services. Robert White, father of John, the emigrant, was guardian and church warden at South Petherton, Somersetshire, as far back as 1578. John received a grant of sixty acres at Salem (now Wenham), Mass., as well as several later grants, and built the first saw and grist mill in Wenham, on Mile river. His son Josiah served as a private in King Philip's war, and in 1704 was sergeant in command of a garrison on the west side

of the Penicook river, called the Neck. Josiah White, the second, served in the colonial war and was a man of considerable prominence in Lancaster. He was a tithing man in Lancaster in 1818, and was one of the first seven selectmen of the town, a position which he held for five years. He was town treasurer for one year, representative to the general court for three years, and deacon of the first church from 1729 until his death, forty-three years later. The third Josiah built the first sawmill in Leominster, the dam of which is still in use. His brother, Jonathan White, was a large land-holder, and one of the first proprietors as well as an officer of the town of Charlemont, Franklin co., Mass. He was commissioned captain in the Worcester regiment of Col. Ruggles which marched for Crown Point in 1755, and he was subsequently promoted to major, lieutenant-colonel and colonel. Luke White served in the war of the revolution in Capt. Warner's company of Col. Marshall's regiment, and later as clerk in the commissary department. John White, father of our subject, was a school teacher and a manufacturer of lumber and veneering. He removed to Chautauqua county, N. Y., in 1843. The son received his education at the public schools and the James-town (N. Y.) Academy. He began his business career in partnership with two Jenner brothers, wih whom he purchased a tract of pine near Youngsville, Pa., in 1868. Two years later, in association with R. A. Kinnear, he opened a lumber yard in Brady and one in Petrolia, Pa.; he bought the Arcade mill, in Tidioute, Pa., in 1874, and started a lumber yard in Scrubgrass, Pa., and in 1878 bought a stave, heading and shingle mill in Youngsville, Pa. He was peculiarly successful in all these ventures, and he further increased his interests when in 1880, with E. B. Grandin, J. L. Grandin, Capt. H. H. Cumings, the late Jahn L. and Livingston L. Hunter, of Tidioute, Pa., he organized the Missouri Lumber and Mining Co., one of the pioneer companies in the exploitation and development of the yellow pine industry. The mills and offices of this company were located at Grandin, Mo., for over twenty years until their removal to West Eminence, Mo. In 1892 it was decided to remove headquarters to Kansas City, Mo., and Mr. White opened offices there that year. He has been general manager of the company since its formation and has been its president for a number of years. In 1899 he was associated with Oliver W. Fisher and others in starting the Louisiana Long Leaf Lumber Co., with mills at Fisher and Victoria, La., of which he has been secretary and director since its formation. He organized the Louisiana Central Lumber Co., with mills at Clarks and Standard, La., in 1901, and became its president, a position he still holds. He is also president of the Forest Lumber Co., which owns a line of retail yards; secretary-treasurer and general manager of the Missouri Lumber and Land Exchange Co., Kansas City, Mo.; and vice-president of the Grandin Coast Lumber Co., which has extensive holdings in the state of Washington. In addition to his big lumber interests, Mr. White has been identified with several other successful enterprises. In 1874 he founded at Youngsville, Pa., the ''Warren County News,'' a weekly, which he afterward, in connection with Mr. E. W. Hoag, purchased outright and moved to Tidioute. During 1886-1907 he was president of the Bank of Poplar Bluff, Mo. He is a director of the New England National Bank of Kansas City, Mo., and vice-president of the Fisher Flouring Mills Co., with mills at Seattle, Wash., and Belgrade, Montana. In 1882 Mr. White organized the first lumber manufacturers' association in the southern states (now the Yellow Pine Manufacturers' Association), and for the first three years served as its president. He is now a director of the Yellow Pine Manufacturers' Association and a member of the board of governors of the National Lumber Manufacturers' Association. He is deputy governor-general of the Missouri Society of Colonial Wars; fourth vice-president, from Missouri, of the Sons of the Revolution; life member of the American Academy of Political and Social Science, the Holstein-Friesian Association, the New England Historical and Genealogical Society, and the Heath, Mass., Historical Society; director of the National Conservation Association and the American Forestry Association; member of the Virginia, the "Old Northwest," of Ohio, the Missouri, and Harleian (London, England) Historical societies; member of Trans-Mississippi Commercial Congress for 1912-14; trustee of the Kidder Institute and of Drury College of Springfield, Mo.; and a member of the National Geographic Society and American Society of International Law. He is also a member of the International Society for the Prevention of Pollution of Rivers and Waterways and the American Academy of Political Science of New York city. Mr. White was president of the board of education of Youngsville, Pa., from 1876 to 1883. He served in the Pennsylvania house of representatives in 1878-1879, and was a member of the committee of seven elected by the Pennsylvania legislature in 1879 to prosecute cases of bribery. In November, 1905, he was appointed by Pres. Roosevelt his personal representative to investigate affairs on Cass Lake (Minn.) Indian reservation and report as to whether the reservation ought to be opened up in part for settlement. Pres. Roosevelt also appointed him a member of the forestry department on the commission on conservation of natural resources in 1907, and in 1909 he was appointed a member of the state forest commission by Gov. Hadley, of Missouri. Later he became aid-de-camp, with the rank of colonel, on the governor's personal staff. He was chairman of the executive committee of the first, second and third national conservation congresses and was elected president of the fourth national conservation congress at Kansas City, Mo., September, 1911. Mr. White has long been interested in genealogical research. In 1909 he published "Genealogy of the Ancestors and Descendants of John White of Wenham and Lancaster, Mass., 1574-1909," in four volumes, and "Genealogy of the Descendants of Thomas Gleason of Watertown, Mass., 1607-1909," and "The Barber Genealogy, 1714-1909." He has delivered numerous addresses on conservation of the forests and other natural resources, some of which have been published in pamphlet form and freely circulated by the conservation congresses, Trans-Missouri congress and lumber associations. Mr. White is a 32d degree Mason, and a member of the Commercial, Mid-day, City and Knife and Fork clubs of Kansas City. He resides in Kansas City and has a fine farm and summer residence at Bemus Point, Chautauqua co., N. Y. He was twice married; first, July 22, 1874, to Arabell, daughter of Daniel Washington Bowen, of Chautauqua county, N. Y., by whom he had two children: John Franklin White, deceased, and Fanny Arabell, wife of Alfred Tyler Hemingway, general manager of the Forest Lumber Co., Kansas City, Mo.; second, Dec. 6, 1882, to Emma, daughter of Benjamin Baird Siggins, of Youngsville, Pa., by whom he

had three children: Emma Ruth, Jay Barber White, deceased, and Raymond Baird White.

WALKER, James Monroe, lawyer and railroad president, was born at Claremont, N. H., Feb. 14, 1820, son of Solomon Walker and Charity (Stevens) Walker. His parents removed to Farmington, near Detroit, Mich., while he was still a boy, and he was educated at Oberlin College and the University of Michigan, being graduated at the latter in 1849. During his senior year he studied law and after graduation he continued his law studies in the office of Judge Robert Wilson at Ann Arbor. Soon after his admission to the bar in 1851 he was elected prosecuting attorney of Washtenaw county and also became local attorney for the Michigan Central railroad, at the same time laying the foundation of a large private practice. Removing to Chicago, Ill., in 1853, he became attorney for the Michigan Central railroad and soon afterward was appointed general solicitor for the road. Here he formed the law firm of Sedgwick & Walker, which afterward became Walker, Van Arman & Dexter, and finally Walker, Dexter & Smith. His general practice became increasingly large, but he was obliged to abandon it in 1868 owing to the pressure of more important affairs. Acting for the Boston company which controlled the Michigan Central, he purchased the right of way for the Chicago, Burlington and Quincy railroad, and, on the completion of the road, became its attorney, counselor and general solicitor. For a time he was acting president of the Leavenworth, Lawrence and Galveston railroad, and in 1870 succeeded James F. Joy as president of the Chicago, Burlington and Quincy. He resigned the presidency of the road in 1875, but remained its legal adviser until his death. In the meantime he had negotiated for its absorption of the Burlington and Missouri River railroad and other important acquisitions and changes in the railroad property owned by the Boston syndicate. He also organized the Illinois stock yards and the Kansas City stock yards, and was president of both from their inception until his death, and was president of the Chicago and Wilmington Coal Co. Mr. Walker was a man of fine taste and of great erudition. He read everything that he found time to read, whether it lay in the line of his special profession or in the broader field of general literature. He was a lawyer of rare attainments, and was possessed of a mind stored with all sorts of legal knowledge. Rev. William Alvin Bartlett, of Chicago, said of him: "His intellect was trained and subtle. He had an intuitive perception of essentials. His keen genuineness would winnow out artifice and deceit. The richer qualities of the man were only displayed at home. He was possessed of a rare literary taste. A discriminating critic, he was a lover of good literature and of the men who make it. His æsthetic nature, aspiring and gratified in rare paintings, warmed and gladdened his sterner gifts. He was a refined Christian gentleman. He thought deeply and built upon the foundation of Christian principle. He had a womanly purity of character, transparent as light in all that related to the high moralities." At a meeting of the Chicago bar, Judge C. B. Lawrence said: "Mr. Walker possessed unusual logical power, exceedingly clear perceptions in regard to the intricacies of a lawsuit, and was so conscientious in his duties to his clients, and in what he deemed his duties to the court, that I imagine he never came before a judge to make an argument without a thorough preparation and a complete and exhaustive study of his case. He was not an eloquent advocate, but a most clear, keen and accomplished reasoner, having all his facilities ready at command, never betrayed into an illogical position, and was a valuable assistant to the bench in the administration of justice, the highest position the lawyer can aim at or occupy." Mr. Walker was married Dec. 5, 1855, to Ella, daughter of John Pitt Marsh, of Kalamazoo, Mich., and had three children: Mary Louise, Wirt Dexter and James Ransom Walker. He died in Chicago, Ill., Jan. 22, 1881.

PEARL, Raymond, biologist, was born at Farmington, N. H., June 3, 1879, son of Frank and Ida May (McDuffee) Pearl, grandson of Eleazer and Barbara Ann (Pendleton) Pearl, great-grandson of Peter Pearl, and great-great-grandson of Eleazer Pearl. He was graduated at Dartmouth College in 1899. He was assistant in zoology in the University of Michigan until 1902, when he was advanced to instructor in zoology, and in 1906–07 held the same position in the University of Pennsylvania. In 1907 he became head of the department of biology in the Maine Agricultural Experiment Station, ranking as professor of biology in the University of Maine, and still holds these positions. During 1901–02 he was engaged in biological researches on variation in fishes, in connection with the biological survey of the Great Lakes by the U. S. Fish Commission. In 1904–05–06 he was awarded grants for research on variation in organisms from the Carnegie Institution of Washington. These researches were chiefly on heredity and plant and animal breeding. They resulted in the discovery of the existence of homogamy in the conjugation of paramecium, an account of which was first presented to the Royal Society of London in 1905 and subsequently confirmed by Jennings of Johns Hopkins University; the laws of variation and correlation in human brain weight; the laws of growth and differentiation in Ceratophyllum and the discovery of the mode of inheritance of fecundity in the domestic fowl. Dr. Pearl may be accepted as one of the foremost experts in the United States on poultry breeding, and for some time has served in such a capacity to the U. S. department of agriculture. He was a non-resident lecturer at the Graduate School of Agriculture, Ames, Ia., in 1910, and at Lansing, Mich., in 1912. He is the author of "Variation and Differentiation in Ceratophyllum" (1907); "Variation and Correlation in the Crayfish" (with A. B. Clawson, 1907); "Diseases of Poultry" (with F. M. Surface and M. R. Curtis, 1915), "Modes of Research in Genetics" (1915), and more than 150 articles in various scientific publications, including domestic and foreign magazines, technical journals and Bulletins of the U. S. department of agriculture. He was associate editor of the "Journal of Applied Microscopy" during 1900–05; the "Zoologischer Jahresbericht" in 1906–07; "Biometrika" (London) during 1906–10, and since 1910 has served in the same capacity with the "Zentralblatt f. Zoologie, Allgemeine und Experimentelle Biolgoie." In 1914 he became assistant editor in charge of experiment station contributions to the "Journal of Agricultural Research," published by the U. S. department of agriculture. Dr. Pearl received the degree of Ph.D. from the University of Michigan in 1902. He is a fellow of the American Association for the Advancement of Science; member of American Society of Zoologists (secretary eastern branch 1911, president 1913); Society of Experimental Biology and Medicine; Boston

Society of Natural History; Society for the Promotion of Agricultural Science; American Breeders' Association (chairman animal section 1913); American Philosophical Society; American Society of Naturalists (president in 1916); the International Association of Poultry Instructors and Investigators; American Association of Instructors and Investigators in Poultry Husbandry (president 1909), and honorary member of the Imperial Society of Rural Aviculture of Russia. He is also a member of Phi Beta Kappa, Sigma Xi, Phi Kappa Phi, and Alpha Zeta, honorary Greek letter societies. He was a delegate to the seventh international congress of zoology, and to the first international eugenics congress, and was a representative from the United States on the permanent international eugenics committee. He was married, June 29, 1903, to Maud Mary, daughter of James Lloyd DeWitt, of Sandusky, O., and has one daughter, Ruth DeWitt Pearl.

HANNA, Louis Benjamin, banker, and tenth governor of North Dakota (1913–16), was born at New Brighton, Pa., Aug. 9, 1861, son of Jason R. and Margaret A. (Lewis) Hanna, grandson of Joshua and Susan Hanna, great-grandson of Benjamin and Rachel Hanna and great-great-grandson of Robert Hanna, a native of Scotland, who emigrated about 1757 and settled in Pennsylvania. Marcus A. Hanna, U. S. senator from Ohio, was his cousin. His father was an iron manufacturer in Pennsylvania, and during the civil war served as captain of company C, 63rd Pa. Vol., and later as lieut.-colonel in the 143rd Pa. Vol. His boyhood years were spent in Pennsylvania, Massachusetts, New York and Ohio, and he received his education, for the most part, in the public schools of New York city and Cleveland, O. After farming for a year in Hope, N. D., he removed to Page, N. D., where he engaged in a general merchandise, lumber and grain business. In 1886 he established a private bank which met with initial and continued success. It was incorporated as the First National Bank of Page in 1900, and he has been its president since its organization. Later he became interested in the First National Bank of Fargo, of which he is also president. He was one of the incorporators and president of the Fargo Street Railway Company, afterwards known as the Fargo and Moorhead Street Railway Company, organized in 1905 with a capital stock of $300,000. He is an owner of the celebrated Carrington and Casey farm in Foster county, one of the largest farms in North Dakota. His political affiliation is with the Republican party. He represented the eleventh district, Cass county, in the state assembly in 1895, 1897 and 1899, and served as state senator from the ninth district, comprising the city of Fargo, during 1905–09. He was chairman of the Republican state central committee for six years. As a member of the sixty-first and sixty-second national congresses, he was a member of the agricultural committee and the committee on Indian Affairs. On the latter he was instrumental in opening for settlement under the homestead law a million acres of land on the Fort Berthold reservation. In 1912 he was elected governor of North Dakota and was re-elected two years later. During his administration the state legislature passed an act to prevent procreation by confirmed criminals, insane, idiots and defectives; a bill to regulate the practice in district and supreme courts; an inheritance tax law, and a bill establishing teachers' insurance and retirement funds. The gracious manner, cordial treatment, straightforward methods and honesty

JAMES M. WALKER
RAILROAD PRESIDENT

WILL C. MACFARLANE
ORGANIST

LOUIS B. HANNA
GOVERNOR

RAYMOND PEARL
SCIENTIST

M. H. Post

of purpose of Gov. Hanna have made a deep impression upon those with whom he has come in contact. His winning, pleasing personality attracts men to him, and no man in the great Northwest enjoys a wider or more intimate circle of friends. He is a Mason and belongs to the Order of Elks, Woodmen and Moose. He is also a member of the Loyal Legion. He was married at Minneapolis, Minn., Nov. 18, 1884, to Lottie L., daughter of Albert Thatcher, of North Adams, Mass., and has three children: Jean E., Dorothy L. and Robert L. Hanna.

SPRY, William, third governor of Utah (1909—), was born in Windsor, England, Jan. 11, 1864, son of Philip and Sarah (Field) Spry. He received his education in the common schools of Windsor and later of the state of Utah, to which his parents emigrated as converts of the Mormon church when he was eleven years of age. At the age of thirteen he began work as a stable boy and afterward became a railroad section hand and striker in the blacksmith shop. He was subsequently employed in the hide and wool business. Upon reaching his majority he went into the South as a Mormon missionary, and for six years was engaged in missionary work for the Mormon church. Returning to Salt Lake City he was connected with the Zion's Co-operative Mercantile Institution for two years and then took up farming and stock-raising in Tooele, Utah. In 1894 he was elected collector of Tooele county, a position which he held until it was abolished by the legislature. In 1902 he was elected to the Utah legislature from Tooele county, and two years later he became state chairman of the Republican party. He was appointed a member of the State Land Board in March, 1903, and served as its president, resigning in February, 1906, to take charge of the U. S. marshal's office for the district of Utah, to which he had been appointed by Pres. Roosevelt in January of that year. He was elected governor of Utah in 1909 and was re-elected in 1913 to serve until 1917. During his administration the legislature passed a law providing for the commission form of government for all cities of the first class. It also enacted a child labor law and a law prohibiting the selling or giving away of cigars, cigarettes or tobacco in any form to persons under twenty-one years of age except upon a physician's prescription. Gov. Spry was married, July 10, 1890, to Mary Alice Wrathall, of Grantsville, Utah.

MACFARLANE, Will C., organist and composer, was born in London, England, Oct., 2, 1870, son of Duncan and Eliza Macfarlane. When four years of age he came to the United States with his parents, attended the public schools of New York, and studied music with his father and with Samuel P. Warren. During 1880–85 he was chorister at Christ Church, Fifth avenue, New York, and as early as 1886, when but sixteen years old, made his début as a concert organist at Chickering Hall. Since then he has toured the country, giving concerts in the principal cities of the United States. He has held prominent positions as organist and choirmaster, notably at Temple Emanu-El and St. Thomas's Church, New York, which positions he resigned in 1912 to become municipal organist of Portland, Me. This position he now holds (1916), and to him is accorded the distinction of being the first organist engaged directly by a municipality in the United States. His compositions include songs, anthems, part-songs, organ music, a Lenten cantata, "The Message from the Cross," and an operetta, "Little Almond Eyes." His setting of Katherine Lee Bates' patriotic hymn, "America, the Beautiful," has had nation-wide usage. In 1897 he received the Clemson gold medal, awarded by the American Guild of Organists, and in 1911 and again in 1914 he was awarded the W. W. Kimball prize by the Chicago Madrigal Club. The honorary degree of Master of Arts was conferred on him by Bates College in 1915. He successfully passed the fellowship examination in the American College of Musicians, and is one of the founders of the American Guild of Organists. Mr. Macfarlane's musical education was entirely acquired in New York city, and it is his pride to be able to demonstrate that a thorough musical education is attainable without having to go abroad for it. He was married, June 2, 1896, to Madeleine, daughter of Dr. David H. Goodwillie, of New York.

POST, Martin Hayward, physician and surgeon, was born in St. Louis, Mo., Mar. 31, 1851, son of Truman Marcellus and Frances Post. His father was a pioneer Congregational minister. He received his preliminary education in the public schools and at Smith Academy, and was graduated at Washington University in 1872, being the honor man of his class. For a period he was principal of the Blow School, Carondelet, then began the study of medicine, and was graduated M.D. at St. Louis Medical College, now the medical department of Washington University, in 1877. He became an interne at the St. Louis City Hospital, and worked in general surgery with Dr. John T. Hodgen after opening his own office for general practice. He was assistant to Dr. John Green for three years, after which he studied with Donders and Snellen at Utrecht, and received instruction in operating from Nettleship. He was on the active medical and consulting staff of St. Louis City Hospital, Female Hospital, St. Luke's Hospital, Missouri Baptist Sanitarium, Protestant Hospital, Barnard Free Skin and Cancer Hospital, and the St. Louis Eye, Ear, Nose and Throat Infirmary. He was president (1914) of the American Ophthalmological Society, and member American Medical Association, American College of Surgeons, American Academy of Medicine, St. Louis Academy of Science, St. Louis Ophthalmological Society, and past chairman of the ophthalmic section of the St. Louis Medical Society. He was an honorary member of Phi Beta Kappa fraternity, and was a member of the University, St. Louis Country and Round Table clubs. He was a member of the Missouri Association for the Blind, and was interested in every movement for the prevention of blindness. He was appointed by the governors of both political parties for more than twenty years as consultant for, and a member of the board of managers of, the Missouri School for the Blind. His numerous publications are contained in the volumes (1885-1913) of the "American Journal of Ophthalmology" and in the "Transactions of the American Ophthalmological Society." His dominant personal characteristics were his friendliness, his cordiality, his sincerity and eminent practicality. He possessed great originality in operative emergency, prompt initiative concerning new methods, and although a conservative operator he was daring when necessary. He was married (first) at Louisville, Ky., to Mary, daughter of William Tyler. She died Jan. 2, 1888, and he was married (second) Jan. 4, 1906, to Mary Brown, daughter of Edward A. Tanner, of Jacksonville, Ill., who survives him, with four children, two by the first and two by the second marriage: M. Hayward, Jr., Lawrence T., Edward Tanner and Frederick Woodford Post. Dr. Post died at Castle Park, Mich., Sept. 1, 1914.

CRANDALL, Floyd Milford, physician, was born at Belfast, N. Y., May 2, 1858, son of Charles Milford and Deborah (Wood) Crandall. His first American ancestor was Rev. John Crandall, a native of Wales, who came to America in 1634 and settled in Boston, Mass.; from him the line of descent is traced through his son Joseph, who married Deborah Burdick; their son Joseph, who married Ann Langworthy; their son Joshua, who married Abigail Crandall; their son Peter, who married Nancy Bliven, and their son Benjamin, who married Anna Van Campin, and was the grandfather of the subject of this sketch. His father, Charles Milford Crandall (1826-67), was a prominent physician of western New York who took a deep interest in the movement to improve the condition of the insane poor of the state, and Willard Asylum for the Insane is largely indebted to him for the law that gave it existence. His professional knowledge made him an important factor in reorganizing the health department of New York city and in reforming the quarantine laws of the port of New York. He was a member of the Council of Hygiene of New York city, a trustee of the asylum at Binghamton, and shortly before his death was made a state commissioner of public charities. But his greatest public service was his work in behalf of the New York soldiers during the civil war. For two months of the summer of 1862 he served as a volunteer surgeon with the army of the Potomac; after the battle of Fredericksburg, in the following December, he again gave his services to the men in the field, and in the summer of 1864 he spent many weeks of service in the military hospitals of Nashville and Louisville. Actuated by his army experience he initiated a movement in 1863, which was promptly supported by the State Medical Society and was enacted into law by the legislature, under which liberal appropriations were made and competent medical agents were stationed at various places in the South, whose sole duty it was to look after the interests and welfare of the sick and wounded soldiers of New York state. During the last three years of his life he was a member of the New York legislature. The son, Floyd M. Crandall, received his early education at the Genesee Valley Seminary, and after graduating at the Genesee Normal School became principal of the former institution in 1879. Having determined to follow the medical profession, he entered the University Medical College of New York, and was graduated in 1884, the second prize man in his class. He was immediately appointed upon the staff of Bellevue Hospital and became house physician in the following year. Upon leaving the hospital in 1886 he engaged in private practice in New York. During 1886-89 he was attending physician to the outpatient department of Bellevue Hospital, and in 1889 was appointed attending physician to the Northwestern Dispensary. He was visiting surgeon to the Skin and Cancer Hospital during 1890-95; visiting physician to the Minturn Hospital, 1897-1900; to the Infants' Hospital, 1895-98, and to the Children's Hospital, 1895-98, and since 1898 has been consulting physician to the New York city children's hospitals and schools. In college work he passed through the various grades of instructor, lecturer, and adjunct professor in the New York Polyclinic. He was early (1889) given a position on the staff of the "New York Medical Journal"; was managing editor of the "Gaillard Medical Journal," 1894-95, and was for six years editor of the "Archives of Pediatrics," then the only magazine in the English language devoted to the diseases of children. He was assistant editor of Sajous' Cyclopædia in 1900, and is the author of about sixty monographs and papers on medical subjects and of a book entitled "Modern Methods of Preventing Disease" (1903), which has won many flattering commendations from medical authorities. He is also the author of articles in Foster's "System of Therapeutics," Hare's "System of Therapeutics," Starr's Cyclopædia of Pediatrics," Carr's "Practical Pediatrics," and Keating's "Cyclopædia of Pediatrics." For ten years he has contributed annually to "Progressive Medicine," and for several years has written largely upon the legal and civil relations of the medical profession. In 1906 Dr. Crandall served upon the hospital commission appointed by the mayor of New York, and in the following year he was appointed upon the New York state board of medical examiners. He has been active in medical society work from his earliest years of practice, and has been at various times recorder of the American Pediatric Society and member of its council; chairman of the pediatric section of the New York Academy of Medicine, and chairman of the committee on admissions; and president of the West End Medical Society (1895), the Society of the Alumni of Bellevue Hospital (1911) and Medical Society of the County of New York. In 1893 he was one of the English-speaking secretaries of the Pan-American Medical Congress. In addition to the societies mentioned, Dr. Crandall is a member of the American Medical Association, being a member of the house of delegates (1906-9), the American Congress of Physicians and Surgeons, the National Association for the Prevention of Tuberculosis, the American Society for the Study of Epilepsy, the New York State Medical Society (member of the house of delegates, 1906-11), the New York Pathological Society, the National Geographic Society, the New York State Historical Society and the Civil Service Reform Association. Portrait opposite page 385.

CARTER, William, manufacturer, was born at Alfreton, Derbyshire, England, Feb. 25, 1830, son of John and Mary (Carey) Carter. He belonged to a family of textile manufacturers and his early education included learning the trade of a knit-goods operative. He began his business career as an employee of a mill in Nottinghamshire. In 1857 he came to the United States and secured work as a journeyman stocking-maker first in New York and later in New Hampshire, and still later in Massachusetts. In 1860 he located permanently in Needham, Mass., where he purchased a small hand-frame and began business for himself manufacturing cardigan jackets. In 1869 he formed partnership with John and Mark Lee to manufacture knit-goods, under the firm name of Lee, Carter & Co. The company produced a fine line of fancy stockings and other goods, and was successful until the financial panic of 1878 caused a failure. Undaunted by this setback, Mr. Carter subsequently resumed the business. His sons, William H. and Horace A. Carter, joined the firm and, in 1902, it was incorporated as the William Carter Co., with Mr. Carter president. The business expanded steadily, until now it occupies a foremost place in its line in the United States. The factories at Springfield and Needham are equipped with hundreds of improved knitting, sewing and other machines for producing men's, women's and children's underwear to the value of $1,750,000 annually. From the beginning Mr. Carter carefully considered the welfare, comfort and health of his millhands, realizing that this was a means of

WILLIAM CARTER

CHARLES M. CRANDALL
PHYSICIAN

FLOYD M. CRANDALL
PHYSICIAN

ZENAS E. NEWELL
BANKER

HENRY DUVEEN
ART DEALER

raising the standard of manhood and womanhood among his employees. He was one of the first manufacturers to grant regularly the Saturday half-holiday. He constructed and built homesteads, introduced landscape gardening, provided playgrounds and adopted the newest safety devices to prevent accidents. Mr. Carter served as selectman, member of the school board and water commissioner (president). In 1895 he was elected to the general court, in which he was active in promoting important improvements at Highlandville, now Needham Heights. He is a member of Norfolk Lodge, F. and A. M.; Newton Chapter, R. A. M., and Gethsemane Commandery, Boston Chamber of Commerce and for years a member of the Ancient and Honorable Artillery Company, of Boston. He was a charter member of the Home Market Club, Boston. For years he has been a trustee of the Methodist Church of Needham Heights, and he has been likewise active in the benevolent and philanthropic work of other denominations. His entire life has been a living exemplification of honesty, truthfulness, fidelity and consecration to duty. His rugged, genial character, his simple tastes, his retiring nature and his broad, human sympathy and quiet democracy have won for him a high place in the esteem of his fellow-men. He was thrice married: First, at Gedling, England, 1853, to Hannah, daughter of Joseph Truman, of Carlton. She died in 1862 and he was married (second) at Newton Centre, 1863, to Martha, daughter of Mark Lee, of England, and sister of his former business partners. She died in 1873 and he was married at Brookline, Mass., in 1874, to Jane G., daughter of Jonathan Avery, of Needham. By the first union he had one child: Frank C.; by the second he had four: William H., Mary Elizabeth, John J. and Horace A., and by the third union, Lucie Avery and Roscoe A. Carter. All five sons are associated in the William Carter Co.

NEWELL, Zenas Edgar, banker, was born in New York city, Oct. 8, 1842, son of Zenas and Eliza (Sneden) Newell. His earliest paternal American ancestor was Thomas Newell, a native of Hertfordshire, England, who emigrated early in the seventeenth century and settled in Connecticut. His wife was Rebeckah Olmstead, and from them the line of descent is traced through their son Samuel and his wife, Mary Hart; their son Thomas and his wife, Mary Lee; their son Elihu and his wife, Esther Langdon; their son James Harvey and his wife, Rachel Paddock, who were the grandparents of Zenas Edgar Newell. Thomas Newell, settler, was first identified with Farmington in 1640; subsequently he became one of the eighty-four proprietors of Farmington, Conn., and later located the town of Mattatuck, now Waterbury. Samuel Newell (1660-1753) held the military rank of ensign. The father (1813-98) of the subject was a prominent and successful dry goods merchant of New York city, and was one of the founders of the Carmine Street Presbyterian Church. He was all his life actively identified with that communion, as were all of his ancestors in the direct line. Zenas Edgar Newell was educated at the Sing Sing Military Academy, after which he entered the employ of the East River National Bank, New York, in 1859. At the beginning of the civil war the 22d regiment, N. G., N. Y., was organized as a home guard to protect the United States treasury, New York. Company E was, for the most part, composed of the officers and employees of the different banks, although the entire regiment was made up mainly of busi-

ness men. He became a charter member, enlisting as a private in company E. When the regiment was called to the front in 1862 he saw service in Baltimore and at Harper's Ferry. In the following year his command was on guard service at Harrisburg; was in reserve at Gettysburg, and followed the retreating Confederates as far as Frederick, where it was ordered to New York to assist in the suppression of the draft riots, and subsequently to guard the Croton aqueduct. After the war he returned to the East River National Bank, but in 1865 entered the service of the Bank of America. At the request of the president of the East River National Bank he returned to that institution as cashier in 1867, being the youngest bank officer at that time in New York city. He continued in that capacity for forty-five years, impaired health necessitating his resignation Jan. 1, 1912. During 1882-83 he served as a member of the nominating committee of the New York Clearing House Association, and during his entire career in banking circles he was highly respected and was widely known. Ever active in civic and municipal affairs, he was a school trustee in South Orange, N. J., during 1898-99, and a member of the building committee when Columbia High School was rebuilt. During his entire life he was identified with the religious activities of the Presbyterian Church. He was superintendent of the Sunday-school of the Eighty-sixth Street Presbyterian Church, New York; was for ten years superintendent of the Sunday-school of the Springfield (N. J.) Presbyterian Church; was the organizer and superintendent of a Sunday-school at Old Short Hills, N. J., and was elder in the First Presbyterian Church, Yonkers, N. Y. His political affiliation was with the Republican party, and he was an advocate of sound money. He was a member of the Metropolitan Museum of Art, the American Institute, Philharmonic Society, New York, and a governor of the South Orange (N. J.) Field Club. His favorite pursuits were fishing, driving and bowling. The dominating characteristics of Zenas E. Newell were a strict integrity, quickness to discern the right and wrong of a question and promptness to act in any emergency. He had little patience with the man who was tardy either in fulfilling a business engagement or in performing any other obvious duty; but he was possessed of a great kindliness of heart, and was ever ready to aid the needy and deserving, even to the extent of great self-sacrifice. Added to this were an untiring devotion to business cares and a strong appreciation of the responsibilities that rested upon him. He was a man of unusual exactness and extremely methodical. He was married in New York, Jan. 15, 1874, to Anna Cornelia, daughter of Samuel Sneden, a celebrated shipbuilder of New York and Greenpoint, who built many vessels during the civil war. She survives him, with six children: Charles Zenas and Harvey Edgar, mechanical engineers; Anna Louise, Agnes Cornelia, Helen Mary and Elsie Sneden. He died at Yonkers, N. Y., Dec. 20, 1912.

DUVEEN, Henry, art connoisseur, was born at Meppel, Holland, Oct. 26, 1854, son of Joseph and Eva (Van Minden) Duveen, and brother of the late Sir Joseph Duveen. He was given a liberal education and completed his studies at the French College in Meppel in 1868. He soon mastered several languages and became a proficient scholar. Later his father removed to Amsterdam, placing Henry at the Van Gelder Institute, where he took up the study of art, and then joined his brother, Joseph, who three years previously had gone to

Hull, England, and opened an art store. This was the beginning of the famous firm of Duveen Bros., organized in Hull, England, in 1874. In 1879 the headquarters was transferred to London, and was most successfully managed by Joseph (afterward Sir Joseph) Duveen, who later was ably assisted by his eldest son, Joseph Duveen, Jr. Mr. Duveen's extensive and liberal education helped him to acquire an extensive knowledge in the art world, and he is to-day a well-known authority on all subjects pertaining to antiques and objects of art. In 1877 the brothers decided to open a branch house in New York city, and Mr. Henry Duveen went to America to take charge of it. He carried with him some of the best examples of fine old art in furniture, tapestries and paintings. He was the pioneer in introducing to the art connoisseurs of the new world the rare handiwork of previous centuries. He found it necessary to develop a taste for such antiques, and it fell upon his shoulders to educate the American public in the æsthetic value of old art objects. In the first years of the venture the public was not sufficiently educated in works of art, but Mr. Duveen believed in the ultimate success of his venture, and having the courage of his convictions he persisted in his efforts until he had the satisfaction of placing his wares in the homes of the first families of the metropolis. It was through Mr. Duveen that the late James Garland made his great collection of porcelain china, from whose heirs it was afterwards purchased by J. Pierpont Morgan. The latter added many costly specimens, until it is now valued at $3,000,000, and it has been placed in the care of the Metropolitan Museum of Art for safekeeping. Some of the notable collections that his firm has purchased during its career were the Hainauer collection, purchased in Berlin in 1906 for $1,500,000; Rudolph Kann collection, purchased in 1907 for $5,000,000, and the Maurice Kann collection, purchased in 1909 for $2,500,000. The famous wing in the Tate gallery, London, was presented to the English nation by Sir Joseph Duveen. After the latter's death his four sons, Joseph, Louis, Benjamin and Ernest Duveen, constituted the firm, and these four, together with Henry Duveen, the subject of this sketch, are now in the present firm. The firm of Duveen Bros. occupies the foremost place in its special line, and has won a reputation that extends over the entire world. In recognition of all that the brothers have done for the advancement of art, the French government in 1902 made Mr. Henry Duveen, the subject of this sketch, a chevalier of the Legion of Honor, and in 1907 he was decorated with the Cross of the Red Eagle by the German emperor, while King Edward of England conferred the honor of knighthood upon the late Sir Joseph Duveen in 1908. Henry Duveen was married, Aug. 16, 1882, to Dora, daughter of Beare Falcke, of London, and has one son, Geoffrey Duveen, a resident of London, who is married to a daughter of Isaac Lewis, the famous South African magnate.

WINSHIP, Charles Newell, manufacturer, was born at Needham, Mass., Nov. 4, 1863, son of Francis and Catherine (Fitzgerald) Winship. The first member of the family to settle in America was Edward Winship, who came to this country from England in 1635 and settled at Cambridge, Mass. James Winship, the fourth in descent from Edward, served throughout the revolutionary war, and it is related that at one time his wife on the approach of the British fled with her children to a log hut in the woods, where she spent the night running bullets for the revolutionary soldiers. Charles N. Winship was educated in the public schools of Wellesley Hills, and at the age of fourteen obtained a position as utility boy in the Dudley Hosiery Mills at Newton Lower Falls. Within eighteen months he was given charge over the knitting machine, which he operated for two years, after which he went in the same capacity to the Lawrence Mills at Lowell, Mass. From Lowell he went to the Allston Mills at Cottage Farms, Mass., where for three years he was supervisor of the knitting department. He then took charge of the knitting department of the Vesta Mills at Providence, R. I., and after a year and a half there returned to the Allston Mills, which had changed hands in the meantime. There for eight months he managed the plant in co-operation with Miss Elizabeth Boit. Then Mr. Winship and Miss Boit formed a partnership and organized the Harvard Knitting Mills at Cambridgeport. In 1889 they removed to Wakefield, where they established a factory on the third floor of Wakefield Block. The unusual knowledge of the business possessed by both partners, the thoroughness of their methods and the high standard of quality which they set before them from the beginning brought very rapid success and the equipment and staff were continually added to from the start. Its growth was such that within a few years they were forced to erect the present plant near the Wakefield station of the Boston and Maine railway. In 1903 another building was secured, until at the present time the business requires a floor space of six and a quarter acres to furnish the product necessary to fill its orders. The mill operates 550 knitting machines, 450 sewing machines, with a capacity for manufacturing 1,800 dozen garments a day, and employs 950 hands. The top floors of the buildings are used for winding and knitting; the second floors contain the sewing rooms, and the first floor is devoted to the final finishing and shipping. In the manufacture of its goods the Harvard Knitting Mill uses cotton, silk and worsted and consumes 3,000,000 pounds of yarn yearly. There are three brands of goods for which the mill is famous, the "Harvard Mills," "Merode" and "Forest Mills," and its distributing agents are Lord & Taylor, of New York, and Brown, Durrell & Co., of Boston and New York. The company's products have the reputation of being among the finest and best offered to the trade, the mixtures having a particularly high reputation, in the opinion of many good judges being superior to anything of the kind manufactured in this country. No more eloquent testimony to the high quality of these goods can be adduced than the fact that the output of the factory has increased with such marvelous and steady rapidity from the very beginning, and that the goods are in increasingly strong demand among dealers all over the United States. Mr. Winship is one of the leading citizens of Wakefield and since his residence in the town has been prominently identified with all its social, philanthropic, religious and educational interests. He is president of the Wakefield Board of Trade, a trustee of the Beebe Town Library, and a member of the Wakefield Lodge, Knights of Columbus. He was married, Feb. 1, 1887, to Mary Ellen, daughter of Michael and Margaret (Maloney) Burke, of Needham, Mass. They have three children: Charles Francis, Edward Newell and Walter Boit Winship.

BOIT, Elizabeth Eaton, manufacturer, was born at Newton, Mass., July 9, 1849, daughter of James Henry and Amanda Church (Berry) Boit.

Charles N Winship

Elizabeth E Bott

Her father was an engineer and for many years a paper manufacturer at Newton Lower Falls. Miss Boit was educated in the public schools of Newton and at Lasell Seminary at Auburndale. At the age of eighteen she obtained a position as time-keeper at the Dudley Hosiery Knitting Mill at Newton, she soon won promotion to the post of assistant forewoman, from which she was shortly afterward advanced to that of forewoman, and within five years she was in full charge of the finishing department of the factory. When Mr. Scudder established the Allston Mills at Allston, Mass., for the manufacture of hosiery and children's scarlet-wool goods, he appointed Miss Boit superintendent of the new business, and she held that position until the property was sold five years later. She then formed a partnership with Charles N. Winship, who was foreman of the knitting department in the Allston Mill, and in 1888 the firm of Winship, Bolt & Co. established the Harvard Knitting Mill at Cambridge, Mass. In the following year they moved to Wakefield, where they occupied one floor of the Wakefield Block. The firm had a very small capital to start with, but the thorough knowledge of the business possessed by both partners and the high standard which they adopted gradually brought success. The finances of the business as well as the general superintendency of the finishing department are in the hands of Miss Boit, while Mr. Winship attends to the knitting and other branches of the work. Miss Boit is the only woman in the United States and probably in the world who is actively engaged in conducting a large and successful textile fabric manufactory, yet she finds time from her exacting business duties to devote to many interests which are usually looked upon as more within a woman's sphere. She is treasurer of the Aged Women's Home and of the Kosmos Club (a local literary organization), and is actively associated with several other bodies, notably the Ladies' Aid Society of Massachusetts. She is especially interested in the welfare of young girls, particularly those in her employ, and avails herself of every opportunity to further the progress and well-being of the wage-earners of her sex.

BROUSSARD, Robert F., U. S. senator, was born on his father's plantation, new Iberia, La., son of John D. and A. E. (Gonsoulin) Broussard. He was educated at Georgetown University, Washington, D. C., and was graduated in the law school of the Tulane University of Louisiana, at New Orleans, in 1889. He began the practice of his profession in New Iberia and acquired an extensive business throughout the state. He served one term as district (prosecuting) attorney of his district, and although he was re-elected, he resigned to enter congress. He was for twenty-five years a member of the Democratic State Central committee of Louisiana. He served in the U. S. house of representatives for eighteen years—from the 55th to the 63d congress, both inclusive, having been elected to the 63d congress after his election to the U. S. senate. He was nominated for the U. S. senate at the general Democratic state primary in January, 1912, and this nomination was confirmed by the legislature of Louisiana by his election to the senate in May, 1912, for the term beginning Mar. 4, 1915. He was married Jan. 12, 1898, to Marrette Applegate, of New Orleans, La.

NILAN, John Joseph, seventh Roman Catholic bishop of Hartford, Conn., was born at Newburyport, Mass., Aug. 1, 1855. In 1870 he went to Nicolet College, Nicolet, Can., and after being graduated in 1875, entered St. Joseph's Seminary, Troy, N. Y., where he made his theological course and was ordained as priest for the diocese of Boston Dec. 31, 1878. His first mission was at Framingham, followed by service at Abington and at St. James' Church, Boston, until 1892, when he was appointed pastor of St. Joseph's Church, Amesbury, Mass., where he remained eighteen years. He beautified and improved this church and its connected buildings, and built a splendid Gothic chapel at Salisbury Beach. Bishop Tierney of Hartford died in October, 1908, and there was a long delay in the selection of his successor, the choice finally being Father Nilan, who was consecrated Apr. 28, 1910. To the administration of the diocese he directed the same successful qualities of administration as had marked his career as a pastor, especially in providing for the spiritual direction of the many French-Canadians, Poles and Italians added yearly to the congregations of the diocese and in increasing the school facilities of the 40,000 children under his care. There are 445,000 Catholics in the diocese, attended by 389 priests, with 410 churches, chapels and stations. The institutions include four day nurseries, two orphan asylums, five hospitals, two homes for the aged and ninety-three schools and academies.

SMITH, Gerrit, inventor, was born in Providence, R. I., Aug. 18, 1838, son of Ruben and Lovey (Baxter) Smith. He attended the public schools in his native town, and when sixteen years of age entered the service of the Western Union Telegraph Co., of which he became electrical engineer, remaining in the company's employ for fifty-four years, and retiring on a pension in 1905. He was the inventor of the quadruplex system of telegraphy. His invention increased the service of the telegraph companies many times, and he spent many years in Europe introducing his invention. He was also instrumental in introducing the Wheatstone system of telegraphy into the United States. During the civil war he was in the secret service of the Federal government, and had charge of a corps of telegraph operators. Mr. Smith was an interesting writer upon subjects pertaining to telegraphy, being the author of "Looking Backward Sixty Years," an account of his life and experience in connection with the Western Union Telegraph Co., which appeared in the "Telegraph and Telephone Age" in March, 1914. He was married Dec. 17, 1868, to Mary Ellis, daughter of Stephen Spock, of Astoria, L. I., and their children were: Charles Elias and Mary Lovey Smith, the latter the wife of Edgar Paterson Foster, of Amityville, L. I. He died in Amityville, L. I., May 4, 1915.

BENNETT, George Slocum, financier, was born at Wilkes-Barre, Pa., Aug. 17, 1842, son of Ziba and Hannah Fell (Slocum) Bennett. His first American ancestor was James Bennett, who came from England and was made a freeman in Concord, Mass., in 1639; from him and his wife Hannah Wheeler the line of descent is traced through their son Thomas and his wife Elizabeth Thompson; their son Thomas and his wife Sarah Hubbard; their son Deliverance and his wife Mary Biggs; their son William and his wife Abigail Hickock; their son Thaddeus and his wife Mary Platt, and their son Platt and his wife Martha Wheeler, who were the grandparents of George S. Bennett. Ziba Bennett was founder and head of Ziba Bennett & Co., the largest general merchandise business in the Wyoming valley. He founded the private banking house of Bennett, Phelps & Co., of which he was the active head until his death, and was one of the founders and president of the Wyoming Bank, president of the Wilkes-Barre Bridge Co., and the Hollenback Cemetery Association. He was a member of the Pennsylvania assembly in 1833, and was associate judge of Luzerne county in 1842. George Slocum Bennett was graduated at Wesleyan University in 1864, receiving the degree of A.M. in 1867. Entering his father's banking house of Bennett, Phelps & Co., he took an important place in the business life of Wilkes-Barre, and became one of the most able and successful financiers in the state. He was president of the Wyoming National Bank; manager and treasurer of the Wilkes-Barre Bridge Co.; manager of the Hollenback Cemetery Association; president of the Wilkes-Barre Lace Manufacturing Co.; treasurer of the Sheldon Axle Co., and a director of the Wilkes-Barre Gas Co., the Hazard Manufacturing Co. and the Wilkes-Barre Water Co. He loomed large in the civic, religious and philanthropic life of Wilkes-Barre and was an active force in every movement for the moral and material betterment of the city. He was a member of the city council and the board of education; trustee of the First Methodist Episcopal Church; superintendent of its Sunday-school; president of the Wilkes-Barre Y. M. C. A., and a member of its board of managers; member of Wilkes-Barre school board in 1870-73, and 1879-82, and its president in 1883; manager and vice-president of the Wilkes-Barre City Hospital; secretary of the Luzerne County Bible Society; president of the board of trustees of the Wyoming Seminary, Kingston, Pa.; trustee of Wesleyan University, Middletown, Conn., and Drew Theological Seminary, Madison, N J.; delegate to the M. E. general conference in 1896, and a member of the Wyoming Historical and Geological Society of Wilkes-Barre. A memorial resolution of the death of Mr. Bennett, adopted by the directors of the Wyoming National Bank, says in part: "His long experience in banking, his conservatism, intelligence, high sense of honor, and noble character, eminently fitted him for the position he so faithfully and forcefully sustained, and which aided greatly in maintaining the high standards and position of the bank. Mr. Bennett's interest in and labors for the welfare of our community raised him to the front rank of our citizens, and his loss to the many varied and important financial and charitable institutions with which he was connected is most serious and far reaching. Beyond and above all this, his work and love for his church and the religious life for which it stands—to which he consecrated his best efforts, and in which he achieved his noblest success—has made his loss more heartfelt and irreparable." Mr. Bennett was married at Kingston, Pa., Sept. 7, 1871, to Ellen Woodward, daughter of Rev. Reuben Nelson and had three children: Martha Phelps, wife of Lawrence Bullard Jones; Reuben Nelson and Ziba Platt Bennett. He died at Wilkes-Barre, Pa., Jan. 2, 1910.

MYERS, George Smith, tobacconist, was born at Flint Hill, Mo., Aug. 4, 1832, son of George Myers, a well-to-do planter of Virginia, who moved his family to Missouri shortly before the son's birth. His grandfather was George Myers, a native of England, who came to the United States in the latter part of the eighteenth century and settled in Virginia, where he acquired a large estate in Albemarle county. George Smith Myers attended private schools, receiving the best education that the times afforded. He began his business career in the employ of a tobacco manufac-

turer at Wentzville, Mo., and when he was eighteen years of age he was sent to Louisiana, Mo., as superintendent of a tobacco factory at a salary of $500 a year, which was a large stipend for those days. He made a trip to California about this time for his health, and after spending a year on the Pacific coast returned by way of Cape Horn. He then formed a partnership with James T. Drummond, and established the Myers & Drummond Tobacco Co. at Alton, Ill. In 1872 he removed to St. Louis, Mo., and within a year purchased the interest of Henry Dausman in the tobacco business of Liggett & Dausman, and the firm name thereafter was Liggett & Myers. Mr. Myers brought to the new undertaking a thorough mastery of all the details of the tobacco manufacturing business. He had a natural bent for mechanics, was thoroughly practical, and was endowed with traits of perseverance, energy, industry and ambition. His mechanical ability resulted in the invention of various labor-saving machines which improved and simplified the manufacture of tobacco. Under his general management the firm of Liggett & Myers grew rapidly, and became recognized as one of the foremost manufacturers of tobacco in the United States. The company was incorporated in 1878 as the Liggett & Myers Tobacco Manufacturing Co. It added new factories from time to time as the business expanded, until in 1897 it erected what for many years was the largest tobacco factory in the world. The development and upbuilding of this industry made the city of St. Louis one of the tobacco centers of the country, an achievement that may be credited to Mr. George Smith Myers more than any other one individual. In 1899 the Continental Tobacco Co. (afterward the American Tobacco Co.) purchased the Liggett & Myers Tobacco Co. at a price considered exorbitant at the time, but subsequent events proved that it was about the best investment that the American Tobacco Co. ever made. When this sale was consummated Mr. Myers retired from all business activities, and thereafter devoted his time and attention to the management of his various estates and to the development of real estate holdings in both St. Louis and Kansas City. He owned a large game preserve, Teton Lodge, comprising several thousand acres at the foot of the Teton mountains in Idaho, where he usually spent several months each summer with a company of congenial friends hunting large game. At his beautiful country place at Glendale, Mo., he maintained a pack of foxhounds, and he was also the founder and first president of the Quiver Shooting Club, one of the most exclusive hunting clubs of St. Louis. He was identified in many ways with the growth and development of the city of St. Louis, and owned several model farms in St. Charles county. He was a director of the Union Trust Co., as well as of most of the leading banks of St. Louis. He also maintained a winter home at Redlands, Cal., where the last years of his life were spent. Mr. Myers was married June 21, 1865, to Mary B., daughter of Alexander and Eleanor Buchanan, of Troy, Mo. She died in 1900, leaving three daughters: Georgie Estell, wife of Herbert Coppell, of New York; Mildred M., wife of John S. Cravens, of Pasadena, Cal., and Robert Tansey, wife of William Downey, of Canada. Of high aims and large views, Mr. Myers had marked personal characteristics which commanded great respect in the community in which he dwelt. Conspicuous among these were his ambition to succeed, his perseverance and application in the conduct of his business, and a capacious, energetic and firm mind. In a published interview which he gave out in 1900 he said: ''I do not know that as a young man I felt that I would make a big fortune. I was little concerned about money. I was in love with my business and it satisfied me. I believe money will come to any man who loves his business and finds satisfaction in it to the exclusion of worry whether he will or will not be a rich man. I was determined to make my business the biggest of its kind. Determination in business is half the battle.'' He died at Redlands, Cal., Aug. 29, 1910.

SMITH, J[onas] Waldo, engineer, was born in Lincoln, Mass., Mar. 9, 1861, son of Francis and Abigail Prescott (Baker) Smith. His first American ancestor was John Smith, who was a proprietor of Watertown, Mass., in 1636, and was admitted freeman in 1637; from him and his wife Isabella, the subject of this sketch is descended through their son Thomas and his wife, Mary Knapp; their son Jonathan and his wife, Jane Peabody; their son Zechariah and his wife, Susanna Grout; their son Jonas and his wife, Thankful Fiske; their son Zechariah and his wife, Sarah Bemis; their son Jonas and his wife, Abigail Fiske, and their son Francis and his wife, Abigail Prescott Baker. Jonas Smith, 1st, was in the revolutionary war and served as second lieutenant in Capt. Caleb Brooke's company in 1776-77. Jonas Waldo Smith was educated in the public schools of Lincoln, and at the age of sixteen secured a position in the local water-works, where a year later he became chief engineer. That one so young and without technical training could hold such a position is strong evidence of his unusual ability. This first work convinced him of the value of a more technical education and he resigned his position to take a two-years' course at Phillips Exeter Academy. After an interval as assistant engineer of the Essex Co. of Lawrence, Mass., he entered the Massachusetts Institute of Technology, and was graduated C.E. in 1887. During his vacations he worked with a number of water companies, particularly the Holyoke Water Power Co., with whom he remained for three years after his graduation. In 1890 he became connected with the East Jersey Water Co., under Clemens Herschel, and upon the latter's retirement, ten years later, was appointed chief engineer. During this period he was identified with a number of important water system installations. He was resident engineer in charge of the construction of four reservoirs and the dam on the Pequannock watershed, now a part of the Newark water system; had charge of the construction of the water purification plant at Little Falls, one of the best known of its kind in existence; was engineer and superintendent of the Passaic Co. of Paterson, and was engineer of both the Montclair Water Co. and of the Aquacknonk Water Co. of Passaic. The plant of the Passaic company for filtering and purifying a municipal water supply was a step far in advance of anything previously undertaken, and, indeed, no better or more successful system has yet been installed elsewhere. In 1903 Mr. Smith was appointed chief engineer for the aqueduct commission of New York city and had charge of the completion of the famous Croton dam, which is one of the greatest masonry dams in the world. When the New York state legislature, in June, 1905, passed an act providing for an additional water supply for New York city, Mr. Smith was selected as chief engineer of the board of water supply under the new law. This, the greatest water supply project in the world, provided for carrying water from the Catskill mountains to New York city in an aqueduct seventeen feet in diameter, capable of supplying 500,000,000 gallons of water per day. It included the building of four high reservoirs. The Ashokan reservoir, which is thirteen miles west of Kingston, N. Y., and its tributary watersheds of Esopus and Catskill creeks cover an area of 255 and 163 square miles, respectively. The reservoir, formed by the building of the Olive Bridge dam and a number of dikes, is approximately twelve miles long by one mile wide, with a maximum depth of 190 feet. When full, the surface of the water is 500 feet above sea level. Leading from the Ashokan reservoir is the Catskill aqueduct, into which, through future developments, may also empty the Lackawax reservoir (supplied by the Rondout watershed, having an area of 176 square miles), and the Prattsville Reservoir (supplied by the Schoharie watershed of 228 square miles), the aqueduct bringing the water to Storm King, four miles above West Point, then under the Hudson river in a tunnel to Breakneck mountain, from Breakneck mountain to Kensico reservoir, and from the latter to Hill View reservoir in Yonkers, just north of the city line. The most difficult tunnel to bore was the one under the Hudson river between Storm King and Breakneck mountains. Here Mr. Smith found it necessary to cut through solid rock at a distance of 1,100 feet below the surface of the river. The Catskill aqueduct is about ninety-two miles long, fifty-five miles being cut-and-cover, thirty-one miles tunnels and six miles of steel pipes. The tunnel from Hill View reservoir passes under the Borough of Bronx, the Harlem river, the Borough of Manhattan and the East river and terminates in Brooklyn. At the Brooklyn terminal water is piped to Queens and to Richmond, the pipes to the latter being of cast iron, crossing the Narrows and discharging into an equalizing reservoir at Silver Lake, 225 feet above sea level. The tunnel is circular in section, reducing from fifteen feet to eleven feet in diameter, lined with concrete, and varying from 200 to 750 feet deep in solid bed-rock. It thus passes far below all subways and building foundations. About every 4,000 feet connections were made to the present distributing system, through controlling valves set to furnish the water at a lower pressure than that in the tunnel. The total cost of the entire system as completed, including the development of four large Catskill mountain watersheds, as needed by the growth of the city of New York, the necessary reservoirs, aqueduct and all appurtenances was $176,000,000. This project was one of the most difficult engineering feats ever attempted and may be compared in size and importance to the construction of the Panama Canal. Mr. Smith is a quiet, unassuming, extremely hard-working man. He possesses the characteristics, notable in all great executives, of being able to keep in intimate touch with the smaller details of his complex work. His temperament is strenuous both in work and play, and his recreations are all of the most vigorous outdoor kind. He is a member of the American Society of Civil Engineers, the Institute of Civil Engineers of Great Britain, the American Society of Mechanical Engineers, Municipal Engineers of the City of New York, Century Association, Engineers' Club, Hardware Club, Technology Club, New England Society, Hamilton Club of Paterson, N. J.; Franklin Institute of Philadelphia, New England Water Works Association, American Water Works Association and the New York Chamber of Commerce. He is the author of a number of papers on technical subjects delivered before engineering bodies, the most notable being ''Flow of Water Through 30-inch Gate-Valve,'' before the American Society of Civil Engineers. He is unmarried.

NOYES, Edward Alling, banker, was born at Eastport, Me., Oct. 6, 1839, son of Joseph Cobham and Helen M. (Alling) Noyes, and a descendant of Rev. William Noyes, the earliest known ancestor of his immediate family. William Noyes, a native of England (1568), was graduated at Oxford, and was rector at Cholderton, where he died in 1622. His fourth son, Nicholas, sailed with his brother for New England on the ship Mary and John in 1633, and landed at what is now Ipswich, Mass. Nicholas' wife was Mary Cutting, and the line of descent is traced through their son Cutting, who married Elizabeth Knight; their son Joseph (the first of the family to settle in Portland, Me.), who married Jane Dole; their son Josiah, who married Mary Lunt; their son Joseph, who married Mary Cobham, and their son Jacob, who married Ann Jones, and was the grandfather of the subject of this sketch. The father, Joseph C. Noyes (1798-1868), was a prominent merchant and shipchandler of Eastport and Portland; he served in the 25th congress, being the first Free Soiler from eastern Maine, and was called the ''Star in the East.'' His son, Edward Alling Noyes, was educated in the public schools of Portland. He acquired a thorough knowledge of the banking business as clerk in the Portland Savings Bank under the direction of his father, who was the bank's treasurer. He was there for four years, and in 1863 transferred his services to the National Traders' Bank, of which he was teller for five years. Upon the death of his father in 1868, he returned to the Portland Savings Bank as assistant treasurer, and in 1877 was elected treasurer, a position he still holds. The Portland Savings Bank is one of the leading institutions of its kind in Maine. During Mr. Noyes' long administration as treasurer the bank's deposits have increased from $4,320,000 in 1877 to $13,984,000 in 1912. The bank has been administered for the growth of the community. A storage warehouse, the Wadsworth apartment house and Keith's Theater have been built on land belonging to the bank, and the banking building made fireproof. The loans on mortgages of real estate increased from $1,251,000 in 1877 to $2,549,000 in 1912. Mr. Noyes has been president of the Western Maine Music Festival Association for thirteen years. He was first librarian of Portland public library, without pay, 1867-78; has been its treasurer since 1872, and was instrumental in procuring and building the stack room for the library. He is also president of the Savings Bank Association of Maine and the Portland Safe Deposit Co., and a director of the Union Mutual Life Insurance Co. He was elected a member of the city council of Portland in 1882, serving four terms, and since 1904 has been a member of the commission of cemeteries and public grounds. Mr. Noyes was married in 1863 to Julia Augusta, daughter of John Edwards, and granddaughter of Lieut. Thomas Edwards, the first judge advocate-general of the revolutionary army. Mrs. Noyes died in 1907, leaving five children: Charles Edwards, Helen A., wife of Winthrop Jordan; Joseph Cobham, Julia Edwards and Sidney W. Noyes.

EASTON, Edward Denison, lawyer and organizer of the talking machine business, was born at Gloucester, Mass., Apr. 10, 1856, son of Denison Mitchell and Mary (Lyle) Easton. The first of his family in America was Joseph Easton, who

came from England in 1633 and settled at Newtowne, afterwards called Cambridge, Mass. Mr. Easton's father (1823-1903) was a school teacher, and subsequently a real estate agent up to the time of his death. The son was educated in the public schools of Arcola and Paterson, N. J., until the age of fifteen, when he began his business career. He was stenographer for several New York newspapers, and served for nearly two years as reporter and assistant editor of the Hackensack (N. J.) ''Republican.'' In 1873 he was appointed stenographer of the U. S. lighthouse board in Washington, and in this capacity he early reached the head of his profession, earning with his pen the phenomenal sum of $30,000 in one year. He reported the Guiteau trial, the Star Route trials, and nearly every event of national importance for fifteen years, including debates in congress and the proceedings of congressional committees. He was the first official reporter of the interstate commerce commission. Meanwhile he took up the study of law at Georgetown University, and was graduated in 1889 with the degree of LL.M. He became a member of the bar of the supreme court of the District of Columbia, making corporation law a specialty. About this time his attention was attracted to the possibilities of the phonograph as an adjunct to business in the matter of committing to that instrument translations of stenographic notes for the use of the transcriber, but the tinfoil which incased the cylinder proved unsuitable for such practical work, and the project was held in abeyance until the problem was solved by the invention of Messrs. Tainter and Bell of the wax cylinder device, whereon could be engraved the markings produced by the vibrations of the diaphragm. With this missing link supplied a practical talking machine was realized, and Mr. Easton then abandoned his shorthand business to take up the development and prosecution of the talking machine business. He was one of the original stockholders of the American Graphophon Co., which was organized on May 15, 1887, and in 1889 he organized the Columbia Phonograph Co., which became the largest distributors of talking machines in existence. In 1893 a coalition was formed between the American Graphophone Co., the owner of the patents, and the Columbia Phonograph Co., and Mr. Easton, as president and counsel for both companies and the largest stockholder, came into control of the market. The American Graphophone Co. owns in Bridgeport, Conn., the greatest factory in the world devoted to this purpose, another in London, England, and record making plants not only in the British metropolis, but also in Paris, Vienna, Milan, St. Petersburg, City of Mexico, Tokio and Peking, where records of the great artists are made, and where the most famous bands, orchestras and instrumentalists play for an audience which embraces the entire world. Besides the instrument used primarily for amusement, the American Graphophone Co. also manufactures the dictaphone, a machine that has been adopted by many of the largest business houses for correspondence. This machine has been brought to an astonishing degree of perfection. Accuracy, speed, independence, privacy, economy, convenience and division of labor are some of the advantages of the dictaphone which are claimed by its makers. The company has sales depots and agencies in all the principal cities of the world, and owns fundamental patents, under the license of which Edison as well as every other lawful manufacturer of talking machines now operates. The old methods

J. WALDO SMITH
CIVIL ENGINEER

EDWARD D. EASTON
MANUFACTURER

EDWARD A. NOYES
BANKER

JOSEPH P. IDDINGS
SCIENTIST

of making records have been superseded by a new and better process, so that instead of duplicating mechanically from a master record, they are now moulded in what are known as metal masters. This, however, refers only to cylindrical records. The disk records are stamped under a very heavy hydraulic pressure. Up to a certain point the processes are identical. The song or speech or brand selection is first taken in wax, and these "wax-masters," so called, are plated with metal, in one case forming a copper mould in which thousands of cylindrical records are cast, and in the other a metal disk from which as many copies —millions if necessary—are made by stamping them. Mr. Easton was president of the Volta Graphophone Co., the Burt Manufacturing Co., the Eaglesmere Co., and the Waterpower Securities Co.; and vice-president of the Hackensack Hospital Association. He was twice married: first in Washington, D. C., Jan. 26, 1876, to Hattie Kaldenbach, who died in 1881; and second in Washington, D. C., May 24, 1883, to Helen Mortimer, daughter of Dr. John P. Jefferis. He has one son, Mortimer Denison Easton, and four daughters: Hattie, wife of C. W. Woddrop; Mary, wife of Earl Godwin; Florence Lyle and Helen Easton. He died at Central Valley, N. Y., Apr. 30, 1915.

IDDINGS, Joseph Paxson, scientist, was born in Baltimore, Md., Jan. 21, 1857, son of William Penn and Almira (Gillet) Iddings, and a descendant of Richard Iddings, a Quaker, who came to America near the end of the seventeenth century and died in Chester county, Pa., in 1726. The line is traced through Richard's son William and his wife, Mary ————; their son William, who married Hannah Lewis; their son James, who married Mary Pierce and their son Caleb Pierce, who married Harriet Hill Jackson, and was the grandfather of Prof. Iddings. He was graduated Ph.B. at Sheffield Scientific School, Yale University, in 1877; took a post-graduate course in analytical chemistry while serving as assistant in surveying and mechanical drawing at Sheffield; was a student in economic geology and assaying at Columbia University under Prof. Newberry, and then went to Heidelberg University, where he studied microscopical petrography with Rosenbusch. In 1880 he was appointed assistant geologist on the U. S. geological survey, and as assistant to Arnold Hague was engaged in field work with Charles D. Walcott in the Eureka district, Nev. He made a special study of igneous rocks of the Eureka district, reviewing the microscopical petrography of igneous rocks of Nevada and Utah which had been previously studied and described by Zirkel, and studying and describing the volcanic rocks of the Pacific coast volcanoes which had been collected by Arnold Hague and S. F. Emmons, and those of Salvador, collected by Goodyear. During 1883–90 he made a study of the geology of the Yellowstone National Park, in association with Arnold Hague, W. H. Weed and G. M. Wright. His studies were directed particularly to the crystallization of spherulites and lithophyses in obsidian, and to the crystallization of magmas as intruded bodies of various kinds, especially within conduits of ancient volcanoes, and the comparison of these forms of crystallization with those of chemically similar magmas that had solidified as extrusive lavas. During 1888–92 he was geologist of the survey. In 1892 he was appointed associate professor of petrology at the University of Chicago, which included also the teaching of mineralogy. In 1895 he became pro-

fessor of petrology and held that chair until 1908. In that period, in association with Whitman Cross, L. V. Pirsson and H. S. Washington, he developed a quantitative system for the classification of igneous rocks based on their chemical and mineral compositions, and proposed a systematic nomenclature for the resulting divisions and subdivisions of rock magmas, and a possible system for the nomenclature of the crystallized rocks. In the pursuit of his special studies Prof. Iddings has visited Great Britain, central Europe, Norway, Finland, Russia, Trans-Caucasia, Japan, Manchuria, China, the Philippine Islands, Dutch East Indies, New Zealand, Australia, Tahiti, the Leeward or Society Islands, and the Marquesas, collecting material for microscopical and chemical investigation. Besides his official reports for the geological survey, he has written papers on the petrography of the rock collections made by him, and general discussions on the character of prismatic and other forms of parting in bodies of igneous rocks; on the crystallization of igneous rocks in general; on their mineral and chemical composition, and on phases of the problem of petrographical provinces, or the geographical distribution of igneous rocks, and he published an abridged translation of Rosenbusch's book on the microscopical characteristics of rock-making minerals. He is the author of: "The Quantitative Classification of Igneous Rocks" (with Whitman Cross, L. V. Pirsson and H. S. Washington, 1903); "Rock Minerals" (1906); "Igneous Rocks" (1909; and "The Problem of Volcanism" (1914). He received the honorary degree of Sc.D. in 1907 from Yale University. Prof. Iddings is a member of the National Academy of Sciences and the American Philosophical Society, a fellow of the Geological Society of America and the American Association for the Advancement of Science, and a foreign member of the Geological Society of London, the Scientific Society of Christiania and the Société Française de Minéralogie. He is unmarried. Portrait opposite page 390.

JOHNSON, Richard W., soldier, was born near Smithland, Livingston co., Ky., Feb. 7, 1827, son of James and Louisa (Harmon) Johnson and a descendant of James Johnson, who came from England in 1648, having procured a grant of land either from the Crown or from Lord Baltimore, for the purpose of planting. The family has contributed much to the civic, scientific and national life of America and includes such noted names as Vicepres. Johnson, Reverdy Johnson, William Cost Johnson of Maryland, Richard W. Johnson, late senator from Arkansas; W. H. and R. M. Johnson of Mississippi, and Dr. John M. Johnson of Atlanta, Ga. Richard W Johnson, the subject of this sketch, was graduated at the United States Military Academy in 1849 and assigned to the 6th infantry. He was promoted second lieutenant, 1st infantry, June 10, 1850; first lieutenant, 2nd cavalry, Mar. 3, 1855, and captain Dec. 1, 1856. In 1849-61 he served on frontier and scouting duty, mainly in the Southwest, and was engaged in numerous skirmishes with the Indians. At the beginning of the civil war he was employed in guarding the upper Potomac and took part in the action at Falling Water, Va., July 2, 1861. He was appointed lieutenant-colonel of the 1st Kentucky cavalry and volunteers (Federal army), Aug. 28, 1861, and on Oct. 10 of the same year was commissioned brigadier general of volunteers. In the Mississippi campaign (Oct., 1861, to June, 1862) he commanded a brigade and participated in the battle of Shiloh and in the siege of

Corinth. He commanded a division of the army of the Ohio in the Tennessee campaign and distinguished himself at the battles of Stone River, Liberty Cap, Chickamauga and Missionary Ridge, receiving the brevets of lieutenant-colonel and colonel for his gallant services. He was in command of a division of the 14th corps of the army of the Cumberland in the Georgia campaign and took an active part in all the engagements up to and including the battle of New Hope Church, May 28, 1864, where he was severely wounded. At the battle of Nashville, Dec. 15-16, 1864, he commanded a division of cavalry and displayed great ability and gallantry, for which he was breveted major-general of volunteers and brigadier-general United States army. He was then assigned to the staff of Gen. George H. Thomas and served as provost-marshal-general and acting judge-advocate of the military division of the Tennessee (1865-66), doing much to ameliorate conditions between the warring factions. On March 13, 1865, he received the brevet of major-general, United States army, for gallant and meritorious services in the field during the war, and on Jan. 15, 1866, he was mustered out of the volunteer service. He served as acting-judge-advocate of the department of the Tennessee from August, 1866, until March 15, 1867, and of the department of the Cumberland until Oct. 12 of the latter year, when he retired from active service with the brevet rank of major-general. He was professor of military science at the University of Missouri in 1868-69 and at the University of Minnesota in 1869-70. General Johnson was the author of "A Soldier's Reminiscences in Peace and War," "Life of General George H. Thomas," "Pistol Practice," "History of Fort Snelling" and various magazine articles. He was married first, at Mendota, Minn., Oct. 30, 1850, to Rachel E., daughter of Gen. James Steele, by whom he had three sons: Alfred Bainbridge, Richard W. and Henry Sibley; second, at Catasauqua, Pa., Feb. 14, 1894, to Julia Macfarlane, daughter of James Clinton Carson, by whom he had one son, John Macfarlane. General Johnson died in St. Paul, Minn., Apr. 21, 1897.

JOLINE, Adrian Hoffman, lawyer, was born at Sing Sing (now Ossining), N. Y., June 30, 1850, son of Charles Oliver and Mary (Hoffman) Joline; grandson of John Joline, of Princeton, N. J., and a descendant of Andre Joline, a Huguenot, who settled in New York. His father was adjutant of the 2d Ohio volunteers in the Mexican war and brevet colonel in the civil war; and his mother was the daughter of Dr. Adrian Kissam Hoffman and a sister of Gov. John T. Hoffman. Dr. Hoffman was the grandson of Martinus Hoffman, of Red Hook, and Alida Livingston, whose father, Philip Livingston, was the son of Robert Livingston, Lord of Livingston Manor. Mr. Joline was prepared for college at Mount Pleasant Academy, Sing Sing, and under the private tuition of Rev. James I. Helm. He was clerk of a military commission at Norfolk, Va. (1863), and in 1864 clerk of a military commission which sat at Fort La-Fayette. In 1866-67 he was employed in the street commissioner's office and the mayor's office in New York city. Entering Princeton College in 1867, he was graduated in 1870 with the degree of A.B., and received the degree of A.M three years later. He studied law at Columbia College Law School, was graduated LL.B. in 1872, and began his practice with ex-Judge William H. Leonard. In December, 1875, he became connected with the well-known firm of Butler, Stillman & Hubbard, of which William Allen Butler (q. v.) was senior partner. He was made a member of that firm in 1881 and in 1896 the firm name was changed to Butler, Notman, Joline & Mynderse. Two years after the death of Mr. Butler he organized the firm of Joline, Larkin & Rathbone on Jan. 1, 1905, which still continues. After 1884 Mr. Joline's practice related principally to railway and other corporations. He was one of the counsel for the Central Trust Co. of New York, and had charge of most of that company's litigations. He was associated as junior or leading counsel with many reorganizations of railroads and other corporations, and was counsel in a large number of suits relating to the foreclosure of railway mortgages throughout the country. He was one of the counsel for the Equitable Life Assurance Society in 1905, and for some years the New York counsel of the Missouri, Kansas and Texas Railway Co., as well as general counsel of the Toledo, St. Louis and Western Railway Co. Having served as a director of the Missouri, Kansas and Texas Railway Co., he became chairman of the board in 1906, and was president of the company during 1906-09. He was also a director of many other companies. In association with Douglas Robinson he was appointed receiver of the Metropolitan Street Railway Co. in New York city in September, 1907, and was engaged in operating that road until Jan. 1, 1912. Mr. Joline was a lawyer of thorough learning and sound qualities who achieved a foremost place before the American bar. For many years he collected autograph letters and manuscripts of distinguished people, and had a list of over 14,000 signatures and autograph letters. It embraced a complete set of the signers of the Declaration of Independence, including a letter of Hart, but signatures only of Lynch and Gwinnett; all the presidents and vice-presidents of the United States, with several letters of Washington; letters from every cabinet member, and practically all the members of the Continental congress; letters or signatures of all the kings of England from Henry VII., including a letter signed by Henry VIII., written to Pope Clement VII., on May 27, 1553; and of all the kings of France from Charles VI.; the manuscript of a short unpublished story of Charlotte Bronte and of a book of her poems; the manuscript of Barry Cornwall's "Life of Charles Lamb"; a novel of Alexander Dumas'; manuscript of Southey's "Curse of Kehama" and of Moore's "Epicurean"; letters of Charles and Mary Lamb, Byron, Wordsworth, Shelley, Keats and other British authors and poets, and of Admiral Nelson; the generals of the American revolution, and all the prominent generals and officers of the civil war. He wrote a book on his hobby entitled, "Meditations of an Autograph Collector" (1902), and was also the author of "Diversions of a Book Lover" (1903), "At the Library Table" (1910), "Edgehill Essays" (1911), and several other books, privately printed. He delivered a course of lectures before the School of Business Administration of Harvard University on "The Method and Conduct of the Reorganization of Corporations," in 1909 and in 1910. The degree of LL.D. was conferred upon him by Princeton University in 1904. Mr. Joline was a member of the American Bar Association, New York State Bar Association, Bar Association of the City of New York, of which he served as vice-president and chairman of the executive committee; Virginia Historical Society, New Jersey Historical Society, Historical Society of the City of New York, American Historical Society, and numerous societies in

ADRIAN H. JOLINE
LAWYER

GEORGE R. BUCKMAN
BANKER

STEPHEN BIRCH
MINING ENGINEER

EDWARD PRICKETT
MANUFACTURER

New York city, and of the Century, University, Grolier, Barnard, Princeton, St. Elmo, and Down Town clubs, Caxton Club and Dofob's of Chicago, and the Bibliophile Society of Boston. He was married, July 12, 1876, to Mary E., daughter of Francis Larkin, of Ossining, N. Y. Mr. Joline died in New York city, Oct. 15, 1912.

BUCKMAN, George Rex, banker, was born in Montgomery county, Penn., Nov. 26, 1853, son of Albert and Emily (Rex) Buckman. He was educated in the public schools of Philadelphia, and was graduated at Philadelphia High School. Desiring to learn the machine business, he apprenticed himself to Messrs. William Sellers & Co., the well-known machine tool makers of Philadelphia. His health failed in 1879, and removing to Colorado Springs, Colo., he became interested in this famous health resort and its growth and development. He was one of the organizers of the Colorado Springs chamber of commerce and was its secretary from 1891–96. In 1896 he joined the banking firm of William P. Bonbright & Co. of New York and became a partner in 1904. He is a member of the El Paso Club of Colorado Springs, and the Cheyenne Mountain Country Club. He was married July 27, 1899, to Gertrude, daughter of Martin Luther Wolffe, of Cambridge, Mass.

BIRCH, Stephen, mining engineer, was born in New York city, March 24, 1872, son of Stephen and Emily (Marshall) Birch and grandson of Stephen Birch, who came to the United States about 1840, and died shortly after, leaving an orphan son, Stephen (father of our subject). On his mother's side, he comes from the family of Chief Justice John Marshall, of Virginia. Stephen Birch was educated at Trinity School, New York city, and at the New York University. After a period of engineering work under William Barclay Parsons, he entered the School of Mines at Columbia University and finished his course in 1898. Immediately afterward, he made a tour of inspection of mining properties in the West. Upon his return he was commissioned by H. O. Havemeyer to examine mining lands in Alaska, and the result of his report was the purchase of the Bonanza property (Kennecott Mines), by Havemeyer, Norman Schultz, and James H. Ralph. He was one of the first to recognize the splendid natural resources of Alaska, and a large part of its very rapid development is due to his recommendation. He opened the first large copper mines and built the first concentrating plant in the Copper river country at Kennecott. He also developed and put on a producing basis the Beatson Copper Mines, located on Latouche Island, Alaska. When the Alaska Development and Mineral Co. was organized as a holding company for all the mines and plants of the Morgan-Guggenheim Syndicate, Mr. Birch was made vice-president and general manager, the president being William Pierson Hamilton of J. P. Morgan & Co. Mr. Birch has spent every summer for fifteen years in Alaska, giving his personal attention to the development of mineral property. In addition to his copper interests in Alaska, he is vice-president of the Braden Copper Co., whose mines are located in Chili, South America, and controlled by the Guggenheim interests, and he is director of the Northwestern Commercial Co., the Northwestern Steamship Co., the Alaska Steamship Co., the Copper River and Northwestern Railway Co., vice-president and general manager of the Kennecott Mines Co., and president of the Beatson Copper Co. He is a member of the Engineers, Columbia University, Riding, Sleepy Hollow Country Club,

City and Recess clubs of New York city, and the Rainer Club and Seattle Golf and Country Club of Seattle, Washington.

WHITNEY, Willis Rodney, chemist, was born in Jamestown, N. Y., Aug. 22, 1868, son of John Jay and Mrs. Agnes (Reynolds) Tew Whitney. His technical training was obtained at the Massachusetts Institute of Technology, where he was graduated in 1890. After teaching at the institute as assistant professor of theoretical chemistry, he went to Germany to take a special course at the University of Leipsic, where he received the degree of Ph.D. in 1896. Returning to the United States he was assistant professor in the Massachusetts Institute of Technology until 1904; was non-resident associate professor of theoretical chemistry during 1904–08, and since 1908 he has been non-resident professor of chemical research. In collaboration with Prof. Arthur A. Noyes he developed a recovery process for alcohol and ether from collodion, a discovery which practically insured the commercial practicability of the present photographic film. In 1901 he was appointed director of the research laboratory of the General Electric Co. at Schenectady, N. Y. This was a new office with the General Electric Co., and in fact was one of the earliest of its kind in the history of manufacturing. He was given free rein in planning the details and organizing the work, and beginning with a small staff of assistants he has developed the laboratory into one of the most important departments of the business, employing the services of over 200 scientists and assistants. It has attained a world-wide reputation in the realm of science. In his scientific researches, Dr. Whitney has made a special study of chromium sulphate compounds, colloids and the corrosion of iron. In 1915 he erected a wireless telephone system, connecting the Schenectady plant with the Pittsfield plant of the General Electric Co., embodying a number of new principles of his own invention. He has published many technical papers of scientific value, the more important of which are a translation of Le Blanc's "Electrochemistry" (1906), "Solubility Determinations," "Colloids," "Corrosion of Iron," "Chemistry of Light," "Carbon Brushes," "Vacua," "Phenomena of Catalysis." In 1915 he was appointed a member of the U. S. Naval Consulting Board. He is a member of the American Association for the Advancement of Science, the American Institute of Electrical Engineers, the American Institute of Mining Engineers, the American Chemical Society, of which he was president in 1910; the American Electrochemical Society, of which he was president in 1911; the American Academy of Arts and Sciences, the American Physical Society, the British Institute of Metals, the Mohawk Golf Club and the Chemists' Club of New York. He is a director of the Mercy Hospital, Schenectady, and a trustee of the Albany Medical College. In 1916 he was awarded the Willard Gibbs medal by the American Chemical Society. He was married June 24, 1890, to Evelyn B., daughter of J. Harvey Jones, of Jamestown, N. Y., and has one daughter, Evelyn Agnes, wife of Van Alstyne Schermerhorn.

HOLLOWAY, Ward Beecher, merchant and promoter, was born at Nittany Hall, Centre co., Pa., Jan. 6, 1864, son of Joseph K. and Mittie (Brown) Holloway, and a descendant of Joseph Holloway, who emigrated from England in 1700 and settled in Chester county, Pa. Joseph Holloway's wife was Hannah Ball, and the line of descent is traced through their son William and his wife Mary, their son Joseph and his wife Rachael, and their son John B. and his wife, Margaret Painter, who were the grandparents of the subject of this sketch. His father was a practicing physician. Ward B. Holloway was educated in the public schools of Akron, O., and Oberlin College. He studied pharmacy in Philadelphia and subsequently took a course at the Eastman Business College, Poughkeepsie, N. Y. He began his business career as a pharmacist in Akron, O., but shortly thereafter removed to Williamsport, Pa., where, for a brief period, he conducted a drug store. Entering the employ of the Rochester Brewing Co. as its Lock Haven representative, he established a bottling works in that city with such success that his firm sent him to Williamsport to establish a central Pennsylvania agency, with branches at Hazleton, Mahanoy City and other points, to supply the trade in numerous smaller towns in that section. His untiring efforts, his remarkable activity and the apparent simple ease with which he secured new trade while holding and increasing the old did not pass unnoticed. Recognizing his unusual abilities the Rochester Brewing Co. sent him to Boston to assume entire control of its Eastern agency, and he served several years in that capacity with a continuation of the success that marked his efforts in Pennsylvania. In 1898 he organized the Harvard Brewing Co., of Lowell, Mass. The ultimate success of this company was more than its promoters had anticipated, and soon their product was in such demand that this model plant was enlarged several times, and is to-day one of the most complete and modern breweries in the East. At the time of his death Mr. Holloway was treasurer and general manager. In 1901 King C. Gillette, of Boston, invented a safety razor. He took his patents to Mr. Holloway and the latter organized the company for its manufacture. In a short time he became known as one of the most liberal and energetic advertisers in America. In 1906 his expenses in this direction alone were more than one million dollars—but the outlay of that enormous sum brought big results. Mr. Holloway was secretary and treasurer of this concern, and at the time of his death factories for the manufacture of ''the Gillette razor'' were located in Boston, Montreal, Berlin, London and Paris. He had also numerous mining and banking interests. He was a thirty-second degree Mason, member of Adelphi Lodge, South Boston; Brotherhood Patriotic Order of Elks and Knights of Pythias. His personal attainment was very great, for he added to a singular symmetry and elevation of character an unusual intellectual culture. His literary taste was unfailing and his reading thorough and extensive. His influence over others was great, and he inspired much affection from all with whom he came in contact. His liberality was marked, and many general charities profited during his lifetime by his lavish generosity. He was married in 1884 to Katherine C., daughter of John Chatham, of Lock Haven, Pa., who survived him with two children, Ethel and Leona Holloway. He died in Santa Barbara, Cal., Jan. 4, 1909. Portrait opp. p. 392.

BRYANT, William Sohier, otologist, was born in Boston, Mass., May 15, 1861, son of Henry and Elizabeth Brimmer (Sohier) Bryant. The family is descended from Rollo through Count Godfrey Brion. The founder of the family in America was William Bryant, who settled in Boston about 1677. Henry Bryant served in the French army in Algiers and in the 20th Massachusetts regiment as surgeon during the civil war. Afterwards as brigade surgeon he was stationed at Washington, D. C., where he organized the Clifton and Lincoln hospitals. Dr. Bryant received his preparatory education at St. Paul's School, Concord, N. H., and under tutors. He was graduated at Harvard University in 1884 and received the degree of A.M. and M.D. in 1888. He began his professional work in the Boston Eye and Ear Infirmary, and was the first to give post-graduate instruction in otology at the Harvard Medical School. He was appointed aural surgeon at the Boston dispensary, assistant in anatomy and otology at the Harvard Medical School, and assistant aural surgeon to the Massachusetts Charitable Eye and Ear Infirmary. He resigned these positions in 1897. Being a member of the Massachusetts national guard, at the outbreak of the Spanish-American war in 1898 he was commissioned by Gov. Wolcott first lieutenant and assistant surgeon in the 1st Massachusetts heavy artillery. In July, 1898, he received a commission from Pres. McKinley as major and brigade surgeon, and was assigned to duty with the 7th army corps, commanded by Maj.-Gen. Fitzhugh Lee, in camp at Jacksonville, Fla., and attached to the staff of Brig.-Gen. William A. Bancroft. During his military service he filled various medical positions: was brigade-surgeon of many brigades, commandant of division hospital and chief surgeon of division, and chief surgeon of the U. S. forces at Savannah, until he was discharged from the service in 1899. From 1903 to 1905 Dr. Bryant was instructor in otology at the College of Physicians and Surgeons, New York; afterward clinical assistant in the department of otology, Vanderbilt Clinic, New York; assistant surgeon, St. Bartholomew's Clinic, New York; clinical instructor and attending surgeon, otological department, Cornell University Medical School; physician in class of nose, throat and ear diseases at the Presbyterian hospital, New York, and adjunct professor in the department of diseases of the ear, New York Post-Graduate Medical School and Hospital. He is now consulting otologist of the Manhattan State Hospital and senior assistant surgeon to the aural department of the New York Eye and Ear Infirmary. He was a member of the Boston Society of the Medical Sciences, the Boston Society for Medical Improvement, the International Congress of Arts and Sciences in 1904, the Seventh and Eighth International Otological congresses, the Fourth and Fifth Pan-American Medical congresses, the Fifteenth and Sixteenth International Medical congresses, and the Fifth, Sixth and Seventh congresses of American Physicians and Surgeons. Dr. Bryant is a member of the American Academy of Opthalmology and Oto-Laryngology, the American Laryngological, Rhinological and Otological Society, the American Medical Association (ex-chairman of the section on laryngology and rhinology), the American Otological Society, Massachusetts Medical Society, Association of Military Surgeons of the United States, New York Otological Society, New York Academy of Medicine, New York Physicians' Mutual Aid Association, New York State Medical Association, New York County Medical Association, Medical Association of the Greater City of New York, Clinical Society of the Presbyterian Hospital, Boston Society of Natural History, Manhattan Medical Association, and American Association for Sanitary and Moral Prophylaxis. He is also a member of the Loyal Legion, Military Order of Foreign Wars, Naval and Military Order of the Spanish-American War, Spanish War Veterans, Sons of Veterans, Sons of the Revolution, Massachusetts Society of the Cincinnati, Knights Templar, Thirty-second Degree Mason, Mystic Shrine, Harvard Club of

New York city, Huguenot Society of America, New England Society of New York, Society of Colonial Wars, Society of Mayflower Descendants, and of the Delta Kappa Epsilon and Zeta Psi fraternities and Porcellian Club. Dr. Bryant has followed the clinical side of otology most energetically, with the gratifying result of improved methods in the medical management and surgical treatment of suppurative and non-suppurative diseases of the middle ear, especially in middle ear catarrh, otosclerosis, middle ear suppuration and mastoid surgery. He has devised an operation for the radical cure of chronic suppuration with the preservation of the middle ear structures and the auditory functions. Dr. Bryant was the first to describe the values in the veins of the human intestines. He has done original work in studying the function and anatomy of the Eustachian tube, and has proposed a theory of sound-perception in opposition to the theories of Helmholtz and various other histologists and physiologists. He is recognized as a leading authority on his specialty, and is the author of ''Diseases of the Nose, Throat and Ear'' (1909), in conjunction with Dr. Charles Huntoon Knight. Dr. Bryant was married Sept 1, 1887, at Orange, N. J., to Martha Lyman, daughter of James Sitgreaves Cox, and has six children: Mary Cleveland, Elizabeth Sohier, Alice de Vermandois, Julia Cox, Gladys de Brienne and William Sohier Bryant, Jr.

FOSTER, Thomas Sampson, merchant and capitalist, was born at Leavenworth, Kan., Feb. 16, 1861, son of John McCullough and Letitia L. (Sampson) Foster, grandson of Samuel Davis and Martha (McCullough) Foster and great-grandson of Alexander Foster, a native of county Londonderry, Ireland, who came to America in 1793 and settled first in Lancaster county, Pa., and later in Pittsburgh. His father (1832-99) was a pioneer settler in Kansas, who carried freight between Leavenworth, Kan., and Denver, Colo., before railroads were built. He was one of the first lumbermen to begin the development of the yellow pine timber resources of the South. Thomas S. Foster was educated in the public and high schools of Leavenworth. He began his business career in his father's lumber yard at Irving, Kan., in 1879, and the ability, intelligence and energy he displayed led to the establishment of other yards at Leonardville and Colby, Kan. In 1885 he was given an interest in the business, the firm name becoming John Foster & Sons. In 1889 headquarters were established in Kansas City, Mo., and the business was incorporated as the Foster Lumber Co. In 1890 Thomas S. Foster opened a branch office in Houston, Tex., from which he conducted a large wholesale lumber business throughout the South and in Mexico. Later he individually acquired extensive timber holdings in Walker, Montgomery and San Jacinto counties, Tex.; built a sawmill, and in 1904 organized the Walker County Lumber Co., with headquarters at Elmina, Tex., and of which company he was president and principal owner. He established the town of Fostoria, Tex., and erected a large mill there for the Foster Lumber Co., of which he was also president. He operated a branch of this company at Houston, known as the Trinity River Lumber Co. He was vice-president of the Thompson-Tucker Lumber Co., Houston, and the Gebert Shingle Co., Ltd., New Iberia, La., being president of the latter when he died. He was a director of the Merchants' National Bank, Houston. Foremost in the development of the yellow pine industry in Texas, no one was more prominent in the

banking, commercial and manufacturing interests of the gulf coast country than Thomas S. Foster. Of a reticent disposition and slow to act, he brought deep thought to bear upon every detail which occupied his mind, and was as firm as adamant after he had once reached a conclusion. Modest and unobtrusive, he had a quiet force of character and discriminating judgment which made him a man of efficiency and dowered him with the elements that command and assure success. He kept faith with his fellow-men and acquired his wealth with clean hands and by honest methods, leaving behind him a record that is a heritage of incalculable value to friends, associates and family. During his lifetime many philanthropic and educational activities profited by his unostentatious generosity. He was especially interested in the Couros Normal and Industrial College and the Austin College, both in Texas. Pre-eminently a family man, his happiest moments were spent in his home, where, amid the surroundings of refinement and cultivation he so much appreciated, it was his pleasure to entertain many thoughtful and brilliant persons. He was a member of the Blue Hills and Mid-Day clubs, Kansas City, and the Houston and Country clubs, Houston. He was married, first, in Topeka, Kan., Nov. 17, 1889, to Addie, daughter of Albert Miller, of Whites Valley, Pa.; she died in 1894, and he was married, second, in Fort Worth, Tex., Dec. 22, 1897, to Florence Myers Wilson, of Minneapolis, Minn., daughter of Robert Henry Stewart Myers, of Shelbyville, Ill. He is survived by his wife and one daughter by the first union, Letitia Jane, wife of Robert E. Campbell, of Cleveland, O. Thomas Sampson Foster died in Kansas City, Mo., Oct. 30, 1913.

GREENE, Myron Wesley, banker, was born in Monroe county, N. Y., Nov. 26, 1864, son of Ira W. (1832-1905) and Hester Ann (Ruliffson) Greene. His earliest paternal American ancestor was John Greene, of Quidnessett, R. I., and the line of descent is through his son, also named John; his son John, who married Ann Hill; their son Nathan, who married Huldah Bowen; their son Jabez, who married Abigail Wilcox; their son Nathan, who married Mariah Green, a descendant of John Greene of Warwick, to which line Gen. Nathanael Greene belonged. Nathan Greene was the grandfather of Myron Wesley Greene. In the war of the revolution Samuel Greene, of Rhode Island, sent eight sons into the conflict, a record no one else ever equaled, and Joseph Greene, of New York, volunteer, twelve years old, was the youngest soldier of the same war. The Greene family, so closely identified with the early history of Rhode Island, have enjoyed more state and civic honors than any other family within its borders, there being more Greenes in the state than of any other name whatever. Mr. Greene's father, Ira W. Greene, for a long period conducted business as a farmer and dealer in live stock, coal and produce. He was a man of distinguished presence and commanding influence in politics, and for twenty-five years served as superintendent of the Sunday-school and president of the board of trustees of the Rush Methodist Episcopal Church. Myron Wesley Greene was graduated at the Genesee Wesleyan Seminary, at Lima, N. Y., in 1887, and he became an active member of the Genesee Lyceum Society, and is now president of its board of trustees. He is treasurer of the Alumni Gymnasium Association of the seminary, and president of the Alumni Association since 1910. His interest in the seminary is further evinced by the fact that he maintains a scholarship prize and a prize to members of the Lyceum Society for public speaking. In 1887 he entered Syracuse University, where he pursued a scientific course, and the following year matriculated at Williams College in the class of 1890. Upon the completion of his education he entered the Bank of Honeoye Falls, N. Y., where he remained until 1892, when he became connected with the Rochester Trust and Safe Deposit Co., with which he continued until 1899. He then established on his own account a private banking and investment enterprise, dealing in government and municipal bonds, and as a financier has won a reputation for keen discernment and sound judgment. Mr. Greene is a member of the Investment Bankers' Association of America, the Zeta Psi Fraternity of North America, of which he was grand officer in 1909-10. During his term of office he visited practically every college of importance in the United States and Canada, delivering numerous public addresses, and presiding at the international convention held in San Francisco in 1910. He has been president of the Zeta Psi Alumni Association of Rochester, N. Y., since the date of its organization in 1905. He also belongs to the Frank R. Lawrence Lodge No. 797, F. & A. M., and Hamilton Chapter No. 62, Royal Arch Masons. He is a worthy representative of an honored family, patriotic in his devotion to American interests, and loyal in his support of those measures and movements which he deems beneficial to the city, government or nation. Mr. Greene was married, April 27, 1900, to Nancy Laura, daughter of George W. Lancaster, of Leadville, Col., and has five children: Lancaster Myron, Norvin Ruliffson, Zeta Priscilla, Nathan Ira and Myron Wesley Greene, 2d.

MELL, Patrick Hues, engineer and educator, was born at Penfield, Ga., May 24, 1850, son of Patrick Hues and Lurene Howard (Cooper) Mell. The first of his family in America was John Mell, a native of England, who emigrated to the American colonies in 1677 and settled in Charleston, S. C. The line is traced through their son Thomas, who married Mary Boswood; their son William; his son William, who married Sarah Hues; their son Benjamin, who married Cynthia Sumner, and was the grandfather of our subject. Patrick Hues Mell, Sr. (q. v.), was a distinguished Baptist clergyman and third chancellor of the University of Georgia. The son received his preliminary education under the direction of his father, and was graduated at the University of Georgia in 1871. In 1872 he took a post-graduate course in civil and mining engineering. In 1880 his alma mater conferred upon him the degree of Ph.D., and he received the degree of LL.D. from the University of South Carolina in 1905. He began his professional career in 1874 as state chemist of Georgia. After practicing as a mining engineer for a year, in 1878 he became professor of geology and botany in the Alabama Polytechnic Institute (Agricultural and Mechanical College of Alabama), a position which he filled until 1902. In the latter year he became president of the South Carolina Agricultural and Mechanical College (Clemson Agricultural College), and held that office until 1910. During 1884-93 Prof. Mell was director of the Alabama weather service. In this capacity he devised a system of signal flags designed to indicate the coming changes in weather. A square white flag was to indicate clear or fair weather, a square blue flag, rain or snow, and a black triangular flag, for the temperature. The

triangular flag placed above either of the others meant a rising temperature, and below them a fall in temperature; no temperature flag meant stationary temperature. A fourth flag was soon after introduced by the weather department in Washington, comprising a square white flag with a square black center, used to indicate a cold wave, or the approach of a sudden and decided fall in temperature. His flags were first used in September, 1884.

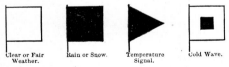

Clear or Fair Weather.　　Rain or Snow.　　Temperature Signal.　　Cold Wave.

As the Washington weather office telegraphed the weather predictions each morning the flags were displayed on public buildings, railway stations and other convenient centers of communication. The railways in Alabama, Georgia and Mississippi readily co-opciated with him in displaying these weather predictions. On Mar. 1, 1887, the chief signal officer adopted Prof. Mell's weather signals for the entire United States, and they are in use at the present day. He was director of the Alabama agricultural experiment station during 1898-1902. Meanwhile his prestige as an educator was such that he was invited in turn to become president of Mercer University, the North Georgia Agricultural College and the University of Florida. In 1909 he was president of the college section of the American Association of Colleges and Stations. He is a fellow of the Geological Society of America and the American Association for the Advancement of Science, and a member of the National Geographical Society, the South Carolina, Alabama and the Southern historical societies, Sons of the Revolution and Sons of Confederate Veterans. He is the author of "Auriferous Slate Deposits of Southern Regions" (1881), "Southern Soapstones and Fireclays" (1882), "Microscopic Study of the Cotton Plant" (1892), "Improvement of the Cotton Fiber" (1894), "Life of Patrick Hues Mell, Sr., LL.D." (1895), "Botanical Laboratory Guide" (1895), "Revision of Mell's Parliamentary Practice" (1896), "Revision of White's Gardening for the South" (1901), "Industrial Education in the South" (1906), "Clemson Agricultural College—The Work Accomplished in Seventeen Years" (1907), "Administrative Methods in American Colleges" (1909), "Biological Laboratory Methods" (1910) and a "History of Georgia" (1913). He has also written many magazine and newspaper articles on literary, educational and scientific subjects. He was married June 15, 1875, to Annie R., daughter of William N. White, a prominent writer on agricultural and horticultural subjects, of Athens, Ga.

AULD, Robert Campbell, editor and author, was born in London, England, Apr. 5, 1857, son of Patrick Campbell and Mary (McCombie) Auld. His preliminary education was received at Ayr Academy, in the schools of Aberdeen, Scotland, and under private tutors. He passed through Stewart's College, Edinburgh, and matriculated at the University of Aberdeen, intending to adopt a scientific career. But, called to act as secretary to his uncle, William McCombie, M.P., his attention was directed to stock-breeding. He visited America in 1880, and in 1884 took up his permanent abode in this country, residing for a time in Michigan, where he engaged in experimental breeding. Finding that its true principles had

MYRON W. GREENE
BANKER

PATRICK H. MELL
SCIENTIST

ROBERT C. AULD
EDITOR AND AUTHOR

CHARLES B. DAVENPORT
BIOLOGIST

yet to be studied out, he devoted himself to that object, combined with literary pursuits, in Chicago. He contributed articles on "Hornless Ruminants" to the "American Naturalist," in which he also advocated a means for the preservation of the American bison. In 1896 he became an associate on the editorial staff of the "New American Supplement to the Encyclopædia Britannica," and contributed an article on "The New Heredity." Removing to New York city in 1901 he edited and published "Public Improvements," contributed to the "Current Encyclopædia," and wrote articles on the origin and natural history of speech to the "Encyclopædia Americana." During 1904-05 he was revising editor of the "American Supplement of the Encyclopædia Britannica," and later became associate editor of the "Alcolm Magazine." In 1911 he edited the "Encyclopædia Digest" and in 1912 was appointed associate editor of the "Standard Illustrated Book of Facts." He published for a time the "Magazine World," and subsequently was associate editor of "Current Topics." He formed the children's committee which aided in presenting the pageant, "Around the World in Search of Fairyland," in Central Park, in August, 1912, and in the same year he founded and incorporated the Human Welfare League. In 1913 Mayor Gaynor appointed him a member of the committee of one hundred to consider the question of the celebration of the three-hundredth anniversary of the beginning of the city as the commercial metropolis of the new world. During the summer of 1913 he inaugurated a school of social welfare in connection with the Y. M. C. A. (Harlem branch), lecturing on "Character," and was one of the organizers of the first church eugenic class ever formed, that of the Mount Morris Baptist Church of New York, lecturing on "Mendelism and Heredity." He published, 1911, "How to Breed the Human Race," and has written authoritatively on eugenics and kindred subjects for the newspapers and magazines. He is a fellow of the Zoological Society of London and a member of the Travel Club of New York.

DAVENPORT, Charles Benedict, biologist, was born in Stamford, Conn., June 1, 1866, son of Amzi Benedict and Jane Joralemon (Dimon) Davenport. His father (q. v.) was a teacher, genealogist and agriculturalist, and his mother was a daughter of John Dimon, carpenter and builder, and a granddaughter of Judge Teunis Joralemon, a leading citizen of Brooklyn, N. Y. His earliest paternal American ancestor was the Rev. John Davenport, a noted English divine, who sailed from London to Boston, Mass., in 1637, and later settled at New Haven, Conn., of which he, with Theophilus Eaton, was a founder. He married Elizabeth Wolley, and the line is traced through their son John, who was a judge at New Haven, and married Abigail, daughter of Abraham Pierson, first president of Yale College; their son John, who married Martha Gould; their son John, who married Sarah Bishop; their son John, who married Deborah Ambler; their son John, who married Prudence Bell, and their son William, who married Abigail Benedict, and was the grandfather of the subject of this sketch. Charles B. Davenport was graduated (B.S.) at the Brooklyn Polytechnic Institute in 1886. He was a member of the engineering corps engaged in the survey of the Duluth, South Shore and Atlantic railroad for some months, but an innate love of the study of animals led him to resign to go to college. In 1888 he became an assistant in

zoology at Harvard and was instructor in the same subject there during 1891-99. He was assistant professor of zoology and embryology at the University of Chicago in 1899-1901 and associate professor and curator of the zoological museum of that university in 1901-04. Since 1898 he has been director of the biological laboratory of the Brooklyn Institute of Arts and Sciences. Shortly after the Carnegie Institution was established, in 1902, with its comprehensive plan and wide field for scientific investigation, it was decided to establish a station devoted to experimental evolution at Cold Spring Harbor, Long Island, a site that provided a great variety of conditions for studying different habitats and easily accessible to visitors. It was necessary that the person in charge of this work should be possessed of wide erudition, large experience and originality of thought and initiative, and Dr. Davenport was chosen to be the director. He spent the winter months of 1903-04 in New York, arranging for the opening of the establishment. The success of the station has been largely due to the wise foresight with which the preliminary steps, under his supervision, were taken. The subjects of study have been variation, inheritance and adjustment, as exhibited in animals and coordinately in plant life. Dr. Davenport's work has been especially upon the breeding of domestic animals and the study of mollusca and bryozoa. Experiments are made in the breeding of domestic animals to test the validity of the theory of unit characteristics, neighbors also co-operating in this work. Cows, sheep, goats, cats, poultry and canary birds are bred and cross-bred and results carefully noted. There is also a large botanical department in which these fundamental questions are studied in their relation to plants. Many details of the work fall to the care of Mrs. Davenport, who has been of great assistance to her husband in his studies and experiments. Although he has given particular attention to experimental morphology, statistics of variability, the rôle of water in the growth of organisms, the acclimatization of organisms to poison, heat, etc., and kindred questions in regard to the lower animals, he has not limited himself to this field. In 1910 he organized the Eugenics Record Office, a clearinghouse, at Cold Spring Harbor, for data on inheritable traits of American families, and to give advice to individuals on marriage and to states on defective communities. An important result already attained has been the discovery of the method of heredity of epilepsy in man, how it is produced, and how in later generations it may be prevented. He discovered the method of inheritance of eye color, hair color, skin pigmentation, etc., in man. These investigations have led Dr. Davenport to agree that there is good ground for belief that the germ-plasm is not affected by the soma, which is a theory accepted by leading students of biology. His work has played a leading part in the development of the "presence and absence" theory of heredity and of the rôle of chemical inhibitors in heredity. Dr. Davenport has been associate editor of the "Journal of Experimental Zoology" since 1898 and of the "American Breeders' Magazine" since 1910. He edits the "Memoirs and Bulletin of the Eugenics Record Office," of which eleven parts have appeared. He is the author of "Graduate Courses—a Handbook for Graduate Students" (1893); "Experimental Morphology" (part I, 1897, part II, 1899); "Introduction to Zoology," with G. C. Davenport (1900); "Statistical Methods in

Biological Variation'' (1904) ; ''Inheritance in Poultry'' (1909) ; ''Inheritance of Characteristics of Fowl'' (1909) ; ''Eugenics'' (1910) ; ''Elements of Zoology'' (1911) ; ''Heredity in Relation to Eugenics'' (1911), and ''Heredity of Skin Color in Negro-White Crosses'' (1913). He is also a frequent contributor to biological journals. Dr. Davenport is a brother of Henry Benedict Davenport, president of the Home Title Insurance Co.; of William Edwards Davenport, poet and head worker in the Italian settlement, Brooklyn, N. Y., and of Frances Gardiner Davenport (Ph.D.), author, historian and investigator in the department of historical research, Carnegie Institution of Washington (D. C.), also half brother of the late John I. Davenport, U. S. chief supervisor of elections, New York city. He is a fellow of the American Academy of Arts and Sciences, the American Association for the Advancement of Science (vice-president 1900-01) and the New York Zoological Society; member of the National Academy of Science, of the American Philosophical Society, American Society of Zoologists (president (1902-03), American Breeders' Association (secretary of eugenics section), American Society of Naturalists (secretary 1899-1903, vice-president 1906). Society of Experimental Biology and Medicine, Boston Society of Natural History, the New York Academy of Medicine and the Washington Academy of Science. He is also a member of the Huntington Country Club. Dr. Davenport was married June 23, 1894, to Gertrude, daughter of William and Millia (Armstrong) Crotty, of Burlington, Kan. She was born at Asequa, Col., Feb. 28, 1866, and, after graduating at the University of Kansas in 1889, and acting as instructor of zoology and anatomy there for three years, took a post-graduate course in zoology at Radcliffe College. She is engaged in original research work in biology at Cold Spring Harbor and is the author of various scientific works. They have had three children: Millia Crotty, Jane Joralemon and Charles Benedict Davenport, all living. Portrait opposite page 396.

SMITH, Edgar Fahs, provost of the University of Pennsylvania, was born at York, Pa., May 23, 1856, son of Gibson and Susan (Fahs) Smith. His preliminary education was obtained at the York County Academy, where he was subsequently a teacher. He entered the Pennsylvania College at Gettysburg in 1872, and was graduated there two years later with the degree of B.S. He took special courses in chemistry under Woehler and Huebner, and mineralogy under Von Walterhausen at the University of Goettingen, Germany, receiving his doctor's degree in 1876. In the autumn of that year he became assistant in analytical chemistry to Prof. F. A. Genth, of the Towne Scientific School of the University of Pennsylvania, and remained in that position until 1881, when he was elected Asa Packer professor of chemistry at Muhlenberg College, Allentown, Pa. After serving five years as professor of chemistry in Wittenberg College, Springfield, O., he returned to the University of Pennsylvania as professor of analytical chemistry. Upon the reorganization of the department of organic and industrial chemistry in 1892, he was placed in charge of it, and under his supervision it has become one of the country's most prominent branches of scientific learning. Many students who have attended Dr. Smith's lectures have attained eminence as teachers of chemistry or as chemical experts in various commercial fields. Dr. Smith has pursued many lines of original investi-

gation in chemistry and is probably best known for his achievements in electro-chemistry, especially the application of electricity to analytical chemistry. His methods of determining metals in an electrolytic way have been established as uniformly accurate. His ''Electro-Chemical Analysis'' (1894) has been translated into German, French and Chinese, and is everywhere regarded as an authoritative treatment of the subject. He has conducted noteworthy researches upon molybdenum and tungsten, and has written over 200 papers incorporating the conclusions of his investigations in organic, inorganic and analytical chemistry, in electro-chemistry and the composition of minerals. For several years he served as a member of the committee on papers and publications issued by the American Chemical Society. Besides his ''Electro-Chemical Analysis,'' mentioned above, he is the author of ''Classen's Quantitative Analysis'' (1878) ; ''Oettel's Electro-Chemical Experiments'' (1897) ; ''Oettel's Practical Exercises in Electro-Chemistry'' (1897) ; ''The Chemical Analysis of Urine,'' with Dr. John Marshall (1881) ; ''Richter's Inorganic Chemistry,'' 5th edition (1900) ; ''Richter's Organic Chemistry,'' 3d edition (1900) ; ''Experiments for Students in General Chemistry,'' with Dr. Harry F. Keller, 5th edition (1902) ; ''Elements of Chemistry,'' 3d edition (1911) ; ''Chemical Experiments—Shorter Course'' (1913) ; ''Theories of Chemistry'' (1913) ; ''Elements of Electro-Chemistry'' (1913). Since 1910 he has been provost of the University of Pennsylvania, and in this capacity he sustains close personal relations with the members of the faculty, the administrative officers and the entire student body, the members of which feel that in him they have a warm friend. He is never too busy to see them. His office is open at all times to the young men, scores of whom come to see him daily, and no student ever leaves his office without feeling encouraged and uplifted. He is deeply interested in the athletics of the university, and is popular with the alumni of the institution. He has received the following honorary degrees: Sc.D., University of Pennsylvania, 1899, University of Dublin, 1912; LL.D., University of Wisconsin, 1904, University of Pennsylvania, 1906, Pennsylvania College, Gettysburg, 1906, Franklin and Marshall College, 1910, Rutgers College, 1911, University of Pittsburgh, 1912, University of North Carolina, 1912, Princeton University, 1913; L.H.D., Muhlenberg College, 1911. Dr. Smith is a member of the National Academy of Sciences, the American Chemical Society (president 1898), the American Association for the Advancement of Science (vice-president 1898), the American Philosophical Society (president 1902-07), the Wistar Institute (president) and the Deutsche Chemische Gesellschaft. He served as a member of the chemical jury of awards at the Columbian Exposition in 1893, as a member of the United States assay commission in 1895 and again in 1901-05, and as adviser in chemistry at the Carnegie Institute in 1902. He was one of the founders of the Pennsylvania chapter of the Phi Kappa Psi, and one of the organizers of the Pennsylvania chapter of the honorary fraternity of Sigma XI. He also founded the fraternity magazine, ''The Shield.'' He is a member of the Robert Morris, Rittenhouse, University and Franklin Inn clubs, and of many of the university societies. He was married Apr. 15, 1879, to Margie A. Gruel, the daughter of John Gruel, of Gettysburg, Pa.

Edgar Fahs Smith

GASTON, William Alexander, lawyer and financier, was born at Roxbury, Mass., May 1, 1859, son of William and Louisa (Beecher) Gaston. Jean Gaston was one of the French Huguenots who were driven from home because of their religious opinions, and sought refuge in Scotland. His grandson, John Gaston, was the founder of the family in America, coming to the colonies between 1720-30, and settling in Voluntown, now Sterling, Conn. The line of descent is traced through John's son John and his son Alexander, who married Kezia Arnold, and was the grandfather of the subject of this sketch. His father, William Gaston (q. v.), was governor of Massachusetts during 1874-76, and his mother was a daughter of Laban S. Beecher, of New Haven, of the famous family of that name. William A. Gaston was educated at the Roxbury Latin School, and was graduated at Harvard College in 1880. During his college career he was enthusiastically interested in outdoor sports and college athletics, and retained for many years his connection with the University Athletic Association. Following the footsteps of his father he chose the legal profession, and after taking a two-years' course at the Harvard Law School secured his first practical experience in his father's law office in Boston. Being admitted to the bar in 1883, he entered his father's law firm of Gaston & Whitney. Upon Mr. Whitney's retirement, Frederick E. Snow was admitted, the name being changed to Gaston & Snow. Another change was made in 1898, when Richard M. Saltonstall became a partner, the firm name being Gaston, Snow & Saltonstall. Gov. Gaston retired from active practice in 1891. The firm made a specialty of corporation law, and has acted as counsel for many large industrial concerns in Boston. William A. Gaston has long been favorably known in financial circles, where his conservative judgment, prudence and sterling integrity have given him a high place among Boston's financiers. When the charter for the Boston elevated railroad was granted by the state legislature, Mr. Gaston became interested in this property, and it was largely due to his executive ability that various financial difficulties were solved and the legal technicalities overcome. He early came to the conclusion that in order to become successful the new company should control the surface lines of the West End Co., and as a result the elevated road took a ninety-nine years' lease of the West End system. Mr. Gaston was made president of the new company, and although not a railroad man in the strict sense of the word, he conducted the road for six years with marked success, and to the entire satisfaction of the stockholders, the patrons and the employees. He was for many years a director and member of the executive committee of the National Shawmut Bank, one of the largest financial institutions in New England, and has been its president since 1907. He is also president of the Boylston Market Association, vice-president of the Real Estate Exchange and Auction Board, director of the Commonwealth Trust Co., the American Trust Co., the Civic Federation of New England, the E. Howard Clock Co., the Fore River Shipbuilding Co. and the Massachusetts Bonding and Insurance Co. He is also a trustee of the Institution for Savings in Roxbury and the Central Building Trust. In politics Mr. Gaston is a Democrat. He served on the staff of Gov. Russell during the three years of his administration, and in 1902-03 was the Democratic candidate for governor of Massachusetts. He was delegate-at-large from Massachusetts to the national Democratic convention in St. Louis in 1904, and was the nominee of the Democratic members of the Massachusetts legislature for United States senator in 1905. He is a member of the Roxbury Military Association, counselor and director of the American Civic Association, director of the Safe Roads Auto Association, formerly a member of the board of overseers of Harvard University, and also a member of the Bostonian Society, the Massachusetts Horticultural Society, the Massachusetts Society for the Prevention of Cruelty to Animals (director), the Boston Elevated Mutual Aid Society, of which he has been vice-president since 1900, and the Somerset, University, Algonquin, Democratic, Exchange, Tennis and Racquet and Harvard clubs of Boston, Country Club of Brookline and the Recess and Harvard clubs of New York. Personally, Mr. Gaston is a man of high intellectual attainments. He combines the traits of his paternal Huguenot ancestry with the rugged characteristics of the Beecher family, from whom his mother came. He was married Apr. 9, 1892, to Mary Davidson, daughter of Hamilton D. Lockwood, of Boston, Mass., and has two sons, William and John Gaston, and two daughters, Ruth and Hope Gaston.

WILKENS, Henry A. J., mining engineer, was born in Baltimore, Md., Nov. 18, 1868, son of Henry and Therese (Geyer) Wilkens. His father, a native of Germany, came to the United States in 1855, and was engaged in the shipping business in Baltimore and Bremen, Germany, for thirty years. The son was educated at private schools in Baltimore and Bremen, and was graduated at Lehigh University in 1887 with the degree of B. S., receiving the degree of E. M. in the following year. He took a post-graduate course at the Freiberg (Germany) School of Mines in 1889, and upon returning to the United States accepted a position as engineer with the Lehigh Zinc Co., at Bethlehem, Pa. In 1889 he became connected with the Empire Zinc Co., of Joplin, Mo., and during 1889-91 was superintendent of the Gold King Mining Co., of San Diego county, Cal. He was assistant superintendent of the Lehigh Zinc and Iron Co., at Franklin Furnace, N. J., during 1891-94. For two years (1894-96) he was general manager of the Wetherill Separating Co., with headquarters in New York city. In 1896 he entered the service of the New Jersey Zinc Co. and became manager of their Western works and mines. While with that company he was responsible for many innovations and efficiency methods introduced in practice and management, notably the contact acid process, then first introduced in the United States. In 1908 he engaged in general practice as consulting engineer in New York, and for the next three years secured various commissions in South America, the United States and Europe. In February, 1912, he became president of the Mines Management Co., of New York, whose object is the supplying of a competent organization for the examination, valuation and management of mining properties. He is still (1916) its president. Mr. Wilkens has contributed a number of articles on technical and mining subjects to various periodicals, and has read a number of papers before professional and scientific societies. He is joint author, with H. B. C. Nitze, of "The Gold Mines of the South Appalachian System" (1894), which was the result of surveys and examinations made in 1894, and which was published by the Geographical Survey of North Carolina. Mr. Wilkens is acting consulting engineer of the Suriana Mining and Smelting Co., of Mexico, and a director of this and the Achotla Mines Co., of Mexico; the Wetherill Separating Co. and the Mines Management Co. He is a member of the American Institute of Mining Engineers, the Mining and Metallurgical Society, the Society of Chemical Industry, the American Chemical Society, Verein Deutscher Chemiker, the Engineers' Club, the Chemists' Club, the Players, New York Athletic Club, Midday Club, Whitehall Club, all of New York city; the Rittenhouse Club, of Philadelphia, Pa.; the University Club of Denver, Colo.; the University Club of the City of Mexico, the Oakland Golf Club of Long Island, and several clubs in Europe. He is unmarried.

GIBBONS, John Francis, manufacturer, was born in Baltimore, Md., Feb. 5, 1849, son of Samuel Smith and Sarah A. (Jillard) Gibbons. His father was a sea captain, born in 1814 and died in 1850, and his mother was the daughter of John J. Jillard. Mr. Gibbons was graduated at the University of Maryland in 1867, and immediately entered upon a business career as traveling salesman for John Grafflin, of Baltimore, Md., manufacturer of bags. He remained with this house until 1874, and then entered the employ of George H. Grafflin, a brother of his former employer, who was in the fertilizing business. This was destined to be Mr. Gibbons' life work. In 1880 he went into business for himself by organizing the Flamingo Guano Co., and in 1890, with Dr. Gustav A. Liebig, he formed the Liebig Manufacturing Co., which used a by-product of the Standard Oil Co. Mr. Gibbons was enabled to form a very valuable connection with the Standard Oil people, and was engaged in business with the Standard Oil Co. for many years. In 1898 he organized the American Agricultural Chemical Co., and was its president until 1907. Mr. Gibbons was a member of the Manhattan Club and Larchmont Yacht Club, the Maryland Club of Baltimore, Md., and the Cuttyhunk Fishing Club of New Bedford, Mass. He was married Oct. 20, 1874, to Ellen Nora Hayward, daughter of Jonas H. and Mary A. Hayward, in Baltimore, Md., and had three children: Nora H., Liebig Wallis and Douglas Gibbons. Liebig Wallis Gibbons is president of the Central Manufacturing Co., in Cincinnati, and Douglas is in the real estate business in New York city. He died in New York city, June 5, 1909.

FINCH, William Rufus, editor and diplomat, was born in Walworth county, Wis., Dec. 14, 1847, son of John Reynolds and Lydia Ann (Rogers) Finch. His father was a farmer. He was educated in the public schools, and at the age of sixteen he began his newspaper career at Sparta, Wis. His rudimentary education was supplimented by a course of constant and enthusiastic study, and his love for books and good reading was life-long. He became well-informed on all subjects and attained an unusual intellectual culture. In 1861 he moved to La Crosse, Wis., where he became connected with the "Republican." He remained with that newspaper until it was merged with the "Leader," under the title of "Republican and Leader," in which he acquired a controlling interest, and was for many years its editor and publisher. In that capacity he wielded a great influence in local and state politics throughout southern Wisconsin, and his powerful editorials attracted attention far beyond the territory of his newspaper organ. He was considered a great asset to the Republican party, and his good work won for him, in 1893, the ap-

pointment of collector of customs at La Crosse, a position he held for two years. In 1897 he was appointed envoy extraordinary and minister plenipotentiary of the United States to Paraguay and Uruguay, remaining in the diplomatic service in those countries until 1905. He was a member of the Masonic lodge of La Crosse, and of the I. O. O. F. He was known to all for his literary acquirements, his singular elevation of character, his fearlessness, and his honesty. He was a man of matchless courage, positive in his convictions, and was bold in their advocacy. He was a natural leader, and no man ever evinced a more thorough understanding of the duties of citizenship. As a diplomat he enjoyed an enviable record, and was highly esteemed in the South American countries to which he was assigned. He was married in La Crosse, Wis., Nov. 2, 1897, to Lillie Martinette, daughter of David S. Law, a lumberman. She survives him with two children: Emita Law and Mary Lillie Finch. He died at La Crosse, Wis., Aug. 9, 1913.

HOLBROOK, Theodore Lewis, manufacturer, was born in Boston, Mass., Jan. 11, 1839, son of Theodore and Rachel Bradbury (Smith) Holbrook. He was educated in the public schools of Boston, and at Hopkins Academy, Hadley, Mass., and began his business career with his father, then a lumber merchant of Chicago. He held a clerkship in the Chicago postoffice for six years, after which he was transferred to the money-order office of the U. S. postoffice department, Washington, D. C. Subsequently he became a general agent of the department, and was assigned to various parts of the South during the reconstruction period. In this work he was eminently successful, and he wrote several books covering his wide experience in postal matters. In 1878 he was appointed general manager of the Washington (D. C.) Brick Machine Company, which had been organized three years before, and which was in a state of insolvency. Within a few years Mr. Holbrook succeeded in paying off the mortgage, bonds and debts, in acquiring new and valuable tracts within the corporate limits of the district, and in paying eight per cent. dividends. Eventually the company was reorganized as the New Washington Brick Company, and he was made president, a position he held until his death, annually increasing the efficiency of the works and the financial prestige of his company. He was possessed of a degree of mental, physical and vital energy that made it impossible for him to be subordinated in his surroundings. His mind grasped large commercial affairs with celerity, and in his many undertakings he always acted with conviction. He was a man of decided and attractive personality, large and benevolent purpose, and really useful accomplishment, who won and retained, during his long and busy life, a high and honored place in the community. His maxim was to deal honestly, live simply, work intelligently, and trust the rest to Providence. Personally he had endowments morally, as well as intellectually, of a high order. The loftiest principles, not merely of integrity, but of honor, governed him in all of his transactions. He was modest, unassuming, kind-hearted and sincere— a well-informed, beautifully-mannered, sagacious gentleman. He was married in Washington, D. C., Sept. 28, 1887, to Catherine, daughter of John Robinson, of Washington, D. C., who survived him with three children: Catherine Theodora, Dorothy Ashley and Julia Peck Holbrook. He died in Washington, D. C., June 9, 1912.

HENRY A. J. WILKENS
MINING ENGINEER

JOHN F. GIBBONS
MANUFACTURER

WILLIAM R. FINCH
DIPLOMAT

THEODORE L. HOLBROOK
MANUFACTURER

GLENN H. CURTISS

CURTISS, Glenn Hammond, inventor, was born at Hammondsport, N. Y., May 21, 1878, son of Frank R. and Lua (Andrews) Curtiss, and grandson of Rev. Claudius Gustavus Curtiss, a Methodist minister, and his wife, Ruth Bramble. When young Curtiss was four years old his father died, and while attending the common schools he earned his living by selling newspapers. He early displayed a bent for mechanics and mathematics, and a forecast of his later accomplishments was his early efforts at rapid propulsion. He was the swiftest hand-sledder among his playmates; he rigged up a skate sail with which he outdistanced all his companions on the ice; with the bicycle he became the speediest rider in the section. He opened a bicycle repair shop at the age of seventeen, and began experimenting with engines and motor-cycles until he perfected the now famous Curtiss motor-cycle. In 1902 he established the G. H. Curtiss Manufacturing Co. to produce his machines and he gained a reputation throughout the country as a racer. He won the championship at the first meeting of the Federation of American Motorcyclists at Yonkers, N. Y., in 1905; in the following year he established a world's record for single-cylinder motorcycles, at Providence, R. I., covering a mile in 56⅖ seconds, and in 1907, at Ormond Beach, Fla., he established another world's record with a two-cylinder motor, going ten miles in eight minutes and 54⅖ seconds—a record which remained unbroken for seven years. He then constructed a forty horsepower, eight-cylinder motor for a Dr. Silverton of Milwaukee, Wis., and proved it the fastest in the world, traveling with it a mile in 26⅖ seconds, or 137 miles an hour. All these efforts were but the preparation for his coming career as a "bird man." The strength and lightness of the Curtiss motors attracted the attention of Capt. Thomas S. Baldwin, who was building a dirigible balloon on the Pacific coast and was unable to obtain a satisfactory motor. Capt. Baldwin commissioned Curtiss to construct an engine suitable for aeronautical purposes, and when the engine was finished and the trial flights began, Curtiss accompanied Capt. Baldwin in the balloon and frequently took a turn at steering it. The success of the first Curtiss aerial motor attracted many other builders of dirigible balloons to the Curtiss workshop, as well as inventors of aeroplanes, and Hammondsport soon became the recognized center of aeronautical experiments. He attached his engine to a crude form of aeroplane, with which he made flights around Hammondsport, and now organized the Curtiss Aeroplane Co. of Buffalo, N. Y. (1907), of which he is president, Harry C. Genung, vice-president and G. Ray Hall, secretary. With Baldwin's assistance he built his first flying machine under a commission from the United States government, using a water-cooled motor of his own construction. In November, 1907, the National Aerial Experiment Association was organized by Dr. Alexander Graham Bell and a number of others, with headquarters at Hammondsport and Mr. Curtiss as director of experiments. Under the auspices of the association the aeroplane, "White Wings," or "Drome No. 2," was built, in which he made several successful flights in the summer of 1908. This was followed by "Drome No. 3," or "June Bug," with which on July 4, 1908, he won the first aviation prize offered in this country for the first machine that would fly one kilometer in a straight line, and known as the "Scientific American" trophy. The "June Bug" had two supporting planes and was driven by a twenty-five horsepower, air-cooled motor, and weighed with the aviator 651 pounds. In March, 1909, the Curtiss motor works at Hammondsport were taken over by the Herring-Curtis Co., capitalized at $300,000, of which he was vice-president and general manager, and the first aeroplane built by the company was purchased by the Aeronautic Society of New York in June of that year. In that year also he conducted a training school for aviators under the auspices of the Aero Club of America. That club induced him to try for the James Gordon Bennett cup. Hurriedly building a new machine, he took it to France without having assembled the parts, and pitting himself against the most skillful aeronauts in the world, won both the Bennett cup and the Prix de la Vitesse. His machine was the lightest of all the entries, the total weight being 716.5 pounds, and his greatest speed was 46½ miles per hour. He was the only amateur who succeeded in landing at his starting point after each flight. In the same year he won the principal events at Brescia, Italy, including the Tour de Brescia for the fastest flight of fifty kilometers. At Los Angeles, Cal., in the early part of 1910 he made several records for quick starting and speed, leaving the ground in 5⅘ seconds from the time of starting the motor; later in the year he reduced this record, at San Antonio, Tex., to 4⅕ seconds. At Los Angeles also he made the longest flight in the air that had been recorded up to that date, passing around the course thirty times, a distance of 48 3-10 miles, in 1 hour, 16 minutes and 34 seconds. In December, at the same place, he traveled aloft with a passenger at the rate of fifty-five miles an hour. But his great achievement that year was his flight from Albany to New York, May 29, 1910, by which he won the New York "World" prize of $10,000. He made two stops, one at Poughkeepsie and one at Spuyten Duyvil, the official end of his journey, finishing the trip at Governor's Island. He covered the entire distance (150 miles) in 2 hours and 51 minutes. His aeroplane was equipped with floats placed under each wing as a precaution against falling into the river, and the development of this idea led to the perfection of a hydroaeroplane, or flying boat, which we find first suggested in patent specifications by Hugo Matullah of New York in 1899. Since then Curtiss has devoted much time to the perfection of the hydroaeroplane. In 1911 he showed a machine of this type, which was built for the United States navy, at San Diego, Cal., with a biplane equipment, and with floats instead of the usual landing skids, but provided with wheels also for use on land. On Oct. 17–21, 1911, mail was carried in one of these machines down the Mississippi river, from Minneapolis to Rock Island, a distance of 314 miles. Later he abandoned floats and used a true boat body. For this development of the hydroaeroplane Curtiss received the Aero Club of America trophy in 1911, and in 1912 for the flying boat, another distinct kind of craft that could be used both above and on the water, that could be moored at anchor in fairly rough water, that could be hoisted in or out of the water with an ordinary crane tackle, and could travel as much as 300 miles in the air. After he had perfected this machine it was accepted for service in the United States military and naval departments. As no machine has yet appeared which claims successfully to avoid an infringement upon the Wright patents, the contentions of the Wright company having been upheld by a recent decision of the court of appeals which requires that all companies using the Wright

patents shall pay a license therefor, it will be of
interest to note some of the features wherein the
Curtiss biplane differs from the Wright biplane.
(See Vol XIV, pp. 56–57). The Wright machine
is driven by two propellers, each about 8½ feet
in diameter, placed at the rear of the planes, the
driving chains running through steel guiding-tubes.
It is mounted upon skids, because of the possibility
of alighting upon rough ground without danger.
The curve of the surface of the planes is very
nearly the arc of a circle. The single propeller
of the Curtiss biplane is about six feet in diameter,
with blades six inches wide, and is mounted upon
a vanadium steel crankshaft. The machine is
mounted upon wheels. A skid is attached to each
end of the lower plane to protect it from breaking should the end of the plane strike the ground
in alighting. The surface of the planes of the
Curtiss machine is a parabolic curve. The surfaces
are made of Baldwin rubber silk stretched to the
tightness of a drumhead. A horizontal rudder, 24
square feet in size, is placed ten feet in front of
the main plane, and a smaller horizontal rudder,
which divides a vertical rudder of the same size,
is placed ten feet in the rear. Stability is secured
by movable surfaces at either extremity of the
main planes, which are operated by the aviator
bending his body to the right or left as the machine keels over through cables attached to a
curved rod which fits closely to the aviator's shoulders. The engine is a four-cylinder, vertical and
water-cooled, of Curtiss' own make, and the total
weight without the aviator is 85 pounds. There
are other minor differences between the Wright
and Curtiss biplanes, in details of frame work,
fittings, etc. With the exception of the Wright
brothers none other than Glenn Curtiss has done
so much for the science af aviation in America,
and if his life is spared, further developments of
first importance may be looked for from him.
Besides making a large number of flights in
America and Europe, he has been actively engaged in the commercial side of aviation. The
Curtiss Aeroplane Co., mentioned above, has turned
out a comparatively large number of aeroplanes
of both land and water types, and aeroplane motors for private individuals, for the United States
government and for governments in Europe. In
1916 it was sold to New York capitalists and
reorganized as the Curtiss Aeroplane & Motor Corporation, with a capitalization of $9,000,000, and
of which Mr. Curtis is president. He is the author
of "The Curtiss Aviation Book" (1912), in collaboration with Augustus Post.

DURANT, William Crapo, manufacturer, was
born in Boston, Mass., Dec. 8, 1861, son of William
Clark and Rebecca (Crapo) Durant. His grandfather, Henry H. Crapo, was governor of Michigan in 1864–69. He was taken to Flint, Mich.,
by his parents when he was nine years old. At
the age of seventeen he went to work in his grandfather's lumber mills, where he was employed first
as a mill hand and later in the office. When he
was twenty-one he accomplished the reorganization
of the Flint City Water Works Co., and succeeded
in making it an efficient and prosperous enterprise.
So successful was he in this undertaking that the
reorganization of several other corporations was
placed in his charge. Subsequently he founded
the Durant-Dort Carriage Co., and began the manufacture of road carts. Foreseeing that the high-
priced carriage would be supplanted by low-priced
vehicles, he entered the field with a general line
of buggies, and so well was his judgment justified
that the output of the Durant-Dort Co. grew

within a few years to 50,000 vehicles a year.
Eventually the output of the company reached
100,000 a year. While he was in the carriage
business, Mr. Durant bought hickory forests in
Arkansas and Mississippi, so that he might have
command of all the hickory he required, and established his own plants for the manufacture of
springs, axles, wheels and varnish. This foresight
which had led him to create a revolution in the
carriage trade made him one of the first to enter
the automobile field. He began by organizing the
Buick Motor Co. in 1904, and showed at once his
exceptional courage, optimism and enterprise by
clearing over seventy acres of oak forest at Flint,
Mich., and erecting thereon what was then the
largest automobile factory in the world. In the
first year the plant turned out sixteen cars, in the
next year 500, and in 1915 the output was 60,000.
So remarkable was his success that during the
panic of 1907, when industry all over the country
was fighting desperately for a mere existence, he
kept 13,000 men busy in one plant, and continued
adding to the buildings and equipment. In 1908
he organized the General Motors Co., combining
the Cadillac, the Oldsmobile, the Oakland, the
Buick, the Northway Motor Co., the Weston-Mott
Co., the Jackson-Church-Wilcox Co., and a number
of subsidiary companies manufacturing accessories.
The General Motors is the holding company, and
each of its units is, from the operating point of
view, an entirely separate and independent organization. At the end of the first year (1909) the
company showed a profit of $9,721,973.91. In 1910
its profits were $11,090,762.72. In that year Mr. Du-
rant refinanced the General Motors Co. by a loan of
$15,000,000 to extend the activities of the com-
pany. Money was then rather scarce, and there
was considerable doubt in the financial world as
to the stability of the automobile industry. He
succeeded, however, in making the loan for a
five-year period, and a voting trust was created.
After the voting trust had completed its term, Mr.
Durant resumed control of the company. In the
meantime, he had perfected his ideas of a medium-
sized, dependable car at a moderate price, which he
named the Chevrolet, the success of which has been
so rapid that the Chevrolet Motor Co. is now shipping cars to all parts of the world, and in spite
of immense manufacturing facilities, is unable to
keep up with the demand. Besides the original
plant at Flint, the Chevrolet Motor Co. has subsidiary or allied factories either in operation or in
process of construction at New York City, Tarrytown, N. Y.; St. Louis, Mo.; Oshawa, Ont.;
Oakland, Cal.; Minneapolis, Minn.; Kansas City,
Mo.; Fort Worth, Tex.; and Atlanta, Ga. The
capital of the Chevrolet Co. was increased from
$20,000,000 to $80,000,000 as a preliminary to an
exchange of stock with holders of General Motors
Co. stock. The General Motors Co. and the Chevrolet Motor Co., each founded and controlled by Mr.
Durant, are two of the greatest enterprises
of their kind in the world, and their development
in so short a period of time, is one of the most
remarkable incidents in the history of American
industry. In the business world, his most marked
characteristic is held to be his genius as a manufacturer, distributor and financier; he is said to
be one of the greatest salesmen America has produced. Personally, he is a pleasant, popular, like-
able person, free from poise, keenly interested
in work, sensitive, responsive, sympathetic, generous, and thoroughly human. He is pleasant and
affable in manner, kindly in his attitude to everybody, and very easy of approach. Mr. Durant

WILLIAM C. DURANT

Henry Woodhouse

has two children by his first marriage: Margery, wife of Dr. E. R. Campbell, of New York, and Russell Clifford, of Los Angeles. His present wife was Catherine Lederer, of Marshall, Mich.

WOODHOUSE, Henry, author, publisher and aeronautical authority, was born in Turin, Italy, June 24, 1884, son of Ludwig Casalegno, a prominent manufacturer. He took the name Henry Woodhouse for a nom de plume, and subsequently adopted it legally. He was early thrown on his own resources, his father having died before the son finished his schooling, leaving a wife and seven children, and his business affairs involved. Going to France he was able to settle his family affairs and accumulate a capital of $25,000 when twenty-eight years of age. He early developed a taste for literary work, and having traveled extensively through France, Switzerland, England and Belgium, he improved every opportunity for studying modern languages and science, especially economics, sociology and aeronautics. He came to the United States in 1904 and took out his naturalization papers in 1909. Almost immediately after his arrival in this country he became a contributor to such periodicals as "Collier's Weekly," "McClure's," "Metropolitan," "The Independent" and "World's Work." There was a growing demand for articles on aeronautics, and he wrote largely on that topic, in one year averaging 3,000 words a day for the entire year. In 1911, with Robert J. Collier and Henry A. Wise Wood, he founded the aeronautical monthly magazine "Flying," of which he became managing editor. He contributed to "Flying" many instructive and timely articles; he prophesied the development of military aeronautics, the extensive employment of aeroplanes by armies and navies in future wars, and the development of the hydroaeroplane, with which Glenn H. Curtiss had just begun to experiment. Being a deep student in economics and sociology, he pointed out the uses of aircraft to solve problems of transportation. As early as 1912 he urged the employment of aeroplanes as mail carriers between points inaccessible by rail. The science was then in its infancy; fatal accidents were numerous, and the general public was skeptical of the practicability of aviation. The aeronautical authorities of the country told him he was ahead of his time, and his associates advocated the suspension of "Flying," but Mr. Woodhouse was firm in the belief that the aeroplane had come to stay. He had the courage of his convictions and continued the periodical at his own expense. "Flying" is to-day, with a circulation of fifteen thousand, the foremost authority on the subject of aviation in the United States. Always well-informed, optimistic and far-seeing, he rendered valuable service to the science by encouraging and advising inventors, aviators and workers in the aeronautical field. His early articles on military aeronautics stand as prophecies fulfilled. He had made a careful study of the military institutions in the United States and Europe. What appeared to be over-estimation in 1910–13 regarding the value of the aeroplane for military service, reads to-day like sane interpretations of the trend of events. Before the European war he was an active peace worker and wrote articles and spoke on the subject, expressing his belief that the factors which would bring world-peace would be aerial transportation and wireless intercommunication, causing the intermixing of people and their interests, just as the railroad, the telegraph and the telephone brought more closely together the people of the North and South in the United States, thereby eliminating the differences caused by the civil war. But after the outbreak of hostilities in 1914 he became an ardent advocate of the national defense movement, and was active in urging upon the American public by voice and pen the seriousness and importance of a stronger national defense. He was the founder of the National Aeroplane Fund; a permanent delegate to the Conference Committee on National Preparedness, and was one of the committee of one thousand appointed by Mayor Mitchel of New York. In 1915 he founded the "Aerial Age," a weekly, and he is president of the Aerial Age Co., Inc., and also the Flying Association, Inc. He is a member of the Aero Club of America, of which he is a governor, the Economic Club, the National Arts Club, the National Geographical Society, the Authors League of America, the League for Political Education, the Twilight Club, the National Security League, the Patriotic Education Society, of which he was a founder, the Navy League, and also of the National Institute of Efficiency; an honorary member of the Aero Club of New England; a director of the American Society of Aeronautic Engineers, and one of the founders of the Aeronautic Federation of the Western Hemisphere. He was a delegate to the second Pan-American Scientific Congress in 1916.

MALLORY, Ezra Andrews, manufacturer, was born at Great Plains, Conn., June 4, 1820, son of Ezra and Eliza (Andrews) Mallory. He was descended from Peter Mallory, a native of England, who was among the early settlers of New Haven, Conn., being one of the signers of the plantation covenant in 1644; the line descending through his son Thomas, who married Mary Umberfield; their son Daniel, who married Abigail ————; their son Daniel, who married Sarah Lee, and their son Samuel and his wife, Hannah Hull, who were the grandparents of Ezra Andrews Mallory. His father was a pioneer hat manufacturer of Danbury, Conn., and the son learned his father's trade, and continued the business at the latter's death. In 1860 he purchased the present site of the factory of E. A. Mallory Sons, and entered into partnership with P. A. Sutton, forming the firm of E. A. Mallory & Co. Four years later he became associated with his brother Samuel, who retired in 1866, and Mr. Mallory continued the business alone until 1872 when he admitted his son, Charles Arthur Mallory, and in 1886 another son, William Ezra Mallory. He retired in 1897. He was married, Oct. 16, 1843, to Hannah, daughter of William Mallory, of Wilton, Conn., and left two sons: Charles Arthur and William Ezra. He died in Danbury, Aug. 15, 1902.

MALLORY, Charles Arthur, manufacturer, was born at Great Plains, Conn., Oct. 16, 1850, son of Ezra Andrews and Hannah (Mallory) Mallory. In 1869 he entered his father's hat manufactory as an apprentice, was employed in the office and various departments of the concern, and worked at the bench to learn the practical side of the industry. In 1872 he became a partner in the business, and in 1886 his brother, William Ezra, also entered the firm. His father died in 1902, and in 1904 the business was incorporated as E. A. Mallory Sons, Inc., with Charles A. Mallory, president, and William Ezra Mallory, secretary and treasurer. The making of fur hats requires more careful attention to the minutest details than the manufacture of any other wearing apparel used by man. The process in the Mallory plant is as follows: When received at the factory the animal skins are sorted, brushed and plucked of the hair. The fur, after being treated with a solution of nitric acid and quicksilver, is cut from the skin, and then fed into a blowing machine to clean it and remove any stray pieces of pelt, dirt, hair, or other foreign substance. In the forming department the fur is weighed to the fraction of an ounce, to the proper weight intended for each hat, and is then carried to the forming machine—an endless apron upon which the fur for each hat is spread, leading to a series of swiftly revolving pickers and brushes, a powerful fan beneath a perforated cone upon which the fur is drawn and held in place by the suction of the fan, until the whole hat is formed on the cone, when it is carefully covered with cloths and dipped into warm water, to make it hold together sufficiently to enable the operator to slip it from the cone. This makes a conical-shaped hat body, many times larger than its ultimate size. It is now hardened by a process of careful manipulation to knit the delicate fabric together slightly to prevent it from breaking in handling. In the sizing department the hat bodies, still in the large cone shape of very thin fabric, are carefully shrunken by continual rolling, squeezing and dipping in hot water by hand and machinery, until reduced or felted to their proper size, but still retaining the cone shape of much thicker and firmer fabric. The edges are then trimmed and notched to suit sizes, the hat dyed, and dipped in shellac for stiffening. The next step is the stretching and blocking out of the hats according to the size and style wanted. Finishers now place them upon wooden blocks, and by expert manipulation of pouncing paper to remove the rough surface, and the application of leur, heated by contact with electric stoves, the crowns and brims of the hats are reduced to a fine, smooth surface, after which a delicately adjusted machine cuts each brim off to the width desired, and another machine curls and shapes the brim. The edge of the brim is then bound, bands, bows and leathers are attached, after which the brims are shaped over wooden flanges with electrically heated heavy sand bags, until the proper roll and style is attained, and the finished hat is ready for packing. In 1908 Mr. Mallory and his associates conceived the idea of waterproofing or cravenetting a felt hat, and since then both stiff and soft styles, waterproofed, constitutes about half the product of the factory, which is 60,000 dozen hats per year. The Mallory firm was one of the first of the large manufacturing concerns which inaugurated a system of selling direct to the retailers. Mr. Mallory is president of the Danbury Hospital, and has been a member of its board of directors since 1899. He is a director of the City National Bank and is president of the Associated Charities. In politics he is a Republican, and in religion a Congregationalist. He is a member of the Danbury Club, the Automobile Club of America, and the Danbury Auto Club. He has been twice married: (1) Sept. 16, 1873, to Ella L., daughter of Dr. William H. Rider, of Danbury. Mrs. Mallory died in March, 1899, leaving two children: Harry B., and Clara J., wife of Mathias C. Loewe, of Danbury; and he was married (2) June 24, 1911, to Marion, daughter of Frederick Warner Tweedy, of Danbury.

GRIFFITH, Armond Harold, art director, was born at Knightstown, Ind., June 11, 1860, son of Collins William and Katherine (Conway) Griffith. His first American ancestor on the paternal side was William Griffith, who came over from Cardigan, Wales, about 1720, and settled at Chester, Pa. From him the line of descent is traced through his son, Griffith, who married Gwendolin Thomas; their son, John, who married Elizabeth Howells; their son, William, who married Ellen Cadwallader; their son, William, who married Sally Morris, and their son, Eli, who married Rachael Patten, and who was the grandfather of the subject of this sketch. Collins W. Griffith, the father (1825-69), was a lawyer by profession and a man of unusual intelligence and ability, and under his personal tutelage the son was chiefly educated. Of a roving, restless disposition, his early life was spent in divers occupations and in extensive travel. He made an excursion throughout Germany and Egypt while in his teens; he lived with gypsies in Spain and with the peasants in Bavaria; he studied art for a time in the Latin quarter in Paris, and returning to the United States, traveled with a theatrical troupe; sold goods on the road and accompanied an itinerant photographer through Yellowstone National Park. In that period of wandering he acquired a fund of information and a degree of polish which, together with the literary and art-loving traits of his family, were to prove of incalculable value in his subsequent career. Drifting to the city of Detroit, Mich., about 1890, Prof. Griffith was offered a small salary to become secretary to the directors of a newly organized art museum. He accepted the position and the work proved to be most congenial. In a remarkably short time he not only mastered all details of management, but displayed so much originality and developed such an intelligent comprehension of the requirements of a municipal art museum, that in 1893 he was made acting director. Since 1905 he has been director. Originally the Detroit Art Museum was a small affair, consisting of two rooms and little in them, the entire property and contents being valued at less than $100,000. Under Prof. Griffith's able direction the institution has grown to be one of the most notable in the United States, because of the practical good it is doing to the community in which it stands. At the present date (1916) the museum building, erected in 1886, contains twenty-two rooms, and holds valuable collections of ancient and modern paintings, sculptures and oriental specimens, with a property value of $400,000. A characteristic feature of the museum is a series of Sunday lectures which have been delivered by Prof. Griffith during the winter months for the past fifteen years to enthusiastic audiences that packed the auditorium at every meeting.

EMERSON, George Harvey, soldier and capitalist, was born at Chester, N. H., Feb. 18, 1845, son of Nathaniel French and Clarissa (Goodhue) Emerson. His earliest paternal American ancestor was Michael Emerson, who came from England and settled at Ipswich, Mass. His wife was Hannah Webster, and from them the line of descent is traced through their son Jonathan and his wife, Hannah Day; their son Samuel and his wife, Sarah Ayers, to their son John and his wife, Elizabeth French, who were the grandparents of George Harvey Emerson. He received his preliminary education in the public schools, and at the age of seventeen enlisted as a private in the 43d regiment, Massachusetts volunteer infantry, for the civil war, serving eleven months. In 1864 he entered Harvard University and spent one year in the scientific department. Crossing overland to the Pacific coast, he began his business career in 1866 at Coos Bay, Ore., in the service of Capt. A. M. Simpson, an extensive lumberman of those days, and later was given charge of a sawmill at

GEORGE H. EMERSON

Gardiner City, Ore. After some years he engaged in the book and stationery business at San Jose, Cal., continuing in that capacity until 1881, when he became the partner of Capt. Simpson in the lumber industry. He then went to the Grays Harbor country, and for more than a quarter of a century was an influential factor in developing that industry in western Washington. Purchasing a large timber tract where the city of Hoquiam now stands, he built the first sawmill of importance between the Columbia river and Puget sound and shipped the output to the California market by water. This mill, with others at South Bend and Knappton, Wash., were merged in 1886 into a corporation called the North Western Lumber Co., capitalized at $1,000,000. Mr. Emerson managed the Hoquiam end of the enterprise. Subsequently he and Charles H. Jones purchased the Hoquiam interests of Captain Simpson and he eventually became vice-president of the North Western Lumber Co. He was also president of the Grays Harbor Tugboat Co., vice-president First National Bank of Hoquiam, Hoquiam Water Co., and a director in the Grays Harbor Land Co., F. G. Foster Co., Lamb Timber Co., Metropolitan Bank, Seattle; Metropolitan Building Co., Seattle, and the Lumberman's Indemnity Insurance Co. He was a member of the Benevolent and Protective Order of Elks. Throughout his life he had been prominent in the discharge of civic obligations, concerning which he had cherished ideals, but he was absolutely without personal ambition. He had served as mayor of Hoquiam, and had declined the Republican nomination for governor of Washington. In 1896 he was a delegate to the Republican national convention in St. Louis. He held membership in the Rainier Club, Seattle. His influence upon the industrial and commercial life of the Northwest was necessarily widely felt. A man of extraordinary acumen, keen and quick preception, of resistless energy and irreproachable honesty, his counsel was courted and his advice sought by many a business or financial institution among whose directories his name never appeared. He was married at Chelsea, Mass., Feb. 9, 1868, to Elizabeth, daughter of Luke Damon, of Chelsea, Mass. She survives him, with two children: Alice (Mrs. Frank H. Lamb), and Ralph D., of the Aloha Lumber Co., Aloha, Wash. He died in Seattle, Aug. 2, 1914. Portrait opp. page 406.

AMMONS, Elias Milton, twenty-seventh governor of Colorado (1913–15), was born on a farm near Franklin, N. C., July 28, 1860, son of Jehu R. and Margaret C. (Brendle) Ammons. His family was among the first white settlers of North Carolina. When he was ten years of age his parents went to Colorado and settled on a ranch in Jefferson county. In early boyhood he was obliged to contribute to the support of the family, and when only eleven years old was employed in a woolen factory. While attending the public schools of Denver, he secured what jobs he could to help pay expenses. In 1880 the Denver "Tribune" sent him to Breckenridge, a mountainous district of the state, to write articles about the mines, and while there he added to his income by hunting wild game. His eyesight, which had become impaired by illness, was almost destroyed through a hunting accident; he was shot in the temple by a companion and lay several hours unconscious in the snow. The confining work in a subsequent position of city editor of the Denver "Times" nearly destroyed the little sight that remained to him, and he was compelled to abandon journalism. Turning to farming he settled with a partner on

eighty acres in Douglas county, and engaged in cattle raising and farming with fair success for twenty-five years. He was the organizer of the Denver Stock Show Association in 1905, and served as its first president. In 1909 he was made a member of the board of directors of the Colorado Agricultural College, which then had less than 200 students, and through his efforts it has become one of the great agricultural colleges of the country. His political activities began in 1890, when he was appointed clerk of the district court of Douglas county, Colo. He was a member of the state house of representatives during 1890–94, serving as speaker during the last two years, and he was in the Colorado senate during 1898–1902. He was twice the unsuccessful candidate for lieutenant-governor, but in 1912 was elected governor of the state on the Democratic ticket. The important legislation enacted during his administration provided for a complete new system to secure equal taxation in the state; a banking department which effectually put a stop to the agitation over the banking system of the state; a complete new centralized highway deparment; a more satisfactory insurance code; the establishment of a public utilities commission; a new law controlling the operation of coal mines, said to be the best of the kind in the country; the establishment of civil service in all state departments; the headless ballot; the regulation of hours of labor for both men and women; home rule in local and municipal matters; the recall of elective officers, including judges, and the recall of certain judicial decisions. Probably more constructive legislation was passed during Gov. Ammons's administration than during any other in the history of Colorado. In September, 1913, a serious strike occurred among the miners in the southern coal fields of the state, which took on a national importance as a result of the inability of the state authorities to control the situation and prevent riot and bloodshed. A number of men were killed in the clashes that occurred between the strikers and strike-breakers, and in October Gov. Ammons was obliged to order out the militia. He used his best efforts to secure a settlement of the matters in dispute but without success. In the spring of 1914 Federal troops were sent to the scene. After several attempts at mediation had failed, Pres. Wilson appointed a commission which submitted a plan for settlement, but it was rejected by the mine operators. The strike was finally ended in December, 1914, when the strikers went back to work without gaining their point. Gov. Ammons is president of the Farmers' Life Insurance Co., director and general manager of the Middle Park Land & Live Stock Co., president of the National Western Stock Show Association and the Grand County Fair Association, and a member of the Grange, Farmers' Union and Sons of Colorado. His clubs are: Stockmen's, Democratic, Colorado Traffic and Denver Athletic. He was married Jan. 29, 1889, to Elizabeth Fleming of Denver, Colo.

CARLSON, George Alfred, twenty-eighth governor of Colorado (1915——), was born at Alta, Buena Vista co., Ia., Oct. 23, 1876, son of Charles August and Louisa Piternilla (Gustafson) Carlson. His father, a native of Hallan, Sweden, came to America in 1872, settling in Johnstown, Pa., where he engaged in the coal mining business. The son was educated in the Colorado Agricultural College, the Colorado Normal School and Colorado State University, being graduated at the last in 1902. Having decided to follow the legal profession, he took the regular course at the Colorado

School of Law and received his LL.B. degree in 1904. He practiced his profession for one year at Lewiston, Ida., and then settled permanently in Fort Collins, Colo. He served as deputy district attorney for two years, and as district attorney of the 8th judicial district of Colorado during 1908-15. In 1914 he was elected governor of the state. Some of the distinctive accomplishments of his administration were the re-establishment of law and order following the miners' strike, the enactment of a state-wide prohibition law, the enactment of laws establishing a system of workmen's compensation and an industrial relations commission, a law providing for a state survey commission to investigate all state departments and institutions for the purpose of recommending legislation and constitutional amendments that would place the state government upon a more efficient basis, the improvement of the state's credit by establishing the principle that a legislature should not make appropriations to exceed available revenue. Gov. Carlson is a member of the Masonic order, the Young Men's Christian Association, the Phi Beta Kappa and Sigma Nu fraternities, and the Denver Athletic Club. He was married Aug. 29, 1906, to Rose Lilly, daughter of John Alps of Loveland, Colo., and has four children: Elaine, Bessie, George Alfred Jr., John Swink and Juanita Carlson.

BLAKELOCK, Ralph Albert, artist, was born in New York city, Oct. 15, 1847, son of Ralph and Caroline (Carey) Blakelock. His father, a native of England, was a homeopathic physician of excellent standing in his profession, but with a reputation for eccentricity. The son was graduated at the College of the City of New York in 1867. His parents intended him for the medical profession, but his love of painting and music led him to become an artist. He was almost wholly self-taught, and his art is the result of many experiments. His early work is therefore crude, but his progress was rapid, and at his best, he ranks as one of the foremost American landscape painters, particularly in evening and moonlight scenes. A trip to the far West, where he studied the life of the Indians, gave him the material for many of his best pictures. He was by nature a dreamer, a poet and mystic, making use of natural forms with which to express himself, and through these his moods and inspirations were expressed in an imaginative synthesis of color and harmonies. He is essentially a tone painter who sees in nature the means of attaining emotional effects rather than a subject to be literally transcribed. But had he not sought as he did for the splendor of color, he would still have been a remarkable artist through the emotional and imaginative character of his work, which manifests itself more in the unconsciousness of his design than in his color. His theme is usually the forest primeval with mysterious glades, peopled by Redmen. Mr. Blakelock married early, had a large family, and found it increasingly difficult to obtain even the bare necessities of life. In a hopeless struggle for existence, during which he sold many charming little canvases as low as two or three dollars apiece, his mind became unbalanced, he was sent to an institution for the insane, and was forgotten for years. As is frequently the case with those who labor in the field of art, many years elapsed before his undoubted genius won that public recognition which was denied him in the days when he needed it most. His paintings have increased in value with each change of ownership until one, "The Brook by Moonlight," was purchased by the Toledo (O.) Art Museum in 1916 for $20,000. The titles of his paintings include: "The Mountain Defile"; "Ecstasy"; "The Brook by Moonlight"; "Moonlight"; "Indian Encampment"; "Pegasus"; "An Indian Girl"; "Shooting the Arrow"; "Evening Landscape"; "Wayfarers at Eventide"; "Entrance of the Forest"; "Near Cloverdale"; "Forest Interior"; "A Farmhouse"; "Moonrise at Sunset"; "The Pine Dancer"; "Sunrise, Donner Lake"; "In the Gloaming"; "Evening at the Spring"; "One Scalp"; "The Pipe Dance"; "Seal Rocks"; "Nature's Mirror"; "The Captain"; "Early Evening." It is said that the painter's daughter, Marian, who is insane in the State Hospital at Poughkeepsie, N. Y., had naturally imbibed some of the superficial characteristics of Blakelock's manner, but stopped painting when she found that her work was being sold as her father's, thus guarding the public from deception and upholding the honor of his name. Blakelock was a skillful musician, a great lover of nature, and very domestic in temperament. In 1900 he was awarded an honorable mention at the Paris Exposition in 1913, was elected an associate of the National Academy of Design and in 1916 a full member. He was married in 1869, to Cora W., daughter of George W. Bailey, a manufacturer of Brooklyn, N. Y., and their surviving children are: Carl E., Marian, Ralph M., Louis R. and Allen; Mary, wife of Harry Vedder; Ruth and Douglas Blakelock.

DUBOIS, Augustus Jay, civil engineer and educator, was born at Newton Falls, O., Apr. 25, 1849, son of Henry Augustus and Catherine Helena (Jay) Dubois, grandson of Peter and Mary (Van Voorhes) Dubois, great-grandson of Pieter and Jaunetje (Burhaus) Dubois and great-great-grandson of Jacques DuBois, a French Huguenot refugee from Leyden who settled at New Platz, N. Y., in 1675. He was a great-grandson of John Jay, the first chief justice of the United States. He was educated at Hopkins Grammar School, New Haven, Conn., and was graduated at the Sheffield Scientific School of Yale University with the degrees of Ph.B. in 1869, C.E. in 1870 and Ph.D. in 1873. He then studied mechanics for two years at the Freiberg (Saxony) Mining School. During 1874-76 he was professor of civil and mechanical engineering at Lehigh University, Bethlehem, Pa., and in 1877 he became professor of mechanical engineering at Sheffield Scientific School. In 1883 he was transferred to the department of civil engineering as professor of civil engineering and head of the department, a position he held until his death. Prof. Dubois was a pioneer in the subject of stresses in frame structures, and his book, "The New Method of Graphical Statics" (1875), was the first full presentation to American engineers of a new method of investigating engineering problems—one that is now included in the curriculum of all engineering institutions. He also wrote a translation of "Weisbach's Mechanics of Engineering" (1877-78) and Rontgen's "Principles of Thermodynamics" (1879); and "A New Theory of the Suspension System with Stiffening Truss" (1882); "The Strains in Framed Structures" (1882), which is the best and most complete treatise on the subject in English, and is a standard work among all engineers; "The Early History of the Steam Engine" (1884); "Science and the Supernatural" (1886); "Formulas for the Weights of Bridges" (1888); "Science and Miracle" (1889); "Science and Religion" (1894); "The Elementary Principles of Mechanics" (1894-95); and "The Mechanics of Engineering" (1902). He was a member of the national societies of civil,

GEORGE A. CARLSON
GOVERNOR

RALPH A. BLAKELOCK
ARTIST

AUGUSTUS J. DUBOIS
CIVIL ENGINEER

JOSEPH E. RANSDELL
U. S. SENATOR

Fritz von Frantzius

mechanical and mining engineers and the Society of Naval Architects and Marine Engineers. He was married in New Haven, Conn., June 23, 1883, to Adeline, daughter of Arthur Blakesley, of New Haven. In Prof. DuBois was combined to an unusual degree the analytical and logical mind of the mathematician with the imagination and artistic sense of the poet. As the natural fruit of this unusual combination, there appeared from time essays keenly analytical and logical in construction, but charming in their beauty and style, stimulating in their originality of thought, and marked throughout by a high purpose. Many of these essays were on different phases of the subject of science and religion, and these to a large extent are summarized and embodied in his essay, "The Religion of a Civil Engineer," which appeared in the "Yale Review" for July, 1913. He died in New Haven, Conn., Oct. 20, 1915.

RANSDELL, Joseph Eugene, U. S. senator, was born in Alexandria, La., Oct. 7, 1858, son of John Hickman and Amanda Louisa (Terrell) Ransdell. He was educated in private schools in Alexandria, and was graduated at Union College, Schenectady, N. Y., in 1882. He began the study of law under Judge J. W. Montgomery, and was admitted to the bar in 1883, opening an office in Lake Providence, La., for practice. While engaged in a general practice, he gave much attention to criminal law, and also was largely identified with land and succession matters. In 1884 he was elected district attorney of the 5th judicial district of Louisiana, and served in that capacity for twelve years. He was a member of the fifth Louisiana Levee Board during 1896–99, and represented East Carroll parish in the state constitutional convention of 1898. In the following year he was elected to the 56th congress to fill the unexpired term of Hon. S. T. Baird, and on this occasion he gave up the practice of law, and devoted himself thereafter to his congressional duties and the management of his cotton plantation, which he has been conducting for twenty years. In congress he was especially active in behalf of legislation for waterways, and has served as president of the national rivers and harbors congress from 1906 to date. This congress was organized in Baltimore, Md., in October, 1901, largely as a protest against the action of Sen. Carter of Montana in talking to death a river and harbor bill during the last two days of congress, closing Mar. 4, 1901. It is a voluntary organization, composed of commercial, manufacturing and kindred organizations, waterway improvement associations, corporations and individuals engaged in commercial or industrial enterprises. Its object is to collect and distribute data regarding the scientific improvement, development and uses of rivers, harbors, lakes and canals, and to disseminate this knowledge through printed circulars and reports to the end that the public may be educated to the importance of waterway development for navigation and commerce. Little interest was taken until January, 1906, when a convention was held in Washington, largely at the instigation of Sen. Ransdell, who was chairman of the board of directors with full power to carry on the work. The influence of this organization upon the policy of our national congress is reflected in the increased appropriations, which in January, 1906, amounted to $20,000,000 on an average per annum, while in recent years they have been increased to over $35,000,000 per annum. Sen. Ransdell has made for many years a close study of flood control of the Mississippi river, which in the section below Cairo causes incalculable damage by

overflow. Through his efforts large appropriations were made by congress for dredging the river, building levees, and otherwise guarding against the floods and consequent damage due to the spring freshets. In 1912 he was nominated to be U. S. senator and was elected by the state legislature to succeed Hon. Murphy J. Foster, taking his seat Mar. 4, 1913, for a term of six years. He received the degree of LL.D. from Union College in 1907, and also from Notre Dame University and St. Charles College in 1914. Sen. Ransdell was married at Lake Providence, La., Nov. 15, 1885, to Olive Irene, daughter of James Powell. Portrait opposite page 406.

VON FRANTZIUS, Fritz, banker and broker, was born at Sawdin, West Prussia, Germany, May 17, 1865, son of Arthur and Ida (Ehlert) Von Frantzius. He has two distinguished progenitors on the paternal side: Theodosius Christiam Von Frantzius, a merchant prince of the free Hausa town of Danzig, who was said to be the richest man in Danzig, and Augustin Ritt, court painter of Catherine the Great, Paul I and Alexander I, at St. Petersburg, called the greatest miniature painter of Russia. He was educated at the Royal Gymnasium at Marienwerder, and Graudenz, West Prussia, and began his business life in an export and commission house in Berlin. Coming to America in 1888, he secured employment as a bookkeeper in the Lipps & Sutton Silk Mills at South Bethlehem, Pa., and later with the Matthiessen & Hegeler Zine Co., La Salle, Ill. After serving as bookkeeper with J. F. Wollensak, hardware specialties, Chicago, 1897, he went with S. E. Gross and Sam Brown, Jr., as salesman in the real estate business. In 1899 he established business as a banker and broker under the firm name of Von Frantzius & Krusemark, which in 1901 became Von Frantzius & Co. Mr. Von Frantzius is a member of the New York and Chicago stock exchanges, the New York Cotton Exchange and the Chicago Board of Trade. He also belongs to the Illinois Athletic Club (life), Press Club (life), Deutsche Pressverein, Germania Club, Germanistic Society (life), Austro-Hungarian Benevolent Association, German-American Historical Society (life), Field Museum (life), Art Institute (life), Friends of American Art (one of its founders), Municipal Art League (life), Palette and Chisel (life), Public School Art Society (life), Chicago Association of Commerce and Association of German Authors in America. He is an art critic and a collector of art, including paintings and vases, being the possessor of the famous paintings "Salome" and "Saharet," by Franz von Stuck; his dominating characteristics being his artistic taste as well as a resistless energy and impetuous generosity. He donated to the Field Museum two Imperial Chinese art treasures in jade and a complete Japanese coin collection of about 800 pieces, to the Art Institute of Chicago he gave Schramm-Zittau's famous painting, "Geese at Play," Franz von Stuck's "Amazone" in bronze and other objects of equal worth, and to the Germania Club he gave a lifesize painting of Emperor William II, by Frank A. Werner. As an art critic he wrote "Overrated Paris" and "Florabust" for "Fine Arts Journal," the former being quoted extensively in art journals and newspapers. He is also the author of an introduction to the opera "Salome," and a pamphlet, "Germans as Exponents of Culture" (1914), in answer to an article by Prof. Brander Matthews of Columbia University. He was vice-president and director of the Chicago Singverein, and director of the German Aid Society of Chicago and German Altenheim. Mr. Von Frantzius was twice married, first, Sept. 28, 1893, to Margaret Sieber, daughter of Dr. Wilhelm Sieber, of Berlin, and has two children: Hans Peter and Annemarie Von Frantzius; and second, June 23, 1913, to Clarissa Saharet, a famous dancer, from whom he was divorced Dec. 1, 1913.

DARLINGTON, James Henry, P. E. bishop, was born in Brooklyn, N. Y., June 9, 1856, son of Thomas and Hannah Anne (Goodliffe) Darlington, grandson of Peter and Maria (Wilde) Darlington and great-grandson of Peter Darlington, who came to this country from Yorkshire, England, and established a paper mill, one of the first in this country, at Salisbury Mills, near Newburgh, N. Y. His father was a member of the New York bar for forty years. He was graduated at the Uni_ versity of the City of New York in 1877, and at Princeton Theological Seminary in 1880, pursuing also the course in philosophy and receiving the degree of Ph.D. In 1881 he became assistant to Rev. Alfred H. Partridge, of Christ Church, Brooklyn, taking deacon's orders in January, 1882, and being ordained priest by Bishop Littlejohn in November of the same year. Upon the death of Mr. Partridge, in 1883, he was elected to the vacant rectorship, and under his administration the church became a center of great usefulness, exerting a marked influence upon the spiritual upbuilding of Brooklyn. Through the forcefulness and clearness of his preaching he was for many years one of the mission preachers of the Parochial Mission Society, and his pulpit powers brought to him calls to the rectorship of numerous influential churches elsewhere. He continued as rector of Christ Church twenty-four years, and in 1905 was consecrated bishop of Harrisburg. He was chaplain of the 47th regiment of the National Guard of New York for eight years, was archdeacon of Northern Brooklyn for three years, and was appointed lecturer in New York University. For several years he was a trustee of Rutgers Female College, New York, and in 1910 was chaplain of the Masonic Grand Lodg of Pennsylvania. He is the author of "Pastor and People" (1912), also of sermons on various subejcts, and is editor of "The Hymnal of the Church," "In Memroiam" and "Little Rhymes for Little People." Bishop Darlington is chaplain-general of the Huguenot Society of the United States, member of the Transatlantic Society, National Geographic Society, Knights Templar and Scottish Rite Masonic bodies, Society of Colonial Wars, Sons of the Revolution, Historical Society, St. Andrews Society of Pennsylvania, St. Nicholas Society of New York, University Club, and the Westminster Club of London. He received the degree of D.D. from the University of New York in 1895, and that of LL.D. from St. John's College, Annapolis, in 1905, and from Dickinson College in 1907. He was married, July 26, 1888, to Ella Louise, daughter of James Sterling Bearns, a banker of Brooklyn, N. Y., and they have five children: Henry V. B., Gilbert S. B., Eleanor T., Elliott C. B. and Kate Brampton Darlington.

COLT, Le Baron Bradford, jurist and U. S. senator, was born in Dedham, Mass., June 25, 1846, son of Christopher and Theodora G. (De Wolf) Colt. His first American ancestor was John Colt, who came to this country with Rev. Thomas Hooker in 1636 and settled in Hartford, Conn., two years later. From John Colt and his wife, Mary Fitch, the line of descent is traced through their son John, who married Mary Lord; their son Benjamin, who married Miriam Harris; their son Benjamin, who married Lucretia Ely; their son

Christopher, who married Sarah Caldwell; their son Christopher, who was the father of Le Baron B. Colt. The second Benjamin Colt was a colonel in the revolutionary army and one of the foremost patriots in the state of Maine. James Benajmin Colt, the famous senator and author of the treatise "On Government," and Samult Colt, the inventor of the revolver which bears his name, were uncles of Sen. Colt. He was graduated at Yale College in 1868, and at the Columbia Law School in 1870. After traveling for a year in Europe he began the practice of law in Chicago, Ill., where he remained until 1876. In that year he removed to Providence, R. I., and for five years was associated in partnership with Francis Colwell, afterward city solicitor of Providence. During 1879–81 he represented Bristol in the Rhode Island general assembly, and in the latter year was appointed U. S. judge for the district of Rhode Island by Pres. Garfield. In July, 1884, he was appointed U. S. circuit judge for the first judicial district, which included Maine, New Hampshire, Massachusetts and Rhode Island. A circuit court of appeals, to relieve the work of the U. S. supreme court, was formed in 1891 and Judge Colt was appointed presiding justice. His career on the bench was notable for his decisions on patent cases, among which were the Edison-Baker suits and the famous Bell telephone suits. The most remarkable of the latter concerned the Berliner long-distance telephone patent owned by Alexander Graham Bell, in which the decision of the court of appeals that Berliner was not the inventor of the long-distance telephone was written by Judge Colt. During his judicial career he had to construe at different times all the schedules of all the tariff acts, and he possessed a knowledge of the tariff equalled by few public men. In all his cases he showed a comprehensive knowledge of the questions involved, due partly to his very wide general information and partly to the thoroughness with which he studied the matters to which the cases that came before him related. He was one of the most brilliant figures on the bench of the United States courts. He was so at college, and on account of his unusual ability was admitted to membership in the Greek letter fraternity, Psi Up_ silon, and the senior society, Skull and Bones. The skill with which he dissected the intricate points in patent cases evoked the admiration of the lawyers who heard him. He gave considerable time to the study of the method and development of American institutions and law, the growth of federal and democratic forms of government, and the study of philosophical history and the historical method of the development of the institutions and laws of the United States. In January, 1913, he was elected U. S. senator from Rhode Island to succeed Sen. Wetmore, and his term will expire in 1919. His public addresses have stamped him as not only an orator of marked ability but a man of great learning and erudition. A collection of them was published in book form, and they are among the best examples of that sort of literature that have appeared in recent years. He received the degre of LL.D. from Columbia Univrsity in 1904 and from Yale in 1905. He was married, Dec. 17, 1873, to Mary Louise, daughter of Guy Ledyard. of Chicago, and has five children: Theodora, wife of Edwin A. Barrows; Emily, wife of Andrew Weeks Anthony; Mary L., wife of Harold J. Gross; Beatrice and Le Baron Carleton Colt.

COLT, Samuel Pomeroy, president of the United States Rubber Co., was born in Paterson, N. J., Jan. 10, 1852, son of Christopher and Theodora G. (De Wolf) Colt, and brother of Senator

James H. Darlington

SAMUEL P. COLT
MERCHANT

LE BARON B. COLT
U. S. SENATOR

THOMAS J. WALSH
U. S. SENATOR

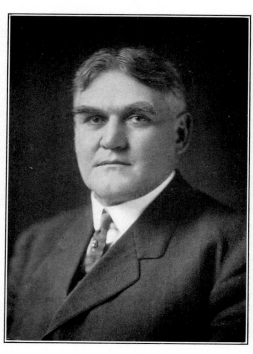

MARTIN G. BRUMBAUGH
GOVERNOR

Le Baron Bradford Colt (above). He was graduated at the Massachusetts Institute of Technology in 1873. After a year spent in traveling in Europe, he took up the study of law at the Columbia Law School, New York, was graduated in 1876, and opening a law office at Providence, R. I., soon acquired an extensive practice. In 1876, 1877, 1878, and 1879, he was a member of the Rhode Island general assembly and during 1879–85, he was assistant attorney general. Fore some time, Col. Colt had made a careful study of the manufacture of rubber. The possibilities of the industry struck him forcibly and the history of its rapid development pointed clearly to a place among the great industries of the world—a position which it by no means occupied at the time he first became interested in it. The history of the rubber industry in the United States is extremely interesting. The first rubber seen in America was brought by Yankee sea-captains plying between Salem and South American ports. They had no idea that those lumps of black gum were of any particular value; indeed, they often used them as ballast. But about 1820, some forgotten seaman took to Salem and Boston as a speculation a number of rubber shoes made by the Indians along the Amazon. People quickly discovered that those shoes kept out the wet, and, crude as the shoes were, there was soon a lively demand for them at four and five dollars a pair. This suggested to the astute Yankee mind that if rubber shoes were worth so much and raw rubber was worth practically nothing, it would be a good business venture to secure the gum and make the shoes themselves. When they had made the shoes, however, they discovered that they melted in summer and froze in winter. So some of the best brains in New England set to work on the problem of preparing the gum rubber in a way to make it of practical value. It was not until 1842, however, that Charles Goodyear (q. v.), a Connecticut Yankee, discovered the secret of vulcanizing it, and that discovery marked the beginning of the rubber industry. The first company to enter the field was the Candee Rubber Co., of New Haven, Conn., which started with an output of one hundred pairs of rubber shoes a day, which was soon increased to 30,000 pairs a day, the full capacity of the factory. This was followed by the Goodyear Co., afterward the Wales-Goodyear Shoe Co., of Naugatuck, Conn., and the proceedings were enlivened by a spirited and famous lawsuit over the Goodyear patent rights in which Daniel Webster took one side and Rufus Choate the other. Webster finally won the suit for Goodyear. The Boston Rubber Shoe Co. was founded in 1853 and became the largest manufacturer of rubber footwear in the country. Its supremacy was soon disputed by the Woonsocket (R. I.) Rubber Co., which made a specialty of rubber boots, and was probably the largest existing manufacturer in this line. Then followed the American Rubber Co., formed at East Cambridge, Mass., in the late seventies. The companies named were the only outstanding ones in the industry until the reorganization of the National Rubber Co., by Col. Colt in 1888. Four years later he consolidated a number of rubber companies into the United States Rubber Co., whose capital stock was increased in 1905 from $50,000,000 to $75,000,000. The company manufacturers not only rubber boots and shoes, but a variety of other rubber goods, and as an indication of its size it may be stated that its mills employ over 20,000 men in Massachusetts, Rhode Island and Connecticut, and produce over 200,000 pairs of rubber boots and shoes per day.

Originally its legal adviser, Col. Colt afterward became a member of its executive committee, and in 1905 was made president, a position he still holds, the other officers being James B. Ford, vice-president; Lester Leland, second vice-president; John J. Watson, Jr., treasurer. Col. Colt was married Jan. 12, 1881, to Elizabeth M., daughter of James Russell Bullock, a judge of Rhode Island, and has two sons, Russell Griswold and Roswell Christopher Colt. He is a member of the Metropolitan, New York Athletic, Republican and Lawyers clubs of New York, and the Hope and Squantum clubs of Providence.

WALSH, Thomas James, lawyer and U. S. senator, was born at Two Rivers, Manitowoc co., Wis., June 12, 1859, son of Felix and Bridget (Comer) Walsh. His parents, both natives of Ireland, were pioneers in that portion of the state, his father being active in all movements for the advancement of the town in which he lived for over forty years, particularly in the improvement of the public schools. He was educated in the public schools of his native town. He taught as principal of several high schools in the state, and while so engaged pursued advance studies so diligently that he was awarded a life certificate on an examination covering all branches included in the usual college course. He studied law in the University of Wisconsin, and upon receiving his LL.B. degree in 1884 immediately began the practice of his profession at Redfield, S. Dak., in association with his brother, Henry Comer Walsh. In 1888 he was a delegate from South Dakota to the Democratic national convention held in St. Louis. In 1890 he removed to Helena, Mont., and opened an office for the practice of his profession, forming a partnership in 1907 with Col. C. B. Nolan under the name of Walsh & Nolan. Mr. Walsh has been very successful as a trial lawyer, a large part of his practice consisting of cases into which he was called by other attorneys. He was nominated for congress on the Democratic ticket in 1906, but was defeated. Twice he represented Montana in the national convention of the Democratic party, at Denver in 1908 and at Baltimore in 1912, on both occasions serving on the platform committee. In 1910 he was a candidate for U. S. senator in opposition to Hon. Thomas H. Carter. The campaign waged by Mr. Walsh resulted in the selection of a Democratic legislature in a state strongly Republican. Owing to internal dissensions a deadlock was created in the legislature and continued throughout the sixty days term until on the very last night of the session the legislature elected Hon. Henry L. Myers. Two years later he was again nominated for the United States senate by the Democratic party, and in the election which followed he received the highest number of votes cast for any candidate. Sen. Walsh was president of the Public Library Board of Helena, and is a member of the American Bar Association, the Montana Club of Helena, the Silver Bow Club of Butte, and the Rocky Mountain Club of New York city. He was married Aug. 15, 1889, to Elinor C. McClements of Chicago, Ill., and has one daughter, Genevieve Arlisle, wife of Emmett C. Gudger, paymaster of U. S. Navy.

BRUMBAUGH, Martin Grove, educator, was born in Huntingdon county, Pa., Apr. 14, 1862, son of George Boyer and Martha (Peightal) Brumbaugh. His ancestors on both sides were of German extraction, mostly adherents of the Tunker faith, and settled in Pennsylvania about the middle of the eighteenth century. He was educated in the public schools of his native county and at Juniata

College, Huntingdon, Pa., where he was graduated in 1881, and after a year of study in the higher mathematics at the State Normal School, Millersville, Pa., was professor for one year (1882–83). For six years thereafter (1884–90) he was superintendent of schools for Huntingdon county, and then, resuming systematic study, was a post-graduate student at Harvard College (1891–92) and at the University of Pennsylvania (1892–94), receiving the degrees of A.D. in 1893 and of Ph.D. in 1894. In 1893 he was elected president of Juniata College, but declined it to accept the chair of pedagogy at the University, to which he was formally chosen in 1894. During 1895 he studied at the University of Jena. He remained at the head of Juniata College until 1906 when he was appointed superintendent of schools of the city of Philadelphia. In addition to his other occupations, Dr. Brumbaugh was for six years (1886–1891) state conductor of teachers' institutes for Louisiana, and lecturer in teachers' institutes in Ohio, Pennsylvania, New Jersey, Maryland, Delaware, Kentucky and Indiana. He was, in 1898, elected president of the Pennsylvania State Teachers' Association, and among other connections, is a member of the Pennsylvania Historical Society and the Pennsylvania German Society. For several years he has been a regularly appointed minister in the church of the Christian Brethren (Tunkers), and has written "Juniata Bible Lectures" (1890); "Stories of Pennsylvania" (1893); "History of the Church of the German Baptist Brethren" (1895); "Liberty Bell Leaflets" (1894); "The Making of a Teacher" (1905), and "Life and Teachings of Christopher Dock" (1906). He enjoys an international reputation as an authority on pedagogy and his lectures on the subject have been widely published and quoted. He was the first commissioner of education for Porto Rico during 1900–02. In 1913 he was a candidate for governor of the state on the tickets of the Republican, Keystone and Personal Liberty parties, and although ex-Pres. Roosevelt actively supported Vance McCormick, the Democratic candidate, Dr. Brumbaugh was elected. The degree of LL.D. was conferred upon him by Franklin and Marshall College in 1902, and by Pennsylvania College in 1908, and the degree of Litt D. was given him by Lafayette College in 1915. Dr. Brumbaugh was married July 30, 1884, to Anna, daughter of Edwin Konigmacher, of Euphrata, Pa., and has two children.

BROSSART, Ferdinand, fourth Roman Catholic bishop of Covington, Ky., was born in Bavaria, Germany, Oct. 19, 1849. He was brought to America when two years old by his parents, who settled first in Cincinnati, O., and then moved to Campbell county, Ky., where his boyhood was spent. His classical studies were made at St. Mary's Seminary, Cincinnati, O., whence, in 1869, he went to the University of Louvain, Belgium, for his theology. Illness prevented his ordination until Sept. 1, 1872. Bishop Maes appointed him rector of the cathedral, Covington, and vicar-general of the diocese in 1888, and on the death of that prelate in 1915 he was made administrator of the diocese, and on Nov. 30 was appointed bishop by the pope in succession to Bishop Maes. The construction of beautiful Gothic cathedral of Covington was completed under his supervision. He published a translation of Denifle's "Humanity" and contributed frequently to a number of publications. He always took an active interest in civic affairs, serving as vice-president of the Covington Park Commission as a member of the National Civic Federation. He also distinguished himself by heroic work, minister-

ing to the people of Cynthiana during a cholera epidemic, and again at Lexington, where there was an outbreak of small-pox, and the unfortunate victims in both instances were abandoned by all others in a panic-stricken community.

DICK, George Frederick, soldier, was born at Tiffin, O., Feb. 22, 1829, son of John Adam and Anna Elizabeth (Dinkleburg) Dick. His father, who held a government office in Bavaria, came to America during the Prussian revolution of 1826, and became editor of a German newspaper in Cincinnati, O. The son, after a public school education, engaged in the tobacco business in Attica, Ind., conducting also a store at Bloomington, Ill. At the first call for troops by Pres. Lincoln in 1861, he organized a company which became company D, 20th regiment, Indiana volunteer infantry, and he was chosen captain. It participated in the engagements between the Merrimac, Cumberland and Congress, and in May, 1862, took part in the capture of Norfolk, Va. He was acting major of his regiment during Pope's Peninsula campaign, winning distinction at Fair Oaks, the Orchards, Seven Days Fight, Manassas Plains and Chantilla. He was commissioned lieutenant-colonel of the 86th Indiana volunteer infantry in 1862, and was transferred from the Eastern to the Western Army. In January, 1863, he was promoted to be colonel, and later was assigned to the command of the 2d brigade, 3d division, 21st corps, of the Army of the Cumberland, with which he remained until the end of the war. He fought with distinguished gallantry during the three days' battle of Chickamauga, and at Missionary Ridge he led his men up a precipitous hill of 1,200 feet in the face of a leaden hail from the Confederate rifle pits that crowned the summit. It was the colors of the 86th Indiana which were first planted on the summit of Missionary Ridge. The flag of the regiment, containing eighty-six bullet holes and with staff broken by other shots, is now in the state house at Indianapolis. Speaking of this assault, in which five color-bearers were killed, Gen. Gordon Granger, the corps commander, said: "I am constrained to express my own admiration for your noble conduct, and I am proud to tell you that the veteran generals from other fields who witnessed your heroic bearing, placed your assault and triumph among the most brilliant achievements of the war." Entering on the Atlanta campaign in May, 1864, he led his men in all the important battles of the expedition, including Resaca, Peach Tree Creek, Atlanta, Lovejoy Station and Jonesboro. In 1865 Col. Dick was brevetted brigadier-general by congress for meritorious services on the field. During the war service he took part in 105 minor and major engagements, including, besides those already mentioned, Second Bull Run, Stone River and Kenesaw Mountain. He was thrice wounded in action. He conducted a wholesale cigar and tobacco business at Bloomington, Ill., until 1873, when he was appointed postmaster of Bloomington and held that office until 1885. Gen. Dick was one of the organizers and a director of the People's Bank of Bloomington, and an organizer and vice-president of the McLean County Bank. He helped to organize the local post of the G. A. R., and was a member of the visiting committee of the Soldiers' Orphan Home of the national organization. In civil life, as on the field, the conduct of Gen. Dick was characterized by courage, loyalty, integrity and strict adherence to the highest standards of honor and duty. He was a member of the Military Order of the Loyal Legion, the

Geo. F. Dick

Charles L. Bernheimer.

Veterans' Union, the Odd Fellows; was past grand commander of his Masonic lodge, and represented his district in the Grand Lodge of Ohio, Indiana and Illinois. He was married (1) in Cincinnati, O., July 14, 1853, to Anna Mayers of Cincinnati, by whom he had one daughter, Ella B., wife of George B. Miller; (2) at Bloomington, Ill., Aug. 8, 1881, to Emma Rankin Kimball, of Whitefield, N. H., who survives him with three children: George Frederick, Carl Rankin and Harry Kimball. Gen. Dick died at Bloomington, Ill., Nov. 12, 1914.

CUSACK, Thomas Francis, fifth Roman Catholic bishop of Albany, N. Y., was born in New York city, Feb. 22, 1862, son of James and Honora (Boland) Cusack. He was graduated at St. Francis Xavier's College, New York, in 1880, and made his theological course at St. Joseph's Seminary, Troy, where he was ordained priest May 30, 1885. After work in several country parishes he was appointed by Archbishop Corrigan superior of the Apostolate Mission Band, which had for its special work the giving of missions to non-Catholics, and continued in this position with very great success for seven years. On Mar. 9, 1904, the pope, at the request of Archbishop Farley, appointed him auxiliary bishop of New York and titular bishop of Themiscyra, and he was consecrated Apr. 25, 1904, and made pastor of St. Stephen's Church. Bishop Burke of Albany having died Jan. 20, 1915, Bishop Cusack was transferred to fill the vacancy in that see July 13, 1915. His Catholic population numbered 205,000, with 242 priests, 263 churches, fifty-four schools and 21,000 pupils.

BERNHEIMER, Charles L., merchant, was born at Ulm-on-Danube, Württemberg, Germany, July 18, 1864, son of Leopold M. Bernheimer, a merchant. He came to America in 1881 and began his business career as an office boy with Adolph Bernheimer, a wholesale dry goods merchant of New York. He is now president of the Bear Mill Manufacturing Co., the successors of the firm with which he began business. The founders of his present business, the Bear Mill Manufacturing Co., were Bernheimer Brothers, who came to America in 1837 from South Germany. As chairman of the committee on arbitration of the New York Chamber of Commerce he was active in the men's clothing strike during the first three months of 1913 in an effort to conciliate and reconcile the differences between the manufacturers and some 110,000 workmen on strike. The principles laid down by him on behalf of his committee during the strike for a basis of settlement were practically those finally accepted by both ides. The activities of this arbitration committee are not confined to labor disputes, but embrace mediation, conciliation and arbitration of business disputes between merchants in this or in any other country, whether members of the Chamber of Commerce or not. After the fifth international conference of chambers of commerce had urged on its numerous constituent bodies the establishment of a system for the settlement of international controversies, private or public, as chairman of the committee of arbitration of the New York Chamber of Commerce, he submitted to that body a report containing an outline of an international plan. It aims to secure a standard clause in all contracts between merchants carrying on international business, wherein the parties pledge themselves to submit differences to the arbitration tribunal of a chamber of commerce or like body named therein. The next step is for these bodies to agree to enforce, with all legal and moral means in their power, the decisions of their respective arbitration tribunals. Where no legal means of enforcement are available, the commercial organizations bring pressure to bear on the party against whom an award has been announced who fails to comply with the award. Charges are preferred to any trade organization to which he may belong, a record of awards is communicated to all the bodies represented, with names of those refusing compliance and their reasons, if any, given for the refusal. Such procedure necessarily affects the reputation and standing of parties to arbitral contracts, gives them ample opportunity to be heard, but visits them with the disapproval of their business associates if deserved. Thus common interests, common standards of conduct, common views of business morals and methods are developed, and the commercial world tends to become one community, and its orderly, peaceful administration tends to become more practicable. He assisted the Chamber of Commerce of the United States, of which he is a member, to formulate a plan for international arbitration between it and the Buenos Aires Chamber of Commerce, so that disputes between merchants of those countries may be settled amicably and expeditiously. Mayor Mitchel appointed him a member of the council of conciliation in 1915 to effect a settlement in the disputes in the cloak, suit and skirt industry. With Dr. J. L. Magnes and Dr. Henry Moskowitz he organized the council of moderators to prevent disputes and strikes in the men's clothing industry. He was treasurer of the Citizens' municipal committee, the so-called committee of 107, or Fusion committee, during the municipal campaign of 1913, resulting in the election of John Purroy Mitchel for mayor of New York, and a near approach to a nonpartisan city administration. He was chairman of the committee on private banks in the commission to revise the banking laws of the state of New York. This was the so-called Van Tuyl commission. His committee had also charge of the laws relating to savings and loan associations, personal loan associations, small loan brokers, credit unions, mortgage loan and investment companies, and to formulate the law to create the Land Bank of the State of New York, a central institution for the liquification of long-term farm mortgages. (See Glynn, Martin H., p. 231.) Besides the chambers of commerce mentioned above, he is a member of the Safety First Society (president 1916), Safety First Federation of the United States, the Merchants' Association of New York, Board of Trade and Transportation, in which he is also a director; American Geographical Society, American Museum of Natural History, Metropolitan Museum of Art, vice-president Republican Club of New York, Century, and member of the City, Country and Hollywood Golf clubs, also of most of the important charitable, benevolent and philanthropic societies of the city. He was married in New York city, Nov. 3, 1893, to Clara, daughter of Jacob Silberman, a silk manufacturer of Paterson, N. J., and has two children: Helen Amailie, wife of Stanley J. Halle, and Alice Martha Bernheimer.

SABINE, Wallace Clement, physicist, was born in Richwood, O., June 13, 1868, son of Hylas and Anna (Ware) Sabine. He was graduated at the Ohio State University in 1886, and then studied at Harvard University, where two years later he received his master's degree. In 1889 he was appointed an assistant in the department of physics at Harvard, and after passing through the grades of instructor and assistant professor was in 1905 given the Hollis chair of mathematics and natural philosophy. At the same time he was made dean of the Lawrence Scientific School, which since 1909 has been the School of Applied Science of Harvard, and of which he remains dean. The arduous duties of teaching and of administration have left Dr. Sabine but little time for research, but the following publications show the line of thought that he has pursued when opportunity and time were favorable: "The Optical Advantages of the Ultra Violet Microscope" (1906), contributed to the "Journal of Medical Research"; "Architectural Acoustics" (1906), which appeared in the Proceedings of the American Academy of Arts and Sciences; and his retiring address before the American Association on "Melody and the Origin of the Musical Scales" (1908), which was published in "Science." He is also the author in book form of "A Laboratory Course in Physical Measurements" (rev. ed., 1906). The degree of Sc.D. was conferred upon him by Brown University in 1907. He is a member of the American Physical Society, and a fellow of the American Academy of Arts and Sciences, and the American Association for the Advancement of Science.

APPLEGATE, John Stilwell, lawyer, was born in Middletown township, Monmouth co., N. J., Aug. 6, 1837, son of Joseph Stilwell and Ann (Bray) Applegate, and a descendant of Thomas Applegate, who came from England in 1635 and settled first at Weymouth, Mass., and later at Gravesend, L. I. He was graduated at Madison University, afterwards changed to Colgate University, Hamilton, N. Y., in 1858. Subsequently he studied law, was admitted to the New Jersey bar in 1861, and since then has been engaged in the practice of his profession at Red Bank, N. J. For many years he has stood among the leaders of the bar in his state. He has been connected with a large number of notable cases and has acted as counsel for some of the most important private and corporate interests in New Jersey. He practised, during 1875–79, with Henry M. Nevius, and during 1884–1901 with Fred W. Hope. Since 1901 he has been in partnership with his son, John S. Applegate, Jr., under the firm name of John S. Applegate & Son. Apart from his professional work he has been prominently identified with many important activities. He was elected school superintendent of Shrewsbury township in 1862, and was re-elected three times. During the civil war he rendered valuable service in recruiting troops in his district, and otherwise contributed valuable support to the national government. As special deputy of the Union League of America he organized a number of chapters of that order in New Jersey. In 1865 he was a member of the Republican state committee and took an active part in the gubernatorial campaign of Marcus L. Ward. He was a leading factor in the incorporation of Red Bank in 1871, became a member of its first council, and was elected president of the council in 1872. In 1881 he was elected to the state senate. Among the laws for which he stood sponsor was one providing that the public printing should be awarded to the lowest bidder, and one authorizing the smaller towns and villages to construct and maintain water works. Under the latter act he was appointed a member of the first board of water commissioners of Red Bank in 1884, on which he served until his resignation in 1905. In this capacity he was instrumental in inaugurating the water system of Red Bank. For some years he was president of the first Building & Loan

Association in the Atlantic shore region of New Jersey. In 1875 he initiated a movement that resulted in the institution of the Second National Bank of Red Bank, which he served as president from its organization until he resigned in 1887. He was elected president of the New York & Atlantic Highlands Railroad upon its organization in 1882, and held that office until the road was merged with the New Jersey Central Railroad system. For many years he has been a director of the Red Bank Gas Light Co. He is president of the Monmouth County Historical Association and the Monmouth County Bar Association; trustee of the Monmouth Battle Monument Association; life member of the New York Genealogical and Historical Society and the Delta Kappa Epsilon Club of New York; honorary member of the Regimental Association of the 157th New York volunteer regiment, and a member of the New Jersey State Chamber of Commerce, the American Bar Association, the New Jersey Historical Society, the New Jersey Society of the Sons of the American Revolution and the Phi Beta Kappa Society. For over fifty years he has been a member and president of the board of trustees of the First Baptist Church of Shrewsbury at Red Bank. Colgate University conferred upon him the honorary degree of LL.D. in 1904. Mr. Applegate is the author of "The Life and Service of George Arrowsmith" (1893) and a "History of the Monmouth Bar" down to 1861 (1911), besides a number of historical and literary addresses. He was married in 1865 to Deborah Catharine, daughter of Charles Gordon Allen, of Red Bank, N. J., and has three children: Annie, wife of Charles H. A. Wager; John Stilwell, Jr., and Katharine Trafford, wife of Francis J. Donald.

BARTLETT, Willard, jurist, was born at Uxbridge, Mass., Oct. 14, 1846, son of William O. and Agnes E. H. (Willard) Bartlett, and grandson of Dr. Samuel Willard, who was a representative from Worcester county, Mass., to the convention which met in Boston in 1788, to consider the question of adjusting or rejecting the Constitution of the United States. In 1857 the family removed to Brookhaven, Suffolk co., L. I., where his father, a distinguished lawyer of the New York bar, had purchased a farm of about 1,000 acres. Willard Bartlett was prepared for college at the Columbia College grammar school and the Polytechnic Institute, Brooklyn, and was graduated at Columbia College in 1869, having in the meantime studied law and been admitted to the bar the previous year. After graduation he practiced his profession with Elihu Root until 1883, and acquired a large practice, not only in the second judicial district, but in many parts of the country. He was justice of the supreme court of New York, second judicial department, from 1884 to 1906; justice of the New York term, New York city, from 1887 to 1889; justice of the appellate division of the supreme court, Brooklyn, from 1896 to 1906, and has been associate judge of the court of appeals since Jan. 1, 1906. In November, 1913, he was elected chief judge of the court of appeals. Since 1898 he has been professor of medical jurisprudence in the Long Island College Hospital. Among the important cases in which Judge Bartlett has been engaged were the investigation at Washington for the house committee on naval affairs into the condition of the navy department; the Lawrence interstate extradition case, in which it was first authoritatively settled that one judge was not bound by the decision of another judge refusing to discharge a prisoner on habeas corpus; the Kemble

WILLARD BARTLETT
JUDGE

JOSEPH H. KASTLE
CHEMIST

EZRA S. TIPPLE
CLERGYMAN

FRANCIS E. LEUPP
EDITOR AND AUTHOR

libel suit, involving William H. Kemble's "addition, division and silence" letter; the defense of Gen. William F. Smith, in which Mr. Bartlett successfully asserted the right of the accused officer to be represented by counsel, and the trial of the New York police commissioners. In 1891 he gave his decision in the famous suit of William Ziegler against Mayor Chapin, and also presided at the trial of John Y. McKane, and the eighteen inspectors of election and Constable Jamison, all of Gravesend, and all charged with conspiracy. In his manner and movements Judge Bartlett is methodical and prompt; in speech he is deliberate but not slow; on the bench he is precise without being tedious, expository but not obtrusive. His knowledge of the law is comprehensive and his administration of it is accurate. His diction is exceptionally clear; as a public speaker he has achieved distinction; he is widely read in general literature; is particularly interested in the theater, and as a traveler has visited many countries. During 1871–73 he was dramatic critic of the New York "Sun," and subsequently a contributor of editorial articles on legal topics; during 1873–76 he was editorial reviser of the "American Cyclopedia." In politics he is a Democrat. He is a member of the Sons of the Revolution, Society of Colonial Wars, Long Island Historical Society (president); and of the University, Century (New York), Brooklyn and Hamilton clubs. He received his degree of LL.B. LL.D. from Hamilton College in 1894, and from from New York University in 1868, and that of New York University and Columbia University in 1904. He was married Oct. 26, 1870, to Mary Fairbanks Buffum, of Brooklyn, N. Y.

KASTLE, Joseph Hoeing, chemist and educator, was born in Lexington, Ky., Jan. 25, 1864, son of Daniel and Thane (Vallandingham) Kastle. He was graduated at the State College of Kentucky in 1884, receiving also the degree of M.S. in 1886. Meanwhile he had entered the Johns Hopkins University, where he pursued higher studies in chemistry, from which he received the degree of Ph.D. in 1888. Returning to his alma mater, he was professor of chemistry until 1895, when he was called to Washington to become chief of the division of chemistry in the hygienic laboratory of the U. S. Public Health and Marine Hospital Service. To this work he devoted four years of his life and then accepted a call to the chair of chemistry in the University of Virginia, a chair long noted for such famous occupants as Robert E. Rogers, J. Lawrence Smith and John W. Mallett. In 1911 he returned to Kentucky to become research professor of chemistry in the Agricultural Experiment Station of the state university at Lexington. Since 1912 he has been director of the Kentucky Agricultural Experimental Station and dean of the College of Agriculture of the State University. Very early in his career he developed remarkable ability for original research, especially in that department of organic chemistry pertaining to animal processes and compounds. Among his earlier papers are "On the Vital Activity of the Enzymes" (1901); "The Inactivity of Lipase Towards the Salts of Certain Acid Ethers in the Light of the Theory of Electrolytic Dissociation" (1902); and "A Method for the Determination of the Affinities of Acids Colormetrically by Means of Certain Vegetable Coloring Matters" (1905), the last two of which were published in the "American Chemical Journal." During his connection with the Public Health Service his papers appeared chiefly in the bulletins of the Hygienic Laboratory

and among these were "The Influence of Chemical Constitution in the Lipolytic Hydrolyses of Ethereal Salts" (1906); "The Toxicity of Ozone and Other Oxidizing Agents to Lipase" (1906); "A Test for Saccharin, and a Simple Method of Distinguishing Between Cumarin and Vanillin" (1906); "The Conduct of Phenolphthalein in the Animal Organism" (1906); and "On the Stability of the Oxidases and Their Conduct Towards Various Reagents" (1906). He also contributed "Phenolphthalin as a Reagent for Oxidases and Other Oxidizing Substances in Plant and Animal Tissues" (1907) to the "Journal of Biological Chemistry," and "On the Available Alkali in the Ash of Human and Cow's Milk in its Relation to Infant Nutrition" (1908); and "On the Use of Nitrous Acid, Nitrates, and Aqua Regia in the Determination of the Mineral Constituents of Urine" (1908) to the "American Journal of Physiology." His other papers contributed to the hygienic bulletins are "Chemical Test for Blood" (with bibliography, 1909); and "The Oxidases and Oxygen Catalysts Concerned in Biological Oxidations" (1909). Most of his later papers appeared in the "American Chemical Journal," and among his many titles may be mentioned "Peroxidase Accelerators and Their Possible Significance for Biological Oxidations" (1908); "On the Decomposition of the Leucosulphonic Acids of Rosaniline Hydrochloride and Crystal Violet in Aqueous Solution" (1909); "On the Preparation of Certain Sulphonic Acids in the Free State" (1910); "On the Conversion of Benzenesulphonedibromamide into Dibrombenzenesulphonamide by Means of Concentrated Sulphuric Acid" (1911); "A Study of Orthoaminoparasulphobenzoic Acid with Special Reference to Fluorescence" (1911); and "On the Experimental Illustration of the Law of Definite Proportions Through Combustion of the Halogens with Finely Divided Silver" (1911). The foregoing have all appeared under his own name, but there are likewise numerous papers of joint authorship representing work inspired by him and carried out under his supervision. Of this character is "The Relation of Calcium to Anaphylaxis" (1913), which appeared in the "Journal of Infectious Diseases." Dr. Kastle is also the author of a textbook on "The Chemistry of Metals" (1900). He is a member of the Society of Biological Chemists and of the American Physiological Society. He was married, June 18, 1895, to Callie Warner, of Lexington, Ky.

LEUPP, Francis Ellington, editor and author, was born in New York city, Jan. 2, 1849, son of John P. and Emeline (Davis) Loop, and grandson of Hon. Henry Loop, who was a son of Capt. Peter Loop, a soldier in the revolutionary war. The family name was earlier spelled "Leupp" and many members of the last three generations have returned to that form. He was graduated at Williams College in 1870 and entering Columbia Law School, received the degree of LL.B. in 1872. After a year of literary work for the magazines, he became an assistant editor of the New York "Evening Post" in 1874, then in charge of William Cullen Bryant, but upon Bryant's death in 1878, he removed to Syracuse, N. Y., to take editorial charge of the "Herald" of that city, in which he had become a stockholder. In 1885 he removed to Washington, D. C., and having retained in the interim his connection with the "Evening Post" as correspondent and editorial contributor, continued in that capacity in Washington. He was identified with civil service reform in the early stages of the movement, and when the leading papers devoted to this reform were combined in one entitled, "Good Government," he became its editor, continuing as such until its removal to New York city in 1895. His interest in the Indian question dated from his first editorial work. He served on the U. S. Board of Indian Commissioners during 1895–97, and in 1905 was appointed U. S. commissioner of Indian affairs. During his administrative term he inaugurated many changes and reforms for the welfare of the Indians that had far-reaching results. He brought the entire service under the civil service rules. He established an employment bureau for Indians who preferred other kinds of work to farming, inducing contractors, railway companies and others to give Indian laborers a trial. He obtained the first appropriation for fighting the trachoma epidemic among Indians and organized a systematic campaign for its treatment; reorganized the medical service, placing it under a specially appointed director and making every reservation superintendent a health officer with full power to enforce rules for sanitation; established sanitarium schools for tubercular Indian children; admitted white children to the little Indian schools on the frontier, thus bringing the races into friendly companionship in childhood, and increased the number of day schools on the reservations, introducing open-air schools wherever the climate would permit. He obtained the first appropriation for suppressing the liquor traffic among Indians; encouraged the development of the natural resources on the reservations, such as water power, mineral deposits and timber industry; liberalized the conditions of trade, discouraging the running of book accounts at the stores, and instructing Indians how to do their own banking; extended the outing system at the schools so as to put the young people into mechanical shops as well as on farms and in families; in brief he tried to treat the Indian like other men, to individualize him just as the Caucasian is individualized, and to give him all the liberty he can enjoy without trespassing upon the rights of others. His administration of more than four years was the first of that length to be free from a hostile Indian outbreak of any kind. Mr. Leupp is the author of "How to Prepare for a Civil Service Examination" (1898); "The Man Roosevelt" (1914); "The Indian and His Problem" (1910); biography of William H. Taft for Scribner's, "The Presidents of the United States" (1914), "In Red Man's Land" (1914), "A Day with Father" (1914), and "Walks About Washington" (1915), and many magazine and cyclopedia articles. He is a member of the Sons of the American Revolution and of the Cosmos and Gridiron clubs. Williams College conferred upon him the honorary degree of LL.D. in 1910.

TIPPLE, Ezra Squier, clergyman, was born at Camden, N. Y., Jan. 23, 1861, son of Martin and Sarah Elizabeth (Squier) Tipple, and grandson of Rev. Ezra S. Squier, a distinguished minister of the old Black River Conference. His boyhood was spent at Camden, where he received his early education in the high school. Later he studied at the Classical School of Rome, N. Y., and was graduated at Syracuse University in 1884. Subsequently he entered the Drew Theological Seminary, where he was graduated in 1887. From Syracuse he obtained the degrees of A.B., A.M. and Ph.D., the last two on examination in English literature; in 1899 he received the degree of D.D., and in 1913 the degree of LL.D. Upon completing his theological course he joined the New York conference of the Methodist Episcopal church. His entire active

ministry has been spent in New York city. His first charge (1887-1892) was St. Luke's Church, for many years the wealthiest of the denomination, and in 1892 he became pastor of Grace M. E. Church, adding 1,000 members and erecting a new edifice that increased the property value to $250,000. In 1897 he was appointed over St. James', one of the oldest and most widely known of Methodist churches in New York, and during the fourth year of his pastorate there he was asked to undertake the organization and executive management of the New York "twentieth century thank-offering movement." This was a project to secure at the beginning of the century a special fund of $1,000,000 as a thank offering for the blessings of the nineteenth century and as an earnest of the denomination's faith and purpose in New York. The money was to be devoted to the liquidation of the mortgage indebtedness of the Methodist churches in New York city, the partial endowment of the New York Deaconess Home and St. Christopher's Home for Children and the enlargement of the fund for aged and infirm ministers. The methods employed were almost entirely originated by the executive secretary, Dr. Tipple. In 1904 $1,032,000 had been received and many results obtained of infinitely greater value than any monetary consideration. During his ministry in New York Dr. Tipple's interest and co-operation were freely given to philanthropic and educational enterprises generally. He has been closely identified with the deaconess movement of the Methodist Episcopal church from its inauguration in 1888, was secretary of the New York Deaconess Home, a member of the advisory board of St. Christopher's Home for Children and of the Gospel Mission to the Tombs. In 1905 he became professor of practical theology at Drew Theological Seminary, and in 1912 he was elected president of the seminary, succeeding Rev. Henry Anson Buttz. He is a trustee of Syracuse University, a member of the board of managers of the Missionary Society of the Methodist Episcopal church and trustee and recording secretary of the board of education of the church. He has contributed widely to the religious press and is the author of: "Heart of Asbury's Journal" (1905); "The Minister of God" (1906); "Drew Sermons" (first series, 1906; second series, 1907); "Drew Sermons on the Golden Texts" (1908, 1909, 1910); "Life of Freeborn Garrettson" (1910), and "Some Famous Country Parishes" (1911). He is a fluent speaker with a rare vein of delightful spontaneity and a commanding presence. He is a member of Phi Beta Kappa and Delta Upsilon. Dr. Tipple was married at Detroit, Mich., June 24, 1897, to Edna Estelle, daughter of A. E. F. White. Portrait opposite page 413.

LAMAR, Joseph Rucker, associate justice U. S. supreme court, was born in Ruckersville, Ga., Oct. 14, 1857, son of James S. and Mary (Rucker) Lamar, and a descendant of Thomas Lamar, a Huguenot, who settled in Maryland in 1663. Descendants of this Thomas Lamar removed to Georgia in 1755 and have played a prominent part in the public life of the nation, the most notable of the family being Lucius Q. C. Lamar, who was U. S. senator and justice of the supreme court of the United States, and Mirabeau B. Lamar, who was Sam Houston's successor as president of the independent republic of Texas. Joseph R. Lamar received his early education at Martin Institute, Jefferson, Ga., Richmond Academy, Augusta, Ga., the Penn Lucy School near Baltimore, Md., the University of Georgia and Bethany College, being graduated at the last in 1877. Subsequently he attended the law school of Washington and Lee University, and was admitted to the bar in 1879. He began practice in Augusta, Ga., and was soon ranked among the leading lawyers of the state. Though he "specialized in general practice," to use his own words, he was perhaps best known as a corporation lawyer, and largely represented railroads and other great corporations, arguing many cases involving important and difficult questions before the supreme court of Georgia. During 1886–89 he sat in the Georgia legislature, representing Richmond county. His service in the legislature led to the passing of several important laws, of which he was the author. In 1893 he was appointed a member of the commission of three to revise the legal code of Georgia. His particular province was the preparation of the text of the civil code, and his masterly completion of his task brought wide attention to his work. Of the statutes he prepared the best known are the Eminent Domain Act, the Auditors' Act, the Assignment Act, and the Practice Act. In 1901 he was appointed to fill out an unexpired term as associate justice of the supreme court of Georgia. He was elected to that office in 1903 and served until ill-health induced him to resign in 1905 when he resumed his law practice in Augusta. While connected with the Georgia supreme court he was the author of more than 200 opinions which are embraced in six volumes of the Georgia Report. The reader of these opinions will be impressed with the learning of the writer and the terse and striking form of expression conveying satisfactory and convincing reasoning. In 1910 Justice Lamar was appointed to the supreme court of the United States by Pres. Taft. His opinions on that bench were finished examples of legal logic, distinguished alike for their brevity of statement, clearness of expression and simplicity of style. In 1914 Pres. Wilson appointed him senior commissioner of the so-called A B C Conference on the Mexican situation, which met at Niagara Falls. During 1905-10 he was chairman of the board of examiners on applicants for admission to the bar of Georgia. Justice Lamar was married Jan. 30, 1879, to Clarinda, daughter of W. K. Pendleton, president of Bethany College, and is survived by two sons: Philip Rucker and William Pendleton Lamar. He died in Washington, D. C., Jan. 2, 1916.

CHOATE, Leander, capitalist, was born near South Bridgeton, Me., Nov. 17, 1834, son of Nehemiah and Rebecca (Kimball) Choate. His earliest paternal American ancestor was John Choate, who came from England prior to 1643 and settled at Ipswich, Mass. Ebenezer Choate, grandfather of Leander Choate, served for three years in the continental army during the revolutionary war. The subject of this sketch was educated at the district schools and by his mother, an experienced teacher. After some time in the employ of Choate & Tolman, wood and coal dealers of Lynn, Mass., he purchased a parcel express route between Boston and Charlestown, which he conducted until 1857. In that year he removed to Wisconsin, where he was engaged as overseer by a lumber firm. In 1862 he formed a partnership in the lumber business with James M. Bray, under the firm name of Bray & Choate, which continued almost half a century. The firm had mills on the Wisconsin and Oconto rivers and at Choate, Mich., the town being named in honor of Mr. Choate. Within twenty-five years the average annual cutting of the firm approximated forty million feet. At this period the policy of the junior partner, upon whom the burden of managing the diverse interests of the company had

fallen, was to buy timber for holding rather than for marketing. In addition to these lumbering operations, he was at one time president of the Wolf River Lumber Co., the Oshkosh Log and Lumber Co. and the Choate-Hollister Furniture Co.; vice-president of the H. W. Wright Lumber Co., the Merrill Boom Co., Merrill, Wis., and the Sanford Logging Co., and was intimately associated also with the affairs of the Oshkosh Waterworks Co. and the Wisconsin Electric Railway Co. At his death he was president of the Oshkosh Savings and Trust Co., the Davis-Hansen Co., the Co-operative Coal and Ice Co., the Oshkosh Grass Matting Co., the Wegner Fuel Co., the Coal Briquette Machine Co., and the Oshkosh Clothing Manufacturing Co., and vice-president of the Oshkosh Logging Tool Co., and the Oshkosh Muslin Underwear Co. He was likewise interested financially in the Wolf River Paper and Fiber Co., Shawano, Wis., and the Schmit Brothers Trunk Co. He was president of the Commercial National Bank of Oshkosh, the National Bank of Manitowoc and the First National Bank of Stoughton; vice-president of the First National Bank of New London, and director of the Marine National Bank of Milwaukee and of the First National Bank of Marshfield, Wis. He was a trustee of the Oshkosh Public Library and the First Congregational Church, and a member of the Benevolent and Protective Order of Elks. He was a man of exceptional strength, energy and persistence, scrupulously honest in all his dealings, and withal a generous, whole-souled, tolerant, gentle man, sensitive and modest in disposition and conduct, who did much good unostentatiously and possessed the affection and esteem of everybody who came into contact with him. Mr. Choate was married, Dec. 19, 1858, to his cousin, Adeline Pratt, daughter of Alden Choate. He died at Oshkosh, Wis., Oct. 18, 1909.

ASHURST, Henry Fountain, U. S. senator, was born in Winnemucca, Nev., Sept. 13, 1874, son of William Henry and Sarah Elizabeth (Bogard) Ashurst, and a descendant of Josiah F. Ashurst, who was a pioneer settler in the Virginia colony in 1741. His father was a pioneer and prospector, who removed from Nevada to Arizona shortly after the son's birth, and the latter was educated in the public schools of Flagstaff. At the age of fifteen he became a cowboy, and for three years rode the range in Coconino, Navajo and Apache counties, but the wild life of the plains was distasteful to him; he was ambitious for a professional career, and embracing every opportunity to improve his education, spent two years in the Stockton Business College of Stockton, Cal., after which he took a course in law and political economy at the University of Michigan (1903-04). He began the practice of his profession at Williams, Ariz., in 1904, and was admitted to practice before the United States supreme court in March, 1908. Early in his career he became interested in politics. He had not been long in Williams when he was made justice of the peace, and at the age of twenty-one, announcing himself as a candidate for the territorial legislature, stumped the surrounding country in his own behalf, and surprised his hearers by the extent of his knowledge and familiarity with the political questions of the day. Despite his youth, his victory at the ensuing election was described as a landslide. He was re-elected two years later, being chosen speaker of the house of representatives, and he is said to be the youngest man who ever held such a position in the United States. In 1902 he was elected to the territorial senate. He also served twice as district attorney of Coconino country, 1904–08. He was one of five Democratic candidates for the United States senatorship in 1911, and at the general election held in December of that year received the votes of the people, and in the following March was elected senator by the unanimous vote of the first legislative assembly of the new state. Sen. Ashurst is of a studious nature, fond of reading, and is an orator of force and ability. He was married Mar. 2, 1904, to Elizabeth McEvoy Rence, of Flagstaff.

PILLSBURY, Walter Bowers, educator, was born at Burlington, Ia., July 21, 1872, son of William Henry Harrison and Eliza Crahtree (Bowers) Pillsbury, and a descendant of William Pillsbury, who came from England in 1642, settling first near Boston and subsequently at Newburyport, Mass. He was educated at the public schools of Mt. Pleasant, Ottumwa and Oskaloosa, Ia., and Fullerton, Neb., at Penn College, Oskaloosa, Ia., and at the University of Nebraska, being graduated at the last in 1892. During 1893–96 he attended Cornell University, where he received the degree of Ph.D. in 1896. He also spent two summers and one period of eight months in study and travel abroad, attending the University of Wurzburg during the summer of 1902. After his graduation at the University of Nebraska, he taught mathematics for a year at Grand Island College, Neb., and during 1895–97 he was assistant in psychology at Cornell University. Subsequently, until 1900, he was instructor in psychology at the University of Michigan, where he became assistant professor in 1900, junior professor in 1905, and professor in 1910. He has taught several summer sessions at Columbia University and was non-resident lecturer there during the first semester of 1908–09. In the summer of 1910 he lectured at the University of Chicago. Besides teaching, he has done important original work, especially in the investigation of the reading processes, the sources of the sensation of movement, and mental fatigue. He is the author of "L'Attention" (1906), which was translated into Spanish, and published in an enlarged edition in 1908; "The Fundamentals of Psychology" (1916), and with Prof. Titchener he translated Külpe's "Outlines of Philosophy" (1897). Prof. Pillsbury was president of the Western Philosophical Association in 1907 and of the American Psychological Association in 1910, and he is a member of these and of the American Physiological Society and the Phi Beta Kappa and Sigma Ki fraternities. He is unmarried.

FREER, Charles Lang, manufacturer and art patron, was born at Kingston, N. Y., Feb. 25, 1856, son of Jacob R. and Phoebe Jane (Townsend) Freer, of French-Huguenot ancestry. His first American ancestor was one of the original patentees of New Paltz, N. Y. He early developed a love of nature, and while still a youth in Kingston sought life in the country, spending two summers at hard work on a farm of rare natural scenic beauty. After a public school education he entered the employ of a cement manufacturing company near his home. At the age of eighteen he became accountant and paymaster of the Ulster and Delaware railroad, his duties requiring him to make frequent trips through the Catskill Mountains. Thus his early working years were spent in an environment of natural beauty, and its influence helped to develop an appreciation of the beautiful in years to come. When twenty-one years of age he became accountant and later treasurer of a small railroad in Indiana and three years later he

engaged in the manufacture of railway cars and equipment under the name of the Peninsular Car Works in Detroit, Mich. He acquired a small interest in the business, was made its secretary, and during the next twenty years accumulated a considerable fortune. Upon the organization of the American Car and Foundry Co. for the purpose of manufacturing railway cars and supplies on a large scale, his company was one of thirteen taken over, and he retired from active business. Thenceforth he devoted his time to indulging his hobby for art and to increasing his collection of paintings and etchings which had already became famous. As early as 1880 he had begun collecting prints by American painter-etchers, to which was added by degrees the work of a few leading American painters, including Whistler. When specimens of early Japanese art were offered for sale in America, he determined to make a study of that field and to add a choice and select representation of Japanese art to his collection. Thus the Freer art collection is confined almost entirely to American and Asiatic schools. His great desire was to unite modern work with masterpieces of certain periods of high civilization harmonious in spiritual and physical suggestion, having the power to broaden aesthetic culture and the grace to elevate the human mind. By 1905 nearly 2,000 objects of American and Oriental art had been acquired. In a letter to Pres. Roosevelt, dated Dec. 14, 1905, Mr. Freer offered to present his entire collection to the Smithsonian Institution or the United States government, and to bequeath the sum of $500,000 with which to erect a building for the future care and exhibition of the collection. The appropriation for the building has since been increased to $1,000,000, and it is to be an annex to the National Art Gallery but under the administration of the Smithsonian Institution. This arrangement did not preclude the right to make additions during his lifetime, and he has since visited Asiatic countries, Egypt and the nearer East and secured from native collectors and dealers many unique objects. The Freer collection contains about 1,200 specimens of the work of Whistler, including the complete woodwork and all of Whistler's decorations of the famous Peacock room taken from the London residence of F. R. Leyland. It is the largest collection of Whistler's art in existence, comprising the best of his oil paintings, water colors, pastels, etchings, lithographs, pencil drawings and sketches, and wood engravings. It also contains some of the best work of John S. Sargent, Abbott H. Thayer, T. W. Dewing, D. W. Tryon, Gari Melchers, Winslow Homer and Childe Hassam. It has over 1,000 Chinese and Japanese paintings, representing the period from the tenth to the nineteenth century, and including such masters as Ririomin, Sesshu, Sesson, Motonobu, Tanyu, Koyetsu, Sotatsu, Korin, Kenzan, Hoitsu, Okio and Hokusai; an exceedingly rich collection of nearly 1,500 pieces of ancient pottery from China, Corea, Japan, Egypt, Persia and Rakka, comprising vases, jars, bowls, bottles, dishes, tiles, plaques, figures, incense boxes, etc.; 150 specimens of stone and wood sculpture from China, Japan and Egypt; 300 specimens of jade and lacquer from the Far East; some 700 Egyptian art objects. Mr. Freer is a member of the Grolier and Players' clubs of New York city, the Caxton Club of Chicago, Ill., the Copley Society of Boston, Mass., and the Yondotega, Witenagemote, Detroit, University and Lake St. Clair Fishing and Shooting clubs of Detroit, Mich. He is unmarried.

THE NATIONAL CYCLOPÆDIA OF AMERICAN BIOGRAPHY.

INDEX

VOLS. XIV, (SUPPLEMENT I.) AND XV.

NOTE: This index is a combination of the Biographical subjects, cross-reference topics and lists of official names, which in the Conspectus and Index Volume covering the first thirteen volumes of the Cyclopædia are grouped separately. With the publication of additional books, it is the intention to make a second Conspectus Volume, in which these various classifications will be separated.

Black-face type indicates the biography subjects; light-face type, the cross references and topics.

Where there are several cross references to a subject in the same volume, the volume number is given in the first reference only.

The lists of official names, such as state governors, college presidents, presidents of societies and U. S. representatives abroad, are continuations of the same lists in the Conspectus Volume from the year 1906, hence some of those names are to be found in the earlier volumes.

A.

Alexander, John W., wife of, **XV. 250, Alexander.**
Alexander, William C., president Equitable Life Assurance Society, **XV. 249, Alexander.**
Aley, Robert J., mathematician, **XV. 13.**
Algeciras, Morocco, conference of European powers at, **XIV. 171, White;** part of U. S. at, **7.**
Alger, Philip R., naval officer, **XV. 118.**
Alger, William R., clergyman, son of, **XV. 118, Alger.**
All Souls Church, Chicago, Ill., **XIV. 161, Jones.**
Allegheny Observatory, director of, **XIV. 376, Schlesinger.**
Allen, Charles F., educator, **XIV. 138.**
Allen, Charles M., educator, **XIV. 138, Allen.**
Allen, Dudley Peter, surgeon, **XIV. 245.**
Allen, Joseph W., soldier, **XIV. 256, Allen.**
Allen, Peter, physician and surgeon, **XIV. 245, Allen.**
Allen, William F., metrologist, **XIV. 255.**
Allison, Edward P., partner of, **XV. 352, Page.**
Allison, William B., statesman, **XV. 130, Rich.**
Allston Club, Boston, Mass., **XIV. 239, Low.**
Almanacs, collection of, **XV. 19, Huntington, H. E.**
Almeda Gardner Industrial School, Mississippi, organized, **XV. 161, Pond.**
Alternating currents, development of, **XV. 75, McAllister; 340, Emmet, W. L.**
Althoff, Henry, bishop, **XV. 243.**
Altman, B., & Co., merchants, New York, **XV. 183, Altman.**
Altman, Benjamin, merchant, **XV. 188.**
Altman Foundation, **XV. 188, Altman.**
Aluminum, process of making developed, **XV. 82, Bradley; 131, Cowles.**
Aluminum Company of America, **XV. 131, Cowles.**
Amber, substitute for, invented, **XV. 331, Baekeland.**
Amberg, John W., iron merchant, **XIV. 360, Amberg.**
Amberg, William A., merchant, **XIV. 360.**
Amberg File and Index Co., **XIV. 360, Amberg.**
American Academy of Art, Rome, Italy, **XIV. 316, Boring;** director of, **XV. 201, Millet.**
American Academy of Medicine, presidents of, **XIV. 424, Hawley; X. 284, Wood; XIV. 232, Davis; XV. 353, Wilbur.**
American Agricultural Chemical Co., **XV. 400, Gibbons.**
American Amateur Athletic Union, **XV. 54, Sullivan.**
American Anthropological Association, presidents of, **X.** 349, McGee; **III.** 102, Putnam; **XII.** 509, Boas; **XVI. ——,** Holmes; **XV.** 32, Fewkes; **XIV.** 353, Dixon, **X.** 51, Hodge; founder of, **XIV.** 121, Kroeber.
American Anti-Boycott Association, **XV. 373, Loewe.**
American Antiquarian Society, presidents of, **I. 199, Hale; XIV. 101, Lincoln.**
American Association of Anatomists, presidents of, **XIV. 49, McMurrich; XV. 172, Harrison, XI. 56, Donaldson.**
American Association of Obstetricians and Gynecologists, president of, **XIV. 279, Dunning.**
American Association of the Red Cross, **XV. 315, Barton.**
American Bankers' Association. presidents of, **XIV.** 189, McMichael; **XV.** 65, Pierson; secretary of, **XV. 322, Farnsworth.**
American Bar Association, presidents of, **X.** 122, Parker; **XIV.** 410, Dickinson; **XII.** 30, Lehmann; **XIV.** 332, Libby, **XVI. ——,** Gregory; **XII.** 530, Kellogg; **XIV.** 433, Taft; **12, Root.**
American Boiler Co., **XIV. 337, Pierce.**
American Bridge Co., **XIV. 147, Steele.**
American Can Co., **XV. 215, Norton.**
American Car and Foundry Co., **XV. 416, Freer.**
American Cement Co. of New Jersey, **XV. 112.**
American Chemical Society, presidents of, **XIV.** 132, Hillebrand; 207, Bogert; **XV.** 393, Whitney; **XIV.**

206, Bancroft; **XV.** 64, Little; **XII.** 362, Richards.
American Cigar Co., **XV. 111, Sylvester.**
American Climatological Association, president of, **XIV. 125, Otis.**
American Colonization Society, account of, **XIV.** 176-177, Appleton; presidents of, **XIV.** 249, Smith; 176, Appleton.
American Dermatological Association, president of, **XIV. 345, Corlett.**
American District Telegraph Co., organization of, **XIV. 74, Fearons.**
American Dyewood Co., **XIV.** 466, Baldwin; 467, **Baldwin, W. M.**
American Electrochemical Society, presidents of, **XIV.** 206, Bancroft; 350, Burgess; 92, Acheson; **XV.** 393, Whitney; 330, Baekeland.
American Exchange National Bank, New York, president of, **XV. 93, Clarke.**
American Federation of Men's Church Organizations, president of, **XV. 119, Loring.**
American Fire Insurance Co., president of, **XV. 216, Montgomery.**
American Folk-Lore Society, presidents of, **XIV.** 120, Kroeber; 353, Dixon.
American Forestry Association, presidents of, **XIV.** 27, Wilson; 454, Guild; **XV.** 114, Drinker.
American Forestry Congress, **XIV. 430, Peaslee.**
American Gas Furnace Company, **XIV. 495, Reichhelm.**
American Graphophone Co., **XV.** 390, Easton; recording department of, **XV. 372, Emerson.**
American Guild of Organists, founders of, **XV.** 364, Brewer; 383, Macfarlane.
American Gynecological Society, presidents of, **XIV.** 240, Maury; 426, Cleveland; 144, Baldy.
American Historical Association, presidents of, **X.** 45, Baldwin; 442, Jameson; **XII.** 253, Adams; **XI.** 394, Hart; **XIII.** 174, Turner; **XIV.** 1, Roosevelt; **XIII.** 217, McLaughlin.
American Indians. See Indians.
American Institute of Architects, presidents of, **XIV.** 311, Day; **XI.** 327, Gilbert; **XIV.** 344, Cook.
American Institute of Chemical Engineers, president of, **XV. 331, Baekeland.**
American Institute of the City of New York, president of, **436, Ely, Nathan C.**
American Institute of Electrical Engineers, presidents of, **XIV.** 240, Stott; 208, Sheldon; 526, Ferguson; 520, Stillwell; **XV.** 225, Mershon; 84, Carty.
American Institute of Homeopathy, **XIV. 283, Runnels.**
American Institute of Mining Engineers, presidents of, **XIV.** 70, Gayley; **I.** 244, Hunt; **X.** 152, Hammond; **XIV.** 508, Brunton; **X.** 227, Kirchhoff; **XV.** 66, Thayer; **XIV.** 190, Saunders.
American Institute for Scientific Research, **XIV. 48, Hyslop.**
American Institute of Social Service, organizers of, **XIV. 219, Tolman.**
American Laryngological Association, presidents of, **XIV.** 188, Knight; **XV.** 56, Casselberry.
American Library Association, presidents of, **XIV.** 340, Andrews; 339, Bostwick; **XII.** 262, Hodges.
American Locomotive Co., organized, **XIV, 525, Fisk.**
American Magazine, founders of, **XIV. 59, Baker.**
American Malt Corporation, **XIV. 479, Sully.**
American Mathematical Soc., presidents of, **XIV.** 382, White; 499, Fine.
American Medical Association, presidents of, **XIV.** 207, Mayo; 156, Bryant; 506, Burrell; 528, Gorgas; **X.** 24, Welch; **XIII.** 602, Murphy; **IX.** 345, Jacobi; **XII.** 207, Vaughan; **XV.** 129, Blue, R.
American Museum of Natural History, collections of birds and mammals, **XIV.** 281, Sennett; meteorites in, **61.**

American Museum of Safety Devices and Industrial Hygiene, **XIV.** 219, Tolman.

American National Red Cross, **XIV.** 406, Taft; **XV.** 315, Barton.

American Olympic Committee, president of, **XV.** 202, Thompson.

American Oriental Society, presidents of, **VI.** 423, Toy; **XI.** 96, Lanman; **XIV.** 476, Hopkins; **VIII.** 147, Ward; **X.** 400, Bloomfield; **X.** 101, Moore; **XI.** 372, Jastrow; **XIII.** 550, Jackson.

American Peace Society, presidents of, **XIV.** 185, Coues; 417, Burton.

American Philological Association, presidents of, **XIV,** 312, Merrill; 484, Kelsey; **X.** 469, Gildersleeve; **XI.** 75, Shorey.

American Physical Society, president of, **XV.** 195, Merritt.

American Psychological Association, presidents of, **XIV.** 269, Angell; **X.** 328, Marshall; **XIII.** 551, Stratton; **XV.** 416, Pillsbury.

American Public Health Association, presidents of, **XIV.** 472, Westbrook; 181, Robinson; **X.** 226, Hering.

American Railway Association, **XIV.** 256, Allen.

American Rubber Co., **XIV.** 452, Evans.

American Sabbath Union, **XIV.** 172, Crafts; 477, Mott.

American School of Osteopathy, Kirksville, Mo., **XIV.** 451, Still.

American Sheet and Tin Plate Co., **XIV.** 442, Leeds.

American Shipbuilding Co., president of, **XIV.** 496, Brown.

American Society of Biological Chemists, president of, **XV.** 334, Osborne.

American Society of Civil Engineers, presidents of, **XIV.** 306, Stearns; 205, Benzenberg; **XI.** 475, MacDonald; **XV.** 208, Bates; **XI.** 339, Bensel; **XV.** 237, Endicott; **XII.** 276, Swain; **XV.** 235, McDonald.

American Society of Irrigation Engineers, president of, **XIV.** 365, Carpenter, L. G.

American Society of Mechanical Engineers, presidents of, **XIV.** 521, Taylor; **II.** 243, Hutton; **XIV.** 419, Holman; **XV.** 41, Westinghouse; 188, Meier; 294, Hartness; **IV.** 552, Brashear.

American Society of Naturalists, presidents of, **XIV.** 49, McMurrich; **XII.** 343, Morgan; **XIII.** 125, McDougal; **XII.** 351, Conklin; **XV.** 172, Harrison; **XIV.** 479, Lillie; **XV.** 382, Pearl.

American Society of Orificial Surgeons, **XIV.** 233, Runnels.

American Society for Psychical Research, objects of, **XIV.** 48, Hyslop.

American Society of Zoologists, president of, **XIV.** 479, Lillie, F. R.

American Sociological Society, president of, **XV.** 9, Giddings.

American Steel Manufacturers' Association, president of, **XV.** 377, Huston, A. F.

American Steel and Wire Co., **XV.** 306, Baackes.

American Strauss, sobriquet, **XIV.** 518, Englander.

American Surety Co., N. Y., **XIV.** 126, Lyman.

American Surgical Association, presidents of, **XIII.** 88, Vander Veer; **XIV.** 245, Allen; 207, Carmalt; 370, Nancrede; **X.** 283, Matas; **XI.** 230, Gerster; **XIV.** 207, Mayo.

American Swiss File & Tool Co., **XIV.** 495, Reichhelm.

American Telephone and Telegraph Co., **XV.** 321, Bethell.

American Tobacco Co., **XV.** 291, Hill; 388, Myers.

American Unitarian Association, missionary supt. for, **XIV.** 453, Wendte.

American University, Wash., D. C., **XIV.** 435, Hamilton.

American Wine Growers' Association, organized, **XIV.** 294, Emerson.

American Woolen Co., presidents of, **XV.** 320, Ayer; 321, Wood.

Ames, Charles Gordon, clergyman, **XIV.** 262; son of, 500, Ames.

Ames, Charles W., publisher, **XIV.** 500.

Ames, David, **XIV.** 201, Ames, Oliver, (1st).

Ames, Frederick L., manufacturer, **XIV.** 202.

Ames, John, man'f'r., **XIV.** 201, Ames, Oliver, (1st).

Ames, Louis Annin, merchant, **XV.** 262.

Ames, Oliver (1779), inventor and manufacturer, **XIV.** 201.

Ames, Oliver (1807), manufacturer and capitalist, **XIV.** 201.

Ames, Oliver, & Sons, shovels, **XIV.** 201-202; Ames.

Ames, Winthrop, theatrical manager, **XV.** 176.

Ammons, Elias M., governor, **XV.** 405.

Amory, Charles W., capitalist, **XV.** 37.

Amory, John J., manufacturer, **XIV.** 239.

Amory, William, capitalist, **XV.** 37, Amory.

Amory Mills, Manchester, N. H., **XV.** 37, Amory.

Amoskeag Cotton Mill, Manchester, N. H., **XV.** 37, Amory.

Amoskeag Manufacturing Co., **XV.** 37, Amory.

Anaconda mine, president of, **XV.** 66, Thayer.

Anatomy, early school of, in Philadelphia, **XV.** 261, Lawrence.

Anderson, Abraham A., artist, **XIV.** 259.

Anderson, Joseph G., R. C. bishop, **XV.** 368.

Anderson, Larz, diplomat, **XV.** 349.

Anderson, Nicholas L., soldier, **XV.** 349, Anderson.

Anderson, William F., bishop, **XIV.** 486.

Andrew, A. Piatt, economist, **XV.** 326.

Andrews, A. H., & Co., school furniture, **XIV.** 260, Andrews.

Andrews, Alfred H., manufacturer, **XIV.** 260.

Andrews, Champe S., lawyer, **XIV.** 293.

Andrews, Chauncey H., manufacturer, **XIV.** 191.

Andrews, Clement W., librarian, **XIV.** 340.

Andrews, Constant A., banker, **XIV.** 323.

Andrews, Herbert L., merchant, inventor, **XIV.** 260.

Andrews, L., & Sons, N. Y., **XIV.** 323, Andrews.

Andrews, Robert E., partner of, **XV.** 97, Edwards.

Anesthetic, new, discovered, **XV.** 354, Meltzer.

Angel of the Battlefield, **XV.** 314, Barton.

Angell, James R., psychologist, **XIV.** 269.

Aniline colors, manufacturers of, **XIV.** 99, Stone.

Annin & Co., New York, flags, **XV.** 262, Ames.

Ansel, Martin F., governor, **XIV.** 373.

Anshutz, Thomas P., artist, **XV.** 279.

Anthony, S. Reed, banker, **XV.** 140.

Anthracite coal strike of 1902, **XIV.** 6; 13; 37; 450, Truesdale; commission to settle, **XV.** 126, Mitchell.

Anthropology, researches in, **XIV.** 121, Kroeber; **XV.** 32, Fewkes.

Anti-Saloon League, **XIV.** 98, Patterson; 272, Baker.

Anti-Trust law, federal, suits under, **XIV.** 408, Knox.

Apartment houses, pioneer architects of, **XV.** 361, Hubert.

Apparitions, scientific investigations of, **XIV.** 48, Hyslop.

Appendicitis, authorities on, **XIV.** 315, McBurney; **XV.** 210, Kelly.

Apple, Henry H., educator, **XIV.** 345.

Apple King, **XV.** 153, Wellhouse.

Applegate, John S., lawyer, **XV.** 412.

Appleton, Samuel E., clergyman and philanthropist, **XIV.** 176.

Aquadag, lubricant, invented, **XIV.** 94.

Aquarium, New York, **XV.** 284, Damon.

Aransas Pass, Tex., founder of, **XV.** 118, Wheeler.

Arbitration of boundary dispute between Brazil and Argentine by United States, **XV.** 100, Uhl.

Arbitration, international, conferences on, **XV.** 38,

Baldy, John M., physician, **XIV.** 144.
Balke, Julius, manufacturer, **XIV.** 294, Bensinger.
Ball, Jonas, daughter of, **XV.** 35, Baker.
Ballenger, Edgar G., physician, **XV.** 134.
Ballinger, Richard A., lawyer and secretary of the interior, **XIV.** 413; 31.
Balloons, ascensions of, **XIV.** 190, Saunders; experiments with, **XV.** 3, Rotch; 401, Curtiss.
Baltimore, Md., U. S. appraiser at, **XIV.** 402, Sharretts.
Bananas, extent of the sale of, **XIV.** 350, Baker.
Bancroft, Edgar A., lawyer, **XIV.** 373.
Bancroft, Joseph, & Sons, cotton mills, **XV.** 371, Bancroft.
Bancroft, Samuel, manufacturer, **XV.** 371.
Bancroft, Samuel, **XV.** 15, Huntington.
Bancroft, Wilder D., chemist, **XIV.** 206.
Bancroft, William P., **XV.** 371, Bancroft.
Bankhead, John H., senator, **XIV.** 210.
Banking, study of foreign system of, **XIV.** 227, Conant; 431, Andrew.
Bank of California, San Francisco, **XV.** 238, Keene.
Banks, Charles E., author, **XIV.** 99.
Banks, James, patriot, **XIV.** 482, Reynolds.
Banks, manufacture of furniture for, **XIV.** 260, Andrews, A. H.; legislative provision for guarantee of deposits of, 466, Haskell; land, first in United States, **XIV.** 232, Glynn.
Bannin, Michael E., merchant, **XIV.** 468.
Bar iron, manufacture of, **XV.** 66, Vance.
Barber Asphalt Co., A. L., **XV.** 109, Henry.
Barber, Donn, architect, **XIV.** 379.
Barbour Bros. Co., thread mfrs., **XV.** 79, Barbour.
Barbour, Erwin H., geologist, **XIV.** 278.
Barbour, James J., partner of, **XV.** 132, Knight.
Barbour, Robert, manufacturer, **XV.** 79, Barbour.
Barbour, Thomas, manufacturer, **XV.** 79, Barbour.
Barbour, William, manufacturer, **XV.** 79.
Barclay, John C., inventor and teleg. mgr., **XIV.** 75.
Barker, James M., jurist, **XIV.** 494.
Barlow, Charles, merchant, **XIV.** 187.
Barnard, Kate, reformer, **XV.** 110.
Barnes, James, author, **XIV.** 437.
Barnes, W. H., banker, **XIV.** 169, Williston.
Barnum, P. T., associate of, **XV.** 284, Damon.
Barr, William, merchant, **XIV.** 522.
Barr, William, Dry Goods Co., St. Louis, Mo., **XIV.** 522, Barr.
Barrett, William E., journalist and congressman, **XIV.** 172.
Barrow, David C., educator, **XV.** 138.
Barrymore, Ethel, in vaudeville, **XV.** 297, Keith.
Bartlett, Robert A., member of Peary north pole expedition, **XIV.** 61.
Bartlett, Willard, jurist, **XV.** 412.
Barton, Clara, humanitarian, **XV.** 314.
Barton, Enos M., capitalist, **XIV.** 110.
Barton, Thomas P., diplomat, **XIV.** 365.
Baseball, promoter of, **XV.** 178, Brush.
Bassett, Thomas J., president of Upper Iowa University, **XIV.** 292, Shanklin, W. A.
Batavia, N. Y., State School for the Blind, **XV.** 54, Fuller.
Batchelder & Lincoln, shoe jobbers, **XIV.** 333, Lincoln.
Bates, Charles A., financier, **XV.** 74.
Bates dredge, inventor of, **XV.** 81, Bates.
Bates, John C., soldier, **XIV.** 34.
Bates, Lindon W., engineer, **XV.** 81.
Bates, Margaret Holmes (Ernsperger), author, **XV.** 74, Bates.
Bates, Onward, civil engineer, **XV.** 208.
Bates, William W., shipbuilder, **XV.** 81, Bates.
Battell, Robbins, philanthropist, **XIV.** 254.
Battery, storage, invented, **XV.** 334, Perret.

Battle, Elisha, **XV.** 97, Battle.
Battle, George Gordon, lawyer, **XV.** 97; partner of, 13, O'Gorman.
Battle Creek, Mich., mfrs. at, **XIV.** 287, Post.
Bauer, L. A., magnetician, **XIV.** 186.
Baxter, Nathaniel, Jr., capitalist, **XV.** 318.
Bay State Co., **XV.** 301, Sullivan.
Beach, Harlan P., missionary and author, **XIV.** 120.
Beach, Henry H. A., surgeon, **XV.** 164.
Beach, Mrs. H. H. A., musician, **XV.** 164.
Beach, Rex E., author, **XIV.** 58.
Beaman, Charles C., lawyer, **XV.** 167.
Bear Mill Manufacturing Co., **XV.** 411, Bernheimer.
Bearns, James Sterling, daughter of, **XV.** 408, Darlington.
Beatty, Alfred C., engineer, **XIV.** 238.
Beatty, John W., art director, **XIV.** 88.
Beaupré, Arthur M., diplomat, **XIV.** 338.
Beaver, James A., sister of, **XV.** 157, White.
Bed, folding, inventor of, **XIV.** 204, Woodruff.
Becker, Francis Louis, musician and inventor, **XV.** 51, Becker.
Becker, Gustav L., musician, **XV.** 51.
Bedel, Timothy, soldier, **XIV.** 135.
Bedell, Gregory T., clergyman, **XV.** 262, Grant.
Bedford, Edward T., merchant, **XIV.** 504.
Beebe, J. M., merchant, **XIV.** 66, Morgan.
Beebe, Morgan & Co., dry goods merchants, **XIV.** 66, Morgan.
Beekman, Charles K., lawyer, **XIV.** 306.
Behan, Kate W., philanthropist, **XIV.** 314.
Behan, William J., merchant, **XIV.** 314.
Behrman, Martin, mayor, **XIV.** 371.
Belasco, David, playwright, **XIV.** 83; 82, Warfield.
Belgium, U. S. ministers to, **XII.** 452, Bryan; **XV.** 349, Anderson; 45, Marburg; **XIV.** 463, Whitlock.
Bell, Alexander Graham, inventor, **XV.** 401.
Bell, James F., soldier, **XIV.** 152.
Bell, James S., miller, **XV.** 41.
Bell, Joseph E., clergyman and classical scholar, **XIV.** 393, Bell.
Bell, Lilian, author, **XIV.** 393.
Bell, Samuel, merchant, **XV.** 41, Bell.
Bell Telephone Co., **XIV.** 216, Dougherty; **XV.** 322, Bethell; manufacturing department of, 123, Thayer.
Belle Meade stock farm, **XIV.** 411, Dickinson.
Belleville, Ill., R. C. bishop of, **XV.** 243, Althoff.
Bells, church, first in America, **XIV.** 247, Hanks.
Belting, manufacture of, **XIV.** 387, Ladew.
Beman, Solon S., architect, **XIV.** 304.
Benjamin, Judah P., partner of, **XV.** 161, Micou.
Bennett, George S., financier, **XV.** 387.
Bennett, John E., soldier and jurist, **XIV.** 335.
Bennett, James Gordon, prize cup for aviation, **XV.** 401.
Bennett, Ziba, merchant and banker, **XV.** 387, Bennett.
Bennington & Rutland railway, president of, **XIV.** 322, McCullough.
Bensinger, Moses, merchant, **XIV.** 294.
Bensley Water Co., San Francisco, Cal., **XV.** 303, Shafter.
Benson, Frank W., governor, **XIV.** 439.
Benton, Guy P., educator, **XV.** 171; **XIV.** 292, Shanklin, W. A.
Benzenberg, G. H., civil engineer, **XIV.** 205.
Berg, Per T., engineer, **XIV.** 514.
Bergengren, Anna (Farquhar), author, **XIV.** 137.
Bernheimer, Charles L., merchant, **XV.** 411.
Bethell, Union, merchant, **XV.** 322, Bethell.
Bethell, Union Noble, vice-president American Telephone & Telegraph Co., **XV.** 321.
Bethlehem (Pa.) Bach Choir, **XIV.** 355, Wolfe.
Bethlehem Steel Co., **XIV.** 69, Schwab; 521, Taylor.

Beverly, Mass., United Shoe Machinery Company's plant at, **XV.** 197.

Beyer, Henry G., surgeon, **XIV.** 250.

Bible, specimen of Guttenberg, **XV.** 19, **Huntington,** H. E.; rare editions of, **XV.** 194, **Thomas;** translated into Gilbertese, **XIV.** 98, **Bingham.**

Bickmore, Albert S., naturalist, **XV.** 284, **Damon.**

Bicycle, improved, **XIV.** 63; early speed records, **XIV.** 163, **Brown; XV.** 401, **Curtiss;** inventor of saddle for, **XV.** 282, **Veeder.**

Biddle, Clement, patriot and soldier, **XIV.** 134; daughter of, **XV.** 305, **Cadwalader, Sr.**

Bierce, Ambrose, journalist and author, **XIV.** 180.

Bifocal lens, inventor of, **XV.** 330, **Powers.**

Big Four railway, **XIV.** 442, **Leeds; XV.** 233, **Ingalls.**

Big Rapids, Mich., Ferris Institute in, **XV.** 213.

Big Stick, sobriquet, **XIV.** 9.

Bigelow, Maurice A., biologist, **XV.** 344.

Billiard tables, mfrs. of, **XIV.** 294, **Bensinger.**

Billings, Frederick, lawyer and R. R. pres., **XIV.** 380.

Bingham, Hiram, missionary, **XIV.** 98.

Binney, Horace, daughter of, **XV.** 305, **Cadwalader.**

Biological Society of Washington, D. C., president of, **XIV.** 130, **Stejneger.**

Biology, researches in, **XV.** 382, **Pearl;** 397, **Davenport.**

Birch, Stephen, mining engineer, **XV.** 393.

Birchard, Matthew, jurist, **XV.** 53.

Birds, authority on, **XIV.** 281, **Sennett;** collection of, **XV.** 70, **Frost.**

Bishop, Charles R., manufacturer, **XIV.** 276.

Bishop Steel Works, Newark, N. J., founded, **XIV.** 276, **Bishop.**

Bismarck, N. Dak., R. C. bishop of, **XV.** 248, **Wehrle.**

Bispham, David, in vaudeville, **XV.** 297, **Keith.**

Bissell, John W., president of Upper Iowa University, **XIV.** 292, **Shanklin, W. A.**

Blackstone, T. B., railroad president, **XIV.** 141.

Blair, Charles A., jurist, **XV.** 48.

Blair, Henry A., banker and financier, **XIV.** 427.

Blakelock, Ralph A., artist, **XV.** 406.

Blandy, Charles, partner of, **XV.** 209, **Shipman.**

Blass, Robert, singer, **XIV.** 485.

Blavatsky, Helena P. H., theosophist, **XV.** 336.

Bleaching, improved methods of, devised, **XV.** 40, **Matthews;** factory for, **XV.** 85, **McKenzie.**

Blease, Cole. L., governor, **XV.** 276.

Blenk, James H., archbishop, **XIV.** 237.

Blind, New York State School for, **XV.** 54, **Fuller.**

Blind deaf mute, **XV.** 177 **Keller.**

Blind senator, **XIV.** 323, **Gore.**

Bliss Co., E. W., machinery, **XV.** 20, **Bliss.**

Bliss, Eliphalet W., manufacturer, **XV.** 20.

Bliss-Leavitt torpedo, **XV.** 21, **Leavitt.**

Blodgett, Delos A., wife of, **XV.** 220, **Peck.**

Blood, device for measuring the circulation of, invented, **XV.** 240, **Keyt.**

Bloomfield, Maurice, sister of, **XIV.** 192, **Zeisler.**

Bloomfield-Zeisler, Fannie, pianist, **XIV.** 192.

Bloomingdale, Joseph B., **XIV.** 323, **Andrews.**

Blue, Rupert, sanitarian, **XV.** 129; brother of, 128.

Blue, Victor, naval officer, **XV.** 128; brother of, 129.

Boardman, Waldo E., dentist, **XIV.** 338.

Boat operated by wireless electricity, inventor of, **XV.** 106, **Hammond.**

Boats. See Ships.

Bodine, Samuel T., capitalist, **XIV.** 311.

Boettger, Henry W., silk finisher, **XV.** 211.

Boettger Silk Finishing Co., **XV.** 211, **Boettger.**

Bogalusa, La., architect of, **XIV.** 316, **Boring.**

Bogart, John, wife of, **XV.** 373, **Jefferis.**

Bogert, Jan Louwe, pioneer, **XIV.** 207, **Bogert.**

Bogert, Marston T., chemist, **XIV.** 207.

Bogert's Point, **XIV.** 207, **Bogert.**

Boggs, William R., soldier, **XV.** 323.

Boiler plates, original method of making described, **XV.** 376, **Huston, C.**

Boilers, steam, invented, **XV.** 156, **Sergeant;** improvements in, 189, **Meier.**

Boit, Elizabeth E., manufacturer, **XV.** 386.

Boit, James Hy., engineer and manufacturer, **XV.** 386-387, **Boit.**

Boltwood, Bertram B., chemist, **XV.** 138.

Bonaparte, Charles J., attorney-general, **XIV.** 22.

Bonaparte, Jérome Napoléon, son of, **XIV.** 22.

Bonaparte, Napoléon, brother of, in America, **XIV.** 22, **Bonaparte.**

Bonnell, Edwin, banker, **XV.** 63.

Bonsal, Stephen, author and journalist, **XIV.** 420.

Book-plates, artistic, **XIV.** 44, **French.**

Booth, Ballington, philanthropist, **XIV.** 54.

Booth, Mary Ann A., microscopist, **XV.** 107.

Booth, Mrs. Ballington, philanthropist, **XIV.** 54.

Booth, Samuel C., scientist, **XV.** 107.

Boothby, Alonzo, surgeon, **XIV.** 203.

Boots, pioneer manufacturers of, **XIV.** 397, **Phelps; Dodge;** see also Shoes.

Borah, William E., senator, **XIV.** 216; **XV.** 298, **Hawley.**

Borden, William, promoter, **XIV.** 365.

Borden, Ind., founded, **XIV.** 365, **Borden.**

Borglum, Gutzon, sculptor, **XIV.** 80.

Boring, William A., architect, **XIV.** 316.

Borland, John J., merchant, **XIV.** 512.

Borup, George, member of Peary north pole party, **XIV.** 61.

Boston, Mass., Emmanuel Episcopal Church in, **XIV.** 84, **Worcester;** Home for working men and women in, 96, **Charpiot;** engineer of the tunnels in, 164, **Carson;** architect of Christian Science Church in, 305, **Beman;** engineer of water-works in, 306, **Stearns;** Second Church in, 394, **Horton;** First Methodist Episcopal Church in, 435, **Hamilton;** street railways of, **XV.** 133, **Kimball;** 399, **Gaston;** Back Bay Improvement in, 350, **Chandler;** R. C. archbishop of, **XV.** 295, **O'Connell;** R. C. auxiliary bishop of, 368, **Anderson;** First National Bank in, 379, **Wing;** National Shawmut Bank in, 399, **Gaston;** West End Co. in, 399, **Gaston.**

Boston American, editor of, **XV.** 351, **Edgerly.**

Boston College of Oratory founded, **XV.** 351, **Edgerly.**

Boston Commercial Bulletin, founder of, **XIV.** 454, **Guild.**

Boston Common, architect of fountains and gates for, **XV.** 33, **Lowell.**

Boston Evening Record, **XIV.** 172, **Barrett.**

Boston Museum of Fine Arts, architect of buildings of, **XV.** 33, **Lowell.**

Boston Public Library, mural paintings in, **XV.** 280, **Abbey.**

Boston Recorder, religious newspaper, **XIV.** 264, **Willis.**

Boston Symphony Orchestra, **XIV.** 445, **Higginson.**

Boston tea party, **XV.** 335, **Rotch.**

Boston University, president of, **XV.** 194, **Murlin.**

Bostwick, Arthur E., librarian, **XIV.** 339.

Botanical library presented to University of the South, **XV.** 91, **Gattinger.**

Botanical Society of America, presidents of, **XIV.** 468, **Earle; XIII.** 478, **Atkinson; XIV.** 483, **Ganong.**

Botany, researches in, **XIV.** 468, **Earle;** 483, **Ganong; XV.** 149, **McWilliams.**

Boughton, George H., artist, **XV.** 190; 280, **Abbey.**

Bowditch, Henry I., associate of, **XIV.** 189, **Knight.**

Bowen, Henry C., daughter of, **XV.** 116, **Holt.**

Bowen, John W. E., educator, **XIV.** 361.

Bower-Barff process, introduced in iron work, **XIV.** 299, **Poulson.**

Bowerman, George F., librarian, **XIV.** 327.

Bureau of Steam Engineering, chief of, **XV.** 355, Rae.
Burford, John H., jurist, **XIV.** 432.
Burgess, Charles F., chemist and electrician, **XIV.** 350.
Burgess, Gelett, author, **XIV.** 144.
Burgess, Neil, in vaudeville, **XV.** 297, Keith.
Burke, John, governor, **XIV.** 449.
Burke, Thomas C., jurist, **XIV.** 449, Burke.
Burleigh, Clarence B., journalist, **XIV.** 377.
Burnett, Henry L., soldier and lawyer, **XIV.** 272.
Burns, William J., detective, **XV.** 49.
Burns National Detective Agency, **XV.** 50, Burns.
Burr, Willard, composer, **XV.** 286.
Burr, William H., member isthmian canal commission, **XIV.** 5.
Burrage, Robert L., physician, **XV.** 127.
Burrell, Frederick A. M., merchant, **XIV.** 79.
Burrell, Herbert L., surgeon, **XIV.** 506.
Burrows, Julius Cæsar, defeated for re-election to U. S. senate, **XV.** 221, Townsend.
Burrows, W. R., engineer, **XV.** 108, Walker.
Burton, Charles F., law partner of, **XV.** 271, Parker.
Burton, Charles G., lawyer, **XIV.** 325.
Burton, Charles S., physician, **XIV.** 284, Burton.
Burton, Clarence M., lawyer and historian, **XIV.** 284.
Burton, Marion L., educator, **XIV.** 113.
Burton, Oliver M., manufacturer, inventor, **XV.** 230.
Burton, Theodore E., sen., **XIV.** 417; 148, Johnson.
Busch, Joseph F., bishop, **XV.** 272.
Bush, Irving T., president of Bush Terminal Co., **XIV.** 102.
Bush, Rufus T., merchant, **XIV.** 102.
Bush, W. H., & Co., piano manufacturers, **XIV.** 245.
Bush, William H., manufacturer, **XIV.** 245.
Bush, William L., manufacturer, **XIV.** 245.
Bush & Gerts Piano Co., **XIV.** 245, Bush, W. L.
Bush Temple of Music, Chicago, Ill., **XIV.** 245, Bush.
Bush Terminal Co., N. Y., **XIV.** 102-103, Bush.
Bushnell, Charles F., mfr., **XV.** 374, Griswold.
Bushwick Avenue Cong. Church, Brooklyn, N. Y., **XIV.** 140, Clark.
Busse Coal Co., Chicago, Ill., **XV.** 67, Busse.
Busse, Fred A., mayor, **XV.** 67.
Butler, Ellis Parker, author, **XIV.** 179.
Butler, William A., manufacturer, **XIV.** 337. Pierce.
Butler, William Allen, lawyer, partners of, **XV.** 103, Stillman; 104, Mynderse; 392, Joline.
Button, self-fastening, inventor of, **XV.** 361, Hubert.
Byers, Samuel H. M., soldier and author, **XIV.** 150.
Byllesby, Henry M., electrical engineer, **XV.** 310.
Byllesby, H. M., & Co., engineers, **XV.** 310, Byllesby.
Byrd, Adam M., lawyer, **XV.** 156.
Byrnes, Thomas, police official, **XIV.** 308.
Byrt, Arthur William, clergyman, **XIV.** 282.

C.

Cabinet letter file, inventor of, **XIV.** 360, Amberg.
Cablegram service, improvement in, **XIV.** 371, Ward.
Cableways, invented, **XV.** 31, Miller.
Cabot, Arthur T., physician and surgeon, **XV.** 46.
Cabot, Godfrey L., manufacturer, **XIV.** 251.
Cadman, S. Parkes, clergyman, **XIV.** 268.
Cadwalader, John, jurist, **XV.** 305.
Cadwalader, John, soldier, son of, **XV.** 305.
Cadwalader, John, lawyer, **XV.** 305.
Caisson system in foundation construction, **XV.** 80, Kimball.
Caldwell, George B., president of Sperry & Hutchinson Co., **XV.** 360.
Calhoun, William J., lawyer and diplomat, **XIV.** 429.
California, Indian tribes of, **XIV.** 121, Kroeber; land fraud cases in, investigated, **XV.** 49; legislation affecting Japanese in, 134, Johnson; authority on Spanish land grant, laws of, **XV.** 309, Haight; governors of, **XIV.** 374, Gillett; **XV.** 133, Johnson.

Callaghan, Bryan, judge and mayor, **XV.** 347.
Campbell, Bulkley & Ledyard, lawyers, **XV.** 328, Campbell.
Campbell, Henry M., lawyer, **XV.** 328.
Campbell, James V., jurist, **XV.** 328, Campbell.
Campbell, R. O., Coal Co., **XV.** 175, Campbell.
Campbell, Richard O., mine operator and capitalist, **XV.** 175.
Campbell, Thomas M., governor, **XIV.** 43.
Campbell, William H., inventor, **XV.** 134.
Campbell Printing Press & Manufacturing Co., **XIV.** 270, Wood.
Canada, commission established for settling disputes with, **XIV,** 15; national conservation conference with, 31.
Canals, organization to promote improvement of, **XV.** 407, Ransdell. See Panama and Cape Cod canals.
Candy, manufacturers of, **XIV.** 192, Gunther; **XV.** 96, Huyler; **XV.** 116, Heide; 368, Intemann.
Cane-sugar industry, promotion of, **XIV.** 422, Kelly.
Canevin, John F. R., R. C. bishop, **XV.** 187.
Canneries, in Maine, **XV.** 222, Fernald.
Cannon, revolving, mfr. of, **XV.** 183, Whitney.
Cannon, Le Grand B., daughter of, **XV.** 374, Griswold.
Cannon, Walter B., physiologist, **XV.** 287.
Cans, machines for making, invented, **XV.** 21, Leavitt; 215, Norton.
Cape Cod canal, builder of, **XIV.** 122, Degnon; engineer of, 218, Parsons.
Cape Morris K. Jesup, Greenland, named, **XIV.** 61.
Cape York, meteorites, discovered, **XIV.** 60, Peary.
Capper, Arthur, governor, **XV.** 275.
Capper building, Topeka, Kas., **XV.** 275, Capper.
Capper's Weekly, **XV.** 275, Capper.
Car. See Cars.
Car rail, Johnson's, invented, **XIV.** 148.
Car spring, invented, **XV.** 356, Shaw.
Caramel candy, originated, **XIV.** 192, Gunther.
Carbon bisulphide industry, **XV.** 132, Cowles.
Carbon black, mfr of, **XIV.** 251, Cabot.
Carbon tetra chloride, process of making invented, **XV.** 40, Matthews.
Carborundum, produced in electric furnace, **XIV.** 93; **XV.** 131, Cowles.
Carborundum Co., Niagara Falls, **XIV.** 94.
Carlson, Androv, inventor and mfr., **XV.** 269, Stromberg.
Carlson, George A., governor, **XV.** 405.
Carmack, Edward W., senator, **XIV.** 484, Patterson; **XV.** 27, Lea.
Carmalt, William H., surgeon, **XIV.** 207.
Carnegie Institute, Pittsburgh, Pa., illus., **XIV.** 88; account of art department, 88, Beatty.
Carnegie Institution, **XV.** 397, Davenport.
Carnegie Museum, Pittsburgh, Pa., collection of minerals in, **XV.** 372, Jefferis.
Carnegie Steel Co., Braddock, Pa., **XV.** 45, Jones.
Carpenter, Fanny H., lawyer, **XIV.** 323.
Carpenter, Louis G., engineer, **XIV.** 365.
Carpenter, William L., jurist, **XIV.** 364.
Carrel, Alexis, surgeon and physiologist, **XV.** 301.
Carrere & Hastings, partner of, **XV.** 323, Brainard.
Carriages, manufacture of, **XV.** 402, Durant.
Carroll, William S., lawyer and diplomat, **XV.** 256.
Carroll, James, surgeon, **XV.** 61, Lazear.
Carroll, John P., bishop, **XV.** 262.
Carruth, William H., educator and author, **XIV.** 486.
Cars, inventor of sleeping, **XIV.** 203, Woodruff; first made of steel, **XIV.** 277, Swensson; heating system, **XIV.** 293, Gold; designer of Pullman, **XIV.** 305, Beman; manufacturer of axles, **XIV.** 147,

Chippewa Falls, Wis., lumber mill at, **XIV.** 52, **Weyerhaeuser;** McDonell Memorial High School at, **XV.** 141, **McDonell.**

Chisholm, Hugh J., financier, **XIV.** 154.

Chittenden, Charles C., dental surgeon, **XIV.** 227.

Chittenden, Nelson, dentist, **XIV.** 227, **Chittenden.**

Chloroform, new process of making, **XIV.** 159, **MacKaye, James.**

Choate, Charles F., lawyer, **XIV.** 253.

Choate, George, physician, **XIV.** 253, **Choate.**

Choate, Leander, lumber merchant, **XV.** 415.

Choate, Mich., named for, **XV.** 415, **Choate.**

Choctaw Indians, **XIV.** 248, **Owen.**

Chouteau, Harrison & Valle Iron Co., **XV.** 268, **Harrison.**

Christian Commonwealth, Columbus, Ga., **XV.** 367, **Albertson.**

Christian Evangelist, periodical, **XV.** 367, **Long.**

Christian Intelligencer, church newspaper, **XV.** 203, **Drury.**

Christian Science Church, Boston, Mass., consulting architect of, **XIV.** 305, **Beman.**

Church furniture, manufacture of, **XIV.** 260, **Andrews, A. H.**

Church of the Ascension, New York city, history of, **XV.** 262, **Grant.**

Church of Pilgrims, Brooklyn, N. Y., **XIV.** 113, **Burton.**

Cigars, improvement in the manufacture of, **XIV.** 45, **Hammerstein.**

Cincinnati, O., political corruption in, exposed, **XIV.** 403; Herron Seminary, **XV.** 285, **Herron.**

Cincinnati Art Museum, a founder and president of, **XV.** 234, **Ingalls.**

Cincinnati, Indianapolis, St. Louis & Chicago railway, **XV.** 233, **Ingalls.**

Circulation of blood, device for measuring invented, **XV.** 240, **Keyt.**

Circuit breaker, inventor of, **XV.** 4, **Leonard.**

Citizens' Industrial Association of America, **XIV.** 318, **Kirby;** 373, **Van Cleave.**

Civic reform, advocate of, **XIV.** 455, **Zueblin;** campaign for, **XV.** 65, **Crane.**

Civil engineering, advances in, **XIV.** 40, **Goethals;** 205, **Benzenberg;** 289, **Thomson;** 306, **Stearns; XV.** 208, **Bates;** 236, **McDonald;** 319, **Gaillard;** 389, **Smith;** 406, **Dubois.**

Civil service reform, **XIV.** 3; league to promote, 22, **Bonaparte.**

Civil war, first women nurses in, **XV.** 314, **Barton.**

Claflin, H. B. Co., dry goods, **XIV.** 302, **Eames.**

Clairvoyance, scientific investigation of, **XIV.** 48, **Hyslop.**

Clark, Champ, congressman, **XIV.** 171.

Clark, Charles H., author, **XIV.** 400.

Clark, Cyrus, **XIV.** 476, **Hopkins.**

Clark, Edgar E., member of coal strike commission, **XIV.** 6; 55, **Parker.**

Clark, Frank King, musician, **XIV.** 376.

Clark, Frederic S., manufacturer, **XIV.** 173.

Clark, James B., congressman, **XIV.** 171.

Clark, John L., clergyman, **XIV.** 140.

Clark, Joseph B., clergyman, **XIV.** 349.

Clark, Thomas F., telegraph official, **XIV.** 73.

Clark, Walter E., governor, **XIV.** 85.

Clark, Walter G., engineer, **XIV.** 261; 260, **Parker.**

Clark University, president of, **XIV.** 367, **Crogman.**

Clarke, Dumont, banker, **XV.** 92.

Clarke, George W., governor, **XV.** 257.

Clarke, Lewis L., banker, **XV.** 93, **Clarke.**

Claxton, Philander P., commissioner of education, **XV.** 270.

Clay, Brutus J., diplomat, **XIV.** 442.

Cleft palate, appliance for, invented, **XV.** 109, **Baker.**

Clearing houses, conference of, **XV.** 322, **Farnsworth.**

Cleaveland, Parker, daughter of, **XV.** 351, **Chandler.**

Clemson Agricultural College, president of, **XV.** 396, **Mell.**

Cleveland, Anthony Benezet, educator, **XIV.** 426, **Cleveland.**

Cleveland, Clement, surgeon, **XIV.** 426.

Cleveland, Grover, **XV.** 100, **Uhl.**

Cleveland, O., mayor of, **XIV.** 149, **Johnson;** first bank in, **XV.** 226, **Kelley, A.;** shipbuilding in, 277, **Coffinberry;** R. C. bishop of, **XV.** 10, **Farrelly.**

Cleveland Iron Mining Co., **XIV.** 357, **Mather.**

Cleveland ligature passer, inventor of, **XIV.** 427, **Cleveland.**

Cleveland Museum of Art, **XV.** 226, **Kelley, H. A.**

Cleveland Ship Building Co., **XV.** 277, **Coffinberry.**

Cleveland surgical table, invented, **XIV.** 427, **Cleveland.**

Cliff dwellings, Colorado, exploration of, **XV.** 32, **Fewkes.**

Clinedinst, Benjamin W., artist, **XIV.** 416.

Clocks, first tower in America for, **XIV.** 247, **Hanks;** self-winding, electric, invented, **XV.** 161, **Pond;** improvements for, invented, 265, **Locke.**

Close, Evangeline Leona (Lewis), musician, **XV.** 146, **Close.**

Close, Stuart, physician, **XV.** 145.

Clouds, measurement of, **XV.** 2, **Rotch.**

Coal, production of, **XIV.** 191, **Andrews;** 211, **Olcott, R. M.;** 389, **Baker;** 456, **Jones;** 498, **Robbins; XV.** 343, **Bullitt;** in Pennsylvania, **XIV.** 368-69, **Coxe; XV.** 213, **Taylor;** in Norway, 295, **Longyear;** dealers in, **XIV.** 369, **Coxe; XV.** 175, **Campbell;** machinery for, **XV.** 359, **Finch.**

Coal dust engine, inventor of, **XV.** 22, **Fessenden.**

Coal Strikes. See Anthracite coal strike and Colorado.

Coaling ships at sea, device for, **XV.** 31, **Miller.**

Coast and geodetic survey, transferred to the department of commerce and labor, **XIV.** 19.

Coast guard, U. S. health protection of, **XV.** 129, **Blue, R.**

Cobb, William T., governor, **XIV.** 378.

Cockcroft, James, physician, **XV.** 67, **Cockcroft.**

Cockcroft, James, publisher, **XV.** 67.

Cochran, George I., lawyer, **XIV.** 284.

Cochrane, Alexander, manufacturer, **XIV.** 493.

Cochrane, Edward G., telegraph official, **XIV.** 274.

Cochrane, Hugh, manufacturer, **XIV.** 493, **Cochrane.**

Cochrane Chemical Co., **XIV.** 493, **Cochrane.**

Coddington, Wellesley P., clergyman, educator, author, **XV.** 88.

Code, maritime, author of, **XV.** 375, **Walton.**

Cody, Hiram H., jurist, **XIV.** 69, **Gary.**

Coe Brass Co., **XV.** 216, **Seymour.**

Coe College, president of, **XV.** 200, **McCormick.**

Coffee, dealers in, **XV.** 25, **Arbuckle.**

Coffin, William C., civil engineer, **XIV.** 73.

Coffinberry, Henry D., ship-builder, **XV.** 277.

Cohan, George M., actor, **XV.** 285.

Cohan, Jerry J., actor, **XV.** 285, **Cohan.**

Cohan, Josephine, actress, **XV.** 285, **Cohan.**

Coins, collection of, **XIV.** 133, **Nichols.**

Cold Spring Harbor, L. I., biological experimental station at, **XV.** 397, **Davenport.**

Cold storage industry, development of, **XIV.** 343, **Wills.**

Coleman, Charles P., merchant, **XIV.** 327.

Colgate University, president of, **XIV.** 496, **Bryan.**

College of the City of New York, president of, **XV.** 207, **Mezes.**

Collier, Price, clergyman and historian, **XV.** 232.

Collier, Robert J., editor and publisher, **XV.** 403, **Woodhouse.**

Collier's Weekly, **XV.** 80, **Nast.**

Colombia, friendly visit of Secretary Root to, **XIV.**

14; fruit products of, imported, 350, **Baker**; U. S. ministers to, 261, **Barrett**; **XIII.** 512, **Dawson**; 495, **Northcott**; **XV.** 58, **Russell**.

Color photography, **XIV.** 457, **Wood**; **XV.** 78, **Ives, F. E.**; 78, **Ives, H. E.**

Colorado Agricultural College, **XV.** 405, **Ammons**.

Colorado Central railroad, promotor of, **XV.** 228, **Teller**.

Colorado, cliff dwellings in, **XV.** 32, **Fewkes**; marble quarries in, 75, **Bates**; 154, **Meek**; gold mines in, **XIV.** 508, **Brunton**; **XV.** 191, **Walsh**; coal miners' strike in, 405, **Ammons**; governors of, **XIV.** 114, **McDonald**; 502, **Buchtel**; **Shafroth**; **XV.** 405, **Ammons**; **Carlson**; U. S. senators from, **XV.** 228, **Teller**; **XII.** 85, **Guggenheim**; **XIV.** 522, **Hughes**; 502, **Shafroth**; political progress of, **XV.** 405, **Ammons**.

Colorado Fuel & Iron Co., **XV.** 154, **Meek**.

Colorado river, diversion of, **XIV.** 197.

Colorado Smelting Co., South Pueblo, Colo., **XIV.** 222, **Eilers**.

Colorado-Yule Marble Co., **XV.** 74, **Bates**; 154, **Meek**.

Colored Methodist Episcopal Church, first bishop of, **XIV.** 316, **Miles**.

Colorimeter, universal, invented, **XV.** 78, **Ives, F. E.**

Colt, Le Baron B., jurist and U. S. senator, **XV.** 408.

Colt, Samuel P., president U. S. Rubber Co., **XV.** 408.

Colton, Arthur W., author, **XIV.** 187.

Columbia motor carriage, invented, **XV.** 137, **Maxim**.

Columbia Phonograph Co., **XV.** 390, **Easton**.

Columbia University, N. Y., School of Journalism of, **XV.** 306, **Williams**.

Columbian University, president of, **XIV.** 515, **Needham**.

Columbus, Ga., Christian Commonwealth in, **XV.** 367, **Albertson**.

Columbus, Miss., Mississippi Industrial College at, **XV.** 326, **Kincannon**.

Combustion, authority on, **XV.** 179, **Lucke**.

Comegys, Benjamin B., banker and author, **XV.** 254.

Comegys, Cornelius P., son of, **XV.** 254, **Comegys**.

Comegys, Joseph P., brother of, **XV.** 254, **Comegys**.

Comer, Braxton B., governor, **XIV.** 91.

Commerce and labor, U. S. department of, established, **XIV.** 6; 19; secretaries of, **X.** 42, **Straus**; **XIV.** 414, **Nagel**.

Commercial Bulletin, Boston (Mass.), founder of, **XIV.** 454, **Guild**.

Commercial Cable Co., **XIV.** 371, **Ward**.

Commission form of government, introduced, **XV.** 37, **MacVicar**.

Commonwealth Edison Co., Chicago, Ill., **XIV.** 334, **Insull**; 526, **Ferguson**.

Commonwealth Electric Co., **XIV.** 334, **Insull**.

Communistic Society, in Georgia, **XV.** 367, **Albertson**.

Comparative religion, investigations in, **XV.** 194, **Gray**.

Compass, gyroscopic, inventor of, **XV.** 23, **Sperry**.

Compensating voltmeter, inventor of, **XV.** 225, **Mershon**.

Compound sphymograph, invented, **XV.** 240, **Keyt**.

Compressed-air condenser, inventor of, **XV.** 22, **Fessenden**.

Compressed-air pumps, manufacture of, **XIV.** 191, **Rand**.

Compressors, air, manufacture of, **XIV.** 191, **Rand**.

Comstock, Anthony, reformer, **XV.** 241.

Comstock, Louis K., engineer, **XIV.** 129.

Comstock, William, **XIV.** 129, **Comstock**.

Comstock Lode, Nevada, **XV.** 238, **Keene**.

Conant, Charles A., banker and economist, **XIV.** 227; 64, **Jenks**.

Concordia, Kan., R. C. bishop of, **XV.** 250, **Cunningham**.

Concrete-Cement Age, journal, **XV.** 112.

Concrete houses, improved methods of construction, **XV.** 220, **Lambie**.

Confectionery. See candy.

Confederate Soldiers' Home, Mississippi, **XV.** 333, **Brewer**.

Conger, John H. B., merchant, **XIV.** 304, **Marten**.

Congregationalist, newspaper, **XIV.** 264, **Willis**.

Congress, single-tax propaganda in, **XIV.** 148, **Johnson**.

Conklin, Roland R., financier, **XV.** 108; 346, **Jarvis**.

Conley, William H., manufacturer, **XIV.** 72.

Connecticut, governors of, **XIV.** 524, **Woodruff**; 474, **Lilley**; **X.** 45, **Baldwin**; **XV.** 106, **Holcomb**.

Connecticut Historical Society, **XIV.** 254, **Battell**.

Connecticut Mutual Life Insurance Co., **XIV.** 167, **Wells**.

Connecticut School for Imbeciles, **XV.** 235, **Knight, H. M.**

Conservation of natural resources, **XIV.** 7-8; 31.

Consolidated and McKay Lasting Machine Co., **XV.** 197.

Consul-general, duties of, **XIV.** 53, **Riddle**.

Consular service, reorganized, **XIV.** 14.

Consumers' League, **XV.** 53, **Nathan**.

Continuous performance entertainment originated, **XV.** 297, **Keith**.

Continuous rail joint, inventor of, **XIV.** 480, **Fearey**.

Converse, Frederick S., composer, **XIV.** 356.

Converter, first synchronous, built, **XV.** 82, **Bradley**.

Cook, Frederick A., explorer, **XIV.** 261, **Parker**.

Cook, Mrs. George Cram, author, **XV.** 64.

Cook, Walter, architect, **XIV.** 344.

Cooke, Jay, partner of, **XV.** 193, **Thomas**.

Cooking range, inventor of, **XIV.** 240, **Chilson**.

Cooking utensils, process of enameling, invented, **XIV.** 396, **Grosjean**.

Cooley, Edwin G., educator, **XIV.** 136.

Coolidge, Louis A., journalist and treasurer, **XV.** 198.

Coolidge, T. Jefferson, wife of, **XV.** 38, **Amory**.

Cooper Hewitt lamp, invented, **XIV.** 470, **Hewitt**.

Cooper, Hugh L., engineer, **XV.** 142, **Value**.

Co-operative home colony, **XIV.** 320, **Sinclair**.

Cope, Walter B., jurist, **XV.** 278.

Cope, Warner W., son of, **XV.** 278, **Cope**.

Copeland, Royal S., physician, **XV.** 358.

Copper, first smelting works for, **XIV.** 166, **Pearce**; process of welding on steel, discovered, 342, **Monnot**; Lake Superior, 359, **Santon**.

Copperas, manufacture of, **XIV.** 101, **Lincoln**.

Copyright, authorities on the laws of, **XV.** 77, **Cox**.

Corbett, Timothy, R. C. bishop, **XV.** 247.

Corbin, John, author, **XIV.** 422.

Corcoran, W. H., partner of, **XV.** 229, **Riggs**.

Cord, manufacture of, **XIV.** 113, **Holmes**.

Cordier, Auguste J., manufacturer, **XIV.** 396.

Corey, William E., manufacturer, **XIV.** 71.

Corlett, William T., physician, **XIV.** 345.

Cornell, Alonzo B., brother of, **XV.** 139, **Cornell**.

Cornell, Ezra, son of, **XV.** 139, **Cornell**.

Cornell, Oliver H. P., engineer, inventor, **XV.** 139.

Corning, Erastus, Sr., manufacturer, **XV.** 374, **Griswold**.

Corn Products Refining Co., president of, **XIV.** 505, **Bedford**.

Corona Kid Manufacturing Co., **XIV.** 489, **Baker**; plant of, illus., 489.

Corporations, bureau of, transferred to the department of commerce and labor, **XIV.** 19; first commissioner of, 27, **Garfield**.

Corporation law, authority on, **XV.** 328, **Campbell**.

Corpus Christi, Tex., R. C. bishop of, **XV.** 137, **Nussbaum**.

Corsets, manufacturer of, **XV.** 127, **Marble**.

Cortelyou, George B., financier, **XIV.** 18.

Cosgrove, Samuel G., governor, **XIV.** 447.
Cosmopolitan magazine, owner of, **XIV.** 450, Hearst.
Costa Rica, fruit products of, imported, **XIV.** 350, Baker.
Cotter, James E., lawyer, **XIV.** 313.
Cotter, Joseph B., R. C. bishop, **XV.** 332.
Cotton, dealers in, **XV.** 258, Brown; 262, Cutler; manufacture of, **XIV.** 116, Whitman; **XV.** 37, Amory; 230, Burton; 321, Wood; 371, Bancroft; loans on, in the South, **XV.** 273, O'Neal.
Cotton goods, bleaching, dyeing and finishing of, **XV.** 85, McKenzie.
Cotton States Exposition, architect of, **XIV.** 298, Gilbert.
Couch, Joseph J., inventor, **XV.** 256.
Coues, Samuel Elliott, merchant and philanthropist, **XIV.** 185.
Court of Claims, chief justice of, **XIV.** 96, Peelle.
Couzins, Phoebe, lawyer, **XV.** 348.
Covington, Ky., R. C. bishop of, **XV.** 410, Brossart.
Coward, James S., merchant, **XIV.** 188.
Coward Good Sense Shoe, trade-mark, **XIV.** 183, Coward.
Cowell, Benjamin, jurist, **XV.** 347, Hitchcock.
Cowdin, Elliot C., merchant, **XIV.** 127; daughter of, 17, Bacon.
Cowenhoven tunnel, Colorado, builder of, **XIV.** 503, Brunton.
Cowles, Alfred H., metallurgist, **XV.** 131.
Cowles, Edwin, son of, **XV.** 131, Cowles.
Cowles, Eugene H., metallurgist, **XV.** 131, Cowles.
Cowles Electric Smelting and Aluminum Co., **XV.** 131, Cowles.
Cox, Archibald, lawyer, **XV.** 77.
Cox, James M., governor, **XV.** 274.
Cox, Rowland, soldier, lawyer, **XV.** 76.
Coxe, Alexander B., merchant, **XIV.** 368.
Coxe, Charles Sidney, **XIV.** 368, Coxe.
Coxe, Daniel, **XIV.** 368, Coxe.
Coxe Brothers & Co., coal merchants, **XIV.** 369.
Coyle, John G., surgeon, **XIV.** 343.
Crafts, Frederick Augustus, clergyman, **XIV.** 172.
Crafts, Leo M., physician and surgeon, **XV.** 57.
Crafts, Sara Jane, author, **XIV.** 173, Crafts.
Crafts, Wilbur F., clergyman and author, **XIV.** 172.
Craftsman, The, art magazine, founded, **XIV.** 291, Stickley.
Cragin, Edwin B., physician, **XV.** 189.
Craighead, Edwin B., educator, **XIV.** 143.
Cram, Goodhue & Ferguson, architects, **XV.** 328, Cram.
Cram, Ralph A., architect, **XV.** 327.
Crandall, Charles M., physician, **XV.** 384, Crandall.
Crandall Floyd M., physician, **XV.** 384.
Crane, Caroline Bartlett, minister, **XV.** 64.
Crane, William M., manufacturer, **XIV.** 321.
Crapsey, Algernon S., clergyman, **XIV.** 174.
Crawford, Corie I., governor, **XIV.** 200.
Creelman, James, journalist and author, **XIV.** 236.
Cremation, early advocate of, **XV.** 171, Le Moyne.
Crematory, first, in United States, **XV.** 171, Le Moyne.
Crew, Henry, physicist, **XV.** 60.
Crile, George W., surgeon, **XV.** 259.
Crocker, Charles, pioneer, **XV.** 16.
Crockery, dealers in, **XV.** 173, Cauldwell.
Crogman, William H., educator, **XIV.** 367.
Crookstown, Minn., R. C. bishop of, **XV.** 247, Corbett.
Cross (Charles) Whitman, geologist, **XV.** 214.
Crossfield, Richard H., educator, **XIV.** 416.
Crossland, J. R. A., diplomat, **XIV.** 471.
Crothers, Austin L., governor, **XIV.** 180.
Croton dam, New York, engineer of, **XV.** 142, Value; 389, Smith.

Crowninshield, Frederic, artist, **XIV.** 417.
Cruger, Mrs. Stephen Van R., author, **XIV.** 160.
Cruikshank, John M., editor, **XV.** 125.
Cuba, under U. S. military rule, **XIV.** 6; postal system established in, 29, Bristow; administration of the affairs of, by the United States, 32-33, Magoon; fruit products of, imported, 350, Baker; provisional government established in, 405; legal adviser of, 429, Calhoun; attitude of United States toward, **XV.** 228, Teller; National Bank of, 108, Conklin; 346, Jarvis; filibustering expeditions to, 312, Boynton; U. S. ministers to, **XIV.** 432, Morgan; **XII.** 2507, Jackson; **XIV.** 338, Beaupre.
Culebra cut, Panama canal, **XV.** 319, Gaillard.
Cummings, J. Howell, merchant, **XIV.** 359.
Cummings, John, **XIV.** 359, Cummings.
Cunningham, John F., R. C. bishop, **XV.** 250.
Cunningham, R. M., gubernatorial campaign of, **XIV.** 91, Comer.
Currency, emergency law of, 1908, **XIV.** 20, Cortelyou; reform of, 227, Conant.
Current Opinion, magazine, **XV.** 268, Wheeler.
Curry, Samuel S., educator, **XIV.** 302.
Curtis, Charles, senator, **XIV.** 416.
Curtis, Charles M., partner of, **XV.** 105, Saulsbury.
Curtis, Cyrus H. K., **XV.** 195, Kotzschmar.
Curtis, H. Holbrook, physician, **XIV.** 376.
Curtiss Aeroplane Co., **XV.** 401.
Curtiss, Glenn H., inventor and aviator, **XV.** 401; 7, Langley.
Cusack, Thomas F., R. C. bishop, **XV.** 411.
Cutler, S. Newton, merchant, **XV.** 262.
Cutlery, manufacturer of, **XIV.** 276, Bishop; 398, Kastor.
Cutting, R. Fulton, financier, **XV.** 183.
Cutting, W. Bayard, lawyer, **XV.** 183.
Cyclometer, inventor of, **XV.** 282, Veeder.

D.

Daily, John E., banker, **XV.** 372, Halsey.
Daily Advertiser, Boston, Mass., **XIV.** 172, Barrett.
Daily Capital, Topeka, Kans., **XV.** 275, Capper.
Daily News, Dayton, O., **XV.** 275, Cox.
Daily Times, Dubuque, Ia., **XV.** 130, Rich.
Daingerfield, William P., sister of, **XV.** 239, Keene.
Daggett, John, soldier, **XV.** 348, Hellier.
Dale, Thomas N., geologist, **XV.** 152.
Dallas, Tex., R. C. bishop of, **XV.** 283, Lynch.
Dallin, Cyrus E., sculptor, **XIV.** 478.
Dalton, Edward B., memorial to, **XIV.** 445, Higginson.
Damon, William E., naturalist, **XV.** 284.
Danbury, Conn., hat factories in, **XV.** 373, Loewe; 403, Mallory.
Daniel, Joseph J., daughter of, **XV.** 97, Battle.
Darlington, James H., P. E. bishop, **XV.** 403.
Dartmouth College Alumni Association of N. Y., **XIV.** 193, Mathewson.
Dashiell, William W., mfr., **XIV.** 120.
Davenport, Amzi B., educator and agriculturist, **XV.** 397, Davenport.
Davenport, Charles B., biologist, **XV.** 397.
Davenport, Frances Gardiner, brother of, **XV.** 398, Davenport.
Davenport, Gertrude Crotty, biologist, **XV.** 398, Davenport.
Davenport, Henry Benedict, brother of, **XV.** 398, Davenport.
Davenport, John I., brother of, **XV.** 398, Davenport.
Davenport, William Edwards, brother of, **XV.** 398, Davenport.
Davidson, Anstruther, scientist, **XIV.** 117.
Davidson, James O., governor, **XIV.** 109.
Davidson College, Davidson N. C., **XV.** 141, Smith.

Drugs, law to regulate purity of, **XIV.** 28; manufacturers of, 146, **Weightman**; 193, **Eimer**; 347, **Metz**; 377, **Nichols**; dealers in, 336, **Noyes**.
Drury, John B., clergyman, editor, **XV.** 203.
Drury College, presidents of, **XIV.** 463, Kirbye; 188, George.
Dry blast, for manufacturing iron, **XIV.** 71, Gayley.
Dry-goods, dealers in, **XIV.** 214, Jackson; 224, Poor; 228, **Farwell**; **XV.** 188, Altman.
Dry-plate, inventor of, **XV.** 330, Baekeland.
Dubois, Augustus J., civil engineer, **XV.** 406.
Dubois, Edward C., jurist, **XIV.** 524.
Dubuque (Ia.), bridge at, **XIV.** 349, Horton; Daily Times, **XV.** 130, Rich; archbishop of, 208, Keane.
Duffy, James A., R. C. bishop, **XV.** 234.
Dun & Co., R. G., **XIV.** 188, Barlow.
Duncan, Isadora, in vaudeville, **XV.** 297, Keith.
Duncan, Louis, electrician, **XIV.** 145.
Duncan, Thomas, clergyman, **XIV.** 145, Duncan.
Dunfee, John, contractor, **XIV.** 504.
Dunn, John Wesley, merchant, **XIV.** 380.
Dunne, Edmund M., bishop, **XV.** 325.
Dunne, Finley Peter, humorist, **XIV.** 53.
Dunning, Lehman H., physician, **XIV.** 279.
Duplex apartment houses, invented, **XV.** 362, Hubert.
Duplex Metals Co., **XIV.** 342, Monnot.
Dupont, Aime, artist, sculptor, **XV.** 135, Dupont.
Dupont, Mme. Aime, photographer, **XV.** 134.
du Pont Powder Co., **XV.** 260, Haskell.
du Pont, Victor, daughter of, **XV.** 105, Saulsbury.
Durand, E. Dana, statistician, **XIV.** 177.
Durant-Dort Carriage Co., **XV.** 402, Durant.
Durant, William C., manufacturer, **XV.** 402.
Durfee, William P., acting president of Hobart College, **XV.** 312, Powell.
Duryea, Jesse T., physician, **XIV.** 421.
Dutch Millionaire, **XIV.** 275, Philipse, Frederick, Sr.
Dutcher, E. C., inventor, **XIV.** 386, Draper.
Dutcher, W. W., manufacturer, **XIV.** 386, Draper.
Duveen, Henry, art merchant, **XV.** 385.
Duveen Bros., art dealers, **XV.** 386, Duveen.
Dwight, Theodore F., wife of, **XV.** 350, Loring.
Dyar, Harrison Gray, scientist, **XIV.** 97.
Dyar, Harrison Gray, Sr., inventor, **XIV.** 97, Dyar.
Dyer, George R., banker, **XIV.** 137.
Dyes, manufacture of, **XV.** 323, Kalbfleisch.
Dykeman, George R., car mfrs., **XIV.** 203, Woodruff.
Dykers, John Hudson, daughter of, **XV.** 246, De Navarro.
Dynamo, improvement in, **XV.** 338, Montgomery.
Dynamometers, inventor of, **XIV.** 435, Emery.

E.

Eads, James B., engineer, **XV.** 321, Donovan.
Eames, Edward E., merchant, **XIV.** 301.
Eames, John Capen, merchant, **XIV.** 302.
Eames, William H., dental surgeon, **XV.** 99.
Earl, Edward, banker, **XIV.** 103.
Earle, Frank H., engineer, **XIV.** 418.
Earle, Franklin S., scientist, **XIV.** 468.
Earle, George H., **XV.** 98, Battle.
Earle, John W., merchant, **XIV.** 270.
Earle, Mortimer L., philologist, **XIV.** 246.
Earthquakes, at San Francisco, **XIV.** 152, Bell; 197; authority on, **XV.** 334, Perret.
Eastern Argus. Portland, Me., establishment of, **XIV.** 264, Willis.
Eastern Oregon, P. E. bishop of, **XIV.** 499, Paddock, Robert L.
Easton, Edward D., merchant, **XV.** 390.
Easton, Pa. silk factory at, **XIV.** 215, Simon, R.
Eaton, Russell, **XIV.**, 377, Burleigh.
East river bridge, New York, **XV.** 290, Rea.
Eberhart, Adolph O., governor, **XIV.** 165.
Eclectic School of Medicine, founded, **XV.** 259, King.

Ecuador, U. S. ministers to, **XIV.** 428, Lee; 114, Fox.
Eddy, Henry T., mathematician, **XV.** 331.
Eddy, Spencer, diplomat, **XIV.** 395.
Edgar, James C., physician, **XIV.** 131.
Edgerly, Julian C., editor, **XV.** 351.
Edison Electric Co., Los Angeles, Cal., **XV.** 257, Sinclair.
Edison, Thomas A., assistant of, **XV.** 218, Hammer.
Education, science of, **XIV.** 252, Brown; public school lectures, 366, **Leipziger**; progress of, 516, **McPherson**; in the South, 415, **Ogden**; Peaslee method of, 429, **Peaslee**; in Alabama, **XV.** 102, **Tutwiler**; musical theories of, 51, **Becker**; Raja Yoga (theosophical) system of, 338, **Tingley**; U. S. commissioners of, **XV.** 1, **Harris**; **XIV.** 252, **Brown**; **XV.** 270, Claxton.
Edwards, John H., clergyman and author, **XIV.** 220.
Edwards, Samuel, jurist, **XV.** 97.
Edwards-Stanwood Shoe Co., **XIV.** 397, Dodge.
Edwards, Tryon, clergyman and author, **XIV.** 155.
Efficiency engineering, science of, **XIV.** 521, Taylor; **XV.** 82, Emerson.
Eger, Charles M., manufacturer, **XIV.** 300.
Egypt, consul-general to, **XIV.** 53, Riddle; American telegrapher in, 370, **Ward**; diplomatic agent to, **XV.** 311, Penfield.
Eilers, Anton F., metallurgist, **XIV.** 222.
Eimer, August, chemist and pharmacist, **XIV.** 193.
Elasticity, experiments in, **XV.** 21, Fessenden.
El Caney, Cuba, battle of, **XIV.** 35, Bates.
Election law in Mississippi, **XIV.** 518, Noel.
Electoral commission, **XIV.** 28.
Electric beacon, highest, erected, **XV.** 22, Sperry.
Electric car heaters, **XIV.** 293, Gold.
Electric carriage, invented, **XV.** 23, Sperry.
Electric cautery, throat operations, **XV.** 200, Lincoln.
Electric clock, self-winding, invented, **XV.** 161, Pond.
Electric elevator, principle of control of, invented, **XV.** 334, Perret.
Electric furnace, **XIV.** 93; inventors of, **XV.** 82 Bradley; 131, **Cowles**; experiments with, **XIV.** 93.
Electric hoists, manufacture of, **XV.** 31, Miller.
Electric lighting, researches in, **XIV.** 260, Parker; tower for, 458, **Adams**; improved forms of, invented, 261; **Parker**; **Clark**; 470, **Hewitt**; for railways, **XV.** 3, **Leonard**; introduced in London, Eng., **XV.** 218, Hammer.
Electric motor, invented, **XV.** 334, Perret.
Electric motor control, invented, **XV.** 4, Leonard.
Electric rectifier, inventors of, **XIV.** 470, Hewitt; **XV.** 338, Montgomery.
Electric shock, resuscitation from, **XV.** 354, Meltzer.
Electric sign, flashing, originated, **XV.** 218, Hammer.
Electric Smelting and Aluminum Co., **XV.** 132, Cowles.
Electric traction, development of, **XIV.** 63; 145, Duncan.
Electric Vehicle Co., **XV.** 137, Maxim.
Electrical apparatus, manufacture of, **XV.** 42; 123, Thayer.
Electrical street railway cars, designed, **XV.** 23, Sperry.
Electricity, advances in, **XIV.** 63; 93; 106, Stone; 145, **Duncan**; 293, **Gold**; 261, **Parker**; **Clark**; 470, **Hewitt**; **XV.** 4, **Leonard**; 18; 22, **Sperry**; 42; 75, **McAllister**; 82, **Bradley**; 157, **White**; 211, **Riker**; 219, **Hammer**; 225, **Mershon**; 257, **Sinclair**; 340, **Emmet**, W. L.; adapted to mining operations, **XIV.** 508, **Brunton**; alternating current introduced, **XV.** 42; applied to elevators, 89, Baldwin.
Electro-chemistry, researches in, **XIV.** 93; 206, Bancroft; 350, **Burgess**; **XV.** 318, **Baekeland**; 398, Smith.
Electrostatic machines, operation of, **XIV.** 208, Sheldon.

Fernald, Bert M., governor, **XV.** 222.
Fernald, Keene & True Co., canners, **XV.** 222, Fernald.
Fernald, Merritt C., educator, **XIV.** 138.
Ferrin, Augustin W., editor and publisher, **XV.** 62.
Ferris, Helen Frances (Gillespie), educator, **XV.** 214, Ferris.
Ferris Institute, Big Rapids, Mich., **XV.** 213, Ferris.
Ferris, Woodbridge N., governor, **XV.** 213.
Fertilizer, artificial, **XIV.** 368, Stockbridge; manufacture of, **XV.** 400, Gibbons.
Ferullo, Francesco, musician, **XV.** 186.
Fessenden, Reginald A., electrician and inventor, **XV.** 21.
Fessenden wireless telegraphy, **XV.** 22, Fessenden.
Few, William P., educator, **XV.** 196.
Fewkes, Jesse W., ethnologist, **XV.** 32.
Fielder, James F., governor, **XV.** 114.
Fields, Lew, comedian, **XIV.** 317.
Files, manufacturer of, **XIV.** 495, Reichhelm.
Filibustering expeditions, **XV.** 312, Boynton.
Filing devices, inventor of, **XIV.** 360, Amberg.
Finance, authorities on, **XIV.** 18, Shaw; **XV.** 181, Morgan; 265, Hamlin; 322, Farnsworth; study of foreign systems of, **XIV.** 64, Jenks; 227, Conant; **XV.** 326, Andrew; relief fund established by the secretary of the treasury, **XIV.** 18, Shaw.
Finch, Irving A., manufacturer, **XV.** 359.
Finch, William R., editor and diplomat, **XV.** 400.
Finck, Henry T., author, **XIV.** 153.
Fine, Henry B., educator, **XIV.** 499.
Finley, William W., R. R. president, **XIV.** 441.
Fire Alarm System, inventors of, **XIV.** 76, Barclay; **XV.** 161, Pond; manufacturer of, **XIV.** 309, Stover.
Firearms, manufacture of, **XIV.** 490, Smith, L. C.; **XV.** 183, Whitney.
Firefly, studies of, **XV.** 78, Ives, H. E.
First National Bank, Boston, Mass., **XV.** 379, Wing.
First National Bank, Fargo, N. Dak., **XV.** 382, Hanna.
First National Bank, Page, N. Dak., **XV.** 382, Hanna.
Fisher, Irving, economist and statistician, **XIV.** 86; **XV.** 69, Ley.
Fisher, Lucius George, manufacturer, **XIV.** 119.
Fisher, Lucius G., Jr., manufacturer, **XIV.** 119.
Fisk, Clinton B., soldier and reformer, **XV.** 324, Russell.
Fisk, Eugene L., **XV.** 69, Ley.
Fisk, Everett O., educator, **XV.** 368.
Fisk, Harvey & Sons, bankers, **XIV.** 525, Fisk.
Fisk, James, partner of, **XV.** 312, Boynton.
Fisk, Pliny, financier, **XIV.** 524.
Fisk Teachers' Agency, Boston, Mass., **XV.** 369, Fisk.
Fiske, Horace S., editor, author, educator, **XV.** 130.
Fiske, John Billings, clergyman, **XV.** 130, Fiske.
Fitch, Clyde, dramatist, **XV.** 192.
Fitch, William G., **XV.** 192, Fitch.
Fitzbutler, Henry, physician, **XIV.** 317.
Fitzpatrick, Thomas B., merchant and manufacturer, **XIV.** 114.
Flagler, Henry M., financier, **XV.** 10.
Flagler, John H., manufacturer, **XIV.** 312.
Flagler, John H. & Co., iron and steel, **XIV.** 312, Flagler.
Flags, manufacturers of, **XV.** 262, Ames.
Flannels, manufacture of, **XIV.** 116, Whitman.
Flashing electric sign originated, **XV.** 218, Hammer.
Fletcher, Charles, merchant, **XV.** 321, Wood.
Fletcher, Duncan U., senator, **XIV.** 464.
Fletcher, Frank F., naval officer, **XV.** 144.
Fletcher, Henry P., diplomat, **XV.** 342.
Fletcher, Horace, dietetist, **XIV.** 39.
Fletcherism, theories of, **XIV.** 40, Fletcher.
Flint, Charles R., merchant, banker, **XV.** 321, Wood.

Flipper, Joseph S., A. M. E. bishop, **XIV.** 348.
Florida, agricultural experiments in, **XIV.** 368, Stockbridge; development of, **XIV.** 440; **XV.** 10, Flagler; 345, Huidekoper; governors of, **XIV.** 59, Broward; Gilchrist; U. S. senators from, **XIV.** 236, Bryan; 388, Milton; 464, Fletcher; Ocean railroad in, **XV.** 10, Flagler.
Florida Coast Line Canal & Transportation Co., **XIV.** 440.
Florida East Coast Railway Co., **XIV.** 440; **XV.** 10, Flagler.
Floss, silk, importer of, **XV.** 230, Burton.
Flour, manufacturer of, **XV.** 41, Bell.
Flour sieves, first made in the U. S., **XIV.** 391, Gilbert.
Floyd, Edward E., merchant, **XV.** 173.
Fluting machine, invented, **XV.** 156, Sergeant.
Flying, aeronautical magazine, **XV.** 403, Woodhouse.
Flying boat, perfected, **XV.** 401.
Flying machine. See Aeroplane.
Folding bed, inventor of, **XIV.** 204, Woodruff.
Ford, Henry, manufacturer, **XV.** 58; 271, Parker.
Ford, Sewell, author, **XIV.** 140.
Ford, Thomas, inventor, **XIV.** 141, Ford.
Ford, Thomas P., man'fr. and inventor, **XIV.** 141.
Ford Motor Co., Detroit, Mich., **XV.** 59; 271, Parker.
Ford pump regulating valve, inventor of, **XIV.** 141, Ford.
Fordham University, presidents of, **XIV.** 487, Pettit; 438, McCluskey.
Forest Lumber Co., **XV.** 380, White.
Forestry, school of, founded at Yale, **XIV.** 32, Pinchot; scientific, 30-31, Pinchot; 195, Sudworth.
Formaldehyde, manufacture of, **XV.** 180, Hasslacher.
Forman, Justus M., author, **XIV.** 424.
Fort, John Franklin, jurist and governor, **XIV.** 123.
Fort Snelling, construction of bridge at, **XIV.** 349, Horton.
Forwood, William H., surgeon-general, **XV.** 148.
Foss, Eugene N., mfr. and governor, **XV.** 339.
Foster Lumber Co., **XV.** 395, Foster.
Foster, Reuben, **XV.** 344, Huidekoper.
Foster, Thomas S., merchant, **XV.** 395.
Foster, William T., educator, **XV.** 300.
Foundation construction, new method of, adopted, **XV.** 80, Kimball.
Foundation for the Promotion of Industrial Peace, **XV.** 126, Mitchell.
Four Cohans, The, actors, **XV.** 285, Cohan.
Fox, John, Jr., author, **XIV.** 90.
Fox, Joseph J., R. C. bishop, **XV.** 214.
Fox, Philip, astronomer, **XIV.** 513.
Fox, Williams C., diplomat, **XIV.** 114.
Foy, Eddie, in vaudeville, **XV.** 297, Keith.
France, U. S. ambassadors to, **XIV.** 171, White; 16, Bacon; **XIII.** 68, Herrick; financial loan to, **XV.** 181, Morgan.
Frank, Melvin Porter, lawyer, **XIV.** 249.
Franklin, Benjamin, manuscript of autobiography, **XV.** 19, Huntington, H. E.
Franklin College, president of, **XIV.** 496, Bryan.
Franklin and Marshall College, president of, **XIV.** 345, Apple.
Freeman, John R., advisory committee on Panama canal, **XIV.** 41, Goethals.
Free Religions Association of America, president of, **XV.** 273, Holmes.
Freer, Charles L., mfr. and art collector, **XV.** 416.
Freer collection of art, **XV.** 416, Freer.
Freight, regulation of, **XV.** 234, Ingalls.
Freight subway system, in Chicago, **XIV.** 400, Wheeler; 401, Jackson.
French, Asa, jurist, **XIV.** 257.
French, Edwin Davis, engraver, **XIV.** 44.

French, William M. R., artist, **XV.** 266.

Fritz, John, medal, American recipients of, **XV.** 41, Westinghouse; **VI.** 221, Bell; **III.** 441, Edison; **IX.** 44, Noble; **I.** 244, Hunt; **XII.** 8, Douglas.

Frost, Albert H., mfr. and ornithologist, **XV.** 70.

Frost, Thomas G., lawyer and author, **XIV.** 431.

Frost Veneer Seating Co., Newport, Vt., **XV.** 70.

Fruits, tropical, trade in, **XIV.** 350, Baker.

Fuller, Gardner, educator, **XV.** 54.

Funston, Frederick, **XV.** 144, Fletcher.

Fur hats, process of making described, **XV.** 404, Mallory. See Hats.

Fur seal industry, **XIV.** 412, Hitchcock; U. S. commission to investigate, 130, Stejneger; controversy with Japan over, **XV.** 265, Hamlin.

Furnaces, automatic, invented, **XV.** 215, Norton.

Furman University, president of, **XIV.** 523, Poteat.

Furnace water-back, inventor of, **XIV.** 201, Ames, Oliver (1st).

Furniss, Henry W., diplomat, **XIV.** 443.

Furniture, office, **XIV.** 260, Andrews; craftsman, 291, Stickley.

G.

Gadski-Tauscher, Johanna, singer, **XIV.** 500.

Gaillard, David Du B., military engineer, **XV.** 318.

Galvenometer, inventor of, **XV.** 265, Locke.

Gamage, Frederick L., educator, **XIV.** 162.

Gamewell & Co., fire-alarms, **XIV.** 309, Stover.

Gammon Theological Seminary, Atlanta, Ga., **XIV.** 361, Bowen.

Ganong, William F., botanist, **XIV.** 483.

Garden, Mary, singer, **XV.** 209.

Garden City, L. I., St. Paul's School, **XIV.** 162, Gamage.

Gardiner, Asa Bird, lawyer, **XIV.** 332.

Gardiner, Charles P., lawyer, **XIV.** 385.

Gardiner, Edward G., biologist, **XIV.** 204.

Gardner, Almeda, Industrial School, Mississippi, organized, **XV.** 161, Pond.

Gardner, Henry J., partner of, **XV.** 245, Stone.

Gardner, Obadiah, U. S. senator, **XV.** 230.

Gardner, Stone & Co., commission merchants, **XV.** 245, Stone.

Garfield, James A., son of, **XIV.** 27.

Garfield, James R., secretary of the interior, **XIV.** 27.

Garman, Harrison, naturalist, **XIV.** 460.

Garretson, Garret J., jurist, **XIV.** 238.

Garside, J., manufacturer, **XIV.** 276, Bishop.

Gary, Elbert H., lawyer and financier, **XIV.** 69; 395, Pam.

Gary, Frank Boyd, senator, **XIV.** 123.

Gary, F. F., physician, **XIV.** 123, Gary.

Gary, T. P., surgeon, **XIV.** 123, Gary.

Gary, William T., soldier and jurist, **XIV.** 123, Gary.

Gary, Ind., founded, **XIV.** 70, Gary; 72, Corey.

Gas, long-distance pipe system for, **XIV.** 243, Guffey; for Pittsburgh, Pa., **XV.** 42; Regulator, inventor of, 156, Sergeant; stove, inventor of, 356, Shaw; manufacturer of, **XIV.** 321, Crane.

Gas Engine & Power Co., boat builders, **XIV.** 239, Amory.

Gas engines, authority on, **XV.** 179, Lucke; inventor of, 366, Rice.

Gas fixtures, manufacturer of, **XIV.** 451, Enos.

Gas furnace, manufacture of, **XIV.** 495, Reichhelm; for dentistry, invented, 331, Land; Siemens, development of, 313, Flagler.

Gas-meter, inventor of, **XV.** 356, Shaw.

Gas and Oil Combustion Co., **XV.** 179, Lucke.

Gaston, William, governor, son of, **XV.** 399, Gaston.

Gaston, William A., lawyer, banker, **XV.** 399.

Gate, automatic, invented, **XIV.** 511, Manlove.

Gates, Charles W., governor, **XV.** 104.

Gates, Eleanor, playwright, **XV.** 263.

Gates, John W., financier, **XIV.** 67; **XV.** 370, Marshall.

Gate valve, inventor of, **XV.** 143, Lunken.

Gattinger, Augustin, physician and botanist, **XV.** 91.

Gauge, mercury steam, inventor of, **XV.** 356, Shaw.

Gavin, Michael F., physician and surgeon, **XV.** 303.

Gayley, James, metallurgist, **XIV.** 70.

Gazzam, Joseph M., lawyer, **XV.** 40.

Gazzam, William, **XV.** 40, Gazzam.

Gearin, John M., senator, **XIV.** 475.

Geer, G. Warren, partner of, **XV.** 253, Baare.

Geddes, James, philologist, **XIV.** 184.

Genealogy, American, authorities on, **XIV.** 285, Burton; 398, Putnam.

General Chemical Co., **XIV.** 377, Nichols.

General Electric Co., research laboratory of, **XV.** 393, Whitney.

General Motors Co., **XV.** 402, Durant.

Geneva, treaty of, **XV.** 316, Barton.

Genial Larry, sobriquet, **XIV.** 234, Jerome.

Geological Survey, U. S., **XIV.** 130, Smith.

Geology, investigations in, **XIV.** 130, Smith; 267, Hill; 276, Owen; 284, Landes; 282, Spencer; **XV.** 152, Dale; 214, Cross; 391, Iddings.

George, Henry, theories of, advocated in congress, **XIV.** 148, Johnson.

George, Joseph Henry, clergyman and educator, **XIV.** 188.

George Washington University, **XIV.** 515, Needham.

Georgetown College, Riggs Memorial Library presented to, **XV.** 229, Riggs.

Georgia, account of Episcopal diocese of, **XIV.** 438, Reese; governor of, **I.** 183, Smith; P. E. bishop of, **XIV.** 438, Reese; state geologist of, 282, Spencer; legal code of revised, **XV.** 415, Lamar.

Georgia Central railroad, president of, **XV.** 217, Gordon.

Gerber, David, lawyer, **XIV.** 363.

Germany, U. S. ambassadors to, **XV.** 100, Uhl; **XII.** 244, Hill; **XIII.** 598, Leishman.

Gibboney, David C., lawyer, **XIV.** 415.

Gibbons, Abram, iron mfr., **XV.** 376, Huston, C.

Gibbons, John F., manufacturer, **XV.** 400.

Gibbs, Willard, medal, recipients of, **XII.** 362, Richards; **XV.** 330, Baekeland; **IX.** 240, Remsen; **XII.** 284, Noyes; **XV.** 339, Whitney.

Gibson, John B., jurist, **XIV.** 338.

Gibson, William, physician, **XV.** 261, Lawrence.

Giddings, Edward Jonathan, clergyman, **XV.** 9, Giddings.

Giddings, Franklin H., sociologist, **XV.** 9.

Gilbert, B., inventor, **XIV.** 391, Gilbert.

Gilbert, Bradford L., architect, **XIV.** 298.

Gilbert, Edwin, manufacturer, **XIV.** 391.

Gilbert & Bennett Mfg. Co., wire screens, **XIV.** 391, Gilbert.

Gilbert Islands, missionaries to, **XIV.** 98, Bingham.

Gilbertese Bible, **XIV.** 98, Bingham.

Gilchrist, Albert W., governor, **XIV.** 59.

Gillett, James N., governor, **XIV.** 374.

Gillette, King C., mfr., **XV.** 394, Holloway.

Githens, J. C., inventor, **XIV.** 191, Rand.

Glaciers, discovered in Greenland, **XIV.** 60, Peary.

Glaspell, Susan, author, **XV.** 64.

Glass, Joseph S., R. C. bishop, **XV.** 296.

Glassware, dealers in, **XV.** 247, Dean.

Glen Iris, New York state park, **XV.** 325, Letchworth. W. P.

Globe Ship Building Co., Cleveland, O., **XV.** 277, Coffinberry.

Gloucester, Mass., experimental laboratories at, **XV.** 105, Hammond.

Glue, machinery for making, **XIV.** 470, Hewitt.

Glynn, Martin H., governor, **XV.** 231.

Goddard, Henry H., psychologist, **XV.** 236.

H.

Hague, The, international peace conference at, XIV. 6.

Haight, Fletcher M., lawyer and jurist, XV. 309, Haight.

Haight, George W., lawyer, XV. 309.

Haight, Mary Ellen (Setchel), XV. 309, Haight.

Haight, Samuel C., partner of, XV. 309, Haight.

Haight, Samuel S., lawyer, XV. 309, Haight.

Haines, John M., governor, XV. 8.

Hair mattresses, originator of, XIV. 391, Gilbert.

Haiti, U. S. minister to, XIV. 443, Furniss, Henry W.

Hale, Philip, music critic, XIV. 462.

Hale, William B., author, editor, XV. 182.

Half-tone process, invented, XV. 77, Ives.

Hall, Charles M., inventor and mfr., XV. 131, Cowles.

Hall, George H., artist, XV. 170.

Hall, John Manning, railroad president, XV. 227.

Hall, John W., musician, XIV. 325.

Hall, Lucy M., physician, XV. 304, Mosher.

Hall, Luther E., governor, XV. 135.

Halpine, Charles G., daughter of, XV. 162, Faure.

Halpine, Margaret G. (Milligan), daughter of, XV. 162, Faure.

Halsey, C. D., & Co., bankers, XV. 372, Halsey.

Halsey, Charles D., banker and broker, XV. 372.

Halsey, F. A., inventor, XIV. 191, Rand.

Hamill, Hugh, principal, Lawrenceville School, XIV. 516, McPherson.

Hamill, Samuel M., principal Lawrenceville School, XIV. 516, McPherson.

Hamilton, Franklin E. E., clergyman, XIV. 435.

Hamilton, Frederick W., clergyman and educator, XIV. 436.

Hamilton, Philip, pen-name, XV. 361, Hubert.

Hamilton, Samuel K., lawyer, XIV. 235.

Hamilton, William P., banker, XV. 393, Birch.

Hamilton coupon, system of profit sharing, XV. 361, Caldwell.

Hamlin, Charles S., financier, XV. 265.

Hammer, steam, inventor of, XV. 356, Shaw.

Hammer, William J., electrician, XV. 218.

Hammerstein, Oscar, impresario and theatrical manager, XIV. 45.

Hammond, Graeme M., neurologist, XV. 199.

Hammond, John Hays, mining engineer, son of, XV. 105, Hammond.

Hammond, John Hays, Jr., inventor, XV. 105.

Hammond, William A., son of, XV. 199, Hammond.

Hammond destroyer, torpedo, XV. 106, Hammond.

Hampden-Sidney College, presidents of, XIV. 471, McAllister; Graham.

Handicraft, revival of, XIV. 291, Stickley.

Hanks, Benjamin, XIV. 247, Hanks.

Hanks, Charles S., lawyer and author, XIV. 247.

Hanly, James F., governor, XIV. 219.

Hanna, Edward J., archbishop, XV. 147.

Hanna, H. H., XIV. 64, Jenks.

Hanna, Jason R., manufacturer and soldier, XV. 382, Hanna.

Hanna, Louis B., banker and governor, XV. 382.

Hanna, Marcus A., XIV. 148, Johnson.

Hannah, Jane O., singer, XV. 91.

Hanover College, president of, XIV. 169, Mills.

Hanover National Bank, New York, president of, XV. 268, Woodward.

Harahan, James T., railroad president, XV. 162.

Harbison, Samuel P., mfr., philanthropist, XIV. 229.

Harbison-Walker Refractories Co., XIV. 229, Harbison.

Harbors, improvements of, XV. 81, Bates; organization to promote improvement of, 407, Ransdell.

Hardenbergh, Augustus A., banker, XIV. 461.

Harding, Alfred, bishop, XV. 258.

Harding, W. P. G., member of Federal Reserve Board, XV. 265, Hamlin.

Hardware, manufacture of, XV. 324, Letchworth.

Harkness memorial chapel in Western Reserve University, XV. 357, Severance.

Harlem, N. Y., pioneer settler in, XIV. 208, Bogert.

Harpster, John H., missionary, XV. 153.

Harriman, Edward H., financier, XIV. 196.

Harriman, Hiram P., jurist, XIV. 273.

Harriman, Tenn., founded, XV. 324, Russell.

Harriman & Co., bankers, New York, XIV. 196.

Harrington, Emerson C., governor, XV. 135.

Harrington & Goodman, importers, XV. 174, Goodman.

Harris, Abram W., educator, XIV. 138.

Harris, Andrew L., governor, XIV. 226.

Harris, Merriman C., M. E. bishop, XIV. 122.

Harris, Sam H., theatrical manager, XV. 286, Cohan.

Harris, Thomas, colonist, XV. 1.

Harris, William L., artist, XV. 257.

Harris, William T., philosopher and educator, XV. 1.

Harrisburg, Pa., tin plate works at, illus., XIV. 396; new state capitol at, illus., 443; P. E. bishop of, XV. 408, Darlington.

Harrison, Edwin, capitalist, XV. 268.

Harrison, Ross G., anatomist, XV. 172.

Harrod, Benjamin M., member isthmian canal commission, XIV. 5.

Hart, William, method of art instruction, XIV. 46, Whittemore.

Hartford, Conn., R. C. bishop of, XV. 387, Nilan.

Hartley, Frank, surgeon, XV. 224.

Hartley-Krause cure for neuralgia, XV. 224, Hartley.

Hartmann, Wm. L., surgeon, XIV. 462.

Hartness, James, engineer and inventor, XV. 294.

Harty, Jeremiah J., archbishop, XV. 45.

Harvard Brewing Co., XV. 394, Holloway.

Harvard Knitting Mills, XV. 386, Winship; 387, Boit.

Harvard Union, XIV. 445, Higginson.

Harvard University, gift of "Soldiers' Field" to, XIV. 445, Higginson; president of, 81, Lowell; first professor of meteorology in, XV. 3, Rotch; gift of books to, XV. 12; Widener, Harry E.; architect of buildings of, 33, Lowell.

Harvey, Edwin B., physician, surgeon, XV. 276.

Harvey, Lorenzo D., educator, XIV. 87.

Harvey Society, founder and first president of, XV. 89, Lusk.

Harwood, Herbert J., merchant, XIV. 391.

Harwood, Joseph A., manufacturer, XIV. 390.

Harwood Mfg. Co., XIV. 391, Harwood, J. A.

Hasbrouck, Henry C., soldier, XV. 356.

Hasbrouck, William C., lawyer, XV. 356, Hasbrouck.

Haskell, Charles N., governor, XIV. 465.

Haskell, Jonathan Amory, merchant, XV. 260.

Hasslacher, Jacob P. M., manufacturer, XV. 180.

Hastings, Frank S., financier, XIV. 255.

Hats, manufacturers of, XIV. 359, Cummings; XV. 373, Loewe; 403-404, Mallory.

Hats, fur, process of making described, XV. 404, Mallory.

Hattie, Aunt, pen-name, XIV. 154, Baker, H. N. W.

Haupt, Louis, physician, XV. 111.

Havemeyer, Henry O., competitor of Arbuckle, XV. 25.

Hawaiian islands, missionaries to, XIV. 98, Bingham; sugar introduced in, 457, Wood.

Hawley, Donly C., physician, XIV. 424.

Hawley, James H., governor, XV. 297.

Hawn, Henry G., elocutionist, XIV. 282.

Hay, John, daughter of, XV. 35, Wadsworth.

Hay, Marion E., governor, XIV. 448.

Hay-Pauncefote treaty, XIV. 5.

Hayden, Charles, banker, XIV. 328.

Hayden, Stone & Co., bankers, XIV. 328, Hayden.

Hayes, John L., lawyer and economist, XIV. 233.

Hayford, John F., civil engineer, XIV. 371.

Hazen, Allen, advisory committee on Panama canal, **XIV. 41, Goethals.**

Health, protection of, by U. S. government, **XV. 129, Blue, R.** See Public Health.

Healy, George P. A., artist, **XV. 317.**

Hearst, William R., publisher, **XIV. 450;** policies of, attacked, **15.**

Heath, Alvan M. C., **XIV. 162, Heath.**

Heath, D. C., & Co., president of, **XIV. 136 Cooley.**

Heath, Frederic C., physician, **XIV. 162.**

Hebrew literature, authority on, **XV. 284, Sulzberger.**

Hebrew Technical Institute, organized, **XIV. 366, Leipziger.**

Hecker, Frank J., member isthmian canal commission, **XIV. 5.**

Heckscher, August, merchant, **XIV. 177.**

Hecla Iron Works, New York, **XIV. 299, Poulson.**

Hedstrom, Oscar C., inventor, **XV. 180.**

Heffron, Patrick R., R. C. bishop, **XV. 139.**

Hegeman Drug Co., **XIV. 313, Flagler.**

Heide, Henry, manufacturer, **XV. 116.**

Heine Safety Water-Tube Boiler Co., **XV. 189, Meier.**

Hektoen, Ludvig, pathologist, **XIV. 167.**

Helena, Mont., R. C. bishop of, **XV. 262, Carroll.**

Helicon Home Colony, **XIV. 320, Sinclair.**

Helion lamp, inventors of, **XIV. 261, Parker; Clark.**

Hell Gate bridge, designer of, **XIV. 492, Lindenthal.**

Hellier, Charles E., lawyer, capitalist, **XV. 348.**

Hemenway, James A., senator, **XIV. 187.**

Henderson, William J., author, **XIV. 346.**

Heney, Francis J., lawyer, **XV. 50, Burns; 133, Johnson.**

Henri, Robert, artist, **XV. 146.**

Henri, Marjorie (Organ), artist, **XV. 147, Henri.**

Henry, O., pen-name; **XV. 170, Porter.**

Henry, Philip W., civil engineer, **XV. 109.**

Henry, William, manufacturer and jurist, **XV. 109, Henry.**

Henson, Matthew, member of Peary north pole party, **XIV. 61.**

Hepburn, A. Barton, banker, **XV. 30.**

Heredity, studies in, **XV. 397, Davenport.**

Heresy, trials for, **XIV. 175, Crapsey.**

Hero, George A., merchant, financier, **XV. 196.**

Herrick, Elias Hicks, broker, **XIV. 121.**

Herron, Joseph, educator, **XV. 285, Herron.**

Herron, William C., capitalist and philanthropist, **XV. 285.**

Herron Seminary, Cincinnati, O., **XV. 285, Herron.**

Hewitt, Peter Cooper, inventor and engineer, **XIV. 470.**

Heyward, Duncan C., governor, **XV. 284.**

Hibben, John G., president of Princeton University, **XV. 199.**

Hicks, Benjamin D., banker, **XIV. 507.**

Hickey, Thomas F., R. C. bishop, **XV. 58.**

Higgins, James H., governor, **XIV. 402.**

Higginson, Henry L., banker and philanthropist, **XIV. 445.**

High school law in Virginia, **XIV. 105, Mann.**

Highways. See Roads.

Hill, Albert Ross, educator, **XIV. 428.**

Hill, David B., **XIV. 517, McLaughlin.**

Hill, Edward B., musician and editor, **XIV. 182.**

Hill, Frederic S., author, **XV. 38.**

Hill, George W., merchant and banker, **XV. 290, Hill.**

Hill, James J., railroad president, **XIV. 197;** associate of, **XV. 150, Kennedy.**

Hill, Percival S., merchant, **XV. 290.**

Hill, Robert T., geologist, **XIV. 267.**

Hill, Thomas, **XIV. 182, Hill.**

Hill & Cutler, Boston, Mass., **XV. 262, Cutler.**

Hill View Reservoir, N. Y., water system, **XV. 389, Smith.**

Hillebrand, William F., chemist, **XIV. 132.**

Hinchman, Frederick B., partner of, **XV. 307, Pilat, C. F.**

Hinitt, Frederick W., educator, **XIV. 472.**

Hispanic Society of America, founder of, **XV. 19, Huntington, A. M.**

Histology, advances in, **XV. 6, Quincy.**

Hitchcock, Frank H., postmaster - general, **XIV. 412.**

Hitchcock, George, artist, **XV. 347.**

Hitchcock, Gilbert M., U. S. senator, **XV. 284.**

Hitchcock, Samuel J., founder of Yale Law School, **XV. 347, Hitchcock.**

Hitchcock, Winchester, soldier, **XV. 119, Loring.**

Hitt, Robert S. Reynolds, diplomat, **XIV. 477.**

Hoadly, George, partner of, **XIV. 512, Lauterbach.**

Hoadly, Lauterbach & Johnson, lawyers, **XIV. 512, Lauterbach.**

Hobart College, presidents of, **XV. 311, Stewardson; 312, Powell;** William Smith College for Women, **316, Smith.**

Hoboken, N. J., tunnel connection with New York, **XIV. 465, McAdoo.**

Hoch, Edward W., governor, **XIV. 426.**

Hodge, William T., actor, **XIV. 384.**

Hodges, George H., governor, **XV. 292; 121, Major.**

Hodges, H. F., member of isthmian canal commission, **XIV. 40, Goethals.**

Hodgman, Daniel, rubber manufacturer, **XIV. 324, Hodgman.**

Hodgman, George B., merchant, **XIV. 324.**

Hodgman, George F., **XIV. 324, Hodgman.**

Hodgman Rubber Co., **XIV. 324, Hodgman.**

Hodgson, Richard, **XIV. 48, Hyslop.**

Hoff, Olaf, engineer, **XIV. 419.**

Hoffman, John T., sister of, **XV. 392, Joline.**

Hoisting engines, manufacture of, **XV. 31, Miller.**

Hoists, electric, manufacture of, **XV. 31, Miller.**

Holbrook, Theodore L., manufacturer, **XV. 400.**

Holcomb, Marcus H., governor, **XV. 106.**

Holden, Edgar, physician, **XV. 91.**

Holland, John P., inventor, **XV. 4.**

Hollander, J. L., appointed special agent to Santo Domingo, **XIV. 15.**

Hollins, Gerald V., banker and broker, **XV. 372, Halsey.**

Hollis, Henry F., senator, **XV. 272.**

Holloway, Ward B., capitalist, **XV. 393.**

Holm, Charles F., lawyer, **XIV. 242.**

Holman, Minard L., engineer, **XIV. 419.**

Holmes, Gideon F., manufacturer, **XIV. 112.**

Holmes, Howard C., civil engineer, **XIV. 194.**

Holmes, John Haynes, clergyman, **XV. 273.**

Holmes, William, telegraph tariff expert, **XIV. 77.**

Holt, Byron W., economist, **XV. 62, Ferrin.**

Holt, Hamilton, editor, **XV. 115.**

Holyoke, Mass., Whiting mills at, **XIV. 481, Whiting.**

Holyoke National Bank, **XIV. 481, Whiting.**

Home Missionary Society, secretary of, **XIV. 349, Clark.**

Home for Working Women, Boston, Mass., **XIV. 96, Charpiot.**

Homeopathic school, **XIV. 133, Nichols.**

Homeopathy, **XV. 146, Close.**

Homer, Louise, singer, **XIV. 217.**

Honduras, ministers to, **XIV. 428, Lee; 428, Dodge; 429, Brown; 118, McCreery.**

Honore, Henry H., daughter of, **XV. 94, Grant.**

Hope Halls of the Volunteers of America, **XIV. 55, Booth.**

Hopedale, Mass., Draper Co., works, illus., **XIV. 386.**

Hopewell, John, merchant and mfr., **XIV. 168.**

Hopi Indian songs, studied, **XV. 32, Fewkes.**

Hopkins, Archibald, soldier and lawyer, **XIV. 182.**

Indians, California, **XIV.** 121, **Kroeber**; Choctaw, 248, **Owen**; campaign against, 1874-75, 340, **Baldwin**; university courses in their languages, 353, **Dixon**; patron of, 407; authority on, 507, **Emerson**; Lake Mohonk Conference of Friends of, **XV.** 38, **Smiley**; languages of, catalogued, 55, **Pilling**; welfare of, promoted, 414, **Leupp**.

Induction furnace, inventor of, **XV.** 22, **Fessenden**.

Industrial Education, National Society for the Promotion of, **XIV.** 252, **Brown**.

Industrial exposition committee of U. S. senate, **XV.** 145, **Martine**.

Industrial peace, movement for, **XIV.** 7.

Industrial Temporary Home for Working Men, Boston, Mass., **XIV.** 96, **Charpiot**.

In-er-seal, trade-name, **XV.** 292, **Green**.

Inertia, study of, **XV.** 22, **Fessenden**.

Infectious diseases, investigations in, **XIV.** 167, **Hektoen**.

Ingalls, Melville E., railroad president, **XV.** 233.

Ingersoll, Edward, soldier, **XV.** 47.

Ingersoll-Rand Co., drills, **XIV.** 190, **Saunders**; 191, **Rand**.

Ingersoll Rock Drill Co., **XIV.** 190, **Saunders**; **XV.** 246, **De Navarro**.

Ingersoll, Simon, inventor, **XV.** 156, **Sergeant**.

Inland waterways commission, member of, **XIV.** 210, **Bankhead**.

Insanity, experts on, **XV.** 92, **Jelly**; 199, **Hammond**.

Institute of Musical Art, New York City, **XIV.** 90, **Kneisel**; 259, **Goetschius**; 434, **Niessen-Stone**.

Insufflation, intratracheal, originator of, **XV.** 354, **Meltzer**.

Insull, Samuel, capitalist, **XIV.** 334.

Insurance companies, investigation of, in New York state, **XIV.** 38, **Hughes**; uniform code of laws proposed, 165, **Johnson**; legislation against, **XV.** 121, **Major**.

Intemann, Ernest A. G., merchant, **XV.** 368.

Interior, department of, reorganized, **XIV.** 27, **Garfield**; secretaries of, 27, **Garfield**; 413, **Ballinger**.

International Acheson Graphite Company, **XIV.** 94; plant of, illus., 95.

International arbitration, conferences on, **XV.** 38, **Smiley**; for. merchants, 411, **Bernheimer**.

International conference on sugar bounties held at London, **XIV.** 171, **White**.

International Council of Unitarian and other Religious Liberals, **XIV.** 453, **Wendte**.

International court of justice, for Central America, established, **XIV.** 15.

International Exchange, Commission of, **XIV.** 64, **Jenks**.

International law, authority on, **XIV.** 12, **Root**; **XV.** 375, **Walton**.

International Monetary Conference of 1898, president of, **XIV.** 18, **Shaw**.

International Paper Co., **XV.** 155, **Chisholm**.

International Peace. See Peace.

International Peace Congress, second, **XIV.** 6; 419, **Grammer**.

International Reform Bureau, Washington, D. C., **XIV.** 173, **Crafts**.

International Steam Pump Co., **XIV.** 380, **Dunn**.

International Sunshine Society, **XIV.** 289, **Alden**.

International Women's Suffrage Alliance, **XV.** 341, **Catt**.

Interoceanic canal. See Panama canal.

Interparliamentary union, requests peace conference, **XIV.** 6.

Interrupter, electrical, inventor of, **XIV.** 470, **Hewitt**.

Intratracheal insufflation, originator of, **XV.** 354, **Meltzer**.

Inventors' Guild, president of, **XV.** 331, **Baekeland**.

Investment Bankers' Association, **XV.** 361, **Caldwell**.

Iowa, governor of, **XV.** 257, **Clarke**; U. S. senators from, **XIII.** 176, **Cummins**; **XV.** 90, **Kenyon**; chief justices of, **XIV.** 464, **McClain**; **XII.** 373, **Ladd**; **XIII.** 24, **Deemer**.

Iowa State College of Agriculture and Mechanic Arts, Ames, Ia., president of, **XV.** 299, **Pearson**.

Iron, first manufactured in America, **XIV.** 64, **Jenks**; adaptation of the Siemens gas furnace to the manufacture of, 313, **Flagler**; manufacture of, **XIV.** 189, **Abeel**; 312, **Flagler**; 357, **Mather**; 496, **Brown**; **XV.** 45, **Jones**; 66, **Vance**; 70, **Whittemore**; 130, **Willard**; 163, **Brown**; 268, **Harrison**; 300, **Kimbark**; 518, **Baxter**; 327, **Burden**; 374, **Griswold**; 375, **Lukens**; 376, **Huston**.

Ironton, O., founder of, **XV.** 130, **Willard**.

Irrigation engineering, instruction in, **XIV.** 365, **Carpenter**.

Irrigation of western lands begun, **XV.** 350, **Loring**.

Irving National Exchange Bank, New York city, president of, **XV.** 65, **Pierson**.

Irwin, Wallace, author, **XIV.** 184.

Islip, N. Y., original proprietor of, **XIV.** 297, **Nicoll**.

Isthmian canal. See Panama canal.

Isthmian canal commission, members of, **XIV.** 5; 40, **Goethals**.

Italy, ambassadors to, **XIV.** 171, **White**; **XII.** 196, **Griscom**; **XIII.** 598, **Leishman**; **XIV.** 182, **O'Brien**; I. 209, **Page**.

Ives Daylight Producer, inventor of, **XV.** 79, **Ives**.

Ives, Frederic E., inventor, **XV.** 77.

Ives, Herbert E., inventor, **XV.** 78.

Ivorydale, architect of town of, **XIV.** 304, **Beman**.

J.

Jackson, Elihu E., governor, **XV.** 48, **Jackson**.

Jackson Bros. Co., lumber mfrs., **XV.** 48, **Jackson**.

Jackson George W., engineer, **XIV.** 401.

Jackson, Henry C., merchant, **XIV.** 214.

Jackson, J., banker, **XIV.** 251, **Cabot**.

Jackson, Mandell & Daniell, dry-goods, **XIV.** 214, **Jackson**.

Jackson, Patrick T., mfr., **XV.** 46, **Cabot**.

Jackson, William P., U. S. senator, **XV.** 48.

Jackson Park, Chicago, Ill., **XV.** 300, **Kimbark**.

Jacob Tome Institute, Port Deposit, Md., **XIV.** 139, **Harris**.

Jacobs, Charles M., engineer, **XIV.** 208; 446, **McCrea**.

Jamaica, fruit products of, imported, **XIV.** 350, **Baker**.

James, Ollie M., U. S. senator, **XV.** 332.

Jameson, Horatio G., physician, surgeon, **XV.** 36.

Jamestown exposition, director of sanitation at, **XV.** 129, **Blue, R.**

Jamieson, Walter W., physician, **XIV.** 477.

Japan, agricultural experiments in, **XIV.** 368, **Stockbridge**; commercial cable system extended to, 371, **Ward**; friendly mission to, 405; legislative discrimination against in California, 375, **Gillett**; missionaries to, 122, **Harris**; war with Russia terminated, 6; U. S. ambassadors to, **XII.** 196, **Griscom**; **XIV.** 20, **Wright**; 182, **O'Brien**; **XII.** 452, **Bryan**; **XV.** 349, **Anderson**; fur seal fisheries controversy, **XV.** 265, **Hamlin**; collection of art from, **XV.** 416, **Freer**; California legislation affecting natives, 134, **Johnson**.

Jarvis, Samuel M., capitalist, **XV.** 345; 108, **Conklin**.

Jefferis, William W., mineralogist, **XV.** 372.

Jefferson, Joseph, 2nd, in vaudeville, **XV.** 297, **Keith**.

Jefferson College, La., president of, **XIV.** 237, **Blenk**.

Jelly, George Fred'k, physician, **XV.** 92.

Jemison, Mary, Indian captive, **XV.** 240.

Jenks, Jeremiah W., political economist, **XIV.** 64.

Jenks, Joseph, pioneer, **XIV.** 64, **Jenks**.

Jennier, nom-de-plume, **XV.** 345, **Gorrie**.

Jennings, Frederick B., lawyer, **XIV.** 503.

Kinnicutt, Francis P., physician, **XV.** 255.
Kinnicutt, G. Herman, **XV.** 95, Kissel.
Kinsman, Frederick J., P. E. bishop, **XIV.** 274.
Kirby, John, Jr., manufacturer, **XIV.** 318.
Kirbye, J. Edward, educator, **XIV.** 463.
Kirkland, Archie Howard, entomologist, **XIV.** 433.
Kirksville, Mo., American School of Osteopathy at, **XIV.** 451, Still.
Kissel, Gustav E., banker, **XV.** 95.
Kissel, Kinnicutt & Co., bankers, **XV.** 95, Kissel.
Kitchin, Claude, congressman, **XV.** 66.
Kitchin, William H., lawyer and planter, **XV.** 66, Kitchin.
Kitchin, William W., governor, **XIV.** 461.
Kites for meterological purposes, first used, **XV.** 2, Rotch.
Kittanning, Pa., destruction of Indian Village at, **XIV.** 125, Armstrong.
Kittredge, George W., civil engineer, **XV.** 73.
Kitty Hawk,, N. C., experiments in aviation at, **XIV.** 56, Wright.
Kneisel, Franz, violinist, **XIV.** 89.
Knight, Clarence A., lawyer, financier, **XV.** 132.
Knight, Edward J., P. E. bishop, **XIV.** 438.
Knight, Fred'k I., physician, **XIV.** 188.
Knight, George H., physician, **XV.** 235.
Knight, Henry M., physician, **XV.** 234.
Knight, Jesse, jurist, **XIV.** 213.
Knit-goods, manufacture of, **XV.** 384, Carter; 386, Winship.
Knowles, Horace G., diplomat, **XIV.** 487.
Knowles, Richard G., actor, **XIV.** 301.
Knox, Philander C., lawyer and statesman, **XIV.** 408.
Konti, Isidore, sculptor, **XIV.** 493.
Kotzschmar, Hermann, musician, **XV.** 195.
Koudelka, Joseph M., R. C. bishop, **XV.** 147.
Kozlowski, Edward, R. C. bishop, **XV.** 309.
Kroeber, Alfred L., anthropologist, **XIV.** 120.
Kuhn, Loeb & Co., bankers, **XIV.** 190, Kahn; 196.
Kümmel, Henry B., geologist, **XIV.** 280.
Kunitzer, Robert, physician, **XV.** 205.
Kymograph, improved, devised, **XV.** 288, Porter.

L.

Labor, decision of courts involving rights of, **XIV.** 403.
Labor unions, crimes of, **XV.** 50, Burns; prosecuted for boycotting, 373, Loewe.
La Crosse, Wis., Republican and Leader, **XV.** 400, Finch.
Ladew, Edward R., manufacturer, **XIV.** 387.
Laemmle, Carl, moving pictures, **XV.** 362.
Lafayette College, president of, **XV.** 205, Mac-Cracken.
Laflin & Rand Powder Co., **XV.** 260, Haskell.
Laidlaw-Dunn-Gordon Co., **XIV.** 380, Dunn.
Lake, Simon, inventor, **XV.** 5.
Lake Erie, geological researches of, **XIV.** 282, Spencer.
Lake Mohonk, N. Y., fresh air home for children at, **XV.** 25.
Lake Mohonk Conference of Friends of the Indians, **XV.** 38, Smiley.
Lake Superior, geological researches of, **XIV.** 282, Spencer; copper deposits of, 359, Stanton.
Lake Torpedo Boat Co., **XV.** 6, Lake.
Lakes, organization to promote improvement of, **XV.** 407, Ransdell.
Lalance & Grosjean, enamel ware, **XIV.** 396, Cordier; factories of, illus., 395; 396.
Lamar, Joseph R., associate justice U. S. supreme court, **XV.** 414.
Lambie, Frank D., merchant and inventor, **XV.** 220.
Lampblack, mfrs. of, **XIV.** 251, Cabot.

Lamps, electric, improvements in, **XIV.** 261; Parker, 470, Hewitt.
Land, Chas. H., dentist, **XIV.** 331.
Land bank, first in United States, **XV.** 232, Glynn.
Land office at Washington, commissioner of, **XIV.** 414, Ballinger.
Land registration, Torrens system of, described, **XV.** 296, Sheldon.
Land system of dentistry, originator of, **XIV.** 331, Land.
Landes, Henry, geologist, **XIV.** 284.
Landscape architecture, **XV.** 33, Lowell; 307, Pilat.
Lane, James Warren, **XV.** 20, Bliss.
Lane, Levi C., surgeon, **XIV.** 341.
Lane, Wolcott G., lawyer, **XV.** 336, Tracy.
Lane Medical Library, California, **XV.** 354, Wilbur.
Langley, John W., chemist and electrical engineer, **XV.** 8; brother of, 7.
Langley, Samuel P., scientist, **XV.** 7; brother of, 8, Langley.
Langley's law in aerodynamics, **XV.** 7, Langley.
La Porte, Ind., pioneer settler in, **XV.** 326, Andrew.
Lap robes, manufacture of, **XIV.** 168, Goodall.
Lark, The, periodical, illustrations for, **XIV.** 47, Peixotto; editor of, 144, Burgess.
Laryngology, specialist in, **XV.** 56, Casselberry.
Lathes, manufacture of, **XV.** 182, Whitney; inventor of, 294, Hartness.
Latimer, Thomas, physician, **XV.** 26, Howard.
Lauterbach, Edward, lawyer, **XIV.** 512.
Law, international, authorities on, **XIV.** 12, Root; **XV.** 375, Walton; Encyclopædia of, 67, Cockcroft.
Law, military, in Pennsylvania, **XIV.** 230, Rogers.
Law Reporter, magazine, established, **XV.** 350, Chandler.
Law and Order Society of Philadelphia, Pa., **XIV.** 415, Gibboney.
Lawler, John J., R. C. bishop, **XV.** 73.
Lawrence, Abbott, daughter of, **XV.** 2, Rotch.
Lawrence, Jason V. O., physician, **XV.** 261.
Lawrence, Mass., worsted manufacturing establishment at, **XV.** 321, Wood.
Lawrenceville (N. J.), School, **XIV.** 311, Mackenzie; 516, McPherson.
Layng, James D., R. R. official, **XIV.** 95.
Lazear, Jesse W., scientist, **XV.** 60.
Lea, Luke, U. S. senator, **XV.** 26.
Leach, Frank A., public official, **XIV.** 333.
Lead, S. Dak., R. C. bishops of, **XV.** 73, Lawler; 378, Stariha.
Leadville, Colo., founded, **XIV.** 365, Borden.
Leaf tobacco, authority on, **XV.** 111, Sylvester.
Leaming, Thomas, lawyer, **XV.** 137.
Leather, manufacture of, **XIV.** 387, Ladew; corona kid, 489, Baker.
Leavitt, Frank M., inventor, **XV.** 20.
Leavitt, Humphrey H., jurist, **XV.** 21, Leavitt.
Leavitt, John McDowell, educator, son of, **XV.** 21, Leavitt.
Lectures, public, in New York public schools, **XIV.** 366, Leipziger.
Lee, Charles A., physician, **XV.** 116.
Lee, Joseph W. J., diplomat, **XIV.** 428.
Lee, Margaret, author, **XV.** 304.
Lee, Higginson & Co., bankers, **XIV.** 445, Higginson.
Leeds, William B., capitalist, **XIV.** 442; 65, Moore.
Leggett, Henry T., artist, **XIV.** 523.
Lehigh University, president of, 1905, **XV.** 114, Drinker, H. S.
Leipziger, Henry M., educator, **XIV.** 366.
Leisser, Martin B., artist, **XIV.** 175.
Leiter, Levi Z., **XIV.** 228, Farwell.
Leland, Lester, manufacturer, **XIV.** 478.
Leland Stanford Junior University, president of, **XV.** 353, Wilbur.

LeMoyne, Francis J., physician, **XV.** 171.
Lenox College, Hopkinton, Ia., patron of, **XV.** 165, Doolittle.
Leonard, H. Ward, electrician, inventor, **XV.** 3.
Leonard, Ward, Electric Co., **XV.** 4, Leonard.
Lepidoptera, authorities on, **XIV.** 97, Dyar; **XV.** 71, Smith.
Lesley Cement Laboratory, University of Pennsylvania, **XV.** 112.
Lesley, James, banker, **XV.** 111, Lesley.
Lesley, James, merchant and editor, **XV.** 111-112, Lesley.
Lesley, Robert W., manufacturer, **XV.** 111.
Leslie, Mrs. Madeline, pen-name, **XIV.** 154, Baker, Harriette N. W.
Letchworth, Josiah, mfr. and capitalist, **XV.** 325; brother of, 324.
Letchworth, William P., manufacturer, philanthropist, **XV.** 324; brother of, 325.
Letchworth Park, N. Y., **XV.** 325, Letchworth, W. P.
Letter files. See Filing devices.
Letts, Frank C., merchant, **XIV.** 378.
Leupp, Francis E., editor, author, **XV.** 413.
Leventritt, David, lawyer and jurist, **XIV.** 310.
Levy, Joseph L., rabbi, **XIV.** 423.
Levy court, Washington, D. C., **XV.** 124, Brown.
Lewis, J. Hamilton, U. S. senator, **XV.** 63.
Lexow committee of N. Y. legislature, **XV.** 254, Goff.
Ley, Fred T., contractor, **XV.** 69, Ley.
Ley, Harold A., contractor and philanthropist, **XV.** 69.
Libby, Charles R., lawyer, **XIV.** 332; partner of, **XV.** 346, Symonds.
Libel, suit brought by fugitive slave for, **XIV.** 226, Lothrop; brought by U. S. government, 22, Bonaparte.
Liberati, Alessandro, musician, **XIV.** 218.
Liberia, historical account of the republic, **XIV.** 177, Appleton; ministers to, 206, Smith; 471, Crossland; 421, Lyon.
Liberty National Bank, New York, president of, **XV.** 67, Schenck.
Library classification system, originator of, **XV.** 32, Parker.
Library for schools, first established, **XIV.** 134, Baldwin.
Licensed Association of Automobile Manufacturers, **XV.** 59; 271, Parker.
Lidgerwood Manufacturing Co., New York, **XV.** 31, Miller.
Lieber, Hugo, manufacturing chemist, **XV.** 179, Lucke.
Lieutenant-general of U. S. army, **XIV.** 151, MacArthur.
Life Extension Institute, **XV.** 69, Ley.
Life insurance, issued by banks, **XIV.** 299, Brandeis; investigation of companies, 38, Hughes; re-organized in New York state, **XV.** 250, Alexander.
Life-raft (mattress), inventor of, **XV.** 230, Burton.
Life-saving service, U. S., **XV.** 129, Blue, R.
Life's farm, for children, donor of, **XIV.** 391, Gilbert.
Ligature passer, invented, **XIV.** 427, Cleveland.
Liggett, John T., life insurance, **XIV.** 367, Liggett.
Liggett, Louis K., merchant, **XIV.** 367.
Liggett & Meyers, tobacconists, **XV.** 388, Myers.
Light, researches on, **XV.** 78, Ives, H. E.
Lighthouse board, transferred to the department of commerce and labor, **XIV.** 19.
Lighting fixtures, manufacturers of, **XIV.** 451, Enos.
Lightning arrester, inventor of, **XIV.** 76, Barclay.
Lilley, George L., governor, **XIV.** 474.
Lillie, Frank R., zoologist, **XIV.** 479.
Lincoln, Abraham, letters and manuscripts, **XV.** 19, Huntington, H. E.

Lincoln, Joseph B., merchant, **XIV.** 333.
Lincoln, Joseph C., author, **XIV.** 90.
Lincoln, Rufus P., physician, **XV.** 200.
Lincoln, Solomon, lawyer, **XIV.** 295.
Lincoln, Waldo, manufacturer, **XIV.** 101.
Lincoln, Neb., First Nat. Bank of, **XIV.** 425, Perkins.
Lindenthal, Gustav, civil engineer, **XIV.** 492; 446, McCrea.
Lindsay, John D., lawyer, **XV.** 159.
Lindsey, Ben. B., jurist, reformer, **XV.** 183.
Lindsey, William, merchant and author, **XIV.** 129.
Linnæan Society of New York, president of, **XIV.** 281, Sennett.
Linsley, John H., physician, **XV.** 370.
Lister, Ernest, governor, **XV.** 340.
Little Arthur D., chemist, **XV.** 64.
Little Giant, rock drill, invented, **XIV.** 191, Rand.
Little Rock, Ark., R. C. bishop of, **XV.** 370, Morris.
Little Theatre, New York city, **XV.** 177, Ames.
Livermore, Abiel A., author and educator, **XV.** 255.
Locke, John, scientist, **XV.** 264.
Lockjaw, remedy for, discovered, **XV.** 354, Meltzer.
Locomobile Co. of America, **XV.** 211, Riker.
Loeb, Louis, artist, **XIV.** 469.
Loewe, Dietrich E., manufacturer, **XV.** 373.
Loew, Marcus, theatrical manager, **XV.** 310, Zukor.
Log-skidding cableway, inventor of, **XV.** 31, Miller.
Lomax family, genealogy, compiler of, **XIV.** 326, Lomax.
Lomax, Joseph, lawyer and journalist, **XIV.** 326.
London, England, incandescent electric lighting in, **XV.** 218, Hammer.
Long-Bell Lumber Co., **XV.** 367, Long.
Long, Franklin B., architect, **XV.** 278.
Long, John Luther, playwright, **XIV.** 83, Belasco.
Long, R. A., & Co., lumber dealers, **XV.** 367, Long.
Long, Robert A., lumberman, **XV.** 367.
Long Island City, Sunnyside yard of the Penn. R. R., **XIV.** 446, McCrea.
Long Island railroad, engineer of the terminal of, **XIV.** 209, Davies; taken over by the Pennsylvania railroad, 446, McCrea.
Longyear, John M., capitalist, **XV.** 295.
Longworth, Langdon R., physician, **XV.** 265.
Longworth, Nicholas, philanthropist and pioneer, **XV.** 349, Anderson.
Loomis, Charles Battell, humorist, **XIV.** 476.
Loomis, Elisha S., mathematician and genealogist, **XV.** 186.
Loomis, John Mason, merchant, **XV.** 186, Loomis.
Loomis, William S., editor and financier, **XV.** 86.
Loomis Institute, Windsor, Conn., **XV.** 186, Loomis.
Lord, Franklin B., lawyer, **XIV.** 491.
Lord, Day & Lord, lawyers, **XIV.** 491, Lord.
Lorenz, Julius, musician, **XIV.** 318.
Loring, George B., agriculturist and diplomat, **XV.** 349.
Loring, Hollis, jurist and merchant, **XV.** 119, Loring.
Loring, Victor J., lawyer, **XV.** 119.
Lorimer, William, senator, **XIV.** 91.
Los Angeles, Cal., street car lines in, **XV.** 18; destruction of Times building, **XV.** 50, Burns; Edison Electric Co. in, 257, Sinclair.
Los Angeles Fellowship, **XIV.** 178, Mills.
Lothrop, Alvin M., merchant, **XIV.** 319, Woodward.
Lothrop, Samuel K., clergyman, **XIV.** 226, Lothrop.
Lothrop, Thornton K., lawyer, **XIV.** 225.
Louisiana, new constitution of, **XV.** 135, Hall; reclamation of swamp lands in, **XV.** 196, Hero; 243, Wisner; governors of, **XIV.** 104, Sanders; **XV.** 135, Hall; U. S. senators from, **XV.** 407, Ransdell; 387, Broussard; chief justice of, **XII.** 103, Monroe.
Louisiana Central Lumber Co., **XV.** 380, White.
Louisville, Ky., R. C. Bishop of, **XV.** 224, O'Donaghue.

Maxim, Sir Hiram S., son of, **XV. 137, Maxim.**
May, Charles Hy., physician, **XIV. 206.**
May Frederick, son of, **XV. 240, May.**
May, Fred'k J., physician, surgeon, **XV. 240.**
Maynard, Mass., carded woolen plant at, **XV. 321, Wood.**
Mayo, Charles H., surgeon, **XIV. 206; 207, Mayo.**
Mayo, Henry, navigator, **XV. 44, Mayo.**
Mayo, Henry T., naval officer, **XV. 44.**
Mayo, William J., surgeon, **XIV. 207.**
Mayo, William W., surgeon, **XIV. 207, Mayo.**
Mays, John, partner of, **XV. 20, Bliss.**
Meacham, Franklin, surgeon, **XV. 309, Meacham.**
Meacham, Franklin A., physician, **XV. 309.**
Mead, Albert E., governor, **XIV. 447.**
Meadville Theological School, president of, **XV. 255, Livermore.**
Meany, Edward P., lawyer, **XIV. 467.**
Meat packing industry, **XIV. 303, Swift;** government investigation of, 27, **Garfield;** 320, **Sinclair.**
Mechanical engineering, advances in, **XIV. 419, Holman;** 521, **Taylor; XV. 41, Westinghouse;** 188, **Meier;** 294, **Hartness.**
Medical service, United States, account of, **XV. 129, Blue, R.**
Medicine, advances in, **XV. 89, Lusk;** 129, **Blue, R.;** 135, **Reinhardt;** 204, **Pearce;** 259, **King;** 264, **McNutt;** preventive, authorities on, 129, **Blue, R.;** 135, **Reinhardt;** Eclectic School of, founded, 259, **King;** Case System of Teaching, 287, **Cannon.**
Medium, spiritualistic, investigations of, **XIV. 48, Hyslop.**
Meech, Ezra, daughter of, **XV. 244, Warner.**
Meek, Channing F., merchant, **XV. 153.**
Meeker, Charles A., dentist, **XV. 221.**
Meerschaert, Theophile, R. C. bishop, **XV. 346.**
Meier, Edward D., engineer, **XV. 188.**
Meigs, Arthur V., physician, **XV. 217.**
Mekeel Isaac A., publisher, **XV. 83.**
Mell, Patrick H., scientist, **XV. 396.**
Mell, Patrick H., clergyman, son of, **XV. 396, Mell.**
Meltzer, Samuel J., physician, **XV. 354.**
Melville, George W., engineer, **XV. 42.**
Memphis, Tenn., yellow fever epidemic in, **XIV. 20, Wright.**
Menocal, A. G., civil engineer, **XIV. 354.**
Menominee iron range, **XV. 295, Longyear.**
Men's International Theosophical League of Humanity, **XV. 338, Tingley.**
Mercer University, president of, **XIV. 459, Smith.**
Merchants' Association of N. Y., **XIV. 468, Bannin;** account of, 390, **King;** presidents of, 390, **King; XII, 129, Towne; XV. 127, Marble.**
Merchants' Refrigerating Co., **XIV. 343, Wills.**
Mergenthaler Linotype Co., **XIV. 440.**
Meritas, oilcloth, **XIV. 249, Hunsicker.**
Merrill, Elmer T., philologist, **XIV. 312.**
Merrill, Charles W., engineer and inventor, **XV. 102.**
Merrill, James Cushing, jurist, **XV. 246, Merrill.**
Merrill, James Cushing, surgeon and ornithologist, **XV. 246.**
Merritt, Ernest G., physicist, **XV. 195.**
Mershon, Ralph D., engineer, **XV. 225.**
Mesa Verde, Colorado, ruin in, **XV. 32, Fewkes.**
Mesaba iron range, Minnesota, **XV. 295, Longyear.**
Metabolism, authority on, **XV. 89, Lusk.**
Metallurgy, advances in, **XIV. 342, Monnot;** 71, **Gayley.**
Metals, processes for welding, discovered, **XIV. 342, Monnet;** machines for working, invented, **XV. 216, Seymour;** pyro-electric reduction of, **XV. 131, Cowles.**
Metcalf, Victor Howard, sec. of the navy, **XIV. 25.**
Meteorites, discovered in Alaska, **XIV. 60-61.**
Meteorology, advances in, **XV. 2, Rotch;** 396, **Mell.**

Meters, water, invented, **XV. 156, Sergeant.**
Methodist Episcopal church, refuses ordination to woman preacher, **XIV. 456, Shaw;** thank offering for, **XV. 414, Tipple.**
Methodist Episcopal church, colored, first bishop of, **XIV. 316, Miles.**
Methodist Protestant church, first woman ordained in, **XIV. 456, Shaw.**
Metropolitan Museum of Art, New York, gifts to, **XIV. 67;** exhibition of German art at, 213, **Reisinger;** Brown collection of musical instruments, **XV.** 160, **Brown;** Abbey drawings at, 281, **Abbey;** Altman collection, 188, **Altman.**
Metropolitan Opera Co., **XIV. 258, Dippel.**
Metropolitan Street Railway Co., New York city, **XV. 11, Widener.**
Metropolitan Street Railroad Co., Washington, D. C., **XV. 124, Brown.**
Metropolitan Temple, New York city, **XIV. 268, Cadman.**
Mettauer, John P., surgeon, **XV. 315.**
Metz, Herman A., chemist, **XIV. 347.**
Mexican Central Railway Co., **XV. 212, Wade.**
Mexico, ambassador to, **XV. 342, Fletcher.**
Mexico, national conservation conference with, **XIV.** 31; monetary reform for, **XIV. 227, Conant;** controversy with, **XV. 44, Mayo;** disturbances in, **XV.** 144, **Fletcher;** ambassadors to, **XIV. 166, Thompson; XII. 126, Wilson; XV. 342, Fletcher.**
Meyer, George A., merchant, **XIV. 413, Meyer.**
Meyer, George von L., diplomat and secretary of navy, **XIV. 413.**
Meyers, Sidney S., lawyer. **XV. 100.**
Mezes, Sidney E., educator, **XV. 206.**
Miami, Fla., development of, **XV. 10, Flagler.**
Miami University, Oxford, O., president of, **XV. 171, Benton.**
Michael, Arthur, chemist, **XV. 172.**
Michener, Ezra, physician, botanist, **XV. 247.**
Michigan, naval brigade organized in, **XIV. 26, Newberry;** lumber interests in, **XIV. 50, Stephenson;** historian of, **XIV. 285, Burton;** municipal reforms in, **XV. 65, Crane;** governor of, **XV. 213, Ferris;** U. S. senators from, **XIV. 483, Smith; XV. 220, Townsend;** chief justices of, **XIV. 364, Carpenter; XII. 457, Grant; XV. 48, Blair; XII. 113, Montgomery; VII. 102, Moore.**
Michigan State Agricultural College, Lansing, Mich., **XV. 244, Miles.**
Micou, Paul, physician and lawyer, **XV. 161, Micou.**
Micou, Richard W., clergyman, educator, **XV. 161.**
Micou, William Chatfield, lawyer, **XV. 161, Micou.**
Microscope improved, **XV. 78, Ives, F. E.;** objects of, photographed, 265, **Longworth.**
Middlebury College, president of, **XIV. 509, Thomas;** Warner Hall at, **XV. 245, Warner.**
Midway, boulevard, Chicago, Ill., **XV. 300, Kimbark.**
Miles, Manly, naturalist and agriculturist, **XV. 243.**
Miles, William H., bishop, **XIV. 316.**
Milford, Conn., a founder of, **XV. 113, Platt.**
Milham, Willis I., educator, **XIV. 430.**
Milk, scientific study of, **XV. 217, Meigs.**
Military law in Pennsylvania, **XIV. 230, Rogers.**
Miller, Adolph C., member of Federal Reserve Board, **XV. 265, Hamlin.**
Miller, Charles, merchant, **XV. 345, Huidekoper.**
Miller, Frank E., physician, **XIV. 296.**
Miller, Spencer, engineer, **XV. 31.**
Millet, Francis D., artist, **XV. 201; 280. Abbey.**
Milligan, John, jurist, legislator, **XV. 219.**
Milling machines, manufacture of, **XV. 182, Whitney.**
Millis, William A., educator, **XIV. 169.**
Mills, Benjamin Fay, clergyman, **XIV. 178.**
Mills. Charles de Berard, writer and philanthropist, **XV. 374, Mills.**

Mills, Harriet May, reformer, **XV. 374.**

Milton, William H., senator, **XIV. 388.**

Milwaukee, Wis., municipal improvements in, **XIV. 205, Benzenberg; R. C.** auxiliary bishop of, **XV. 309, Kozlowski.**

Milwaukee Free Press, proprietor of, **XIV. 51, Stephenson.**

Miner, Thomas, physician, **XV. 261.**

Mineralogy, researches in, **XV. 214, Cross; 372, Jefferis.**

Minerals, collections of, **XV. 107, Booth, S. C.; 372, Jefferis.**

Mines Management Co., New York, **XV. 109, Henry; 399, Wilkens.**

Mining engineering, advances in, **XIV. 508, Brunton; XV. 393, Birch.**

Mining machinery, manufacture of, **XIV. 191, Rand;** inventor of, **XV. 22, Sperry.**

Minnesota, lumber interests in, **XIV. 52, Weyerhaeuser;** legislation in, **165, Johnson; Eberhart;** governors of, **164, Johnson; 165, Eberhart.**

Minnesota Institution for the Feeble-Minded, **XV. 235, Knight, H. M.**

Mint, U. S., duties of superintendents and directors of, **XIV. 334, Leach;** records of, **XV. 326, Andrew;** directors of, **XIV. 333, Leach; XV. 326, Andrew.**

Missions, in Gilbert Islands, **XIV. 98, Bingham;** in Japan, **122, Harris;** chair of the theory and practice of, **120, Beach.**

Mississippi, governors of, **XIV. 518, Noel; XV. 333, Brewer;** U. S. senator from, **XV. 107, Percy;** Confederate soldiers' home in, **XV. 333, Brewer.**

Mississippi, State University of, **XV. 333, Brewer.**

Mississippi Industrial College, Columbus, Miss., **XV. 326, Kincannon.**

Mississippi River Boom and Logging Co., **XIV. 52, Weyerhaeuser.**

Mississippi River, flood control of, **XV. 321, Donovan; 407, Ransdell.**

Missouri, governors of, **XIV. 475, Hadley; XV. 121, Major;** U. S. senator from, **XV. 99, Reed.**

Missouri Lumber and Mining Co., **XV. 380, White.**

Mr. Dooley, pen-name, **XIV. 53, Dunne.**

Mrs. Madeline Leslie, pen-name, **XIV. 154, Baker.**

Mitchell, Samuel C., educator, **XIV. 88.**

Mitchell, John, labor leader, **XV. 126.**

Modern Language Association of America, presidents of, **XIV. 229, Elliott; 437, Gummere; 204, Todd; 399, Scott; 230, Warren; IV. 538, Learned; VI. 326, Matthews; XIII. 583, Mott; XIII. 539, Grandgent.**

Modern Woodmen of America, **XV. 271-72, Root.**

Modjeska, Helena, son of, **XV. 68, Modjeski.**

Modjeski. Ralph, civil engineer, **XV. 68.**

Moffett, Cleveland, author, **XIV. 381.**

Molitor, David A., civil engineer, **XV. 160.**

Monaghan, John J., R. C. bishop, **XV. 148.**

Monekey, Charles, inventor of monkey-wrench, **XV. 216, Seymour.**

Monetary commission, Indianapolis, **XIV. 227, Conant;** national, **XV. 326, Andrew.**

Monetary science, **XIV. 227, Conant.**

Monette, John W., physician, **XV. 4.**

Monkey-wrench, Acme, inventor of, **XV. 216, Seymour.**

Monnot, John F., metallurgist, **XIV. 342.**

Monnot copper-clad steel, **XIV. 342, Monnot.**

Montana, governors of, **XIV. 431, Norris; XV. 241, Stewart;** U. S. senators from, **XIV. 107, Dixon; XV. 48, Myers; 409, Walsh.**

Montgomery, John J., scientist, inventor, **XV. 338.**

Montgomery, Thomas Harrison, scientist, **XV. 216.**

Montgomery, Thomas Harrison, Sr., **XV. 216, Montgomery.**

Moody, Dwight L., **XIV. 228, Farwell.**

Moody, John, financial expert, **XV. 62, Ferrin.**

Moody Magazine and Book Co., **XV. 63, Ferrin.**

Moody, William Henry, jurist, **XIV. 21.**

Moody's Magazine (financial), **XV. 62, Ferrin.**

Moon, studies of the motion of, **XV. 24, Brown.**

Mooney, Edmund L., partner of, **XV. 209, Shipman.**

Moore, Henry, **XV. 358, Russell.**

Moore, Martin, clergyman, **XIV. 264, Willis.**

Moore, Nathaniel, **XV. 159, Robinson.**

Moore, Risdon, legislator, **XIV. 364, Deneen.**

Moore, William, manufacturer, **XV. 158.**

Moore, William Henry, financier, **XIV. 65.**

Moorhead, Miss., founder of, **XV. 161, Pond.**

Morehead, John H., governor, **XV. 230.**

Morgan, David E., jurist, **XIV. 499.**

Morgan, Edwin V., diplomat, **XIV. 432.**

Morgan, George W., daughter of, **XV. 277, Coffinberry.**

Morgan, J. P., & Co., bankers, **XIV. 66; 16, Bacon; 78, Steele, C.; XV. 181, Morgan.**

Morgan, J. S., & Co., bankers, **XIV. 66, Morgan.**

Morgan, John H. A., entomologist, **XIV. 439.**

Morgan, John Pierpont, Sr., financier, **XIV. 66; 37; 197; XV. 386, Duveen.**

Morgan, John Pierpont, Jr., financier, **XV. 181.**

Morgan, Junius Spencer, banker, **XIV. 66, Morgan.**

Morgan breed of horses re-established in the U. S., **XIV. 29, Wilson.**

Morgan library, New York city, illus., **XIV. 67.**

Morgenthau, Henry, lawyer, ambassador, **XV. 363.**

Morley, Frank, mathematician, **XV. 147.**

Moroccan conference of European powers, **XIV. 171, White.**

Morocco, U. S. minister to, **XIV. 408, Dodge.**

Morrill geological expeditions, director of, **XIV. 278, Barbour.**

Morris, Hugh M., partner of, **XV. 105, Saulsbury.**

Morris, John B., R. C. bishop, **XV. 370.**

Morris Brown College, Atlanta, Ga., **XIV. 348, Flipper.**

Morse, Jay C., iron merchant, **XIV. 487, Mather.**

Morse, Robert M., partner of, **XV. 348, Hellier.**

Morton, Julius D., banker, **XIV. 24, Morton.**

Morton, Paul, financier, **XIV. 24.**

Morton, Samuel G., daughter of, **XV. 216, Montgomery.**

Moses, Adolph, lawyer, **XIV. 394, Pam.**

Moses, Charles M., public official, **XIV. 338.**

Moses, George H., editor and diplomat, **XIV. 115.**

Moses Brown School, Providence, R. I., principal of, **XV. 38, Smiley.**

Mosher, Eliza M., physician, **XV. 304.**

Mosquitoes, authority on, **XIV. 97, Dyar;** yellow fever spread by, **XV. 61, Lazear;** efforts to destroy, **71, Smith.**

Motor boat, hydroplane, constructed, **XIV. 470, Hewitt.**

Motor carriage, Columbia, invented. **XV. 137, Maxim.**

Motor and Accessory Mfrs., **XV. 101, Meyers.**

Motorcycle, inventor of, **XV. 401;** manufacture of, **XV. 180, Hedstrom.**

Motors, electric, invented, **XV. 42, Westinghouse; 334, Perret.**

Mott, George S., clergyman, **XIV. 477.**

Mottier, David M., botanist, **XV. 191.**

Moulton, Augustus F., lawyer, **XIV. 337.**

Moulton, Barron Clinton, partner of, **XV. 119, Loring.**

Moulton, Loring & Loring, lawyers, **XV. 119, Loring.**

Mount, Shepard A., painter. **XIV. 457, Mount.**

Mount, Wallace, jurist, **XIV. 505.**

Mount, William S., artist, **XIV. 457.**

Mt. Etna, eruption of, predicted, **XV. 335, Perret.**

Mt. Huascaran, Peru, ascent of, **XV. 152, Peck.**

Netherlands, U. S. minister to, **XIV.** 338, Beaupre; I. 252, Bryce; VII. 291, Van Dyke.

Nethersole, **Olga**, in vaudeville, **XV.** 297, Keith.

Neuralgia, first successful cure for, **XV.** 224, Hartley.

Neuropathology, study of, **XV.** 76, Schlapp.

Nevin, William George, R. R. manager, **XIV.** 279.

Nevius, Henry M., lawyer, **XIV.** 433.

New Amsterdam, first official map of, **XIV.** 18, Cortelyou.

New Bedford, Mass., founder of, **XV.** 335, Rotch.

Newell, Zenas E., banker, **XV.** 385.

Newell, Thomas, settler, **XV.** 385, Newell.

New England Agricultural Society, established, **XV.** 349, Loring.

New Hampshire, governors of, **XIV.** 100, McLane; 498, Quinby; U. S. senator from, **XV.** 272, Hollis.

New Imperial University, Peking, China, **XV.** 20, Martin.

New Jersey, Raritan 'River Railroad, **XIV.** 418, Earle; state geologist of, 280, Kummel; destruction of mosquitoes in, **XV.** 71, Smith; direct primaries in, 145, Martine; dental societies organized in, 221, Meeker; governors of, **XIV.** 123, Fort; **VIII.** 176, Wilson; **XV.** 114, Fielder; U. S. senators from, **XIV.** 305, Briggs; **XV.** 145, Martine; chancellor, 61, Pitney.

New Jersey Zinc Co., **XIV.** 177, Heckscher.

New Jerusalem church, **XIV.** 348, Reed.

New Orleans, archbishop of, **XIV.** 237, Blenk; mayors of, 314, Behan; 371, Behrman; New Orleans Dry Dock and Ship Building Co., **XV.** 196, Hero.

New Paltz, N. Y., founded, **XV.** 356, Hasbrouck.

Newport News, Va., developed, **XV.** 17, Huntington, C. P.

News League of Ohio, **XV.** 275, Cox.

New Washington Brick Co., **XV.** 400, Holbrook.

New York city, Boys' Club, **XIV.** 198; builder of theaters in, 45, Hammerstein; commissioner of immigration for, 369, Williams; designer of bridges for, 492, Lindenthal; detective bureau, 308, Byrnes; Grace Church, 35, Potter; improvements in park system of, 382, Willcox; J. P. Morgan & Co., bankers, 66; Lyceum Theatre, Madison Square Theatre, 158, MacKaye, Steele; Manhattan Opera House, 45, Hammerstein; Metropolitan Temple, 268, Cadman; Nassau Bank, president of, 103, Earl; National Park Bank, 224, Delafield; Poor, E. E.; 379, Barber; new system of warehouses in, 102-103, Bush; Pennsylvania railroad station, illus., 446, McCrea; postmaster of, 382, Willcox; public libraries, 339, Bostwick; public lecture system of, 366, Leipziger; Rapid Transit Commission of, engineer of, 218, Parsons; rapid transit in, 145, Duncan; 209, Jacobs; 465, McAdoo; **XV.** 11, Widener; reforms in police department, **XIV.** 4; 308, Byrnes; settlement work in, 353, Hunter; 382, Willcox; first steel skeleton buildings in, 298, Gilbert; subway system of, 63; tunnel under, for Pennsylvania railroad, 492, Lindenthal; university settlement in, 353, Hunter; history of National City Bank of, **XV.** 28, Stillman; 29, Vanderlip; Chase National Bank, 30, Hepburn; Chamber of Commerce, president of, 30, Hepburn; Chamber of Commerce, arbitration committee of, 411, Bernheimer; public playgrounds advocated in, 54, Sullivan; Emigrant Savings Bank, 102, McMahon; Provident Loan Society of, 150; Little Theatre, 177, Ames; Sydenham Hospital in, 205, Kunitzer; originator of night court in, 208, Whitman; Navarro Apartments, 246, De Navarro; 361, Hubert; account of the Church of the Ascension, 262, Grant; Union Trust Co. in, 282, King; Rockefeller Institute of Research in, 302; School of Journalism in, 306, Williams; St. Thomas's Church

in, architect of, 328, **Cram**; first apartment houses in, 361, Hubert; water supply of, 389, Smith.

New York state, constitutional convention of 1893, **XIV.** 12, Root; legislative insurance investigation, 38, Hughes; oldest church in, 275, Philipse, Frederick, Sr.; Philipseborough, manor of, 275, Philipse, Frederick, Sr.; public utilities, state control of, 382, Willcox; salt industry in, **XV.** 319, Gouinlock; regents of the University of, **XV.** 83, Alexander; 209, Shipman; governors of, **XIV.** 436, Odell; **XIII.** 551, Higgins; **XIV.** 38, Hughes; **XV.** 26, Dix; **III.** 369, Sulzer; **XV.** 231, Glynn; 207, Whitman; U. S. senators from, **XIV.** 12, Root; **XV.** 13, O'Gorman; 34, Wadsworth; chief judge of 412, Bartlett.

New York American, **XIV.** 450, Hearst.

New York Arion Society, conductor of, **XIV.** 318, Lorenz.

New York Central & Hudson River Railroad, **XIV.** 63; presidents of, 41, Brown; 42, Newman; chief engineer of, **XV.** 73, Kittredge.

New York Clearing House Association, president of, **XV.** 268, Woodward.

New York Connecting Railroad, **XV.** 290, Rea.

New York Herald, managing editor of, **XIV.** 444, Chambers.

New York Journal, **XIV.** 157, Brisbane; 450, Hearst.

New York Life Insurance Co., **XIV.** 508, Weeks; **XV.** 34, Perkins.

New York Lubricating Co., **XIV.** 120, Dashiell.

New York, New Haven and Hartford Railroad, **XIV.** 63; 492, Lindenthal; **XV.** 227, Hall.

New York public library, **XIV.** 339, Bostwick.

New York Society for the Prevention of Cruelty to Children, president of, **XV.** 169, Lindsay.

New York Society for the Suppression of Vice, **XV.** 241, Comstock.

New York State Woman Suffrage Association, **XV.** 375, Mills.

New York Tanning Extract Co., **XIV.** 467, Baldwin, W. M.

New York Telephone Co., **XV.** 84, Carty; 322, Bethell.

New York World, libel suit against, brought by U. S. government, **XIV.** 22, Bonaparte; prize for aviation, **XV.** 401, Curtiss.

Newark, N. J., Bishop Steel Works, **XIV.** 276, Bishop; Tea Tray Co., 304, Marten.

Newberry, Oliver, manufacturer, **XIV.** 26, Newberry.

Newberry, Truman Handy, secretary of the navy, **XIV.** 26.

Newman, William H., railroad president, **XIV.** 42.

Newspaper, first religious, in U. S., **XIV.** 264, Willis.

Niagara Falls, manufacturers at, **XIV.** 93; **XV.** 142, Value; geological researches of, **XIV.** 282, Spencer; factories in, illus., 94; 95.

Niblick, pen-name, **XIV.** 247, Hanks.

Nicaragua, U. S. ministers to, **XIV.** 487, Knowles; 495, Northcott; route for canal proposed in, **XIV.** 354, Menocal.

Nichols, Charles F., physician, **XIV.** 133.

Nichols, James E., merchant, **XIV.** 329.

Nichols, William H., chemist, **XIV.** 377.

Nichols Chemical Co., **XIV.** 377, Nichols.

Nichols medal, recipient of, **XV.** 331, Baekeland.

Nicoll, Anable, Lindsay & Fuller, lawyers, **XV.** 169, Lindsay.

Nicoll, De Lancey, lawyer, **XIV.** 297.

Nicoll, Matthias, mayor of New York, **XIV.** 297, Nicoll.

Nicoll, Solomon T., merchant, **XIV.** 297, Nicoll.

Nicoll, William, **XIV.** 297, Nicoll.

Niessen-Stone, Matja von, singer, **XIV.** 434.

Night court, New York city, originator of, **XV.** 208, Whitman.

Night riders, Kentucky, **XIV.** 266, **Willson.**

Nilan, John J., R. C. bishop, **XV.** 387.

Niles-Bement-Pond Co., XV. 182, **Whitney.**

Nixon, George S., senator, **XIV.** 443.

Nobel prizes, American recipients of, for peace, **XIV.** 1, **Roosevelt;** 12, **Root;** for physics, **XII.** 100, **Michelson;** for medicine, **XV.** 301, **Carrel;** for chemistry, **XII.** 362, **Richards.**

Noel, Edmund F., governor, **XIV.** 518.

Noiseless steam exhaust, inventor of, **XV.** 356, **Shaw.**

Norfolk, Conn., Robbins preparatory school at, founded, **XIV.** 254, **Battell.**

Norris, Edwin L., governor, **XIV.** 431.

Norris, Frank, author, **XV.** 378.

Norris Iron Co., XIV. 204, **Woodruff.**

North American conservation conference, XIV. 31.

North American Civil League for Immigrants, XV. 249, **Kellar.**

North American Trust Co., XV. 108, **Conklin;** 346, **Jarvis.**

North Billerica, Mass., Talbot Mills at, **XIV.** 173, **Clark.**

North Carolina, governor of, **XIV.** 461, **Kitchin.**

North Dakota, governor of, **XIV.** 449, **Burke; XV.** 382, **Hanna;** U. S. senator from, **XIV.** 489, **Johnson;** chief justice of, 499, **Morgan.**

North Easton, Mass., developed, **XIV.** 202, **Ames, F. L.**

Northcott, Elliott, diplomat, **XIV.** 495.

Northcott, Robert S., soldier, **XIV.** 495, **Northcott.**

North Pole, discovery of, **XIV.** 61.

Northern Pacific Railway, XIV. 197; 380, **Billings;** corner in stock of, 16, **Bacon.**

Northfield, Vt., public library presented to, **XV.** 198, **Brown.**

Northway, Stephen A., lawyer, **XV.** 351.

Northway, Zenas, soldier, **XV.** 351, **Northway.**

North Western Lumber Co., XV. 405, **Emerson.**

Northwestern Telegraph Co., XV. 136, **Simmons.**

Northwestern University, president of, **XIV.** 139, **Harris;** settlement work of, 454, **Zueblin;** medical school of, **XV.** 55, **Casselberry.**

Norton, Edwin, manufacturer, **XV.** 215.

Norton, John N., clergyman, author, **XV.** 355.

Norton, Roderick N., president of Upper Iowa University, **XIV.** 292, **Shanklin, W. A.**

Norwich, Conn., American Thermos Bottle Co. in, **XV.** 108, **Walker.**

Notman, John, lawyer, **XV.** 103; partner of, **XV.** 392, **Joline.**

Notre Dame University, president of, **XIV.** 473, **Cavanaugh.**

Nova Scotia, gold mines in, **XV.** 227, **McClure, C. F.**

Noyes, Arthur A., chemist, **XV.** 393, **Whitney.**

Noyes, Daniel R., merchant, **XIV.** 335.

Noyes, Edward Alling, banker, **XV.** 390.

Noyes, Joseph C., merchant and congressman, **XV.** 390, **Noyes.**

Noyes Brothers & Cutler, drugs, **XIV.** 336, **Noyes.**

Nussbaum, Paul J., R. C. bishop, **XV.** 137.

Nutrition, authority on, **XIV.** 39, **Fletcher.**

O.

O. Henry, pen-name, **XV.** 170, **Porter.**

Oberlin College, Severance Chemical Laboratory of, **XV.** 357, **Severance.**

Oberlin Telegraph Institute, organized, **XV.** 161, **Pond.**

O'Brien, Edward C., diplomat, **XIV.** 492.

O'Brien, Morgan J., jurist, **XIV.** 449.

O'Brien, Thomas J., lawyer and diplomat, **XIV.** 182.

Ocean City, N. J., founder of, **XV.** 5, **Lake.**

O'Connell, Denis J., R. C. bishop, **XV.** 65.

O'Connell, William H., cardinal, **XV.** 294.

O'Day, Daniel, manufacturer, **XIV.** 175.

O'Dea, Edward J., bishop, **XIV.** 527.

Odell, Benjamin B., merchant, **XIV.** 436, **Odell.**

Odell, Benjamin B., Jr., governor, **XIV.** 436.

Odell, George W., organ builder, **XIV.** 115.

Odell, J. H. & C. S., organs, **XIV.** 115, **Odell.**

Odell, John H., manufacturer, **XIV.** 115, **Odell.**

O'Donaghue, Denis, R. C. bishop, **XV.** 224.

Office furniture, manufacture of, **XIV.** 260, **Andrews, A. H.**

Ogden, Herbert G., lawyer, **XIV.** 330.

Ogden, Herbert G., Sr., engineer, **XIV.** 330, **Ogden.**

Ogden, Jonathan, merchant, **XIV.** 415, **Ogden.**

Ogden, Robert C., merchant, **XIV.** 415.

O'Gorman, James A., judge and senator, **XV.** 13; partner of, 98, **Battle.**

Ohio, early physician in, **XIV.** 245, **Allen;** governors of, 444, **Pattison;** 226, **Harris; XIII.** 279, **Harmon; XV.** 274, **Cox; XVI. Willis;** U. S. senator from, **XIV.** 417, **Burton;** state bank organized, 226, **Kelley, A.**

Ohio canal, XV. 226, **Kelley, A.**

Ohio Female Seminary, president of, **XIV.** 278, **Wood.**

Ohio river, improvements by the U. S. government, **XIV.** 40, **Goethals.**

Ohio Wesleyan University, XIV. 42-43, **Welch.**

Oil, transportation of, **XIV.** 175, **O'Day;** development of lands, 243, **Guffey; XV.** 239, **Brown;** 370, **Marshall;** as fuel on steam vessels, 356, **Shaw.**

Oil cup, inventor of, **XV.** 143, **Lunken.**

Oil switch, electric, inventor of, **XV.** 340, **Emmet, W. L.**

Oildag, lubricant, originated, **XIV.** 94.

Oklahoma, governors of, **XIV.** 465, **Haskell; XVI. Cruce;** U. S. senators from, **XIV.** 248, **Owen;** 323, **Gore;** chief justices of, 432, **Burford;** 496, **Williams;** constitution of, **XV.** 110, **Barnard;** R. C. bishop of, 346, **Meerschaert.**

Olcott, Henry S., theosophist, **XV.** 337, **Blavatsky.**

Olcott, Jacob Van Vechten, congressman, **XIV.** 210.

Olcott, R. Morgan, merchant, **XIV.** 211.

Olcott Coal & Iron Co., XIV. 211, **Olcott, R. M.**

Olcott, W. Va., founded, **XV.** 211, **Olcott, R. M.**

Old Clock on the Stairs, original of poem by Longfellow, **XIV.** 293, **Gold.**

Old Colony Steamboat Co., president of, **XIV.** 253, **Choate.**

Old Vermont brigade, XIV. 265, **Stoughton, C. B.**

Oldham, William F., M. E. bishop, **XIV.** 336.

Oliver, James E., mathematician, **XIV.** 342.

Olympic games, XV. 54, **Sullivan;** patron of, **XV.** 202, **Thompson.**

Omaha, Neb., R. C. bishop of, **XV.** 45, **Harty.**

Omaha, Neb., World-Herald, **XV.** 284, **Hitchcock.**

Omniscope for submarines, inventor of, **XV.** 6, **Lake.**

O'Neal, Edward A., son of, **XV.** 273, **O'Neal.**

O'Neal, Emmet, governor, **XV.** 273.

Oneonta (N. Y.), Herald, **XIV.** 247, **Fairchild.**

Ophir Co. gold mine, **XV.** 227, **McClure, C. F.**

Ophthalmology, specialist in, **XV.** 143, **Strawbridge.**

Orange, N. J., Seguin Physiological School at, **XV.** 151, **Seguin.**

Oratory, study of, **XIV.** 302, **Curry.**

Ordnance, improvements in, **XV.** 118, **Alger;** 144, **Fletcher.**

Oregon, governors of, **XIV.** 135, **Chamberlain;** 439, **Benson; XVI. West;** U. S. senators from, **XIV.** 475, **Gearin;** 135, **Chamberlain;** land fraud cases investigated, **XV.** 49, **Burns.**

O'Reilly, Charles J., bishop, **XV.** 3.

O'Reilly, James, R. C. bishop, **XV.** 206.

Ores, methods of treating, improved, **XIV.** 508, **Brunton.**

Organ, municipal, at Portland, Me., **XV.** 383, **Macfarlane.**

Peddie Institute, Hightstown, N. J., **XIV.** 464, **Swetland.**

Peelle, Stanton J., jurist, **XIV.** 96.

Peerless oil (petroleum), **XIV.** 102, **Bush, Rufus T.**

Peixotto, Ernest C., artist and author, **XIV.** 47.

Pell, S. Osgood, real estate, **XIV.** 499.

Pemberton, Henry, Jr., chemist, **XV.** 69.

Pencil factory, first in the United States, **XIV.** 267, **Faber.**

Pencils, process of making described, **XIV.** 267, **Faber.**

Pendelton, Edmund, author, **XV.** 245.

Penfield, Frederic C., diplomat, **XV.** 311.

Penholders, first factory for making, **XIV.** 267, **Faber.**

Penn, William, **XIV.** 497, **Weiser.**

Pennington, James W. C., clergyman, **XIV.** 307.

Pennock, Isaac, iron manufacturer, **XV.** 375, **Lukens;** 376, **Huston, C.**

Pennsylvania, coal strike in, 6; coal lands in, 191, **Andrews;** 368-369, **Coxe;** state superintendent of public instruction of, 214, **Schaeffer;** military law in, 230, **Rogers;** new state capitol of, illus., 443; governors of, **XIV.** 443, **Stuart; XV.** 409, **Brumbaugh;** originator of public school system of, 210, **Vaux;** coal operations in, 213, **Taylor;** natural oil industry in, 239, **Brown.**

Pennsylvania railroad, introduction of sleeping cars on, **XIV.** 203, **Woodruff;** tunnels for, 209, **Jacobs;** 492, **Lindenthal;** bridges built for, 372, **Richards;** entrance to New York, 446, **McCrea;** new station at N. Y., illus., 446; presidents of, **XIV.** 446, **McCrea; XV.** 289, **Rea.**

Penology, authorities on, **XV.** 210, **Vaux;** 365, **Whitman.**

Penrose, Boies, partner of, **XV.** 352, **Page.**

Pens, gold, manufacturers of, **XIV.** 374, **Aikin.**

Peoria, Ill., R. C. bishop of, **XV.** 325, **Dunne.**

Percy, Le Roy, U. S. senator, **XV.** 107.

Perfumes, manufacture of, **XIV.** 173, **Palmer;** 278, **Hudnut.**

Periscope, inventor of, **XV.** 6, **Lake.**

Perkin medal, American recipients of, **XII.** 354, **Herreshoff; XIV.** 92, **Acheson; XIII.** 94, **Hall; XIV.** 70, **Gayley; XII.** 148, **Hyatt; V.** 176, **Weston; XV.** 330, **Baekeland.**

Perkins, Charles E., railroad president, **XIV.** 425.

Perkins, George H., daughter of, **XV.** 349, **Anderson.**

Perkins, George W., financier, **XV.** 33.

Perkins, Stephen George, memorial to, **XIV.** 445, **Higginson.**

Perky, Henry D., associate of, **XV.** 154, **Meek.**

Peroxides, manufacture of, **XV.** 180, **Hasslacher.**

Perret, Frank A., volcanologist, **XV.** 334; 69, **Ley.**

Perry, Nora, poet, **XV.** 116.

Persia, U. S. ministers to, **XIV.** 131, **Pearson; XII.** 250, **Jackson; XV.** 358, **Russell;** studies of language of, **XV.** 194, **Gray;** financial adviser to, 303, **Shuster.**

Peru, friendly visit of Secy. Root to, **XIV.** 14; U. S. ministers to, **XIII.** 309, **Combs;** 79, **McMillin.**

Peter Cooper Fire Insurance Co., **XIV.** 436, **Ely.**

Petroleum, manufacture of, **XIV.** 102, **Bush, R. T.**

Petrology, researches in, **XV.** 214, **Cross.**

Pettit, George A. J., educator, **XIV.** 487.

Pettit, Henry C., lawyer, **XV.** 379.

Pettit, John Upfold, congressman and jurist, **XV.** 379, **Pettit.**

Pharr, Henry N., planter, **XIV.** 212.

Pharr, John N., planter, **XIV.** 211; 136, **Williams.**

Phase rule, in physical chemistry, exponent of, **XIV.** 206, **Bancroft.**

Phelps, Charles H., merchant, **XIV.** 396, **Phelps.**

Phelps, Edmund J., merchant, **XV.** 155.

Phelps, Erskine M., merchant, **XIV.** 396.

Phelps & Dodge, shoes, **XIV.** 396, **Phelps;** 397, **Dodge.**

Philadelphia, Pa., opera house, **XIV.** 45, **Hammerstein;** First National Bank, 189, **McMichael;** Law and Order Society, 415, **Gibboney;** development of street railways in, **XV.** 11, **Widener;** branch of Free Library in, **XV.** 12, **Widener, P. A. B.;** R. C. archbishop of, 222, **Prendergast;** early school of anatomy in, 261, **Lawrence;** Chambers Presbyterian Church in, 299, **Chambers.**

Philadelphia & Reading Railway, **XIV.** 37.

Philadelphia Rapid Transit Co., **XV.** 11, **Widener;** counsel for, 137, **Leaming.**

Philadelphia School of Anatomy, **XV.** 261, **Lawrence.**

Philip Hamilton, pen-name, **XV.** 361, **Hubert.**

Philippine commission, **XIV.** 20, **Wright; XV.** 104, **Elliott.**

Philippine islands, **XIV.** 152, **Bell;** insurrection in, 13; code of statutes for, 13; governor-general of, 20, **Wright;** naval base of United States at, 21, **Moody;** administration of, 35, **Bates;** military governor of, 151, **MacArthur;** monetary system of, investigation of, 227, **Conant;** operations against the Moros in, 340, **Baldwin;** disposition of friars' land question in, 404; reforms in, 404; R. C. archbishop of, **XV.** 45, **Harty;** American legislation for, 303, **Shuster;** sanitation in, **XV.** 309, **Meacham.**

Philipse, Frederick (1626), pioneer, **XIV.** 275.

Philipse, Frederick (1695), jurist, **XIV.** 275.

Philipse, Frederick, Jr. (1720-85), **XIV.** 275, **Philipse, Fred. 2d.**

Philipseborough, manor of, **XIV.** 275, **Philipse.**

Phillips, Alexander H., principal Lawrenceville School, **XIV.** 516, **McPherson.**

Phillips, David Graham, author, **XIV.** 47.

Phillips, James, Jr., merchant, **XV.** 321, **Wood.**

Phillips, William, diplomat, **XIV.** 330.

Philology, advances in, **XIV.** 230, **Elliott.**

Philosophy, early American exponent of, **XV.** 2, **Harris.**

Philosophical Society of Washington, president of, **XIV.** 186, **Bauer.**

Phonograph, used to study Indian music, **XV.** 32, **Fewkes;** improvements in, 22, **Fessenden;** 390, **Easton.**

Phosphorescence, researches in, **XV.** 78, **Ives, H. E.;** 195, **Merritt.**

Phosphorus, new method of making, **XV.** 132, **Cowles.**

Photo-engravings, process of making perfected, **XV.** 77, **Ives.**

Photography, advances in, **XV.** 77, **Ives, F. E.;** 78, **Ives, H. E.;** adapted to anatomy, 223, **McClellan;** applied to microscopic objects, 265, **Longworth.**

Photography, color, invented, **XIV.** 457, **Wood; XV.** 78, **Ives.**

Photometer, inventor of, **XV.** 79, **Ives.**

Phyfe, William H. P., author, **XV.** 296.

Physics, researches in, **XIV.** 457, **Wood.**

Physiology, advances in, **XIV.** 309, **Mall; XV.** 288, **Porter; MacCallum, W. G.**

Pianos, manufacture of, **XIV.** 245, **Bush;** 524, **Mason.**

Pickands, James, iron merchant, **XIV.** 487, **Mather.**

Pickands, Brown & Co., iron merchants, **XIV.** 496, **Brown.**

Pierce, William K., manufacturer and financier, **XIV.** 337.

Pierce, Butler & Pierce Manufacturing Co., **XIV.** 337, **Pierce.**

Pierson, Lewis E., banker, merchant, **XV.** 65.

Pike's Peak, cog road up, **XV.** 136, **Simmons.**

Pilat, Carl Francis, landscape architect, **XV.** 307.

Pilat, Ignaz A., landscape gardener, **XV.** 307.

Piles, Samuel H., senator, **XIV.** 389.

Price, McCormick & Co., cotton brokers, **XIV. 281,** Price.

Princeton Theological Seminary, president of, **XV.** 254, Stevenson.

Princeton University, president of, **XV. 199,** Hibben; director of observatory of, **XIV. 499,** Fine.

Printing ink, carbon black used for, **XIV. 251,** Cabot.

Printing telegraph, **XIV. 76,** Barclay.

Prison, first conducted exclusively by women, **XV.** 304, Mosher.

Private Hospital Association, founders of, **XV. 168,** Walker. _ _

Proctor, Fletcher D., governor, **XIV. 448.**

Proctor, Joseph, actor, **XV. 47.**

Proctor, Vt., marble quarry at, **XIV. 448,** Proctor.

Profit-sharing plan, **XV. 60,** Ford.

Prohibition, in Oklahoma, **XIV. 466,** Haskell; in Mississippi, **518,** Noel.

Prospect Park, Brooklyn, N. Y., chief engineer of, **XIV. 49,** Martin.

Proteins, investigations regarding, **XV. 334,** Osborne.

Protestant Episcopal church, patrons of, **XIV. 66,** Morgan; **XV. 194,** Thomas.

Prouty, George H., governor, **XIV. 448.**

Providence, R. I., auxiliary R. C. bishop of, **XV. 243,** Doran.

Provident Life Assurance Co., **XIV. 117,** Woodruff.

Provident Loan Society of New York, a founder of, **XV. 150.**

Prudential Insurance Co., chief medical director of, **XV. 127,** Burrage.

Pruyn, John V. L., daughter of, **XV. 266,** Hamlin.

Pruyne, Peter, daughter of **XV. 300,** Kimbark.

Psychology, researches in, **XIV. 270,** Angell; **521,** Hudson; **48,** Hyslop; **XV. 205,** Thorndike; **416,** Pillsbury.

Public health, labor's interest in, **XV. 24,** Nelson; promotion of, **69,** Ley; **129,** Blue, R.; **370,** Linsley.

Public health service, United States, account of, **XV. 129,** Blue, R.

Public Service Commissions, New York, **XIV. 39,** Hughes; **382,** Willcox.

Public utilities, New York, state control of, **XIV. 382,** Willcox.

Pullman, George M., **XIV. 203,** Woodruff.

Pullman, Ill.; architect of, **XIV. 304,** Beman.

Pullman cars, designer of, **XIV. 305,** Beman.

Pumps, compressed-air, improvements in, **XIV. 141,** Ford; **191,** Rand; steam, **XV. 156,** Sergeant.

Pure food law of 1906, provisions of, **XIV. 28;** exposures resulting in its passage, **320,** Sinclair.

Putnam, Eben, author, **XIV. 398.**

Pye, David Walter, merchant, **XIV. 355.**

Pyne, Percy R., **XV. 28,** Stillman.

Pyramidal roof truss, inventor of, **XIV. 316,** Boring.

Pyro-electric reduction of metals, **XV. 131,** Cowles.

Q.

Quadruplane, flying machine, inventor of, **XV. 274,** Sellers.

Quaker Blues, **XIV. 134,** Biddle.

Quimby, Silas E., clergyman, **XIV. 321.**

Quinby, Henry B., governor, **XIV. 498.**

Quincy, Henry P., physician, **XV. 6.**

Quincy Mansion School, Wollaston, Mass., **XV. 68,** Willard.

Quinine, introduced into the United States, **XIV. 146,** Weightman.

Quinine king, sobriquet, **XIV. 146,** Weightman.

R.

R. & G. Corset Co., **XV. 127,** Marble.

Race horses, famous, **XIV. 505,** Bedford; **XV. 239,** Keene.

Radio-activity, study of, **XV. 193,** Bumstead.

Radio telegraphy, experiments in, **XV. 106,** Hammond.

Radiodynamic torpedo, inventor of, **XV. 106,** Hammond.

Radium, researches on, **XV. 139,** Boltwood.

Rae, Charles W., naval officer, **XV. 355.**

Rail-joint, continuous, inventor of, **XIV. 480,** Fearey.

Rail Joint Co., factory at Troy, N. Y., illus., **XIV. 480.**

Railroads, development of, **XIV. 37,** Baer; **42,** Newman; **196; 420,** Spencer; **425,** Perkins; **440,** Bradley; **441,** Finley; **446,** McCrea; **450,** Truesdale; **460,** Stilwell; investigations of, **247,** Hanks; interlocking signals for, **XV. 42;** in the South, **344,** Huidekoper.

Rails, first made of steel in America, **XV. 374,** Griswold.

Railway gate, inventor of, **XV. 139,** Cornell.

Railway tickets, various forms of, invented, **XV. 134,** Campbell.

Railway trains, electric lighting for, invented, **XV. 3,** Leonard; air brake for, **42,** Westinghouse.

Raincoats, manufacture of, **XIV. 324,** Hodgman.

Raja Yoga Academy, Pt. Loma, Cal., **XV. 338,** Tingley.

Ralston, Samuel M., governor, **XV. 142.**

Ramapo Water Co., **XIV. 468,** Bannin.

Ramsay, Francis M., naval officer, **XV. 122.**

Ramsay, George Douglas, soldier, **XV. 122,** Ramsay.

Rand, Albert T., **XIV. 191,** Rand.

Rand, Jasper R., manufacturer, **XIV. 191.**

Rand Drill Co., **XIV. 191,** Rand.

Randall, Edwin M., Jr., clergyman, **XIV. 385.**

Randolph, Isham, advisory committee on Panama canal, **XIV. 41,** Goethals.

Randolph-Macon College, medical department of, **XV. 316,** Mettauer.

Range lights for navigation, proposed, **XV. 144,** Fletcher.

Ranger, Henry W., artist, **XV. 269.**

Ransdell, Joseph E., U. S. senator, **XV. 407.**

Rapid transit, experts on, **XIV. 209,** Jacobs; **63.** See also Boston, Chicago, Los Angeles, New York city and Philadelphia.

Rapid Transit Commission of New York, engineer of, **XIV. 218,** Parsons.

Rappold-Berger, Marie W., singer, **XV. 203.**

Raritan River railroad, **XIV. 418,** Earle.

Raven, Anton A., insurance president, **XIV. 435.**

Raven, John H., educator, **XIV. 436,** Raven.

Raymond, James I., merchant, **XIV. 383.**

Rea, John, soldier and congressman, **XV. 289,** Rea.

Rea, Robert L., physician, **XIV. 511.**

Rea, Samuel, railroad president, **XV. 289.**

Reading, Pa., pioneer of, **XIV. 497,** Weiser.

Reading, Pearson B., pioneer and soldier, **XV. 368.**

Reading Co., Philadelphia, **XIV. 37.**

Real estate, promoters, **XIV. 344,** Storer; **460,** Ely; **499,** Pell.

Reaping machine, early form of, invented, **XIV. 203,** Woodruff.

Receiver, wireless telegraph, inventor of, **XIV. 470,** Hewitt.

Reclamation of swamp lands in Louisiana, **XV. 196,** Hero; **243,** Wisner.

Recorder, The Boston, religious newspaper, **XIV. 264,** Willis.

Records, for phonographs, how made, **XV. 391,** Easton.

Rectifier, inventors of, **XIV. 470,** Hewitt; **XV. 338,** Montgomery.

Red Cross, American National, **XIV. 406,** Taft; **XV. 315,** Barton.

Redlands, Cal., development of, **XV. 38,** Smiley.

Reed, Elizabeth A., author, **XV. 229.**

Reed, James, clergyman, **XIV.** 348.
Reed, James A., senator, **XV.** 99.
Reed, James H., lawyer, **XIV.** 408, Knox.
Reed, Myrtle, author, **XV.** 229.
Reed, Simeon G., founder of Reed College, **XV.** 301, Foster.
Reed College, Portland, Ore., **XV.** 301, Foster.
Reese, Frederick F., P. E. bishop, **XIV.** 438.
Reformed Episcopal church, **XV.** 298, Sabine.
Refrigeration, artificial development of, **XIV.** 343, Wills; **XV.** 179, Lucke.
Registered cable addresses, system of, introduced, **XIV.** 371, Ward.
Reichhelm, Edward P., mechanical engineer, **XIV.** 495.
Reid, Daniel G., **XIV.** 65, Moore; 442, Leeds.
Reinhardt, George F., physician, educator, **XV.** 135.
Reisinger, Hugo, merchant, **XIV.** 213.
Religion, comparative, investigations in, **XV.** 194, Gray.
Religious newspaper, first in U. S., **XIV.** 264, Willis.
Remington typewriter, **XIV.** 270, Earle.
Remondino, Peter C., physician, **XIV.** 279.
Republican and Leader, La Crosse, Wis., **XV.** 400, Finch.
Reservoirs, authority on, **XIV.** 306, Stearns.
Respiration, artificial, method of, **XV.** 354, Meltzer.
Reynolds, James B., physician, **XIV.** 482.
Reynolds, Stanchfield & Collins, law firm, **XIV.** 360, Stanchfield.
Rheostat, inventor of, **XIV.** 76 Barclay.
Rhetoric, study of, advanced, **XIV.** 399, Scott.
Rhode Island, governors of, **XIV.** 402, Higgins; **XV.** 114, Pothier; U. S. senator from, 408, Colt; chief justices of, **XIV.** 241, Douglas; 524, Dubois.
Rice, Alice Hegan, author, **XIV.** 484.
Rice, Cale Young, poet and playwright, **XIV.** 485, Rice.
Rice, Mrs. Isaac L., reformer, **XIV.** 508.
Rice, John V., Jr., inventor, **XV.** 366.
Rice, Victor M., educator, **XIV.** 178.
Rich, Jacob, journalist, **XV.** 130.
Richards, Joseph T., engineer, **XIV.** 372.
Richards, Laura E., author, **XV.** 176.
Richardson, George F., lawyer, **XV.** 168.
Richardson, Harry A., senator, **XIV.** 310.
Richardson & Robbins, manufacturers, **XIV.** 310, Richardson.
Richmond, Charles A., educator, **XIV.** 187.
Richmond, Va., R. C. bishop of, **XV.** 65, O'Connell.
Richmond & Danville railroad system, **XV.** 344, Huidekoper.
Riddle, John W., diplomat, **XIV.** 53.
Rideout, Henry M., author, **XIV.** 485.
Ridgeway, Mich., Hall Memorial Library, **XIV.** 102, Bush, R. T.
Riebenack, Max, R. R. official, **XIV.** 300.
Riggs, Elisha F., banker, **XV.** 229.
Riggs, George Washington, banker, **XV.** 229, Riggs.
Riggs & Co., bankers, Washington, **XV.** 229, Riggs.
Riggs Memorial Library, Georgetown College, **XV.** 229, Riggs.
Riggs National Bank, Washington, **XV.** 229, Riggs.
Right Relationship League, **XV.** 368, Albertson.
Riker, Andrew L., electrical engineer, **XV.** 211.
Rio Grande river, canyons of, explored, **XIV.** 267, Hill.
Riordan, Patrick Wm., R. C. archbishop, **XV.** 248.
Riter-Conley Co., **XIV.** 73, Conley; Coffin.
Rittenhouse, Elmer E., **XV.** 69, Ley.
River and harbor improvements, **XV.** 81, Bates.
Riverside, Cal., Sherman Institute at, **XIV.** 407.
Riverside Home for Crippled Children, New York, **XV.** 25.

Rivers, organization to promote improvement of, **XV.** 407, Ransdell.
Roach, John, son of, **XV.** 286, Roach.
Roach, John B., ship-builder, **XV.** 286.
Roach, John & Son, **XV.** 286, Roach.
Roads, improvement of, **XV.** 104, Gates; 121, Major.
Robbins, Francis L., merchant, **XIV.** 498.
Robbins, James M., mfr., **XIV.** 310, Richardson.
Robbins, Thomas Burr, coal operator, **XIV.** 498, Robbins.
Robbins preparatory school, Norfolk, Conn., founder of, **XIV.** 254, Battell.
Roberts, John Marks, jeweler, **XV.** 125, Roberts.
Roberts, Steele F., jeweler, **XV.** 125.
Roberts & Sons, E. P., jewelers, **XV.** 125, Roberts.
Robinson, Edward A., poet, **XV.** 240.
Robinson, Edward Mott, merchant, **XV.** 128, Green.
Robinson, Franklin C., chemist, **XIV.** 181.
Robinson, John H., clergyman, **XIV.** 232.
Robinson, John N., financier, **XV.** 159.
Robinson, Wallace F., manufacturer, **XV.** 197.
Rochester, N. Y., R. C. bishop of, **XV.** 58, Hickey.
Rochester, Minn., St. Mary's hospital and clinic at, **XIV.** 207, Mayo.
Rock drill, inventors of, **XIV.** 191, Rand; **XV.** 156, Sergeant; 256, Couch; 366, Rice.
Rock Island system, **XIV.** 65, Moore.
Rockefeller, John D., capitalist, **XV.** 10, Flagler.
Rockefeller Institute for Medical Research, New York, **XV.** 302; 354, Meltzer.
Rockford, Del., cotton mills in, **XV.** 371, Bancroft.
Rocky mountain geology, authority on, **XV.** 214, Cross.
Rode, Paul Peter, R. C. bishop, **XV.** 98.
Rodney, Richard A., partner of, **XV.** 105, Saulsbury.
Roebling's, John A., Sons Co., **XIV.** 305, Briggs.
Roessler & Hasslacher Chemical Co., **XV.** 180, Hasslacher.
Rogers, H. H., **XIV.** 475, Hadley.
Rogers, John I., jurist, **XIV.** 230.
Rogers, Robert C., poet, **XV.** 281.
Rogers, William A., merchant, partner of, **XV.** 163, Brown.
Rogers, William A., educator, **XV.** 182, Whitney.
Rogers, Brown & Co., iron, **XV.** 163, Brown; 285, Herron.
Rome, Italy, American Academy in, **XIV.** 316, Boring; **XV.** 201, Millet.
Röntgen rays, investigations of, **XV.** 30, Goodspeed; 193, Bumstead.
Roof truss, pyramidal, inventor of, **XIV.** 316, Boring.
Roosevelt, steamship, **XIV.** 61.
Roosevelt, Edith Kermit, **XIV.** 10.
Roosevelt, Theodore, 26th U. S. president, **XIV.** 1; averts crisis with Japan, 375, Gillett; coal strike commission appointed by, 55, Parker; efforts to nominate for vice-president, 23, Payne.
Roosevelt, Theodore, Sr., merchant, **XIV.** 1.
Root, Elihu, statesman, **XIV.** 12.
Root, Joseph C., capitalist, **XV.** 271.
Root, Oren, educator, **XIV.** 12, Root.
Rope drives, improved pulley for, **XV.** 31, Miller.
Rope, manufacture of, **XIV.** 113, Holmes.
Rosary, The, poem, author of, **XV.** 281, Rogers.
Rose Polytechnic Institute, president of, **XV.** 331, Eddy.
Rosengarten & Sons, drugs, **XIV.** 146, Weightman.
Rotary engine, inventor of, **XV.** 41, Westinghouse.
Rotch, A. Lawrence, meteorologist, **XV.** 2.
Rotch, Benjamin S., merchant, **XV.** 2, Rotch.
Rotch, Joseph, founder of New Bedford, Mass., **XV.** 335, Rotch.
Rotch, William, civil engineer, **XV.** 335.
Rotch, William J., capitalist and mayor, **XV.** 335, Rotch.

Sprague, Ralph, colonist, **XV. 244, Sprague.**

Sprague, Warner & Co., wholesale grocers, **XV. 244, Sprague; 245, Warner.**

Springfield, Mass., armory at, **XIV. 201, Ames, Oliver (1st)**; growth of, **XV. 48, Ingersoll.**

Springfield, O., Daily News, **XV. 275, Cox.**

Spring for cars, invented, **XV. 356, Shaw.**

Spring pawl washer, inventor of, **XV. 356, Shaw.**

Spry, William, governor, **XV. 383.**

Squier, Ezra S., clergyman, **XV. 414, Tipple.**

Stage, double, for theatre, invented, **XIV. 158, Mac-Kaye, Steele.**

Stanchfield, John B., lawyer, **XIV. 360.**

Standard Bleachery, **XV. 85, McKenzie.**

Standard Oil Co., **XIV. 102, Bush, R. T.; 111, Tarbell; 175, O'Day; 504, Bedford; XV. 10, Flagler; 28, Stillman; 357, Severance;** convicted of rebating, **XIV. 7;** government investigation of, **27, Garfield;** suit against, **475, Hadley.**

Standard Oilcloth Co., **XIV. 249, Hunsicker.**

Standard time, originator of, **XIV. 256, Allen.**

Stanford, Leland, **XV. 16.**

Stang, William, R. C. bishop, **XV. 39.**

Stanley, William, electrical engineer and inventor, **XV. 42.**

Stannard, Monroe, **XV. 182, Whitney.**

Stanton, John, capitalist, **XIV. 359.**

Stanwood, Isaac A., manufacturer, **XIV. 167.**

Star in the East, sobriquet, **XV. 390, Noyes.**

Star Fire Brick Works, **XIV. 229, Harbison.**

Stariha, John N., R. C. bishop, **XV. 378.**

Starrett, Helen (Ekin), educator and author, **XV. 278, Starrett.**

Starrett, Theodore, builder, engineer, **XV. 278.**

State, reforms in department of, **XIV. 14;** secretaries of, **12, Root; 16, Bacon; 408, Knox; IX. 467, Bryan.**

State insurance laws, uniform code of, suggested, **XIV. 165, Johnson.**

Statistics, bureau of, transferred to the department of commerce and labor, **XIV. 19.**

Steam boiler feeder, inventor of, **XV. 356, Shaw.**

Steam boilers, invented, **XV. 156, Sergeant.**

Steam plow, inventor of, **XIV. 204, Woodruff.**

Steam pump, inventor of, **XV. 156, Sergeant;** regulating valve for, inventor of, **XIV. 141, Ford.**

Steam trap, inventor of, **XIV. 141, Ford.**

Steam turbine, improvement of, **XV. 42;** verticle shaft, inventor of, **XV. 340, Emmet, W. L.**

Steam vessels, oil fuel on, **XV. 356, Shaw.**

Stearns, Frederic P., civil engineer, **XIV. 306;** advisory committee on Panama canal, **41, Goethals.**

Stedman, Arthur W., merchant, **XIV. 125.**

Steel, manufacture of, **XIV. 68-71; XV. 163, Brown; 300, Kimbark; 318, Baxter; 374, Griswold; 377, Huston, A. F.;** framework of buildings first made of, **XIV. 298, Gilbert;** process for welding copper and silver on, discovered, **342, Monnot;** increased cutting efficiency, **521, Taylor;** improved methods of manufacture, **XV. 45, Jones.** See Iron.

Steel castings, first in U. S., **XV. 41, Westinghouse.**

Steel rails first made in America, **XV. 374, Griswold.**

Steel traveller, invented, **XIV. 277, Swensson.**

Steele, Charles, financier, **XIV. 78.**

Steele, Frederick M., manufacturer, **XIV. 147.**

Steele, Henry M., civil engineer, **XIV. 78.**

Steele, Isaac N., lawyer and diplomat, **XIV. 77.**

Steele, John N., lawyer, **XIV. 77.**

Steffens, Lincoln, journalist, **XIV. 455.**

Stein, Robert, **XIV. 184, Geddes.**

Stejneger, Leonhard, naturalist, **XIV. 130.**

Stephenson, Benjamin F., physician and soldier, **XIV. 111.**

Stephenson, Isaac, senator, **XIV. 50.**

Stephenson Training School, Marinette, Wis., **XIV. 51, Stephenson.**

Stereogram, parallax, invented, **XV. 78, Ives, F. E.**

Stereotypy, automatic, machine for, **XIV. 271, Wood.**

Sterling Coal Co., **XIV. 389, Baker.**

Sterling, Thomas, U. S. senator **XV. 287.**

Stetson, Francis L., lawyer, **XIV. 503.**

Stetson, Lemuel, lawyer and congressman, **XIV. 503, Stetson.**

Stetson, John B., & Co., hats, **XIV. 359, Cummings.**

Stetson, Jennings & Russell, lawyers, **XIV. 503, Jennings.**

Stevens, S. S., manufacturer, **XV. 62, Thompson.**

Stevens & Thompson, Paper Co., **XV. 62, Thompson.**

Stevenson, J. Ross, theologian, **XV. 254.**

Stevenson, Robert Louis, author, **XIV. 459, Osbourne.**

Stewardson, Langdon C., president Hobart College, **XV. 311.**

Stewart, Alexander, lumberman, **XV. 190.**

Stewart, Austin, abolitionist and author, **XIV. 308.**

Stewart, Samuel V., governor, **XV. 241.**

Stewart Lumber Co., **XV. 191, Stewart.**

Stickley, Gustav, craftsman, designer and publisher, **XIV. 290.**

Stickney, Austin, educator, **XV. 351.**

Stickney, Joseph T., author and educator, **XV. 352, Stickney.**

Stickney, William, member of provincial congresses, **XV. 351, Stickney.**

Stieglitz, Julius O., chemist, **XV. 56.**

Still, Andrew T., osteopathist, **XIV. 451.**

Stillman, Alfred, **XV. 103, Stillman.**

Stillman, James, financier, **XV. 28.**

Stillman, Thomas E., lawyer, **XV. 103.**

Stillwell, Lewis B., electrician, **XIV. 520.**

Stilwell, Arthur E., financier, **XIV. 460.**

Stilwell, Hamilton, financier and promoter, **XIV. 460, Stilwell.**

Stimson, Benjamin, **XV. 95, Kissel.**

Stockbridge, Horace E., agriculturalist, **XIV. 368.**

Stockslager, Charles O., jurist, **XIV. 200.**

Stockton, Charles S., dentist, **XV. 204.**

Stoeckel, Gustav, craftsman, designer and publisher, **XIV. 290.**

Stoeckhardt, Carl G., theologian, **XV. 126.**

Stone, Carlos M., jurist, **XV. 136.**

Stone, George F., merchant, **XV. 245.**

Stone, Isaac F., manufacturer, **XIV. 99.**

Stone, John Stone, inventor and electrical engineer, **XIV. 106.**

Stone, Matja von Niessen, singer, **XIV. 434.**

Stone, William W., merchant, daughter of, **XV. 252, Post.**

Stone system of wireless telegraphy, **XIV. 106, Stone.**

Stone Telegraph and Telephone Co., **XIV. 106, Stone.**

Storage battery, inventor of, **XIV. 63; XV. 334, Perret.**

Storer, John H., capitalist, **XIV. 344.**

Stott, Henry G., electrical engineer, **XIV. 240.**

Stoughton, Bradley, metallurgist, **XIV. 265.**

Stoughton, Charles B., soldier, **XIV. 264.**

Stoughton, Edwin H., soldier, **XIV. 265, Stoughton.**

Stoughton, Henry E., lawyer, **XIV. 264, Stoughton.**

Stoughton, Thomas, **XIV. 265, Stoughton, C. B.**

Stover, Joseph W., merchant, **XIV. 309.**

Stoves, improvements in, **XIV. 240, Chilson;** manufacture of, **372, Van Cleave.**

Stowers, Charles M., president of Upper Iowa University, **XIV. 292, Shanklin, W. A.**

Strawbridge, George, physician, **XV. 143.**

Street railways, in Philadelphia, Pa., **XV. 11, Widener;** in Boston, **399, Gaston;** in Massachusetts, **301, Sullivan.**

Strikes, anthracite coal miners, in Pennsylvania, **XIV. 6; 13; 37; 450, Truesdale; XV. 126, Mitchell;** in Colorado, **XV. 405, Ammons;** organized efforts to prevent, **411, Bernheimer.**
Stringer, Arthur, author, **XV. 293.**
Stromberg, Alfred, electrician, **XV. 269.**
Stromberg-Carlson Telephone Manufacturing Co., **XV. 269, Stromberg.**
Stromberg Electric Co., Chicago, Ill., **XV. 269, Stromberg.**
Stromboli, eruption of, **XV. 335, Perret.**
Stuart, Archibald, congressman, **XV. 333, Stuart.**
Stuart, Edwin S., governor, **XIV. 443.**
Stuart, Henry C., governor, **XV. 333.**
Stuart Land & Cattle Co., Virginia, **XV. 333, Stuart.**
Student Volunteer Movement for Foreign Missions, **XIV. 120, Beach.**
Sturgeon Bay and Lake Michigan Ship Canal, **XIV. 51, Stephenson.**
Sturtevant, B. F., Co., **XV. 339, Foss.**
Sturtevant, Benjamin F., manufacturer, **XV. 339, Foss.**
Subaqueous tunneling, method of, invented, **XIV. 419, Hoff.**
Submarine, inventors of, **XV. 5, Holland; 6, Lake;** telephone for, **22, Fessenden.**
Submarine tunnel, invented, **XV. 6, Lake.**
Subterranean tunnel bridge, orginator of, **XIV. 209, Jacobs.**
Subways. See Tunnels.
Success Magazine, founder of, **XIV. 269, Marden.**
Sudbury aqueduct, construction of, **XIV. 306, Stearns.**
Sudworth, George B., dendrologist, **XIV. 195.**
Sugar, manufacture of, **XV. 25, Arbuckle; 242, Sco-vell;** international conference on bounties on **XIV. 171, White;** expert on, **343, Wiechmann; 422, Kelly;** industry introduced in the Hawaiian Islands, **457, Wood.**
Suicide, statistics of, compiled, **XV. 303, Gavin.**
Sullivan Anne M., educator, **XV. 177, Keller.**
Sullivan, James E., promoter of athletics, **XV. 54.**
Sullivan, Patrick F., financier, **XV. 301.**
Sully, Wilberforce, lawyer and financier, **XIV. 479.**
Sulphate of magnesium, anesthetic properties of, discovered, **XV. 354, Meltzer.**
Sulphuate of quinine, introduced, **XIV. 146, Weightman.**
Sulzberger, Abraham, philanthropist, **XV. 283, Sulzberger.**
Sulzberger, Mayer, jurist, **XV. 283.**
Summa, Hugo, physician, **XIV. 237.**
Sumner, Charles, private secretary of, **XV. 167, Beaman.**
Sun, studies of, **XIV. 224, Poor, C. L.; XV. 8, Langley.**
Sunday-school books, publishers of, **XV. 373, Wilde.**
Sunday School Society, Boston, Mass., **XIV. 394, Horton.**
Sunny Jim, sobriquet, **XIV. 407.**
Sunnyside Yard of the Pennsylvania railroad, L. I. City, **XIV. 446, McCrea.**
Sunshine Society, International, **XIV. 289, Alden.**
Superior, Wis., R. C. bishops of, **XV. 147, Koudelka; 269, Schinner.**
Surgeon-general, United States army, **XV. 148, Forwood.**
Surgery, advances in, **XIV. 240, Maury; 268, Green; 283, Runnels; 370, Nancrède; 427, Cleveland; XV. 46, Cabot; 87, Willard; 139, Kinloch; 179, Albee; 210, Kelly; 240, May; 265, Longworth; 301-2, Carrel; 316, Mettauer;** instruments for, invented, **XV. 139, Kinloch;** method of preventing shock in, **260, Crile.**
Surgical instruments invented, **XV. 139, Kinloch.**

Surgical table, Cleveland, **XIV. 427, Cleveland.**
Swanson, Claude A., governor, **XIV. 104.**
Swayne, Charles, impeachment charges against, **XIV. 374, Gillett.**
Sweden, U. S. minister to, **XIV. 186, Graves.**
Swedenborgian church, **XIV. 348, Reed.**
Sweet Marie, original of song, **XV. 285, Warman.**
Swenson, Emil C. P., engineer, **XIV. 277.**
Swetland, Roger W., educator, **XIV. 464.**
Swift, Gustavus F., merchant, **XIV. 303.**
Swift, William, merchant, **XIV. 303, Swift.**
Swift & Co., packers, Chicago, **XIV. 303, Swift.**
Switch, oil, inventor of, **XV. 340, Emmet, W. L.**
Switzerland, U. S. ministers to, **XIV. 442, Clay; XII. 108, Swenson.**
Sydenham Hospital, New York, **XV. 205, Kunitzer.**
Sylvester, Allie L., manufacturer, **XV. 111.**
Sylvester, Lewis, **XV. 111, Sylvester.**
Symonds, Joseph W., lawyer, **XV. 346.**
Symonds, William Law, clergyman and author, **XV. 346, Symonds.**
Sysonby, race horse, owner of, **XV. 239, Keene.**

T.

Tabernacle, Chicago, **XIV. 228, Farwell.**
Tachometer, inventor of, **XV. 282, Veeder.**
Taft, Helen Herron, XIV. 406.
Taft, William H., 27th U. S. president, **XIV. 403;** chosen by Theo. Roosevelt for president, **8.**
Taggart, William R., lawyer, **XIV. 75.**
Talbot, Isham, senator, **XIV. 151.**
Talbot, Thomas, manufacturer, **XIV. 173, Clark.**
Talbot Mills, North Billerica, Mass., **XIV. 173, Clark.**
Tapestries, collection of, **XV. 12, Widener, P. A. B.**
Tappan, A., merchant, **XIV. 187, Barlow.**
Tarbell, Ida M., author, **XIV. 111.**
Tariff commission, permanent, advocated, **XIV. 319, Kirby.**
Tarrytown, N. Y., founder of, **XIV. 275, Philipse, Frederick, Sr.**
Taylor, David W., naval constructor, **XV. 87.**
Taylor, Edward R., lawyer and mayor, **XV. 309, Haight.**
Taylor, Frederick W., mechanical engineer, **XIV. 521.**
Taylor, Moses, merchant and banker, **XV. 28, Stillman.**
Taylor, William H., financier, **XV. 213.**
Taylor, William S., **XIV. 266, Willson.**
Taylor & Brunton Sampling Works Co., **XIV. 508, Brunton.**
Tea Tray Co., Newark, N. J., **XIV. 304, Marten;** plant, illus., **304.**
Teachers' College, University of Missouri, **XIV. 428, Hill.**
Telautoprint, inventor of, **XV. 338, Montgomery.**
Telegraphy, printing device invented, **XIV. 76, Barclay;** early experiments in, **97, Dyar;** development of, **XV. 136, Simmons; 161, Pond; 387, Smith;** Wheatstone system introduced, **XV. 387, Smith.**
Telegraphy, radio, experiments in, **XV. 106, Hammond.**
Telegraphy, wireless. See Wireless Telegraphy.
Telepathy, scientific study of, **XIV. 48, Hyslop.**
Telephone, improvements in, **XIV. 106, Stone; 440, Bradley; XV. 84, Carty;** anti-induction wire for, **XIV. 93;** wireless, **106, Stone; XV. 22, Fessenden;** for submarines, invented, **22, Fessenden;** automatic exchange, invented, **42;** relay, invented, **219, Hammer;** spread of the industry, **XIV. 216, Dougherty; XV. 269, Stromberg.**
Telescope, turret equatorial, inventor of, **XV. 294, Hartness.**
Teller, Henry M., U. S. senator, **XV. 228.**
Temperance, advocate of, **XV. 299, Chambers.**

Transylvania University, **XIV.** 416, Crossfield.

Trask, Spencer, partner of, **XV.** 140, Peabody.

Trask, William, colonist, **XIV.** 451, Enos.

Traveller, steel, invented, **XIV.** 277, Swensson.

Treasury, accounting system of, changed, **XV.** 265, Hamlin.

Treasury, secretaries of, **XIV.** 17, Shaw; 18, Cortelyou; 409, MacVeagh; **XIV.** 465, McAdoo.

Trees, studies of, **XIV.** 195, Sudworth; 30-32, Pinchot.

Tribune, Chicago, Ill., **XV.** 29, Vanderlip.

Tricycle, steam, first constructed, **XIV.** 163, Brown; illus., 163.

Trinity College, Durham, N. C., president of, **XV.** 196, Few.

Trinity College, Hartford, Conn., architect of, **XV.** 80, Kimball.

Trowbridge, Samuel B. P., architect, **XIV.** 213.

Trowbridge, William P., civil engineer, **XIV.** 213, Trowbridge.

Troy, N. Y., Rail Joint Co., works at, **XIV.** 480; Burden Iron Co. at, **XV.** 327, Burden.

Trude, Alfred S., lawyer, **XIV.** 132.

Truesdale, William H., railroad president, **XIV.** 450.

Trusts, prosecutions under the Sherman law, **XV.** 90, Kenyon.

Tuberculin, first brought to United States, **XV.** 370, Linsley.

Tuberculosis, prevention of, **XV.** 46, Cabot; efforts to cure, **XIV.** 84, Worcester; 124, Otis; **XV.** 370, Linsley.

Tucker, Anthony, & Co., bankers, **XV.** 140, **Anthony.**

Tucker, W. A., associate of, **XV.** 140, **Anthony.**

Tuckerman, Charles K., diplomat and author, **XIV.** 426.

Tuckerman, Edw., first insurance president in U. S., **XIV.** 426, Tuckerman.

Tucson, Arizona, R. C. bishop of, **XV.** 122, Granjon.

Tufts College, presidents of, **XIV.** 436, Hamilton; XIII. 110, Bumpus.

Tulane University, president of, **XIV.** 143, Craighead.

Tunnel, submarine, invented, **XV.** 6, Lake.

Tunnels, in Boston, **XIV.** 164, Carson; Pennsylvania railroad, construction of, 209, Jacobs; 446, McCrea; 492, Lindenthal; new method of building, invented, 209, Jacobs; 419, Hoff; freight, in Chicago, 400, Wheeler; 401, Jackson; in New York city, 209, Jacobs; 217, Parsons; 465, McAdoo; Cowenhoven, (Colo.), 508, Brunton; subaqueous, 289, Thomson.

Turbine, steam, development of, **XV.** 42; 340, Emmet, W. L.

Turkey, ambassadors to, **X.** 42, Straus; VIII. 129, Rockhill; **XV.** 363, Morgenthau.

Turner, J. Spencer Co., **XV.** 249, Brinckerhoff.

Turner, Thomas M., merchant, **XIV.** 399.

Turner, Vines E., dentist, **XIV.** 180.

Turner & Seymour Manufacturing Co., **XV.** 216, Seymour.

Turret equatorial telescope, inventor of, **XV.** 294, Hartness.

Tuttle, Ezra B., banker and merchant, **XIV.** 146.

Tutwiler, Henry, educator, **XV.** 101, Tutwiler.

Tutwiler, Julia S., educator, **XV.** 101.

Twentieth Century Magazine, **XV.** 367, Albertson.

Twine, manufacture of, **XIV.** 113, Holmes.

Typewriter, improved, **XIV.** 97, Brown; SmithPremier, 490; **Smith;** for telegraphing, 76, Barclay.

U.

Uhl, Edwin F., lawyer, diplomat, **XV.** 100.

Ulrich, Edward O., assistant of, **XV.** 122, Schuchert.

Uncle Ike, sobriquet, **XIV.** 51, Stephenson.

Underground transportation. See Tunnels.

Underwood, Frederick D., railroad president, **XIV.** 513.

Uneeda Biscuit, trade-name, **XV.** 291, Green.

Union, W. Va., founder of, **XIV.** 293, Andrews.

Union Carbide Co., **XV.** 132, Cowles.

Union College, president of, **XIV.** 187, Richmond.

Union fire alarm system, **XV.** 161, Pond.

Union Hardware Co., Torrington, Conn., **XV.** 216, Seymour.

Union League Club, N. Y., presidents of, **XIV.** 498, Sheldon; 12, Root.

Union Pacific railroad, **XIV.** 196-197; 202, Ames, O.; **XV.** 16; 150, Kennedy.

Union Stock Yards, Chicago, Ill., **XIV.** 303, Swift.

Union Switch and Signal Co., **XV.** 42.

Union Theological Seminary, N. Y., president of, **XIV.** 220, Brown.

Union Trust Co., New York, **XV.** 282, King.

Union Typewriter Co., **XIV.** 490, Smith, L. C.

Uniontown, Pa., First National Bank of, **XIV.** 432, Thompson.

Unit of electrical measurement proposed, **XV.** 132, Cowles.

Unitarian Church, post-office mission of, **XIV.** 453, Wendte; missionary of, 510, Douthit.

United Booking Offices, **XV.** 297, Keith.

United Charities building, New York, **XV.** 150.

United Cigar Stores Co., **XIV.** 307, Wise.

United Drug Co., **XIV.** 367, Liggett.

United Dyewood Co., **XIV.** 467, Baldwin, J. C., Jr.

United Fruit Co., **XIV.** 350, Baker; 351, Keith; 351-352, Preston.

United Mine Workers of America, **XV.** 126, Mitchell.

United Piece Dye Works, **XV.** 211, Boettger.

United Pipe Lines System, **XIV.** 175, O'Day.

United Publishers Corporation, **XV.** 81, Nast; 84, Mekeel.

United Shoe Machinery Co., **XV.** 197-198.

United States, terminates Russo-Japanese war, **XIV.** 6-7; settlement of Alaska boundary dispute, 11; reorganization of war department, 14; endeavors for universal peace, 15; department of commerce and labor, 19; naval base at Philippine islands, 21, Moody; cruise of battleship fleet around the world, 26, Metcalf; 30, Sperry; forest policy established, 31, Pinchot; policy regarding insular possessions, 32, Magoon; fur seal investigation commission, 130, Stejneger; Yellow Fever Commission, **XV.** 61, Lazear; naval construction bureau, **XV.** 88, Taylor; arbitrates boundary dispute between Brazil and Argentina, 100, Uhl; public health service, 129, Blue, R.; naval observatory, 145, Updegraff; army medical school, 148, Forwood; first creamatory in, 171, Le Moyne; commissioner of education, 270, Claxton; Red Cross in, 315, Barton; commissioner of agriculture, 349, Loring; commissioner of Indian affairs, 414, Leupp; National Art Gallery, Freer gift to, 416. For U. S. government departments, see under their respective names.

U. S. Military Academy, superintendent of, **XIV.** 494, Scott; artichitect of new buildings, **XV.** 328, Cram.

U. S. Philippine commission, member of, **XV.** 104, Elliott.

U. S. Rubber Co., **XIV.** 452, Evans; **XV.** 409, Colt.

U. S. Savings Bank, organized, **XIV.** 323, Andrews.

U. S. Smelting, Refining and Mining Co., **XIV.** 452, Evans.

U. S. Steel Corporation, history of, **XIV.** 65-72; **XV.** 33, Farrell; iron deposits leased by, 295, Longyear.

U. S. supreme court, associate justices of, **XIV.** 299, Brandeis; **XV.** 61, Pitney; 414, Lamar.

United Telephone Co., **XIV.** 216, Dougherty.

Unity, magazine, **XIV.** 161, Jones.

Universal Brotherhood and Theosophical Society, **XV.** 338, Tingley.

Universal City, Cal., **XV.** 363, Laemmle.

University of Alabama, president of, **XIII.** 101, Denny; women first admitted to, **XV.** 102, Tutwiler.

University of California, department of music, **XIV.** 335, **Wolle**; infirmary established in, **XV.** 135, Reinhardt; president of, **IV.** 480, Wheeler.

University of Chicago, extension work, **XIV.** 454, Zueblin; president of, **XI.** 67, Judson.

University of Cincinnati, **XV.** 331, Eddy.

University of Denver, chancellor of, **XIV.** 502, Buchtel.

University extension work, Chicago, **XIV.** 454, Zueblin.

University of Georgia, chancellor of, **XV.** 138, Barrow.

University of Illinois, loans to students, **XV.** 115, McKinley.

University of Maine, history of, **XIV.** 138-140; library building of, illus., 138; presidents of, 138, Allen; 138, Fernald; 138, Harris; 139, Fellows; **XV.** 13, Aley.

University of Minnesota, **XV.** 236, Vincent; 331, Eddy.

University of Mississippi, **XV.** 333, Brewer; 326, Kincannon.

University of Missouri, president of, **XIV.** 428, Hill; observatory, **XV.** 145, Updegraff.

University of Nebraska, chancellor of, **XIV.** 473, Avery.

University of Pennsylvania, first non-resident trustee of, **XIV.** 447, McCrea; Lesley Cement Laboratory, presented to, **XV.** 112; provost of, **XV.** 398, Smith.

University of Pittsburgh, chancellor of, **XV.** 199, McCormick.

University settlement, N. Y. city, **XIV.** 353, Hunter; Chicago, 454, Zueblin.

University of the South, botanical library presented to, **XV.** 91, Gattinger.

University of the State of New York, regents of, **XV.** 83, Alexander; 210, Shipman.

University of Tennessee, herbarium of, **XV.** 91, Gattinger.

University of Texas, president of, **XV.** 206, Mezes.

University of Vermont, library of, **XIV.** 380, Billings; president of, **XV.** 171, Benton.

University of Wisconsin, state tax for, **XIV.** 33, Spooner.

Updegraff, **Milton**, astronomer, **XV.** 145.

Upper Iowa University, Fayette, Iowa, presidents of, **XIV.** 292, Shanklin, W. A.; **XV.** 171, Benton.

Uruguay, friendly visit of Secy. Root to, **XIV.** 14; U. S. ministers to, 492, O'Brien; 432, Morgan; **XV.** 400, Finch.

Utah, P. E. bishop of, **XV.** 374, Spalding; governor of, 383, Spry.

V.

Vacuum bottle, manufacture of, **XV.** 108, Walker.

Vahey, **James H.**, lawyer, **XIV.** 199.

Value, **Beverly R.**, civil engineer, **XV.** 142.

Valve, gate, inventor of, **XV.** 143, Lunken.

Van Briggle, **Artus**, painter and potter, **XIV.** 242.

Van Briggle Pottery Co., **XIV.** 242, Van Briggle.

Vance, **James N.**, financier, **XV.** 66.

Van Cleave, **James W.**, manufacturer, **XIV.** 372.

Vanderlip, **Frank A.**, financier, **XV.** 29.

Van Every, **John B.**, telegraph official, **XIV.** 73.

Van Rensselaer, **Marianna (Griswold)**, art critic and author, **XIV.** 338.

Vantine, **A. A.**, & Co., **XIV.** 383, Raymond.

Vassar College, president of, 1915, **XV.** 206, MacCracken, H. N.

Vaudeville entertainment introduced, **XV.** 297, Keith.

Vaughan, **Sue Landon**, patriot, **XIV.** 128.

Vaux, **Richard**, father of, **XV.** 210.

Vaux, **Roberts**, penologist, **XV.** 210.

Veeder, **Curtis H.**, inventor and mfr., **XV.** 282.

Veeder Manufacturing Co., **XV.** 282, Veeder.

Velvets, dealers in, **XV.** 224, Schoolhouse.

Velox, photographic paper, inventor of, **XV.** 330, Baekeland.

Veneers, manufacture of, **XV.** 70, Frost.

Venetian red, manufacture of, **XIV.** 101, Lincoln.

Venezuela, diplomatic difficulties with, **XIV.** 15; U. S. chargé d'affaires, 77, Steele; special envoy to, 429, Calhoun; U. S. minister to, **XV.** 58, Russell.

Vera Cruz, Mexico, seizure of, **XV.** 44, Mayo; 144, Fletcher.

Vermeule, **Cornelius C.**, engineer, **XIV.** 105.

Vermilye, **Washington R.**, **XIV.** 455, Mackay.

Vermilye & Co., bankers, **XIV.** 455, Mackay.

Vermont Academy, **XV.** 68, Willard.

Vermont, improvement of highways in, **XV.** 104, Gates; State Laboratory of Hygiene, 370, Linsley; governors of, **XIII,** 296, Bell; **XIV.** 448, Proctor; Prouty; **XV.** 104, Gates; U. S. senators from, **VIII.** 325, Stewart; 329, Page.

Vermont Marble Co., **XIV.** 448, Proctor.

Verona lock-nut washer, inventor of, **XV.** 356, Shaw.

Vessey, **Robert S.**, governor, **XIV.** 200.

Vice, New York Society for the Suppression of, **XV.** 241, Comstock.

Viceroy's University, Wuchang, China, **XV.** 20, Martin.

Viele, **Herman K.**, author, **XIV.** 147.

Vincent, **George E.**, president University of Minnesota, **XV.** 236.

Vincent, **John H.**, son of, **XV.** 236, Vincent.

Vineland, N. J., school for feeble-minded at, **XV.** 236, Goddard.

Virginia, education in, **XIV.** 105, Mann; governors of, **XIV.** 104, Swanson; Mann; **XV.** 333, Stuart.

Virginia Hot Springs, development of, **XV.** 234, Ingalls.

Vogue, periodical, **XV.** 80, Nast.

Volcanic Research Society, **XV.** 334, Perret.

Volcanoes, studies of, **XV.** 334, Perret.

Volplane, inventor of, **XV.** 339, Montgomery.

Volunteers of America, **XIV.** 54, Booth.

Volunteers Prison League, **XIV.** 54, Booth, Maud B.

Voltmeter, compensating, inventor of, **XV.** 225, Mershon.

Von Frantzius, **Fritz**, banker, **XV.** 407.

von Niessen-Stone, **Matja**, singer, **XIV.** 434.

Voorhees, **Foster M.**, governor, **XIV.** 399.

Vosburgh, **George B.**, clergyman, **XIV.** 357.

Vroom, **Garrett D. W.**, jurist, **XIV.** 442.

W.

Wade, **Levi C.**, lawyer and railroad president, **XV.** 212.

Wade & Brackett, lawyer, **XV.** 212, Wade.

Wadsworth, **James W.**, soldier and congressman, **XV.** 34, 35, Wadsworth.

Wadsworth, **James W., Jr.**, senator, **XV.** 34.

Wadsworth, **Joseph**, **XV.** 233, Doherty.

Waggoner, **Clark**, journalist, **XIV.** 243.

Wagner, **Charles**, manufacturer, **XV.** 187.

Wagner Leather Co., **XV.** 187, Wagner.

Wagoner, **George**, **XIV.** 383, Wagoner.

Wagoner, **George W.**, surgeon, **XIV.** 383.

Waldo, **Samuel L.**, artist, **XIV.** 104.

Walker, **Charles H.**, architect, **XIV.** 285.

Walker, **David**, abolitionist, **XIV.** 306.

Walker, James M., lawyer and railroad president, **XV.** 381.

Walker, John B., surgeon, **XV.** 168.

Walker, John G., member isthmian canal commission, **XIV.** 5.

Walker, Matthew H., banker, **XV.** 61.

Walker, R. J. C., **XIV.** 146, **Weightman.**

Walker, William B., manufacturer, **XV.** 108.

Wallace, Charles W., philologist, **XV.** 299.

Wall paper, manufacture of, **XV.** 26, **Dix.**

Walsh, David I., governor, **XV.** 99.

Walsh, Louis S., R. C. bishop, **XV.** 252.

Walsh, Thomas F., miner, capitalist, **XV.** 191.

Walsh, Thomas J., U. S. senator, **XV.** 409.

Walton, Clifford S., lawyer, author, **XV.** 375.

War, secretaries of, **XIV.** 403, **Taft;** 20, **Wright;** 410, **Dickinson.**

Warburg, Paul M., member of Federal Reserve Board, **XV.** 265, **Hamlin.**

Ward, George G., electrician, **XIV.** 370.

Ward Leonard Electric Co., **XV.** 4, **Leonard.**

Warehouses, **XIV.** 117, **Woodruff;** new system of, in N. Y., 102-103, **Bush.**

Warfield, David, actor, **XIV.** 82; in vaudeville, **XV.** 297, **Keith.**

Warman, Cy., author, **XV.** 284.

Warner, Ezra J., merchant, **XV.** 244.

Warner, Joseph, 3d, banker, **XV.** 244, **Warner.**

Warner Hall, Middlebury College, **XV.** 245, **Warner.**

Warren, Frederick M., educator, **XIV.** 230.

War ships, U. S., construction of, **XV.** 88, **Taylor.**

Washburn-Crosby Co., flour manufacturer, **XV.** 41, **Bell.**

Washer, Verona lock-nut, spring pawl, invented, **XV.** 356, **Shaw.**

Washington, George, manuscripts of, **XV.** 19, **Huntington, H. E.**

Washington, (state), geological survey, **XIV.** 284; **Landes;** land fraud cases in, investigated, **XV.** 49; lumber industry in, 405, **Emerson;** governors of, **XIV.** 447, **McBride; Mead; Cosgrove;** 448, **Hay; XV.** 341, **Lister;** U. S. senators from, **XIV.** 389, **Piles;** 393, **Jones; XV.** 211, **Poindexter;** chief justices of, **XIV.** 505, **Mount; V.** 441, **Dunbar.**

Washington, D. C., International Reform Bureau at, **XIV.** 173, **Crafts;** electric traction, 145, **Duncan;** commissioner of general land office at, 414, **Ballinger;** American University at, 435, **Hamilton;** P. E. bishops of, 433, **Brent; XV.** 258, **Harding;** Metropolitan Street Railroad Co. in, 124, **Brown;** hygienic laboratory in, 129, **Blue, R.;** first private conservatory in, 149, **McWilliams.**

Washington and Lee University, president of, **XV.** 141, **Smith.**

Washington Park, Chicago, Ill., **XV.** 300, **Kimbark.**

Washington University, St. Louis, Mo., first to admit women to the law course, **XV.** 348, **Couzins.**

Watch-dog of the treasury, **XIV.** 523, **Whittlesey.**

Water-back, furnace, inventor of, **XIV.** 201, **Ames, Oliver (1st).**

Water meters, invented, **XV.** 156, **Sergeant.**

Waterbury Brass Co., Waterbury, Conn., **XV.** 216, **Seymour.**

Waterways, expert on, **XV.** 81, **Bates.**

Water works, authority on, **XIV.** 306, **Stearns;** for New York city, **XV.** 389, **Smith.**

Watkins, Thomas H., member of coal strike commission, **XIV.** 6; 55, **Parker.**

Watson, William, jurist, **XV.** 141, **Smith.**

Watt-lumen, standard of light, proposed, **XV.** 78, **Ives, H. E.**

Wau-be-ka-chuck, Indian name for James S. Sherman, **XIV.** 407.

Wave meter, inventor of, **XV.** 22, **Fessenden.**

Wa-Wan Press, Newton Center, Mass., founded, **XV.** 359, **Farwell.**

Weather forecasts, distribution of, **XIV.** 28; local, **XV.** 2, **Rotch;** 396, **Mell;** flags devised for, **XV.** 396, **Mell.**

Webster, F. S., naturalist, **XIV.** 281, **Sennett.**

Webster-Powell, Alma (Hall), singer, **XIV.** 329.

Weeks, Bartow S., partner of, **XV.** 98, **Battle.**

Weeks, John W., U. S. senator, **XV.** 115.

Weeks, John W., soldier and congressman, **XV.** 115, **Weeks.**

Weeks, Rufus W., actuary, **XIV.** 508.

Wehrle, Vincent, R. C. bishop, **XV.** 248.

Weightman, William, manufacturer, **XIV.** 146; daughter of, **XV.** 311, **Penfield.**

Weiser, Conrad, pioneer, **XIV.** 497.

Welbourn, Oclasco Carlos, physician, **XIV.** 275.

Welch, Herbert, educator, **XIV.** 42.

Welch, John J., financier, **XIV.** 506.

Welfare work for employees, **XV.** 60, **Ford;** 197; 377, **Huston, C. L.**

Wellhouse, Frederick, agriculturist, **XV.** 153.

Wellman, Arthur H., lawyer, **XIV.** 108.

Wellman, Joshua W., clergyman, **XIV.** 108.

Wells, Daniel H., actuary, **XIV.** 167.

Welsh, John, daughter of, **XV.** 143, **Strawbridge.**

Wendte, Charles W., clergyman, **XIV.** 453.

Wentworth, Charles F., partner of, **XV.** 328, **Cram.**

Westbrook, Frank F., physician and educator, **XIV.** 472.

Wesleyan University, Middletown, Conn., president of, **XIV.** 292, **Shanklin, W. A.**

Wesleyana, collection of, **XIV.** 435, **Hamilton.**

West End Co., Boston, Mass., **XV.** 399, **Gaston.**

West Virginia, claim of, against federal government, **XV.** 343, **Chilton;** U. S. senators from, **XV.** 343, **Chilton;** III, 202, **Goff.**

Western Colorado, P. E. bishop of, **XIV.** 438, **Knight.**

Western Electric Co., **XIV.** 110, **Barton; XV.** 123, **Thayer.**

Western Grocer Co., **XIV.** 378, **Letts.**

Western Reserve University, Harkness memorial chapel in, **XV.** 357, **Severance.**

Western Union Telegraph Co., **XIV.** 73-76; 361, **Wilbur;** 440.

Westinghouse Electric and Manufacturing Co., **XV.** 42.

Westinghouse, George, inventor and manufacturer, **XV.** 41.

Westinghouse, Mrs. George, XV. 43.

Westinghouse, Henry Herman, inventor, **XV.** 42.

Weston, Edward, assistant of, **XV.** 218, **Hammer.**

Weston, Joseph, soldier, **XV.** 348, **Hellier.**

Weyerhaeuser, Frederick, lumber merchant, **XIV.** 52.

Weyerhaeuser Syndicate, **XV.** 52, **Weyerhaeuser.**

Wharton, Edith, author, **XIV.** 80.

Wharton, John A., lawyer, **XV.** 238.

Wheatland, Pa., development of, **XIV.** 191, **Andrews.**

Wheatstone system of telegraphy introduced, **XV.** 387, **Smith.**

Wheeler, Edward J., editor, **XV.** 268.

Wheeler, Thomas B., jurist, **XV.** 118.

Wheel-hub, iron, invented, **XIV.** 201, **Ames, Oliver (1st).**

Wheeler, Albert G., capitalist, **XIV.** 400.

White, Edwin, artist, **XIV.** 58.

White, Henry, diplomat, **XIV.** 171.

White, Henry S., educator, **XIV.** 382.

White, J. G., & Co., engineers and contractors, **XV.** 157, **White.**

White, J. G., Management Corporation, **XV.** 158, **White.**

White, James Garrard, educator, **XV.** 313.

White, James Gilbert, engineer, **XV.** 157.